THE POLITICAL AND STRATEGIC HISTORY OF THE WORLD: FROM THE ORIGINS OF GOVERNMENT TO THE PRESENT

VOLUME I

FROM ANTIQUITY TO THE DEATH OF
THE EMPEROR AUGUSTUS CAESAR

EARLIEST TIMES TO 14 A.D.

Also by Conrad Black:

Duplessis, updated and retitled, *Render Unto Caesar*

A Life in progress

Franklin Delano Roosevelt, Champion of Freedom

Richard M. Nixon, A Life in Full (published in the U.K. and Canada as *The Invincible Quest*)

A Matter of Principle

Flight of the Eagle, The Strategic History of the United States

Rise to Greatness, the History of Canda From the Vikings to the Present

Backward Glances

The Canadian Manifesto

Donald J. Trump, A President Like No Other

Forgotten History

THE POLITICAL AND STRATEGIC HISTORY OF THE WORLD:

FROM THE ORIGINS OF GOVERNMENT TO THE PRESENT

VOLUME I

FROM ANTIQUITY TO THE DEATH OF THE EMPEROR AUGUSTUS CAESAR

EARLIEST TIMES TO 14 A.D.

CONRAD BLACK

Copyright © Conrad M. Black, 2023

All rights reserved. No part of this book may be reproduced in any form or by any means, electronic or mechanical, without permission in writing from the publisher except by reviewers who may quote brief passages in their reviews. Maps and illustrations are sourced from Wikipedia Commons unless otherwise indicated.

Published by New English Review Press
a subsidiary of World Encounter Institute
PO Box 158397
Nashville, Tennessee 37215
&
27 Old Gloucester Street
London, England, WC1N 3AX

Cover Art and Design by Kendra Mallock

ISBN: 978-1-943003-87-7

Library of Congress Control Number: 2023944912

First edition

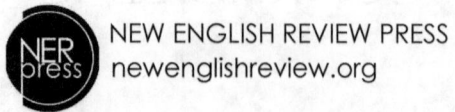

NEW ENGLISH REVIEW PRESS
newenglishreview.org

For my dear and very distinguished friends of over forty years in each case,

Henry A. Kissinger

and

Norman Podhoretz

CONTENTS

PREFACE   xv

INTRODUCTION for Thorough Readers
    Connecting the Old Testament to History
        The Early Jews and Other Semites   21

PART I – The Origins of Government
    From Earliest Times to the Fifth Century B.C. in the West
    and the Third Century B.C. in the East   29

ONE – The Jews from Antiquity to the Fifth Century B.C.
    Moses, David, and Solomon
        1. The Early Jews   31
        2. Philosophical and Theological Influence of the Early Jews   34
        3. The Jewish Struggle for Palestine   36
        4. The Assault and Oppression of Israel by the Philistines   39
        5. The Kingdom of Israel, Saul, and David   37
        6. King Solomon   44
        7. Other Contemporary Middle Eastern Peoples   47
        8. The Disunion and Subjugation of The Jews   48
        9. The Jews in the Late Persian Empire   49

APPENDIX A – An Outline of the Intricate History of Non-Jewish
        Ancient Mesopotamia   57

TWO – Ancient Egypt from the Fifth Millennium to the Eleventh Century B.C.
    The Thutmose and Ramessid Pharaohs
        1. The Earliest Dynasties   67
        2. Senusret III and Amenemhet III   71
        3. The Hyksos   73
        4. Ahmose, the Expulsion of the Hyksos, the Ahmenhotep
            and the Thutmose Pharaohs   76
        5. Ikhnaton and Harmhab   87
        6. The Ramessid Kings   90
        7. The Decline of Egypt   100

THREE – Babylonia and Assyria from the Second Millennium to the
    Eighth Century B.C.
    Hammurabi, Tiglath-Pileser, and Nebuchadnezzar
        1. Babylonia and Hammurabi   103
        2. Hittites, Kassites and Philistines   110

3. Assyria I: Tiglath-Pileser and Shalmaneser	113
4. Assyria II: Sargon, Sennacherib and Ashburnipal	117
5. Babylonia II: Nebuchadnezar	115

APPENDIX B – Assyria's Later Warlords   131

FOUR – The Beginnings of India and China from Antiquity to the
       Third Century B.C. (India) and the Second Century B.C. (China)
       Gautama (Buddha) and Confucius
1. Early India	139
2. The Aryan Invasion of India	141
3. Social and Religious Developments	144
4. India's First Unification	147
5. China, the Beginnings	151
6. Chou Culture	156
7. The Ch'in Unification of China	159
8. Western Han	162

FIVE – The Early Greeks from the Fifteenth to the Sixth Centuries B.C.
       Homer, Draco, Solon, and Cleisthenes
1. The Hellenization of the East	167
2. The Flowering of the Greeks	176
3. The Rise of Athens	186
4. The Greeks of Asia Minor, Egypt and Italy	199
5. The Rivalry between Athens and Sparta	206

**PART II – The Persian Empire and The Golden Age of Greece
           550-358 B.C.**   213

SIX – The Rise of Persia and the Invasion of Greece, 550-445 B.C.
      Darius, Xerxes and Themistocles
      Marathon and Salamis
1. The Persians	215
2. Preparations for War with Greece	229
3. War between Greece and Persia - Marathon	235
4. The Death of Darius and the Persian Invasion of Attica	242

SEVEN – The Age of Pericles and Cimon
        the Ascendency of Athens and the Start of the Peloponnesian War
        from the early Sixth Century to 445 B.C.
1. Sicily and Carthage	255
2. Athens after the Persian War	262
3. The Periclean Age	270

EIGHT – The Peloponnesian War II
    The Death of Pericles, 445 to 420 B.C.
    Archidamus and Brasidas
        1. The Thirty Years Peace, 445 B.C.   285
        2. The Breakdown of the Thirty Years Peace   294
        3. The Archidamian War 431-421 B.C.   304

NINE – The Syracusan Disaster and the Fall of Athens, 420-399 B.C.
    Alcibiades and Socrates
        1. The Peace   324
        2. The Sicilian Disaster   333
        3. The Fall of Athens   342
        4. Hellenistic Cultural Influence and the Death of Socrates   364

TEN – The Revival of Athens, Rise of Thebes and the Decline of Persia
    Xenophon, Lysander, and Epaminondas, 399-358 B.C.
        1. The State of the Western World in 400 B.C.   373
        2. The Decline of Persia   374
        3. The Odyssey of Xenophon   379
        4. Turmoil in Persia   381
        5. The Decline of Sparta, Renascence of Athens,
            and Rise of Thebes   388
        6. The Apparently Final Descent of Egypt   405

Part III – Sicily (410-290 B.C.) and Macedonia (358-275 B.C)
    Dionysius, Timoleon, and Agathocles
    Philip and Alexander the Great   411

ELEVEN – The Rivalry of Sicily and Carthage, 410-290 B.C.
        1. Syracuse, Carthage and the Battle for Sicily   413
        2. Carthage in Spain   423
        3. Sicily After Dionysius   426
        4. Timoleon   430
        5. Agathocles, Sicily and Carthage   435

TWELVE – Philip of Macedon, 360-336 B.C.
    Philip and Demosthenes
        1. The Rise of Philip of Macedon   447
        2. The Emergence of Macedonia as the Greatest Power in the
            Eastern Mediterranean   456
        3. Macedonian Dominance of the Hellenic World   466
        4. War Between Macedonia and Athens   471

THIRTEEN – Alexander the Great, 336-323 B.C.
    1. The Invasion of Persia   481
    2. Alexander the Great II: The Battle of Gaugamela and the
        Death of Darius III   498
    3. Alexander the Great III: India   503
    4. Alexander the Great IV: The Return   515
    5. Alexander the Great V: Death and Assessment   519

FOURTEEN – The Wars of Succession to Alexander I: 323 to 308 B.C.
    1. Greece in the Last Years of Alexander –
        Eumenes and Antigonus   523
    2. Opening skirmishes   534
    3. The First War of the Diadochi, 322-320   536
    4. Second War of the Diadochi 318-315   543
    5. The Third War of the Diadochi, 314-311   551

FIFTEEN – The Wars of Succession to Alexander II: 308-275 B.C.
Seleucus and Ptolemy
    1. The Fourth War of the Diadochi, 308-301   562
    2. The Fifth War of the Diadochi –
        The Struggle for Macedonia, 298-285   572
    3. The Sixth War of the Diadochi –
        Lysimachus and Seleucus, 285-281   581
    4. The Invasion of the Gauls   588

PART IV – The Rise of Rome
From Its Origins to Roman Dominance of the Mediterranean
Seventh Century B.C. to 180 B.C.   593

SIXTEEN – From the Birth of Rome to Control of Central Italy
    Antiquity to 292 B.C.
Romulus and M. Furius Camillus
    1. The Latin and Etruscan Origins of Rome and the
        Roman Kings   595
    2. The Early Roman Republic   601
    3. The Gallic Invasion, Disaster and Recovery   608
    4. The Roman Conquest of Central Italy   618

SEVENTEEN – The Pyrrhic Wars, the Roman Federation
The Roman Rivalry with Carthage the First Punic War – 292 to 240 B.C.
Pyrrhus, Gaius Duilius, and Hiero
    1. Pyrrhus and Roman Expansion over Central Italy   625
    2. Pyrrhus at Large   628
    3. The Roman Federation   635

    4. The Struggle for Supremacy Between Rome and Carthage
       The First Punic War   638

EIGHTEEN – The Supreme Struggle for the Mediterranean
    The Second Punic War, 240-201 B.C.
  Hannibal and Publius Scipio Africanus
    1. Roman-Carthaginian Relations After the First Punic War –
       Sardinia, Corsica, and Sicily   658
    2. The Carthaginian Reconquest of Spain and the
       Rise of Hannibal   660
    3. Rome, Northern Italy, and the Gauls   663
    4. Hannibal's Invasion of Italy   668
    5. Hannibal and Fabius   679
    6. Cannae   681
    7. Roman Recovery   683
    8. Spain and Italy   689
    9. Publius Scipio and Roman Victory in Spain   694
    10. The Last Phase of the Second Punic War in Italy   698
    11. The Last Battles, Zama   702
    12. Peace in the West   709

NINETEEN – Rome Turns to the East—The Temptation of the
    Former Macedonian Empire
  Philip V of Macedon, Antiochus III, Ptolemy IV, 253-215 B.C.
    1. Rome, Illyria, and Macedon   712
    2. War Between Rome and Macedonia   718
    3. Egypt, Greece, and Syria, From the Wars of the Diadochi
       to the End of the Second Punic War   726
    4. The Third Syrian War and War of the Brothers   730
    5. Antiochus III and the Fourth Syrian War   734

TWENTY – The Triumph of Rome in the East, 215-155 B.C.
  Flamininus, Philip V, and Antiochus the Great
    1. Rome at the End of the Second Punic War   740
    2. War With Macedonia   750
    3. Rome and Antiochus   756
    4. The Contest between Rome and Antiochus in Greece   762
    5. Renewed War in Greece   767
    6. The Deaths of Antiochus, Philopoemen, and Philip V
       and the Decline and Fall of Macedonia   776

PART V – The Crisis of the Roman Republic 787

TWENTY-ONE – Digesting an Empire, Strengthening Frontiers, and the Third Punic War, 155-140 B.C.
Cato and Massinissa
- 1. The Eastern States — 789
- 2. Rome and Spain — 797
- 3. The Final Destruction of Carthage — 803
- 4. The Conquest of Cisalpine Gaul and Liguria — 808

TWENTY-TWO – The People and the Generals
The Tragedy of the Gracchi and the Rise of Gaius Marius, 140-100 B.C.
- 1. The Roman Republic in the 130s B.C. — 812
- 2. The Gracchi — 815
- 3. Tiberius Gracchus — 819
- 4. Gaius Gracchus — 827
- 5. Frontier Wars and the Origins of Gaius Marius — 835
- 6. The Jugurthine War and the Rise of Gaius Marius — 841
- 7. The Mortal German Threat and the Triumph of Marius — 847

TWENTY-THREE – The Social and Mithridatic Wars
the Rise and Dictatorship of Lucius Cornelius Sulla, 115 B.C. to 78 B.C.
- 1. The Legacy of the Gracchi and Social Wars — 851
- 2. The Social War — 853
- 3. The Rivalry Between Sulla and Marius — 860
- 4. The Mithridatic Empire — 861
- 5. Sulla's Campaign in the East — 867
- 6. The Death of Marius and Sulla's Return — 871
- 7. The Dictatorship, Retirement, and Assessment of Sulla — 876

TWENTY-FOUR – War in Spain
The Rise of Gnaeus Pompeius Magnus and
Marcus Tullius Cicero, 78-62 B.C.
- 1. Sertorius — 881
- 2. Caesar, Crassus, Pompey, Cicero and the War of the Gladiators — 884
- 3. Suppressing the Pirates — 890
- 4. Pompey's Campaign in Asia Minor — 892
- 5. Pompey, the Jews, and Egypt — 895
- 6. Pompey's Asian Settlement — 898
- 7. Political Developments in Rome in Pompey's Absence: The Catilinarian Conspiracies — 901

TWENTY-FIVE – The First Triumvirate, Caesar in Gaul, Crassus in Parthia
   Crossing the Rubicon, 62-48 B.C.
   1. Cicero's Moment and Pompey's Return   910
   2. The First Triumvirate and Caesar's Consulship   912
   3. Caesar and Clodius   914
   4. Disagreements in the Triumvirate   918
   5. Caesar's Gallic Wars   920
   6. Britain and the First and Second Revolts of the Gauls   924
   7. Vercingetorix and The Third Gallic Revolt   930
   8. Rome After Luca and Crassus and the Parthian Disaster   935
   9. The Descent to Civil War   941

PART VI – The Triumph of Julius and Octavian Caesar   949

TWENTY-SIX – Caesar, Pompey, and the Civil War, 48-46 B.C.
   1. The Civil War in Italy and Spain   951
   2. The Civil War in Africa and on the Adriatic Coast   956
   3. The Decisive Battle: Pharsalus   961
   4. Caesar and Cleopatra in Egypt   965
   5. Cleaning up Asia and Africa   968

TWENTY-SEVEN – Gaius Julius Caesar:
   Dictatorship, Assassination, Vengeance, and Succession, 46-37 B.C.
   The Ides of March and Philippi
   1. The Dictatorship   976
   2. The Ides of March   982
   3. Avenging Caesar   987
   4. The Second Triumvirate, Proscription, and Philippi   996
   5. The Division of Spoils Between the Victorious Triumvirs   999
   6. The Parthian Invasion   1005

TWENTY-EIGHT – Octavian Caesar
   Mark Antony and Cleopatra, 37 B.C.-2 A.D.
   1. Eliminating Sextus Pompeius   1011
   2. The Invasion of Parthia   1016
   3. Preparing for the Showdown   1020
   4. Actium   1029
   5. The End of Antony and Cleopatra   1032
   6. The Triumph of Octavian   1036
   7. The Imperial Republic   1040

TWENTY-NINE – The Augustan Empire, 27 B.C.-14 A.D.
    1. Restructuring the Roman State   1048
    2. The Roman Frontiers in the Late Augustan Years I: Egypt, Syria, and Armenia   1056
    3. Judea   1064
    4. Spain, Africa, and Northern Frontiers   1069
    5. Germany   1072
    6. Commerce and Integration of the Roman Empire in the Augustan Era   1077
    7. Augustan Social Policy   1080
    8. Death, Legacy, and Assessment of Augustus Octavian Caesar   1082

THIRTY – CONCLUSION   1086

INDEX   1091

ACKNOWLEDGEMENTS   1151

PREFACE

THE REASON FOR WRITING a political history of the world in three solid, but not herniating, volumes is that when that history is generally confined to an outline of the development of techniques of government and the evolution of political society with the waves of ethnic and sectarian influences spreading out from the cradles of recorded history in the Middle East and South and East Asia, with emphasis on the decisive personalities who have led peoples and societies in novel directions, the task is considerably more manageable than prior histories indicate. People who aspire to a grasp of the whole history of the world without becoming monastic recluses for twenty years can do so: such histories need not be 20 or 30 volumes.

As an entire social and cultural history is not attempted here, the narrative is obviously extensive, but definitely of manageable length, and conveniently divisible into defined subjects and periods. The process can be seen to be an evolution of governmental techniques and principles, with some backsliding and renovation, but in a discernible pattern of more competent and broadly even more humane, government. This is not a process of repetitions of cycles of rise and decline, though the temptations of that system of presentation are evident. In fact, the frequent rather flippant comparisons of modern states and empires with Rome or the cycles of Chinese history are largely false, and the resemblances are superficial. Rather, man has generally grown politically wiser and more efficient, though scientific, and other progress has sometimes notoriously been applied by objectively oppressive and even evil regimes to tighten their control over their societies temporarily.

The power of political ideology and universal human objectives have repeatedly been conjoined with material and scientific progress to provide the raison d'être of successive important political societies. Clannishness, tribalism, and nationalism have consistently alternated with universalist proclaimed goals in motivating and justifying political expansion. While there is a pattern of increasing political sophistication, the narrative is influenced at every stage and raised far above a mere chronology by the endless vagaries of the conduct and talent of individual influential historic personalities. By emphasizing the human drama of noteworthy individuals and the strategies devised for such expansions of dynastic or national influence, political societies have generally become more sophisticated, conceptually and methodologically. None of this requires oppressive length to explain. Influence of individual people in the course of political and institutional development demarcates much of the history of the world and is seen as an always interesting succession of exceptional, or at least exceptionally important, people succeeding and contesting with each other for influence on the political evolution of all the world's societies and peoples and countries. Told properly, it is at least a very interesting story.

Readers will discover, presumably to their pleasure, that as presented, the history of the world is no more an inert mass of random happenings than it is a robotic and determinist repetition of the cycle of energetic and then gradually more dyspeptic political systems. Rather, the history, or at least the political and strategic history of the world, is an always interesting sequence of talented and highly motivated individuals, always distinguishable from any preceding individuals, refining and adapting political techniques of popular advocacy and administrative methods to strategies of personal and collective self-interest. This process is almost never dull and presented in this way, and not as the drudgery of mere and repetitive chronology, the political and strategic history of the world is varied and unpredictable, though there are many resemblances of people and events. It is also a pleasure to encounter the real circumstances of Armageddon, the Pyrrhic victory, the wealth of Croesus, the Gordian Knot, and Nero helping to extinguish the fires rather than fiddling, and many similar episodes that remain commonplace as fragments.

Readers will also note the greater historic importance of men of action over the sages, like Plato and Cicero, whose meddling in government was largely ineffectual. The Greeks also will seem slightly less majestic than they are usually portrayed-because of their endless addiction to internecine war and their ingratitude at any favours proffered by foreigners, especially Rome.

Readers are advised in many places that the next part of the story is rather complex and repetitively intricate, and while it must be included as a bridge to their consequences, in several chapters, especially complex and not overly consequential periods are placed in long appendices or designated sections following the chapter, preserving them for the most enterprising readers but not over-straining the narrative. The objective is to provide the necessary but never to entrap the reader in thickets of extraneous or excessively obscure events.

Eras that are comparatively static and unoriginal have been got through quite quickly, as a political history does not require a laborious record of every change of officeholder or minor military operation. The arresting personalities and seminal events in the political development of mankind provide a rich descriptive canvas, but not, unlike mere and compendious chronologies, a morass of laborious and mechanical events and people. Approached as it is here, the entire political history of the world is a self-sustaining panoply that is much less overwhelming than previous multi-volume chronologies on this vast subject. The greatest drama of modern times, the Second World War, can most interestingly be appreciated by considering the struggle between totalitarian and democratic states in the rivalry and shifting arrangements between the leading personalities of the time, as success in the Manichaean struggles required intermittent co-option by the democratic leaders of some dictators against others: Franklin D. Roosevelt, Winston Churchill, Charles de Gaulle, Adolf Hitler, Joseph Stalin, and Mao Tse-tung, as well as a large and interesting cast of secondary political personalities and military chiefs.

This book makes it clear that from earliest times, people wished to organize their lives in living communities and accepted that some level of authority had to be established and respected to achieve that purpose. Nomadic groups, even though they attacked established cities for centuries, ultimately wished some form of defined territorial existence and government, part of it urban, for themselves. We will see that even the more belligerent tribes, though attracted by the wealth and ease of urban settlements in the gentler climate of the Mediterranean, compared to the steppes of Russia and the barrenness of the Urals and of Mongolia, were motivated at first by a desire to pillage, and only later to settle, produce their own food, and create towns and cities that presented much more diverse opportunity for leisure. By this process, successive invaders were absorbed, softened, and ultimately civilized, whether in Egypt, Greece, China, India, or ultimately, Western Europe.

It is also discernible throughout the period, from approximately the last 3000 years before the birth of Christ and in the 2000 years since then, that all societies, barbarous or civilized, have been religious. Almost all of them endured considerable competition between secular and religious leaders, though some were more successful than others at uniting them.

The enduring importance of Israel and the Jews comes from their monotheism, and from their intermittent belief that their leader was Jehovah himself, who not only enlightened the Jewish people by revelation and periodically occupied the minds of its great men, but also is considered to be present but invisible in many of the supreme councils of the Jews. The prevalence of God for every function and principal initiative in nature competing with other sets of gods in other municipalities sometimes just 10 miles away, though usually in larger areas of religious belief—entire very small countries, gradually reduced the credibility of the concept of these multiplicities of gods and the credulity of their adherents. It was clear by the beginning of the Christian Era that throughout the Roman world, the proliferation of gods was regarded with substantial skepticism, at least by the intellectual leaders of society. Yet even the greatest leaders, Alexander the Great, and Julius and Octavian Caesar, were careful to appear as communicants in their national religions. But it appears that the readiness of those religions to elevate them to a status of partial deities, which their prodigious terrestrial achievements conferred upon them, may have been at least as great a motivation for their religious practice as the fervour of their own belief.

The advances generated by urbanization will be clear and unsurprising to the reader, and while the primitiveness of science and particularly medicine, by contemporary standards, is very striking, it must also be said that technologically and architecturally, the more sophisticated ancient societies were astonishingly advanced. Suez was a canal under the more ambitious pharaohs and Persian kings, though it was not capable of accommodating immense vessels such as go through the Suez Canal today (and, of course, did not then exist). The sophisticated new financiers of Rome in the late Second Century B.C. built fabulous estates on the Bay of Naples with wood-fired hot water-heated swimming pools. The construction of the Great Pyramid at Giza, albeit by slave labor, remains a wonder of the world. The basic stone blocks weighed 2.5 tons each and it remains a mystery how they were moved into place. The roads and aqueducts and eventually even sewage systems of the

Romans were astonishingly advanced, and the great monumental cities: Babylon, Athens, Alexandria, and Rome were magnificent, aesthetically and in their scale even by modern standards..

The West has traditionally been gulled by the pretense of the Chinese in particular to be senior to us as a civilization and more prodigious in its early accomplishments. Neither was the case, and Chinese and Indian society seem to have been so violent and so abused by their leaders that religions and philosophical schools of religious conviction intruded heavily into the secular domain and distracted both peoples with totemistic religiosity and with a religious counter-culture of extreme poverty and abstention.

The *Cambridge Ancient History* (*CAH*) has often been used for outlines, heavily supplemented by its bibliography and very many other works published in the 91 years since the publication of the edition I used. A perusal of the chapter end-notes might incite the suspicion that this volume is partly a condensation of the first ten volumes of the *Cambridge Ancient History*; that impression is deceiving. Other sources, taken as a whole, are much more important, but everything relevant to this project from the *CAH* is here, whatever its source. As the *Cambridge Ancient History* is a large collection of sequential essays largely taken from longer works by the contributing historians, the particular author is named in each case. The extensive chronicle found here is a matter of agreed historical fact and only direct quotes or, where appropriate, disputable interpretations, are the subject of footnotes. No good purpose would be served by deluging readers with a forest of redundant and recondite references. These can be unearthed in the cited works.

It will be clear at the end of the first volume of this work that the populations and circumstances are ripe for a new religious concept. Up to this point, religion had chiefly consisted of making sacrifices in the hope that they would propitiate the divine powers that be, who would then favour the supplicants. It is from this perspective easy to see why the world was ready for a religious conception of a single, universal, and omniscient God who produced the creation for a positive purpose and looked more benignly upon all those endowed with the spiritual life of people than had previously been assumed. Egyptian, Jewish, Greek, and Roman gods were more afflicted by unbecoming characteristics than the Christian God who eventually emerged. Once this new orthodoxy was enunciated, allegedly by the long-awaited Messiah, and interpreted and transmitted by talented disciples, the ancient religions were virtually all eliminated except for Judaism, and the influence upon the conduct of peoples and governments by religious leaders grew very substantially, though the competition between religious and secular leaders continued, intensified, and has not ceased.

Volume II will recount how the theocracy contributed, both constructively and reactively, to the Renaissance, the establishment of the nation state, the age of exploration and colonization, the Reformation and Counter-Reformation, and subsequent volumes will coherently explain the rise of nationalism, democracy, totalitarianism, and the epic armed struggles of modern history. It is a sequence that possesses an identifiable logic of its own and at every stage new developments grafted themselves on to the repetition of a familiar cycle.

All of the volumes in this book may be considered stand-alone descriptions of defined periods in world political history. Any and all of them may be read at different times, in any order, and over any reasonable length of time without the narrative breaking down because of interruptions or variations from the actual sequence of events. In a word, the basic history of the world's peoples is a much less intimidating and implacable subject than it has previously been seen to be.

It is the purpose and intention of this book to make the entire subject, and the principal component parts of it, more accessible and readable than they have been.

Conrad Black   Toronto, August 2022.

INTRODUCTION
FOR THOROUGH READERS

CONNECTING THE OLD TESTAMENT
TO HISTORY
❦
THE EARLY JEWS AND OTHER SEMITES

THE REAL BEGINNINGS of European government were less in the primitive tribal organizations of the Celts, Germans, Gauls and the many other tribes, clans, and bands of Western Europe than in the Middle East, where, at the crossroads of three continents, Western Civilization began. Neither the discernible development of anthropology nor the earliest fruit of imprecise archeology are recounted in this presentation of the ebb and flow of peoples and governments and the complicated and fissiparous course from the ancient Egyptians, Hittites, Babylonians, Jews, and other Semites into the recognizable, ancient, medieval, and modern world. The Semites are generally seen as the Aramaeans (Syrians) to the north, Phoenicians and Hebrews on the Mediterranean, Arabs to the south, and the Babylonians and Assyrians in the east. They all resided between the Persian Gulf, Egypt, the Mediterranean and the mountains of what are today Turkey, Armenia, and Iran. Most of these peoples, being on territory open to the mass movements of three continents, were frequently overrun and inundated with invaders and migrant peoples; only Egypt, with natural sea frontiers, retained comparative geographic and demographic continuity. The routes of caravans from the Arabian Peninsula to upper Egypt and the Mediterranean met the routes from Persia, Mesopotamia (now Iraq but in early times, Babylonia and Assyria), around Gaza, Sinai, and Israel. Palestine was Israel and part of Jordan and Lebanon, a broken and in places arid country, and Syria was agriculturally richer. The Phoenicians in what is now Lebanon and Israel, being on narrow land on the Mediterranean took naturally and early to maritime trade and eventually colonization.

Cities and towns, and even oases on the rich, crossing trade routes arose and many were very prosperous, attracting armed assault from rival or less prosperous tribes or communities, generally on no motive that was pretended to be more than avarice. This was the forerunner for national rivalries, ethnic or sectarian abrasions, and the casuistry of modern international justification of armed aggression. Syria and Palestine were the particular fulcrum of activity and have exercised a substantial influence, extending far from their own modest circumstances for more than four thousand years. Damascus may claim to be the oldest still-functioning western city, and in the Seventh and Eighth Centuries A.D., was the capital of the Omayyad caliphate which extended from India and across North Africa and into Spain.

The word Semite originated with Shem, one of Noah's three sons.[1] The names of Noah's early descendants are used in the identification of many ancient peoples. His grandsons Dorus and Aeolus and great grandsons Ion and Achaeus are the source of the names of Greek (Hellene) branches: Dorians, Aeolians, Ionians and Achaeans. Genesis[2] credits Noah with the discovery of how to produce wine from grapes. Canaan was supposedly cursed and condemned to be Shem's servant but became the father of some of the Phoenicians and Hittites, and his territory was to the south of Sidon and east of the Dead Sea. Shem was not only Noah's son, but a descendant of Eber (hence Hebrew). Yahweh, or Jehovah, is referred to as the God of Shem, which means that he was not the God of Israel only, and another son of Noah, Ham, is held to be the father of Cush (Ethiopia), Mizraim (Egypt), and Canaan. Where Canaan fell afoul of Shem, Japheth was Shem's protégé, and his lands were to the north and extended as far as Greece. Shem's realm also extended along the main post road from Susa to Sardes.[3] Generally, Japheth had the (cold) north, Shem the (changeable) centre, and Ham the (hot) south. Cush's son Nimrod is credited with founding Babylon and Assyria.

All of this falls well short of modern standards for documenting history and is a mélange of legend, lore, and alleged Revelation. There has been an immense amount of scholarly examination of ancient writings and archeological remains and widely differing recitations of inherited beliefs, but from any angle, the expression Semite has a very uncertain and varied original meaning, though in modern parlance, it generally refers only to the Jews, other than in specialist scholastic circles of people steeped in the mists of antiquity. The principal Semitic languages are Babylonian and Assyrian (almost identical), Phoenician, Hebrew (Canaanite and Moabite), Aramaean (Syriac) and South Arabian. The relationship of all of them is somewhat like that between the Latin-originated languages—French, Spanish, Italian, Portuguese, and to a point, Romanian.

Victorious invaders of Semitic lands, such as Kassites and Philistines, adopted the Semitic languages of those they conquered, in the pattern of Chinese and post-Roman Empire eras, where the militarily more powerful were the culturally less sophisticated of the protagonists. In the brief overlordship of occupied nations by Germany and Russia in and after the Second World War, there was a start at this, but it was rarely successful as the conquests were not durable. The more ardent French proponents of almost unconditional surrender to Nazi Germany, whose early appearance of crisp, strong, disciplined, and well-uniformed military invincibility intimidated much of Europe, thought that after a period of submission, French cultural superiority and refinement would seduce the German conquerors. Of course, the issue was never tested.

Although the Semitic peoples did not depart their regions of origin in great

---

1 Genesis 9-11.
2 Genesis 5:29, 9:20 et seq.
3 *Cambridge Ancient History* (CAH), I, p. 185 (S.A. Cook).

numbers as the Indo-European peoples did, they exercised an immense influence through Phoenician maritime and commercial activities throughout the Mediterranean and Black Seas and along the Atlantic coasts of Spain, Gaul, and North Africa. Eventually, of course, the spread of the Judeo-Christian and Islamic religions conferred upon the area between what are now Turkey, Egypt, Arabia, and Iran and Armenia, an unparalleled influence that has profoundly marked the entire world, apart only from the remotest regions of China.

There is a portrayal of Phoenician sea commerce in Ezekiel.[4] There were pre-Israelite peoples as there were pre-Phoenician mariners, "Byblos-farers," but our knowledge of them is very sketchy. The Semites were always limited in their penetration of Egypt, "the wilderness of the land of Egypt,"[5] and only really permeated Egypt with the Islamic conquest of the Seventh Century A.D. Even after that event, Egypt has always been susceptible to overtures from other powers to separate itself from other Near Eastern countries.

The Semites never made any headway in Asia Minor, now the Anatolian section of Turkey. After reaching twenty-five hundred feet above sea level in Syria, said Hogarth, "the Arab tongue is chilled to silence."[6] Most successful invaders of Semitic countries have been "Semitized," though there was a profound exchange and blending of cultures with the invading Sumerians. Egypt, Crete, Asia Minor, and Iran have all had a lasting impact on the Semites. But even Mongols, Turks, and Persians were to some extent Semitized as occupiers. The only conquering influence that put down roots among the original Semites was that of the Arabs, though the Euro-Americans may still contend, even though European occupation of the Semitic lands was essentially confined to the inter-war period, and such western influence as there is has not been by outright occupation and acculturation.

It has often been concluded that the Semitic area that has been defined has been altered by and had to assimilate five successive waves of migrant invasion, such as afflicted Europe at the end of the Western Roman Empire. It is generally assumed that the invaders had always been motivated by natural calamities, but it is quite possible that the wealth of the area was a magnet to less fortunate groups within striking distance, and for most of history, at least on the Eurasian land mass, there have been tribes or whole races that for long periods moved nomadically for spontaneous reasons. The first of these waves was an invasion of Mesopotamia and northern Syria from an uncertain source that settled its initial character (for purposes of discoverable history) in around 4000 B.C. A thousand years later came Canaanites carrying an Amorite influence. A thousand years after that came the Aramaean influx bringing the Hebrews and the people of Ammon, Edom, and Moab. A thousand years later came the Nabataeans, and about fifteen-hundred years later, there was, in the Seventh Century A.D., the Mohammedan tidal wave. These developments are unlikely to have been so definable and symmetrical, and some of the more fierce inundations by primitive desert tribes into the Fertile Crescent remained unassimilated, including, to a considerable extent, the Bedouins (who, though a minority, rule

---

4 Ezekiel 26.
5 Ezekiel 20:36.
6 CAH, I, p. 192.

the Kingdom of Jordan today). This pattern of warrior tribes and nations conquering more degenerate and culturally refined peoples has recurred, all over the world. Not only the relatively uncultured belligerence of Sparta and some other Greek city states, but in India and China, and also the experience of the central and eastern barbarians of the early Christian Era in Europe. But the Mongols, the Turkish invasions of the Balkans, the antics of the later unified Germans, much of the tribal history of Africa and the Americas, and even outbursts of militant Islam around the turn into the third Christian Millennium may be taken as illustrative of this tendency.

Genealogy of the Old Testament

It would have been absurd if the Semites had not been the initiators of Judaism, as they were. It is traditionally ascribed to Moses or Abram, and it has been claimed that the worship of Jehovah began with Enos, the grandson of Adam. Judaism gradually developed into henotheism or monolatry; the worship of one God was where Judaism generally rested for many centuries before taking the final step to monotheism, which explicitly rejects any lesser or other Gods, but not the worship of other individuals (such as Christian saints). Atheism was very rare in the ancient world, and the natural psychological tendency of everyone was to resort to worship of some kind, in recognition of the imperfectability of man and the inevitability of death.

Christianity eventually developed out of Judaism and was for at least a couple of centuries considered by the Romans to be a branch of Judaism. In the first centuries of Christianity, anti-Semitism was generally an attack upon Jews. The Semitic conception of the deity was not necessarily of an especially kindly or merciful, or even particularly ethical God, but of a frightening and somewhat unpredictable and even implacable God. The character of the deity became gentler and more fully anthropomorphic under the Christians, following the visitation of the proclaimed Messiah. The Jewish God was often nasty, as when he hardened Pharaoh's heart, and sometimes devious, as when he tempts man to sin. As God sometimes seemed to scorn the law, early Semitic societies developed the role of chief of the clergy, usually a high priest, in parallel with the secular leader, though in some Semitic societies, the two offices were combined in the same person, often, as in medieval and modern times, quite uneasily.

Religion was often identified with intellectual activity, and the divination of God's will through the examination of animal livers contributed to knowledge of anatomy, as divination through astrology encouraged an enhanced grasp of astronomy. The Semites parted company on the issue of another world or life, where Egyptian belief preceded and presaged Christian belief in the afterlife. The Egyptian King Ikhnaton in the Fourteenth Century B.C. presented a trial "doctrine" of monotheism, but did not claim to believe it and his new doctrine was inundated and drowned by Egyptian cultic custom (Chapter 2).

Jewish temples became centres for social work, counseling, and even banking ("the money-changers"), as well as worship. The prophets of Israel were practical in their judgments, like Solomon, who was gnomic—as in the reflections upon the ant and the rock badger.[7] Because of their geographic position, interaction with other assertive though often relatively primitive cultures, and because of the commercial raison d'être of their communities, the Semites became transactional. The perception of material and intellectual sharp trading, though it was usually based on envy and malice, began early and has persisted, and has intermittently been amplified over thousands of years by the oppression of Semites, especially Jews, but also Lebanese and Palestinians, which has obliged them to be unusually agile to survive and flourish.

Polygamy was generally seen as irreconcilable with a close family life. In the early ancient era, the Semites had their own Gods for each tribe and sometimes each town, and these Gods intervened as partisans of the group that worshipped them. There were implicit skirmishes between the Gods of tribes or peoples that contended on earth, like the ascending leagues of competitive sports. Attempts at sacred literature were very uneven, sometimes inspirational, as in countless places in the Old Testament, but running to argumentative pedantry and just dullness, as in Isaac of Antioch's gigantic 2,137-verse poem about a parrot proclaiming God's holiness.[8]

Because of the nomadic and constantly unsettled nature of early Semitic existence, the early Semites were energetic and intelligent, but moody, impulsive, stubborn, often hidebound in fact. There was a greater tendency to dogmatic stubbornness and then resignation than to improvisation, as developed in Indo-European

---

7 Proverbs, vi.
8 CAH, I, p. 204 (S.A. Cook).

cultures slightly later. The Semites were the cradle of Western Civilization, but their Golden Age was long before the arising among them of the Christians.[9]

The sociological divisions among the early Semites are not unrecognizable today. Cain was a farmer who seeded and harvested, while Abel was a pastoral shepherd; Jacob was averse to agricultural toil and was the subject of a curse, from which he was only emancipated by the intercession of Noah the comforter, discoverer of wine; Esau lived from hunting. The ideal life was one of ease under one's own vine and fig tree. Blessings and curses are agricultural in nature, and "Israel could boast of occupying cities it had not built and vineyards it had not planted."[10] The Bedouins, as they were nomadic traders who had little notion of fixed assets and immoveable property, were a sort of communist aristocracy.

Marriage could either be female adherence to a subordinate role to a husband-protector, or her continued residence with her own family, but with visits by lovers and her husband. Harem-mothers were recognized as powerful women. "Mana" was the intervention of God or Gods who were held always to reveal their intentions to the prophets. There was no conception of an absolute beginning of life, or of its end. The basic elements pre-existed and no effort (that has come down to us) was made to grasp the temporal or spatial limits of the cosmos. The Semitic religions addressed man's need to reconcile himself to his own relative insignificance, formalize notions of destiny and luck, and create cross-supporting structures of government and religious leadership to help stabilize and make more durable the leadership of emerging communities and societies.

The entire conception of the earliest world history is Semitic. We don't know where history starts and lore leaves off. Biblical history represents the arrival of Abraham and his followers in Palestine as a decisive turning point, but not the beginning of history. The period from the Creation until Abraham is a very grey zone in Semitic history. More is known of Egypt, the Sumerians, and South and East Asia, but Abraham begins Semitic history.

Scientific analysis suggests that if anything like the Flood occurred, it would have been earlier than the Biblical implication that it occurred in the Twenty-Fourth Century B.C. There allegedly followed an attempt to build a tower to heaven (Babylon's immense E-temen-ana-ki, "the foundation stone of heaven and earth"). Yahweh came down to see the "brazen-doored sanctuary of Zeus-Belus" and then scattered the presumptuous race of pre-Israelites, and the tower became known as Babel "because Yahweh did there confound the language of all the earth."[11] In fact, Babel meant "gate of God" and did not come from "balal," the Hebrew word "to confound." Thus, do myths arise and take hold forever. The base of the tower remains, almost four-hundred metres square. At about the same time as Hammurabi and the Golden Age of Babylonia and the XIIth Dynasty of Egypt, around 1900 B.C., Abraham opened the history of Israel. Syria and Palestine do not seriously enter into fully believable history until the Sixteenth Century B.C.

---

9 CAH, I, pp. 204-5 (S.A. Cook).
10 Deuteronomy 6:11.
11 Genesis 11:7.

Mesopotamia

The plain between the Armenian slopes, which are the source of the Tigris and the Euphrates, and the 800-mile wedge between those rivers, was the cradle of Babylonian civilization. Many of the storied cities of the ancient world were here, between the modern Baghdad and Basra, including Babylon and Susa (which was actually 50 miles east of the Tigris and 200 miles southeast of Baghdad). In this area, on the two main rivers and smaller rivers that flow into them, modern archeologists have found evidence of a good deal of extensive and imaginative works of irrigation and canalization. As far back as can be discerned, and blending into legend, the Sumerians arose in Neolithic times near the confluence of the Tigris and Euphrates, about a hundred miles from the Persian Gulf. Around 5500 B.C., Susa had risen as a substantial capital, and with stout walls and multi-story structures by about 4000 B.C. The Sumerians wore sheep's fleeces, while some other contemporary peoples have left clear evidence of woven linen. (North American readers might want to remember that the natives Europeans found in this continent in the Fifteenth Century A.D. did not weave and had little agriculture or permanent buildings and were mainly nomads.) In the Twenty-Second Century B.C., scholars at Isin, in this Tigris-Euphrates area, constructed a dynastic table that enumerated one-hundred and thirty-four kings from the Flood to the eleventh king of Isin in 2198 B.C. The first dynasty was centered on Kish, about nine miles east of Babylon. A good deal of this alleged historical sequence is wildly implausible, with reigns of seven-hundred and twenty and six-hundred and thirty-five years, and lesser periods, but the contention of the authors of the tablets where this chronology was recorded was that it had been twenty-five or twenty-six thousand years since the Flood. But the later details must be somewhat reflective of historical facts. There were some exercises in symbolism that are still used, such as the image of an eagle killing a snake (the flag of contemporary Mexico).

The next dynasty was at Erech to the south and had a distinctly Sumerian character. The chronologies of the times contain more fantastic reigns of up to four-hundred and twenty years, but also produced the great literary epic of Gilgamesh, in twelve tablets. This was a semi-divine king with an imputed reign of one-hundred and twenty-six years. He was a despotic ruler at first, but his mother, a sun-goddess, sent a rival, Enkidu, to harass him and they were eventually reconciled and made war successfully against the northern oppressors of Erech, led by the God Khumbaba in the cedar mountains of Elam. The succeeding dynasty, farther south on the Euphrates at Ur, was altogether Sumerian, clearly the rising Semitic subgroup. The recorded reigns of these kings were mainly of believable duration, and there followed a jumbled sequence of short-lived and contending dynasties including Akshak on the Tigris and Opis, and there was at least one revival of government at Ur. The first reliable date in Sumerian and Babylonian history was the Akshak Dynasty that began at about 3200 B.C.

What was really happening was a town or city with an unusually ambitious warrior-leader extending his municipal sway out from the city for a time and memorializing the regime with the habitual grandiosity of empire, but quickly fading as the only raison d'être of its ephemeral prominence was the aptitude for conquest and government of one person, or even, as with the Hyksos, improved military equipment and attack techniques. Kish was the principal of these cities, and it became a generic word for empire in Sumerian times, as Athens, Rome, and Paris eventually became emblematic of learning, empire, and style: the Athens of the South (Nashville), a new Rome (London, New York), the Paris of South America (Buenos Aires), and so forth. The leading city of the area oscillated for a few centuries between Kish, Ur, and Maer in the north, and Akshak. The whole era was highlighted by a clash between the Sumerian and the various Semitic groups with which they warred and intermingled.

They developed close political relations over two thousand years, and the Semites were culturally overwhelmed by the Sumerian influence, the progress of whose written language can be followed in the gradually greater sophistication of successive eras of tablets and engravings. The Semites accepted the Sumerian religion, while the Assyrians, though intermittent rivals in control and influence of the Middle East, contested material and military matters fiercely and often successfully, but allowed their feebly held and tokenistic religious practices to be subsumed in Sumerian religious lore.

The complicated and sanguinary history of early Mesopotamia, an almost incomprehensible sequence of treacherous and barbarous acts involving people and places with unfeasible names, appears in some detail for the more intrepid readers, as an Appendix at the end of Chapter 1.

PART I

THE ORIGINS OF GOVERNMENT

FROM EARLIEST TIMES TO
THE FIFTH CENTURY B.C. IN THE WEST

AND THE THIRD CENTURY B.C. IN THE EAST

CHAPTER ONE

THE JEWS FROM ANTIQUITY
TO THE FIFTH CENTURY B.C.
✿
MOSES, DAVID, AND SOLOMON

Abraham by Guercino (1591–1666)

Moses by Guido Reni (1575–1642)

1. The Early Jews

JEWISH TRADITION, as revisited and composed in the Sixth Century A.D., holds that Israel and the Jews began with Abraham, the last of the patriarchs, and tenth generation descendant from Noah, who was himself a direct descendant of Adam. This was mentioned in the Introduction. From Abraham and Sarah of Hebron, founders, or progenitors of all the Judeo-Christian and Islamic religions and peoples, came Isaac, founder of Beersheeba, while Abraham's nephew, Lot, was the father of Moab and Ammon. Abraham made the Covenant of the Jewish people with God. In response to the summons of Jehovah (Yahweh will be called by His English name throughout this work), Abraham entered into Canaan, and to Shechem and then to Bethel and the south. Abraham's grandson, Jacob, settled among the Aramaeans, south of Damascus. He eventually returned with his children from Aramaean wives and went to Shechem and then to the south, and finally, fleeing famine, into Egypt.

The twelve tribes of ancient Israel were all named after different sons of Jacob, and the pharaohs of Egypt enslaved and oppressed the Jews. Jehovah sent Moses, a fugitive from the pharaoh, who was tending the flock of his father-in-law, Jethro, to deliver the Jews from bondage. He and his brother Aaron led the exodus from the "house of the slaves," as the pharaoh had initially agreed, when asked by Moses to release his people, and then changed his mind. Moses was assisted by miraculous events to make good their escape, concluding with the parting of the waters of the Red Sea, and the Jews arrived in Sinai, where the covenant of the Jewish people with Jehovah was solemnized. This was the beginning of Judaism and all its subsequent beliefs and practices. (There is some evidence that there was a natural partial recession of the waters of the northern Red Sea. This might have facilitated the flight of the Jews.)

Intelligence expeditions directed by Moses gleaned from Palestine information that made the Jews fearful to enter into that more fertile territory and for the proverbial forty years, until most of the elders had died, and Moses, accompanied now by a younger generation of bolder Jewish leaders, made an indirect approach by proceeding southeast to the top of the Gulf of Aqaba, and then wheeling north and west and seizing the land promised to their ancestors between the Jordan River and Gilead and Mt. Hermon.[1] Moses made a second covenant with God, in the last days of his life,[2] and at Gilgal, Joshua led the younger generation of male Jews in what became the national Jewish rite of circumcision.[3] Dealing with aroused enemies and the treachery of defecting allies, Joshua captured Jericho, Bethel, Jerusalem, Hebron, and other centres. Joshua attacked south and captured all Palestine as far as Gaza and all the Land of Goshen as far as Gibeon, and in a northern campaign as far as Lebanon and Mt. Hermon. Joshua arranged to divide all the territory west of the Jordan River among the twelve tribes. Joshua died after a third covenant at Shechem, and a new generation succeeded that had no knowledge of Jehovah, who became the God of Israel, and Israel became the people of Jehovah.

The Israelites settled into their new territory, but bore then, as they have all through the time since, many sorrows and afflictions. Canaanites and other Palestinian peoples attacked relentlessly, and the trials of Israel were well launched. They have not ceased. The unity of the tribes sundered but was restored by common enemies which disputed Israel's right to be present between the Jordan River and the Mediterranean, though the tribe of Judah was dissentient, and some of the others were tepid in their adherence. These fissiparous and argumentative traits too, survive.

In the Philistine oppression, the mighty and rambunctious Samson, of the tribe of Dan, the prophet Samuel, and Shamgar are the early saviours. Saul founded the Israelite monarchy, but was almost instantly contested by David, but the whole issue is the subject of sharp debate in Jewish history. Some claimed that Saul was selected by God to save Israel from the Philistines, and others that Samuel of Ephraim saved the Israelites from the Philistines and that a king was demanded to be raised up but that this offended those that considered Jehovah to be a terrestrial as well as a heavenly king. (This belief must have led to intense metaphysical debate.) David was the alleged candidate of Jehovah and, in any case, after Saul was defeated by the Philistines at Mount Gilboa, David emerged to rout the Philistines and liberate Israel again. David's coronation was at Hebron, and he then captured Jerusalem from the Philistines and Jebusites. (We are now at about 1000 B.C.) David made Jerusalem the

---

1 Deuteronomy 3:8 et seq.
2 Deuteronomy 19:1; 2 and 5.
3 Joshua 5; Genesis 17:29; 9:20 et seq.

capital of the Jews, pacified the surrounding areas, and began work on the Temple, which was completed by his son, the equally famous King Solomon. When Solomon died, the united kingdom of Israel broke apart and Judea in the south seceded from the control of Jerusalem, which was itself controlled for a lengthy time by the Samaritans, and Judea professed to be the home of the Jewish people. (The Samaritans did not enjoy at the time such benign public relations as they acquired a millennium later with Jesus Christ as their supporter.)

The Old Testament history of this time cannot be taken as rigorously authentic, but there are many aspects of it that are based on serious scholarship and accurate reflection of known historic developments. The Old Testament account is generally taken as an heroic historic Jewish narrative with an uncertain amount of truth to it, but there is no remotely comprehensible alternate history available. The word Jew is derived from the Roman word Judea, the southern kingdom of Judah which seceded after the death of Solomon and included the tribes of Benjamin, Judah, and Levi. The Pentateuch (Torah—the books of Genesis, Exodus, Leviticus, Numbers, and Deuteronomy) appears to conflate some parts of the story, though many descriptive parts are accurate and conform to known history, including use of weapons, and the evolution of early Egyptian society, which is somewhat documented.

Elements of Jewish history that can be confirmed prior to the emergence of that people into the fairly clear light of known history between 1200 and 1000 B.C. include the strong Egyptian influence in contemporary Palestine and the accurate reflection of early Israelite and Hebrew cultural conditions and traditions. As well as can be reliably determined, the family of Jacob "went down into Egypt" and the list in Genesis 4 corresponds to the known Israelite tribes, "the children of Israel."[4] Jacob died after seventeen years in Egypt, and the size of the Israelite community that survived him is impossibly large if the Old Testament accounts[5] are taken literally but was certainly considerable.

There was a numerous enough group of Jews to make the strategically inspired sweep east and then north and west to invade Palestine, but it would seem that they were the tactical hammer to the anvil of a significant number of Jews who had remained behind in Palestine and made a sort of pincers movement to unite the forces of Jewry and impose themselves on the whole territory, the occupation of "the promised land."[6] There is considerable doubt about whether the Land of Goshen was in Egypt, and there are several somewhat different accounts of the progress of Abraham and his family toward or into Egypt.[7] The traditions of those Jews who did go down into Egypt and those who did not but awaited their returning and now distant cousins, bifurcated considerably, a fact that can be deduced by scrutiny of the Pentateuch, but which is not acknowledged in it.[8] The wandering Jews do

---

4 Genesis 46.
5 Numbers 26.
6 Genesis 12:8 et seq.
7 Genesis 12, 20, 26.
8 CAH, II, pp 359-360.

seem to have come by Kadesh, "the well of judgment."[9] It is not clear[10] whether the father-in-law of Moses, or Moses himself, procured assistance in fleeing Egypt. Here are invoked the ark,[11] the pillar of cloud and fire,[12] the angel,[13] and the Divine Presence.[14]

The story of the Golden Calf also arose.[15] The Levites rebelled against this cult of materialism, and its posterity has been a source of division in the Jewish community ever since. The worship of the Golden Calf, ascribed to both the first king of the schismatic north and to Aaron (brother of Moses), led to a second Covenant, when Moses broke the tables of the Decalogue (Commandments) and produced a more traditional edition of it. This caused the people to discard their jewelry and fineries.[16] This supposedly caused Moses to pitch the Tent of Meeting, not the Tabernacle, but a sanctuary guarded by Joshua. This was produced, it is said,[17] after Jehovah's refusal to accompany the heretical Jewish people. Then was the Ark made and the Tablets placed in it.[18] This is assumed to be the explanation for the self-forsaken jewelry's reallocation to the henceforth splendid Tabernacle.[19] Israel was partially composed of Edomites, but the leadership, Jacob and his family and wives, Leah and Rachel, appear to have been Aramaean.[20] The centuries-later distinction between Aramaean and Arab tribes east of the River Jordan was also rather fuzzy. It can be safely recorded that the subsequent torment and complexity of Jewish life and development are well presaged in the tangle of the accounts of their ancient forebears.

2. Philosophical and Theological Influence of the Early Jews

The gate cannot be closed on the semi-prehistoric elements of the Old Testament without a respectful look behind at the mighty power of much of what it attests—though much may be lore, it has been no less influential on the Western mind and evolution of the organization of Western Civilization, for that. Man grasped his role as a participant in an immeasurable environment and quickly and spontaneously submitted to worship of whatever authority there might be in the cosmos, given the presumed omnipotence and permanence of the creative and at least intermittently intervening force and the fragility of mere man. God was one and a little like a man contemplating a vast ant-hill, but with the authority of creation and the ability to judge each individual morally, and the apparent disposition to occasional Revelation.

---

9 Genesis 14:7.
10 Exodus 38, Deuteronomy 9:9.
11 Numbers 11:33.
12 Numbers 14:14.
13 Exodus 14:19; 33:34.
14 Exodus 33:14.
15 Exodus 32, Deuteronomy 9:20.
16 2 Kings 33:6, 32:2.
17 2 Kings 33:7-11.
18 Deuteronomy 10.
19 Exodus 15-31, 35-40.
20 Deuteronomy 36:5.

All this added, in this comparison, to man's superiority over the common, worthy ant. Man made, through the period purportedly described by the Old Testament, the distinction of what he knew from what he could not, imperfectly, of course, as ignorance can never be measured by the party that is ignorant. Obviously, as time progressed, more was learned in every field, though the effect of learning more was as much to enlighten men of the extent of their ignorance as to seem to approach the finite plenitude of knowledge.

The first great sense of man's role was a recognition that we are participating in some vast canvas, a perception that, as far as we can judge, is not appreciated by any other creature. Second, and indicative of the nature of discovery to reveal even greater proportions to the unknown than was brought to light, was the distinction between what lasts and what dies, and the virtues of procreation and spiritualism as, apart from their other satisfactions, a rebellion against death. Next came a symbolization between the cosmos and the world with the common trait and necessity of social organization and governance. This was first an attempted replication terrestrially of a presumed or ostensibly revealed cosmic organization. Second, which enters usually when societies disintegrate, whether from internal or external reasons, or both together, men tend to assume they have offended the cosmic order and that the forces of disintegration prevail, and reinforcement must be sought from other-worldly inspired insight and determination.

People must ultimately defer to terrestrial facts, at least practically, however inconvenient and disappointing. But in the embracing of symbolization that is completely intangible, there emerges "the rich flora, luxuriant, bewildering, frightening, and charming, of the tales about gods and demons and their ordering and disordering influences on the life of man and society."[21] The Old Testament led the way in chronicling man's acceptance of the absolutely unbridgeable gap between the human and the divine, apart, possibly, from supplication and in the hereafter. Thus did the tendency become heresy for exceptional men to incite the living, with varying degrees of resistance and spontaneity, to proclaim their leaders to be Gods.

And thus arose the immense cult and body of belief that the link between God and man was not broken, only altered to a regime of inanimate passage that could yet be assisted by supplication and the elevation heavenward by elections of the deceased to exalted status (e.g. and i.e., sainthood). When the full acceptance of this passage to a people in worshipful communion with God is made, as it was by the Jews, and then by the Christians, the impact on the world was an instrument of mass and even universal reconstitution. It was the unique achievement of the Jews to effect that step, which with Messianism could take hold of almost all mankind, intellectually and psychologically, and retain its intellectual and philosophical suzerainty for millennia, and perhaps forever. The Jews did not recognize the Messiah, when most of the ancient West ultimately believed that He had come and gone. But they composed and kept alive a story of the Creation and of the birth and progress of man, imperfect in all respects except legitimacy, to the present. For this, and for their failure to recognize what most Jews and most others in the West recognized as the Son of God when He came, the Jews have earned great homage, and have paid a

---

21 Voegelin, Eric, *Order and History*, p. 7.

back-breaking, almost terminal but never soul-destroying, price. We shall return often to the influence upon human history of this strain of imaginative monotheism.

3. The Jewish Struggle for Palestine

Following the circuitous return of the Jews from Egypt to Palestine (a brilliant if protracted strategic master-stroke by Moses), there was a great deal of skirmishing with the natives of Palestine, and successes and set-backs of the individual tribes of Israel. Many famous names and places were involved: Joshua, Ephraim, Benjamin, Gideon, Ammon, Joseph, Judah, Simeon, and Samson, and Bethel, Gilgal, Manasseh, Gilead, Dan, Beersheba, and Shiloh. None of this fabled activity, many elements of which can be verified, need concern us here, as internecine fluctuations of the Jewish tribes. The salient outcome was that the Jews, more or less in unity, established themselves in Palestine, inter-married with the locals fairly extensively and were entrenched atop and athwart the rich trade routes in all directions toward Egypt, Ethiopia, Phoenicia, Asia, Arabia, Europe, and Asia Minor. Saul attempted to exterminate the Gibbeonites.[22] David captured Jerusalem from the Jebusites,[23] and Solomon completed David's conquests and fortified many Israeli towns.[24]

The Song of Deborah,[25] the earliest known example of Jewish literature, is of uncertain authorship, doubtful accuracy, and has probably been altered from the original. It describes the disorder and unarmed condition of the Jews retreating from Egypt. Deborah and Barak (of northern Palestine) rallied the itinerant Israelis from their apathy and demoralization,[26] and they defeated those who would harass them en route. The kings of Canaan, under Sisera, tried to stop and repulse the Jews at Taanach, on the Kishon. The Jews won decisively, which is traditionally ascribed to the intervention of Jehovah as ruler of Israel.[27] Sisera allegedly fled and took refuge in the tent of a Kenite woman, who, after she had sedated him, slew him as he dozed by driving a steel spike through his head. This is portrayed as treachery[28] in the Song of Deborah (which means "bee" and Barak means "lightning" in ancient Hebrew). This victory opened the Promised Land to the Jews. There followed the prolonged effort to establish a kingdom of the Jews. Gideon of Oprah and the tribe of Manasseh (names that reverberate in modern American history and culture) raised the northern Jewish clans and cleared much of Palestine for Jewish occupancy and settlement. Gideon, who was rivaled as a contemporary Jewish hero by Ephraim, declined the kingship of Israel, which was proffered by his followers, because Jehovah was king.[29] When Gideon died of natural causes, Abimelech, the son of one of Gideon's Schechemite concubines, became king and massacred the

---

22 2 Samuel 21:2.
23 2 Samuel 5.
24 Kings 9:20, et seq.
25 Judges 5.
26 Judges 8:5-9.
27 Judges 5:26.
28 Judges 4:19 et seq.
29 Judges 8:23.

competing princes, except for Jotham, the youngest. Jotham denounced the usurpation of the "low-born thorn-bush" and proclaimed himself the "choice of the Cedars of Lebanon." A revolt occurred, the headship of the Jewish tribes involved swayed in the balance, and Abimelech appeared to prevail but was slain at Thebez. Jotham's curse was fulfilled, although as usual in these ancient internecine struggles, the vindicated party predeceased his chief enemy.

4. The Assault and Oppression of Israel by the Philistines

The Philistine (Palestinian) oppression followed.[30] The Philistines had iron weapons and had effectively disarmed the Israelites.[31] The surrounding and displaced tribes and peoples were not slow to try to undo the Jewish advance and entrenchment in this most strategic place. Canaanites and Palestinians beset the Jews (as they still do), and Israeli unity was sundered and restored in cycles, faithless suffering alternating with miraculous deliverances. The tribes separated acrimoniously and reunited, as necessary, though Judah was generally absent.[32] The tyranny of the Philistines was followed by the rampaging of Samson of the tribe of Dan, and the prophet Samuel of Ephraim, who rescued Israel from the Philistines.[33] These are among Israel's better-known saviours. It was of the nature of Jehovah, what became known as Yahwism, that Jehovah, God, could become a man and be the king with divine powers, and then depart again to be an intangible God. The Jews never claimed that their God was greater or less than the Gods of others in his virtue, but he was greater in his universality. The Jewish God tolerated the gods of others but was the God of all; the elaboration of this status naturally involved a good deal of theological explication. When the Jews prevailed, either Jehovah had descended to lead them within the body of their king, or the gods of the enemies were vexed with their own worshippers. When the political situation demanded, Jehovah, a little like some Egyptian concepts, could enter and occupy the mind of a Jewish leader, as he was deemed to have done with Moses when he led the Jews out of captivity and through the desert to within sight of the promised land. But that superhuman genius and spirit then departed but was never inaccessible.

It was the arrival of "the people of the sea," as the Egyptians called them, the beginnings of the Hellenization of Asia Minor, and the arrival simultaneously and after of the Philistines that reduced the Hittites to a few towns, such as Aleppo and Carchemish. This broke Egyptian control of Palestine, though the façade of Egyptian sovereignty continued for a time, as the Aegean migrants were not especially ambitious about setting up new states, only expelling those who were in their way and more or less gently asserting their dominion over the rest. It was the vacuum of the former authority of Egypt in the region that invited and facilitated the Jews in moving north and west to the occupancy of the land that had, they believed, been promised to them.

---

30 Judges 10.
31 Judges 5:8; Samuel 17:7.
32 Judges 5.
33 1 Samuel 9:12.

From 1190 B.C. on, one of the most strategically desirable regions in the world was a power vacuum with open doors to all points of the compass. This was the context for Israel's pursuit of its providentially imparted destiny, for the spread of Greek civilization, for the rise of Phoenicia, for the arrival of the Philistines, the resurrection of Babylon, and the return in strength of the Assyrians. The Philistines assimilated with the Canaanites, though they dominated them, and were less numerous than the Israelis, but better organized politically, until Israel was endowed with a Jahwist king, who, by his achievements and bearing, attained to the stature and moral authority of the divine. Gaza was the only one of the principal Philistine centres that continues to be a recognizable city today. The Jews and Philistines contended in what are now Israel, Palestine, Lebanon, and South Syria. The Philistine city states evolved into a small empire between 1150 and 1050 B.C. It is broadly sketched (and none too sympathetically) in Judges 13-16 with the stories of Samson. In the first phase, the Philistines spread over Judah, and the Dan (Samson's people) retreated to the north.

Peoples bunched together, vying for the earthly rewards of those who controlled the Middle East or key parts of it. They recognized the existence of the gods of neighbouring peoples, and although they did not believe in them, conferred a certain status on them. Yet Jehovah, though the Jews recognized the gods of other peoples, was held by the Jews to be universal, and the only god of Israel. In this there was not only monotheism, but the notion of the Chosen People, the Royal Priesthood, the One True God, the Messiah, and the "turgid experience of divine force."[34] Jehovah is generally thought to have directly animated Saul, but deserted him, as, the legend has arisen, the terrestrial Saul thought he, and not Jehovah, was the king. It required the threat of the extinction of Israel at the hands of the Philistines for the crystallization of this concept of Jehovah. Unfortunately, very little that is reliable is known of the rise of Saul. And even the reign of David, though there is no doubt that it occurred, rests mainly on the historically disputable accounts of the Old Testament.

In the first half of the Eleventh Century B.C., the Philistines fought with the tribes of Benjamin and Ephraim. This led to the Jewish national disaster, in which the Philistines captured the Ark, and the capital of the Jewish confederacy, Shiloh, was occupied and destroyed by the Philistines.[35] The Philistines ruled partly directly and partly through cooperative Jewish governors. Apparently, one person elevated to this role was David, who governed Judah, supposedly in the Palestinian interest. There was clearly great unrest, as the well-armed Philistines tried to disarm the Jews by deporting all blacksmiths and ironmongers.[36] The Aegean arrival of the original Philistines which threatened Israel with extinction was necessary to galvanize Israel to a fierce struggle for survival and integrality. The chieftains of the Jewish clans were inadequate to assure Israel's survival, and the need became urgent for a national saviour.

---

34 Voegelin, Eric, *Israel and Revelation*, p. 221.
35 Judges 15-17; 1 Samuel 4-6.
36 1 Samuel 7:19-22.

Saul founded the monarchy and routed Israel's enemies at first.[37] But he legendarily angered Jehovah, the ostensible king of Israel, and he was crushed by the avenging Philistines. There are royalist and non-royalist versions of the rise of the monarchy. The royalist version credits Jehovah (Yahweh) with the elevation as well as the destruction of Saul. According to this account, Saul's father, Kish, sent Saul out to recover two donkeys he had lost. Saul came upon the seer Samuel, who had been visited by Jehovah the day before and told to expect Saul, and to inform him that he was the savior of Israel from the Philistines, to anoint him and send him to Gibeah to overthrow the Philistines' monument to their conquest, the stele.[38] As Saul approached Gibeah, he encountered a band of musical prophets and Jehovah entered Saul and transformed him. This was the origin of his kingship; his anointment as the Messiah. Given the various fantastic elements of this chronicle, it is little wonder that another version of the rise of Saul arose, and there is an immense amount of Jewish legendary controversy over the entire question of the emergence of Saul.

The anti-royalist version of his rise is that Samuel was a prominent seer and revered prophet, who had effectively led a government of the tribes of Israel by theological and equitable judges. The cupidity of Samuel's sons caused the elders of Israel to approach Samuel and request the selection of a king, to govern justly, and a meeting of the clans and tribes gathered and a very complicated system of successive elections to narrow down the number of candidates occurs, and from this process, Saul emerged as the candidate-presumptive of Jehovah. According to this theory, Jehovah professes to feel slighted by the election of a king over his prophetic theocracy, but on Samuel's plea, pardons Israel and allows Saul to rule after the new king and the whole people have made a vow of submission and obedience to God (Yahweh-Jehovah).

Obviously, all of this has to treated with caution, but the most important practical result of the rise of Saul as a durable political development was the symbol of spiritual control of secular leadership. This led to various forms of divided rulership and fused capacities in monarchs as religious leaders, which continues yet in the status of the British monarch as supreme governor of the established church and of the Roman Catholic pontiff as head of the diminutive Vatican state. In the Seventeenth Century, the British King James I (uniting of the thrones of Scotland and England) asserted his right and duty not to descend to the guilt of Saul and to act as "head of the tribes of Israel" in correcting the errors of his people. In elevating a king, the problem arose of whether Israel had ceased to be the chosen people of Jehovah. Related problems persist in Israeli politics, society, and Jewish theology. Israel did continue, more or less, on the path to traditional nationhood until the Prophetic Revolt in the Eighth Century B.C.

5. The Kingdom of Israel, Saul, and David

It is alleged that Saul, while victorious against the Moabites, Ammonites,

---

37 1 Samuel 14:47-51.
38 1 Samuel 9:1-16; 10:1-9.

Edomites, Philistines, and Amalekites, failed to carry out the word of Jehovah as transmitted by Samuel, who continued as the Jewish religious leader, to kill all of the Amalekites. (He killed all but the king, but that exception supposedly alienated Jehovah and the conditions of his assumption of the secular kingship.) This produced the condition of the charismatic war leader who loses his charisma.

Saul had initially been impressed by David, son of Jesse, a Bethlehem landowner, and a friend of Saul's son Jonathan, who was a successful warrior, because of David's talent as a harpist. He sometimes attended Saul's court by invitation, still a shepherd for his father, and his harp-playing placated Saul, who had moments of acute tension. Saul gave him his daughter by marriage, on David's production of an adequate number of Philistine foreskins to betoken their death in battle.[39] David became a popular hero when he was the only person who accepted the invitation of the Philistine warrior Goliath to single combat and felled him with one projectile from his slingshot. A popular song was "Saul has slain his thousands and David his ten thousands," and Saul became progressively more jealous of David, and set out, first to send him on dangerous missions from which he might not return, and then in hot pursuit himself, to kill him. (David would use the same tactic himself, sending someone he wanted killed on a dangerous mission—Uriah the Hittite, because David coveted his wife, Bathsheba. Uriah was killed and David took his widow as one of his eight wives, i.e., harem members.) David evaded Saul and then confronted him and persuaded Saul to accept reconciliation.

But while Saul had been chasing David, his kingdom had been invaded by the Philistines, and he moved to repulse them. On the eve of the Battle of Mount Gilboa, he sought guidance from the witch of Endor, who reminded him of Samuel's prophecy that he would lose his kingdom. So he did, at Gilboa, where the Philistines practically annihilated the Israeli army, and Saul perished. His son Jonathan, a much admired historic and folkloric figure for his lack of envy of his friend David, perished with him in total defeat. Saul is deemed to have ruled from about 1020 to 1004, B.C. David assumed the throne by popular acclamation, and it fell to him to lead the resistance to the Philistines, who now controlled all Palestine west of the Jordan River.

David appeased the leader of the southern enemy, Gibeon, and handed over seven members of Saul's family for the vengeance of the Gibeonites.[40] Impenetrable hyper-pre-Byzantine complexities are unreliably alluded to in the scriptures between Shiloh and Bethel and involving elements of the tribes of Judah and Benjamin south of the Joseph tribes and an Edomite (descendants of Esau)—Reubenite (descendants of Jacob and Eleah)—Judean bloc of tribes.

The young King David emerged to defeat the Philistines, and free Israel. There comes now the flood-tide of ancient Jewish history, with the epics of David and Solomon, father and son. As we have seen, he was a friend of Saul's son Jonathan. They became so intimate, it was said[41] that Jonathan "loved David as himself." It is unlikely, however, that their relations were ever at the point conjectured by French novelist

---

39 1 Samuel 18:18-27
40 2 Samuel 21.
41 1 Samuel 17:1.

André Gide, that Jonathan was an effeminate quasi-sex slave of the mighty David (a thought more likely induced by Gide's own proclivities than by any real insight).

Rather, he is remembered for all time as a loyal and devoted friend, with no homo-erotic implications. Saul became concerned that David and Jonathan might try to usurp the throne, and turned upon them both, at one point seeking to put Jonathan to death for violating Saul's prohibition against eating before sunset when he consumed some honey[42] and on another occasion throwing a javelin at him.[43] Jonathan and David both fled, and made a covenant at their last meeting. Jonathan was reconciled with Saul, and as they both died at the Battle of Mount Gilboa,[44] David was the natural and popular successor. Proclaimed and installed as king of Judah at Hebron, David led an Israel that was both north and south of Jerusalem, a Canaanite enclave in the midst of his territory. Jerusalem was an anomaly, as well as an ancient goal of the Jews. David fought his way north and captured Jerusalem from the Jebusites in about 1000 B.C. David made Jerusalem the Jewish capital, and began the construction of the Temple, the long-sought climax of the affirmation of Judaism, and this work was taken in hand and completed under David's equally renowned son, Solomon. Jerusalem is a natural fortress site on elevated hills, and it formed the natural centre of the Jewish state.

He made it the capital of Israel, a fact from which an immense torrent of human history flows yet.

For almost a century (c. 1020—c. 931 B.C.), under Saul, David, and Solomon, Jehovah was present, and it was widely and is proverbially believed, ruled through these very famous kings. Thereafter, he was not, and the Prophets who began as diverse national ecstatics, eclipsed the kings in the chronicles of the Old Testament and, as far as can be ascertained, in contemporary opinion and practice. The great Jewish theologian Maimonides wrote in the Mishneh Torah of the "optional wars" conducted by kings "to enhance their greatness and prestige." But the wars were not optional if Israel was to survive, and it was in these circumstances that the roles of the terrestrial kings were assumed.

During his difficulties with Saul, David had found refuge for a time in Gath, and once he had enthroned himself, his Hittite guard was his ultimate elite unit of military security. He also recruited those "in distress, in debt, and everyone who was discontented...he was captain of...about 400 men."[45] David certainly promoted his cronies and lieutenants well beyond the standards of objective merit. Saul's entourage was packed with members of the tribe of Benjamin, abjuring them that "the son of Jesse" (David) would not make them all landowners and army commanders.[46] David appears to have exempted his home province of Judah from the taxes he imposed on the rest of Israel and to have stuffed the ranks of his state with cronies and been rather profligate with public money in the enrichment of his entourage.

David built a splendid palace and court. He did retain Saul's cousin, Abner, for a

---

42 1 Samuel 14:24.
43 1 Samuel 20:33.
44 1 Samuel 31.
45 1 Samuel 22:2.
46 1 Samuel 22:7.

time, as his principal general, and accepted the establishment of Saul's son Ishbaal as the Israeli king east of the Jordan in Mahanaim. After seven years, there was the inevitable falling out between the house of Saul and King David; Abner was murdered by David's chief general, Joab, the Benjaminites murdered Ishbaal, and in person delivered his severed head to David as an act of adherence and obeisance. David righteously executed them as murderers of Ishbaal, retained Joab in place, and was accepted as king of a united Israel without further bloodshed.

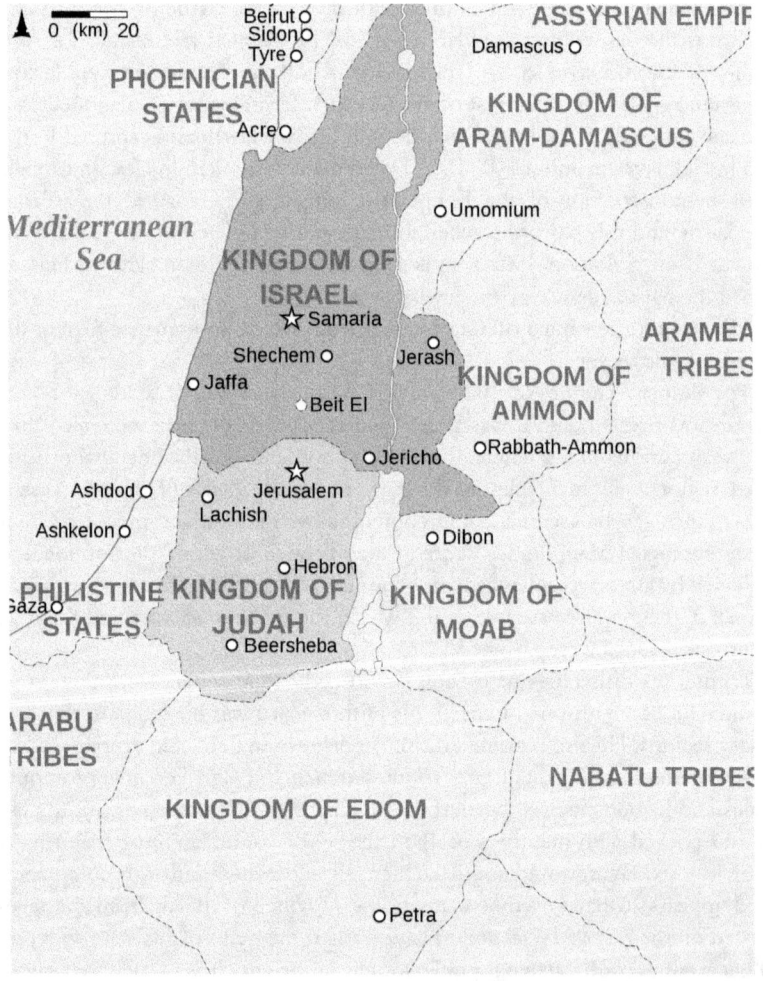

Kingdoms of Israel and Judah

David ruled from approximately 1004 to 966 B.C., and he gradually extended his realm to include Edom in the east and Damascus in the north. The basic problem that he faced was that Palestine had poor soil, little seacoast, and the Jews were not a seafaring people. The territory, though at the crossroads of the world, was too poor to sustain a rich court and a happy people, as could the well-irrigated river kingdoms of Egypt and Mesopotamia. David's personality, his victories, handsome appearance, prowess as a womanizer, virtuosity as a musician and showman, all made him popular, but in time, his largesse to his entourage and his own tribe created a considerable souring of the well of public approval.

There is much conjecture that there was a widespread reaction against the treatment of Uriah the Hittite, and the king's allegedly cavalier attitude toward the death of Uriah and Bathsheba's child. David emerges from as much analysis as the very thin reliable accounts of him furnish, as a rather callous and amoral person, at some dramatic remove from the fearless and righteous and artistic youthful hero and model king that has curled up the chimney from the Biblical lore composed many centuries ex post factum.

And as generally happens in dynastic matters, the heirs and relatives of the deposed, in this case the house of Saul, always lurked, sinister and vindictive, in the shadows of ancient Israel. The legitimacy of the Davidic line was compromised by a series of violent or otherwise untoward events: the murder of David's eldest son, Amnon, by another son, Absalom;[47] the emergence of a faction led by Adonijah, David's fourth son;[48] the rise of a harem candidate in Solomon who was anointed by David as his heir; and the murder of Adonijah after David's death.[49] David preserved his claim to the succession to Saul by keeping Michal (Saul's daughter) prominent in his harem, and was a skilled political manipulator of the disparate factions of Israel and Judah, of different tribes, clans and dynasties, but his rule was always fragile and was maintained chiefly by his political guile backed by his intimidating eminence as a military commander and even, as Goliath discovered, a single combat warrior. Withal, though there were many challenges and commotions, David maintained his alleged pact with Jehovah, and held himself out to be a pious guardian of God's grant to him of rulership over the chosen people. He was undoubtedly a talented, formidable, and clever leader.

In the conquest of Jerusalem, David faced, like all the conquerors in the Middle East, the task of synthesizing the religion he espoused with that of the Canaanite occupants of the newly conquered territory. Jerusalem's god had essentially the qualities of Yahweh, but was deemed to be the supreme God of the universe, "the summus deus of a cosmological empire."[50] David effected this, and the 103rd to 110th Psalms, the Psalter, are known as the Imperial Psalms and date from Davidic times and are a testament to his unification of the priestly and kingly powers of a king acting in accord with the rule of Jehovah—the Yahweh of Israel with the Jebusite El Elyon. This was what became known as a berith—the transmutation of a great human figure into the agent of Yahweh and was known as the David Covenant in Jewish religious tradition, succeeding the Sinai Covenant of Moses. Even in the King James Christian Bible of the Seventeenth Century A.D., the Hebrew expression "Yahweh is king" is translated as "The Lord reigneth," perpetuating the boxed

---

47 2 Samuel 12:15-18.
48 1 Kings 1:5-10.
49 1 Kings 1:11-53; 2:12-25.
50 Voegelin, Eric, op. cit. p. 273.

compass of the monarch's relationship with the Almighty. The Jews had already, in the time of David, developed very substantially, both structurally and laterally, from their origin as nomadic tribes. They were now a well-organized imperial nation with a sophisticated culture that had broadened ethnically by the absorption of the Canaanites and the people of Judah.

6. King Solomon

Despite all the skullduggery in his family and harem, David was succeeded, as he ultimately intended, by his equally renowned son, Solomon. David as king was represented by some of his more enthusiastic followers as Messianic, which meant sufficiently divine that he fulfilled and united in himself the position of King of Israel, with the powerful tradition that that role must remain empty of human claimants, since the kingship of Israel was the role of Jehovah Himself. Whether David himself advanced this theory is not clear, but it was in any case an opportune political science initiative to unify the candidates for the throne in a single human, whose successor would maintain this temporal and spiritual unity.

Solomon, whether from reasons of faith or political astuteness, treated the great high priest Zadok with formidable deference, assumedly to appease those who thought (like the assassins of Julius Caesar nine hundred years later) that he was putting on the airs of a deity. Solomon's fiscal and artistic efforts on behalf of the Temple were to some extent replicated twenty-five centuries later in the creation of St. Peter's Basilica, and may be said, on behalf of the Pagans, to have been contemplated also by Hitler and his architect Speer, in the mighty monuments of the planned city of Germania, to be superimposed on Berlin in gigantic proportions. Solomon was somewhat notorious for his personal extravagance, as well as his high judicious intelligence.

According to legend, Solomon was David's second son with Bathsheba. His first son having allegedly died in infancy as a punishment of David for sending Bathsheba's husband, Uriah the Hittite, to his death, and Solomon was the reward for David's repentance. (These legends assumed a significance regardless of whether there was any truth to them.) He became David's favourite son after Absalom's treachery was exposed and punished. A further coup was attempted by another son, Adonijah, but was foiled and Solomon executed his brother.[51] Adonijah had been supported by David's longstanding senior general, Joab, whom Solomon also executed at the start of his reign. There is plenty of support for Solomon's historic status as a prudent and perceptive judge and ruler, but he also had to be severe at times, and rather ruthless in keeping the divisive forces of his society in check, especially under the pressure of his own extravagance. Solomon was only about fifteen when he became king but moved as deftly as Octavian after the murder of Julius Caesar, or as Stalin after the incapacitation of Lenin, and his political sagacity helped create the young king's reputation for high intelligence and judgment. He purged his father's entourage, quite summarily executing and banishing those he suspected, and packed the ranks with people he considered reliable. His judgment was generally vindicated.

---

51 1 Kings 1:5-53; 2:13-23.

Solomon considerably expanded his army, and greatly expanded David's commercial relations with the king of Phoenicia, Hiram of Tyre, effectively establishing a joint venture in which Hiram's mariners (with a Jewish contingent in one of that extremely talented people's few ventures into maritime activities) journeyed to Ophir and other exotic places in India or Africa, bringing back gold, silver, sandalwood, pearls, ivory, apes, and peacocks. Hiram handled the transport and Solomon the distribution. According to First Kings,[52] he collected forty-thousand pounds of gold from this source in one year ($1.35 billion in contemporary money), with only a fractional cost of goods and services. After completing the Temple where Yahweh would dwell and the Ark repose, he built an immense and sumptuous palace for himself, a formidable defensive wall around Jerusalem, and many aqueducts and other noteworthy construction (though no remains of his Temple or palace have been discovered).

In no previous era had the Middle East's status of world crossroads been so diligently exploited, as commercial relations extended through much of the Mediterranean and Black and Red Seas, and East Africa and Arabia and India. Solomon was so renowned that he received a visit from the Queen of Sheba, an opulent monarch of a trans-Red Sea kingdom covering what is now Yemen, Djibouti, Eritrea, Somalia, and part of Saudi Arabia and Ethiopia. He proved to be a king of both luxurious tastes and humanistic instincts. It was claimed that Solomon had seven-hundred wives and three-hundred concubines; even allowing for greater exaggeration than usual in the legendary accounts of these ancient times, he must have had an immense and opulent court, an astounding number of accessible and generally submissive women, and a huge stable of fine horses and chariots. He married the Egyptian pharaoh's daughter for political reasons and lined the front ranks of court ladies with other foreigners. Naturally, some of the king's habits attracted criticism, and Jewish scriptures are very critical of him morally, while respecting his wisdom and even his meritocratic grandiosity, up to a point. In First Kings 11, he is criticized for his polygamy, especially with non-Jews and resulting ecumenism, and idolatry, and he is censored in First Kings 10:14 for violating Deuteronomy.[53]

David and Solomon, stripped of all unsubstantiated legend, stand as talented and compelling kings. It must be said that their conquests and consolidations were in some measure facilitated by the decline of the neighbouring peoples and their regimes, especially the Egyptians. But the Jews waited their turn and took their chance when it came. David was a great leader who united and strengthened and expanded the Jewish territory and their realm, took Jerusalem, rescued the Jews from the danger of the Philistines, and solidified the legend of the Jewish Yahwist kingship, which was incubating and very precarious at the end of Saul's life and reign.

If David established Israel, it was Solomon who was recognized and courted by the world. He built a navy and extended Jewish influence to the Euphrates, a limit it has never approached since. "Judah and Israel dwelt safely, every man under his vine and under his fig tree, from Dan even to Beersheba, all the days of Solomon."[54] He

---

52 1 Kings 1:10-14.
53 1 Kings 10:14; 17:16-17.
54 1 Kings 4:21-25.

was a great entrepreneur, and not only the maritime trade developed with the seafaring Phoenicians, but such discoveries as King Solomon's mines (generally thought to be Edomite copper mines near Eilat in the Persian Gulf). Enterprise rather than oppression and embezzlement were the main source of his legendary wealth. Solomon remains one of the few prominent historical personalities renowned for both his wealth accumulation, and culture and scholarship, a status aspired to by some modern kings and lions of finance, such as J.P. Morgan. Solomon epitomized the traditional criteria of male success—political power, personal wealth, high scholarship, a demiurgic sex life, and general popularity. He is a Jewish prophet, despite the prophets' wariness of him, and a senior prophet in Islam, where his name, Suleiman, has been borne by some of the greatest figures of Muslim history.

Solomon's consorting with foreign women, for whom he built religious edifices in Jerusalem, and his broadening of foreign contacts for the Jewish people, did not weaken what had always been a tribal religion, but the prophets were always wary of dilution of the Covenant. The prophets were essentially preachers, and there have been few preachers in history as successful. Amos, Isaiah, and Jeremiah had denounced officialdom and proclaimed that all men were equal, and by the end of Solomon's reign, the Jewish prophets were armed with arguments against an omnipotent king but armed also with the ultimately irresistible argument for a universal, merciful, just, stern but forgiving God, risen from the originally local cult of Yahweh.

Legend would hold that Solomon would be punished for his extravagance, materialism, and exaggerated and polyglot sex life, by the secession of Judah from Israel when he died and the loss of ten of the twelve tribes of Israel in that schism. They would not accept Solomon's son, Rehoboam, whose authority was accepted in Judah, but the northern kingdom of Israel went its way, taking ten of the tribes of Israel, led by the Samaritans; the Jewish world became a fragmented and vulnerable theocracy, and assumed a secondary and almost invisible role for nearly a thousand years, and was revived in its importance by its prescience, or at least credibility, in prophecy, not for any secular distinction.

The status of Saul as a rallying figure in Jewish history, of Jonathan as a saintly and brave prince, of David as warrior, man of culture, and ruler, and of Solomon as consolidator of church and state of a united historic people, and permanent exemplar of judicious rule and majesty; remains, after more than three thousand years, one of the best-known and most brilliant chapters of a few associated individuals in human history. It is probably rivaled only, if at all, in the human pantheon, by the founders and conservators of the United States of America (Washington, Franklin, Jefferson, Hamilton, Adams, Madison, Jackson, and Lincoln).

The literature created by historians and prophets in the monarchic century of Saul, David, and Solomon (1020-931 B.C.) was able to survive in Judah even after ethnic Israel had been dispersed and scattered. A unique path of the Jews of death and survival was begun that has continued to contemporary times. The Yahwist confederacy of Canaan gave rise to the charismatic kingship of Israel, and that gave way to a reassertion of the priesthood. In the post-monarchical Jewish era, as is clear from all accounts of the life of Jesus Christ a thousand years later, the high priests had usurped the position of the Israeli royal or secular authorities and ran the temple in a rather unecclesiastical manner. The priesthood deposed the kings, and the Messiah debunked the priests. But the charismatic royal tradition, though it would lapse for a millennium, never vanished, but rather sired the expectation of the Messiah, the Godly king made man. The Jews had fashioned a religious conception, which when convincingly personified, though it was not specifically Jewish, would uplift and shake the whole world.

7. Other Contemporary Middle Eastern Peoples

A brief summary from the fragments of authenticated history that are available should be made to outline the evolution and condition of the neighbors of Israel. At the end of the Fifteenth Century B.C., the Mitanni kingdom (largely influenced and penetrated by the Hittites) was the leading northern state in what is now the Middle East and was beating back the Assyrians into what is now Syria, Turkey, and Iraq. Assyrians were fierce, and their fortunes depended, over many centuries, on the strength of their military leadership and the condition of their military hardware and war-making tactics. Their permanent objective was to fight their way through to the Mediterranean and help themselves to maritime and crossroads trading prosperity. The quest for wealth and dependence on military leadership command ability and weaponry are not objectives or factors of success that have evolved unrecognizably these thirty-five hundred years. The Mitannians and Hittites fell back in the Thirteenth Century B.C., the Assyrians and Babylonians reasserted themselves in the Twelfth Century, and the Assyrians wore down the forces standing between themselves and the Mediterranean. In between the supremacy of the Mitanni and Hittites in the north in the Fifteenth Century and the Babylonian and Assyrian revivals three hundred years later, Syria and Palestine were left comparatively undisturbed and it was the first golden age of Israel.

It was in this period that the Phoenicians and Philistines entered known history. The Phoenicians are generally but not universally thought to have migrated from the Persian Gulf, especially Bahrain, to the Eastern Mediterranean shore. The Philistines are generally but not with certainty thought to have been Aegeans who landed in Egypt and also gravitated to the Eastern Mediterranean and gave their name to Palestine and were the greatest local enemy of the early Israelites.

Egypt entered a period of decline at this time, and we shall record the principal developments of all of these major groups in order. Ikhnaton had floated his idea of monotheism, but did not try to promulgate it officially in Egypt. The wealth and power of the priests on behalf of all the Gods of Egypt gained strength as the power of the pharaohs after Ramses III (1186-1155 B.C.) declined. The Phoenicians and numerous maritime Philistines established themselves in the Egyptian port cities and the Nile Delta. Northern Egypt was prosperous, semi-autonomous, and of diverse ethnicity as the pharaonic Egyptian state receded up the Nile. At roughly the same time, the Iron Age had an impact in Syria as profound as the Industrial Revolution had on Nineteenth Century (A.D.) Britain.

The Philistine influence in Israel displaced the Egypto-Hittites, who, as uncircumcised (a defining distinction in these times), comparative outsiders, were gradually expelled or subordinated in Israel. Phoenicians occupied the coastal cities of what are now Israel, Lebanon, and Syria, and the Philistines (very roughly-Palestinians) rivalled the Jews in Canaan, Judea, Israel, and what has intermittently been known as Palestine. Both the Phoenicians and Philistines are deemed to be Semitic peoples, and their progress will be summarized shortly. Our purpose here is to get all the relevant groupings, peoples, states, and coherent tribal or semi-national entities and kingdoms up to a starting line of about 1000 B.C., when the political progress or fate of all can be recounted with relative confidence.

The Phoenicians generally held the seacoast, with intermittent Israeli and Philistine windows on the Mediterranean. The Philistines were usually anchored to the sea at Gaza and their territory (then as now) proceeded inland from there. Phoenicians, Philistines, and Jews, though uncoordinated between each other and even among themselves, were all engaged in mastering and even expunging Egyptian influence in what is now Israel and Lebanon. When the Israelites, fleeing Egypt by their circular route, entered Palestine from the east, they were not only reunited with the Jews who had never gone to Egypt proper, but began mingling and inter-marrying, at first somewhat peaceably, with the Philistines. This may be taken as the beginning of the Palestinian and even Israeli-Arab problem, and lent it the initial character of a civil war, always and ever since, rendered more intense and implacable by the ancient intimacy of the combatant protagonists.[55] From surviving accounts, we can detect the fluctuating relationships between Jews and Philistines, and the division, sharper even than rural-urban differences of perspective in modern times, between the high-walled, relatively cosmopolitan city-dweller, and the nomadic or agrarian country in, by the standards of the place and time, what were wide open spaces. There seem to be some natural phenomena that lend very measured partial credence to inveterate traditions, such as the crossing of the Red Sea on foot (unusually low water), and the fall of Jericho's walls before Joshua (an earthquake), but as in many areas, we have no ability to demarcate between outright fiction, partial fact, and the miraculous. The fuzzy historical unreliability of the origins of deep-seated Middle Eastern problems naturally makes their current resolution even more difficult. The same real estate has been occupied by too many peoples too historically intertwined, still aggressively claiming ownership with some historic rights to uphold.

8. The Disunion and Subjugation of The Jews

During the lengthy gestation of this world-shaking cataract of events and personalities, the Jews fell on evil days. Judah was left with Jerusalem and the south and the Davidic dynasty. But Israel set out to organize itself as a state in the northern two thirds of what had been Solomon's empire. Jeroboam had been a capable young official under Solomon, who delegated him to supervise the construction of one of the forts of Jerusalem. He fell in with malcontents complaining about Solomon's extravagance but was denounced and fled to Egypt until Solomon died in 931 B.C. Jeroboam returned and gained control of a secessionist Israel, after Solomon's suc-

---

55 Deuteronomy 23:16 et seq., Judges 3:5-7; Psalms 106:34 et seq.

cessor, Rehoboam, declined the request for reduced taxation made on behalf of the northern tribes. Rehoboam, counselled by his cronies to show no weakness, instead promised to raise taxes and collect them with more frequent floggings of reluctant taxpayers. Rehoboam managed to maintain his throne for eighteen years in what was not a happy or united kingdom, and was succeeded by his son Abijah. Jeroboam successfully led the northern tribes out of the Davidic empire, and he continued on his throne, which he placed at Sechem.

The internecine struggle between the tribes and clans began again with rejuvenated vigour and bitterness. Jeroboham's son, Nadab, lasted only two years before he was assassinated by Baasha of Issachar, who systematically murdered all of Jeroboam's surviving family and reigned uneasily and fractiously for a little over twenty years. He was succeeded by his son Elah, but he was also assassinated after two years by another military faction leader, Zimri, general of chariots. But his commander, Omri, disapproved this enterprise and seized power himself, Zimri perishing in the flames that engulfed the official palace, after only one week of ostensible rule. The Omride dynasty was comparatively successful, prevailed in a civil war of four years (in a country only about twenty miles by fifty miles), and then continued for another forty years, to 841 B.C. The Omrides were then overthrown and mainly executed by another general, Jehu. His dynasty proved more durable, lasting until 747, before it was overthrown. The whole tumultuous epoch reached a climax of ephemeral regimes violently crushed from within, the official leadership being renewed by ever more frequent armed palace insurrections and righteous executions at a steadily brisker pace until the whole enterprise was abruptly reduced to dust by the grim tornado of the returning Assyrians in 721 B.C. The northern tribes were effectively evicted and exiled by the Samaritans in the Eighth Century B.C., and Judah professed to be the heir and continuator of all Israel, though Jerusalem was in the hands of the Samaritans.

9. The Jews in the Late Persian Empire

The Jews were ostensibly slumbering under Persian rule. During the lengthy Persian occupation of what is now Israel, the Jews were gathered in part of the fifth satrapy in the Great King's empire and did nothing to incite external interest. Sharing the satrapy were Palestine, Syria, Phoenicia, and Cyprus. Herodotus did not mention them once and contemporary writers took no notice of them. This was the period of post-exilic Judaism, which, while it passed unnoticed at the time, would have an immense impact on the future of the whole world. The Pentateuch emerged as the ark of Mosaic history, the time and covenants and commandments of Moses, the beginning of the history of Judaism from which came Christianity, with the emergence of a plausible Messiah, and even of Islam.

The books of Ezra and Nehemiah are our principal record between the capture of Jerusalem by the Babylonian Nebuchadnezzar in 586 B.C. (Chapter 3) and the return of the Jews from their Biblical captivity to Jerusalem under Cyrus I of Persia (538 B.C.). Heggai and Zechariah, c. 520 B.C., reveal that the number of returning exiles was small and that the Davidic Zerubbabel headed a much more significant political and religious movement than had long been perceived. Our next historic glimpse of the Jews comes sixty years later from Ezra, who was (458 B.C.), allowed by Artaxerxes to return to Jerusalem accompanied by a body of lay and clerical followers, with expensive adornments for the temple, and considerable powers to rule in the name of the Great King. Ezra appears to have persuaded the Great King of the rightful and reliable attachment of the Jews to their homeland in and around Jerusalem, as Moses did with Pharaoh.

Ezra returned as a pioneer, with authority to reestablish Judaism, instruct the people about it with the Torah as his text and to appoint judges for all Jews "beyond the river," which presumably meant between the Jordan River and the Mediterranean. This generosity of the King of Persia is in stark contrast to the fiercely hostile attitude to neighboring groups, Syrians, Phoenicians, Egyptians, and others, and also contrasts with the hostility of the Persian Xerxes, and the escape from the massacre during the reign of Xerxes that was engineered by Esther, Xerxes' wife. According to the Old Testament, Esther turned the tables on the Great King's adviser, Haman, who had erected a tall gallows on which to hang Jews for banquet entertainment, but which was used instead, after a formidable bridal forensic performance by Esther, for hanging Haman instead. The Jews, allegedly, were permitted to kill anyone who was tormenting them, and they killed tens of thousands of hostile neighboring groups (but, obviously, not Persians). This image is renowned, and George Washington famously said he wished to send much of the Continental Congress to Haman's gallows for execution.

To recent times, Persian attitudes to the Jews have oscillated wildly: the late Shah was most friendly to them and the subsequent regime of the ayatollahs extremely hostile. It has never been clear whether there was any sectarian aspect or political tactics behind the actions of Xerxes and Artaxerxes. In Esther's time, Xerxes was contending with an insurrection in Babylon, and may have wished to be conciliatory to other elements in the empire while he administered suitable punishment to Babylon (a city frequently in need of strict correction, even from its own rulers).

Ezra's mission was a zealous one, and not entirely successful. He began by expelling from the Jewish community any non-Jewish wives. This was a Jewish problem then, as it remains, but Ezra's solution to it was so draconian, it roused great resistance. (Draco was a Greek legislator of the Sixth Century—Chapter 4.) As Ezra was wrestling with the reassertion of Jewish tradition, Nehemiah was struggling to rebuild and fortify Jerusalem. Nehemiah was the cup-bearer of the Great King at Susa, and it is rumored, a eunuch. But he was very distressed by the ruined and ransacked physical state of Jerusalem, and gained Artaxerxes' approval, in 445, to rebuild the city. In just seven weeks, he had urged the civil population, in a torrent of energy, to rebuild the outer walls. The Ammonite Tobiah and the Arabian Gashnu were, with Sanballat, the leaders of the anti-Ezra liberals and Samaritans. They accused him of bribing prophets to hail him as the king.[56]

At this point, the suspenseful chronicle is interrupted, and Ezra reappears, having successfully imposed a stern religious practice. This was drawn up in a proclaimed covenant requiring the avoidance of intermarriage, and of trading on the Sabbath,

---

56 Nehemiah 8-10.

the observance of the Sabbatic year, and the forgiveness of debts every seven years (which would reduce any economy to chaos) and regulations for the maintenance of the temple. The collective determination was expressed "never to forsake the house of our God."[57] Nehemiah appears to have prevailed, as Jerusalem was repopulated and building continued energetically. Their determination entrenched in the Deuteronomic Law,[58] the Ammons, Moabites, and other strangers were put at arm's length and segregated. The Persian influence that conferred additional rights for women was fiercely opposed by Ezra, in keeping with Jewish tradition. Ezra was authorized by Artaxerxes to revisit Jerusalem in 433 and was appalled by rampant intermarriage, the profanation of the Sabbath, and the deemphasis of the Hebrew language. Also, the High Priest Eliashib was married to an Ammonite who had been installed in a temple chamber.

Nehemiah was also generous to the poor and ran an efficient and completely honest administration throughout his twelve years and seems to have been popular and was admired by Malachi. Nehemiah's rule ended with the particularly acute split between the Judeans and Samaritans. Not long after his time, the Samaritan leader Sanballat tried to heal the schism by marrying his daughter to the prominent Judean priest Manasseh, but this enflamed further resentment, and the Samaritan community of Jerusalem withdrew to Samaria. The Samaritans did eventually accept the Pentateuch, the legal books of the Old Testament (and again the first five books of the Torah).

Nehemiah was an ambitious collector of ancient documents, including many letters of David, a forerunner of Judas Maccabaeus, the great Judaic collector of books, scrolls, and letters. There is a great deal of conjecture, embellishment, and exaggerated lore, as well as outright gaps in Jewish history in the latter Persian days. There is fragmentary evidence that Artaxerxes stopped the reconstruction of Jerusalem for a time, when anti-Jewish advisers told him of the potential of Jews for trouble-making and rebelliousness. Certainly, when the sections of the Persian Empire started to come unstuck and revolt, Judea cannot have been completely unaffected, though the Jews liked the Persians better than their immediate neighbours. The revolt of Evagoras in 389, the uprisings in Phoenicia and Palestine that followed, and the tumultuous events in Egypt up to 342, would have generated repercussions all around the Jewish world. A substantial Jewish historical narrative only really resumes with the Maccabees (Antiochus Epiphanes), in 175 B.C., and the Hasmonaeans who followed them.

Phoenician maritime aptitudes gave cities, especially Tyre and Sidon, a particular influence. Tyre had ancient connections with Jerusalem. Sidon was generally more powerful, other than following the severe crushing of their revolt in 345-344 B.C. Sidon was a larger, more cosmopolitan, and more philhellene city. By the mid-Fourth Century B.C., Arabs were becoming more prominent and are frequently mentioned in narratives of the time. They steadily infiltrated most of the Levant and Syria and ultimately Egypt. A tight political connection between Judah and Samaria tended to aggravate the frictions between them, but they were both threatened and crowded

---

57 Deuteronomy 23:3-6.
58 Joshua 15:13; Numbers 27:21.

at times by their Phoenician, Syrian, and Philistian neighbours, especially in Edom, the focal point of the richest trading routes, in south Palestine and around Gaza.

Nehemiah's Judah is a small unit between Jericho, Keilah, Beth-sur, and Mizpah; it seems that this was a truncated Israel, reduced to its tightest, most rugged, and defensible core. It appears that Nehemiah's Jerusalem, in 445, had suffered some recent natural disaster. It became the custom, and this was almost certainly not the first occurrence of it, to attribute such grievous misfortunes, natural calamities, and onslaughts from other peoples to the sinfulness, irreligiosity of the people, the habitual improvisation of zealous clergy (and in recent times, ecologists). In Jewish tradition, the Jews' general confession to shortcomings led to Jehovah's intervention and then promise of a redeemer. Edomite aggression against Israel is identified as evidence that Jehovah hated Esau and loved Jacob.

Judah at the time of Nehemiah and after was quite decimated and was buttressed by the Edomites including Caleb and Jeremeel. It appears that Edom attacked Judah after its devastations, possibly under the influence of the Nabataeans, and reduced Judah to the borders outlined, and had Abraham in their custody (in Hebron). Only the patronage of Jehovah, the subject of much supplication, sustained the morale of Judah in these testing times, travails that seemed not to spare the Jews for long throughout three thousand years.

The Edomite Caleb seems to have been more important than he is portrayed by those chroniclers who emphasize the primacy of the Ephraimite Joshua, himself subordinate to the high priest.[59] In reward for his faith in Yawveh, Caleb was promised Judah as it was when he arrived there from Edom, while the pagan interlopers who had diluted the faith and piety, as well as the ethnicity of Judah, were anathema. The triumph of the high priest Zadok over the corrupt and unfaithful Levites[60] is a central part of Jewish lore and faith. The prophets came to believe, for some time, and stipulated in Deuteronomic literature that Jerusalem was the only place where Jehovah could be worshipped. This contributed to the very high exclusiveness of Judaism: it shaped the biblical accounts of the Jewish people but did not ultimately contain the jurisdictional ambitions of the Jews.

Jewish exclusivity came into conflict with the acknowledgement, and then the assertion, that Yahweh was not only the god of all activity, that he was not the god of Israel alone,[61] and that he was greatly admired by the Gentiles.[62] The Persian worship of a heavenly god to some extent smoothed the way forward for the Jewish universal god among the Persian dominated peoples. The whole idea of every community having a god for every function was bound to come to grief before much more time had elapsed.

The Semites in general, and perhaps the Jews most of all among them (though the Lebanese Christians of modern times were challengers), were highly motivated and financially motivated—their religion was connected with their financial apti-

---

59 Ezekiel 44:6-16.
60 Isaiah 65:10.
61 Malachi 1:11.
62 Deuteronomy 28:12-24; Jeremiah 29:7.

tudes and ambitions.⁶³ Jewish prosperity has always incited envy, and the fact that Semites are generally more self-conscious than Indo-Europeans made them more exclusive, and the combination of exclusivity and collective self-focus with the growing concept of a universal god, made many leaders of Jewish thought think in terms of a Zion uniquely endowed with divine truth, and of a chosen people deserving deference, and of Jerusalem as the world's religious centre. "Whoso of all the families of the earth goeth not up unto Jerusalem to worship the King, the Lord of Hosts, there shall be no rain."⁶⁴ With this there came the idea of a priestly nation with magic rituals, the personal treasure of its god. Thus were universality and exclusiveness reconciled, but on a basis that was bound to antagonize others. The grandiosity and legitimacy of the Judaic concept and belief was fortified by the prophetical teaching of Isaiah and others.

The Book of Job presents the Jewish conception of God and man's relations with Him in particularly vivid terms. Job, a prosperous and respected man, is punished beyond endurance, although he is unaware of any personal misconduct or sinful thoughts that could merit such severity. His condition is aggravated by the conviction of his friends that he is being justly punished. Gradually, Job grasped the concept that God was omnipotent but not necessarily always just, and that it was only when he became completely resigned to his own insignificance and the unmediatable supremacy of God that alleviation of such injustice would be possible. This was what occurred, including the noteworthy promise that Job could sire a stupefying number of children in the very long life that now opened to him. Job found his consolation in his new knowledge of avoidance of being self-centred. There is the problem of the suffering servant; Job and Israel faced the problem of virtuous conduct and basking in the benign attention of Jehovah (Yahweh) and now unable to find a religious or philosophical place for terrible misfortune, until man's (and Israel's) relationship with God is recalibrated.

The great priestly text and achievement was the Pentateuch, the first five books, easily distinguishable narratives and laws in Genesis, Exodus, Leviticus, Numbers, and Deuteronomy. History is marked by the figures Adam, Noah, Abraham, Jacob, and Moses; and the gradual self-revelation of God: Elohim, El Shaddai, Yahweh. It comes to the Sinaitic laws, the formation of the Congregation of Israel, and the theocracy emerges. The Pentateuch ("P" in ancient sacred texts) is an inner core of repeated narratives and laws in the Pentateuch. It memorializes religious practices as ordained by God with precision and as compulsory; the patriarchal figures become less anthropomorphic and accessible and convey "The Word" of God: "And God said..." Festivals are divine commands. The High Priest became the head of the people, with almost kingly power, as Yahweh was taken to be the head of the people and their religion and their state.

The strength of the theocracy resided in the power of faith and convictions: withholding tithes and sacrifices was dangerous.⁶⁵ The temple ritual removed sin, which whether sinful or in ritual shortcomings, struck Jews in the sensitive place of

---

63 Zachariah 14:17.
64 Malachi 3:17.
64 Malachi 3:8-12; Judith 11:13.

their prosperity. The Day of Atonement provides the solution to sin and forgiveness. God will not destroy a wicked world as was foreseen.[66] He has an eternal covenant with man,[67] and sacrifice is the means to achieve the divinely appointed method for the restoration of holiness, which provides the only way for the theocracy of Israel to attain their highest ambition and purpose of being the people of a holy God. Since Yahweh possessed Israel altogether, offerings of first fruits and other sacrifices and rituals were a sort of symbolic rent and tribute to the omnipotent God. A wide latitude in conduct was accorded within this framework of practical organization, cloaked in strict and fervent piety, which was profoundly spiritual and ritually meticulous, yet freely accorded.

The Jewish exiles in Babylonia who claimed a spiritual superiority,[68] and their return to become the elite of what had become a population of mixed blood, are vital elements in the rise of Judaism. The Pentateuch eventually emerged as a compromise between the strict priestliness of the P and the more popular and expansive lore of secular Judaism. Within these sacred texts, there has been ample room for extremely spirited debate on finer points these twenty-five hundred years. The ambitious philosophical conceptions and scholarly and rigorous historical analysis have gained almost universal intellectual admiration, even from thoughtful atheists. The deliverance from the Egyptian bondage, the long journey to the Promised Land, the rivalries, strife, and covenants are all presented in their historical context in a way that has profoundly influenced every substantial subsequent culture and has been imprinted on the human mind throughout the world. The Pentateuch begins with Elohim and Man. But God, who destroys a sinful world, is replaced by Yahweh, Jehovah, the God of Israel, who was appreciated and respected, if not worshipped, by others. When man presumptuously raises up a tower to reach heaven, the human races are scattered, and Abraham appears and the chosen people emerges. The question of whether it was a prophet-people of missionary ambitions or a priest-people dispensing ritualistic salvation has not been resolved; other than that in practice, it has been both.

The Samaritans accepted the Pentateuch, the supreme achievement of the entire Persian Age, and not only in Israel; and they were happy to help rebuild the Temple of Jerusalem. In fact, the Pentateuch was, soon enough, all that united the people of Judah and Samaria. It must be said, in the now arcane debate of the merits of the two Jewish entities, that it was the exclusiveness of Jerusalem and its theological elaborations that projected the tiny Jewish people in the hinterland of the vast Persian Empire to a gigantic role in the development of the civilization and culture of the West and ultimately of all mankind.

They were the fighters and martyrs, from the Maccabees to the Warsaw Ghetto and the founders of modern Israel, that preserved and made heroic the heritage and genius of Israel, her prophets, psalmists, theologians, and the conservators and propagators of Jewish religion and history. Looking at the full canvas of Jewish history up to this time, it is not entirely surprising that the immense intellectual treasure

---

66 Genesis 6:7; 8:21 et seq.
67 Isaiah 54:9.
68 Jeremiah 24:1-10; Ezekiel 11, 33.

of Israel would be realized by a movement that was as proselytizing as Judaism was restricted.

Nor, in hindsight, was it surprising that this movement would spontaneously believe and incite ultimately almost unanimous belief in the known world that the Jewish Messiah had come, and that this movement would initially be largely composed of Jewish Messianists; and that it would then intermittently torment the recusant continuing Jews, who were unmoved by this mighty and almost universal religious updraft.

Invisible as it may have been to all but the most perceptive, Western civilization in the middle of the Fourth Century B.C. was ready for monotheism, and ready for heroic national leadership, and a much wider arc of military operations. Then would come the men and the moments; an unforeseen sword-bearing political messiah (Alexander the Great) would precede by a few centuries a plausible, and within a few more centuries, almost universally worshipped, divine Messiah. Military, political, and sectarian frontiers would soon be greatly extended.

Then, as in recent times, the sorrows of Israel were proverbial, but the determination and genius of the people of Israel proved equal to undreamed of misfortune, and they will reappear, in tragedy and in great accomplishment, at intervals through all the rest of history.

APPENDIX A

AN OUTLINE OF THE INTRICATE HISTORY OF NON-JEWISH ANCIENT MESOPOTAMIA

(ONLY FOR THE MOST PERSEVERING READER)

ALL WE KNOW OF early Sumerian history is from the cities that have been unearthed. The tomb of the oldest historic ruler of Lagash, Nina, has been found at Ur and dates at about 3100 B.C. It was carefully constructed of hand-made brick. The clay writing tablet seems to have been developed about a century before this. The very ancient city of Shuruppak, on the old course of the Euphrates about fifty miles north of Lagash, was the home of Ziudsudu, hero of the Flood story (apart from Noah), and the Semitic version credits him with the Ark. Shuruppak vanished from history between about 2380 B.C. and its Nineteenth Century A.D. excavation. Shuruppak, Eridu, Larak, and Sippar are the only cities mentioned as having existed before the Flood. All legal documents found here and in nearby places are in Sumerian, indicating that Lagash kings ruled from Kish around 3000 B.C. Ur-Nina (c. 3100) is the first Sumerian city-king who has left any significant record of himself. We have likenesses of him and of the king being tendered a cup of some beverage by his butler Anita. He appears to have had a long and tranquil reign. Subsequent fragments of haut-reliefs and pottery indicate prolonged war between Kish and Lagash.

It is not proposed to visit upon even the persevering reader the incomplete toings and froings within a small space that in these early times were earth-shaking events, one of the frequent plots of which was the strife between the king and the patesi—the priest-king. Again, this practice would ramify very widely in succeeding centuries and civilizations. Archeological evidence of a rampant inferno that appears to have burned most of the population of two adjoining cities to death has been found about thirty miles northeast of Lagash. Vast temples were built, exceeding in lavishness and proportion preceding or competing kings, like the Great European Powers of the Twentieth Century steadily building larger, faster, and more magnificent ocean passenger liners.

Ur-Nina was followed by Eannatum, and he by Entemena. One of the latter king's innovations was to affix to a contract the personal seals or a fingerprint of every member of a signatory town, the beginning of crude fingerprinting, and of adding to the contract the clause that if the contract is complained of falsely and in an evil manner, the complainant shall be executed by being run through with a sword. Entemena's high priest, Dudu, was a figure of legendary character and integrity, an almost Solomonic figure whose name adorned all official weights and measures, confirming that the role of the religious leadership moved forcefully into the realm of commerce, where it has intermittently remained, often with storied and violent consequences in many times and cultures.

In the aftermath of Entemena, one of the first of the historic type of the strong queens—mannish in bearing but feminine in character—arises, Baranamtarra, wife of a patesi and a very powerful and esteemed queen regent, as was Queen Shagshag, wife and heir of King Urukagina of Lagash. These two Elizabethan or Maria Theresan figures (they were too upright to be Cleopatran) were legendary figures in Sumeria and succeeding regimes in Mesopotamia and far around for many centuries. Most of these cities seem to have had reasonable civil rights and some sort of adjudication of disputes to discourage and replace instant recourse to tests of violence.

Urukagina and Shagshag were particularly liberal and thoughtful rulers, discouraging exploitation and mistreatment of the poor, forbidding usury, and providing assistance for widows and orphans. Entemena also forbade the promiscuity of married people, providing for adult female incitements of adultery to be punished by the offending woman having her "mouth smashed with a burning brick." (Despite such correctional flourishes, history has reckoned him a popular and progressive ruler.[1]) This high moralism was yet in keeping with his reforms, an area where he is generally recognized as a pioneer in government. He even produced what is often represented as the first code of laws, though it was rudimentary and only a few of its provisions survive.

The benign rule of Urukagina and Shagshag was ended by Lugalzaggisi, patesi of Umma, who conquered Lagash and pillaged it. "Blood flowed in her sanctuaries and fire consumed her splendid buildings. Silver and precious stones were taken from her temples and grain from her fields."[2] Though they were defeated, Urukagina and his queen emerged as durable heroes in ancient Mesopotamia for governing altruistically and sharing the fate of their subjects in being conquered and murdered by an odious tyrant. It was widely believed among Urukagina's countrymen that as Lugalzaggisi had sinned against the local God Ningirsu that he was doomed. His unhappy new subjects would not have long to wait for the redemption of their prophecy. All would be put right, according to widely circulated prayers, in the next life, which would take place below, in the bowels of the earth, not in the heavens as subsequent religions have envisioned.

The course of even the main rivers, Tigris and Euphrates, meandered around over the centuries, altered by canal construction. The constant city in these sanguinary chronicles of endless combat for many centuries is the religious centre Nippur. Kish, Lagash, Ur, and the others fought for occupation of it. At Adab, twenty-five miles south of Nippur, an exploration team from the University of Chicago found the sort of bricks of Ur-Nina's period at a depth of ten feet. Ten feet below that were limestone paving blocks from the period before brickmaking was discovered

---

1 *Cambridge Ancient History* (CAH), I, p. 382 (Stephen H. Langdon).
2 Ibid., p. 388 (Stephen H. Langdon).

(other than in baked mud). And twenty-eight feet farther down but at the same site were found wheel-made pottery and fragments depicting four-stage ziggurat buildings, but not the taller seven-stage buildings from 2700 B.C. on.

All the central and northern Sumerian cities between Lagash and Akshak worshipped earth deities, while in the south were the sky-God at Erech, the Sun-God at Larsa, and the Moon-God at Ur. Even far-sighted people at the time must have grasped, though it might have been severely punishable heresy to say so, and in any case, we have no record of it, that no such system of municipal Gods was remotely plausible. Man was just getting his concerns about mortality, fallibility, and his ignorance of the prelude and sequels to life and the dimensions of the universe off his chest and was embracing whatever was locally customary in terms of worship to deal with it. The greatest Sumerian theological figure was Ninana, the Queen of Heaven and Goddess of Battle, who had graduated over time from Goddess of the vine, and whose name in common reverential repetition became Innini.

Erech, one-hundred and twenty miles south-southeast of Baghdad, was one of the greatest of the early Babylonian cities, and it has been extensively excavated. Even in the times of the renowned Greek astronomer, Strabo, Erech retained its school of astronomy, one of the most famous in the world for more than tweo-thousand years. Larsa was only fifteen miles from Erech and was renowned as the centre of worship of the Sumerian Sun God, Babbar. Only fifteen miles southwest of Larsa was Ur, sometimes the capital of the principal Mesopotamian state but the permanent centre for the worship of the Moon God. Entemena's very ambitious canal connecting the Tigris and the Euphrates passed adjacent to Ur. These were the city states and corresponding religious cults when Lugalzaggisi of Umma conquered Lagash and laid waste to it in 2897 B.C.

Lugalzaggisi has left an inscription that turned up on excavated vases, in which he claims to be the protégé and champion of a series of Gods from around Mesopotamia, and explicitly claims divine sponsorship (as was customary in these times). He united almost all of Mesopotamia, having come from Elam somewhat to the east, and claimed to rule between the Mediterranean and the Persian Gulf. This was an exaggeration, because of his tenuous connection to the Mediterranean, but this was an ambitious empire for the time. He sent an expeditionary force at one point to the Mediterranean and glimpsed what was effectively considered in Mesopotamia at this time to be the Western extent of the world; as the new "lord of Erech and king of Ur," Lugalzaggisi had launched himself from his position as patesi (high priest) at Kish. He ruled his empire for twenty-five years and built a statue of himself at the great temple at Nippur, confirming early on the tendency of men to take the place of Gods when they think a vacancy is available.

As the unhappy subjects in Lagash had foreseen when their generous monarchs Urukagina and Shagshag had been overthrown and executed by Lugalzaggisi, the new conqueror was almost effortlessly overwhelmed and crushed by Sargon, founder of the Semitic Dynasty of Agade, in 2872 B.C. Sargon had Lugalzaggisi put in stocks and tethered, whipped along the road back to Nippur, where he was executed in proximity to the repurposed statue he had commissioned to himself when he elected himself to join the Gods. (So he did, in a fashion.) Throughout the period of this ancient history, and even in the most refined polities, it was rarely far from the royal throne to the gallows or headsman's block. All laurels and crowns and headgear that were emblematic of royal and God-given authority were worn uneasily, unless the wearer was impetuous or naïve, in which case he was apt to be disposed of quickly.

Sargon was a foundling from a poor mother and father he did not know and was abandoned in a reed basket on the Euphrates and was found and raised by an irrigator, Akki. He eventually became a cup-bearer and gardener to the king and was promoted on merit and anointed royal successor. There are other legends, including that he was a shepherd. He was a believer in divinations through the examination of livers, and some of his life can be pieced together from the Assyrian and Babylonian records of noteworthy liver divinations.

Sargon ascribed his success to the interventions of Ishtar, the Semitic Goddess of Agade, identified with the Sumerian Inini, Goddess of Battle. His crushing of Lugalzaggisi was the opening of his career as a conqueror, and it was a considerable achievement. Lugalzaggisi had rounded up a league of about fifty towns and cities that made common cause with him, despite his severity, as the strongest leader of a common defence against an aroused and renascent Kish. He washed his spears in the sea (Persian Gulf), always a ceremonious pleasure for warlords from the interior, and rebuilt Kish, which had badly deteriorated when its paramountcy had passed. Sargon conquered the Elamite cities, including Susa, and then turned westward and cut a swath to the Mediterranean, and seems even to have led a raiding party to Cyprus.

The great series of ever-greater conquests along the Mediterranean littoral had begun and would continue for five-thousand years. He seems to have held everything from Phoenicia (Lebanon) to Armenia and Iran, and to the northern line of the Arabian Peninsula and the border of Egypt. Sargon divided his empire into districts of ten-hour marches (regardless of sectarian or ethnic divisions) and made the "sons of my palace," as he delicately put it, the governors. The Elamitic land (now part of Iran), Kazalla, flared into revolt, and Sargon crushed it ruthlessly, reducing the capital, also Kazalla, to ashes and rubble, allegedly even destroying the birds' nests.[3]

He did not have a relaxed old age. All his governors revolted at once and attempted to besiege him in Agade, but he beat them off, defeated them in detail, and undiminished in his zeal by the fact that most were kinfolk, wrought the customary mortal revenge on most of them. His golden years were next disturbed by the Hittites, putting in their opening appearance and attacking Sargon in northern Mesopotamia. The Hittites were another wandering and war-like Asiatic people drawn by the widely fabled wealth of the Tigris and Euphrates valleys and the crossroads trade routes of Phoenicia and the approaches to Egypt. Sargon had not lost his gift for command in battle and gave the Hittites, who would be back, but not against this adversary, a good thrashing. Sargon's reign was glorious but bloody, and he was a better conqueror than a ruler. Even after all his victories, he died with a new general uprising sweeping his domains. His memory was honoured, as the "King of Univer-

---

3 Ibid., p. 407 (Stephen H. Langdon).

sal Dominion" but without overflowing affection.

Sargon was officially succeeded by his son Rimush, who waded through blood to a throne with both Sumeria and Elam (southwest Iran), in revolt. Rimush suppressed those provinces, and then Ur and Umma, which had also risen, and then the feisty Elamites again. Every time Rimush turned his back on one part of his inherited empire, the parts of the empire where he was not present burst into rebellious flames, and even more vigorously than under Sargon. There was no institutional structure or constructive record of governance to secure any public order, only the king's physical ability to overpower one or two provincial uprisings at a time. Rimush also called himself the ruler of all the lands from the Persian Gulf to the Mediterranean, as Sargon had, and the rule of Rimush was even more contested and precarious. He threw in the title "Smiter of Elam and Barakhshi" to boot. Rimush was murdered by his "sons of the palace," children and senior bureaucrats and officers, who smote him with their large and splendid seals of office, as had been foreseen by scrutinizers of liver omens.[4]

The succession to Rimush went to one of his brothers, also a son of Sargon, Manishtusu. Manishtusu was successful for a time, and was a considerable general, before Naram-Sin made his move. Manishtusu continued the practice of his brother and father of moving around the empire crushing whomever was in turbulent revolt. This led him to the rout of a league of thirty-two southern cities in an uprising in what is now southeastern Iran and close to what is now Afghanistan. In 2260 B.C., Manishtusu was murdered by his entourage, as Rimush had been. Manishtusu is considered by many to be a nephew of Rimush rather than his brother, but as soon as Manishtusu was disposed of, Naram-Sin, either his brother or nephew, set out to take over and extend the entire kingdom, which Manishtusu had succeeded in extending to the east and south, pillaging silver mines at the western extremity of the Indian Ocean. Naram-Sin would prove the greatest of the Sargonic kings, though they had all been pretty capable army commanders and rudimentary despotic monarchs.

Naram-Sin began his reign, as his predecessors had, going in forced marches around his empire, pummeling dissident tribes and regions into resubmission. He brought captured kings back to his temple city in humiliation as Sargon had whipped Lugalzaggisi in stocks and chains along the road to his own temple. Naram-Sin was soon deified, as was the custom with kings in this time in Babylonia. The theological basis of this was that the kings were supposedly born of virgin mother-goddesses. This was the forerunner of the concept of the Virgin Birth, and the fact that the kings in this dynasty were also high priests facilitated the rapid ascent to deification, as long as the candidate-deities were militarily successful. Only anti-theistic people create overly fallible gods, as Richard Wagner did. Naram-Sin expanded his kingdom and added Syria, Samarra, and other areas east of the Tigris to it. One of the kings Naram-Sin captured and humiliated was Mannu-Dannu ("Who is King"), who had apparently been king of what is now Oman and the Emirates on the southern end of the Arabian Peninsula. On his return from conquering these kings and regions, and as was also the tradition in this dynasty, Naram-Sin found Elam and Sumeria in

---

4 Ibid., p. 409 (Stephen H. Langdon).

revolt and made short work of these impertinences. A good deal of sophisticated statuary was carved and crafted to memorialize this king and demonstrate that the Egyptian talents in this field had been largely replicated in Mesopotamia. Naram-Sin acquired a formidable reputation as a builder of temples, and such was his power and prestige that most of the last half of his reign was comparatively peaceful, and he was succeeded by his son Shargalisharri.

At his succession, Sumeria apparently rose in revolt again. The new king managed to suppress that uprising, but then the sinister Hittites put in an appearance on his eastern borders. He withstood them, but the presence of large masses of marauding Hittites would prove an unfortunate omen. Shargalisharri devolved administration in the provinces by patesis, the high priests, ruling in his name and remitting tribute to the emperor as Nafam-Sin and Shargalasharri wished to be called, who trained and maintained his army to deal with the frequent revolts. Like his predecessors, when Shargalasharri was old and less energetic, several provinces raised the standard of rebellion, and his successors, none of whom had any stability or security, were unable to deal with the disaffection and the Sargonic Empire swiftly disintegrated.

Sumeria became again the leading member of the units of the former empire, but it exercised no suzerainty over the other provinces, and they were all now vulnerable to the marauders in the east. The Hittites of Gutium could not now be kept out of Mesopotamia, and they were a terrifying occupier.

"The royalty was taken to the hosts of Gutium, which has no king...So direful was the rule of Gutium...So detested was the name of Gutium in Sumeria, it was known as the habitation of the pest."[5] Approximately one-hundred and twenty-five years was taken up with the pillage and oppression of Sumeria and Akkad, and the partially Hittite occupiers set up a capital at or near the present Iraqi city of Kirkuk. Eventually, as with most conquerors of culturally more advanced peoples, the hordes shaped up somewhat and their principal leader, Sium, who apparently ruled for thirty-five years, permitted the provinces to be ruled by patesis (high priests) in his name, with comparative liberality. The end of this interlude saw some revenant prosperity and a few fine stone public buildings and excellent statues (of the rulers of course, and their Gods, whom they unsurprisingly resembled).

The part of Shargalisharri's domain that was centered on Lagash was not occupied by the Gutium Hittites. In the Twenty-First Century B.C., Ur-bau, an enlightened patesi, ruled Lagash successfully, and some statuary of him and his era remain. Lagash and its immediate neighbours seem to have navigated this time fairly peacefully, as its population became quite cosmopolitan, with Semites, Hittites, Sumerians, and a motley of others mixed together. Gudea was the high priest and he achieved great and lasting renown as a scholar and propagator of Sumerian literature. He eventually assumed considerable temporal influence and cleaned up Lagash and its outward moral decadence, expelling designated evil wizards. Religious practice was required more frequently, and Gudea extended his authority to the cedar forests of what is now Lebanon and to silver mines near Agade.

Gudea asserted a somewhat equitable justice system, restraining the rich from

---

5 Ibid., pp. 423-4 (Stephen H. Langdon).

exploitation or mistreatment of the laboring class. It was a time of ambitious sculpting and statue-making, and surviving examples are fairly numerous and of quite sophisticated quality. Gudea appears to have ruled for approximately forty years, and was technically a subject of Gutium, but that baleful regime is never mentioned in Gudea's surviving archives, and obviously the grip of the Guteans was weakening after nearly a century of enslaving, oppressing, and robbing the Sumerians. Finally, the Sumerians arose, and their leader, Utukhegal, sent the Gutians and Hittites packing in a painful and retributive expulsion, the last of their kings, Tirigan, having resisted, was taken prisoner. He was brought to Utukhegal, made to kneel before the Sumerian leader, and Utukhegal put his boot on Tirigan's neck. It was one of the memorable scenes of the ancient world, and Tirigan, the last of the feared and hated Guteans, became a name synonymous with both evil and failure.

The Sumerians proceeded in what is now a historical silence for about fifty years until the rise of their greatest leader, Ur-Engur, in 2475 B.C. In a memorial, it was claimed that he was such a charismatic leader that "Those whom he plundered followed with him in tears." Even by the normal hyperbole of obsequious inflations of the qualities of ancient leaders on the crowded up-ramp to self-deification, this is fulsome. It is not clear how he achieved the rout of the usual factions, the conquest of the normally more militant Semites, and the headship of all Mesopotamia, sending ships to places "that were unknown." But apparently, he did.[6] Ur-Engur rebuilt temples throughout his reign and kingdom, including at Nippur, where many of his predecessors had been both elevated and humbled. He subdued the Semitic capital of Kish, and his son became the high priest at Erech, and from all accounts it was a period of prosperity and good government. He set about building defensive walls, especially at Ur. (Such walls have almost never succeeded, though they can delay invasions and sieges for a time.)

Ur-Engur built a prodigious palace at Ur and held his court in the throne room, as a proclaimed God of Heaven and Earth, and king of Sumeria and Akkad, amid the apparently fabulous treasures that he had sacked in his foreign conquests and exactions. The law of the Empire imposed heavy religious tribute on all parts of the prospering empire, it evidently being easier to collect tax if it is being paid to God than to the national treasury, even if the treasury receives the divinely collected deposit as terrestrial trustee. Granaries and stockyards and storehouses had to be constructed near Nippur to receive the immense quantities of sacrificial tribute that poured in.

Ur-Engur was succeeded by his son Dungi, who was also a gifted ruler, in 2456, and ruled for the apparently reliable and formidable period of fifty-eight years. Even Ur-Engur and Dungi had problems with the northwestern tribes, and Dungi was conducting punitive assaults and suppressions against them in the fortieth year of his father's dynasty. On such occasions, he was not a merciful God-king, and burned and pillaged, razed vast acreages to the scorched earth, and wasn't squeamish about ordering the instructive and deterrent massacre of anyone he suspected of taking up or even encouraging the taking up of arms against his godly and royal authority. On the other hand, proud Susa, another ancient capital, when approached by Ur-Engur,

---

6 Ibid., p. 435 (Stephen H. Langdon).

preemptively submitted, swore worship and allegiance, and was treated with great courtesy and respect, and with neither rapine nor triumphalism— an in-gathering of civilized peoples under the temporal and moral authority of the greatest man visible on the earth.

There is a little more evidence of the fate of the surrounding provinces, such as Lagash, and the story is generally one that supports the narrative of Ur-Engur's benignity and universally recognized distinction. In his theological activities, the most noteworthy aspect of Ur-Engur's reign, apart from his own popularity as a venerated deity, was the emergence among the pantheon of the most prominent Sumerian deities of the nature goddess, Gula-Bau-Ninkharsag, who was a sorrowful provider of spiritual unguent to all the woes of man, and the source of fruitfulness and abundance, and was also the wellspring of mercy who could placate and calm other deities who were angry, belligerent, and vengeful. She was worshipped throughout Mesopotamia. The whole concept of religion was becoming more sophisticated and generalized, but the vulnerability of these ancient theological beliefs to messianic monotheism that is stern yet forgiving and egalitarian in spirit is obvious in retrospect. Besides what has been mentioned, there was a multiplicity of other cults and deities, a little like the cult of saints in the Christian Era, though generally more fantastic in the claims made for the adored and worshipped subject-deities.

Babylon first became prominent under the kings of Ur, and the first prominent figure in the city was Arshikhand; he was the high priest in the latter years of Dungi and on into the time of his successor, Bur-Sin. Babylon, unlike Susa, did not take agreeably to the yoke of the kings of Ur, and the central government, though it stopped short of plundering Babylon, did that city no favours as it rose. Dungi extended the empire through Syria and into Cappadocia, in what is now Anatolia, Asian Turkey. It seems that Dungi and the Western Semites (probably the Amorites) were, like the Assyrians from the east, attracted to the gold and silver mines of Cappadocia, which was occupied by a commercially agile people of traders and merchants. These elements mixed and were soon joined by the Hittites, a crossroads of people at a centre of resources; a combination of circumstances that possessed the elements of combustion. Bur-Sin was followed by Gimil-Sin and then Ibi-Sin, and they reigned a total of about fifty years, but the dynasty in Ur was loosening, and restless elements on the fringes of the empire were gnawing at it. Under Ibi-Sin, the whole structure crumpled and caved in, in a pattern that was already familiar and would prove to be timelessly recurrent.

Ibi-Sin died in control of Sumeria, but little else. The Elamites of what is now western Iran put in one of their cameo appearances in Mesopotamia (which continues under Iran at time of writing), and penetrated the walls and canals that the Ur Dynasty had erected, and overthrew the royal house of Sumeria. Ur was sacked and Sumeria thoroughly conquered and humiliated, and Ibi-Sin was placed in fetters and flogged along the road to the Elamite capital of Anshan. He died in captivity, in 1940 B.C., in circumstances unknown to posterity, but as he was officially lamented by the continuing followers of the cult of Ur; he was presumably executed when all propaganda value had been extracted from his downfall and humiliation.

What occurred was a peculiar twist of the intense relationships between all the forces contending in and around the ancient crucible of Mesopotamia. The Sumerian people vanished as a distinct ethnicity, but their culture prevailed among their conquerors and some of their neighbours, as if there were an ethno-cultural relay race in which Sumerians passed the torch of their civilization to more robust and determined racial groups to carry it forward. The Sumerian religious notion of God-men as saviours continued and evolved, and the Sumerian law codes, though less comprehensive than more or less contemporary efforts by some of the Semites, especially the Jews, were more merciful and forgiving. And this trait, though it was often suppressed and forgotten, was never out of mind and did return, doing honour to its long departed authors.

The Sumerian penetration of Mesopotamia and Egypt is generally regarded as the birth of modern Western civilization, and Sumerians were the most humane and imaginative of the early peoples. There are many traces of their pictographic writing and cylindrical seals in pre-dynastic Egypt and much evidence of their symbolism, such as man wrestling with a fierce animal such as a lion or large serpent, in the earliest arts and crafts of Egypt and Mesopotamia.

This was the first people with no war-like ambitions, though not without warrior aptitudes when the cause justified it. They steadily improved their land, and their engineering triumphs of irrigation as early as the Fifth Millennium B.C. are among the wonders of applied science. They also, as has been lightly mentioned, advanced religious speculation from rank surmise and invention to serious consideration of plausible spiritual speculation and moral philosophy. And though they were the apogee of the human God worshipped as a deity and accorded absolute obedience as king, they also reflected profoundly on human fallibility and its consequences. The Sumerians had been gradually forced southward to the lower Tigris and Euphrates, preventing immigration and confining them to less fruitful terrain. They had little aptitude for extreme heat, unlike the Semites who fairly steadily encroached upon them, despite their generally inferior culture.

CHAPTER TWO

ANCIENT EGYPT FROM THE FIFTH MILLENNIUM TO THE ELEVENTH CENTURY B.C.

✤

THE THUTMOSE AND RAMESSID PHARAOHS

Thutmose III (circa 1479 –1425 B.C.)

Ramses II (circa 1250 B.C.)

1. The Earliest Dynasties

P REDYNASTIC EGYPT is something we have been made aware of by prodigious archeological discoveries. The First Dynasty seems to have followed the union of Upper and Lower Egypt and agreement on a calendar in the middle of the Fifth Millennium B.C. The known history consists chiefly of pottery and archeology, which, with a great deal of lore, is not sufficient to be appropriately recounted in a narrative of the political history of peoples and states. The IInd Dynasty kicked off in about 3350 B.C. with the kings Hotepsekheumi, Reneb Kakau, and Neneter Banantirurenebis who are claimed to have commended the worship of the bull, who is referred to as a sun-god. These kings were from northern Egypt. The IIIrd Dynasty, the Memphites, began in about 3200 B.C. with a southern Egyptian, Khasekhemui, who announced on his numerous surviving monuments that he had conquered the north, the lower Nile. His son Zoser is the first renowned Egyptian king, who reigned for twenty-seven years and had as his first minister, Imhotep, who was also the king's architect and physician. He was eventually deified by subsequent generations as the patron of science. Zoser is buried in the step-pyramid of Memphis. The IIIrd Dynasty ended with the great king, and at about this time, Egypt emerged as the most advanced civilization in what was then the world known to the West. Babylonia was a competitor, but distinctly inferior in the arts and sciences, architecture and construction techniques. Snefru unified Egypt from Sinai and the isthmus at Suez to Lower Nubia, with his capital near the present Cairo, and with the whole country organized in coherent provinces. This was about 3100 B.C.

The IVth Dynasty popularized the full-sized pyramids which grew steadily larger, in a posthumous competition. The names of their occupants were written all over public monuments in clear hieroglyphics extolling their achievements. The kings were worshipped as living gods. There was a matriarchal system in succession to property, though a father could make specific bequests. When meritocratic men made their way to the kingship, they generally married a royal princess, to maintain what was often the fiction of the transmission of the royal blood of Re, the Sun God deemed to be the mother of Egypt (as Jehovah was said to be the husband of Israel). These familial metaphors continued to abound, as France is referred to traditionally in the Roman Catholic Church as the Elder Daughter of the Church, and England is the Dowry of Mary.

It became the custom to build mighty but at first, simple, temples of stone, although opulent residences, even the royal palaces, were of brick, and most buildings of bricks of mud. Law, though not codified, existed, and was imposed by the kings, governors and counsellors, the latter very numerous, and many of the king's entourage were priests. This, in practice, only meant that they were charged by the king with conducting sacrificial and other spectacles of veneration to the king and other deities. Snefru's successors, Khufu, Khafre, and Menkaure, built the pyramids at Gizeh, near Cairo, the Great Pyramid being virtually the life-work of Khufu, better known by the name Herodotus gave him, of Cheops. The Great Pyramid was an astonishing achievement: four-hundred and fifty feet high in perfect symmetry built of limestone blocks, each weighing two and one half tons. The entire structure necessitated the carving, transport, and precise insertion of five-million, seven-hundred and fifty thousand tons of limestone. Khafre (twenty-eight years), Rededef (what was then considered the short reign of eight years), and Khufu (fifty-six years), was a distinguished near-century of Egyptian history. Under Khafre, Egyptian painting reached a high level of sophistication, as did many crafts, and sculpture of this period is among the masterpieces of all history, and many examples are preserved, especially in the Cairo Museum. Menkaure reigned for about twenty years, and was followed by Shepsekaf, who was less noteworthy than those who preceded him, though government was largely in the hands of the talented prince and son-in-law Ptahshepses, who carried on after the king died in 2970 B.C. The Vth Dynasty from Heliopolis overthrew the Memphites, but their chief minister carried on under the new king, Userkaf, presaging modern legendarily agile high office-holders like Talleyrand and Gromyko and J. Edgar Hoover.

The Vth Dynasty (2965-2825 B.C.) is chiefly known for the institutionalized worship of the Sun God, with a powerful official insinuation that the kings were at least kinfolk of the Almighty, as well as high priests of Re. Userkaf, after some level of civil rivalry and strife (which tended to be quite sanguinary in these times), was followed by his brothers, Safure and Neferirikere, all uniting the kingship with the rulership of the state religion (largely dedicated to organized thanksgiving for the governmental aptitudes of the king). The design and decoration of temples became ever more magnificent, but the pyramids were rather smaller than Cheops and his family had conceived, and much of the interior was composed of rubble, with only a limestone face. Some Egyptologists have considered this to be a sign of the onset of decadence.[1] There were local high priests, who exercised great authority, and in Memphis and some other cities, he was known as the "Great Chief of the Artificers." The great burial sites were attended by priestly treasurers, who assured their maintenance and the regularity of posthumous offerings. These tombs became steadily more elaborate with passing Dynasties, with paintings on walls, furniture, including a stone bed, for the comfort of the physical "double" of the deceased, and the process of mummification began in the VIth Dynasty and grew swiftly and was taken up even by commoners with the means to afford it.

There survives some literature from this era, as society became reflective and better organized and more given to writing down laws and practices. Schools were set up, usually around the temples, mainly for the sons of the wealthy but with some meritocratic aspect. Here and generally, there was a good deal of recourse to correction and family and civic punishment by thrashing the buttocks of children and wives, and the flogging of servants and slaves. From here, it was a short step to the removal of limbs or eyes in judicial or even arbitrary sentencing, and summary public executions were routine. Figures of authority had practically unlimited power to maintain order as severely as they pleased. Thus was society ordered with the ever-present penalty of varying levels of physical violence. It was primitive and harsh by modern standards, but at least there was an education system and a consensus to devote a good deal of attention on education, science, and culture. In the midst of the VIth Dynasty, explorations were conducted toward what is now Somalia, and dwarfs were found and brought back, and were taught to dance in festivals and much appreciated.

Pepi II Neferkere was the seminal king of the VIth Dynasty, as he probably ruled longer than anyone in history, ascending the throne at the age of six and occupying it for ninety-four years until his death shortly after his one-hundredth birthday (2738-2644 B.C.). His reign was a protracted disaster, as he squandered the treasury, allowed the quality of ministers and governors and prophets and priests to decline and tolerated an increasing rot of official corruption and incompetence. Pepi II pushed the southern frontier farther south, past the cataracts and well into what is now Sudan, and opened what would prove to be a very contested and often savage relationship with the negroes of north central Africa. Shortly after Pepi II finally expired, a full-scale war broke out between the Egyptians and the blacks in South Sudan, and this conflict has been waged intermittently ever since, nearly five-thousand years, the most recent severe outburst resulting in the international conviction of the leader of Sudan of genocide, and the internationally recognized secession of South Sudan.

---

1 *Cambridge Ancient History* (CAH), I, p. 286 (H.R. Hall).

Chaos and prolonged civil war ensued on the death of Pepi II, and his heirs were not competent to restore the prestige and power of the royal house. The only interesting person among Pepi II's successors was Neterkere, a man, who nonetheless may have been Nicrotis, made infamous by Herodotus, who presented Nicrotis as a woman, who in revenge for the murder of her brother, invited all those she believed complicit in the murder to a great banquet in a vast underground dining room, and murdered them all by introducing the Nile into the room in a torrent from a disguised conduit, and then committed suicide, avenged. The evidence that Nicrotis existed is not conclusive, but Herodotus made her one of the notorious figures of ancient history.

There was a prolonged war between Northern and Southern Egypt. The two sides moved up and down the Nile, often on large river boats constructed of Phoenician (Lebanese) cedar. Finally, after decades of savage warfare up and down the country, the Thebans of the south prevailed over the Memphites and Heracleopolites and stabilized Egypt after nearly three-hundred years of very destructive civil strife. The Theban ascendancy is known as the XIth Dynasty, and it began with King Intef the Great of Increasing Life, Son of the Sun, in 2375 B.C.

The succession was fairly regular and Egypt (which at this time was in fact southern and middle Egypt only) got back on its feet, and the leading figure of the XIth Dynasty, Nebhapetre, reigned from 2290 to 2242 B.C. Art and sculpture, long lapsed in the shambles of intra-Egyptian strife, began to re-emerge in high-quality artistic creations. We know almost nothing of his actual rulership, but to judge from posthumous memorials, he appears to have commanded the respect of the governing class. It was in this Dynasty that Karnak became the principal temple of the country, and the great works of Luxor started to rise. Karnak venerated the human-headed God Min of Coptos, theoretically the beginning of the Copts and of the worship of a quasi-anthropomorphic God, and Amenemhet, the founder of the XIIth Dynasty (reigned from 2212 to 2182 B.C.), made him the principal deity of Egypt, king of the gods.

This was government by Thebans and families from south of Thebes, who built a new capital between Memphis and Heracleopolis. Amenemhet and his successors, Senusret III and Amenemhet III, were extremely distinguished rulers by the standards of any country or era. They were of partly south Sudanese (black) ancestry and fought vigorously and successfully on all of Egypt's frontiers and were great builders of monuments of many kinds, enlightened and judicious rulers, spontaneously worshipped by their subjects. Amenemhet I began the system of co-regency, by which his chosen successor ruled with him for a time, to try to assure a smooth succession without a civil war as frequently followed the death of a king in these early days of organized government. Amanemhet I left "The Instructions of King Sehetepibre," renowned in subsequent Egyptian history as a manual of good sense in how a king must govern. The Instructions recommend altruism, constructiveness, avoidance of favoritism, and the avoidance of any friends or clique around the king—all must be treated equally and fairly or factionalism and disloyalty will ensue. A written description of the death of Amanamhet I survives: "Departed the God into his horizon. He ascended to heaven, he joined the Sun; the divine limbs were mingled with him that begat him. At the court was silence, the great double doors were closed, the court sat mourning, the people bowed down in silence."[2]

The red granite obelisk of his much beloved successor, Senusret III, remains at Matarieh. He expanded his realm into Ethiopia and was a formidable warrior, but battles with the southern negroes were constant (as they still are) and see-sawed back and forth between the cataracts of the Nile. The negroes were fierce and well-organized and though feared and hated, were respected. These kings all enforced tighter discipline on the provincial prince-governors, gradually centralizing the kingdom. Senusret I was memorialized in ten large white limestone figures that remain in the Cairo Museum. His successor, Amenemhet II, in the recurrent pattern not to be cast aside for many centuries, was murdered by the palace guard (2115 B.C.). Senusret II co-reigned and reigned from 2118 to 2099 B.C.

2. Senusret III and Amenemhet III

In this and succeeding reigns, such was the prosperity of Egypt that it attracted a good deal of Semitic immigration. There was something resembling diplomatic relations with a number of foreign governments, including Crete, Phoenician cities, and the leading Bedouins. The great King Senusret III reigned from 2099 to 2061B.C., is reckoned a monarch of epochal talent and distinction, and he expanded Egyptian rule into Nubia, defeating the blacks, and into Palestine. At Wadi Halfa, by the second cataract, he erected a statue of himself that presaged Ozymandias: "And on the pedestal these words appear:" (after stating that no negro shall pass north of that boundary) "I am the king and what I say I do." This statue is not here "from any desire that you should worship it, but that ye should fight for it."[3]

There came then the greatest of all the kings of the well-cast XIIth Dynasty: Amenhemet III (reigned 2061-2013 B.C.). This king was known as "the good God" and ruled in peace for forty-eight years. He devoted himself to works of irrigation and diversion of the Nile and nearby lakes to expand the cultivable area and enrich the soil. He also combated flooding with an ingenious curved dam that regulated substantial flows of water into the Nile. He also enhanced the exploitation of copper and turquoise in Sinai, and in governmental matters, he replaced the local governors with less authoritative mayors and centralized power in the hands of his council. So exemplary was this monarch that everything in Egypt, the economy and the social and political stability of the country, rested on the king's prestige and acuity, and when he died, the regime was vulnerable to internal fissures and if any arose, aggressive neighbours.

His successor, Amenemhet IV, and his successor, Queen Sebuknefrure, were not competent, and the queen married the founder of the XIIIth Dynasty, Khutouire Ugafa, who was considered inadequately regal by the proud Thebans, who presented a rival monarch, and the customary process of disintegration followed. Khutouire had a plethora of ephemeral successors, and while Thebes managed a coherent state in southern Egypt, northern Egypt dissolved into quarrelling fragments

---

2   CAH, I, p. 304 (H.R. Hall).
3   CAH, I, p. 308 (H.R. Hall).

for the delectation of a determined invader, and by the slow-moving standards of ancient Egypt, did not have long to wait for him. Because of her long fertile valley and rich agriculture, Egypt was always in danger of invasion by fierce military peoples, who regularly arose or arrived at the hinge-point between Africa and Asia.

Egypt, in these times, was self-sufficient in all but wine, heavy timber, and oils, that were imported from Syria and Phoenicia, and paid for with grain and Nubian gold. Egyptian life, over thousands of years into the early Twentieth Century, changed very little for the average person. The arrival of Christianity and then of Islam had little impact on the national personality. Amenemhet I had abolished private wars and imposed general order, and centralized government under his viziers and myrmidons; a middle class of free townsmen and larger farmers developed, and tax collectors and law courts answerable directly to the king's bureaucracy were established throughout Egypt. The kings were generally careful to assure that none of their viziers became excessively powerful. The viziers were assigned around the kingdom and could enforce the king's rule with military powers, and there was rarely much agitation from the king or his entourage to err on the side of mercy. The principal weapons were bows and arrows and short swords, and bronze gradually replaced copper. The Thebans adapted the chariot from the Hyksos (who were about to erupt into Egypt), but continued to be more expert and practiced in moving soldiers on the Nile and in the Red Sea and striking amphibiously in the flank or back of adversaries. They only graduated to up-to-date land forces when finally stirred to drive the Hyksos across Sinai and pursue and annihilate them.

The later Egyptian navies were as good as the Greeks'. The Egyptians were slow to adopt the wheel for transport or for making pottery, but advanced in glazing pottery and glass-blowing. Furniture and the decorative arts and crafts advanced very swiftly, especially in funerary matters and the elaborateness of tombs. Tombs had detailed painted interiors and sculpted wooden effigies of servants and others, who were to turn into replications of real people when the deceased reached the next life. Likenesses of the dead were painted on top of the thick linen and cotton embalming, which also had a coat of stucco. Eventually, some "answerers," as they were called, were put to death, and then recreated as wooden statues in the tombs of their masters. Mummification developed gradually.

Egyptians invented linen, and the upper classes were proud of their cleanliness and absence of facial hair and considered foreigners to be unclean as well as uncouth. Eventually, the great figures of Egypt were buried in carved-out caves bordering on the Nile or its tributaries, though the kings continued to be buried in pyramids. The camel was disdainfully regarded as a Bedouin animal and was only later adopted in Egypt. Osiris, the God of the Nile and of fertility, gradually emerged as the chief of gods and the most generally worshipped. Somewhat later than in this era, priestly colleges developed around the various temples, but the Egyptian religion was never very centrally controlled until the time of the Christians many centuries later. Monotheism was still distant in Egypt.

3. The Hyksos

After about a century of disorganization, Canaanite migrants established a realm of their own in the Nile Delta around 1800 B.C., and it functioned beside the crumbling XIIIth Dynasty in northern Egypt, which was constantly rent by internal rivalries. In a pattern that would be repeated twenty-five hundred years later in Western Europe and several times in China, Indo-Europeans made their debut in the Middle East around the start of the Twentieth Century B.C., and Aryans, originally from central Asia, moved through Anatolia and into northern Syria and the kingdom of Babylonia.

A domino process, based on superior military abilities, enabled the Aryans, the Hittites, because they introduced the horse to the region, and hitched them to war chariots, to descend with unheard-of speed upon Babylon, crush the Babylonian forces, and seize and brutally sack Babylon in 1926 B.C. The Babylonians had chariots drawn by donkeys, and the Egyptians had donkeys but had not hitched them to chariots, only ploughs. The Hittites struck with the effect of Nazi Panzers in 1939 and 1940 when, as Mr. Churchill wrote, "The Germans broke up the little countries like matchwood,"[4] and then completely defeated and humiliated France. The Hittites withdrew to Anatolia after pillaging everything valuable that was moveable in Babylonia, and their place was taken by the equally fierce and more sedentary Kassites, who remained in authority in Babylon for 600 years. These events will be described in the next chapter. The Hittites and Kassites drove large numbers of Syrians and Canaanites and adventurous Aryans south, and they easily poured through "the Prince's Wall," the traditional unimposing line of defense of the Nile Delta. This mélange of opportunistic groups roughly formed the Hyksos, a destructive and very aggressive people who could not resist the rich, plump, sitting duck of Egypt, and they stormed into northern Egypt in horse drawn chariots, brandishing bronze scimitars. The Egyptians had no possible response to such a formidable and rapid invasion, and were easily and completely beaten and conquered in the north, though the Thebans rallied bravely and contested southern Egypt for some time, emulating the weapons and tactics of the invader as best they could. It was a grim time in Egyptian history, a dark age of several centuries, in which the Hyksos plundered and enslaved the countries under what they called the XVth and XVIth Dynasties. These were naturally expunged in Egyptian history when that country finally threw off the Hyksos yoke. The Hyksos never enjoyed or deserved a day of general popularity or even spontaneous acceptance in Egypt.

There was a series of Hyksos kings, but the Egyptians ultimately succeeded in erasing from memory even a record of the names of most of them. The personalities of the Hyksos era that are remembered are the leading figures of the Resistance, and it must be said that the Egyptians, after their initial subjugation at scimitar-point in the north and fighting retreat to a state of quasi-acquiescence in the Theban south, mounted and sustained an indefatigable movement of national reassertion. King Sekenenre I the Great, of Thebes, began the War of Liberation

---

4   Cable of Prime Minister Winston Churchill to U.S. President Franklin D. Roosevelt, May 15, 1940. Kimball, Warren F., *Churchill and Roosevelt, the Complete Correspondence*, I, p. 37.

toward the end of his reign, in about 1615 B.C. About ten years later, Sekenenre the Great and Victorious ascended the Theban throne and escalated the assault on the hated Hyksos, after a brief truce. The peace allegedly ended when the Hyksos king, Apopi III, complained without success about the noise of Sekenenre's hippopotami, roaring in their royal tank in the night; the noise apparently carried through the night air and disturbed the sleep of the Hyksos king, which was preposterous in fact, and only a pretext.[5]

This final war of liberation continued intermittently for forty years, Sekenenre III was killed in battle, and his wounds were identifiable when his mummified corpse was discovered in the Nineteenth Century. The renewed war began badly for the Thebans. Eventually, the succeeding Theban king, Kames, routed the Hyksos from Memphis, and his successor, Ahmose, came north into the Nile Delta and then besieged the Hyksos remnant and its diehard followers in the south Negev Desert at Sharuhen, and after a siege of three years, in 1575 B.C., subdued the Hyksos. Ahmose repulsed a final counter-attack from Palestine when he was absent in the south beating back the Nubians. Thus did the iniquitous tyranny of the Hyksos end and the prosperous XVIIIth Dynasty of Egypt's New Kingdom under Ahmose, began.

The legend of power had foreseen foreign conquest and prolonged strife and subjugation, culminating in liberation and the coming of a Messiah who would rule. Ahmose was somewhat believable in that exalted role. Nubia, rich in gold, ostrich feathers, and slaves, which had been temporarily liberated by a spirited slave revolt, was reconquered, and placed again under a regime of strictly enforced slavery.

It is generally agreed by scholars of the ancient world, and has been since Plato, that Egyptians were extremely conservative and unimaginative, had no philosophical interests at all, and were preoccupied with the pursuit of pleasure, material prosperity, the enjoyment of the arts, agriculture, and practical disciplines such as mathematics and engineering. They were interested in religion, but not theology, and while their astronomy was commendable, their medicine had some strong points but was intruded on by the always vivid Egyptian love of magic.[6]

The Egyptians had a uniquely large number of gods—every animal, human activity, all great geographic and planetary entities, and all natural acts, had their gods, as did deified personifications of work or attitudes, and immensely prestigious people. In the predynastic period of ancient Egypt, there were many tribes, each with their own gods, but they gradually meshed, more or less together into Northern and Southern Egypt, though only after a very long period of fluctuatingly intense warfare.

Extravagantly rich legends developed about the principal Egyptian gods—Plutarch's account of Osiris and Set being perhaps the most famous. These gods were brothers. Set was wicked and lured Osiris into a coffin with his face carved on it, then nailed it closed and threw it into the Mediterranean. The coffin washed up at Byblos (Syria), where an Erica tree grew up around it. The tree was chopped down and used as a pillar in the royal palace, where Osiris' faithful wife, Isis, and sister found it and took it back to Egypt. Set, while hunting by moonlight, came upon it

---

5 CAH, I, p. 314 (T.E. Peet).
6 CAH, I, pp. 326-7 (T.E. Peet).

and scattered the bones so widely that innumerable claims of being part of Osiris' skeleton arose, like alleged pieces of the original cross three thousand years later. When Osiris' son Horus, of whom Set was unaware, grew to be a man, he thought to avenge his father, sought out Set and engaged in combat. Horus lost an eye, but he castrated Set. Osiris was immortalized as God of the Nile.

The Egyptians regarded life as a physical fact and appearance, a totemic attachment to one of the subjects of godliness: another animal phenomenon of nature or activity, and an after-life, which was often pre-replicated in advance in this life. Salutations often referred to distaste for death and public statements often emphasized what might be taken as obvious, that the individual issuing the decree, was alive. Those who had died were held, like gods, still to be alive, but in a less real manner, but with needs that had to be addressed. There was an elaborate ceremony conducted, sometimes at intervals for years, for prominent people in which fully dressed, corpses were placed at a table within the tomb, incense was burned, water poured, food placed within the corpses' mouths, and there was even some form of ablution, following which a modified and forcibly somewhat stilted banquet ensued. It was a formidable imposition of the will not to die over the objective perceptions of the physical capabilities of a corpse. Death was, in a more physical way than subsequent religions held, a continuation of life. The feted corpse is assumed to have ascended from his tomb up the shaft to the offering room where these banquets occurred. These comforts of a ceremonialized pretense that the dead had not died existed only for the wealthy. This continuous partial life coexisted with a complete and happy life in the next world.

While these practices continued, the faith grew that gods returned and were active in human form, Osiris being the most prominent. Various kings were deemed to be the revenant Osiris. Gradually, these two religious views came together, and there were degrees of death and resurrection, generally according to the merits of the deceased in real and common life, both for good and evil. The total of Egyptian literature from the Archaic period is very sketchy and consists of some chronicles of the more difficult periods in early Egyptian history, and the customary lamentations of all societies of the fragility of human virtue and the sinfulness and shortcomings of society. With the Middle Kingdom, starting in 2400 B.C., prosperity returned to Egypt and feudalism prevailed, not altogether unlike Western Europe three thousand years later.

Osiris became steadily more preeminent among the deities, a development that could be interpreted as a gradual evolution of Egyptian theology toward monotheism. And there developed, contemporaneously with the levitation of Osiris, and as in other religions, a perceived relationship between one's moral and ethical conduct in the terrestrial world and that person's reception and station in the after-life.

However, this progress, if it may be so considered, was countered by an increasing recourse to a form of fortune, based on slavish adherence to rote in invocation of the gods, and called "hike," which could make up for ethical lapses and turned the moral and theological (as gods possessed hike also), into a crap-shoot based on the mechanical recitation of dogmatic formulas, and was even then, unpredictable. This inevitably led to a corrupt clergy, an erratically motivated populace, and a framework for Egyptian civilization that was intellectually and morally vulnerable. Obviously, no serious culture could be indefinitely sustained on this concept of cosmic organization. This was the state of Egypt at about 1600 B.C.

4. Ahmose, the Expulsion of the Hyksos, the Ahmenhotep and the Thutmose Pharaohs

Egypt, though its western neighbours are not populous and are confined to a narrow shore, and the Red Sea protects the east, has always been vulnerable to attack from the northeast across Suez and from the Upper Nile to the south. Ahmose (1580-1557 B.C.) expelled the Hyksos, who had grown fat and unfocused in the plush occupation of Egypt, and turned to deal with the south, causing the customary uprising of his rivals and enemies in northern Egypt. Ahmose fairly effectively dealt with them, but it was the traditional shuttle-cock of the ancient world of factional and tribal leaders marching back and forth and from side to side assailing the always numerous chiefs unreceptive to their preeminence. Apart from ethnic and tribal distinctions, there was little to distinguish the more from the less successful except their numbers, military skill, or sophistication of weapons. Religion was not an unusually powerful weapon, and ideology, as it has emerged in the modern world, had not really been devised. Ahmose seized all the property of the aristocracies and tribal leaders who had opposed him, apart from the Theban al-Kalb dynasty, which was permitted to retain its land. But apart from this, the landed nobility was crushed, impoverished, and scattered, and the absolute primacy of the pharaoh was established. Egypt was his property.

The struggle to expel the Hyksos, a genuine national liberation movement, had made much more motivated warriors out of the previously rather easily distracted Egyptians. With Ahmose, the Egyptian army became the premier institution in the country and was relatively well organized into two armies—in the Nile Delta, and farther south to protect from the always nasty elements bubbling up from the Sudan and Ethiopia. The Egyptian army learned of and emulated the quiver from eastern invaders, and this gave them a technical advantage in planning and synchronizing barrages of arrows. And the craftsmen of Egypt, learning from their former Hyksos conquerors, designed and built powerful, fast-moving, and elegantly designed chariots. The pharaoh became an itinerant administrator who knew the need for being seen all over his jurisdiction and dealing with local grievances promptly and justly, to build loyalty to the absolute central monarchy.

The ruler had also to maintain control of his religious officers, and this imposed a double burden. Despite the energy and aptitudes of Ahmose, who must be reckoned a great monarch, he soon had to appoint two viziers to deal with administrative matters. It was a laborious process of constant touring and managing and preemptively stamping out incipient disloyalties as well as outbreaks of administrative incompetence and clerical heresy. The key was material prosperity, as it generally remains in government, and the pharaoh had to ensure flood and drought control, efficient agriculture and its distribution, encourage handicrafts, and the avoidance of exploitive and confiscatory taxation.

In some respects, the requirements of government have evolved little, whether changes are effected democratically or with unformalized violence. The treasury, in the first official utilization of this expression, was called The White House. In general, taxes were in kind and of twenty per cent of all production, including cattle, all grain, wine, oils, honey, and textiles, as well as luxury goods, such as perfumes and sophisticated fabrics. (At time of writing, corporate taxation in the United States is twenty-one per cent.) Egypt was an administrative pioneer in the collection of taxes, as the Greeks and even the Romans did not have tax collectors, an institution whose rise and self-assertion the West was spared until the nation-state, three-thousand years after Ahmose.

The southern vizier was effectively the treasurer and minister of revenue, and he was the minister of justice as well, ultimately presiding over all courts through an appeals process that would only occasionally be evoked to the pharaoh himself. In practice, most courts were presided over by priests, on the theory that their inspired vision and spirituality produced a sense of equity. As always in doling out judgeships, notions of avocational impartiality were generally illusory. The status of the viziers was unique, and explains the Jewish veneration of Joseph, as their champion in this great office. The pharaoh's words on the induction of Joseph, though their entire authenticity could be questioned, are entrenched in Jewish and Judeo-Christian history and "show a spirit of kindness and humanity and exhibit an appreciation of statecraft surprising in an age so remote. Such was the government of the imperial age in Egypt."[7] This ruling clerisy of Egypt was formed of former land-owners dispossessed comfortably by the king in its higher brackets, while the lower echelons were composed of the old middle class. The middle class of merchants and craftsmen also survived and prospered. The wealth of the temples, endowed by the rulers to reinforce the concept of their providential emergence and divine right, assured that there would be a refinement of the qualifications and selection process for this occupation, which soon became a thoroughly learned profession.

The entire priesthood was soon assembled in one sacerdotal organization. At Thebes, the Holy See of Egyptian religion, the high priest was known as the "Divine Consort" in reference to the high priest's wife, who enjoyed the official dignity of the "chief concubine of God." She led the ceremonial choirs and was personally entrusted with stewardship of much of the treasury of the temple. The Egyptians showed themselves insightful in inter-sexual official relationships and worldly in judging the influence of women and the ability to assert it. With this rise and veneration of the clergy and the spiritual in formal funerals, the assumed prodigies of the honoured dead were no longer emblazoned only in the inside of the coffin but were also inscribed on papyrus rolls left in the coffin. All manner of slippery clerical wheezes crept in. Statuettes bearing the implements of menial agricultural labour were put in the tomb with the deceased, to assure that they would not in the hereafter be sentenced to manual labour.

The priests retained, however, the ability to confer a permanently virtuous status on the deceased in exchange for material preferments conferred on the priests. Spectres of Reformations were early visible. The ancient Egyptian *Book of What is*

---

7   Breasted, J.H., *A History of the Ancient Egyptians*, New York, 1908, pp. 238-246.

in the Nether World, and *Book of the Portals*, presage and confirm that "grotesque creations of the priestly imagination finally gained the credence of the highest circles."[8] The corruption of the priesthood is a perennial and permanent saga, and contemporary outrages would perhaps be less vehemently denounced if the ancient traditions and temptations of those empowered to mediate between terrestrial and godly and miraculous life, and the extent to which their clergy were also compromised, were better known. All people, including those who would interpose themselves between God and men, are sinners. The greater sin has been in representing them as supermen while in function. When men are elevated to sainthood while executing a worldly office, the results are almost indistinguishable from the pagan exaltation of political leaders such as Tiberius and the lesser Caesars, Robespierre, Hitler, Stalin, and Mao Tse-tung. Ahmose was a great king, and his embalmed body reposes yet in the Museum of Cairo.

His successor, Amenhotep I, after belligerent skirmishing from the Nubians in the south, occupied upper Egypt to the Middle Kingdom frontier at the second cataract of the Nile, decisively defeated the Nubians, and constituted a new southern province that herded and conveyed the customary tax and tribute to the pharaoh each year. At the same time, Amenhotep had to brush the Libyans back from the Western Nile Delta, to which, when no one was looking, they were always attracted by the rich soil, an irresistible temptation to a desert people. Amenhotep also led his army into Asia and as far as the Euphrates, before retiring, apparently undefeated. Amenhotep reigned about ten years and was succeeded by the immortal King Tut—Thutmose I, the comparatively low-born husband of a cousin of Amenhotep, a woman whose name was also Ahmose.

In his second year as king, Thutmose conducted a severe subjugation of the Nubians, seizing the Plain of Dongola, building a formidable fortress there, and extending his writ to the fourth cataract. This area became known as the Kush. The Nubians were divided into a number of powerful nomadic tribes, and the elimination of them would have required an open-ended invasion of the bowels of Africa in pursuit of the retreating Nubians. Thutmose contented himself with capturing and executing one of the most powerful and troublesome chieftains and proceeding home at a leisurely pace in the royal Nile barge, with the Nubian chief's bound body tied and hung head down over the prow of the ship in a macabre bowsprit indicative of the pharaoh's authority. Thus did Thutmose return to Thebes.

With these matters stabilized, Thutmose proceeded into Asia, retracing Amenhotep's progress to the Euphrates (which Thutmose already claimed to have ruled in large tablets he commissioned on the Nile at Tombos). He then proceeded fairly effortlessly up the Mediterranean coast to Syria, asserting his sovereignty as necessary, but generally received with submission. Syria and Palestine, between the sea and the desert, was about four-hundred miles from south to north, and only about eighty miles from west to east. Ancient Palestine, with few harbours, a great profusion of limestone, and cut transversely by the steep ridge of Carmel, and up the middle by the Jordan Valley, was an unlikely place for such fierce claims of contested nationhood as afflict it yet. This corridor, joining Asia and Africa and connecting them

---

8 Engraved on the Tombs of the XIXth and XXth Dynasty Kings at Thebes, CAH, II, p. 52.

to Europe, was becoming steadily more contested as it became an ever-more well and richly travelled crossroads. The Hyksos had begun what was essentially piratical aggression but were succeeded by more substantial empires seeking to impose themselves. The indigenous population of the corridor, Aramaeans in the north and Canaanites in the south, formed many small city-states and had little aptitude for government. It was, and long remained, their lot to be sequentially dominated by greater powers approaching from all directions. Each city-state had its own royalty and religion, replete with its own gods, but there was a great deal of inter-marriage and movement between and among the constituent communities as greater powers came and went. The Middle East has not changed unrecognizably in the intervening millennia.

The leading town in the Syria-Palestine corridor in the Sixteenth Century B.C. was Kadesh, where the last vestiges of the Hyksos had mixed with the many other groups that milled about where the routes from three continents came together. Cuneiform was imported as a written language from the Hittite communities and Babylon, and the handicrafts of Egypt and the Near East and the Aegean and Crete were exchanged and replicated, and commercial hints of the distant civilizations of India and China sometimes appeared. The Semites proved with infinite practice to be skilled traders, and in general, less civilized tribes and peoples were attracted by the luxury and sophistication of Egypt, Babylonia, and Syria. They asserted their military prowess and expertise at inventing and adapting weapons to intimidate and subjugate more advanced civilizations, which absorbed the military lessons and eventually expelled the invaders, after they had lost their barbarous edge wallowing in the wealth of their conquests. Egypt, in particular, went through several of these cycles.

The Semites of what is now Lebanon became the Phoenicians and expanded the commerce and culture of these crossroads communities out into the Mediterranean, and became one of the Western World's earliest sea-powers by the Twelfth Century B.C., along with the Cretans, and to some extent the Egyptians. The Phoenicians sailed ever farther into the Mediterranean and into the Black Sea and up the Nile to Thebes, and moved the wares and crafts of all the bazaars they visited around the range of their commerce. Harbours were worked up at strategic points along the Eastern Mediterranean littoral, including Simyra, Beirut, Byblos, Sidon, and Tyre.

The next group of outsiders to press into the region was from ancient Iran and established the Aryan kingdom of Mitanni between the Euphrates and the Orontes in Syria and effectively cut Babylon off from the western states and peoples with which it had traded and communicated, beginning the decline of Babylon. Thutmose I eventually found himself and his army at the border of the Mitannis. In the ensuing armed struggle, Thutmose was wholly successful, but did not try to press the eastern borders of his empire beyond the Euphrates, declaring himself, in tablets and addresses to and by his subordinate clergy, the master of the world to the extent of where the sun shone, which even many of his unworldly subjects must have recognized as what was already the hyperbole of kings in a practice that never, in subsequent ages, has lapsed for long.

Having repulsed and soundly beaten the Mitanni interlopers, Thutmose returned to Egypt and buckled down to serious monument and temple-building and other self-celebratory public works. He and his architect, Ineni, expanded the Middle Kingdom temple at Thebes with a large, covered approach fronted by two great stone pylons and an immense bronze and gold-inlaid door, and upheld by mighty Lebanese cedar columns. He did a similar fix-up on the temple at Abydos of Osiris, kitting it out with silver and gold furniture, and ordained that this temple should receive offerings to be rendered in grief and respect at his own passing, which, at least actuarially, approached.

His end may have been accelerated by the prior death of his wife, Ahmose (an extraordinarily perverse coincidence), descendant of the house that had led the expulsion of the Hyksos and the liberation of Egypt, which raised a prolonged delirium of grateful thanksgiving. Their only surviving child (of five) was a daughter, `1Makere-Hatshepsut, and popular and court sentiment notwithstanding, the pharaoh's immense prestige and success, and Egypt's aversion to the notion of female rule, required him in his prime to proclaim Hatshepsut his heir. It is not clear from reliable records how his end came, but if it were not natural and peaceful, that would probably have been widely recorded.

There was a second and third Thutmose, the former quite inadequate and swiftly disposed of, but the third, heir via an inconspicuous concubine named Isis, put up a spirited fight. He had become a priest at Karnak, where he secured the support of the clergy for his eventual candidacy, and he seems to have married Hatshepsut, and to have staged a carefully prepared and flawlessly executed coup d'état on May 3, 1501 B.C., and was widely proclaimed pharaoh. Young Thutmose was not a good sharer and confined his wife to the title "chief royal wife." Of course, this was not acceptable, and she gradually surpassed him, and emerged as the pharaoh, realities of gender notwithstanding. Hatshepsut emerged as the first great known queen of history. She and her scheming court now ruled, and Thutmose III faded temporarily into obscurity.

Hatshepsut chiefly concerned herself with her own authority in Egypt and with being a relatively enlightened monarch. She gave great attention to her own and her father's tombs, which were constructed on an immense scale and with great opulence in the Valley of the Kings tombs, two miles to the west of the Nile, near Thebes, and with extravagant efforts to prevent easy discovery and vandalization. Hatshepsut did a good deal of temple and monument-building, including obelisks to herself ninety-seven and one half feet tall. But her empire frayed at the edges, and she aged and was outlasted by the imperishable Thutmose III, who emerged from her sepulchral shadow, but by this point, all the Asian domains inherited from Thutmose I were on the verge of revolt except southern Palestine, which had had a particularly vivid experience of Egyptian military severity under the Pharaoh Ahmose.

Kadesh was feeling the pulsation of Syrian nationalism and the Mitanni were contemplating a rematch. Thutmose III set out from Egypt on April 19, 1479 B.C., at the head of an army of about twenty-five thousand and was met at Megiddo, Armageddon to history, about ninety miles beyond Gaza, two weeks later, by an army of comparable size, composed of various disgruntled Asiatics, commanded by the

King of Kadesh. In a bold move that would have been disastrous facing a more alert opponent, Thutmose advanced at the head of his army, and they threaded a narrow pass in single file and emerged above Megiddo and he deployed his army in a wide arc. The Asiatics interposed themselves between Thutmose and Megiddo, but when the Egyptians charged, led by the pharaoh in his ornate chariot, they broke and fled and were hauled up over the walls of Megiddo by the populace, lowering lines of rope and clothing.

Thutmose would have completely eviscerated the broken opposition army if he had been able to keep his soldiers on task and they had not been distracted by looting the chariots and other valuable objects their enemies had abandoned in their headlong flight. As it was, they captured the tent of the King of Kadesh (with his cowering son in it), and a great many prisoners, nine hundred and twenty-four chariots, twenty-two hundred and thirty-eight horses and much valuable loot. Thutmose invested the city, and though the King of Kadesh fled, the pharaoh had most of his family and the allies in the revolt come forward in utter submission to resume their status as conquered people as the siege of Megiddo continued for several months until it surrendered, yielding up immense wealth, including an ebony statue of the King of Kadesh.

Thutmose moved north and reorganized his empire, replacing the rebellious dynasties with rulers in whom he had more confidence, whatever the lack of enthusiasm for Egyptian rule of the local populations. In a great act of piety, Thutmose contributed a number of cities he had recaptured and surrounding rural areas with large herds, and which yielded rich harvests, to the God Amon, passing a huge and self-sustaining fortune to the priesthood. Thutmose greatly expanded the temple at Karnak, even beyond the munificence of his late wife. It remains at Thebes, a timeless marvel, around a great colonnaded hall of fifty-thousand square feet.

Thutmose then set out on an ambitious and ingenious amphibious campaign, in which he avoided baring his left flank to the Phoenicians as he proceeded northward up the spine of Palestine to deal with Kadesh once and for all. He landed in northern Phoenicia, supplied himself from the sea, and subdued the Phoenician cities from the north and attacked Kadesh and faced down the Mitanni from the west, when all were anticipating his approach from the south. His army again seized a great amount of treasure, and his soldiers again lost their discipline in plunder, celebration, and drunkenness, but the Phoenician cities, with a few brief sieges to complete the process of persuasion, capitulated abjectly. Thutmose returned again to subdue Kadesh at last, which required a lengthy siege, at the end of which there had been stirrings of renewed revolt on the Phoenician coast which he had again to suppress, first at Arvad, and the following year, the thirty-second of his reign (including the co-monarchy), and again for an entire campaigning season. He returned on yet another campaign the following year, disembarked at Simyra, captured Aleppo, and hammered the Mitanni. He plundered the Euphrates valley, as the Egyptian army had been doing intermittently for fifty years, going back to Thutmose I. He also added the great oases of western Egypt to his territory. They contained rich vineyards and were among gold fields that produced six to eight hundred pounds of gold to the pharaoh's treasury every year. The oases also gave ample protection against encroachment on the Nile by the desert tribes, who were ungrateful for the Egyptian king's appropriation of their resources and territory.

The pharaoh was everywhere victorious, hosted an immense elephant hunt in Syria, and got his army to safe and comfortable winter quarters. Even the Hittites paid him tribute, out of respect, not subservience, making one of their first official appearances as a government. New columns were raised to him at Karnak—some of these columns survive, but not in Egypt. Istanbul, Rome, London, and New York prominently display columns of tribute to Thutmose the conqueror and ruler. His fourth Jubilee celebration columns, which stood on either side of the approach to the sun-temple of Heliopolis, still retain their grandeur—one on the Thames Embankment in London and the other in Central Park in New York, attesting alike, after thirty-five hundred years, to the stature of the great pharaoh in the modern metropolises on each side of the Western Ocean.

Thutmose III gave perhaps the first lesson of Western history in the importance of sea power. He required all the Phoenician ports to retain adequate stores for his army, so he could arrive within a few days sailing from Egypt at any of the Phoenician ports and proceed quickly inland, subduing a rebellious Syrian or Palestinian entity swiftly and from any and all sides. Holding the scepter of the seas enabled the pharaoh effectively to dominate Cyprus and the Aegean islands, which acknowledged his ultimate authority. From the fourth cataract of the Nile to the Aegean and from Libya to the Euphrates was an ambitious empire for the time, composed of a multiplicity of tribes and races, and controlled almost entirely by the constant application of military force abetted by the rewards of a wide commerce. With a canal connecting the Red Sea to the Nile Delta and Mediterranean, Egypt not only sat in strength and comparative security at the meeting of continents and waterways connecting Eurasia and Africa, she was the dominant cultural and political force of the known world. The Hittites were beyond the frontiers; Assyria was in its infancy, and Babylon had atrophied. Such agglomerations of disparate peoples as Thutmose ruled flourish under very talented rulers but cannot long survive the absence of one.

The rich trade of the entire Mediterranean now came in elaborate Levantine galleys up the Nile to Thebes. Astoundingly opulent cargoes of exquisitely carved ivory and ebony, gold and silver, gems, fragrances, exotic woods and artifacts of immense value and quality, and slaves from exotic places of great strength and great beauty became for the pharaoh and his entourage the wages of empire and victory. Thutmose developed the habit of returning to Thebes each winter after another successful campaign and throwing himself with undiminished energy into the administration of Egypt and the steady construction of fine buildings and monuments and temples. Two years away from the Euphrates (the crossing of which stirred an obsessive pride in the pharaoh somewhat as Napoleon and Hitler conceived of the Volga thirty-five centuries later) facilitated delusions of local independence. In his thirty-fifth year on the throne, he returned and dealt so harshly with the Mitanni and other susceptible elements that they remained quiescent for seven years. Thereafter, for the next several years, apart from chasing the wily Bedouin tribes across the Jordan, he essentially conducted campaigns that were inspections, with rewards and punishments meted out without the need of combat or repression.

In his forty-second year as pharaoh and now in his seventies, the great king was affronted by a general uprising in Syria and parts of Phoenicia, led, as always, by Kadesh, still the relic of Hyksos militarism and animosity. In this autumn of his days came the final reckoning with the Hyksos. Thutmose landed his army northwest of Kadesh, cut it off from the north, and approached from the north, putting towns and villages to fire and sword. The Kadesh army met him before the walls of their city and tried to distract the stallions of the Egyptian cavalry with a mare, but Thutmose's old comrade-general Amenemhab pursued the mare on foot and rendered her uninteresting to the Egyptian horse with his sword, presenting the Pharaoh with the mare's severed tail. (The same trusty officer had severed the trunk of a threatening elephant during the celebratory elephant hunt several years before.) Thutmose prevailed again, captured most of the Kadesh army, and he required the complete self-abasement of Kadesh, which surrendered meekly after a brief siege following the decisive defeat of its army. The renown of Thutmose III was very great and widespread, and the lore of his campaigns has permeated general literature-such as the capture of Joppa recreated in "Ali Baba and the Forty Thieves." (As with the subsequent Trojan Horse, Egyptian soldiers were insinuated into the town of Joppa in large parcels born by donkeys, and then captured the town from the inside.)[9]

In the fifty-third year of his reign, Thutmose III made his son (by an obscure wife subsequent to Hatshepsut-Mekere), Amenhotep II, his co-regent. The following year, in the spring of 1447 B.C., Thutmose III died, a universally revered and admired ruler, whose legend has endured (as his body is preserved also). His stature as a conqueror somewhat resembles that of Alexander the Great and Napoleon, and as a durable ruler, somewhat that of Augustus. Being more ancient than and somewhat superseded by them, he is not as well-remembered in the West, but stands undoubtedly as one of the gigantic figures of world history. He was the first person to build a real empire in the West, and the first hero of the whole known world. "His commanding figure, towering over the trivial plots and schemes of the petty Syrian dynasts...clarified the atmosphere of oriental politics as a strong wind drives away the miasmic vapours."[10]

Entirely predictably, the news of the death of the Great King excited the always latent ambitions of the tributary kingdoms (they were not, in more modern parlance, provinces) to slough off the onerous annual tribute that had been enforced by the pharaoh and his army and was never considered by those that paid it anything but extortion, theft, and blackmail. Amenhotep II was under no illusions about what he faced, and without waiting for confirmation of rumours that the Asiatic jurisdictions of the empire had risen in revolt, he entered Asia by land rather than sea as his father had done, as he assumed the revolt was general and could not be easily isolated. He turned north through Palestine and met an army of most of the Lebanese ports and principalities at Shemesh-Edom and smashed the enemy. He bore northeastwards into the Euphrates valley and surprised and captured seven of the rebellious dynasts at Tikhsi and continued on to the end of his father's and grandfather's advances, rescuing a frontier garrison that had been besieged in the

---

9   CAH, II, p. 84 This exploit was reenacted fictitiously in "Ali Baba and the Forty Thieves." (J.H. Breasted).
10 CAH, II, p. 87 (J.H. Breasted).

revolt. Other cities opened their gates as he approached, and in the early test of his strength, resistance collapsed.

The new pharaoh's return was a triumphal march, as he brought with him over five-hundred of the rebellious North Syrian lords and two-hundred and forty of their women, and four-fifths of a ton of gold tribute and fifty tons of copper. He completed his journey home to Thebes on the royal barge and embellished on the precedents of his forefathers. He bound the seven kings he had captured at Tikhsi and hung them by their ankles upside down over the bow in a row like spinnakers, their heads almost skimming the water. His countrymen appreciated the spectacle, and he then executed the hapless kings in what purported to be a religious sacrifice of thanksgiving, and then hung their corpses on the walls of Thebes, except for one. This last dead king he transported with him to the south as a cautionary sign to the Nubians of what they could expect if rebellion got the better of them. Kush got the hint and accepted the yoke of the pharaoh, while profiting from the trade with Africa and Abyssinia. Amenhotep II reigned peacefully after this for 25 years and died of natural causes in 1420 B.C. Buried with him in the Valley of the Kings tombs (where he remains, mummified, despite intrusions, the last being in 1901 A.D.) was his bow, which he claimed no one else could draw, on which was engraved, after his name, the description: "Smiter of the Troglodytes, Overthrower of Kush—Hacker of their cities, the Great Wall of Egypt and Protector of His Soldiers."

He was succeeded by Thutmose IV, who had to make the customary coronation visit to "Naharin the wretched" (the Euphrates), and subdue the restless marches of the empire. Practically all the Asiatic parts of the Egyptian empire revolted whenever a pharaoh died and at intervals while they lived. Thutmose IV adopted a new policy of seeking an ally in the north, as the Hittites (the Kheta) were starting to flex their muscles. The pharaoh selected the Mitanni, notwithstanding the fierce and longstanding animosity between them and the Egyptians, and requested the daughter of the Mitanni king, Artatama, as a bride. This was agreed, after some hesitation, and the young lady duly arrived for her royal assignation, and eventually presented the pharaoh with his successor, Amenhotep III. The reign proceeded, fairly peacefully, but Thutmose IV died in 1411, after completing, in memory of his grandfather, the tallest of all the Egyptian obelisks, at Karnak. It is one hundred and five feet and six inches tall, and stands now, as it has for many centuries, before the Lateran Palace in Rome.

Amenhotep III, as often happens in dynasties, was not as talented a warrior or ruler as the greatest of his predecessors, though he was capable, and he was the most opulent. There were not all the usual uprisings of the Asiatics, perhaps because of the relatively new alliance with the Mitannis, who had previously specialized in stirring up the Syrians and Phoenicians almost as a matter of course at each pharaonic passing. He did have to deal with the Nubians, another rite of passage, but these were just tribes of bandits who had no ability to challenge the pharaoh's army for control of the upper Nile. He made the Mitanni alliance closer, and a correspondence of some intimacy survives between Amenhotep III and Artatata's grandson, Tushratta. Syria and the Lebanese coastal cities were quiescent, and the empire was relatively serene. Civilians could travel through Palestine and Phoenicia in reasonable safety, and commerce across the Indian Ocean started to be a factor in the economy of Egypt and the tastes in jewelry and fabrics of its upper classes. Greek trade and cultural influences also took their place in Egypt, and Aegean, Cretan, and Greek traders became a familiar feature of life in Thebes.

Large numbers of slaves were admitted to Egypt and centrally settled around the kingdom as unskilled labour. Many became tax-paying serfs, as money flooded into the royal treasury and the commercial classes, increasingly culturally diverse as they were. The intermarriage of the serfs with the natives changed the physical and psychological character of Egypt, and as generally happens, immense enrichment was not always as wisely or tastefully deployed as it might have been. Opulence and extravagance became visible and omnipresent, in apparel, residential dwellings, public monuments, and adornments of all kinds. architecture, which had long been sophisticated, became magnificent and often on a gigantic scale.

Egypt became extremely advanced in engineering, mathematics, astronomy, anatomy, medicine, and all building trades and arts and crafts, as well as sculpture, painting, glass-making, tapestry, and from the relative fragments we have, literature as well. Here was the birth of European cathedral and basilica architecture. Luxor and Thebes grew toward each other and joined and were accorded a majestic unity of monumental buildings, grand boulevards, and spacious gardens. This was perhaps the second, after Babylon, of the mighty capitals of the Western world. But it was on a much greater scale than Babylon and was more prodigally sumptuous and classically distinguished than anything the urban world would see for a long time.

Court festivities, hunts, and spectacles all assumed astounding proportions. The pharaoh was claimed to have killed over a hundred lions, and hundreds of dangerous wild boar. With his opulence and love of the spectacular, Amenhotep III had a popular touch and unapologetically married women with no connection to the nobility. The mystery, remoteness, and semi-divine nature of the monarchy was inevitably seriously diluted. For a time, this evolution in the institution of the monarchy and of Egyptian life generally went well, but administration became more lax, the bonds of empire slackened, other kings became less deferential. In embracing the Mitanni, Amenhotep III renounced crossing the Euphrates, and lost some of his deterrent strength opposite those who coveted the great Egyptian inter-continental intersection. Some of his vassals began negotiating and maneuvering for their own account in a way previous pharaohs would not have tolerated, and the Hittites attacked the Mitanni, who resisted successfully and drove the Hittites off. The pharaoh's alliance policy appeared to have been vindicated, but the potential vulnerability of Egypt became more evident. The pharaoh sent troops to deal with uprisings around Damascus, but did not go himself, as his illustrious ancestors had done. His absence from Syria for years on end, as he luxuriated in the splendor of his capital, contributed to the relaxation of his authority in the Asian vassal states. Most of these were restive by the time Amenhotep the Magnificent, as he was known (a foretaste of Louis XIV), died, in 1375, after a reign of thirty-six years. (It was during his reign that Moses departed Egypt with his fugitive co-religionists, already accustomed to persecution.)

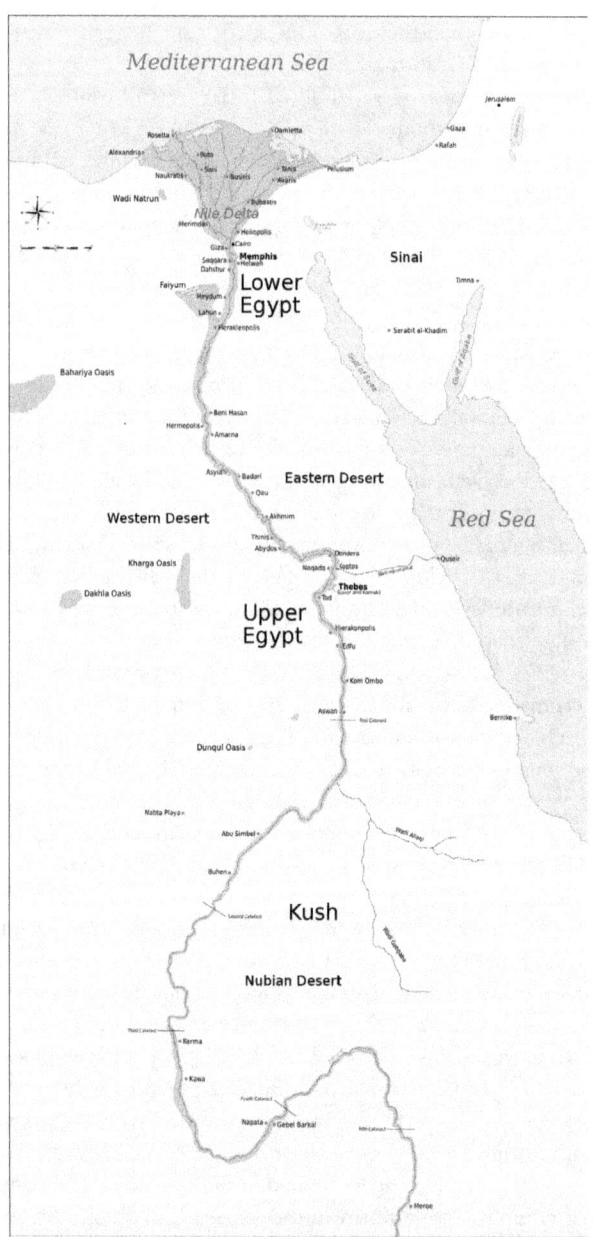

Map of Ancient Egypt, showing the major cities of the Dynastic period (c. 3150 BC to 30 BC).

5. Ikhnaton and Harmhab

Amenhotep IV faced the subtle and implacable task of managing a transition in the economy and ethnicity and sociology of Egypt as its monarchy evolved, and the restlessness of vassals and pressures on the frontiers challenged the empire. The external pressures and internal stresses were both made more difficult to manage by the tensions within the country, and the new pharaoh had no qualifications to address the problems, nor the rare natural instinct to lead a beleaguered empire, and did not have a reliable and disinterested group of royal advisers—rather his mother and his wife and a learned priest—not at all the opportunists, superannuated servitors, and shameless courtiers who cleave to many inexperienced inheritors of great office. The young pharaoh had a philosophical mind and was a discriminating and disciplined thinker. He pursued intellectual and moral objectives with sincerity and intellectual curiosity and acuity. These were admirable aptitudes and motives, but not the dispositions immediately needed to preserve the empire of his forefathers. He was, in some respects, the most admirable and intellectually distinguished of all the pharaohs in the several thousand years of that kingship, but he was not a man for his times.

The growth of the empire had rendered implausible and obsolescent the ancient Egyptian religion of a sun-god of national scope. The natural reservoir of the superstitious and supplicative tendencies of ignorant masses might be satisfied with such a facile and simple deity, but the intellectual vigour any robust religion requires could not possibly be satisfied with such a truncated concept of cosmic forces. The new pharaoh, like other intelligent and worldly Egyptians, saw both the intellectual necessity and the practical potential for a more metropolitan religious conception. The impracticality and illogic of multi-theism was increasingly evident, and the pharaoh was increasingly vested with the moral authority of a monotheistic deity, even as the proclivity to worship him was mitigated by public familiarity with the formerly impossibly inaccessible king. The Egyptian words for the sun and the sun-god ceased to be the same. The gradual shift in the fundamental nature of the state religion naturally aroused schisms and animosities, as only the infelicitous combination of religious dogma and clerical ambition can produce.

The pharaoh was only eighteen-years-old at the outset of his reign and he started into these vehement theological matters at once. References to a multiplicity of gods had to be avoided, and a great deal of official nomenclature implying polytheism, in the names of pharaohs and elsewhere, had to be altered. Because his name meant polytheism (Amon), this was changed, and changed in the temples and gravestones of the nobles—the old terminology was relentlessly effaced, presaging the Stalinist practice of repressing all references to purged individuals and their air-brushing out of official photographs. An understandably fierce resentment arose, which was precisely what the unsettled and materially challenged empire did not need, but which the Egypt as the Western world-leading state, politically and culturally, did need. The old Egyptian religion could not be defended and was not accessible to the cultures that Egypt claimed, even if only by the fiat of military domination, supplemented by Egypt's grandiosity, to rule. The rise of Egypt as a world power outstripped its evolution as a sophisticated culture of which its subjects could approve. Amenhotep IV changed his name to Ikhnaton, meaning God is satisfied (i.e., a singular God). It was a bold stroke, but the entire empire was rendered unstable.

An impossible state of affairs resulted. The royal palace had been clumsily purged of references to the previous Amenhoteps, and the great temples and obelisks stood out on the skyline but were not the centres of public worship that they had been. For a very young man and new king, Ikhnaton embarked on a very bold and comprehensive plan. He deserted Thebes and Luxor and established three capitals for the empire, one in Nubia, one in Syria, and one on the northern Nile delta, Akhetaton. The pharaoh dedicated this new capital as the property of the one God. It was a little like modern countries: Canada, Australia, Turkey, India, Brazil, Pakistan building new capitals, but with a religious rather than a political purpose, and more in the act of flight than of renovation.

Ikhnaton knew enough about politics to know that he had to try to entice the higher clergy with him. His counselor Eye, a senior priest as well, in a considerable display of multi-tasking, master of the royal horse and husband of the king's nurse, and his chief generals and the pharaoh's other principal aides were very richly rewarded for supporting the king in the reformation he was trying to conduct. The king gave the effort at evangelization to the logic of a god for all under the same secular jurisdiction his most ardent and complete attention. He wrote a number of hymns that were used in the temples, and which showed some talent for poetic composition as well as ecclesiastical persuasion.

It must also be emphasized that Ikhnaton's worship of a single God was based on a poetic insight into God's presence in nature and was accompanied by his own pursuit of a life of simplicity. He dismantled the mighty edifice of pharaonic pomp and circumstance and ate and acted humbly. He added something about "living in his daily life" in all public references to himself. He anticipated Judeo-Christian deism and emphasis on the glories of nature. He wrote of the lilies being "drunken" in the radiance of God, where birds lift their wings "In adoration of the living God," and where the divine light causes the fish "in the midst of the great green sea" to leap from the water to glimpse God's universal light. Ikhnaton was more a prophet than a ruler, in some ways more like modern national leaders and intellectual innovators such as Gandhi, Walesa, and Mandela, and though his views did not immediately prevail, and unlike those men, he did not see his efforts crowned in victory. He did foresee and proclaim the mightiest and most universal concept of all: a single, universal, Godly, just, creator. It required fourteen-hundred years and the arrival of someone claiming to be God's son, and eventually largely accepted in that Messianic role, to entrench Ikhnaton's concept in worldwide belief.

Such a religious reformation could have been assumed not to be conducive to the young pharaoh's attendance to the practical and rather grubby problems of holding his inherited empire together, a task which had absorbed the entire military and political skills of his ascendants. He was initially greeted with respect from those who had known his antecedents. The Hittite and Mitanni leaders wrote cordially and solicitously. The Hittites had gathered in tribes behind them, learned lessons from the defeats they had suffered at the hands of the Egyptians and their Mitanni allies of convenience and had become a very formidable rival to Egypt, poised on the northern edge of the wobbling Syrian vassal states. At this improvident point, the Mitanni king, Tushratta, who had been a reliable ally, was murdered by one of his sons, and that people was convulsed in civil strife and the Hittite king took advantage of conditions to offer his daughter in marriage to one of the Mitanni faction-heads, assisted him in becoming the Mitanni king who then shifted his regime's loyalty from Egypt to the Hittites.

It was a strategic disaster for Egypt, compounded by the treacherous desertion of some of the Syrians, who normally waited for the death of a pharaoh to defect. There were Egyptian loyalists who cried out for help to Ikhnaton, who dithered, sought more information, and allowed himself to be deceived by treacherous, double-dealing Syrian princes, and was completely diffident as his empire started to decompose with increasing speed. Southern Palestine started to crumble as well, as ancient foes, regularly chastised by Ikhnaton's predecessors, came out of the undergrowth, and became agents of the Hittite-Mitanni alliance. Egyptian loyalists fled for their lives and with no shoring up from the pharaoh and his army as in olden time, the Asiatic empire was a house of cards and collapsed accordingly.

Ikhnaton was strangely passive—his enlightened religious preoccupations were no excuse for a complete lack of any personal, dynastic, or national sense of self-preservation. In fact, the pharaoh's domestic position was also severely enfeebled, as his authoritarian suppression of all the symbols and public references to the old religion provoked a religious civil war and the disaffection of much of his army, navy, and bureaucracy. The veterans of the glorious campaigns of the past were particularly outraged at Ikhnaton's complete inability to respond to the imperial crisis and his other-worldly and repressive preoccupation with spiritual divinations. His initial reasoning on the limitations of the Egyptian sun-god was its lack of universality that could enlist the fidelity of conquered people, but now there was scarcely an empire left to be concerned about and Egypt itself was asunder in its religious adherence.

One of Ikhnaton's most prominent supporters, Harmhab, a supporter of the pharaoh's religious views but above all a patriotic Egyptian, rallied the dissident officers and exploited the imperial crisis and menace at the borders and within the state to arrange peace with the refractory priesthood while he urged the pharaoh to abdicate in favour of his son-in-law (as he had no son). Ikhnaton did so and departed his new capital and died shortly after, not evidently violently. He was unceremoniously buried after dying aged about thirty, yet after sixteen years as king. On the canvass of history, he deserves and enjoys considerable distinction, but as pharaoh, he was an almost unmitigated failure. He was a brave soul and mind, an individualist and internationalist, and the world's first substantial monotheist, who received no recognition, nor any treatment except to be reviled, until Hebrew prophets and scholars referred to him politely nearly eight hundred years later. There was something of a Gorbachev aspect to Ikhnaton, as well as an element of Ozymandias, when one visits his abandoned capital, still very discernible and overwhelmingly forlorn, even by the unpromising standards of ancient ruins. But Ikhnaton was more than either Gorbachev or Ozymandias because of his spirituality and his status as a pioneer of almost all successful religious activity of the last two millennia of human activity. He saw, in a sense, the promised land, and so did those who followed him, but none of them lived to realize their dreams. Yet they were ultimately realized and triumphed throughout the world for many centuries, and are formidable, yet challenged only by anti-theists, not by other religious denominations.

Another son-in-law of Ikhnaton, Tutankhamon, soon replaced his brother-in-law and acquiesced in the reassertion of the old religion. The priesthood now ran the creaking empire, in alliance with a clique of officers and civil servants and courtiers (generally the same occupation). Tutankhamon was a figurehead pharaoh for about seven years but is the most famous pharaoh because his tomb was discovered intact in 1922 and with all the articles buried with him. The discovery was a massively publicized sensation all over the world; this was the renowned King Tut.

Eye briefly followed, but then came Harmhab, the restorer, the Thermidorian figure who generally emerges after a state of chaos, a Bonaparte or Thiers, or what many Germans thought they were getting with Hitler: someone to bring an end to a complete civic breakdown and quickly organize an eleventh-hour response to an acute national crisis. Well regarded as a long-serving high functionary by the officers and the priests, he won immediate approval as ruler and had a spontaneous mandate to prevent the complete collapse of the empire, as people who have not sought great office do when they accept such burdens in great emergencies. He took the treasury in hand, reorganized the senior ranks of the army and agreed on a common front with the priests and reopened all the temples on traditional lines but with no vengeance against the followers of Ikhnaton, though evidence of that pharaoh was effaced. He enacted strict statutes against abuse of public office. Those tax-collectors convicted of extortion were subject to having their noses cut off and banished to a desolate desert outpost. Those who stole animals or hides from herdsmen were subject to a hundred strokes of a cane or lash. He toured the entire country, reorganizing the administration, rewarding the honest and rooting out the corrupt. Harmhab reigned for thirty-five years and got Egypt back to prosperity and national cohesion. He was unable to regain Syria, but retained southern Palestine, and achieved a durable cease-fire with the Hittites. He was succeeded by Ramses I in 1315 B.C.

6. The Ramessid Kings

Ramses I began the immense colonnaded hypostyle of Karnak (a name revived by many modern comedians, including American night-time television host Johnny Carson), but he was elderly and brought in his son Seti as co-regent, and after a year, Seti became pharaoh. He turned at once to restoration of the recently imperiled empire. The Bedouins, the fierce nomads of the east bank of the Jordan, had attacked the Palestinians who were tumbling pell-mell back into Egypt. Seti led the Egyptian army back into Palestine and Syria, returning to Megiddo and crossing the Jordan (despite its immense renown, the Jordan River is only about fifty feet wide in most places), and then turned westward and restored Egyptian authority in southern Lebanon. He cleared the southern Phoenician ports and received pledges of allegiance (for what they were worth) from many of the Phoenician princes and southern

Syrian dynasts. It was the first appearance of an Egyptian pharaoh at the head of his army in this region in over fifty years, and he restored his tactical ability to bring his army back into play in this theatre by sea. Seti returned overland to Egypt, where a huge official welcoming party cheered heartily as the pharaoh's ornate chariot, leading the army, appeared, with conquered Syrian dynasts plodding resignedly in front of Seti's chariot, prodded, and lightly whipped to keep them moving and fully conscious of their conquered and abased status.

Seti spent the next year clearing the Libyans away from the western Nile Delta and returned to Asia the next year to try to regain Egypt's position in the north. He pushed through the buffer tribe of Amorites, captured Kadesh yet again and broke even in heavy skirmishing with the Hittites, who now threatened the entire region. He negotiated a treaty with the Hittites, and although they could not be trusted, it at least was a mutually respectful document that implicitly acknowledged that Egypt remained a serious power in the region. Seti spent most of his energies thereafter in public works and monuments, roads, and canals, and reinvesting in the revenant prosperity of his empire. He died peacefully at the head of a contented and stable empire in 1292 B.C., and was followed by his son Ramses II, who on learning of the pharaoh's death, executed a well-planned coup against his elder brother, and smoothly replaced him in the succession, as Seti was laid to rest in a magnificent alabaster tomb, where he remains yet, identifiable from his bones as a tall and powerful man in his day.

Ramses II embarked at once on a comprehensive plan to consolidate gains under Seti and retrieve Egypt's status at the height of its power. He went at once to Thebes and cemented relations and a common imperial policy with the leaders of the army, clergy, and clerisy, packing in unquestionable loyalists where appropriate. He ordered the viceroy of Kush to reopen the Nubian goldfields to help replenish the imperial treasury and seized several of the Phoenician ports to enable him to make an amphibious strike at the flank of the lost Syrian provinces, as Thutmose III had done. Although this gave Ramses II some strategic flexibility, it also gave the Hittite king, Mutallu, the time to demand levies of all his vassal tribes and peoples and organize a defence in depth. Ramses likewise demanded and received contributions of soldiery from Nubians, Palestinians, and others, and both armies numbered about twenty-thousand. Incited by claimed Bedouin deserters from the Hittite forces, Ramses believed that Mutallu had withdrawn his army to Aleppo. Ramses strung his army out on a route of march, took the vanguard with his household troops, and rushed northwards to invest Kadesh, yet again in its blood-stained history.

The Bedouins were agents of the Hittite king and Mutallu moved his forces to the east of Kadesh as Ramses moved up on the west, and the Hittite king kept his army invisible to Ramses by keeping the city of Kadesh between them in Ramses' army's line of sight. Ramses' reconnaissance unit brought in two Asiatic spies, who after savage torture, confessed the position of the Hittite army and the mortal danger in which the pharaoh now found himself. He called at once for the nearest division in his train to close up, but it was already attacked by the Hittite main army in overwhelming force and was sliced to small units and annihilated. Some units were able to flee north in rout and warn Ramses of what had happened and arrived in his camp with the Hittite chariots in hot pursuit. The Egyptians beat off the immediate pursuers, and with unflappable coolness, the pharaoh organized his forces and struck back. He made some headway but saw the strength of the reinforcements approaching the Hittite front, regrouped and attacked to the south east where Hittite lines were thinner, and did great damage to the Hittite flank as he pushed them up against the Orontes River and smashed units of Mutallu's household, killing his scribe, charioteer, chief bodyguard, and brother. The king of Aleppo had to swim for his life and barely survived.

Mutallu, though hard-pressed by this magnificently impetuous assault, would have been able to pull reinforcements in behind Ramses and destroy most of the Egyptians in a pincer, but as happened with less seasoned troops in the Middle East, especially when mercenaries were involved, Mutallu's forces were so intoxicated by seizing the pharaoh's camp that they reined in their chariots and gave themselves over altogether to plunder. While so engaged, some of Ramses' straggling units from the line of march, forewarned and incited to haste by Ramses' messengers, fell on Mutallu's main army as it ransacked the pharaoh's camp and baggage trains, and massacred much of it.

This substantially reduced the Hittite advantage, and the battle resumed on a less one-sided basis, though Mutallu inexplicably held back his eight thousand infantry who had not yet been blooded on the day and were fresh troops. Ramses was still outnumbered, but not too one-sidedly and he led his own forces in a succession of chariot charges that did honour to the most valorous traditions of the greatest pharaohs. As the sun started to sink, his final division on the ill-fated march arrived by forced march and drove the main force of the Hittite army within the walls of Kadesh. Ramses' losses had been greater than Mutellu's, but he held the field at the end of the day and had been memorably courageous and effective in extricating himself from what could have been an unmitigated disaster. Ramses made no effort to besiege Kadesh and returned to Egypt in an attitude of confected triumph, but to the always wavering Asiatic states for whose suzerainty Egypt was now contending with the Hittites, it was not clear which was the wave of the future in the region. Certainly, Harmhab, Seti, and Ramses II had restored Egypt as a serious power. Ramses spent several years reasserting himself in Palestine and around the Sea of Galilee. It was hard slogging, but Ramses took back southern territories as the Hittites continued to creep south from Kadesh. The desperate struggle at Kadesh achieved a folkloric quality, deservedly, like Caesar at Elysia and Napoleon at the Beresina.

Ramses II continued the struggle to regain Egypt's position for about fifteen years when the political realities of this always embattled region put a rod on the back of the belligerent Hittites. Mutellu died, just as the Assyrians, who had long lurked on the edge of the world crossroads, building and periodically testing their strength, crushed the Mitanni and emerged in strength on the eastern flank of the Hittites. Mutellu's successor, Hattushil, immediately saw the wisdom of ending the struggle with Egypt, a relatively civilized country and reasonable leader compared to the Assyrians. As with the barbarians on the borders of the Roman Empire more than a thousand years later, groups of Asiatic marauders appeared in sequence, and the next were always to be more savage than the group that preceded them.

The Assyrian king, Shalmaneser I, arrived in great strength, and with flared and flaming nostrils on the far bank of the Euphrates and Hattushil, in instantaneous recognition of the long-concealed fraternity of the Hittites and Egyptians, negotiated a treaty of "permanent peace" which was delivered in form to be signed by Ramses II in 1272 B.C. The Hittites had been transformed from the hammer of the north against Egypt to the contents of the sandwich between Egypt and Assyria. The treaty confirmed boundaries, promised eternal peace between the parties, made a defensive alliance that each would come to the aid of the other in case of attack by a third party, and invoked a thousand gods on each side as enforcers. (Ikhnaton's monotheistic influence had been eradicated.) The wives of Ramses and Hattushil began a warm correspondence ("Dear Sister'), and thirteen years later, in 1259, Hattushil made a state visit to Egypt as his daughter replaced "Dear Sister' as the wife and queen of the pharaoh. This great occasion was the forerunner of spectacular public state visits of the future, such as the German emperor Wilhelm II to his grandmother, Queen Victoria, in 1899, of Edward VII to Paris in 1906, Hitler to Mussolini in 1936, King George VI and Queen Elizabeth to President Roosevelt in 1939, and President Nixon to China and then the Soviet Union in 1972. Ramses II was able to complete his long and successful reign in peace.

With Ramses II, the centre of Egypt was drawn north to the Delta, as the focal point of Egyptian life and commerce shifted toward the Eurasian crossroads. Ramses left behind at Thebes the greatest room of the ancient world, the colonnaded temple begun by his grandfather at Karnak, and the greatest monolithic statues ever created, including one of himself which weighed a thousand tons. As Egypt flourished and slaves and serfs were imported to do the heavy construction and mining and work in the marble quarries, the country became more dependent on mercenaries from the lean and hungry Asiatics, coveting the stupefying wealth of Egypt. Palestine and part of Syria remained in Egyptian possession, and the empire to the south and west had not contracted. There were magnificent spectacles throughout the calendar as cities and provinces and tribes arrived bringing tribute and were greeted in pharaonic ceremonies designed to overawe the vassals and subjects.

Following the extirpation of Ikhnaton's heretical usurpation, the old religion was reimposed, but with little vitality, and was further compromised by being united with the deification of the pharaoh. Every temple was now also a residence of the pharaoh, as his spiritual presence might alight there at any time, even if he was physically situated far away. In all of the circumstances, the priesthood did not have the moral authority of earlier times. The heresy had been suppressed, but the religious mind of Egypt had been permanently distracted and partly demotivated. The retention of dogma is, in practice, impossible, when it has been contested and resides only on force and habit. But the demystification of the priesthood and the elevation of the royal house to divine spiritual status made the priesthood an ever more powerful bulwark of the throne. What it lost in spiritual adherence it may be said to have replaced in wealth and political influence, and the high priests and great temples were gradually better provided for over the one hundred and fifty years after Ramses II.

The Ramessid kings were, in any case, very materialistic and acquisitive, and the temples came to contain all manner of hokey pretexts for soliciting contributions to the pharaoh for favours he had allegedly conferred or would perform if suitably worshipped and tangibly rewarded. It must also be said that with the materialization and secularization of the state religion, there also arose, as an undetected currant from Ikhnaton, the urge to silent, unostentatious worship to a disinterested God who would hear and answer the supplicant. With the vulgarization and greater ostentation of the Ramessid religion, there flowed ever more widely the encouragement of unspoken faith—direct communication with the deity, or combination of deities, in prayer based on faith and virtue and without liturgy or ceremony. This would prove, after some centuries, an overpowering and irresistible force. It, like so much else, began in Egypt.

Egypt, through luxury, the absence of foreign invaders, and an unaccountable political and religious hierarchy, was gradually drifting from the pioneering intellectual qualities and patriotic militarism that built and maintained and resurrected it, to a self-indulgent, ethnically diluted, rentier state built on slave labour and racial insolences, morally directed by a visibly corrupt clergy in the name of a self-engorging royal kleptocracy, and defended by mercenaries of steadily less indefectible loyalty. Ramses led a lascivious private life, with an immense harem and over one hundred and fifty children. He maintained them all as a royal family and many proved talented soldiers, and administrators who were admired for their human qualities. But he outlived many of them, and the whole administration became less vigilant, with the usual resulting encroachments in the Western Desert and the upper Nile. The pharaoh became sedentary and unresponsive, and perhaps somewhat senile, yet on he lived and reigned. Finally, in his nineties, and after sixty-seven years of rule, he died in 1225 B.C. (none too soon for the stability of the spavined regime). His was an epochal time and passing; as with Augustus, Charlemagne, Louis XIV, Victoria, and Franz Josef, at his mighty obsequies, a whole era and a civilization were laid in his magnificent sepulchre with him.

The entire strategic equation in the Middle East was altered by the thrust downwards through the Balkans of the Greeks, pushing the Aegean population off-shore and increasingly off the Aegean islands and to Asia Minor and what are now Turkey, Syria, Lebanon, Israel, and Egypt. The Greeks quickly became a dominating seafaring people, the Aegean became more active and with more itinerant traders than ever, and Egypt's status as the Eastern Mediterranean's greatest naval power, always the ultimate pillar of Egyptian strength, deteriorated. This pattern of irresistible migratory waves had occurred intermittently for centuries, as has been recorded, up to the Hittites and Assyrians, and would ultimately be resumed in overwhelming numbers and military strength. But in this case, it was coming from the north and northwest, and the Greeks, even then, were not unsophisticated. This migration of the Greeks had been gradually proceeding for about eight hundred years, and for a time, the movements of the Greeks were the greatest demographic pressures on the Eastern Mediterranean; but the Middle East cross-roads was a magnet that attracted populations from all directions.

Ramses II was succeeded by his thirteenth son, Merneptah, who was already elderly, probably nearly seventy, and he didn't have the energy to push back the

Libyans, much less resume the attempted reexpansion of the empire. Despite his generous shipment of grain to the Hittites when they were afflicted by famine in Merneptah's first year as pharaoh, he discovered the Hittites were assisting the depredations of the Libyans and helped to incite the revolt of the Palestinians and coastal towns, right down to Askalon, the gateway to Egypt. In a formidable performance for the new but geriatric pharaoh at the head of an army that had not lifted a spear in anger or even in formation for decades, Merneptah led his army to the prompt and harsh subjugation of all the rebellious towns and areas, executed the ring-leaders, flogged the suspect, required mass acts of submission, generally rubbed the disaffected populations' noses in their indiscipline, and for good measure and to send a calculated message to the ungrateful who would betray him, sacked a few Hittite border forts and towns. A siege and complete destruction of the rebarbative city of Gezer required an additional campaigning season. All in all, it was a stylish performance, and the message was received.

However, by the time that frontier was reasonably laid-low and ship-shape, the Libyans had escalated their customary infiltrations into the western Nile Delta to a full-scale offensive that had brought them up almost to Heliopolis. It was none too soon for Merneptah to move his now battle-refamiliarized army back to the west, as these crafty and fierce Berbers were now only about fifty miles from the pharaoh's palace. The delays imposed on Merneptah were in some respects a blessing as the Libyan leader, Meryey, who launched a combined military invasion and demographic migration, as he had inflated his ambition to imagine that he could permanently occupy Egypt right up to the western debouches of the Nile. He brought his queen, family and court, such as these desert people had, with him in his army of about twenty-thousand, allegedly including for the first time in these conflicts, some Europeans (Etruscans, chased to sea by the Greeks). Merneptah organized his army, now crisply trained and battle-hardened, and rudely intercepted Meryey and his army and civilian occupation force almost as they reached one of the pharaoh's western Delta estates. Merneptah and his army fell upon Meryey on April 15, 1221 B.C., and an intense battle ensued which lasted for six hours.

From this perspective, it can be seen that the Egyptian empire was in the latter part of its cycle, but this day was a glory of its autumn. Merneptah kept his infantry at close quarters in mortal combat most of the day—no Libyan disengagement was possible though the Libyans slowly retreated. As the retreat quickened and the fear and fatigue of the enemy became clear to a seasoned commander, Merneptah brought forth his massed archers and they fired a rapid sequence of withering blasts of arrows directly into the Libyans. Then Merneptah, as greater commanders would do in subsequent centuries, from Alexander the Great and Julius Caesar to Napoleon and William Tecumseh Sherman, set his charioteers and cavalry and reserves on the back and flanks of the enemy, and ran them down, overwhelmed and slaughtered them. Meryey made his escape, fleeing as he saw his line start to waiver after a few hours, but he had brought his entire household, including valuables, furniture, carpets, jewelry, as well as his whole family and entourage. The pharaoh captured all of it and all of them, except for six of Meryey's sons who died in the battle their father fled. About nine thousand of the Libyans and their allies were killed and about an equal number captured. Everything of value in the baggage train and equipage of the Libyans was carted back to the pharaoh, including nine-thousand copper swords, and what was left was torched in a mighty bonfire.

The immense loot was piled onto donkeys and led to the pharaoh's palace, and among the evidences of the bone-crushing victory of Egypt were small mountains of severed hands and legs and occasionally moldering heads of the deceased enemies. Merneptah assembled his nobles in the great hall of his palace and read them a dispatch from one of his officials from the western edge of Egypt. Meryey had been overthrown and banished and his policy repudiated, and the Libyans affirmed solemnly that there would be no more depredations of Egypt from that quarter. It was a great victory, though these victories now were on Egypt's frontiers and not in distant lands of pharaonic conquest. Rounding things out, Merneptah sent a force south to put the Nubians in their place, though their offenses had not been especially troublesome, and the pharaoh's army was not seriously resisted.

Merneptah, all in all, had been a distinguished pharaoh, but given his age, as there was not time to excavate an entire tomb for himself, he rather gauchely and cheesily cannibalized the magnificent tomb of Amenothep III. This was not well-viewed. He followed in the footsteps of his father, Ramses II, in stealing marble and monuments and emblems from the tombs of his own father and others. Ramses II, who had been egregious in these matters, had left behind a monumental request that his own memorials not be tampered with, but Merneptah ignored this. The fixation of the Egyptian kings and nobles on their deaths and memorials was understandable, and in some ways (embalming, decoration), it was original. But the practice of raiding the tombs of previous pharaohs to engross their own and then asking that their tombs be left untroubled revealed the corruption of the system. Nor, perhaps, would there have been such a preoccupation with tombs so elaborate that they constituted and reinforced a pretense that the deceased was not really dead, if Egyptian religion were not so polytheistic and evidently pecuniary and memorial, and not, as Ikhnaton had wished, more spiritual and egalitarian. (The discovery of the tomb of Merneptah disconcerted the claims of those who held that since he was thought by many to be the pharaoh of the Israelite exodus, he must have drowned in the celebrated crossing of the Red Sea.)

The death of Merneptah, after a successful reign of about ten years, gave rise to the rending struggles for power that often attend the decline of a dynasty and its jurisdiction when an elderly ruler passes on. Initially, there were two contenders to succeed, Amenmeses and Merneptah-Sipta. The first was a distant collateral relative who was easily eliminated by Siptah, a court politician of skill and complete unscrupulosity. His power base was on the border of and in Nubia, which furnished him a quantity of gold which he used to grease his candidacy. His viceroy there, Seti, was so essential to Siptah's role, and so steeped in the intrigues of the court, that he supplanted Siptah after a few years, removing the rug from under him. He showed some aptitudes for kingship, despite the customary morbid and even necrophilic preoccupation with tombs, his own and others.

But the court atmosphere of seething nobles, a reign of courtiers and favour-seekers, ambitious generals and admirals and high priests, and the generally sleazy and unpatriotic nature of conspiracy-plagued Egyptian court patriotism compromised by endless dealing with foreign rivals, dissident minorities, and frontier charlatans representing themselves as saviours and conciliators, made it impossible for anyone but the most steady and sure character to prevail; the foregoing was not a fair description of Siptah II. He soon vanished, precipitating a state of official chaos. All central power disintegrated, leaving authority devolved unofficially to local nobility and regional leaders and priest and army detachment commanders. It was an almost spontaneous atomization of the empire that proceeded so quickly and far, it reveals how skeletal the central pharaonic state had become under the focused but leisurely and interminable rule of Ramses II, which despite his merits, was little uplifted by the venerable Merneptah.

What followed was just an ignoble snake-pit of equal but equally unworthy contenders for the succession. Mountebanks and charlatans succeeded each other every few days, claiming the emblem or legitimacy of rule, but none of them could achieve any such status without a cohort of military bully-boys to intimidate court scribes and officials, who then recruited less irritating, but not more talented, claimants of pharaonic legitimacy. Each of these factions claimed to expropriate great estates, dispossess rivals, and reduce drastically the number of individuals to whom it was acceptable to make spiritual or tangible offerings in the temples.

The best of the candidates to emerge from this convulsing matrix of instant suitors for the imperial dignity, one Setnakht, surged to the fore, sword in hand, in about 1200 B.C., to be done with a Syrian usurper who was pillaging the temples and simply using the remnants of the central state as a fulcrum for robbery. Despite the colossal defeat of the last Libyan effort under Meryey, the Libyans again sensed their chance, and their customary infiltration of the western Nile Delta began all over again, fortified now by the migrating Aegeans, who included what became the Philistines, who poured into Lebanon. Setnakht did reestablish the pharaonic state, a prodigious feat given the dissolution that had occurred, but he died in 1198, and left the unsteady throne to his son, Ramses III, who proved a vigorous ruler. He reorganized the military but was by now largely dependent on mercenaries from the frontiers. The Aegean fugitives, including some Philistines, were in the custom of maritime raiding up the western Nile, in cooperation with the Libyans, who had crept back since the drubbing given Meryey. They staged a coordinated amphibious assault in 1194, but Ramses III smashed them even more decisively than had Merneptah twenty-eight years before, killing twelve thousand, five hundred, and capturing most of the rest. The prisoners shambled along in chains for review by the pharaoh and public, the mockery of the Egyptian populace. Most were delivered into slavery, but a number were made human sacrifices to the post-Ikhnaton Amon, God of Gods. The Pharaoh boasted, "A woman might walk abroad as far as she wishes with her veil raised without fear of molestation."[11]

There was great rejoicing in Egypt at the destruction of the Libyan-Aegean force, but more sinister was the Aegean Philistine army and navy advancing like a plague down the eastern shore of the Mediterranean through Syria and the ports of what is now Lebanon. An immense migration descended and seemed fixated

---

11 CAH, II, p. 173 (J.H. Breasted).

on a holy mission of seizing Egypt, as the Hyksos had done. Ramses III prepared thoroughly for this onslaught and led the Egyptian fleet. He had loaded the decks of his ships with crack Egyptian archers. The Egyptian navy approached and raked the decks of the enemy with arrows before the ships could directly engage, and the invading vessels were resistless against Egyptian boarding parties. The Aegean navy was completely destroyed, and on land, the attempted migration was a debacle; Ramses defeated the military units which could scarcely maneuver among the two-wheeled ox-carts carrying the families and property of the migrants, and the Egyptian victory on land was even more decisive. Ramses ordered that civilians be treated as civilians, but in the melee, the carnage was very great. The invaders returned to the Syrian border, happy enough to have chased off the Hittites. It was another mighty pair of Egyptian victories, but Egypt was still a country with a rotted state, depending on mercenaries to fight for it, with a dynasty whose legitimacy was coextensive with the pharaoh's ability to defeat invaders, and aware that the Aegean wave of migrants was far from over.

The next threat was from Meshesher, king of the western Berbers (Meshwesh), who had attacked the Libyans as they licked their wounds after their last encounter with the pharaoh and forced the Libyans to join them in yet another assault on Egypt from the west. Again, Ramses III led in person and was victorious. The Meshwesh were brave but unsophisticated and were no match for the pharaoh's well-paid and equipped and much-tested legions, even though they were motivated by money and not patriotism. Meshesher was killed. The Libyans reverted to uncoordinated and gradual seepage into the western Delta, not as a military operation, but like contemporary Muslims entering Europe or Central Americans the United States. Ramses III returned to Syria, to strengthen and fortify his frontiers, and administer a sharp rebuff to the Hittites, who were now in decline, squeezed between the aggressive Aegeans and Assyrians and the still-formidable Egyptians.

Ramses III engaged in the now customary public works and encouragements of foreign commerce, and Egypt did not yield its status as the world's crossroads, as intercourse with the northern and western Mediterranean and Africa and the Indian Ocean increased steadily. The Egyptians built ships of over two hundred feet from Lebanese cedar if for river use, and the most efficient of hardwoods for ocean travel. The canal at what is now Suez silted up occasionally but was soon cleared again. At Thebes, Luxor, and Karnak, architecture and construction achieved new prodigies of grandiosity, generally in monumental celebration of the quasi-divine genius of the regnant pharaoh. His tours of his domains were now reviews and verifications of the docility of his neighbor; in a particular flourish, Ramses III had a tame and well-fed lion trot or gallop along beside his chariot, completely unleashed. It was an impressive tour de force. Ramses III was not as effective in bringing the bloated and opulent clergy to heel as he was in subduing foreign opponents. His father, Setnakht, had bought the priesthood off to facilitate getting complete control of the army and clerisy, and individual temples now had their own fleets which removed the tithes and tribute they collected in Egypt to overseas colonies. In a manner that became more familiar in the times of Henry IV and Richelieu, they were "a state within a state," and reducing them to a state of subordinacy was a challenge, at which statesmen became more adept with experience. Ramses III was a pioneer.

A census the pharaoh had conducted in the midst of his reign showed that the temples had one hundred and seven thousand slaves—two per cent of the entire population (seven million people in the United States in 2022), maintained on church property. They worked on sacred real estate totaling fifteen per cent of the arable land of Egypt, or about seven hundred and fifty thousand acres, where they tended more than five hundred thousand cattle. Their combined fleets numbered over ninety vessels, over fifty factories and shipyards, and one hundred and sixty-nine towns, all in a land of only about five and a half million people. There were also jealousies and rivalries between the temples, and the pharaoh subsidized the less patronized ones, dividing conveniently the solidarity of the clergy. But the entire fluid and illegitimate power structure of the late-Egyptian state and church was an increasing vulnerability for the country. Membership in the clergy did not necessarily entail a whit of sacrifice, and it was not an intellectually rigorous calling by subsequent Judeo-Christian, or even Islamic or Oriental standards.

After these many centuries, Egypt, though capable for now of paying mercenaries enough to keep its borders clear, was being hollowed out within. An indication of this was the decadent extent of public holidays and festivities. Every third day was a holiday in honour of Amon, the principal God, whose annual feast was twenty-seven consecutive days, while Ramses III himself, not to be greatly outdistanced by his divine step-brother, was extended from one day to twenty-one days in the course of his reign. The amount of work which was actually done in the Egyptian Empire was reduced to basic agriculture and grandiose public works and the energetic activities of the commercial population. The military were mercenaries, well-paid to wait like firemen until the bell rang, and the religious office-holders were underworked businessmen: masters of ceremony in very profitable pseudo-religious rituals. The power of the high priest of Amon came to rival that of the pharaoh.

Ramses III's authority depended on almost entirely foreign army units and even his household staff was composed of slaves from Egypt's current and previous provinces, particularly Syria, Nubia, and Libya. Ramses III was a cunning internecine politician who possessed other kingly aptitudes, but he was in an increasingly tight corner. His chief civilian advisers were greedy slaves of something less than immaculate loyalty, an army composed almost from top to bottom of soldiers of fortune, and a clergy whose leaders were and regarded themselves as rivals to the authority of the crown. It was, in the abstract and in the light of subsequent world history, an impossible state of affairs.

An ostensibly absolute monarch had taken the throne from his talented father, who had occupied it in a time of chaos; the monarch had organized the country well and led a largely foreign, well-paid force to secure the frontiers, and the chief opinion-formers in the kingdom were a clergy that was at least composed of Egyptians, but exercised a material, let alone moral, influence approximately equal to the king's. Uneasy was the head that bore the crown, and with good reason. The king's strategic entourage measured out their adherence entirely in pecuniary terms. If Ramses wanted any job security, he would have to arouse the patriotic adherence of the masses of Egypt, who were not overflowing with good will to the foreigners around the pharaoh, but thought the priests, though greedy, were at least fellow Egyptians.

The house of pharaoh and all Egypt, the greatest country in the world known to the West, was a powder-keg. The fuse was lit, as often occurred in this form of political science, in the harem: one of the numerous queens, slouching about the harem with many rivals, organized a conspiracy to elevate her son, Pentewere (presumably sired by Ramses III), to assume the throne at once, and the aspiring queen mother attracted the collaboration of the wives of many of the palace guard, and the commander of the Nubian archers, via his sister, who was in the harem. Ramses III would be murdered, Pentewere enthroned, and the high priests more obsequiously deferred to than ever.

Ramses III's spies heard of it, all the conspirators were arrested, but some of the accused managed to arrange a temporary release from custody and visit two of the fourteen special commissioners Ramses appointed to try the conspirators, sincerely commanding them to be scrupulously fair. This was too much, and the fraternizing commissioners had their ears and noses severed, and one of them committed suicide. The trial proceeded, convictions were obtained, and Pentewere, doubtless a dupe, along with his mother and thirty other conspirators, were permitted to commit suicide, as they did to spare themselves execution. Ramses III naturally found it a nerve-wracking experience and died as the trial ended, in 1167 B.C., after a successful, but far from serene reign of just over thirty-one years.[12]

7. The Decline of Egypt

The Egyptian empire now accelerated toward complete collapse. Ramses IV was the first of eight new Ramses in rapid succession. He did commission the Harris Papyrus, one hundred and thirty feet long, loyally detailing his father's achievements, to be placed in his father's tomb. The core of the great papyrus was Ramses III's alleged prayers for the reception of his son, who commissioned the papyrus. This was granted, up to a point, but Ramses IV reigned without real authority for six years, but seems to have died naturally. Ramses V to VIII followed quickly, and little is known of their lives or deaths. But Amenhotep, high priest of Amon, flourished, and in 1132 B.C., we see him receiving from Ramses IX gifts, deferences, and surrenders of tax revenues of immense value. The clergy now was more powerful than the state, and largely had become the state, taking precedence over the pharaoh in the collection of taxes. The high priest, Amenhotep, led the Egyptian people; the pharaoh commanded only the paid foreign army and a claque of foreign slaves in the household. The state had been subsumed and had missed its opportunity to rouse the country in the patriotic interest and overturn the clerical influence. The revolutionaries of France, twenty-nine centuries later, though they made almost every other conceivable tactical error and almost all were publicly executed in relays (in lock step to the guillotine with the higher clergy), did not commit that mistake.

The last Ramses entered upon what was left of his pharaonic functions in 1118 B.C. After five years, a local nobleman in the northern Delta, Nesubenebded,

---

12 In 2011, researchers subjected the mummy of Ramses III to a CT scan and found a gash in his neck deep enough to have been lethal, so it is now thought the assassination attempt was successful.

announced that he had replaced the pharaoh in the region and described himself as a Pharaoh of Northern Egypt. Ramses meekly retreated to Thebes, where he festered, contending unsuccessfully with the high priest of Amon for the headship of a truncated Egyptian state, powerless and anemic for a few years. By now, the Philistines had expelled the Egyptians from Syria, seventy-five years after being soundly whipped by Ramses III. A group of Egyptian officials was seized and detained at Byblos in about 1140 and died in captivity after fifteen to twenty years. In about 1100, the pharaoh gave the Assyrian leader, Tiglath Pileser I, a live Nile crocodile (over thirty feet long and among the world's least domesticated animals), as recognition of his arrival at the northeast gate of Egypt and as able to enter and crush Egypt as had been the Hyksos seven hundred years before. All crumbled in slow-motion sequence: the high priest of Amon declared himself viceroy of Kush, taking over the gold mines and not bothering to consult with the ostensible pharaoh, whose jurisdiction was now reduced to little more than a postage stamp in official Thebes. The high priest also announced himself to be commander of the armies of Egypt, as he took over paying them. The mercenaries who supposedly defended Egypt would acknowledge their paymaster, but it was obvious that they were not going to risk their lives against a powerful adversary for the rich but crooked and unfeasible chief of the licentious and unholy Egyptian clergy.

A series of strong and cunning pharaohs had managed to maintain Egypt as a serious imperial power for about three centuries, even as the population of Egypt lost all the pride and motivation that the people of a Great Power have always required, and still do, to maintain their national status. Military superiority, which Egypt heroically resurrected from the crushing defeat and ruthless occupation by the Hyksos, had armed and furthered the cultural attainments of Egypt and wrested the military leadership of the tri-continental centre of the Western world from the naturally hungrier and fiercer Asiatics; but now, it was over. Egypt was weak and decadent and corrupt and submitted again to the conquest of less enlightened and intellectually accomplished foreigners, failed by its religious leaders and without serious secular leaders. But Egypt retained its status as the greatest culture and civilization of the Western world, which it had held for more than two-thousand years, in itself, a mighty historic achievement, for a while yet as it was trodden down by lesser foes, actual and symbolic philistines and others, until the rise of the Greeks. This chapter of world history, a brilliant and permanently formative one, was not far off, announced by the flight of the Aegeans and Philistines before the southward advance of the Greeks, men of war as well as of high culture.

A pattern and sequence of affairs which would continue and become ever-more elaborate, was now visible in human affairs. People were attracted to the wealthiest areas in terms of accessible resources, and also in terms of the interchange of goods and talents. The peoples that most exploited the human intelligence and broadened it into fields of art and culture and expression were not for long those most adept at war, who were most able and determined to conquer the most desirable populated areas. The cultural leaders established their competitive superiority as warriors and then gave themselves over to the advance of the human intelligence and character, made themselves vulnerable to assault from militarily well-organized and commanded barbarians, who lay about them and then gradually succumbed to the temptations and exaltations of elemental and ultimately, high culture. The Egyptians had had a long incumbency and a prolonged sunset obtained by agile later pharaohs. They had become weak and were crushed, and they were succeeded briefly by their military conquerors, and then by their rightful successors, in battles on the field and of the mind, the Greeks. They, too, would follow a similar trajectory.

Their early times were golden, their middle ages were bronze, the declines were leaden, and the ends ashen, but the process was inexorable, not ignoble, and the creative periods of the cycles, almost all of them, had merit and often grandeur. Approximately, this cycle (often replicated in the lives of noteworthy individuals also) will be recounted again and again, in this summary narrative of human history.

This was the condition of the Western World as the last millennium before the birth of Christ approached. Two peoples emerging, who have survived as small but influential, were particularly worthy of notice and would play an immense part in the development of the world: the Greeks and the Jews. They were argumentative and bellicose, but compulsively ambitious intellectually, and irrepressible. They would have a colossal and permanent influence, and though suppressed for centuries on end and assaulted often, they have proved imperishable. And their influence has only declined as their concepts have been adopted and taken forward by others, who have then, whether in gratitude or not, gone back to free them, Greece and Israel, from bondage and welcomed them back into the West as venerated, if diminutive, nations.

CHAPTER THREE

BABYLONIA AND ASSYRIA FROM THE SECOND MILLENNIUM TO THE EIGHTH CENTURY B.C.

HAMMURABI, TIGLATH-PILESER, AND NEBUCHADNEZZAR

Hammurabi receiving his royal insignia

Border stone - reign of Nebuchadnezzar I

1. Babylonia and Hammurabi

BY 2000 B.C., THE rising city states of Babylon, Isin, and Larsa, to the north of Ur (though Larsa was only twenty miles away), were steadily the subject of Semitic immigration, and they and other neighbouring towns grew competitively, like frontier cities, growing and filling with aggressively ambitious immigrants. The forces that closed in on Sumeria may be broadly grouped as the Amurru camped in the west on the edge of the Arabian Desert. To the north of them was Carchemish, near Aleppo, where Neolithic man adapted copper and then bronze, and where the Hittites had now arrived in all their unpredictable ferocity. This population pressed southwards in gradual encroachments and occasional fierce military sallies, crowding the Amurru and the Sumerians, as well as, directly to the north of the Sumerians, the Subartu, increasingly dominated by the Assyrians, belligerent nomads of a kind that would always under-appreciate and disparage the comparatively effete and thoughtful Sumerians. To the east, and also a source of pressure, were the Elamites.

The fall of Sumeria, and specifically of Ur, was engineered by the king of the Subartu, Ishbi-Girra, to the north, in alliance with the Elamites to the east of Sumeria. With these developments, Larsa, twenty miles to the north of Ur, and Isin, about thirty miles further north, held joint suzerainty of Sumeria. Isin and Larsa started out co-celebrating their victory over Sumeria, happily adopting the local practice of worship of the deified incumbent kings, and inter-marrying the royal families in festive accord. But after a couple of generations, and with increasing Hittite and Assyrian immigration into them, these kingdoms recognized in each other a rivalry. The two states skirmished intermittently for about the second fifty years following the fall of Ur.

Starting about one-hundred and thirty years after the fall of Ur (almost 1800 B.C.), it became a tripartite rivalry as Babylon, edging south and flexing its muscles, crowded both Isin and Larsa, and was soon itself under pressure from the Assyrians. The Babylonian king Sumu-la-ilum, in the first half of the Nineteenth Century B.C., having cooperated with his neighbor, the ancient city of Kish, in joint resistance against Assyrian pressures, suddenly turned on Kish and crushed and subdued his ally. It was a rousing military success, but there was never any explanation of what provoked such a cobra-thrust against a close and cordial ally. (It had the impact at the time in Mesopotamia as the German assault on the Soviet Union had in 1941, less than two years after the Nazi-Soviet Pact.) At about the same time, in a strange inspiration, the king of Isin, Girraimaiti, established his gardener, Enlil-Ibni, as king (prefiguring modern stories like the film *Being There*, based on Jerzy Kosinski's novel, in which Peter Sellers, as the monosyllabic gardener, becomes an influence on the president of the United States). This unlikely king only lasted for six months. In the midst of the Eighteenth Century B.C., Elam overran Larsa, in alliance with Babylon and Isin.

Larsans, by this time, infested Isin, and the lines were being blurred between these peoples. Isin, fearful of the Elamite Larsans, allied itself closely to Babylon. The Elamite Larsan king Rim-Sin started "nibbling" around the edges of Babylon and Isin.[1] Finally, after the aggrandizement of Elamite Larsa after having taken over Erech, Babylon effectively took over Isin, and won the first battle with Rim-Sin, but in about 1710 B.C., Rim-Sin captured Isin. Fortunately for Babylon, its rather quiescent and tentative king Sin-muballit died peacefully and was miraculously succeeded by one of history's great kings, and the first mainly secular person to arrest and hold the attention of the Western world, Hammurabi, for a forty-two-year reign. His name and legend linger still.

He reigned, by the modern reckoning we have been using, from 1792 to 1750. (The older method set all these early dates back by two-hundred and seventeen to two-hunderd and thirty-one years; the explanation is too complicated—a multi-sided historical argument—to be worth recounting here.) Six years after his accession, having stilled unrest and built some fortifications, he attacked Rim-Sin without warning and seized Erech and Isin. All was quiet for four years when he struck again and took Rapikum, leaving Rim-Sin pretty much where he had begun. Hammurabi had befriended and assured the cooperation of a few tribal leaders who had been

---

1 CAH, I, p. 485 (R. Campbell Thompson).

miffed at the belligerence of Rim-Sin. Hammurabi bided his time and was very efficient and constructive as a Babylonian ruler, building canals and public buildings, assuring an equitable distribution of wages, and furnishing Babylon with the instances of a civilized state: organized statutes, and ultimately a law code, cultural assistance, libraries, and places of study of what were becoming the learned professions. In 1763 B.C., as he was preparing to strike Elam, the chief aggressor against Mesopotamia, and although Rim-Sin had promised to contribute an army but not to support Hammurabi publicly, the Babylonian king apparently feared that once engaged with Elam, he would be struck in the back by Rim-Sin (Larsa's population was partially Elamite). He struck Rim-Sin first, overran all Larsa, and captured Rim-Sin, who died in captivity from undisclosed causes. They were unlikely to be natural, but at least Hammurabi did not subject him to a public execution as was standard for defeated kings at the time, as we have seen.

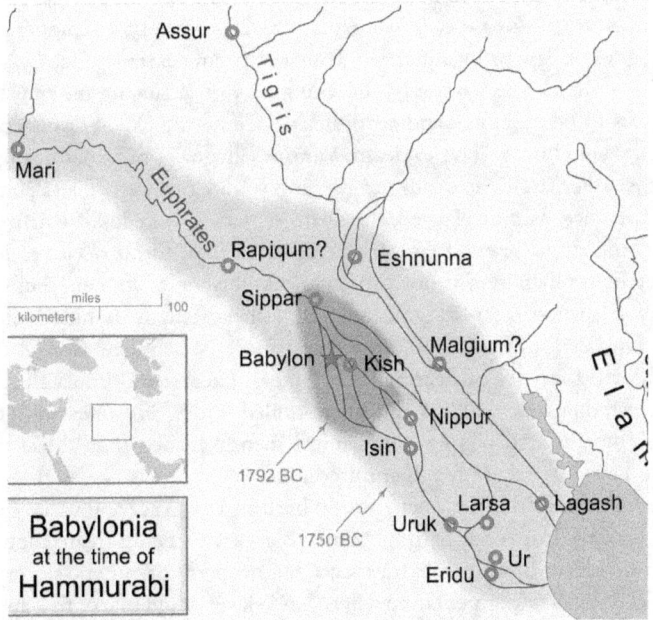

He did, however, appropriate the religious statues in the main temple of Larsa, and had them conveyed to Babylon, where he could refresh himself with contemplations of his conquests. The faithful could conduct pilgrimages to Babylon to continue the practice of their faith. Hammurabi routed the Elamite army, and by a combination of border actions and economic and diplomatic measures, he reduced the aggressive Assyrians to a respectful state of quiet. He then devoted the last decade of his reign altogether to public works and prosperity, especially an immense canal for drought control in Sumeria. He bound his empire together with roads and other canals. There is no doubt that his greatest achievement was the famous law code of two-hundred and eighty-five articles, which he published throughout his kingdom. The laws themselves were partially derived from the Sumerians and from equitable concepts that were frequently enforced at the time, but this was the first serious attempt to assure the rule of uniform laws throughout a large jurisdiction. He would be emulated by many rulers across the ages, most prominently, Justinian and Napoleon, but not excluding such diverse law-givers as Draco and James Madison.

In the times before Hammurabi, the local high priests were also magistrates, but they paid taxes, as well as overseeing the collection of them. With the takeover of Sumeria by Isin and Larsa, the local high priests (patesis) were largely supplanted in the towns and provinces by the mayors, who assumed the powers of magistrates and supervisors of the imposition of all central laws and taxes. Under Hammurabi, the patesis became effectively like modern Roman Catholic parish priests, delivering religion with local liturgical flourishes, but as instructed by the king, in post-Sumerian times, only he was "the favourite of the Gods" and was deified posthumously. There was an appeal court in Babylon. Witnesses were sworn in the name of the Gods and the king, and Hammurabi laid out these matters in his Code. The penalty for perjury was death, as it was for rape, brigandage, burglary, robbery, kidnapping, adultery with a daughter-in-law or by a married woman, extreme extravagance by a wife (for the last three offenses-execution by drowning); a wife arranging the murder of her husband was to be crucified, and a priestess violating the cloister or even entering a wine shop would be burned to death. Various categories of gross negligence and military cowardice drew the death penalty, and so did a variety of less common offenses. In practice, as time elapsed, the death sentences were less frequently carried out, and comparative liberality in sentencing crept in. Ordeals occurred in charges of sorcery or probability but not proof of adultery by a woman. Teeth and eyes were extracted for some offenses, and sixty lashes with an ox-hide whip awaited someone who struck a superior officer, and mere banishment from a city could also be ordered for types of bearing false witness. There were stipulated charges for surgeons, veterinarians, builders and many skilled trades, and fines were common. Completely uneducated people were more leniently treated than those the courts deemed to have less excuse for their misconduct.

Slavery had existed in this society as far back as we can see and was referred to in surviving writings from early Sargonic times. Slaves were better treated and regarded than in more recent times; while they were the property of others, slavery was not along entirely racial or pigmentational lines, and slaves could marry free spouses and their children would be free from birth. They were apt to be slaves by virtue of being prisoners of war (a better fate than simply being massacred), and there was much less stigmatism of assumed inferiority of race or intelligence than in modern slavery. Emancipation was quite frequent and available to slaves who performed good services that were not of Olympian rarity, just good, accomplished workers. Marriage was by contract and not a religious ceremony, though festivities were frequent, but as celebrations, not solemnizations. Concubines could be engaged by married men, but they had rather diminished legal status. Divorce was very unequal—a declaration by the man, but for a woman, unless she could establish adultery, repudiation of a husband was punishable by death or defenestration from a mortal altitude, at the discretion of the magistrate. When the man initiated the divorce, he had to give his wife either the family home or an adequate financial settlement that she could live on. Adoption of children was frequent, largely as a substitute for welfare. So the elderly could live off them in their declining years.

Babylonian religion had the customary multiplicity of Gods, with the principal ones rising and falling in the fluctuations of current opinions. While Hammurabi ruled, his preferred God, Marduk, God of atonement, rose steadily in popularity of worship by his subjects, and was rivalled only by Ashur, God of fortune and prosperity. There were local gods, and they were worshipped in almost diocesan packets. Deities were almost human in their talents and foibles, but they were gifted with tremendous powers in their spheres. No concept of heaven existed, nor any after-life paradise; but man, having been buried, lives on in a seven-walled underground town, where people would continue to live, accommodated in a regime directly proportionate to their virtue while on the surface of the earth. Temples were important, were erected on hill-tops, and around them were conducted a great many occupations. Temple personnel included people to address the personal needs of the clergy, which included a significant number of dedicated and forcibly chaste daughters of the powerful. Improper sexual derogations were punishable by death, though usually, as in all ages, the support of an influential and indulgent father could accomplish miracles for a daughter in distress.

In the records of Hammurabi, we find a temple whose staff included a priest, three brewers, two musicians, a boatman, and a shepherd. Large temples held large herds of sheep and cattle. The shepherds were summoned, sometimes by the king himself, to render account for any unexplained diminution of the animals given to the temple and entrusted to the temple shepherd's care. In a special category were the temple harlots, whose somewhat scandalous conduct was officially tolerated. They were expected to maintain certain standards of restrained promiscuity and tasteful selectivity, in which case they were not penalized for bearing children and owning real property. Here, as elsewhere and always, political acumen was essential to making the occupation a success. Frequenters of the temple could also bring in their newborn to be nursed and suckled by the temple women of lesser rank, a social service, and just one of many offered by large urban temples of Babylon.

Grain rations were issued to the whole population, to avoid speculation, hoarding, and general food shortages (though the management of this system must have been quite heavily abused at times). Land-owners paid a corvee, or taxation in kind imposed on agriculture, to pay for the deployment of soldiers and public security forces and for public works, an area where Hammurabi, like most great rulers, was very active, particularly in canals for drought control, flood control, and transport between the Tigris and Euphrates.

The greatest legend of Babylon was the Epic of Gilgamesh, the king of Erech, whose tyranny was going to be abolished by the divinely sent and inspired Engidu, but they became friends and co-adventurers. The Goddess Ishtar falls in love with Gilgamesh, but her affections are unrequited, and Ishtar's father creates a mighty bull to destroy the two cads, but they slay it. Engidu dies, and Gilgamesh, fearful of the same fate, seeks out Babylon's equivalent to Noah, who was rewarded in Babylonian lore with eternal life as a reward for saving the known world. After a formidable odyssey, Gilgamesh reaches the man-God he is seeking (Uta-Naphistim), who tells him to deep-dive in the ocean for a life-giving plant. He does so but is robbed of it by a snake, and toils on, a mere mortal. There are elements of these happenings and characters in the lore of many peoples, including the Jews, and in Richard Wagner's Ring Cycle. The themes, heroism, comradeship, killing the monster, the temperamental qualities of women, a near-paradisiacal ending and the inevitability of the basic limits of human life, have not much changed.

Hammurabi was succeeded by his son, Samsu-iluna, in 1750 B.C., who established a supposedly maritime kingdom called the Dynasty of the Sea-Country, but this ambition was countered by the arrival of the Kassites, another fierce incoming of savage Asians that materialized improvidently out of the hills of what is now Persia (Iran). (The claim of a sea Dynasty was itself an affectation and referred to the marshes at the mouths of the Tigris-Euphrates near Basra.) The Kassites were attracted by tales of the prosperity and fruitfulness of Mesopotamia, and the urban luxury of Babylon. They were fierce and wild men, who had thirteen-thousand crossbows, and they began encroaching on the western approaches to Babylonia in the last days of Hammurabi, deterred from outright assault, perhaps, by the universal prestige of the Babylonian king, in war as in peace. The Kassites overran all the south between 1742 and 1740 B.C.

However placid the country was under Hammurabi, the Kassites, under their leader Iluma-ilu, seem not to have had much difficulty inciting a revolt across the south, and Samsu-iluna, to deny the Kassites the fortresses, took down the massive walls that had been constructed to protect Ur and Uruk, and made a start on the same object at Isin. Samsu-iluna, with great difficulty, got the better of the Kassites and those they had infected in the south in 1739, though he did not remotely regain all the territory he had lost. The Kassites and their suborned or terrified internal allies did not entirely prevail in their first assault, but they were soon back. The invaders and their allies seized the holy city of Nippur and the ancient capital Kish, and closed in on Babylon itself, when Samsu-iluna died in about 1712, apparently of natural causes, acute nervosity doubtless prominent among them.

His son, Abeshu, ingeniously damned the Tigris near Nippur to flood out the Kassites and their local allies. It did not drive them out but certainly slowed them down, and a stasis settled for some time between the Kassite-occupied Sea Country and the traditional kingdom of Babylon. The Babylonians reverted to being somewhat complacent and lethargic, civilized and with artistic and cultural talents and ambitions, but a sitting duck for these fierce Central and South Asian invaders. The very disagreeable Hittites reappeared, almost alongside the Kassites, from Cappadocia, in about 1696 B.C. This was the end of the First Dynasty of Babylon, under Samsu-ditana. The ravenous and destructive Hittites and Kassites would rampage through and around Mesopotamia for a time, and then the Kassites settled into a gradually more progressive, and replicative Babylonian government, which endured for six centuries. The Babylonians were only good warriors with an inspiring military leader, but they were capable and relatively civilized rulers and had an aptitude for sensible government. They were not finished yet, but as with all these peoples, times of splendor were succeeded by times of humiliation and servility. Some, such as the Egyptians, recurrently regained their status as important countries, but most did not.

Babylon entered a torpor that would last a thousand years before being dispersed into the sanguinary melting pot of Mesopotamia.

Gandash was the first Kassite chief to conquer Babylon, and his successors eventually subdued the so-called Sea Lands to the south. Gandash, as a barbarian, was barely literate and not much versed in the more sophisticated pursuits of cultural Babylonia, but he was not a nihilist or a vandal. After some time, the Kassites at least fostered a normal everyday life for the civil populace, and eventually, the occupiers adopted the Semitic language of the Babylonians and also revived Sumerian and became energetic builders of schools and other cultural institutions. They quite cheerfully allowed their own language to fall into complete disuse. Their greatest additions to Mesopotamian life were the introductions of the horse and of dating events straightforwardly from the reign of the incumbent king. The more ferocious Hittites pressed on Kassite Babylon from the north, and the most ferocious of all the groups then active in subsequent Asia Minor, the Assyrians, were building their empire in what is now Asiatic Turkey and were pressing the Hittites upon the Kassites. An irresistible accordion of coarser and fiercer peoples was compressing the region from present Turkey toward the southern end of the Arabian Peninsula. Babylon, though not autonomous, did not cease to be a great capital. The Semites absorbed Sumerians and were then conquered by the Kassites, who became made-over Babylonians, who, with the Hittites and Egyptians, ruled the area with considerable friction between them but with great and rising sophistication, as the Assyrian marauders hung over the whole Mesopotamian and Egyptian sociological experiment, growing more powerful and dangerous each century.

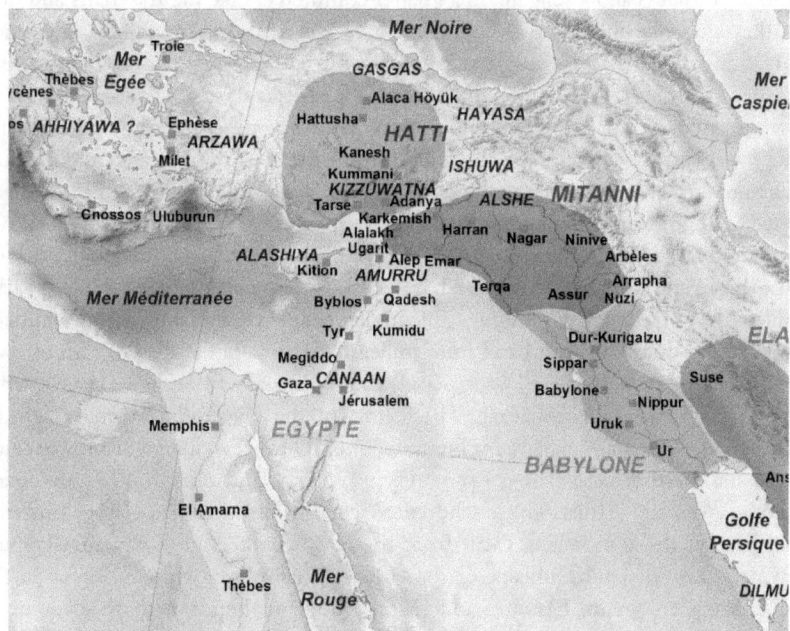

The Middle East in the first half of the Fourteenth Century B.C.

2. Hittites, Kassites and Philistines

The course of international politics in these primitive times were changed, perhaps more than by anything else, by the introduction of the horse. They were infinitely faster and more adaptable to terrain than donkeys and camels, and more easily trained. The Kassites, as has been mentioned, introduced the horse into Babylonia, in the Eighteenth Century B.C., and the Hyksos into Egypt at about the same time. This development approximately equaled the introduction of motor transport and airplanes in modern war and movement of men. Apart from accelerating and expanding transport, the horse also spread cuneiform and a language of general communication. It became a universal language in the Near East, in documents if not speech.

In the Sixteenth Century, the Egyptians and Hittites were the principal nationalities, with the Kassite-Babylonians the third force, and Assyria was a small state, its way to the crossroads of the Western world barred by Mitanni allies of the Egyptians. As the Egyptians and Hittites contested control of Syria and Palestine, Assyria and Babylonia developed, almost ignored, in a secondary theatre. Assyria gradually expanded to the north and restricted the Kassites. About 1400, Egypt accepted into the royal harem a Babylonian princess, at this time the most efficient embassy available between two courts.

The Hittites were, in general, even less culturally substantial than the Assyrians. They were a somewhat heterodox group of tribes on the edge of the centre of the Western world's activities in the Middle East, pushing forward to better their lot with more fertile lands and a tollgate on a greater commerce. Like the Assyrians and others, they were like children pressing their noses against the glass window of a candy store, hungering for admission, and eventually breaking the glass or forcing the door to enter. They were Hattic peoples from Cappadocia, Phrygia, Lydia, Cilicia, and northern Syria, all parts of what is now Asian Turkey, Asia Minor, and almost a catchment for the elements of the region up to the start of the first pre-Christian millennium that were not of Egyptian, Hebrew, Babylonian, Assyrian, or Phoenician heritage. In northern Cappadocia, there are written and archeological evidences of a Hittite monarchy in the Thirteenth Century B.C. The Assyrians dominated much of Asia Minor, and the Hittites retreated as necessary, advanced when possible, and assimilated to some extent. It is impossible to determine whether any of the Semitized Cappadocians of the second and third millennia B.C. were Hittite. We cannot even be confident of whether the Hattic people came originally from the Caucasus, from beyond the Caspian, or from Iran. The history of this era produced what might be regarded as a queue of peoples waiting impatiently for the chance of approaching and fixing themselves on the great maritime and overland trade routes connecting Europe, Asia, and Africa. Those who encroached on the area had also to turn and look back at those crowding them from the rear, whether the Egyptians slapping down the Libyans and Nubians, or the endless skirmishing with and between the Babylonians, Assyrians, Elamites and Hittites, not, for the moment, to dwell upon the Aegeans and Philistines.

The Hattic dynasty reigned in much of Asia Minor around 1450. This was the proto-Hattic period, and it was succeeded by the imperial Hattic period installed by the uneuphoniously named Shubbiluliuma, who succeeded Hattushil in about 1400. Shubbiluliuma appears to have been a somewhat epochal conqueror, throwing off the Assyrian yoke and pressing his claims in North Syria in 1390-1380, and pushing back both the Mitannis and the Egyptians. The Mitanni leader Tushratta, whose efforts have been mentioned, was forced back and had to exchange a very respectable junior position in alliance with Egypt to a more exacting subordinacy to the Hattic state. However, Shubbiluliuma had a greater appetite and returned for a second course, and enforced a suzerainty on a number of border areas with the Egyptians in particular and took over most of north Syria and northwestern Mesopotamia and opposed Tushratta. The Hittites were good and efficient warriors, but they were a sort of no-name conqueror—they didn't really have a serious culture or religion or mode of life but were good and numerous warriors of some ethnic consistency. Shubbiluliuma did make a treaty limiting his incursions on Egypt with Ahmenotep III in about 1345 B.C. He had cleaned up what he could from Ikhnaton's other-worldly conduct of the affairs of the Egyptian Empire. Hattic advances reached their climax at Kadesh (which seems to have been the Sedan—the turning point of Franco-German wars, of the ancient world), and which they held against determined assault by Ramses II in around 1220 B.C.

Shubbiluliuma's heir, Hattushil III, held such sway in Mesopotamia that his correspondence clearly shows that he was of superior wealth and influence compared to the Kassite king of Babylon, and of equal stature to mighty (post-Ikhnatonic) Egypt and the pharaoh, Ramses II. The two made a famous treaty of equivalent forces that reached the reasonable limit of their ability to impose themselves fairly closely to where they met (including at Kadesh). Hattushil was almost certainly moved to compose his differences with Egypt by new pressures from Assyria under Shalmaneser, and the Hattic dynasty and empire mysteriously crumbled shortly after 1200 B.C. when attacked by new waves of foes on the outer rim of the world whose centre was from the mouth of the Nile along the Phoenician coast and inland a little beyond Jerusalem and Aleppo. There are intermittent blank areas all along the eastern and northern frontiers of the countries that comprised the centre of the Middle East throughout this period. The states to the east of the Hattic peoples, Hanigalbat and Kash, were sometimes relatively docile but toward the end of the Hattic period were ferociously independent and ambitious, and undoubtedly played an important part in bringing down the whole Hittite state, restless and migratory and polyglot as it was, fairly early in the Twelfth Century B.C.

The identity of the people who invaded Egypt from the sea in the time of Merneptah remains a mystery. They may have been Aegeans, or Achaeans, a small band of sea rovers, not much anchored anywhere for long. These sea-tribes play a larger role in 1194, when Ramses III repelled their invasion of Egypt, and was supported by significant numbers of Aegeans who had previously migrated to and settled in Egypt. But he only did so after they attacked in Syria and occupied the shoreline and inland to Palestine and got as far east as the Euphrates and south to the border of Egypt where the pharaoh defeated them. They then withdrew to the east and north as the whole area was disrupted by the Philistines pressing southwards with the

Thracian Phrygians pressing them. The Hittite state, which was rather skeletal anyway, was enfiladed, infiltrated, and dismembered in the cross-fire as everyone within range, encouraged by the instability of Egypt, the region's ancient bulwark, pushed aggressively toward the trough of abundance that was the world's crossroads.

The Philistines were conspicuously non-Semitic, which broadly explains the imperishable character the word Philistine has retained of being entirely foreign, hostile, and uncultured. The Palestinians were convinced the Philistines came from Crete, and the whole subject is muddled considerably by the trenchantly advanced opinion of the historian Tacitus, who concluded that the Jews and Philistines were identical. This would be like modern historians confusing Teutons and Slavs. It was in Gaza where Samson brought down the pillars of the temple on the Philistine lords. The waters are further muddied by the assertion of Amos[2] that the Philistines are from Caphtor, unleashing debate that has continued inconclusively for fifteen centuries over where and what Caphtor was. The appearance of the Philistines was distinctive and not similar to that of the Cretans. Wherever they came from, the Philistines seemed to be most comfortable in Egypt, and as long as they did not challenge the regime, were fairly well tolerated there. Many of them settled in Canaan when that was still part of Egypt. The Philistines, to judge from comments by and about Samson, were accomplished at the most brutal sports—death struggles between men and with savage beasts.

The Philistines were uncircumcised foreigners in Judah, and their long dispute with Israel began in these times, and was only resolved, and not permanently, by David. In the territory they occupied, the Philistines disarmed everyone and removed anything that could be turned into a serious weapon, the first known endeavor at civil arms control.[3] The Philistines were so comparatively heavily armed that some parallels have been drawn between the Philistines and the Crusaders, who, two millennia apart, invaded from the West, heavily armed, but were ultimately sent packing, and settled mainly in Philistia, around Gaza in the southwestern Levant.

In the last quarter of the Second Millennium B.C., small states, independent of the greater forces contending around them, emerged at Damascus, and in Israel, Judah, Moab, Edom, and a few others, though their history is very obscure and largely undiscernible. The area was almost continuously contested by Egypt and by the intruding and opportunistic forces to the north and east. The wishes of the local inhabitants, over and among whom the outside nations fought and somewhat inter-married, were of little account, though the Jews, proverbially and notoriously, have proved inextinguishable and the Phoenicians and their successors have also exercised a great influence throughout the Mediterranean and beyond, though not, unlike the Jews, culturally or as a distinct entity. We will resume the history of the development of the Jews from time to time throughout this extensive narrative, but the fact that anyone under the heel of these unsympathetic conquerors coherently endured is an astonishing achievement, and one of which the whole world has been a beneficiary.

Even in these early days, the major powers corresponded, inter-married, and

---

2 Amos 9:7.
3 1 Samuel 8:19.

conducted extensive diplomatic relations. There was elaborate ceremony between them—the Babylonian king was outraged when Ikhnaton sent only five chariots to conduct the Babylonian king's daughter to Egypt.[4] The Amarna letters from around 1350 B.C. give a relatively detailed picture of how these courts functioned; from the Pharaoh Amenhotep III's perspective, trade was very important and empowering; caravan leaders had great wealth and influence. Mohammed himself was one. Even trading posts and key stopping points had some autonomous importance. The oasis of Palmyra in the Third Century A.D. was able to play powers off against each other for a time, and even require the intervention of Rome. And in this age, where the powers of totalitarian rulers are well known and served by advanced technology, it is hard at first to appreciate how comparatively porous and haphazard was the functioning of even the strongest and best-organized regimes. There were always influence-peddlers and courtiers who modified communication both ways between the court and the districts of all of these entities, especially as, once they started to expand, they were occupying the territories of surly masses of foreigners who resented their presence and obstructed the intruders as much as they safely could, or, in extreme circumstances, in open revolt, no matter how unpromising. Uprisings rippled intermittently whenever any of these disputatious and usually naturally belligerent peoples or cities were overly imposed upon by any oppressor.

Even the Egyptians, a society with considerable cultural distinction, unlike the Assyrians, Hittites, or Philistines, rarely made much of an effort to raise the cultural horizons of those whose overlordship they assumed. On the religious front, the Egyptians carried their polytheistic notions, centred on Osiris, Isis, and the others, and gained some adherence to them in Palestine and Syria, but they were not fervent missionaries, and the Jews in particular, for obvious reasons based in monotheism and messianism, would have none of it. The human acceptance of the notion of a deity was almost universal; there was almost no overt atheism, though some notions of divinity were eccentric, ranging from the hedonistic and almost bacchanalian to the austere and vengeful. It was an extensive religious menu, but almost everyone purported to worship something—altogether missing were the notions that there were no spiritual forces at all, that man could perfect himself into a god, or take the place of a god, even among those exalted kings and potentates who managed to graduate to a level of quasi-deity. Many centuries of "progress" were required for those theories to take hold.

3. Assyria I: Tiglath-Pileser and Shalmaneser

In the time of Amenhotep III (1411-1375), embassies were sent to the Assyrians, assuring that Egypt had no ambition to cross the Euphrates. In fact, Egyptians had an aversion to the terrain and climate of the Assyrians, and the pharaoh wished only a peaceful border and cordial relationship. The Kassite kings of Babylon and the Assyrian chiefs vied with each other in the lavish and tangible expression of their desire for friendship with successive pharaohs, and after Amenhotep's daughter became engaged to the son of the Kassite king of Babylonia, the Babylonian king

---

4 CAH, II, p. 297 (S.A. Cook); Ezra 8:21 et seq.

also sought to arrange the marriage of another son to the daughter of the Assyrian King. All these intricate relations were complicated by the habit of the Bedouin tribes who lived between and athwart the three courts of interrupting communications between them. Eventually, the Assyrian princess who married the Kassite prince produced the next king of Babylonia, Kadashman-Kharbe, who administered a harsh military repulse against the rapacious Bedouins and established a highway secured by a linked system of walled blockhouses to secure communications.

Kadashman-Kharbe was murdered by rebellious Kassites in 1368 B.C., in a rising supported by the resentful Bedouins exploiting the king's half-breed status and the recession of Egyptian assertiveness and vigilance due to Ikhnaton's religious upheavals in that empire. The aged Assyrian king, Ashur-Uballit (reigned 1386-1369), responded by marching on Babylon, smashing the revolt, chasing the Bedouins back into the desert, and establishing his grandson Kurigalzu III on the throne. While all this was afoot, and with the vacuum created by Ikhnaton's immobilization of the Egyptian state, the Mitanni leader Tushratta, in loyalty to the Egyptian alliance, as we have seen, had intervened to try to break an attempted siege of the Egyptian-occupied Phoenician city of Simyra, an important Mediterranean port.

And the memorably named Hittite king (though royal institutions were pretty rudimentary in such peoples), Shubbiluliuma, who we have also heard from, attacked the Mittani and helped engineer a coup against Tushratta, who was murdered and succeeded by his son, Artatama. This was the opportunity the Assyrian king Enlil-Narari (reigned 1368-1346) had sought. He attacked the Kassites and decisively defeated Kurigalzu III at Zugagi, and shrunk the Kassite kingdom according to his wishes. Kurigalzu was resistless. Artatama was a Mitanni puppet of the Assyrians, and soon a nationalist resistance arose, which was beaten off, and the Hittite king Shubbiluliuma intervened and put Mattuaza, Tushratta's son, on the throne. The Assyrians soon absorbed the Mitanni ethnically, and this group disappeared. (Reductions of ethnic and irredentist confusion in the Middle East are rare, and are welcome, at least to historians.)

Enlil-Narari's grandson and succeeding king of the Assyrians, Adad-Nirari I (reigned 1305-1277), flexed his muscles and extended his borders to Persia in the east and to the end of the western deserts. (Readers should be grateful for my refusal to mention the adversary leaders, tribes, and geographical areas involved; all have unfeasible names.) The Assyrians and the Hittites then respected the Euphrates as a border between them for many years. "They glared at each other across the river, without venturing to dispute possession."[5] With the death of the Kassite-Babylonian king Kadashman-Turgu in 1277, that kingdom was in a state of general disaffection. This was Assyria's hour. Shalmaneser I, the Assyrian king (reigned 1276-1257), took advantage of the Hittite-Egyptian wars and the exhaustion that followed them to expand his territory. He moved first to the north, into Armenia, and then attacked the Hittites, and captured fourteen-thousand, four-hundred prisoners at Hani, and proceeded west through foothills and skirting the flatlands where the armed opposition was more formidable. There was absolutely no claimed reason to this war except conquest for its own sake—no past grievance to be settled, no ethnic

---

5 CAH, II, p. 239 (R. Campbell Thompson).

quarrel—just a desire to prevail.

Shalmaneser left the Kassites alone and expanded in all directions except the south. And his son, Tukulti-Ninurta (1256-1233), conquered a great deal of territory and people to the northwest, and moved twenty-eight thousand Hattis to the east of the Euphrates, originating a mode of occupational conquest that would be emulated to the end of the Second World War and thereafter. Then, he defeated the Kassites: defeating Kashtiliash III (1249-1242), taking him prisoner, and then tearing down the ramparts of Babylon and killing many inhabitants. He withdrew to build a new capital to celebrate his conquests, disastrously leaving Assyrians in charge of governing Babylon. This Assyrian ruler was driven out by Elamites after eighteen months and sacked by his king and replaced by a couple of Kassites, and in 1233, the tables were turned in the Middle Eastern manner, and Tukulti-Ninurta was overthrown and murdered by his son, as Babylon had a brief sensation of liberty. Several Assyrian kings later, Ninurta-apal-ekur (reigned 1202-1176) regrouped and defeated an attack on Assyria from Babylon led by Meli Shipak II (1202-1188), and after a general melee, the Elamites attacked Babylonia from the east and occupied and sacked Babylon.

It was the end of the undistinguished Kassite era, after five-hundred and seventy-seven years and thirty-six kings. The Kassites accomplished little after introducing the horse and a new calendar and took up the Babylonian gods and cuneiform for themselves. Despite their long incumbency, they were squatters. The succeeding dynasty in Babylon was the Pashe, and they lasted for one-hundred and thirty-three years, in which there was one of the ancient world's most famous rulers, Nebuchadnezzar, and with Hammurabi, Babylonia's premier figure, he defeated the Elamites in a prolonged war but was unsuccessful against the Assyrian monarch, Ashur-Resh-Ishi I (1127-1116). This king defeated Nebuchadnezzar decisively and drove him back to Babylon where he died.

At this point, the Assyrians, another crude and fierce people, profited from the degeneration and moral decay of all the other countries about—Egypt under the later Ramessids, and the Hittites overwhelmed by the barbarians (even by Hittite standards) from the west. Tiglath-Pileser, the Assyrians' great leader, now had his turn. Tiglath-Pileser (reigned 1114-1076) started with two provinces that had revolted against him and raised an army of twenty-thousand to extinguish their independence in 1115. The Assyrian king met them at Commagene, annihilated their army, severed the heads of about ten-thousand dead and piled up their skulls, and whipped six-thousand prisoners along the dusty road back to Assyria. Commagene itself, however, drew the wrong lesson from the Assyrian king's victory and declared that it would pay no taxes to Assyria. Tiglath-Pileser quickly returned and disabused them of any notion of a tax holiday. He smashed their army and captured their king, and much of the population fled in the direction of a jurisdiction they thought might be less authoritarian as Tiglath-Pileser put Commagene to fire and sword. He drove the population into the mountains and then extended Assyria's jurisdiction in all directions. He steadily expanded the grain production of the lands that he occupied, and as he moved north, he also occupied valuable copper and bronze mining areas. He claimed, presumably exaggerating, to have killed eight-hundred lions from his chariot and one-hundred and twenty on foot.

Tiglath-Pileser also came in contact with the Aramaeans, a people, as we have seen, related to the Jews, who operated the trade routes from the Tigris-Euphrates all the way to the Mediterranean in the Levant. It did not take long for the Assyrian king to become intoxicated with the possibilities of wealth creation that this enterprise presented, and he effectively imposed himself on the whole route, taxed the entire commerce, and personally visited Lebanon and Phoenicia, and got as far south as Sidon. He embarked on the Mediterranean, a body of water that naturally astounded him, and harpooned a porpoise, and had models made of porpoises, which festooned his palace. He shipped substantial quantities of Lebanese cedar to Nineveh for the construction of his own palace, and shipped there exotic animals that he learned of, including apes and crocodiles, a yak, and two-humped camels, which he tried to breed, and even fruit trees that had never been seen in the area native to Assyria. Tiglath-Pileser built a formidable capital at Nineveh and had an extensive library of cuneiform tablets, a comprehensive set of statutes. He was a great conqueror and rather a benign ruler, not overly severe and dedicated to improved irrigation and the reconstruction and elaboration of cities, without, except when his authority was defied, excessive extravagance by himself or the royal family. He did capture Babylon near the end of his reign, but was not especially severe and not at all a vandal. But the Assyrian era produced almost nothing durable.

In the last two centuries of the second pre-Christian millennium, there was a flood of disruption over the whole Middle East and southeast Europe. Egypt, after some very long innings, and one miraculous recovery, was again in steep decline. Troy (Chapter 4) had been eradicated; the Hittites, briefly the terror of the region, had been given a good cuffing and slunk off into the east and north. The southern and Aegean Greeks, especially Mycenae, had been reduced to incidental states by the Dorian and other migrations. All was in flux. Phrygia and Lydia, in western Asia Minor, became important powers, receiving Greek migration and extorting tribute from the enfeebled occupants of the Levant and Palestine, and conducting a rich maritime commerce, but their political, i.e., military power, was not going to be adequate if a serious new or revived former force arrived.

Once again, the crossroads of the world was effectively a vacuum. Assyria, after a lapse, was militarily the most proficient of the contending peoples in the area and had only one policy—to conquer, subdue, and extract the wealth from the resources and work of as many people as it could for as long as it could. There was no pious humbug about a civilizing or evangelizing mission; the goal was to dominate and exploit and there was not the least pretense of trying to better anyone's lot except the conqueror, or to lay down the basis of a new and self-sustaining civilization. It was a smash-and-grab carried out because it was possible, so enervated were the local elements that had rebuffed the Assyrians before. But those who congratulated themselves on surviving that onslaught were little prepared for a return. In the West, the Assyrians had vanished altogether, and they were understandably assimilated to other wild and woolly groups that had come snorting out of the eastern or northern undergrowth, but after being more or less roughly handled, had vanished.

The balance of this section of Chapter 3 is a simple recitation of a series of polysyllabically named rapacious warlords reenacting a well-practiced sequence of conquest and eventual subsidence. It added little to the political development of the region but cannot conscientiously be omitted. Those who have not had a surfeit of such activity may read an account of it in Appenndix B at the end of this chapter.

Readers who skip this phase will deprive themselves of some of Assyria's best times as well as the undoubted pleasure of reading of Assyria's permanent disappearance.

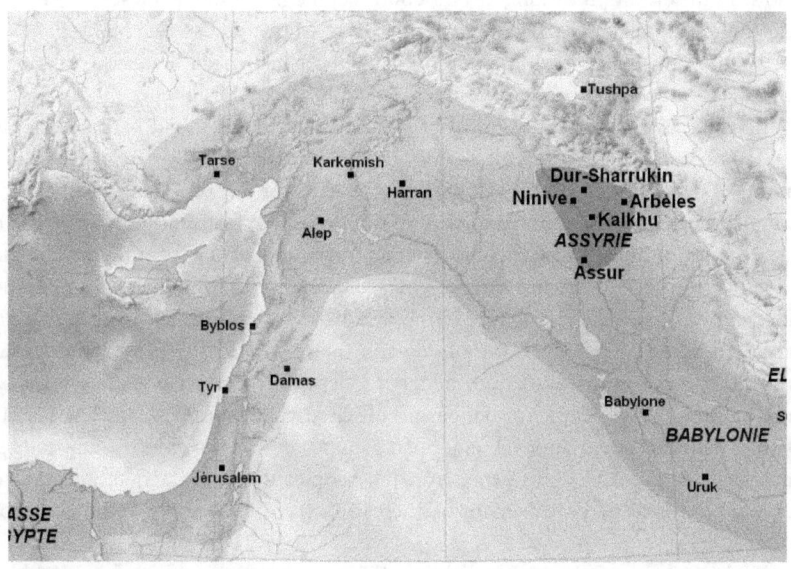

Assyrian heartland and its maximal extension under the reign of Ashurbanipal (668-627 B.C.)

4. Assyria II: Sargon, Sennacherib and Ashurbanipal

Shalmaneser V reigned inconsequentially from 724 to 722 and was succeeded by Sargon II (722-705 B.C.), one of history's great imperial rulers, almost on the same exalted plain as Augustus Caesar. Viewed with perspective, the original Assyrian attempt in the Eleventh Century B.C. to establish a dominion over the whole rich commercial area of the Middle East was too swift and ambitious and could not be maintained against the combined force of encircling neighbours. The return of the Assyrians in the ninth and eighth centuries was more cautiously executed from a stronger base and was then expertly consolidated; eventually, the already well-developed pattern was bound to repeat itself. Unlike Egypt, which was hectored but never overwhelmed from the west and south, the Middle East and Asia Minor and southeast Europe were always subject to the latest and most powerful forces sweeping across the immense and populous mystery of the Eurasian land-mass. The prize of the world's commercial and cultural crossroads could not fail to become steadily more tempting and desirable, and the strength of those peoples and governments seeking control of it was bound to become more formidable and determined until other areas became more magnetic. As Assyria entrenched under Sargon and his successors, the forces of Iran amalgamated and grew and became the immense Persian power; the Urartus were a mere sorbet compared to the barbarian hordes that would emerge from Asia and northeastern Europe in succeeding centuries.

Sargon devised his name "true king" as part of a campaign of legitimization following his elevation as king after a coup d'état against Shalmaneser V, who was murdered in a palace coup, presumably led by Sargon (whose real name has been interred beyond reliable exhumation). Shalmaneser had made the frequent and often mortal error of depriving the over-fed political establishment, clinging to the regime like barnacles in the country's capital, Ashur, of what had been their rights of position, particularly exemption from taxes and conscripted work. This is an admirable idea but one that has been known to lead to serious problems when enacted without proper preparation and insulation of the regime from the surly response of the deprived, and particularly without taking physical distance from them. The king took no such precautions and forfeited his head. Such discontinuities often ramified widely around an ancient kingdom composed of many tribes, clans, and ethnic and special interest groups which were bound to the regime by the most tentative and vulnerable bonds of intimidation, material incentive, or convenience. Assyria had had a number of good warrior-kings and efficient rulers, but it was still essentially a fierce, militarily adept and well-equipped group that had not asserted any cultural, ideological, or managerial influence over the peoples it had invaded and dominated and had no means of enforcement of their will except their military and constabulary prowess.

With the rise of Sargon, Babylonia, Syria, and Palestine, all began wobbling badly and making irritating noises of revolt. In Babylon, the Chaldean leader, Merodach-baladan, declared alliance with Elam in southwest Iran, seized the throne of Babylon, which belonged by right to the king of Assyria, and abruptly seceded from the Assyrian kingdom. Sargon moved against him, but was barred by the Elamites, who saw the Babylonian exodus from Assyria as an opportunity to snaffle up a rich and prestigious nation as a windfall, an ex-gratia gift from whatever they conceived as Providence. Because of the secessions and challenges elsewhere in the Assyrian realm, Sargon was obliged to withdraw—draw a line between himself and Elam, give notice that he did not accept this revolt and usurpation, but defer for, as it turned out, ten years, before the resolution by force of the issue. In Syria and Palestine, the Assyrian authority had been through a patchwork of outright Assyrian provinces and vassal states. And, as usually arises in such uncertain times, the vassals became exceedingly outspoken and prone to agitation.

As might have been, and doubtless was, expected, Hamath, such a tedious opponent of former Assyrian kings, attempted to lead a revolt, inciting Damascus and Samaria, the capital of Israel after the separation from Jerusalem. Here, Sargon was able to intercede at once, in 720 B.C., leading an army of adequate size, professionalism, and concentration of purpose straight onto Hamath. Sargon decisively defeated the upstart, and publicly flogged the Hamathite king within an inch of his life. It was an upliftingly enlightening lesson to all the people whom this severe measure was intended to influence. This was a punishment Sargon announced he would carry out with other rebel leaders, which undoubtedly sharply reduced the number of candidates for such attention.

As rulers of such obscure provenance are apt to do, Sargon rewrote history somewhat, and he recorded historically Shalmaneser's subjugation of Samaria, with his own achievement of the same objective. Samaria had transferred its allegiance from Assyria to Egypt, bringing down the wrath of Sargon, and causing him to lay siege to Samaria and give an unambiguous warning to the pharaoh. While the evidence that the Egyptians had stirred up the revolt in Samaria against Sargon was inconclusive, there is no doubt that Egypt had incited the revolt of a number of the Palestinian and Philistine cities. After the comprehensive defeat of Hamath, Sargon attacked toward the pre-established border between Assyrian and Egyptian influence, and recaptured Gaza after giving a sound cuffing to the Egyptian detachments sent to assure Gaza's independence from the eastern foe. (Some of these activities and the perceptions that inform them have not evolved very quickly.) But Sargon had no real quarrel with Egypt, a country that had comparatively limited aptitude to come across Suez and seriously inconvenience the Near Asian powers. He executed a stylish diplomatic overture and settled relations with Egypt with no rancour or embarrassment to either side.

Urartu (Ararat) was a continuing concern. It was centred in what is now eastern Anatolian Turkey and was continuously expanding to the west and intruding in Syria and to the east where it poured into western Iran and then into Assyrian domains. The areas Urartu was threatening were the principal source areas for valuable metals and for horses for Assyria, and the threat was thus one that required response. In the northwest, Sargon relied on diplomacy as much as a steady military show of strength. Assyria had turned even southern Cyprus into a vassal state, and so along the coast of Asia Minor and into the Levant. The legendary personality who became known as Midas of Phrygia was in Asia Minor (close to where the similarly mythologized Croesus of Hercules had lived). Sargon succeeded in attracting Midas away from Urartu and into alliance with the Assyrians, a considerable accomplishment, which rested on Sargon's superior credibility opposite Urartu, which never seemed to have a discernible policy except to attack to the south as often and strongly as possible.

In the east, Sargon had greater problems with the Urarti, as they actually met and there was frequent fairly light skirmishing, but the northern country was always a threat and always picking the places for it to erupt into Assyrian territory and sabotage or carry off what it could. Sargon determined that a campaign was necessary but calculated very carefully to move due east into uncharted territory and then north and only then to strike at Urartu's capital from the east, where hostile action would presumably not be anticipated. Sargon made the approach, even with heavy chariots, which had to be man-handled along treacherous mountain slopes up-hill and down.

At one point on this tortuous approach, Sargon's way was blocked by the main

Urartian army, and after a march of more than six-hundred miles, the Assyrian army was verging on insubordination at the thought of hurling itself, so far from home, on a feared enemy defending its home ground. Sargon addressed this urgent morale problem by getting into his own formidable war chariot and announcing that he would lead the charge in person and assume that he would have enough loyal followers to make a good fight out of it. As usually happens when serious commanders have done such a thing, the ranks slowly but acceleratingly fell in behind a brave leader prepared to take his chance. The whole Assyrian army charged behind their king, forming up and focusing fiercely as the issue was joined. The Urarti disintegrated under the weight of the mighty charge, were routed and slaughtered. Sargon raided deep into Urarti territory and destroyed everything of the slightest use to an unfriendly country down to the least barn and hovel. He didn't overly spare the civil population either. All crops, gardens, orchards and forests were completely destroyed, granaries were emptied or destroyed, and all bridges, canals, and irrigation systems were blasted, and reservoirs were opened to drain into swamps. An immense quantity of gold, silver, and bronze was seized from Urarti metal-working activities and shipped back to Assyria.

The expedition was a colossal triumph, except that the Urarti, as ferocious and troublesome as they were, provided protection for Assyria and the entire Near East against the Asiatic hordes, who constantly arrived on the flanks of the Urarti and kept them thoroughly preoccupied. Sargon had no useful intelligence on what lay beyond the Urarti and had no idea what a valuable, if frequently marauding, shield they had been against more sinister and formidable possible adversaries beyond the mountains and in the trackless plains and steppes of what became Russia. For the meantime, with Urartu no longer a danger, Sargon was able finally to revisit his ostensibly lost kingdom of Babylonia. He followed Tiglath-Pileser's path down the east bank of the Tigris to disrupt the liaison between Elam and the Chaldeans. The Chaldeans had been pillaging Babylonia and were extremely unpopular, and Sargon had no difficulty exploiting discontent and installing himself again in Babylon, where the gates were thrown open to him. The Chaldean leader, Merodach-baladan, fled for his life to the south, where Sargon followed him and forced him, on pain of his entire home province being laid waste and fearful atrocities on the able-bodied men, to make a humble and submissive peace. As always in these matters, Sargon was as good as his word, and this frontier was quiet for the balance of Sargon's reign and beyond, and Merodach settled in as a contented vassal.

As the oppression of the inhabitants of the capital at Nineveh had been the key to the downfall of Shalmaneser V and of Sargon's overthrow and murder of him, he was careful in seeking a new and less militarily vulnerable capital, to build a new capital at Dur Sharrukin (Fort Sargon), northwest of what is now Mosul, Iraq. This was a magnificently defensible elevated city, and it liberated the regime from the army of factionalists, gossips, and crooked civil servants who teemed in Nineveh. The first of the tribes that swarmed forth, past the collective husk of the defeated Urarti, were the Cimmerians, who flooded into eastern Anatolia and impinged on Assyria from the north and east. Sargon took his main army into Anatolia to give battle in 705, and nothing more is known. The army was not destroyed, but the Cimmerians weren't driven out either. It seems most likely that a stand-off occurred, probably after a severe amount of blood-letting. As Sargon passed mysteriously into history, apparently in battle at the battle of Tabal, his forced migration or deportation of very large numbers of conquered people, perhaps as many as two-hundred and fifty thousand, had been affected, including the selection of a multi-ethnic population for his new capital. He made a thorough job of assimilating conquered peoples and making the Assyrian population as homogeneous as possible and as swiftly as possible. He never took his eye off industries, especially metallurgy, which conferred some technological superiority on Assyria, and on agriculture, where very advanced methods were applied to increase and protect the food supply to the whole empire. He was an enlightened, shrewd, and highly successful ruler.

Now it was the turn of Sargon's son Sennacherib (705-681 B.C.). He is one of the famous ancient rulers because of the Biblical references to his siege of Jerusalem, and Byron's well-known poem about that incident which began, "The Assyrian came down like the wolf on the fold." Sennacherib had been the crown prince for some years and had been assigned to administrative tasks in different parts of the empire by his father, and ascended the throne an experienced, confident, and proven ruler. Unusual for anyone schooled in the Babylonian tradition that mankind had already been given all the knowledge there was and that there was little point in innovation, Sennacherib was an astute and intellectually curious and practical person. Babylonia was the root of such Assyrian philosophical conceptions as developed. He commissioned surveys of forestry and mining resources, and dispensed with historic texts on such matters, which were frequently completely out of date. He also supervised the devising of an intricate water supply system for the palace he built for himself, transferring water by large buckets from wells under cross-beams a considerable distance to their place of use of the water. He introduced the production of cotton to Assyria and personally led the search for underground water sources to assure adequate water supplies for extensive areas of Assyria, facilitating irrigation and canalization. Sennacherib was also the planner for the expansion and refurbishment of Nineveh, and the laying out of the capital within a system of parks that was unique in its time and has been much admired throughout subsequent history. The king oversaw the construction of a peripheral wall forty feet wide at the top, permitting three war chariots to deploy abreast on top of it, and stretching eight miles around Nineveh, with fifteen gates. Sennacherib's palace was two-and-one-half acres in extent, and it was approached by a road of ninety-foot blocks of limestone pavement. Trespassers, in a rule emulated by totalitarian dictators of the Twentieth Century (Hitler and Stalin), were subject to summary execution by impalement.

The Assyrian empire that Sennacherib inherited extended from the edge of Egypt near Suez, north along the Mediterranean coast into Anatolia and Asia Minor, east to what is now northwest Iran, south to the Persian Gulf, and along the northern edge of the Arabian Peninsula. He would be most active in Babylonia and Palestine, where the chief historical source we have is the Old Testament, which of course must always be read with reverent caution. Israel had been reduced to the status of a province in 722 B.C., but early in his reign, Sennacherib had to put down a resistant coalition in an anti-Assyrian league of Judah and some Phoenician and

Philistine coastal cities. This movement was led by Hezekiah of Judah and was supported by Egypt. It became an active rebellion in 701 and Sennacherib was ready: he led his army down the Mediterranean coast, receiving the submission of all cities as he arrived at them. Only Judah and two Philistine cities persisted in their rebellion, awaiting Egyptian aid (an unpromising salvation at the best of times). Egypt did send an army in the direction of its protégés, but it was an insufficient force, and was intercepted and soundly walloped by Sennacherib, whereupon the Philistines surrendered, leaving Judah alone, encircled by the Assyrian king at the head of the Western world's greatest army. Sennacherib subdued the cities and towns of Judah one by one, forty-six fortified cities in all, and the Assyrians captured their populations totaling more than two-hundred thousand. The Assyrians had the technique of meeting in parley before joining combat and speaking Hebrew so loudly that some of the resistant population could hear them. It sometimes rattled those about to be besieged. The siege of Jerusalem began, but Hezekiah submitted and paid a large tribute; this is presented in the Bible as a miraculous deliverance, but Sennacherib had achieved what he wanted and had to deal at once with a Babylonian uprising that was more serious than events in Palestine, and closer to home.

Babylonia had a position opposite Assyria slightly analogous to that which Greece would for a time have opposite Rome, or what 1950s British prime minister Harold MacMillan would claim Britain had vis-à-vis the United States (utter rubbish, in fact); that of the cultural centre of a shared civilization which was, alas, ruled by the newer, stronger, military power. It is the traditional role of the impecunious aesthete reinterpreting history and deluding himself culturally about the present, and Babylon drank that cup to the lees, partly because Sargon had been extremely gentle with a rather submissive Babylon. In 703, Merodach-baladan,[6] having kept his word to Sargon, led a rebellion of his Chaldeans against the Assyrians, raising southern Babylonia. Even Isaiah, who had never advised opposition to Assyria, was a sympathizer. The ancient foe in Elam assisted him and allowed Chaldean raiders to seek safety in Elam after causing havoc in Babylonia. Sennacherib addressed this problem with an imaginative amphibious plan, importing skilled shipbuilders from the Mediterranean cities to construct boats that would transport his armies down the Tigris from Nineveh, move by canal to the more navigable Euphrates, to the Persian Gulf, sailed east and struck the Chaldeans in the back, and then carried havoc into Elamite cities which were completely unprepared.

But Elam was not to be silenced that easily. There was a de facto truce between Elam and Sennacherib until 694 B.C., when Elam counter-attacked against Assyria in Babylon, took Sennacherib's son prisoner, murdered him, and claimed to install a pawn of the Elamites on the throne of Babylon. A civil war between pro-Elamite and pro-Assyrian forces in Babylon ensued, and Sennacherib and the Elamites fought a tremendous battle in 691, which forced the Elamites to withdraw but so exhausted and depleted the Assyrian army that Sennacherib rested and restored his army in place in Babylonia for a year. The Elamite royal family had frequent upheavals and assassinations and was reputed, at the time, to be afflicted by psychopathic insanity. Mad they may have been, but they were formidable warriors.

---

6 CAH, III, p. 48 (Sidney Smith).

Finally, Sennacherib concluded that he had to destroy Babylon itself to eliminate the Elamite faction, and he moved on the ancient capital in 689. He besieged and took the city, sacked and razed it, piled up in public squares the corpses of the inhabitants, who were slain in plentiful numbers on little professed excuse, distributed all valuables among his victorious troops, smashed religious statues, tore down temples, houses, and the walls of the city, and dug canals into the city to inundate it entirely. All temple property was seized. He made such a convincing impression that Bahrein, six-hundred miles away, sent a declaration of submission and substantial tribute.

Eight years later, in 681 B.C., members of a pro-Babylonian faction in Assyria, and they abounded, encouraged by the king's son, murdered Sennacherib.[7] Adrammelech and Sharezer, the elder sons, who had been passed over for Esarhaddon as successor, may themselves have been the assassins. Despite the bad reputation he received from the Bible because of his siege of Jerusalem and sack of Babylon, Sennacherib was an enlightened ruler, and as gentle as he felt was safe, politically. He was popular in his time for assisting the poor, and when, as frequently occurred, he levelled a city, he went to some lengths to distinguish between rebels in revolt and innocent bystanders. This was an approach to rebellion considerably ahead of its time. He was a great builder and improver and, by most criteria, a distinguished and very respected monarch. Sennacherib was followed by his son, Esarhaddon, who had a tumultuous time establishing his legitimacy, and chased his brothers to Urartu where they sought refuge, and murdered their families and supporters left behind at Nineveh where the assassination of Sennacherib occurred. Esarhaddon was obliged constantly to shore up his empire, including in the northwest, where he subdued a revolt on the Gulf of Antioch and captured the two dissident kings, Sanduarri, and Abdi-milkutti, king of Sidon, whom he had to chase to Cyprus and retrieve. Sidon was thoroughly and brutally sacked, and the two kings were involuntary participants in Esarhaddon's triumphal entry into a new city Esarhaddon founded in place of Cyprus, and as a highlight of a large public festivity of municipal founding, the rebellious kings were ceremoniously executed by decapitation.[8]

Esarhaddon showed great ambition in setting out to conquer at least lower Egypt, to extend the borders of the Assyria of his illustrious predecessors, and to punish Egypt for its continuous subsidization and reinforcement of the states and peoples on Assyria's borders and the less compliant of those under Assyrian occupation. It was a formidable task, given Egypt's distance from the Assyrian heartland, and its prestige as the most illustrious of the Middle Eastern countries. Egypt had undoubtedly sponsored the many provocations and rebellions of Hezekiah, king of Judah, and the preternaturally scheming Merodach-baladan. Esarhaddon enjoyed considerable success, but it was an imprudent campaign, a little like Napoleon in Russia; it over-extended Assyria and left the empire vulnerable in the east and north.

Esarhaddon died after a satisfactory launch to this campaign, and after thirteen years of contested rule, leaving his throne to the last great Assyrian king, Ashurbanipal (668-627 B.C.). Esarhaddon had been a benign king, who kept the peace

---

7   2 Kings 19:37.
8   CAH, III, p. 83 (Sidney Smith).

in Babylonia and rebuilt the capital, and was apparently able in most respects, but could never entirely secure his position. He established that his son Shamash-shum-ukin be the king of Babylonia, and his son Ashurbanipal be king of Assyria, and the whole senior ranks of his government had sworn allegiance to these arrangements. Ashurbanipal had been meticulously trained in the kingly arts, which included royal administration, protocol, literary composition and writing, mathematics, and the principal sports, including javelin-throwing, archery, riding, and driving a chariot.

Ashurbanipal inherited a campaign his father had initiated—to invade and take control of the principal populated areas of Egypt. Esarhaddon had been aided by a number of Arab tribes which assisted in crossing the Sinai desert. Esarhaddon took the capital at Memphis and gained professions of submission from the princes of the Delta, but as soon as the main Assyrian army withdrew, these were all rescinded, and the Assyrians were left with little to show for their efforts. Egypt had endured, rebuffed, and temporarily absorbed many invasions and was not going to take first efforts too seriously. In 667, Ashurbanipal returned in person at the head of his main army, and again the Assyrians captured Memphis and the lower Delta without much military opposition. The leading vassal princes were captured, treated generously, and their chief, Neco of Sais, was transported in comfort to Nineveh, where he swore obedience to the Assyrian king and returned to Egypt heavy with honours, including an increased jurisdiction. The independent Egyptian king of the upper Nile at Thebes, Tarqua, came down the river and claiming to be the patriotic native Egyptian ruler, besieged Neco and his army in Memphis. Ashurbanipal had been alerted and approached in forced marches and repulsed Tarqua in 664 and gave chase to him, and captured and sacked Thebes.[9]

At the same time, Ashurbanipal extended his reach into western Asia Minor, at the invitation of Gyges, king of Lydia, where a century later Croesus would rule. Ashurbanipal sent reinforcements that enabled Gyges to prevail over the invading Cimmerians, and he dutifully shared the loot of victory with the Assyrian king. Ashurbanipal's and his father's activities in Egypt had demonstrated that it was too complicated and extensive a task to secure Egypt by durable Assyrian occupation—too much of the army would be tied up in an extremity, and the whole empire would come apart with inadequate garrisons to keep all the constituent peoples and groups in line. Ashurbanipal deputized Neco, whom he had treated so generously, and left him significant rotating frontier forces to deal with contingencies. His trust was not misplaced in Neco, and after he died in 663, his son, Psammetichus, was also a loyal viceroy, until Psammetichus' pride propelled him into an independent posture, in concert with the ingrate Gyges of Lydia, who, untroubled by the Cimmerians, also threw off the Assyrian yoke. Ashurbanipal did not want to commit his main army to these outer peripheral regions again, and largely withdrew from Egypt while signaling to the Cimmerians that they would have no problem with the Assyrians if they wanted to put Gyges roundly in his place. They did so, although Gyges put up a spirited fight, but was eventually slain in battle, though his dynasty persevered.

Ashurbanipal was unable to contribute the necessary forces to deal with either Gyges or Psammetichus, because his brother was under grave threat in Babylon, as

---

9 CAH, III, p. 285 (H.R. Hall).

the Chaldeans and Aramaeans in Babylonia joined with the Elamites on Babylonia's eastern frontier. The Aramaeans and Chaldeans were nomadic and tended to drift across borders and settle and graze where the land was richer than the resistance was tenacious. This led them at times into Elam, where they were not always welcome, but all three groups, and they were all formidable war-making peoples, could agree on their resentment of the Assyrians. Despite Ashurbanipal having sent emergency grain stocks to help Elam deal with a famine at the start of his reign, the Elamites attacked Babylonia, believing that Ashurbanipal was too preoccupied in Egypt to keep them out of Babylon. They miscalculated, and their king died, and a fearful blood-letting ensued in the royal house of Elam. Sixty of the late king's relatives sought refuge in Assyria, and the king declined to extradite them to Elam for execution, citing the "insolence" of the new Elamite king, who had the most absurd name and undignified end of anyone in this section. This was Tempti-Khumma-inshushinak. Learning from intelligence sources that the Elamite king planned to attack him, Ashurbanipal struck preemptively, decisively defeated the Elamite army, captured and executed Tempti, severed his head, slashed it, spat upon it and by some accounts, urinated on it, and stuck it in a tree in the garden in the Elamite capital where he celebrated his victory with a great festivity which was a command performance for what was left of the local nobility and gentry.

The energetic collusion between Elamite and Babylonian factions within the kingdom of Ashurbanipal's brother, Shamash-shum-ukin, led Ashurbanipal astray. In order to maintain his position, bequeathed by their father, Esarhaddon, Shamash was in constant negotiation with the local and intrusive Elamite factions and finally had to ask his brother's assistance, which began the deterioration of their fraternal relations. Transported in his judgment by the intense atmosphere of intrigue and betrayal, Shamash-shum-ukin, in 652, with a factional Elamite army, attacked his brother's Assyrian garrison which sustained him on his throne, bringing Ashurbanipal's wrath down upon him. Ashurbanipal besieged Babylonia, and the venerable city surrendered to Ashurbanipal in 648 after famine had reduced the population to cannibalism.

Shamash-shum-ukin had the decency to commit suicide rather than face his brother after this ghastly familial climax, and Ashurbanipal gave him a dignified and honourable funeral, but was less forgiving of his late brother's factional allies, whom he believed had exploited Shamash-shum-ukin's unworldliness and threatened the Assyrian empire with their childish and treacherous scheming. Accordingly, the Assyrian king set his invincible army on the Babylonian and Elamite factions that had attacked Assyrian forces, routed them, did not take an excessive number of prisoners, and when they captured the factional leaders, Babylonian and Elamite, ignored their pleas for mercy and acts of submission, and summarily executed them in the sight of their surviving erstwhile followers, and then had their corpses carved up and fed to wild dogs, pigs, wolves, and vultures.

Ashurbanipal had made his point in Babylonia and continued to send forces to assist in stabilization in Elam, which was now being pressured by the rising forces of Persia, pressing against Elam and Assyria. Ashurbanipal decided, with some reason, that his diplomacy and by the standards of the times, relatively gentle treatment of dissentient elements, must now give way to a more repressive approach, and in the first half of the 640's, invaded Elam twice and laid waste much of the country. Susa, the capital, was sacked and looted of all treasures. Temples and royal tombs were desecrated and pillaged. The entire civil population was uprooted and deported, with a minimum of human consideration, almost like the Jews in Central Europe three-thousand years later, though not with a similar gruesome and fore-ordained end. "I left the fields empty of the sound of mankind and the tread of cattle and sheep."[10] As a clearance of his enemies, his campaigns were successful, but strategically, like the reduction of the Urartis, it left Assyria's frontier on the east extremely vulnerable to the advancing Persians. Ashurbanipal's empire had achieved an extent of eight-hundred miles by one-thousand miles of historically valuable and contested territory, but encroaching on its borders were very powerful forces from the immeasurable depths of Eurasia.

Despite his other preoccupations, Ashurbanipal managed a further extension of his authority—over the Bedouin tribes of Arabia. He did not, and did not seek to control them entirely, only to shoulder his way into joint control of the rich trade routes from Arabia. Ashurbanipal achieved his ends by sending sufficient forces into the desert to control many of the oases, requiring the Bedouins to compromise with him. He took it upon himself to appoint a king of Arabia, and when this vassal imagined that he possessed more autonomy than the Assyrian king was comfortable with, he seized the so-styled Arabian king and tied him up like a leashed watch-dog, for all his former subjects to behold.

Ashurbanipal reigned thereafter reasonably serenely, until his death in 627 B.C. of natural causes. He left a library of about five-thousand cuneiform tablets, a huge library by the standard of the times, that was unearthed almost intact in the middle of the Nineteenth Century by British archeologists, and it was moved entirely to the British Museum, and is the greatest source extant of ancient Mesopotamian culture. He was undoubtedly a brilliant king, which was, if anything, highlighted by the amazingly swift collapse of his empire within twenty years of his death. In the end, Assyria paid the price of being a warrior state, as strong as the strategic and organizational standards of the commander-in-chief, and bedeviled by the fact that the more severely it punished marauding and trespassing neighbours, the more it opened itself up to the more powerful and efficiently belligerent peoples behind its annoying frontiers. The instinct to clear the frontiers of irritating smaller states that continually harassed and raided was understandable, but it opened wide, with no screen of resistance at all, the borders of Assyria to very powerful and barbarous nations completely unimpressed by the vaunted military traditions of Byron's Sennacherib and other formidable Assyrian warriors.

5. Babylonia II: Nebuchadnezzar

Ashurbanipal's sons succeeded each other after violent internecine struggle, and the empire became ragged and enervated as the Medes and reemergent Babylonians formed an alliance to overthrow Assyria and divide the spoils. The Medes were an

---

10 John Canning, ed., *100 Great Lives of Antiquity*, Methuen, London, 1985, p. 58.

enemy from beyond the borders without the Urartians as a buffer zone, and Babylonia, which Assyria had taken the trouble to preserve, was aroused again and full of vengeance. Psammetichus of Egypt and the Scythians were prepared to support Assyria, not having had the experience of being governed by it, but the civil wars between Ashurbanipal's sons had drained the Assyrian army and deprived it of its former serrated edge as a fighting force, and the Babylonians and Medes had unusually good generals. Gradually, between 620 and 615 B.C., Assyria was hemmed into the quadrilateral of the original dimensions of Assyria. Nabopolassar of Babylonia and Cyaxares of Media attacked simultaneously from opposite directions, and Nabopolassar was able to come up beside the Euphrates and decisively defeat the Assyrians at Kablinu, but the Egyptians arrived and forced Nabopolassar back on Babylon.

Cyaxares was not so easily beaten off and attacked the Assyrians while the Egyptians were pushing the Babylonians back, and managed to persevere almost to Nineveh. On this occasion, interior lines were not an advantage. Cyaxares executed some fine maneuvers and with the Babylonians free of their Egyptian enemies, managed to seize the ancient Assyrian capital of Ashur, and the two vengeful armies brutally sacked Ashur, with a vengeance of centuries of accumulated anger and unquenched greed. Even now, Assyria did not disintegrate. Sin-shar-ishkun, the last Assyrian king, still bravely fighting, defeated Nabopolassar and had a fair chance, even after all the disasters, with Cyaxares, but he was betrayed by his Scythian allies, who took a bribe from Cyaxares, and all was lost. After three fierce assaults, Nineveh fell to the encircling enemies, in July 612. Sin-Shar-ishkun perished in the flames of his capital, a brave and spectacular death, and the storied Nineveh, to which royal city so many had come to be executed as trophies of futile resistance, or if more fortunate, to kneel before the Assyrian kings and pledge tribute and fealty, was sacked and ruined in an orgy of savagery.

The last remnants of Assyria regrouped at the Syrian fortress of Harran. Assyria was finally completely overthrown, defeated, and ground into the dust by Nebuchadnezzar, the new Babylonian king, at Carchemish in 605 B.C. In addition to the great numbers of Assyrians who were massacred, a very large number, especially of skilled craftsmen, were carried off by the Medes. Much of what was most elegant and tasteful in Persepolis and Ecbatana, the Persian and Medean capitals, was wrought by involuntarily transplanted Assyrians and their descendants. Seen all in all, the most durable achievement of Assyria was that it preserved the cradle of Western civilization, Babylon, as a vanquished but unmolested and unextinguished centre, until the Chaldean dynasty led a renascent Babylon to the utter destruction of its benefactor. Assyria was truly dead. "Nineveh ceased to exist. The noise of the rattling of the wheels and of the prancing horses and of the jumping chariots was stilled, and in place of the hum of a populous city, there was but the little plaintive cry of the golden plover in the amber fields."[11]

Nabopolassar was an upstart, a non-royal thruster who led an officers' clique and was always subject to clerical plotting and was in his official utterances obsequiously pious and humble; he even put his sons to work as simple labourers, in his reconstruction and enlargement of the principal Babylonian temple. The priestly party

---

11 CAH, III, p. 207 (R. Campbell Thompson).

in Babylon had great influence, and Nabopolassar devoted great attention to keeping the priests and the clerics on side. He died unexpectedly but of natural causes when only fifty-three, in 605, and Nebuchadnezzar rushed back to assure his succession, but found no attempts at usurpation under way. Nebuchadnezzar quickly confirmed the impression he had already made, as a brilliant general and ruler, the commanding regional figure of the time. At Carchemish, when he was only twenty-nine, he had defeated Pharaoh Necho and brought Phoenicia and Syria back under Babylonian suzerainty, just before his father died, and Nebuchadnezzar had at all times the loyalty of the army, which, if it came to it, was more powerful than the clerisy or clergy.

Jehoiakim, king of Judah, revolted against Babylonian overlordship, gently applied though it had been, and against the well-known advice of Jeremiah.[12] In 597, Nebuchadnezzar besieged Jerusalem and eventually occupied the city, though three months after Jehoiakim had died. Nebuchadnezzar took the late king's wife and son, Jehoiachin, and with them the entire royal family and army, all the craftsmen of Jerusalem and the valuable contents of its temple back to Babylon. This was not the end of it, as Judah, and particularly Jerusalem, rose again, at the approach of the new pharaoh, Hophra (Apries). Jeremiah again warned against rising in revolt,[13] but Zedekiah, the last king of the Jews, ignored Jeremiah, and a desperate and courageous resistance was put up when Jerusalem was again besieged, but the city fell in 587 B.C. Nebuchadnezzar sacked it to its foundations, fired and destroyed it, had Zedekiah's eyes put out after the king had witnessed the execution of his sons, and the entire population was whipped along the long road to Babylon as slaves. Zedekiah died in captivity. This was one of the much depicted acts of modern culture, most famously in the "Song of the Hebrew Slaves," "Il Pensiero," in Verdi's opera *Nabucco*. (The tenacity of the Levant against Nebuchadnezzar's sieges was remarkable; Tyre, which could be supplied by sea, held out for thirteen years and did not surrender.)

Nebuchadnezzar never stopped building his great capital throughout his reign of forty-three years. And he campaigned to a draw with Croesus of Lydia, at the Halys River, in 585, after five years of heavy fighting. The principal military effort of the Babylonian king's later years was against Egypt, a retaliation for Egypt's attempt to frustrate Nebuchadnezzar's reassertion of Babylonian hegemony over Palestine. Hophra conducted a disastrous expedition against the Greeks in Cyrene, and when a revolt, almost certainly materially assisted by the Babylonian king, broke out at home, and Hophra instructed his senior general, Amasis, to suppress it, the rebels purported to elect him pharaoh, and he became the executive regent. The fall of the Egyptian monarch counts as another military triumph for Nebuchadnezzar. He was attacking the Bactrians when Astyages, the Medean king, died. This left Nebuchadnezzar without rival in the world to the full extent known to him. He was not a great patron of culture, other than architecture, and in forty years, he made Babylon the greatest city in history up to that time. Palaces and temples were always under construction or renovation, and his pièce de résistance was the Hanging Gardens of Babylon, one of the Seven Wonders of the World.[14]

---

12 Ibid., p. 212.
13 Ibid., p. 213.
14 Oxford Assyriologist Stephanie Dalley has recently argued that the fabled Hanging Gardens were cre-

Nebuchadnezzar died in September 562 B.C. Under his son Amel-Marduk, Babylon was already seething with revolt and factionalism. Nebuchadnezzar's brother-in-law, Neriglissar, who was wealthy in his own right but greatly enriched himself from his proximity to the king, led a revolt that killed his nephew, the king, in 560. The new king's reign was not serene, and he died after two years, and was succeeded by his incompetent son, Labashi-Marduk. He was murdered after a few months and the new king, Nabonidus, was scholarly and circumspect, but elderly and rather other-worldly. Babylonia and Egypt were disintegrating; Lydia and the Medes were in a cease-fire stand-off, and the rising power was Persia, which was almost at the door of Babylon. Nabonidus engaged in a few activities around the edges of Babylonia, too fearful of the political class in Babylon to spend much time there. He rebuilt a temple in Harran, Syria, and conducted skirmishes at oases on the edge of the Arabian desert, but eventually retired to Babylon. It was in this period that the son of Nabonidus, Belshazzar, conducted a great banquet where an invisible hand wrote on the plaster of the palace dining room wall the words that the prophet Daniel was summoned to translate: "You have been weighed on the scales of justice and you have been found wanting." (Mene, mene, tekel upharsen).[15]

This may be taken as the symbolic end of a much less distinguished period than was covered in the first two chapters, about the Jews and the Egyptians. At this point, in the Middle Eastern countries, as with India and China (Chapter 4), human government had not progressed much beyond rudimentary tribal self-assertion and preliminary efforts to establish rulership on a combined basis of slavery and condoned kingship, combined with the moral and ecclesiastical authority of an official priesthood. In the next chapter, the Greeks give a tantalizing demonstration of greater civic virtue and a more purposeful approach to culture and science.

Jewish folkloric history holds that the message of Belshazzar's banquet was a commentary on the Babylonian kingdom's forcible removal of Jews from Israel and their enslavement in Babylonia. Very soon, the Persian king, Cyrus, arrived at the gates of the city. No resistance was offered; the gates were opened, and Babylonia surrendered quietly and without evident rancor to Persian domination. Cyrus incorporated Babylonia into his empire and issued new coinage for this new province. The religious icons and relics that the Babylonian kings had removed from the temples of conquered territories were restored to them, and Cyrus went to some lengths to claim to be in Babylon under the sponsorship of the Babylonian God Marduk. Belshazzar died mysteriously in the night.

Babylonia would not rise again, but Mesopotamia would remain the cockpit for all nations to fight in. In place of Babylonians and Assyrians, Scythians and Hittites, the Jews, Arabs, and Persians would continue, and the Greeks, Macedonians, Sassanians, Romans, Turks, Crusaders, and finally Germans, British, French, and Americans and Russians would contend and leave traces of themselves there.

---

ated by Sennacherib and located in Nineveh rather than Babylon in *The Mystery of the Hanging Garden of Babylon: An Elusive World Wonder Traced,* Oxford University Press, 2013.
15 Daniel 5:25-28.

APPENDIX B

ASSYRIA'S LATER WARLORDS

(ONLY FOR READERS INTERESTED IN REPETITIVE WARS OF LITTLE LASTING IMPORTANCE)

TIGLATH-PILESER'S DIRECT heirs maintained their positions, in an apparently unbroken line through the balance of the Eleventh Century B.C. and into the Tenth, when all the peoples that Tiglath-Pileser I had subjugated or intimidated or whose wealth and trade he had usurped or appropriated rose apparently almost in unison and severely harassed the former overlord-power. There were steady movements westwards from Semitic tribes, Babylon was invaded by the Chaldeans, and the Aramaeans reasserted themselves from what is now central Iraq all the way to Damascus and Aleppo and they pressed on Palestine and Phoenicia. Prolonged and unceasing invasions and attacks like this always wear down the targeted state, and the ancient civilizations of Mesopotamia were exhausted like Egypt. Nineveh was threatened and somewhat impoverished, and the tribes that the Assyrians had suppressed and largely assimilated were surly and disobedient, but through the Tenth Century B.C., the invasions of marauding Asians subsided and the rebellious and aggressive tribes and peoples between the Euphrates and Palestine settled and were less belligerent. What amounted to a new Assyrian dynasty, though somewhat connected to Tiglath-Pileser I, began with Ashur-rabi in 1001 B.C. and a gradual restoration of order and coherence was effected in the core of the old Assyria.

Tiglath-Pileser II (966-934) was fully worthy of the great name he bore, and Assyria reentered the trade routes and steadily expanded its agriculture and relatively gentle suzerainty of its smaller neighbours. After several decades of this gradual self-strengthening, the Assyrian vocation for outright conquest and plunder asserted itself with, literally, a vengeance. King Adad-Nirari (911-889) conquered as far east as Persia, then turned south and routed the king of Babylon, Shamash-Mudammik, and drove his army down the Euphrates and occupied all of Babylonia that was fortified and economically useful. The several centuries of conflict between Babylonia and Assyria somewhat presaged the struggle between the Gauls and Teutons (French and Germans) for superiority in western and central Europe. The grand prize was the area now occupied by the Tammanai, assisted by the devious and tenacious Aramaeans, just west of the Tigris, and the Assyrian army beset and attacked all around and through this area in campaigns that never paused for more than a few weeks from 907 to 903. Adad-Nirari seized Hanigalbat in 900 and moved on to exact tribute from the leading Aramaean tribes and federations, the Laki and Khindanu. Like a Middle Eastern Frederick the Great, Adad-Nirari had reconstituted Assyria as a powerful but compact state, occupying and steadily building the core of Tiglath-Pileser I's empire. It was an astounding act of national resilience and dynastic self-resuscitation.

With the accession of Tukulti-Ninurta II in 889 B.C., there began yearly campaigns that continued for approximately sixty years, to regain everything that had been lost in the erosion after Tiglath-Pileser I. An ambitious plan, including the steady intimidation and garrisoning of frontier areas and the occupation and administration of the trade routes into Cappadocia (Anatolia) and all the way to the Mediterranean, was successfully pursued. Where on their first eruption to the west, the Assyrians had been generally content to exact tribute and toll-gate commerce, on their second visitation, in greater strength and numbers and less preoccupied than Tiglath-Pileser I had been to show his personal talents as a nimrod and his intellectual catholicity, new Assyrian kings were garrisoning and directly governing an ever larger swath of what is now the Near East—from Persia to the Mediterranean, and into what is now Turkey, and down to the edge of Arabia and the approaches to Egypt. Tukulti-Ninurta proved a formidable strategist: he requisitioned thousands of horses and immense quantities of metal, to build into the Assyrian army a powerful advantage in mobility, logistics, and equipment, and in 885, conducted a ceremonious march around the borders of his kingdom, including trampling through suzerain territories. In his route of march, he shrewdly steered between assertions of force and the ability to expropriate, without vandalizing or plundering on a scale that left the population in desperate revolt or so seething with hate that they would risk everything against the occupier.

Tukulti-Ninurta's son, Ashur-nasir-pal, was the Assyrian king from 884 to 859, and another formidable ruler and conqueror. His first task was to attain a renewed suzerainty over the surrounding tribal areas and continue to retrace the steps of Tiglath-Pileser I. It was hilly and semi-mountainous country, and the occupants were not numerous, but agile and good warriors. But Assyria had achieved a superiority of swiftness of movement that gave them an advantage, and they routed their immediate neighbours, and the Assyrian king dealt with his opponents as his father had, not oppressing the population but harshly demystifying the conquered tribal lords. The most determined of this first tier of opponents, the governor of Nishtun, was publicly whipped to death at Arbela (a town that would take a permanent place in world history five-hundred years later as the sight of the greatest military victory in the history of the world up to that time, by Alexander the Great). This, coupled with the relatively unoppressive nature of the Assyrian overlordship, had the desired effect of cowing the bordering lands into a state of quasi-submission, neither in constant fever of agitation nor altogether docile. This was quite acceptable, and economical of Assyrian military manpower.

In 882, Ashur-nasir-pal moved north in forced marches and assaulted and seized by storm the fortress of Kinabu and roasted three-thousand defenders alive.

He made short work of the Aramaean contingent that attempted to intervene, burning three-thousand of them also. The king accepted without critical comment the rich offerings of his and his family's former enemies. He did this without cordiality or a hint of what his intention might be. In 879, the northern hills required a return from the Assyrian king, who was a good deal less gentle than he had been on his earlier visit. By this time, frontier provinces, their leaders completely unsure of what might next sweep in from the vast Asiatic plains, found Ashur-nasir-pal a fairly safe shelter, and if their chiefs were obstreperous on behalf of their subjects to be tyrannized and exploited and oppressed by their own leaders, dispensing with them was a small sacrifice to gain a more gentle regime from an imperial outsider. The public whipping to death of their former chiefs did not so much stir the passions of revolt as incite the sagacity of survival.

Ashur-nasir-pal moved sharply westward starting in 884, and such was the momentum of this astounding resuscitation of the force of the Assyrians, even the Aramaeans, who had been anticipating unlimited enjoyment of the taxation of the trade routes, offered not only no resistance to the Assyrians, but professed in places to be their collaborators. Ashur-nasir-pal was sufficiently worldly to see this only as a measure of his preeminence in the theatre. Obviously, the Aramaeans would have the grace of conversion at the appearance of a plausible alternative to the Assyrians. Ashur-nasir-pal pressed on irresistibly to the east, across the Euphrates. In 878, a revolt inspired and led by the Aramaeans broke out, and Ashur-nasir-pal had little difficulty snuffing it out. An attempt at revolt by the Sukhu, Laki, and Khinani was attempted one final time (in this sequence) in 877. In 876, the Assyrian King marched unopposed all the way to the Mediterranean. He exacted tribute in an unabashedly confiscatory manner at the tip of the spear and the arrow, and was thus greeted by Tyre, Sidon, Byblos, Tripoli, and Arpad. All was quiet for ten years, when the distant north became impertinent, and Ashur-nasir-pal set forth in his war chariot, took Damdamusa by storm, massacring six-hundred defenders, and crucified three-thousand Amid. The Assyrian king moved his capital from Nineveh to Kalakh, Shalmaneser's capital, and took up residence there in 879. He built a splendid palace of brick, stone, and cedars of Lebanon.

Ashur-nasir-pal was a strong king, who reigned another twenty years, until 859. He kept his army in peak condition throughout this time, and never deserted or failed to take a keen interest in his officers, and his famous and invincible army did not lose its edge. He was generally reckoned a prudent and firm but not gratuitously oppressive king, and was an efficient if not especially amiable chief of his people. He was followed by Shalmaneser III, who reigned from 859 to 824, who continued his father's policy of expanding to the north and west along the trade routes. This required the reduction in detail of some stubborn "tributary" (autonomous) regimes.

Subduing these peoples involved assigning more forces from other occupied and garrisoned areas than was altogether safe and opened a vulnerability to the determined neighboring Urartu tribes. They were apparently Caucasian and from the Biblical Ararat and had adapted the better techniques and weapons of all the major peoples that had come by or over them, and they were tenacious and avaricious. At the beginning of his accession year of 859, Shalmaneser seized and sacked the Urarti fortress city of Sugunia, and then went through the deterrent ceremony of washing the weapons in Lake Van, in sight of the Urarti capital of Van. He returned in triumph to Nineveh (with some two-humped camels as souvenirs) but continued each year to make war on the same elements impeding the way of Assyria along the trade routes, especially the Bit Adini. These campaigns continued for four fierce years, in which the Assyrian king sacked and plundered all the cities and towns that resisted him and killed thousands of people. He finally deported seventeen-thousand five-hundred, the entire surviving army of Akhuni, king of the Bit Adini, to Ashur, and resettled the whole area.

The Assyrians occupied most of northern Syria, and the kings of Damascus and Hamath joined in a confederation composed of twelve lesser monarchs in a pan-Syrian resistance to Shalmaneser, who set out from Nineveh to bring Syria completely to heel in 853. The cities on his route of march submitted, including Aleppo, and the Balikh obligingly overthrew and executed their sheikh in order to surrender to the Assyrian king, who sacked Karkar as he neared Hamath, where battle was joined. The defenders mustered sixty-three thousand infantry, two-thousand cavalry, four-thousand chariots, and one-thousand camels. Shalmaneser inflicted fourteen-thousand dead on his enemies, and they slowly withdrew, but Assyrian casualties were ample enough that no siege of Hamath or hot pursuit was attempted. The following year, Shalmaneser did not return to Syria, but quelled impertinences in Babylonia and formally occupied Babylon with full ceremonious rights of the conqueror, crushed Aramaean settlements along the Euphrates, and generally cleaned house on his other flanks and replenished his forces until returning to the Syrian project in 849. Carchemish was subjugated (as it had been countless times by now, by every passing army in the area for centuries), and Shalmaneser moved northwest to attack Urartu, but the Damascene and Hamathene armies attacked Shalmaneser's communications train; he repulsed them but deferred his supreme assault until 845. In the interregnum, Shalmaneser sacked about one hundred Urartu towns and generally cleared the scrub away, but all knew that the main event was imminent.

The Assyrian king assembled the maximum force he could safely remove from the garrisons, assuring the fealty of the conquered, and crossed the Euphrates into Syria at the head of a mighty force of one-hundred and twenty thousand battle-hardened warriors. He defeated his enemies and pushed them back, but they did not crack and flee or descend into disorder. They conducted a slow and orderly retreat, and tried to tempt the Assyrian king into impetuous over-stretch. Shalmaneser did not take the bait, accepted a partial victory, and withdrew. In the next three years, he moved north to the sources of both the Tigris and the Euphrates and again tidied up Babylonia. As Shalmaneser prepared to come back to Syria, his tactics were vindicated, as the Hamath-Damascus alliance broke down; the king of Damascus was murdered in a coup, and Hamath, in an exhausted and war-wearied state, declined to rise to resist the approach of Shalmaneser in 841. Hazael, the opportunistic king of Damascus, put up a good fight at Mt. Hermon, but lost sixteen-thousand dead in a pitched battle, and retired within the walls of Damascus while the Assyrians subdued and sacked the lesser towns of Hazael's unenthused realm. In these circumstances, Jehu of Israel, and the kings of Tyre and Sidon (effectively municipal rulers of prosperous port towns), came to submit to the authority of the Assyrians. Even Egypt, which traditionally claimed a legitimate interest in Syria, sent an embassy to Shalmaneser highlighted by a number of two-humped Bactrian camels, a hippopotamus, and other exotic creatures for the divertissement of the Assyrian king. He had not completely subdued Damascus, but had reached the Mediterranean in strength, and would remain there.

In 839, Shalmaneser again attacked northward into Syria, with the goal of clearing and securing the caravan route to the sea; the Assyrian king visited the mines of Cappadocia in 837, and he continued his probing marches north and west from 835 to 832. At this point, Shalmaneser III ceased his campaigns of conquest, having gained control of the whole caravan route from Cappadocia to Ashur, and having reduced the Mediterranean coast from Byblos to Tarsus to a suzerain level of submission. His declining years were challenged, but not greatly clouded by the rebellion of one of his sons, Ashur-danin-apal, in 827, and as Shalmaneser III died in 824, many of his influential subjects were in real or threatened revolt against his chosen successor, Shamshi-adad. He died with his kingdom in some internal factional disarray, but with Assyria established as the greatest power in the Middle East. He pushed Assyrian influence out in all directions and left it as the greatest toll-collector on the richest trade routes in the world. The Urartu had not been completely routed from the northern passes, though they were much-chastised and worried, though no less greedy or aggressive, but he left Assyria, however internecine maneuverings among his family might play out, stronger than ever.

Shamshi-adad V succeeded to the throne in 824, but it required until 821 to see off Ashur-danin-apal. The actual authority of Assyria, beyond its own ethnic and tribal bounds, was essentially dependent upon the ability of the Assyrian army to intimidate neighbouring tribes and countries to obedience. This was bound, by its nature, to be a constant challenge, as it had been in this region for many centuries. Obviously, the arts and artifices of rulership had not, at this point, much advanced beyond overrunning weaker neighbors and declaring them to be subordinate and to be required to pay tribute until they thought it safe to rebel. Shamshi-adad followed up the Tigris to its source and struck eastward but was resisted by a formidable coalition of Chaldeans, Aramaeans, Elamites, and Namrites under the flag of rebellious Babylon. The Assyrian king continued in the family tradition, and routed the enemy, killing five-thousand ostensible Babylonians and taking two-thousand prisoners. Shamshi-adad finally, triumphantly, reentered Babylon in 811. He died in that year, and his mother, Sammu-ramat, assured continuity for three years as regent, and secured the immortality of the derived name Semiramis.

Adad-nirari III succeeded to the throne of Assyria and owed to his mother's sagacity the fact that he shortly assumed a stable and settled authority. The Urartu king Menaus clearly posed a serious threat, and rampaged around the northern fringe of Assyria, plundering and intimidating smaller tribes into joining Urartu in its opposition to Assyria. Eight campaigns were fought between these adversaries between 810 and 787, at the end of which the passes in the northern mountains separating Assyria from the Caspian Sea remained in dispute. The Urartu held their own.

In Syria, Hazael's son, Bar-Hadad, succeeded his father as king of Damascus, supported by the almost ubiquitously scattered Aramaeans, set out to punish the apostasy of Hamath from the anti-Syrian bloc; but with Assyrian support, he was rebuffed between 805 and 802, and Bar-Hadad died, leaving an untried son, Mari, to lead the defence of Damascus against Adad-nirari III. Mari surrendered to the Assyrian king, who conducted a civilized triumph, but received the unambiguous tribute and submission of the entire Mediterranean littoral from Egypt to Cappadocia. This was the greatest accretion of influence Assyria had yet achieved, and it would not need to return to its western suzerainties, clients, and ostensible allies until 796, and then only briefly.

Adad-nirari sorted out his relations with Babylon, always too vain to remain subservient for long to any foreign power, and was acclaimed "protector" of a still proudly, but not unlimitedly, independent Babylon. These arrangements gave Assyria the unlimited right to traverse Babylonian territory militarily, but it also facilitated Babylon giving the rugged Assyrian warrior-state the mantle of its relatively more sophisticated cultural and religious views. Adad-nirari has enjoyed a good reputation, not only as a general but as a champion of civilization among his subjects, most of whom were much in need of it. Shalmaneser IV succeeded Adad-narari(782-772), but his reign was disturbed from the outset by the attempt of Argistis I of Urartu to turn the tables on Assyria.

From 781 to 774, Shalmaneser IV assailed Argistis I unsuccessfully, and the Urarti king counter-attacked and narrowly gained the upper hand. Assyrian prestige was slightly clouded and ruffled, but the issue was uncertain and Argistis compromised himself by excessive boastfulness. The Assyrian set-backs in the north naturally caused uprisings in other questionable parts of the empire, including in northern Syria and Damascus, where punitive campaigns punished the recalcitrant. Under the next Assyrian king, however, Ashur-dan (772-754), Assyrian fortunes clearly declined: a number of cities were regained by the Urartu, or had at least come back under their influence. Argistis' son, Sarduris II, regained control of a number of cities, including the ultimate shuttlecock of the region, Carchemish. This returned to Urartu control over the traffic along the trade routes in metal, a very valuable franchise, and any such impairment of the Assyrian connection to Cappadocia and the Mediterranean imperiled the entire regime. There were rebellions in a number of cities which Ashur-dan was only able to subdue in 758. There was also disorder and peril along the southern border. Assyria was never more than military conquest and the subornation by the most unsubtle methods of bribery of local rulers, and little durable loyalty was aroused, though its governance, by the standards of the time, was not overly severe. The Urartu were even able to stir up the Medians, and Ashur-dan left Assyria disorganized, dispirited, and with an empty treasury. His son, Ashur-narari V (754-746), was incompetent and he left Assyria in a parlous condition once more.

All was not lost, however. The colonies that had been established were not uprooted by Urartu, and the military continued to be strong, well-trained, and highly motivated; the problem was with the commanders-in-chief. The Assyrian army continued to be the best in the region, Assyrian governors had been relatively enlightened and competent, and Urartu, especially, would be very vulnerable to a seriously planned and well-led assault. Assyria was no pillar of a new enlightenment, but it was the repose of man's intellect in comparison with its enemies, such as the resourceful but culturally primitive and gluttonously motivated Urartu, who were incapable of any tocsin more uplifting than to kill, sack, subjugate, and wallow in lasciviousness until the gods come for one. No such ethos would cut it for long, when challenged seriously. It all came right for Assyria one more time with Tiglath-Pileser III, who reigned from 745 to 727. He was faced with the tasks of shaping up the bedraggled and disoriented Assyrians, restoring order and (his) authority in Babylonia, regaining control of Syria and the trade routes to the Mediterranean, and driving Urartu back through the passes to the north. The first targets were the inevitable Aramaeans in Babylonia and on its edges.

The king conducted a successful campaign down the eastern bank of the Tigris, clearing away hostile tribes and enclosing Babylonia. He made a peace from strength with the king of Babylonia, Nabunassar, who accepted Assyrian overlordship but was assured in his position, and both sides abided by their agreement. Tiglath-Pileser now turned on Urartu, attacking in strength on the east and west, where the enemy was overstretched, and encountered no resistance in the east but administered a sharp defeat in the west, sending the Urartu reeling backwards and separating them from their erstwhile Syrian allies. The Assyrian king chased the Urartu king, Sardoris, back into his own interior near the Caspian, and he was now free to deal with the Syrians without their having the aid of reinforcements. From 742 to 740, he launched almost continuous offensives in Syria, and rolled up the country, inciting the voluntary submission of Damascus, Tyre, Carchemish, and many lesser cities. In 739, he secured the northern passes from Syria, thus effectively sealing the country off from possible northern intrusion or infiltration. Tiglath-Pileser III conducted another campaign in the east and northeast in 736 and trampled through a large part of Urartu territory. He attacked toward Egypt in 724, going as far as Gaza. In this process, he made himself the master of Philistia and the protector of Israel and Judah from its hostile neighbors. The Assyrians continued to impose themselves on Syria and weed out opposing factions, while in factional struggles in the lesser kingdoms in Syria and the Levant, the partisans of the Assyrians generally got the upper hand. The successful military power in the theatre achieves great natural adherence if there are not the elements of a nativist coalition, and Tiglath-Pileser had skillfully divided and defeated piecemeal many of what might have been the ingredients of such a resistance.

Following the death of the loyal Babylonian king, Nabunassar, in 734, order broke down and Tiglath-Pileser intervened after Nabunassar's son was murdered and cut a mighty swath through Babylonia, deporting approximately one-hundred and seven thousand people in rugged conditions from provincial areas of Babylonia and razing the principal cities to the ground. He eventually elevated himself to the historic kingship of Babylonia in 728, and there was no one to oppose him. Tiglath-Pileser III has always ranked as one of the most remarkable and successful of ancient monarchs. He was not a well-rounded civil governor, but an efficient administrator, bold strategist and invincible general in his severely contested times.

Viewed from a distance, Assyria's chief contribution to history was to conserve the useful, if pretentious and temperamental vessel of civilization, Babylon, well intact, to hand it on in due course to Persia. The kings of Persia also treated it fairly gently and left it for Alexander the Great, whose heirs involuntarily bequeathed it to Rome, which, through its secular and ecclesiastical influence, saw to the conservation of what was worthwhile in Babylon all the way to the modern age.

CHAPTER FOUR

THE BEGINNINGS OF INDIA AND CHINA
FROM ANTIQUITY TO THE THIRD CENTURY B.C. (INDIA) AND THE SECOND CENTURY B.C. (CHINA)

GAUTAMA (BUDDHA) AND CONFUCIUS

Seated Buddha; circa 475 A.D.

Confucius by Qiu Ying (1494–1552 A.D.)

1. Early India

IT IS NOT INTENDED at this point to give more than a concise summary of the development of India and China. Coverage of these vast countries will gradually become more comprehensive as their contacts with the West increase. The purpose here is to provide an insight into their comparative political development. Presenting these facts as comprehensively even as has been done in respect of the earliest known inhabitants of the Middle East would involve an enormous amount of personal and geographic detail requiring heavy usage of inaccessible languages and a colossal labyrinth of details that would be incomprehensible to all but a handful of Western readers. The objective is to present the most seminal protagonists and events and to keep the reader broadly in touch with developments in South Asia and the Far East parallel to developments among the Mediterranean and Near Eastern peoples. In this volume, trading relationships and distant political contact with India will arise and grow and the existence and great extent of China will become generally known to the political leaders of the West. As the narrative continues in the succeeding volume, these and other distant regions will be increasingly in contact with the Mediterranean and Middle Eastern peoples and will be presented with summarized prior histories as they join what was the world known to the West. By the late Middle Ages, this will include the Americas and North Africa and almost all of Eurasia. In the modern sections of this book, from the start of the nation state, all parts and countries of the world will be covered with the detail appropriate to their contemporary relative importance. Though it may not be obvious to the reader, I have gone to some lengths not to mire us in the absurdly obscure and unpronounceable vastness of history; a full immersion in the trackless infinities of southern and eastern Asia would overwhelm the intellectual patience and absorptive powers of all but the most invincible scholars. This work has no such objective.

Contrary to widespread belief in the West, recorded Indian history somewhat predates that of China. And for obvious geographic reasons, India has been engaged with the early Western world much longer than has China. Even in the times already covered in preceding chapters, the myth and lore of India had already stirred the imaginations of the West and had caused the opening, via Arabia and Persia, of minor commercial activities in exotic agricultural products and handicrafts. Indic civilization gradually emerged in the South Asian subcontinent bounded by the Hindu Kush and Baluchistan in the west, the Himalayas on the north, the Burmese mountains to the east, and the Indian Ocean. Doubtless because of the heat of most of India all of the year, the early expansion of population has consistently challenged the agricultural productivity of India for centuries, and water has always loomed very prominently in public thoughts and fears. Hindus have long worshipped "Mother Ganges." In the south, where rivers are sparse, and the population depends on rain, the June monsoon, despite its inconveniences, is greeted as a providential visitation. The great subterranean upheavals that threw out of the Himalayas the watercourses of the Indus, Ganges, and Brahmaputra Rivers, now roughly divide the subcontinent between Pakistan and India and Bangladesh. The Indus River system became the cradle of North Indian culture and, like the alluvial valleys of the Punjab and Sind, have their origins in the "abodes of snow." The original population appears, from Paleolithic skeletal remains and fragments of tools, to have migrated from central Asia between two-hundred thousand and four-hundred thousand years ago, during the second interglacial age.

India appears to have been at least a thousand years behind Egypt and Persia in the transition from primitive hunting to the agriculture of crops, and the relative scarcity of water contributed over many centuries to the immense proliferation of India's proverbial ten-thousand villages. Flood-borne silt was the principal fertilizer, and until the expanding semi-rural population put much of South India under cultivation, the tiger and the rhinoceros were numerous. The disappearance of the long grass drove the rhinoceros out of India, along with lesser game, and the tiger retreated to more remote and less populated regions of the subcontinent.

Archaeological exploration approximately a hundred years ago unearthed the city of Harappa in the Punjab, which seems to have flourished between approximately 2300 and 1750 B.C. and to have attained a circumference of about three and one half miles and a population of about thirty-five thousand. Excavation has revealed what seems to have been relatively solid and well-sewered workers' barracks much more salubrious than the teeming slums of later Indian cities where outcast working families dwelt miserably outside city walls. This society seemed even in these early days to develop into a large majority of laborers, some of them quite skilled and relatively well-paid, a small middle-class of more skilled or managerial people and a very small priestly and warrior elite.

A large archaeological site explored contemporaneously with Harappa about two-hundred and fifty miles upstream from the Arabian Sea on the west bank of the Indus, Mohenjo-Daro, revealed ten cities constructed directly on top of each other apparently over a period of several thousand years. The evolution of living quarters, building materials, tools, and arts and crafts is clearly discernible. The uniformity of building styles and materials and the symmetricality of blocks and streets all suggest that there was some sort of overall municipal authority in each re-creation of the city. While the uniformity of it seems unspontaneous, there remains plenty of evidence of artistic creativity, especially in pottery and engraving. India's original domestic God, Shiva, seems to have been particularly revered for his potent virility, which is celebrated with a great variety of phallic symbols.

A profusion of merchants' seals in all excavated cities revealed that India was conducting a substantial trade with Sumeria by 2300 B.C. By this time, the population along the Indus had begun spinning cotton, and the provision of cotton for clothing domestically and as an export industry continues yet. Weaving cotton soon became and long continued to be India's principal industry. But India was also by this time producing a large quantity of luxury items such as shell and bone inlay goods, ivory objects, imaginative fabrications from peacock feathers, pearls, and sophisticated wood-carvings. We have already seen, in the last section of Chapter 1, that Israel's King Solomon imported peacocks and apes from India. It must have been well before that that the exportation of spices began as well as India's importation of jade, silver, turquoise, tin, and lapis lazuli from Persia and Bactria (Afghanistan). Also, by 2000 B.C., both wild and cultivated rice had become the principal crop along the Indus, along with dates, and sesame and mustard seeds. The dog, cat, camel, sheep, pig, goat, water buffalo, elephant, and chicken had all been domesticated.

Around 1700 B.C., severe floods, and a shifting of course of the Indus inundated Mohenjo-Daro and Harappa. "The city empire with its wondrous citadels was gone, disappearing as dramatically, almost as inexplicably, as it had emerged, washed over by the Indus and its rushing tributaries, like a world of sand-castles reclaimed by a rising tide, its crumbling walls and vague outlines all that remained for the next wave of invading children to occupy."[1]

2. The Aryan Invasion of India

It was not long after these changes in the Indus and other rivers that India became subject to the same barbarian pressures that assaulted Europe and Mesopo-

---

1 Stanley Wolpert, *A New History of India*, Oxford, 1982, p. 23.

tamia. Indo-European speaking semi-nomadic barbarians, many from between the Black Sea and the Caspian Sea but others in the Steppes of what is now European Russia, were driven in huge numbers to the south as they were to the west and to the southwest. It has never been known to what extent they were driven by drought or extreme cold or plague or other disease or assault from Mongols or other aggressive Eastern peoples, and to what extent they were attracted by what in modern parlance are called "greener pastures." But essentially, a very similar phenomenon to that which produced limitless marauding hordes pouring up against or into central Europe and the Middle East also afflicted India. The remarkable work of comparative linguists and philologists, in particular Sir William Jones (1746-1794), a judge of the high court operated by the British East India Company, eventually revealed similarities, especially in geographic, climatic, botanical, and zoological terms between Sanskrit and the Greek, Latin, and Germanic languages. The similarities were extensive enough to establish and justify the concept of a single Indo-European family of languages.

The period of these aggressive migrations into India is known as India's Aryan Age, approximately between 1500 and 1000 B.C. As with Europe and the Middle East, though not to such a pronounced extent, the invading hordes brought with them a civilization considerably more rudimentary than those which they assaulted. The invaders of India lived in tribal villages made of light wood, not brick and without baths or sewers or any identifiable artistic talents, but they had harnessed their horses to chariots and had bronze axes and formidable long-bows: it was the pattern we have so often seen in the West in the first three chapters of primitive societies being militarily more advanced and probably more highly motivated because of their vulnerability to the elements and to each other than the comparatively flaccid and sophisticated societies that they overran. This was not such a contrast in India as it was in Egypt and Mesopotamia and Southern and ultimately Western Europe, but it was very much a parallel and related activity.

There is no archaeological evidence of the Aryan invasion or of the entire Aryan Age, probably because their building materials were so vulnerable to the ravages of intervening centuries. But we do have the "books of knowledge," or Vedas, which were composed and added to by the tribal bards, and they preserve the oral tradition of many of these tribes. They were considered sacred works, and the most renowned that has survived is the Rig Veda, made up of over a thousand Sanskrit poems mainly addressed to the many Aryan gods. This is the preserved origin of the ancient Indo-European literature. While the Vedas provide little history of the Aryan invasion, they do mention victories over darker skinned people attempting to defend themselves within fortresses. Excavations in the early years of the Twentieth Century at the Hittite sites in Cappadocia led to the discovery of tablets recording a treaty between the memorably styled Hittite King Subiluliuma (this is absolutely his final appearance in this book), and the Mitanni King Mattiwaza, in about 1400 B.C. The Aryan invaders were probably an even more influential agent of change in the subcontinent than the British more than two-thousand years later. They came in much greater numbers and with more permanent ambitions, and imposed Sanskrit and a new pantheon of deities, and the patriarchal family and the three-level socioeconomic structure of priests, warriors, and the people.

As far as can be judged, when the Aryans were not subduing the native peoples of India, these natives were like many of the North and South American indigenous people when the Europeans arrived, energetically fighting each other. This constant recourse to war caused the victorious tribes to be enlarged by their conquests and the tribal structures to become more complicated. The kings elevated the priests and the army commanders, and, as in the West, generally tried to retain, though not always successfully, the headship of both the religious and governmental structures, primitive as they were, for themselves. The authority was known as the Raja, and in the final book of the Rig Veda, the structure of four "classes" is summarized by the anatomical source of their work product. Thus are the Brahmans who derive their welfare from their mouths, and there followed in descending the socio-economic ladder, the Kshatriyas—warriors who were sustained by their arms, the Vaishyas, who lived from the ability of their thighs to make them bearers and drawers of essential goods or objects, and last, the Shudras, who lived from the efforts of their feet, preeminently farmers. The most important distinction, however, was skin color, which has continued to define the castes. It does not appear that iron was discovered in India until approximately 1000 B.C., and it caused the gradual emergence of a less relentlessly agricultural economy.

The Vedic Aryans, along with their belligerency, seem to have had the traditional soldiers' appreciation of wine and gambling and in their time, chariot racing, but also of music and song, and they created relatively sophisticated music with lutes, flutes, and drums. Their music and even dances were integrated into religious worship, which continues in Hindu ceremony today. In their musical proclivities, the Aryans and the Indians shared their enthusiasm and merged their instruments. The Aryan religion consisted of the worship of thirty-three identified coequal deities, representing natural phenomena, to whom sacrifices were made for the enjoyment of pleasure and a serene after-life. Eventually, a number of super-deities emerged, as India, like Western peoples, moved towards monistic religion as it progressed determinedly towards monotheism.

As in Europe and the Middle East, the Aryan conquest, or at least occupation of North India, produced a gradual socio-cultural integration between the invading barbaric hordes and the original population. More than a thousand years would be required to complete this process as the geopolitical and cultural centre of northern India moved a thousand miles to the east of the Indus and into the plains of the Ganges. This process was especially aggravated by terrible quarrels between the Aryan tribes themselves; North India knew almost no peace. Such literature and other evidence as there is indicates that there was no move away from monarchical government, and all emphasis was on magnifying the prestige of the king and consistently linking him to the deities.

The two great literary works of this era, the *Mahabharata* and the *Ramayana*, both composed sometime prior to 500 B.C. but not greatly before that date, exalt the virtues of monarchy, provided the king is just and respectable and pious. Court decadence is punished in this literature, and the austerity and simplicity of the sage, especially the hermit sage, is exalted. The widespread clearing of land as the Aryans continued to arrive and move eastwards and to the south, coupled to the Aryans' comparatively sophisticated, adapted methods of agriculture, especially seeding and ploughing with horses, canalization for irrigation and flood and drought control, stabilized the food supply for northern and central India.

3. Social and Religious Developments

The four-level Vedic division of castes also evolved, and blended the Indian notion of castes according to birth with the development of the Aryan-sponsored view that the three upper classes or varnas, the Brahman, Kshatriya, and Vaishiya, were resurrected or twice-born people, while the Shudra were a vast only once-born class of servants, slaves, and peasants, who could be exiled or killed at the whim of the upper groups and who were not even permitted to hear or discuss the Vedic poems and hymns, which, it was feared, could incite revolt. Socioeconomic conditions eventually required the creation of a large class caste inferior even to the Shudra. These were the "Untouchables." Fear of losing power militated against any system of meritocracy or free movement between the groups, and the Indian upper classes by 500 B.C. had adapted their political and social institutions to repress the Untouchables with a thoroughness that made Sparta and its slaves, in comparison, almost a social democracy. Eventually, though gradually, India was consumed in a narcissistic and absurdly obscure system of caste subdivisions.

It was inevitable that any society that attempted to impose such a severe and inequitable social structure and to invoke religious support for a regime so repugnant to the great majority of the population was foredoomed to be a stunted society in political science terms. Each Aryan household had a Sacred Hearth at which sacrificial offerings were supposed to be made five times each day. The great annual religious observance of soma required the wealthy to build huge altars where elaborate ceremonies occurred and were credited with bringing the rain upon which survival depended. For this reason, soma was held each year shortly before the anticipated monsoon. Naturally, when the monsoon came early or a month or more late, it was not only an inconvenience and sometimes the cause of famine, but also raised substantial credibility problems, if not about the deities, about the good standing of the Brahmans who led the observances. By 500 B.C., concepts of ascent to heaven to join the deities and the banishment to a hell that might be so painful that those so consigned reawakened to endure the experience in increments, had taken hold. Cremation became the preferred method of disposing of the physical remains of the deceased.

It was also inevitable that such a demanding religion celebrating an objectionably authoritarian system, vastly more disrespectful of the lower socioeconomic groups than most contemporary notions of slavery in the West, would incite considerable dissent. This was aggravated by the venality and presumption of substantial numbers of the clergy. An intellectual revolt led by the hermit sages of the Gangetic Plains, who wandered about the forests meditating and lecturing selected acolytes, began to surface in about 700 B.C., called Upanishad, meaning "sitting down before," an act of nonviolent protest ever since. The practitioners of Upanishad espoused austerity, honesty, a lack of concern for material things, and the notion of the silent, sacred, devolution of human events, transcending cravings and strivings of the spiritless. It may be imagined that this would appeal to the oppressed, but its limitations as a philosophical blueprint for how a society might function are equally obvious. What was sought was release from the impulsive desire, but this obviously does not have general applicability as an ambition. The notion of it remains with us still and has somewhat penetrated the culture of the West, but it was never going to be the basis for organization of the whole society. The Upanishad view of the world was ultimately too negative for most people. Its mysticism has its appeal, but as one of the most famous hermit sages, Brihadratha, said: "In this ill-smelling, unsubstantial body, which is a conglomerate of bone, skin, muscle, marrow, flesh, semen, blood, mucus, tears, rheum, feces, urine, wind, bile, and phlegm, what is the good of enjoyment of desires?"[2]

The only escape from the unpleasantness and fraudulence of life was knowledge of mystic identity of oneself and all. Controlling the universe only required control of oneself. All action was essentially delusional—this was karma, and every action was deemed to have repercussions immediately or eventually, and to the extent that our karma was evil, we might be condemned to return to the cycle of suffering of another life. If a man was especially evil, he might be condemned to return as a lower species, even a mosquito. The supreme Upanishad objective was the attainment of "a deep dreamless sleep." Yoga featured in the pursuit of it. For all the problems in even the more sophisticated societies of the West, none brought down on itself so unpromising a conception of life as those that were in the last few centuries before the dawn of the Christian Era contesting for the adherence of the Indian subcontinent.

By the Sixth Century B.C., there were sixteen major kingdoms and tribal oligarchies in northern India, from Afghanistan to Bengal. The most powerful were Magadha on the eastern plane of the Ganges, and Kosala, somewhat to the northwest and stretching up to the Himalayan foothills. The Buddha, Sidhartha Gautama, was born in this region in Kapilavastu, in 563 B.C. Gautama was a wealthy tribal prince, but when he was about thirty, he departed his life there and wandered in the manner of the subcontinent for the next six years in the forests of Kosala and Magadha. He then created what has become the religion of Buddhism which advocated a monastic regime of virtue, pacifism, and austerity in opposition to the Brahmin clerical monopoly of magic and wealth. The Buddha encouraged the Kshatriya and Vaishya and effectively opposed the tyranny of the Brahmin. Gautama was supported and patronized from the beginning by the king of Maghada, Bimbisara, who reigned from 540 to 490 B.C. He was naturally not particularly attracted to Brahmin prayers and sacrifices that beseeched the deities for the increased power and wealth of the Brahmans themselves; he naturally found even the Buddha's calls for virtue and austerity preferable to the incumbent religion's supplications for the greater wealth and prosperity of and led by the Brahmans. It is alleged that the Buddha gained the king's favor by responding to a court Brahmin who had demanded that the king sacrifice fifty of his finest goats as "whatever he sacrificed went directly to

---

2 Ibid., p. 47.

heaven," by asking if the Brahmin's father was alive and when informed that he was, asking why the Brahmin did not sacrifice him.

In a nearby deer park, the Buddha was believed to set in motion his "wheel of the law" which set out the four Noble Truths of suffering, which were held to be universal and unavoidable: ignorance; the claim that any unpleasantness if understood could be cured, and in North India, medical insights were comparatively advanced; attachment to the material world in the form of desire, craving; and the fourth Noble Truth was the eightfold path to eliminating suffering by holding, practicing, and following the right views. This would lead to nirvana, literally the snuffing out of pain and suffering. The Buddha spent the next forty-five years preaching these four Noble Truths and gathered such an immense host of disciples and believers that he established a monastic order that flourished and grew and still spans the world. Initially, only men could join and had to take vows of poverty, chastity, and non-violence. (Gandhi took and observed these vows.) In his last years, and not without some skepticism, the Buddha admitted nuns to his religious order, which followed an extremely spartan discipline and tried to survive on the proceeds of mendicancy by assuring those who gave them food that their marriage would be divinely recognized. This challenging form of monasticism achieved great popularity, and it became a powerful countervailing force against Brahmin-ism in North India and obtained considerable political power in Magadha. As often happens, it was ultimately even more widely embraced and more influential in China and Japan than in its country of origin. The Buddha died at the age of eighty of natural causes and with an immense following. His closest collaborators conferred upon him the status almost of deity unto himself, which he firmly rejected.

Another rebellion from Vedic and Brahmin authority was launched by Kshatriya Prince Vardhamana Mhavira (540-468), who, like Gautama, renounced his pleasure-seeking life at the age of thirty to be a wandering contemplative ascetic, with the added flourish that he was, for about ten years, a nudist. He eventually founded a new sect, the Jainas, who adopted and espoused a more extreme regimen than the Buddhists: not only, for a time, nakedness, but also self-torture and even induced death by self-starvation. This was his own method of dying, though his hunger strike endured with slight interruptions for thirteen years before accomplishing its objective. The core of Jainist belief is that everything is animate—even rocks have a soul, though the souls of evidently animate creatures are more complicated. His doctrine was total pacifism. In service to this rather eccentric cult, orders of monks and nuns arose and flourished even though it opposed agriculture, as that activity could kill living objects by plowing. Ironically, and despite Jainist opposition to materialism, the order focused on commercial activities such as banking and other lucrative occupations and became very rich and continues to be so. These sects did not have unlimited appeal, but Buddhism especially has been extremely successful and is in practice somewhat less onerous than its founder advocated. At the least, they weakened the Brahmin strangle-hold on the population and contributed to the assimilation of the Aryans and the Indians whom they conquered when they crossed the Himalayas. By the mid-Fourth Century B.C., communications had developed sufficiently that commerce and other contacts among the northern and central Indian states and tribal entities were such that the will to expand and even unify, from both fraternal and aggressive instincts, began to produce personalities and initiatives of pan-Indian significance.

4. India's First Unification

Magadha continued to be the largest jurisdictional unit within the Indian subcontinent, and there is ample evidence that trade throughout what is now India increased fairly steadily through the Fifth Century B.C. Gandhara, in the northwest of India, Pakistan today, came under the control of the Persian Empire in 518 B.C. and became the twentieth satrapy of Darius' Achaemenid Empire. The capital was at Taxila, near the modern Pakistani capital of Islamabad. According to Herodotus, whose history of the Persian Wars takes a number of extraordinary liberties (including his belief in giant gold-digging ants), this satrapy paid three-hundred and sixty talents annually to the Great King of Persia.

The powerful catalyst in the Magadhan unification of India was the arrival at the Northwest Frontier and penetration beyond it of the demiurgic conqueror Alexander the Great in 326. The Bible provided the authority for John Masefield's reference in his famous poem "Cargoes" to Ophir and ivory, apes, peacocks, sandalwood, and cedarwood, which had all purportedly been brought by sea to contribute to or festoon King Solomon's mighty temple in the Tenth Century B.C. While there may be some inexactitudes in the lore, the exotic wealth of the Indian subcontinent was already known in the more sophisticated localities of the late Old Testament. These may well have inspired Alexander the Great's ambition to discover and seize the wealth of India and to arrive at the Eastern Sea. Alexander crossed the Indus unopposed, and Taxila surrendered to him without resistance. He continued eastwards and, as will be recounted in Chapter Thirteen, crossed the Hydaspes River where the Aryan Rajah Puru barred his way. He had two-hundred elephants, but Alexander was already well accustomed to dealing with elephants, and his cavalry charged around the flanks of the elephants while his archers startled and panicked the great beasts with flaming arrows, and they, in their confusion, joined the charge against their own masters as the Macedonian cavalry slaughtered Puru's flanks while his own elephants crushed his vanguard. The Macedonian infantry was not really needed as the cavalry easily executed a colossal rout on the scale of some of Alexander's greatest triumphs on his route of march across southeastern Asia.

Alexander continued east but as will be described, when he got to the Hyphasis River with his army after a zig-zag march of five years, conquest following conquest in one of the most extraordinary triumphal progresses in all military history, was restless and homesick. According to Justin and Plutarch, the young Chandragupta Maurya, a confident young man claiming the name of Sandrocotus, approached the Macedonian king, who received him out of curiosity, and he interviewed Alexander for a few minutes very respectfully. He was permitted to depart unobstructed. In late July 326, Alexander himself yielded to the intense pleading of his men and began his orderly withdrawal, completely undefeated, in the three-thousand miles and many battles he had fought since crossing the Bosporus five years before.

Little is known of Chandragupta's origins and one school of thought holds that he was mentored by an older Brahmin chief minister Kautilya, who is also credited with being the chief author of at least the early chapters of the *Arthashastra* ("Science of Material Gain"), which was written over approximately six-hundred years starting in about 350 B.C., and contains, among considerably wider contents, cynical tactical advice somewhat like that in Niccolo Machiavelli's *The Prince*, eighteen centuries after the apparent beginning of the lengthy and many-authored *Arthashastra*. It was a multi-layered work, and included a lot of moralistic reflections that were of no interest to Machiavelli, particularly the counsel to avoid the "six enemies:" lust, anger, greed, vanity, haughtiness, and exuberance. (Machiavelli would have no particular objection to those, except perhaps exuberance.)

The *Arthashastra* counsels leaders to control their subjects, especially the prominent ones. At the height of the Mauryan Empire, which included almost all of the present Pakistan and India except the southernmost four-hundred miles of India and contained as many as fifty million people in the early Second Century B.C., it is estimated that the spies, soldiers, police, and civil service of the state totaled perhaps a million men. Taxation by the monarch varied between twenty-five and fifty percent, depending on whether the taxation was applied to harvests, property, designated valuables, or transactions. It may well be imagined that the process of tax collection was authoritarian and seriously tainted by extortion, subornation, and embezzlement.

Most Indians lived in villages and Chandragupta's capital, Patna, seems to have been the greatest city in the world in the late Fourth Century B.C. It was on the south bank of the Ganges and was eight miles long and one and one-half miles wide and was surrounded by a timber wall with five-hundred and seventy towers and a moat nine-hundred feet wide and thirty feet deep. Patna was governed by sixty-five-member councils of elders that divided up various distinct responsibilities. There is considerable evidence of this era, including fragments from the diary of the Greek ambassador, Megasthenes. The ambassador identified seven classes of Mauryan society from royal advisors down through farmers, soldiers, craftsmen, unskilled laborers, and official denunciators. Chandragupta did sign a demarcation treaty with Seleucus Nikator, one of Alexander the Great's senior generals and the ultimately successful contender to take most of the Macedonian Empire, the principal victor of the Diadochi, who fought over Alexander's leavings for forty years (Chapters 14 and 15).

There was a good deal of state-owned enterprise, including all of the mining industry and strategic industries such as shipbuilding and the production of armaments and much of the relatively well-developed textile industry. The Mauryan regime was in some respects a socialized monarchy and enforced comparatively reasonable regulations on working conditions, which also required labourers to be diligent. Levels of compensation arranged downwards from a royal counselor's forty-eight thousand panas (a coin containing 3.5 grams of silver) to one-thousand panas for an engineer or manager or military officer, five-hundred for soldiers and internal spies, one-hundred and twenty for skilled craftsmen, and just sixty panas per year for unskilled labourers. Chandragupta thus created a much more comprehensive and sophisticated state than the rustic and somewhat itinerant tribal-monarchical regimes of preceding centuries. In theory, the king owned all the land, though in practice, concessions substantially mitigated that status.

It should be remembered that the *Arthashastra* was a gradually written compendium of precepts, rules, and insights composed between approximately 350 B.C. and 250 A.D., and what is being described as the latter phase of that development, so almost a thousand years beyond where we have tracked the Mesopotamians, Egyptians, Babylonians, Assyrians, Jews, and Greeks in the opening chapters of this section. The *Arthashastra* also elaborated India's original tradition of foreign policy in which the king's domain was seen as the centre of twelve concentric rings with the adjoining territory being held by enemies, the next ring by friends, and so forth, including spheres of friends of friends out to the last two rings inhabited by what were described as intermediate and neutral kings. Foreign policy was chiefly defined as the prevention of the assemblage of a league of enemies of the king and his allies that could overpower the central authority. Alexander the Great materialized from the realm of the neutral king, and while he galvanized the Mauryan dynasty to build a much more thorough and resilient state than had previously existed in India, by providing the catalytic service that he did and retiring as benignly as he did, Alexander the Great has never been considered as a negative or hostile invader. His effect on India was somewhat like that of the United States upon Japan when it opened the ports of that island country to the world in 1854 under Commodore Matthew Perry.

The unverifiable tradition is that Chandraguptra voluntarily abdicated in 301 B.C. to become a Jain monk in southern India, where he fasted until he died. His son, Bindusara, reigned benignly for thirty-two years and expanded his kingdom to the south and is best remembered for his communications with Seleucus' successor, Antiochus I, from whom he requested Greek wine, figs, and a sophist. Antiochus provided the first two but explained that philosophers could not be sold. The retirement of Chandraguptra to a life of contemplation and austerity somewhat presaged that of the Holy Roman Emperor Charles V to a monastery in 1556 A.D., and even though it was scarcely a Spartan retreat, the retirement of the Roman Emperor Diocletian in 305 A.D.

Bindusara was followed by the very much admired King Ashoka ("sorrowless") from 269 to 232 B.C. This king is better documented than any others in ancient India because he had all of his statutes and many of the events of his reign inscribed in stone that has been preserved or rediscovered, totaling five-thousand words. After faithfully following the *Arthashastra* in making war against "any power superior in might" to eliminate that threat preemptively (a system the Romans would follow for many centuries without ever ascribing to it the weight of divine inspiration), Ashoka professed guilt at his merciless war against Kalinga, which caused immense carnage. He thereafter followed the Buddha's law of pacifism and may even have formally converted to that sect.

For the balance of his reign, Ashoka endlessly professed an implacable preference for nonviolence; he would bear "wrong as long as it can possibly be borne."[3] The endless repetitions of his compassionate nature were generally followed by an admonition to be mindful of his power. It was a deft and effective policy that has

---

3 Ibid., p. 63.

been universally respected in all versions of the ancient history of India. He ruled from Kashmir to Mysore and from Bangladesh to Afghanistan and the only remaining states outside his control in southern India were Kerala, Chola, and Pandya, as well as Sri Lanka. Ashoka's government maintained diplomatic relations with all of its neighbours as well as Antiochus II's Syria, Ptolemy II's Egypt, Antigonus Gonatas' Macedonia, and Alexander of Epirus (Alexander the Great's uncle), all of whom will be suitably covered in Chapters 13-15.

He canceled the annual royal hunt and replaced it with what was called a "pilgrimage of religious law," which he used to visit all of the sections of his empire and for which he enhanced the empire's road network and had shady trees planted all along their routes with hostels at intervals to facilitate safe travel in reasonable comfort. Many emulated the king's vegetarianism, and such was his personality, large numbers of people even outside India adhered to Buddhism because of the great respect in which Ashoka was held throughout the Indian world and neighboring cultures. In approximately 245 B.C., he hosted the Third Great Council of Buddhism at Patna. This was something like the subsequent Councils of the Christian Church and later of the Roman Catholic Church, though it was much less structured. Ashoka is claimed to have built eighty-four thousand stupas, Buddhist reliquary mounds among which were supposedly distributed the ashes of Buddha himself. These were hemispherical mounds of solid stone, some of them very large, and they became centres of worship.

Ashoka withdrew almost completely from public life in the last years of his reign, which ended in 232 B.C. He was undoubtedly a great king and has enjoyed a uniformly appreciative posterity. The Mauryan Empire disintegrated quite quickly after his death, economically and spiritually. The coinage was soon debased and the Empire broken up in civil strife with many contestants for the throne and fragmentation accelerated by resentment of costs of a central government that was deemed to be exploitive and in most regions of the empire, foreign. Regional rivalries flared up and Chandragupta's dynasty collapsed completely and vanished about fifty years after the death of Ashoka, who had shrewdly cultivated and appealed to the shared interests of the different faiths, tongues, and levels of development of the many components of the vast pluralism of the Indian subcontinent. As with the kingdom of the Jews, under Saul, David, and Solomon, even though it was a much less numerous people, the idea of a hereditary king with almost absolute power, including in ecclesiastical matters, could really only continue through three monarchs for about or almost a century.

This survey brings India up to the Third Century B.C. It will be seen that at no point did any part of India approach in political sophistication the notion of citizenship and of comparatively equal rights of most adult males that some of the Greek states and particularly Athens devised. The Mauryans got about as far as Babylonia under its separated twin peaks of Hammurabi and Nebuchadnezzar, and certainly got well past the conquering bellicose warrior kingdoms of which the Assyrians were the most numerous and durable. The early Indian religions were somewhat impractical paradigms of recommended conduct that generally fell short of a consistent system of worship of a divine intelligence that was more than vaguely contemplated. This left the priestly class less powerful than it was in Egypt and many Mesopotamian countries and in Israel, for better or worse. The greatest comparative deficiency of India was the rigorous and anti-meritocratic class or caste system with a large majority of untouchables whose position was even more vulnerable and impotent than that of the slave in most Greek states and certainly in Rome.

At the Golden Age of ancient India, in the time of Ashoka, there was no participatory government and there were no real political institutions apart from the king himself. This was a much inferior level of development to the contemporary Roman Republic which was at this point crushing Carthage as a rival in the central Mediterranean and beginning its swift advance to the status of the greatest power in the world, known and unknown. Sanskrit was a sophisticated language, and it had a considerable literature, though as far as can be determined from those sufficiently learned to comment, it was not as well-developed nor as intellectually ambitious as the Greek or even the Roman worlds. Alexander the Great's Hellenizing mission, had he been able to carry it into India, would certainly have elevated the culture and raised the sophistication and relative liberality of Indian society. India was comparatively advanced in many of the arts including sculpture, but not more so than the Greek world, and it did not have as great a gift for immense works of construction and architecture and the accompanying talents in engineering and mathematics possessed by early Egypt, or contemporary Greece and Rome.

In summary, India in the Third Century B.C. was as advanced in some respects as the Mediterranean world, but was on balance primitive politically and sociologically, and had locked itself into a rigidified class system that would retard socioeconomic and political progress and the creation of a fully integrated and ethnically homogenized state, ultimately producing an excruciatingly complicated and fissiparous sub-continent that was vulnerable to European conquest.

5. China, the Beginnings

Extensive archaeological evidence indicates that the first Chinese people that can be responsibly identified are the Yang-shao in North China around Honan, and the Lung-shan (Shantung) cultures. Both were relatively advanced farming peoples. Both had advanced forms of pottery, but the Yang-shao did not use a pottery wheel and the Lung-shan did. The Yang-shao had domesticated pigs and dogs, and had stone and bone implements and were at their peak between 3000 and 2000 B.C. The Lung-shan had also domesticated horses, sheep and cattle and cultivated silk, where the Yang-shao had confined themselves to harvesting millet, had developed the potter's wheel, and appear to have been at its height in the middle of the Second Millennium B.C. It may be assumed that at around this time, it entered the Iron Age. It was succeeded directly by the Shang civilization, the first in China of which we have any serious historical record. Readers will note that at this time India and more particularly Egypt, Israel, and parts of Mesopotamia appear to have been considerably more advanced than China.

There is an elaborate Chinese mythology that is even today embraced in part to advance the pretense that China is a more ancient civilization than its peers. It early became a Chinese preoccupation to embellish their own history in order to promote the favored national argument that it is the most eminent, numerous, and profound culture. To this end, a rich mythology has been developed and embellished including numerous mythical monarchs deemed to have reigned for millennia and to have given rise to Chinese culture that anti-dates all others. The most famous of the rulers so conceived was Huang Ti, the Yellow Emperor from whom the rulers of the Shang and Chow periods claimed to be descended. And in this mythological era, it is claimed the entire foundations of Chinese culture and civilization were developed. The traditional Hsia dynasty, founded by the legendary Emperor Yu, and which ruled on the banks of the Yellow River for most of the period between the late Twenty-third and mid-Sixteenth Centuries B.C., is generally reckoned as the first major and responsibly outlined Chinese state, a rough Confederation of tribes along the Yellow River. For centuries, most substantial Chinese claimed to be descendants of the Hsia. From this time, Chinese civilization expanded largely with the spread of the peasant farmer from the Yellow River valleys in all directions across China. In this period leading up to the Shang dynasty, there emerged a tribal aristocracy and the transition to a society of various classes.

The current Chinese regime, responding to its Marxist roots, has alleged that China developed layers of economic classes, including slaves at the bottom of the pyramid, and evolved in accordance with the provocations of inevitably insufferable economic injustice. In doing this, it applied Mediterranean societal evolution to China and other parts of the world despite the absence of serious evidence that the Mediterranean model was exactly experienced elsewhere. The Slavic and Germanic tribes evolved into feudalism without ever having a slave society and such prehistoric suppositions are unrigorous. Not altogether unsurprisingly, the People's Republic of China has not yet accommodated this inconvenient gap in the Marxist narrative.

If the Hsia are the first clearly established Chinese dynasty, the first that is known about in some detail is that of the Shang, between approximately 1766 to 1122 B.C.; it centered on Honan, Hupei, Shantung, and Shansi as the capital moved from time to time apparently due to floods of the Yellow River. Though it was somewhat urbanized, it was ruled by a nobility based on a warrior cast which retained a monopoly on bronze weapons and chariots. Like dynasties of both preceding and later eras in the West, its chief raison d'être was expansion, conquest, and the extortion of tribute from adjacent tribes. The invaluable military chariots were also useful for the nobles to indulge their love of hunting. There was a somewhat orderly institution of hereditary monarchy, though succession was from brother to brother, and a permanent small bureaucracy of royal officials. The Shang King managed the traditionally difficult balancing act of being also the religious leader.

The Shang dynasty was Neolithic, and while it was in the Bronze Age, bronze was too expensive to be used in agricultural tools or other items to the benefit of the general population. While the nobility lived with an extravagance unknown in previous ages, there was little progress in the standard of living of peasants farming the customary variety of grains and cattle. The Shang devised a calendar of twelve or thirteen months, each of twenty-nine or thirty days divided into ten-day periods. Archives have been discovered revealing over one-hundred thousand inscriptions of people and events and greatly enhancing our knowledge of the era. The basis of these archives is oracular bones: a question was posed, and the alternative answers were inscribed on the bone, and a heated object was applied to the bone causing it to crack. The decision of the Oracle was the alternative on which the bone cracked. All the Chinese languages at this time appear to have had approximately five-thousand characters, and it has been maintained throughout Chinese history. Though there has been a profusion of spoken dialects requiring interpretation between them, the root of the language has remained unchanged and is traceable back from all of the current spoken versions. The Shang were perhaps the most advanced civilization in all of history in the artistic use of bronze as well as its transformation into weapons, tools, vessels, and artistic decoration.

The Shang religion was mainly the worship of nature and fertility as well as the ancestors of the nobility. The king alone had the right to worship the supreme deity effectively, though the nature cults also embraced a number of local divinities that included the spirits of geographic entities such as rivers and mountains. The large cattle population facilitated sacrifice of those beasts. The Shang Chinese did not stop there, and human sacrifice was a common phenomenon, especially when worshiping ancestors. As we've seen in India, animism was also practiced and continued to modern times, though all ancient Chinese religion was eventually influenced by Buddhism and Taoism and Confucianism. The worship of ancestors, which had been initially largely confined to the nobility, spread throughout Chinese society and has proved a bar to the triumph in China of any single religion. This, in turn, produced some institutional weaknesses to Chinese religion that may perhaps have made it easier for the present totalitarian government and some of its less-authoritarian predecessors to succeed. As we have seen in Europe, the Christian churches have never been stamped out even by the most oppressive totalitarian political systems in all of history.

The five-century rule of the Shang was abruptly ended by an invasion from the West by the Chou tribe in eastern Shensi at a date between 1122 and 1028 B.C., depending on the calendrical system used. The Chou had been a vassal people, somewhat less civilized than the Shang, but eventually, as we've seen elsewhere in this narrative, they had somewhat more advanced weapons technology. In what is also already a pattern, the Chou prevailed by the exploitation of the general discontent among outlying tribes with the tyranny and exploitation of the Shang. The Chou's great mobilizing leader was Wen Wang, and the revolt was affected by his son Wu Wang. The last Shang ruler, Chou Hsin, was portrayed as an unrelievedly oppressive, brutal, avaricious, and incompetent tyrant in the manner reserved previously and thereafter for those subject to dynastic overthrow.

It took more than twenty years for the Chou to impose themselves thoroughly on the Shang, but even then, a revolt supported by some of the Chou royal family occurred, despite the fact that the Chou leadership had installed themselves on the Shang in over one-hundred garrisoned fiefdoms. The Regent for Wen Wang's thirteen-year-old son, Ch'eng, the Duke of Chou, suppressed the uprising, distributed more fiefdoms, and forcibly resettled much of the Shang population. He, like the first two heads of the Chou Dynasty, is generally reckoned an outstanding leader, and his realm was extended to beyond what the Shang had previously held and stretched from Liaoning to the Yangtze and from Kansu to the sea. The regime established was somewhat more sophisticated than the Shang and had a system of conscription and a somewhat more comprehensive civil service. The nobility was more carefully demarcated in degrees of the peerage, and the king ("Wang") continued the challenging balancing act of being also the chief spiritual leader of this vast population, most of whom lived in villages, which were themselves dominated by the fortified towns of the Chou chief lords and their soldiers and functionaries.

Where the Shang had been proto-feudal, the Chou were unambiguously feudal. The kings ostensibly owned all the land, and the peasantry cultivated it, rotating in adjacent units, and most of what was harvested was paid effectively as rent, net of the value of labor, to the presiding lord, and they somewhat resembled serfs but not slaves. To the slight extent that slaves existed in China in this era, it was a phenomenon confined to domestic service.

In another pattern that is already familiar from Europe and India, the Chou Empire was engaged in almost constant skirmishing on all of its frontiers with semi-nomadic tribes. It generally prevailed for some time, but by the Ninth Century B.C., the Chou dynasty was weakening in the customary manner of corruption, oppression, and leading cadres that commanded neither affection nor respect. In 841, Li Wang, an unusually oppressive monarch, was driven from his throne. The final crisis of the dynasty occurred in the reign of Yu Wang, who had managed to alienate the entire vassalage by amusing one of his concubines and provoking himself to laughter, which he had difficulty doing, by setting off false alarms by firing beacons with tops of hay as signals that announced emergencies and caused the soldiery and armed peasantry to come quickly to the king's aid. He continued to do this until one nomadic tribe fiercely attacked him in 771, and he called for assistance in the agreed manner; his call was not answered, and he perished in the attack. His successor, P'ing Wang, was forced to abandon the capital, which was sacked, and the dynasty became an itinerant group of deposed royals, presiding with difficulty over a shrinking kingdom until they were finally reduced to a postage stamp of land in the environs of the ambulatory capital. The fate of China became a matter of dispute between a large number of feudal states struggling to gain central control.

The ensuing period of considerable disarray is known as Eastern Chou and extended from 772 to 221 B.C., and that is divided between what are called the Spring and Autumn (722-481) and the Warring States (403-221). This long period of Eastern Chou was a time of tumultuous activity including intense socioeconomic and cultural development as well as prolonged political confusion and conflict. China got determinedly into the age of iron including for agricultural tools and ploughs and weapons. This vastly increased agricultural production not only through more efficient seeding and harvesting but also improved control of irrigation. The sharp increase in agricultural production generated quick population growth, and by the Fifth Century B.C., the population of China is now estimated to have achieved the formidable total of twenty-five million people, approximately equivalent to India, and well ahead of any Western population at the time, including the Persian Empire (about fifteen million).

These factors of growth also produced larger towns, copper money, and enhanced trade. By the Fourth Century B.C., the traditional villages had been replaced by towns and the ostensible ownership of all land by the king had given way to private property, though land-owning peasants and sharecroppers were a large percentage of the population. Primogeniture ceased to be automatic, and a substantial number of penurious nobles, a phenomenon that would become familiar, resulted. The merchant class became prominent, though it was despised by the patriciate and aristocracy and was at the bottom of Chou society's regard for the classes: first were the "shih"—the nobility, including scholars and high officials; second were the "nung," the peasants; third were the "kung," the skilled tradesmen and artisans, and fourth were the "shang," the merchants and businessmen.

The Spring and Autumn of the Eastern Chou from 722 to 481 BC was a time of almost uninterrupted strife between the approximately one-hundred separate clannish and tribal states composing the Chou Federation. Only fourteen of these were of any real importance, and they absorbed and devoured the rest; and of these, the most aggressive and successful were the Ch'in, Chin, Ch'i, and Ch'u. The struggle between these many similar and contesting states was a prolonged period of ruthless bloodletting with no purpose or inspiration whatever except to crush the small and vulnerable and establish a reputation for seizing and occupying weaker entities. In these respects, China was not particularly more or less distinguished than Europe, the Middle East, or India.

Ch'i was the first of these states to emerge as a coercive aggregator of smaller Chou states in the Seventh Century B.C.; it was a reforming regime under the Duke of Huan (685-643) and his chief minister Kuan Chung. They rallied a number of like-minded states and attacked the state of Ch'u and retained a substantial hegemony over much of eastern Chola for about two centuries. In what today seems like nothing more than a dispute of Orwellian states for control of Oceania, or some such prize, Ch'i was defeated by Duke Wen of Chin, who controlled most of Shensi, Honan, and Hopei. Chin maintained its preeminence for approximately a century though it was almost constantly at war with Ch'u, and after about a century, it dissolved in internal conflict into the states of Chao, Han, and Wei. Chin and Ch'u effectively exhausted each other fatally, and Ch'u was decisively defeated by two less sophisticated coastal states, Wu and Yueh; none of these states was originally ethnically Chinese, all gradually became so.

Wu prevailed over Ch'u, but was then defeated by Yueh, as practically all of China oscillated between consolidation and dissolution, though conflicts were generally conducted by the nobility and career military forces, and the devastation of civilians was, compared to much we have seen and will see elsewhere, relatively restrained. When China graduated into the Warring States period, masses of peasants were conscripted on all sides and hurled into battle as infantry; cavalry replaced the chariots, reflecting the influence of the nomadic barbarians around the fringes of China, and the objective in conflict was escalated to the complete annihilation of enemy forces, though it had not yet reached the point of total war of more modern times, in which the objective was the almost complete destruction of the enemy, military and civilian.

In this mode of war, Ch'in, a frontier state, proved superior to its rivals and emerged as the premier Chinese state in the Fourth Century B.C. Ch'in occupied and absorbed most of Szechuan. Its leaders, Shang Yang and Duke Hsiao, proved capable reformers and rebuilt administration on territorial rather than clannish and aristocratic lines and imposed a severe criminal code and unique system of collective responsibility which included the obligation to spy and denounce. Ch'in was constitutionally declared to be virtually a military state but with private ownership of land and incentives for the development of agriculture, settlement, and light industry. There was an explicitly enunciated hostility and suspicion toward cultural activities. Though it was not a naturally attractive society to live in, it did produce a successful formula for expansion and the ruthless and almost totalitarian methods of Shang Yang and Duke Hsiao (361-338) were reaffirmed even after the Duke had died and Shang Yang was personally overthrown and executed by being torn apart by five horses charging in different directions, following which his entire family was exterminated, albeit less spectacularly. Ch'in then emerged as the most formidable militarist state of the seven principal states in the early Fourth Century: Ch'in, Ch'u, Ch'i, Han, Wei, Chao, and Yen. In the much-quoted phrase of Ssu-ma Ch'ien, "Ch'in conquered as a silkworm devours mulberry leaves."[4] Ch'in became known as the "ferocious beast of Ch'in," and engaged in the wholesale slaughter of tens and sometimes hundreds of thousands of active or deemed enemies, including, in 260 B.C., with the massacre of the entire Chou army, four-hundred thousand men. They were "the Assyrians of East Asia-without the bas reliefs."[5]

6. Chou Culture

Eastern Chou, along with its terrible political convulsions, was an intellectual Golden Age in China; the appalling and violent times motivated many of the most intellectually gifted people to focus on China's social and political problems and to seek a humanistic philosophy with ethical and practical components that might be useful in guiding Chinese society to happier times. Concentrated as they were on the emergencies about them, they paid comparatively little attention to theological or metaphysical questions. The premier intellectual figure at this time and in all of the history of China was Confucius (K'ung fu-tzu), 551-479, the scion of an impecunious Shantung noble family which claimed to be descended from the ancient Shang royal family. Confucius spent some years as a minor civil servant in his home province of Lu and most of the rest of his life wandering from court to court trying to find a Chinese provincial ruler that would implement his suggestions. Essentially, he was urging kings or their chief ministers to behave as he himself recommended and even to the extent that his modest positions could do so, implemented. In this again he somewhat prefigured Niccolo Machiavelli, who wrote for Rodrigo Borgia a modus operandi for statesmen that was admirably suited to Machiavelli himself, but which that member of the Borgia family (unlike his father, Pope Alexander VI) either could not or declined to enact. He even, to some extent, had a career slightly

---

4 Witold Rodzinski, *The Walled Kingdom*, The Free Press, MacMillan, New York, 1984, p. 32.
5 Ibid.

like that of Socrates, though with a happier ending (Chapter 9).

Confucius made no pretense to originality and claimed merely to be deducing and summarizing the qualities most admired in ancient Chinese folklore, based on conservative tradition. He claimed that in olden times, nature and heaven followed a certain path known as the Tao, according to which man knew his place and did not seek to depart, and in the conduct of the state, behaved like a good head of a family, as the state was merely a large family. The ideal was a benevolent patriarchal ruler and what was required was a return to an idealized early past and the cultivation and practice of proper moral and ethical principles. This was the "chun tzu," the superior man: honest, righteous, loyal, forgiving, tolerant, and cultured, gentle and humane. In these respects, Confucius was a meritocrat; he paid no attention to the genealogy of his disciples and was concerned only with their ethical and intellectual qualifications to determine whether they were suitable participants in the sacred trust of rulership. His primacy in Chinese cultural history resides chiefly in his position as China's first educator, and his preamble to his *Analects*, like some of the works of Plato, stands up well even today as a prescription for the character and intelligence of a secular ruler.

Apart from the *Analects*, he is credited with the *Spring and Autumn Annals*, a very simple chronicle of his home province of Lu, a *Book of Songs*, and the *Book of History*, though his authorship of these latter works is the subject of considerable doubt. Confucius continued almost unknown in China for nearly a century until a brilliant disciple, Mencius (371-289), and the time that elapsed between the lives of the two men was an even more difficult and destructive period than Confucius had himself observed. Mencius seems faithfully to have recounted the Confucian theories but to have adorned them with the theory of the mandate from heaven and that the collected wisdom of the ethical nobility was a Chinese version of the Roman concept "Vox populi, Vox dei." The class message of Confucianism was explicitly stated by Mencius in the division of people who worked by using their muscles and those who worked by using their intelligence. The second group obviously had to govern but were obligated to show reasonable humanitarian concern for the welfare of the working people. Mencius is credited with the original formulation of the goodness of human nature, and in this, he presaged Western religion, particularly Christianity, and he advocated the education of everyone in the Confucian virtues to conserve and amplify this innate goodness. Like Plato and St. Paul, he vituperatively attacked the enemies of Confucianism, and his disciples eventually compiled the Confucian philosophy as one of the Four Books.

The most prominent Chinese philosopher of the Fourth Century B.C. was Hsun Ch'ing, though he was something of a Taoist, who took a legalistic approach and was to some extent a materialist and an agnostic who treated the concept of heaven as a sort of deistic notion of nature. He was not an optimist like Confucius or Mencius about human nature but believed that it could be transformed to a benign and Confucian state of uprightness by education. Next to the *Analects*, the most important philosophical Chinese book is *The Way and the Power*, attributed to Lao Tzu. There is extensive historical data but whether Lao Tzu actually existed is not clear, and the date of this book is alleged with equal persuasiveness to have been at many points in and between the sixth and fourth centuries. It rails against the evils of society and advocates retreat into a "natural life." This too may be variously interpreted but could be claimed to include living simply in nature like Henry David Thoreau all the way through to monasticism and even wandering mendicancy. This concept of natural life had a profound and endurable impact on all aspects of Chinese culture and arts.

The greatest rival to Confucianism in these early times was the school of Mo Ti (480-397), which was essentially utilitarian and opposed the extravagant rites that the Confucianists liked and practiced, and opposed the wars of the feudal lords to which he recommended as an antidote defensive and even guerrilla warfare, at which his followers proved very competent. He also produced his doctrine of Universal Love as the best and most intellectually respectable way of disposing of war and social conflict. Eventually, this became more popular and was regarded as more realistic than the Confucian enthusiasm for individual virtue and government as if by family patriarchs. Mo Ti also sought support from the distant past and went even farther back than Confucius by going to periods of ancient lore which had never really been sketched out very much and elaborating for them conditions and attitudes that legitimized his own views. His disciples became China's leading logicians and dialectical philosophers, and they became a disciplined and organized sect which exercised considerable influence for some time.

Not without its ironies, the school that ultimately provided the intellectual basis for the most oppressive period of ancient Chinese history was the Legalists. Despite their somewhat pretentious title, they had no interest in the law as it is conventionally conceived and merely espoused the triumph of the most militaristic and ruthless government. They had no evident interest in intellectual or cultural life, took little trouble to prepare such texts as they published with any style or eloquence and advocated invincible military power and agriculture sufficiently productive and diligent to feed the population, especially the army. The best-known legalist advocate was Han Fei (280-233), who really was an outright Machiavellian though apparently not as talented a writer. He outlined the steps that had to be taken to achieve absolute power and maintain it.

Another influential group was the naturalists, who originated the dual theory of negative and positive principles known as a Yin and Yang, represented as the source of all natural phenomena, and the theory of the five elements: wood, metal, fire, water, and earth, the essential gradients to any natural or human permutations. This was eventually incorporated into Confucian philosophy by Tsou Yen (350-270), the principal founder of Chinese scientific thought. Also published in the Hou era was the *Book of Odes* or *Songs*, an anthology of three-hundred and five Chinese poems written from the Tenth to the Seventh Century B.C. The profound knowledge of these poems was for many centuries regarded as the principal proof of a civilized and educated person. The next important collection of poems, the *Elegies of Ch'u*, was largely composed by the greatest poet of ancient China, almost a Chinese Shakespeare, Ch'u Yuan (343 -280). He was a learned nobleman who tragically committed suicide. There are a number of other books of historical narrative and antique documents though both their authenticity and their authorship have been the subject of a great deal of dispute, and many are indifferently forgeries. But they do provide considerable insight into ancient China. The *Tso Commentary* is a work of undisputed authenticity that is the principal historical narrative for the period 722-468. The combination of all these books and texts does enable us to get a fairly detailed and representative impression of China in most of the First Millennium B.C.

7. The Ch'in Unification of China

The great drive of the warrior state Ch'in for mastery over most of China from the edge of what is now Manchuria south-southwest to include two thirds of what is now Kwangtung, began with the accession as king, in 246 B.C., of the fourteen-year-old Cheng, guided for the first nine years by his chief minister, Lu Pu-wei, a wealthy merchant who was also widely alleged to be the king's biological father. Lu pursued a relatively moderate policy but was implicated in a scandal involving the Dowager Queen Mother, and her power was sufficient to have him banished to a remote province where he committed suicide. Lu is better remembered as an encyclopedist. Following his departure in 237, a group of legalist ministers took over, and campaigns against all of the neighboring states of Ch'in were resumed with a vengeance. Inexplicably, all these natural targets for Ch'in's expansion could not concert on any shared defense, and Ch'in picked them off one after the other: Han in 230, Chou in 228, Wei in 225, Ch'u in 223, Yen in 222, Ch'i in 221. Instead of the Chou technique of distributing fiefs, a system of thirty-six "commanderies" was established, each with a military and civilian governor and a number of prefectures to deal with local matters. Cheng took the position of Emperor of the Ch'in (China), with the title of Shih Huang. The new regime aspired to ten-thousand generations, two-hundred thousand years, but it did last the impressive total of approximately two-thousand years, with wildly fluctuating fortunes.

Private land ownership was favored throughout the country and the entire populations of the conquered states were disarmed. Their weapons were melted down and the metal was utilized for huge bells and statues. It is claimed the one hundred and twenty thousand aristocratic families of the conquered states were forcibly resettled in Shensi, near the Ch'in capital of Hsien-yang. Comprehensive measures of standardization of coinage, weights and measures, trade dimensions—such as the length of axles, and the script of a uniform Chinese language were all imposed. A gigantic palace was built along with two-hundred and seventy other royal residences and an immense mausoleum. An army of forced labor allegedly totaling seven-hundred thousand was pressed into service in refashioning the capital into one of monumental importance somewhat reminiscent of the prior activities of Luxor, Memphis, Athens and subsequently, Rome. It was in this area that the life-size statues of Ch'in warriors were discovered in 1974.

Ch'in authority, almost prefiguring the totalitarianism of the People's Republic of China more than twenty-two hundred years later, was asserted by the proscription and destruction in 213 B.C. of all writings considered to be subversive, leading to the Great Burning of Books, which engulfed *The Odes, The Book of History*, most works of history, and most existing literature. At the same time, approximately four-hundred and sixty traditional scholars were executed. It was one of history's most revolting episodes of officially imposed nihilistic ignorance. Hitler and Stalin were men of considerable cultural latitude in comparison.

More significant and of more durable effect were the campaigns against the fierce and nomadic Hsiung-nu, who were driven out of Shensi, and retired to the Steppes and deserts and foothills of Central Asia. These people were almost certainly the ancestors of the Huns, and this act seems to have propelled the Huns out of China on their long journey of over five-hundred years to western Europe. An army of three-hundred thousand, led by the authentically talented Chinese army commander Meng T'ien, supervised this expulsion and once that had been achieved, a number of walls in northern China were connected and reinforced. This slammed the gate behind the barbarians and the walls extended for fourteen-hundred miles from Kansu to the sea. The wall was principally built by forced laborers and convicts shipped on site in lots of more than one-hundred thousand, and for the most part, perishing miserably at their tasks. While the famous Great Wall of China did pose a significant inconvenience to invaders, it more thoroughly demarcated nomads from settled agriculture on proper farms.

From 221 to 214 B.C., the giant Ch'in army of five-hundred thousand men subdued heavy resistance in the Southwest: Kwangtung, Kwangsi, and North Vietnam. Four new commanderies were set up, and the Chinese policy of mass insertion of their own nationals to dilute and assimilate the local population occurred. The Chinese would employ the same policy in many subsequent centuries including in Tibet in contemporary times. Shih Huang's ambitious military campaigns and monument-building public works drained the treasury, and while millions were engaged in slave labor and hundreds of thousands were conscripted into the military, the economy was terribly depressed, as taxes, both in cash and in the contribution of harvests, increased twenty to thirty-fold. The regime was only kept going by an almost permanent state of martial law which featured twelve different forms of capital punishment, all of them extremely gruesome.

China was in extreme economic distress and suffering from the rigors of an iron despotism when the first emperor, Shih Huang, died in 210 B.C. A disciple of Hsun Ch'ing, Li Ssu, had become Shih Huang's chief minister, and had ruthlessly enacted the Legalist methods outlined. When his patron died, Li Ssu and the chief eunuch, Chao Kao, in one of the best-known incidents of ancient Chinese history, disguised the fact of the emperor's death by having the carriage bearing his corpse followed by a cart of rotting fish, thus disguising the fact that he had died. He and the chief eunuch then betrayed the emperor's son, who had been banished because of his disapproval of The Great Burning of the Books and related measures. In forged letters, the late king ordered him and the general Meng T'ien to commit suicide, which they did. Li Ssu effectively elected and had elevated the infant grandson of the late emperor, but as not infrequently happens in such deadly minuets of authoritarian office, he who seemed to win, lost. The regent for the new infant-emperor, the egregious eunuch Chao Kao, mistrusted his patron and had Li Ssu overthrown and tortured until he confessed, at which time he was publicly executed by being chopped into two pieces more or less at the waist, and his family was rounded up and executed to the third degree of relatives. This macabre operation was concluded in 208 B.C. Chao Kao, having master-minded the betrayal and execution of Li Ssu, was himself murdered, though less painfully than his former master, after about eighteen months. During the "Cultural Revolution" of 1966 to 1976, Lu Ssi was extricated from the mists of antiquity and promoted as a great hero of ancient China. The fact that he was responsible for needlessly inspiring the deaths of many hundreds of thousands of people was lightly glossed over but mainly praised as purposeful statesmanship. He is generally reckoned to have been a cruel and paranoid personality of medium intelligence and "with the face of a jackal and the heart of a wolf".[6]

An authentic popular revolt occurred quite promptly after the death of Chao Kao, and two peasants, Ch'en Sheng and Wu Kuang, incited the initial uprisings in Anhwei. The revolt spread like the proverbial wildfire and although the great Ch'in army defeated successive masses of angry peasants, a state of revolt became general almost throughout China with a great deal of collaboration with the peasants from their former aristocratic landlords. The peasant revolt became an intermittent feature of all subsequent Chinese history, and the Ch'in central authority collapsed in East and Central China. Two popular leaders emerged who completed the downfall of the Ch'in tyranny: Liu Pang and Hsiang Yu. Liu Pang was a cunning peasant, who, by the time revolts against the Ch'in dynasty became general, was a well-known and veteran professional outlaw. In contrast, Hsiang Yu was a dissident military aristocrat, an accomplished officer of imposing stature though cruel and arrogant. He soon gained the leadership of the principal rebel army, and in 207 B.C., Hsiang Yu successfully led his insurgent forces against the beleaguered main Ch'in army.

In another infamous incident of Chinese history, once he had forced the surrender of the main Ch'in army, Hsiang Yu then had it massacred to the last man— approximately five-hundred thousand prisoners of war murdered. While this action proceeded, Liu Pang had largely conquered the Ch'in home areas, and had behaved with commendable moderation in stark contrast to his patrician colleague, but when Hsiang Yu arrived in the same area, with a much larger army than Lu Pang's, he seized the royal family and executed it to the last related person, regardless of age and gender, stole all the royal family's treasures and all the numerous palaces were torched and razed to the ground. There was now obviously going to be a resolution between the two insurgent leaders, and as Liu Pang had less numerous forces, he escaped a showdown and retired to become the king of Han in the southern Shensi and Szechuan provinces as Hsiang Yu became the premier King in East China. A quarrel between the two victorious insurgents was inevitable, however, and it soon became a savage Civil War known as the War Between Han and Chu, and it wrought horrible damage in eastern and central China for five years. Liu Pang, though a less competent general, was a superior politician and he prevailed over Hsiang Yu, who committed suicide after his defeat, and in 202 B.C., Liu Pang ascended the throne as founder of the Han Dynasty which would rule for almost all of the next four-hundred years. The institutions and personnel of the preceding regime had been almost completely eliminated, and the new dynasty maintained the concept of centralized

---

6 Ibid., p. 43.

authority that began again with new personnel and a new but similar governmental structure.

8. Western Han

Liu Pang, better known to posterity as Kao-Tsu, faced a country in chaos. The armed forces were quickly demobilized and the soldiers resettled on the land. This enabled a drastic reduction in the tax burden borne by the peasantry; in 197 B.C., the land tax was set at one-fifteenth of the harvest and was later reduced to one-thirtieth, and the poll tax was diminished. As in all times and among all peoples of all classes, few things build popularity as effectively as tax cuts. In the first seventy years of Han rule, agricultural production increased immensely, facilitating, along with steadily greater use of iron tools and improved irrigation, the growth in the population of China by the end of the pre-Christian Era to a formidable sixty-million people. Textiles also developed quickly and Chinese silk soon made its way all across Asia to the ancient marketplace of the Middle East. Kao-Tsu (Liu Pang) was convinced that the Ch'in dynasty fell, ultimately, because it had no grassroots support and he granted fiefdoms to key generals and clan members. This divided the country into two areas—one under direct central government control, and the other under lords of the designated fiefdoms, but soon Kao-tsu turned against his own officers, including his principal strategist, Han Hsin, deprived most of them of their fiefdoms and many of them of their lives as well, and redistributed fiefdoms to his own family which he redefined with great latitude. He chose the present Sian as the new capital, as from Shensi, "one could hold the Empire by the throat."[7]

It was a novel ruling class that was chiefly composed of peasants who had suddenly become great landowners, a class of agrarian parvenus that soon allocated its newly gained land to tenant farmers and were not slow to replicate some of the methods of exploitation of their former landlords. This new structure obtained in China for nearly two-thousand years. The taxes paid from the same sources as under previous regimes sustained the new dynasty, and while this was not remotely as oppressive a regime as in the Ch'in Empire and previous governments, it still consigned the landowners to centuries of near impoverishment though generally stopping well short of outright famine and with much less provocation or recourse to violent rebellion. The supply of plentiful peasant labor is the chief explanation for why, in the Han era, slavery never developed on a large scale as it did contemporaneously in the Roman Empire.

As we shall see in the Roman Empire, much of the slavery was of conquered people whom the Romans felt were guilty of excessive resistance or bad faith and sold into the ranks of slaves which grew steadily as the frontiers of Rome extended; but as slavery was not a matter of caste or race, and in Rome, it was usually not as despised or servile condition as more modern slavery. In many cases, Roman slaves had similar rights to citizens, except that they could not vote, and in the early years were discouraged from intermarrying with free people. But although Han China was as authoritarian a government as Sparta, it did not, as Sparta did, have to dedicate

---

7 Ibid., p. 46.

its army most of the time to maintaining the huge slave population in a state of unbending obedience. Slaves are not believed to have exceeded one percent of the total population in this Western Han period. The other principal reason why this era in Chinese history was largely spared the blight of slavery was the personalized, almost gardening-like nature of Chinese agriculture, which made the use of slaves a matter of questionable utility. Chinese slavery in this period was almost entirely confined to the household domestic variety.

The new Empire built up its own civil service, approximately one-hundred and thirty thousand officials at the time that the population achieved fifty million. Government was a much less comprehensive range of activities than it has become, that is, mainly defense, police, basic public health, tax collecting, public works, and rudimentary justice and cultural activities, with occasional recourse to stimulus spending, especially when it entailed the increase in agricultural production. The civil service was chiefly filled on a somewhat advanced version of the examination method, and the overwhelming majority of the positions were filled by the families of lesser aristocrats. This continued throughout the Han era and invested that class with a tremendous political advantage in that they naturally tended to govern in the interest which they themselves represented. While ultimate control was highly centralized down to the level of district capitals, beneath that level and apart from taxes, the countryside was largely free of central control: "the government thus was a relatively small, highly centralized body that floated on a sea of isolated peasant communities."[8]

In the disastrous circumstances created by the overthrow of the Legalist Ch'in tyranny, Confucianism made its come-back. Though he was no great admirer of the scholars himself, Kao-tsu, who realized the accuracy of his chamberlain, Lu Chia's, advice that an empire can be conquered, but not ruled, on horseback. But the Confucianism of those who served the Han dynasty and their methods were far removed from the ethical teachings of Confucius and Mencius. The new Confucian spokesman, Tung Chung-shu (179-104 B.C.), professed a composite blend of classical views including the yin-yang and Five Elements with a metaphysical twist connecting natural phenomena and human existence. An inexhaustible storehouse of superstitions instantly materialized.

The Ch'in edict against Confucian literature was revoked in 191 B.C., and the resumption of Confucian study was approved. Confucianism became the credo of the senior stratum of the bureaucracy and of the principal educators. Confucianism became the basis of the curriculum of the Imperial University, founded in 124 B.C., initially with fifty students but it grew gradually to three-thousand students a century later. A thorough knowledge of this distilled Confucianism became a prerequisite for a serious permanent position in government. The inherent gentleness and respectfulness of Confucius gradually reduced social tensions between the emperor and his subjects.

Kao-tsu died in 195 B.C., and his son Hui succeeded him (194-188), but the dowager Empress Lu retained all power in her own hands. She was a fierce and extremely determined woman and remained the real sovereign for fifteen years un-

---

8 Ibid., p. 48.

til her own death in 179. Though she staffed the ranks of government with her closest and most reliable relatives, after she died, Kao-tsu's intimates overthrew the empress's entourage and ruthlessly executed them, and installed the Emperor Wen (179-157), who proved a moderate and frugal ruler, assuring the country's prosperity and stability and amassing the resources needed for the aggressive policies of his grandson, Emperor Wu-ti (140-87). Wu was perhaps the best known Han ruler after Kao-tsu. The first thirty years of Wu's reign were consumed with the struggle against the Hsiung-nu, fierce nomads who had recovered entirely from the defeats they had endured at the hands of the Ch'in. Under their capable and bellicose ruler Mei Tei (Mao Tun), they were constantly raiding North China and threatening all of North China. In 201 during one of his raids, Mei Tei succeeded in surrounding Kau-tsu's army, forcing the Emperor of China to accept the humiliation of heavy payment of tribute, largely in grain and silk to the Hsiung-nu, all sealed by marriages between the families of Mei Tei and Kau-tsu. Although Kao-tsu and his successors continued to pay the tribute, the Hsiung-nu continued to attack, and the emperor and his successors continued to attempt to annihilate the Hsiung-nu.

In 133, an elaborate Han scheme for the capture of the Hsiung-nu leader was foiled, a very long series of extremely costly campaigns was launched and by 119 B.C. had succeeded in forcing the Hsiung-nu northwards, largely by the sophisticated development and deployment of mobile light cavalry. These forces encircled their enemies and constantly harassed them and wore them down, like a swarm of bees buzzing around the heads of a large group of men. The Hsiung-nu did not recover from this terrible war, and after their Empire collapsed into internal dissension in 58 B.C., they no longer posed an urgent threat to the Chinese Empire. It may be that it was not long after this defeat that they began to consider moving westwards towards Europe and the Middle East (with whom China would soon open a trading and sporadic diplomatic contact).

An important milestone in East-West relations began in 138 B.C., when the redoubtable Chang Ch'ien, an official in the Han court, was sent on a diplomatic mission to the Indo-European Yueh-chih, who after the Emperor's defeat of the Hsiung-nu, had themselves been defeated and driven northwards and westwards by the Hsiung-nu, and the Han project was to join with the Yueh-chih in a pincers movement to crush the Hsiung-nu once and for all. Chang Ch'ien was captured by the Hsiung-nu, who apparently treated him well, and after ten years, he managed to escape and make contact with the Yueh-chih, who were now busy conquering Bactria (Afghanistan) and had no interest in the Han proposal. Chang Ch'ien, his mission completed unsuccessfully, was again taken prisoner by the Hsiung-nu, but again managed to escape after two years and returned to the Han court that had sent him thirteen years before, accompanied now by his Hsiung-nu wife, whom he married en route, and one survivor of his original one-hundred-member delegation. This visit produced extensive reports from Chang Ch'ien on intervening territories and peoples and caused the beginning of the Silk Road and a stream of commercial and diplomatic convoys that led to a large Chinese diplomatic and trade embassy to the first Roman emperor, Augustus Caesar, in the middle of his reign (27 B.C.-14 A.D.). Chang Ch'ien led another mission to central Asia in 115 B.C., and in campaigns of

104 and 102, the Chinese conquered all the oases in what is now Sinkiang, and ensuring the Silk Road and other major trading routes across Asia were firmly in Chinese control. This mastery of the Western regions as the Chinese called Central Asia did increase trade, sharply increased cultural contacts with the West, and provided increased impetus for the westward movement of what were known both in China and in the expanding Roman empire at the other end of the Eurasian landmass as barbarians, and which the Chinese were pushing westwards upon the Romans.

Further campaigns in the South beginning in 119 extended the Han Chinese Empire back to Indochina, northern Vietnam. Again, the Chinese had recourse to their policy of physical expulsion of much of the civilian population of the area that they had occupied and the colonization of it by Chinese migrants moved westward for the purpose. The Han was also extended into North Korea in 109 with the establishment of three commanderies there.

As has already occurred before in this narrative of the development of China, the endless effort of expansion had a drastic depressive impact on the economy and squandered previously amassed resources. A severe financial crisis, almost on the scale that brought down the Ch'in Empire, resulted. The Imperial regime sold assets, sold titles to nobles, taxed the large landowners and merchants, and set up state monopolies for the production of iron and salt, whose profits went to finance the aggrandizements of the Han Empire. These measures alleviated the immediate crisis, but the underlying problems awaited Wu-ti's successors.

This financial crisis, generated by Wu-ti's imperialist ambitions, did largely create Han China and drove the barbarians from the East ultimately against the West, but most importantly for China, it produced a great social crisis. The landed estates grew to immense proportions at the expense of the peasants whose socioeconomic condition was steadily subordinated. The government overtaxed the property owners causing them to sell their land and reducing many of them to tenancy or even farm labor, in extreme cases, slavery—noble slaves. The depletion of the landholders further undermined the financial position of the government, because the largest and most powerful landowners were either exempt from taxation or corrupted the tax collection system to produce the same effect. The population continued to grow in the census for 2 A.D. to show almost sixty million people, as great as or possibly slightly more than the population of the contemporary Roman Empire, though the Roman Empire was better organized, more coherent, more prosperous, a good deal more culturally advanced, especially in the Hellenic parts of it, and at this point in the Augustan Empire, as we shall see, a much more sophisticated government administratively and militarily (Chapters 28, 29).

The concentration of land ownership and the pauperization of the peasant masses produced a prolonged feudal cycle in China of peasant rebellions and dynastic collapses. The Confucionists at least stressed the need for concern for the welfare of the underprivileged. It would take China a very long time to get to grips with these issues, and then it would be under the sponsorship of an improbable movement, the Chinese Communist Party. For our purposes now, it is sufficient to note that with India and with China, important cultures had launched themselves, and while they were somewhat in arrears of the most advanced civilizations of the West and Near East, the unknowing competition would remain close enough that it is still a matter of some suspense as this is written. Westerners should, however, beware of the practice of Chinese and the (East) Indians to make exaggerated claims not only of their longevity and durability, but of their levels of sophistication in ancient times. The Egyptians and the Greeks were well ahead of the Chinese and Indians in architecture, mathematics, and most sciences. The Greeks and the Romans were well ahead of them in the sophistication of government and particularly in the application of any democratic concepts. A number of Mediterranean and near Eastern jurisdictions preceded India and China in the development and administration of law.

Indians and Chinese were competitive and ,of course, they were and are numerous. But all Westerners should be cautious about any attempt by the advocates of those civilizations to condescend to the West and the Near East across the range of their accomplishments in ancient times.

We return to the West and to the extraordinarily gifted and influential Greeks, as they build upon their foundations of civic government and of vast intellectual and scientific progress, and struggle for survival successfully against the formidable Persians.

CHAPTER FIVE

THE EARLY GREEKS FROM THE FIFTEENTH TO THE SIXTH CENTURIES B.C.
❦
HOMER, DRACO, SOLON, AND CLEISTHENES

Bust of Homer

Bust of Solon

1. The Hellenization of the East

COME NOW TO THE forefront of this narrative, the Greeks by sea as have the Jews by land, peoples that would be reckoned with; we have already seen the early development of the Jews. Most of coastal Greece and Crete and the Cyclades were dominated by the Mycenaeans in the middle of the Second Millennium B.C., corresponding to the Iron Age, and known mainly from archaeology, called the Shaft Grave Dynasty, because of their burial practices. Their tombs reveal practically all that we know about the Mycenaeans, and they were sophisticated makers of pottery and fabrics, and were succeeded in the Fifteenth Century B.C. by the Bee-Hive Tomb Dynasty. As the words imply, these were more elaborate and populous graves. Mycenae succeeded Cnossus as the leading city in what became Greece at the start of the Fourteenth Century B.C. They built roads and fished extensively, built solid and well-engineered buildings and decorated them and dressed well, but nothing is known of the internecine struggles of Greece or of its political organization. In what is known as the late Helladic period of Mycenae and Thebes

(Greece, but indicating the commercial intercourse with Egypt and the Greek presence there), there was a literate class of writers, but no literature has survived from that time.

Mycenae seems to have begun to decline in the Twelfth Century, possibly after the exertions of the war with Troy, and the volume of Greek migration into Egypt indicates that the Dorian invasion of southern Greece, in addition to burning down many towns, drove many to seek refuge as well as commerce across the Mediterranean Sea.

Despite the demise, the probably violent demise of Cnossus and certainly violent demise of Mycenae, the core of the timeless Greek culture that endures is based on a renascence of the glory of Cnossus and Mycenae; and Homer, who remains after nearly thirty centuries, a giant of world literature on a plain with Shakespeare, Dante, Goethe, and a very few others, is the principal source for that time. He may not be a more accurate (or gifted) historian than Shakespeare, but his account is certainly not outright fiction. Troy was a city in the northwest of what is now Anatolia in Asian Turkey, Asia Minor, the Troad, about fifty miles to the southwest of the opening of what are now the Dardanelles, and beyond to the Sea of Marmara and the Black Sea. The Trojan War is variously placed between the Fourteenth and Thirteenth Centuries, in 1384 by Eratosthenes and in 1250 by Herodotus. The transition from the Bronze Age to the Iron Age in the Twelfth Century coincided with a splendid renaissance which produced the classical Hellenistic culture, one of the richest and most durable of all history, rivalled in fact, in the ancestral world only by the Jews and Chinese.

Reliable history from this place and time really begins around 1250 B.C., shortly after Perseus had ruled Mycenae. Pelops, an Asian, arrived in the west of the Peloponnese, and married and succeeded the king of Pisa and gave the whole area his name. His daughter married the son of Perseus and king of Argos, and the customary disputes between royal relatives (as right up to World War I) divided the Peloponnese, until the grandson of Perseus, Atreus, and his two famous sons, Agamemnon and Menelaus, who married Clytaemnestra and Helen, came to rule most of the Peloponnese. It is even more impossible here than in the tractations of the Old Testament, to separate myth from fact. Thus, Perseus slew the Gorgon Medusa and saved Andromeda from the sea-monster. Minstrels perpetuated these stories, and Homer immortalized them. The labours of Hercules were contemporary with the feats of Jason and the Argonauts. This was the Heroic Age, meaning the time made famous and unforgettable by heroic poetry. Whatever parts of it were true, the Achaeans, northern Greeks, effectively took over Crete and most of Greece as well in the mid- and later Thirteenth Century. In 1223, we find the Pharaoh Merneptah, bedeviled by Libyans, assisted and joined by Achaeans. He did hurl back the Libyans, though their ranks were fortified by a large number of Greeks. Jason's pursuit of the "Golden Fleece," in his ship *Argo*, was based on a desire to conquer and occupy more of the Hellespont (around the passage to the Black Sea which would be so bitterly contested nearly thirty-two centuries later at Gallipoli). Minos, though the historical validation of this is thin, after establishing his kingship on Crete, subdued the Aegean pirates.

In the early Twelfth Century B.C., Agamemnon ruled Mycenae and Corinth and Menelaus ruled Sparta and throughout Lacedaemon. Their relations were good, and opposite third parties, they acted together. Central Greece was dominated by the Boeotians, and immediately north of them were the Locrians, governed by one Ajax (son of Oeleus), while the more famous Ajax (son of Telemon) ruled at Salamis, near Athens. The Achaeans, as has been mentioned, ruled in Crete, which was then implausibly known as the "land of a hundred cities." Achaean dynasties governed in all the principal units of Greece, and the king of Mycenae, starting with Agamemnon, was traditionally the first among ostensible equals.

In these many Greek states, the kings, though supreme, supervised sacrifices to the Gods, towards whom they professed humility. All the Gods of Greece were deemed to live at Mount Olympus, in northern Greece, and to be Gods of the whole world, and not just of a single town or area, though there were gods for separate activities. Zeus was the God of Gods. And decisions of state were taken in consultation with a council and announced to the public in general assembly, though not submitted to a popular vote. A great many issues were resolved in single combat, between city states and within them, even within families. Fights, generally fights to the death, were not at all discouraged nor thought unusual or unseemly. When a man had defeated another, he generally killed him and removed his armour, which in Achaean times was bronze, iron having not yet been adapted to armour.

Education was relatively general, at least to a rudimentary level, and it was very strict for boys and girls. Girls were taught handicrafts and cooking, but also vigorous sports, including boxing and wielding spears and knives. Boys were more culturally developed in some places than others, but all were taught to be disciplined, brave and obedient, and were severely whipped on the buttocks for any shortcomings, almost always with enthusiastic parental approval. The Greek states were generally fairly prosperous, which was due not only to their agricultural talents, including the production of wine, but also to piracy, at which Greece, an early and formidable sea power, was always adept.

The Trojan War, which remains one of the most folklorically storied conflicts of all history, and the first conflict to be so durably recounted, presaged other great rivalries, such as Athens and Sparta and Rome and Carthage. Only the Egyptians and the Hittites could have bothered the Achaean Greeks, and Egypt was not interested in the Aegean, and was in the late second millennium, settling comfortably anyway. The Hittites did not have the luxury of plunging into Europe and were never a maritime power capable of harassing the Greeks on the Aegean, especially after Ramses II had hammered them badly at Kadesh in 1288 B.C. The Hittite retreat after that defeat opened up possibilities for Dardanians, Phrygians, Mysians, Bithynians, and Moesians to cross the Hellespont and settle in northwest Asia Minor. Once established there, these people could, and did, harass the Achaean Greeks. And a rivalry developed.

The Trojans quickly emerged, and were a Greek civilization with Greek Gods and Greek names, and had a strategic location on a promontory and with an agriculturally fertile plain stretching behind them. The power of Troy extended northeast along the coast of Asia, as well as south, and Troy was not so much a city as a fortress, which enclosed a palace. Priam and Paris were claimed to be the founders, and Priam's grandfather, Ilus, lent Troy its name Ilium. The fathers of the town soon established a fair, in which traders of the Eastern Mediterranean could buy, sell, barter, and exchange with those proffering goods from all the trade-routes that crossed in the Middle East. It was a tremendous intercontinental focal point, and raised the status of Troy to immense proportions, though there is no evidence that Troy was a maritime power.

There is great uncertainty about the origins and some of the history of the Trojan Wars, but the most widely accepted version of events is that war broke out between the Achaeans and Trojans in 1192 B.C. when Paris, son of the Trojan king Priam, visited Sparta and seduced Helen, wife of Menelaus, ruler of Sparta and brother of Agamemnon, and bore Helen off to Troy, whither she allegedly went with no great reluctance. Agamemnon asked the unity of all the Greeks in a war of vengeance and virtually all the Greek states agreed and sent an immense armada of which Agamemnon and Menelaus were the principal commanders, but with them were other historic celebrities, including Achilles, son of the king of Phthia (Peleus was the king), and Odysseus, king of Ithaca, Diomede of Argos and both Ajaxes, of Locria and Salamis. They disembarked their forces just inside the mouth of the Scamander River near Troy, including most of the sailors, who could double as soldiers, and invested Troy, which received a good deal of assistance from its neighbours, for nine years. Thracians and Macedonians were in the Greek expeditionary force, and this was effectively a war between those on each side of the Bosporus and of the Aegean Sea.

After nine years, the famous Trojan Horse was advanced and admitted to Troy, as the Greek fleet apparently abandoned its objective and sailed away, but in fact, turned in the night and were admitted to the city by the men hidden in the wooden horse. The victorious Greeks sacked Troy and then destroyed it completely, with minimal concern for the fate of its occupants. According to most accounts, Helen herself, she of the "face that launched a thousand ships" (allegedly 1176 ships, in fact), returned to live happily ever after with Menelaus, forgiven for her lapse of judgment.

Obviously, almost all of this must be received with caution. But that there was a prolonged war and that both sides were widespread confederacies of the opposing and rival sides of the Aegean is not in doubt. The Greek leading families were very ambitious to extend their influence and field of self-enrichment and regarded Troy as not just a rival but an unreasonable obstacle at the gate to the Black Sea, whose commerce Troy monopolized, as it did everything coming north from Asia, Africa, and the Middle East. In this sense, Helen, one of the great legendary women of all history, probably rivalled only by Cleopatra, played a role like Jenkins' Ear in the War of Spanish Succession. (The ear was returned also.)

Apart from other exaggerations, it is unlikely the war continued for nearly ten years, as there is no account of action for the first eight years, and the claim of fifty-thousand Trojan warriors is challenging also, as the physical space of the city is measurable from the remains of its fortifications, and it could not have accommodated so many people, though the Trojan force may not have been entirely within the walls. Lemnos served as the supply point for the Greek invaders, and there is no doubt that the whole effort set the treasuries of Agamemnon and Menelaus back a great deal, but they evidently helped themselves to the spoils. Most of the captured men and women were sold as slaves at the Lemnos slave market.

One of the most storied side-shows was the Greek amphibious raid, led by Achilles, against the island of Lesbos and several towns south of Troy, which the Greeks sacked thoroughly. Homer's *Iliad* is essentially a quarrel over the winnings between Agamemnon and Achilles, and while much of it may have been fiction, this sort of falling out has not been uncommon in modern wars and was routine in the ancient world and is therefore quite plausible. A legend arose that the breach in the walls at Troy, apart from those who rushed in the open gate, was an exploitation of the weakest part of the walls, as legend held that while most of the fortifications had been supervised by the Gods Poseidon and Apollo, a part was human only, and more vulnerable. The ruins bear out that that part was less formidable than the rest, but these divinations of supernatural influences must naturally be read with the customary skepticism.

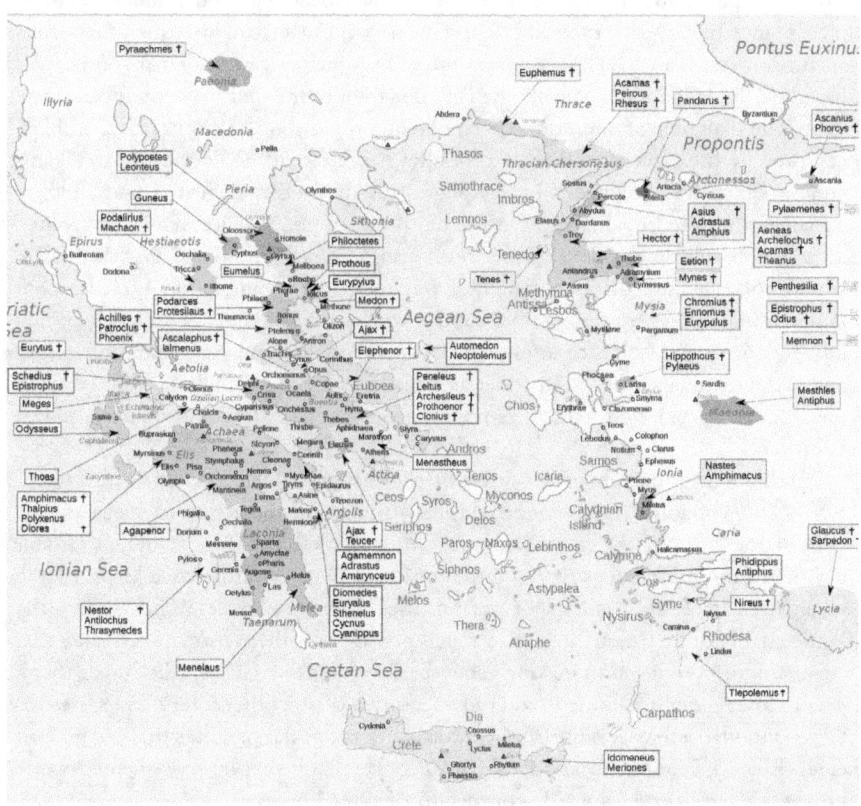

Homeric Greece

What followed has been known as the Aeolic invasion of Asia, as the Greeks poured into Asia Minor, in the absence of any force to restrain them, and, as always, approaches to the great crossroads of the Middle East were a good deal more rewarding than wandering north or east from Greece into the trackless wilderness of the Eurasian landmass. (It would be three-thousand years before European leaders would start complaining about "lebensraum"—room to live.) Thus began the Hellenization of Asia Minor. According to legend, which is not necessarily fictitious, Agamemnon's son, Orestes, married Menelaus' daughter, Hermione, and inherited Sparta and bought Argos. What came next, after a few generations, was the Doric invasion of Greece and the Greek outposts. The Greeks had been so focused on expanding where wealth beckoned, their geographic rear was vulnerable to a new power. This was the same pattern that had produced the Hyksos, Assyrians, and Hittites, and would continue to furnish Asiatic or at least east European invaders intermittently for millennia. The heroics of these pre-Dorian Greeks were preserved by the minstrels who circulated in the Eastern Mediterranean, and, of course, Homer immortalized them.

Although they were written three centuries after the fact, Homer's immortal works of epic poetry, *The Iliad* and *The Odyssey*, have been regarded as literary masterpieces since they were written. Homer was less of a historian, in terms of rigorous accuracy, even than Shakespeare, and the *Iliad*, which is our principal source, was based on the kidnapping of a clergyman's daughter in the ninth year of the siege of Troy. The daughter of the priest of Apollo at Chrysa, not far from Troy, had been captured by the Greeks, and the girl's father, Chryses, offered a ransom to Agamemnon which was declined. Chryses prayed to Apollo for vengeance and a plague descended on the Greek army. On the ninth day of the plague, Achilles convened an assembly of the Greeks and the soothsayer Calchas determined that the plague would not end until Chryses' daughter was returned. Agamemnon agreed except that he insisted that Briseis, another captive who had been taken by Achilles, should be offered instead. A fierce argument between Achilles and Agamemnon ensued, and Achilles finally agreed; Briseis was handed over, but Achilles withdrew from the war, and in one of the most famous legends of all history and folklore, sulked in his tent.

Achilles' mother, Thetis, Goddess of the sea, persuaded Zeus to accord victory to Troy to punish Agamemnon. Achilles' anger and the action of Zeus are the core of the story of the *Iliad*. Zeus waits for a whole day before acting, as Homer elaborates the preferences of the different lesser Gods, and the correlation of the terrestrial forces and their major personalities. The absence of Achilles from the battle enabled the Trojans to put so much pressure on the Achaeans (Greeks) that Agamemnon is reduced to making generous overtures to Achilles, who resists them. The following night, Diomede and Odysseus, two of the other Greek kings, stealthily reconnoitre and ascertain from a Trojan spy they take prisoner that a Thracian chief, Rhesus, is about to arrive to reinforce Troy, and that he has splendid white horses. Odysseus and Diomede contrive to steal the horses.

In the ensuing day's battle, the Trojans, after a close and intense battle all day, minutely described in hand-to-hand as well as general combat, with references to the lesser Gods trying to evade the instructions of Zeus to be neutral, seem on the verge of seizing and destroying the Greek ships (proverbially "launched" by Helen) on the beach where they had landed. Achilles' friend Patroclus beseeches Achilles to intervene, but Achilles still declines, but urges Patroclus himself to lead the resistance, and lends him his own armour to do so. Patroclus stabilizes the fight for the Greeks, but is defeated and killed by Hector, who relieves him of Achilles' armour.

Finally, Achilles' grief for his friend Patroclus and desire for revenge on Hector motivate him to reenter the battle. His mother plays her part again, and Thetis prays to the divine metalsmith and armourer Hephaestus, who forges new amour and produces a magnificent shield for Achilles, who, on the next day, carries the fight to victory for the Greeks and slays Hector in a titanic individual struggle. The *Iliad* ends with a mighty funeral for Patroclus and a visit by Priam, the Trojan king, to redeem the lifeless body of the great Hector.

The Odyssey recounts the mythological return of the king of Ithaca, Odysseus, to Greece. It is a brilliant story that brings in a great deal of local accumulated folklore. *The Iliad* and *Odyssey* were two of the greatest units in what later became known as *The Epic Cycle*, which appeared over a period of about three-hundred years following Homer and down to the Sixth Century B.C. The first of these epics, in chronological order of the tale that was recounted, though long after Homer's works, was *Cypria*, where Thetis married Peleus in a ceremony attended by all the Gods and Goddesses, and Discord gave a prize of a golden apple to the most beautiful Goddess, which Paris awarded to Aphrodite as he carried off Helen as his own bride—an unusual act for a bridegroom to reward someone other than his intended as the most beautiful female present, an act which in lore or fact, could believably be presumed to lead to war as this did—it is little wonder that Helen was seduced by Priam. There followed the *Aethiopis*, which describes the death of the Thracian Amazon queen Penthesilea by Achilles, who, as she dies and removes her helmet "falls in love with her" with, presumably, the normal pre-mortal after-piece. Achilles kills Thetis for his moral reproaches and then goes to Lesbos for purification and returns to settle scores with the Trojan chief Memnon (not related to Agamemnon), beside whom Penthesilea had been fighting Achilles.

One need seek no further to find the inspiration for an immense number of future, desperately intricate and protracted dramas, from the Attic poets to Richard Wagner's Ring Cycle. The authorship of Homer became a subject of as much controversy and dispute, and obviously for a longer time, than the imperishable challenges to the authorship of Shakespeare of all his works. In general, in the one case as in the other, the putative author may be taken as genuine. But in the case of Homer, the argument about authorship rolls into dispute about whether the Trojan Wars occurred and even over whether Troy existed at all. Archeology has established beyond peradventure that Troy existed, and a great many facts described by Homer, in reference to Crete and Mycenae and other areas and cultures between mainland Greece and Asia Minor, have also been substantiated, and these doubts have vanished in all serious academic and historical circles.

Comparative studies of the relationship of national folklore to history, such as the Teutonic kings of the early Christian Era, and early Slavs and Celts, indicate that "If the Aegean area had been in as close geographical contact with the Egyptian

Empire as the Teutonic world was with the Roman Empire, some of these (heroic folkloric Greek) names might have occurred in the historical monuments of Egypt. No other supposition carries any conviction."[1] It must be noted here that after all controversies have been heard and argued out, Homer appears to have lived along the Aegean Sea and in the Ninth Century B.C.

In this Homeric and heroic age, immense and irresistible migratory waves, such as those mounted in the Middle East by the Hyksos, Kassites, Hittites, and Assyrians, descended into Greece and drove the Hellenistic influence out across the Mediterranean and the Aegean, into Asia Minor and Egypt. The Dorians came from the north, from what are now Macedonia and Bulgaria, and drove the Greeks largely into the islands and Asia Minor and mingled with and assimilated those who remained behind in the Peloponnese. The Arcadians and Atticans were left relatively undisturbed, but the Ionians, who were pushed before the human wave of the Dorians, sought refuge in Attica and spread across the Aegean and into Asia Minor. The Aeolians from Salonika removed in large numbers to Lesbos and then into Asia Minor, and the Dorians were wanderers. They were comprised of three tribes, the Pamphylians, Hylleis, and Dymanes, and after overflowing the Peloponnese, occupied Crete, Rhodes, and the southwest of Asia Minor. Here these eventual Greeks remained for twenty-five hundred years. These were the classical Great Migrations.

Since the dates and extent of all these developments cannot be calculated with any precision, we were thrown back to a large extent on the questionable recollections of early historians. Thucydides considered that the Dorian invasion of Greece and the resulting spill-over into the islands, Asia Minor, and Egypt had occurred in the Ninth Century B.C., and there is no good reason to doubt that. Following these population movements, there appears to have been for a couple of centuries a virtual dark age of little intellectual or political development, the stasis of an undisturbed people, with neither invaders pressing upon it nor tempting doors opening to its physical exploration or natural development.

There are elaborate tales of the Dorian, or Heraclid (as Dorian legend claimed descent from Hercules), conquest of the Peloponnese, explicitly asserted by Thucydides and strongly hinted at by Herodotus, as unworthy of belief. The founders of Sparta seem to have happened upon its fruitful valley and from the first were an important power in the Pelopponessus because of their agriculture, and soon, the well-organized society they built up. Dorian Sparta, in Laconia, was surely the Lacedaemon of the *Odyssey*, and archaeological evidence of the veneration of Menelaus remains there. By the Eighth Century B.C., Sparta was an expanding and conquering little nation, led by their splendidly styled king, Theopompus. Men who were free but unpropertied were known as helots and were usually farm labourers.

But the north did gradually, and in separate movements by separate groups, descend to the south of Greece, settling among, assimilating, or forcing out the incumbent peoples. It is impossible to separate lore from fact in the great intricacy and prolonged shifting of population groups around what is today quite a small area. But scores of towns and cities in Greece developed their own personalities and to some extent their own ethnicities. It would be a mistake to consider the Greek

---

1 CAH, II, p. 512 (J.B. Bury).

cities and towns of the mid-first millennium B.C. as culturally coherent, like the conurbations of a modern state like France, or a large state of the United States. For two-thousand years, scholars have tried to trace tribal movements, invasions and migrations, inter-marriages, conquests, assimilations, and expulsions in Greece, and especially in the Peloponnese, and to trace the development of the scores of Greek city states, relying on archeology, folklore, and the divinations and suppositions of Greco-Roman historians.

For our purposes, we will deal with the emergent Greek city states and islands starting about two centuries after Homer, and not venture to mire this narrative in the theorization and surmise of the development of the individual components of classical Greece. The evolving political structures of most of these states are, in any case, almost impossible to discern or follow until the history is better documented. *The Odyssey*, which describes Odysseus' return to Greece (Ithaca) from Troy, does not mention any Hellenic settlements along the way, and Miletus, an unambiguously Greek city in northwest Asia Minor, is represented as speaking Greek with a crude accent and vocabulary. The whole Greek world was in some flux, from Macedonia through the peninsula and Peloponnese and across the Aegean to the shores of Asia Minor.

The initial move to Hellenize Asia Minor began somewhat before the Trojan War and was spontaneous, gradual, and sporadic, and continued for several generations after the Trojan War. Following the Achaean victory over Troy, systematic plans of colonization and transfer of formidable numbers of people to Asia Minor became a matter of policy for many of the states, and the result of over-population at home, but even now, these settlements were from the first autonomous of the home state and the Asia Minor populations became somewhat mixed in terms of their place of origin in Greece. This was known as the Ionian migration. And the first of these settlers were in large measure, from distinct groups, such as veterans of the Trojan War, especially heroes, Amazons, those claiming, in the manner of the time, with some plausibility to be related to the Gods.

The farther these settlers went into Asia Minor or along its coast, the more remote they became from their cities of origin. Following these Dorian groups of settlers, largely from Argos and the Argolid, and the Aeolians came from Thessaly (Salonika) and the north and central Greece. The subsequent Ionian migration settled on the large islands of Samos and Chios, and on the mainland shore opposite them, while the Dorian settlers, if from the south, settled south of Samos in Caria, and the northern Greeks settled in the area of Propontis, on the approaches to the Bosporus and the passage to the Black Sea.

In general, the main Greek penetration of Asia Minor took advantage of the decline of the senior powers of the area, under pressure from the Caucasus and Thrace, after the Twelfth Century B.C. It is generally agreed that the Hellenization of Anatolia and the northern Levant began about 1150, and that these Greek outposts developed culturally more swiftly than the complacent motherland. Thus, Ephesus became a democratic republic among its upper classes in the Tenth Century, while Miletus did not achieve that condition until the Eighth Century B.C. All of these new Greek states in Asia evolved either into democratic rule by free men, or dictatorships operated by large land-owning oligarchs.

Except for the epic struggle with Troy, and an account by Herodotus of Greek colonists forcing the issue with the arrival of Ionians at Miletus, the entire Hellenistic settlements seem to have been a matter of gradual infiltration and not amphibious violence. Each new settlement spun off expansions and satellite settlements, and the Greek presence steadily and organically expanded. It was only when the Greeks started to approach the great Middle Eastern crossroads by encroaching on the northern Levant that the whole project became more complicated and contested.

Pamphylia was undesirable marshland on the coast, and Cilicia is mountainous and commercially uninteresting. Samos settled some people there, and Rhodes managed to put down a couple of outposts on the Lycian coast. The Greeks were established at Ashod (in what is now southern Israel), and by the Sixth Century, the Greeks had established a few settlements in the Nile Delta, and well before that, Miletus had put down settlements on the Hellespont. While this Greek activity crept along the coast of Asia Minor south and east, Greeks, especially from the large islands, settled westwards also, to Sicily and Italy. Between the Eighth and Fifth Centuries B.C., the Greeks were evolving and spreading quickly, and producing a civilization that would profoundly influence the world and still does.

2. The Flowering of the Greeks

From about 1200 to about 950 B.C., after the fall of Troy, there was a long transitional period in which Aegean society gradually broke down, under the intrusion from the north, which became particularly heavy after about 1050. The invaders were Indo-Europeans, and they were neither the start nor anywhere near the end of more than twenty-five hundred years of arrivals in force with a generally aggressive and destructive appetite from more primitive but assertive and culturally unsophisticated societies. They did not entirely subdue the Greeks, but largely overran them, arrested their progress, drove them into the Cyclades and other islands, and propelled them as the "people of the sea" to move to Asia Minor, the Levant, and coastal Egypt. This wave of invaders was broadly referred to as the Dorian invasion; as barbarians go, they were fairly gentle, and did not so much uproot and destroy Mycenaean Greece as take what was valuable, assimilate up to a point, and move on, both forward in the trail of those they had displaced, and backward in the direction of their source. In general, as eminent historian J.M. Roberts put it: "These new people destroyed much and brought little."[2]

They were rugged and adaptable people, many of whom took to seafaring and blended forcefully into the Eastern Mediterranean melting pot. The Doric people founded what became Sparta and also much of Argos, which became for a time the leading Greek city, but in other Greek cities and towns, they just came through, generally taking away with them anything of value. Often, they drove off the occupants they found; more often, they reduced them to serfdom, but in general, they did not massacre them. The Greece that eventually emerged to lead the culture of Western Civilization and leave a permanent imprint on human intellectual and so-

---

2 J.M. Roberts, *History of the World*, Penguin, 1984, p. 114.

cietal development owes something to the Dorians for their vigour, and something also for their civility compared to other waves of barbarians, prior and still to come. In moving through the islands toward Asia, the Dorians displaced the Mycenaean civilization and the fairly sophisticated societies of the Cyclades islands and of Crete, sturdy and enterprising maritime cultures that moved ahead of the invaders or adapted to them.

This period had some of the qualities of a dark age for Greece, as the cohesion of the Greeks was broken down, some cities were so severely disrupted, they lost continuity and much of the period is obscured. It was, in sum, a dismal period for Greece, rather than an unmitigatedly tragic one, and although the Dorians were assertive interlopers, they were not indiscriminately or systematically nihilistic. The claim that they were descended from the legendary hero Heracules may be treated with as much skepticism as the claim of the Phoenicians that they had been implanted in the Levant in 2700 B.C. (an apparent advance on the facts by about six-hundred years). All skilled and artistic traits vanished between 1100 and 1000 B.C. in Greece: carving of gems, painting of frescoes, fine pottery—the Dorians suppressed or scattered any such creativity and continuity was confined to verbal folklore. Enough came through the uneven sieve of Doric passage to enable Homer to write his mighty epics. They, and most of what is alleged about Homer himself, are discounted by serious historians, but some sort of conflict occurred at Troy, and someone known as Homer wrote about them in such majestically elegiacal terms as to put him in the very most exalted rank of the literary culture of the West. Herodotus and Thucydides recounted the Dorian invasion, but it is difficult to tell where history and folklore meet in their narratives of these events.

The dialects cited by Homer reveal full measures of the Aeolian, Ionian, and Arcadian tongues, all of which antedated and were influenced by the Dorians, who chased Greeks of all groups and places into the islands and to Asia Minor, and then followed them, not from animosity, but from the same motive as the Greeks, in search of better homes and richer lives. The Dorians were undoubtedly the creators of the Sparta known to history, the Sparta of which, in the Eighth Century, Theopompus was the great and victorious king, ushering in the brilliant flowering of ancient Greece. Our knowledge of the rise of Greece and particularly of the Hellenization of the Aegean and Anatolian islands and Asia Minor is largely dependent on legends that were passed down to classical Greeks and that sound relatively plausible. Archeology and original writings are not very extensive or reliable. The migration process appears to have been very prolonged, to have begun tentatively and sporadically, gradually developed into colonization, and finally, after the Trojan War, to have become a substantial popular relocation. But, as was mentioned at the end of the first part of this chapter, this strong demographic movement was not an article of policy by the principal city states; rather, it was a spontaneous popular movement where the emigrants did not feel they were carrying the flag of their country of origin, but were rather striking out on their own, albeit in numerous company. The nature of the settlers evolved from exotic people of the Greek world such as those from Crete, and storied veterans of the Trojan War, but the later flood were mainly conventional Dorian or Aeolian Greeks, from Argos or Thessaly. They tended to move laterally, so the Thessalonians were in northern Asia Minor and the Dorians in the southern Anatolian islands and mainland, mirroring Greece itself.

By the middle of this settlement process, distinctions arose in the Hellenic communities of Asia Minor and the Anatolian islands, between oligarchies ruled by large landowners and potential democracies. The first step in the democratization process was always the elevation to the headship of the entity by some elective process, even if only the consultation of the apparently leading personalities or families. Thus, Miletus, on the southwestern mainland, near the large island of Samos, had an elective dictator by the Eighth Century B.C., and this evolved into an elected president of the council. Those settlements, which were more urban and maritime-based, tended not to have the sort of influential class that rural jurisdictions tend to with large and economically dominant landowners. In the development of democracy, as in the flourishing of the arts, the newer, trans-Aegean Greek states moved more swiftly than the Greek cities and islands from which their founders departed.

To a slight degree, this was the dynamism of the comparatively new world that was demonstrated in later migrations, including those of Europeans to North America. The population that was in western Asia Minor prior to the arrival in strength of the Greeks has not come down to us with any clarity. Generally, it was an area that was bypassed by the overland route from the Levant and Palestine to the Bosporus and Europe and was also bypassed by most of the sea-traffic from the Phoenician and Egyptian ports to the main Greek cities. Most activity there was by Phoenician coastal traffic, and the natives were scattered, subjugated, or assimilated, with little cultural trace.

The Dorians drew the shades down on what had been, leading up to and beyond the Trojan Wars, a time of heroes, and of flamboyant living and imperishable legend. It was, as one eminent classicist wrote, "As dark and unproductive as winter (but) full of germination, and in due time there followed the spring and the summer, the Hellenic Renaissance and the Hellenic Prime. In the Peloponnese, the winter belongs to Argos, the spring to Corinth, the summer to Sparta."[3] These were all Dorian cities. The mighty autumnal harvest of renown and achievement and permanence would go to Athens. Argos was the Dorian replacement of Mycenae, though Argos did not remotely enjoy the maritime and commercial and colonial reach or architectural ambition of Mycenae, she was yet the premier city of the Inachus Valley of the Peloponnese. Argos played a leading role in the legends of the Twelve Labours of Hercules and was the source of the heroic Argonauts in the Trojan Wars. Argos eventually fell into a desperate struggle with Sparta for control of the Peloponnese. (This is an adjunct to the Greek mainland that at its maximum extent is only about one-hundred miles west to east, and north to south, though somewhat trapezoidal in shape, and to the west of Athens, from which, along with the rest of Greece, is separated by the Corinth peninsula. Given the immense prominence of the Peloponnese, and Sparta, Corinth, and Argos, in particular, in ancient history and even in contemporary folklore and language, it would be easy to conceive that the Peloponnese was as large as France, if not Australia.) Arcadia is the rather mountainous centre of the Peloponnese.

---

3 CAH, III, p. 543 (H.T. Wade-Gery).

By the Eighth Century B.C., in almost every valley of Greece, the hereditary nobles around a heroic king, or a king whose ascendants were heroic within relevant memory or belief, were simultaneously authors of the evolution of the Greek state, which combined noble kingship, influential elders, and consultation of the citizenry. This was a revolutionary advance from the brutal and elemental structures of the Jews and Egyptians and the transitory and fragile structures of the peoples that occupied or surged into the Middle East. Other characteristics of this state included the worship, at agreed public places, of common gods, a common law, evenly administered in public, and the acceptance of a general mass response to external danger. This led to the hoplite—the citizen soldier, and the hoplite phalanx: massed citizen-infantry, armed with spear and shield, close together and with several rows of depth and flanks protected by similar formations. These proved insuperable for a long time, and when similar armies similarly deployed clashed, as often happened in the Greek internal wars, the result was often very sanguinary and very narrowly determined. This was the Greek Hoplite Phalanx, and its members (and survivors) were the core of the elite rule in the post-Dorian Greek city state. At the same time this method of warfare was adopted, the emerging political society conferred an unprecedented degree of participatory adherence.

Most of the Greek city states were starting to run out of cultivable food. This was the source of Greece's maritime destiny and genius: they had to take to the sea to find the sources of survival. Their commercial astuteness warmly complemented their nautical vocation, need for foreign resources, food and wealth, and domineering and war-like natures.

There was fairly free and undisturbed contact by sea from Sicily and southern Italy, and into the Adriatic, to Egypt, Phoenicia, the Levant, and all the Greeks in Asia Minor, the islands, and Greece herself, and also into the Black Sea. Thus did Greece swiftly and unsought become the centre of the known Western world. It was to the sea lanes what the Middle East was to the land routes. In 734 B.C., the Corinthians founded the trading and agrarian colony of Syracuse, in Sicily, and also of Corcyrus. The Greek states were running short of cultivable land to support themselves and the development of colonial granaries commended itself as policy. The redoubtable Theopompus responded to the Corinthian initiatives in Sicily with the suppression and subjugation of the southwestern corner of the Peloponnese to assure its wheat fields and vineyards to the security of Sparta's food and wine supply.

As the sweep-through of the Dorians subsided, the Greek city states rose again, in a different configuration but in more vigorous form: Argos looked with suspicion and hostility on the rise of Corinth and Sparta. Argos, like Sparta, had retained a traditional hereditary monarchy and King Pheidon of Argos was one of the formidable leaders of the time (early Seventh Century B.C.). Pheidon was a fine military commander, who began to reassemble the kingdom of Temanus, founded two centuries before, by training up his army, awaiting an opportunity, and pouncing on the Spartan army in the pass at Hysiae between the Plain of Thyrea and the Plain of Tegea. Pheidon had the pleasure of giving the Spartan soldiers one of the few thorough defeats in their history, and he did not hear much back-talk from Sparta for the balance of his reign.

Between Argos and Athens, rivalry arose by Athens' encroachment on Aegina, which caused the Aegineans to appeal to Pheidon, and their combined forces annihilated the Athenian army and smashed the Athenian navy. With Sparta, as with Athens, their immense military mystique, earned and maintained valorously in both cases, only took hold after they had been knocked around a bit. Pheidon replied more subtly to the rise of Corinth, at the western end of the isthmus connecting Greece to the Peloponnese, by building up Megara, to the east of the isthmus. Together, Pheidon's Argives and the Megarans established the trading ports of Byzantium and Chalcedon. Pheidon deftly advanced the Argive interest through the championship of these smaller cities that became dependent on his support.

It was through contact with the kings of Lydia in Asia Minor that the Greeks came in contact with coinage, and Pheidon adopted this method of currency, and it swiftly revolutionized commerce throughout Greece and along the Aegean and Mediterranean littoral to Sicily and beyond. Pheidon marched across the Peloponnese to the west and took over by force the presidency of Olympia and the organization of the festival to much more spectacular proportions than it had enjoyed under the Eleans, who had originated the games that attracted pan-Hellenic competition. Boxing, wrestling, the pentathlon and chariot races were added to the original foot-racing, and his status at Olympia made Pheidon the foremost of the Greek leaders.

It is not exactly clear when Pheidon died, but this event presaged the swift descent of Argive influence in the mid-Seventh Century B.C., and the rise of the isthmian tyrants. Pheidon had raised the Dorian era to a revival of the city states and represented a relatively benign, final assertion of the Doric presence in Greece, which died with him, and the strongmen elevated in the leading cities effectively reasserted pre-Dorian Hellenism, blended though it was in many subtle ways by the Dorian experience and intermarriages. The Elians, Elis, rose up against post-Pheidon Argos. (Pheidon's son, Lacedes, was completely inept and had none of the talents required of a successful ruler.) The Eleans started on the northwest of the peninsula, and the poet Pindar wrote, "Fortune gave no small part of the delights of Hellas" to the Eleans (as to Thessaly), who reasserted themselves at Olympia after the demise of Pheidon, and spread into Arcadia in the centre of the Peloponnese. Elis founded the Peloponnesian League and was the largest state in the Peloponnese outside Laconia, where Sparta prevailed. The history of this era is not well or reliably recorded, and we only have some random reflections of Aristotle to go by. Elis allegedly had a council of ninety members which held office for life and conducted what Aristotle called "an oligarchy within an oligarchy," which evolved in the Fifth Century into democracy. "Tyrants" of this era is not a word that connotes erratic and severe despotism as it has come to mean in modern times; it generally means people exercising powers largely irrevocable by legislatures but having attained to their position by some sort of legitimate process, and not, at least automatically, by heredity. It was not a derogatory title—even the supreme God Zeus was referred to as a tyrant. (Like coinage, the word and concept is a contribution to the Greeks by the Lydians of Asia Minor.) The tyrants were, rather, meritocrats raised up by those energized and enriched by increasing commercial velocity after the partial Hellenization of Asia Minor and the burgeoning of Greek shipping and trading, an activity in which the Greeks of the islands and seaports have not ceased to excel to the present time. Tyrants were a transitional regime from the hidebound aristocracies to the early Greek elaborations of democracy.

Pisa was the name given to the site of Olympia, and in 399 B.C., the Spartans, seeking to humiliate Elis, purported to establish Olympia as a separate independent state under the name of Pisa, in order to substitute itself for Elian influence. The games had become the focal point of Pan-Hellenic identity. Versions of these contentious disputes over control of Olympia are furnished variously by the historians Xenophon, Strabo, Eusebius, and others. The Pisatans seem to have presided from the 28th Olympiad in 668 B.C. at least intermittently until 580 B.C., under their own tyrants, especially Pantaleon and Pyrrhus (not to be confused with the Fourth and Third Century B.C. Greek and Albanian warrior-king). The Eleans evicted the Pisatans in 580, but this was the tradition the Spartans claimed to revive in their competition for influence with the Eleans in 399.

Throughout the Seventh Century, the scale of activities at Olympia grew. In addition to the athletic competition, a council house was erected of greater use as an oratorical forum, more like a forerunner of the League of Nations or United Nations than a place of legislation, and a large steadily more opulently decorated temple arose festooned with the benefactions of the city state leaders, competing in their munificence. Even after the construction of Zeus' temple in the Fifth Century B.C., it remained an immense attraction. Olympia thus became a great centre of the most talented athletes, the leading statesmen, and for religious panoplies and devotions. The Olympic games became so important that at one point, a war between some of the contestant countries was suspended by a stand-still truce in place, to enable their athletes to take part.

One of the most illustrious of the early tyrants was Cleisthenes of Sicyon, a city only about ten miles west-northwest of Corinth. (The distances between these Greek cities are astonishingly small considering their universal and permanent renown, as if they were immense domains as far apart as Berlin and Paris.) Cleisthenes reigned in Sicyon between 600 and 560 B.C., approximately. Cypselus and Periander ruled Corinth from about 650 to 580 B.C. and made it the greatest power in Greece, and Periander became the arbiter of Greek affairs, invited by both sides to be the arbiter in the war between Athens and Mitylene. Periander became friendly with the kings of Egypt and Lydia, a formidable achievement of personal diplomacy in such a primitive era. He was hostile, as these holders of the status of Tyrant tended to be, toward the nobility of his city, and generally popular with the new commercial classes and, up to a point and to the limited extent that they had any influence, the popular classes. As the power and capacities of Periander weakened as he advanced through his seventies, the strength of his younger rival, Cleisthenes of Sicyon rose. Periander thought of abdicating, according to Herodotus, but resisted the temptation (as tyrants of all times and definitions usually do). Within ten years of his death, Cleisthenes had built the greatest fleet in the Corinthian Gulf for Sicyon.

Cleisthenes timed his rise to conform with the descent of Periander, and is alleged to have outwitted his brother, Isodemus, for the little-valued headship of

Sicyon. Those who sued for the hand in dynastic marriage of Cleisthenes' daughter ranged from all over Greece, Asia Minor, and Italy, but Cleisthenes selected the distinguished Athenian Alcmeonid, Megacles. He thus made himself the direct ancestor of Cleisthenes the Lawgiver, Pericles, and Alcibiades. It was the crusade of Cleisthenes to exalt the anti-Dorian over the Dorian influence in Greece, and he generally prevailed, but a stand-still eventually arose between the Isthmian cities and the Argives.

In this narrowly balanced struggle between the ultimately war-fatigued Isthmians and Argives, Sparta, growing stronger and ultra-belligerent in temperament, if prudent in state policy, was ready to make its move by about 580. Sparta had occupied Messenia, all of the far southwestern Peloponnese, which gave its leadership enough land to resist the quasi-democratic tendencies of the neighbouring tyrants. The nobles reigned, and this very purposefully fierce state was an outlier in Greece, a strictly disciplined people raised and constantly reconfirmed in a cult of municipal superiority through bravery, sacrifice, and discipline. The young were raised with intense physical training and severe discipline, as was usual in the ancient world, boys and girls, whipped on the buttocks for any derogation from authority, and slaves flogged, and the men remained in the military to the age of sixty. They could marry as adults but did not live with their wives. Women were comparatively respected and powerful, as the severity of their upbringing was deemed to make them more likely mothers of fine warriors, and maternity was highly prized and admired. They had more independence than was usual in these times because they did not live with their spouses. It was a barrack state of almost co-equal sexes, but it generated almost nothing of lasting value except the example of military single-mindedness.

Sparta was astute politically, and bided its time as the struggle between the tyrants and the aristocracies ran its course, though it had to suppress a revolt in Messenia, which was fought out, tooth and nail, despite Sparta's ferocity and determination, for many years, no quarter given or asked. The non-Dorian tyranny had been reinforced in Sicyon under Cleisthenes but had been banished and reviled ten miles away in Corinth. The two great Hellenic sanctuaries were divided also: Delphi, having long favoured the tyrants, was now opposed to them, and Olympia supported them. In this profound and narrow division, after Sparta finally crushed the Messenians comprehensively, it held the balance.

It cast its lot decisively and permanently with rigid authoritarianism. According to the Eunomia, the law entrenching equality, military capability, and austerity as the rule of Sparta, promulgated by the possibly mythical regent Lycurgus, ninety per cent of the population had effectively no rights, and the aristocracy had all the power. But the men lived in barracks, dormitories, into middle age, allowed to frequent their wives for sufficiently short periods that procreation could be reasonably assumed to be the chief conjugal activity. Spartan women, less careworn and as strictly raised as the men, were renowned for their poise, beauty and confidence, and admired by society for their fertility. The Spartans did entertain well, and hunted with great energy, pioneering hunting on horseback. Sparta had its pleasant aspects, but it was a stern, uncreative, and unspontaneous place.

The Lycurgan reform abolished official recognition of the three Dorian tribes, and replaced them with five geographic sections, a formula that was emulated by Cleisthenes, the Athenian law-giver, a century later. It was on this geographic basis that the Spartan army was to be organized and this had the effect of homogenizing differences and strengthening attachments within the institution to which cadets were conscripted at age seven and retained until they were released from reserve duty at age sixty. This was the forge of the finest army in the world. The basis of citizenship in Sparta was that men should own enough land to produce food for themselves and their family—thus, the citizen was able to serve in the army and handle his own mess-bill. As a war-machine, it contained a structural efficiency that has never been exceeded, though a few armies have been as effective, better equipped, and commanded with greater agility, but very few in pre-Christian Greece. This was Sparta: coinage and even the circulation of precious metals was prohibited—it was the complete socialistic society. Land could not be transferred, and society was in stasis, as in a beehive or ant-hill, but it was geared to the expansion of Sparta, or at least its defence with unwavering tenacity. This was one of the few successful societies in history to defy the power of money.

Lycurgus established the government of two kings, from the hereditary elders, the Gerousia with twenty-eight other Gerontes (Elders), apart from the two kings, and the citizenry formed the Apella, the entirety of the citizens. But the Apella had no power and could be dismissed by the Gerontes. But the Apella did elevate five Ephors, representing each district, and these five did effectively represent the mass of citizens opposite the Gerontes, so there was, even in this very severe and collectivized and disciplined state, a significant element of democracy. The Ephorate was created in the late Seventh Century B.C. and did not really assert itself for fifty years, but in 556 B.C., Chilon asserted the prerogatives of the citizens with an articulation that made him as influential in the state as the kings. Sparta's credentials as a strict socialist democracy are presentable, then, as the chief magistrates were chosen by the entire citizenry; the problem with this, by the standards of human political society twenty-five hundred years later, is that ninety per cent of Spartans were not citizens. But it must be conceded that the Spartans, though they derived some of these features from Crete, were pioneers in their level of participation and their effective socialism, vastly exceeding anything accomplished in Marxist times, as well as in building the warrior and garrison state.

But it was a selection of national vocation for Sparta (it can scarcely at this point be described as a municipality). "The city, where life had been as beautiful as anything in Greece, became a barracks; there are no more Spartan poets...or artists...Sparta had none of the splendor of a Greek city: to look at her, said Thucydides, you would never believe the greatness of her people. The discipline impoverished their spirit."[4] Sparta had fine buildings and arts and crafts and a substantial literature, but it all ceased and never recovered. This is the message of bellicose, demonetized, socialism, a lesson that remains relevant, if sometimes unheeded.

Having endowed itself with such a splendid army, Sparta's quasi-democratically chosen but authoritarian leaders naturally desired to use it, as has generally happened with the armies of authoritarian regimes prior to the era of collective

---

4 CAH, III, p. 564 (H.T. Wade-Gery).

security and nuclear arms. Having conquered Messenia and severely repressed an attempted rising there, Sparta, with no reason except that a weaker and prosperous and under-populated area was a neighbor unable to defend itself against such a war machine, selected Arcadia, in the centre of Peloponnese, as its next victim. What resulted was quite unforeseen: despite its un-Spartan character and organization, Arcadia resisted fiercely, and two pairs of Spartan kings, Leon and Agesicles and Alexandridas and Ariston, blunted their spears on the Arcadians (about 590-560 B.C.), and then Sparta, with the pragmatism of Richelieu or Metternich, changed course and made a solemn alliance, "a peace of the brave,"[5] with Arcadia, a refinement of their relations the gallant but hard-pressed Arcadians were happy to make. This was the beginning of the League, where Sparta became the chief among a group of nearby and ambitious states and transformed itself from a ravening wolf among its neighbours to a respected and trusted protector: instead of the conqueror of the sullen and the oppressed, the chief guarantor of the grateful neighbours. Herodotus credits this as the arrival of Sparta as what he called, in his diminutive geographic range, "a World Power," starting in about 560.

This sea-change of policy, the product of enlightened statesmanship of a kind not normally ascribed, then or in all posterity, to a militant warrior-state, took distinct shape with the restoration to Sparta of the bones of the ancient (not to say mythological) hero, Orestes. Orestes was the son of Agamemnon and Clytaemnestra. When Agamemnon returned from the Trojan Wars with his concubine Cassandra, according to Homer, Orestes, absent at the time of the return of his father, returned seven years later and slew both his mother, Clytaemnestra, and the lover Aegisthus whose company she had retained since the return from the wars of his father. Pindar, however, claimed that Orestes' sister, Electra, or Orestes' nurse, Arsinoe, saved Orestes when Clytaemnestra greeted his return by trying to have him killed. Aeschylus, Euripides, and the modern mythologist and classical interpreter and novelist, Robert Graves, all have different views of these events, and the issue of the mortal remains of so mythologized a figure as Orestes cannot become a serious historical episode. However, as was often the case in these times, symbolic issues can easily be seized upon and empowered with a substantial importance. Sparta, with extraordinary political skill for a regime which had delivered itself altogether to the most unsubtle and non-political of political options, managed to represent itself to the Peloponnese as, at the same time, anti-Dorian, and, by the same token, thoroughly Dorian.

This problem was illustrated by the Spartan king, Cleomenes, son of Anaxandridus, on the steps of the Acropolis of Athens in about 505 B.C., when the priestess told him that Spartan foreigners, Dorians, were prohibited. Cleomenes replied that he was no Dorian, but an Achaean. Sparta's problem, as soon came to light, was two-fold. Greeks were too appreciative of culture and hedonism to submit to Sparta, and a few thousand citizens under a fierce monastic and racist rule that eyed all non-co-tribalists with suspicion and retained domestic tranquility by burdening the governing ten or twelve per cent of Spartans with the right and duty to impose themselves with whatever degree of firmness was judged necessary, on nearly

---

5 President Charles de Gaulle, address at press conference, Paris, October 23, 1959.

ninety per cent of the country, a visually almost indistinguishable under-privileged group of the helots, was in no condition to take on the headship of a motley of other Greek states. They were, in any case, little disposed to accept the authority of other municipalities, all headstrong and fractious, the more so for their confined geography. They were, in the circumstances, if anything, even more argumentative and contentious than the Jews, as they were not as threatened by large and hostile contiguities.

Sparta was yet able to exploit the factionalism within the polities of some of its neighbours. In Corinth, the tyrants had been overthrown and expelled, and the oligarchs, fidgeting uneasily in their place, were happy to accept a junior role in alliance with Sparta to outmaneuver Sicyon and give it a good comeuppance. The original Cleisthenes had died, and Sparta was happy and able, by deployment of some of its army, to intervene and expel his less capable successor, Aeschines, and put a docile oligarchy in place. Again, Sparta, for all its humorless ferocity, imposed its will moderately and did not incite extreme resentment. It humbled the mediocre leader of Sicyon and his entourage but did not oppress the city. This was the beginning of a remarkably crafty and successful Spartan policy of expelling tyrants in the cities of the Peloponnese in the name of a more democratic regime, an appeal to pan-Hellenism and partial democracy, rather than self-aggrandizing brute conquest. In contemporary parlance, it was the use of relatively soft power, where the hard power option clearly existed in the mighty Spartan army, but the kings and ephors and gerontes of Sparta knew at all times that it had to maintain most of its army at home to keep the ninety per cent of Sparta who were serfs or slaves, toiling in their socialist boarding school, the lash never far from their backs.

Megara had been soundly defeated by Athens and was smarting in its humiliation. Spartan arbitrators awarded the large, disputed island of Salamis to Athens, and although Megara was able to set up a colony in the Black Sea at Heraclea, she was in an almost permanent state of civil disruption between champions of oligarchy and democracy. Megara had failed to deal with the problems of new wealth and its distribution, either with swiftly maturing democracy as the Athenians had practiced, or with the Spartan model of demonetized socialism, strictly enforced by armed forces controlled by a democratically chosen leadership among the small elite of full citizens. Megara needed the assistance of Sparta against Athens, but this roundel was interrupted in 546 B.C. by the arrival on the Greek horizon of the giant of the near east, Persia, under its great king Cyrus. Croesus, king of Lydia, had skillfully divided the European and Aegean Greeks from the Near Eastern Greeks, made alliances with some of the principal Greek states while subjugating the Greek cities of Asia Minor and exacting tribute from them rather greedily. He issued the most valuable pure gold coinage the western world had seen, the origin of his identification with great wealth. But his activities were interrupted and suppressed by Cyrus, and Croesus was insufficiently strong to resist Persia, and had offended too many of the Greek states to be able to call them for assistance. In any case, at this point, the Greek and Aegean states were happy to take Cyrus' assurances that his interest did not overflow continental Asia. Croesus was captured by Cyrus, who legendarily determined to execute him by fire, but relented and translated the recently great and hugely rich king into an advisor, presumably on Hellenic matters, which, however ardently the Greeks appeased him, appeared to be Cyrus' next likely target.

As Croesus endured his transformative demotion, Sparta determined to settle accounts with Argos over which was the dominant power in Arcadia. Almost simultaneously with the defeat and submission of Croesus was the Battle of the Champions, both in 546, at Thyrea. First, three-hundred outstanding single combat warriors clashed, and then the whole armies of Sparta and Argos, and the Spartans won, avenging their defeat at the hands of Pheidon in the previous century. Full of confidence, the Spartan kings warned Cyrus not to try to cross to Greece. Cyrus responded with a withering rebuke to the effect that the king of Persia would go where he pleased and that there was no force on Earth to stop him. Hubris was forming up on both sides. This was 545, the year of the birth of Cleomenes, son of Anaxandridus II, who would reign from 519 to 490 B.C. and be Sparta's greatest leader. He would be an almost exact contemporary of Darius. The greatest Heroic Age of Greece, surpassing even that of Agamemnon immortalized by Homer, was about to begin.

3. The Rise of Athens

Attica, a thousand square miles at the southeast of Greece, northeast of the Peloponnese across the isthmus guarded by Corinth, was, when its history was first recorded, already a large number of city states. Herodotus and Thucydides are the principal authors of its early history, though their sources are often of doubtful authenticity, and much is mere legend and supposition. Gradually, Athens became the dominant influence throughout Attica. This was the Synoikismos. Thucydides would have us believe that this was a process of voluntary adherence, a triumph of civilization rather than force. The renown of Athens, doubtless generally merited, became so immense because of the survival, as much as the scholarship or literary artistry, of its historians. The Athenian people were divided into brotherhoods, tribes, and clans, with some overlapping between them. According to Aristotle, each of the twelve Attic brotherhoods was divided into thirty clans, so there were 360 family groups in total. It remains a matter of astonishment that the activities of so small a group could remain, after nearly three-thousand years, the subject of such intense interest and study. The real nature of the clans was not genealogical at all, but rather economic: the first clan to make its historic mark was the great landowners. This was the beginning of the Attic nobility, whose power grew as they gravitated toward Athens, reinforcing that city as the political capital of Attica, and strengthening their own ability to influence its government. Like almost all Greek constitutions, Athens had a king and a council at first. None of the recitations of the orderly succession of thirty kings is verifiable or trustworthy.

The first somewhat known Athenian council was the Areopagus, according to Aristotle and others, established by Solon, the principal Athenian ruler after the redoubtable Draco, still renowned as a severe law-giver and prosecutor. The council of Areopagus was undoubtedly deliberative, legislative, and also in part judicial. By a process that will apparently always remain a mystery, by the Seventh Century B.C., the Athenian kingdom had evolved into an aristocratic republic. By that time, the king had evacuated the Acropolis where he formerly lived, and lived in "the king's porch" in Athens' lower town, and was elected by the rest of the council in which he sat for one year at a time. All that really distinguished him from other councilors were ceremonious religious functions (somewhat like the modern British monarch as nominal head of the Church of England), and a status as a judge in criminal cases.

The monarchy was gradually reduced, in a condensed process of what happened in England and some other monarchies. First it was made an elective office, then reduced to one year (in 753 it was limited to ten years and in 683 to one year), and finally the powers were divided up. The devolution of powers began with the appointment of the Polemarch as armed forces commander, and then came the Archon as a sort of prime minister. Different offices were established, and groups of councilors were designated to write and judge laws. Eventually, the Areopagus was entrusted with the election of archons. The ephetae were a tribunal to judge murder cases selected from the councilors. The kolekktretai ("ham-carvers") were a committee of treasury and finance, and the ecclesia were a larger electorate of fluctuating and uncertain authority. Attica long remained involuted and agrarian, with little focus on commerce or maritime activity. By the standards of the ancient world, the rise of Athens as a colonial, maritime, and commercial power was astonishingly swift, catching up with its comparative intellectual sophistication.

A good deal could and has been written about the other Attican cities apart from Athens, but of them all, only Delphi deserves particular mention here. The ability of this little town to become important was due to the renown of its oracle. Divinations were made in every Greek town, but Delphi achieved its prominence and became the spiritual centre of Greece partly because it was near the centre of the Greek areas at an extremely majestic and inspiriting site that delighted pilgrims. It is on an elevated clearing of five acres, standing on a cliff one thousand feet above a canyon, and enfolded by limestone cliffs seven-hundred feet high. But the principal reason for the rise of Delphi was its association with Apollo. Delphi was originally a shrine of a primitive earth goddess and was held to be "the navel of the earth." A Homeric poem from the Seventh Century B.C. holds that Apollo was proceeding from Macedonia to Thessaly and on to Boeotia, came upon Delphi, and ousted the earth mother by slaying her protector and warder, the serpent Pytho. Eventually, he embarked for Crete and rounded up a group of sailors and made them his priests at Delphi. The name Delphi is thought to have been furnished by an ancient sea god of Crete which took the form of a dolphin. Apollo's self-installation appears to have occurred in Trojan times, at the end of the pre-historic age of Greece. The site was threatened by Dorian migration, but Apollo allegedly won over the invaders, who spread Apollo's renown as they moved across the Greek world.

Those who provided Delphic oracular reflections as time passed were very careful not to impose fasts of more than one day per month, nor to risk their credibility on vulnerable predictions. Thus Croesus, king of Lydia, was told that in his conflict with Persia, he would see the "fall of a great kingdom," without specifying that it would be his. The Oracle's soothsayers generally avoided predictions of severely contested outcomes and did not engage in religious chastisements beyond reproaches and admonitions. The slogan of the Delphic Oracle, inscribed at the entry, was: "Nothing Too Much." They almost never criticized other oracles or secular legislators, and sometimes assisted in disseminating public policy. They always championed comparative leniency and were in the vanguard of those calling for emancipation of slaves. The Delphic Oracle's material standards were also exemplary; gifts were generally accepted from respectable people, but not in exchange for approbation or even insight, and in one case, physically expelled a trustee who tried to put the Oracle's services on a commercial basis.[6]

In Homer's time, the temple was renowned; in the Seventh Century, it received pilgrimages from foreign kings, and in the Sixth Century B.C., the king of Egypt (Amasis) was a lead contributor in building a new temple appropriate to a centre of such wisdom and worship. In approximately 590 B.C., a dispute arose between Delphi and the adjoining town of Crisa about the tolls that Crisa collected from pilgrims to Delphi. The Amphictyonic League, initially established by Thessaly but soon dominated by Athens, took Delphi's part in the dispute and Athens was the principal military contributor in the First Sacred War, which followed. The facts of what actually happened have never been well established. But Delphi was separated from Crisa, put under Amphictyonic trusteeship, and the League held two of its four annual council meetings at Delphi. Thessaly prevailed for a time, at Delphi, and presided over the creation and enlargement of the great national Pythian festival, which made Delphi an even rival with Olympia as the principal exposition centre of the ancient Greek world.

At first, the Pythian festival was just a religious ceremony celebrating the victory of Apollo over Pytho; it grew into a singing contest, then other musical and then athletic feats. It never equaled Olympia as an athletic contest, but it surpassed it as a gathering place, when its different activities were all taken into account. But Thessaly was shouldered aside by Sparta and Athens. Delphi continued to flourish; very valuable war offerings—sometimes from contending parties in a conflict—"golden harvests" and other gifts of treasure were made and stored in treasure houses that made Delphi a target for greedy foreign disbelievers.

With the Amphictyonic League, sordid political intrigue was not long in coming, and the First and subsequent Sacred Wars may pass adequately as a preliminary model for some of the religious wars of the Middle Ages. Colonial and large exploratory operations generally sought Apollo's goodwill at Delphi and paid heavily for it. Readers may form their own views of the believability of the insights of the Oracle of Delphi, but Pindar and Plato and most Greek dramatists and thinkers acknowledged Apollo as the font of all wisdom. Delphi achieved great influence as a source of education and in the standardization of Greek religion and ethical concepts, and with the presence there of a sort of national Greek Court to even out some of the mores and folkways of the different Greek areas, and Apollo came to rival the Zeus of Olympia, as a figure of Greek worship and unitary symbolism and spiritual authority.

In the first half of the Seventh Century B.C., Attica was distinguished in Greece for just one achievement: it was a united region, governed under a rather sophisti-

---

6 CAH, III, p. 628 (M. Cary).

cated system by Athens. Attica's only manufactured resource was pottery, an artistic craft in which it did not equal Corinth or a couple of other centres. Most of Attic territory was poor agricultural land from which the peasants eked out their existence. The fertile land was owned by the nobles. Athens competed fairly well in the Olympic games, but it was not at this point a particularly renowned city.

Cylon, an Athenian Olympic champion and young Athenian nobleman, was impressed by the tyranny of his father-in-law Theagenes of Megara. He and some of his young noble friends admired the successful tyrannies of Corinth and other states and schemed to overthrow the Athenian aristocracy. They waited for the distraction of the Olympic games, where Cylon had distinguished himself as a fleet-footed runner, and attempted a coup, with the assistance of Theagenes' hoplites. It was successful at first, and Cylon seized the Acropolis, but the Archon, Megacles, a proud and resourceful aristocrat, sent word out to the countryside, and the rural peasantry revered the king and stormed the Acropolis. Cylon managed to escape to exile, but his followers were massacred. The extent of bloodshed embarrassed and shamed the nobility and the peasantry, and the position of Megacles was not secure.

Eventually, the Alcmaeonidae, the clan of Megacles, were judged collectively guilty of the excessive use of murderous force and tried en masse. The clan was banished, and the dead participants in the suppression of Cylon, including Megacles, had their bones exhumed and disposed of outside Attica. Peace was restored, but the moral authority of the nobles had been badly shaken by the actions of Cylon and Megacles and their followers. The legislator Draco was entrusted, in approximately 621 B.C., with the task of codifying the criminal law and regularizing the justice system to establish a uniform law for all.

Draco ranks with Croesus, Pyrrhus, Helen of Troy, and a few others of the ancient world whose names are known for a single aspect of their lives, even if most people who invoke their names know little about them. Draco personified the judicial severity that was popularly demanded to deter blood feuds and compel the aristocracy to observe common statutes. Blood feuds were entrenched in Attic folklore and society. The spirit of vengeance lived on in the offspring of the mortally wronged. The Areopagus was declared a sanctuary where a justly vengeful man could flee and secure his official innocence of the act he was about to commit. There was a ceremony in which such a person faces the Rock of Offense and then the Stone of Implacability and swears his vengeance, and the council of state determines whether the violence about to occur is blameworthy or justified. Draco legislated this first official doctrine of justifiable homicide. He determined that where a claimed murder of rightful vengeance occurs, the murderer may appeal to a court of Ephetae at the Delphic Oracle, and if upheld, pays no penalty. Draco also established in law the distinction between premeditated and accidental homicide. And he exonerated homicide in exile as long as Attica itself was not defiled and imposed penalties for the crime of blackmail by threatening murder.

Draco created central Ephetae, fifty-one jurors, where the Basileus presided, a primitive chief justice of a mixed court of equity, justice, and ecclesiastical interpretation. Draco is remembered for his stern laws because of the frequent provision of the death penalty for offenses. He allegedly explained that he found robbery deserving of the death penalty and felt therefore obliged to apply it to all equivalent and greater crimes. In fact, his justice system was more subtle than generally believed, and he skillfully wove together the treatment of the grievances of family, society, and the religious establishment, and asserted secular governmental authority. All in all, Draco, if not a progressive, was at least an author of enhanced and even-handed state authority.

By about 600 B.C., Athens was being inhibited in the exploitation of its growing seafaring vocation by Megara's possession of the large island of Salamis in the Saronic Gulf. Given the omnipresence of the sea in and around Greece and the scarcity of arable land and natural resources, nothing was more natural than that Greeks should turn seaward to enhance their fortunes, as they had already done in colonizing the western shore of Asia Minor. At some point in the late Seventh Century B.C., Athens wrested Salamis from Megara, where Theagenes' regime had ultimately collapsed, and launched an expedition to the Dardanelles, to try to secure the gateway to the Black Sea and assure the passage of grain from Black Sea suppliers to supplement uncertain Attican harvests. Specifically, the Athenians attempted to seize the town of Sigeum from the island of Lesbos. The Athenian commander, Phrynon, was somewhat successful, and Athenian possession of Sigeum was upheld in arbitration by the Corinthian tyrant, Periander, though Lesbos subsequently abrogated the agreement and seized Sigeum back from Athens. Athens was moving to protect her trade with Egypt, Cyprus, and Asia Minor and the Levant, but the levies on her agrarian class to man the Athenian fleet were causing unrest as well as the usual challenges to the treasury that heavy military spending generates.

The exigencies of Attica's economic limitations, where even its production of sophisticated pottery, exotic oils, and wine, the principal exports, had not peaked, propelled the Athenians to sea to make money in trade and transport. The wealthy nobles who ran the government and commerce squeezed the agrarian classes, and enforced their rights of credit with a firmness that provoked political unrest, especially as it reduced many small landholders to tenant-farmers, and then even their future labour was pledged to the landlord-creditors. Some even lapsed into slavery and were sold abroad. The economic strains on the impoverished majority turned Athens into a socioeconomic pressure cooker in desperate need of reform. The agent for such change miraculously appeared in the form of Solon.

Where Cylon had been the person who levered his status as an admired athlete into political renown, like cricketer Imran Khan in Pakistan or former footballers Jack Lynch in Ireland and Recep Erdogan in Turkey, and Draco was the Thermidorean restorer of order like Barras after the Reign of Terror in 1794 and Adolphe Thiers after the siege of Paris in 1871, Solon was the patrician altruist, a Roosevelt or Kennedy. Solon was appointed Archon and "reconciler" in 594 B.C. Solon began by abolishing all debts of land-tenant farmers and they were resurrected as freeholders. All enslaved for debt were emancipated at once. And for good measure, he declared debt that led to confiscation of residential property or servitude to be illegal. Simple commercial credit, the owing of money, would remain. Whetted by these measures of relief, the underclass quickly set up a prodigious agitation to seize all the great estates and divide the totality of Athenian land among the adult population in equal lots. Solon would not hear of it, and the agitation for this outcome rallied the aggrieved rich and great landholders who did not enjoy being shorn of their rights of credit, in solidarity behind Solon as the defender of their birthrights. As with astute politicians in all times, Solon judged correctly the point where reforms would slake the temptation to violent revolution of those who were desperate, and where he could then be the champion of the powerful, who, though reduced in wealth, were threatened by unrestrained class war and wealth redistribution. Solon alleviated the crisis but did not remove the potential for future economic discontent. Solon strongly incentivized overseas commerce, to import wealth from elsewhere into Attica on the basis of the shrewdness of Athenian merchants and the intrepidity of its sailors, and he issued a new and lighter coinage to facilitate trade.

There were already the first discoveries of silver in Attica, and these reserves would be steadily expanded and would assist in general wealth creation. Solon also oversaw the development of a new system of weights and measures. A ruler of varied talents, he took Draco's work in hand and codified a good part of law and compiled a code that entrenched rights as well as prescribing penalties for delicts. Solon's code was widely emulated in the ancient world. His code included many practical relationships, such as the obligation of the state to pay five drachmas for anyone who would slay a wolf. Plutarch claims, though this is not entirely substantiated, that Solon codified the rules for the behavior of women in public. He is generally credited with legislating against sexual abuse of children and promoting state-owned brothels to assure reasonable outlets for heterosexual activity.

Among his other initiatives as a law-giver were the rules for admission to citizenship, which had not been standardized, and which included a fast track to citizenship for immigrants with particular skills, such as in arts and crafts. He also legislated against unemployment—to discourage the sloth of the idle rich, but more importantly, to discourage the development of a sullen unemployed mass of demagogically manipulable malcontents. Rules were devised for searching private homes for ill-gotten gains, and householders were within their rights if they killed an intruder. With time, Solon caused all Greece to value legislative precision and the establishment and defence of rights and statutory movement away from the arbitrary rule of the strongest and richest.

Solon really earned a place in the pantheon of great political leaders with his Constitution. As he swept away the past with its primitive laws and inequalities and entrenched exploitation of the poor and set Athens up for a great maritime and commercial vocation, he also installed what would become the institutions of Athenian democracy and the cornerstone of its intellectual primacy, which had barely been hinted at before Solon's time. Athens had been divided into classes: first, the Hippos, those who could afford horses and if mustered, would be cavalrymen. These were the knights. Next came the Hoplites, who would be the heavy infantry in war. These were the Zeugites. Last came the urban and rural labourers, the Thetes. The knights, according to Solon's reforms, would have to have land producing three-hundred units (one-and-one-half bushels of grain or eight-and-a-half gallons of wine or olive oil). A Zeugite's land would have to produce two-hundred units, and the Thetes had less productive land than that, if any. He also exalted specially those whose land produced five-hundred bushels (pentakosiomedimnoi).

Solon's classification of the classes according to their landed wealth was a partial move of meritocracy and democratization, as it replaced the hereditary families, shouldering off the front bench of Athenian governance a good deal of hereditary deadwood. Athens became what is called a timocracy: government by landowners with a sense of honour as the criterion for public policy. This movement to democratization was substantially strengthened by Solon's reactivation of the Ecclesia: the enfranchisement of the Thetes with a right to vote in the Assembly of the Athenian people. This Assembly was not new, but had fallen into disuse, and the prosperous classes effectively side-lined it and promoted their pecuniary interest with comparative disregard for the interests of the people of modest income. In much of Greece, and particularly Attica, the prestige of the aristocracy effectively silenced a concern for the lumpen-underachievers, gradually fomenting a pressure of popular disaffection and anger. Solon may be accurately compared to modern leaders of patrician origin who recognized that contented agrarian and working classes were both just and necessary to the health of the society and the stability of the position of the more exalted socio-economic echelons, such as Franklin D. Roosevelt, and even a Harold MacMillan or Mackenzie King. As Aristotle wrote, the poor came "to have no share in anything," unless they agitate sufficiently to be bought off by the state.[7] Solon did limit the authority of the Ecclesia, but did at least revive the ability of the lower middle and working and agrarian classes to be heard.

Solon's system continued the king as Basileus, who performed a few civil and religious functions. The Polemarch led the Athenian armed forces when the tocsin of war sounded, and the archons directed the government. There were also the stewards or treasurers of the Goddess, who oversaw the state treasury and the valuable offerings of the faithful. The holders of these positions, according to Aristotle, were chosen by lot from among the pentakosiomedimnoi (those with land that produced over five-hundred bushels a year). There is some dispute about how Solon left the election of archons perhaps by direct election from the Ecclesia, with a weighted ballot from the Hippos (knights) and Zeugites (Hoplites). Aristotle alleges that the archons were chosen from among former holders of the office, but this could not have been the whole story, or the office would have eventually become extinct.

The power of the Athenian executive had been historically limited by the Areopagus, a modified supreme court and high prosecutor, a body composed of archons and other present or former high officials, appointed for their lifetimes. This status continued for about a century after Solon, before being modified. While it was removed from current political issues, the Areopagus was replaced as an influence over the enlarged Assembly by the Council of the Four Hundred. The safeguard of the property qualifications for office proved ineffective in the face of severe demagogy and the times that fostered it, and the Council of Four Hundred was not effective in these most testing times in the century after Solon. The Areopagus proved impervious to fashion and corruption, but the legislature was more vulnerable. Where the force of Draco's laws were a reinforcement of the noble judges and

---

7   CAH, IV, p. 49 (F.E. Adcock); Aristotle, *Politics*, Everyman's Library, J.M. Dent, London, 1961, p. 111.

their primacy in Athens, Solon's code was to be administered by and for and under the gaze of all free Athenian men.

Solon also accorded the right to every citizen to claim justice for himself or others to be judged by a meeting of the citizens, known as a Heliaea. This notion of a right of appeal to the public was somewhat continued by the Roman Ius Provocationis, and by the Macedonian right of appeal to the army. Aristotle held that Solon had promoted and safeguarded democracy by three initiatives: the illegalization of loans secured by the debtor's body or its work; the right of anyone to claim redress on behalf of anyone who is believed to have been wronged; and the appeal to a jury court. These were extraordinary advances for the time, and taken as a whole, Solon's reforms were a great advance in government. Solon had intended the maintenance of the primacy of the great landowners, but the rise of the Athenian commercial class, the capitalists, and resulting improvements in the pay of those who toiled, created a much larger electorate and a more perfect democracy than the law-giver had imagined or the world had seen.

Solon was widely urged to take the power and the office of tyrant that the city would surely have proffered, but he declined: "The character which had won him power was proof against the ambition to retain it. Assailed by the hopes and the reproaches, the grievances and the ingratitude of his friends and enemies, he stood at bay like a wolf surrounded by a pack of hounds."[8] He bound his fellow citizens to maintain his laws and went into voluntary exile for ten years. It was a noble career and a noble ending. His economic and legal reforms endured because of their incontestable value. His political institutions were stretched in different directions by succeeding tyrants and demagogues. Fortunately, although there would be ups and downs, Peisistratus and Cleisthenes would build on Solon's work, as Solon had built on Draco's. Athens' neighbours illuminate the success of Athens. In Mitylene, Pittacus established a tyranny that was successful, but not replicable, while in Megara, economic strife led to a bloodthirsty state of terror followed by prolonged civil strife. Solon had set the example of disinterested withdrawl for Diocletian, Charles V, and George Washington, and Athens was about to gain the moral and commercial scepters of the Hellenic world, and an unshakeable civic immortality.

Solon had put Athens in position to play an enhanced role in Greek affairs, and the opportunity came quickly with the attempt by Thessaly to assert influence on Delphi, by aiding that city's attempt to secede from Crisa, which, according to the Delphic authorities, was trying to extract tribute from pilgrims. Sicyon and Athens both joined this movement against Crisa, and Athens sent a force led by Alcmaeon, son of Megacles (whom we last saw being exhumed and reburied outside the wall for excessive force in suppressing the attempted coup d'état of Cylon). This coalition was successful and Crisa was destroyed, and Athens was rewarded by receiving permanently one of the Ionian seats in the Congress of the Amphictyony. But Athenian government reverted to instability in the elections of archons in 590-589 B.C. and 585-584; "anarchy" was written on the lists.

In 582, an eminent hereditary nobleman, Damasias, became Archon, and apparently attempted to extend the length and powers of the office, but was overthrown

---

8 CAH, IV, p. 58 (F.E. Adcock).

after two years and two months, and ten archons were elected. Politics frayed between the party of the Plain (composed largely of big landowners and led by Lycurgus) and the party of the Coast: fishermen, sailors, and craftsmen, led by Megacles (grandson of the first bearer of that name in this narrative), who had apparently made his reappearance in Athens as the ally of the artisans and maritime population; and, as eventually developed, the Hill people, shepherds, herders, crofters, the smaller towns and farmers, led by Peisistratus.

A sign of the disorder of Athens in the post-Solonic years was that it again lost the large island of Salamis, key to sea access to Athens and to Attican maritime commerce generally, to Megara. Megara was soon herself torn politically between nobles and dissident commoners, creating an opportunity for Athens to reassert herself. The war party was led by the young general Peisistratus, who wrote fervently patriotic poems about fighting "clear of the cruel shame" (of Salamis not being Athenian). Athens considered the Megaran repossession illegal, and in that city's time of tumult, Peisistratus led a successful Athenian campaign of repossession, starting with his occupation of the Megaran port of Nisaea. Peace was reestablished by the acceptance by both sides of Spartan arbitration, which returned the island to Athens, allegedly on the Homeric evidence that Ajax, hero of Salamis, fought through the Trojan Wars in the Athenian contingent.[9] The annexation of Salamis was deemed permanent in Athens, and the island was thoroughly colonized and in places fortified. The return of Salamis seems to have occurred in 571, and the rise of Peisistratus was thereafter inexorable, as effective ruler of Athens in its phase of ascent to Hellenic leadership and historical immortality in succession to Draco and Solon. Some of those who would follow him would be even more illustrious.

The population at whose head Peisistratus placed himself was numerous and important enough to influence Athens, and the constituencies of the large landowners and the urban artisans and maritime populations had to make way for them. When Peisistratus was victorious against Megara, his and their time had come. He became an equal faction-head to Lycurgus and Megacles, but was more exalted by his youth and military prowess. Lycurgus was a talented inheritor, Megacles an accomplished political maneuverer. Peisistratus had the talents of the others and was the leading military commander of the time.

Solon could have had Peisistratus in mind when he wrote of the Athenian citizens: "With fox-like gait each one of you walks slily, but collected, all your cunning turns to folly: while you watch the subtle pall of a man's speech, you fail to see the deed that is afoot the while."[10] Peisistratus was granted a bodyguard armed with staves and, on occasion, appeared with apparent wounds and real blood on himself and some of his guard; his guard was increased, and in 560, he staged his coup d'état. (These apparent attacks were presumably staged, and presaged, future staged assassination attempts—most recently Francois Mitterand, later president of France, in 1971.) Solon had warned of it and had lived just long enough to see a tyrant in Athens, before dying at eighty-two, a very good innings for the times.

The leaders of the Plain and Coast, Lycurgus and Megacles, joined forces and

---

9   CAH, IV, p. 61 (F.E. Adcock); Homer, *Iliad*, II, 558.
10 CAH, IV, p. 62 (F.E. Adcock); fr. 8. Diehl, II, pp. 5-8.

undid the nascent tyranny, and drove Peisistratus out of the city, but after a few months, Peisistratus, whose talents ran beyond politics, poetry, and military command to low intrigue, detached Megacles and made Lycurgus the odd man out, and returned to Athens. Peisistratus even returned in a chariot with a voluptuous woman beside him dressed up as Athena and proclaimed to be Athena. Herodotus, while despising such a trumpery, asserts that it is not clear whether Megacles or Peisistratus first had this idea, but it worked, and men of sound mind and some education actually prostrated themselves before the alleged Goddess.

Somewhat more tangibly binding, it was supposed, was Peisistratus' marriage with Megacles' daughter. However, Peisistratus already had his own children and heirs and had no interest in cluttering their lives, and it soon became clear that he intended no children with his new bride. Athena and the still blushing bride were forgotten, Megacles torqued up his alliance with Lycurgus, and they managed to drive Peisistratus out of Athens again. Next to anarchy, this sort of coup-ridden factionalism, which presaged the endless putsches and juntas of modern Latin America, the Santa Anas (seven times president of Mexico), and Perons, was what Solon least wanted.

Peisistratus was not to be seen off so easily. He retired to the northern shore of the Aegean, and settled at Raecelus in the northwest Chalcidic Peninsula, and gained the support of the king of Macedonia. He moved next to Mount Pangaeus, where there were silver mines, and he extracted enough precious metal to raise a mercenary army, and connived with Athens' enemies, Thebes and the Argives, who were not well predisposed to any connection of Megacles and Cleisthenes of Sicyon (the younger Megacles' father-in-law, and not to be confused with the later Cleisthenes of Athens). Peisistratus mustered his riches and forces and strengthened his alliances and maintained and nourished malcontent factions within Athens for ten years, and finally set himself up at Eretria and intensified contact with his own hillside supporters. In 546, he landed at Marathon and was soon met by an instantly conscripted and thrown together army of defence which was untrained and not necessarily hostile to the returning adventurer. Peisistratus cleared the field, near the temple of Athena at Pallene, allowed the enemy army to flee to its homes, and reoccupied Athens. The families of anyone rumoured to be enemies were rounded up and interned at Naxos, which was ruled by a protégé.

Peisistratus now embarked on a wise and judicious dictatorship of nearly twenty years. He used his silver mines to pay for mercenaries, and especially Scythian archers, making their first appearance as special police without the cost of them oppressing the people, whose commerce and welfare he encouraged. He maintained careful diplomatic relations with all Athens' neighbours, and concentrated on building his people's commercial wealth. His foreign policy was an artistic combination of conciliation with near neighbours and rather aggressive imperialism farther away. Megacles and his son Cleisthenes schemed and plotted constantly against Peisistratus, and he always had to be on his toes to avoid their entrapments and deter their courtship of Athens' neighbours.

Peisistratus demonstrated surpassing skill in conciliating Thessaly, still the most powerful Greek state militarily, even naming one of his sons Thessalus. He had longstanding family relationships with Sparta, and managed to placate Corinth, though Thebes was always a challenge. Peisistratus maintained his position in the northern Aegean, where he had lived in exile while mining silver and plotting his return. He recaptured Sigeum, which had been seized by the Mityleneans, and installed his illegitimate son, Hegesistratus, as governor. The retention of this fall-back position would prove very astute, even though it now meant an acceptance of the Persian hegemony over Asia Minor, as that power flexed its muscles and moved steadily closer, both to the Greeks and to the world's crossroads: the Levant, Palestine, Syria, and Israel. Sigeum, apart from its utility in other ways, helped secure the Dardanelles, and the route of grain from the Pontus on the Black Sea to Greece, which was moving from grain to the more profitable production of olive oil and wine.

While Sigeum guarded the Dardanelles on the south, Miltiades, no great friend of Peisistratus, had been recruited by the Dolonci on the advice of the Delphic oracle to become their tyrant in the Chersonese on the northern shore of the Dardanelles. Miltiades built a wall across the isthmus that joins Chersonese to the mainland of Europe but was captured by the Lampsacans while Peisistratus was in exile, but Miltiades was released by the intervention of Croesus, still king of Lydia. Peisistratus set up Lygdamis as tyrant of Naxos, and he and Lygdamis assisted Polycrates to become tyrant of Samos, the large island just off Asia Minor. Peisistratus also strengthened the defenses and physical condition of the Ionian shrine at Delos, inciting much goodwill among the Ionians, and laying the groundwork for the eventual Confederation of Delos.

Apart from anything that affected his dictatorship, Peisistratus did not significantly alter the institutions of Solon's government, and he died peacefully in 527 B.C., secure in his position to the end. He was not a law-giver like Draco and Solon, or a reformer or especially thoughtful ruler like Solon, but he was a shrewd and authoritarian ruler, and an eloquent statesman who raised Athens' status very significantly among the Greek states. He deserves much credit for enabling the emergence of Athens as the immense influence it became and has exercised on the course of Western history. His time has been favorably viewed in Athenian history and his power passed uncontestedly to his sons.

It was in the time of Peisistratus that the greatest organization of the Greek states arose: the Peloponnesian League. Up to this point, Greek states had joined regional Amphictyonies, based on a temple, but the Peloponnesian League was a group of states which shared a connection to Sparta, but were not necessarily coordinated between themselves. Sparta had acquired enough land to satisfy its needs and occupy its available forces and ceased to be a threat to its neighbours, as long as they accepted the primacy of Sparta in exchange for Sparta's protection against outsiders. In 546 B.C., Sparta crushed Argos and thereafter had little to fear from its old rival, but it was concerned about a possible helot revolt.

The treaties that Sparta had with Corinth and other states were permanent, and they mutually reassured each other. This arrangement not only deterred outsiders but cut off the sullen helots from the aid of other states near enough to disturb Sparta. Sparta thus pursued a conservative foreign policy that was not at all impetuous and maintained her position as the leading state in the Peloponnessus. In adopting the policy it did, Sparta closed the gates on any broadening of the cultural or political maturity of their city. Sparta was not to be disturbed by the democratic and artistic notions of other Greek states, especially Athens, and solidified its status as a garrison state, a strictly regimented military dictatorship, excluding even the prospects of ambitious maritime commerce that so enriched the development, materially and culturally, of Athens and other states.

It was still an attractive arrangement for Sparta's immediate neighbours. Sparta did not interfere in their internal affairs and kept outside powers away, as long as these states did not entertain delusions of complete independence or provoke Sparta. The League was Delian in its general loyalties, but not uniracial or intolerant of diversity in matters that did not affect the primacy and cultural and commercial isolation of Sparta, that came through the Sixth Century still without coinage. It was a commune or kibbutz, strictly and honestly ruled, fierce and humorless, but concerned only with self-defence in all respects. The military hegemony of Sparta and the territorial integrity and administrative autonomy of the adherent states, which came to include all of the Peloponnese except Argos and Achaea, were inviolable.

Sparta is historically credited with assisting in the overthrow of tyrants in Corinth and even of Peisistratus' sons in Athens, though not by outright invasion, and it is uncertain how much credence can be safely attached to this lore. Certainly, Sparta had no particular objection to tyrants for dogmatic reasons, though it may have preferred less purposeful regimes in some of the other principal Greek states. The Spartans appeared to regard tyrants as the Holy Alliance of Russia, Prussia, Austria—and as France looked upon liberal states in the decade after Waterloo—a dangerous contagion to be repressed.

Sparta or a majority of the League states could require the activation of a military alliance governing all the states in the League, a formidable coalition. The Lacedaemonians (Sparta) enjoyed great prestige throughout Greece and adjacent areas, and Sparta could occasionally be mobilized to sortie from the territory of the League. In 524, Polycrates, tyrant of Samos, an extremely successful pirate who seized the large island and operated a flamboyant court that patronized writers and the arts, irritated the Great King of the Persians and Sparta's allies in the Aegean. Sparta led a siege of Samos, that was lifted after forty days, and was officially deemed by Sparta to be a warning rather than a failed expedition. But shortly after the withdrawal of the League forces, the Persian satrap at Sardes succeeded by bribery in inciting a revolt in Polycrates' palace guard, and Polycrates was summarily executed before his former subjects by gruesome crucifixion.[11]

Peisistratus had four sons, but only two, as the issue of his principal marriage, were considered to be legitimate: Hippias and Hipparchus. Hippias was the senior and is generally regarded by historians as a competent successor to his agile and cunning father. Of the two, Hippias was the politician and statesman, and Hipparchus was a considerable and cultured patron of the arts, and was indirectly responsible for the founding of the Athenian school of dithyrambic poetry. One of his protégés was the authority on oracles, Onacritus, who gained great renown, but was eventually discovered to have sponsored some fakes among the oracular collections he deposit-

---

11 CAH, IV, p. 75 (F.E Adcock).

ed at the Acropolis and was turfed out in disgrace by his patron. Hippias maintained the influence of Athens in the Dardanelles, sending out Miltiades, grand-nephew of the original Miltiades, when the Athenian hold on Chersonese was threatened and the nephew of the first Miltiades, Stesagoras, was ousted by the Lampsacans. The young Miltiades proved adequately successful.

As Athens gained in prosperity and prestige, and political, commercial, and cultural influence, it became more difficult to maintain the peace based on neutrality toward the surrounding states that Peisistratus had successfully pursued. Thessaly had declined somewhat in influence since its successful leadership of the Sacred War, and Thebes had arisen to contest Athens' preeminence among the Greek city states, apart from the virtual hermit city of Sparta. The Thebans came to regret the assistance they had given to Peisistratus. Sparta was an ally of two states that were commercial and maritime rivals of Athens, Corinth and Aegina, and this caused the gradual deterioration of relations between Sparta and Athens; they became, and long remained, natural rivals in Greece. In 519, Plataea, at the passes which were the hinge between Boeotia and Attica, was threatened by the rising Thebans and appealed to King Cleomenes of Sparta and his Lacaedemonian allies. Cleomenes saw that attempting to assert direct influence north of the isthmus that connected the Peloponnese to Attica could drive Thebes into the arms of Thessaly and Athens. So he urged Plataea to seek the help of Athens. Hippias agreed to assist Plataea; an attempt at mediation by Corinth was rejected by Thebes, as it found against any coercion by Thebes, and it defeated the army of the Boeotian League, which enabled Athens to snap up a useful extension to its northern frontier. This was a considerable success for Athens, but it incurred the wrath of Sparta.

To the east, The Great King of Persia was coming ever closer to the Hellene cities and colonies of Asia Minor, and Hippias tried to entice the son of the Lampsacan tyrant Aeantides, a protégé of the Persian monarch, as the husband of his daughter, Archedice, who became no longer just the daughter of a tyrant, but the wife, sister, and mother of tyrants as well. In 514, an attempted coup against Hippias and Hipparchus was staged by Harmodius and Aristogeiton, two bisexual lovers, as a result of a private feud, mainly with Hipparchus (who was also bisexual, which was not uncommon). They organized a group of assassins and plotted the murder of the brothers at the Great Panathenaic Festival. They killed Hiparchus, but the population did not rise, and Hippias' elite mercenary guard remained loyal and the coup was suppressed. Harmodius was killed in the melee, and Aristogeiton was captured and, in the inevitable denouement of ancient times, was executed but only after being gruesomely tortured.

The whole macabre episode made Hippias excessively suspicious, and he set about disarming the Athenian populace, which was resented and made Athens more vulnerable to invasion. He had only his mercenaries (who, as Machiavelli remarked two-thousand years later, could always be bought by a higher bid) and his Thessalian allies to protect Athens. Cleisthenes—the son of Megacles—saw his chance, and attempted an invasion of Attica, but it was a failure.

This did not quench the vindictive ambitions of the Alcmaeonidae, the clan of Megacles, who had prospered from rebuilding the Temple of Apollo at Delphi after it had burned down in 548 B.C. The construction was on a magnificent scale and raised considerable goodwill among the whole range of Greek states and settlements. Aristotle, in the Fourth Century B.C., promoted the legend that the Alcmaeonidae had, in the course of the reconstruction of the temple, bribed the Pythian priestess and attained the repeated advice to pilgrims that the Alcmaeonidae had to be restored to power at Athens. Historians generally disbelieve this, but it had wide currency as a result of its propagation by such a distinguished source as Aristotle. It is more probable that Spartan influence at Delphi was a more effective anti-Athenian influence. The Athenian appeasement of Persia may have been astute strategically, but at the tactical level, it enabled the Spartan king, Cleomenes, to fan resentment among the Greek states.

The Spartan king dispatched a force to "liberate" Athens from the tyrant in 511, but it was of inadequate size, and Hippias, though unable to intercept the Corinthian or Aeginan fleet that transported the invaders, deployed a thousand Thessalian cavalry and they mowed the invaders down in the country between the point of disembarkation at Phalerum and Athens. The expedition was a disaster, but given Sparta's pride and power and the determination of Cleomenes, it was, as Hippias realized, unlikely to be the last word on the issues between Sparta and Athens.

In 510, Cleomenes himself led a large Spartan army along the isthmus and on toward Athens. On this occasion, the Thessalian cavalry was repulsed by the Spartans and after a sound cuffing on the field, limped homewards, with Thessalian military prestige permanently in tatters. Hippias retreated into Athens, whose fortifications and walls he had presciently reinforced. The Spartans, according to Herodotus, were of no mind for a long siege, but as Hippias was smuggling his children out of the Acropolis and to a safer place, they were intercepted by the Spartans, and in exchange for their release and Hippias' safe passage, he departed for Sigeum, whence Peisistratus had come to found his dynasty. The rule of his house in Athens ended. It had not been undistinguished but was not of the integrity or high-mindedness of Solon, or of the greatest days of Athens that were soon to come.

4. The Greeks of Asia Minor, Egypt and Italy

Greek power and influence outside Greece itself gradually declined after the beginning of the Sixth Century B.C. The Macedonians were starting to press somewhat from the north and the Persians were pushing in relentless strength from the east. And while the Greeks opened many trading ports and colonies in Italy and Gaul and Spain, and their maritime prowess conducted them to Gibraltar ("the Gates of Hercules"), Italy was stirring spontaneously and with less Hellenic assistance than the Greeks and their admirers have claimed. The claim of Horace that "captive Greece took captive her wild conquerors" after the assertion of Roman authority in Greece, three-hundred years after the period we are now discussing, has been overdone.

From the early Fifth Century B.C., the Asian Greek city states were under some sort of hegemony; this afforded Greece a strong protective framework that successfully kept powerful foreigners at bay for several centuries. But there were no such leagues or associations as the Greek states were grouped under, among the extensive

Greek communities in Asia Minor. Our principal source for this history is Herodotus, who was born in Asia Minor, was a refugee in Samos from the Persians, and then moved to an Athenian colony in southern Italy.

During the height of Ionian civilization in Greece in the Seventh Century, Asiatic Greece's eastern neighbor was Lydia, made famous by King Croesus. Lydia's relations with the Greeks fluctuated but were largely determined by their relations with first Assyria to the east, and then the more powerful Persia steadily asserting itself, and in doing so, inviting the Lydians to contemplate the virtues of friendship with the Asiatic Greeks. Throughout the Seventh Century, the Lydians had also to deal with the unruly Cimmerians, who lived near and among them, but whom the Lydians gradually overcame and drove out.

And towards the end of that century, the Medes and Babylonians succeeded in completely defeating and subjugating the Assyrians (Chapter 3) or chasing them northwards. The Medes had only about half the extent of the Assyrians, and the Lydians skirmished with them in attempting to roll the Lydian domains out to the east in a twenty-five-year war that was only concluded when the daughter of the Lydian King Alyattes married the son of the Medean king. Alyattes then turned to the west and managed to persevere to the coast and seize and destroy the considerable Greek city of Smyrna, a much-assaulted fulcrum point of the region, which would be a hazardous bone of contention for the whole three-thousand years of an important Greek presence in Asia Minor.

Croesus followed Alyattes in 560 B.C. and renewed the war against the proximate Greek cities, which had been suspended by a truce after Alyattes was repulsed at the walls of Miletus. Croesus was more successful, and subjugated all the Greek coastal cities, but in 546, the Persians under Cyrus, despite Croesus' mollifications, overran Lydia, defeated Croesus before Sardes, his capital, and besieged him until he surrendered. There are competing and unverifiable stories of what came next, as was mentioned earlier in this chapter. Either Cyrus executed Croesus by burning him and there is a depiction of this on an exquisite contemporary ceramic vase at the Louvre. Less likely, but a persistent alternative, is that Croesus managed to sign on as a prominent confidant of the Great King, or, shorn of his legendary wealth and power, Croesus became an adviser to Cyrus, respected and comfortable.

All Lydia became a Persian satrapy, and the Greek cities were ruled with a fairly light hand by pro-Persian tyrants appointed by Cyrus. Although Cyrus and his successor, Darius, elevated Greeks to important public offices, the Greeks were, as always, proud and rebellious, which caused the Persian monarch to favour Phoenician maritime commerce to their Greek rivals. Aided by the Athenians, the Greek cities eventually rose in revolt, and were briefly independent again, but were shortly suppressed by the great Persian juggernaut. Led by the Athenians, the looming contest between Persia and the Greek states and leagues was billed, somewhat simplistically, as a contest between despotism and democracy, or mindless oriental mammon and vulgarity, and high culture. There was a tincture of truth to this, but the Greeks were neither as virtuous nor the Persians as odious as was implied.

The other regional power that managed yet another renascence was the long slumbering Egypt, which had languished, an unconquered backwater, but with its pride and much of its distinction intact, and was brought back to life by the Saite dynasty of Psammetichus I, who had become pharaoh in 663 B.C. His successor, Necho, defeated the pro-Babylonian king of Judah at Megiddo (Armageddon), where Thutmose had defeated the King of Kadish in 1479 (Chapter 2). He sent a tribute of thanksgiving to the temple of Apollo at Miletus, thus inciting a great deal of goodwill among the Greeks. When the next pharaoh, Psammetichus II, invaded Ethiopia, he invited and received substantial Greek participation, and a stone remains, from Abu Simbel, attesting to the Greek presence. For one-hundred and fifty years, Greek mercenaries were the chief buttress of the Saite dynasty, and their rapacity brought a revolt against the subsequent pharaoh, Apries (the Biblical Hophra), in 566. Yet the Greek mercenaries, wallowing in the opulence of the lower Nile, soldiered on, living liberally off their hosts to the point that Pharaoh Psammetichus III was a virtual figurehead for his Greek throne protectors. Egypt became a province of Persia, a force that now seemed unstoppable, a little like, though comparatively much more benign than Hitler's German Reich in 1940. The Greeks were somewhat replicated by Churchill's Britain, but there were no great allies on the horizon such as the United States and Soviet Union to take on the burden of counter-attack, if the initial assault on the citadel of civilization could be repulsed.

Of the Greek cities of Asia Minor, Miletus was the most important, though it vacillated constantly between strength and acute civil strife. Thrasybulus was the first outstanding leader of Miletus, who reduced the city to faction by persecuting the nobility and was in no condition to defend it against Croesus and then Darius. The next strong ruler, Histiaeus, had befriended and helped the Great King during Darius' campaigns in Scythia and Thrace, and asked the reward of the gift of the rich area of Myrcinus. This aroused Darius' suspicion, and he removed him to a luxurious exile in Persia. However, Histiaeus assisted in fomenting a Greek revolt in Asia Minor in 499, known as the Ionian Revolt, which was crushed by the Persians over the next four years. Histiaeus became a pirate in the Black Sea, but abandoned this occupation when the advance of the Persian forces made his position at Byzantium vulnerable. He joined the Greek revolt but was captured, and the Persian satrap, Artaphernes, who had encountered him before, was afraid that if he were sent back to Susa, Histiaeus would manage to talk his way back into the confidence of Darius, so he executed Histiaeus and sent his head to Darius. The Great King retained sufficient respect for his old friend that he gave a ceremonious burial to his severed head. Despite political tumult, Miletus maintained its status as a centre of commercial prosperity and of learning and science. Thales, Anaximines, and Anaximander gained lasting and widespread renown for their scientific research. Miletus developed a very profitable commerce with Sybaris, the greatest Greek city in southern Italy, but when the sybarites were invaded and defeated by the Crotonians in 510, the twinning of the cities ended.

After Miletus, the greatest of the Greek states of Asia Minor was the island of Samos. The preeminent figure in the history of that state was Polycrates. Samos and Miletus had long been rivals, and when Miletus was completely subjugated by Persia, Polycrates, who had established himself as tyrant of Samos, announced that his government was leading the Greek resistance to further westward expansion of the Persian Empire. He set up a thalassocracy, a league of the islands in the Samian archipelago, and purported to lead and enforce a blockade against Persia. This had some semblance of success while the Great King was preoccupied with other fringes of his empire, but when Cambyses had dealt with other areas and successfully invaded Egypt and announced construction of a Mediterranean fleet, Polycrates revealed himself as a complete mountebank and unilaterally proclaimed alliance with Persia and sent an expeditionary force of soldiers to collaborate in the conquest of his erstwhile Egyptian ally. Cambyses set up one of his satraps to pretend to be disaffected and to invite Polycrates' collaboration with promises of an in immense reward. The Samian tyrant took the bait, was seized on landing and brutally executed with no pretense, not so much as a sentence of accusation, of due process.

Polycrates had left a rather limited man named Maeandrius behind to mind the regime, who set out to democratize the tyranny, but soon thought better of it. As he was attempting to reverse policy, Polycrates' brother, Syloson, who had been disembarked from government by Polycrates and who had become friendly with the Persian crown prince, Darius, persuaded the Persians to assist his assumption of power. Maeandrius fled to Sparta where he passed the remainder of his days in obscurity, while Sylosan and his Persian masters committed such massacres that Samos became temporarily semi-depopulated. Herodotus is the source of most of this history and wrote that his interest in Samos was due to its remarkable achievements in building tunnels and viaducts under a mountain in a great feat of engineering and diligent labour, and in building an extensive mole to expand the harbor, and in building a magnificent temple. These were undoubtedly prodigious works, initiated by Polycrates, who despite his treachery, retains a little of the charm of the rascal, who paid the full penalty for his skullduggery.

The only mainland Greek City in Asia Minor that rivalled Miletus was Ephesus. From 600 B.C. on, this city had a series of tyrants of whom the most notable may have been Melas, son-in-law of the Lydian king, Alyattes. His son, Pindarus, alienated Lydia, now governed by Croesus. When Alyattes died, there was a contest for the throne of Lydia between Croesus and his half-Greek half-brother, Pantaleon. The Melian house in Ephesus supported Croesus' rival, while other wealthy factions in Ephesus effectively bankrolled Croesus, who, when victorious, attacked Ephesus in vengeance. Pindarus did the honourable, and in some measure the prudent thing, and retired to the Peloponnese advising his fellow citizens to place themselves under the protection of Artemis, the goddess to whom the great temple so admired by Herodotus had been raised up. Croesus accepted all this in good heart, and Ephesus flourished in the Lydian orbit, but was governed rather democratically by Arstarchus, an Athenian whom the elders of Ephesus recruited from Athens, and who was an admirer and emulator of Solon. It was like the Swedes recruiting Napoleon's Marshal Bernadotte to be their king when the throne was vacant in 1810 because he had treated Swedish prisoners kindly. Ephesus declined the sinister Persian invitation to join in the attack on Croesus and Lydia, out of loyalty, but soon had to accept the overlordship of the Great King. The city retained some autonomy, and the intellectual life was relatively vibrant, especially the rather mordant satiric poet Hipponax (who was eventually expelled by the tyrannical government of Comas and

Athenagoras) and the philosopher Heraclitus, who spent his whole life (535-475) in Ephesus. (His unflinching attachment to his city, despite his worldliness, was a little like that of Immanuel Kant to Königsberg, twenty-three centuries later.) Hipponax referred to one influential Ephesian worthy as a "mother-fucker…a crack-brain (whose birth had been bungled by) the navel-snipper" (midwife). It is little wonder that he didn't really fit in.

If the Greek world was composed of Aeoliians, Ionians, and Dorians, and we have seen most of the Ionians and Dorians, the Aeolians varied widely from the very agrarian north of Greece to the maritime-oriented inhabitants of Mitylene, on the island of Lesbos. In 600 B.C., it was one of the most sophisticated centres in all of Greece. Its most illustrious citizens, all active at this time, were the lyric poets Alcaeus and Sappho, identified with love between women although they also fancied men, including Alcaeus, and the statesman Pittacus. Alcaeus and Pittacus had led a political upheaval to depose the Mitylene tyrant, but Alcaeus favoured the return of the nobility and Pittacus, a democrat, prevailed and was entrusted with direction of a Solonic regime, and he did largely follow the same lines. He practically eliminated drunkenness as an excuse for a wrongful act, and he intervened to restrain the cost of funerals. (Then, as twenty-five hundred years later, when the same subject attracted the derogatory interest of Aldous Huxley and Jessica Mitford.)

A rivalry developed between Mitylene and the Athenian branch city of Miletus as they sparred for control of the Hellespont. Pittacus successfully led Mitylene in a war with Athens, dispatching the Athenian general in single combat. Periander, tyrant of Corinth, as has been recorded here, acted as arbitrator and Sigeum related to Mitylene until Peisistratus seized it, as has been narrated. Pittacus was accorded a ten-year mandate as tyrant but to install a Solonic moderate democracy. Alcaeus and Sappho were both banished in this period. Sappho went to Sicily (writing a harp-accompanied love poem about the ferry-captain Phaon), and Pittacus faithfully executed his mandate. Mitylene flourished and he was a much-admired figure when he retired after his allotted ten years, though he enjoys much less renown in modern times than the two poets whom he banished, and the renown of Sappho and her female disciples show that women had an opportunity for professional success and recognition in Mitylene with few parallels anywhere until modern times.

Of the Dorian settlements in southwest Asia Minor, the most distinguished was Halicarnassus, though several on Rhodes and Cos, in the Dodecanese, were also noteworthy, though the Dorians also put down settlements in Sicily. Thus, did Western Civilization, as it was slowly emerging, led by the Egyptians and Jews, and now the Greeks, spread from the Near East and Egypt, and then Greece and Asia Minor, into the Black Sea and Italy, the Western Mediterranean and Gaul, Spain, and the southern Balkans. The Cyclades, fabled islands, were too far apart and without resources, except for seafaring (and recently oil tanker-owning) men, to be coherent, and all in all, without enough mass to influence the sway of events between larger contending entities.

By 600 B.C., the Greeks, albeit without much solidarity between them, set themselves up on both sides of the Hellespont linking the Mediterranean and Black Seas. We have seen the activity at and around Chersonese and Peisostasrtus' assistance to the Dolonci, and the duplicitous but enterprising role of the two Miltiades. The problem with all the Greek initiatives in Asia Minor and its adjoining islands was that they could not be sustained or protected against the Persian king, or later, the Romans, the followers of the Prophet Mahomet, or the British and French. A prosperous Black Sea trade caused the establishment of trading posts to beyond Crimea. Byzantium, founded by Megara about 660 B.C., was the principal centre throughout, as it remains (Istanbul), nearly twenty-seven centuries later.

The Greeks also had a durable presence in Egypt. The late Pharaoh Necho led the Greeks (not many Egyptians) on the expedition which overthrew Josiah,[12] and it was from their encampment on the Nile at Daphnae that Jeremiah and his co-religionists and countrymen sought refuge from Nebuchadnezzar[13] and received it, until the Babylonian king assaulted Egypt and led the Jews away, in one of the most famous deportations in all history, to Babylon. This camp on the Nile, at Daphnae, was thus the first place and time for substantial direct intercourse between the Jews and the Greeks, two of the most influential and enduring peoples of the whole earth and all its history. Greece was more interested in the fact that at Daphnae, Greek and Egyptian history became more closely connected, and this opened the way to a vital connection between these countries and peoples. Pythagoras and Solon were both prompted to visit Egypt by this connection, and at the intellectual and commercial levels, there was a good deal of cross-pollenization between them as early as the Seventh Century B.C.

The Greeks first established what were intended to be permanent settlements about thirty miles west of the Nile Delta on the Mediterranean coast about 630 B.C. The arrival of the Greeks naturally produced some misgivings among the natives. In about 570 B.C., the Cyrenaicans invited the Greeks, wherever they might be, to come to Cyrenaica and participate in a distribution of land. Their first ruler was Battus I. The native Cyrenaican town of Barca began, after a fierce dispute between Arcesilas the Cruel (II), and his brothers. Arcesilas was murdered and a usurper's claim to the throne was only averted by the astute dowager queen, Eryxo, who arranged the succession for her son, Battus the Lame (Battus III), who had been a gentle but effective, almost constitutional monarch of Cyrenaica. Arciselas III, with the help of the ubiquitous Polycrates, always ready to stick a wrench into the most serene political landscape, became the tyrant of Cyrene. He was staying with his cousin, Alazir, king of Barca, out of mistrust of his own people and palace guard, when both kings were murdered (c. 510 B.C.). Women played an uncommonly prominent role in the development of this area, and the mother of Arcelas III, Pheretime, secured the aid of a Persian army to punish the assassins. The army of the Great King razed Barca to the ground, and the queen mother massacred or mutilated the entire ostensible leadership of the country. When Cambyses conquered Egypt, both Cyrene and Barca obediently prostrated themselves before the Great King.

Throughout the Sixth Century B.C., the greatest Greek cities in Italy were Croton and Sybaris, whose populations may have exceeded one-hundred thousand. Mediterranean currents and weather gave these cities a natural advantage, in the

---

12 CAH, IV, p. 87 (P.N. Ure).
13 Ibid., p. 107 (P.N. Ure).

gulf between the heel and toe of the foot of Italy, near the modern port of Taranto. Sybaris became one of the greatest of all Greek cities, as Italy was only twenty miles wide at that point in the upper toe of the country, and it was economic to transit goods across the narrow connection to the southwest of Italy and Sicily. These two cities had a practical monopoly over the Etruscan-Ionian trade, which had become very extensive. Sybaris staged regional games modeled on those of Olympia, almost as elaborate, and held concurrently. Croton had a higher altitude and somewhat cooler climate than Sybaris and became a centre of medical studies in the Sixth Century. Taranto, which remains today the principal base of the Italian navy, became one of the great Dorian cities in the early Greek maritime expansion and retained that status for centuries, until it was incorporated into the domains of the rising power of Rome. Farther west, Marseilless (Massilia), had been founded by the Greeks in the late Seventh Century B.C., and remains the second city and greatest seaport of France, and in all the Mediterranean is rivalled only by Genoa as a great seaport.

In all of these Greek communities outside Greece itself, in Asia Minor, North Africa, Italy and the Western Mediterranean, there were vibrant commercial and cultural activities as civilization that began in the Middle East and was joined and enriched by the successive waves of Aeolian, Ionian, and Dorian Greeks spread more widely almost every decade, propelled by the sails and oars of Greek and Phoenician sailors. Maritime activities kept the Black Sea, Levantine, Greek, and Egyptian seaport cities in steadily more ambitious and intimate contact with the ports of what are now Italy, France, and Spain. The self-defined civilized world had burst out of its tight cradle between the Mediterranean and Red Seas and was growing rapidly. Even as city states reached the apogee of their cultural and martial achievements, newer and large political structures, more closely resembling, but surpassing Egypt when it stretched from the Nile Delta to Ethiopia, were already in various states of development: Persia, Macedonia, Rome. The great development of trade, industry, and arts and crafts in the Seventh Century B.C. generated a demand for a vast expansion of the skilled labour pool, and large numbers of agrarian labourers toiling in pitiable and immemorial conditions were attracted to the cities, where they enjoyed higher incomes, more varied career prospects, a diverse society, and the pleasures and opportunities afforded by the teeming urban marketplace of activities and ideas. This was bound to change political arrangements, and the system of tyrants proved to be a transitional form of government between the more or less absolute monarchies that were the original governments of civilization, and the somewhat democratic forms that succeeded the tyrannies. On installation, tyrants had some call on popular support, even if only among more influential classes of citizens, the same echelons of society that initially conducted the democracies.

The rising demand for manual labour and skilled labour reduced the power of the landlords over the landless, and the new urban working class became the source of the power of many of the tyrants: vintage demagogues among whom were some sincere and efficient promoters of the general and common interest. The wealth of new commerce and proliferation of ready labour contributed to and was fed by a great advance in urban public works: aqueducts, bridges, harbor expansions, stadia, temples and other public buildings, and the nature of society and politics evolved together. Greek contact with Egypt and some of the Asians assisted in the growth of Greek learning, culture, and scientific research, and their commercial wealth also enticed the great Asian states to aspire to conquer and control Greece. As the world changed, it moved past the practicality of the small Greek states. As the Persians encroached on Greece from the east, the Greeks spread a new and metropolitan culture throughout Italy and into France and Spain. Imports from Greece spread from Marseilles up the Rhône and other rivers throughout most of what is now France. The subsequent and even modern world—everything that preceded the age of exploration and the colonization of the Americas and Africa—was starting to appear in skeletal outline.

In the aftermath of the expulsion of Peisistratus' heirs from Athens, the leading figure in Greece was the Spartan king, Cleomenes, who appeared earlier in this chapter. He was another of the ancient world's astonishing figures; he inherited the throne by complete accident of seniority and was universally judged less talented than the younger Doreius, he was intermittently mad, and became a conspicuous drunkard, but is generally reckoned, even by the antagonistic Herodotus, to have been a general and ruler of high intelligence and ability, although he ultimately committed suicide. He has certainly been defamed by the Athenian and pro-Athenian historians, including Herodotus, and seems to have reigned approximately from 520 to 489 B.C.

5. The Rivalry between Athens and Sparta

In the aftermath of the ouster of Hippias, Athens was contested between the Peisistratid faction, the old clans and nobles led by Isagoras, and the imperishable Alcmaeonidae, whose popularity had risen because of the role they played in forcing out Hippias and the Peisistradic faction. Their leader was the second Cleisthenes, grandson (via his mother Agariste) of Cleisthenes, tyrant of Sicyon. Cleomenes, who had, as has been described, played an important role in turfing out Hippias and his faction, assumed and wished that there would occur in Athens what generally followed other Spartan interventions to dispose of Greek tyrants: the replacement of those regimes with the ascent of the aristocratic party, which would be altogether deferential, or even subservient, to the wishes of Sparta, the grim, strict guardian and enforcer of much of Greece. Cleomenes favoured Isagoras and his followers, and for three years after the flight of Hippias, Isagoras ruled precariously. The role of citizenship had been arbitrarily altered after the overthrow of the Peisistradists, disenfranchising many of them, which enabled Isagoras to prevail narrowly over Cleisthenes. Cleisthenes was a powerful rival, and he effectively set himself at the head of all factions except the Spartan-sponsored traditionalists of Isagoras with a proposed new constitution.

Herodotus and Aristotle disagree on the sequence of these events, and it seems that probably Cleisthenes called generally for the support of Alcmaeonidae, and others, causing Isagoras to solicit on his own account and without authority to do so from all Athens, the support of Cleomenes. Isagoras proposed that Cleomenes demand the expulsion of the Alcmaeonidae because they were afoul of the curse that had been placed upon them because of their wrongful, or at least overly harsh, suppression of the conspiracy of Cylon in 632 B.C. Cleomenes supported this and appeared in person in Athens to demand the exile from Athens of seven-hundred families who were deemed the principal supporters of Cleisthenes. This was effectively demanding the excise of a large slice of the city's most distinguished people. Cleomenes and Isagoras demanded that the Council of Athens be shrunk to exclude all those not in the party of Isagoras, and the Council, in the highest Athenian tradition to be amplified yet, declined. Cleomenes and Isagoras then seized the Acropolis, but Isagoras had made himself a pawn of the Spartan king and sacrificed much of his Athenian adherents. Cleomenes had over-confidently brought with him only a small force, and when the Athenians revolted against his demands for a shrunken and obedient Council, the Spartan king consented to withdraw after only two days in the Acropolis, on the condition of a safe-conduct for himself and his entire force of two-thousand, which was granted. Isagoras slunk away with his Spartan master, but his supporters who had taken part in seizing the Acropolis were seized and publicly executed in short order. The triumphant resistance recalled Cleisthenes at once, and he returned at the head of the seven-hundred families who had just been expelled. It was 510 B.C.

Thus began Cleisthenes' benign rule of Athens, which was, effectively, a resumption of meliorist Solonic reform and prudent governance. The electorate was reorganized from clannish to geographic lines, though in a confusing manner. His motive appears to have been to weaken the power of ancient clannish authority and to admit a large number of worthy Atticans, previously excluded from the prerogatives of citizenship. His reforms thus resembled in some measure the British First Reform Act of 1832, which broadened the franchise and standardized the number of electors in the parliamentary districts. It was completely misunderstood and misrepresented by Herodotus, who had no understanding of constitutional matters, but was faithfully recreated by Aristotle. The Greek city state, including Athens, had not previously been conceived as an aggregation of citizens and others, but as a grouping of ancient clans, and Cleisthenes reorganized Athens as a political entity united by the collective interest. This had the ancillary benefit of admitting to citizenship those who did not have entirely Athenian ancestry. This liberality of admission to Athenian citizenship was only revoked fifty years later by the greatest democratic statesman of the ancient world, Pericles. Cleisthenes' reforms were designed to bury and make incapable of resuscitation the traditional divisions of the plain, the hills, and the coast. The unit of local administration was changed from the tribal naucracy to the geographic deme, whose president, an alderman or city councilor, was the demarch. It was a profound and enlightened reform that was long overdue, and greatly enhanced Athens as a standard-bearer of democracy.

Cleisthenes renovated the old Solonic Council, which had had four-hundred members, one-hundred from each of the four Ionic tribes, and refashioned it as a council of five-hundred—fifty from each of the demes, or roughly, clans. They were selected by drawing lots, and the demes conformed fairly closely to the size of the populations they represented, and no one could hold the position more than twice in their lives. The Athenian year was divided into ten periods of thirty-six days, but councilors sat for one of these periods (called prytanys) annually. As there seemed to be about thirty-thousand adult male citizens in Athens at this time, about a third of them were cycled through this council, and its proceedings were open to all. In theory, the council had an almost unlimited legislative and administrative jurisdiction. In the circumstances, it must be said that the Cleisthenean system did create a politically sophisticated and informed populace, and drew heavily on the citizenry, as opposed to an elite political class, to govern.

Another of Cleisthenes' innovations was the notion of official ostracism. Once a year, an Ostracophoria was held, in which at least six-thousand citizens had to participate for its proceedings to have any effect. At this occasion, any citizens could write (on a broken piece of pottery) the name of anyone he wished to have ostracized, and the citizen against whom most votes for ostracism was cast would be exiled for ten years. There was no confiscation of property, and when he returned, it was to the full possession of his rights. This was undoubtedly a measure designed to prevent the return of a tyranny. The partisans of the exile Hippias, son of Peisistratus, still had a large following in Athens, and this kept him at bay while opinion cooled. (Aristotle's claim that this measure was designed to get rid of the resident leader of the Peisistratid party, Hipparchus, a cousin of Hippias, appears to be inaccurate, as Hipparchus was not ostracized until 487 B.C., twenty years after the proclamation of this constitutional feature.) The last Peisostratid suspect to be accorded this treatment was the astonishingly durable and energetic Megacles, current bearer of the name and son of Peisistratus' rival and sometime ally, who was literally sent away in 486. There was no serious temptation to tyranny as Peisistratus had practiced it, after this time. Hereafter, ostracism was not so much a preventive measure against relapse into tyranny as a tool in the political bag of tricks of each party and faction. Pericles' father, Xanthippus, who had married Cleisthenes' daughter, Agariste, was ostracized in 484. It would be utilized a number of times against powerful Athenian figures whose only effective failing was not to have quite enough support as their chief opponent but was effectively in disuse during and after the time of Pericles. The unjust imposition of ostracism would, at times, reduce Athens to violent reprisals: when Cimon was ostracized in 461, his chief adversary, Ephialtes, was assassinated.

In coming years, various additional reforms were added to what Cleisthenes had facilitated. The army was reorganized into ten sections supposedly on tribal lines, and the position of archon was made subject to drawing lots rather than election. This method of filling public offices was eventually extended throughout the government, and if it seems quaint today, it is the same principle of drawing jurors, or military conscripts: in a smaller population, with women and slaves excluded, it was based on an egalitarian evaluation of the aptitudes of the people. Each section of the army had a regiment of hoplites and a cavalry squadron. The polemarch ceased to be the commander of the army and this post was given to the Strategos autokrator.

Cleisthenes had certainly installed himself as a popular and effective legitimate ruler of Athens, but he was under no illusions that he had seen the last of Cleomenes. Hippias, four years before, had defeated the small Spartan force that had been sent as a deterrent to him under Anchimolius by the Spartan king; Hippias had rebuffed it, but was shortly defeated, faced down, and thrown out of Athens by Cleomenes at the head of his main army. Cleisthenes had a good idea of what would happen next and there seems no doubt that he was prepared to ask the assistance of the Great King and invite Persia across the Aegean to intervene in favour of Athens against the Peloponnesian League if Cleomenes mobilized it. (In this, Herodotus appears to be incontestable.[14]) Cleisthenes apparently sent emissaries to the satrap at Sardes, capital of what was now the Persian province of Lydia, and formerly the capital of Croesus and the other Lydian kings. It is inconceivable that he would have imagined that the Great King would come to the aid of the mere, if distinguished, Greek city state of Athens. What ensued was a series of ironies. The Persian governor at Sardes told the emissaries of Cleisthenes that if Athens was prepared to concede "earth and water," i.e., territory and harbor rights, Persia would extend her protection but not otherwise. The emissaries took it upon themselves to accept these conditions (though it is hard to credit that they would have done so with no authority—here Herodotus may be partisan against Cleisthenes, as he was an admirer of the Megaclean Alcmaeonidae).

Cleisthenes had apparently assumed that when his emissaries returned, Cleomenes would be at the head of the Peloponnesian armies and almost at the gate of Athens. That was a reasonable supposition, but in fact, Cleomenes had devised an astute strategy of attacking Attica on three sides, but his Corinthian allies abruptly defected for reasons having nothing to do with Athens, and Cleomenes' co-king of Sparta, Demaratus, deserted Cleomenes for intra-Spartan political reasons, and Cleomenes returned to Sparta, undefeated but without giving battle at all. In these conditions, Cleisthenes apparently took his distance from emissaries he claimed had exceeded their mandates and these dutiful ambassadors were warmly excoriated by the newly democratized Cleisthenean Council. Corinth appears to have been motivated by commercial reasons and did not want to alienate Athens while it was in intense commercial conflict with Athens' perennial enemy Aegina, on the theory that the enemy of the enemy is a friend. The question is why Corinth sent its armies to the field before deciding to desert Sparta and it has never been answered.

Although the Corinthians and Spartans had withdrawn, the Thebans (Boeotians) and Chalcidians remained to be dealt with. The Athenian army followed an imaginative counter-attack plan, advancing unexpectedly and swiftly to intercept the more distant Chalcidians, defeating them, and then striking the Boeotians in the flank as they rushed to the aid of the Chalcidians, defeating them. It was a great victory, and the Athenians may have taken as many as a thousand prisoners, whom they held until they were ransomed at a handsome value, and after a considerable delay. The chains in which the prisoners were held were on permanent subsequent display at the Acropolis, where Herodotus saw them. Thebes contemplated resumption of war with Athens, and sought the alliance of Aegina, then Greece's greatest naval power, and received encouragement from the Oracle of Delphi. It's overture to Aegina was based on the mythological kinship of the Theban and Aeginan nymphs. But Aegina, in the less ethereal world, wanted no part of war with Athens and re-

---

14 CAH, IV, p. 168 (E.M. Walker).

sponded with a reference to send images of the tutelary deities of the states; not something one could transmute into an instrument of war.

Two years later, Cleomenes returned to the task and convened the Peloponnesian League at Sparta and asked for unanimity in effecting the defeat and humiliation of Athens and the reinstallation of Hippias as tyrant. This was a complete turnabout, as it was Spartan intervention that had driven Hippias out. Sparta sought the establishment of an Athenian regime subservient to Sparta, and with it, the harsh discouragement of a spirit of democracy that was offensive to Spartan pursuit of dictatorship. Beyond this was a broader issue; Athens' recent victories had crowned its pioneering democracy with great prestige and a natural following, and what was emerging was a contest between fair Athens, free and creative and spontaneously artistic in culture as in politics, and Sparta, formidable also in its sleek, disciplined austerity: the human spirit unbound against the human spirit strictly disciplined and focused. Now it was Cleomenes who was trying to operate the Peloponnesian League like the post-Waterloo Holy Alliance, intervening around Europe to suppress democracy. Once again, Cleomenes was frustrated in his ambitions, as Corinth again declined to join any such effort, as it had declined before.

Cleomenes concluded, after his alliance was again immobilized by Corinth, that he must pursue his goal in increments, and began with the project of humbling Argos, Sparta's ancient rival which it had defeated before, but which lingered yet, a threat if it joined forces with any other serious opponent. To achieve his ends, the Spartan king saw that he would have to defeat Argos itself, with no assistance from the Peloponnesian League; a win–double, if it worked—raising the status of Sparta and demonstrating the dispensability of its inconstant allies. Again, Cleomenes devised an ingenious strategy, advancing almost to Argos from one side and then retiring and approaching from another. Battle was joined a few miles from Argos, at Sepeia. It was a complete and quick Spartan victory, one of the most decisive in Greek history; the Argives suffered six-thousand dead, a very heavy toll by the standards of war in Greece. Cleomenes did not besiege or make any attempt to capture the enemy capital, though he could certainly have done so had he wished. On his return, in the always grudging and belligerent Greek manner, Cleomenes was put on trial for his throne and conceivably his life for not having captured the enemy capital. In fact, as he usually did, Cleomenes made exactly the right decisions. The Argives sued for peace, Sparta had proved her point, and all back-talk in the Peloponnesian League against her stopped. In accepting the tacit submission of the Argives without sacking their capital or massacring civilians, Cleomenes triumphed in the forum of Greek opinion, having taken all the laurels to be had on the field of battle. The Spartans thought better of convicting their king, the success of his strategy was acclaimed, and as he raised up Sparta to unchallenged supremacy in the Peloponnese, he added another large cubit to his own stature and was henceforth enabled to govern almost alone.

Hippias had returned to Sigeum but never ceased to scheme for his return to power in Athens, under any conditions and any sponsorship, from Sparta as a bulwark against the Persians, or from Persia to penetrate the European Hellenic homeland, or even just from the Athenians themselves, with whom he retained substantial

The Early Greeks from the Fifteenth to the Sixth Centuries B.C. 211

popularity. Everything goes silent in Athenian history for about a decade on both sides of the turn from the Seventh into the Sixth Century B.C. Cleisthenes, a popular, talented, and respected leader, simply vanishes. As far as anyone knows, Cleisthenes died of natural causes and has always been recognized as a signal reformer and propagator of democracy and justice.

We have arrived at the point where Persia becomes an overwhelming presence in the life of Greece, and Chapter 6 will deal with the rise of Persia and that great empire's involvement with Greece, one of the most celebrated contests in the whole history of the world, and the brilliant summit of Greek history.

PART II

THE PERSIAN EMPIRE
AND
THE GOLDEN AGE OF GREECE
550-358 B.C.

CHAPTER SIX

THE RISE OF PERSIA
AND THE INVASION OF GREECE, 550-445 B.C.

DARIUS, XERXES AND THEMISTOCLES
MARATHON AND SALAMIS

A relief stone of Darius the Great

Bust of Themistocles

1. The Persians

PERSIA SUCCEEDED ASSYRIA as the great power of the Middle East and of Western Asia. The conquests of Cyrus and Cambyses endangered and then engulfed the previous substantial power of the Medians, Babylonians, Lydians, and ultimately Egypt. Persia more or less gently absorbed the Asiatic Greeks and Phoenicians, and contemplated Greece itself, across the Aegean and the Hellespont (Greek bridge). What soon loomed was the distinct possibility of Persia establishing herself as the dominant power of southeast Europe, her tentacles stretching out across and along both shores of the Mediterranean. In the Western Mediterranean, the Greeks, well-settled in Sicily and southern Italy; the Carthaginians (initially a Phoenician colony in what is now Tunisia); and the Etruscans—the principal early occupants of central and northern Italy, were becoming rivals in the Western seas and shores as Persia eased itself up to the eastern littoral of the Mediterranean.

The Medes were the first Aryans of world historical importance, but the related Persians were the West's first world power. In the astonishingly short space of thirty years, they achieved this with a series of conquests more rapid than anything that had been seen before, and was only subsequently equaled by Alexander the Great, the Arabs in the generation following the death of Mohammed, and by Genghis Khan, Napoleon, and Hitler in the speed and extent of their conquests. The swift sequence of the Persian defeats of Astyages the Mede in 549 B.C., Croesus of Lydia in 546, the capture of Babylon in 538, and of all lower Egypt in 525 gave Persia a greater empire than anything previously achieved by anyone west of China. Unlike Alexander and the others mentioned above, the Persian Empire endured intact for over two centuries. The other great individual conquerors were either defeated or their empires disintegrated shortly after their deaths, and though the Arab Islamic empire lasted a little longer, its unity was broken in less than one-hundred and fifty years.

Persia was practically unknown until the succession of Cyrus, Cambyses, and Darius (559-487 B.C.) made it in one full lifetime the greatest empire in all non-Chinese history up to the pinnacle of Rome under Julius and Augustus Caesar and again in the Second Century A.D. Ezekiel seems to have mentioned the Persians twice, though this is not certain,[1] and they may have come from a region the Assyrians called Parsua, southwest of the Caspian Sea, and occupied the territory where they are still situated (Iran). So placed, Persia was a fertile country that produced resolute people, but was inaccessible as the centre of an empire composed of the ever-more distant conquests of its talented rulers. Cyrus began as king of Anshan, connected ethnically and otherwise to Elam and Susa, and Anshan was considered by Sennacherib to be an enemy state, allied to Elam.

The first task of Cyrus as king of Anshan was to assert himself over the other peoples of the plains of Iran, especially the Medians and Persians, and he began with the Median king Astyages (with whom Greek writers claimed he was related by marriage in some way), and in 549, he overwhelmingly defeated Astyages by suborning parts of his army and exploiting disaffection, which caused the Medians to surrender in their thousands. Astyages was captured and brought before Cyrus, who treated him civilly and contrary to the usual custom of the time, did not execute him in front of his former followers. Cyrus entered and occupied the Median capital of Ecbatana and exported its treasures to Anshan, but did not otherwise pillage the capital or disturb its population. There was some shuffling of officers and positions, but government was made more efficient and there was no reduction at all of the status of the Medes. They were no more a conquered people than were the English after the ascent to the throne of the Dutch King William III in 1687, following the so-called Glorious Revolution, in which King James II was betrayed by his own daughters. (Those who are not arch-Protestants might apply other adjectives to the change of royal house, but it was not oppressive of the average English person or family.)

Croesus, king of Lydia, was in no doubt of what the rise of Persia and its approach toward Lydia portended. He had no confidence that Cyrus would abide by the longstanding border of the River Halys, which had demarcated the Medes from the Lydians since 585. In 547, Croesus, who was not just idly rich, but an industrious

---

[1] Ezekiel 27:10.

and unscrupulous political maneuverer, as we have seen already, made alliances with Egypt, Babylonia, and the Spartans, to try to patch together some collective security against the Persian emperor. In 546, Croesus, having got mixed messages from several oracles about his possible success in taking the field preemptively against Cyrus, charged across the Halys like a fire-horse into Cappadocia and captured the city of Pteria after a considerable siege. Cyrus attempted against Lydia to replicate his feat in raising the Medes against Astyages, but Croesus ran a tighter ship, and his Ionian subjects, who were the subjects of Cyrus' solicitude, generally liked Croesus. There was nothing for it but for Cyrus to cross the Halys and give battle. He and Croesus fought a severe but even match to a draw, near Pteria, and as winter approached, Croesus fell back to his capital at Sardes, and stood down his Babylonian and Spartan allies, and saved himself the cost of expensive mercenaries, charging by the month while sitting out the winter well-bundled-up against the nasty desert winds.

Croesus bade his allies to be ready for decisive action in the early spring and settled into the luxury of his legendary opulence for the winter. The ingenious Cyrus then ignored the calendar and attacked in full strength. Croesus responded boldly and fought hard, deploying his cavalry with determination, but Cyrus rebuffed his outnumbered army, captured him, seized Sardes, and again treated the population with exemplary gentleness. It remains a matter of conjecture how Croesus ended his life. It was generally put about that he had been executed, but without excessive preliminaries and without any public embarrassment. We do not and never will know, but at least there was no public denigration of Croesus, who deserves to be remembered for more than his wealth, which was, at the least, the fruit of his ingenuity and diligence, not of rapine and gluttony. As has been mentioned in Chapter 5, he may have served as a counselor to Cyrus and died naturally.

Thus did the Great King, as the Persian ruler was now known, heave up at the shores of the Mediterranean, the avenue to the half of the known world that Cyrus did not already dominate. Still showing unprecedented moderation for an "oriental" conqueror, Cyrus agreed that Miletus could enjoy the same status as subordinate but autonomous with Persia as it had enjoyed with Lydia. With Lydia, Cyrus was absorbing a jurisdiction that had been profoundly influenced, and in places, peopled, by the Greeks. It would not be possible, even if it were desirable, to homogenize these people with the Persians and Medes at whose head Cyrus was. Cyrus respected the Greeks culturally but was coming overland to their maritime presence and was culturally somewhat repelled by their commercial avarice and materialism generally.

Sparta, which had no currency and was essentially a large and powerful and entirely independent and dominant commune, should have been inoffensive to Cyrus on commercial grounds; it did not really rally to Croesus, though it had made purposeful noises, but did suggest to Cyrus a sort of (to pluck a phrase from twenty-four centuries later) Monroe Doctrine to govern the Greek states of Asia Minor. The proposal did not reflect the correlation of forces and Cyrus declined, but he demonstrated his regard for Greek cultural and intellectual weight by leaving the Greek communities of which he became suzerain undisturbed, and by soliciting the counsel of Greek oracles. The Persian Empire was to Greece something the Western world had not seen before: a respectful adversary to which submission had its temptations: it did not disturb or affront the Greeks and relieved them not only of the dire burden of self-defence against such a powerful adversary, but of defence against anyone else, once in the orbit of the Great King.

It must be said that in a sense, Persia's time had come, not because it was Persia, but because communications, trade, exploration, had made possible larger units of government. Persia presaged larger empires than had been imagined before, spanning continents and facilitating the bazaar of cultural and commercial interchange. The Greeks were an antique political model: little states and leagues of little states, a little like the United Kingdom and British Commonwealth in 1940-1941, magnificent against an infinitely more barbarous adversary than Persia was to the Greeks, inspiring an heroic underdog resistance, but without the alliance of two emerging giants (the United States and the U.S.S.R.), who would lead the defeat of the barbaric enemy but divide the world between themselves in the aftermath of the conflict. Greece, like Churchill's Britain, would earn the military and cultural homage of all, but it operated on a scale that fell behind these new super-states. What the British would manage but the Greeks did not was an elegant, almost imperceptible transition from world Great Power to principal and much respected senior ally of the new Super-Power. This study will get to all of these cycles and patterns in their turn.

Although neither Egypt nor Babylon, though recruited as allies by Croesus, lifted a finger to help him, though they were full of encouragement as the Lydian king was overrun, captured, and died in captivity; the fact that they had been nominal allies was noted by Cyrus, who did not need much encouragement to set his sights on another potential subject state. Egypt and Babylon had not committed the presumption of Sparta by proposing a no-conflict line between parties of very uneven military strength, but nor did they comport themselves as the decrepit sitting ducks that in comparison to Persia, they were.

Cyrus paused for a few years to consolidate what he had, settle all parts of the Persian Empire down, and then, with no hint of provocation, nor any motive except superior strength, asserting himself, he attacked Babylonia in 540. Once again, there were disaffected elements among the opposition, but to an unprecedented degree. It was barely twenty years since the end of the reign of the remarkable and much-admired Nebuchadnezzar, but his successors had fragmented and alienated their inheritance, and Cyrus was endorsed as he approached by the leaders of huge factions. It is a wonder that so astute a statesman as Croesus (though he was more a clever adventurer than a statesman) could have attached any credence to alliance with such a weather-vane regime as then prevailed in Babylon.

Babylon knelt before the conqueror and assumed a submissive posture with almost no visible dissent or even displeasure. It was a nationality with no sense of legitimacy that, in fact, resented the offense to its religious beliefs of the Babylonian ruler Nabonidus (who had taken the idols out of the provincial temples and placed them in Babylon, in order to try to assure loyalty to himself, but accomplished the reverse). It was thus an extremely uneven contest, and the great Babylonian state and empire passed almost silently and without demurral under the firm but civilized domination of the Persians. Cyrus redistributed the religious statuary and iconography to their original sites, and was duly admired for that. Cyrus took over the palace of the Babylonian kings and Babylon became a co-capital of the entire Persian Empire, thus raising its status by the stratagem of crumbling before and capitulating to the invader. The Persian attack on Egypt was left for Cyrus' heir Cambyses, and Cyrus spent the last decade of his reign presiding over and still extending his vastly expanded domain. All accounts agree that he was on his northeastern frontier when he died, beating off attempted incursions from the Massagetae, a nasty tribe that occupied a sizeable plain east of the Caspian Sea.

In general, and for many centuries, the natural demographic flow was from east to west. China and India had their civilizations, cursorily described in Chapter 4, as can be detected already from the patterns described; those in the area of the central crossroads of the world, in the Middle East, were under constant pressure from the east and northeast, and for a time, from the northwest, by the antecedents of the Greeks (Aeolians, Ionians, and Dorians). The aggressive advances from the east and north were from fierce and rugged nomadic peoples, whose success largely depended, apart from their number, on the skill and originality of their assault techniques. As early as the Thirteenth Century B.C., the Hyksos successfully overran mighty and complacent Egypt with better war chariots and swarmed over the country and occupied Egypt for one-hundred and fifty years, until they had been worn down and absorbed by Egyptian decadence, at which time, they were summarily routed from their debauchery and thrown out of Egypt, bag and baggage. The bum's rush was a sumptuous departure compared to the disembarkation of the Hyksos once they had plumbed the lascivious depths of Egypt.

China and India cast off recalcitrant conquered groups or irritating neighbours, and they tended to surge toward the much-rumoured luxury and wealth of the West. This long remained the prevalent demographic current, from the east and north to the rich, balmy, and fabled crossroads of the Middle East. And from the Middle East and the Aegean, the trend was the same—to settle in the Western Mediterranean, and ultimately along and across the Western Ocean. Except for some cultural fineries, almost nothing was known in the West of the strength and maturity of the East, but the dangerous advances of powerful minority elements of Central Asia and the Far East and the sub-continent awakened the leaders of the West. After the sudden dramatic crumbling of the Assyrians and then the Babylonians, and the arrival of mighty Persia on the Aegean shore, facing Greece, the Greeks had some idea of what to expect. They were divided into states that seemed ludicrously small by the standards of the Persian Empire and the Great King, now Cambyses, but faced with such a threat, Greece united to defend their Hellenic homeland. Nothing could be done to prevent encroachment in Asia Minor and some of the nearer islands, but Persia would soon discover that Greece was not another decadent or easily intimidated oriental despotism.

Amasis, a relatively talented Egyptian king, ruled for forty-four years and died just as Persia was fetching up at the Asian gateway to Egypt. Amasis was a Hellenophile, and married a Greek wife (in addition to having married the daughter of the pharaoh whose house he deposed, Psammetichus II). Amasis also increased the number of Greek mercenaries who protected his rule and drew them in around his capital at Memphis. From this perspective, it is obvious that however prosperous and culturally accomplished Egypt was, the governance of it was unstable. No serious regime, before or since, maintained itself against serious opposition by recourse to mercenaries.

As the Persian menace loomed, under Cyrus' son and heir, Cambyses, Amasis forged alliances with Croesus (Lydia), Polycrates (Samos), and Nabonidus (Babylonia), but they weren't reliable, either personally, or in their ability to stay out of the Persian orbit, and Amasis' reliance on Greek mercenaries was not popular in Egypt, where Greek commercial acumen was resented. In the Persian conquest of Syria and assertion of suzerainty over Phoenicia, Persia effectively gave itself control of the Phoenician fleet, with which Cambyses threatened Egyptian control of Cyprus, Amasis' principal addition to the Egyptian Empire, which had afforded some security from marauding Asians. Cambyses also used this naval force to persuade Polycrates of Samos, who, as we have seen, was a scoundrel at the best of times, to turn his coat and forsake Egypt.

Phanes of Halicarnassus, the chief of the Greek mercenaries in Egypt, shortly after the death of Amasis and the succession of Psammetichus III, deserted to Cambyses with invaluable intelligence on the state of Egyptian defence. The high priest, who, in a unique Egyptian state structure, was also the grand admiral, arranged the idleness of the navy in the event of a Persian approach by sea.[2] This was all the encouragement, apart, no doubt, from a hefty bribe and dire threats from Persia for Polycrates to change sides, and Egypt's position instantly became untenable. Cambyses, at the head of the main Persian army, proceeded along the coast road from Gaza into Egypt, guided by Arabs across the desert, and met the Egyptian army at Pelusium. The Egyptians and their Greek allies put up a respectable fight but were outnumbered and less well-armed, and when their resistance finally gave way, it quickly turned into a rout.

The wreckage of the Egyptian army made a last stand at Memphis which was besieged. The Persian ambassador was murdered and Cambyses, when Memphis fell, wrought a terrible revenge, executing Psammetichus' sons and daughter and thousands of others of the nobility, before the public of the Egyptian capital. Psammetichus himself was taken in an itinerant public spectacle to Susa in chains, and according to some accounts, was allowed to live after Cambyses had his eyes put out. He tried to raise a revolt, and when this was apprehended, he managed to commit suicide by drinking poisoned bull's blood, shortly before he would certainly have been publicly executed. Cambyses undertook an expedition, according to Herodotus, of fifty-thousand people toward Cyrenaica, but they withdrew after being engulfed by a sandstorm, and he plunged into Ethiopia at the head of his troops. This was not a great success either, though he did succeed in moving the southern border of Egypt well to the south, easily exceeding the Assyrian penetration of Ethiopia a century before.

The population of Egypt again accepted the foreign yoke with the slightly majestic and stoical resignation of Nile oxen pulling a plough. Persia held Egypt in its grip for over a century, a greatly more significant incumbency than that of Esarhaddon and Ashurbanipal of Assyria, who held sway in Egypt for only a few years,

---

2 The great French Seventeenth-Century statesman, Cardinal Richelieu, was also Director of Navigation.

and of Nebuchadnezzar, who had arrived just forty years before but never really occupied any substantial part of the country.

It was thirty years before there was even a significant rebellion in Egypt, and it was put down. Cambyses was recalled to Persia in 522 because of some civil strife that constituted a threat to the throne. He died en route, allegedly from a wound of a knife or his sword, self-inflicted, but according to most accounts, accidentally. Darius succeeded him as king and continued his conciliatory policy in Egypt. Darius extended his empire west along the Mediterranean into Cyrenaica and transported the population of Barca to the opposite end of the Persian Empire, to Bactria, south and east of the Black Sea (Afghanistan). Darius, like Cambyses, took the title king of Egypt, and took an Egyptian name and purported to rule in the name of the Egyptian God Re. Darius reopened the canal that connected the Mediterranean and Red Seas, which Necho had unsuccessfully attempted a century before. Even today, the Suez Canal has no locks as the two seas are only a maximum of eight feet different in height, but it was a remarkable feat for the Sixth Century B.C. Persia took an annual tribute of seven-hundred talents from Egypt, as well as sizeable quantities of fish and grain, but they cannot have weighed heavily on the population, which was proliferating quickly.

Cambyses was recalled to Persia in 522 because the Magian, Gaumata, claimed to be Bardia, the brother of Cambyses, whom Cambyses had slain, but had withheld this fact from any publicity. It thus appeared to be an attempted coup by the king's brother, rather than a complete usurpation by a dishonest clergyman. There was disaffection around the court because of Cambyses' prolonged absence at the head of a very large army. When apprised of the gravity of this attempted seizure of his throne, which enjoyed some success in Persia itself and in Media, Cambyses began his return to Persia in some haste, in the course of which, as has been mentioned, he died. There has been speculation ever since these ancient times that Cambyses committed suicide when he learned of the proportions of Bardia's revolt, but that is unlikely. Darius, who succeeded to the throne and was a very distinguished monarch, has generally written the received history, and he was in little sympathy with Bardia.

Darius' father Hystaspes, a relative of Cyrus the Great, father of Cambyses and the real Bardia, and the powerful satrap of Bactria and Persis, was not challenged in his position by Bardia (Gaumata). The new self-proclaimed king did purport to suspend wars of expansion for three years and the taxes that they necessitated, as the financial and human cost of these wars was unpopular as was the absence from their families of scores of thousands of young men. Cyrus and Cambyses had already, at least for a time, satiated any Persian national hunger for the glory of their nation's conquest. Much less clearly popular was Gaumata's destruction of many of the Persian temples, but it is not possible to be confident whether he was affronting the religion of the Persians themselves, more or less, than he was relieving the peoples conquered by the Persians of the unpleasant presence of Persian temples whose presence they considered a sectarian imposition in the first place.

Darius generally conceded that Gaumata was adequately popular in the empire and had played his cards astutely in lining up the ruling elites behind him. But he also stated that he was enabled to govern and to be believable as king because "The people feared him for his tyranny."³ In fact, Gaumata seems to have tried, as a Mede, with some success, to have played off the conquered areas of the Empire against the misgivings of the Persians, though Gaumata falsely claimed to be a Persian. Darius arose to challenge Gaumata (Bardia), who never acknowledged publicly that he was not the scion of the Persian house at all, and even this breach with Gaumata did not provoke Gaumata to try to remove Darius' father, Hystaspes, indicating that his control was fragile, as the civil divisions opened up. Darius cut the contest short by arranging a meeting with Gaumata in which Darius was accompanied by five other prominent Persians, Intaphranes, Otanes, Gobryas, Hydarnes, Megalbyxos, and Ardumanish, and Darius stabbed Gaumata to death and announced that he was the rightful king.

The kingdom Darius had seized was seriously divided, and in danger of falling apart. All of the main sections of the Persian Empire except Persia itself were to some extent subject to revolt. None of these movements was very advanced, and Darius moved swiftly to suppress them in their infancy. Susiana and Babylon were both in open revolt, and Darius sent his army into Susiana, the cornerstone of Cyrus' empire, and seized the rebel leader, Ashina, and brought him to Darius, who personally executed him, and was becoming something of an expert at this grim practice. The uprising in Babylon was more serious, and Darius invaded the province, where an imposter claimed to be the son of Nabonidus, the last independent king of Babylon. Darius had already announced his status as king of Babylon, a state brought back to life again.

The Babylonians seemed to accept him, and Darius invaded Babylonia with most of his army, having spent two months cleaning up Media after he had slain Gaumata. Nidintu-bel (the real name of Nabonidus II) tried to prevent Darius from crossing the Tigris, but was unsuccessful, and then tried to stop the Persians from fording the Euphrates, but the experienced Persian army was larger and better trained and officered and made the crossing successfully, and Nabonidus was shortly barricaded into Babylon and besieged. He had had no opportunity to prepare the city for a siege, and was unable to resist for long. Babylon fell, and Nabonidus shared the customary penalty of being put in chains and summarily and publicly executed, though on this occasion, Darius appears to have been content to leave the mortal blow to a subordinate.

Darius remained in Babylon for a few months, while other provinces erupted. Susiana started up again, but the locals themselves put a stop to the attempted coup of Martiya, and he was personally disposed of with his fellow conspirators even before Darius, who was leaping from province to province like a famished cat, could get to the site of the uprising. Darius carried on, almost directly, to Media, where a very serious and widespread revolt had begun shortly after Darius had killed Gaumata and departed that province for Susiana. The leader of this endeavor was Fravartish, who claimed kinship with Cyaxares of the old Median royal family, which had been evicted by Cyrus. (In Persia as in the Hellenic world, these deposed royal houses never went away for long—even if they were all killed, someone would arise and claim to be the surviving legitimate claimant.) Fravartish was recognized

---

3 CAH, IV, p. 175 (G.H. Gray and M. Cary).

as legitimate by Parthia and Hyrcania, despite the fact that Darius' father, Hystaspes, was a neighbouring satrap.

At the same time as the uprising in Media, a national revolt arose in Armenia, where Darius dispatched two of his senior generals, Vaumisa and Dadarshi. With some difficulty, these men invaded and effectively occupied a substantial part of Armenia (Dadarshi was an Armenian loyal to Darius), but they waited for their final offensive to coordinate it with Darius' assault on the Median rebels. He sent another general, Hydarnes (one of the cabal, which accompanied Darius in the assassination of Gaumata), ahead of him, and he drew in skirmishing on the border of Media, and awaited the Persian king. Darius himself attacked Media in the summer of 521, and was met by Fravartish, who put up a respectable fight but was ultimately routed by the Persians and fled to eastern Media. Darius occupied the Mede capital, Ecbatana, and imposed his rule, while Fravartish was pursued and captured and brought in chains to Ecbatana, where the most elaborate form of the customary punishment was carried out: the purported descendant of Cyaxares was first mutilated and then publicly executed.

Darius' father, Hystaspes, partially settled disturbances in Parthia and Hyrcania, though Darius had to send him reinforcements. The general Dadarshi moved on to Bactria and suppressed a localized rebellion there and another claimed heir of Cyaraxes, one Citrantakhma, tried his hand at revolt in Sagartia, and received the customary reward of being mutilated and publicly beheaded at Arbela, in Assyria (again, a city to be made immortally famous by Alexander the Great two-hundred years later). Darius was holding his own, but the rebellions did not cease: the Persian nomadic tribes renounced their allegiance to Darius and proclaimed Vahyazdata of Tarava as their king; he was emulating the late Gaumata and claimed to be Bardia, son of Cyrus and brother of Cambyses, explicitly confirming that Gaumata had been a fraud. Darius despatched another of his generals, Artavardiya, to deal with this irritant, which he did, and the new Bardia and his chief colleagues were all publicly decapitated. A second Babylonian revolt occurred in 521, led by yet another claimant to be Nabonidus (although he was an Armenian named Arakha), to whose elimination Darius assigned Intaphrenes, another comrade from the murder of Gaumata. Arakha shared the fate of the other rebels.

It must be said that these repeated executions, some of them preceded by barbarous mutilations, did not seem to have much of a deterrent effect, and it is startling to see how comprehensively fragile the Persian Empire was. Once everything was settled and the forces of the empire marshalled and in hand, the monarch at the head of it all was entitled to be called the Great King; Persia was a grouping of states and peoples of a strength and wealth unprecedented in the Western world, but the internecine problems and almost incorrigibly fissiparous nature of the component parts made administration immensely more complicated than had been the previous empires over which the Persian hegemony was constructed. In Persia itself, there were still disaffected remnants of the pre-Cyrus era and of other branches of Cyrus' family. The Medes harboured factions of the Cyaxares family and other notables who resented being subordinated to Persia, and the Armenians tended to side with the Medes for the furtherance of their own autonomous claims. In Babylonia, there were still nostalgic longings for the independence of Babylonia and its reemergence, as it had already managed once, as an important sovereign power.

Egypt, Phoenicia, Syria, and Lydia were quite quiescent. The Persian Empire had arisen very quickly and exclusively on the basis of military conquest and efficient and ruthless but not culturally oppressive administration. It was a new kind of state on a new and larger scale, but it still had problems of internal homogenization and integration on the same immense scale of its diversity, aggravated by the rapid assembly of the Empire on the basis of military conquest alone, with not the slightest pretense to a civilizing mission. In this respect, the Persians were more like the Assyrians and even the Hittites, and not the Egyptians, Babylonians, Greeks, and Jews, all of whom were bearing some level of cultural or religious enlightenment with them.

Having generally shaped up the empire of Cyrus, with Cambyses' valuable addition of Egypt, Darius had to strengthen internal administration, which had been severely frayed by the two-year, province-by-province reconquest of half of what he thought he was inheriting when he slew Gaumata. Charlatan though he was, the false Bardia turned the majestic succession of the dynasty of Cyrus the Great first into a farce and then into a desperate scrimmage. Darius began, as soon as no open revolt was in progress, by dealing with two satraps whom he considered untrustworthy: Aryandes, satrap of Egypt, and Oroites, satrap of Sardes, were both deemed by the new Great King, flexing his muscles after the bracing suppression of a pandemic of insurrection, to have given him no assistance when he needed it, and so to be loyalty risks. It is impossible from this distance to adjudicate the merits of Darius' grievances, and he resolved them in his now thoroughly tried and tested manner: he went personally to Egypt in 517, accompanied by a contingent of forces, and with no pre-declared intention of anything unusual—just an introductory royal tour, Aryandes was seized and executed, though apparently by straightforward decapitation with a minimum of explanation and no preliminary torture or dismemberment.

With Oroites, it was entirely the personal skullduggery and chicanery of the satrap that had been the problem. This, it will be remembered, was the person who lured the wily and unscrupulous Polycrates to Sardes and then murdered him. When his turn came, Darius sent an assassin to dispose of Oroites and then sent Otanes (another of the loyal gang of henchmen present at Darius' murder of Gaumata) to Samos to install Syloson, Polycrates' brother, as ruler, as a Persian vassal. These political families never were gone for long, unless the chain was broken by exterminating the whole family, as Cambyses did with Psammetichus III (or, two-thousand, four-hundred and fifty years later, the Bolsheviks did with the Romanovs).

The last of these revolts that greeted Darius' self-proclamation of his kingship by right of legitimacy expressed through the murder of the interloper Gaumata was in Susiana itself, and was not one of the more challenging convulsions that required the Great King to stamp them out. Darius delegated the suppression of it and the administration of the now traditional summary public execution of the ring-leaders to subordinates, in 518, as he was already engaged in an expedition of vengeance and intimidation against the Scythians. These were another fierce and numerous nomadic people that descended from the rugged vastness of the steppes, as the Hittites,

Urarti, and Assyrians and others had and would, and struck fear and inflicted rapine on the frontiers of the great empires of the Near East, and encroached as far as they could before, if it were capable of it, the incumbent organized state repulsed them. The Scythians were habitually to the north of the Black Sea but came round the eastern end of that sea to infiltrate and assault the Persian Empire along its eastern shore. Darius wished to leave the Scythians in no doubt that his was not a regime with which they could take liberties.

The Scythian expedition of 516 was an immense undertaking, the first direct attack of Asia upon Europe, though in its scale, it had some of the early features of the modern French and German invasions of Russia, though Darius was not so impetuous as Napoleon or Hitler. It also had some of the exploratory character of Julius Caesar's excursions into Germany and Britain, though it was in greater strength. Darius employed a fleet drawn up from his Greek subjects that numbered up to three-hundred vessels, and he embarked an army of perhaps eighty-thousand. Darius commanded personally and crossed from Asia to Europe on a temporary bridge constructed across the Bosporus by the Greek engineer, Mandrocles of Samos. He pressed on through Thrace and along the northern shore of the Black Sea, crossing the Danube near its mouth and into Scythia, where no invader had ventured—the Scythians did the invading.

The intervening tribes and peoples on the Great King's route of march were astonished by the size and strength of his forces and paid him every deference. There was no raiding in the rear or tormenting of outliers or stragglers. It has never been entirely clear what Darius' motive was in launching such an immense foray early in his reign into an almost unknown area, whether he was just conducting reconnaissance in great strength, warning barbarians not to provoke him, seeking riches, especially precious metal sources, or engaging in outright exploration, or a combination of these. He crossed the Danube on another bridge built by Greek engineers and carried on to the Don and then the Volga, and then apparently turned north into the trackless vastness of the Eurasian steppes. This resembled the Bactrian Prairie where Cyrus had fought his last and not very satisfactory campaign. The Scythians would have no part of a direct battle with such a great and battle-tested army, and drove their herds away to the north and east, leaving only squalid and abandoned farm-houses and villages for the Persians to torch. The Persian pursuit, even by the advance cavalry, never came across a large body of Scythians. Thus passed the summer of 516.

Encountering nothing of interest and no organized opposition, the Great King retired in order, having got dangerously far from his empire. In his retreat, the Scythian cavalry appeared and became a serious nuisance. Conscious of the slipping calendar and the approaching weather, Darius accelerated his withdrawal. He held his army together but had to leave some supplies and even some of the more serious sick behind, to the mercies of those he had come to discipline. Darius was also disconcerted by reports that the Greeks, whom he had left behind to guard the passage over the Danube, were being incited and incentivized to disaffection by the timeless scoundrel Miltiades, tyrant of the Chersonese, to detach their ships and leave Darius to try to cross the Danube without transport and with the Scythians on his rear. The equally agile survivor, and more practical Histiaeus of Miletus, whom we also encountered earlier, reminded Miltiades that the result would be either an unholy vengeance inflicted by Darius, if he survived, or an open door to Thrace and Asia Minor for the Scythian marauders if they defeated the Persian king. Miltiades thought better of his enticements, masqueraded as the soul of solidarity with the Great King (who was not deceived), but who got his entire army intact across the Danube and out of danger.

Less reliable and perceptive Greeks had sabotaged his bridge across the Bosporus, but Darius was able to use his navy to make an orderly return to Asia, and he never set foot in Europe again. Darius assigned one of his generals, Megabazus, to scorch the earth from the Sea of Marmara along the Black Sea coastline for a hundred miles or more. Darius represented his incursion as a successful disruption and cautioning of the Scythians, and a show of strength opposite the Greeks, but it was generally recognized as strategically unsuccessful and a demonstration of the limitations of the Great King's reach. It must be said that although it was not by any normal measurement a successful operation or one that justified the deployment of such force, it was still a show of great confidence by a leader who only a couple of years before had been scrambling around his realm brutally suppressing uprisings and publicly executing a considerable swath of the Persian Empire's ostensible officialdom.

Darius next turned his restless and acquisitive attention to the East, to Gandara and Sattagydia, territories Cyrus had appended to the Persian Empire that thus extended it to the northwestern frontier of India. This province was the richest source of all for taxes and tribute to the central treasury and extended modestly beyond the headwaters of the Indus River, to the east of the present Afghanistan. The innovative extent of this immense empire so hastily assembled can be grasped from the fact that it now comprehensively extended, which is to say, the same central authority's writ ran throughout the expanse between what is now central Libya in the far west, northern Ethiopia and northern Arabia to the south, the Aegean Sea and some of its islands and the Black Sea in the northwest, Armenia and the Caucasus and the Caspian to the north, and the northwest gates of the Indian sub-continent to the east. This vast empire opened the first Suez Canal and conducted trade that connected Western Europe, east central Africa, the whole Mediterranean and Black and Caspian seas areas, to India overland and across the Indian Ocean, and even to China via ancient Eurasian trading routes. As Rome, Great Britain, Russia, and the United States would subsequently do, Persia had created a functioning jurisdiction of greater extent than had ever existed on earth, except for China, with whom the first contacts were being tentatively made at a great remove.

Cyrus was a great general, Cambyses a competent general but mediocre politician, a fatal shortcoming in these times; Gaumata was an agile politician but not a general at all and not with enough panache to make up for his incandescent illegitimacy and imposture. Darius was a brilliant politician, a very capable administrator, and a competent general. He had the confidence and judgment to make inadequate deference to him, within the original Persian Empire or on its frontiers, a capital offense, and loyalty to him a passport to place and fortune, and to impose that dual policy with such astute judgment that, instead of eliciting a successful revolt or putsch or just an assassination, as even so very great a leader as Julius Caesar did nearly five hundred years later, he hammered the constituent parts of Persia together and ruled with unwavering judgement and authority for nearly forty years.

The Persian Empire may be seen as the first attempt, other than in east or south Asia, to bring a great range of races and tribes and nationalities and religions together in an integrated, functioning jurisdiction. The hereditary principle which was the basis of the rule of the family of Cyrus within Anshan was continued. This was the house of Achaemenes. Darius restored its right, though he was a descendant of a cousin of Cyrus but secured his legitimacy by marrying a daughter of Cyrus, Atossa. Their son, Xerxes, would succeed to the throne of the Great King. Primogeniture was not the rule: Darius would have had to defer to his father, and Xerxes was the eldest son of Darius, but the oldest of Darius with the youngest daughter of Cyrus. The legitimacy of the Achaemenes was the legitimacy to select the heir within the family but to keep it in the family. The Achaemenes claimed their election to the throne was by the God of Anshan, Ahura-Mazda, but as each new race or people was added by fiat of being militarily overrun and the leading resisters submitting, or being executed, usually in public ceremonies to reinforce the roughest and most physically expressive notion of legitimate succession, the Persian king would assert that he was also the king of the new Persian province in question as the elect of that people's God. Otherwise, Persian arms would not have been successful, and the former king would not be submissive, or if not submissive, sidelined by the act of separating his head from his shoulders.

Thus, Cyrus was called to the throne of Babylon by the Babylonian God Marduk; Cambyses and Darius claimed the sponsorship of the Egyptian God Re. The Great King cumulated his titles, like the modern British monarch or the pope ("of the United Kingdom...and of the British Dominions, Realms, and Territories Beyond the Seas, Emperor of India, Defender of the Faith" etc.; and "Vicar of Christ, Rector of the World on Earth, Patriarch of the West, Primate of Italy, Bishop of Rome," etc.). In cooperative places, the royal families continued as local nobles arrayed beneath the Persian royal house, but with pride of place in the absence of the Great King, at least in protocol terms, even if the Great King's satrap exercised authority. In practice, this would depend on the reliability of the local nobles. The reliable royal vassals, as in the cities of Phoenicia, would continue to be kings, but kings subject to the "King of Kings, the Great King."

It seems pretty simple from this vantage point of the Twenty-First Century, but it was a comparatively dynamic and innovative system. It was an absolute monarchy, where there was no authority that could vary the orders of the monarch. But in practice, going back to the pre-Cyrus kings of Anshan, the local nobles were welcomed to give their opinions, and these were weighed seriously and taken into account. The king had official counselors, and there were state departments, and a mixed jurisdiction between what was determined in the capital of the empire and what was left to the provinces, even though the provinces were usually nominal kingdoms. And there were special royal commissioners sent to one of the component provinces to deal with a particular problem, if it seemed to be beyond the abilities or jurisdiction of local government. As far as is known, there were no constitutional texts that recorded all these offices and jurisdictions; it just developed pragmatically, and precedents developed.

The Persians showed an almost overpowering tolerance of the religious personnel and practices of the components of the empire. They encouraged local religious practice and heavily subsidized the construction and improvement of their temples. Both Cyrus and Darius approved the reconstruction of the Jewish Temple at Jerusalem. Under both kings, the Persian treasury paid for the magnificent resurrection of the Temple as a reduction in the tax that would normally be collected from the Jews. The Persian government even paid for the cost of sacrifices made in the temple for the life of the king. This generosity to religions within the empire was very pronounced and included an immense donation (three-hundred talents of frankincense) at the altar of the Greek Gods, and Cambyses and Darius went to extraordinary lengths to assure the prosperity of the main Egyptian houses of worship and of the priests.

The Persians themselves were substantially exempted from taxation, a privilege of being a member of the dominant people within the empire. The Persian kings built their palaces and tombs within the territory of Persia itself, on a grand scale, certainly, but not as astonishingly grandiose as the pharaohs. Cyrus decreed that his tomb, which still largely exists, be built at a palace which he called Pasargadae, after his family's name. This was the Rheims or Westminster of the Achaemenidae, although Darius and his successors built and focused on Persepolis. They could not, however, have made of any place in Anshan the administrative capital of so vast an empire as they now ruled. Susa became the capital, two-hundred miles south of Ecbatana (the Median capital, and two-hundred and twenty-five miles east of Babylon, but three-hundred miles northwest of Persepolis). The cadres of the military and the bureaucracy were fed and renewed by specialized schools that emphasized physical prowess to some degree but with nothing like the mechanical insistence on physical strength and durability of Greek schools, nor anything like the harsh discipline of Spartan schools.

The Persian Empire was divided into twenty satrapies. This method of government had been originated by Cyrus, who named about thirteen satraps, and was expanded and standardized by Darius. Satraps were generally prominent citizens of the province, of which type Darius' father, Hystaspes, was a notable example. The positions had indefinite terms, and the satraps were invited to "imitate" the Great King. They had very wide powers in civil matters and almost equally extensive in military affairs, which were essentially public order and safety and the suppression of any form of insurgency and primary response to external military threats if the satrapies were on the frontiers of the empire.

The satraps also managed the finances of the territories they governed. The central government would fix a sum each province had to remit to the Great King, and the satrap was responsible for finding and sending it. The satrapy of India had gold miners and was assessed forty-six hundred and eighty talents, the highest total of any. Charges on the provinces were also paid in kind, and these varied widely.

Three types of charges are identified:[4] land taxes, payments in kind, and tolls on the empire's road network (one of the reasons for the successful governance of so vast an empire). The payments in kind went largely to the Persian army to feed it. To the extent that Herodotus may be believed (limited but probably reliable here), Babylon paid for four months of the year for the Persian army and the rest of the satrapies in Asia paid the rest.

Apart from some border skirmishing and the great war to come with the Greeks, Persia was a peaceful empire after Darius dealt with the upstarts and secessionists in the first few years of his regime. The historically unprecedented road network served commerce as well as military security and administrative unity. Persia made cultural progress by leaps and bounds once it became an imperial power. It had been a robust but simple people, more civilized than the fierce nomadic tribes that harassed and pierced the northern borders, but primitive for a settled people. Babylonians, Egyptians, and the Greeks swiftly imparted to Persia arts and crafts it had not had, but impressed the Persian ruling class, from the Great Kings down, with the prestige, credibility, and necessity for a great people to have a vital culture. Writing was picked up from Babylon, and cuneiform was modified to Persian usage. The Persian government picked up the Aramaic language for communication with the western part of its empire. In architecture and art, rapid progress was made, initially more or less imitative of the Babylonians, but soon and steadily more original. The Persians developed more slender columns and buildings that were more graceful, if less massive, than the Babylonian. Persia's efforts in the arts were a commendable start but have not had, and were not intended to have, any permanent influence beyond Persia's borders.

Persia's principal religious figure was Zoroaster. He was not a Persian, but neither his country nor approximate date of birth are known. He seems to have lived in the Seventh Century B.C. and to have believed in a "Wise Lord" rather than gods of individual faculties, activities, or places, though he was not declared a monotheist as the Jews were. The Persian royals do not seem to have been much affected by Zoroaster and clung to a multiplicity of gods which straddled with monotheism by declaring their Persian God Ahura-Mazda, first among gods.

2. Preparations for War with Greece

The known Western world was now effectively divided between the unruly but brave and generally cultured Greeks and the more primitive peoples of southwestern Asia and the Middle East, gathered forcibly into the great unitary empire of Persia. It was of the nature of the times and places that conflict impended, a conflict that would have a great influence on the history of the whole world, and an influence that lingers yet, still disputed. Persia was, in fact, a military dictatorship, and the Great Kings—Cyrus, Cambyses, and Darius— were constantly at war, assuring order within their borders and extending those borders as far as possible. Darius, especially, had some notions of government, and the operation of so large and far-flung a state caused the spontaneous creation of some interesting cultural achievements

---

4 Ezra 4:13, 20; 7:24.

and a lively commerce, as the Persian Empire was placed entirely on top of the most prosperous trading area of the world.

What was lacking at this critical stage in Persian development was a king who would strive to build the political and cultural infrastructure of this most diverse empire, as Ramses II, Nebuchadnezzar and even Ashurbanipal and, up to a point, Solomon, had all done in their component parts of what was now the Persian Empire. The apparently irresistible urge of Darius was to expand farther; the manageable borders of the empire had been achieved at all points of the compass except northwest, and Darius had already found the Greeks "the most restless of neighbours and the most useful of subjects."[5]

Greco-Persian relations were aggravated by Greeks who had been exiled or who had fled Greece and were seduced by the prospect of returning to Greece in a Persian war chariot, or at least the baggage train of the Great King. Hippias was an example of this, the ex-tyrant of Athens and son of Peisistratus who was championed for a time by Darius' brother, Artaphernes. The antics of these exiles incited the belief in the Persian capital that Greece was more profoundly divided than it really was on the issue of a Persian presence in European Greece. The major Greek cities which had set up colonies and affiliated towns in Asia Minor were fairly resigned to the inevitable facts of the correlation of military forces on the mainland of Asia and adjacent islands. They had seen Persia snaffle up Lydia and other supposedly strong states easily and were not to go to war with the Persian giant except as a matter of self-preservation. Here again were slight parallels, at least in British perceptions, with Britain when it faced Hitler in 1940. Of course, Persia was nothing like as comparatively evil as Nazi Germany, but neither was Britain as alone as the Greeks were. In 1940, there were two other Great powers, beside Germany and Great Britain, whose dispositions would ultimately be determining, and the British had reason to hope, as came to pass, that if they could prevent the Nazis from over-running their island home, they would soon be in an invincible coalition (with the U.S.A. and U.S.S.R.). There was no way for the Greeks to prevent a Persian invasion, and no one but themselves to repel the invader.

The beginning of the epochal Greco-Persian conflict was what has been known as the Ionian Rebellion, which began in 499 B.C., from an absurd sequence of events. As has been recounted, the Greeks didn't seriously resist the fairly gentle subjugation of the Persians in Asia Minor and off-shore and thought better of sabotaging Darius' route of retreat across the Danube and out of Scythia. "Their uprising against the Persians at first sight appears like an attack upon a wolf by a sheep."[6] We have Herodotus' account of all this, and though he is at his most gossipy and unreliable, we can at least piece it all together. Aristagoras, tyrant of Miletus and another of these scoundrels who scurried between the Greeks and Persians opportunistically, was asked by fugitives from the island of Naxos to sponsor them in retaking their island, and as Aristagoras coveted Naxos himself, he argued their case opposite Darius' brother and governor of Lydia, Artaphernes (just mentioned as the champion of Hippias, and a go-to person for displaced Greeks). Aristagoras sketched

---

5 CAH, IV, p. 215 (G.H. Gray and M. Cary).
6 Ibid., p. 216.

out a very plausible strategic argument for Artaphernes of how convenient it would be for Persia to use Naxos as the stepping-off point for a capture of the Cyclades islands, giving them a strong avenue toward a landing in strength in Greece without too hazardous an amphibious journey for a sizeable army and without recourse to the lengthy overland route. It was a little like the island-hopping strategy of General Douglas MacArthur and Admiral Chester W. Nimitz in the Pacific theatre of World War II (from Guadalcanal in the Solomons two-thousand miles to the Philippines and from Midway twenty-five hundred miles to Iwo Jima and Okinawa).

Artaphernes signed on to this and successfully proposed it to his brother, Darius. Artaphernes organized in his own satrapy a fleet of two-hundred sail, twice what Aristagoras had recommended (in for a drachma, in for a talent), and a cousin of Darius and Artaphernes, Megabates, was placed in charge, with Aristagoras as deputy commander. This was where the imperial plan came unstuck. The two chiefs quarreled en route because Megabates wanted to give a proper naval flogging to a protégé of Aristagoras who had not mounted his watch properly. Aristagoras was the ground forces commander, but he protected the offending man and the Great King's brother, in vengeance, sent word to the Naxiotes of the imminent attack. Aristagoras' soldiers, deprived of surprise, were unable to break the resulting siege at Naxos after four months, and the mission returned unsuccessful. Although the king's brother was responsible for this fiasco, which was not a fillip to Persian prestige, it was, given relations, Aristagoras who feared the vengeance of Darius.

At this timely moment, Aristagoras received a message from his fellow scoundrel Histiaeus, who was comfortably detained at Darius' court but was pining for an Ionian insurrection that would acclaim him back as a liberator from the Persian yoke. He ingeniously sent Aristagoras a message, tattooed on the scalp of a slave, who was kept until his hair had grown back and made the message, an incitement to rebellion, undetectable. The slave was instructed to say to Aristagoras: "Please to shave my head." He did so, and this was all the encouragement Aristagoras needed. His friend the geographer Hecataeus warned Aristagoras and his friends that Persia was too powerful and that what they were contemplating would be a disaster. Aristagoras was chiefly concerned with saving himself, though he should have thought of that before preventing that a sailor be flogged, as was normal for such a dereliction as he had committed. (It was a humanitarian intervention entirely at odds with Aristagoras' usual cynical nature.)

In a formidable act of utterly rank opportunism, Aristagoras now declared that he had renounced his status as a tyrant in favour of Athenian democracy, an elective leadership, and that he sought the reform or overthrow of all the tyrants in Greece. Many of the tyrants whom he targeted had been in the expedition to Naxos, and had not departed Miletus, and they were all arrested and informed that they had been sacked as tyrants, enabling the egregious Aristagoras to strut and preen throughout Ionia as the agent of democracy. In his mad and desperate egotism, Aristagoras had declared war on the Great King with a particularly personal affront; the deposed tyrants were all vassals of Darius, and while their private loyalty to the Persian throne might not have been impenetrably solid, a recognition of the balance of forces in play and the rude disembarkation they had just received from the sponsor of the mission to which they had committed themselves made of them a legion of fervent supporters of the Great King. All of Ionia and the island of Lesbos were thus apparently at war with the Persian king, who could rightfully claim that the Greeks had instituted hostilities, although Athens, Sparta, Corinth, and the other Greek cities had had nothing to do with it. Neither the Persians nor, except for a few playwrights, the Greeks, were encumbered with a rollicking sense of humour, and this was, up to this point, a hilarious farce that Aristagoras was trying to present as an epochal, ground-breaking, and spontaneous triumph of human freedom of Solonic proportions that would presage 1776, 1789, and 1848. The Great King saw it differently. Of course, Aristagoras was going to do this anyway, and Histiaeus' cryptogram cannot be seen as anything more than timely and ingenious tinder to start the bonfire Aristagoras had determined to begin.

The reason for the dramatic rallying of the Ionian states to the tocsin sounded by Aristagoras had little to do with the herald of democracy himself, who was a notorious roué, but was successful because it was timely. Tyrants were long out of fashion, and Athens was showing the way to a more creative and contented society, and it was also a time of some economic distress, as the wares and manufactures of the Greek city states were superior to what came from Ionia, and the great Ionian market at Naucratis in Egypt had sharply diminished since Cambyses had taken over Egypt for the Persian empire. So these states were susceptible to such a call, and as is always the pattern, when the standard of democracy is raised, no matter how imprecisely, it tends to gain great popular acclaim. The Persians were taken by surprise and left the new democrats of Ionia undisturbed over the winter of 499-498.

The Ionians took advantage of this respite to resuscitate the Ionian Confederacy, that had lapsed, and even agreed on a common system of weights and measures. Aristagoras had a peppy and chipper group of allies, and this emboldened him to visit the Greek mainland and canvass support. The response was tepid, which was not surprising given Aristagoras' general implausibility, but if the Greek city states had rallied then and fought the Persians in Ionia and before they could set foot in Greece, it would have been much more advantageous than simply sitting idle, as the Persians, with full provocation, turned their overwhelming strength on this congeries of vulnerable enclaves and islands.

When Aristagoras got to Sparta, he allegedly tried to bribe Cleomenes, the stern and vehement Spartan king, with a bribe of fifty talents (although Sparta had no currency and recognized none). At this point, legend and Herodotus claim that Cleomenes' young daughter Gorgo (subsequently queen of Sparta) warned her father not to trust anyone who would try to bribe him, and the negotiations failed. Aristagoras had also supposedly misrepresented the proximity of Persian riches and under-estimated the size and competence of the Great King's army, though this could hardly have been unknown to the king of Sparta. Aristagoras was more successful in Athens, where there was great hostility to Persia, and Artaphernes in particular, for befriending Hippias. He received promises of support from Athens and also from Eretria, but nowhere else, but Aristagoras did show considerable tactical astuteness in opening hostilities with a surprise offensive, using Athenian and Eritrean naval contingents, they landed amphibiously in Lydia and besieged most of the capital of Sardes.

One may imagine with what lack of amusement the Great King learned that one of his satrapies was under invasion and its capital under siege, with his representative, his brother, Artaphernes, in this case, barricaded into the citadel. This deferred the anticipated attack on Miletus, but Persian reinforcements on a huge scale were proceeding in forced marches to assist the king's brother. The Ionians set off a considerable fire in Sardes, and destroyed the Lydian national sanctuary of Cybebe, rousing Lydian sentiment in support of Persia and against the Greeks. The expeditionary force was roughly handled as it withdrew, but the bold stroke at Sardes did stir up a number of other Greek states in Asia Minor and broadened the revolt that Persia had now to put down. The misfortune with the religious sanctuary of the Lydians also furnished the Athenian and Eritreans the excuse to withdraw from the mission, leaving the Ionians to face the wrath of the Great King unassisted.

But the tide was still running in favour of Aristagoras, as an Ionian fleet cruising up the coast as far as the Bosporus raised all of the states along the Mediterranean in revolt. At this point, Histiaeus offered his host Darius his mediation, as if there were substantive disagreements at the root of this essentially ethnic conflict. This is an indication of the serious military conditions that had been enflamed against the Persians, but Darius and his counsellors devised a plan that started with the invasion of Cyprus and would effect a mighty pincers attack on the disaffected region. The Greeks defeated the fleet of the Persian allies, the Phoenicians, but on land, the Persian forces that had been landed defeated the Greeks, who fell out among themselves in the midst of battle with the enemies. The Persian land campaign in Asia Minor in 497 had a more uneven result. The Persians under the aggrieved Artaphernes did quite well in the Hellespont, and a number of the smaller towns fell, but Miletus, Ephesus, Byzantium, and the other large centres, held out. But in Caria, the Persians started well and literally had the Carians on the run, when, with ineffable Greek cunning and bravery, they turned on their pursuers in a night operation and severely defeated the Persian operation, stalling the Persian offensive and giving heart to the whole Greek rebellion and resistance.

The years 496 and 495 could have been used by the Ionian rebels to strengthen their position, as it was obvious that the king of Persia would be back. Darius, who took eighty-thousand of his best troops on a wild goose chase into Scythia, was not going to tolerate with folded arms a revolt of many of his most prosperous cities. When the Persians advanced into Caria, the Milesian leaders panicked and contemplated evacuating to their islands (as if Darius did not have a fleet that could have followed and subdued them). Histiaeus had also overplayed his hand as a mediator, a service the Persians apparently sought at this point. He went to Sardes, capital of Lydia in 496, and tried to win over Artaphernes' staff with a tremendous show of reconciliation. But Artaphernes deeply resented his busybody attempts at mediation, which he saw as hardly disinterested, as he accused Histiaeus as having "stitched the shoe which Aristagoras put on,"[7] and he pounded the table and pawed the ground sufficiently vigorously to cause Histiaeus to withdraw, go through the Persian lines to Chios, and to try to revive discussions with his faction at Sardes.

---

7 Ibid., p. 225.

His rascality was so profound, he at the same time represented himself to his Chian hosts as, and as Aristagoras had accused him of being, the instigator of the Ionian revolt. We were now down to a contest between two of the ancient world's most egregious scoundrels. Histiaeus persuaded the Chians to conduct him to the insurgent headquarters at Miletus. Instead of embracing Histiaeus, who was finally forced to choose between the sides that he was alternately claiming to support, and could have been useful in fighting the Persians, they rejected him, and he had no option but to patch together a trivial third option of privateering. The Lesbians gave him a small squadron of adventurers, and with these, he interdicted Greek ships coming from the Black Sea and operated out of Byzantium. Having set out to establish himself as a liberator of the Ionian Greeks, Histiaeus was now obstructing the flow of vital food and other supplies from the Black Sea to the Ionian cities and islands in revolt. He had at least survived Aristagoras, who had taken a stand in Thrace and been massacred with almost all of his followers by the Thracians in 497 B.C. Histiaeus had no time for the instantly disintegrating and recongealing politics of Asia Minor.

The Great King took an inexplicably long time to deal with this upstart threat from a bunch of unruly and absurdly argumentative Greeks, but at length, he was ready. The Persian fleet was apparently defeated off Cyprus, and their local army was defeated in Caria and that inflicted a further delay, but in 494, the Persians prepared a new offensive. A Persian fleet was partially checked by a naval force from Lindus, on Rhodes, but the Persian fleet pressed on to Miletus, while Artaphernes promised Milesian territory to a neighbor and besieged Miletus by land. The Greeks, ever fractious, especially when they felt they had the upper hand, were divided, and only eight of the Ionian states, led by Miletus, Samos, Chios, and Lesbos, gathered to resist the Persians and assembled a fleet of perhaps four-hundred ships. The Persians, having the advantage of not being a coalition, tried to bargain and pry away some of the constituent Greek states, but at the outset, they all acquiesced in the command of Dionysius of Phocaea; but after a week of maneuver at sea, the Persians succeeded in detaching some of the participants in the combined Greek fleet, and in the ensuing action at Lade, off Miletus, the Samians were induced by Persian blandishments to defect from the line, and the Lesbians, under attack from two sides, bolted with them, and the Persians gained a great triumph. Dionysius fled with his contingent and transformed himself into a buccaneer in the Western Mediterranean; the Persians stormed Miletus from land and sea and subdued it, and also suppressed the revolt in Caria.

In 494 and 493, the Phoenicians received the surrender of the Greek insurgents in the Aegean and the Propontis (Bosporus). Miltiades, another resourceful adventurer with more lives than a cat, returned to Chersonese, while the ineffable Histiaeus returned to the Aegean, and with the support of the Lesbian fleet, regained Chios and raised the standard of Greek resistance there. He put up a commendable fight against the Phoenician allies of the Great King, but was run down and captured while foraging in Aeolis, and was handed over to the persistent Artaphernes. This much-beset but tenacious satrap, fearing that if Histiaeus could get an audience with Darius himself, he could reingratiate himself with the Great King, murdered him as if in combat. The removal of such a resourceful adventurer clarified the issues locally.

The Persians, unaccustomed to dealing, either diplomatically or in combat, with such courageous warriors and compulsive factionalists as these Greek islands and cities, engaged at first in "unwonted acts of frightfulness"[8] and transplanted much of the population of Miletus to farthest Mesopotamia, and the coastal part of Miletus was razed so severely it was never rebuilt, and the main Milesian temple at Branchidae was burned to the ground and its foundations unearthed and pulverized. The Persians gave Samos a pass because of its timely defection but conducted a manhunt through the islands for other enemies among the Greeks, who were, as always, courageous and fierce, when they were not rebellious and treacherous. Darius himself, once involved in the details of the campaign aftermath, though one who did not hesitate, as we have often seen, to execute summarily any resisters, had mercy on the Greeks, for tactical reasons as well as out of respect for the fact that ceremoniously killing them didn't necessarily persuade the survivors to be more cooperative.

Artaphernes, a vigorous survivor, ruled moderately in Lydia, and even legislated a rather generous land reform. In 492, Darius sent his son-in-law Mardonius to the Ionian and Hellespontine towns and islands and ejected all the tyrants and established democratic regimes everywhere except in Chios and Lampsacus. This policy had a remarkably conciliatory effect, and the beneficiaries of it became reliable subjects and allies of the Great King. This was, in some respects, the most brilliant administrative achievement of Darius, who must be reckoned one of the very great rulers of the ancient world.

Yet while Asiatic Greece was pacified, it declined, economically and culturally, and the constructive fermentation of its competitive, enterprising, and always vigorous societies gave way to lassitude, which only ended and became once more the vigour of olden times, when it was freed of constraint and encouraged to be the cutting edge of Hellenism by Alexander the Great, the sublime conqueror of pre-Roman times, almost two centuries later. But the sacrifice of the Ionians was not in vain. From this severe war, the European Greeks learned the necessity of unified command and control of the sea, which made them an infinitely more formidable protagonist when, at length, the Persian Empire set its sights upon European Greece as the target of its restless and far from barbarian militarism. One of the great showdowns of world history was almost at hand.

3. War between Greece and Persia - Marathon

In the spring of 493 B.C., the Persians sailed northwards from Miletus, and shore parties scooped Chios, Lesbos, and all the cities on the Ionian mainland and Hellespont, as they meekly surrendered to the Persian and Phoenician amphibious forces. They flushed Miltiades out of the Chersonese with five triremes and chased after him. He made a stand at Cardia and then fled on to Athens, where his arrival precipitated a political crisis. Athens was trying to decide whether to resist the Persians, which would have required requesting the assistance of Sparta, and that might

---

8 Ibid., p. 227.

have led to Sparta's demand for an end to Athenian democracy, but accepting the hegemony of the Great King would have been an act of more complete submission to a more powerful and foreign master than Sparta. Mardonius, the son-in-law of Darius, having distinguished himself in the Ionian actions, was the supreme Persian commander. He persevered through bad weather at sea, and a Phrygian night attack at his base camp, in which Mardonius was himself injured.

In Athens, Miltiades had impeccable credentials as an opponent of Darius, and was an authentic Athenian nobleman, and well-credentialed opponent of Cleisthenes and his democracy and his heirs. And Miltiades was in good standing with the maritime and merchant class of Athens, as Chersonese was a trading-based entity. With this backing, he ran as the anti-democratic candidate for the popularly elected office of General. This was really a referendum on whether Athens would preemptively submit to Persia or lead the resistance to Persia on the Greek mainland. If the policy of the majority would be submission to Persia, the man of the hour would be the displaced Hippias, who had sought and received Persian protection. The agrarians, the old followers of Peisistratus, were for Hippias and peace with the Persians and avoidance of anything to do with Sparta. The Patricians and the merchants stood to lose the most from Persian mastery and (like much of the British and French upper classes in the 1930s, who somewhat admired Hitler's installation of a disciplined regime) saw advantages in a Spartan alliance and would not be too upset to see a curtailment of democracy.

The merchant class was further outraged at the abandonment of the Ionians, and Miltiades was elected General. But his opponents, the Alemaeonid nobility, now cooked up a charge of having conducted a tyranny in Chersonese (which was no business of Athens if true), and sought to negate his election. This is all a bit rich, given the support the agrarians gave Peisistratus and now his son Hippias, tyrants par excellence. The goal was to disqualify his election on the ground that his performance at Chersonese showed he did not respect democratic principles. This gambit failed and Miltiades was confirmed in his election as general.

Mardonius mopped up Thrace and gathered the Macedonians back into the fold, and Persia was now not only at Athens' door by sea, but hovered just to the northeast. The Great King considered that Persian prestige and self-interest generally required that Athens be soundly punished for its insolence in supporting the Ionians. Darius and his court also wanted to administer a good thrashing to the Cyclades for their support of the Ionians, and especially to Naxos, where the trouble began. The Persians made extensive preparations and built transports to conduct a large army, and Artaphernes, son of the satrap at Sardes, and another vintage court loyalist, was entrusted with command of the expedition. The fleet had about one-hundred and forty ships. They landed first at Naxos, where the population fled from the city into the interior and the Persians severely sacked the town, and moved through the Cyclades, exacting acts of submission in exchange for light treatment, and at Delos presumably under the influence of Hippias, were particularly respectful, and made a powerful offering of incense at the temple of the Delian God. This great armada moved through the northern Cyclades requiring delegations of volunteers for the mission of humbling Athens. Artaphernes made landfall on the mainland at

Carystus, where the population refused to betray their Athenian and Eritrean allies, and the Persians successfully besieged the city and scorched the countryside until resistance could not be continued and obedience, however doubtfully, was pledged.

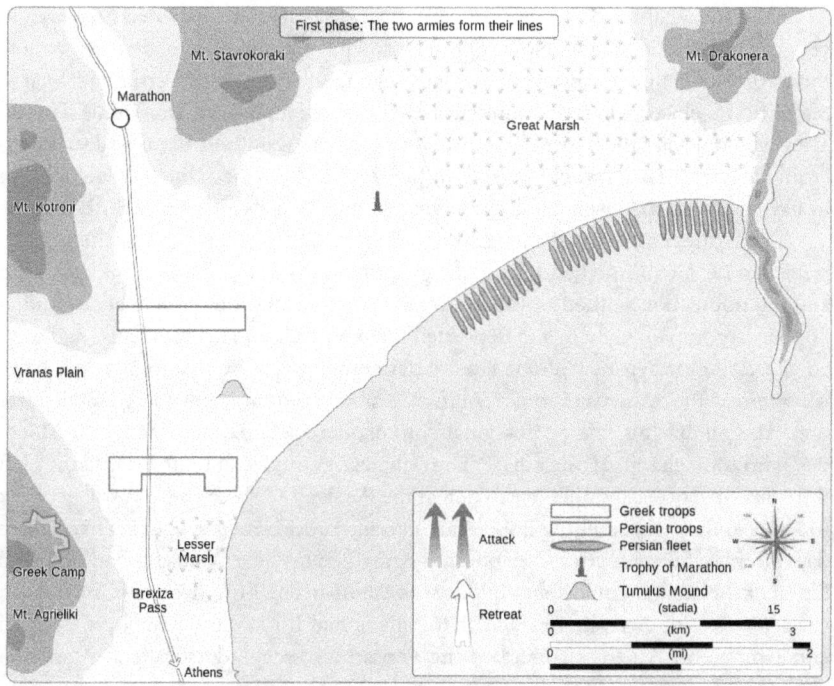

Battle of Marathon- the two armies form their lines.

Artaphernes moved on to Eritrea, which could only muster three-thousand hoplites and six-hundred cavalry and called for aid, pledging to resist to the end. Athens promised assistance, but produced none, and an endless dispute has arisen, involving the historians Herodotus and Thucydides as well. Athens voted to help Eritrea but seems to have awaited the assurance of Spartan assistance, and Sparta delayed because of religious prohibitions of departing the city for battle in a period of the full moon. It is elsewhere suggested that Athens offered her Chalcidian settlers, three- to four-thousand able-bodied men nearby as reinforcements, though there is no evidence that they participated, and it has been suggested that over the longer term, the Athenian merchant class was quite content to have Eritrea and Naxos razed to the ground and commercially eliminated. Herodotus is more unreliable than usual on this point, in his labored apologia for the Athenian non-appearance. Athenian forces did march out ostensibly to the aid of Eritrea, led by the Polemarch Callimachus. The march to Eritrea was rerouted on news of a Persian army advancing from the south to strike the Athenian force on the flank or rear. What ensued was one of the most famous battles in the history of the world, at Marathon.

The two armies faced each other for eight days while the rest of the disembarked Persian force subdued Eritrea, and the Athenians waited for the Spartans. The Persians had their backs to the sea, from whence they could be supplied, and the Athenians were on slightly higher ground facing them, with the main road leading south to Athens on the Persian left and the Athenian right. The Persian plan was to sit tight until Artaphernes had smashed Eritrea, at which time he could go by sea to very near Athens, which would not have an adequate army of defenders, and where the parties of Hippias and Miltiades, advocating alliances with Persia and Sparta, respectively, closely divided opinion, and the presence of an irresistible Persian army would decide the issue. If the Athenian army at Marathon attempted to counter-march, the Persians would strike it in the rear. At Marathon, the Athenians seem to have had ten- or eleven-thousand men, and the Persians about fifteen-thousand.

The Eritreans mounted a tenacious and brave defence, but two treacherous citizens had been suborned and opened a gate to the Persians. The city was destroyed and the population herded onto transports for deportation to Asia. The scoundrel Hippias accompanied them and deposited them on an island, to be fetched and driven like cattle to their new abode later. Artaphernes was now free to attack Athens. This forced the Athenians to act. Miltiades favoured attack, but the generals were divided, Callimachus, the professional commander (polemarch), sided with Miltiades, who took charge of the attack. The Athenians could wait until Artaphernes left the ruins of Eritrea and then try to defeat the Persians at Marathon and still get back to Athens; they waited in the hope that Spartan reinforcements would arrive. Three days after the fall of Eritrea, Artaphernes embarked his men. Miltiades had prepared his tactical plan and could wait no longer for reinforcements. Given that the Persian cavalry was with Artaphernes and that Athens had no cavalry, Artaphernes could either move on Athens or increase the Persian advantage drastically at Marathon and try to destroy the Athenian army there before the Spartans arrived, if they were coming. The Battle of Marathon was initiated by the Athenians on September 21, 491 B.C.

The plain of Marathon was about a mile square; the Athenian army came forward from its encampment and deployed to the left and right to face the Persians. The Athenian infantry were superbly trained and were thought by their commanders to have some advantage over the more polyglot Persian infantry, but Miltiades justly feared the Persian archers, whose fire could be withering if the Athenian army could not come to grips with their enemy quickly enough. Because the Athenians had to stretch their forces out to ensure there was no space to be outflanked, and both armies rested on the north on a small river and on the south by a marsh, this left the Athenian centre thin-just four soldiers deep, where both flanks were eight men deep. Miltiades made a virtue of this thin centre. The whole Athenian army advanced on the double through the heavy shower of archery and joined battle all along the line. As Miltiades and Callimachus had foreseen, the Athenian centre gave way, but the soldiers backed onto the flanks of the Greek right and left rather than retiring backwards, the Persians poured into the gap, and the Athenians overwhelmed the Persian flanks and closed behind the Persians, driving some into the sea and chasing others inland. The Athenians slaughtered many and advanced into the water to try to seize the Persian ships and burn them. The Persian commander, Datis, got his main force back to the sea and embarked most of them but suffered a heavy defeat. The Athenians only managed to get seven of the Persian ships, but they killed sixty-four hundred Persians to fewer than two-hundred Athenian dead, but the brave Polemarch, Callimachus, and the brother of the dramatist Aeschylus, Cynegirus, were among them. (Cynegirus was killed trying to board a Persian ship—his hand was severed by an axe as he tried to grapple his way aboard.)

Artaphernes had elected to come to Marathon before Athens, and his advance ships approached as Datis' vessels began to withdraw. The whole battle began at about 8 a.m. and was over by noon, and the entire Persian squadron, both Artaphernes' force and Datis' seriously mauled army, headed for Athens to try to reach there before the Athenian army could make the march back after its hard morning of mortal combat. Both the Persian fleet and the Athenian army reached Athens the next day. The victory at Marathon had silenced the patrician and agrarian enemies of Miltiades, and Artaphernes recognized that it would be impossible to attack Athens in these conditions. For good measure, the Spartan vanguard arrived in Attica, three-thousand impressive warriors only a few hours from Athens.

The Persians withdrew, the Eritreans were picked up off their island drop-off (Aeglea), and Darius resettled them near Susa, where they long remained, a Greek-speaking community in Iran. The Persians should not have divided their army and should not have bothered with Eritrea until they had dealt with Athens. The transmutation of Marathon into a long-distance run is due to the heroics of the courier Philippides, who was dispatched to Sparta to seek assistance and made the journey of one-hundred and fifty miles, much of it in hilly country, in forty-eight hours. Marathon did not end the war—it assured that the forces of the Great King would be back in greater strength, but it electrified much of Greece and emboldened the Hellenic world to resist Persian hegemony. There was naturally much legend, imputations of divine protection, and the general narrative that Marathon was a sacred place "Where sons of Athenians laid the resplendent foundation of freedom."[9]

Miltiades, the surviving hero of Marathon, led an expedition of seventy vessels against the island of Paros, which is adjacent to Naxos. The plan was to build an outer ring of defence in the Cyclades and start by building on the outrage of Naxos at having been thoroughly sacked by the Persians on their way to Marathon. The Parians put up such a stout resistance that Miltiades, who was wounded, abandoned the siege after twenty-six days and returned to Athens. His enemies, his great and immense services notwithstanding, put him on trial for his life, although gangrene had afflicted his wound. He was convicted of campaign errors in the Parian operation, but only fined fifty talents, which was paid by his son, as Miltiades died soon after the trial, at the end of 491. This revealed one of the unattractive aspects of the Greek nature; even those who had rendered immense service to the state and people of Athens were apt to be overthrown, tried, exiled, or even executed regardless of past service and sometimes after a very defective judicial process. The Greeks were often envious and always argumentative and fickle, less attractive qualities to go with their great courage and intellectual curiosity.

An informal war, known as the "Unheralded War," took place between Athens

---

9 Ibid., p. 252 (E.M. Walker).

and Thebes' ally, Aegina, that was conducted by skirmishing only and antedated the first Persian War. It was only resumed about thirty years after Marathon, but the poor relations between the two states complicated questions of Hellenic unity while the Persian threat overhung all Greece. When Darius sent heralds to the various Greek states demanding earth and water as indicative of a desire to keep peace with Persia and avoid an anti-Persian coalition, Aegina submitted, with the excuse that it lived entirely on its commerce with the east and that Persia could therefore reduce Aegina to starvation without any direct act of war. Doubtless Aegina's haste to submit to Persian domination was accelerated by its desire not to make common cause with Athens.

This was a splendid diplomatic breakthrough for Persia, to crack Greek solidarity, and Athens responded by asking Sparta to exercise its role of leader of the Peloponnesian League to be the guardian of the Panhellenic interest: to support Athens and compel Aegina to do so also. Cleomenes had indeed gained such an eminent place for Sparta by the crushing defeat of Argos at Sepeia in their Peloponnesian showdown in 494 described above. More surprising than the appeal is the fact that Cleomenes, showing again his statesmanlike talents, rose above the rivalry between Athens and Sparta, and above Sparta's solidarity with Aegina as a Dorian oligarchy and Peloponnesian ally that had lent its fleet to Sparta in the Argive War, to embrace the higher interest of all Greece. This was complicated, as Cleomenes went to Aegina and demanded that it end its feuding with Athens and rescind its promised submission to Persia. Cleomenes' fellow king of Sparta, though junior to him, Demaratus, with whom he had disagreed before, advised the Aeginans in dispute that Cleomenes had the authority to make his request to desist, which required Cleomenes to return to Sparta unsuccessful. He now exploited the rumour that Demaratus was of illegitimate birth and therefore ineligible to be king. This issue was submitted to the Delphic Oracle, which found for Cleomenes; Demaratus was deposed and replaced by Cleomenes' acolyte, Leotychidas; Cleomenes returned to Aegina fully empowered and arrested ten members of its oligarchical government, such was Sparta's authority, and deposited them with the Athenians to ensure Aeginan obedience to the will of Sparta and Athens.

These being Greeks, this was not the end of it. Demaratus fled to Persia where he was warmly received by Darius, who gave him extensive estates in the Troad (near where Troy had been), and they remained with his family until Roman times. But Demaratus' partisans in Sparta had Cleomenes formally reproached for inducing the Delphic oracle corruptly to find against Demaratus. This charge was judged to have merit, the Delphic official who had been Cleomenes' agent, and the priestess herself, Perialla, were sacked and Cleomenes removed, first to Thessaly and then he tried to return to Sparta. Sparta welcomed him back, but at this point, Cleomenes became somewhat deranged, and while in the care of relatives, he committed suicide with a knife. He had been a wise and astute ruler. But he was also violent and unscrupulous. Spartans were always fierce, but Cleomenes was an over-achiever.

These events swung Sparta and Aegina back into line with Persia. Leotychidas was now the king, but the Spartans reversed his policy, and he was sent on behalf of Sparta and Aegina to deal with the Athenians. The Aeginitans managed to intercept an Athenian ship carrying dignitaries to a nearby festival and seized the passengers as hostages to trade for their hostages that Cleomenes had taken and entrusted to the Athenians. Aegina, an island, had a superior navy to Athens, so the only methods available to Athens were diplomatic, and Athens negotiated with the democratic opposition leader in Aegina, Nicodromus, whom they would assist to stage an uprising. In fact, Aegina was not remotely fertile ground for democracy, as there was a merchant ruling class, and a vast proportion of the population that were actually or effectively slaves. The Athenian-sponsored uprising was put down by the Aeginitans without great difficulty, though Nicodromus and some of his followers escaped and launched a guerrilla movement from nearby. The Athenian fleet, reinforced by twenty Corinthian vessels (seventy ships altogether), arrived, and the Aeginitans put to sea and directly into battle. The engagement was effectively drawn, but after a few weeks, in a match-up, the Aeginitans soundly defeated the Athenians and captured four of their ships with their crews. This was naturally not an acceptable outcome for Athens, so the war had to go on. This was an absurd state of affairs, as Greece prepared to be assaulted by the Great King, who threatened the independence of all the Greeks—Aeolian, Ionian, and Dorian.

Finally, in 482 B.C., Themistocles persuaded the assembly; instead of distributing the profit the state treasury had raised from the silver mines at Laurium, they agreed to build a new fleet of two-hundred modern triremes. The main motivation for this great construction program, somewhat presaging what occurred in Britain and Germany before World War I and in Japan and the United States before World War II, was not to humble Aegina, but to lead the defence against mighty Persia. The political condition of Athens at the approach of the supreme test with Persia was chiefly divided between four parties: the aristocratic party under Miltiades, the radical party under Themistocles, the Alcmaeonidae under Aristides and Xanthippus, and the exiles and their partisans, led by Hippias, leader of the Peisistratic party. In foreign policy, Miltiades and Themistocles worked together. Themistocles must have supported Miltiades in the Parian operation, and the firing and then death of Miltiades would have put his faction largely in the hands of Themistocles, but his rival Aristides was elected to the archonship in 489. Aristides had been a close comrade of Cleisthenes, and he retained the effective headship of the Alcmaeonid Party. Themistocles fought a relentless and ingenious war of intrigue and maneuver to regain the preeminent position in the Athenian state. In 487 and 486, he secured the ostracism of Hipparchus and Megacles (the latter being generally credited with the signal that diverted the Persian army toward Athens and away from the tired Athenians at Marathon). Themistocles was working with great assiduity, and he managed to force the exile of Xanthippus in 484 and of Aristides in 482. He was turfing out his rivals (like, but not as lethally, as Stalin removed from the post-Lenin Soviet Politburo, first Trotsky, then Kamenev and Zinoviev, and then Rykov, Tomsky, and Bukharin—all of them executed except Trotsky, who was banished, then assassinated).

While he was achieving this, Themistocles also remodeled the constitution in 487-486 to permit one-man rule and assumed that status himself. Drawing lots replaced elections in choosing the archons in 486. In an astounding triumph of the fluid Athenian system, Themistocles also secured the creation of the office of commander-in-chief, strategos autokrator, and his election to fill that post in 480. And in that same year, he secured from the assembly the construction of the ultra-modern two-hundred-trireme fleet. In anticipation of the approach in great strength of the Great King, Themistocles had repositioned Athens from a land to a sea power, equipped it, banished his opponents, created the position of, in effect, military dictator, and secured the position for himself. Other times and nations have found the man for the crisis: Lincoln, Roosevelt, Churchill, de Gaulle, but not the removal of rivals, relaunch of the system, creation of the supreme office, redirection of the country altogether between being a land and a sea power, and then the assumption of supreme civil and military authority himself. Themistocles' political achievement was profoundly historic, before his exercise of the office he created to conduct the defence he planned, and vastly transcended the political machinations that made the Hellenic deliverance possible.

4. The Death of Darius and the Persian Invasion of Attica

The political agility and strategic genius were not the only good fortune that Greece and particularly Athens enjoyed in the decade after Marathon. Darius took the matter in hand with his great thoroughness and talent at military organization on a grand scale, aiming at the suppression and occupation of all of Greece, under no delusions that the Greeks would roll over as easily as the Egyptians or Babylonians. But in 486, uncharacteristically, Egypt rose in revolt, and then, later in the same year, Darius died, of natural causes (he who had summarily executed so many rivals), after a formidable and very successful reign of thirty-six years. He remains yet one of the great monarchs of world history. Darius' son, Xerxes, succeeded as Great King and such had been the authority of Darius, there was no instability at all, at first. It was not in the slightest reminiscent of the frightful fissures and serial revolts that erupted as Darius was trying to squash opposition following the death of Cambyses, and deal with the carnival imposture of Gaumata (Bardia). However, the Egyptian uprising (and even the Babylonians became a bit restless and needed to be put firmly in their place) took Xerxes several years to deal with and to complete the preparations his father had put in hand to settle affairs with the Hellene states. The Greeks, always aggressive and rather cocky, took the unexpected delay in the return of Persia to be a sign of weakness.

Xerxes approached by land. He marched through Cappadocia (Anatolia, today Asian Turkey) and crossed the Hellespont by bridge systems designed and constructed by an engineering corps led by the Greek Harpalus. The main rivers of Thrace were also crossed by pontoon bridges. A canal was even built at one point in Thrace to facilitate the movement of the Persian navy. The whole expedition was a remarkable feat of logistics, as extremely ambitious, even if ultimately unsuccessful invasions (such as Napoleon's and Hitler's of Russia), often are. The highway constructed in Thrace for this route of march continued in operation for generations and was by far the best and straightest road in the entire region for centuries.

The local inhabitants were awe-struck by the scale of preparations and the size of the Persian army, with all its baggage trains. Huge stores of grain and other foodstuffs and drink were created at intervals. When the vanguard of the army reached the frontier of the Persian Empire near the demarcation between Macedonia and Greece, a third of it was sent forward to clear forests and extend "the King's way." "Xerxes with titanic might ignored the divinely ordered constitution of the world; his army marched across the sea, and his navy sailed through the dry land."[10]

The Great King spent the winter of 481-480 B.C. at Sardes, the Lydian capital, and sent emissaries to invite the states of Greece except Athens and Sparta and their closest allies, with whom he assumed he was already at war, to recognize his sovereignty and provide food for his passage. Over three-hundred boats were required to make the bridges at each river crossing, and they then resumed their status as transport vessels. The king only came with the military units from the eastern provinces; the rest arrived by sea and formed a gigantic force: one-hundred and eighty thousand combatants in the expeditionary corps, with another one-hundred and eighty thousand support troops, and probably two-hundred thousand or more civilians in various occupations, and approximately seven-hundred and thirty ships.

The Greeks had not been idle while the numberless hordes of the Great King approached. (The Persian Army was composed of forty-six different peoples.) A League was formed under the presidency of Sparta. Intense and generally successful efforts were expended to patch up any disputes between Greeks; Athens and Aegina were reconciled, and it was agreed that anyone who joined the Persians would suffer confiscation of property and one tenth of the spoils would be donated to Delphi. The northwest was thinly represented, and Argos abstained, still smarting from the whipping it had received from Sparta. The Persian armies were now on the borders of Thessaly, so the adherence of Boeotians and Thessalians was a great benefit to the Greeks, denying as it did, a straight pass-through for the Persians to the Peloponnese and Attica. Crete abstained, the Cyclades was lukewarm, and Syracuse, which was then perhaps the greatest Hellenic power in the world, was heavily engaged with the Carthaginians and could not spare any attention to Greece. (The westward spread of Greek and Phoenician influence in the Mediterranean would bear prodigious fruit in the immediately following centuries.) Spies were sent to report on Persian preparations, but they were apprehended. Xerxes treated them gently and allowed them to see much of the vast extent of Persian preparations and to go home and tell those who sent them how gigantic were the forces of the Great King.

Though command on land and sea was entrusted to the Spartans, Themistocles personally had more influence than anyone on strategic planning. The entire League, committing all the manpower it had, could not muster a force more than half the size of the Persian army that was about to be upon them. But that army was too large to be sent by sea, and would have to come overland, apart from possible diversionary or supportive amphibious attacks. Since the Greeks were not numerous enough to meet the Persian army head on, they would have to hold the passes through the rocky north of the country in great strength and try to keep the invader back at the bottle-necks. Some of these, particularly the pass at Thermopylae and the Isthmus of Corinth could be turned by sea; and on the water, the Greeks could put up a more even contest, but they were still outnumbered. Abandoning all Greece

---

10 Ibid., p. 269 (J.A.R. Munro).

except the Peloponnese was not a viable strategy, as it would have meant asking more than half the League, including Athens, to sacrifice themselves for the safety of Sparta and its immediate allies. The calculation was made that the Persian fleet must be divided and defeated in stages, to prevent it from forcing the way of the great Persian army into the Peloponnese, and to do this before the Persian army had advanced far into northern Greece, thus, to hold the whole League in line and in support of the strategy. Anything that contemplated taking the full weight of the Persian force at one show-down, on land or sea, made a Persian conquest of all Greece probable, and anything that asked one part of Greece to sacrifice everything for another part would enable Persia to divide and conquer. The farther north Greece could take its stand, the more allies would be retained. The strategy was thus elaborated to defend the passes at Tempe and Thermopylae, forcing Xerxes to use his navy to outflank the northern defenders, and there to try to divide the Persian navy and defeat it in separate actions, making all Greece impregnable. It was an intricate and exacting strategy.

The Thessalians soon asked for assistance, as they were facing Xerxes, and Themistocles and a Spartan polemarch, Evaenetus, were sent to Thessaly's assistance with a sizeable fleet carrying ten-thousand hoplites. Themistocles was the chief author of the strategy and was the naval commander of this expedition; his Spartan colleague commanded the land forces. It started badly, as the Thessalians produced only their aristocratic cavalry in their own defense, indicating that Thessalian political opinion had been divided by appeasers of the Persians. Evaenetus reembarked his troops, but Themistocles, burdened with the implacable task of wringing unity from a congeries of argumentative and self-interested Greeks, managed to reconstruct a consensus to try to hold the pass at Thermopylae, effectively writing off Thessaly.

While shoring up support for the stand at Thermopylae and while angling for a favourable test of naval strength, both Themistocles and the Athenian agrarians, who wanted a united army to fight to the death with the whole invading force, sent to Delphi for oracular confirmation of their views. The Pythia Aristonice advised them to "Go to the ends of the earth and school your hearts in woe." When Timon sponsored a return to Delphi as suppliants seeking a more favourable counsel, he at least got a recommendation to avoid ground combat and focus on the sea. This gave Themistocles enough of what he needed to build a consensus on, but the whole process was vitiated. The Delphic Oracle was overseen by the Amphictyonic Board, and from six to nine of the twelve nations represented had already largely prostrated themselves at the feet of Xerxes. Themistocles knew this and the assumption must be that he only made a request of Delphi to try to get something less unhelpful than what the request from the Athenian Agrarian Party was likely to elicit. He was successful in this. This episode illustrates that while religious authorities are frequently unreliable in secular matters, "The policy of la haute finance is seldom heroic."[11]

Themistocles prevailed, and by a majority of votes, in one of the important decisions of all human history, the League determined to stand and fight at Thermopylae and Athens said it would devote its entire navy to try to deny Persia the ability to strike an amphibious blow in the back of the allies; and while the help of

---

11 Ibid., p. 283.

the allies would be gratefully received, that was Athens' policy whether it had supporters or not. The aged king of Sparta, Leonidas, departed for Thermopylae with four-thousand of his best troops, including the royal guard. There were contingents of Thespians, Thebans, Phocians, Locrians and Trachinians, and they numbered about ten-thousand men. They were not numerous for their task, but they were front-line troops, and their experience and their valour were assured in advance of being at the highest level. The Athenian navy was repositioned to Artemisium and was joined by contingents from Sparta and other states, to total three-hundred and twenty-four triremes and nine pentecontes. In theory, the Spartan admiral Eurybiades was the supreme commander, but given that Athens supplied two thirds of the ships, Themistocles was the tactical commander. After all their debating and toing and froing, the Greeks arrived just in time to mount a defence at Thermopylae. The defection of Thessaly and the overtures they were receiving from some of the Delphic states must have given the Persians a sense of over-confidence or they would have moved more swiftly to occupy the northern passes and place their navy at the entry to vital waterways.

First blood was drawn in the naval action at Artemisium. The fleets first became aware of each other's presence when Persian reconnaissance vessels and Greek scouts chanced to encounter each other. The fleets maneuvered at a distance for several days, unsure of the other's exact size and whereabouts, and the Persians were hoping to avoid a major battle altogether if the army was able to force the northern passes. The Persian fleet took a nasty knocking around in sudden storms, and a number of ships were lost on reefs and forced to ground. They finally attacked the Greeks in their anchorage at Artemisium. The Greeks were ready and expecting them, and their fleet was in a concave arc, the whole fleet side-by-side facing forward and at a signal charged stem to stern against the Persians and Phoenicians, even more crowded together and facing in. Wild hand-to-hand combat ensued across the whole of the fleets as the ships became entangled. Then Greeks narrowly got the best of it, as they retained the harbor, and the Persians withdrew and lost more vessels, but the Athenian fleet lost seventy vessels. The Egyptians, who were more heavily armoured, were the most distinguished section of the Persian squadron, while the Athenians were the strongest fighters among the Greeks. It was their initiative. Themistocles technically had been victorious, but his allies and many of the Greeks were dissatisfied with such severe losses leading to an ambiguous result.

Before the Persians had retired from the horizon, news had arrived from Thermopylae. As the navy had waited, hoping for news from Thermopylae that would make it unnecessary to attack the Greek fleet, Xerxes himself waited several days before Thermopylae in the hope that his navy would have so damaged the Greek fleet that he could transport his army by sea around the passes. The Persian generals clearly saw the strength with which the passes were guarded and recognized the challenge facing them. Frontal assaults on such determined enemies in strong positions would be very costly. The Persian general Hydarnes, on a tip the Persians had had of a hidden secret path that went round the defenders' left flank and led back into the Greek rear, led the light guard, the Immortals, on this fourteen-mile walk through very difficult country on a dark night.

They encountered the Phocians, whose general responded peremptorily and then withdrew to cover his own unit's line of retreat if necessary, and the devil take the Greek army under Leonidas that was about to have the Immortals arrive on their rear on the day of battle. Advised by deserters and scouts of the movement in his rear, Leonidas called a council of generals, and it was determined to allow Sparta's allies to withdraw, as the Phoci had done. Both sides were still hoping for good news from the naval engagement at Artemisium. The Spartans, and the Thebans who were there essentially as hostages and whose solidity could not be relied upon, remained. Leonidas and the other generals may have thought a Greek naval victory was still possible, and in the aftermath of events, a great manufacture of implausible excuses for the conduct of most of Sparta's allies occurred. The likeliest explanation for the allied flight was that they thought they would be caught in a pincers movement and wished to escape the trap. On the day, either the 21st of July or 19th of August, 480, Leonidas met the Persian army and fought until he died, and as Hydarnes arrived, the Spartan survivors, in perfect order, retreated to a knoll, where a statue of a lion now stands in honour to Leonidas and his men. Overwhelmingly outnumbered, they fought with perfect courage and determination to the last man. No one surrendered.

The Persians occupied Artemisium, as the Greek fleet withdrew, and Xerxes himself invited his sailors across to look at the Greek dead at Thermopylae. The northern Dorian Greeks had gone over almost en masse to the Persians. Some looting and razing of Phocian towns occurred as the Persians resumed their advance into Greece, but Xerxes stopped it and insisted on civilized treatment of all Greeks. He had lost two brothers, sons of Darius, at Thermopylae, and could not fail to be impressed by the valour of the Spartans, and the Athenian navy had acquitted itself also with great honour. The Persians were naturally not disrespectful of Delphi—the Persians were traditionally respectful of the religions of conquered people, but, as has been mentioned, the Delphic authorities had already made their peace with the Great King and had done their reasonable best to assure that Greece passed smoothly into servile domination. Greek religious apologists, led in the vigour of their pious imaginations by Herodotus, have confected the myth that Delphi's deliverance was an act of divine intervention. The truth lies in ecclesiastical hypocrisy and material greed, protected by the superstitious humbug of tradition. In words made famous five-hundred years later, the money-changers were running the temple.

The extreme emergency that had now arisen elevated Sparta and Athens to a joint leadership of the defence of the Peloponnese and Attica. The Greek fleet took up its position in the Gulf of Salamis. The entire Peloponnesian army went to the Corinthian Isthmus. There was little doubt that a much larger force than that deployed by Leonidas would replicate, if necessary, his feat of heroism in keeping the Persians out of the Peloponnese. The Spartan army and the Athenian navy were now the last ditch defence of Greece; and the Spartan plan to hold the Corinthian Isthmus, left Athens at high risk of occupation by the Persians, now descending to southern Greece in great strength. Athenian civilians were evacuated to the Peloponnese in large numbers, and the Athenian army, the junior service of Athens at this time, was deployed to resist the Persian advance into Attica and toward Athens. Themistocles had more trouble than ever before persuading his countrymen to be prepared to lose their city to Persian occupation temporarily. He did what he could with the Delphic Oracle's advice to have faith in "wooden walls" which Themistocles represented as the navy. The Court of Areopagus assured eight drachmas to every sailor, and provision was made for the evacuation of all women and children to Peloponnesian centres (mainly Troezen, the now friendly Aegina, or Salamis). A garrison was left in the Acropolis. The Athenians were well aware that Athens was Xerxes' chief target.

In the isthmus, roads were broken up and covered with obstacles, a wall was hastily constructed, along with trenches, breast-works, and positions for archers to surprise advancing forces with showers of closely targeted arrows. The Athenians hastily added what they could to their fleet and deployed three-hundred and seventeen ships to the Gulf of Salamis. What the League of Greek states had lost in the flaking off of the appeasers and defeatists, it had apparently more than made up for with the total war mobilization of Sparta and Athens and their closest allies and the mass determination to follow the heroic example of the late Spartan king if necessary and fight to the last man.

Xerxes arrived at Athens in mid-September, having brushed aside or driven back to the Corinthian isthmus the Athenian army that was left alone to try to protect Athens while Sparta led the defence of the Peloponnese. Despite having been effectively declared an open city (like Paris in 1940 and Rome in 1944), the resistance at the Acropolis was of Leonidian tenacity. The Persians fired arrows that were on fire at the wooden palisades, but the defenders rolled rocks and boiling oil down on the Persians. They fought desperately and rejected the king's terms, transmitted by the Peisistratidae (outright traitors in the end). Finally, Persians managed to climb up the back of the Acropolis and were able to open one of the gates. The defenders were overwhelmed, but they too, fought to the last man. The siege had lasted about three weeks. Xerxes burned out the Temple of Athena. He sent a courier to announce at Susa the achievement of his supreme objective and the revenge for the defeat at Marathon. Xerxes invited the return of the Athenian exiles, some of whom had assisted him, but none came. They doubtless wished to see how the Persian invasion ended. The Greeks had evacuated Athens; they would not be defeated as an entire people without an appalling bloodbath, such as even the armies of Cyrus and Darius had not seen. Two days after the fall of the Acropolis came the Battle of Salamis.

Despite the Persian penetration of Attica on land, it had lost two-hundred and fifty ships to storms and skirmishes and to the fierce battle at Artemisium, and with the Phoenicians and lesser maritime allies combined, had about three-hundred and fifty triremes, which was perhaps fifty more than the Greeks, but a hodge-podge of allies and vessels, and with a proximity of supply advantage for the Greek fleet. Xerxes was not going to try to force the Corinthian isthmus without an amphibious force to make it a pincers attack. The Persian fleet could not undertake such a mission and retain enough vessels to have any confidence of preventing the Greek fleet from destroying the Persian navy in two bights, stranding the amphibious force and leaving the Great King a long way from home with the prospect of the kinfolk of Leonidas nipping at his ankles all the way to Asia Minor. Wintering in Attica was out of the question and a logistical nightmare. The Persians blockaded the Greek fleet in the commodious anchorage at Salamis, but as time passed, the Persians had much more difficulty feeding their sailors than the Greeks did, as they were well taken care of from shore. In these circumstances, Xerxes called for a round-up of any possible allied ships and wrung seventeen vessels from the Hellespont and a few from the more susceptible Cyclades. The Greeks were warned by spies, deserters, and observers of the strengthening of the Persian fleet and called a counsel of war. The fall of the Acropolis, and the unlimited valour shown by the Athenians there and by the Spartans at Thermopylae, stirred all Greece. There were many different arguments, from lingering defeatism to Corinthian panic for a full land offensive to prevent Xerxes from doing to Corinth what he had done to Athens. The news of Persian naval reinforcements created a consensus that something had to be done, lest Persia have the forces to blockade Salamis and escort an amphibious landing on the Peloponnese.

The decisive moment had come, like Gettysburg in the U.S. Civil War, both battles of the Marne in World War I, and the Battle of Britain in World War II. And the man of the hour had come as the hour struck. Themistocles told them that if the Greek fleet came out now for any purpose other than to defeat the Persian navy and strike from Xerxes' hand the possibility of an amphibious landing south of the Isthmus, the Greek fleet would break up. The Athenian bulk of the navy would transport the women and children of Athens to the Athenian colonies in Italy, which were flourishing, and the devil take their so-called Greek allies who twiddled their thumbs while the Athenians gave up their city to the enemy in the common cause and fought to the death in the Acropolis. The pompously self-styled League, which had so far generated nothing but the bravery and sacrifice of Athens and the Spartan king, now had, he explained, their last, best, and only chance. This time there was no temporizing with symbolic gestures of coalition such as imagining that the fleet commander was the worthy Spartan Eurybiades as at Artemisium. He, Themistocles, had devised a plan for sending one part out of Salamis by one side, drawing the Persian fleet to deal with it, while sending the main Greek fleet out from behind the other end of the island of Salamis and striking the Persian navy in the flank and rear and rolling it up, and achieving a decisive margin of strength over Persia at sea before its reinforcements from the Hellespont and Cyclades could arrive, and then breaking them up like kindling as they arrived. It was one of history's most perfect examples of the coming together of one man at the focal point of disparate events allowing the application of decisive force at a decisive fulcrum point, determining a vastly consequential history. (This was a concept most directly identified by Napoleon, who was an intimate student of all the Greek and Persian wars, and all the major conflicts between them, and he applied their lessons in the great campaigns and battles in which he was himself the chief protagonist.) As usually happens on such rare moments, the person with the carefully thought-out option and the forensic talent to argue for it fluently and eloquently prevails: you can never defeat something with nothing. Themistocles, at the hour when all the traditions and culture and political sophistication of the more intellectually fertile and better organized elements of Greece were in mortal peril and their fate and future hung by a thread, was the only one among them who had a plausible plan for salvation. He received the mandate to save the Hellenic peoples.

Themistocles sent his sons' tutor, Sicinnus, to masquerade as a deserter and go on the day after the fall of the Acropolis (September 22) to the Persian headquarters at Phalerum, near the Athenian port of Piraeus, and to tell the highest ranking Persians to whom he could gain access that the Greeks intended to escape from Salamis the following night; he was unsure of their destination. Herodotus claims that there was an additional suggestion that Athens might be prepared to treat with the enemy. It is unlikely that Sicinnus said anything of the kind, or that Xerxes or his senior advisers would have been disposed to believe that, given the sacrifices the Athenians had recently made to the cause of resisting Persia. But Xerxes and his admirals approved dispositions of their fleet to interdict the escape of the Greek vessels, and Xerxes (like Stalin twenty-four hundred and twenty years later) made it clear that those responsible for allowing the escape of Greek vessels would forfeit their heads to the executioner. (Stalin only said they would be shot; a fate many shared.)

In an elaborate ruse, the Greek fleet sounded its departure with horns and a chanted paean at sunrise, and, invisible to the Persians, started toward open water, emerging from the easterly point of Salamis Island, Point Barbara. They emerged scarcely a mile in front of the Phoenician fleet, and feigning surprise (which was preposterous since overland observers on Salamis Island could have confirmed the position of the enemy), fell back—actually rowed backwards a little. This was the key moment: Themistocles was enticing the Phoenicians, as well as the Ionian section of the Persian fleet to the east of the small island of Psyttaleia, to come into the channel after them, believing the Greeks, from their behavior, to be unawares. As the Persian navy surged into the inlet and set upon the Greek vanguard, the Greek rear was able to strike heavily at the left flank and rear of the Phoenicians, who were too committed to their course to turn easily. Themistocles led his own Athenian fleet, recently built, directly against the Phoenicians, who, compressed by fighting the Athenians on two sides, the Spartans in front, and their Ionian-Persian allies on their right, were heavily engaged in front and flank, and soon in the rear also. The Persian ships had no room to maneuver, and their central vessels had no one to fire their arrows or projectiles at, as they had friendly craft on their sides and a very narrow range of fire forward and astern. An immense melee ensued.

Xerxes watched the action from a hill and was disconcerted as it unfolded. There were Persian highlights, as when Artemisia, Queen of Halicarnassus, chased closely by an Athenian ship, made her escape by ramming and sinking her own vessel and maneuvering around the wreck and escaping her pursuer. (It has been suggested that the vassal, Damasithymus, in the ruined ship, was a nuisance to the queen politically as well.) The Persians fought well, but from the moment they fell into the trap so ably created and baited by Themistocles, they were fighting for survival. At terrible cost, they managed to get their ships turned about and retained the mass and force to fight their way clear of the confining waters and back into the open sea, leaving a great many floating wrecks behind. There were not in these times the chivalrous practice of rescuing survivors, and the Greeks, left in control of the battle area, meticulously slaughtered survivors in the water or on floating wrecks, until nightfall. Xerxes lost another brother, Ariabignes, the admiral commanding the Ionian half of the Persian fleet. There are only estimates of the cost of the fighting, but it seems that the Persians lost two-hundred ships, to about forty for the Greeks.

The reinforcements that arrived in the next two days from the Hellespont and the Cyclades might have brought Persian strength up to about parity with the Greeks, but the balance of naval power had shifted dramatically. The Great King's fleet had been badly beaten and was demoralized, missing many of its best ships and crews and officers, and the Greek part of his navy, now better than half of it as the Phoenicians had taken heavier losses, could not be considered reliable. They might not have the stomach to slug it out as underdogs against Themistocles and Eurybiades, who, in all respects, now had the wind in their sails. It was the end of September, and Xerxes could not leave his huge army, gathered from throughout his empire, sitting in front of the Corinthian isthmus in winter quarters.

He had sacked Athens, taken the Acropolis, slain the Spartan king, more than redeemed the reverse at Marathon, and enhanced his own prestige by intimidating or suborning or soundly beating and punishing at least half of Greece. His navy was composed of Phoenicians and Greeks, and had acquitted itself well at Artemisium, and had fought honourably at Salamis, even if its admirals had been foxed by Themistocles. Xerxes retired, half-satisfied and half-disappointed, but not at all humiliated. (Hitler's position after the Battle of Britain was less sustainable—he had promised victory in the air and the Germans had been defeated by the British—there were no allies involved, and the German air force resorted to night terror-bombing and appeared to be whipped beasts, defeated in fair combat despite a numerical advantage and reduced to murdering civilians indiscriminately.) Xerxes was in a position occupied many centuries later by Louis XIV, Napoleon, and Hitler—supremacy on land, but with a strategic position seriously diminished by not having the scepter of the seas.

As is traditional in such circumstances, efforts were made to over-dramatize success and inflict humiliation on Xerxes, now the beleaguered favourite seen off by the scrappy underdog. Herodotus confected from whole cloth the claim that Themistocles seriously considered attacking Xerxes' pontoon bridges in Thrace and the Bosporus. The Persian fleet had retired to these areas, and Xerxes had spare pontoons and an immense army that could have gone farther inland, if necessary, to return to Asia. He did not retire as Napoleon and Hitler did from Russia after a mortifying attrition or defeat. He had taken very few casualties, his army had endured no defeats or hardships, and Greece had taken a great deal more damage than Persia in the campaign; its victory was that it had survived. The Great King reached the Hellespont in forty-five days, in mid-November. He divided his army into three: a substantial force was left with Mardonius in Thessaly, in good quarters and in full communication with the Empire, a third under Artabazus in Thrace, and the last third returned to Sardes with the king, who after a period of administrative and strategic reorganization, retired in the orderly course with a modest internal force to Susa. There had been the customary uppity impertinences from Babylonia, but these had been dealt with by the forces in the garrison there, and Artabazus was required to smack down some insurrectionist activity on the route of march, and did so effectively, executing the ring-leaders in the manner of the house of Darius, but his attempt to bring his siege of Potidaea to fruition by trying to infiltrate a battalion under the sea wall at low tide was a costly fiasco, as the tides had been miscalculated and his men drowned.

Mardonius was left with about one-hundred and twenty thousand men in Thessaly, many of Xerxes best units, though not the Immortals, who remained with the king, and also some less reliable Greek units who rejected the leadership of Sparta and Athens. This was a formidable force, but Xerxes himself, with two-hundred thousand men, did not try to force his way into the Peloponnese, which had been further strengthened after the Persian withdrawal of its main force. There was no longer an amphibious option after Salamis. Mardonius hatched a plan to try to induce the Athenians, who were still cleaning up the Acropolis and the rest of Athens after the Persian visit, to change sides and lend him their fleet. This would certainly have made an amphibious landing behind the fortified lines of the isthmus a hot prospect, but it is hard to believe that Athens would entertain such a prospect after recent events and the prodigies it had expended in saving the Spartan League from invasion.

Themistocles had, as the Athenian system provided, handed over control of the military affairs of Athens to his political opponents, Aristides and Xanthippus. Aristides was a leader of the Agrarian Party, which had grievances against Sparta, and there was considerable sentiment in Athens that their city had taken the brunt of the Persian invasion and sacrificed itself for the Spartans and their allies and had received very little thanks for their efforts. In 479 B.C., Mardonius sent Alexander of Macedon, who was well-known and regarded in Athens, on a mission to the new Athenian government; he offered complete remission of penalties imposed by Persia, alliance with the Great King, and Persian assurances of restitution of territory and assistance in any reasonable accretion of territory it sought, in exchange for the use of the Athenian navy. Though the sources for the claim are unreliable, it is likely that Sparta became concerned at their vulnerability to a Persian-Athenian rapprochement and made competing offers.

Athens had lost two harvests, and its land as well as its capital had been scorched and there seems to be little doubt that the Athenian leaders demanded not just assistance from the granaries of the Peloponnese, but practical military alliance to repel the Persians and remove the constant and close threat of Persian reoccupation, against which, at this point, Athens would be resistless. Aristides and Xanthippus may be assumed to have obtained satisfactory assurance from Sparta that a trans-Hellenic offensive was about to take place to push the Persians back from the edge of Attica.

It seems, though the evidence is incomplete, that Mardonius devised another plan for fragmenting Sparta's Peloponnese alliance by hiving off the brooding and resentful Argives, and storming into the Corinthian isthmus at one end of it while Sparta was distracted with intra-Peloponnese tribulations. Mardonius broke his Thessalian camp and moved south in forced marches, gathering Greek allies as he approached, but before he got to the isthmus received a messenger from Argos who advised that the advance guard of the Spartan army had left Sparta and made for the isthmus and that there was nothing the Argives could do to stop them. Mardonius, who was undoubtedly ingenious and persistent, devised his next plan, which was to do what he could to incite Athenian impatience at its allies skulking behind the isthmian barricades while the Athenians still had burnt-out farmlands and a city in ruins, as its supposed allies, whom it had rescued from Persian invasion, cowered behind their barricades. Mardonius wanted to draw the Spartan army out of the isthmus where he could attack and destroy it in the open field.

On receipt of the Argive message, Mardonius marched into Attica and effortlessly reoccupied Athens in June 479. He sent another emissary to the Athenians at Salamis, inviting the Council of Five Hundred to reconsider its position. This overture was so unsuccessful that the Council lynched one of its members who favoured acceptance of the Persian offer, and the women present (generally spouses of the five-hundred) went their men one better. After the Council lynched the member who supported compromise with the Persians, the women, without further formalities, and without interference, stoned the wife and children of the inopportunely conciliatory Council-member to death. These murders were also retroactively declared to have been just and righteous executions of traitors. Although the Athenian government clearly had matters in hand despite the distressed condition of Athens and Atticus, it sent Cimon, Xanthippus, and Myronides, three prominent civic leaders, to Sparta to urge the launch of the long-promised counter-offensive, doubtless suggesting that otherwise the party that favoured the appeasement of Persia might gain the upper hand. The Spartans were in the midst of the Hyacinthia festival, but after letting the envoys cool their heels for ten days, they dispatched forty thousand soldiers to the Isthmian boundary and sent the envoys back with assurances of Spartan solidarity.

In fact, Sparta had to be mindful of manpower requirements to bring in the harvest and was not seduced by any strategic argument to venture north to meet Mardonius, rather than awaiting him at the now well-fortified Isthmus. The Spartans had their own grievance at Athenian lack of naval cooperation, but the two cities, yielding to the pressure of the Persian presence that mortally threatened them both, cooperated and prepared for a full joint offensive once the harvest, which the Athenians depended on no less than the Spartans, had been gathered into the granaries. Pausanias, who was the regent for the underage Spartan king Pleistarchus, assembled an army, of which about forty-thousand Spartan hoplites (armoured troops) and helots was the core, and which totaled between eighty- and one-hundred and twenty thousand, including a large corps of support and service units from the helotry.

Mardonius, if Herodotus is to be believed, had burned what was left of Athens and sacked and scorched Attica, as part of a campaign to lure the Greek army into Attica. The Greeks were not able to reply to the Persian cavalry, so Mardonius dangled himself as bait before Pausanias, hoping to draw him away from the isthmian fortifications, enabling his cavalry to cut off the Spartan retreat. Mardonius built a stockade on friendly Theban territory, in case of need for a place of retreat. Mardonius and Pausanias conducted an intricate war of maneuver for some weeks, with the Spartan careful not to become completely separable from his isthmian fortress. Mardonius launched his cavalry under Masistius against what seemed the weakest exposed part of the Greek formations, but Aristides' archers in the vanguard, rushed to fill the void and Masistius was unhorsed when an arrow struck his mount, and he was killed in single combat. The Persians made a determined effort to retrieve their commander's corpse, but were unable to do so, and his body was paraded in a cart along the front of the Greek line, to encourage the Peloponnesian and Athenian soldiers. His armoured courselet later was a main attraction in the refurbished Acropolis.

The partial victory over the renowned Persian cavalry emboldened Pausanias to move northwest, and both armies moved along opposite sides of the Asopus River for several days. The Greek army suffered water shortages (there was little to be had in the parched Asopus in August), and the Persian cavalry harassed any exposed Greek units. There were difficulties of communications between the Athenians and Spartans and some allegations of skullduggery, and the Persians were able to exploit a gap between the two armies and fell upon the Athenian army divided into three groups, near Plataea. The advantage was at first with the Persians, and it joined in close combat with the Spartan army, Mardonius leading his forces on his white charger. Courage was conspicuous and uniform on both sides, and the entire main battle devolved to intense hand-to-hand combat. The issue was determined in favour of Pausanias and the Spartans when Mardonius was killed by bowmens' arrows. The Persians fought to the end, but this section of their army was almost completely killed, though Spartan casualties were heavy.

Several miles away, the Athenians were engaged with the Boeotians, the only Greek ally of the Persians that showed any disposition to fight. The Athenians, buoyed by the news of the victory of their Spartan allies and sensing a chance to regain Athens with some security to rebuild it, gradually got the upper hand, and the Boeotians withdrew. The Persian cavalry was able to prevent a rout and slaughter of the retreating Persians, and despite the terrible casualties taken by the main army, the balance of the Persian and allied forces regained the wooden fortress they had built for just such a contingency. The secondary Persian army however, under Artabazos, who had disapproved of Mardonius' conduct as impetuous, with some reason as it turned out, on seeing the other Persians, whom he was advancing to assist, in retreat, turned and departed in forced marches for the Hellespont, washing his hands of Greece and the whole business.

The Athenians and Spartans laid siege to the improvised Persian fortress, which was defended valiantly by the defeated army, but the Greek tide was now inexorable. Artabazos could have saved his comrades, but without him, they did not have the manpower to hold the perimeter, and the Athenians slaughtered virtually everyone. From the entire Persian host, apart from Artabazos, at least fifty-thousand perished, and only about three-thousand stragglers survived. It was a stunning defeat for the Great King, though he himself was not implicated or dishonoured by it. But Persia had been evicted, flung out of Greece like whipped animals. It was a mighty Greek victory, and an altar was erected to Zeus the Liberator, and the Eleutheria Festival, at the initiative of Aristides, was established. It was an instructive battle: Mardonius had maneuvered skillfully, and the Greeks were over-exposed in Attica. Mardonius attacked at the right moment and led his attack personally and bravely but did not count on the almost super-human discipline and fortitude of the Spartans, who drew Mardonius' large force into entire combat, and overwhelmed it when Mardonius himself was killed and his brave troops became demoralized and discoordinated. Artabazos wrote the death warrant for the surviving army, but was rewarded by Xerxes for saving his army with the satrapy of Hellespontine Phrygia, which he occupied comfortably for about twenty-five years.

To make the shambles of Persia's Greek adventure complete, on the same day as the Battle of Plataea, the Greek naval fleet, having regrouped after Salamis, attacked the Persian navy which Xerxes had withdrawn to Mycale, in Asia Minor just east of the island of Samos. At the approach of the Greek fleet, the unreliability of the Greeks who had allied themselves with the Persians became clear, and the Persian admirals sent the core of their navy, the Phoenicians, to the Levant; the rest of the navy was beached to try to shift the impending battle to the land. The Greeks accepted this challenge, disembarked at least twenty-thousand men at Samos, though many were sailors taking up land combat from scratch, but they were sufficiently motivated and numerous that they pierced the Persian fort where the remnants of their grounded sailors had gathered, and in the custom of the time, massacred the defenders practically to the last man. With this victory, an Ionian revolt against the Persians began, as the debacle Xerxes had sustained achieved ever greater proportions.

The Greek council of admirals debated at Samos the issue of whether to take the Athenians' Ionian kinsmen back from Asia Minor to Attica and expel the "Medizers" (those Greeks who had sided with the Persians), in effect engaging in a large-scale population transfer. The Spartans and other Peloponnesians wanted to get back home and demobilize. There was no thought of trying to contest any part of Asia itself with the Great King, stinging defeat though the Greeks had inflicted on him. The transfer of these peoples was the Spartan proposal to assuage the Athenians, without having to continue the war with Persia. Themistocles had proposed this the year before (and this was effectively what was done twenty-four hundred and two years later in 1923 A.D., when the Greeks were driven out of Asia Minor by the great modern Turkish leader, Kemal Ataturk).

The Athenian leader Xanthippus led the entire expedition to Sesta in the Bosporus to recover the cables that Xerxes had used to tie his transpontine bridge together. This involved besieging a Persian force in Sestos, where the Persians resisted stoutly. The siege proceeded for about two months, to November. Leotychidas took his Spartans and their allies home, but Athens continued the siege until late October when "the garrison had been reduced to eating their bed-straps," and the Persians evacuated the fortress-town of Sestos on the landward side. The principal defender, Artayctes, was overtaken and crucified, and the person who had tried to remove the cables, Oeobazus, was burned alive as an offering to the God of the Apsinthians, Pleistorus. The cables, a great war trophy, were transported back to Athens by Xanthippus and displayed in the Acropolis, like the standards of France's enemies in the modern Invalides in Paris.

Thus ended one of the most momentous and celebrated military campaigns in all of history.

CHAPTER SEVEN

THE AGE OF PERICLES AND CIMON
THE ASCENDENCY OF ATHENS
AND THE START OF THE PELOPONNESIAN WAR
❦
FROM THE EARLY SIXTH CENTURY TO 445 B.C.

Bust of Pericles

Bust of Cimon

1. Sicily and Carthage

THE SCHISM BETWEEN Sparta and Athens would broaden and lead to the most dramatic internecine struggle in Greek history, involving the most illustrious Greeks of all. But before getting to that, it is appropriate to bring in the progress of Greek and Phoenician activities in Italy and North Africa, as civilization spread westwards along both the northern and southern shores of the Mediterranean. In the closing decades of the Eighth Century B.C., Greek settlers landed and put down roots in significant numbers in Sicily, which was mainly inhabited by two tribal peoples with accidentally similar names. The Sicels who gave their name to the island, were in the eastern and central part of Sicily, and they had banished to the west the Sicans. The Greeks also found an even earlier tribe, the Elymians, in small numbers, but more numerous and vigorous were the Phoenician colonies that had begun to be established in the Eleventh Century B.C.

The Phoenicians had gone as far west as Gibraltar by 1000 B.C. and had opened up a flourishing commerce with the Tarshish, the most advanced of the tribes of Iberia, who developed and successfully operated, from Cadiz, near the mouth of the Guadalquivir River, the silver, copper, and lead mines of Andalusia. The Tarshish, on their own initiative, had opened a flourishing trade with the inhabitants of what are now Ireland and the French province of Brittany, in tin and amber. The Phoenicians traded the wares and products of their own arts and crafts for these precious metals and minerals and were for some centuries the principal agents in the commercial exploration and social and economic modernization of Western Europe. Cadiz was the first Phoenician settlement in Spain, and because they were astute traders who generated prosperity, the Phoenicians were not molested or resented. They claimed no mission to civilize, unlike, up to a point, the Greeks.

Of greater political significance were the extensive settlements Phoenicia made in the Eleventh and subsequent centuries, B.C., in what is now Tunisia. This was the beginning of Carthage. As the Greeks became more numerous in Sicily and spread along its coast, the Phoenicians huddled at the western end of Sicily, according to Thucydides (who is generally more rigorous than Herodotus but was no more a mind-reader), to be a commercial station between Spain and the Levant. Some rivalry started to develop between the Phoenicians and Greeks in Sicily, but the Greeks were much more colonial settlers, while the Phoenicians were essentially always traders (a vocation that remains with the Christian Lebanese today, the heirs of the Phoenicians in the Levant and throughout the western world). In the Eighth and Seventh pre-Christian centuries, there was little for the Phoenicians and Greeks to quarrel about, but with the threats to the original Phoenician cities in the Levant, and the rise of Greek claims to commercial hegemony in Sicily, some natural antagonism arose between the two groups of relative newcomers in the central Mediterranean.

By the middle of the Sixth Century B.C., Tyre had been besieged three times. She withstood the onslaught on her island, but in 669 B.C., Tyre accepted the suzerainty of the Assyrians, under Esarhaddon, but continued the inter-continental commercial shipping business without much interference—the Assyrians knew nothing of maritime matters. When the Babylonians took over Nineveh in 611 B.C., the Phoenician cities regained enhanced independence, as the Babylonians were less dominating than the Assyrians and no more attuned to maritime matters. Apries of Egypt rudely interrupted this equilibrium in 588 B.C., and he occupied Tyre for two years until he was unambiguously evicted by Nebuchadnezzar in 586, which began a Babylonian siege of Tyre that continued for thirteen years. Tyre finally capitulated, but Babylonia was also overrun and there was extensive civil factional disorder in Tyre until the arrival of the Persian army in 539. Sidon surpassed Tyre in influence and commercial activity in this period of overall Persian rule, and as a consequence, more Phoenician mariners and traders, fatigued and inconvenienced by the recurrent arrival of Asian warlord monarchs, moved to Carthage, the greatest of the Phoenician cities in North Africa. The gravitation of the Phoenicians to Carthage and some lesser Phoenician-originated cities prefigured to some extent the rise of America, Canada, and Australia in the Eighteenth to Twentieth Centuries, though

Great Britain, as an island kingdom, was much more insulated than the Phoenician cities from the depredations of those powers that rose to control of the adjacent land-mass of Western Europe.

Carthage became a catchment and a magnet for the more creative and ambitious people of Tyre and Sidon, fatigued and distracted, as much of the European flood of immigration to the Americas and Australasia would be more than two thousand years later, by the wars and pogroms of Europe, as well as by comparative socio-economic stultification. The attractions of the prosperity and democracy of the frontier had asserted their dominion in the human mind, and have not relinquished it. Carthage was a fine port with an agriculturally rich adjacent hinterland and steadily rose in population and prosperity for several centuries. She gradually supplanted the Levantine Phoenicians in the commerce with Spain and the western ocean. She did negotiate a treaty with the rising Italian city of Rome in 508-7 B.C., dividing the Western Mediterranean between them, under which Carthage monopolized the Spanish trade. A rivalry between these cities was already foreseeable. Tarshish had a phil-Hellenic king, Arganthonius (Silver-man), for a substantial part of the period between 700 and 550 B.C., but after the Battle of Alalia in 535, in which Carthage, aided by the premier Italian people, the Etruscans, defeated the Greeks. They closed the Western Mediterranean to them. At this point, Tarshish disappears from history, and it appears that Carthage took over a complete commercial monopoly with Spain, in the Mediterranean and the Atlantic.

The Greeks had begun their colonization of Sicily in 735 B.C., and it continued aggressively for more than a century, until the Greeks occupied almost all the more desirable sites on the island. This was almost as ambitious a project in its time as Spanish, Portuguese, British, French, and Dutch colonial and commercial missions across the Western Ocean and across the Pacific twenty-two to twenty-five centuries later. And they were undertaken for similar motives—commercial prosperity for the trading sponsors, and a flight to comparative safety and absence of Old World strife for the settlers and immigrants. The latter aspect of the allure was even more pronounced with the Phoenicians, as their homeland was constant prey for a succession of Asian powers that occupied or oppressed them. It was the Phocaeans, of northern Greece, who had the distinction of founding Massilia, in 600 B.C., which from its first years to the present time, as Marseilles, has constantly been one of the greatest seaports in the entire world.

Through the Seventh Century B.C., the Phoenicians and Greeks in the Western Mediterranean avoided eachother and each was satisfied to build up their trade and populations where they had arrived first. The first dispute between them that we know about was in 580 B.C. when the Greeks started to try to push the Phoenicians out of the northwest corner of Sicily. The effort was a complete fiasco, and had been launched by mainland Greeks, not the Greeks of Sicily. Almost the only Sicilian Greek leader whose name has come down to posterity is Phalaris (c. 615-554 B.C.) the tyrant of Acragas, who seized power by impressing the community with his religiosity by building a temple to Zeus, but is known as the most cruel person of the mid-Sixth Century of any nationality or people. His particular specialty was throwing opponents into a hollowed out bronze bull and roasting them within, their screams taking the place of the roar of an angry bull. His conduct was repugnant to everyone, and he was eventually seized and executed, to general celebration, in the last enactment of the gruesome and macabre ceremony he had conceived. At Catana, however, not very far from Acragas, the people elevated a relatively democratic ruler, Charondas, who was revered in the ancient world, even by Plato, as a civilizing legislator on the same plane as Solon.

The beginnings of substantial conflict in the western or central Mediterranean seems to have come with the rise of Carthage, and aggressive actions by that city, led by Malchus (no conceivable ancestral relationship to the assistant to the high priest whose ear St. Peter severed nearly six-hundred years later in Israel), against Greek Sicilian cities. Malchus pushed the Greeks back slightly but then sought easier conquests in Sardinia but was defeated and died in the endeavor. He was a followed by Mago, who decreed that Carthage's armies would henceforth be composed of subject soldiers or from dependent peoples in Carthage's orbit. This eliminated the problem of the army periodically refusing to be merely the bill-collectors of the Carthaginian oligarchs; they did not mind that, but when issues of survival against mortal rivals arose, this was not the best use of the armed forces. (Neither, it ultimately became clear, was relying on mercenaries.) The Battle of Alalia united the Carthaginians and the Etruscans (including Romans), against the Greeks; the new world against the old, in a pattern that would recur. Even though the results of the naval battle of Alalia were ambiguous, that battle effectively marked the beginning of the retreat of the Greeks in the Western Mediterranean and the rise of the Carthaginians and Italians: Etruscans, Etrurians, and ultimately, and soon, the Romans.

An eccentric Greek, Dorieus, half-brother of Cleomenes, king of Sparta, talented but impulsive, found it intolerable in the shadow of Cleomenes and engaged in private colonial expeditions, starting in Libya, and after being dislodged by Carthage, on to Sicily. These were not operations sanctioned, even unofficially, by the Spartan state. Dorieus was striking out as a private freebooter. It was a mad enterprise, and the Phoenicians and Carthaginians made short work of it. Dorieus was killed, but given military honours, and one of his lieutenants, Philip of Croton was reckoned the most handsome man in the known world, and a gallant warrior (like his chief), and Philip was given a formidable tomb. Some of the survivors of this hare-brained endeavor attempted other colonizations and occupations in Phoenician Sicily but were crushed and executed by the Carthaginians and Phoenicians with an efficiency that would have impressed the usurpers' Spartan kinsmen.

The real drama in Sicily at this time was caused by the astounding rise of Syracuse, which in the Seventh Century B.C. spread across a considerable part of southern Sicily. Syracuse had effectively ceased, by its size and relative security from foreigners or antagonistic Hellenes, to be a colony or anything but a rival to the principal states of Attica and the Peloponnese. Though this parallel could be overstated, something a little like the rise of New York opposite London occurred, including the spontaneous growth of a powerful spirit of complete independence. A Syracusan city, Camarina, arose nearby but full of pride and friskiness, purported to rebel against Syracuse and was crushed. Another city allied to Syracuse that was also sensing its enhanced strength from steady immigration and trading profits, was

Gela, which also began spreading its influence to the west. Its king, starting in 492, was Hippocrates, one of the great names of Sicilian history. His accession (from the murder of his brother, Cleander, apparently without the complicity of Hippocrates) corresponded with the Persian suppression of the Ionian revolt, which Athens had incited but for the fomenting and support of which Sparta had no enthusiasm. (This successful reassertion of the authority of the Great King, while it did not expunge the humiliation of his forces, though not of Xerxes personally, did mark the reestablishment of the perimeter of the Persian empire and the determination and capacity of its king to assert and defend it.) There thus was driven from Asia Minor and the Ionian and Aegean islands, a substantial number of Greeks who chose not to live in the shadow of Persian oppression, nor even to join in the clangorous and ever-changing politics of Attica and the Peloponnese and moved straight on to Sicily. Hippocrates did his best to entice such susceptible fellow Greeks (again, not unlike the techniques for attracting immigration from central and eastern Europe by the Americans and Canadians, over a million a year between them, for nearly forty years between the U.S. Civil War and Canadian Confederation and the start of World War I).

Hippocrates, unprovoked, now made a bold stroke for what was becoming the supreme Hellenic prize: Syracuse itself. He had been complicit in the rather shabby affair of the Sicilian city of Zancle, of which Hippocrates was the overlord. The townspeople wished to invite the migration of some Ionians being oppressed or threatened by the Persians and a number of Samians and Milesians responded. A competing ruler to Hippocrates, Anaxilas of Rhegium, enticed the Samians and Milesians to come to Zancle, whose army was absent battling irreducible Sicels (Sicilian natives). The discreditable theory is that the Rhegian king (Anaxilas), assuming that he could, to his own account and benefit, convert a number of migrating families fleeing a war zone, to be his agents in order to secure his suzerainty over the city, Zancles (Messina), to which he had invited them. The ancient world is even more rich in sleazy and outrageous acts of mountebanks, sharpers, tyrants (by our contemporary definition), scoundrels, and demagogues, than are modern times, but this was, in all of ancient Greek history, i.e., the history of a people with a well-developed sense of ethics, a low moment. Before long, the Zancleans rebelled, Hippocrates subdued them, and placed his agent, Cadmus, in charge of the partially Samian Zancle.

This utterly squalid enterprise, a pastiche of fraud, repression, and hypocrisy transparent to the entire Mediterranean world, from the capital of the Great King to the Rock of Gibraltar, yet emboldened Hippocrates to have a stab at taking over Syracuse, which had a status in the Greek world a little like New York in the English-speaking world at the end of the U.S. Civil War, awaiting the arrival of the Statue of Liberty. Unimaginably, Hippocrates took this shabby initiative as his cue to try to seize Syracuse itself. Corinth and its associate city, Corcyra, intervened to dissuade Hippocrates, and gave him Camarina and a prisoner exchange that got him safe return of his prisoners of war. Hippocrates shortly found himself crowded in popular esteem by his most gifted general, Gelon, who succeeded Hippocrates when he died of apparently natural causes in 485 B.C. Gelon was possessed by an even greater ambition to gain control of Syracuse, which had been suffering considerable internecine fractiousness, than had animated Hippocrates.

In the internal disturbances at Syracuse, the local oligarchs had been turfed out of power and physically banished and were eager to ally their continuing influence with Gelon, on the supposition which he encouraged, that he would restore them. Gelon engaged in a massive build-up of Syracuse, such a huge expansion that it was in grievous need of more inhabitants. These were forcibly transferred from other near-by towns, and Syracuse expanded its territory about five-fold, and its population almost as much. One of the cities virtually depopulated and its population transferred to Syracuse was Camarina, which had provoked Gelon's wrath by deposing and murdering the strongman that Gelon had installed there. Megara was a somewhat distinguished neighbouring city to Syracuse that Gelon had taken against because it had effectively consented to the overlordship of Camarina, and that city had required and received the execution of the supposed tyrant of Megara, Glaucus. This swift expansion of the role and attitude of Syracuse presaged serious problems between the Greeks and the Carthaginians.

Sicily quickly developed rather complicated politics (and they have remained so ever since); when Gelon had imposed himself successfully upon Syracuse, he strengthened his primacy on the island by contacting a double marital alliance with Theron, the comparatively civilized and benign eventual successor to Phaleris as tyrant of Acragas. Theron married Gelon's niece, and Gelon himself married Theron's daughter. As these were the two most powerful cities in Sicily, this act effectively united the rest of Sicily against them. And it did not require demiurgic imagination for the opposition to the Syracuse-Acragas alliance to invite Carthage to come to their assistance. Not surprisingly, the resourceful Anixalas, king of Rhegium, became the agent of this concept. Since being faced down by Hippocrates over Zancles, he had awaited the hour of his revenge, and when Hippocrates died, he seized Zancles, put the Samian fugitives there in their palace and annexed the city, changing its name to Messina. At the double-connubial entanglement of Gelum and Theron, he invited Carthage into Sicily to make a spheres of influence agreement with him over the whole island. Anaxilas torqued the business up, in the manner of the times, by marrying the daughter of Terillus, tyrant of Himera, which clearly signaled that that important city had rallied to the philo-Phoenician and pro-Carthaginian cause.

Theron, with Gelon's support, moved swiftly to evict the newlywed tyrant of Rhegium's father-in-law, Terillus, from Himera. Anixalas, as had been his habit throughout his career, was not slow to see his opportunity: he described the ouster of Terillus as a casus belli against Carthage, handed over most of his family (for whom his paternal affection was unlikely to have been unlimited) as hostages to assure his constancy and pledged to be the Carthaginian semi-autonomous governor of as much of Sicily as Carthage was prepared to assist him in conquering.

Theron and Gelon had overplayed their hand. It was 480 B.C., and to add to his discomfiture, Gelon had just received special ambassadors from Athens and Sparta asking for a contribution to the defence of Greece against the Persians. He assured them that he would normally have rallied to the call of mother countries, but that this was rendered impossible by the flagrant stab in the back by Carthage and its insidious agents in Sicily. Instead of the military reinforcements the Athenians, who were about to sacrifice their city to the heavy-handed marauding of the Great King, and their Peloponnesian allies were seeking, he sent Cadmus, a scoundrel by nature and the former interloper-tyrant of Zancle, to Delphi, heavy-laden with cash, to inquire frequently of the likely outcome of the epic contest beginning, and to be prepared to placate Xerxes with a large cash gift, should military events commend such a step.

Of course, the Persian invasion of Greece unfolded in such a way as to permit Cadmus, doubtless after dealing himself a portion of the pious ecclesiastical tribute entrusted to him, to return from Delphi, his embassy of rank opportunism an undoubted success. There were, however, some risks in the fact that Syracuse had not lifted a finger to assist the mother states in their hour of maximum need. They were still heavily engaged with the Great Persian adversary of the entire Greek and Phoenician worlds, but lashing out at Syracusan ingratitude would not be a primary motive for the Greeks, until the timing and correlation of forces for such a venture was almost unbelievably inopportune.

A theory has arisen among ancient historians that there was a coordination of attacks between Persia and Carthage, but this is unlikely, because Carthage, though independent of its Phoenician antecedents in mind and fact, had absolutely no reservoir of goodwill for Persia, nor any particular antagonism to Greece. Carthage's rivalry, a mortal combat, was with a state that had not yet really revealed itself, though its approach was perceptible. In the late summer of 480, the Carthaginians took the bait and embarked an immense naval and military force for Himera. There is considerable debate about the number of soldiers embarked, but it was something on the order of one-hundred thousand men and a fleet, including transports, of two-thousand ships commanded by Carthage's leader, Hamilcar; an astounding force for what was still casually regarded in the Levant as an only relatively recently self-emancipated state. It is surprising that Gelon did not try to intercept this force (although the weather was unfavourable, and sank almost all the ships carrying the cavalry). Again, inexplicably, Gelon and Theron did absolutely nothing to impede the landing of Hamilcar's great force right beside Himera. Hamilcar was completely unmolested, landed his entire force from beached triremes (very vulnerable if there was a hostile force around on land or sea), set up a commodious camp, did a bit of reconnaissance and skirmishing, and then Hamilcar in person led a direct assault upon Himera. Theron instantly grasped that he could not deal with such an opponent on his own, and as Hamilcar limbered up, Theron urgently appealed to Gelon, who was ready for the call and sent cross-country, a force of about fifty-thousand infantry and five-thousand cavalry. This would make it a much closer match for the disposition of Sicily.

Hamilcar astutely made a great act of obeisance and worship to the Greek God Poseidon in his naval camp. He set out to be thoroughly unterrifying. What ensued was one of history's great surprises. Hamilcar had sought Greek advice on how best to propitiate the Poseidon and had requested a cavalry contingent from his Greek Sicilian ally Selinus. This letter was intercepted by the forces of Gelun, and the Selinuntine horse were replaced by Syracusans, in a double reversal of the Trojan

Horse: the infiltrators came as invited allies and instead of emerging from the horse, they rode their horses: Hamilcar was murdered at once on the reviewing stand, like Egyptian President Sadat in Cairo twenty-three hundred and sixty-six years later. (Herodotus has produced a wildly improbable story that a disappointed Hamilcar had immolated himself in the great roast.) The Carthaginian fleet was burned on the beach, and the entire invasion mission was a mortifying disaster. Only one ship returned safely to Carthage and the Carthaginians were so shaken that they manned their barricades on full watch day and night for years, and their aggressive tendencies were restrained for a full seventy years. The Carthaginian soldiers were mainly rounded up and sold (at rich prices) as slaves and reassigned to Libya, though Carthage was able to redeem and retrieve most of them.

Gelon, full of surprises, and of perhaps unexpected statesmanlike aptitudes, made a generous peace with Carthage, and then with Anaxilas. One might have thought that they had crossed swords so often their rapport might have been negligible, but Gelon was magnanimous, Anaxilas acknowledged his primacy throughout Sicily. Buoyed by this great victory, Gelon accepted, after a day of doubtless fairly genuine and deserved acclamation as a great and wise ruler, elevation to the kingship of Syracuse. In all the Greek world, there was no greater position, in fact, even if, after the repulse of Persia, the rulers of Athens and Sparta had pride of place for national reasons. For a colonial city, Syracuse had become a great western polar attraction in the Greek world, again, somewhat like America, twenty-two hundred and fifty years later.

2. Athens after the Persian War

After inciting the Ionian revolt and defeating the remnants of the non-Phoenician squadrons of the Persian navy at Sestos, the Athenians, as has been recounted, made for the Bosporus, where they wintered uncomfortably, while the Spartans returned to the Peloponnese. In the mind of the Athenians, they had doubly sacrificed for the common cause—in permitting their capital, without serious resistance, to be sacked and burned by the Persians twice and the Acropolis befouled by the barbarian, and in going to extreme lengths to make another Persian landward invasion of the Hellenes, across the Bosporus very difficult (by destroying much of the Persian fleet and chastening the rest, and by seizing the cables laboriously created to hold a bridge from Asia to Europe). The Spartans appreciated what Athens had done for the common Hellenic good but felt that the Persian king's highway from the Bosporus to Thessaly, still a pro-Persian government, was still intact—a straight, fine road to the gateway to Greece, and the Spartans prepared a mission to detach Thessaly from Persia. Athens had been assisting kinsmen in Sestos and the Ionian islands, and Sparta felt fully entitled to pursue its own interests, confluent with those of Greece as a whole, in Thessaly. In fact, the Spartan king, Leotychidas, tried to bribe the Lacedemonian (Spartan) faction in Thessaly, but he failed to change the government and his mission, unlike the Athenian efforts in the Bosporus, was a failure.

The latent escalation of the rivalry between Athens and Sparta for the headship of all Greece was ratcheted up by the proposal of Sparta in about 479 B.C., that all

Greek cities renounce fortification of their capitals. This was the most rampantly self-serving nonsense, as Sparta, supreme power in the Peloponnese, girt by the sea and accessible overland only by the wasp-waisted Corinthian isthmus, while Athens, as recent events had shown, was a sitting duck for an invader of Attica unless it was heavily walled and fortified, as its rightfully Nelsonian hero, Themistocles, was constantly urging in his postwar role. (It is doubtful that Admiral Lord Nelson, had he survived Trafalgar, would have been as politically motivated and as astute as Themistocles.) Themistocles caused the Athenian state to designate him, with Aristides and Abronichus, to be a mission to Sparta to discuss the proposal of not having walled cities in the Hellenes. It was something like the effort in modern arms control, to limit anti-missile defence systems. It was arranged that Themistocles would precede his colleagues, while Athens made a massive municipal effort to put up fortified walls. News of these events naturally reached the Spartans and their interrogation of the distinguished but hardly pacifistic Athenian emissary became very insistent. Themistocles urged the dispatch to Athens of a Spartan delegation to check the intelligence reports they were receiving for themselves, sent a side-message back to the government in Athens to send on his two negotiating colleagues, but to delay the departure of these Spartan monitors from Athens. Joined by his colleagues on the Athenian negotiating team, Themistocles dragged his heels as a negotiator, invoking every conceivable dilatory nonsense, until he was advised that the reconstruction of the fortifications of Athens were effectively complete. At this point, with King Leotychidas still in Thessaly, he threw down the mask, told Sparta that there would be no such agreement as far as Athens was concerned, that the Spartan motive for requesting it was entirely self-serving, and that the Athenian "negotiating" team was leaving, on confirmation of which fact the Spartan emissaries in Athens verifying the state of Athenian refortification would, of course, be released. Themistocles, by his services to all Greece, and by his comradely respect for Sparta and the Spartan leaders he had known, always found a friendly faction in Sparta. Whatever differences of national interest there may be, great military leaders in a common cause always retain a significant measure of goodwill in the camps of their formerly allied rivals, as Wellington did in France, Marshal Soult in Britain, and Eisenhower and Zhukov did reciprocally, from 1945 to 1955.

In 478, Pausanias was entrusted with command of a fleet that was to take back Cyprus for the Hellenes, as the four main islands off the shore of Asia Minor, Samos, Lesbos, Chios, and Rhodes, had all been liberated from the Persians. This mission was successful and from here, the Greek fleet sailed to the Bosporus and seized Byzantium. This was becoming more irritating than the Great King had to endure without riposte. He may by now have been philosophical about ceasing to be the overlord of a congeries of quarrelsome and chronically rebellious Greeks, but he was not prepared, nor in any such vulnerable position, as to endure gratuitous provocations on the mainland of Asia. Furthermore, Pausanias, unlike Themistocles, seems to have been transported to heights of self-importance by his back-to-back victories at Plataea and Byzantium. He decided that it was his destiny to unite the Persian and Greek worlds that he had done so much to keep apart and sought the hand in marriage of the daughter of the Great King himself.

Xerxes, doubtless bemused, if not astonished, played this along as Pausanias recruited a Persian bodyguard and disported himself in Persian costume, and descended into a treasonous correspondence with Xerxes, in which he offered to become Xerxes' agent in the subjugation of all Greece to the will and suzerainty of the Great King. He was recalled in alarm to Sparta and stripped of his command, but acquitted of the charge of outright treason, of which there was inadequate proof, and he was permitted to return to Byzantium in a private capacity, though the Spartan court must have known that by this time he was capable of any mischief. Dorcis was sent out to replace Pausanias, but the Greek allies were so outraged at Pausanias' lapse of loyalty and judgment, they demanded a change of the nationality, as well as the person, in command.

Athens had the largest Greek navy and had provided most of the ships and all of the tactical and strategic genius (Themistocles) in the repulse of the Persians, had the close relationship with the Ionians, and Pausanias had embarrassed Sparta by his betrayal and his Ruritanian self-important charade, so the change to Athenian command was natural, but it was also a humiliating rejection of Sparta. And, whatever the facts, Sparta did not endure humiliations with equanimity. Leotychidas had been found wanting and Pausanias an embarrassment. In Sparta there was a pro-Athenian, semi-isolationist (i.e. confined to the Peloponnese) party, and a more adventurous one. The first of these had been embarrassed when Themistocles engaged in his diplomatic chicanery while Athens was refortified and had sent to the Bosporus and had to recall Pausanias, and had to accept the non-installation of Dorcis. This sequence of events strained the primacy of that political faction in Sparta, and the alternative was a faction hostile to Athens, worldlier in its ambitions but more parochial in its attitudes. For the time being, the Delian Confederation was formed under the presidency of Athens. For her sacrifices, bravery, and leadership in victory over mighty Persia, Athens had earned that status. But proud Sparta was sullen, always a dangerous state of affairs in Hellenic affairs.

The Confederation of Delos was consecrated at the Temple of Apollo at Delos and contributions to its maintenance of the constituent members were deposited there, where its synods (executive council meetings) were held. The Confederacy was really a treaty between Athens and the associated states. There was an elaborate ceremony of exchange of oaths and adherence to the treaty, in which a large quantity of iron was hurled symbolically into the sea—the symbolism being that the alliance would remain solid until the submerged iron rose to the surface of the Mediterranean. It was an offensive as well as a defensive alliance, and its pledged objective was to retaliate effectively for the losses that the Persian invasion of Greece had inflicted. At least this was the account of Thucydides (who had exclusive primary sources to work from). The allies bound themselves either to provide their agreed quota of ships and men for a war of revenge on Persia, or to pay the cash required to maintain that quota instead. Synods met as necessary and served as a forum of appeal from the assessments of Athens and had some level of overall supervisory authority. Despite its evident utility, the Confederation of Delos would not have been successful, and might not have taken the form it did, if the Athenian fleet were not commanded by so honorable and diplomatically adroit a man as Aristides. The

Athenians were better at collegial arrangements than the Spartans, being less authoritarian in their own organization, more dependent on allies to assist them in their relatively exposed position in Attica, and more accustomed to seeking and working with more or less equal allies. And Aristides was the ultimate warrior-diplomat, a forerunner of emollient coalition-leaders such as Foch and Eisenhower.

There were two structural weaknesses in the Delian League: Athens alone decided which states would be required to contribute ships and men or money to different campaigns, and it was not decided in advance whether each state had the right to withdraw from this alliance at its pleasure and autonomously. The one-sidedness of this arrangement illustrates the immense prestige that Athens had earned, and the respect Sparta had squandered, in the fact that such an arrangement got off the ground at all. Had the right of secession been denied at the outset, no such numerous a Confederation as was established would have been made. The acceptance that Athens alone could decide when a withdrawal was acceptable, effectively meant that any move to secede amounted to an act of rebellion, against which Athens possessed the right to apply the full enforcement powers of the whole Delian League. Athens had the power not just to enforce adherence but to declare the penalty for any such attempt, effectively converting itself into the hegemonic power of southeastern Greece.

The Delian Confederacy, in practice, divided into five groups in matters of assessment: the islands, Thrace, Hellespont, Ionia, and Caria. These jurisdictions were quite fuzzy for some time; except for Rhodes and some other islands, the Persians retained their control over Caria. Some of the other areas were aspirational: the Delian League held Thracian Chersonese, and even Themistocles had, for a time, to accept grants to Lampsacus and Myus to be at the disposition of the Great King. The Delian Confederacy was an incremental, gradual enterprise. And it was preeminently a monument to Themistocles, though he was not allowed to participate in it. The Delian League and Confederacy was the culmination of Themistocles' strategy, his naval policy, including building the port at Piraeus, his victories as an admiral, his grand strategy for Athens to take the headship of a victorious Greece protecting its Ionian kinfolk, all of this reached its apotheosis in the Confederation of Delos.

Themistocles completed the reconstruction plan of Athens with an element of assured invincibility, with the massive expansion and fortification of Piraeus, and its access to Athens ten miles away protected by a wide road bounded by high thick walls for all its distance. Thereafter, all we know of Themistocles politically is that, in Plutarch's words, "The people having had their fill of Themistocles." It was like the electoral defeat of Winston Churchill in 1945. Henceforth, as long as Athens kept her command of the neighbouring seas, given the strength of her fortifications and of those that protected the access to Piraeus, she was invincible.

The success of Themistocles, whatever his immense services to the state, frightened the aristocracy, and the response arose from the marriage of Cimon, a thrusting meritocrat, with Isodice, granddaughter of the endlessly self-replicating Megacles. Cimon also married off his sister to a son of the wealthiest man in Athens. Cimon, by some combination of recognized merit and distasteful subornation, had himself appointed commander-in-chief of Athenian forces in 476 B.C., and held that position until 462. Plutarch provides the most believable account of the rise of Cimon, who was more sociable than Themistocles because Cimon could sing and play the harp, and he was also, like Themistocles, one of Athens' greatest military commanders. He was to become a rival to Pericles, who possessed cultural and oratorical advantages, but their rivalry sharpened Athenian public life at the height of its greatness, like those between Pitt the Younger and Charles James Fox, Thomas Jefferson and Alexander Hamilton, and Benjamin Disraeli and William Ewart Gladstone.

By early 476, Pausanias had been removed from Byzantium and the Delian Confederacy had secured the free passage through the Bosporus of all trade, and especially of grain and wheat from the Black Sea to Greece. It was obvious that the logical sequel would be the attempted expulsion of Persia from Thrace. With the Greeks in control of the Bosporus, the Persian presence in Macedonia and Thrace was isolated and vulnerable, unless Xerxes had a surge of revitalized interest in transpontine matters. Asia Minor was secure and the islands were in the hands of Athens' Ionian allies, so there was a plausible demarcation between the Greek states and the Persian empire, in which the Persian position in Europe was anomalous. Cimon set out to eliminate this Persian presence in 476. He was successful except Doriscus was never captured, and Eion put up a resistance that inspired the admiration of the known world and may have been the finest hour of Persian martial bravery in its entire history.

The Persian commander, Boges, resisted a siege through a harsh winter for which Greek soldiers were not well prepared, and finally, when the population was largely dead of starvation, he killed his family and harem and slaves as mercifully as he could, threw all precious metals and gems into the Strymon River, fired up a prodigious funeral pyre, and leapt onto it. Thucydides, who was not overly generous in his treatment of Persians, rendered Boges respectful homage. Cimon continued his campaign to uproot the Persians from Europe, but the historical record is sketchy. One of his early objectives was the rocky island of Scyros, a centre of piracy which menaced the sea lanes for everyone at the approaches to the Dardanelles. It was Dolopian and independent but Cimon went through the formalities of gaining a clear moral justification for attacking it (that he would do so was something of an innovation and indicated the extent to which Greece had become, even in modern terms, a somewhat civilized place—no Asian state had ever given an ethically serious reason for initiating hostilities against another. Apart from its threat to international navigation and commerce, Scyros had defied an edict of the Delphic Oracle to return the bones of Theseus, the mythical co-founder of Athens, supposedly buried at Scyros. Scyros had also ignored a demand of the Amphictyonic League (which oversaw the Oracle of Delphi), that Scyros pay reparations for some acts of piracy committed against some Thessalian ship-owners. Cimon quickly overwhelmed the island, expelled its inhabitants, and repopulated it with Athenians. Rugged and barren as it was, there was not an unlimited legion of revanchists seeking its repossession.

Cimon proceeded next against Carystus, the southern section of the island of Euboea. It was composed of Dryopians, unlike any nearby state, and had been roughly treated by Themistocles after the Battle of Salamis, and refused to join the Confederacy of Delos, which it regarded as a disreputable front for Athenian aggression and perfidy. The real motive for this action was to round out and homogenize, in political terms, the states near Athens; there was no trace of moral provocation as there had been with the buccaneers of Scyros, and the conquest was easy and the inhabitants gently treated. The only real penalty Carystus paid was that it was a coerced member of the Delian Confederacy, and in moral and constitutional terms, this was a decisive and portentous step.

The Confederacy of Delos began to define itself not as a league of voluntary comrade-states, but in some measure as also a league of dragooned and reluctant allies. The next step, in Cimon's strengthening of the League, toward the removal of Persia from Europe, was the suppression of the almost inexplicable attempt of Naxos to secede from the Delian Confederacy. It had joined the Confederacy in a spirit of vengeance against Persia for having sacked and burned the town of Naxos on their way to their rendezvous with the Greeks at Marathon. It is not clear why Naxos purported to secede from the Confederacy, but it was easily suppressed. The relevance of this was that it reinforced the evolving status of the Confederacy of Delos as less of a confederation and more of a compulsory recruitment and retention of states to the will of Athens and its closest allies, whether the local populations and legislatures wished it or not. In fairness to Athens, that city had paid the maximum price for the absence of a common front when the Great King attacked, and had contributed most, in men and human sacrifice and in genius of tactics and strategy to the repulse of the Persian threat. But it was still a qualificative demotion of the spirit and essence of an all-for-one-one-for-all alliance of voluntary partners.

In 467 B.C. the decision was made to take the counter-offensive after Salamis to the next step, and to try to dislodge the Great King from the overlordship of the Greek states of Asia Minor on the shores of the Aegean. This was, on its face, a bold stroke. Xerxes had lost the game with Greece in Greek territory but trying to throw him back in Asia Minor was a premature move, unless the Greeks could act very boldly and were assured of a sluggish response by the Persians, who became more powerful and heavily entrenched the closer one came to their place of origin. Cimon assembled a fleet of two-hundred triremes and reduced the fortresses defended by Persians; the unfortified towns apparently slipped their loyalty of convenience to Persia and adhered to their conscription, as dues and forces-contributing members of the Confederacy of Delos. As generally happens with aggressive military campaigns, the criteria for eligibility of invaded territories for reunification with the invading power, became steadily less convincing.

The Confederacy of Delos started with outright Greek coastal towns but pressed inland to communities that owed no more ethnic or cultural loyalty to Greece than to Persia and regarded both of them as interlopers, or even occupiers. In the summer of 466 B.C., the Persians finally responded to this incursion, and a fleet largely composed of Phoenician vessels, of about two-hundred triremes was assembled at the mouth of the Eurymedon River in Pamphylia, and with a considerable land force, was commanded by Ariomandes. There are competing versions of the engagements that followed. The narrative of Diodorus credits the Athenians with the capture of one-hundred Persian vessels in a decisive naval engagement off Cyprus, and the use of many of these ships to convey a Greek army in captured and adapted Persian uniforms, a giant amphibious Trojan Horse, past the Persian sentries at the mouth of the Eurymedon and into the Persian camp, where they suddenly erupted in violent combat and were joined by an overtly Greek force arriving in hot pursuit. This is exceedingly far-fetched, and more likely is the version of Plutarch, taken from Callisthenes, which holds that Cimon attacked in the conventional manner, after winning the naval engagement off Cyprus, though not as decisively as Diodorus had claimed, but won a decisive victory, and then succeeded in capturing most of the force of eighty Phoenician vessels the Persian commander had been anticipating. It was, by either account, and certainly no less by Plutarch's, one of the great victories of Greek arms, on land and sea, and secures Cimon a place of great distinction in the pantheon of Greek warriors.

Next to Marathon and Salamis, this was the greatest feat of arms of Athens. Cimon, cementing his claim on being one of history's great military commanders, knew when to stop and declined to advance further into the occupation of places where the Delian Confederacy would merely have been the military governors of sullen and hostile people. In this knowledge of where to stop, Cimon puts himself in the rarest company in the history of grand strategy, realizing, like Julius and Augustus Caesar, Richelieu and Bismarck and unlike Napoleon and Hitler, how to avoid becoming over-extended. Cimon rounded out his brilliant campaign, with a victory over the remaining Persian fleet as he found it and defeated in detail the Persians in Thrace and their steadily more demoralized allies. In 465, the island of Thasos, which was a wealthy trans-shipment point for the mines of Mt. Pangaeus, since the times of Peisistratus, followed the precedent of Naxos in going into revolt. The versatile Cimon shut this down, after a siege of two years, and imposed a severe peace, in which Thasos gave up its fleet, an indemnity, tribute, and watched as its fortifications were completely destroyed. This would be a powerful deterrent, as it was intended to be, against the temptation of others to rebellion, even though in the midst of Thasos' agony, Sparta had promised to assist it. Sparta was unable to do so because of the great earthquake at Sparta and the revolt of the helots, in 463. Sparta's response, like the spirit of Thasos' resistance, did not bode well for the future of the Confederacy of Delos.

In fifteen years of the Delian Confederacy, Cimon had cleared the Persians out of Europe, the Ionian Islands, and almost all the coast of Asia Minor from the Bosporus to Lycia. While the arrangement remained a confederation, it had aspects of being an Athenian Empire; Athens possessed most of the naval strength and provided the military and statesmanlike leadership and enjoyed immense prestige for its sacrifices and victories in the Persian Wars. Withdrawal from the Delian Confederacy was, in practice, almost like secession from an empire, and the theory of collegiality was seriously strained by the overbearing influence Athens exercised. We have seen that already some of the members had thoughts of Spartan intervention. As long as Athens led successfully and was not too oppressive, the Confederacy would be viable, but the potential problems were discernible.

It is not clear to us exactly how the standardization of judicial matters could be enforced, but in theory, the laws of the whole Confederacy were effectively identical, except for Chios and Lesbos, and the appellate process, though limited, was on a confederal basis. Nor do we know how many of the members, by 463, had been demoted to the less privileged status of members because of failure to provide their allotment of naval vessels or tax revenue. Cimon encouraged some degree of substitution of tribute instead of ships, as it made the navy more efficient and raised Athens' comparative superiority in arms and enforcement capability and projection of political influence. In Athenian domestic politics, Cimon was diplomatic and conciliatory in imposing penalties on delinquent subscribing states, and only slowly and with reluctance demoted allies to subjects. There were more authoritarian voices in Athens, and this would soon come between Cimon's successor as leader of the Athenian Conservative Party, Thucydides of Melesias (not the historian) and Pericles, the man synonymous with the Golden Age of Greece, whose time was about to come.

The rise of Athens coincided with a decline of Sparta's status. Pausanias played his part in this, and after his expulsion from Byzantium, he had removed to a place in the Troad (near ancient Troy), where he conducted mischief with Artabazus, the satrap of Dascylium, a propontine town. This became notorious and the ephors of Sparta recalled him again. He returned and was imprisoned, but soon released for a lack of conclusive evidence against him. However, the government of Sparta received word that Pausanias had been participating in a scheme to raise the helots in revolt and to enable the kings to dismiss the ephors (magistrates). The ephors waited for an unusually long time before moving to arrest Pausanias, who was tipped off that he was about to be taken into custody and fled for refuge to a sanctuary attached to the temple of Athena. The ephors walled up the temple to starve Pausanias out, and he eventually consented to be removed when he was on the brink of death. He died on the steps of the temple, of his accumulated weakness and famine. But the lesson of the episode was that Pausanias retained a considerable following grateful for his past services and especially his victory at Plataea, and many who resented that the victor of Plataea had been recalled to preserve an alliance with Athens.

The fall and death of Pausanias was connected to the fate of Themistocles, who had rendered comparable or even greater services to Greece than had Pausanias and had not so evidently taken leave of his position and loyalties. It appears that Themistocles' political agitation had resulted in his being officially ostracized in about 471, and he removed to Argos. Documents unearthed in the papers of Pausanias were alleged to have connected Themistocles with the conspiracies of Pausanias with the Persians, and possibly against the Spartan constitution also. Spartan envoys were sent to Athens to demand the prosecution of Themistocles, apparently for complicity in the plot against the ephors, and also, to some extent, in improper discussions with the Persians, what was known as the crime of "medism:" illicit alliance with the Medes—Persians. (Themistocles' enemies in the Conservative Party in Athens were more than pleased to take up these charges and he was accused of impeachable offenses and summoned to trial before the Assembly.) Themistocles did not respond to the charge and vanished from Argos. He fetched up in Corcyra, where the authorities were afraid of the joint wrath of Athens and Sparta, and he narrowly escaped to Molossia, where the king, Admetus, with whom he had had some disagreements in the past, had the generosity to have him conducted through mountain passes to Macedonia, where he embarked by ship for Ephesus, still in the hands of the Persians, narrowly avoiding capture at sea by the Athenian fleet blockading Naxos. From here he wrote to the new king of Persia, Artaxerxes, following the murder of Xerxes by his household, and Artaxerxes' success in a series of intrigues and murders in the palace of the Great King. Themistocles proceeded then to the Persian capital at Susa and promised to assist and advise in a Persian return to Greece. Artaxerxes received him warmly, accepted his offer and gave him custody of three Persian cities, but Themistocles was still planning his revenge and Persia's and enjoying his luxurious exile, when he died of natural causes in 459, mourned by the Persian king. He was sixty-four. (Plutarch claimed that he ceremoniously committed suicide rather than sully his glory as a Greek, but there is no real evidence of this.)

This episode illustrates the trait of the Greeks to renounce their heroes, and up to a point, the same case could be made about Pausanias. But Pausanias was only a soldier, though a capable one who rendered immense service at a decisive time. Themistocles was a great and decisively victorious admiral, and a great statesman also, and his death in exile is a human and, in some respects, a national tragedy, although he was well treated and much honoured in Persia. (It was a little like Winston Churchill seeking asylum in an unoccupied Germany after 1945 would have been.)

While the dramatic flight of Themistocles was in progress, Sparta's position as leader of the Peloponnese was seriously threatened. Argos had made alliance with Tegea and assisted it in rising against Sparta. Argos did not attempt a full revenge for the Battle of the Champions and the Spartan humbling of Argos almost a hundred years before. Sparta won narrowly at Tegea, and then decisively at Dipaea in 469 B.C. (Where the Argive army was not present). This enabled Sparta to reassert itself as the premier Peloponnesian state. Argos had not made a maximum effort, and most importantly for Sparta, the Athenian government and leadership of the Confederacy of Delos were at this time in the hands of people who strongly favoured a solid and trustworthy peace of mutual respect between the two greatest Greek states.

3. The Periclean Age

In 463, after he had secured the fall of Thasos, Cimon, in keeping with the unattractive Greek habit of persecuting their great men, was brought to trial, because of the official audit of his spending and income while conducting the siege. Traditional histories of Greece dismiss this as illustrative of the corruption of the demagogues.[1] Cimon was a wealthy man which makes it unlikely that he accepted, as was alleged, a bribe from Alexander of Macedon. The point of the recall was, now that Cimon had performed successfully all the military services that could reasonably be asked of him, to test the strength of the Conservatives and the so-called Democrats. Elections to the Assembly were personal and regional and not strictly partisan, and such esoteric matters as these tested the strength of the government. In this case, it was a test of the strength of the coalition of historic, wealthy, patrician, and even noble Athenian houses. What made this one of the turning points in Athenian history was

---

1 CAH, V, p. 68 (E.M. Walker).

that Pericles, a rising and already respected coming figure in Athenian politics, played a role, albeit a small one, in the prosecution. Cimon was acquitted, and the fact that he should be tried at all, after his immense services to the nation, and by a political riff-raff in a forum that scarcely made any pretense to being judicial, was an outrage. That the man who would soon assume a role as great as any, and rivalled by very few in Hellenic history, should have been associated with such a spurious endeavour, only illustrates the inadequacy of these earliest democratic forms of government. But the abstract significance of the trial was that the aristocratic houses couldn't hold the line in Athenian public policy any longer. Aristides, who rightly enjoyed immense prestige, both for his talent as a civilian and military leader and for his "ostentatious probity" was dead; Xanthippus, the leader of the Alcmaeonidae, was also dead, and Pericles was his son, and this event showed that Pericles had, in modern parliamentary parlance, crossed the aisle. While he was changing the course of his father's house, he was adhering to the policy of his mother's uncle, Cleisthenes, and voting for reform. It was an institutional shortcoming that such a turn in the tide of political sentiment should take the form of a spurious and politically inspired trial of one of the great servants of Athens.

The struggle for the control of the political direction of Athens was now well underway, and the leader of the opposition to the aristocratic Conservatives was Ephialtes, and Pericles was, for the time being, his deputy leader. It would be, as only the Greeks and Jews of early western peoples could make of political disputes, an intense and intricate struggle. The superficial similarity of these political contests in Athens and a few of the other Greek states, and the great stature of some of the protagonists, have got for Athens, in particular, and the Greeks of this era in general, an extraordinary historic prestige. No one has the right, academically or morally, to try to debunk that prestige. It should be kept in mind that the modern proponents of this philo-Hellenic view: the Whig utilitarians like Macaulay, the classicist romantics like Byron, classical scholars prominent in the public life of modern Britain, like W.E. Gladstone, Harold MacMillan, and Enoch Powell, have all romanticized and projected ancient Greece well beyond what it objectively deserves. The Greeks of that time were quarrelsome, corrupt, loquacious, and ultimately almost a complete failure, even against the relatively benign Macedonians and then Romans, and certainly against the decivilizing waves that followed. They were narrow-minded, unworldly squabblers, but they were splendid. They were the first people to inspire the world with any notion of democratic government, the serious rule of law in any sense that held out the slightest hope of general equality before the law, and of orderly changes of government with some reference to popular preferences. And they produced an era of great cultural and scientific advancement in a society that respected and encouraged those advances, even as they persecuted some of the authors of that progress. In a word, ancient Athens is much idealized and much exaggerated; but compared to anything that preceded it and most of what followed for two millennia (apart from Rome at its best, and leaving aside Rome's incomparable aptitude to expand and rule), it was a remarkably sophisticated and virtuous place and time. The trial of Cimon presaged a comprehensive legal and pseudo-legal attack on the ruling class of Athens. Imperfect as it was in abstract law, it was preferable to the contemporary alternatives for regime change, such as the recent murder of the Great King of Persia, Xerxes, by assassination with the complicity of an evil eunuch. In other states, as we have seen, changes of rule tended to be even more generally violent and to make no pretense to any legitimizing criteria such as competence, probity, and last of all, popular approbation.

The next test in the collective determination of Athenian public policy was in a completely unforeseeable call for help from Sparta. Although the long-standing rivalry between Athens and Sparta was involved, this would be a test of the balance of influence and power between the aristocrats and the middle class, a criterion that two-thousand years later became the principal issue in all advanced countries, and several centuries later in most countries, almost regardless of how advanced they were. In 464 B.C., Sparta suffered a very severe earthquake that allegedly killed up to twenty-thousand people and brought down all but a few buildings in the city, which was a good deal less monumental than Athens. The official Spartan view, showing their primitive conception of how the world functioned, held that the terrible earthquake was the punishment of the god Poseidon for the violation of his sanctuary at Taenarus, an offense for which a group of helots were seized, and following a summary proceeding of no legal credibility, were executed. Taking their cue from these spurious legal proceedings, the helots of Sparta rose in revolt, the great majority of the population, and advanced on the devastated city, provoking a general uprising against the outrageous structure of the Spartan state, where over ninety per cent of the population were slaves and serfs. The earthquake was generally regarded by the malcontents as a Godly invitation to rise up. The young king, Archidamus, lived up to the highest traditions of his courageous city, was unflinchingly calm, and received some aid at a timely moment from the old treaty-partners the Mantineans, and the advance on the ruins of Sparta was at least decisively repulsed. The insurgents were driven back and forced to take refuge on Mt. Ithome, which had steep cliffs on all sides and could be held indefinitely, as long as the defenders were well-stocked. The Spartan armed forces, for all their talents, were not good at siege-warfare, and they were facing an irreducible target and put out a call for assistance to the Peloponnesian allies, and others, in particular Athens, which had eliminated some very well-entrenched and redoubtable besieged cities.

It was in the spring of 462 B.C. that the Spartan request for assistance came before the Athenian assembly. Ephialtes and his democratic followers, led by Pericles, didn't see the benefits of assisting Sparta in its time of greatest need, in exchange for favours to be named later, an arrangement that Sparta would almost certainly have honoured and would have been a huge prize for Athens to have in its hand. Ephialtes and Pericles for a variety of reasons, had long hoped for, and were now eager to help bring about, a severe humiliation for a regime that they regarded as retrograde, ignorant, and contemptuous of the whole notion of human rights, though well-organized, courageous, and not to be underestimated.

Against them, in the Assembly of Athens, was the large bloc led by Cimon, who was not without eloquence, and argued powerfully that Greece should not, as a political entity, be allowed to become lame, and that Athens should not vote to cast aside its "yoke-fellow" in pulling the Greek states through all the internal and external crises. It was again illustrative of the deep-seated respect that Cimon personally enjoyed, and the policy of alliance with Sparta, however strained, also enjoyed among clear-headed Athenians, that Cimon carried the bill fairly easily. Cimon carried the assembly, which voted four-thousand hoplites, Sparta's and Athens' universally feared elite troops, under the command of Cimon himself, to assist the Spartans. Cimon, along with a number of other allies to whom Sparta had appealed, threw in whole-heartedly with Sparta. But their participation did not lead to the swift capitulation of the besieged, and in a singularly ill-considered gesture, the Spartan authorities concluded that Athens was just playing games and cranking up to betray Sparta, and they expelled Cimon and the Athenians, bag and baggage. This was obviously the end of the Athenian-Sparta alliance and it was judged by the assembly of Athens and by Cimon to have been a mistake to uphold their treaty with Sparta.

The effect of the dismissal of Cimon was electrifying in Athens; the Democrats took over almost effortlessly, and Athens withdrew from the anti-Persian Confederacy (having joined it in 481 B.C.), and immediately concluded alliances with Thessaly and Argos, Sparta's long-standing rival. In 461 B.C., Cimon was ostracized from Athens, completely unjustly, but as a bellwether of where the political winds were blowing, and his party was unable to prevent the crowning triumph of the opposition: the overthrow of the Areopagus, the supreme executive authority of the country. The traditional pro-Periclean denigration of Cimon's policy is unjust. It was as a member of the anti-Persian League that Sparta appealed to Athens and in that capacity that Cimon replied. Persia was not a threat anymore, because the alliance had been successful. That did not mean, as subsequent events were to confirm, that the alliance with Sparta had no value, even if it still had legitimacy. Cimon's enemies, including Pericles, for all his virtue and historic approbation, did not realize the gravity of the step they were taking.

Cimon's basic theory of the desirability of the two great Greek powers, Athens and Sparta being in alliance, was sound. The arguments against Sparta are ex post facto unverifiable claims by Thucydides that Sparta had already vitiated the treaty by promising to invade Attica, which they would have done if they had not been levelled by an earthquake. That is rank conjecture. There were some abrasions in the alliance but there is no reason to believe that they could not have been smoothed over. On this occasion, the Athenian leaders did something that four-hundred years later would be called crossing the Rubicon. They did not judge the consequences of their actions as well as Julius Caesar would, and even he died prematurely and violently as an ultimate consequence of his move.

A few months after the ostracism of Cimon, Ephialtes, having carried out his reform of the Areopagus (the conservative council of ex-archons), was assassinated, by Aristodicus of Tanagra on behalf of one of the secret societies that pursued the interests of the oligarchs in the Fifth Century in Athens when those interests were generally in retreat. With this, Pericles assumed the leadership of the democratic and reform elements of Athens and will become one of the most eminent statesman to appear in this lengthy narrative. The case can be made, and to some extent I will try to make it, that Pericles has been somewhat overrated, but no case can be made that he was not a man of extraordinarily high abilities, intelligence, culture, and in most respects, integrity. As has been recorded, his mother was an Alcmaeonidae and niece of Cleisthenes (and great granddaughter of Cleisthenes the tyrant of Sicyon), and her father was Xanthippus, commanding Athenian admiral at Mycale. His principal teachers were Damonides, musician and musical theorist, and the philosopher, Anaxagoras of Clazomenae. Damonides was something of a political scientist and while it would be unrigorous to credit him with forming Pericles' democratic views, he may perhaps be credited with encouraging them.

Anaxagoras would have seconded, if he did not incite Pericles' almost agnostic religious views. Pericles seems to have accepted a level of spirituality to be abroad in the world but regarded the oracles and their personnel as outright charlatanism and a retrograde and frequently financially corrupt force in society. Like many political leaders, from Jefferson to Churchill and beyond, Pericles believed enough to be a passenger with the adherent majority, enjoyed enough of the ceremony to be in Churchill's phrase reflecting modern ecclesiastical architectural idiom, "a buttress but not a pillar," and for expedient reasons, he avoided waging war on the religious practices of Athens, though he considered most of it to be a superstitious, light-fingered trumpery.

This was obviously the case, and with all the religious views that we have seen to this point, the only one that contained any kernel of serious believability was Jewish messianic monotheism; the rest were municipal gods of all activities and parts of the universe, terrestrially represented by a clerisy whose intellectual and pecuniary integrity, with the rarest exceptions, could not be vouched for or believed in by any serious person. This, even more than the impermanence and weakness of the political institutions unless they were defended by the prevailing force of arms, was the greatest weakness of the political societies that had developed in the previous twenty centuries in the Middle East and Southeastern Europe. The institutions of state were at risk one minute after the force that had upheld them was absent, and no seriously educated person could attach any credence at all to anything any religious spokesman uttered beyond velleities and platitudes about the general desirability of good conduct. Pericles was careful, as were many who followed him these twenty-five years, not to allow his religious skepticism to surface as a barrier to the adherence of the masses whose support he sought and needed.

In all respects, a more formidable pedigree than Pericles could scarcely be found. His only rivals as galvanizing statesmen in Fifth Century Greece were Themistocles, whose intelligence may have been as high as Pericles, but he was less educated and as a meritocratic parvenu, had neither the social and political finesse of Pericles nor a very leakproof notion of ethics; and Alcibiades, who was a well-born and refined person, but unscrupulous and rather louche. They were all brilliant, but Pericles had the most even and stable personality, and the most unimpeachable ethics, though the Athenian (and generally Greek) nature of impugning the integrity of even their most disinterested and great men, created problems for everyone who rendered some service to the state. It must be emphasized that we are considering only Pericles' competence as a national leader; as a military leader, he was definitely inferior to Themistocles, Cimon, and Alcibiades, all of them talented to sublime as military commanders. (In this time, little distinction was made between leading a government and an army or navy, and practically no distinction was made between naval and army commanders, though their skills are certainly not interchangeable, but they were thought to be so for a long time.)

Pericles possessed, throughout his career, a rigid ascetic devotion to his duty. He was not overly sociable, did not steep himself in luxuries, or depart from a frugal life at all. Pericles was reckoned by a wide margin to be the greatest orator of his time, with a technique that was simple and unaffected enough to rally the whole multitudes without demagogic techniques or intonations that would rankle with the better educated. It was understood at all times that Pericles spoke fearlessly and thoughtfully for the whole country as he saw Athens' interest and that he was above pandering to any interest but that of the state as a whole. The era we are now entering is rightfully known as the Periclean Age, and the talents of Pericles have been put forth here in superlative terms in advance of the recitation of the events of his brilliant career, but he does raise this peculiar Greek phenomenon of a great man whose greatness is based more on his qualities and what he might have done than on his actual attainments. Ultimately, Pericles was not successful, where that cannot be said of Themistocles or Cimon.

Greek history, especially as transmitted by Nineteenth and Twentieth Century British historians, is like the cricket game where the losers get the applause as they leave to the applause of the winners, and the winners leave relatively unapplauded. Pericles was great and even magnificent, but he was not especially successful. If the same criterion were applied to modern times, Napoleon would be unquestionably the greatest leader in the history of the world (and he may be), ahead of Lincoln and Roosevelt and Churchill and de Gaulle, and they would be just a nose ahead of Stalin and Hitler. The tendency of the British, including their historians in particular, to see the Greeks as romantic precursors to themselves, has somewhat skewed modern perceptions of Greece as a whole, and of some of its leading historical personalities. But this take on history, that the world advanced swiftly in a small place to achieve most of what an enlightened society could be, and that then Greece was supplanted by a second-rate knock-off but brandishing the power of a much stronger originating entity, and then that history went blank for over a thousand years, is tinged by self-service, and always has been with British historians. This view holds that Britain, in particular, emerged from the swamp of the Dark Ages, and regained the civility, culture, and civic virtue of Athens, added a great empire, but was also, after many historic vicissitudes heroically resisted, surpassed by a larger, more vulgar power, which it was Britain's mission to help to guide in the paths of historical and cultural righteousness, if not sophistication.

This is the core of accepted modern history in the British and British-influenced world, and there are elements of truth and at least of plausibility to it. But it is also fashioned from a subtle, almost persuasive egotism that has been one of the great weapons of British civilization. The problems with this school of history are that Greece was not quite so exalted, and that Britain was not quite so surely the national and cultural heir of Greece, and the United States was not as morally compromised or governmentally as uncivilized as Rome, let alone inferior to Britain, for this theory to hold. It is a fine attempt at a rationale for the world's development, but it doesn't work. The Greeks, Romans, British, and Americans were or are, magnificent sections of world history and will be so presented, but the history of the world cannot honestly be contorted to produce Britain, like a golden egg, as the most perfect society in history with the unquestionable pedigree of descent from a pristine and flawless Periclean Athens. That such a narrative has been so admirably argued and well-received is a part of this history, but it is not sufficiently accurate to be presented here otherwise than as a fore-warning. Where the greatness of Pericles is unchallengeable is in the cultural flowering and institutional progress of Athens while Pericles ruled it. He gave his name, uncontestedly, to an age, and it was a great age.

The alliance that Athens made with Argos and Thessaly in 462 was certainly designed as a provocation to Sparta and a signal that Athens was prepared to go to war with the Peloponnesian League. It is not obvious why Pericles considered this to be in the Athenian interest. There had been friendly relations between Argos and Persia, ultimately for reasons deemed to be useful to Persia's advance in Greece, no doubt, but this initiative invited Persian alliance with Athens, a grievous breach in Hellenic solidarity at a time when Persia, though unchallenged in its own seat, was a much-diminished threat to Greece. It seems that the Argive embassy and the Athenian delegation, led by Callias, son of Hipponicus, arrived simultaneously at Susa to negotiate their arrangements with the new Great King, Artaxerxes, in 461. But Persia, though the reception of the two delegations was exceptionally cordial, could not accept alliance with any Greek state without walking back the reversals Persia had sustained in Asia Minor. Artaxerxes was prepared to leave it at tribute from the newly liberated Hellenic states of Asia Minor, but that was the least he could accept, and Athenian pride in their recent victories in that theatre prevented any consideration of such a concession. Thus, the democrats of Athens, now led by Pericles though it is not clear that he was the author of these developments, had produced a configuration of states in which the democratic Greek states now faced imminent war simultaneously with Sparta and Persia, and without Sparta being sullied in pan-Hellenic eyes by overt collaboration with the Great King, the supreme ogre. The Athenian democrats had blundered, Ephialtes was dead, and Pericles was going to have to try to sort this out.

The alliance with Argos and Thessaly was expanded to include Megara, a wise move, as that state had been encroached upon by Corinth and sought Athenian protection and Megara had the fine army to help hold the isthmus and gave the formidable Athenian fleet a port in the Gulf of Corinth. Unfortunately, it also assured the hostility to Athens of Corinth. Athens distinctly took the headship of the alliance and replicated what Themistocles had done in building walls to protect the road between Athens and Piraeus and did the same in connecting Megara and its port of Nisaea, and Athens effectively occupied, as a benign invitee, much of Megara. In the initial engagements between the two sides in what was now the First Peloponnesian War, the Athenians lost a minor engagement with Corinthian land forces, but more than balanced that with a successful exchange with a Peloponnesian fleet off Aegina. This propelled Aegina, which had almost all its maritime commerce with the East-Ionia and Asia Minor, right across the path of the Athenian navy, into the alliance with Sparta and there was soon a major naval battle off Aegina, in which the almost unbeatable Athenian navy severely defeated the Peloponnesian fleet, sinking or capturing seventy of their ships, to relatively few Athenian loses. The Athenians were thus able to land a large siege force against Aegina. The war had started well for Athens.

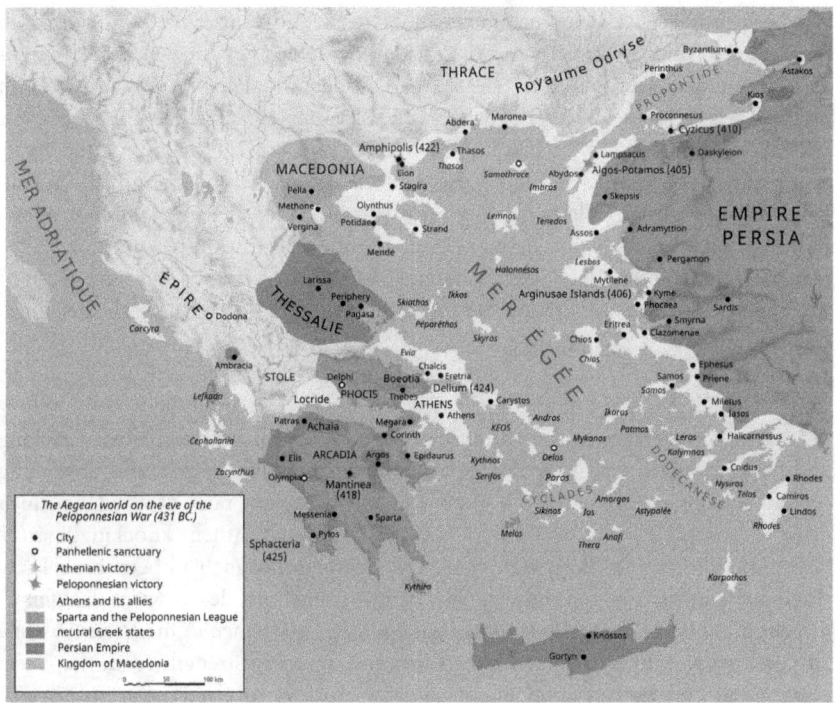

The scope of operations of the First Peloponnesian War was quickly escalated to include Egypt. The Libyan leader, King Inaros, had effectively revolted against Egyptian hegemony and had invaded Egypt and penetrated up to what later became Alexandria, and rallied a large section of the ancient realm of the pharaoh to his control. The Persian government had not been overly severe, but by this time the Egyptians had largely settled into the role that they have occupied for most of their subsequent history, as cynical connoisseurs of foreign rule, and the Libyans, whom Egypt has always regarded with some disdain, if they wished to engage the expeditionary forces of the Great King, were entitled to some encouragement. Inaros was in acute need of an ally with a strong navy. Athens was urgently solicited and responded and, believing that a sharp snap across the nose of the Great King might impart to the Persians the advisability of caution in Greek matters, sent her fleet of about two-hundred vessels, standing out of Cyprus, up the Nile, where they disembarked forces and assisted the Libyan king in taking over most of the capital of Memphis.

The Persian response was to send an embassy to Sparta under Megabazus, offering a large financial incentive to induce a Spartan invasion of Attica. In classic manner, the Spartans accepted the bribe but managed to find reasons not to invade Attica. This opened as a clear victory for Pericles, but he was over-extended: Athens had no ability to counter a serious effort by the Great King to restore his position in Egypt, and he could not leave fifty-thousand sailors and soldiers indefinitely in a country peripheral to the balance of forces within the Hellene world. Pericles was besieging Aegina while maintaining an extensive force in Egypt and helping to garrison the isthmian approaches to Attica in the defense of Megara. The Spartans and Corinthians saw this more clearly than, apparently, Pericles did, and Corinth attacked Megara directly, overland. Despite being acutely stretched for forces, the Athenian commander in the Isthmus, Myronides, conscripted reserves of the overly young and overly elderly, and threw them into battle against the Corinthians at Hallieis, and won a clear victory, another great feat of Athenian arms—reserve troops hastily thrown together defeated a seasoned army. With the Athenians as with the Spartans, at sea and on land, they were great fighters who earned and have received the highest historical admiration for their valour in combat, through all the subsequent centuries.

Sparta had finally to take action. The Athenians had been defeated diplomatically but had regained any lost ground by creating a severe problem in the strategic rear of the Persian Empire after the rebuff of diplomatic overtures, detaching and besieging into near-starvation Sparta's new-found ally Aegina, and now using second-echelon troops to give a good rebuff to the first rank of the Corinthian army. If Sparta did not intervene to stop this process of Athens knocking Sparta's allies around, it could all go very awry. The Boeotian League had been completely discredited and left in full disarray by Thebes' scandalous desertion of her fellow Greeks and her ineffectual but somewhat energetic assistance to the Persians while all Greece was under threat of armed invasion in heavy strength from the Great King. What Pericles had done, in considerable measure reversed the strategic position of the Athenians in A.D. 1941. On that occasion, the British leader, Winston Churchill, though threatened by four German and seven Italian divisions in Libya and western Egypt, sent substantial forces to assist the Greeks and Cretans, when the Germans eventually arrived there. The Greeks, in 1941 A.D. were defeated, with their British allies, and the allies were chased out of Greece and Crete. As it turned out, this enabled the Germans to launch a reinvigorated charge against the British defending the Suez Canal and the oil fields of Arabia and Iraq. But it also delayed by six weeks the German attack on the Soviet Union. These secondary theatres and incidental tactical considerations can ramify very widely.

Returning to Fifth Century B.C. Greece and Egypt, Sparta became convinced of the necessity of cultivating a serious and war-making ally of Sparta against Athens north of Attica, to divert the attention of Athens even further. It started in Boeotia. Sparta seized upon a squabble between small states in the Boeotian League to intervene with a large army there. The League had been a serious entity, with Thebes at the head of it, but Thebes' medism (again collusion with Persia) had completely discredited it and the whole enterprise of a League fell apart. The dispute which

Sparta invoked as an excuse to intervene was between Doris and Phocis, and Sparta came to the aid of Doris, which, as it was in the vanguard of the Dorian invasion of the Hellenes, Sparta claimed, somewhat dubiously, as its mother-state. This was a deft strategic and political move. Sparta was able to deliver across the Corinthian Gulf in the absence of the Athenian fleet, an army of fifteen-hundred of its formidable Lacedemonian hoplites and ten-thousand troops from among its allies in the Peloponnesian League, under the command of Nicomedes, regent in Sparta for the adolescent King Pleistoanax. The invasion force was much greater than necessary to assist Doris, and Nicodemus put Thebes back on its feet morally, shaped it up militarily and assisted in renovating its fortifications. Sparta now dominated Greece to the immediate north and down the isthmus to the west and South of Athens, and Nicomedes moved his forces up to the northern border of Attica, with Athens still distracted in Egypt and Aegina. Athens was now also busily engaged in enacting Themistocles' plan for the "long walls" protecting the roads from Athens over four miles to Piraeus and nearly three miles to the reserve anchorage at Phalerum. If these works could be completed, Athens would be invulnerable as long as her navy was preeminent, and that fact would require an immense effort, a long time, and one-sidedly good fortune to reverse. Strategically, the Hellene world was dividing into two camps, the impregnable land-power and the impregnable sea-power, somewhat like the position of England at times between the fifteenth and twentieth centuries, opposite, successively, Spain (and the Holy Roman Empire), France, and Germany, in the eras of the Spanish Armada, Trafalgar, and Jutland.

The secret societies who had murdered Ephialtes were still active in Athens on behalf of the conservative elements, and continued to be so hostile to Pericles and his democrats they did not hesitate to engage with Athens' mortal enemies. They managed to contact Nicomedes, but the Athenian rumour-mill aroused Pericles and his democratic allies, and they managed, allegedly (by Thucydides) to assemble and launch against the Spartan army in Boeotia an army of fourteen-thousand. If this figure is accurate, a significant number of them must have been veterans of the heroic battle at Halliesis against Corinth, and many Argive and Thessalian allies; no smaller force would stand a chance against Nicomedes' powerful and seasoned army. The two armies met at Tanagra in the spring of 457 and had a prolonged battle with heavy casualties on both sides. The Spartans ultimately prevailed, but only because of the desertion of the Thessalian cavalry, and neither side was in any condition to rejoin battle the next day. The Athenians retreated slowly and in good order, allowing the Spartans to regain the Peloponnese overland, giving the Megarian countryside a good burning and sacking on the way through. No force presumed to try to molest the retirement of Nicomedes. While the Spartans had technically won, they did not humble or intimidate the Athenians, and having raised up Boeotia, they left it to the mercies of the Athenian army, battle scarred, but master of the region after the Spartan withdrawal. Pericles, despite the risky strategic course he had followed, remained a successful war leader, and was strengthened opposite the conservatives, whose dalliance with the enemy was thoroughly publicized and rather implausibly disputed.

The most interesting element of apparently believable lore generated by this campaign is that Cimon, four years into the ostracism imposed by Pericles and Ephialtes, materialized on the Athenian route of march and volunteered to fight as a common soldier, he who had led the Athenian army to many of its greatest victories. The Council, dominated by Pericles, declined, but his friends took his suit of armour and set it up and fought to defend it from the Spartans all day, though their casualty rate was about ninety per cent, and the suit of armour was retained by the Athenian army. It is claimed by some but disputed by others that Pericles commuted Cimon's ostracism, but in either case, this episode raised Cimon's prestige to new heights and effectively silenced his enemies.

Boeotia, in the wake of the whirlwind visitation from the Spartans, was sharply divided between the federalists, led by a somewhat revitalized Thebes, supported by the oligarchic parties governing the adherent states who looked to their powerful kindred spirits in the patrician dictatorship of Sparta, and the anti-federalists, who did not want their civic freedom or comparative autonomy diminished by the Thebans as enforcers for Sparta, and sought the protection of Athens. Just sixty-one days after the Battle at Tanagra, the Athenians, commanded by Myronides, thoroughly defeated the Theban-led federalists, who crumbled and were routed. This was another great victory for Pericles, and the entire oligarchic and pro-Spartan project in Boeotia was in shambles. Most of the oligarchic states overthrew their governments, gently in some cases, and with the contemporary recourse to summary public executions of the recently powerful in others. Even Thebes was taken over by the local democrats. Pericles rounded out this phase of the struggle with Sparta by reducing Aegina to submission and integration into the Delian Confederacy as a heavily-taxed subject-ally, and the long walls protecting the roads that connected Athens to its ports were completed. At this point, Pericles had won every round: with the third Athenian army, he had effectively held his own with the Spartans and caused them to abandon their strategic enfilade to the north with nothing to show for it but a good looting of rural Megara, and had brought all of Boeotia into line, and soundly whipped the Aeginans. His domestic conservative enemies were sullen, discredited, and almost inaudible, and Athens had fulfilled the Themistoclean project of self-defense with massive fortifications and protected access to its navy, which held the sceptre of the whole Mediterranean. To rub Sparta's aquiline Hellenic nose in the maritime power of Athens, Pericles sent the Athenian fleet, with boarding parties, under the general Tolmides, around the Peloponnese in 455 B.C. He landed shore parties to destroy a major Spartan arsenal at Gytheum, burned large swaths of productive agrarian land, and brought Achaea and a couple of other places into the Delian Confederacy. It was literally a tour de force (that to some degree inspired, though it was more successful than the Elder Pitt's "descents"—amphibious raids on France in the Seven Years' War, twenty-two centuries later). Athenian fortunes were at flood tide, but they would not long remain there.

After Megabazus' effort to bribe Sparta to invade Attica in 459 had been rejected, the Persian king and court regained their traditional pride and determined to reassert their hegemony in Persia. In 456 a large army was raised under Megabyxus, and despite the very narrow land access to Egypt from Palestine, he succeeded in getting his whole army into Egypt and marching to the relief of the beleaguered

Persian garrison besieged in the White Castle in Memphis. The inept Greek commander, Charitimides, retreated to the island of Prosopitis, formed by a canal between two branches of the Nile. After a blockade of eighteen months, in which the Greek garrison was protected by the Athenian fleet preventing Persian vessels from crossing the canal, Megabyxus managed to drain the canal, stranding many Greek ships, stormed the island and smashed the Athenian army in Egypt. Only a small force escaped. And a naval relief force that had been sent, unaware of the turn of fortunes, sailed into a trap and was eviscerated by the Phoenician fleet in one of the mouths of the Nile. The Great King was well served by Megabyxus, who quelled the Egyptian insurrection, received the surrender of Inaros, who, following a supposed breach of his surrender terms, was crucified. Only one Egyptian prince, Amyrtaeus, hung on in a wild and marshy part of the Nile Delta called "the Fens." The Athenian expedition to Egypt, which had been so successful for several years, was the greatest disaster in Athenian history up to that time. The effort of Thucydides in particular, to downplay it with a very brief summary, cannot conceal that the six-year expedition had cost Athens and her allies two-hundred and fifty ships and fifty-thousand men. These were huge losses to the small and compact Greek states, and it is a wonder that Pericles' prestige was such, astonishingly, that his incumbency survived such a crushing and humbling defeat, especially given the shabby treatment Athens meted out to its most victorious commanders, Themistocles and Cimon.

Even before this catastrophic news reached Athens, the Periclean government had thought it prudent to move the treasury of the Confederation of Delos from Delos to Athens, from concern for a possible raid by the Phoenician fleet, again contending for mastery in the Eastern Mediterranean after the reversals sustained by the Athenian navy. Athens had sent a force through Boeotia to kick Thessaly back into line, as the desertion of its cavalry at the battle of Tanagra, which was all that prevented a great Spartan defeat, had not been forgotten. Athens was supporting the monarchical party in Thessaly, which was opposed by the oligarchy of the Knights, and the two sides were closely divided. The Athenian premise was that their forceful intervention would tip the scales in favour of their local allies, Thessaly would rally and the whole Boeotian League and the alliance with Thebes would be solidly established as a northern bulwark of Athenian influence. The Athenians were seeking to establish Orestes on the throne, but while waiting for this hoped for consummation, Orestes had been forced into exile. The Athenians met the oligarchic Thessalian army near Pharsalus (which would enter history prominently four centuries later because of Julius Caesar). The Thessalian cavalry, who had deserted at Tanagara, were masters of their home ground and rolled up the Athenian hoplites. The Athenian army was obliged to retreat, in good order and not severely defeated, but mission unaccomplished. Pericles now personally led a smaller expedition, of only about a thousand men and narrowly defeated a small force of Sicyonians, but was not successful in his object of taking Oeniadae in Acarnania. His mission was unsuccessful but made the point that Athens had yielded none of its ambitions for respect in the Hellenic world, even if its foray into Egypt had ended ignobly and at great cost. Athens remained a great Hellenic power, and Pericles' position appeared to be unshaken in Athens.

There was a de facto truce in Greece for several years. Cimon's ostracized condition ended in 451, and he returned to Athens and resumed his dispute with Pericles. To shore up his position, Pericles adopted two laws designed to reinforce the democrats: henceforth jurors would be paid, and electors in civic elections in order to be able to prove they were Athenian, would have to prove that both their parents were Athenian. Pericles, though hard-pressed by Cimon, was able to hold his position, despite the setbacks he had suffered. But in foreign policy, Cimon was successful. Athens did not have an entirely coherent system of government, as one faction might command the support of the Assembly in foreign affairs and another in domestic. This was in fact, what occurred. Cimon negotiated a five-year truce with Sparta, while severing the alliance with Argos, which, as part of the same intricate negotiations led by Cimon, concluded a thirty-year truce with Sparta. But in 450, the Assembly approved the construction of a fleet of two-hundred vessels to replace those lost in the Egyptian misadventure, and to reopen the war with Persia under Cimon's command. It was Cimon's view at all times that Athens should focus on beating back Persia and defending her interests against Persia in Asia Minor, Thrace, and the Aegean, and not squander her energies and resources in Hellenic internecine warfare. These arrangements constitute a serious rejection of Pericles, and also show that the return of Cimon in Athens strengthened the hand of the Spartan moderates in Greek policy. Unmistakeably, this rolling back of the clock in foreign and security policy was a sharp rejection of Pericles, but his retention of his control over domestic policy indicates just as clearly his popularity as a reform leader in Athens.

In 450, Cimon sailed at the head of two-hundred triremes, Athenian and allied, and stopped in Cyprus to stamp out a rebellion at Citium, in the southeast of Cyprus. He sent sixty of his ships on to assist Amyrtaeus, who was still holding out in the Fens. So a spark of the Egyptian intervention was kept alight. Cimon died, late in 450, and it is not clear if this was from wounds or natural causes. The mission to wrest Cyprus from Persia was abandoned, but the next year, the Athenian fleet decisively defeated a joint Phoenician and Cilician fleet at the Cypriot Salamis, and a Greek army was also victorious. The Persian control of Cyprus continued, but as a final service, Cimon had restored Athens' prestige as a naval power, and partially reversed the debacle in Egypt and the setback in Thessaly. The death of Cimon effectively ended conflict with Persia, but on a basis of mutual respect and a clear demarcation of influence. Pericles had learned that war on two fronts was beyond the resources of Athens and attrition seems to have satisfied both the great Athenian democrat and the Great King, that the interests of the two powers should be left where they were. Athens would take no aggressive actions against Cyprus, Cilicia, Phoenicia, Egypt, or other Persian positions, and Persia would send no fleet into the Aegean. There were subsequent claims that a treaty existed which formalized these conditions, but there is no real evidence of that and the balance of historical opinion is that peace arose from the withdrawal of contending forces and the acceptance of a military status quo, not diplomacy.

Athens' problem was no longer Persia. Sparta remained unsatisfied and the empire in northern Greece that Athens had hastily assembled in Boeotia was far from secure. It all started to come unstuck with what was grandiloquently called the Sacred War. The control of the Temple of Delphi was always contentious in Greece, and the Phocians claimed it as an administrative responsibility of theirs as Delphi was ostensibly on Phocian territory. Practically all other Greek states opposed this and after the Phocians formally occupied the precincts of the Temple in 448 B.C., the Spartans dispatched an army across the Gulf of Corinth and briskly chased off the Phocians. The Spartans professed to be acting for all Greeks and they promptly withdrew. This motivated Pericles, who should have learned to be more careful, to lead an Athenian army, picking up Phocians as he went, to reinstall Athens' Phocian allies, at Delphi. None of this violated the Five-Year truce between Athens and Sparta, as they were not engaging each other, but it assured that at the expiry of the five year term, matters could deteriorate quickly.

In fact, it all went downhill ahead of the lapse of the treaty. In Thebes, Athens' monarchic protégés so mismanaged the country that the oligarchs rose up and overthrew them and welcomed in all the other dispossessed oligarchs whom Athens had evicted in Pericles' swift reassembly of the Boeotian League. An insurrection, planned at Thebes, began to ripple across Boeotia, starting with the northwest, bordering Phocis, where mixed Boeotian oligarchic forces seized the cities of Orchomenus, Chaeronia, and others. The Athenian Assembly, despite eloquent warnings from Pericles that they did not appreciate the gravity of conditions in Boeotia, dispatched the workmanlike Tolmides one more time, but with only a thousand youthful troops and a couple of hundred token allies, to deal with a state of regional disaffection that would require a much stronger force to stabilize. Tolmides performed well, took back and garrisoned Chaeronea, and then prudently withdrew. But he was overtaken by a larger insurrectionist force, was slain in battle at Coronea, where the Athenians were severely defeated and most of his diminutive army was captured. The Assembly, unrepentant at having authored this famous scheme, contrary to the warnings of Pericles, promised to evacuate all of Boeotia in exchange for the return of their prisoners—most of them the sons of noble Athenian families. With the Athenian withdrawal, the remaining Boeotian allies renounced alliance with Athens, even Phocis, to whose assistance Pericles had just come. Athens' northern Greek empire simply collapsed like a house of cards in a few days and with no direct application of force necessary.

The Five Years' Truce expired in 446, and Sparta and her allies had already prepared their response to events. Euboea, just north east of Athens, revolted en masse; Pericles took the main Athenian army to suppress this very serious threat. As he did so, and by careful prearrangement, Megara rose, massacred the Athenian garrison, and drove the Athenians out except for a couple of small towns. The news from Megara arrived before Pericles had got the main Athenian army to Euboea, and the remaining army units in Athens were sent to Megara but were clearly inadequate in number to face the task, and withdrew with difficulty by a circuitous route, harassed by the soldiers of disaffected former vassal states. Pericles had no choice but to abandon hope of subduing Euboea, when further news arrived that the (mainly Spartan) Peloponnesian army, under Spartan King Pleistoanax had already begun to invade Attica. Athens itself remained impregnable because of its fortifications, including its port cities, and its navy remained invincible in Greek and Aegean waters, but the supplementary position Athens had built up, effectively from its principal role in the repulse of the Persians, was being spontaneously sloughed off like the winter coat of an animal.

At this critical point, Pleistoanax and his advisor, appointed by the Ephors, Cleandridas, withdrew. It was alleged in Sparta that Pericles had bribed them, and the war party secured the forced abdication of the king and the exile of Cleandridas. However, the terms reached between Pericles and Cleandridas, which secured a relatively free hand for Athens opposite her neighbours but restored an effective joint-leadership of all Greece by Athens and Sparta was preserved into what became the Thirty Years Peace. This was Pericles' finest hour: his diplomacy gained a peace more favourable than conditions on the ground appeared to warrant, and taking up his military command, he led the Athenian army, five-thousand hoplites, fifty triremes, and a support train into Euboea, and ruthlessly suppressed and disciplined the entire island. He banished the entire aristocracy of Chalcis, and annexed appreciable territory from Histiaea, the leading towns of Euboea. Pericles the democrat had shown his versatility. Athens and its immediate vicinity was safe and sound, even if the Boeotian enterprise was in shambles. Thirty years of peace were declared to ensue between Athens and Sparta, starting in 445 B.C.

CHAPTER EIGHT

THE PELOPONNESIAN WAR II
THE DEATH OF PERICLES, 445 TO 420 B.C.
❦
ARCHIDAMUS AND BRASIDAS

Archidamos, 1629 woodprint   Brasidas by Walter Crane (circa 1900)

1. The Thirty Years Peace, 445 B.C.

THE PEACE CONFERENCE met at Sparta and the negotiations do not seem to have been unusually arduous. It was agreed that Athens would abandon her landward empire. The two ports in Megara, Pegae and Nistaea, as well as Achaea and Trosezen in the Peloponnese, were a particular irritant to Sparta. But Sparta recognized without reserve or exception Athens' entire empire in the Aegean. This fact, coupled to the impregnability of Athens and its ports, fortified as they were, and by Athens' continuing maritime dominance assured that it emerged from a harrowing and dangerous conflict still as a coequal lead state of the Hellenes, and completely untouched in sea-girt areas of its greatest interest. (Any Athenian interest in the Peloponnese was entirely designed to keep Sparta on its back foot; Athens had no other interest in that area.) To the annoyance of Corinth, Athens retained the fortress town of Naupactus dominating the entrance to the Gulf of Corinth, and Aegina continued to pay tribute to Athens, though nominally autonomous. Neither Athens nor Sparta would assist factions in revolt in the others' allied states; neutral states were free to join either party's confederacy, and differences between the contracting powers would be settled by arbitration. Euboea, despite having rendered great service to the Peloponnesian League by its timely and tenacious revolt, was abandoned entirely to the mercies of Athens, which assured a harsh retribution for Euboea's almost mortal stroke.

The Thirty Years Peace was undoubtedly a humiliation to Athens when compared to its former status, but it secured it a strong position and was a considerable achievement for Pericles, especially as his impetuosity had generated the rockslide of negative events which was ended by the treaty. For so talented a statesman to imagine that Athens could fight Sparta and Persia at once was an astounding lapse of judgment. The error was compounded by the misplaced conceit of imagining Athens capable of durably sustaining an empire on the mainland of Greece. Errors of this sort of strategic over-reach would recur constantly in subsequent centuries. Louis XIV, Napoleon, the German Emperor Wilhelm II, Hitler, and the Soviet Union would all be examples of either carrying on major wars on two or more fronts at once, or generally overstretching their natural powers of control of peoples or countries against their wishes.

Democracy, as it was practiced in Athens, was still a novelty in Greece; and as in all the intervening centuries, the democratic states assumed that once other countries were aware of the availability of democratic freedoms, they would opt for them. The Jacobins assumed that all Europe would rise and overthrow the nobility and the ecclesiastical leadership of their countries as the French people in full exaltation of soul counter-attacked the armies of royalists and mercenaries that harassed them. The democratic spirit fired the French with almost super-human courage and tenacity but did not affect the enemy very much. The egalitarian and fraternal spirit of the French was veritably unstoppable when commanded by a military genius, as it was by Napoleon.

In the case of Athens, some historians have made the case that if the Athenian mission in Egypt had been commanded by the almost invincible Cimon, instead of the inept and slothful Charitimides, Egypt could have been durably ruled by Athens and even Sparta would have had to defer to Athens as the premier Hellene state.[1] But Egypt has never been ruled by foreigners indefinitely and particularly not by a small number of foreigners relative to the population of Egypt. The whole concept was strategically insane. After the Aegean had been secured, all Athens' efforts at expansion should have been down the Mediterranean to the west, where it would not have been demographically disadvantaged. Twenty centuries later, the British would realize this and populate North America across the western ocean, rather than trying to occupy parts of Europe (though they would squander most of this also in mismanaging the American colonies).

In about 447, as Pericles was about to begin construction of the Parthenon, he invited delegates from all Greek states to come to a Congress to discuss the

---

1 CAH, V, p. 92 (E.M. Walker).

reconstruction of all temples that had been destroyed in the late war with Persia. The Greeks of Italy and Sicily were not included, as they naturally were unaffected by the war with Persia. Pericles was much admired in Athens for this gesture, but he must have known that it would be demeaning to Sparta to attend, and effectively recognize the convening power of Athens over the whole Hellenic world, and for the purpose of assisting in reparation for the damage done by Persia in areas outside the Peloponnese, which Sparta did not claim or admit to be any of its business.

While this was an overly grandiose idea, Athens had consolidated the Confederacy of Delos into an empire. The Synod of the League of Delos had ceased to meet, the treasury had been moved from Delos to Athens, and the board of the Hellenotamiae had been converted into a magistracy of Athens, and the jurisdiction of Athenian courts now extended through the entire confederacy. It had been a smooth and elegant accretion of status from a city state to a maritime empire, and Themistocles, Cimon, and Pericles, in particular, deserve the credit for it. Only Chios, Samos, and Lesbos were still autonomous. It must be said that Athens was an exemplary colonial power. Admittedly, the challenges of assimilation are trivial where a state is enveloping descendants of its countrymen and there is a common culture, language, and ethnicity. That being said, Athens spread democracy throughout its Aegean empire wherever it did not already reside, and it stamped out piracy, which had plagued much of the Aegean, and it kept out the Persians, of whom a number of the affiliated states did not have pleasant memories. (As soon as Athens' preeminence ended, the long-extinct pirates miraculously revived and terrorized the Eastern Mediterranean until suppressed by the Romans.)

Great democrat though Pericles was, he had his authoritarian moments. The Athenian legal system was not infrequently used by Athens to remove recalcitrant local leaders, sometimes hauling them into court in Athens on thoroughly spurious charges. Pericles also claimed that as long as Athens kept Persia out of the area of the so-called Confederacy, it had no obligation to explain what it did with the tribute it received. This would be the arrangement with a province of a federal country, but as the position adopted by a state that was still the first among supposed equals in a confederation, it was high-handed, though in practice, not a bad deal for the subject states and not something they had the ability to do much about.

Pericles was always careful to ensure that no member of the Delian Confederacy had a just grievance for revolt. There was the problem of the cleruchies; colonies within the territory or adjacent to and competing with the member states of the Confederacy. This was an institution that dated back to Pericles' distinguished kinsman Cleisthenes, but Pericles refined it to be a method for relief of unemployment in Athens—simply shipping the unemployed out to virgin territory, and for the occupation and development of strategic sites around and for the monitoring of the Athenian Empire. Naxos, Andros, and Chersonese in Thrace were among the early recipients of such settlements, and they became quite widespread. The people involved remained Athenian, and thus were exempt from local tax, and were often seen as spies from the central government or even outright forces of observation, if not oppression, subtle or otherwise. At the least they were seen as privileged interlopers, and resented as recipients of privileges always are.

While Pericles' record as a national statesman of Athens in strategic and foreign questions had been mixed, his astute grasp of the requirements for the defence of Athens, only twenty-five years after Athens herself had been occupied and largely destroyed, was exemplary. His grasp of the potential for further extension of Athenian influence was inflated, as if, and this is not speculation about the reasons for certain misjudgments, he thought Athenian military supremacy among the Hellenic states was equivalent to its cultural superiority. But it must also be said that uneven though his judgment was in these matters, he largely redeemed his strategic miscalculations, at least up to this point, with surpassing diplomatic skill and a sure touch at rousing popular and general support from his countrymen for the sacrifices and exertions necessary to furnish the national determination to pursue successfully Athens' vocation as leader or co-leader of the Hellenic world. And in fulfilling this role, Athens secured for itself an indelible and it must be said, a glorious, chapter in the entire history of mankind. Vastly more numerous civic, tribal, and national populations have striven much longer in the same pathways without remotely approaching the military glory, cultural primacy, or sophistication of government and political society that Athens, in particular among the Greek states, gave to the world.

Even though the democratic participation in government in Athens did not extend to women, or the servile majority, and was confined to no more than twenty per cent of the adult population, it was extraordinarily innovative, and must be taken as the origin of the democracy that now prevails in the world, though it lapsed for many centuries. Variants of that Athenian model were revived and amplified unimaginably to Periclean Athenians, by the gradual devolution of powers from the Crown to the people in Great Britain and its Commonwealth, by the revolutionary propagation of the rights of all men in liberty, equality, and fraternity of the French (with a good deal more discontinuity of application even than in Athens), and finally by the mighty promotional proselytization, backed by irresistible economic, military and popular cultural strength, of the colossal United States of America.

Between the arrival of the Great King's army in the Acropolis and the rise of Pericles, there were two important political developments in the evolution of Athenian democracy. The performance of the Areopagus, the forum of former archons, had been so distinguished and courageous in the abandonment of Athens to the Persian invader in the framework of the larger Greek national interest, that the authority of this otherwise rather arcane and obsolescent body had been circumscribed, but revived. And in recognizing the selfless bravery of the Athenian people altogether, in making such great sacrifices so courageously in the face of the Persian invasion, Aristides opened the archonship to all four of the old Solonian classes of citizens, a conspicuous enlargement of the eligible pools for the selection of the leaders of Athens. The Areopagus was effectively transformed into a supreme court, but its political authority, which had largely lapsed anyway, was distributed to the Council, the Assembly, and the popular law courts. It was a mark of the revived distinction of the Areopagus that membership was automatic for retired archons, but that tenure was for life.

Athenian historians regarded it as the turning point in the history of their democratic institutions that the Areopagus, this ancient institution of the elders of Hellenic life and wisdom, was reverently revived to recognize its traditional virtues, but rolled back to an appellate function to make way for the inexorable forces of democracy. This was the reform of Pericles' immediate predecessor, Ephialtes, and the combined juridical elevation of the Areopagus with its jurisdictional restriction not only affronted conservative sentiment but also shocked traditional religious feeling and took a long step toward the secularization of temporal authority.

Prior to this, the whole aura of the Areopagus was shrouded in imputed ecclesiastical insight and inspiration. Athens, the modern reader must keep in mind, not only had none of the formally enunciated powers of government of the United States and other modern republics, but almost none of the officially solemnized stages of evolution of continuous jurisdictions, such as Great Britain, the Netherlands, and Switzerland, that gradually broadened powers and democratic safeguards down to the people. This redefinition of the role of the Areopagus would be revisited in harsher times; this was an important step in Periclean times. The reform of the archonship extended it to the third Solonian class, after Penticosiomedimni and the Knights, which were the Zeugitae; and even the lowest class, the Thetes, were, in practice, admitted to vote and had other prerogatives of citizens, though this occurred before it was formally proclaimed. The principal of equal eligibility for all, took hold and was a fundamental principle of evolved Athenian democracy.

Despite the comparative liberality of Athenian democracy under Pericles, as it was a non-constitutional system, rights could be radically altered, and the system of government profoundly overhauled by laws passed in a very populist and informal manner. In Periclean times, any citizen could propose a law, he could also be prosecuted for advocating adoption of a law or amendment of an existing law that was deemed to derogate from the law or to affront the public interest. As we celebrate Athenian democracy and see elements of the highest contemporary civic virtues so long ago, we cannot fail to note the vulnerability, unevenness, and manipulability of Athenian institutions. At its best, it was an astoundingly prescient and virtuous political society, fully worthy of the elegiacal paeans of adoration of the full range of enlightenment and modern commentators, from utilitarian Whigs like Macaulay, romantics like Byron, great liberals like Gladstone, susceptible French republican idealists like Rousseau, and hugely knowledgeable contemporary American republicans like Victor Davis Hanson.

Of even greater significance in the development of democracy was Pericles' grant of payment for jury work in 450. Since all were eligible for such work, paying everyone was of great assistance to the less affluent. At about the same time, as has been mentioned, Pericles restricted the franchise to only those both of whose parents were citizens. This had the effect of reducing the number of citizens by about five-thousand.[2] This was, in fact, a reactionary move, but by the standards of the time, it was not undemocratic. Pericles strengthened the democratic state, at least notionally, by refining the electorate to make it more highly prized and immune from truckling and pandering by demagogues. Modern democratization has tended to be identified with the broadening of the franchise, as in the successive British Reform Acts from 1832 to 1885.

---

2 Ibid., p. 102.

Plato, fifty years later, charges Pericles with having corrupted Athenian democracy by paying those attending the Assembly (jurors and, partially, legislators). Plato claimed that this made the citizens "indolent, cowardly, greedy of filthy lucre, and loquacious."[3] He is to some extent supported by Aristotle, who claimed that twenty-thousand people derived their income from this source, which, if true, meant approximately a third of the ostensible work force. Aristotle and Plato railed against what Aristotle called a "nation of salaried paupers." This was excessive, as the number twenty-thousand also included members of the army and navy, whose numbers were reduced when the country was militarily inactive, and when no conflicts impended, they largely concerned themselves with suppressing piracy at sea and assuring the safety of roads and land borders.

The receipt of what amounted to a minimum wage for attending sessions of the Assembly cannot have appealed to young men of any ambition or talent, and would do quite well, even by very modern and contemporary standards, as a reward for the attention and engagement of the aged. In fact, it constitutes a very imaginative innovation in work-fare, not much followed by posterity, but comparable to all but the most creative modern versions of workfare, such as Franklin D. Roosevelt's vast Tennessee Valley Authority and Civilian Conservation Corps, and Dwight D. Eisenhower's Interstate Highway Program. Plato frequently exaggerated, and his appreciation of recent history and of contemporary events, like many Intellectuals in all subsequent eras, were frequently overstated and other-worldly. Pericles was not above vote-buying, and no significant percentage of politicians before or since, have been, and as a benefit system, this one was original and constructive. Even if half of those who attended sessions of the Assembly for the fee did so because they needed the money, that does not vitiate the quality of their participation in those sessions or incite the inference that the deliberations and conclusions of those sessions were negatively affected thereby. (Plato is scarcely a logical source for charges of loquacity, even when directed against defendants who were not his peers.) There seems no doubt that Pericles' initial motive in paying the attenders at the Assembly was to incentivize participation in civic activities. That it also became a form of welfare for the unemployed is true and must have been foreseeable, but that it was intended as a benefit system to rival the attractions of real work for those capable of working, is completely unsubstantiated and unlikely. As politicians go, Pericles was relatively principled.

The most noteworthy change to the political state of Athens in Periclean times was the rise of the Demagogues. It is a testament to the liveliness of Athenian democracy that the arrival of people whose talent and eligibility for influencing the course of public life was their ability to stir mass opinion by their oratory. In an undemocratic system, the ability of people to stir listeners by their forensic and oratorical talents are only decisive in closed proceedings of small numbers, and a mere fillip to public morale beyond that. Up to and including Pericles, it was the custom in Athens that whoever was the leader of the state was also the General, which in practice required that he be a member of the old families of Athens which all had a tradition and knowledge of military life, if not any aptitude for military strategy

---

3 Ibid., p. 104.

and tactics.

In the early years of the Peloponnesian War, in the relatively accessible democracy of Athens, a new type of public figure emerged who was naturally and sociologically dangerous to an elitist like Pericles. Tradesmen and skilled craftsmen, rather than learned or patrician men, pushed forward into public discussion. The patrician generals were rural aristocracy, fairly similar to the long rule of the landed aristocracy in Britain. As in Britain, after the First Reform Act of 1832, the aristocrats remained in power, Whig peers like Grey, Melbourne, and Palmerston, before the less well-born exploited demographic facts and emerged: Peel, Disraeli, and Gladstone. Something similar, toute proportion gardée, can be said for the United States: eventually, the Virginia plantation owners and learned Boston lawyer-academics who founded the country (Washington, Jefferson, Madison, Monroe, and Adams, Franklin and Hamilton were exceptions) gave way to the frontiersman and General Andrew Jackson, and then to men of rather average birth, until the Roosevelts, more than sixty years later. The socioeconomic origins of the president have not much mattered after that, and have oscillated.

In Athens, the first demagogue who became prominent was Cleon, though to some extent Eucrates and Lysicles had preceded him. These men were noteworthy because their more modest socioeconomic origin, as craftsmen, made them more practical in their appreciation of public opinion, and they were urban, unlike the Periclean and previous holders of that office, who were ample rural landowners, ambassadors from the era when the wealth and wisdom of the state rested on those who grew the most. The eminent rural families had produced Miltiades, Cimon, Xanthippus, Pericles, Thucydides (of Melesias), Aristides and Ephialtes. Only Themistocles had come from outside that background and had been promoted and deferred to when the state needed his service, and dispensed with like a used antimacassar by an exalted dowager when they did not. These demagogues were opponents of the government; they were not just rural relatives annoyed at having been bested in small and exclusive groups like children sulking after a sports prize day.

The demagogues did not particularly seek an office, and generally did not have one, other than as members of the Assembly—the same status as any other citizen who was not dodging his civic responsibilities. Yet, it was of the nature of the Athenian democracy that such a person, by the lucidity of his views and power of his articulation could exercise enormous influence. In Athens, anyone could introduce and speak for a measure, and this was not an accessibility to popular influence that was replicated in the world for many centuries. These demagogues were not elected by anyone; they were citizens who dropped by the assembly of a day, got something off their chests, and if they were plausible and persuasive, could suddenly have great influence, as some did. If carried by the Assembly, a demagogue's bill or motion could prevail. There was no sober upper house or wise holder of the veto, though the Council could amend it, and even send it back. These were not, in modern parliamentary terms, confidence motions. Rejection of a measure from the General or one of his colleagues, did not require a change or test of regime, and the demagogues, even if they eventually derailed a legislative project, had no right to substitute one of their own for it.

The rise of these demagogues exposed one of the most serious failings in the Athenian system. Though all civil and military officials had to account for themselves at the end of each year, those who vociferously advocated policies that were adopted but did not themselves execute those policies, were never accountable for the consequences of their actions, if the actions they championed were unsuccessful. Hugely successful servants of the people and state of Athens, including Themistocles, Miltiades, Cimon, and eventually Pericles himself, were all tried and to some extent punished for their unsuccessful initiatives, despite their glorious prior service. The demagogues thus enjoyed the power often in modern times attributed to the most powerful media owners or personalities.

It is clear from Thucydides (II, 14), that in Periclean times the Athenian majority was still rural, and was essentially conservative-minded, as the contemporary plays of Aristophanes indicate. The small farmers and tenant farmers tended to follow the lead of the noble landowners. But in sessions of the Assembly, for obvious reasons of proximity, the urban masses predominated, which conferred on the demagogues who were so skilled at whipping them up, a considerable influence, with no attached responsibility. The practice of paying "jurors" (those who attended the Assembly) naturally swelled the urban ranks, while the distant farmers found even the incentivization of attendance inadequate to compensate them for the much more difficult journey that they had to make, separating them from their livelihoods to be present.

Prior to the Fifth Century B.C., Athens was predominantly a land rather than a sea power, and the strength and defence of the state depended on the hoplites, who were mainly drawn from the countryside. When Themistocles refocused Athenian military strategy on naval power and fortified Piraeus and access to the ports, the professional armed forces shifted to mainly naval, and most sailors were recruited in the port cities, importantly altering the composition of the front-line defenders of the Athenian Empire, whose Ionian islands furnished a large share of the men of the Athenian navy. The consequences of this would become very clear after the reversals in Sicily of the Third Century B.C., when Isocrates, recognizing the primacy of the plebeians of the maritime communities, called for the disbandment of the empire in the Ionian and Aegean islands. In proposing this, he was seeking a retrenchment to an Athens governed in theory by the conservative agrarian classes. But in fact, given the limits, already mentioned, of the rural population at the Assembly, by the great landowners, they could be relied upon to avoid the temptations of seeking regional hegemony and would be content to achieve and protect the autonomy and prosperity of Athens, with no imperialist, civilizing, or Hellenic defence destiny thrust upon her. In its odd way, the whole concept of the sovereignty of the people reached its most democratic expression in this time in Athens. The rule in the law-courts of the urban masses added judicial dominance to their control of legislation. and judicial decision-making. Because the urban masses controlled the courts and because they were in constant session and were such reliable sources of personal income, they really largely ran the state. This was, given the uneducated condition of these people, a bold introduction to the whole idea of popular government. It was not especially successful, and was, in any case, capable of being subverted, frustrated, or over-turned, but it was a beginning of a concept of political organization that has gone on to considerable recognition and practice in our times.

Even in a political history, a few paragraphs should be devoted to the pioneering role of Greek development of Fifth Century Athenian drama. Homer had given Achilles the character of a tragic hero, and from this the many variations of tragedy quickly appeared: misunderstandings leading to one party being placatory and the other vindictive, and then changing roles, and death almost always being premature, self-inflicted for reasons of misperception, or glorious failure. The gods, with human failings, as in Wagnerian operas in the Nineteenth Century, are scarcely recognizable as gods to those of the Judeo-Christian tradition of monotheism: "Credo in unum Deum, Patrem omnipotentum." Greek and other pre-Judeo-Christian deities are fickle, fallible, numerous, and sometimes hag-ridden, spiteful, envious, and even gullible. Their status as gods is to those of the later Western and Middle Eastern traditions, incongruous—they are rather like men, only more indestructible. The power of and recourse to prayer was a constant—man recognized his inferiority, vulnerability, and shortcomings, but walked far less humbly with his God than did the Jews and would the Christians and Muslims.

The Aeschylean trilogy evolved: three acts, wrath, escalating tension, and death, with a quiet end. In Aeschylus' *Agamemnon*, Clytaemnestra's wrath when her husband kills her child, which is "Terrible, abiding, unforgetful," until she kills him in his moment of triumph. In the second act or movement, she is killed by her own son, and in the last the Furies intervene and escalate the bad blood into a cosmic struggle pitting groups of gods against each other, until the intervention of Athena to bring peace and reconciliation. The Homeric method built competing themes and alternated between them, as in a symphony, and Aeschylus built upon this technique. Music accompanied the plays and powerful and evocative recourse to poetry was frequent, and of great literary virtuosity, with Aeschylus as it was with Homer. (The author accepts the word of classical scholars as I do not know any Greek beyond a few letters.) Peisistratus added drama to his great festivals of religious devotion, processions, athletics, and celebration, and he established dramatic prizes for dramatists and actors, even awards for esoteric specialties, such as goat-singing. Aeschylus also dramatized great historic events and personalities, as Shakespeare and French dramatists, like Corneille, would do.

Aeschylus (523-456 B.C.) and Sophocles (496-406, and artistically productive through his eighties), engaged in decades of amicable competition, like two matadors, and this further raised public interest in the theatre and the careers that theatre generated. Aeschylus and his brother fought bravely in the Persian War, and it has been mentioned that his brother (Cynaegeirus) suffered the severance of a hand, at Salamis. Aeschylus was inducted into the ancient cult of Demeter, in which inductees were imparted secrets about the after-life under bonds of absolute secrecy, and was accused of violating the vows of secrecy in his dramas, and put on trial for his life. He was acquitted, partly because of the testimony of his brother, who showed the stump of his arm to the jury. In his production of *The Persians*, a war epic, in 472, Pericles himself appeared. Aeschylus died in Sicily, allegedly because he remained outside most of the day after a dream had warned him he would be killed by a falling object; after a local large vulture that picked up tortoises and cracked them by dropping them from a height on rocks to shatter them, mistook the glabrous head of the playwright for a rock. The Assembly of Athens at once, on the death of Aeschylus, established an elaborate annual drama festival in his honour. Henceforth, Sophocles and Euripides (480-406) engaged in cordial combat for dramatic prizes and the acclaim of audiences for more than fifty years. Sophocles was more austere than Aeschylus or Euripides, and his gods were pagans. Euripides was more moralistic and altruistic and traded somewhat a homilistic championship of benevolence for the violence and passion of war, with all its cynicism and cruelty.

Though there were many other talented Attic playwrights of the Fifth Century, it is generally reckoned that the great masters of Athenian drama were Aeschylus, Sophocles, Euripides, and the comic playwright, Aristophanes (446-388). This, obviously, was a different genre, but the Greeks showed a fine sense of humour, and his comedies achieved great popularity. Aristophanes himself referred to the tragedians jocularly as "Choirs of chattering swallows, pests of art," and modestly excluded himself from any right to be considered in the same company as the other three, but posterity has regarded him more kindly. These four men, in particular, added immense cultural prestige to Athens, and when coupled to the self-sacrificing valour and victories of deliverance at Salamis and the later Persian Wars, and to its extraordinary implementation of democratic rule many centuries ahead of almost all other jurisdictions in popular government, this gift for drama sharply raised the eminence of Athens in the Hellenic world.

2. The Breakdown of the Thirty Years Peace

The Thirty Years Peace was a recognition by Pericles, in particular, that Athens was exhausted from trying to assign to its limited free population the heavy burdens of maintaining its expanded Greek territory and its adjacent empire, much less also engaging in adventurism in Egypt and the Peloponnese. Pericles used this period, which he had sought and artfully arranged in a considerable feat of diplomacy, to consolidate Athenian interests to a tenable perimeter. The demarcation of interests left Sparta preeminent on land and Athens at sea, and the general lack of aggression in Sparta, a self-contained and unadventurous society, in politics, expansion, and all forms of culture and commerce, but made of fierce warriors, made it possible to achieve an understanding with Athens. The Athenians were much more outward-minded, commercial, culturally creative and spontaneous, but their extreme exertions after their great services to the Hellenic world in the Persian Wars, trimmed their ambition. Coexistence, the object of the Thirty Years Peace, looked attainable.

Although Athenian maritime ambitions and post-Themistoclean aptitudes had led Athens to impetuous over-stretch, readers should note how vastly and swiftly the maritime activities of, particularly the Athenians and Phoenicians, had spread Western civilization. Until almost half-way through the last pre-Christian millennium, the Western world was essentially the overland crossroads between Asia, Africa, and Europe in what are today Syria, Lebanon, Israel, Jordan, and northeast Egypt, and the repulse, or endurance and partial absorption of waves of fierce nomadic tribes and peoples from north and east of the great crossroads. With the emergence of the modern Greeks from the Aeolian, Ionian, and Dorian swarms, and the persistence of the Phoenicians in exploring, colonizing, and trading with the Mediterranean peoples, the crossroads of the world was swiftly expanded to include about half of the Mediterranean, and the Phoenician settlement and colonies in North Africa and Spain and the Greek states in Sicily, especially, grew very quickly and came to rival the mother states, in a manner that somewhat presaged the rise of the Americas when it became a commonplace to cross the Western Ocean and populate the farther shores.

Athens had had the ambition, cloaked in commercial appetite and the civilizing mission of a flourishing and very advanced culture, to expand without limits, but had painfully learned the practical limits of its abilities. Sparta had gained what its army could have won for it without a real battle, but it suffered from the anomaly of having an army that all feared, but that, because of the overwhelming domestic majority of the slave population, the Spartan government was afraid to send far from Sparta's precincts. It was an "army her enemies could not face and Sparta dared not use."[4] the military party in Sparta chased out the prudent King Pleistoanax and sent him into exile, but did not change his cautious policies.

Pericles was the subject of considerable disappointment, and he had miscalculated in over-extending Athens, but had recovered with ingenuity under great pressure, the traditional criterion of able leadership. He now directed the exploitation of Athens' protectorate over the Aegean, and heavily taxed the many Aegean states it had liberated and protected. Pericles believed in the political superiority and civilizing influence of Athens, but he was not averse to extorting generous tribute in recognition of it and of Athens' great contribution to saving all the Hellenes from the imperialism and avarice of the Persians. He also led the policy of reinvesting the surplus of empire in the magnificent construction of buildings and monuments to celebrate the greatness of Athens.

The immense Parthenon was begun in 447 B.C. Within three years, the Athenian treasury was stretched and Pericles proposed the allocation of tribute from the states defended by the Athenian Navy to assist in the construction, which roused a direct challenge from the aristocratic party, now led by the well-tried wheel-horse of Athenian politics, Thucydides of Melesias, who summarized his opposition in the statement that the component states were paying for their defence against Persia, not for Athens "to deck herself like a courtesan with thousand-talent temples."[5] Thucydides was acting on behalf of all his fellow members of the aristocratic parties throughout the Athenian Empire, and in February 443, the Athenians voted a straight choice between Pericles and Thucydides, and Pericles won, his autocracy was confirmed (democrat though he was), and his adversary was ostracized.

The Parthenon was almost completed in 438, and the splendid statue by the great sculptor Phidias of Athena, in gold and ivory, was completed and installed. The population was fully employed in these great public works, which extended to the Propylaea, the monumental gateway to the Acropolis, and to new walls all the way to Piraeus, and a great strengthening of that city's fortifications, and extension

---

4 Ibid., p. 166 (F.E. Adcock).
5 Ibid.

of its port. Sheds were built for the triremes, which in their strength and numbers were the supreme engine of Athens' authority and power (like the British Dreadnaughts before World War I, and the American Nimitz-class aircraft carriers in the late Cold War), and much expanded commercial facilities as well. Almost all of this was completed within ten years of the opening of the thirty years peace, in 435. Hereafter, Pericles was more concerned with building up a great reserve for military contingencies at the end of the Peace.

Such was the prestige of Athens in the Eastern Mediterranean that the Libyan king Psammetichus spontaneously delivered forty-five thousand bushels of grain for delivery among the Athenian population, gratis, presumably to strengthen official bonds in the event of a Persian threat (though Pericles had made it pretty clear that he was not touching the mainland of Asia again). In 451 B.C., Athens had legislated the requirement that citizenship meant that both parents had to be citizens. This was one of the greatest of Pericles' errors, as five-thousand people were struck off the roles, and the strength and extent of Athens depended on the number of her citizens. This was an error that Rome, already rising to a local importance in central Italy, would not replicate.

Pericles pursued a policy of rigorous and onerous collection of tribute, inciting some resentment among the so-called allies in Ionia, the Hellespont, Thrace, and the Islands. But Pericles observed the terms of the truce strictly as Athens had been in desperate need of peace, with the end of casualties and the expenses and dislocations of war. The one area where Athens could still expand at will was in the west—down the Mediterranean toward Gibraltar. Pericles responded to invitations to send colonists to Sybaris in southern Italy, where a quarrel arose with the original population, which was driven out by the new arrivals. There was room and need for more colonists, and Pericles threw this open to all Greece, and the resulting migration was only about forty percent Athenian. Pericles retained alliances with Rhegium and Leontini, Chalcidian cities with which he worked to counter-balance the ever-rising strength of Syracuse, which was closely allied with Corinth and was raising a very considerable naval force.

In 441, the large island of Samos, which had a fleet and had retained its independence, moved to secede from the alliance. Samos had had a dispute with Miletus over Priene, a small settlement on the mainland of Asia Minor, and Miletus, getting the worst of the struggle with the larger Samos, appealed to Athens for assistance. Pericles himself set out in command of a substantial fleet, and he overthrew the oligarchic government of Samos, straightened out the dispute with Miletus and returned to Athens, mission accomplished, as he thought. The Samian oligarchs had withdrawn at the approach of Pericles, and took refuge with the Persian satrap at Sardes, Pissuthnes, the nephew of the Great King. They were permitted to recruit mercenaries, and they regained control of Samos, drove out the democrats, and renewed the war with Miletus, imagining that Pericles would not respond quickly. This was a miscalculation, and Pericles returned at once and met the Samian fleet of seventy ships off the island of Tragia, fourteen miles south of Samos. Pericles got the better of it, but part of the Samian fleet withdrew into Samos. Pericles laid siege to Samos, and because he correctly assumed that appeals had been made to the

Great King, he took a large part of his fleet to stand off the port where the Persian Mediterranean fleet was laid up at Caunus, where he could interdict hostile Persian or Phoenician naval movements. In his absence, the Samian scholar and philosopher Melissus, roused the Samian fleet and they broke the blockade and reinforced their island with stores and provisions for two weeks, until Pericles returned, and was joined by further reinforcements from Athens and loyal parts of the Alliance, and after eight months, Samos was starved into surrender, in 439.

Pericles imposed a fairly severe peace—the walls of Samos were destroyed, its fleet surrendered, an island detached, and heavy fines imposed. Pericles had demonstrated the sea power of Athens: the Persians had not stirred though their assistance was beseeched. The aid of Sparta and Corinth was urgently sought, and they considered the appeal but didn't do anything. Pericles delivered a famous eulogy for the Athenian war-dead, saying that the spring had been taken out of their lives. In the Samian revolt, only Byzantium had overtly sympathized, and it had quickly withdrawn its disaffection. It was alleged that Pericles had said that it had taken Agamemnon ten years to reduce Troy and he had subdued the greatest of the Ionian states in just nine months. Athens allies were fearful, but they were discontented.

Athens easily put down minor outbursts of disaffection in the Hellespont but chose to overlook delinquency in tribute from some of the Carian towns in the southwest. Along the Strymon River to the northeast of the Chalcidic peninsula, Athens found its allies being pressed both by the Thracian Empire of King Teres to the east and by Macedon, always a looming presence, to the north. Athens established the port of Elon and the city of Amphipolis to tax the export of mining and forest products, as well as grain. Teres' empire of Thrace extended east to the Danube, and was a natural ally of Athens, but both felt threatened by the Macedonians (with good reason, as time would reveal). Athens also reopened its trade with the Olbia, the Cimmerian Bosporus, starting with Crimea. This was mainly the access to wheat and other grain from what is now western Russia and Ukraine. This trade had lapsed during the Persian wars but was now reopened—Athens was concerned above all other strategic matters with securing access to a stable food supply. As Athens grew in population, its rural areas turned more to olive trees and less to wheat and barley, and the strain on access to grain was a vulnerability that Athens looked to its fleet, as with all strategic concerns, to make good. Pericles' many expeditions of cleruchies (colonists), relieved the demographic pressure on Athens to some extent, but the continuous arrival of rural migrants and people from the empire attracted by Athens as the great metropolis of the time made the food supply a constant concern.

Large grain-houses at Piraeus had constantly to be replenished. It was Athens' policy to avoid interfering in Egypt and Libya or provoking Persia. Syracuse could be a supplier, but Syracuse was a Corinthian colony, though by now, probably larger than Corinth, so it was not a reliable source of supply. Nor were the Odrysian Thracians, who could neither be coerced nor trusted. But with the elevation of a new chief, Sitalces, in 431, Pericles struck up ever more intimate relations with him. Grain was shipped to Piraeus in large quantities, and Athenian drama and pottery and other wares became popular in Crimea. It was at this time that the Parthenon was completed, the supreme monument to Periclean arms and culture, and to Pericles himself. Thucydides (the historian), did for Pericles effectively what Shakespeare would do for Elizabeth I, putting noble and aphoristic words in his mouth, but in the one case as in the other, the admiration was not unearned. In Greece, nay-sayers and the irreverent were never silent. At this mighty triumph of Periclean splendor was completed, the crowning work of Phidias being the statue of Athena, Phidias was accused of embezzling the gold and ivory with which he constructed the statue and was driven into exile. Pericles was at the centre of a brilliant social circle such as usually attends upon all leaders who are successful and wish to memorialize their accomplishments. His courtesan, Aspasia, was respected for her wit and intelligence, as well as her physical allure, and Pericles' closest friends appear to have been the philosopher Anaxagoras, and the musician Damon, both of whom were driven from Athens at times prior to the completion of the Parthenon.

It was of the nature of Greece that however quiescent the Greeks might be as Athens unveiled more monuments to its own greatness, the forces of envy, schism, and back-biting were never far away. All was quiet in the Peloponnesian League; Sparta had no complaints with Athens, and Corinth, a commercial rival, might have wished to reverse the balance of prosperity and naval might that was in Athens' favour, but there was no obvious way of doing this. The most immediate grievance of Corinth was against her recalcitrant colony, Corcyra, which had declined to assist the colonists of Epidamnus, a settlement which Corinth and Corcyra had collaborated in establishing. Corinth responded to the Epidamnian appeal and Corcyra revolted against this act of overlordship and demanded the withdrawal of the forces Corinth had sent. The Corinthians relished the opportunity of putting fractious Corcyra soundly in its subordinate place and noisily began full war preparations.

This got the attention of the Corcyreans and with the encouragement of Sparta, Corcyra sent envoys to Corinth offering arbitration by agreed Peloponnesian states but declining to concede in advance and stating that if forced to war by Corinth, Corcyra would seek allies where it could, Athens being implied as a potential intervenor. Corinth wouldn't compromise and dispatched a fleet of seventy-five triremes, thirty Corinthian and the rest its allies, and were met by eighty Corcyrean craft, though generally less formidable vessels. But the Corcyreans forced battle on the Corinthian fleet near Leucimne, and narrowly defeated the Corinthian fleet, which lost fifteen triremes. On the same day, Epidamnus surrendered to the Corcyrean siege. The Corcyreans took the Corinthians at Epidamnus prisoner, as well as a number of Corinthian sailors, but executed the allied sailors for what they held to be the illegal and treacherous intervention of the allies of Corinth in a quarrel that was no concern of theirs. Corinth spent the next year preparing a decisive counter-stroke and recruited mariners and oarsmen throughout the sea-faring Hellenic world. Athens made no effort to restrain this practice among its Ionian allies.

By 433, the Corcyreans were finally alarmed at the scale of the Corinthian war preparations and sent envoys to Athens to seek the assistance of that country against Corinth. The Corinthians sent envoys requesting Athenian neutrality. The Athenian Assembly heard the presentations of both groups of envoys. The arguments of the two sides were weighed on grounds of justice and expediency. Athens was free to ally with Corcyrea under the terms of the Thirty Years Peace; Corinth's claim of past services to Athens was vitiated by the fact that it had entered the war against Athens twenty-seven years before. On that occasion, Athens forged an alliance with Megara, which Corinth regarded as a casus belli and it began the First Peloponnesian War. Evaluation of expedient concerns was more complicated. The Corinthian argument was for an agreement between the two imperial states to uphold each other in their respective spheres, to which the Corcyreans countered that if they were subdued by Corinth and the Corcyrean fleet captured, Corinth, whether it professed to be an ally of Athens or not, would be a mortal threat to Athenian naval supremacy, and would control all traffic to the Western Mediterranean from Greece. Public opinion appeared to uphold the Corinthians narrowly, but the government's decision, presumably formulated by Pericles, was that Athens would accept Corcyra as an ally, but only in a defensive alliance. An offensive alliance, committing Athens to make war on Corinth, would violate the terms of the Thirty Years Peace. But Pericles knew that this decision made war with Corinth inevitable and knew that once war had broken out between two of the three principal Greek states, the possibilities of a general conflagration were probable. (The whole process strangely presaged the toppling into war by triggering successive alliances of World War I in 1914.)

The Corinthians were undeterred by Athens and when its modern fleet of one-hundred and fifty ships sailed, this was a cause for Corcyra to invoke the new alliance. Athens waited and then sent two squadrons a few days apart, ten triremes and then twenty triremes, to complement the Corcyrean fleet of one-hundred and ten ships, though many were aged and under-manned. All the forces engaged; they were Greeks after all, and doughty fighters. The Athenians had to await attack on their new ally before they could claim any treaty legitimacy in engaging the Corinthians. Pericles's tactics in sending a small force and waiting to do even that, was that any sinkages between the Corinthian and Corcyrean fleets would strengthen the superiority of the Athenians, as long as the Corinthians did not win a swift and complete victory. The Athenian judgment was that thirty triremes would provide the margin of victory, and the dispatch of a modest force was an act of panache, which often typified the bold Athenian touch that combined courage, calculation, and flair.

The Corinthian and Corcyrean fleets met in September 433, off the island of Sybota, and the first ten Athenian triremes were present. The Athenians remained inactive until the Corinthians had forced the Corcyrean fleet to retreat, and then the ten Athenian triremes intervened, in full conformity with their defensive alliance, and covered the retreat of the Corcyreans. Towards the end of daylight, the Corinthians formed up to inflict a full defeat on their enemy, but the second Athenian squadron hove into view, and the Corcyrean fleet and first Athenian squadron rowed slowly backwards until the reinforcements would be in line. The Corinthians hesitated, fearing it could be the vanguard of the main Athenian fleet; both fleets remained at sea overnight and the next morning the Corcyreans with both Athenian squadrons in support, offered battle, and the Corinthian fleet retired.

It was a partial Corinthian victory, an unambiguous but honourable Corcyrean defeat, and a striking illustration of the prestige of the Athenian navy, that it could turn a battle and compel retreat on Corinth with a relatively modest reinforcement of its new ally. Athens had jousted with Corinthian vessels, however, though the two states had not been at war, and technically, the Thirty Years Peace was breaking down after just twelve years. The Athenians could claim a tremendous display of their prowess, and did, and their sailors loudly disparaged the ships and tactics of their Peloponnesian analogues, allied and opposed. In all of the circumstances, even at this initial stage, this intervention must be counted as imprudent by Pericles. Sparta declined the importuning of Corinth, because Pericles had acted within the terms of the Thirty Years Peace, but Corinth was seething with renewed hatred of Athens, and it was a sufficiently important state to be able to upset the entire flimsy structure of peace if it was as disruptive as possible. The Corinthian government went prowling around the Hellenic world seeking a cause that could be aggregated up into a casus belli that would bring the great power of Sparta into play against Athens.

A possibility presented itself at once in the Athenian activity against the Chalcidians. The founding of Amphipolis and Eoin referred to eight paragraphs above, irritated the crafty and ambitious Macedonian king, Perdiccas, who was doubly annoyed with Athens because Pericles had been encouraging a furtive insurrection against Perdiccas by his brother Philip, aided by the Macedonian factional warlord Derdas. This caused Perdiccas to begin inciting the Chalcidic towns that Pericles had rather cavalierly reduced to a state of suzerainty. Among the affected states, an old Corinthian colony, Potidaea, was discontented because Athens had doubled its tribute for defending it against the Persians, whose arrival had ceased to be a serious threat.

Potidaea, under intense Corinthian and more subtle Macedonian incitement, prepared to launch a revolt against Athens. The Athenians were aware of this and demanded the giving over of hostages and the demolition of part of the walls of the town. Potidaea sent envoys to Athens with entreaties and protestations of goodwill, as Corinth was not ready to give active support, particularly, as they had promised, aid from the usually almost comatose Peloponnesian League. Finally, after months of shilly-shallying, the Athenians became explicit in their demands of the Potidaeans. At this point, the loquacious and imaginative envoys of Potidea who had been spinning yarns of goodwill for Pericles and his government, departed for Sparta to try their salesmanship there. They found the Spartan ephors inclined to war with Athens, and firm in their promises of support for the Potidaeans. When the grim men of Sparta spoke in such terms, they could be relied upon, and while they were not a significant naval power, they were the terror of the land of Greece and could mobilize a great deal of support. With this encouragement, Potidaea went formally into revolt against Athens and raised most of the other Chalcidian centres with them.

Pericles dispatched a fleet and a thousand hoplites under the command of Archestratus in July 432, to reign in Potidaea. Pericles must have realized that he was ending the Thirty Years Peace seventeen years early and was likely to find Athens at war with Corinth, Sparta, and Macedonia at once. In the initial phase, his tactics were astute: he could impose a siege on Potidaea that could not be lifted during the winter, and the Peloponnesian League would take until the spring to be organized to do anything. The fervently hostile and bellicose Corinthians, however, were ready and eager and at the news of the Chalcidian revolt sent two-thousand Peloponnesian volunteers under the distinguished Corinthian statesman, Aristeus. Pericles sent a further two-thousand men under Callius, with forty ships, but he was too late to intercept the Corinthian force. Callius managed to assuage Perdiccas, and advanced on Potidaea, defeating the Corinthians and forcing them into the besieged city. The siege for the winter began but Sparta was now left with the choice of leading the Peloponnesian League against Athens, and presumably her allies, or facing the complete defection of Corinth, which had been Sparta's most important ally. There was little doubt that Sparta would feel moved to respond, and it must, even at this early point, be said that Pericles alit into war rather light-heartedly, given the strength of his enemies and the stakes in such a war.

Pericles believed that his best course for avoiding a general war was an early and heavy blow against Corinth. He started with a decree of the Athenian Assembly excluding Megara from any Athenian, Attican, or allied port or market. Athens had never avenged the revolt of Megara and massacre of Athenians in 446. This was designed as a show of force, to display the ability of Athens to shut a hundred harbours at once to an enemy. Corinth would be next, but was so full of hate, it had committed its stroke, Sparta was not much concerned with maritime affairs, but it had no direct grievance with Athens, and no need to prove its military capabilities. Pericles was now sixty and if it were to come to another decisive test, he wanted to be able to meet the supreme challenge with the Peloponnesians while he was still fit to do it. He had no confidence in the democracy that might follow him, subject to the influence of the demagogues, to devise and implement a sensible policy for Athens. The case can be made that he semi-deliberately provoked this early end of the Thirty Years Peace because he wanted a more durable resolution of Pan-Hellenic affairs while he was still in a fit state to achieve it.

The Corinthians had stirred up every nearby state that had any grievances against Athens, including the Aeginetans, who resented being told by Athens that they had no right to trade with their Megarian neighbor, and the Megarians were themselves naturally fuming against the blockade that the Athenians had imposed on them. The Corinthians presented to the Peloponnesian League meeting that was convened in Sparta, that if Sparta would not lead in these circumstances against Athens, the aggrieved allies of Sparta would have to seek leadership elsewhere. There were also Athenian envoys present, who though they had no standing to engage in the debates of Sparta, asked and were accorded the right to put Athens' case. They confirmed that under the terms of the Thirty Years Peace, they could and were prepared to submit all contentious matters to arbitration. They otherwise stood firmly on their rights and gave no quarter about their preparedness to defend their position by war if necessary. But they were somewhat placatory to the Spartans and at pains to make the point that they intended no offense to Sparta, whose rights and distinction were unchallenged and respected by Athens.

The peace party in Sparta was led by the king, Archidamus, who warned that Athens was an extremely formidable adversary, and that Sparta should not go to war with Athens if it had not committed a direct affront to Sparta. He recommended that Sparta prepare for war but test the sincerity of Athens in its envoys' promise of arbitration. This was complicated by the absence of any state of sufficient importance to have the standing to arbitrate, but perhaps a Triumvirate of Sparta and two other neutral states could have been arranged. This was not pursued, as the war party prevailed, led by the ephor Sthelaidas, who declared that Athens had violated the truce and that Sparta "must stand by her friends."[6]

This was not the end of the issue, however. The Peloponnesian League had to be convened and a majority had to approve going to war. The Spartans repaired to consult Apollo at the Delphic Oracle and received the response that if they fought with all their might, "They would win, and he himself would assist them." It is indicative of Pericles' lack of thoroughness at this decisive point that he had not taken adequate precautions to assure that Delphi was not in the ranks of the enemies of Athens. The adequate majority of the Peloponnesian League voted for war in November 431. There then began an intricate pre-war dance of protocols and formalistic grievance. The League called for the rejection by Athens of the Alcmaeonidae, effectively Pericles, whose position in the Assembly was too strong for that, as the assembly confirmed. Athens replied with the request that Sparta approach the issue with clean hands by repenting the killing of helot suppliants and the death of Pausanias at Spartan hands. Sparta replied disingenuously that war could be averted if Athens ended the siege of Potidaea, restored autonomy to Aegina, and ended the blockade of Megara. Athens brought formal charges against the Megarians which they claimed justified the blockade and rejected the other demands of the Peloponnesian league. Sparta replied by sending three envoys to Athens with the message: "The Lacaedemonians (Peloponnese) desire the peace to continue and it would continue, if you leave the Greeks autonomous."[7] The response of Pericles, who was sustained by the Assembly, was that Athens could never accede to the threat of force and cannot retain its alliance by fear. Athens was prepared to accept an arbitration, but until this took place, they would continue to besiege Potidaea and blockade Magara. With this, diplomacy ended and war involving almost all Greece was certain. Pericles must bear the responsibility for the war that followed. By modern standards there was no clear casus belli, and it should have been possible to negotiate a resolution without pushing Athens or Sparta beyond the boundaries of what their alliances required of them. This did not happen, and the war came.

The ancient anti-Periclean claim that he set Greece ablaze from vulgar personal vanity, is unjust and unproven. But the fact remains that it was an incorrect decision, and Pericles should, for the sake of Athens, not have embarked on a course that finally roused the hibernating bellicosity of Sparta at the head of a very powerful coalition. Pericles had labored mightily and successfully to make Athens the star that illuminated all Greece and much of the known world, and he committed it all to grave risk for no remotely adequate reason. What did Athens stand to gain in such a war, which under any plausible scenario, would be very long and difficult? There was nothing in it for Athens except to make a point, and there were painless ways to do that. The wisdom of stirring Corinth up to such a fever of hate is also questionable.

The beginning of the war was provided by Thebes, which aspired to unite all

---

6 Ibid., p. 188.

7 Ibid., p. 189.

Boeotia and make it fully resistant to Athenian pressure. To do this, Thebes attacked the Athenian ally Plataea. Like most Greek cities, Plataea had a faction that would betray the city to an enemy to achieve power themselves. The Thebans contacted the right agents, who left the gates open for the entry in dead of night for three-hundred Thebans in March 431 B.C. Having declared to the populace what they had done, the Thebans awaited the dawn, but the Plataeans realized how small was the force that purported to have occupied them and prepared an attack. They stormed the market where the Theban force was concentrated in the midst of a teeming rain, with the air empurpled by the war-cries of the Plataean women who pelted the Theban intruders with roof tiles. The Plataeans and their wives killed or forced the surrender of the Thebans, including a group that had broken through what they thought was an external gate but only led into a building.

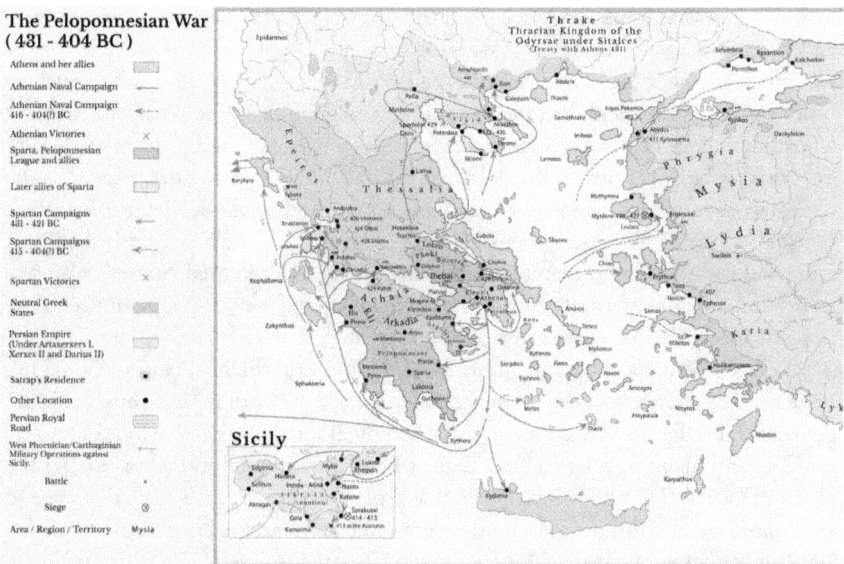

Source: Evonne Stella De Roza for the World History Encyclopedia[8]

The Plataeans took as many as possible prisoner, as hostages in the negotiations that were assumed to be about to begin. A macabre farce had begun and continued, as the main Theban force, fighting its way through the torrential rains, learned of the misfortunes of the advance unit, and started rounding up Plataean country-folk as hostages to trade with the Theban prisoners who had been taken at Plataea. The Theban army withdrew on the understanding that their comrades in the hands of the Plataeans and the country people the Thebans had taken into custody would be reciprocally spared. The Plataeans spent two weeks gathering in what they would need for a long siege and then murdered the Theban prisoners. This ensured a Pan-Hellenic war. The Athenians had sent an urgent embassy to Plataea telling them to protect the Theban prisoners until wider arrangements could be explored, but

---

8 https://www.worldhistory.org/image/12079/map-of-the-peloponnesian-wars-431-404-bce/

the Plataean blood was up. The Athenians took all the Boeotians they could find into custody, as likely sympathizers with Thebes, and sent a garrison to help defend Plataea and removed all civilians within the ample walls of Athens. The war was on.

3. The Archidamian War 431-421 B.C.

Apart from Argos, Sparta's ancient enemy, and most of Achaea, the Peloponnese rallied to Sparta's call to arms. The Peloponnesian armies gathered at the Isthmus, twenty-four thousand hoplites and a large number of less trained and well-armed forces. The Boeotians and Phocians and Locrians produced ten-thousand hoplites and a thousand cavalry. The Peloponnesians mustered a navy of about a hundred triremes, but many were not first class ships or men. Athens, apart from all that was needed to man the walls and fortifications of Athens and Piraeus, had thirteen-thousand hoplites; Pericles had laid up six-thousand talents as a war reserve, and Athens derived tribute of six-hundred talents a year and the Athenian navy was much stronger than its adversaries and could secure its empire and the revenue produced in tribute there, and the city's supply of grain from the Black Sea. Corcyra and a number of other states remained faithful to Athens. The Peloponnesian hoplite army would over-power the Athenians if they met as two entire armies, as the Athenian navy would dispose of its enemies. But the Spartan-led land forces were unlikely to be able to seize Athens itself. Spartan hopes for alliance with the Great King and for naval reinforcements from Sicily were disappointed. Sparta's plan was to invade Attica in strength and destroy Athens' rural areas and agriculture, in the hope of luring the Athenian army out to combat.

Pericles' plan was to maintain his forces within the Athenian perimeter and use his naval superiority to destroy the trade and fleet of Corinth and thus bankrupt Sparta's chief ally. The Corinthians cherished the hope that its allies would focus on building and manning a larger fleet than Athens possessed, but this was asking too much of heavily land-bound states. Pericles' plan was to use his naval advantage to send shore parties into the Peloponnese unpredictably and generate havoc in the villages and agricultural areas of his enemies, while Athens defended itself from direct assault. The Athenian army was powerful, other than in comparison with Sparta's, and opportunities might arise for sudden sorties from Athens.

The Peloponnese was expected to grow weary of the struggle, as they could not interdict Athens' commerce or seize its empire, could not attack Athens itself, and could not defend the entire coastal perimeter of Sparta's allies from the marauding of the Athenian navy. Pericles had a credible strategy, somewhat emulated by Frederick the Great in the War of the Austrian Succession. Athens had interior lines and naval superiority (in Frederick's case this rested with his British ally). His strategy was sensible, but his actions beg the question of why he got so prematurely into war with Sparta and its allies at all. The peace had another sixteen years to run. It has been mentioned that Thucydides and others speculated that Pericles saw his life ending within ten years and did not trust his successors to be adequately vigilant to the requirements of Athenian security. Leaders who move too quickly because of concerns about their own mortality (as Hitler did, for no obvious reason—he was only fifty when he started World War II) are generally prone to make mistakes. Pericles, talented statesman though he was, was not immune to this problem.

Archidamus II, one of Sparta's greatest kings, who ruled from 476 to 427 (one of the longest reigns of ancient times, apart from a couple of fantastic pharaonic kingships), led his alliance's forces into Attica. Before doing so, he sent envoys to Athens offering peace for fairly minor concessions but was rebuffed. No one could accuse this judicious and very capable monarch of impetuosity, vainglory, or indifference to the human and material cost of war, especially with such a formidable adversary. The human qualities of Pericles and Archidamus gave this conflict an escalated level of tragedy. Pericles declined to be drawn into combat in open Attican country, painful though the spectacle of the wanton destruction by his enemies was. Athens moved its herds to Euboea, where they were expected to be safe, and brought in all the crops and fruit in their territory. A long war portended.

The Athenian spirit of high bravery and originality was contained in deference to strategic realities, and the Peloponnesian claim to seek the liberation of the Athenian empire (which was assembled and held together by fear of the Persians), was exposed as pious claptrap. There were great demonstrations within Athens to go out and fight when the people saw from the walls the fire and smoke arising from their fields, but Pericles withstood the agitation. The Peloponnesian army was too large to remain where it was for long, especially after it had scorched the earth, and it was very expensive to retain, roaming about in the complete absence of an armed enemy, or even a civil population. After a month, the Peloponnesian army returned across the Isthmus. The damage to rural Attica was severe, but the fertility of the land was not affected, there was almost no loss of life on either side, and nothing of military significance had been achieved.

Athens had returned the Spartan visit to Attica, with a fleet of one-hundred triremes, supplemented by fifty Corcyrean ships, carrying a thousand hoplites and four-hundred bowmen, who were disembarked at various points along the Peloponnesian coast, who ravaged a good deal of country. On this expedition the one reversal the Athenians suffered was at Methone, where one Brasidas "chanced to be in the neighbourhood." He showed an almost Napoleonic cunning and determination which marked him for promotion and this most spontaneously original soldier of un-Spartan regimental qualities, would, by the strength of his genius and leadership, shift the correlation of forces in this long war. The Athenians, especially in dealing with the Spartans, were accustomed to having the advantage of innovation and improvisation in military matters. Brasidas was a completely unforeseeable force for change. Elsewhere, the Athenians were entirely successful, including in the success of their Messenian allies, old enemies of Sparta, who sacked the town of Pheia. The Athenian fleet proceeded on to even greater success against Corinth, capturing a number of the western dependencies of Corinth. The Athenian navy caused havoc in all the littoral of Sparta's allies and on balance, avenged, simultaneously, the Spartan spoliation of Attica. Pericles wrought a particular vengeance on Megara, personally leading the Athenian army after the Peloponnesians had retired, and joining with the Athenian fleet, scorched all of the Megarid hinterland and returned triumphant to Athens.

At the same time, the Athenians continued their siege of Potidaea. The unscrupulous Macedonian king Perdiccas was now allied with Athens and assisted the Athenians in destroying and pillaging the Chalcidians. The alliance with the Thracian king Sitalces, who had minimal contact with and no concern for the Peloponnese, continued and was an assurance of the reliability of Athens' grain and other trade with the Black Sea. At the end of the first year of the resumed war, Pericles' strategy had been generally confirmed. Pericles fully retained his preeminence among Athenians as he rendered the year-end homage to the fallen dead. Thucydides "in phrases unmarred by the bitterness of defeat or the memory of crimes and follies... described the Athens for which men lived and died...If Athens was the school of Greece, she was a hard school and taught much that was evil. It is not easy to forget the cost to Greece of all this greatness, or the justice of the nemesis that struck Athens down, but it remains true that nothing greater than Periclean Athens had ever yet been achieved by the mind and will of man."[9]

In the second year of the war, disaster befell the Athenians. The plague descended on the city and sickness and demoralization swept Athens. Archidamus led the Peloponnesian army into central Attica as had been anticipated, and in June 430, just before the outbreak of the plague, the Athenian navy, one-hundred and fifty triremes carrying four-thousand hoplites and three-hundred cavalry, personally commanded by Pericles, landing at Epidaurus with the hope of rousing the Argives to war in Sparta's rear. They were disappointed in this, and in their ambition to incite a disaffected faction within Epidaurus to betray the city. They continued on, sacking coastal towns and eventually reinforced the investment army at Potidaea. The plague was among the embarked soldiers and the fleet returned, having thus lost to disease one-thousand and fifty of the four-thousand hoplites. In Athens the plague continued through 430 and 429, seemed to subside, and returned in 427. Three hundred of the Athenian cavalry and forty-four hundred of the hoplites were laid low by the pestilence. The Athenian army was substantially reduced and the navy though less severely afflicted, was filled with many islanders who refused to go to port at Piraeus. At least Attica was now protected from invasion because of the epidemic, but the war-making capabilities of the Athenian navy and army were reduced. The mastery of the seas was retained but not the ability to roam and raid at will the Peloponnesian coast.

The morale of Athens, normally so indomitable, was shaken. There was no shortage of people seeing the plague as a celestial chastisement of the city and especially of its ruler. Remembered now was Apollo's promise at Delphi to assist the Spartans. In their beleaguered state, Athens sent envoys seeking peace, but they were rebuffed by Sparta, which wished to allow the plague to do its work at no cost to itself. Pericles sternly convened the Assembly, took full responsibility for everything except the plague and eloquently urged his countrymen to honour their heritage by redoubling their resolve in the face of adversity. This sufficed to see off those demanding peace at any price, but Pericles was unable to deal with a charge of misuse of funds (malversation). He had held the chief office for fifteen years and did not have a complete account of all that had been transacted. He was convicted but only

---

9 CAH, V., p. 200. (F.E. Adcock).

fined fifty talents, and he only surrendered office for a few months, until public anger, like a Greek summer storm, subsided.

But Pericles himself, suffered deeply. His two legitimate sons died in the plague, and although he was reelected General in 429—a considerable testament to his prestige, given the dire circumstances of Athens at the time—he died after three months. There was no natural or logical successor, and no Athenian combined Pericles' skills as a military commander, diplomat, and master of administration, especially finances. Pericles is one of history's compelling and imposing figures. His talents were very great, and his stature was such that he personifies the golden age of Athens. But in some respects, he must be considered an early Gorbachev: he impetuously pushed Athens into an avoidable war where the outcome was always uncertain, for no justifiable reason. Sparta was happy to divide the Hellenic world with Athens, and confine itself to the Peloponnese, where Athens had no particular interest. Instead, he embarked on a very dangerous war which he could have foreseen he personally would not survive. No one could blame the plague on him, and he faced up to it bravely, but his insouciance in plunging into war mid-way through the Thirty Years Peace he had skillfully negotiated, left his achievements and the fate of Athens in very uncertain hands.

At this stage, there was no faction of Athenian opinion that favoured peace at any price. There was an aristocratic party with little popular support but was furtively hoping for a return of their fortunes after the long night of Periclean democracy. The cost of the war was chiefly being carried by the wealthy and the agrarian population whose land had been ravaged by the Peloponnesian invasions of Attica. The seafarers, craftsmen in the shipbuilding and naval maintenance industries and the large class engaged in external commerce, were relatively unaffected or even prosperous. The reduction of population effected by the plague, grim though it was, alleviated unemployment. Those connected to Athens' naval and maritime commercial activities wanted the war conducted aggressively, taking full advantage of Athenian superiority at sea. The more conservative groups, more inconvenienced or even impoverished by the war, wished to proceed cautiously.

There was no audible defeatism, a remarkable fact given the depredations of the plague, which would have worn down the morale of a less resilient people. The leader who cautiously emerged was Nicias, who conducted a defensive policy for several years as Athens recovered from the devastation of the plague. Most of the navy was occupied at Potidaea, and the Spartans attempted to detach Zacynthus from its alliance with Athens by landing shore parties that burned its crops in the fields, but they were not successful. Athens did send a squadron under the capable Phormio, to Naupactus at the head of the Gulf of Corinth, to prey on Corinthian commerce, which proved quite successful. Sparta tried to send envoys to the Great King, guessing that old enmities between Persia and Athens could be rekindled. Because of Athenian control of the sea approaches to the Persian Empire, the envoys proceeded overland via Thrace, and attempted to detach the Thracian king, Sitalces, from his alliance with Athens, but Athenian ambassadors were installed at the king of Thrace's court, and he handed the Spartan delegation over to the Athenians, who brought them back to Athens as prisoners. After interrogation, and contrary to Greek custom, on the ground of Peloponnesian mistreatment of neutrals, the envoys were executed.

The fiasco of the Spartan mission to Thrace demoralized the Potidaeans, and they requested terms to end the siege. The Athenians, for whom the winter in this comparatively inclement place had been very challenging, dispersed the population safely, but when their land forces attempted to subdue the Chalcidians and Boettians, the Athenians were defeated and lost three generals and four-hundred and thirty men, and abandoned the entire operation. It was a tenuous action under the best of circumstances, given the fickle untrustworthiness of the Macedonian King Perdiccas, who was actually assisting the Peloponnesians in Acarnania. The Athenians devised an ambitious plan by which Sitalces, king of Thrace, and Athens would jointly attack Perdiccas and install his nephew, Amyntas, as king. Sitalces arrived with a very large army and overran most of Macedonia, but the Athenians, who had promised to join him with a large fleet and substantial army, sent only ambassadors with gifts. There has never been a serious explanation of this un-Athenian defection. Thucydides, something of an official chronicler, wrote that Athens had no faith in Sitalces, but that is completely inadequate. Instead of Perdiccas being replaced by his nephew, the Macedonian king married his daughter off to Sitalces' nephew, Seuthes, and Macedonia and Thrace enjoyed cordial relations afterward, and all were antagonistic to Athens.

Thus, Athens retained the Chalcidian coast, but its position in northeast Greece was tenuous after this. matters did not go better in the northwest, where Athens' allies, especially Corcyra (where this improvident war essentially began), required a lot of assistance. Phormio could hold Naupactus indefinitely and interdict commerce into the Gulf of Corinth, but Corcyra was unreliable and fraught by internal political strife, which was not a recent development and incites further questions about Pericles being drawn into such a conflict by so unstable an ally. Because of the plague and increasing financial burdens, Athens did not have the resources to extirpate Corinthian influence in the northwest completely, and if Corcyra deserted Athens, even Naupactus and control of the gulf of Corinth might not be tenable. In 429, the Ambraciotes appealed to Sparta for a force that would assist them in detaching Zacynthus from its alliance with Athens. Sparta saw the virtues of this plan and dispatched Cnemus, their admiral who had assailed the Zacynthans the year before and a pincers movement was attempted. He executed his landing well and the Spartans and some barbarian allies progressed through part of Acarnania, but then were rebuffed, and their Ambraciotean allies did not appear, and Cnemus had little choice but to retreat.

The Peloponnese did not do well by sea either as they sent a fleet of forty-seven triremes crowded with an invading army and tried to sneak past Phormio's twenty triremes, which were in battle condition. Phormio detected the movement, surrounded the larger Corinthian and allied fleet and gradually hemmed them in until, as he expected, the wind changed, and the Peloponnesian ships jammed each other and the Athenians attacked and sank twelve of the ships with considerable loss of life and scattered the rest. The whole operation had got off to a very bad start for the Peloponnese, by land and by sea. At this point, the Spartan commissioners told their generals and admirals to regroup and raise their game. In particular, one of the commissioners, Brasidas, as we have seen, was a man of great ability and boldness and would succeed Pericles as the principal figure in the pan-Hellenic struggle. His arrival at a position of decisive influence would prove a severe inconvenience for Athens.

Phormio foresaw a reinforced attack from the Peloponnesians and urgently requested reinforcements to his modest fleet of twenty triremes. Athens sent twenty more triremes at a leisurely pace, stopping first at Crete in a fruitless effort to subdue a city there (Cydonia). Before this force could come to Phormio's assistance, that doughty admiral found himself invested at Naupactus by seventy-seven Peloponnesian triremes fitted for naval battle. After a week of maneuver, the Peloponnesians attacked and split Phormio's forces in two. Eleven of Phormio's ships retreated into Naupactus, and the others were deliberately grounded. One of the first group rowed around an anchored merchant vessel and rammed its pursuer, and the balance of the group took advantage of the astonished Peloponnesians, who momentarily slacked on their oars, and chased them away from Naupactus, sinking six of them, and then recovered most of their grounded vessels, which the Peloponnesians had started to try to tow away. It was, despite the odds of nearly four to one against, an Athenian victory and a reaffirmation of superior Athenian seamanship. Finally, the additional twenty triremes arrived and Phormio was able to badger the larger Peloponnesian fleet into the Gulf of Corinth and bottle them up there. The Spartan commander, Cnemus, docked his ships at Corinth, led his men overland to Megara, and took to the sea in forty rather overaged Megarid triremes and tried to surprise Piraeus. It was a bold counter-move, but the Athenians by night beacons signaled a warning, which was received in time at Piraeus for the Athenian fleet to put to sea and chase off the Peloponnesians.

Perdiccas had advanced a thousand men to join Cnemus, but they quickly grasped what had happened to Cnemus and retired without encountering any Athenians and Perdiccas pretended he had never taken up arms against Athens and responded to developments by professions of affection to Athens. Phormio returned overland to Athens in 428 after a remarkably successful campaign against heavy odds in the northwest but in the ghastly and ungrateful moralism the Athenians inflicted on their greatest men, instead of a hero's welcome, he received an auditor's inquisition and he was accused of embezzlement and disgraced. This was the reward of Themistocles, Cimon, and even, up to a point, Pericles. It was one of the most unattractive traits of the Athenians, a sort of narrow Protestantism, to borrow from the terminology of belligerent and unworldly zeal twenty centuries later.

The Athenians had done well but the combination of the plague's thinning of their ranks and the excessive caution of the central command had deprived their brave forces of the decisive victory that would have forced Corinth out of the war. Archidamus set out to neutralize Plataea as it barred the road from Thebes to Attica. He did not take his army back into Attica for fear of the plague, which though it was declining, was still a hazard. The Plataeans received a generous offer of respected neutrality but relying unwisely on Athenian promises of assistance (which were not honoured), Plataea loyally resisted, and held out against siege and blockade bravely for nearly three years, until forced to surrender.

In 428 the Peloponnesian army returned to Attica to destroy the crops, and Mitylene, the principal city of Lesbos, was cranking up to secede from the Athenian alliance. It had retained its autonomy, had its own navy and did not pay tribute, but its secession could still be a heavy strategic blow to the solidity of Athen's position in the Ionian islands. It was a gentle oligarchy, and although Sparta had withheld its support when it had received overtures in the days of peace, Sparta and Boeotia were prepared to assist Mitylene now. Other, more pro-Athenian cities on Lesbos warned Athens of what was afoot, as they feared that if Mitylene dispensed with Athens, it would move to dominate all Lesbos. The whole Hellenic world was a mass of concentric circles of varying sizes and always conflicting jurisdictions; there was little sense of unity to any of it. Some of the divisions were of the ancient Aeolian, Ionian, and Doric origin, some were between democratic and oligarchic states, and some were just civic rivalries.

Mitylene strengthened its fortifications and imported grain for a siege and recruited mercenaries to top up their own army. Athens dispatched a fleet of forty triremes under Cleippides, who had originally been destined for the Peloponnese, which forced the Mitylenean fleet into harbor. Cleippides set up a camp, but not having the land forces to impose a siege, negotiated an armistice to allow the Mityleneans to show their good faith (which would be a challenge given their real intentions). Mitylene managed to slip out a vessel carrying emissaries to Sparta to ask for military assistance, while Cleippides called for reinforcements from the loyal neighbouring states in the Ionian islands.

The Mitylenean envoys to Sparta asked the admission of their city as a member of the Peloponnesian Alliance, and were, in classic Greek manner, allowed to plead this case before the Pan-Hellenic audience at the Olympian Festival. They persuaded the Spartans to send the bedraggled fleet that Phormio had roughly handled in the northwest, by moving it overland, a prodigious labour, to the other side of the Isthmus, and calling for support from its Peloponnesian allies. The Spartan hoplites, having spent a month destroying any crops in Attica, were busy harvesting their own, and Spartans though they were, took their time rallying to the colours, since Sparta itself was not under threat.

The Athenians outsmarted the whole business, by bringing forward their reserve fleet of one-hundred triremes and filling out the manpower shortages caused by the plague with zeugite and metic hoplites acting as rowers. While the Peloponnesian land forces, including Sparta's reluctant agrarian harvesters, gathered at the isthmus, Athenian shore parties burned their crops and trees, reciprocating the damage they had wrought in Attica. The Peloponnesians did not dare to come out to challenge the main Athenian fleet (though, and the Spartans had no way to know this, it was largely manned by amateurs). They gave up the whole effort and the swiftly mobilized army returned dejectedly to their burnt-out homesteads. Athens still possessed the confidence and panache to outwit and face down its enemies, at least at sea.

Athens still had to squash the Mitylenean rebellion and thus discourage sequels. The eyes of the Ionian islands were on Mitylene to see how efficient Athens was at enforcement. A number of cities in Caria and Lycia had refused to pay tribute and had killed the Athenian general Melesander and the demagogue Lysicles when they went forth to collect it. The Ionian was a powder keg and Athens had to douse it down with cold water. For the first time, Athens imposed a property tax on itself, which was onerous, given that the crops had been destroyed, and a thousand hoplites were sent out, rowing themselves to the islands of combat to economize, and as leader it elevated Cleon: "insensitive, unscrupulous, plausible, vain, resolute, and violent."[10] Cleon exploited the patriotism of the wealthy whom he so heavily taxed in the emergency, and engaged in outright terrorism of the so-called allies who wobbled with Athens under such pressure and the Great King quiescent.

The mission against Mitylene was led by Paches, and he scattered his enemy before him when he landed and drove them all inside Mitylene and began the siege, as Cleon threatened his other ostensible allies with horrible fates if they defected at this point with Athens beleaguered. The Spartan emissary Salaethus had arrived and urged the Mityleneans on, assuring them that the arrival of a Peloponnesian fleet and relief force was imminent. They held out into 427, and the Peloponnesians invaded Attica again and attacked the local food and wine supply in the fields, and a Peloponnesian fleet of forty vessels commanded by the Spartan admiral Alcidas managed to leave port undetected and sneak around the Athenian naval screen on its way to Mitylene. But the Mityleneans had reached such a point of famine that they determined to attack the Athenian lines besieging them. This bold and desperate gamble was about to occur when it circulated that the oligarchic governors were not sharing the people's rations and were quite well fed themselves while the common people were to go out and fight to the death in most unpromising circumstances. They thought better of this, and the oligarchs sued for peace. The Athenians were not overly severe, but Salaethus was sent back to Athens as an illegal interloper and executed.

The Peloponnesian fleet arrived a week after the surrender of Mitylene. Alcidas might still have salvaged a victory if he had attacked Paches' fleet while most of its crew was ashore accomplishing its hoplite duties, but he was a cautious Spartan rather than a bold Athenian and he withdrew, and barely made port ahead of Paches who gave chase. Once again, and by a hair's breadth, Athens, by its boldness and improvisation, even under less talented and confident leadership than Pericles had long provided, had eked out a victory. The other Ionian states, who had sat on their hands waiting to see how the Mitylenean initiative worked out, remained in the Athenian orbit. All saw that the assurances of assistance by Sparta were hot air and the maritime authority of Athens was not to be doubted.

Cleon persuaded the Assembly to approve the slaughter of male Mityleneans of military age, but the next day, that savage verdict was reversed following the eloquent argument of one Diodotus, who never arose in Athenian history again, but persuaded the Assembly that any such action would rouse the whole Athenian Empire and alliance to revolt as soon as such a step seemed possible to be successful. Diodotus made the point that if even the democrats of Mitylene, who had risen up against their leaders, were murdered, Athens would have no support whatever in its Empire and would deserve none. He was sustained by a slender majority. The news

---

10 Ibid., p. 216.

of this decision of the Assembly arrived in Mitylene in the midst of the reading of the original decision of the Assembly and was received with considerable relief. The ringleaders of the Mitylenean revolt were executed, and the walls of the city were demolished, and its fleet was handed over. An Athenian garrison was awarded most of the arable land and its former owners henceforth cultivated it for the benefit of their Athenian landlord.

Paches had carried out his mission well and added to his success by stopping at Notium to put down an attempted secession by an anti-Athenian faction. But Paches suffered the fate of many victorious returning Athenian commanders. At the end of his year as General, he was accused of malversation (embezzlement) in Mitylene, and in the midst of the court stabbed himself to death with his sword. His principal durable contribution to Athens was that it was decreed that henceforth defendants should be brought to court in fetters, to prevent spontaneous suicides. In this Stalinist finale of envious national ingratitude, Paches ended his very considerable service to the hard-pressed Athenian state from which he deserved better.

The successful suppression of the Mitylene affair was uplifting to the Athenians, still recuperating from the ravages of the plague, and while it fortified its empire in the Ionian, it left Athens again under-garrisoned in the northwest, and incapable of fulfilling its promises to the faithful Plataeans. Well into the second year of the siege of Plataea, with no Athenian relief in sight, half the Plataean garrison elected to try to slip through the ranks of the surrounding Spartans and Thebans, and successfully did so, but the half that chose to remain, though they had rations to hold out longer with diminished numbers, surrendered in August 427. The Spartans would have been fairly merciful, but the Thebans were understandably riled at the Plataean massacre of the Theban prisoners four years before. Two hundred Plataeans and twenty-five Athenians were executed, and the women were sold into slavery. After a year, Thebes razed Plataea to the ground and declared its former area to be Theban property. Athens, in the least gesture it could make in the circumstances, made the surviving Plataeans Athenian citizens, still a coveted status.

The next pillar of the Athenian position in the northwest to wobble was Corcyra. It was now in a state of divided opinion between the local democratic forces who wanted to maintain the Athenian alliance, and the aristocrats who wanted strict neutrality and peaceable relations with Corinth. Both Athens and Corinth, in the summer of 427, had ships bearing envoys in the harbor of Corcyra, and both groups were ardently courting the Corcyran factions. Corinth had released back to Corcyra two-hundred and fifty aristocratic elders it had taken captive in the action at Sybota in 433. Peithias, the democratic and pro-Athenian leader in Corcyra, was impeached for alleged treason, but succcessfully rebutted the charge and counter-claimed against his accusers by declaring that five of the wealthiest aristocrats, had cultivated grapes on sacred territory dedicated to Zeus. He managed to secure their conviction on this rather odd charge, and heavy fines were imposed. In the rough and tumble of municipal politics in Corcyra at the time, the matter was not allowed to rest there. The aristocrats stormed the council chamber and killed Peithias and sixty of his followers. Peithias' surviving allies appealed to Athens. The Athenians took the envoys the aristocratic party of Corcyra sent them captive as well as other Corcyrans of that faction they could lay hands on, while the aristocrats rammed through the thinned-out Council a state of unilateral legislated neutrality for Corcyra in the current conflict. The aristocrats really had worked themselves into a lather and they imported eight-hundred mercenaries from the mainland of Greece and set them on the known democrats in Corcyra, but with this, the slaves of Corcyra revolted in favour of the democrats and turned the tide in three days of house-by-house street fighting.

The democrats and slaves were about to deliver the coup de grace to the aristocrats when the Greek commander at Naupactus in the Gulf of Corinth, Nicostratus, arrived and attempted to impose a peaceful resolution based on Corcyra's continuing to honour the alliance with Athens. The democrats, for understandable reasons, no longer trusted the aristocrats in any agreement, and asked that they be imprisoned in some of the Athenian triremes. Nicostratus declined to do this but evacuated the leaders of the aristocratic faction to an isolated island. The Peloponnesian commander in the unsuccessful mission to the Aegean, Alcidas, arrived; he forced the rickety Corcyran fleet to beat a retreat home, but the part of his fleet detailed to take care of Nicostratus again learned how determined and precisely aggressive Athenian warships and their crews could be. Nicostratus prevailed and Alcidas, ignoring the advice of the gifted Brasidas, landed ineffectually near Corcyra, but was soon obliged to retire at the report of the approach of Athenian reinforcements. With this decisive turn, the Corcyrean democrats massacred their opponents in the most savage manner, going through the city rooting out and murdering suspects.

The Athenian commanders, Nicostratus and Euremydon, did not feel it was their place to intervene. Thucydides describes vividly how the factions in Greek city states can quickly metamorphose into gangs of savage beasts showing none of the humanity or civility of Hellenic culture and civilization. His reaction was something like that of observers astonished and horrified at the infamies committed by the Nazi rulers of the country of Goethe and Beethoven nearly twenty-three hundred years later. The factional struggle in Corcyra continued for several years, until the aristocratic party managed to return to Mt. Istone, a few miles south of Corcyra, where in 425 they were attacked by an Athenian squadron proceeding toward Sicily, and handed over to the Corcyran democrats on a promise of humane treatment. They were tricked by the Corcyran democrats into attempting to escape, which was seized upon as an excuse to violate the promise of civilized treatment and massacred with the most appalling barbarity; and the women were sold into slavery. With this, the focus of Athenian activity, fatefully, turned to Sicily.

The politics of Sicily were already at this early date, quite complicated. Syracuse was the rising power and was the leader of the Dorian cities in Sicily and was accordingly allied and in some kinship with the Peloponnesians, especially Corinth. Its Sicilian rivals were Leontini and Rhegium, which were Ionian cities and loosely in league with several Ionian members of the Athenian empire, as well as Chalcidian cities in Sicily and Camarina. By 427 there was open war between the Siceliote Dorians led by Syracuse, and Ionians of Sicily. Syracuse gained the upper hand, causing Leontini to send envoys led by the renowned sophist Gorgias, to ask the assistance of Athens. After some deliberation, the Athenian government determined that there was a danger in Syracuse overpowering the Ionian states of Sicily and then being lured into the Hellenic lists on the side of its mother-city Corinth. For this reason, and on a limited mission to reconstruct a balance of forces within Sicily, Athens dispatched a squadron of just twenty ships under Laches and Charoeades. The Athenians also reasoned that if they could stoke up the war in Sicily, the manhood of that island would be drawn into war and away from agriculture and the ability of Sicily to provide grain for the Peloponnese would decline.

The strategic conception was sensible, but the correlation of forces was slightly miscalibrated. The Athenian squadron went to Rhegium and gained control of the Straits of Messina. But Charoeades was killed in battle and Laches was unable to prevent a steady, slight, but growing edge to the Sicilans by the end of 426. Pythodorus was sent out with a small contingent of troops and forty triremes and Laches, who had performed well on a challenging mission was submitted to the customary ingratitude of his country and prosecuted for embezzlement, but he was sustained by the court. Pythodorus was only an average commander and lost control of Messana and the Straits, though in the ground fighting, the allies of Athens gained some ground. The forty triremes that were to follow Pythodorus were detained in home waters through 425.

The Athenians had outsmarted themselves by their disingenuous pursuit of a drawn battle for preeminence in Sicily. Its Ionian allies realized that they were just being used to keep Syracuse out of the war between Athens and the Peloponnese, and, conveniently, at the head of Sicilian affairs at this point was an astute statesman, Hermocrates, who saw that Syracuse's best interests would be served by making a reasonable peace in Sicily, as long as Athens was obliged to withdraw from the island. This was concerted at a conference in 424 in Gela (Sicily) and the Athenians were more or less politely informed that their presence in Sicily was no longer necessary. Their new commanders, Eurymedon and Sophocles, as well as Pythodorus, returned and were a great public disappointment, as the unscrupulous Cleon and the egregious demagogue Hyperbolus (his name gave rise to the word hyperbole because of his demagogic excesses, and was even employed by U.S. President Trump as he described his frequent recourse to self-serving exaggeration as "constructive hyperbole") had whipped Athenian opinion up to expect a great triumph in the West. The three expedition leaders had at least extracted a promise from all the principal Sicilian states to avoid meddling in Greek affairs. In 422, Cleon sent Phaex to Sicily on a diplomatic mission to see if any advantageous diplomatic arrangements could be made there but he returned empty-handed.

In 427-426, just as it was getting back toward full strength, Athens was struck by a limited revival of the plague. This fact and the expenditure of about two thirds of the great fiscal reserve Pericles had laid up, compromised the Athenians again, but their spirit did not flag, and they had so far more than held their own against a powerful if somewhat disjointed coalition. In the Athenian election of 426, the cautious Nicias was succeeded by the more courageous and militarily professional Eurymedon, and Laches, despite his persecution for embezzlement, was restored to command. Athens was opting for a more aggressive prosecution of the war. But the young Aristophanes attacked Cleon so fiercely as a warmonger in his play, *The*

Babylonians, produced at the Great Dyonesia of 426, that he was summoned before the Council and barely avoided a severe chastisement. Cleon and his faction were over-confident.

The wise and respected Archidamus died after his reign of nearly fifty years, in 427, and his son Agis was inexperienced. The seasoned Pleistoanax returned and was in placatory mood. Sparta had suffered no defeats in war but had not accomplished anything, and Sparta took advantage of an earthquake that narrowed the invasion route to Attica. In 426, the ephors sent envoys to Athens proposing a peace that it is assumed was essentially a confirmation of the status quo. But Cleon and his belligerent claque dismissed them. Pericles had more or less blundered into this war, but he would certainly have taken advantage of this opportunity to restore the peace. In 426 there was some indecisive campaigning in the northwest. The Athenian admiral Demosthenes failed to reduce the island of Melos and tried unsuccessfully to bring the Boeotians to battle. He was urged by his Acarnanian and Corcyran allies to try to crush the strategically located city of Leucas, which would have greatly enhanced the Athenian position in the northwest, but he found a lengthy siege unappetizing.

Instead, Demosthenes devised an imaginative plan for attacking Boeotia. The disappointed Acarnanians returned home, and Demosthenes invaded Aetolia, but with inadequate forces and was driven off by the Aetolian javelin-throwers. He lost one-hundred and twenty hoplites and was forced to retire to Naupactus but did not return to Athens as he well knew the welcome that awaited defeated homecoming Athenian commanders (worse even than for the victorious ones). The Aetolians, on the heels of their repulse of the Athenians, successfully asked for assistance from the Peloponnesians and the Spartan general Eurylochus appeared before Naupactus with three-thousand hoplites in September 426. Demosthenes rose admirably to the challenge, wheedled a thousand hoplites out of the disappointed Acarnanians, and with them successfully defended Naupactus. Undismayed, Eurylochus pressed on toward Amphilochia in tandem with the Ambraciotes. The Acarnanians were aroused and placed all their forces under the command of Demosthenes, who commandeered an Athenian fleet of twenty ships carrying the generals who had been appointed to replace him after the Boeotian fiasco, but Demosthenes soundly defeated the Peloponnesians and Ambraciotes, Eurylochus was killed, and the Peloponnesians negotiated their own retirement and deserted their Ambraciote allies, whom Demosthenes further defeated and humiliated, before returning to Athens in triumph after all. Demosthenes would have done better to focus on Leucas, but as it was, Corinth had been weakened and the formerly irreducible prestige of Sparta had suffered from its desertion of its Ambraciotic ally. The plague had finally ended, and Athens was in high morale after five gruelling years of this absurdly needless war.

The Peloponnesians opened the campaign of 425 with another invasion of Attica, now plague-free, while sending a fleet of sixty triremes to assist the exiled aristocratic party of Corcyra, and the Athenians responded by sending out Eurymedon, Demosthenes, and Sophocles, the General for the coming year. The mission was to break up the Peloponnesian effort around Corcyra and then proceed to Sicily, but Demosthenes could detour further and harry the Peloponnesian coast if he saw the opportunity to justify such a mission. Just as the fleet received an urgent request for assistance from Corcyra, a storm drove the fleet into Pylos on the west coast of the Peloponnese, which is where Demosthenes had hoped to operate from anyway. While the storm blew itself out, the Athenians fortified Pylos with timbers and stones at the narrow land entrance to the peninsula, and Messenians were dispatched into the western territory of the Peloponnese to destroy the crops and take full advantage of the absence in Attica of the Spartan army (which wasn't maintained at home at all times to ensure against a revolt by the ninety-five per cent of the population consisting of slaves. The rigorous life of the Spartan has been mentioned—the strict state of the Spartan slave may be imagined). When the storm subsided, Sophocles and Eurymedon pressed on to Corcyra, leaving Demosthenes with only five triremes.

Demosthenes began successfully; the Spartans withdrew from Attica, and the fleet that had been sent by the Lacedemonians (Peloponnesians) to Corcyra also withdrew. A couple of Messanian privateers with some hoplites joined Demosthenes, but he was about to face attack from the fleet withdrawn from Corcyra and the main Peloponnesian army. He would be heavily outnumbered by land and sea, and this time he would be facing Brasidas, who was as bold and tenacious as Demosthenes. There were two walls, one rather weak, at opposite ends of the little Pylos peninsula, which was only about half a mile long. Demosthenes dug in as best he could and prepared personally to lead the defense in the more vulnerable southern section with about sixty hand-picked veterans, where an attack by sea might be expected, and the northern section of Pylon was held by six-hundred hoplites against an anticipated land attack. The Spartans quickly attacked at both ends, Brasidas leading the seaward invasion. It was almost hand-to-hand combat between the two talented commanders. Demosthenes got the better of it, and Brasidas was wounded, but only evacuated after losing his shield. The Spartans attacked again, but were again unsuccessful, and then the Athenian fleet arrived from Corsyra, and after giving the oarsmen overnight to rest, Sophocles and Eurymedon attacked the Peloponnesian fleet in the close waters near the shore and won a decisive victory, isolating the shore party of about five-hundred hoplites and helots the Peloponnesians had left on the island of Sphacteria just one-hundred and fifty yards south of Pylos. The Spartans had sent for timber to build siege engines, but now were isolated and vulnerable.

This was such a startling reversal, the Spartan high command traveled across the Peloponnese to see for themselves what condition their forces were in. They had suffered such a set-back, they negotiated a local armistice while they sent a peace overture to Athens. They would temporarily hand over their ships in the squadron that had returned from Corcyra to the Athenians, and the Athenians could patrol the coast but not land, and the Peloponnesian forces on Sphacteria would receive an adequate ration (twice what their attendant helots would receive), and there would be a stand-still cease-fire in place until the envoys returned from Athens. The envoys, once at Athens, proposed not only peace, but alliance. This was an astounding turn of fortune, attributable altogether to the military genius and aptitudes of the Athenians, commanders and the ranks. The Spartans were certainly disposed to make large concessions, albeit mainly at the expense of her allies. But Cleon led the Athenian side and tried to dictate a peace that was more humiliating to Sparta than was justified by the correlation of forces. Cleon insisted on public negotiations, which Sparta could not accept, because if it became publicly known the allied territory Sparta was prepared to give away to Athens, the allies would withdraw, and Sparta would be left at war with Athens and with no allies to assist it.

The talks broke down, and it was up to Cleon to try to enhance by arms the condition of Athens so that such one-sided terms as he was trying to impose could be wrung from a further test of arms. The whole policy was unsound, as Pericles would have judged. Cleon was refusing an advantageous peace and an alliance with Sparta that would make Athens impregnable, in order to try to regain the extremities of Athenian influence that had been established in the latter Periclean era to be beyond Athens' ability durably to retain. The Athenians invoked a very dubious pretext to avoid giving back the Peloponnesian fleet of which they had been given temporary custody, a sizeable bloodless victory. Time passed and the conditions were never ripe for an attack on the Peloponnesian force on Sphacteria. They were supplied by swimmers and small craft that were able to come ashore in relatively high winds that prevented the Athenian ships from interdicting them. With autumn, it would be impossible to maintain the siege of the island. In the Athenian Assembly, a strenuous debate between Nicias and Cleon reached a climax when Nicias, who had advocated peace, offered to retire prematurely as General and yield his place to Cleon to personally lead the assault on Sphacteria. A fire on the small island revealed that the Spartan hoplites had been deserted by their helots.

Cleon arrived with reinforcements and Demosthenes had already devised a plan. The Athenians managed to land eight-thousand men on Sphacteria and pressed the four-hundred and twenty Spartan hoplites back into primitive fortifications at the north end of the island. After days and nights of hand-to-hand combat, the Messenians managed to climb round behind the Spartan defenders, who had fought with the courage of the highest and noblest Spartan tradition. As the commanding officer of the Spartans had been killed and his deputy, incapacitated, the acting commander asked for a cease-fire to seek leave to surrender from the mainland. This was granted and the authorities approved surrender provided Sparta was not thereby dishonoured. No one could claim the Spartan performance had been anything less than heroic, and Cleon and Demosthenes knew that Spartan prisoners were much more valuable to them than Spartan corpses, and the action ended. Valorous though they had been, it was a Pan-Hellenic eye-opener that any Spartans ever surrendered. Cleon and Demosthenes returned to Athens in triumph.

Athens' prestige was again at a peak; in fact, its achievement in getting the better of so powerful a coalition without the benefit of a brilliant leader like Pericles was an even greater achievement: all countries will prosper under inspired leadership, only the greatest can succeed with leadership of ordinary or indifferent quality. Cleon doubled the tribute to his allies, and none revolted, though it is doubtful that all paid the increased amounts. The war was not started by Athens' allies, nor in their interests, but it was in their interests for Athens to succeed and up to this point, there had been no contribution of money or men to assist them, and the sailors from the empire that Athens had employed, to reduce the impact of the plague, had been paid fairly. Now was the time for a collective effort.

The Athenians held the Spartan prisoners from Sphacteria and promised gentle treatment of them if Attica were not violated. In this way, at no cost, the Athenian defensive perimeter was moved outwards from the city walls to the borders of Attica and Athens was more supreme at sea than ever after snatching the Peloponnesian fleet that had been dispatched to Corcyra. Athens also had Sparta on its back foot for domestic reasons. Having set up the Messenians at Pylos, whence they established a shelter on the adjacent Peloponnesian mainland for defecting helots, Sparta was afraid to send the helots out to gather in the crops for fear of a general revolt. This idea of fortified places from which to harass the enemy's food supply and incite slave revolts, inadvertently devised by Demosthenes and transformed by him into a distinct victory, was now integrated into Athenian strategy.

The cautious Nicias, now in the shadow of Cleon (although Nicias was the better strategist and a man of considerable integrity, unlike his rival, a rabble-rousing scoundrel), still had some months to run in his term as General and to try to get up-sides with Cleon, he took to sea with eighty ships and two-thousand hoplites, two-hundred cavalry and contingents from several allies and set sail for Corinthian territory with a view to replicating Pylos. He was only partially successful. The Corinthians deployed their army all along their sea-coast. Nicias landed at Solygeia but was attacked before he was solidly established. He narrowly won the ensuing engagement but withdrew anyway and went on to Crommyon at the other end of Corinthian territory. He ravaged the surrounding country and departed without waiting for serious resistance, and alit this time on the isthmus joining the Methana Peninsula to Epidaurus and Troezen, outside Corinthian territory but in a place that would be very inconvenient to those enemy states. The whole mission was a modest success.

Aristophanes attacked Cleon in his play, *The Knights,* and emphasized that Pylos was the success of Demosthenes and not Cleon. This was all the encouragement Cleon needed to try to appease the Athenian love of bold strategic conception and military leadership. There were several co-equal generals elected for 424, including Nicias, returned to office, along with Demosthenes, Aristides, Autocles, and Demodocus, as well as Eucles, and of all people, the historian Thucydides. Elected General-in-chief was Pericles' nephew, Hippocrates. This was the group that under Cleon was to press forward the Athenian drive to a great victory. Nicias embarked again, this time for the island of Cythera, off the southeast tip of the Peloponnese, which Sparta garrisoned as a station against pirates and a destination on the trade routes. Nicias was justly regarded as an expert in amphibious landings, and many of these sea-borne attacks were very sophisticated military operations for the times—some were studied in preparation for the great World War II landings in Sicily, Normandie, Iwo Jima, and Okinawa. He had sixty triremes, two-thousand hoplites and some cavalry and allied forces. He seized the island without undue difficulty, an event which further rattled Sparta, and then wrought havoc on the coasts of Sparta's allies Epidaurus and Limera and then attacked the Aeginetans at Thyrea, where they were protected by a Spartan garrison. The Athenians overpowered and drove off the Spartans, slaughtered their Aeginetan enemies from previous wars, and sent a number back to Athens to be publicly and ceremoniously executed. Gentle democratic

Athens was not above reflexive and tactical recourse to obscene barbarity.

At this point, the news of the conference of Gela reached Athens, which, in Sicilian affairs, was, as has been described, a set-back. The problem had been the inability of Athens to get clear of the Peloponnesian conflict sufficiently to send substantial assistance to reinforce its side in Sicily. It had injected enough to be regarded as an intruder by Syracuse and its allies, but not enough to be effective, a position the full danger of which would become clear soon enough. The incoming Generals in Athens in 424 set their sites now on the Megarid, which was very vulnerable, and beyond it, to avenge itself on Boeotia, which had inflicted the deepest wounds of rank disrespect on Athens, under the domination of Thebes. The Athenians had long blockaded the southern Megarian harbor of Nisaea, and the northern harbor of Pegae was held by exiles, and the burden of war had become generally insupportable to the Megarians. Megara was ruled by democrats, who were natural allies of Athens, and they made overtures to Hippocrates and Demosthenes, and arranged for the isolation of the Peloponnesian garrison of Nisaea, by seizing the long walls between the port and Megara and opening the gates into the city to the Athenians. (This was a complete betrayal of the Peloponnesian Alliance, an action that was habitually hazardous.) The long walls were occupied, the Spartan Garrison in Nisaea surrendered, but the promised coup within Megara did not happen.

Now the leading personality of the Spartan counter-attack, Brasidas, who has put in cameo appearances already, moved to the forefront. He was nearby, preparing an expedition against Thrace, and sent a message to the Boeotians to meet him at Tripodiscus, seven miles from Megara, which he reached himself with a hodgepodge of forces hastily rummaged together, after an overnight march. Within Megara, the two conflicting sides agreed, with consummate cynicism, to await the decision between the Athenian and Spartan-led forces, to decide which side would be honoured and which betrayed, by what would, ipso facto, become the governing faction in Megara. The Boeotians arrived a few hours later with twenty-two hundred hoplites and six-hundred cavalry. There was an indecisive cavalry skirmish, and then Brasidas, with six-thousand hoplites, awaited the Athenians, but Demosthenes and Hippocrates, having cleared the Spartans out of Nisaea, considered they had rendered Megara unsustainable, and were unimpressed by the degree of their solidarity, took their small victory and prudently withdrew. It was not a mistaken decision, but notwithstanding their very limited success, they continued the plan to attack Boeotia. Here again, Athens would be dealing with its enemy's unfaithful subjects and nominal allies.

There were pro-Athenian exiles in Phocis and in Orchomenus which promised to assist the invasion of Boeotia by helping to seize the border city of Chaeronea; Siphae on the Crisaean Gulf promised to open itself to Demosthenes who would arrive from Naupactus with forty ships and contingents of allied forces. On the same day that Demosthenes arrived at Siphae, Hippocrates would cross the eastern border and seize the great sanctuary of Apollo at Delium. The Athenian enterprise would depend on the spread of anti-Theban strength and sentiment within Boeotia, the maintenance of secrecy and surprise, precise coordination, and indifferent leadership on the other side. Demosthenes was obliged to spend considerable time patching up allies and reassuring them about the intention of each other. The Acarnanians and Aetolians needed reassurance about the Agraei. Brasidas' march on Thrace also delayed matters and obliged Athens to send a small fleet under Thucydides of all people, and Eucles, to protect Athenian interests in Thrace (an inadequate force led by inadequate commanders on a dubious mission).

To compound the mounting difficulties, Demosthenes arrived early at Siphae, and departed, and was rebuffed in an improvised landing at Sicyon. The wheels had come off the Athenian plan, but Hippocrates went ahead with the occupation of Delium, and spent several days fortifying the Athenian position. These were in satisfactory condition after three days, and hearing nothing, Hippocrates assumed that the overall plan had gone awry and started down the road to Athens with the draftees first, followed by the seven-thousand hoplites and a thousand cavalry, when he learned that the Boeotian army was assembled with apparent intent to prevent his safe return to Athens, they had gathered on short notice at Tanagra. Many of the Boeotians were for allowing the Athenians to leave their territory undisturbed, but the Theban commander, Pagondas, wouldn't hear of it. The armies met about a mile from Delium. The Athenians were outnumbered in light troops but even in hoplites and close-in cavalry and held a strong defensive position. Pagondas proved a very able commander and enfiladed the Athenian left and as the Athenians pushed back the Boeotian left, causing the whole front to move counter-clockwise, the Theban cavalry was able to get behind the Athenian right and the battle became a rout. Hippocrates and nearly a thousand of his hoplites died and the remains of the army retreated into Delium, or escaped through mountain passes and took back the unhappy news to Athens. After sixteen days, in which the Boeotians managed to set fire to much of the improvised fortification of Delium, the Athenians took to the boats and most escaped, but the Athenian army had suffered a severe defeat, exemplified by the death of the general in chief and nephew and heir of the great Pericles. It was a debacle.

Now came the hour of Brasidas. Athens had ignored its position in the northeast since the failure of Sparta to detach the Thracian king, Sitalces, from his Athenian alliance, described above, but the determined Brasidas decided that it was time to have another try in the northeast. Athens' complete ignorance of the northeast and inactivity there, even diplomatically, and Cleon's high-handed increase in the assessment of tribute, bred some hostility and the chronically unreliable Macedonian king, Perdiccas, was envious and suspicious of the string of Athenian victories, and very amenable to a promising anti-Athenian scheme, should one arise and the tide of fortune turn. This left an opportunity and the Macedonians and Chalcidians jointly approached Sparta and proposed a combined mission towards and perhaps against Thrace. Brasidas led a motley and small army through Thessaly, that was pro-Athenian, kept his distance from the shifty Perdiccas, and arrived in Acanthus. There he occupied the principal lands of its vineyards before the grape-harvesting season, and persuaded the Acanthans to desert Athens and enjoy real freedom with Sparta. On this news, Athens declared war on Perdiccas, and Eucles and Thucydides were instructed to protect Athenian interests in the northeast. Thucydides was partially of Thracian origin and had reason to expect a welcome from the Thracian king, Sitalces. But unfortunately the king of Thrace died, fighting the northern tribe of the Triballians, and the succession went not to his son Sadocus, but to Perdiccas' son-in-law, Seuthes.

Eucles and Thucydides trusted to the Thracian winter to shut down the Spartans, but Brasidas ignored the weather and descended on Argilus, where he already had agents in the towns. He offered exceedingly generous terms and Eucles was not an eloquent or persuasive rival and Argilus and Amphipolis had surrendered to Brasidas before Thucydides arrived with reinforcements. Thucydides did beat off an attack on the port of Eion. The territory where Brasidas was now free to intervene provided Athens both ample tribute and timber for ship-building, and this was now in jeopardy as winter finally slowed down even Brasidas. He did manage some advances along the coast, and seized the city of Torone, reducing the Athenian presence to little more than the well-garrisoned Potidaea. Thucydides was recalled but Brasidas' request for reinforcements from Sparta were not answered, as King Pleistoanax was a pacificator, as were most of the ephors. The Spartan government wished to exploit Brasidas' victories rather than build upon them.

The series of defeats, from Delium to Torone, broke Cleon's influence and elevated the advocates of peace in Athens, and Nicostratus was elected as General to replace Hippocrates; a one-year cease-fire in place pending negotiation of a durable peace was agreed. The Spartans were aiming to secure Pylos and the return of their prisoners, and the Athenians wanted Brasidas off their back in the approaches to Thrace. Before the news of the truce arrived, Brasidas had taken the city of Scione, and garrisoned it, and was close to Potidaea and the possible complete expulsion of Athens from the area. The two sides disagreed on the applicability of the armistice to this area, though it was in force everywhere else. The Athenians, on a motion of Cleon's in the Assembly, planned to retake Scione and put the inhabitants to death for their betrayal. This was naturally a contentious issue. Brasidas stirred up an oligarchic revolt in Mende and that city seceded from the Athenian alliance. Brasidas was apparently compelled by Perdiccas, who had been supplying Brasidas' forces and called in his credit to require Brasidas to bring his army with him for an attack on Arrhabaeus. Before this expedition reached its destination, the egregious Perdiccas deserted Brasidas and retreated toward Macedonia, leaving Brasidas outnumbered by the Lynecestians and Illyricans. Brasidas made his peace with them, but plundered Perdiccas' baggage train, and Perdiccas completely deserted Brasidas and resumed peace with the Athenians, who had by now recaptured almost all of Mende with a large force commanded by Nicias and Nicostratus. They were generous to the civil population, and Perdiccas prevented reinforcements from reaching Brasidas.

The armistice continued to 422, but the negotiations for a durable peace were acrimonious, and accomplished nothing. The belligerent Cleon was reelected General and planned to replicate in the northeast his success of 425, and especially to recapture Amphipolis. Athenian diplomacy had aligned some support of Boettaeans and Perdiccas purported once more to be an Athenian ally. Cleon departed Athens in early September with a substantial force and regained Torone and a number of neighbouring cities. He drew up to Amphipolis, and his men, who disliked Cleon and did not want an inclement Thracian winter, required him to do something, so he feinted toward Amphipolis and Brasidas emerged and defeated Cleon. The talented and brave Brasidas performed a double service for Athens, as Cleon was killed while fleeing and Brasidas was himself mortally wounded in victory.

With the death of Brasidas, the peace party was strongly in control in Sparta, with Pleistoanax still harassed by claims that he had bribed the priestess at Delphi to furnish the assurance that Apollo had promised a Spartan victory. (In religion as in other spheres, the old tricks are the best tricks.) The families of the Spartans taken prisoner at Sphacteria were agitating incessantly for their return. The thirty years of peace was almost at an official end, which would enable Argos to join with Athens and stir up anti-Spartan feeling among the lesser Peloponnesian states, who were not enchanted by the progress of the war. On the Athenian side, the death of Cleon was also timely, as most of his demagogic promises of easy and overwhelming victory were buried with him, and Athens was certainly ready for peace also. In 422-421 there was intense toing and froing of envoys between Athens and Sparta, as elements of a peace agreement were hammered out. Sparta was, as is generally the case, prepared to sacrifice the interests of its allies, but did not want this fact known until the peace was concluded, which tended to protract the discussions. But Sparta, as the Athenians were well aware, was also anxious to conclude peace with Athens before the peace with Argos officially ended. Argos would not dare to antagonize a Sparta that was not encumbered with a war with Athens but might be more than willing to join the Athenian side in such a war.

Aristophanes wrote one of his comedies, *The Peace*, for the Great Dionysia of 421, which highlighted the terrible damage done by wars between the Greeks and effectively rejoiced in the deaths of Brasidas and Cleon, and somewhat mocked the skullduggery and dilatoriness of the negotiators. Sparta, to force the issue before Argos was relieved of its obligation to observe the peace, announced a general mobilization of a Peloponnesian army to return to Attica and to construct a large fortification athwart the road system to and from Athens. Within a few days of the opening of Aristophanes' play, in March 421, the Athenian and Spartan negotiators reached agreement and Sparta summoned the Peloponnesian League and revealed what had been concluded with Athens. It was in the end, not onerous to any party and reflected the general recognition of the point Aristophanes had made that war among the Greeks, especially for ten years as this resumption of war had taken, was weakening all of Greece, and the only beneficiaries of this could be the Macedonians, Thracians, and Persians, as well as the new states in the West, in Sicily, North Africa, and Italy. The Delphians, who despite suggestions of corruption of the clergy, had in secular matters been rigorously neutral and placatory, were rewarded with independence from the Phocians (who were shifty and inconsistent). The Lacedaemonians and Athenians and all the respective allies concluded a peace this time for fifty years, and all states were restored to where they were at the start of the Archidamian War. All disputes henceforth would be settled by arbitration.

There were special arrangements for cities in the approaches to Thrace that had seceded from the Athenian alliance before the resumption of war, or had revolted from it with Sparta's assistance and had not been subdued. Athens regained Amphipolis, to which it attached great strategic and sentimental importance, and a number of other nearby cities were deemed to be neutral but could, of their own will and not by coercion, join or rejoin the Athenian alliance if they wished, but would not be in alliance with Sparta. Athens was given a free hand to deal with any other state in its empire and alliance as it wished. All that Athens had actually lost in the long and demoralizing war, amplified in its severity on the Athenian side by the plague, were Amphipolis and Panactum, which an internal faction had betrayed to the Boeotians, and Athens recovered both. There was a complete exchange of prisoners, and Athens restored to Sparta a number of strategic points around Sparta that the Athenian navy had taken and used to harass and generally irritate Sparta and her allies. Sparta effectively abandoned any championship of the interests of Corinth, which had been a loyal ally. Athens and its northwestern allies had overwhelmed a number of the allies of Corinth and Sparta did not lift a finger to restore them to their ante bellum status. The Acarnanians and Amphilochians had already withdrawn from the war and had helped themselves to occupation of some dependencies of Corinth, which was free to try to recover them if it wanted, but without any assistance from Sparta or the other Lacedaemonians, or any assurance of non-intervention by Athens. Corinth was, in any case, exhausted and in debt.

There was no mention of restoring from Athenian control Nisaea, the port of Megara. That city too, which had fought bravely and at great cost to itself alongside Sparta, was put over the side; it could get by as best it would, in a truncated condition. Boeotia regained nothing of what it had lost. The true copies of the agreement were to reside in the three religious centres: Delphi, the Isthmus, and Olympus, and in the Acropolis and the Amyclaeum of Sparta. All parties were to renew their oath to uphold the agreement solemnly every year, but Athens and Sparta alone had the right to agree amendments, whenever they wished and without preestablished limit to the scope of amendments.

This was the final confirmation of the statecraft of Pericles, who, had he lived longer, would have ended the war after the victory at Pylos. Athens had gained the recognition of her power, and whatever envy or back-biting other Hellenic states might feel or be tempted to commit against Athens, this very costly war had drained away the spirit and resources for internecine Hellenic conflict. Corinth was like the latter Austro-Hungarian empire of the early Twentieth Century, it brought on a war, and was decimated by the war it had itself begun. Sparta could return to its isolation, unchallengeable in the Peloponnese, and self-sufficient, but fully occupied grimly keeping its slaves under control. Athens, on the heels of its brilliant victories against Persia, and in the Peloponnesian war, had forged its position as the premier Hellenic state by attrition, both of war and of pestilence. Peace came upon an exhausted Greece.

CHAPTER NINE

THE SYRACUSAN DISASTER AND THE FALL OF ATHENS, 420-399 B.C.

ALCIBIADES AND SOCRATES

Alcibiades being taught by Socrates by François-André Vincent, 1776

1. The Peace

PEACE DID NOT COME as easily or completely as was hoped. The treaty was written so that Sparta would make restitution first, and they couldn't make good on two commitments: to restore Amphipolis and to get their reluctant and in some cases legitimately aggrieved, allies to ratify the treaty. A Spartan officer, Clearidas, the successor to Brasidas, was in command of a Lacedaemonian army in Amphipolis, but when Clearidas was ordered to surrender the town to the Athenians, in un-Spartan manner, he refused, as he did not approve of the treaty (any more than Brasidas would have) and took the position that he could not deliver Amphipolis to the Athenians against the wishes of the townspeople. Sparta tolerated this insubordination and gave Clearidas leave to return and make his case, whereupon Sparta withdrew its garrison from Amphipolis, relieving it of non-compliance opposite Athens in respect of Amphipolis, but had no means to deal with uncooperative (former) allies. Athens was in some measure the victim of its own success, very hard-won as it had been. Sparta could only deliver the concessions in the so-called Thrace-ward areas if its alliance held together, and its three principal allies, Corinth, Megara, and Boeotia, unconditionally refused to ratify the treaty of peace or pay any attention to its provisions, though most of the Peloponnesian states did adhere to it. Athens regained Corcyra and the principal ports and bases that could control and monitor shipping to and from the Adriatic and the Western Mediterranean. Corinth suspended hostilities with Athens but did not make even a truce. Athens declined to give Nisaea back to Megara, and was under no treaty obligation to do so, unless Thebes gave Plataea back to Athens. Thebes wouldn't hear of it and gained control of the Boeotian League, which almost alone in the Hellene world had had a splendid war: protected by Peloponnesian armies, it had pillaged Attica for ten years, and had lost considerable respect for Athens after the fiasco at Delium, and thought it could fend off the Athenians unaided. It declined to return Athenian prisoners and only observed a truce in renewable periods of ten days.

The peace between Sparta and Argos expired, and Argos was now a loose cannon—bound to no one but still fired by its burning hostility to Sparta. Sparta found itself deserted by its three principal allies, unable to fulfill its treaty obligations to Athens, which altogether held five per cent of Sparta's citizens prisoner, and with legitimate concerns for a general defection of the Peloponnesian states. Sparta was beset, yet it remained the greatest land power in Greece and had not been defeated, other than, in some respects, diplomatically. Even without Pericles, Athens was worldly, confident, had the elan of democracy, the elevation of intellectual creativity and its spontaneous energy had been fully a match for Sparta's discipline. After the war of two coalitions, and the bitter disappointment of the key members of the Spartan coalition, the forces of disunity created a fluid political condition that was potentially dangerous for Sparta, stretched as it was demographically and socially, while Athens, though enervated, was under no threat and remained in undisputed possession of the scepter of practically the entire Mediterranean. It was the first of those historic turning points where suddenly the best course was for two of the greatest powers, longstanding foes, to stand the diplomatic order on end and embrace. Athens and Sparta suddenly discovered the virtues of rapprochement, as in modern times, Hitler and Stalin did in 1939, and Richard Nixon and Mao Tse-tung did in 1972. The stupefaction of the engaged world was equivalent in each case.

The shift shook public opinion in both states, as animosity between them had obviously achieved a highly vitriolic state after so many years of mortal and ruthless combat, but neither had been humiliated and they were able to construct (again, as in Chapter 5, footnote 5) what Charles de Gaulle called, in Algeria in 1959, after many years of savage fighting, including the murder of women and children and the torture of prisoners, "a peace of the brave." The two parties could meet as patriots, courageous and proud peoples, and above all as Greeks, and started to recall and venerate the days of Cimon, when they fought side by side against the common

Persian enemy. In May of 421 B.C., after a very brief negotiation, Athens and Sparta agreed an alliance for fifty years, in which each side would come to the aid of the other with full military support if it were attacked and that in such an eventuality, neither would make peace without the agreement of the other. As is usually the case in such sudden shifts of alignment between great powers, it made perfect sense.

For Sparta, alliance with Athens almost certainly staunched any Peloponnesian desertion, and for Athens, alliance with Sparta assured that Attica would not be troubled by Peloponnesian intruders, enabling Athens to concentrate on regaining what had been lost in the Thrace-ward territories and generally sorting out any problems that had arisen during the frightful decade of constant and sometimes precarious war, and the ravages of pestilence. Argos would not now take up arms against Sparta, nor would the Peloponnesians, though unimpressed with Sparta's conduct of the late war (in strategic terms—no one could ever find fault with Spartan war-making). Argos wouldn't move, and neither would the other malcontents. Corinth and Megara, battle-weary and reduced; and even cocky Boeotia, had to be careful, faced with the joint force of the two great Hellenic powers.

Withal, the alliance got off to a slow start. The Athenians released the Spartan prisoners from Sphacteria, but the effect was not a relaxation of Spartan coolness to Athens—after the end of this restraint that Athens had so successfully imposed on Sparta, instead of getting quickly into the spirit of the new arrangements, Sparta became rather abrasive in demanding the withdrawal of Athens from Pylos. In the still ambiguous circumstances, Athens could not continue to promote a revolt of the Spartan helots there (having pledged to assist in the repulse and defeat of any enemy of Sparta). But it evacuated the renegade helots from Pylos, as well as the Messenians, but replaced them with Athenian troops. This dramatic turn in the alignment of the Hellenic states would have to be achieved in stages. This Spartan reticence was unsuccessful policy all round: Athens went no further down the road of collaboration, and under Argive enticements, the Peloponnesian League effectively disintegrated. Sparta could take care of itself, and had nothing to fear from Athens, but its status as chief state of the Peloponnese was whittled down appreciably.

Argos hated the Spartans, and was more democratic, but not as democratic as Athens, and very divided internally between conflicting ideas in foreign relations and domestic political organization. It had sat quiescent and watchful for thirty years but was completely unprepared to step forward and try to lead even itself in a coherent direction of independence from the new Hellenic world of an alliance between the two principal states, even if the alliance was off to a shaky start. Argos, as a relatively democratic state, was attractive to the Mantineans, but the Megarians and Boeotians were repelled by it. Given the ambiguities of Argos, just awakening from its long slumber, Corinth, hot with the spirit of war and the ferocity of being betrayed, took on the task of organizing a third force in opposition to the Athens-Sparta tandem. Corinth asked for a commission of twelve Argive citizens that could secretly conclude treaties with any state except Athens or Sparta. Any alliance with either of those states could only be made with general agreement of the Argive people. At the same time, Corinth convened a council of all states that were prepared to come together in a block that would be outside the orbit of Athens and Sparta. They sought a league of all those states which had rejected the peace. Sparta denounced this as sacrilege, as the Peloponnesian Congress had the pledge of all members to abide by its decisions unless prohibited from doing so by the "hindrance of Gods own heroes." What undercut Corinth's effort was the refusal of the Boeotians and Megarians to join it.

What occurred was a gradual aggregation of an alliance of a third force. Singly, Corinth, the Chalcidians, and Mantinea joined with Argos, some motivated by hostility to Athens, some to Sparta. As an alliance, it was a pantomime horse, but Tegea balked, and Megara and Boeotia hesitated. Boeotia was anti-democratic and was only interested in alliance if convinced that Athens and Sparta together would take up arms to force Boeotia to give up what it had gained in the Archidamian War. Short of that, it would sit on its hands. Sparta was again in a quandary, as it did not want to join Athens in crushing the renegades, because Sparta would only benefit from the defeat of Argos, while Athens would pick up what it wanted in the northeast and northwest, and gain immensely from the humbling of Corinth, its closest maritime rival, albeit a distant one. In the Spartan elections at the end of 421 (amid an extremely circumscribed electorate), two of the five ephors publicly advocated renouncing the peace with Athens. Diplomacy became terribly confused, as a treaty was advanced involving all the malcontent third parties, but it was dependent on the adherence of Boeotia, whose council would not touch it because they were not aware that the whole plan would require Argos to join them and that Sparta was assumed to be ready to break the Athenian alliance. With so little actually assured, Sparta was left with no alternative but to stick with its new alliance and retrieve the Athenian prisoners from the Boeotians as well as the handing over of Panactus by the Boeotians to Athens, which would trigger the restoration to Sparta of Pylus by the Athenians.

Boeotia stipulated that its terms to accede to this were a separate alliance of Boeotia with both Athens and Sparta. Sparta went ahead on this basis, and its envoys arrived in Athens with the returning Athenian prisoners that had been held by the Boeotians. Unfortunately, instead of handing Panactus over to Athens, the Boeotians fired and levelled it, and so the fact that Sparta had made a side-alliance with Boeotia was hard to reconcile with the treaty between Sparta and Athens, and instead of welcoming the Spartan envoys accompanying the liberated prisoners, the Athenians dismissed them after a tongue-lashing on the theme of Spartan non-compliance and general diffidence and unreliability, and refused to relinquish Pylos. However, Boeotia upheld the Spartan alliance, and the effort to set up a rival alliance to Athens and Sparta collapsed. Sparta had done well to seal an alliance with Boeotia, and Argos sent envoys to Athens to try to recreate its former alliance with that city, who arrived just before special Spartan ambassadors empowered to resolve all outstanding issues with Athens, and to assure their hosts that the alliance with Boeotia was in no sense hostile to Athens.

Athenian opinion was divided; to the citizens it seemed that Sparta should be required to unloose its vaunted army on its former allies who were under-performing. But the cautious but astute Nicias, still the Athenian chief, remonstrated that it would be folly to undo the results of a war that had ended so well for Athens, and that the dissolution of the old Spartan coalition was worth as much to Athens as Sparta's specific performance on its peace treaty with Athens. However, this latest practice of Sparta of rebuilding relations with its former allies without requiring them, as they had pledged to do, to restore to Athens what Sparta had promised, complicated Nicias' life considerably. Nicias agreed with his opponents in Athens that Sparta must be made to maintain the pressure on its erstwhile allies.

The leader of the opposition to Nicias in Athens now, Cleon dead, was only briefly the well-named Hyperbolus, but quickly became Alcibiades, who won election as a general in 421. He was, like Pericles, an Alcmaeonid. Alcibiades was a dashing and handsome and eloquent young man in an era when the precocity of youth was admired and not repressed. Alcibiades fascinated his elders, including Socrates, and developed simultaneously as a soldier and strategist, and as an orator and politician. In his eloquence and egotism, as in his military talents, he somewhat prefigured Charles de Gaulle and Douglas MacArthur. For all his talent and personality, his character was vain and vulnerable to flattery and excessive praise.

For all his energy and charisma, he could not gain and hold the support of the people. He had exploited the death of Cleon to push himself forward as the person to lead relations with Sparta, as his grandfather had been the Spartan ambassador in Athens, but Nicias was left in charge of negotiating with Sparta. Alcibiades responded with a demonic fury to upset the peace. He managed to cajole the Spartan ambassadors into renouncing the plenipotentiary status they had been accorded by their government, Alcibiades whipped up such public antagonism toward Sparta (which he had started out a few months earlier championing as the man who could make the Grand Alliance of Athens and Sparta work), he almost succeeded in getting an anti-Sparta alliance with Argos approved. Nicias was hard-pressed but managed to get himself vested with authority to give Sparta what amounted to an ultimatum: Sparta could rebuild Panactum, restore Amphipolis, and renounce the alliance with Boeotia, or Athens would enter into alliance with Argos.

In these circumstances, the anti-Athenian party gained the upper hand in Sparta and Nicias received no concessions at all. Sparta confirmed its signature to the treaties but nothing more and rested in comparative security in its alliance with Boeotia. In response, in July 420, Athens revived its alliance with Argos, and added Mantinea and Elis in what purported to be a quadruple alliance of one hundred years. Though it was a defensive alliance, that was not entirely clear, as Elis and Mantinea were at war with Sparta. Fifteen months into the Athens-Sparta alliance, it was not faring well. Athens had made arrangements with other democracies, as Sparta had with the undemocratic Boeotia. Still security prevailed over political community in the intricate diplomatic roundel that followed the Archidamian War. As always, all states follow their interests.

In Athens, a struggle for preeminence took place between the rather wise and cautious Nicias, a man of peace, and the impetuous warmonger Alcibiades, who sought nothing less than the complete destruction of Sparta. Athens starved the city of Scione into surrender, and as the peace with Sparta authorized Athens to deal with the reduced city as it wished, the adult male population was immediately executed, and the women and children sold into slavery. Even Alcibiades could not complain about excessive civility in this case. Athens returned the Sphacterian Spartans, and great efforts were deployed to restore the damage and agricultural fertility of war-ravaged Attica. In 419, Nicias and Alcibiades were both elected general, and Alcibiades set out around the Peloponnese trying to recruit allies for Athens in what was quite plainly an anti-Spartan cause. He managed a couple of minor successes but was faced down by a strong Corinthian-Sicyonian force when he started to build a fortified settlement at the exit from the Gulf of Corinth. But he next urged the Argives to join him in a contrived quarrel with Epidaurus, a loyal ally of Sparta, which mobilized its entire army and moved it to the frontier, where it remained for the Carnean month, in which believers were obliged to refrain from war. Just as that month ended, Nicias generated a peace initiative, and all the cities sent ambassadors to Mantinea. Corinth declined to negotiate until combat between Argos and Epidaurus ceased, and Nicias prevailed upon the Argives to withdraw. The conference resumed but did not reach agreement. Alcibiades crossed the Saronic Gulf with a thousand hoplites, but the Spartans, though mobilized, did not move; the Lacedaemonians established a garrison to assist Epidaurus defensively in 418 B.C. Alcibiades had the effrontery to have affixed to the copy of the peace treaty at the Acropolis the assertion that the Lacedaemonians (Spartans) "have not kept their word." But at this late stage, Nicias carried the day and the Athenians rallied to the lesson of the latter Pericles and Delium: not to incur certain losses for a result that would be hazardous to achieve and unlikely to be durable even if successful.

Alcibiades was not reelected general in 418, but Nicias and Nicostratus and Laches were. With this assurance of Athenian moderation, Sparta waited to high summer and then a grand force of twenty-thousand hoplites from Sparta and many of its allies, perhaps ten-thousand more lightly armed men and at least five-thousand cavalry, under the Spartan King Agis, met ten-thousand Argive, Elean, and Mantinean hoplites at Methydrium. Just as they were on the verge of combat, two pro-Spartan Argive statesmen, Thrasyllus and Alciphron, on their own authority, advanced to meet Agis, and said Argos was ready for peace. Agis, also on his own authority, for the whole Spartan alliance, granted a cease-fire for four months. during which time, a treaty was to be concluded. Agis was severely criticized, especially by his allies, for squandering an opportunity to annihilate the combined army of three members of the Quadruple Alliance, albeit the missing member, Athens, was much the most powerful. In Argos, the military party apparently did not know how much stronger Agis' army had been than theirs. A force of a thousand Athenian hoplites and three-hundred cavalry under Nicostratus and Laches did arrive after the armies had stood down, but they were treated very discourteously. Alcibiades accompanied them and finally got to address the people of Argos and said that they had no right to withdraw from the alliance with Athens. As the Argives almost certainly mistakenly believed that they had been cheated of a great victory, and were furious at the aristocratic peace party, Alcibiades was sustained and Argos decided not to conclude a treaty but to resume a policy of war with Sparta, starting with the seizure of Orchomenus, which capitulated quickly. The Eleans now proposed an insane initiative: the recapture of Lepreum. This was too dangerous an enterprise for all three Elean allies, but Elia was able to secure the capture of Tegea through the actions of a fifth column within, as was frequently possible in these terribly factionalized inter-municipal conflicts.

Agis, though much criticized, yet, gained in Sparta the general adherence for a mission of punitive vengeance; and Sparta, as always, mobilized very quickly. The king was accompanied by a council of ten popularly selected advisers to ensure there was no repetition of the truce at Methydrium. Agis was, in fact, a talented, though unorthodox, military commander. He attacked uphill at Alesion, and just before his forces came to grips with the enemy, he withdrew, and set his army to work diverting a river into Mantinean lowlands, where it would do much damage. This lured the Eleans down from their elevated redoubt to an open plain, where the numbers were more even than at Methydrium, and there was a more substantial Athenian contingent. Agis outmaneuvered his opponents, the secondary Argive units broke and fled, and the Spartans won a decisive victory. The Athenian cavalry cut its way through encircling Spartan cavalry, enabling most of the Athenians to escape, though two of the elected generals, Laches and Nicostratus, were killed. The Quadruple Alliance lost eleven-hundred soldiers to three-hundred Spartans, and Agis, still seeking a reestablishment of the peace that had been agreed upon for fifty years just three years before, did not seek a blood bath against his retreating enemies. He did not try to discommode the retirement of the Athenians, who would, in any case, as they maintained their formations, have exacted a terrible toll on Sparta's army in a fight to the finish. At a stroke, Spartan military prestige was fully restored.

In the aftermath of the debacle at Mantinea, the Quadruple Alliance repaired directly to the reduction of Epidaurus and surrounded it, but only the Athenians did a professional job of building fortifications of investment, and the whole enterprise dissolved in the disunity of the feckless and now threadbare alliance. All the parties withdrew, and Epidaurus was not disturbed further. The real vulnerability of the Quadruple Alliance, the so-called Confederacy (though it was nothing of the kind), was the pro-Spartan party in Argos, that had intervened with Agis at Methydrium. After the rout at Mantinea, the aristocratic party in Argos got tenuous control of the state, when, apparently by prearrangement, Agis advanced to Tegea and sent an emissary to Argos telling the Argive leaders they had a choice between peace and war, and not long to decide.

The aristocrats made their move, dispensed with the unbidden advice of Alcibiades who had arrived to champion the alliance with Athens, and flipped Argive foreign policy, repudiated its treaty with Athens, Elis, and Mantinea, and signed a fifty-year alliance with Sparta. (It was the Greek custom to sign truces and peaces for extraordinary lengths of time, but they generally only lasted as long as the ruling faction within each contracting state considered them to be in their interests.) In order to give this arrangement some chance of durability, Sparta made a generous preemptive concession to Argos: that if it should be determined that the Peloponnesian Alliance as a whole should engage in war, Sparta and Argos jointly would decide what contingents should be requested of all of the allies. Argos had leap-frogged Corinth as the principal ally of Sparta. It was further agreed between Sparta and Argos that they would declare war on Athens if Athens did not depart the Peloponnese, and they agreed not to "conclude peace or wage war with anyone except together." The two foes of the last century were suddenly joined at the hip. It was an arrangement as reliable as the immobility of fortune.

This sea-change created a sequence of events that reinforced Sparta's suddenly strengthened position. Athens abandoned Epidaurus and did leave the Peloponnese (where its ambitions were very limited and intermittent anyway). Mantinea made a thirty-year alliance with Sparta, and the inimitable Perdiccas of Macedon, one of the most inveterate opportunists ever to lead any state in all history, joined the Sparta-Argos alliance, without officially abandoning his alliance with Athens. In light of this, the Chalcidians defected from Athens and joined the Argos-Sparta alliance (mainly to try to deter Perdiccas, certainly not out of any fealty to their new allies). The dramatic shift in fortunes did not reflect an underlying shift in the correlation of forces, just the weakness of the other Hellenic states apart from Athens and Sparta, while confirming the unfathomable venality of Perdiccas. Athens itself had not been defeated; it withdrew in good order at Mantinea, after its so-called allies had been soundly defeated by the Spartans.

Athens had made a mistake in imagining that anything could be done with an alliance with such unstable and ineffective states as Argos, Mantinea, and Elis. The effective architects of this moderate set-back for Athens were the rambunctious and superficially talented Alcibiades, and the aristocratic party in Argos, that had been waiting like a cobra for one false step by its democratic Argive fellow citizens to do a bunk on the rickety Confederacy. Alcibiades had tried to plunge into war, and Nicias had ensured that Athens did not really commit itself to war with Sparta. In this vortex, the pressure placed on the Quadruple Alliance revealed that alliance as a feeble, and artificial celebration of a fleeting and shallow concordance of interests between the parties. Alcibiades had many of the less attractive traits of Cleon.

It was sorted out in Athens by a showdown between Nicias and Alcibiades, as they both ran again for general, but they agreed on a vote for ostracism. But at a strategic moment, Alcibiades suggested that he and Nicias both urge their supporters to vote for both of them and that the leading demagogue apart from Alcibiades, Hyperbolus, be ostracized. This is what happened in 417: nothing was solved, although the technique of ostracism for the resolution of such problems was discredited and abandoned. Sparta's diplomatic victory seemed greater than it was; in Greece, the balance of power, with so many states and such shifting political sands all the time, depended on the always mobile correlation of forces. Sparta could only prevail over those states with oligarchic governing parties which were effectively dependent on Spartan support. Argos, which had been the chief check on Spartan overlordship of the whole Peloponnese, had crumbled from its role as a perceived check on Spartan authority, even when it had only been neutral. Now that Argos had become Sparta's junior partner, everything, politically in the Peloponnese, came loose, especially in Argos itself. The democrats in Argos, were profoundly aggrieved and constantly tormented and oppressed, and they plotted a counter-coup with the courage and determination which Greek democrats perfected to a unique degree. They waited until Sparta would be completely absorbed in its religious and athletic celebrations in July 417, then rose up. Fighting raged throughout Argos, and the Spartans tarried so long leaving their festival that when they finally sent a contingent as far as Tegea, they met a delegation from Argos that told them the democrats had won and that the oligarchic and aristocratic leaders had been killed or expelled. If there was to be a direct intervention in Argos, it would have to be by the entire Peloponnesian League, which met in Sparta and heatedly debated the subject, with the Argive democrats there also to argue their case. When the Congress voted to intervene in Argos to restore the aristocrats, the Corinthians walked out and refused to have anything to do with the coercion of Argos.

The inexhaustible Alcibiades joined in the internal Argive debates and carried the move for Argos to a return to alliance, this time for only fifty years, with Athens. Even the Argives now recognized that they were too divided and bypassed by time to cleave to anything more than their autonomy, which would be much better and more enthusiastically preserved by the Athenians than in any alliance with Sparta. Argos, with Athens' assistance, started to build "long walls" around the road to the sea, to facilitate Athens' supply of Argos, if the need arose (which it almost surely would). But the Spartans invaded in 416 and tore the uncompleted walls down themselves. The Argives replied with a raid into Phlius, a pro-Spartan neighbor, and hundreds of oligarchic sympathizers were deported by Alcibiades. For two years, the Athenians and Spartans vied for preeminence in Argos; it was to this pitiful state as a pawn scrapped over by Athens and Sparta, that Argos had been reduced. In 414, Argos responded to the Spartan interventions which had inflicted much damage on the Argive countryside, by laying waste and plundering the Lacedaemonian land of Thyrea.

By this time, the Athenians had pursued their fateful interest in Sicily, where they had already come close to over-stretching themselves. Especially when Alcibiades was around, they imagined themselves to be invincible. This was far from the last time that a state would be so profoundly seduced by its ambitions masquerading as its destiny. The Athenians had plenty of naval strength to put down shore parties at intervals along the Peloponnesian coast. This gave the Spartans all they needed to tear up the most sensible act of diplomatic statesmanship that had been engaged in in Greece since the prime of Pericles: the fifty-year alliance, which had lasted for only seven years, and was observed for only two years. The peace between Athens and Sparta, however, was not deemed to be violated.

In 420 B.C., Nicias, who had concluded that the future of the tides of war depended on a reassertion of Athens' position in Thrace, felt the rebellious Chalcidians deserved a good chastisement and set out to give it to them with, as he imagined, Athens' always reliable ally, Perdiccas, king of Macedon, who was, in fact, already in alliance with Sparta. Once embarked on this venture and realizing the proportions of the treachery he faced, Nicias cobbled together a neutral truce with the Chalcidians, and set out to teach Perdiccas a lesson that would be long remembered. Perdiccas got no assistance from either the Spartans or the Chalcidians, as everyone now realized that the Macedonian scoundrel was no use to anyone as an ally, given his incorrigible chicanery, so he professed alliance yet again with Athens, as Nicias now sought recovery of Amphipolis, but was not able to achieve it. Nicias had begun a blockade when word arrived of setbacks in Sicily.

In fact, Athens had not really committed unreservedly to any of these ventures and had just been dabbling. Apart from Alcibiades' permanent war party, the Athenians had generally returned to what many regarded as their higher vocation of beautifying and monumentalizing Athens and of encouraging the highest culture and greatest festivals the Western world had ever seen. At the same time, a traditionalist spirit, nationalistic and conservative, was abroad. Protagoras was indicted for impiety, Diagoras outlawed for atheism, and Alcibiades was mocked theatrically for vulgarity and debauchery.

The competition between Nicias and Alcibiades continued, as Nicias made an extravagant act of devotion at Delos, while Alcibiades was everywhere at Olympus, entering seven contenders in the four-horse chariot races of 416. He had Euripides compose an ode to victory for him. All these activities reminded even the belligerent Alcibiades of the virtues of peace. It was a good deal more enjoyable and reliably uplifting to have competing teams in chariot races and to patronize the poets and playwrights of Athens, than to fight in mortal combat with the grim and forceful Spartans. Athens gradually reduced the tribute exacted from its allies and the constituents of its empire, and began to build up its reserves, even as it returned to the construction of ambitious public monuments in Athens. In 416, to make a point, Athens punished the small Doric community of Melos, which had not paid any tribute to Athens for nine years. Melos made the grievous mistake of trusting to its good relations with Sparta and the Peloponnesian League to assure its safety. Alcibiades successfully championed exemplary punishment: Melos was invested, surrendered, and the adult males in the traditional Greek manner, were executed in front of their families and the families were sold into slavery. For all Athens' high-mindedness, it was still a part of a horridly barbaric civilization that spent most of its energies in internecine strife.

Athens was at its peak, despite the failings and compromises that were evident. It had become distracted by Sicily and drawn into Sicily. In its exalted state among the diminutive but talented and sophisticated Greeks, Athens had lost somewhat a full sense of its limitations, even though they had been demonstrated several times, not by lack of courage or training, but by, as Pericles had warned, the limits of Athens' power to impose itself on a known world that was steadily growing because of the curiosity and valour of men, especially Greek men, though, as always, they had their rivals. Most dangerously, they also had their always fluid intra-Hellene disputes.

2. The Sicilian Disaster

A dispute arose in 416 between two Hellenic Sicilian cities, Athens' ally Segesta, and Syracuse's ally Selinus, over precise border areas, compounded by problems generated by inter-marriage, of a fanatical and violent character for which Sicily eventually became world famous. Acragas and Carthage declined to assist Segesta, and in desperation it sent envoys to Athens, where their principal argument, apart from the existence of an alliance, was that if Syracuse dominated all Sicily, its kinship with and loyalty to Corinth could lead to an immense strengthening of the Peloponnesian states and a mortal threat to Athens. The Athenians sent observers to determine the state of the war and the veracity of Segesta's claims to be able to finance its own war effort, including an allied contribution.

The Sicilian Expedition

The Athenian government had no idea that Sicily's population was now larger than that of the Peloponnese, and that the great majority were Greek. It was not widely known that Syracuse had a population as great as Athens, and there was anyway, as there long persisted between Western Europe and North America, a certain snobbery (it lingers yet). There was a good deal of restless and expansionist agitation in Athens, especially among younger men, who were frustrated at the cautious and pacific policies of Nicias and had not experienced the extreme danger and tension of the most difficult periods of the Peloponnesian and Archidamian Wars. While some Athenians looked upon Sicily as a theatre of expansion, it was more generally thought of as ensuring a balance in the correlation of forces in Sicily, as had generally been accomplished, at great cost, in eastern Hellenic areas, and an opportunity for vastly increased trade. There was thus general support for a policy of some expansion to the West, though to varying extents and for differing reasons.

Alcibiades, predictably, saw it as a splendid chance for derring-do, especially when the exploratory mission to Sicily returned with sixty talents (the cost of maintaining a fleet of sixty ships for a month) and confirmed (they were hoodwinked on this point) that the Segestans had the means to pay for a lengthy campaign. Athens voted to send a fleet of sixty vessels with the mission of aiding Segesta against Selinus, to restore Leontini, and to advise the Segestans on how to resolve Sicilian issues in the best interests of Athens. Three generals were sent as co-commanders: the inevitable Alcibiades, equally tenacious Nicias, and the less well-known Lamachus. This reflected political divisions in Athens, including differing views on what the mission was supposed to achieve. It was clear that unity of command would be a challenge. Nicias warned of yielding to the war-lust of inexperienced and often profligate youth, and of engaging in a grand mission at a distance when Athens had formidable enemies near it which would lunge at any opportunity created by a reversal. If there were not a reversal, Nicias reasoned, it would create an immense problem of overreach to maintain order in Sicily, putting Athens in a permanent state of vulnerability opposite any combination of Sparta, the Boeotians, the ineffable Perdiccas of Macedon, and the still powerful and dangerous Persia.

Nicias said that it was unwise to embark on anything remotely as ambitious and hazardous as was contemplated while there were still members of the existing empire in a state of revolt. Alcibiades successfully responded to this argument by saying there was an opportunity to overawe and effectively dominate all Sicily tipping the balance in Greece in Athens' favour, and that if Athens just rested on its oars, it would grow soft and under-motivated and would be endlessly hectored and badgered by insolent challenges from other Hellenic states. Nicias next tried the tactic of insisting that a much larger mission was called for, hoping to persuade his countrymen that so large a mission was unwise. In this way, the Athenian force was raised to one-hundred triremes and five-thousand hoplites, and the whole surplus in the treasury, three-thousand talents, and Nicias himself was given the distinct authority to conduct the operation. He was hoist on his own petard, and instead of his requirements scuttling the operation as he had hoped, it ensured that if anything went awry the proportions of the disaster would be almost unlimited.

Just before this huge expedition was going to set sail, a far-reaching act of impious vandalism struck Athens, and almost all public likenesses of Hermes, of which there were a great many in shrines and public squares, were smashed. Alcibiades' enemies accused him of inciting such behavior in the youth, and he was personally accused of having conducted an extreme sacrilege in a private home, with a burlesque of the sacred Mysteries of Eleusis. Alcibiades was irreverent and headstrong, and the vandals might have been followers of his, but it is unimaginable that he would have countenanced such a profane act. He demanded an immediate trial if he were accused of anything, but this was blocked by the demagogues, Androcles and Peisander, and Alcibiades was obliged to set sail with the fleet in June 415. He was popular in the army, but in his absence from Athens, his political position could erode quickly if things went badly.

There was a grandiose and moving departure process at Piraeus, as a huge throng on shore, after all the ships were ready and the trumpet had sounded, recited the usual prayer, and the vessels raced out in perfect order and formation. It was an awesome sight. They stopped at Aegina and then Corcyra, and then proceeded across the Mediterranean toward Italy, the full fleet, with allied contingents, now one-hundred and thirty-four triremes, including forty carrying the hoplites, and one-hundred and thirty supply ships, carrying a total of twenty-seven thousand men, twenty-thousand of them sailors. Apart from shelter and water, no further port welcomed them. At Rhegium, they were permitted to land and revictual, but the gates of the city were not opened to them. This was not a good omen, and the impression created by it, was supplemented by the squadron of three vessels that had been sent ahead to Segesta from Corcyra, and had come part way back to reveal that the Segestan emissaries who had assured Athens of the financial solidity of Segesta were victims of a hoax and that apart from thirty additional talents that remained, the Segestan government possessed no additional cash reserves.

A council of war was convened. Nicias was for moving at once to intimidate Selinus, which had started the disturbance, and forego grander ambitions. Lamachus wanted an immediate assault on Syracuse, and Alcibiades wanted to sail around the island trying to round up allies. Lamachus had insufficient influence to prevail, and his idea of an assault on Syracuse with such a diminutive land force would not have had good prospects anyway, but he did cast the balance for Alcibiades, as he thought Nicias' idea was too defeatist. Messana, Naxos, and Camarina refused, Catana admitted the Athenians, but only after their forces had infiltrated a back-gate while the whole town was in the public square listening to Alcibiades' sales pitch.

They returned, almost empty-handed, to Catana, where a boat from Athens awaited them, requiring the immediate return of Alcibiades to Athens to face a charge of sacrilege. As had been feared, Androcles and Peisander and other rivals, had pulled the rug out from under him in his absence. Alcibiades was a vainglorious and unstable man and, in some respects, an outright scoundrel, but he was talented and patriotic and courageous, and had been voted co-commander of this mission. Recall of this disruptive kind was illustrative of the nastiest of Athenian official and popular vengeance. Politics never ended, even in the face of foreign enemies, and the greatest were if anything, less immune to it than the less exceptional figures.

In the absence of the mission to Sicily, a couple of alternate theories had developed about who was responsible for the desecration of the statues and busts of Hermes, but a partial confession seemed to establish that it was a group not connected to any of the co-commanders, and the guilt of the culprits was slightly diminished by the fact of drunkenness. But the group that committed the burlesque of the Mysteries of Eleusis had been prosecuted, all except Alcibiades. The febrile atmosphere was enflamed by minor Lacedaemonian and Boeotian military maneuvres, which caused a general mobilization in Athens, for a few days. The whole Athenian community dreaded the conduct of Alcibiades should he triumph in Sicily, and an indictment was brought against him by Thessaly, the son of Cimon, who also knew something about the ingratitude of the Athenian Republic. Alcibiades was permitted to return on his own ship, escorted by the vessel that had been sent to fetch him, but he parted from the other ship and went to Elis, and received a safe conduct to Sparta. On this news, he was sentenced in absentia to death in Athens. For the most distinguished state in the Western world, it was an absurd state of affairs.

Nicias was now effectively in control, and he made for Segesta. He collected their remaining thirty talents, some of the hoplites created some consternation by marching overland back to Segesta, sacked one small town, but were rebuffed at Himera, and actually thrown back from the walls of Hybla. The effect of this very irresolute handling of this great but unbalanced force—much larger than was necessary on the sea, but of insufficient strength on land, was to inflate the complacency of the Syracusans. Syracuse's politics were at least as chaotic as those of Athens: popular opinion was influential and subject to unpredictable and diametrical changes. The leader of the popular factions was Athenagoras; he had never believed that the Athenian force was particularly directed at Syracuse, as he considered that any such move would be insane and have no chance of success.

The aristocratic leader, Hermocrates, at the early stage, as the Athenian fleet approached, had more respect for Athens than Athenagoras did, but saw this as an opportunity to unite pan-Sicilian opinion against the Greeks. He promoted a call for insular union and a combined naval force to confront the Athenians before they had deployed their fleet strategically, but he was unable to generate any enthusiasm in any quarter for such a policy. The numerous (fifteen) generals professed to have everything under control and Athenagoras and his followers were confident and relaxed. Once the Athenians got to Rhegium and started to redeploy, Syracusan opinion became much more concerned, and forces were dispatched around Sicily, firming up relations and putting observation points and small garrisons around the island.

When the Greek fleet arrived at Syracuse, the Syracusans kept their modest fleet safely in port, and the Athenians only sent a reconnaissance squadron into the main harbor, which made an incoherent proclamation and withdrew. They also chased out a small Athenian landing party, and as time went by without the Athenians actually doing anything, the Syracusans moved from complacency to aggressive confidence and launched an overland attack on Catana, the Athenian base of operations in Sicily. Nicias had enticed this and sent his full force by sea overnight and into the Great Harbour at Syracuse and disembarked his entire force on the south side of it, while much of the Syracusan army was on a wild goose chase to Catana, whence it returned by forced marches. Nicias had succeeded in landing unopposed and closed up the harbor completely. But it is not clear what he thought he could accomplish with only about seven-thousand men trained in land warfare. The Syracusan army appeared just to the south of Nicias and he attacked them before they had sorted out their positions. The Syracusans had about twelve-hundred cavalry, but Nicias skillfully made it difficult for them to make headway. Though pushed back, the Syracusans fought bravely and used their cavalry to shore up weak patches in the infantry. A tremendous electric storm startled horses and less experienced Syracusans, and the Athenians won on the day, but it was not a rout, and the Syracusans retired in good order and barricaded themselves into the Olympeium, the city's nearest fortification. Having won the battle and killed a few hundred of the enemy, Nicias reembarked his entire force and sailed back to Catana.

Nicias appears to have hoped that his victory would shatter Sicilian solidarity (Segesta, the origin of the war seems to have almost vanished from anyone's thinking). Winter was approaching and Nicias did not in these circumstances want to embark on a siege. In any case, his minimal cavalry (thirty horse) was a very serious liability. He also seems to have hoped that he had given the aggressive party, now presumably a little less bellicose since the apostasy of Alcibiades, enough to enable to bring the mission back ostensibly victorious. But Androcles and Peisander were now in the ascendant in Athens, in the absence if Nicias, and they voted Nicias three-hundred talents and sent him two-hundred and fifty cavalry and thirty mounted archers, with orders to subdue Syracuse.

This was an early classic case of what became known in the Pentagon (U.S. Defense Department) in the late Twentieth Century as "mission creep." The whole point of it kept moving around. It was at this point not clear what grievance Athens had with Syracuse or what it was doing in Sicily at all. The Syracusans were not in the least demoralized and spent the winter of 415-414 strengthening walls and obstacles between all the peaks and cliffs around their city of one-hundred thousand. They knew that they could not survive a successful siege for long—their population was too large to be supplied by anything that could be laid up now, and almost nothing would come in by water—no one underestimated the efficiency of the Athenian navy. The Syracusans streamlined their command, and Hermocrates, and two others received general command. He and Athenagoras tentatively cooled their rivalries in the public interest, a state of political maturity that eluded the much more sophisticated Athenians.

The Syracusans succeeded in dissuading other Sicilians from entering the lists on the side of Athens, and they had an even greater diplomatic success in Greece. The Corinthians still hated Athens and were happy to help. Sparta, which the Syracusans urged to reopen war with Athens was much less enthused. The Syracusan argument was that if Athens prevailed in Sicily, it would become an incomparable super-power in the Hellenic world and would easily assert itself over the Peloponnese. This argument was especially well and persuasively advanced by Alcibiades, who was envenomed with hatred of his native city, and was even more dangerous in this role than he was when he was just a loose cannon in the common cause in Athens. Sparta declined to create a diversion in Attica, but did agree to send a general, Gylippus, a very talented commander, with a Corinthian contingent, and Gylippus would take charge of the whole Syracusan resistance.

The reinforcements from Athens only arrived in the spring and Nicias was able to supplement them with four-hundred cavalry from Segesta and Naxos, so he had about eight-hundred in all. The objective of the other Sicilian states was to be with the victor and wait to see who that was, so at least neither side had the benefit or handicap of a landslide in one direction of the Sicilian states. Carthage continued to decline any involvement. Nicias and Lamachus launched their offensive in May 414. The Syracusans had strengthened defences in the port, if the Athenians were tempted to approach by their original route and had also got well along in establishing anti-cavalry defences at the logical points on the landward side. But they had not completed that task and they were in no position to sustain a long siege, given the requirements of the civil population.

It opened well for Athens. Nicias and Lamachus came by sea and landed just northwest of Syracuse, disembarking their entire force, and moving quickly to the still uncompleted part of Syracusan land-ward defences. The defenders came forward as quickly as they could but could not plug the line that had been breached and tumbled backwards within the city walls, and with the Athenians in possession of a fortified height of land overlooking the city. The Athenian commanders and their elite forces moved very quickly to build a wall of circumvallation to the west of Syracuse, sealing the city off completely, as it was effectively, by the Athenian fleet at sea. The Syracusans attempted a cavalry attack on the construction crews but were beaten off, and then attempted to build their own wall that would cross the path of the Athenian wall, but the Greeks launched a surprise pincers attack at the early afternoon time of comparative rest, and rolled up the entire Syracusan line and inflicted significant casualties and occupied the whole Syracusan counter-line.

The Syracusans attempted a further interruption of the rapidly extending siege wall, but this was defeated by Lamachus leading an amphibious counter-attack that struck the Syracusans in the back and flank. It was a fierce fight, in which Lamachus, who had shown himself a capable general, was slain, and even Nicias, recovering from influenza but at an under-defended forward point, only evaded capture by firing some lumber for siege engines while calling urgently for reinforcements. It was now clear that Athens was going to impose a virtually air-tight siege, and it was already in negotiation with the inevitable faction of disloyal Syracusan renegades who almost always surfaced in any siege in the ancient world. There was vivid discussion in Syracuse, finally, about why they were being besieged and taking casualties while their forces were being commanded by a Spartan. Hermocrates was abruptly dismissed.

The Athenians had wasted a lot of time redefining their mission, coping with political cross-currents and finally equipping themselves properly for a land campaign. They had won the first season, but with a Spartan commander and some assistance from Athens' Hellenic rivals; Syracuse was far from subdued. Lamachus, though he had always warned of the dangers of the mission, had commanded very ably and was now much missed. Even Alcibiades would have infused more energy into the effort than Nicias, whose caution was aggravated by his infirmity, though he remained a wise and skillful leader. The death of Lamachus and arrival of Gylippus made a great difference, as leadership almost always does in military matters. Gylippus was cut from the same cloth as Brasidas, and he set off with only four ships, got through the Straits before Nicias could have him intercepted, and landed at Himera, where he was greeted as a liberating hero. He converted some of his sailors to soldiers, armed by the Himeraeans, and set off across Sicily with three-thousand somewhat miscellaneously derived but enthusiastic soldiers, including a hundred cavalry. The Spartans slipped a vessel through the blockade into Syracuse with news of approaching help, but Gylippus fell completely unexpected on the back of the Athenian siege army and joined the Syracusans. In a quick sequence of actions, Gylippus turned the tables on Nicias and besieged the Athenians, though their naval superiority could assure supplies.

At this point, after sixteen rather unrewarding months, the Athenians were suddenly hemmed in by the Syracusan cavalry and their sailors were under steady attack by Spartan and Syracusan archers. The allied contingents started to slink away, and Nicias was aware that Spartan naval reinforcements were en route. In October 414, Nicias sent an extensive message home explaining his weakening condition and increasing vulnerability, which would be very difficult to deal with come the spring. He recommended that the entire enterprise be abandoned, while it could be done without serious losses, or if it were to be continued, that it be very heavily reinforced, to have any chance of success. In either case, he pleaded ill health (very honestly), and asked to be relieved of command.

Proud Athens would hear of none of it, and retained Nicias in place, but sent their most resourceful general, Demosthenes, and the talented Eurymedon with substantial reinforcements, starting with ten new ships and two-thousand seamen. Sparta, responded as Athens raised the ante, by taking the advice of the Argives (formerly among Athens' most loyal supporters), and invaded Attica, ravaging and pillaging and even installing some fortified places in Attica: the Peloponnesian War opened up again in March 413. Hermocrates reappeared as a strenuous leader of the Syracusan navy, which was supplemented by Corinthian vessels, and shaped into a force of seventy ships. Hermocrates worked hard on talking his crews into the theory that the Athenians were not invincible.

Gylippus and Hermocrates organized a coordinated attack: the Syracusan navy would press a two-pronged assault on the storage base of the Athenian navy and Gylippus, on a signal from Hermocrates would attack from the landward side, to the south of the harbor, where he had stealthily moved his whole force during the night. The Athenians made a very spirited effort to intercept both Syracusan fleets but being outnumbered by ten ships in each of the two actions, gradually gave way, and as they did so, Gylippus launched his entire force on the Athenian rear and overwhelmed the principal fort the Athenians had built for their protection. A terrible disaster threatened the Athenian forces, but in their highest tradition, they suddenly got the better of the Syracusan naval squadrons by sheer skill and boldness of seamanship, got both Syracusan fleets in confusion and jostling each other, and snatched out a victory. The Syracusans retired, having lost eleven ships to only three Athenian, but on land, Gylippus had seized the main Athenian warehouse, including the sails for forty triremes. Athenian casualties were not severe, but their position was now very truncated and unpromising. Athens' prestige was shaken.

Nicias tried hard to exploit his naval victory, but the Syracusans retreated entirely into port and put stockades in the water to protect themselves. The Athenian navy was now confined to waters so narrow, its greatest strengths of maneuver and formation were not useful to it. Gylippus brought up reinforcements by land, though Acragas would remain neutral to the end and would not allow him to cross its territory. Nicias also succeeded in rousing Sicilian states to harass Gylippus' forces, killing eight-hundred of his hoplites as they marched across Sicily. But several states did rally to Syracuse and made good Gylippus' losses. Finally, in August, Gylippus attacked all around the land perimeter of the Athenian position, which Nicias quickly perceived to be a diversion, as the main attack came by sea. The Athenians responded quickly to this and repulsed the attack, without heavy loss on either side. The same occurred two days later. But the next day, a Corinthian captain, Ariston, proposed and executed a plan for attack and retreat, quick refreshment for his crews, and then a surprise return to attack later in the day. They took advantage of the heavier prows they had added to their vessels and got the better of the Athenian navy, an almost unheard-of result. The condition of the Athenian expeditionary force was extremely serious when Demosthenes and Eurymedon finally arrived.

The Spartans occupied Decelea, in Attica, only fourteen miles from Athens, but as long as Athens ruled the waves, the city was in no danger. Sicily only engaged a quarter of Athen's army, and her naval supremacy would continue unless the entire fleet sent to Syracuse was lost. They replied to the Spartan invasion of Attica, with amphibious landings near Cythera, where they hoped to provoke a slave revolt, always a fear of the Spartans. Demosthenes and Eurymedon had collected forces along their progress, from Chios, Zacynthus, Cephallania, Naupactus, Acarnania and Corcyra, and several other points, and a fleet of seventy-three triremes, bearing five-thousand hoplites and three-thousand archers arrived with a full commissariat in July 413. Demosthenes assumed command from the exhausted Nicias. Demosthenes struck at once, trying a daring night action to envelop the Syracusans. It succeeded at first and made good progress, but Gylippus brought his main forces up in good order and bright moonlight, and the two lines of fighters became completely enmeshed in a chaos of hand-to-hand combat and eventually the defenders repulsed the Athenians, and the Athenian and allied retreat became disorderly and Athens suffered an immense disaster.

Demosthenes proposed a complete withdrawal, when a significant part of the army and almost all the ships could be extracted, or at least a retirement to Catana, where they could maintain themselves. But Nicias rose from his illness and demoralization and claimed that the Syracusans were in worse condition and there was no need for hurry, and he claimed to be in discussion with the peace faction in Syracuse that was on the verge of betraying the city. Disease from the swamps that were in the middle of the uncomfortable Athenian position had afflicted a large number of the Athenians, and it was a steadily less battle-worthy force. After about a month of this, not even Nicias could propose deferral of departure, but he took the eclipse of the moon to be a celestial requirement to remain twenty-seven days, as soothsayers recommended.

On the intelligence that the Athenians had been at the point of departure, Gyllipus determined to strike, and attacked the Athenian navy in the narrow waters of the Great Harbour of Syracuse. Skiffs sped up under the Athenian ships' oars and fired javelins through the oar-portals, disrupting the crews. Eurymedon led the Athenians and tried to outflank the Syracusans. He was unsuccessful and the Syracusans tried to drive the Athenians on to the shore, and attacked on land toward the shore as well, and even dispatched a fireship among the Athenians. The Athenians fought bravely, as always and saved many ships, and badly defeated the overland attack, but they had been defeated, Eurymedon was killed, and the Syracusans now had the stronger sea force. The Athenian position was desperate and further threatened by the Syracusan construction of impediments to depart the anchorage, by tying sundry craft together and narrowing the exit from the harbor. Demosthenes contracted his land perimeter and jammed his vessels with soldiers and archers, and aimed at grappling the Syracusan ships and conducting a land battle at sea. They charged for the open sea and the Syracusans were waiting for them; the Athenians made some progress but were beset from all sides and faced the bottle-neck of the contracted harbor exit. The Athenians sunk more Syracusan ships than they lost, but they could not break away. Nicias and Demosthenes were agreed on trying again at once, but the sailors and soldiers were for trying their luck on land.

The resourceful Hermocrates bluffed them into thinking their route was blocked, and they delayed thirty-six hours packing up and preparing. They advanced in two hollow squares, Nicias and Demosthenes commanding. The dead, wounded, sick, and all the ships were left behind. They managed to make about eight miles and then found their progress blocked by larger and more heavily armed forces on several sides. They escaped overnight. Leaving diversionary fires, but after two days' march, with Nicias four miles ahead of Demosthenes, both squares were overwhelmed by surrounding forces much more numerous and better armed. Demosthenes' force, on promise of their lives being spared, surrendered, six-thousand men. Nicias fought his way to the River Assinarus and his men tried to escape across it, but many were slaughtered, and finally, with no hope, Nicias surrendered. There were only a thousand survivors. A total of seven-thousand, including Nicias and Demosthenes were marched back to Syracuse. The two generals were executed, it was a particularly tragic end for Nicias who had presciently seen the potential for disaster from the start and long opposed it. The men imprisoned in very crowded and unhealthy circumstances, where most died within six months, and a very few were sold into slavery.

It was an overwhelming, bone-crushing defeat. As Thucydides wrote: "There was no department in which the beaten were not utterly beaten, no misery from which they were spared. Their destruction was total in the fullest sense of the word. Ships, army, everything was lost. Of the many that went forth, few returned home."[1] It was a disaster greater than those of Napoleon and Hitler in Russia more than two thousand years later. So distinguished a state had never and even today has rarely immolated itself so swiftly and inadvisedly. Athens would try to regroup, but it was finished as the leading state in the known world, and there was nothing to replace it. "Mere anarchy was (to be) loosed upon the world."

3. The Fall of Athens

When the proportions of the astounding defeat Athens had suffered were known in Greece and generally in the Eastern Mediterranean, and Near East, Athens was effectively deserted, with varying degrees of pleasure, and by former friends in haste to feast on the carcass of the battered Athenian Empire, as is the nature of the world and of human society. The Athenians briefly feared the appearance of the Syracusan navy off Piraeus, but Syracuse had bought its victory very expensively and was interested in the conquest or suzerainty of Sicily, although it did send twenty-two triremes to join other anti-Athenian forces. Various former allies and studious neutrals defected and swarmed about like vultures, or at least flies, and the Empire of Athens was almost completely unreliable. Even Persia, which Athens had flung out of Europe, contemplated some share of spoils for itself, inert and almost moribund though Persia had become. Sparta was challenging Athens as a sea-power and commissioned a hundred new triremes. Athens itself, governed now by a board of ten "advisers" under no illusions about the gravity of their country's failure in Sicily, was imposing special taxes and rebuilding the damaged navy. To finance the

---

1 CAH, V, p. 311 (W.S. Ferguson).

reconstruction of their navy and replenish their treasury, Athens imposed a five per cent tax on all commercial navigation through the Ionian. This was widely seen as an effort (which it was), to make Athens' loyal or at least uncomplaining allies to pay for the disaster for which the Athenians alone were responsible.

A secession movement in the Empire, took like wildfire, starting in Euboea, Lesbos, Chios, and Erythrae, which contacted the durable King Agis now sitting in Decelea, menacingly close to Athens, or Sparta directly. They all avowed the desire to rise up against Athens as soon as the universally anticipated Peloponnesian fleet appeared in Ionian waters. Darius II, now the Great King, or the heir to the more rightful bearers of that title, also contacted the Spartan government, seeking to evict Athens from the cities in Asia Minor that it had taken from Persia in 448. A plan was concerted in which the Peloponnesian fleet was to make a stately tour of liberation through Ionia, and then to Lesbos, and on to the Hellespont, graciously relieving everyone of the insufferable burden of the Athenian association which all of them were happy enough to have and pay for when it was their security against the Persians, pirates, and general armed discord.

The Spartans were importuned with such fervor to act that they moved twenty-one ships across the Isthmus and sent them toward Chios, in July 412, but the Athenians intercepted them and forced them to ground in a deserted harbor where they were blockaded. Then the Athenians had the pleasure of soundly repulsing the Syracusan squadron, but a Lacedaemonian squadron persevered to Chios. In the intricate and always vindictive manner of Hellenic affairs, this squadron was inspired and led by none other than Alcibiades, much more filled with (not entirely incomprehensible) vindictive and treasonable hate than Themistocles had been fifty years before. Alcibiades' enthusiasm was supplemented by his desire to escape the hostility of Agis, who was, to say the least, shirty over the fact that Alcibiades, irrepressible in all things, had seduced his wife, 'lese-majeste' as well as ingratitude to one's host. Chios, Erythrae, Clazomenae, Ephesus and Miletus all announced their secession as Alcibiades and his nominal fleet commander, Chalcideus, sailed from one Athenian Empire member to the next. At Miletus, a treaty of alliance with Sparta against Athens was agreed, and in it Sparta acknowledged the right of the Persian king to retake all of Asia Minor, and, by liberal interpretation, some of the Ionian states who imagined they were seceding from the Athenian Empire to enjoy the independence they had rarely, and not recently had. The Spartans did not inform their new allies and protégés that they had practically signed some of them over to the Persians (a fate whose contemplation could quickly revive nostalgia for Athens). The enemies were tripping over each other's feet in their haste to cast off the Athenian yoke and complete the humiliation of their former esteemed leader of the Hellenic states and chief defender against the Persians. Lebedus, Aerae, Lesbos, Mitylene, and Methymna all revolted at the suggestion of a roving squadron from Chios.

They were like children loose in a candy store, while the Athenians, Spartans, and Persians prepared their separate designs for asserting themselves. The relatively gentle yoke of Athens was not to be cast away that easily. Athens struck back and as each group of new ships under their emergency naval replacement plan was finished, they sailed for the rebellious islands of Ionia. Chalcideus and the ineffable Alcibiades were blockaded into Miletus, and the Athenians based themselves in Samos. To secure its loyalty, they adroitly granted it autonomy, assured the complete victory of the democratic party of Samos and executed the leading nobles with minimal formality, and exiled the rest without the right even to inter-marry with non-nobles. Desperate times call for desperate measures. Mitylene and Methymna were retaken, and the Chian navy given a good beating.

The naval offensive in Ionia weakened the Athenians to the point that the fleet that was blockading the Peloponnesian fleet, couldn't prevent its escape. Under the Spartan admiral Astyochus, it made for Chios but was defeated by the Athenians on sea and land, and the Chian population was seething with rage at its rulers who caused them to be shut up behind fortress walls while the Athenians plundered the island. The Athenians used new vessels laid down and finished since the Syracusan disaster, to besiege and invade Miletus. Inspired by the Persian satrap in Caria, Tissaphernes, the defenders tried to evict the Athenian amphibious force but were defeated. A fleet based on twenty-two Syracusan triremes under the durable Hermocrates arrived, though the Spartan Theramenes was the combined fleet commander. The Athenians prudently withdrew to Samos unharmed and concentrated their forces there, but at the cost of the Argives, who had not fought well at Athens' side, going home in a huff and effectively quitting the alliance (of which they had been inconstant members).

There was a good deal of coming and going as miscellaneous squadrons of ships joined Athens' enemies, but the Athenian shipyards and seafaring population kept arriving in greater force also. The Athenians departed and then returned to Chios, where the Athenians incited a revolt of the Chian slaves, seventy-five per cent of the population, while barricading the population and its Spartan defenders into the main town, and the Athenians again ransacked the island. The Spartan commander, Pedaritus, was reduced to ruthlessly subduing his disgruntled allies and ostensible hosts, while all of them squabbled and jostled in a state of increasing famine. The slaves returned to their purported owners the savagery they had long endured from them and conducted a vicious and bloody guerrilla war against their erstwhile masters, heartily encouraged and abetted by the Athenians. Pedaritus finally in desperation came out and gave battle but was killed and his army defeated, as the famine of the resisters became almost unendurable by the spring of 411. Leon was appointed to replace Pedaritus, and slipped through the Athenian blockade to assume his bedraggled command. He dared a naval battle, which was drawn as night fell and forced disengagement. The Athenians retained their position on Chios until 406, but ended the blockade and concentrated their fleet elsewhere.

The whole Ionian struggle was reduced to a crass bidding war for mercenaries by the Persian governor Tissaphernes. Theramines had a Spartan fleet of seventy triremes but most of the crews were mercenaries and Sparta had no money. The Spartan admiral was only enabled to make good part of the arrears of pay that had already accumulated by plundering a few small islands and he beseeched the Persians for enhanced assistance. Persia's animosity was to all Greeks, and they did not particularly prefer the Spartans to the Athenians, other than in the sense that the Athenians had encroached upon the Great King's position in Ionia and Asia Minor.

Tissaphernes, with or without prompting from his monarch, thought better of a straight subsidy to one faction in the Greek struggle, and agreed to pay from his own resources for the Spartan fleet while it was deemed to be acting in the interests of the King of Persia, but he would determine when that was, and he was only prepared to pay at half the scale that the mercenaries had signed on for.

The Persian satrap (grandson of Hydarnes, one of the original six accomplices in the violent coup of Darius I), effectively assumed control of the extent of Spartan naval activity in Ionia. Tissaphernes quickly realized that the best course for Persia, given its ambition to take back what it had lost, or at least some of it, was to promote a prolonged and enervating war between Sparta and Athens and their respective supporting states. The progressive enfeeblement of the Hellenes who had, united, inflicted such a terrible defeat on Xerxes, was a dazzling prospect. He aimed for the exhaustion in men and money of both navies, to enable Persian retrieval of the Hellenic usurpation of Persian territory in Asia Minor and the Aegean.

Tissaphernes' principal adviser in Hellenic matters was none other than the irrepressible Alcibiades, who, having aroused Spartan reservations about his loyalty, had narrowly escaped the execution of the order given to Astyochus by the Spartan government to murder him, and fetched up at the palace of Tissaphernes offering his services as the world's leading expert on the correlation of forces in the Hellenic struggle. At this point, he hated Sparta more than Athens, as Athens had not actually tried to put him to death. Alcibiades calculated that if he persuaded, or could represent himself as having persuaded, the Persians to favour the Athenians over the Spartans, he could assure himself of recall to Athens and, in his ever-ambitious imagination, even to leadership of that state, especially in light of the calamitous end of his rival Nicias. To the extent he was successful, he was certain to part company with Tissaphernes, as the Persian interest lay in a war of mutual enfeeblement between the two Greek sides, facilitating Persia's resumption of all of what it considered itself to have been wrongly deprived.

Astyochus, on receiving reinforcements, instead of trying to relieve Chios, which he judged too risky, attacked to the south and began intercepting grain-carrying ships from Egypt to Athens. This quickly produced an Athenian squadron which chased off or sunk the commerce-raiders, and a Spartan riposte, and a good deal of naval maneuvering but no definitive engagement. Through it all, Tissaphernes steadily reduced his payments to the Spartans, whose crews were sluggish and frequently failed to man their oars. It was far from the selfless and almost demiurgic heroism of Sparta's greatest days and lore. The Spartans sent commissioners to sea with full powers to reach a binding agreement with Persia, and, if necessary, to overrule Astyochus. The parties met at Cnidus and although Alcibiades was claiming on behalf of Tissaphernes that Persia wished to liberate all Greeks from Athenian dominance, the Spartans, through their plain-spoken leader, Lichas, said that Sparta would not accept the apparent terms of the existing agreement that Persia was free to occupy all Hellas except the Peloponnese, and wished to make a definitive demarcation of spheres of influence and commitment to alliance to reach it. Tissaphernes abruptly broke off negotiations and departed. This cut off all assistance and created a mutinously unhappy atmosphere in the ships of fabled Sparta.

The Spartans had a stroke of luck when the aristocratic party on Rhodes seized power and joined with Sparta, enabling Astyochus to disembark many of his sullen (unpaid) crew who had been conducting a shipboard work to rule and defying officers, and to replace them with hearty and motivated men of Rhodes, whose government also gave Astyochus a good dollop of cash. The Athenians arrived too late to kick their subjects in Rhodes back into line, but from Samos harassed everything Rhodes and Sparta were trying to do. Astyochus quickly went through the money Rhodes had given him, and was in a desperate condition, back to crews too discontented for him to put most of his ships to sea.

In the aftermath of the overwhelming disaster Athens sustained in Sicily, Peisander and Androcles were turned out of office, and the whole democratic system so susceptible to the claims of demagogues, fell into some disrepute. The state elected a council of ten elders, including the poet Sophocles, a colleague of Pericles, but the new regime did bring one-hundred and fifty new triremes fully manned into the line in one year, a naval building program proportionately greater than anything Britain managed in response to Germany before the First World War or than the United States managed in its immense naval construction program of 1939-1942. In 412-411, Athens, the proverbially virtuous and stable democracy, was being bled white financially by the costs of a war of survival. Tribute had been raised in the empire to intolerable levels and at home to a point that was impoverishing the wealthiest families. About twenty-thousand slaves defected in Attica and this closed many mines and rolled back agriculture and other commerce. All the wealth Athens had accumulated over its long rise and generally prudent management was being expended. The war profiteers had generally moved beyond the reach of the Athenian tax-collectors. To some degree Athens was the victim of believing in its own propaganda and self-regard about disinterested public service and democratic rule.

Effectively, the longer and greater the cost of the war, the louder and more insistent became the demand of the monied elements of Athens to determine how their taxes were deployed. In these circumstances, the state was resistless against the logic of these demands, and money began to define the limits of what Athens was prepared to fight for, just as Sparta had to consider to what extent it would mortgage itself to the Persians, with whom it had less affinity than with its great but Hellenic rival, Athens. There arose a national Athenian desire for a more effective strategic management: the rich were being taxed out of their wealth and the lower income groups were providing most of the armed forces and taking most of the casualties. In these very difficult times, there was a form of symmetry in the rise, within Athens, of the fortunes of Alcibiades. Scoundrel though he was, he had been stabbed in the back when he was preparing to lead the attack on Syracuse, and his response was understandable. His desertion of Sparta for Persia was not anything that the Athenians looked upon askance. He was the last leader they had had who had any claim to the aura of success.

At this point, the politics of Athens degenerated into the lowest and most contemptible squalor of opportunistic faction and scheming. Phrynichus purported to take the part of the democrats, evoking the most admirable democratic traditions, but really trying to feather his own nest and frightened by the possible return of the avenging Alcibiades for reasons that concerned his own wellbeing and had nothing to do with the merits of different political options. In his desperation, Phrynichus tried to enlist Astyochus to get rid of Alcibiades, Astyochus informed Alcibiades, who by the narrowest of margins failed to have Phrynichus seized and put to death. It was to this instability that Athenian democracy had now descended. Finally, the people were consulted, and they voted to send Peisander as a plenipotentiary to represent the interests of all classes in Athens and to try to work out all issues with Alcibiades and with Tissaphernes. Peisander was received by Tissaphernes, who used Alcibiades as his translator, and it quickly emerged that the satrap of the Great King demanded that all Ionia be ceded to Persia, as well as the right to send fleets of whatever size wherever the Persians wished in the Aegean, This was completely out of the question: Athens would have to be completely prostrate before it would consider such an arrangement, and the negotiators retired to Samos, where there had been an informal agreement of the local leadership in favour of Alcibiades. This was now abandoned as Alcibiades, not for the first time, had overplayed his hand.

Athens had had extra-legal societies, clubs they were called, of dubious people, fixers and thugs who undercut law enforcement and the courts, and were opposed to the democrats, and were composed in considerable measure by the dissolute scions of the oligarchy. They were known to exist but the extent of them was not known. War-time, with its shortages, corruption in defence procurement, and manpower shortages, as well as the stress and joylessness of war itself, especially when the war is not going well, caused the activities of these clubs to intensify, including by the commission of wanton acts of nihilistic vandalism, such as the smashing of the statues of Hermes. On that occasion, it was declared to be only one club that was the culprit, not the whole network of them, which had become extensive and sinister. The leader of this underworld was the shadowy figure Antiphon, a political boss and fixer. Alcibiades, though officially a democrat, was a hero to the clubs, and he presumably incited them to murder Androcles, who had secured his prosecution and exile. The object was to terrorize the democrats, and to some extent it was successful.

When Sparta had run out of money and could no longer pay its sailors, Tissaphernes was concerned that the Spartan admiral, Astyochus would plunder Persian coastal territory to pay his hungry sailors, and Persia made a formal treaty in April 411, to pay the Spartans at a respectable wage per sailor, but only to a certain number of ships, and only until the Persian (Phoenician) fleet arrived in Greek waters. In this way, Tissapohernes continued the policy of promoting the continued war between the Greek states without either Athens or Sparta gaining mastery of all Greece. The various anti-democratic forces of Athens planned to restrict the electorate to those who could afford to serve Athens in war without pay, and the public payroll would be cleared of large numbers of court and festival officers and other civil servants, to free up more of the budget for war.

To institute this authoritarian regime of austerity and much more focused war-making, a Council of Four Hundred, mainly oligarchic benefactors, was contemplated. Athens handed over a number of the units of its empire to local groups and individuals who were known to crave independence. The Athenians assumed that this concern for independence would dissuade them from giving themselves over to Sparta. It was a big gamble, but Athens could not extract any more tribute from these areas and it was burdensome to try to defend them. Every aspect of the Athenian Empire was now under intense pressure. Peisander rounded up supporters around the Empire and three-hundred prominent citizens of Samos announced the establishment of an oligarchic or aristocratic regime on Samos and murdered the demagogue Hyperbolus, who had been living on Samos. They joined Peisander's movement, descended on Athens to replicate there the installation of oligarchies he and his associates had set up elsewhere.

A large public assembly was held more than a mile outside the city walls of Athens, where the hoplites and cavalry Peisander had rounded up could predominate and the urban masses would not trouble to attend or be encouraged to do so. Athenian democracy was abolished, all the beneficiaries of government jobs and benefits were dismissed, the death penalty was ordered for anyone who tried to restore democracy. Citizenship was confined to five-thousand relatively well-to-do people and all revenues were to be consecrated to the war effort. It was a sequence which long foreshadowed both the ignominious self-termination of the French Third Republic at Vichy in 1940, and the German declaration of "total war" by Hitler and Goebbels in 1944. (Vichy and the Nazis were modern anti-democratic regimes of different levels of fervor.)

The Council of Four-Hundred was chosen at the same assembly by the tribal councils of Athens. After all these measures, they marched on Athens to effect a coup d'état. The people, in one of democracy's finest stands, rose in resistance, the generals Leon and Diomedon, joined and led them. And a number of other determined democratic officials rounded up loyal soldiers and sailing crews in port who were reliable democrats and prepared a serious resistance of the Periclean political heritage.

The Four-Hundred, with concealed arms and large groups of followers idling quietly by in case of need, broke into the Council Hall, gave the incumbents their attendance fees for the balance of the legislative session and dismissed them. The new regime announced itself in terms of comparative civility and to this point, there was no violence at all. All of the five-thousand "active citizens" were deemed to be councilors. Officially, a modest restraint of democracy had been instituted in order to prosecute the war more efficiently, following which, liberality would be reestablished. However, the reign of the Four-Hundred was a disastrous failure. The democratic soldiers and sailors at Samos or Athens, failed to negotiate a peace with Sparta, failed to stabilize what was left of the empire or reinvigorate the war effort, and most of the Athenian fleet mutinied (like the German navy in 1918). Reports of what was happening in Athens were reported in wildly lurid exaggerations in Samos, and the loyal sailors and soldiers thought their wives and families were being abused. Only the intervention of the distinguished democratic loyalists Thrasybulus and Thrasyllus, prevented a massacre of the anti-democratic forces of Samos, which would have facilitated the massacre of everyone of all factions by the nearby Spartan fleet.

These resisters did uphold Athenian traditions and it was determined to consider that Athens had temporarily seceded from the Athenian empire, which would be continued by Samos and the Athenian ships in Ionia. Astyochus threatened battle while Samos appeared to be divided but withdrew when a united Athenian fleet came out to challenge him. At this point, Tissaphernes, learning of the strife in Athens and fearing that Sparta might win a decisive victory, cut off wages to the Spartan navy again and Astyochus was reduced to sending a third of his fleet to join in the Spartan assault on Thrace, which had been adequately funded to pay those sailors. This had the effect of restoring the naval advantage in the Aegean to the democratic Athenians. The Council of Four-Hundred in Athens was essentially talking to itself. Most of the squadron sent to Thrace was driven back by storms, but those that persevered joined with rebellious elements within Byzantium and wrenched that city from Athenian control.

At this extremely tense and confused point, Thrasybulus had the inspired thought of recalling Alcibiades, who was still friendly with Tissaphernes. He declaimed the preposterous improvisation that Tissaphernes was now in secret alliance with Athenian democracy, calculating that Sparta would be so enraged by his betrayal of them that even the cautious Astyochus would venture into battle with the Athenian fleet. In a particularly splendid flourish, he claimed that Tissaphernes had declared that if Alcibiades were at the head of Athens, Tissaphernes would back the Athenians financially "even if he has to sell his own bed."[2] Alcibiades declined to go at once to Athens, as he had set a defeat of the Spartan fleet in the Aegean as his first goal. The Spartans now mutinied, in rage at lack of payment and when Astyochus tried to rally them with appeals to ancient Spartan courage in war to a large number of idle sailors refusing to go to sea, he only escaped being stoned to death by his men by taking refuge in an altar.

The Spartans then incited the populations of Miletus and several other places to expel and rough up the Persian garrisons there. Tissaphernes, who seemed, despite Alcibiades' influence, to be self-taught in political chicanery in the same school as the Macedonian scoundrel-king Perdiccas, declined to order reprisals against Sparta, though he went personally to Sparta to defend his conduct against the charges of the ubiquitous Hermocrates. After that, he summoned the Phoenician fleet of a formidable one-hundred and forty-seven vessels to Aspendus in Asia Minor and went there but did not move from there. He hoped the Athenian-Spartan conflict might so enervate Greece that he could take over all the Hellenes, as Xerxes had aspired to do.

When Alcibiades retuned, in his capacity as General of Athens (given him with questionable legality by Thrasybulus, he found emissaries from the Council of Four-Hundred. The angry democratic Athenian sailors wanted to lynch them and return at once to their families in Athens, but Alcibiades wisely calmed them down by saying that Athens was in no danger but that if the fleet returned now, all of the Aegean would be lost to Sparta. This was sound advice and was heeded. He told the Four-Hundred's representatives, that they had to go peacefully and the former council of five-hundred restored, and these emissaries should return and urge their moderate colleagues to conciliate the Athenian democrats and he would try to stabi-

---

2 Ibid., p. 334.

lize matters in the Aegean. He went first to see Tissaphernes and solemnly assured him that Athens was not about to fold. Tissaphernes took his word for it and sent the Phoenician navy back to the Levant.

The Council of Four-Hundred imagined that they could arrange peace with Sparta on the basis of the solidarity of anti-democratic and aristocratic government. (The Spartans were not sufficiently commercially minded to be impressed by an oligarchy.) But Sparta was so encouraged by Athenian divisions and squabbles, they demanded complete surrender of the Empire and Athens retaining only municipal autonomy. This was out of the question, but as their position eroded, the most unscrupulous of the leaders of the revolt and the installation of the Four-Hundred, sent what was supposed to be a final embassy to Sparta, led by the gangster Antiphon and the unreliable Phrynichus. They were really trying to deliver Athens to Sparta while assuring their own position. The usurpation supposedly by aristocrats had taken only a few months to degenerate into treason by thugs, while the egregious Alcibiades emerged as the Athenian redeemer. There was a symmetry to this, as he had pushed Athens into the Syracusan disaster in the first place.

Sparta had assembled a large fleet at Las in southern Laconia, to go to the assistance of the long-prepared revolt against Athens in Euboea. This was a second Attica, in terms of agriculture and manpower for Athens, and such an achievement by Sparta would be another very heavy blow to Athens. The oligarchs at the head of the Council of Four-Hundred had swiftly made arrangement with like-minded elements in Euboea, but as was predictable, and as with other governments in Greece, autonomy and the desire to be on the winning side weighed more heavily than the system of government. The Euboeans began building a fort immediately to the west of Piraeus, supposedly to resist the Samian rebels, but in fact to assist the Spartans in starving Athens into submission. Theramenes rose to the extreme peril of the occasion and connected this sinister activity to the so-called peace mission of Antiphon and Phrynichus to Sparta.

The weakness of the Council of Four-Hundred was exposed when opponents assassinated Phrynichus in the market place, and after the Spartan fleet arrived at Epidaurus and began the conquest of Aegina, Theramenes and Aristocrates denounced the treason that was afoot, raised a revolt of the soldiers and the population of Piraeus, proclaimed the government of the five-thousand and not just the Four-Hundred, and demolished the beginnings of the nearby fort west of Piraeus, threatening access to that port. Theramenes and Aristocrates led their large Piraean following on Athens. The regime gave way and agreed that the five-thousand should be publicly identified and not just as they had been, a government by a secret society, and that it should reform the manner of selection of the Four-Hundred, as, effectively, an upper house. The oligarchs folded, a little like the failed coup against Soviet President Mikhail Gorbachev in 1990, and the forces of Theramenes and Aristocrates marched on Athens somewhat as Mussolini did on Rome in 1922. A date was agreed of the many Athenian factions to meet in full public view in the theatre of Dionysus to concert on what amounted to a new constitution to heal the rifts in the political life of Athens.

The main Spartan fleet came to Megara to be ready to intervene directly in

Athens, and then, on the day of the great public meeting in Athens, it sailed at a stately pace to Salamis, site of the greatest of all Athenian triumphs. On this news, thousands of Athenian men marched to Piraeus to man the ships and forts of the town and prepare to defend Athens. The Spartan fleet sailed to Oropus to support the pro-Spartan party in Euboea. The Athenians in their righteous zeal dispatched a fleet of undermanned ships, with untrained crews, and in insufficient strength to contest Euboea with Sparta and its local allies who had prepared their stroke months before and rose in revolt.

The brave but unready Athenians were decisively defeated, an unprecedented fate for an Athenian naval squadron, though explicable in these circumstances. If the Spartans had then attacked Piraeus, the fleets holding the empire largely in place would have had to return to protect Athens and the Athenian Empire, still being energetically defended, against the restless natives and the Spartans with intermittent Persian assistance, would have been forfeited. The Spartans missed the chance, and then, having swanned around the Aegran quite successfully, they blundered into a fierce storm and lost most of the fleet to angry nature. Euboea, however, revolted successfully, amputating a primary Athenian source of grain, men, and money.

The upshot of the Athenian governmental meetings was, Thucydides and Aristotle agreed, the finest government Athens had ever had: amendments to the laws of Solon were voted systematically and after due deliberation. All freeborn men were citizens, but only those capable of bearing arms were "active" citizens, and there proved to be nine-thousand. All, on achieving the age of thirty, were unpaid councilors. The nine-thousand were too unwieldy a group to meet as one, so they were divided into four and each met once a week with fines for non-attendance, and each of the four had plenary powers for a year and the sequence of councils was chosen by lot. Half the magistrates were chosen by election and half by lot, and committees among them administered the great religious festivals, and became Hellenic treasurers. It was an improved system, produced better coordination between government departments, better public participation from a more qualified electorate, and reduced the vulnerability of the system to the often irresponsible activity of demagogues. The democracy was extended by the fact that each councilor in office could invite in another to assist in an important proceeding, broadening and strengthening the government. The General could only hold office for one year and then would have to step down for three years. Themistocles and Pericles would not have been able to render the service they did.

It was a good governmental system, as was Napoleon's when he returned from Elba, and built a democracy and announced that the restored Empire was a republic, and like Napoleon's last government, it would not be durable. Antiphon, though treacherous, is generally reckoned extremely cunning, sincere in his distaste for democracy, and the first of the great Greek orators. He was arrested and Thucydides regards his speech in his own defence the greatest ever given by a person in such a position. His talents were feared more than admired and he was so intelligent and persuasive, public opinion regarded him with ingrained hostility. His eloquence was complimented by those who judged him, but he was convicted of treason and executed, in 411.

The focal point of the struggle between Sparta and Athens now shifted to the Hellespont, where the Spartans sought to cut off the grain supply of Athens in the Black Sea countries. The Spartan admiral for 411-410, Mindarus, now that Sparta had finally realized the game of Tissaphernes, relied on his own means, and Mindarus abandoned the Ionian islands and states, and by luck and boldness, slipped past the Athenian navy, which concentrated at Elaeus under the now well-tried Thrasyllus and Thrasybulus. Some of the Athenian states on the Black Sea littoral had already risen in revolt and any concept of Athenian security required the reopening and securing of the trade routes from the Black Sea to Piraeus. An initial fleet engagement between the two navies in the Dardanelles, resulted in a clear Athenian victory in September 411 B.C. The Spartans, being so close to land, managed to escape without a gross disparity in losses but there was no doubt of the result, and it was a very invigorating outcome for the still hard-pressed Athenians.

The Athenians reopened the access to the Black Sea and suppressed one of the revolts but were recalled by the Spartan fleet's raid on the Athenian base at Elaeus. Another main fleet engagement took place in November 411, at Abydos, and this time a very close fight was turned into a decisive Athenian victory by the timely arrival of Alcibiades. Much of the Spartan navy tried to save itself by running aground. They saved the crews, but the Athenians towed thirty of their ships. Alcibiades tried to bring Tissaphernes into the Athenian fold, but the negotiations ended their close relationship and Tissphernes forcibly detained Alcibiades at Sardes for thirty days when, ever resourceful, he managed to escape. The Athenian navy dispersed to various locations for the winter.

Theramenes sailed from place to place trying to overthrow disaffected regimes and intimidate others, but was summoned by a message from Thrasybulus to the Hellespont. Alcibiades was gathering the whole Athenian navy for a showdown with Sparta. Alcibiades had eighty-six ships to sixty for the Spartan admiral, Mindarus, but he kept part of them back and approached under cover of a rainstorm as the Spartan fleet engaged in maneuvering exercises to practice for combat, which fell upon them very suddenly. This was the Battle of Cyzicus. Alcibiades' hidden squadron cut off retreat and virtually the entire Spartan fleet was sunk or run up on shore and burned or towed away by the Athenians. Alcibiades landed some of his men on shore to pursue the Spartan sailors and Mindarus died conducting a rear-guard land action.[3] The Syracusan squadron was burned by its crew, and though Hermacrotes survived, he was sent into honourable retirement. It was very late, but a sweet victory for Athens and an astounding turn of events in the spectacular career of Alcibiades.

In the aftermath of this great victory, the entire class of which the citizen crews of the Athenian navy were members was enfranchised, and the Council was reduced to five-hundred. Theramenes, as he was now in opposition politically, remained abroad for a time and the head of the government became Cleophon, a manufacturer of lyres, and specialist in public finance. Cleophon sympathized with his opponents and governed with exquisite integrity and moderation, providing a dole for

---

3 This was the only time in recorded history when a fleet commander in a major engagement started out on his bridge and ended by dying while considering a retreat on land pursued by his erstwhile naval adversary.

the poor of all classes and resuming public works as workfare projects for the unemployed, especially in completing the Erechtheum, a splendid temple on the north side of the Acropolis. Cleophon shaped up Athens' finances quickly enough that he and Alcibiades elected to continue the war, although a tolerable peace could have been had. The report sent to Sparta of Cyzicus was "The ships are lost. Mindarus is dead. The men starve. We don't know what to do." Having received this news, Sparta sent its leading Philo-Athenian, Endius, another friend of Alcibiades, to Athens to offer a peace that would leave everything as it was. This would accept Athens' loss of Euboea, Andros, Rhodes, Chios, Thasos, Byzantium, a number of other places and almost the entire coast of Asia Minor. The wise course would have been to take the offer and consider it as a ten-year armistice which could be used to rebuild and to conduct energetic diplomacy, as the Spartans had demonstrated that what was on offer was not subordinacy or liberty, but subordinacy to Athens or to Sparta. The Athenians were haughty and often guilty of hypocrisy and arbitrariness, but they were a gentle and humane yoke compared to the humorless and severe men of Sparta. Peace would have allowed Athenian diplomats time to disassemble the opportunistic alliance between the eastern and western Greeks and the Persians, but Athens felt the power of their renascence. The war continued.

Alcibiades spent the summer of 410 taking back some of the lost or defected Black Sea and Bosporus towns but did not have enough soldiers to invest Byzantium or Chalcedon, so he built a fort beside Chalcedon, and left Theramenes there with a strong squadron to assure that Athens controlled the waterway to the Black Sea. In 410, the Spartan king Agis had marched from Decelea to the walls of Athens and then quickly retreated when Thrasyllus brought out the Athenian army to do battle. This emboldened the Athenian leaders to set about regaining lost ground. In the spring of 409, Thrasyllus was sent to Ionia with fifty ships and one-thousand hoplites. He landed near Ephesus, defeated the Milesians, plundered Lydia and took other towns around Ephesus, but failed to take Ephesus itself, because of the intervention of Tissaphernes, now so distrusted by those he had betrayed that he could no longer pay surrogates and had to do his own fighting.

Alcibiades fixed the winning of the Bosporus as his goal for the 408 campaign. He started with Chalcedon. The crafty satrap of Hellespontine Phrygia, Pharnabazus, undertook to send ambassadors to Susa to try to negotiate peace with the Great King, an opportunity the Athenians eagerly embraced. If they could detach Persia completely from Sparta, they might recover their threadbare empire quite quickly. Alcibiades' siege of Byzantium was not at first successful, but because the governor, Clearchus, reserved almost all the rations for the garrison, the famished and angry townspeople took advantage of the absence of Clearchus (who was beseeching the assistance of Pharnabazus), to introduce the Athenians into the city. This was another great win for Alcibiades and the Athenian food supply was again entirely safe. Alcibiades returned a hero to Athens, with a hundred talents of tribute, and he was absolved of past conduct and installed as war chief for the following year. Thrasybulus regained Thasos, and opposing navies were not to be found in the Ionian and Aegean, and Sparta again offered peace. Sparta had not been completely idle and unsuccessful. Corcyra reestablished the oligarchs and declared its neutrality, and

Sparta finally recovered Pylos, and the Megarians retook Nisaea.

For Athens, disaster now, very unpredictably, struck again. Tissaphernes was discredited in Susa for the failure of his policy to assist Sparta, and Darius determined that he would put the full weight of his Empire behind Sparta, as the only one of the two Greek combatants which could only keep a fleet at sea with full Persian assistance. He wrenched the matter out of the hands of satraps, Tissaphernes and Pharnabazus. in particular (approximately equal in their limitless rascality), and gave it to his son, Cyrus, who became governor general of Asia Minor. Cyrus met the envoys Pharnabazus sent, at Gordium, a city to be made immortal in the coming century by Alexander the Great. Darius gave Cyrus five-hundred talents to use to rebuild the Spartan fleet. The Athenian ambassadors were detained. A heavy fate awaited plucky, brave, and cerebral Athens, as proud Sparta defiled the honour of all the Hellenes by making itself the Medist pawn of the ancient foe Persia, against whom Sparta had first gained immortal glory at Marathon. It would be a shabby end to one of Western history's distinguished chapters.

The assault on Athenian democracy had severely weakened Athens. The soldiers who had remained in Athens under the Four-Hundred had the right to speak in debates in the Assembly or to be members of the Council. Those who had been deprived of full citizenship in the shrinkage to five-thousand exacted their revenge on those who had demoted them. The hunt for the mutilators of the likenesses of Hermes was a very disruptive and extra-legal affair, with the political clubs and vigilantes, lawlessness and unfounded rumour exalting and punishing scores of people, most of them completely innocent. Any service to an undemocratic movement within Athens was henceforth a capital offense, and anyone reasonably apprehended as having anti-democratic intentions could be slain with impunity.

The popular courts were now the only courts of authority in such matters and the fabric of Athenian political society had been so profoundly riven that even the most unoffending and loyal aristocrats were suspected of being traitors. Something slightly foreshadowing the Reign of Terror in France in 1793-1794 occurred, though the leaders of those clamouring for retribution were not of the quality of Danton and Robespierre, and were rather "acrid politicians and sycophants, headed by Epigenes, Demophantus, and Cleigenes."[4] Extraordinary penalties were devised, such as banishing accused people from certain places or disqualifying them from some activities. So many people were being assessed fines and so much money was being transferred in bribes, ordinary property values fell, and there was a heavy cloud of fear and denunciation over all Athens.

The supreme test of Athens, against unfavourable odds, began in 407. Alcibiades had emerged as the most talented Athenian leader, and in the supreme struggle that loomed, the less salubrious aspects of his tortuous past were overlooked. Unfortunately for Athens, Sparta put up at this time one of its greatest leaders, Lysander. Tissaphernes warned Cyrus of the dangers of making the greatest Greek land power the greatest Greek sea power also, but Cyrus had been installed by his father, the Great King Darius, to smash Athens. The Persians had failed to defeat the Greeks as a whole people, so they would start over and defeat the strongest with

---

4 Ibid., p. 351.

the aid of the second strongest and work down. Alcibiades had one-hundred ships and an amphibious army of fifteen-hundred hoplites and one-hundred and fifty cavalry. Lysander was not only a capable general but an astute courtier and diplomat and was exactly the person to impress the Persian prince as someone upon whom he could place his bets. Cyrus gave Lysander the money to pay arrears of wages to his sailors and raise his fleet to ninety ships. With this threat on his flank, Alcibiades had to abandon the attempted suppression of the revolt at Andros, He spent the winter at Samos, and was suffering from desertions and inertia, while Lysander was still building his forces with Persian money.

Alcibiades struck out on land to assist Thrasybulus in subduing Phocaea, but he left his fleet in the hands of Antiochus who disobeyed Alcibiades' orders and committed his fleet in successive units in combat with Lysander's fleet and suffered the loss of fifteen vessels. Alcibiades hastened back and shaped the Athenian fleet up and offered battle to Lysander, who withdrew. He was facing the problems Napoleon would face after 1813: he could win but he did not have sufficient forces or enough talented and loyal subordinates to fight on a number of fronts at once and was always rushing to where the greatest crisis arose, dictated to by improvident events. This was enough to undercut Alcibiades in Athens, where, for notorious reasons, he was not widely trusted. He was not reelected one of the ten generals in 406, feared for his life if he returned to Athens or remained without official authority with the fleet. He had bought a couple of castles in Thrace some years before for just such an occasion as this, and repaired to his estates on a commandeered trireme, and settled in to nibbling a little territory away from the Thracians., while the life and death struggle of Athens, Sparta, and Persia unfolded. He was Athens' most swashbuckling and astute leader of his times, but his unscrupulous methods and inconstant personality left him with no one to lead and no state to serve.

As Alcibiades departed centre-stage, so, for a time, did Lysander as, in the absurd Greek manner, his term as state admiral (nauarch) ended. He gave back to Cyrus the unspent balance of funds he had received, to ensure that his successor, the young but traditional Spartan, Callicratidas, had to go cap-in-hand to Cyrus, which he did. The experience of waiting so long in Cyrus' ante-room was enough to convince him that intra-Hellenic conflict was ultimately suicide for all and that no outsiders, and certainly not the Persians, should be relied upon to intercede in Greek affairs. He saw Cyrus as a leopard in the Hellenic tent, filled with alternately warring and slumbering Greeks, mindless of their impending fate. He was a plain and young man, but of good judgment. He departed Sardes without having gained an audience. Callicratidas collected more ships from Rhodes and Chios and concentrated his forces at Miletus. From there, having built his fleet to a formidable one-hundred and seventy ships, he stormed and captured Lesbos.

Alcibiades was replaced by Conon, who found the Athenian fleet so diminished and demoralized, he decommissioned about thirty vessels, so the remaining seventy were fully manned and equipped and reasonably purposeful, though seriously outmanned by their enemy, though this was a condition Athens had known before. The Spartan king, Agis had invaded Attica again and even attempted unsuccessfully to storm Athens by night, but was repulsed. In these circumstances, Athens was in no position to assist Conon, who began plundering towns in Asia Minor to pay his men and bring his fleet back to full strength. The Spartan fleet caught up with him and chased him into Mitylene, losing thirty of his seventy triremes and many of the others grounded, though recoverable. He beat off heavy enemy assaults, and on the news of Spartan success, Cyrus rushed to the aid of Callicratidas' victory with unsolicited grants of money, having declined even to meet him when he had come to ask the prince's assistance.

Athens was in an objectively desperate condition, but the people did not falter. Besieged, its fleet immobilized if not destroyed, maximum taxation was imposed, silver and gold from the temples and greatest statues were melted into coins; copper coins were used as substitute currency to be redeemed later. All able-bodied men, nobles, citizens, sub-citizens, slaves, were hurled into ships and one-hundred and ten ships were manned and put to sea within thirty days and sailed to the rescue of Conon at Mitylene, and were joined en route by forty ships of still loyal allies. The great battle that ensued in the Arginusae Islands in August 406, was a fierce and at first, closely matched struggle, the greatest there had ever been between Greeks. Eight of Athens' generals were present, each commanding fifteen ships. The Spartans were outnumbered, as Callicratidas left his slower ships behind, and he attacked in a single file, aiming to have his column turn swiftly and attack or ram Athenian ships from the side. The Athenians had adopted a hedgehog formation of staggered rows of ships and resisted successfully. The battle turned when the Spartan commander fell off his ship when it rammed an enemy vessel, and he drowned. Some confusion resulted and the Athenians, risking everything on the battle and with the fervor of a popular force fighting for their personal and national lives; the Spartan fleet lost sixty-nine ships, twelve of which were captured by the Athenians, but the casualties were very serious on the Athenian side also, almost fifty ships, but Sparta's were much greater, Conon was liberated and replaced the lost ships with the remains of his own fleet, and five times as many Greeks died, mainly Spartans, than Sparta had citizens. Athens had survived a hair-raising climax again.

In the astonishing Greek manner, the eight victors in this battle were charged with failure to rescue the Athenians who had been plunged into the sea when their ships were sunk, or to have pursued and completely destroyed the enemy. In the anti-aristocratic mood of Athens, and given that the crews included a great many common people and slaves (all of whom were emancipated), the public mood was vengeful rather than grateful. The initial hearings in the Council went well for the eight generals, where their excuse for failure to rescue their comrades was blamed on heavy weather that came up; the real problem was the absence of a united command that would have detailed some ships to pick up survivors of both fleets and the rest to give chase (although that probably would not have succeeded because of the greater speed of the Spartan ships). After holding their own at this session, the generals' fate was then adjourned until after the Festival of Kinsmen, where the widows and families of the dead dressed in black and shaved their heads. Theramenes, who had some concerns with being singled out by the mobs for some of his previous activities, invited the mourning families to the resumed trials before the Council. An emotional orgy occurred and it was demanded that there be an immediate vote of the people—acquittal or immediate execution. Another demagogue of the now familiar type, Callixenus, whipped up the mob, carried the Assembly against the traditions of appeal, reflection, mitigating circumstances, and the right to individual trials, put through a motion providing for direct popular decision of the life or death of the accused, with only Socrates, who would have his own experiences of Athenian justice soon enough, dissenting. Those responsible for one of Athens' greatest victories in the most dire and fateful conditions, for saving Athens from destruction, were, albeit by a narrow vote, summarily executed, including Thrasyllus as an accomplice, he who had done as much as anyone to restore democracy in Athens and save Athens from its external enemies, and the eight victorious generals (admirals on the day), including Pericles, son of the great ruler.

Athens had lost confidence in its leaders, but not in itself. Sparta had sent Callicratidas to humble Athens so Sparta could be liberated of Persia. Now the Spartans had again realized that they could only continue the fratricidal struggle with Athens as paid surrogates of Persia for the ultimate triumph of Persia over all the Greeks, an end Sparta had done its full share to avoid. The current condition of the Greeks was in shambles: the Athenian navy was supreme, but to pay itself, was plundering the islands and Asia Minor, including many of its former allies, and occasionally its beleaguered persevering allies. The defeated Spartan navy, without Persian subsidies, was immobilized at Chios and the crews of the Spartan ships were toiling like share-croppers in the fields of the Chian estate-owners to feed themselves. With great difficulty were the Spartans dissuaded by their commanders from massacring the impudent Chians. With the great struggle between Athens and Sparta drawn, and the Athenians having again shown their surpassing bravery, cool heads in both cities saw they were just blooding each other and enervating all Greece for the delectation of the traditional Persian enemy. Sparta offered a peace in which it would evacuate Decelea and apart from that both states would retain what they had.

The Athenians confirmed the accuracy of the saying of Euripides that those whom the Gods would destroy, they would first make mad. Cleophon was the principal Greek leader, one of history's everyman leaders, apparently even an exemplar of the Orwellian ideal of a government of decent men, a Gerald Ford (without a Kissinger and Rockefeller to help him), or a more assertive John Major. But in his ordinariness he was a viral carrier of the fatal madness that now gripped Athens, victorious in arms but in the death-throes of strategic insanity. Cleophon mounted the podium wearing his battle armour at the Assembly after the Spartan peace proposal was presented, and said Sparta must release all the cities its Persian-financed fleet had pried loose from Athens. A moron could see that this would revive the Spartan-Persian alliance, which Athens could not hope to defeat again, given the correlation of forces, but great Athens, the beloved of historians and romanticists, was possessed by a suicidal urge. Sparta, having regained Persia's favour, returned more in sadness than in anger, to the Great King's prince, as the only way to end the Greek death agonies. Cyrus asked for the reappointment of Lysander, whom Sparta was happy to elevate. Sparta had the man for the time and Athens did not. Sparta being the unworldly, unsubtle, altogether Spartan place that it was, harboured many who suspected the ambition and the chicanery of Lysander, but after the rebuff from Cleophon, at least in Sparta, sanity prevailed. The only way to end the desperate and now almost terminal struggle of the Hellenes was to accept Persian aid to crush Athens and then to try to rebuild Greece.

Lysander went to Ephesus, and as Darius was dying and Cyrus was at his deathbed, and on his assumption of the greatest office in the known Western world, the new Great King gave Lysander access to the entire flow of revenues from Asia Minor. Lysander doubled the number of his triremes with Cyrus' largesse, and filled his ships with happy well-paid oarsmen, including many deserters from the Athenian ships. Lysander gained control of Miletus through treachery with the local patriciate and assisting in the massacre of the leaders of the popular party. Lysander assessed the strategic correlation of forces accurately and determined to avoid the big battle, where the almost super-human elan of the Athenians and their long mastery as seafarers made them almost insuperable at times and use his greater resources to harass and enervate the edges of the shrinking Athenian perimeter, requiring them to engage in a great deal of unproductive scrambling between contested areas. Again, the campaign on the Rhine in 1814, and the Athenians had no one like Napoleon to win all the battles and make a good fight of it week after week. Lysander concerted his broad design with Cyrus, to spare him impatience, and then, after a couple of feints, made for the Hellespont and seized Lampsacus. From this critical point, he proposed to interdict the grain ships that conveyed much of Athens' food supply (and almost all of it when the Spartans were encamped in Attica) from the Black Sea to Athens.

Athens compounded its problems by sidelining its best leaders, Theramenes and Thrasybulus, whose ambition was suspected (this from the former, admittedly grudging, followers of Alcibiades, whom they should have recalled). Of their generals, only Conon and Menander were qualified for such an office, and neither was the equal of Lysander. The Spartans now had the mass, the money, and the leader, every advantage in such freighted times. Even the comedian, Aristophanes (in his poem "Frogs") urged Athens to set aside its snobbery and raise the banner for all who would fight on its side, and to forgive the scoundrels and get the most talented leaders. Athens severed the right hands of captured enemy sailors and even Philocles (one of the over-promoted generals) executed the entire crews of two enemy triremes that were captured. In the summer of 405 B.C., Athens had enrolled more than thirty-thousand non-citizens in their forces.

When they realized that Lysander was at Lampsacus athwart Athens' food supply route, the Athenians sailed, practically all their large fleet, to deal with him. Lysander stayed in port, and the Athenians sailed back and forth offshore. Alcibiades, who lived nearby came down to warn them not to confuse Lysander's tactics with fear, that he was plotting a surprise, and that they should withdraw to Sestos where they would be safe in a harbor and had supplies. He was insultingly dismissed. Unknown to the Athenians, Lysander had the Athenian fleet imperceptibly followed and saw where it went to forage and feed itself, and on the fifth day, Lysander slipped out of port, surprised the Athenian fleet that at day-break was almost entirely ashore except for Conan and one squadron, and destroyed almost the entire Athenian fleet. He sank or captured one-hundred and sixty triremes, and as retribution, executed all of the three-thousand Athenian sailors whom his shore parties rounded up. It was an irretrievable disaster. Athens now had no navy, no food supply, no money, terribly depleted forces, and the only military and political leaders of any stature that were left were mistrusted by the people and not allowed to occupy positions of influence. Athens had systematically done everything it could to ensure its abject humiliation and overwhelming defeat. It only remained to receive the bone-crushing humiliation that awaited it, with almost the whole world applauding—it had come to this.

Conon went to Cyprus but sent back the news of the disaster in a dispatch boat, the Paralus. It arrived in Piraeus after nightfall, and a moan went up that spread by word of mouth along the walled road to Athens. No one slept that night; all knew what was coming. But the Athenians did not flinch. Lysander wisely began by telling all Athenians not in Athens, they could return to Athens or share the fate of the Athenians he had recently captured. Nostalgia for the homeland predictably caused a mighty influx of Athenian expatriates, whom Athens had to admit but could not feed. King Agis moved forward from Decelea and closely invested the city by land, while Lysander herded the shiploads of fugitives ahead of him and blockaded Piraeus with a fleet of one-hundred and fifty vessels. Athens gave citizenship to all who had lost it, all who had served Athens, the whole population of the still loyal island of Samos, and the whole city prepared for attempted starvation and a fight to the death. It was assumed that if Athens fell, and whenever it fell, the adult males would be summarily executed, and the women and children sold into slavery. For all her enlightenment, this had been the Athenian practice; it could not doubt the fate that awaited it.

Athens tried to open negotiations, but Sparta required the dismantling of the walls between Athens and Piraeus. A councilor, Archestratus, was imprisoned for suggesting acceptance and Cleophon demanded the death penalty for anyone who advocated surrender. The resourceful Theramenes got himself set at the head of a mission to explore further possibilities with Sparta. In fact, he pretended to be detained by the Spartans, but was just waiting for famine to induce greater flexibility in the Athenian civic mind and then to negotiate for the creation of a new government in Athens, in modern terms, his was an almost Petainist mission, though one justified by war conditions, unlike Petain's. In fact, in several ways, the desperate factional maneuverings in the Athenian political community resembled slightly analogous scrambling in the more tense moments of the Third and Fourth French Republics. The attempted Union Sacree (the just phrase of French national unity in World War I) cracked apart after three months of diminishing rations and increasingly frequent death by malnutrition and violence provoked by the desperation of implacable hunger. All factions understood that Athens was about to be subjugated by Sparta, the principal point of disagreement was what form of government the survivors in Athens would have. It was assumed, accurately, that Sparta and Lysander in particular, were not in favour of Athenian democracy, and to cater to this wish the political clubs quickly came back to furtive life and activity and claimed to have elevated five ephors (a Spartan title) beneath whom were knights, who were military officers favourable to anti-democratic political intrigue. (The comparison with the last days of the French Third Republic, and even with Weimar Germany, remains valid. Some of the actions and circumstances of Petain, Weygand, Hindenburg, and Ludendorf were prefigured here, and the reference will be taken up when this narrative gets to those men in the last volume.)

The anti-democratic party prevailed as the condition of Athens became more desperate and Cleophon, who had sabotaged the last opportunity of peace with honour, accused the anti-democrats of being a rag-tag of traitors and cowards, very bravely (and not altogether unjustly) and was arrested, given a drumhead trial and summarily executed. Reckless and brave in life, he died bravely; his honour intact, though his judgment was inadequate to the high positions he occupied. Theramenes was the only substantial Athenian who saw things clearly and made a serious effort to salvage something from what would soon become the complete extinction of Athens if some cord could not be pulled with the proverbially unremitting Spartans. He was given a formal assignment to make peace, which meant, as everyone knew, the acceptance of whatever terms Sparta stipulated, short of instant mass suicide instead of waiting for starvation to achieve that end.

These terms had already grown harsher since Theramenes' original peace-feelers. Lysander demanded in the name of Sparta the complete dismantling of the fortifications and walls of and to Piraeus and the limitation of Athens to twelve triremes. This was actually somewhat generous, and when this was submitted to the Spartan allies, the Corinthians and Thebans in particular demanded that the city be razed, and the population scattered as slaves. Sparta would not hear of such a fate for a people and state that had done so much to save Greece from the Persians (Sparta's ally and paymaster at the moment), to be destroyed. Not to over-stress these comparisons, but it was slightly like Hitler ordering that the statue of Foch at the place of the Armistice of 1918 not be damaged, even as his railway car where the armistice was signed was removed to Germany, and his sending the coffin of Napoleon's son from Vienna to be buried with his father at the Invalides in Paris. (These were Hitler's only kindnesses to France.)

Lysander also required that Athens become an ally of Sparta and commit to contribute forces to Spartan causes when required. Theramenes in particular saw that the only way for Athens to have a future was to accommodate the existing facts and tuck in under the wing of the most magnanimous and much the strongest of the other Greek states. The fluidity of fortunes, as they did much later between France and Germany, would produce opportunities for the bettering of Athens' lot, from a more equal alliance to revanchisme. But for now, Athens was so desperate, Theramenes' terms were considered a deliverance from war, famine, and pestilence, and the demolition of walls began with celebratory musical accompaniment.

A new chapter opened in the life of Athens, in which the exiles, many of them reasonable people who had fallen out of favour but some the ethical dregs of Athenian public and commercial life, returned. The most noteworthy of these was the protégé of Alcibiades, Critias, an energetic and talented scoundrel of the kind that tend to turn up at the darkest hours of great peoples. He had been, like Alcibiades, a chum of Socrates and an alleged participant in the mutilation of the Hermae, and was a talented writer of prose and poetry, and a persuasive public speaker. His loyalty to Alcibiades was not requited and that unhappy episode seems to have soured whatever scruples he ever had. He had been exiled by Cleophon, and when he returned with the other Athenians escaping the promised vengeance of Lysander to ensure that all the starving Athenians were in one pustule, he became the most merciless enemy of the demos, quickly took over the direction of the political clubs, and emerged as the hard-line rival to the more moderate Theramenes, a democrat but one who recognized Sparta had to be accommodated.

Because of the difficulty of really stamping out democracy in Athens, especially to the satisfaction of the Spartans, Theramenes judged it wise to wait for the complete reduction of Athens' fortifications until he promulgated a new constitution. In this delay, a democratic counter-plot arose from the irrepressible recesses of Athenian democracy, and the Council approved the rounding up and impeachment of a group of allegedly seditious democrats. As in the inauguration of the Four-Hundred seven years before, the public meeting was held outside the walls of Athens and was overseen by a sizeable detachment from Lysander's garrison. A motion by one of Critias' followers was introduced to amend The Ancient Constitution. Theramenes intervened in support of this, and then Lysander himself intervened and said that as Athens had failed to meet the prescribed and agreed timetable for demolishing the walls to and of Piraeus, it could only avoid the consequences of this delinquency by changing governments. The Thirty were thus constituted, ten named by Theramenes, ten by the ephors put forward by Critias, and ten elected by the eligible electors present. Once in office, the Thirty took their time writing constitutional amendments but aggressively cleansed the city, in drastic terms, of the generally identified low-lives of political corruption, sycophancy, and treachery. As generally happens in such revolutionary movements, and as in Paris in 1793 and 1794 and in St. Petersburg in 1917 and 1918, the movement is always to the revolutionary extremes before Thermidorean reaction takes hold. The democratic leaders were publicly executed with minimal pretense to due process. Inadequate continuators though they were, they surrendered the greatest traditions of Athens to the headsmen's axes. The regime had three-hundred floggers to whip those guilty of non-capital offenses, but against the judgment of Theramenes, who remained a moderate as he had always been, the Thirty asked for seven-hundred Spartan enforcers, who bivouacked in the Acropolis and did as asked or as their Spartan commander, Callibius, pleased.

It was here that Critias made his move. Like Robespierre and Lenin (except France was victorious in 1794, and Russia was at least at peace with Germany in late 1917), it was the hour of the advocate of taking matters to their logical conclusion. Anyone who could conceivably be an alternate pole of authority, or a mere non-adherent of stature, was to be eliminated. Critias wished the Thirty to rule absolutely and be unanswerable to anyone (except Sparta). Theramenes, one of the leaders of the Revolution of 411, was for the ultimate authority of a larger group—it had been a down-sized political citizenry of five-thousand at that time. Critias proposed that the sovereign electorate be three-thousand, eliminating most of Theramenes' followers from his proposed slate, the others were disarmed with the active assistance of the Spartan garrison, and then a preposterous law, again presaging the French Committee of Public Safety, that entitled the Thirty to put to death anyone they regarded as a loyalty risk. The practice became to delegate the more moderate members to identify and take into custody the designated victims. Socrates ignored this. Nicias' son, Niceratus, was one of those identified, seized and executed. Within a few months, the total of those put to death in this way was over fifteen-hundred; it was the most pitiful and execrable end imaginable to Athenian democracy.

Theramenes, the last personification of the dignity and courage of the Athenian state, objected to all this, knowing the risk he was taking. Theramenes won the argument before the five-hundred, but Critias had him stricken from The Three Thousand and then on behalf of the Thirty, where he had a majority, pronounced the sentence of death on Theramenes. Because of his station, the sentence was to be by the consumption of hemlock. In the distinguished final curtain call of any vestige of Athenian democracy, Theramenes jauntily raised his cup to "the gentle Critias." Alcibiades and Thrasybulus were both also exiled, and Lysander required passage of an Athenian law that would impose heavy penalties on any state that harboured Athenian political fugitives. Alcibiades realized at once what his former protégé had in mind and hurled himself on the mercy of Pharnabazus, a man as cynical and opportunistic as Tissaphernes or even Perdiccas, and in any case a satrap of the Great King who was backing Lysander at the moment. And with slight apparent regret, Alcibiades was delivered over to the agents of Lysander and precipitated into eternity, unceremoniously slain. By this time, the Greek cities were becoming disgusted by the humiliation and self-humiliation of Athens. Argos was the first to admit Athenian political refugees, but even Thebes soon followed, and Thrasybulus, who had done the Athenian democracy much service, found safety there, the great survivor of Athenian politics in the end. Continuing our projections into Western European political and military matters twenty-three centuries later, Thrasybulus was to some extent a de Gaulle figure, as he shortly led a force of seventy men in December 404, into Attica from Boeotia and seized an unassailable (except by stealth), mountain fortress (Phyle on Mount Parnes).

Critias set the apparatus of his puppet state against this and started to build a wall around Mount Parnes to starve Thrasybulus out, as Athens itself had been starved into submission. But he was confounded by a heavy snowstorm and the whole ignoble effort to invest Thrasybulus had to be abandoned. This fine thrust of Thrasybulus summoned a wave of seven-hundred miscellaneous volunteers, to show what free men can do. The Thirty asked the aid of Sparta, as Thrasybulus' volunteers became numerous enough to require him to pillage the neighboring countryside. Thrasybulus, a felicitous combination of Themistocles, Robin Hood, and Ho Chi Minh, routed the Spartan garrison and cavalry. At this, Critias reached farther into his bag of tricks and attempted bribery of Thrasybulus, but he was not having it. Athenian heroism was inextinguishable (as Romans, Turks, and Nazis would discover). Critias and his henchmen, noting the fragility of their position, selected Eleusis as a place of retreat should they lose control in Athens, and uprooted the actual population, and bound themselves by a heinous criminal act, by massacring the entire population, which had given no offense whatever. Instead of uniting a solid phalanx of a complicit Athenian majority, it irreversibly alienated Athenian opinion and Critias was now a very precarious tyrant.

Critias was steadily revealing himself as lacking the stature and judgment of a serious leader, and only that of a dispensable tool of foreign enemies of Athens and domestic traitors, an intelligent and energetic man not anchored to anything solid or reliable, even an acute sense of self-preservation. Critias simultaneously had the Thirty expel to Piraeus all the unprivileged people not identified clearly with the regime in Athens who had not left already. After only four days, Thrasybulus led his men, now more than a thousand, into Piraeus and effectively took possession of it and marched toward Athens. Critias saw the menace and led a force of nearly ten thousand out of Athens at once to suppress this threat, which had been expanded from the ranks of those evicted from Athens. Critias, in his febrile concern at his evident vulnerability, charged uphill at Thrasybulus and his followers in the citadel of Munychia (where the exurban political assemblies had been held in 411 and 404), and were mown down by Thrasybulus' archers. Critias and several of his principal collaborators were killed in the action, dying more bravely than they had governed. The Thirty were finished and disintegrated after only eight months of odious incumbency.

The survivors among the Three Thousand allowed the defeated forces to withdraw to the depopulated Eleusis, and a Council of Ten was installed, including a couple of the former Thirty. There then began an absurd and demeaning tripartite, intermittent civil war; the Ten, knowing that Sparta would support their resistance to Thrasybulus, held their corner, while Thrasybulus held Piraeus and the remnants of the Thirty were in Eleusis. Sparta had no interest in intervention as any internecine Athenian conflict served their purposes. There was intermittent skirmishing, but Thrasybulus grew steadily in strength, as the serious and virtuous patriot of the three contending factions, and he steadily trained his forces into a real army. By mid-403, he was able to close in on Athens and invest the city, leaving the oligarchic remnants no alternative except to appeal to Sparta, which naturally responded. Because of the nature of envy and faction in Greek cities, and Sparta was not much less blameworthy than Athens in these matters, at this decisive point, Lysander, the foremost military commander Sparta had had, greater even than Brasidas, was undercut domestically and recalled. At the time of his recall, he was blockading Piraeus with forty triremes under his brother Libys, and was organizing an army from Eleusis, with one-hundred talents he had received from Sparta to stamp out that hardy perennial, Athenian democracy, yet again.

Lysander has benefited from Macaulay's glorification of him; competent though he was as an admiral and general, he was a wicked man who terrorized all populations that came under his control. Wherever he conquered, he established despotisms run by the most dubious and cruel elements, who would so alienate the people they ruled, the tyrants would be entirely dependent on Lysander. His chosen henchmen were "blind fanatics or mere adventurers, the scum that bubbles up in the cauldron of civil war."[5] His word was worthless, and he squandered the last best chance of achieving genuine Greek unity under Spartan leadership, with the possibility of the major component states free to develop their personalities while maintaining a coherent pan-Hellenic confederation that would have a chance of repulsing the Persians and Macedonians. Greece had had its last chance.

---

5 CAH, VI, p. 28.

In the changed political climate of Sparta, King Pausanias prepared to occupy Attica, but Corinth and Thebes, finally grasping that Sparta completely dominating Athens with the Persians supporting them could be extremely dangerous, refused to join Pausanias' mission. They wanted Boeotia to dominate Athens. Sparta's greatest and most victorious leader had been sidelined and its alliance was crumbling. Serious Athenian statesmen such as Theramenes and Thrasybulus could have taken advantage of this. Pausanias made informal contact with respectable elements in Athens and professed a policy of reconciliation.

The democratic forces in Piraeus refused to listen to Pausanias and he was forced to fight a serious action to bring them to a more reasonable stance. The Ten proposed a peace directly to Sparta rather than to their king who, with his army, was now before Athens, and in their proposed terms, they explicitly handed over the right of Sparta to determine the Athenian government. Events had now reached the astonishing stage where Sparta would not touch such a hot poker and left it to Pausanias to negotiate and enforce the terms he thought appropriate. Pausanias' terms astounded Athens by their generosity and did great honour to Sparta: amnesty and restitution of position and property for everyone (apart from the Thirty, Ten, Eleven, and the temporary regime in Piraeus, unless they gave a proper accounting for their actions); and any Athenian who wished to move to Eleusis was free to do so.

The men of Piraeus marched into Athens right after Pausanias had departed, and made sacrifices at the Acropolis. But they had to swear to the Lacaedemonians present that they foreswore revenge, no matter how dreadful the outrages they had suffered. Archinus became the leader of Athenian moderates, and blocked Thrasybulus' attempt to extend the franchise to everyone who fought with him. But Athens did revert to democracy and readopted the Periclean Law of 451 B.C. and other measures to safeguard democracy. After its overwhelming defeat by Sparta, Athens had chiefly inflicted damage on itself.

But this horrible and humiliating chapter of Athenian history had a rather happy ending. A number of amendments and laws were passed to eliminate anomalies, compensate the wronged and make Athens' institutions more efficient without becoming less democratic. There was some skirmishing with Eleusis, but in 401, the entire Thirty were ambushed by Athenian forces, and, in the manner of the time, bound hand and foot and bent over a row of chopping blocks and beheaded as quickly as the corpses could be thrown aside to make way for the next culprits. With this conflict ended, Athens was united; bygones were bygones, and no more general settling of scores occurred. All Athens voted thanks to the men who had restored democracy, and Sparta, contrary to all expectations, was allowing Athens to be Athens.

4. Hellenistic Cultural Influence and the Death of Socrates

We cannot depart Greece to review what had been happening elsewhere without a brief summary of Greek cultural influences. Unlike most important civilizations, Greece's cultural influence became stronger even as its political importance declined. The attempts of the Ionian philosophers to make the world intelligible spread throughout the Greek world and beyond, and the era from the middle of the Sixth Century to the beginning of the Fifth Century (550-400) B.C. was one in which Greek scholars in the humanities and sciences and mathematics were toiling uninterruptedly to install reason and rationalism in place of cant, obscurantism, superstition, and unrigorous supposition and folklore. It was sometimes erroneous and unjustifiably dogmatically advanced, as new discoveries, real and illusory, often are. But it was an unprecedented advance in the intellectual development of mankind, easily exceeding Greece's political contribution to the world, though here again, Athens' influence in its near-invention of a plausible concept of democracy is also almost beyond estimation. The genius of the ancient Greeks was not in commerce or international statesmanship, or theology; it was in the intellectual humanities and in science, and it gives Greece a unique and perpetually honoured place in human history.

Primitive but pioneering scientific research flourished, especially in Ionia, and for over a hundred years after about 530 B.C., what became known as Greece's Age of Illumination prevailed in intellectual circles and was generally devoted to the pursuit of reason, prefiguring somewhat the modern Age of Reason in the Eighteenth and Nineteenth Centuries, A.D. and accordingly much praised by classicists of the modern Age of Reason. The Pythagoreans discovered that the earth is round. The Sophists, in the early years of this period, were an informal association of learned men who rented themselves out as tutors and formed itinerant universities. The basis of their fraternity was the subjectivity of knowledge: that what appeared to one person to be beautiful or efficient or otiose could with equal legitimacy be seen otherwise by an equally perceptive person. This, philosophically, began the process of deconstruction of dogmatic conventional wisdom, and was perhaps, the beginning of relativism, which has fluctuated in fashion and intellectual respectability over the centuries and reached particular prominence in recent and current times.

The intellectual flourishing of Athens was undoubtedly encouraged by Pericles, who cultivated and conversed knowledgeably with intellectual leaders in many fields. The much-overdone Periclean ideal of the philosopher king, most notably espoused by Plato, has been a popular concept in enlightened and even just meliorist circles for many centuries. Pericles, as has been mentioned, was particularly friendly with the scientist Anaxagoras (a little as Winston Churchill was with Lord Cherwell), and Damonides, the musicologist, and both were widely believed to have advised Pericles in some policy matters. This notion of Pericles the comparative democrat and patron of intellectualism, advanced learning and lofty concepts, has prevailed over the objective facts that he was something of a Mikhail Gorbachev figure though also a part-time warmonger, in that he initiated the Peloponnesian War which ultimately reduced Athens to meek submission to Sparta and the end of proud Athens as light unto the world, though he had the good fortune to die before the suicidal Sicilian enterprise, which he might well have avoided, was launched.

The transformation of Athens to an officially progressive and intellectually curious society and one that rather vigorously promoted an ambitious Hellenizing influence throughout the Greek and adjacent world, provoked immense discontent and suspicion in traditionalist circles, with predictable political frictions. Athenian leaders of the old school, like Cimon, plain soldiers and civil office-holders were easily offended by the airs and worthiness of the arriviste Periclean eggheads. The ancient charge of impiety, a civic offense from olden times, was frequently dusted off and hurled at any of the new wave of academical leadership that put a foot wrong, or sometimes even if they had not. There have been many recurrences of this phenomenon in later centuries, such as libertarian concepts that preceded and accompanied and were carried across Europe by the French Revolution, and the teaching of scientific rather than scriptural doctrines of creation, evolution, and other key phenomena of human development.

The study of astronomy, which was a legitimate subject for the less developed Egyptians and had been for many centuries, was significantly advanced by Anaxagoras and others who undermined the concept of a solar deity. Anaxagoras was indicted for impiety and blasphemy and condemned to death, chiefly because of his well-known friendship with Pericles, and all Pericles could do was facilitate his escape to Lampsacus, where he lived happily ever after. Damonides was ostracized. Pericles' own companion, Aspasia, a sister-in-law of Alcibiades, lived with Pericles from 445 to 429, when Pericles died, and bore him a son, the younger Pericles, who eventually became an Athenian general. (See preceding section of this chapter.) She was accused of impiety but was acquitted. It is not known when or how her life ended.

Posterity has naturally emphasized the extraordinarily advanced aspects of Greek civilization, as well as the heroism of Greek defence against Persians and of Athenian combat with less enlightened states, both Greek and altogether foreign. A particular benefit to the cause of Greek historic prestige has been the tendency of the British, as they emerged as the world's most prestigious empire after the Napoleonic Wars, to consider the Athenians, sea-faring and democratic, to be precursors of themselves, and to champion the cause of the liberation of the Greeks from the Turks. All this has sentimentally magnified Greek and especially Athenian historical prestige, but that should not prevent us from rendering great homage to the startling precocity of aspects of Greek civilization. The Greek Age of Illumination reached its coruscation in the period approximately between 430 and 400 B.C., and its most eminent figures were Socrates, Euripides, Plato, Aristotle, Aeschylus, Sophocles and Thucydides. Thucydides was essentially an atheist and a misogynist, which did not impair his talents as a historian, though he was in that capacity frequently unrigorous. But he was a pioneer of critical history, not merely a chronicler. Euripides seems also to have been an atheist, or at least an agnostic, and was openly skeptical of oracles, and doubtful of the justifiability of slavery.

Socrates, as all the world knows, is one of history's most famous thinkers and cultural figures. He was always an eccentric, subject to spells or trances, where he would stand oblivious to what was going on about him, and hearing "monitions" from his inner self. He served in several military campaigns, including Potidaea in 432 B.C. and always acquitted himself very well: intelligent, unflappable, and utterly indefatigable, even in the severest conditions and foulest weather. He became something of a disciple of Zeno in his youth. Archelaus was his principal tutor and once well into his twenties, he became the convener of a group of sprightly minds, a little like the circles that in more recent times assembled around Montaigne, Goethe, Dr.

Johnson and Benjamin Franklin. Socrates and his circle were generally known, not necessarily respectfully, as "the Thinkers." Socrates was bemused when one of his disciples, Chaerephon, asked the Delphic oracle if anyone was wiser than Socrates and was assured that no one was. Socrates always disparaged his own talents and erudition, but he was somewhat friendly with Pericles. Apart from Plato, the most illustrious of his followers was Alcibiades, with whom Socrates shared a profound mistrust of democracy. Like some great statesmen of modern times who were also eminent scholars, such as Richelieu, builder of the modern French state (and to a considerable extent the Church also) and founder of the French Academy, and Bismarck, creator and unifier of modern Germany, considered democracy little better than parliamentary hooliganism, in which government, statecraft, was inevitably squandered to the squabbling and demagogy of democratic confusion and contumely.

Socrates had got through the entire Peloponnesian War unharmed in Athens, despite his well-known and frequently repeated skepticism about democracy. When the Thirty emerged (Section 3), the leaders of the regime assumed they could count on Socrates' support of the oligarchs, but they didn't recognize the importance Socrates attached to the rule of law, impartially imposed. The leader of the Thirty, Critias, and his colleague, Plato's uncle, Charmides, were shocked to discover his animosity. They required that Socrates cease to meet with the circle of impressionable and articulate followers and refrain from criticism of the government. They then sought to assert their authority by requiring Socrates to join an extradition party that was dispatched to Salamis to arrest a dissident, one Leon, and return him to Athens for summary execution, Socrates admirably ignored all this and went home. Fortunately for him, the Thirty were overthrown almost at once on unrelated matters, sparing Socrates likely execution.

Despite this deliverance, a consensus developed in the febrile political atmosphere of Athens as it reeled in defeat and self-doubt, riven by factions after its collapse as the leading Greek state, that Socrates was a danger who must be silenced. He never commented on political matters and was equivocal in his criticism of regimes, although he disliked democracy, he respected democrats who acted on a basis of legitimate legislation. But the democrats felt he had been ungrateful for his liberty and the anti-democrats felt he had betrayed them by his refusal to give them any public or even private encouragement. It was an overheated atmosphere, but Socrates was unflappable as ever, and felt no need to trim and hedge according to prevailing political winds (as Plato did), and was quite relaxed about whether he survived or not.

Anytus, a scrupulous democrat and one of the leading figures in beleaguered Athens after the unlamented disembarkation of the Thirty, determined to compel Socrates' silence, though, again, he never publicly commented on politics, and decided that the best way to do it was with the hackneyed charge of impiety, or irreligiosity. Socrates' skepticism about Athens' official religion was well-known, so Anytus put an obscure but fervently zealous upholder of traditional religion, a little-read poet named Meletus, up to laying the charge against Socrates, and Anytus would have himself nominated prosecutor. Only in its death-throes as a great state would

Athens have resorted to such a shabby assault on the person who is probably, after these twenty-four centuries the most widely and profoundly admired Greek of all history, and one of the giants of the whole history of human civilization.

In laying the charge, Meletus and Anytus commenced a sequence of improvident and outrageous events. The actual charge was two-fold: "Socrates is guilty of not worshipping the Gods whom the city worships, and of introducing religious novelties, and he is guilty of corrupting young men." It was the practice that the court would consist of a large number of jurors, in this case it is thought to have been five-hundred and one citizens, who would have to choose, in the event of conviction, between the sentence asked by the complainant and by the prosecutor, and that substituted by the defendant after conviction. Meletus asked for the death sentence. There is no reason to think Anytus had any interest in executing Socrates, only in silencing him, despite his discretion on public matters; the charge of misleading the bright young men of Athens, including Alcibiades in his time, weighed here, but exile would have been quite sufficient. The arbitrariness of the system and the perversity of the defendant came successively into play.

Plato's *Apology of Socrates* is widely seen as Plato's greatest work, though in fact it was likely Socrates' address to the court, with some editing and additional flourishes by Plato. However they combined, they were both at their most eloquent, lucid, and persuasive. Socrates appears to have been found guilty by a vote of 280 to 221. Socrates conducted his defense with his customary courtesy and fluency, but without a trace of deference to the dangers of his position. It was almost always a defense tactic to bring in the defendant's spouse and family and prey with varying degrees of histrionic theatricality, depending on the gravity of the proceedings and the sophistication of the defendant, on the human and familial decency of such a large jury. Socrates did nothing of the kind and instead assumed a nobler, more detached, and exaltedly philosophical tone in his defense in discussing the sentence.

> Meletus assesses the penalty at death. What fair counter-suggestion then shall I make, Athenians? What do I deserve to suffer or what fine to pay because over my life I have not kept quiet, but have neglected the ambitions that enlist the effort of most people—self-enrichment, management of my own affairs, public office and political associations? I considered myself above such things and instead of devoting my energies to these activities where I would have been no good to you or to myself, I set out to be a benefactor in the most important possible way: by trying to persuade each of you individually not to put any possessions ahead of yourselves—for each among you to be as good and as wise as possible, and to put Athens ahead of any individual part of Athens, and so to regard all matters. What then do I deserve for this? Something good, surely, Athenians, and suitable to me, a poor man because I have been a benefactor and require leisure. What is suitable for such a man is free public accommodation (at the Prytaneum), which I deserve far more than does one of you who has won a horse race or chariot race at the Olympia, because that may make you appear happy, but I cause you to be happy, and the winner of such a race does not need support and I do. So if I am asked what I deserve as the issue of these proceedings, it is free and adequate public accommodation at the Prytaneum.

There may have been some truth, in perfect and impartial justice, to what he said, but Socrates in all his fecund imagination could scarcely have alit upon a counter to a demand for his execution in a more obnoxiously obtuse manner: a partially, objectively justified assertion of immense contempt for the court, but a tactical disaster of Syracusan proportions. A man of his high intelligence must have reckoned that such a haughty address would provoke the maximum penalty. It was 399 and he had had a full life for the times, perhaps slightly over seventy years, and he rightly judged that this trial if it led to his execution would be an indelible and instructive episode through all of succeeding history. With this inauspicious opening, he went on to adumbrate alternatives:

> Perhaps banishment is what you think I deserve. But I would love life indeed, my fellow Athenians, if I thought that you, my fellow citizens, found my lectures and discourses so burdensome and irritating that you wished to rid yourselves of my presence, and that I would be better tolerated elsewhere. A fine life it would be, leaving my native city at my age and thereafter being continually driven out from one city to the next. I know that wherever I am, the intelligent young men will come to listen to me as they have done in Athens, and that if I repulse them, their influential fathers will expel me, and if I please and interest them, their fathers will expel me from envy and fear. Some of you will say: 'Socrates, when you leave Athens, why not be quiet and uncontroversial?' This is what is so difficult to make you understand. That would disobey *the God* [my italics as monotheism is implied and was heresy in Socratic Athens]. Though you will not believe me, I say that it is impossible to keep quiet; failure always to test one's own virtue and consistency reduces life to something ignoble and unworthy of being lived. But you do not believe me. If I was wealthy, I would offer all I have as a fine. Plato and Crito, however, will stand surety for me for a fine of thirty mina [difficult to translate into current currency but perhaps ten-thousand dollars]. They are solvent and so I propose this fine.

This was an astonishing performance and has, as Socrates undoubtedly calculated, reverberated across history. He appears to have determined that either the court would back down and reduce the sentence without his having made any particular plea to do so, or it could put him to death and inflict an intellectual and moral defeat on Athens itself more overwhelming and humiliating than the sequence of military blunders and failures that had brought proud Athens to the point of submission to an unholy coalition of compromised enemies. This sequence was crowned by the shameful and treasonous collusion of Sparta with Persia. Thus, would Athens' humiliation be completed by a self-inflicted mortal wound to its status as a free and ethical and intellectually ambitious society. Of course, this is conjecture, but unless Socrates had taken leave of his senses, of which there is no other evidence, he was inviting the elders of his native city to acknowledge his exaltation above the crude and portentous activities of Athens' legitimate governors or take unto themselves the tragic crime of cultural and civic patricide. He conceived himself as, intellectually and culturally, the personification of Athens, a less militant and pious and more cerebral Joan of Arc, or even an unelected Charles de Gaulle, or he would die for a timeless and insuperable cause—the liberty and integrity and ambition of creative thought, a martyr of a kind often replicated but rarely for such purely intellectual ideals. There have been many such religious victims, most conspicuously and consequentially, Jesus Christ, and modern figures who died deliberately for their beliefs, such as Thomas More, John Brown, and even the erratic Canadian native leader Louis Riel. It is conjecture to judge with any complacency what Socrates was thinking, but it could not have been a mere miscalculation. Self-important and presumptuous though he was, and armed with all the contempt, accumulated and confected, that the impecunious intelligentsia usually affects toward the wealthy, Socrates cannot have been unaware of the impression he would create among all his listeners and the city generally. He must have known that he was judging his judges and so little valued the life that the jurors could extinguish, that he considered it of no account in the balance of stature between himself and those who had his life in their hands.

Just as the trial opened, a garlanded ship had sailed to Delos to pay homage to Apollo at the annual feast in that God's honour, and Athenian law forbade the state to take a life while that mission was in progress. Socrates passed this month in the public prison in chains, but was well and courteously cared for by the warden and received visitors each day, with whom he coolly discussed the philosophic aspect of great and small matters with no sense of perturbation or fear. Crito and others cooked up a scheme for his escape, which could easily have been effected and would probably have been a relief to the authorities, but Socrates would not hear of it. He was above all a legalist and had been condemned within the legal system. If he were to consent to be spirited out now, after the pose he had struck at trial, it would undermine his claim to moral superiority over his accusers and judges. If he were now to agree to flee, he would have been better off to be lofty but not so haughty in addressing the court and to have recommended banishment in place of execution and would almost surely have won that decision. It must be said that the execution, by taking a draft of hemlock which induced gradual paralysis, was entirely painless and occurred in the presence of his friends and was described by Plato in *Phaedo*. This was a clear favor and recognition of Socrates' great stature, as the Athenians, whatever their claims to comparative civil elevation, disposed of common criminals with extreme cruelty, including crucifixion and death by various excruciating methods of torture.

As Socrates presumably foresaw, his friends, Plato in particular, assured that he would be remembered with respect as long as any Greek literature from the time survived. This experience radically altered Plato's life, as the conduct of both the democrats and the oligarchs completely disgusted him and he renounced the political life that had previously been his ambition. He wrote: "Such was the end of our friend, whom I may truly call the wisest, most just, and the best of all the men I have ever known." Plato led the movement to make Socrates immortal as the most insightful, eloquent philosopher of all time. And so, he remains still very widely regarded. Forty years later, in a letter to the friends of Dion of Syracuse, Plato wrote that Socrates' enemies had levelled against him "a most wicked charge and one which was least applicable to Socrates of all men in the world." Socrates was greatly admired by his followers, but was considered an eccentric sophist, and even an innocuous windbag by the population generally; they had no concept of his greatness. In this sense, Plato and the others were like the Disciples of Christ: they made of him, as Napoleon wrote of Christ, "One who passed His years in obscurity, and who died a malefactor's death,"[6] an unquestioned and universally admired figure for all times and nations. His death and the manner of it, as well as the proselytizations of his followers, catapulted Socrates to a higher level of intellectual prestige than he would otherwise have attained. In that sense, Socrates calculated accurately.

It is not clear how great a genius Socrates really was, though that he was a brilliant and magnetic and courageous man is not open to question. Without over-stressing the point, in associating with Pericles, and inspiring the notion that Pericles was a philosopher chief, Socrates and Plato glorified Athens (and Pericles) possibly somewhat beyond what was objectively justified. In opting for the end he did, and in having Plato as custodian and propagator of his legend (apart from the Apostles, the greatest executory publicist until William Shakespeare played that role for Elizabeth I), Socrates moved into the permanent footlights on the great stage of Western civilization's history, as did Plato, who made the undoubtedly wise career move of renouncing politics in favour of this role. (A less successful but noteworthy elevation of a national folk figure was Tolstoi's lionization of General Kutuzov in *War and Peace*.) Completely unforeseeable, even by Socrates and Plato, was that more than two millennia later, an important country whose existence was only whispered of in Socratic times, the British, would excavate the Greeks and recreate them as a forerunner of British national virtues: democracy, integrity, absence of aggression but with a civilizing mission in the world; a great seafaring nation with a vibrant culture, commercially astute and led by courageous and scholarly men. To some degree, many great British leaders, including Russell, Gladstone, Asquith, and Churchill, fulfilled and evoked these values. Disraeli was even more complicated, as he too evoked them with his espousal of "One Nation" at home, "Power and Liberty" in the world, "peace in our time" as policy, and he added the rich ingredient of his scholarly rabbinical background, which Carlyle nastily described as the talents of "a superlative Hebraic conjurer." This narrative, after many turns, will heave up at Victorian and Edwardian times two volumes hence.

The tragedy of Greece was that for all its advances in self-government and civility, and its intellectual attainments and martial bravery, it could never stop for long fighting within itself. No one succeeded in putting up a pan-Hellenic idea that would captivate the imagination of all or develop and expand the bonds of adherence and empire, as the Romans would soon do. Even the Persians, decrepit now compared to the time of Xerxes seventy-five years before, could still imagine exerting themselves over Greece. Yet the hour of Greece was not over. It had no remaining chance to extend its influence militarily, and a tornado was about to sweep through the region: a much more civilized version of the Assyrians and Hittites and others who had come snorting briefly out of the north and east in ancient times and occupied the Middle East up to the Levant and the Bosporus and Egypt. But such was the strength of Greek culture, though it outstripped the military and colonial potential of Greece,

---

6 St. John H. Cardinal Newman, *Grammar of Assent*, Oxford, 1870, p. 490.

that Greek culture would move more swiftly and surely in the baggage-train of more powerful military forces than Greece could muster. But it would be an even greater influence for that and have a permanent impact on the world. Ancient Greece would remain a popular favourite across all succeeding civilizations.

CHAPTER TEN

THE REVIVAL OF ATHENS, RISE OF THEBES AND THE DECLINE OF PERSIA

XENOPHON, LYSANDER, AND EPAMINONDAS
399-358 B.C.

Epaminodas defending Pelopidas
by W. Rainey, 1900

Lysander outside the walls of Athens
19th century lithograph

1. The State of the Western World in 400 B.C.

THE ORIGINAL CROSSROADS of the world, in the Middle East, to the conquest of which the Egyptians and highly organized and militarily advanced tribes from Europe and Asia were attracted, had now spread almost all the way around the Mediterranean, Greece and the Ionian islands, Macedonia, Thrace, and most of Italy. The maritime trade routes throughout the Mediterranean and Black and Red Seas were even more important than the overland routes to East and South Asia. The Greeks, as we have seen, remained bitterly divided and so addicted to internecine war that they had humbled their leading maritime power, Athens, when the formerly rigidly principled Sparta had committed the formerly unthinkable treachery of making itself a satellite of Persia against another Hellenic state. Almost the whole known world was politically exhausted. Persia remained an extensive empire but was regularly riven by royal and provincial or tribal factionalism, and had no political institutions of any merit and no means of maintaining themselves except the imposition of martial force. Greece had bled itself white and barely had the political strength to continue the repression of its inordinately large slave population. Already, the pattern of double concentric waves rippling out from and washing back towards the original centre of civilization was perceptible. The Persians had come from what is now eastern Iran. The Greeks, initially Aeolians, Ionians, and Dorians, came from southeast Europe and with no great homogeneity between themselves. By the beginning of the 5th Century B.C., the Greeks and Persians, with the Phoenician colonies of North Africa and Spain, occupied almost all the territory from what now are southern Italy and Sicily, and Tunisia to the western shores of the Black Sea, well down the Nile, into Arabia, and into Afghanistan. As these civilizations stretched farther out from their places of origin, the magnet of the societies and commerce they were building, in between and along with endless war-making, became ever more attractive to peoples generally inferior in culture and social organization, but often superior in the military arts and weapons, and motivation. The person who has spent the first twenty-five years of his life squatting in tents of animal skins in the Steppes, challenged by blazing heat, bone-chilling cold, and tempestuous winds, could easily develop an unquenchable ambition to live like King Solomon, or a Pharaoh, or the nobles around the Great King.

The bloodletting of the Greeks had thinned their ranks and dulled their edge, as the dishonourable Spartan dalliance with Persia illustrates. Formerly unmonetized Sparta, a sternly organized commune, was awash with the precious metals and the tribute Sparta had won in its later wars, especially what was pillaged by Lysander in his exploits. Corruption was rife among the ephors. The state was slowly rotting, but its basic problem—that ninety-five per cent of its population was composed of slaves—put a permanent check on what it could achieve beyond its immediate borders. And two-hundred and fifty years of sitting like a hen on top of congeries of Near Eastern peoples who did not appreciate or acculturate to them, had made Persia vulnerable. As the known world caused the frontiers of the unknown world to recede, the more militant forces among the unknown or on its fringes, became resistless to the temptations of assaulting the vulnerability of over-burdened or degenerate civilization. In the wings was a cyclonic force of soon-to-be immense military prowess, in Macedonia. And behind it, stirring and growing, and preparing for a vocation of rulership of greater extent and duration than would be seen in the Western world again for more than fifteen centuries after its passage (with the United States of America), was Rome. It was an embryo in the time of Pericles, flourishing but inconspicuous now, but predestined to exercise an influence unlike any other, first temporally and then ecclesiastically, from the Fourth Century B.C. to the present, an unbreakable chord connecting the ancient world to every succeeding epoch the world has yet known.

2. The Decline of Persia

In our extensive preoccupation with Greek affairs (which deserve no less), some other important states and peoples have been briefly neglected. The Persians had learned from their misfortunes at Salamis and Plataea that they should not attempt to invade Europe. It must be emphasized that Xerxes' return to Sardes after Salamis was not an embarrassing flight or rout. His plan of direct invasion had been foiled, but his main land units were undefeated and his chief motive in retiring was to squash a revolt in Babylon, where a local noble, Shamash-erba, proclaimed himself King of the Lands. Xerxes had no difficulty suppressing this impertinence and reduced Babylon's status from a subsidiary kingdom to a mere satrapy. Xerxes destroyed Babylon's fortifications and seized a good deal of aristocratic property. But gradually, what was left in Europe was relinquished between 479 and about 460 B.C. The Hellespont, Byzantium, the Bosporus, Thrace, and Macedonia, all were abandoned, though in fairly orderly manner, or gained their independence. Xerxes' brother, Masistes, satrap of Bactria, also attempted an uprising. Xerxes fancied his brother's wife, and when this became known, Xerxes' wife demanded vengeance on her quasi-niece, which was hideously carried out and caused Masistes to scramble back to Bactria to raise a revolt of self-defence, but he was intercepted and executed.

The central Persian state still possessed the strength to maintain internal order, despite its bloody nose in Europe, but the Great King had proved rather feckless and unsuccessful, and retired to sensuous idleness and decadence at Susa, the setting for the book of Esther. He began an immense palace for himself at Persepolis. It was uncompleted when a courtier, Artabanus, commander of the Great King's bodyguard, having placed his own sons in powerful positions and infiltrated the royal house through his manipulative skills and agility in the royal harem, murdered Xerxes in 465 B.C., with the complicity of a court eunuch. Xerxes was not a successful or talented king, though he was not egregiously incompetent. His loss of prestige and deterioration after the defeat in Greece and retrenchment in Eastern Europe contributed to the mortal squabbling in his family. Persia was the triumph of a smallish people, fierce and well-organized like many preceding intruders upon the Middle East had been, and there was no cultural elevation or community of ethnicity to bind the empire together. And now, the mystique of the Great King had been eroded by military defeat and royal dissolution.

(Xerxes was revived as a household name in the West briefly in 1940 when the renowned aviator and isolationist Charles Lindbergh, campaigning against President Franklin D. Roosevelt's program of rearmament and of all aid short of war to Britain and Canada and the Commonwealth in their resistance to Hitler and Mussolini, likened Roosevelt to Xerxes. This long-forgotten, almost Ozymandian, name, was bandied about for some months, but no one, including Lindbergh, knew much about Xerxes. Roosevelt, who did have a respectable classical education, was bemused by the completely spurious comparison.)

Artabanus clung to power for some months and took the precaution of murdering Xerxes' eldest son, Darius, and defeated the second son, Hystaspes, while the third son, Artaxerxes, pretended to accept the scourge of his family as legitimate while he prepared his stroke. After about seven months, and after resentment of the usurper and his sanguinary methods had gained some currency, Artaxerxes (called Long Hand, but whether from techniques or physiology is not known) struck suddenly and murdered the usurper and defeated and slaughtered his supporters. Legitimacy was restored but the inheritor had to wade through much blood to ascend the throne. Artaxerxes' first task was the suppression of Inaros' revolt in Egypt (Chapters 7 and 8), which required a considerable time and some concessions, but at least it was a reversal of Xerxes' policy of allowing the limbs of the empire simply to fall off. The defeat of the Athenian mission in aid of Inaros (one of Pericles' least intelligent strategic initiatives) did constitute a significant recovery of Persian arms, and something of a revenge against the Greeks. The regime of Psammetichus in Egypt has been mentioned, and at this point it seemed that Egypt was content under a fairly gentle Persian suzerainty. (At time of writing, the antics of the Iranian theocracy indicate a desire to reimpose such a relationship, which might conceivably be possible but for the intervention of far-distant powers, especially the United States.)

Artaxerxes also dealt gently with the Jews, and in 458 B.C., Ezra was permitted by Artaxerxes to return to Jerusalem and refurbish and reopen the Temple and set up Jewish courts that would enforce Judaism on its adherents. This was the beginning of post-exilic Judaism, its reestablishment as an accepted religion in a defined territory for the first time since Nebuchadnezzar had removed the Jews to Babylon one-hundred and twenty years before (586 B.C.). The Persians were thus much friendlier to the Jews than their immediate neighbours (in contrast to current conditions at time of writing), but it is impossible to know to what extent Artaxerxes, who was not a gentle ruler, was motivated by liberality and benignity, and to what extent by a wish to divide his restive subjects more thoroughly by the revitalization of the Jewish community, which could be relied upon to resist neighbourly intrusion and generally distract peoples that might otherwise be tempted by revolt against the new Great King.

Artaxerxes fared less well in Asia Minor and the Aegean and was obliged to yield the islands and the Greek communities in Asia Minor, under the Peace of Callias in 448. Further, he was unable to resist the encroachments of his mother, Xerxes' barbaric widow, Amestris, who even while Xerxes lived sometimes successfully demanded the arrest, torture, and mutilation of people she suspected, sometimes entirely capriciously, of some slight or presumption. At her insistence, Artaxerxes felt it necessary to ignore his covenants with Inaros, whom Amestris had taken against, and to seize him and hand him over to his mother, who tortured him to death in the most disgusting fashion, even by the macabre standards of the time and in a region which had little to learn about bloodshed. This inaugurated the domination of the Persian Empire by demonically overbearing women, which persisted for two generations, and the first result of it was the revolt in Egypt of Megabyxus, who had conquered Egypt for Artaxerxes and made the arrangement with Inaros which Amestris so sadistically violated. Megabyxus more or less held his own, and remained on good terms with Artaxerxes, who reigned for forty years, to 424, but was overly influenced by his mother and wife Amytis, both devious, fierce, and motivated by a relentless and vicious cunning. Artaxerxes was a more capable ruler than his father, but if the Great King was to hold his own in the mobile and pitiless currents of the Near East, steadier and more trustworthy statesmanship would be required.

The immediate aftermath was not encouraging; the new king was Xerxes II, but he was promptly murdered by his half-brother, Sogdianus, who after a few months was overthrown by his half-brother Ochus, who executed Sogdianus by incineration in a large court oven, which became the preferred method for some time afterward for the numerous executions that occurred. Ochus took the kingly title, Darius II. He was brave and decisive, but intimidated and dominated by his wife Parysatis, who was his half-sister, a horrible monster by all accounts. This ghastly regime provoked a depressing sequence of revolts that jumped up like popcorn around the Empire, groaning under the maniacal tyranny of the bloodthirsty Parysatis. The king's brother Arsites rose and both sides employed Greek mercenaries, always a sure sign of popular sullenness; eventually the revolt was suppressed with the usual barbarity and Arsites was tortured to death.

Lydia rose under Pissuthnes, but he was crushed and executed by Tissaphernes, as we have seen, a Persian soldier-politician of considerable ingenuity. He became the Lydian satrap and the brother-in-law of the king's son. A revolt broke out briefly in Media and was crushed without undue difficulty and the ringleaders dealt with in the accustomed manner (this at least was egalitarian as the higher ranks of the royal family down to the peasantry when on the wrong side of the ever-shifting fortunes were dispatched with gratuitous severity). Next came Terituchmes' wide-ranging conspiracy. He was Tissaphernes' brother and the son-in-law of Darius, but he was defeated at close quarters in intra-palace war and intrigue and Parysatis broke even her own past records for extensive and horrible liquidation of real and imagined rivals, poisoning some many years later when she was unable to kill them in hot blood. She was unable to destroy Tissaphernes, who was not implicated in the revolt but that did not acquit him in the febrile mind of Parysatis, but she did succeed in having Darius displace Tissaphernes as satrap of Lydia. He did continue, however, as satrap of Caria and the remaining Ionian cities.

The Persian Empire, heaving and seething at the centre with deranged and murderous intrigue, maintained for a time considerable tensile strength because of the competence of the principal satraps: Tissaphernes, Cyrus, who replaced him in Lydia, Phrygia, and Cappadocia, and Pharnabazus. Darius died, apparently, in a great rarity, of natural causes. Parysatis had borne 13 children, though many were now dead. Arsaces and Cyrus were the two leading candidates. Cyrus was the protégé of Parysatis and when Darius called the two sons to interview them as he was dying, Tissaphernes accompanied Cyrus, pretending not to have been miffed by Cyrus' displacement of him in much of the Lydian satrapy. Arsaces secured the succession, a set-back for Parysatis, but Tissaphernes, taking the offense against Cyrus and Parysatis, falsely denounced Cyrus to Arsaces, who spared Cyrus' life at the fiendishly energetic intervention of Parysatis, but sent him back to Lydia as satrap. Arsaces took the name Artaxerxes II, and was called Mnemon because of his renowned memory. The fight was on. (These events were almost exactly contemporaneous with the last days of the life of Socrates, and it is little wonder that Athens gloried in its humanist gentility; the realm of the Great King was at its core, an unimaginable torture chamber of horrors.)

Cyrus was to prove a man of high quality in many respects, courageous and generous and intelligent, and someone who understood and appreciated the Greeks well, but also the inheritor of the terrible cruelty and savagery of his family. All those who offended him were not only executed but mutilated to death in excruciating pain and dismemberment. And in the deadly game in which he was engaged ex officio, but into which he entered with relish, he had the fatal difficulty of not always being able to distinguish friends from enemies. He set out to conquer the Persian Empire from Cappadocia and recruited substantial numbers of Greek mercenaries, ostensibly to assist in the siege of Miletus. He only discovered very late that his real enemy, and the cunning master of the deadly power game in Persia, was Tissaphernes. Among the Greeks who volunteered as mercenaries was the young Xenophon, another remarkable early historian, but with practical gifts as well, a youthful acolyte of Socrates and an admirer of Sparta, which was not a popular view in Athens in 400 B.C. Cyrus gathered all his forces together and announced a campaign against Pisidias, but Tissaphernes recognized that his true purpose was to overthrow the Great King and hastened to Susa to warn Artaxerxes. Cyrus gathered forces as he went, and met up with his fleet carrying seven-hundred hoplites, commanded by the Egyptian Tamos, at Issus. Cyrus pressed eastwards, and was able, because of unusually low water, to wade across the Euphrates, which was seen as a good omen, as it would in the case of Alexander the Great nearby, sixty-eight years later. Cyrus marched south along the east bank of the Euphrates. They came upon Artaxerxes' army at Cunaxa, forty-five miles north of Babylon.

The two armies were each close to thirty-thousand men; neither was well-trained, but Artaxerxes had more than twice as many cavalry. He was expecting reinforcements but did not want to allow Cyrus to take Babylon, an event that could have started the fall of dominoes within the Empire where all power was now unstable. It was a closely fought battle, but when Cyrus' right advanced and moved farther from his centre, Tissaphernes, as alert a general as he was a politician, hurled his forces into the gap and was followed by Artaxerxes himself with substantial forces. Cyrus recognized the danger and led a brave charge directly against Artaxerxes, accompanied by his entire well-trained guard of six-hundred horsemen wielding heavy swords. Cyrus cut right through to Artaxerxes himself, and lightly wounded him in personal combat, but Cyrus was overwhelmed by the encircling forces and died bravely with most of his own guard. The balance of his army which was in the fray, Greek mercenaries and adventurers who had no interest in the outcome except their own welfare, fled. Cyrus' right, which had detached itself to pursue retreating Persian infantry, returned to the site of the battle in good condition, but with no particular aim, since Cyrus had perished. Artaxerxes demanded the unconditional surrender of the Greeks, which was refused.

There now ensued a struggle for influence over the impressionable king, a much weaker personality than Cyrus. Tissaphernes, his sister, Queen Statira, and the imperishable Parysatis, the blood-thirsty queen mother, divided up their spheres of influence on the king, and there was a redistribution of satrapies; and Tissaphernes, completely effacing the usurpation of the late Cyrus, took back all his satrapies and became the master of the Western Persian Empire. Tissaphernes, with Artaxerxes' blessing, undertook to conduct the Greeks out of Mesopotamia, on condition that they would do no harm on their passage. Tissaphrnes escorted the Greeks up the Tigris and where it reached its principal tributary, the Zab, at which point the Greeks were extremely suspicious that Tissaphernes was leading them into a trap.

Tissaphernes invited the Greek high command to a friendly dinner to iron out any misunderstandings. The Greek commander, Clearchus and twenty-five of his corps commanders attended and all were seized, delivered to Artaxerxes, and murdered in the customarily barbarous manner of the later Achaemenids (Persian ruling house).

3. The Odyssey of Xenophon

The Greek army, decapitated though it was, determined to go on and the young Spartaphilic and Socratic historian Xenophon assumed command of the Greeks and they marched on. This would become one of history's astounding lonely military exercises, like Mao Tse-tung's Long March in China of 1934-35. There were ten-thousand Greeks, including a significant number of women; they burnt their carts and tents and used their horses as pack animals, and beat off harassing attacks as they moved slowly north. They were unable to cross the Tigris because of cavalry formations on the other side, but then struck off north into the hills of Kurdistan. They marched as a hollow square, with Tissaphernes pursuing and picking off stragglers, not trying to kill them all but merely assuring that they all departed his reexpanded satrapy. Xenophon was aiming for Armenia, the source of the Tigris, whence he could strike west to return by land or sea to Greece. They had a sharp exchange with the Carduchians, tortured from a prisoner an alternate route through a pass in the Caucasus, and emerged to face Orontes, Artaxerxes' son-in-law, satrap of Eastern Armenia. He didn't disturb them as long as they kept moving, which they did with the Carduchians returning and Xenophon, with splendid improvisation, repulsed them with a sharp rear-guard defence. The astonishing odyssey continued into a terrible blizzard, which they faced, under-clothed and exhausted, without cover. Prisoners and natives were induced by a variety of means to advise on the best routes; Xenophon sent Cheirisophus ahead with the main body of his still mobile band, and he led rescue parties around in the snow, rounding up frost-bitten, snow-blinded, and demoralized stragglers, fed them, and regained the main force. They were directed safely to underground quarters where the villagers were induced to receive them hospitably and they rested for a week.

A regrettable episode occurred when Xenophon seized the horses of someone whom he was relying on as a guide and the man misled the Greeks. They wasted ten days, but then turned north aiming for the Black Sea. They encountered small settlements of fierce tribesmen, and when they subdued the men of one village, the women murdered their children and then committed suicide. It had become an extended saga. After some more brisk fighting, they found a river that clearly flowed to the sea and followed it without further incident to Trapezus, on the Black Sea. They had wandered through treacherous country and elements nearly a thousand miles, with relatively few losses. They were now really outside the Persian Empire and by the primitive and sparsely populated standards of the region, Xenophon was at the head of a formidable army. He had conducted a self-deliverance that ranks in historical celebrity with Napoleon's astonishing crossing of the Beresina in 1812 as he departed Russia and defeated armies totaling three times the size of his own on both banks of the river.

EXPEDITION OF THE TEN THOUSAND

There now began the last leg of the return of the fabled ten-thousand (reduced to about eighty-six hundred by the trials and privations they had endured). Trapezus gave them a ship which Xenophon dispatched to Byzantium to seek transport. Instead, the Spartan admiral there, Anaxibius, sent back two ships and Xenophon alit upon the tactic of piracy to round up more ships to transport his army. They almost came to grief dealing with one of the local tribes, but Xenophon, short of food, managed to get the women and baggage shipboard and proceeded on by foot a hundred miles west to Cerasus. Here, no longer in danger, discipline dissolved and a good deal of looting and general mistreatment of the local villagers occurred, which Xenophon, with the utmost difficulty, managed to restrain. The next stage of the trek brought them to the land of the tower-dwellers, where the clan chiefs lived at the top of seven-story towers and were not permitted to depart the towers, where they administered justice and laws. This peculiar group had conquered and more or less indentured the iron-mongering Chalybes to work as blacksmiths in the service of the tower-dwellers. Xenophon associated his army with nearby clans who were smouldering with resentment for the tower-dwellers, overran this odd tribe and burned the king alive in his, the highest tower, about a hundred feet tall, and propped on floors of wooden stilts. His tower was a landmark, known to Greek mariners and called by them the Metropolis.

Xenophon adopted the tactic of renting his army out to local tribes as they moved west, and in this way, they continued their march. Xenophon, after considering putting down roots and founding a kingdom which he would rule, and suppressing the resulting revolt, exacted an offer of passage by sea which took them four-hundred miles on to Heraclea, almost within the confines of Greek civilization. The Heracleans resisted the tendency Xenophon's ever-evolving army had now developed of looting and pillaging in order to take home with them as much plunder as they could. There was a good deal of skirmishing with Bithynians, as they were back to the edge of the Persian Empire. After further jousting and jockeying with the Spartan governor of Byzantium, Cleander, who at one point was stoned and fled on foot and threatened to ban Xenophon and his itinerant army from all Greek ports, peace broke out and Xenophon's army and its dependents were ushered out of the city and promised money and food. The gates were locked behind them and Byzantium reneged on its promises. The Xenophonians breached the wall and infiltrated the city and had it at their mercy, but Xenophon sagely persuaded his men (and women), to accept rations and depart peacefully, a wise act. Even this was not the end of the journey. Xenophon led the six-thousand remaining members of his army, a pretty well-trained and rough and ready group by now, in conducting brigandage through the Thracian winter for an improvident local king, Seuthes, sacking neighbouring villages. Here, finally, the Ten Thousand, now about six-thousand, were merged into the army of the Spartan general Thibron.

Xenophon himself was given an estate by Sparta in Elis and lived comfortably there for twenty years writing the books for which he has ever since been famous. Thereafter, he returned, a popular and respected figure, to Athens. His extraordinary career brings to mind Juvenal's famous encomium: "He performed a march without precedent across savage mountains; his reward has been to become a textbook for schoolboys."[1] There has been a good deal of tendentious history written exaggerating Xenophon's remarkable achievement and disparaging the military talent and courage of the Persians. Xenophon wasn't really facing a Persian army and triumphed rather over an extraordinary sequence of improvident events visited on him by numerous scattered and wild tribes. Nor, as has been argued, was Cyrus' invasion of Asia Minor a prelude to Alexander the Great's actions in the same areas more than sixty years later. What did stand out as the principal lesson of Cyrus' experience (and he was much praised by Xenophon, loyal to the man who had recruited him to his mission) was that Persia could not be invaded without a strong cavalry force. Alexander, who was to prove the greatest general in the history of the world up to his time and remains today one of the greatest commanders of all times, fully grasped and applied that lesson. He will come swashbuckling through this narrative three chapters hence.

4. Turmoil in Persia

Most of the Fourth Century B.C. in Persia was the customary struggle in dissolving empires between the central authority and the provinces. There was no unifying ethnic or cultural bond in Persia, and the various ethnicities were bound to be restless unless the government was superbly efficient, and retention of the empire was the best way forward for every constituent province. In the present state of Persian government, this was not a case that could be made easily. Add to the separatist tendencies of the fractious peoples the ambitions of the governors themselves. The more astute among them could harness local discontent to their

---

1 CAH, VI, p. 18 (W.W. Tarn).

own military strength and masquerade as both champions of local government and good government alternatives to the proverbial, if now rather reduced and thoroughly demystified Great King. The Persian government concluded on the basis of recent events that Egypt, which was in an almost constant state of revolt, was the real threat to the integrity of the empire and that the Greeks could be more easily managed. Given Persia's experience in Greece, this was a counter-historical opinion made even more perilous by the fact that the retrenchment of Greek colonies and a diminution of intra-Grecian war-making generated a large number of unemployed, able-bodied Greeks eligible to be recruited as mercenaries. It was an adventurer's life (as Xenophon had most memorably demonstrated) and could furnish a good living, and an improving one, as mercenaries could always switch loyalties for a higher price and if at all successful, had plenty of opportunity to loot and pillage.

The perfect exemplar, more typical and more unscrupulous than Xenophon, as a chief of armies that could be hired or otherwise attracted by outright cupidity, was the ineffable Tissaphernes, who immediately after the battle at Cunaxa set about aggressively looting Greek towns and villages, causing Sparta to declare war on him in 399. And eventually a general melee ensued until the former Persian fleet commander, Conon, returned from Cyprus, joined forces with Tissaphernes's rival, Pharnabazus and gained Artaxerxes' authority to attack Sparta by sea. Pharnabazus visited the Persian court in 398 and was so persuasive that Sparta had to be countered at sea that Artaxerxes financed the construction and manning of a fleet for him, for this purpose, and Pharnabazus established himself at Cyprus, which was practically in the full control of a Greek adventurer of note, Evagoras. Evagoras was a seeker of fortune and a colourful and resourceful brigand who governed so benignly that he attracted a lot of immigration from Greece to Cyprus, and prospered so impressively that he drew an ever-larger number of like-minded men of action and free-booters. His rulership of Cyprus was almost universally praised. Evagoras was ostensibly on a commission from the Persian king, but had not remitted tribute for some time, when the itinerant Athenian admiral, Conon, who sought refuge here after the disastrous Athenian defeat of Aegospotami, persuaded Evagoras of the desirability of action in favour of Athens and against Sparta. Evagoras came current on tribute to Artaxerxes and sent a supporting emissary in the mission of Pharnabazus. The petition from Conon and Evagoras was presented to Artaxerxes by his Greek doctor, Ctesias, and urged that the Persian king support a combined effort by Conon, Evagoras, and Pharnabazus, which Pharnabazus temporarily extended to Tissaphernes, who was battling with Dercyllidas, the Spartan commander in Thrace and Bithynia. There was thus assembled such a coalition of dashing, even stylish, Machiavellian (to adapt a description from two millennia later) scoundrel adventurers as has rarely been replicated at the same time in quadruplicate in all subsequent history.

Sparta retaliated by sending an army under their king, Agesilaus II in 396 to invade Persia. Agesilaus was altogether different from the commanders serving (for the time being) the Persian and Athenian interest. He was a gentlemanly king, just embarking on a reign of thirty-eight years, but a talented general, an experienced and intelligent statesman, and for the times, a civilized and moderate leader, magnanimous in victory and extremely tenacious and forceful when on the defensive. Lysander hurried to Agesilaus' headquarters and tried to gain effective control of operations and entrench a cadre of his favourite officers, but the king declined. Agesilaus was inspired by the example of Agamemnon and tried to offer such a prayer on his departure, but his Theban allies would not allow it, a slight that would be remembered.

It was an unusually talented and picturesque cast of characters in Asia Minor and in the adjacent waters. Agesilaus conquered Lydia, chased Tissaphernes off, proceeded inland to Paphlagonia, and destroyed and pillaged Pharnabazus' satrapy. Tissaphernes made peace with the Spartans, but instantly violated it on the arrival of Persian reinforcements. Agesilaus then expanded his offensive and besieged Tissaphernes in Sardes. He was holding out with difficulty when Agesilaus made his peace with Artaxerxes on the condition which Pharnabazus and the beastly Parysatis eagerly supported—that Tissaphernes be put to death. Parysatis hated Tissaphernes for betraying her favourite son, Cyrus, and Artaxerxes, always malleable, abandoned Tissaphernes who, egregious though he was, had secured the Persian throne for Artaxerxes. The Great King, as the Persian monarch still called himself, sent an emissary with a military escort to see Tissaphernes and they seized and executed him. The deceased was not widely lamented but he was a good exemplar of the Middle Eastern opportunistic faction-head. He was the last of the line of Hydarnes (one last time—one of the six original comrades of Cyrus I).

Pharnabazus now faced the wrath of Sparta, but he lavished his fortune, assiduously extracted from the subjects of his satrapy, to help fund and raise, beyond Evagoras and Conon, a Greek league against Sparta, as in olden Hellenic times. His family, the Pharnacid dynasty, had held the satrapy of Hellespontine Phrygia (across the Bosporus from Istanbul-Byzantium) since 478, and he married Artaxerxes II's daughter, Apama. His heirs succeeded him in his satrapy, which was effectively independent of Persia, and his granddaughter, Barsine, would marry Alexander the Great. He was not a parvenu-adventurer like Tissaphernes, or a career warrior like Conon and Evagoras, but in his diplomatic and political techniques, was cut from similar cloth to Tissaphernes, but was more patrician, and none of the surviving three were quite as maniacally treacherous. In 394, Agesilaus launched an ambitious operation, marching five-hundred miles northeast almost to the Sea of Marmara, and attracting some degree of loyalty from the hill tribes, who were no admirers of the Persians. Agesilaus' campaigns were never more than predatory raids by expanded shore parties, but they protected the Greek towns in Asia Minor from the Persians and showed again the valour of the Greek hoplites. The Greek cavalry, as always, was weak. Agesilaus' successes were, however, blunted on other fronts.

Conon defeated the Spartan fleet off Caunus, and his appearance off Rhodes was sufficient to raise a democratic revolt in that island. This would eventually change the course of the war. Artaxerxes wasn't paying his soldiers of fortune promptly and it was all Conon could do to avoid serious mutinies, but he called upon the king in person and managed to clear up the arears. Agesilaus named his brother-in-law, Peisander, as Spartan admiral, but was obliged by domestic political matters to withdraw from Asia, and at Cnidus in 394, Conon and Pharnabazus completely destroyed the Spartan fleet and Peisander perished in the battle. The result was explained in part by the fact that the Persian fleet of Conon and Pharnabazus was, in fact, manned almost entirely by Greek sailors. Further, Sparta's Asian allies disliked the Spartan authoritarian mode of governing and found their cultural protection more onerous than the relaxed suzerainty of the Persians. In effect, the Spartan effort in Asia Minor was a pallid and belated imitation of Athens. Agesilaus had reestablished Lysander's oligarchic regimes in the territories Sparta occupied in Asia Minor. It was unpopular and after Agesilaus' withdrawal and the destruction of Peisander's fleet, almost all the Greek communities revolted against Spartan domination. In a trice, Sparta's assumption of the role of premier Greek state was dashed, and she was entirely confined again to the Greek mainland.

Pharnabazus was not content with this, and probably Artaxerxes encouraged him, and he sent Timocrates on a diplomatic mission to Sparta, which included stops at Thebes and Corinth, which along with Argos, was always ready to discard Sparta and find any pretext to start quarreling again. The inescapable fact is that the Greeks didn't really like peace. Athens, at the destruction of the Spartan fleet and news of the uprisings against Sparta did not take much prompting before thoughts of a renewed empire and Athenian primacy were reawakened. Thrasybulus and the moderates maintained appearances in Athens and seemed to adhere to the Spartan agreements, but Epicrates and others sent emissaries to the Persian king and more volunteers proceeded to join the colours of Conon. Conon then helped raise the sponsorship of the destabilizing act of reconstructing the Long Walls connecting Athens and Piraeus and restoring that city as a rival to Sparta. In 389, Evagoras, unofficial king of Cyprus, a fervent Hellenizer, revolted officially from Spartan hegemony and with support from Athens and semi-independent Egypt, regained Cyprus, from which he had been expelled.

The Corinthian War broke out in the summer of 395 B.C., when Thebes intervened in a frontier argument between the Phocians and the Locrians, in a manner clearly intended to promote a war with Sparta. Agesilaus' colleague in the kingship of Sparta, Pausanias, gathered together an army quickly and Lysander raised a Phocian army. Pausanias invaded Boeotia much earlier than the Spartans had imagined to be possible, and Lysander was also able to get well into Boeotia. But Lysander soon found himself between the Theban garrison at Haliartus and the Theban army, and his army was driven off with heavy casualties and Lysander perished in battle, an anti-climax to such a prodigious career. (His name had a small return to familiarity in the twentieth century as the small aircraft, needing little space to land or take off, which the British used to maintain communications and traffic with occupied countries in World War II. Among those conveyed in a Lysander between Britain and occupied France was future president Francois Mitterand.) The Athenians sent reinforcements to the Thebans, and Pausanias negotiated a somewhat embarrassing cease-fire and withdrew from Boeotia. In the Greek manner, and despite his royal status, Pausanias was publicly tried and condemned and only escaped execution by fleeing to Tegea.

The quadruple alliance of Corinth, Thebes, Argos, and Athens met at Corinth and agreed a program of seeking other allies, and fairly soon, the Locrians, Euboeans, Acarnanians, Chalcidians, and Thessalians all joined. In the spring of 394, the Boeotians and Argives expelled the Spartans from Pharsalus and Heraclea. A large army composed of units from all over the new confederacy invaded Laconia in the summer of 394 but squandered the advantages of numbers and surprise by dithering, and when battle was joined, it was between armies of about twenty-five thousand men each. It was a complicated engagement, and was about even, after the right wings of both armies closed on the left of the opposing army, making it an immense melee. The Spartans may slightly have got the better of it, and in any case, the confederacy never attempted such a main army engagement with the Spartans again.

It was in these circumstances that Agesilaus was recalled from Asia. On his homeward march, Agesilaus encountered evident mass hostility in Thessaly, where the cavalry hovered on the edge of his column but no attack by either side occurred. In central Greece, Agesilaus received reinforcements and made an incursion into Boeotia, but this was rebuffed by the sturdy Thebans at Coronea. The casualties were about even but the Spartan king abandoned the venture and resumed his march back to Sparta. There ensued an attack by Sparta on Corinth that succeeded in cutting the walls that protected the access to the sea and imposing a siege on Corinth which was only broken when the Athenians, realizing that if Corinth fell, Sparta would again invade and raze Attica and destroy the Athenian food supply, restored the sea access and rebuilt the breached walls. They also sent a flying column of volunteers of the mature and rapacious variety, led by Iphicrates, prototype of a new condottieri-class of semi-autonomous military adventurers in charge of experienced irregular troops. The Corinthian action dragged on to 392.

Conon's visit to Athens not only presaged the restoration of the walls to Piraeus which enabled the city to regain a maritime and imperial presence and import her food supply; and this was promoted by Conon himself, as he regained Athenian citizenship and stayed on in Athens, participating in Athenian politics. More or less on his own authority, he attempted unsuccessfully to negotiate a treaty with the Syracusan leader Dionysius, and did negotiate tentative arrangements with Rhodes, Samos, Ephesus, Byzantium, and several other states. A second league composed of some of the same states was formed and the general policy of the Greek states in the Aegean and Asia Minor, was favorable to Athens, of whose overlordship they had reasonably fond memories, despite the Confederacy having been turned arbitrarily into an empire with centralized Athenian authority.

This effort to treat free allies as colonies must rank as next to the Syracusan disaster the most serious strategic error Athens made in its history. Such was the fluidity of Greek events and the swift changes in forces and interests, the formerly restive League-members were recalling those days with some nostalgia. In general, they disliked the Spartans because of Lysander's corrupt and vicious tyranny (conducted in order to make the nasty local governments dependent on him, with the result they were all overthrown). They felt reasonably comfortable with the Persians, who made no effort to assimilate them, but did periodically exact tribute and weren't reliable defenders against the Spartans. And they generally liked and felt kinship with the Athenians, as long as they were not again subsumed into the grander designs of the Athenian leaders. By 390, the Athenians had gathered a League that included

Delos (a sacred island to all Greeks), Rhodes, Cidus, Carpathus, Eritrea, Lemnos, Imbros, Scyros, Ephesus, Chios, Erythrae, and Litylene. They were small or smallish states, but together constituted a considerable force in Grecian terms.

At this point, Sparta, which for centuries had held itself aloof from such skullduggery, realized it was over-extended and could not maintain itself in Greece without the assistance of Persia. This was, in a way, a death-knell for the noble Greeks, as the execution of Socrates had been. The first time Sparta connived with Persia, the ancient foe of Greece, it had been a scandalous betrayal of the Hellenic world, but an opportunistic stratagem somewhat justified by military necessity, a once-only preview of the Nazi-Soviet Pact, twenty-four centuries in advance. This time, it revealed an addiction to the endless war and scheming of Greece, which through most of its history Sparta had avoided, and it was another betrayal—Sparta could have negotiated a peace with Athens and the other principal states and tried to resurrect a balance between them that would not be conducive to perpetual war. This was the scourge that for all its elevation culturally, Greece could not escape: it was constantly bickering and fighting like a group of scorpions in a bottle and the wars never achieved anything except to prevent over-population.

It must be said that Sparta set about its task with agility. It sent Antalcidas to Tiribazus, the new satrap of Lydia (succeeding Thithrausetes, who briefly followed Tissaphernes), effectively to steal diplomatically what had amounted to the Spartan harvesting of the fruits of the Persian victory over Athens. Antalcidas' embassy competed with that of Conon on Athens' behalf, and his message was generously to offer Persian, rather than Spartan control of all the Greek island and Asia Minor cities, and that Sparta sought nothing more than that they should be peaceably governed and not duped into war-making. Since Sparta had been evicted from most of the states in question, it was not self-sacrificing to make the proposal. But the Spartan emissary claimed that Athens was obviously reviving the Pan-Hellenic anti-Persian stance of Cimon's time. Artaxerxes was in no hurry to move. He had detained Conon when he arrived as an emissary in Sardes, and was arguing against Tiribazus' proposals, without knowing their exact terms. Conon was comfortably detained for a time, but, talented at eluding misfortune as he always was, he escaped and made for his old ally Evagoras, but died of natural causes en route.

The initial reaction of Artaxerxes was to take his time before accepting the Spartan proposals conveyed by Tiribazus, and so Sparta resolved to continue at war with Persia and seek peace with the other Greeks, convening an assembly in pursuit of that object with the theme of "autonomy for all," an unexceptionable concept. Athens was specifically invited to rebuild its walls and reacquire its empire. A classic case of unfathomably stupid Greek obstinacy ensued. Argos was asked to cooperate in freeing Corinth and Thebes was asked to show restraint opposite its neighbor, Orchomenus. The Athenian representative at the meeting, Andocides, returned and advocated acceptance of the Spartan proposal. It was only fifteen years after the disaster at Aegospotami which left Athens with no fleet, no army, and no means of defence at all, in shambles and defenceless. Despite his fine presentation of the terms, the public assembly was disturbed by demands for return of the cleruchies (private sector allotments of land outside Attica). On this nonsense: to fight on until their restoration, peace was rejected and Andocides was packed off into exile with recriminations ringing in his ears as a reward for his work. It was as if Cleophon lived. Thebes had wished to accept the Spartan terms, and Argos could have been brought along, but they all flopped back into the endless, hopeless morass of internecine Greek warfare.

Back to war they went and in 391, Agesilaus, no less formidable than he had been against the Persians in the previous war, again breached the long walls of Corinth to its harbor, and in the following year, 390, he again came across the same walls to interrupt the Isthmian Festival, which was in progress, and displace Argos as the presiding power at the festival. He continued on to seize northern territories of Corinth (Peiraeum and Oenoe), while his brother, the admiral Teleutias, recaptured Lechaeum. At this point, the condottiere Iphicrates, caught a column of six-hundred Spartans without cavalry escort, and killed almost all of them. This had an electrifying effect in reducing the prestige of Sparta, and her allies and auxiliary forces became restless. Boeotia withdrew from its negotiations for a separate peace with Sparta, and Iphicrates retook Oenoe and several nearby places to lift the blockade of Corinth. The venerable Thibron recovered Ephesus in 391 and commenced plundering excursions in Asia Minor but was overwhelmingly defeated and slain personally by the Struthan cavalry. This was the last Anabasis, as incursions into Asia Minor were called. Agesilaus successfully invaded Acarnania in 389, but almost all the Greeks had, once again, exhausted themselves over the temporary occupation of towns of a few hundred people.

Artaxerxes was economizing and laid up most of his fleet, even as Athens had done the same, imagining it could rely on the Persian navy. Sparta took advantage of Tiribazus' subsidy to build up a naval squadron that recaptured Samos and Cnidus in 390. It was planning an attack on Rhodes in 388 when a new Athenian fleet commanded by Thrasybulus appeared. It was on a mission of diplomacy and piracy. Thrasybulus had won back to Athens the Thracian chiefs around Gallipoli as well as Byzantium and Chalcedon and had reopened the trade route between Athens and the Black Sea, its traditional source of food supplies. It was from this low base that Athens had to begin its reconstruction as a great power, and from the demeaning activity of piracy or wasted pillage by shore parties and embezzlement from dependent jurisdictions that Thrasybulus, one of Athens' great heroes, closed his career. He was killed while looting Aspendus in 388, as he was cruising off Delos, intercepting and plundering foreign merchantmen.

Artaxerxes finally accepted the wisdom of Sparta's overture made by Antilcidas to Tiribazus in 390. Evagoras, de facto king of Cyprus, set about establishing his authority over and ability to exact tribute from the lesser surrounding islands that had withheld recognition of him as master of the Aegean. The Persian king, acting through the satraps of Lydia (Autophradates), and Caria (Hecatomnus, successor to Tissiphernes) sent an army and fleet to put down Evagoras. The Athenians, graciously if unwisely, sent out a squadron to help Evagoras, and Artaxerxes handed control of the enterprise to the two trusted satraps, Pharnabazus and Tiribazus. Antalcidas took charge of a squadron composed of Spartan, Persian, other Greek, and Syracusan vessels (twenty ships sent by Dionysius)—a fleet totaling eighty ships.

He blocked the Athenian fleet up in the Dardanelles, and domestic support for this aggressive policy waned, the peace party gained the upper hand, and in 387 Tiribazus, in the Persian king's name, summoned all the warring states to send emissaries to Sardes to hear the Persian king's peace terms. Artaxerxes' peace proposals were reasonable and close to what Antalcidas had suggested in 393: All of Asia Minor and Cyprus were to be protectorates of the King of Persia; Lemnos, Imbros, and Scyros were to remain Athenian, and all other Greek states of every size and place would remain autonomous. The Argives withdrew from Corinth; the Athenians dissolved their Aegean alliances; the Thebans acknowledged the autonomy of the other Boeotians. Once again, a great deal of bloodletting had accomplished nothing. This was the King's Peace and it disguised an accelerating state of deterioration within the Persian Empire (that was slightly less swift than the self-destruction of the warring Greek states).

The King's Peace conferred on Persia the right to intervene at will in Greece and with Spartan complicity pre-arranged, as Persia, though it had been militarily expelled from Greece in the times of Hellenic glory, was now the overlord of the Greeks. It remains a mystery how such a talented people as the Greeks, could so mismanage its affairs. The gradually decomposing Persian Empire had completely outsmarted the Greeks. Greece had just given away a vital part of its heritage, the Greek population of Asia Minor and the adjacent Greek islands. The rise of Persia was attributable to the suicidal intra-Greek bellicosity of the constituent city states. Even in these latest conflicts, the Persian satraps recruited Greek sailors and Greek admirals to command them, and Greek soldiers. Satraps, including satraps seeking the overthrow of the Great King, competed in the recruitment of Greek auxiliaries (mercenaries). The Greeks were superior warriors and Greece was culturally more sophisticated than Persia and made great inroads in many of the more enlightened satrapies. Greeks were more homogeneous than the polyglot ingredients of the Persian Empire, but Persia had greater resources than Greece, and their complete intolerance of any governmental system involving popular consultation was in some respects a comparative strength. (Apart from the obvious strategic differences between a sea and a land power, this would also be the main distinction between post-Cromwell, parliamentary Britain and post-Richelieu absolutist France.)

5. The Decline of Sparta, Renascence of Athens, and Rise of Thebes

Sparta is chiefly responsible for this decline of Greece, by beginning the practice of giving away Greek assets to gain a foreign ally against a Greek opponent. But the other Greek states leapt into the same practice. All these quarrels arose from trivial vexations or unjustified ambition. Sparta did establish a common front of defence opposite Persia and was stabbed in the back by its fellow Greeks for its trouble. "In the fourth century the crime of 'medism' (dealing with the Persians against the interests of other Greeks) became respectable in Greece, and it remained an honour so long as the Mede remained to medize with."[2] Greece and Persia were both exhausted. The consequences of the existence of this large number of unem-

---

2 Ibid., p. 56 (M. Cary).

ployed Greek warriors and sailors were a blight on the known Western world. They were easy hires, without loyalty, recourse to them sharply reduced more productive expenditures such as fine public works and majestic buildings. And these mercenaries became a permanent and powerful war lobby, as traditional patriotism gave way to dependence on unreliable scoundrels.

The erosion of Rome with barbarian influences is notorious, but what preceded it in Greece, with the descent of patriotism and the endless preoccupation with war conducted by a corrupt (if still generally courageous) warrior class, would prove a durable litmus test and yardstick for the imminent collapse of civilizations. In most of the Greek states, although there were reasonable levels of economic prosperity, especially in Athens, the to and fro between democrats and oligarchs was just a naked struggle to stage a coup d'état and then prevent an opposing group from doing the same. Greek democracy was always fragile, but it became a fraud subject to ephemeral overthrow—to the extent it existed at all by the Fifth Century—it became chiefly the right to evict the current government. Historically in such conditions, a vacuum is identified, and a powerful neighbor appears to exploit and fill the vacuum. A person with a good lifespan born at the time of the King's Peace would see the appearance and then the overwhelming triumph of the Deus ex Machina, that would put an end to this incessant squabbling in Greece and the macabre despotism in Persia both tempered and highlighted by assassination.

In 385, Agesilaus reasserted his expansionist policy and demanded that Mantinea demolish its fortifications (to facilitate Sparta's ability to punish it if it wished). On being refused, Sparta besieged it, and dammed an adjacent river and then released the accumulated lake onto the fortifications, which created the access required by the Spartan army to exact obedience from the Mantineans, who were redistributed among nearby towns. In 383, he supported the cause of some exiles from Phlius, a strategically important isthmian town, and forced their elevation to govern the city according to Sparta's wishes. From 382 to 379, he was engaged in successfully beating down the Chalcidian League, which had originally been set up to keep the Thracians out of Greece but became more assertive when the Macedonian state virtually disintegrated into a hodge-podge of fiefdoms after the death of the capable King Archelaus in 399.

Agesilaus next engaged in complicated jousting with Thebes, culminating in unauthorized adventurism by the Spartan general Sphodrias, who took it upon himself to try to seize Piraeus, whose main gate had not yet been rebuilt, though the long walls to Athens had been. He misjudged the time required to make the march, was exposed at dawn and retreated, pillaging Attica as he went. It was an astounding impudence for a general with no authority from his government to instigate a war between Sparta and Athens. Agesilaus pardoned him ex post facto, and this caused Athens to join Thebes in alliance, and war again prevailed in Greece. Agesilaus successfully invaded Thebes in 378 with an army of twenty-thousand, and forced the Thebans into their city, but could not hold the siege and withdrew, scorching the Boeotian earth on his way. The two sides milled about for several years, but Sparta was never able to accomplish anything decisive against Thebes. It was a completely stupid and ineffective act of aggression by the normally sensible Agesilaus and

Sparta withdrew in 373, undefeated, but enabling Thebes to recreate the Boeotian League with enhanced prestige, having seen off the greatest Greek land power.

At the same time, the Spartan navy was surpassed by renascent Athenian naval construction and suffered attrition in a variety of actions. The scales of balance between Greece's two principal city-states were tipping again toward Athens. In this atmosphere of constant war, shifting alliances, and intermittent Persian and Macedonian intervention, Greece was like a tumbler-dryer whose constituent states were enmeshed with each other and constantly alternating in relative position. Athens further benefited from becoming the transporter from the rich wheat-fields north of the Crimea, in what is now Ukraine, and from the export of its own marble, the preferred building and decorative material for the finest housing, public buildings, and monuments. The prosperity of Athens and the horrifying interlude of the Thirty had disabused Athenians of any notions of mob rule or tyrannical government and there was general abhorrence of extremism, presaging in more pristine form, the French Thermidoreans of 1794. And the cultural supremacy of Athens, in Greece and throughout the known Western world continued to rise until it justified Pericles' famous claim that "Athens is the school of Greece."

In 380, Athens' aspiration to reassume the hegemony of Greece was laid out in the pamphlet of Isocrates, the Thomas Paine of ancient Greece, *Panegyricus*, in which he severely attacked the King's Peace. This may be taken as the launch of general advocacy of a more ambitious policy that was formalized in 377, when the bungling and bad faith of the Spartan leadership prompted Athens to invite all Greeks and so-called barbarians except Persian subjects to form a league of mutual defence in support of Greek territorial and cultural integrity. It was clearly aimed at displacing Sparta as the leader of the Greek states. The proposal showed that Athens had learned from its colonization of the late confederacy and proposed an executive in Athens answerable in equal measure to the Athenian council and assembly and a chamber composed of delegates from all the subscribing jurisdictions. Cleruchies would not be asked or tolerated and emphatic safeguards were laid down for the autonomy of constituent states. The problems with this enlightened proposal were that there was no mechanism for assessing the members nor for resolving a deadlock between the two halves of the parliament. Chios, Byzantium, Mitylene, Rhodes, Methymna and Thebes joined Athens at once in what became known as the Second Athenian Confederacy. Euboea and a number of smaller states joined, which Chabrias rounded up by sailing a naval squadron around the north Aegean, like a roving and not completely unthreatening recruiting sergeant. Sparta retained most of its allies and most of the Aegean states remained aloof, as the new grouping prepared to make war on Sparta yet again.

This new recourse to war was conducted mainly by sea in 376, when Spartan advances against Thebes were abandoned and it turned to a direct naval confrontation with Athens. The Spartans sent a fleet of sixty-five ships to interdict the Athenian grain supply coming from the Black Sea and the Athenians and their allies sent under the capable Chabrias, a counter-force of eighty-three ships. Chabrias gained one of the great naval victories of ancient times at Naxos, regaining for Athens long-term naval supremacy in the Aegean. He would have destroyed the Spartan fleet altogether if he had not paused to rescue his own sailors, but his victory rallied Delos and most of the Cyclades island states rallied to the new League. In 375 Chabrias returned to his vocation as a recruiter of allies in the north Aegean, and brought in the Chalcidian League, the states as far as Lesbos and the Sea of Marmara, and signed a treaty with the Macedonian King Amyntas providing Macedonian timber in unlimited supply for the renascent Athenian shipbuilding program. Still in 375, Conon's son Timotheus, somewhat avenging his father's disaster at Aegospotami thirty years before, chased off a Spartan fleet of fifty-five ships off the Acarnanian coast, forcing an invasion fleet destined for Thebes to turn back and rallying Acarnania and several smaller states to the Athenian Confederacy. By this time, the cost of this new war had become so onerous for Athens that it had to demand that the wealthiest of the allies pre-pay their annual assessments. By this time the rationale for the war had largely evaporated, as Sparta had been smacked sharply and retreated back into the Peloponnese, like a turtle retreating into its invincible shell. The Athenians and others felt they were effectively fighting for the Thebans, who were not pulling their weight, but this had not been a successful chapter in the long reign of Agesilaus. Both Evagorus and Pharnabazus seem to have died of natural causes in 374 or 373, closing out the grand guard of scoundrel adventurers, including also Conon and Tissaphernes. They would have many emulators but few more flamboyant or unscrupulous.

Athens offered Sparta peace, which was tentatively accepted, but before terms could be finalized, Timotheus had tried to bring Zacynthus into the Athenian Confederacy, which Sparta considered a provocation as it was an ally of Sparta, and the Spartan instinct for combat was suddenly reinvigorated by the spontaneous offer of aid by the formidable Sicilian leader, Dionysius. The two allies declined Athens' terms and tried a lightning strike on Corcyra as the chief link between them. Timotheus was unable to raise the money from Athens' allies to relieve Corcyra, which the Spartans and Sicilians blockaded. An overland force from Athens was inadequate to the purpose, but the Spartan naval commander embezzled funds from allies and in revenge, the allies allowed themselves to be soundly beaten by a Corcyrean sortie which broke the siege. The Athenians replaced Timotheus with Iphicrates, who was less reluctant to turn the financial screws on non-performing allies and mustered a fleet of seventy ships, fully manned, which relieved Corcyra. But Iphicrates too soon ran out of money. War was too costly for all these Greek states and despite the military, diplomatic, and cultural renascence of Athens, the whole effect of all this renewed internecine Greek warring was to weaken Greece, so it could not soon exploit the deterioration of the Persian state and would be very vulnerable to an attack from the undefended north by a Macedonia in purposeful hands.

By 373 after Timotheus was tried, as Greek commanders, no matter how victorious, generally were, and was acquitted, and Athens and its supposed ally Thebes came to the brink of war over the Boeotian spoils, and all Thessaly came under the domination of the able Jason of Pherae, who withdrew from the Athenian alliance and made common cause with Amyntas of Macedonia, the virtues of peace imposed themselves. Greece was again exhausted. Callistratus became the leader of the Athenian peace party, and the Persian king, who had determined on an effort to subdue Egypt, which he had launched in 385, on request from Sparta offered to mediate peace among the Greeks and this was achieved without much difficulty in 371. Callistratus and Agesilaus and delegates of the other powers met in Sparta and all was agreed, until on the day after signature, the Theban delegate, the about to be renowned general Epaminondas, asked to substitute Boeotian for Theban, thus asserting complete Theban authority over all Boeotia. This was not unreasonable, but Agesilaus pedantically objected and once again logic and good sense were confounded by the almost demented bellicosity of the Greek leadership. This was a serious error by Agesilaus, who was generally quite astute.

The leaders of the Theban government were anxious and discouraged, they were represented as the wreckers of the peace and had no allies, and parts of Boeotia were restless. The Thessalians and Macedonians were untrustworthy and Athens was offended by the Theban courtship with Sparta. The Spartans, convinced of their invincibility on land were eager to mete out a good beating to insolent Thebes. The co-king, Cleombrotus, was authorized by the ephors (what was about to happen was not Agesilaus' gig), to ascertain if Thebes still purported to lead Boeotia and if Thebes was still at the head of a functioning Boeotian League, Cleombrotus was to subdue Thebes at once. There was no consultation with allies as the recently signed treaty had required, and plunged into Boeotia with an army half composed of the forces of disgruntled allies. Cleombrotus moved swiftly along the coast, taking the Thebans by surprise, and turned inland. The Boeotarchs who governed Thebes knew that their allies were wobbling and their countrymen were afraid of another ruinous war, but were confident of their fighting abilities and had a considerable army. They also had as it would turn out, possibly the most capable of all ancient Greek generals, Epaminondas, himself a Boeotarch. He and Pelopidas were entrusted with the defence.

The armies met at Leuctra, a field about a thousand yards wide. The Spartan infantry was massed on Cleombrotus' right twelve deep, and the Theban forces were directly opposite them, but standing fifty deep. The principal armies were the best troops on both sides. There was an opening cavalry duel and Sparta paid the price of not adapting any of the tactics they should have learned fighting Persians and Chalcidians. The Thebans thus pushed the Spartan horse back upon their infantry and their own infantry advanced, masked by the cavalry of both armies. The infantry engaged in intense fighting at close quarters, but the Thebans gradually reduced the Spartan infantry and forced them, by superior numbers, backwards with the Theban cavalry harassing the flanks. The rest of the two armies remained connected to the units that were engaged, so the Boeotians advanced as the Peloponnesians retreated. The Spartans retired in good order and returned to their camp. Only about ten-thousand men were engaged on the two sides, about equally divided, and the Spartans seem to have lost about a thousand dead, including Cleombrotus.

The immediate consequences of the battle were not dramatic. The Spartans were unflappable and called up their entire reserve—as many men as they could spare without losing their ability to suppress the huge slave majority. Agesilaus' son Archidamus was in command and he proceeded toward Leuctra. General Greek reaction was consolable that arrogant Sparta had been put in its place, but envious and suspicious of Thebes. The Athenians hooted at the messenger bearing the good Theban news, and Jason of Thessaly flew to the aid of the Thebans once he had heard of their victory. He was preparing to lead an army through Phocia to Delphi and there to conduct the Pythian army when a court conspiracy suddenly arose and he was murdered. He wasn't much of an ally for Thebes, but for what he was worth, he was gone and Thessaly would not find such an able replacement. The rise of Macedon, under the young King Philip, now began apace.

The ascendancy of Thebes in central Greece began eccentrically with their antics at Delphi, where the sacred structures had been severely damaged by an earthquake. The Thebans didn't assist in the rebuilding of the Temple of Apollo, but they did set up a trophy showcase for their victory at Leuctra, and prevailed upon the governing Amphictyonic Council to impose a fine on Sparta for its invasion of Thebes a decade earlier, and had a section of the local population, who had ostentatiously shown their partisanship for Athens against Thebes in the past, evicted. Thebes then usefully intervened in Thessaly, where the death of Jason of Pherae had unleashed a bloodbath in his own family in the course of which the districts beyond Pherae sloughed off the yoke of central government. Jason's heirs set about reasserting themselves in Thessaly with such brutal severity that the secessionist provinces, in the normal script of incipient Greek conflicts, asked intervention, from Macedon in particular. Amyntas' successor, Alexander II, occupied two Thessalian provinces, but not for the purpose of giving them independence, just to displace the Thessalian tyrant (Jason's fourth brother or nephew, the others having murdered each other). Also, Alexander was a man of psychotic cruelty. At this time, the Thessalian states that had rebelled from Pherae (Jason's realm) appealed, in 369, to Thebes to assist them against the Macedonians. Thebes was militarily engaged in other matters but Pelopidas became the Theban authority on Thessalian matters and dispatched a small force to assist in preventing further Macedonian encroachment as an earnest of future collaboration. He brushed Alexander of Macedon (not the Great, who would be born thirteen years later), out of the provinces he had taken, but quite suavely, and offered to mediate a dispute the Macedonian king was having with Ptolemy of Aloru, one of the great lords of the kingdom.

Northern Greece was terribly tempestuous, the settlement that Pelopidas had sponsored with Ptolemy, was in 368 abruptly rejected by Ptolemy, who murdered Alexander II and set himself up as regent for the deceased king's brother, Perdiccas. Further eruptions in the palace caused Ptolemy's authority to be reduced, and Pelopidas, who really just had the veiled potential intervention of Thebes and his own diplomatic skills and agile personality as cards to play, secured Ptolemy's withdrawal from the provinces of Thessaly that Alexander II had occupied. Ptolemy gave hostages to assure Pelopidas' of his fidelity to the new arrangements, including the late Alexander II's younger brother, Philip. Pelopidas now called upon Alexander of Pherae, still on his throne despite his maniacal tyranny. For this act of diplomacy, Pelopidas paid by being taken into custody, and kept by Alexander in none too commodious circumstances. This led at once to war, but Athens assisted Alexander II. A Theban army was harried by the Athenians and finally was forced to withdraw, and but for the swift elevation of a skilled commander of the forces of Pherae,

Athens could have made it a rout. The Theban soldiers overthrew their officers and replaced them with the talented Epaminondas, unpretentiously serving in the ranks, yet another manifestation of Greek revulsion (and envy) of too much authority or praise for anyone, no matter what services he had rendered. Epaminondas withdrew successfully but returned in 367 and outmaneuvered Alexander of Pherae, compelling him to surrender Pelopidas.

Alexander of Pherae continued to terrorize Thessaly until in 364 the remaining independent states in what had been Jason's kingdom again appealed to Thebes for assistance. Thebes determined to respond in strength, but then reconsidered after an eclipse that was judged to be a bad augury. However, Pelopidas, who had been appointed to lead the excursion, departed anyway at the head of only three-hundred mounted volunteers. He was a virtual T.E. Lawrence of Thessaly and recruited a number of dissident Thessalians as he progressed, and when faced with Alexander at the head of a substantial army arrayed on a ridge, he flung his slight force at him, dislodged the king and set out in hot pursuit. Pelopidas made a supreme effort to engage Alexander in direct personal combat but was slain by the king's guards. However, emboldened by their indomitable leader, the Thebans completed the defeat of Alexander's army. Theban opinion was so aroused by Pelopidas' splendid performance and brave death that they sent a substantial force to Pherae. Alexander surrendered without resistance and was reduced to being the king of the bare-bones state of Pherae, and became a junior ally of Thebes with ambiguous sovereignty. A new league of the component Thessalian states was formed and was allied to Thebes, but while Alexander was actually a reasonably loyal ally to Thebes, the rest of the Thessalians, though they owed their autonomy and comparative independence to Thebes, arrayed themselves with Athens against Alexander, though not specifically against Thebes itself. As always in Greek matters, everyone changed partners as in a Canadian square dance; war was as constant as allies were inconstant, and nothing was ever accomplished in these intra-Hellene wars.

The Spartan alliance and the King's Peace had enabled Artaxerxes II to deal with Egypt, which had been flapping with irritating pretense to independence for many years. He attacked in 385, but two years of fighting were inconclusive (far from a show of strength by the Great King), and Evagoras raised Phoenicia against him. Artaxerxes reoriented his forces against Evagoras and defeated him in the naval Battle of Citium and chased Evagoras into Salamis. But Evagoras played off his opponents against each other (Orontes and Tiribazus, two more veterans of the endless maneuvering and double-dealing in the region). Artaxerxes turned again on Egypt, but changed generals as he felt threatened by the success of his designated commander in Egypt, Datames, and he took over his command and carried out the invasion. Pharnabazus took his place and invaded Egypt in 374, but fell out with the leader of his ubiquitous Greek mercenaries, the also ubiquitous Iphicrates, and the expedition was yet another fiasco in the timeless Egyptian landscape. Persia then renounced its alliance with Sparta and realigned itself with Thebes in 367.

But Datames, after being dismissed for being excessively successful, returned to his satrapy of Cappadocia, beat off desultory attempts by the Persian king to subdue him and then happened upon the deadly threat to the decaying Persian Empire: a coordinated revolt of satraps. Complete disintegration now threatened. Pharnabazus' successor, Ariobarzanes, and Orontes, satrap of Armenia, joined them with the concurrence of Mausolus, satrap of Caria. Most of the Greek cities Persia had taken back in the King's Peace and most of the coastal provinces from Syria to Lydia joined in. And so, eventually, did Tachos, king of Egypt. The Great King was almost cut off from the Mediterranean and Black Seas, and almost half of the Persian Empire was in revolt. That is to say, their governments were; the civil populations, worn down to unfathomable cynicism by centuries of official venality and oppression, rarely exhibited more than a flicker of curiosity about who was ostensibly at the head of the rickety political apparatus that purported to govern them. This was, depending on circumstances, both a strength and a weakness of the regime. Thebes remained inexplicably loyal to the Persian alliance, and Athens and Sparta joined forces one more time and supported the revolt in Egypt. Agesilaus came over to help shape up Tachos' army and the Athenian Chabrias took the Egyptian fleet in hand. Chabrias also gave Tachos a crash-course on how to conduct a shake-down on the wealthy priestly organizations. Thus did he fund his revolt, the traditional official pieties be damned. It would have been fine entertainment if it had not been so violent.

Orontes, being a collateral relative of the Persian royal family, became the nominal leader of the revolt, but none of the regional leaders trusted each other enough to concentrate their forces, and Artaxerxes, despite his cowardice and irresolution, had the conceit of imperial incumbency and had picked up some of the habits of rulership of his forebears: he enticed Orontes back into the family fold with the offer of Mysia (the Hellespontine coast), a considerable accretion to the wilds of Armenia where he had ruled. He arranged the murder by assassination of Datames, and bribed members of Ariobarzane's entourage to deliver the Phrygian satrap to the Great King, who bestirred himself from his lethargy to dispatch the rebellious heir of Pharnabazus in a macabre public crucifixion. In 359, after Tachos ignored Agesilaus' counsel, the Spartans induced the son of Tachos, Nectanebo II, to overthrow his father, who fled to Persia, claiming fidelity to Artaxerxes and blaming any appearance of infidelity on the Greeks (a plausible scenario at the time). The revolt ended in 359; only Paphlagonia, Pontus, and Northern Cappadocia were permanently lost, but the whole Persian state was very wobbly when Artaxerxes II died in 358, in his eighties and after a turbulent reign of forty-six years. He was not a strong or particularly admirable leader, was hag-ridden by his mother and his wife, but he was a survivor, which in his times was the greatest and rarest of all talents. He had considerable ecclesiastical importance, as he imported Asiatic polytheism and fastened it to Zoroastrianism—this was popular for a time, but as the next few centuries would reveal, this was no more a winning sectarian ticket than the Persian royal house now possessed in secular matters.

Thebes was not more coordinated and well-organized in its dealings with Sparta and the other Peloponnesian states than it had been with Thessaly. The Peace of 371, which inaugurated the Pax Peloponnesiaca seemed to gain widespread adherence and was timely after all the exertion of the last fifty years. The treaty more or less reaffirmed the primacy of Athens, but not its overlordship, and it was assumed that Thebes would have no problem joining at least in the spirit of it. But Leuctra had permanently shattered the mystique of Sparta's army. This led to very fractious conditions among Sparta's neighbors; Corinth was well-disposed to Sparta, but Argos, its ancient foe, was raised by demagogues and the leading oligarchs were overthrown and publicly executed in a long orgy of blood-letting among the upper classes again somewhat resembling the French Reign of Terror in 1793-1794. The Mantinean villages into which Sparta had scattered that population after militarily defeating them (387), spontaneously regrouped and reconstituted themselves as a city. The anti-Spartan party at Tegea set up an Arcadian League with a full-time army of five-thousand purposeful men with no love for Sparta.

They were so agitated that in 370 they tried to coerce some neighboring states into their League. This was a clear violation of what had just been agreed and Sparta also violated the agreement by going to war at once in strength and without the treaty-required consultation with the associated states. The Athenian League was finished, after a brief existence, like almost all peace efforts in Greece for centuries. The Arcadians, Argos, and Elis joined forces to fight out again their old grievances with Sparta. Athens had no dog in this hunt and wisely abstained. But Thebes accepted the challenge and joined the anti-Spartan alliance, this time with Epaminondas in command from the start, without having to trek about with the infantry until the nominal commanders had lost the confidence of their soldiers. His associate commander was the able Pelopidas (who would soldier on until 364).

This alliance put together an army of fifty-thousand and launched it toward Sparta in mid-winter. Its arrival in Mantinea caused the venerable Agesilaus to withdraw from Mantinea at its approach. Epaminondas managed his large army through nasty weather in three parallel columns with great precision. The allies insisted on a plundering mission in the rich country of Laconia, collecting significant numbers of Sparta's allies' deserters. Agesilaus was a worthy adversary of the Theban chiefs; his government rooted out the forces of slave and lower class discontent, summarily disposed of ringleaders, and emancipated a substantial number of indentured people in exchange for their service as helots. Sparta had no fortifications, so inconceivable had been the thought of such an attack as this.

His army and position were strengthened as Epaminondas lost forces to the joys of looting and wenching in enemy territory. Agesilaus seemed to win the match, as Epaminondas rightly saw that fighting his way into the city before or after a siege could consume his whole army. No one was in any doubt that the entire free population of Sparta would fight to the death for their city. Such an enterprise would have been a forerunner of the Battle of Stalingrad. Epaminondas withdrew with many wagons of plunder and assisted Messenia in setting up its own state and fortresses. This sliced away almost half of Sparta's territory and perhaps a third of its population, over half of its serfs, so Sparta's "victory" in seeing off Epaminondas and Pelopidas was sharply tempered by the fact that the economic foundation and agricultural self-sufficiency for their long-held position of co-leader with Athens of all Greeks was seriously compromised. As Epaminondas returned to Thebes, the energetic Iphicrates was threatening an invasion of Thebes.

Athens was uncertain what to do, and instead of staying quiet and enjoying the blood-letting between rivals, and especially the shearing of Sparta, it decided to take the field against Theban expansionism. Agesilaus had asked for assistance and Athens sent their full citizen levy to intercept the Theban retreat. It did not actually do this, but hurried the Theban army out of the Isthmus. Naturally, this being Greece, when Epaminondas and Pelopidas returned to Thebes in 369, they were court-martialed and tried for exceeding their authority. The defendants argued their strategic case and the extent of the damage wrought on Sparta at modest cost and they were acquitted. In 369, while Pelopidas was preoccupied in Thessaly as has been described, the states of the anti-Spartan league in the Peloponnese were quarrelling among themselves and feeling uneasy at the prospect of a functioning alliance between Sparta and Athens. Epaminondas was sent to assist Sparta's enemies, but Athens foresaw this move and strengthened Isthmian defences with a powerful force augmented by a Spartan division. This strong a defence had been impenetrable in the Corinthian War, but Epaminondas sensed that the Spartan division was complacent and struck there and broke open the Isthmus and got his whole army in direct contact with the Argives and Arcadians, and Eleans. Their combined forces seized the port cities of Sicyon and Pellene, assuring naval communications. Apparently envisioning permanent arrangements, Epaminondas founded the town of Megalopolis, which was to be the centre of Arcadian activity. Such was his success, as Megalopolis completed a series of forts through Mantinea to Messene, confining realistic Spartan ambitions, that, again replicating many previous such developments, the Arcadians shortly considered Theban sponsorship and even suzerainty to be a burden, and agitated for an end to it to facilitate the Arcadian claim to preeminence in the Peloponnese, even over long-unchallengeable Sparta.

When Epaminondas returned to Thebes at the end of 369, he was not reelected boeotarch (general) and the operations were abandoned, enabling the Arcadians to flex their muscles, and the Arcadians seized Messene and some territory that had been deemed to belong to Elis. This juvenile derring-do stopped short of directly antagonizing Sparta, and the Arcadians were content only to insult former allies. Most of the Hellenic states were now ready for peace, if only to replenish their fortunes, fortifications, navies and supplies of young manhood before having another free-for-all. The Persians in particular wanted Greek mercenaries, which were scarce when all the Greeks were engaged in war with each other. Probably the most powerful Greek of all at this point was Dionysius of Sicily. He made peace proposals in 368 which the Athenians particularly welcomed, and they made Dionysius an Attic citizen in recognition of his efforts and gave him a literary award because of a play he had written (it was a little like Winston Churchill being awarded the Nobel Prize for Literature in 1953.) The other peace-maker was Philiscus of Abydos, an emissary who was sent by Ariobarzanes, satrap of Phrygia, who wished to recruit an entire Greek mercenary division. A peace conference was held at Delphi in 368, attended by all the Hellenic powers, but Sparta sabotaged it by demanding that Arcadia give up Messenia. The Spartans were probably emboldened by the prospect of assistance from Dionysius, who did send a contingent in case of trouble to the Peloponnese, even as he firmed up his alliance with Athens.

The Spartans resumed their desultory war with Arcadia in 367 and closed in on Megalopolis, but soon found themselves nearly surrounded by the Argives and Messenians who came to the assistance of the Arcadians. The near-encirclement was pierced, however, by a bold cavalry charge by the Spartan commander, Archidamus, and Sparta won a great victory, worthy of the best of far-off glories. The celebration in Sparta was one of almost hysterical rejoicing. The city had endured many defeats with unflinching determination; this abrupt turning of the tide of their fortune shattered the stoical Spartan countenance, and induced almost a civic delirium of joy and relief.

In the winter of 366, the Persian king convened another peace conference at Susa, still deferred to as the greatest power in the region, despite the horrible violence that often beset the Persian Empire and the court, where these war-weary Greeks sought the support of the Great King. Greece was reduced to the status of debaters in a contest for the approval of the successor to the king whom the Greeks had defeated when he attempted to conquer Greece. Pelopidas won over the capable Spartan Antalcidas, not just because of his forensic ability. Thebes had been the premier Greek Medist, in times when Sparta and Athens would have considered it treason to make common cause with Persia. Artaxerxes decided for Thebes and Pelopidas returned with an edict that Sparta should relinquish Messenia and Athens should lay up her entire fleet. The Spartan negotiators were executed on their return, for even listening to this outrage (Antalcidas committed suicide to avoid the indignity of public decapitation).

The Greeks shortly realized that unlike the infamous King's Peace of twenty years before (386), the Persian king had absolutely no ability to determine who was occupying what in the Peloponnese nor to decommission the Athenian fleet, which had returned to a powerful and numerous condition. The Thebans, as beneficiaries of the imaginary largesse of Artaxerxes, convened a conference to try to get immediate consent to the peace terms, but this was a complete fiasco. Diplomatic set-backs rained down on Thebes as the inevitable reward for their maladroitness in this area. Formidable warriors, they were utterly incompetent diplomats. Epaminondas, in 366, led a campaign to seize the Achaean coast and dominate the Gulf of Corinth. The Argives cleared a path for him across the isthmus and the skilled Theban general had no difficulty rolling up the coastline. Epaminondas ignored the Theban law that required that all Boeotian refugees be executed. He held that any such policy, or the overthrow of the local Achaean oligarchies, would stir Sparta to action that could not ultimately be contained with Thebes in control of the Achaean coast. The other Boeotarchs who ruled Thebes, took over the occupation in 365 and generated Achaean democratic revolutions. This was a throw-back to Lysander, and was an equivalent debacle. Oligarchic counter-revolutions swept the area and they quickly negotiated direct alliances with Sparta. At the same time, Arcadia and Athens transformed their alliance into one of reciprocal military assistance. The Thebans warned against this, and sent Epaminondas, who was a considerable orator in addition to being the greatest general of the time, and he and Callistratus debated before the Arcadian congress at Megalopolis (a city which Epaminondas had founded), like Antalcidas and Pelopidas debating at Susa. Callistratus prevailed.

The Athenians celebrated their success by now debating openly in their Assembly the wisdom of taking over Corinth by force, a debate of which the Corinthians naturally soon became fully aware. When an Athenian fleet arrived "to assist Corinth against her secret enemies" (a preposterous effrontery to one of Greece's eminent states), the fleet was rebuffed and not admitted to harbor. But the Corinthians botched the after-game by turning over command in the Isthmus itself to a complete scoundrel named Timophanes, who immediately declared himself tyrant of the area where he was supposed only to be a local governor taking orders from Corinth. Fortunately for the Corinthian cause, Timophanes was promptly murdered by a group of palace malcontents led by the tyrant's brother, Timoleon. With this, Corinth almost unilaterally withdrew from the war, which had become one of "mere brigandage."[3] The Corinthians made the distinguished decision to maintain neutrality, ignoring Thebes' efforts to take against their longstanding Athenian enemy, which had just been caught red-handed trying to seize Corinth with a coup de main. When most of these Greek states were not at war, they were betraying each other in diplomatic skullduggery. In the Greek context, the stand of Corinth was a noble one.

The Greeks could not resist the temptations of war for long. In 365, Elis decided to enforce a Persian allocation to the Eleans of some territory on their frontier with Arcadia. With aid from Athens, the Arcadians soundly defeated the Eleans and chased them inside their own borders, seizing Olympia and Pylos. Elis exploited the uniform Greek enthusiasm for war by recruiting Sparta and Achaea. The Achaeans posted a garrison in the Elean capital of (also) Elis, and the Spartans erupted into Arcadia and threatened Megalopolis. The Arcadians called upon their allies; the Athenians had the restrained intelligence to honour their agreement not to go to war with Sparta, but the Argives and Messenians and Thebans all responded, though the Thebans, despite their disastrous previous interventions in the area, were more interested in taking tenable territory for themselves than assisting the Eleans in their ill-considered recourse to war against Arcadia, a stronger power than Elis. The Arcadian allies stayed in the field only long enough to subdue the town of Cromnus, while the Arcadians took back Olympus and set it up in a miniature state, but their benevolence and legitimacy were sullied by resumption of the not unprecedented practice of removing the treasures from the sanctuary, ostensibly on loan. The Arcadian leaders were to a large extent complying with the wishes of their army, which enjoyed plunder more than combat but was prepared to do enough of the second to achieve the first, and enough of the first to provoke the second.

Finally Mantinea objected in the Assembly of the Arcadian Federation to the pampering of the army and to its rapine and sacrilege. The Assembly was moved by the Mantineans to abolish the grant to the Arcadian army and seek its demobilization and replacement by a "white guard" of unpaid volunteers. The Assembly offered peace to Elis, based on giving it back Olympia, and the battered Eleans accepted it with relief in 362. Greece being as it was, this could not be the end of this chapter; peace did not break out that easily. The ousted Arcadian government appealed to that most susceptible Hellenic power Thebes, as skilled in war as it was incompetent in diplomacy. A small Theban force was sent to Arcadia and its leader

---

3 Ibid., p. 96.

turned up the at the signing of the peace and arrested as many of the Assembly members as he could find but missed the Mantineans. Faced with the choice of backing down or striking hard, Thebes, under the customary bellicose influence of Epaminondas, outstanding military commander as he was, mobilized its allies and prepared for a comprehensive attack on all of Arcadia. This started out as Elis trying to steal a bit of border country from Arcadia, and at what was supposed to be a general pan-Hellenic signing of peace; outrages were committed that plunged most of Greece into war for no plausible and identifiable reason. The southern members of the Arcadian Federation, along with the Argives and Messenians, sided with Thebes, and the northern members, along with Elis, Achaea, Athens, and Sparta, supported Mantinea. Corinth was neutral, but almost all Greece was at war. The two sides appeared to be of about equal strength.

Epaminondas mustered his forces before his opponents and came through the isthmus without difficulty, but his plan to lay in wait for the Athenian contingent to arrive was frustrated by Athens' use of the sea route to deliver her land forces to the side of its Arcadian allies. Epaminondas then made a sudden dash for Sparta, whose capture would have been a huge morale boost for the Theban-Arcadian side. Half Sparta's army was already at Mantinea and the other half, under Agesilaus, was just close enough to turn back to defend Sparta. Epaminiondas prudently judged not to attack Agesilaus barricaded into Sparta with a respectable army and his next gambit was to send his Theban and Thessalian cavalry to disrupt the harvesting of crops in Mantinea. Epaminondas was again frustrated, however, by the Athenian cavalry. Xenophon lost a son in the action, but with customary Greek resignation, did not even put this fact in his history of the time. Epaminondas now abandoned Tegea, the possession of which enabled him to control the Isthmus, and allowed his enemies to concentrate at Mantinea and determined on a major battle, if he could force one, to determine the winner of this intractable (and completely pointless) war.

The two armies, each of about twenty-five thousand men, met outside Mantinea, and Epaminondas employed essentially the same tactics that had served him at Leuctra: He loaded up the strength of his left wing with his massed Boeotian infantry corps, drawn up in a spear-headed formation while his centre and right tapered backwards as they got farther from the left, and he set his cavalry and javelin-throwers forwards from both ends of his army to enfilade any advancing enemy on the wings. He deftly executed a skillful deception by having his left wing veer further left to indicate he was deferring battle and setting up camp. Much of the left wing of his army appeared to be at ease, and not in formation at all, inducing the Mantineans to retire from the field assuming danger was deferred. At the right moment and having rehearsed it, Epaminondas ordered his army to regain formation and attack at once. The Boeotians on the left breached the lines of the Spartans and the Mantineans and the defenders started to break up. But at this critical moment, Epaminondas was struck dead by a distant archer-marksman. His army without him and with no designated successor, was incapable of decisive action. Part of the Boeotian left drifted across the battlefield and was roughly handled by the Athenians. Only an hour away from a decisive victory, this was denied Epaminondas and the battle became a draw and the Theban-led force withdrew, carrying in grief the body of their leader as they retired.

Epaminondas was undoubtedly one of the great generals of the ancient world, and probably ranks only behind Alexander the Great in pre-Roman times as a brilliant war planner and executant. But his strategic vision was flawed; he had no diplomatic talents to build upon his military superiority, unlike such future great generals as Julius Caesar. He overthrew Spartan supremacy in the Peloponnese but had nothing to replace it. He seemed oblivious to Thebes' limitations in resources and demography, groomed no successor, and had little pan-Hellenic sentiment, nor any grasp of a general policy for the Greeks, as Pericles, and even to a degree, Agesilaus (who continued to soldier on) had. Epaminondas' final words were reported to be a counsel to seek peace at once, which, without him, Thebans were happy enough to do. Sparta refused to sign the resulting peace because it could not abide the notion of Messenia being independent. All the other Greek states subscribed and Sparta wasn't initiating war with anyone, and the peace came, again.

Finally, at this late date, Greece had effected a Greek league of cities, pledged to avoid aggression and to assist all others in the event of aggression, rather than one city after another getting to the precarious position of strongest Greek state and then being pushed off by the next competitor. Athens, Sparta, and Thebes, in particular, had played starring roles in this cavalcade of several centuries. The Athenian maritime league was the only instrument immediately available for the coordination of action between the states. But it did not contain all the Greek states, only applied to naval affairs, and unfortunately, in the inveterate Greek manner, the Athenians had not learned the lessons of their Confederacy and tried to convert their naval superiority from a source of gratitude for its allies to an instrument of aggrandizement. Calistratus, the formidable orator, was an advocate of cautious alliance building and general renovation, but was harassed by more aggressive political rivals. The Athenians were perhaps the first society to elevate the criminalization of policy differences, a practice that has intermittently plagued the United States. Callistratus orated and argued his way out of a charge of treason for having lost the town of Oropus, and after a few years was charged with having "misadvised the demos," and went into exile. This was obviously an asinine charge, and essentially just an opinion sampling among the voting elite, but it served the Greek mania for punishing and belittling even successful statesmen and military and naval commanders. It was a society which, for all its prescient respect for liberty of expression and judicial regulation, circumscribed rights by allowing due process to rely as much upon the hot-blooded Mediterranean currents of envy and opportunism as upon any notion of fundamental justice, as the fates of many, including Themistocles, Pericles, Socrates and (later) Demosthenes attested.

Callistratus was succeeded by the dashing soldier of fortune Timotheus, an excellent man to command risky and imaginative operations, an adventurer, but not a statesman to pull all Greece together as Macedonia, Sicily, Carthage, and young Rome, grew and flexed their muscles, and Persia, edgy and unstable, yet retained great wealth and political strength. Despite the shambles of his campaign in 373, in 366 Timotheus was sent out into the Aegean with a powerful fleet and orders to roam about and feel free to throw his weight around as long as Persia was treated respectfully. Timotheus, as could be predicted, ignored this last caution. At this point, as has been described, Persia was in a somewhat tumultuous condition and the fractious Egyptian leader Nectanebo II had repulsed an attempted Persian reconquest largely consisting of Greek mercenaries in 374 under Pharnabazus and Iphicrates. The uprisings in Phoenicia and Cilicia against the Persian king, followed by the revolt of Datames in Cappadocia and insurrections in Armenia, Caria, and Lydia, had severely challenged the central authority of Persia. To the cavalier mind of Timotheus, nothing was more logical than to exploit this condition, and even the sober and very experienced Spartan king Agesilaus threw in his lot with Ariobarzanes and tried to drum up support for the rebels. After the Mantinean campaign, he assisted Nectanebo in Egypt, and ended his long career fighting effectively along side the Egyptian independentists, raising revenue for Sparta without directly implicating his country in combat with Persia.

Timotheus, after a siege of ten months, conquered Samos in 365 for Athens, and sufficiently befriended Ariobarzanes that he gave him the strategic Hellespontine port of Sestos. He next went to the Macedonian coast, where Iphicrates had wasted four years, and benefited from the scoundrel-regent Perdiccas' desire for Athenian recognition after his murder of the regent Ptolemy and assumption of the kingship, and Potidaea and a number of other towns from the Chalcidian League. In 364, Timotheus had been momentarily defeated by the Thebans, under the overall command of the ubiquitous Epaminondas, who reasoned that the only way to topple Athens was to defeat it at sea, and secretly and swiftly constructed a fleet of a hundred vessels that took Timotheus by surprise.

The Thebans compelled the handing over of Byzantium. In 362, Alexander of Pherae, now a pawn of Thebes, made hit and run descents around the Cyclades and caused the Athenians some inconvenience and embarrassment. It can easily be discerned that although all Greece supposedly desired peace and comparative union, their Greek hearts and souls were easily captured by the love of combat, despite four centuries of evidence that it never accomplished anything for long. According to the Homeric culture and notwithstanding the admiration for humanist Athenian culture, war was held to be the noblest, most necessary, and distinguishing of human activities. And it practically never ceased, until peace was imposed from outside. The Greeks took back most of Gallipoli, and Euboea in 357, extending themselves as far as they could. But Timotheus had killed the second Athenian Confederacy as Pericles and Cleon had strangled the first. The military panache of Timotheus was so costly that the second Athenian Confederacy was in any event, bankrupt. In less than a decade, what started out as a unifying and benign Pan-Hellenic defensive alliance to protect all Greeks from all outsiders, had been effectively farmed out to Algerian brigands and shore raiders and had mightily antagonized most of those whom it was supposed protect.[4] Callistratus, a demagogue but a man of judgment, was in exile, and Agesilaus, a reasonable man without great animus to Athens, was raising money for Sparta in Egypt and assuring the vindictive animosity of whoever might become the next leader of a united Persia.

---

4 Ibid., CAH, VI, p. 107.

When Artaxerxes II died in 358, his son, Artaxerxes III (known as Ochus), engaged in the family practice of murdering his brothers and established himself properly as king. He immediately addressed the greatest internal problem of the dynasty: the ability of satraps to conduct their own wars, and he ordered the demobilization of the satraps' armies. Artabazus, who succeeded on the execution of his father (Ariobarzanes), refused to comply, as did Orontes. Artabazus' brother-in-law, Mentor of Rhodes, was the commander of the Greek mercenaries employed by the new king of Egypt, Nectanebo II, and he stood his ground for several years, with the support of first Athens, then Thebes. But that support was suddenly withdrawn, and Artabazus fled in 353 to Macedonia, which was now emerging as the new regional force that the clear-sighted might see, with the right leadership, could put an end to the macabre and decadent farce of Greco-Persian politics and diplomacy. (The right leadership, Crown Prince Alexander of Macedon, was born in 356.) Orontes seems, again, to have been bought off, and Artaxerxes III judged himself capable of subduing Egypt. He attempted an invasion in 351, but this came to grief on the coastal road to Egypt near Gaza, and he withdrew. This abject failure caused risings again around the empire. Orontes raised his standard of revolt, as did Cyprus and Phoenicia—the ancient city of Sidon had been harshly treated by the Persians and rose violently. Nectanebo II sent the Sidonian leader, Tennes, four-thousand Greek mercenaries under Mentor of Rhodes.

Artaxerxes (Ochus) again gained the support of Thebes, by giving that city a sizeable grant of money to help fight the Sacred War, and, ominously modest assistance of Philip of Macedon also, as Macedonia started to exert an influence a little like Greece and Persia had at times asserted in the affairs of each other. Ochus isolated Orontes, another of these regional survivors who at one time or another was the ally and enemy of everyone, sometimes more than once in both roles in the same general conflict. He lost Mysia, which had been the bribe to detach him from the satraps' revolt, but scrambled, by the skin of his teeth, back to Armenia, and regrouped for the next round of intrigues. Cyprus was overrun by eight-thousand Athenian mercenaries hired by the Great King, who took personal command of the suppression of Sidon, which repulsed the initial Persian attacks. He finally prevailed in 345, sent a generous selection of the comelier women to his harem, but Tennes had apparently betrayed Sidon whose inhabitants burned down their city and perished in the municipal furnace. (This may be taken as one of the first examples of this form of collective suicide, which has found modern cultic emulation, especially in Jonestown, Guyana, site of the famous pre-incendiary consumption of Kool Aid in 1978.)

Predictably, Mentor, the Rhodian adventurer and mercenary leader, accepted the retainer of the Great King, who, in 343, prepared another invasion of Egypt, more thoroughly than the first. He had rounded up 10,000 Greek soldiers, authentic men at arms and not just unenthused mercenaries, from Thebes, Argos, and the Asiatic Greek towns. And he secured the promise of benevolent neutrality from Athens. Nectanebo held the eastern tributary of the Nile as his line of defence, manned almost entirely by Greek mercenaries. Ochus had the judgment to allow his Greek generals to command the combined Greco-Persian army, while the king of

Egypt reserved command of his Greek mercenaries to himself. Naturally, the Persian side prevailed and Nectanebo abandoned his positions before the invaders had really crossed the eastern (Pelusiac) Nile. The Egyptian king fled south to Memphis, and then to Ethiopia, where he lived out his days in obscurity as an exile. (Egyptian legend held that he avenged himself on Persia by fathering Alexander the Great, who was already 13 years old when the Persian invasion was launched.) Ochus occupied the populated parts of Egypt but brought completely unnecessary trouble on himself by ransacking the temples and killing the sacred Apis calf.

Mentor and his colleague, Bagoas, now became the most powerful men in the Persian Empire, surpassing the Great King, as regional military commanders (and the Christian religious leader) would eventually surpass in power and authority the western Roman emperors. Artaxerxes II (Ochus) gave Mentor the satrapy of the Asiatic coast and he reduced a number of the petty dynasts in the area. Bagoas was commander of the palace guard and effectively the grand vizier to the Great King. Macedonia, led by King Philip, was now putting irresistible pressure on the northern Greek states, but Artaxerxes ignored their ever more urgent calls for assistance. This was a grievous strategic error, as only a shoulder-to-shoulder coalition of all the Greeks and Persians and Egypt would have any chance of arresting the advance of the Macedonians once, under Philip and his son Alexander, it developed momentum. Mentor died peacefully, and while in an intimate relationship with Artabazus' comely daughter Barsine, who would eventually share the bed of Alexander the Great (the two memorably portrayed in the film of the Macedonian conqueror's name, by Claire Bloom and Richard Burton).

In perfect Persian tradition, to be emulated often in Roman and other histories, in 338 Bagoas, head of the palace guard, poisoned the Great King, who was succeeded by his son Arses. Artaxerxes III had been a successful and clever king, but had completely failed to see the approaching Macedonian danger, and Persia unto itself certainly, as would soon be demonstrated, did not possess the skill, official courage, or energy to resist the Macedonian tornado that was now on the near horizon. The macabre Persian court farce played out: Arses was poisoned by Bagoas in 336, and Bagoas set up Darius III, a cousin, to be a cat's paw for himself. Darius' principal achievement in his career, and it was a great imperial service though too late to be more than a palliative, was to poison Bagoas. The Greek mercenaries and the inconstant alliances between Persia and various of the Greek states had started the rapid spread into Asia Minor of Hellenistic cultural influences. Persia was in some respects becoming more civilized, just as its blood-stained Achaemenid royal state ripened to fall. It had become so primitively odious, from this distance, it looks like a rotten riff-raff awaiting their executioner, or a gang of grossly misbehaving Dickensian schoolboys waiting to be caned.

Greece was in theory in a healthier state, but it had all gone horribly wrong when Athens converted its confederacy into a tyranny based on the application of Athenian force. The Peloponnesian War gorged Greece almost mortally, both by attrition and by the moral corruption that led Sparta to debunk the entire point and value of the Greek victory in the Persian Wars, by conspiring with Persia to defeat Athens. Despite the efforts of especially British Hellenophiles to glamourize ancient

Greece and minimize the self-inflicted damage of their endless internecine conflicts crowned by the obscene alliance with Persia and collective partial surrender to it in the King's Peace, it remained vital and capable of great things. Greek, and particularly Athenian, culture was rightly preeminent and spread quite quickly in Asia Minor as the ramshackle Persian state rotted, but the squabbling mass of Greek towns and the putrid corpse of Persia were no longer adequate. Improved roads and more sophisticated ships encouraged larger political units. Human progress could no longer be squandered in absurd Greek quarrels or stalled by Persian despotism. It was time to clear it all away and build larger political units. The Western world had moved beyond the Greeks and Persians and could no longer be dominated by them. As with the various waves of people that swept through the Middle East for more than fifteen-hundred years, and the Aeolians, Ionians, and Dorians who swept over Greece, it was time for a dramatic change to a higher level and scale of military operations and government. It would not now be long in coming.

6. The Apparently Final Descent of Egypt

Back, one last time as a principal nation, to Egypt. For readers punch-drunk from the squalid, treacherous, often brave quarrels of Greece, Persia and Egypt, a brief resume ensues for those who might find it useful. In the last reconquest of Egypt by Persia, under Artaxerxes, a large number of Persian officials crowded into the country to collect taxes. The Great King was, as has been recounted, not the awe-inspiring figure of the known world that he had been, and was much dependent on the revenues of Egypt, which continued, because of the fruitful Nile Delta, to be a very rich country. The continuing waves of Jewish, Syrian, Babylonian, Syrian, and Greek traders and primitive capitalists helped to dilute Egyptian nationalism in some ways, while augmenting the country's resentment at its exploitation. The Egyptians were not integrated into the Persian Empire at all and there is little record of Egyptians gravitating upward in the Persian government. The lengthy war between Persia and Athens and its allies sharply reduced the Greek commercial presence in Egypt for a time, the trade with Arabia, the Levant, Asia Minor, the Aegean islands and the hinterland of the Persian Empire continued unabated by endless wars in the area.

Xerxes made no effort to be popular in Egypt, as Cyrus had, and was referred to in Egyptian posterity as "that scoundrel Xerxes."[5] His death in 465 B.C. was the occasion for yet another Egyptian revolt under Inaros, son of Psammetichus (Chapter 3). The Persian viceroy and his tax-collectors were expelled and the modest Persian garrison was barricaded into Memphis, which controlled all traffic north down the Nile or overland to the Delta. This throttled any coordination between northern and southern Egypt, where the Persians may be assumed to have been no more beloved of the Egyptian and Ethiopian populace than they were in the Nile Delta. Inaros appeared to have run out of steam with his revolt as the Persians desultorily organized yet another mission of suppression, when an Athenian fleet of two-hundred vessels arrived off the coast of Cyprus under the ultimate command of Cimon, anxious to inconvenience the Persians in any possible way and to revive the Greek commercial

---

5 Ibid., p. 138 (H.R. Hall); CAH, III, p. 315 (H.R. Hall).

presence in Egypt. Much of what follows was summarized from the Greek and Persian angles already in this chapter.

The Greek galleys came brazenly up the Nile (a considerable feat of persevering navigation against the current of one of the world's greatest rivers), disembarked enough Greek hoplites to give the Persian commander, Achemenes, a thorough defeat at Papremis, before slaying him. (This was a more seemly and a braver death than the summary proclamation of disgrace as the defeated general, with hands bound behind him was bent over a chopping block in a public square and decapitated, as if this would somehow redeem the military defeat. In the ancient world, survival of such a defeat was seen as cowardice, confirming the assumption that cowardice, as well as stupidity, was the reason for the defeat.) The Athenians sent Achemenes' corpse to the Great King as an intimation of the outcome of the military contest in Egypt. The remnants of Achemenes' army fled on foot to Memphis, but arrived there more or less simultaneously with the intrepid Athenian naval squadron, and surrendered. (Memphis was close to the modern city Cairo). This was referred to in the second section of this Chapter.

Artaxerxes was distracted with domestic strife and engaged in what would be called the Byzantine maneuver (when Byzantium grew into the eminence to be synonymous with political and commercial complexity) of sending the satrap Megabazus to Sparta to incentivize a Spartan attack on Athens that would require Athens to withdraw its expeditionary force from Egypt. However, as was recounted earlier in this chapter, Artaxerxes was in his way a formidable and tenacious continuator of the zigzag Persian royal line, and when he got the upper hand over his disaffected subjects, he dispatched Megabyxus, satrap of Syria, and Artabazus, satrap of Hellespontine Phrygia and nephew of Hystaspes and first cousin of Darius I, at the head of more than one-hundred thousand men, to retrieve the wayward Egyptian crown jewel of the Persian Empire. Such a force had no trouble chasing the Greeks out of Memphis and besieged them in the island of Prosopis for eighteen months, damming and draining the canal up-river until the Persian army could walk to the fortress and stormed it successfully. The tide of fortunes had turned decisively since the ignominious failure of Achemenes just five years before (459): the Greeks were killed or captured and only a few survived, the entire six-year operation had been a complete failure; Inaros, the king of Libya who had started it all, was captured and crucified. The only continuing armed resistance was by the fenmen, under their king, Amyrtaeus, who were invincible in the fen-marshes, as the only people who knew where dry land existed and were extremely ferocious, unlike most of the population of naturally prosperous Egypt. Egyptian affairs drifted sleepily along until 404, when the grandson of the said Amyrtaeus, and bearing the same name, emerged from his tenebrous fens and launched yet another revolt against the Persians.

He conducted an ineffectual guerrilla war for six years, and was then killed by Naif'aurud (the Greeks called him Nepherites), a more representative Egyptian, who led a widespread revolt. In 396 the Great King assembled a fleet of three-hundred vessels in the Phoenician ports, to deliver an invading force to the Nile Delta, but Conon, the adventurous Athenian admiral and the inevitable Evagoras, urged the Persian king to use the great armada against Sparta instead. The Spartans suspected such an initiative and opened negotiations with Nepherites to strengthen this disturbance in the strategic rear of Persia. Nepherites sent five-hundred thousand bushels of grain as an encouragement to the Spartans, but the ships were intercepted by Conon and never reached Sparta. After about four years, Nepherites was mysteriously followed by Muthes, who only lasted about a year and was deposed and replaced by Hakori, whom the by-now skeptical Greeks called Achoris (no official Greek intervention in Egypt was ever successful). Hakori was soon to prove the most substantial leader Egypt had had in many decades.

There was a tortuous progress toward the Peace of Antalcidas in 386 (The King's Peace). Hakori died in 378 and was succeeded by Nepherites II, who was soon assassinated, along with his son and the last two native Egyptian kings to rule the whole land, succeeded: Tachos and Nectabano II. The XXXth Dynasty; all of this was succinctly earlier recounted in this chapter. Persia's last assaults on Egypt came in 374, 351, and 344. The old warhorse and schemer Pharnabazus, reinforced by the ingenious and courageous condottieri Iphicrates, attacked with, it was semi-believably alleged, two-hundred and twenty thousand men and three-hundred ships. Iphicrates led an amphibious attack in the Nile Delta and proceeded to invest Memphis. Pharnabazus would not let Iphicrates attack at once because he feared the Athenians would take the conquest for themselves and required him to wait until the arrival, overland, of the great Persian army. By the time it heaved into sight of Memphis, that city had been admirably fortified and could not be taken by storm.

The seasonal rains came and reduced the whole area to a swamp and the invaders withdrew. Iphicrates, disgusted, returned to Athens and Pharnabazus returned to the Great King with his tail between his legs and was lucky to keep his head on his shoulders. Nectanebo reigned undisturbed for another eighteen years and died peacefully in 361. Then came Pelopidas' attempt to gather all the Hellenic parties together under the mediation of the Great King at Susa. The Greeks were unanimous in being unimpressed with the Persian capital and with the Great King. One grumbled that the "Famous golden plane-tree would not give enough shade for a lizard."[6]

It was after this farce that the revolt of the satraps occurred: Datames, Orontes, Mausolus, Ariobarzanes, Autophradates, and others rose up and the son of Nepherites II, Tachos, joined in, even though Egypt was not at this time under Persian occupation, and as was described cursorily above, this murderous but farcical melee enervated Persia and Egypt, and the Greek interveners until 359. The most distinguished participant had been Agesilaus, the redoubtable Spartan king, who commanded Spartan forces (Greek mercenaries made up most of the armies on all sides) and was energetic and effective, and was generously rewarded.

He died on his way home, laden with treasure and plunder for Sparta, aged 84, after a tumultuous reign of forty-one years. Agesilaus had deposed his supposed ally, Tachos, whom he found insufferably quarrelsome, and Tachos fled to Susa, claiming to have been loyal at all times to Artaxerxes, who was succeeded by his son, Artaxerxes III (Ochus) in 358. The treachery of Tachos of Sidon, betraying his own people, who burned their city and themselves rather than be captured, was mentioned

---

6 CAH, VI, p. 150.

above, as was the fact that justice, in a sense, was done: Ochus rewarded Tachos for his munificent treachery by executing him to general relief throughout the Hellenic and Persian worlds, decrepit as they now were. Ancient Egypt, the first of the great civilizations, had finally dwindled into a torpor even more profound and less agitated than that of Persia. It could only be penetrated by a profound shock of unheard-of force. That would come ten years later with the arrival of Alexander the Great.

Looking back at the eight centuries of Egypt since the priest-kings, some similarity with China, can be discerned. Too much has been made of the theory that civilizations have the same cycle of rise, maturity, and decline, and sophisticated and durable civilizations like India, China and Egypt cannot be usefully compared to ephemeral militarily superior tribes like the Assyrians. And India and China have never lost their immense scale and ultimate unconquerability. China revives after periods of decay, and China's fortunes undulate over the ages. We are witnessing in this chapter the end of Egypt's important stature as a country, even though the diligent reader will recall many occasions when Egypt was overrun by outsiders by land and sea, and there would be many more in the intervening centuries. At time of writing, she is culturally the premier Arab country, and one of the leading Muslim countries, but only a middle power in international terms and significantly dependent on direct and indirect assistance from the United States and Saudi Arabia. But up to this point, the similarities between Egypt and China, and to some extent India were quite striking: solid and conservative peasant countries with strong intelligentsias that weathered repeated invasions that overran their defenses and allowed the invaders to ransack national treasures and rule the capitals arbitrarily for a while, but they were always absorbed by the more numerous Chinese, Indians and Egyptians as they settled into the comparative civility and opulence of the native elites, after the fatigue of occupation vigilance for a few generations. And then they were themselves assimilated, overthrown, or expelled. Such were the sagas, in Egypt's case, of the Hyksos, Philistines, Libyans, Assyrians, Ethiopians, Greeks and Persians, and there would be more. China had comparable experiences with Scyths, Tu-Chi, Hungnu, Khingans, Mongols, Manchus, and Japanese. The experience of India was somewhat similar though complicated by two-hundred and fifty years of the British Raj. The more durable conquerors gave the Egyptians and Chinese a ruling class and aristocracy. To a large extent in the history of both those countries, neighbouring peoples drifted en masse into Egypt and China attracted by the wealth of their more fertile areas, and by the attainments and luxury of their civilizations. Some comparison could be made, tenuously, with the contemporary trend of masses of impecunious and uneducated people to swarm across the southern border of the United States, and of Muslim peoples into Western Europe, though their numbers and level of sophistication, in the one case as in the other, and despite alarms, are insufficient to effect any significant alteration to the governing regimes. These are resistible or assimilable masses of migrants, not armed invasions.

In subsequent centuries, Egypt became depressed and dulled by constant foreign rule, and it descended into "humourless, semi-idiotic, religious delirium and fanaticism, and the dirtier, the stupider and the more delirious a man was, the holier he was deemed to be"[7] by the most primitive and cynical elements of society. These traits were not distinct to Egypt and China, but the manner of their endurance of frequent invasions and oppressions, and the patience of their peoples with frequently oppressive misgovernment were comparable. India endured less frequent invasions, and was a less homogenous people. Egypt's religion became altogether funerary, and the mournful babbling of the bereaved was a greater matter of familiarity for centuries than the elegant literature of the XVIIIth Dynasty when Amon-Re was worshipped. "Osiris-Apis was naturally identified with Hades (hell), and with its Greco-Roman 'fake' mysteries, which brought hierophants of Isis to Delos and to Rome and made the great mother-goddess of a great and ancient people become one of the attractions of a second-rate seaside resort like Pompeii. So Egypt perished., but Qualis Artifex! On her death-bed she was a sham and a poseuse" (and has largely remained so, at least until quite recently), "but what had she not been in her young days: the mother of the arts."[8] Without knowing it, like Greece, and Persia, Egypt was waiting for a new conqueror, who would vastly transcend this dreary and repetitive pattern of the greedy and often brutish avarice and brigandage of bellicose invaders; a great, enlightened, and over-powering hero. The time of Alexander the Great was now imminent in the Fourth Century Before Christ.

---

7 Ibid., p. 164.
8 Ibid., p. 166.

PART III

SICILY (410-290 B.C.) AND MACEDONIA (358-275 B.C)

DIONYSIUS, TIMOLEON, AND AGATHOCLES
PHILIP AND ALEXANDER THE GREAT

CHAPTER ELEVEN

THE RIVALRY OF SICILY AND CARTHAGE, 410-290 B.C.

Coin of Dionysius I

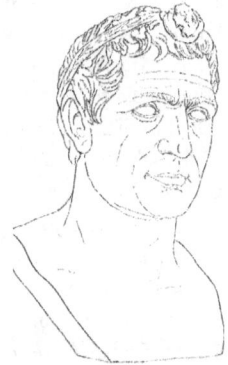

Drawing of possible a bust of Agathocles of Syracuse

1. Syracuse, Carthage and the Battle for Sicily

REVERTING TO SYRACUSE'S total and crushing defeat of Athens in 413 (Chapter 9), Syracuse had avoided the temptation of trying to dominate the other Greek states, as Athens and Sparta and Thebes and groups of others had been attempting for over two-hundred and fifty years. Syracuse did continue, as we have seen, to support its allies and repay their powerful assistance, and particularly to participate in the destruction and humbling before its near neighbours, of Athens. Syracuse sent naval units to assist Spartan and Persian efforts to extirpate Athenian enclaves and interests in Asia Minor. Hermocrates, who had been a very effective leader of the Syracusan defence in the late war in Sicily, was the expeditionary force leader. In proper Greek fashion, While Hermocrates was soldiering with distinction on a fully authorized mission, his chief political opponent at home, Diocles, managed to have him censured and banished. However, Diocles did elevate and refine the democracy of Syracuse, reducing the authority of the military, choosing magistrates by lot, and raising the power of the somewhat democratically elected Assembly.

The great local Western Mediterranean rival of Syracuse, Carthage, in what is now Tunisia, had been defeated by Syracuse at Himera in 480 B.C., and had stayed away from Syracuse for most of the rest of the Fifth Century, partly because of distractions from African tribes harassing the approaches to Carthage. When one of the Sicilian cities requested Carthage's assistance against a Syracusan protégé-state, Carthage accepted. An immense force was put together to revive the rivalry with Syracuse for preeminence in Sicily. The time was judged appropriate, with Syracuse fatigued by its exertions with Athens and with a significant part of its forces absent in Greek waters and states. Mercenaries from Spain and a muster of Libyan forces brought the Carthaginian army to one-hundred thousand men who could be conveyed in a giant fleet of fifteen-hundred transport vessels, escorted by sixty warships. Preparations were completed in 409 and Hannibal, grandson of Hamilcar, who had fallen at Himera and was bent on national and family revenge was named the commander. This Hannibal was several generations before the renowned Hannibal, all were members of the Barca family (meaning "thunderbolt"), Canaanites who had emigrated from Phoenicia to its colony at Carthage in the Sixth Century B.C.

Hannibal landed in Sicily, and took and sacked Selinus, joined now by considerable forces of Sicilian allies. He had begun to besiege Himera when Diocles arrived to relieve the city. Diocles thought better of a full confrontation with Sicily's largely unwelcomed visitor and sent ships to evacuate the population. Half were evacuated but just before the returning fleet could enter the harbor of Himera and take off the remaining half of the Himereans, Hannibal's Spanish troops broke through the city walls. The entire remaining population was massacred, and a numerous group of selected officers and officials were tortured to death before the conquering army at precisely the point where Hannibal's grandfather had died. The city was completely destroyed. Personally satisfied with his mission, Hannibal left a large part of his army to support his allies and returned to Carthage.

It was precisely at this time that Hermocrates returned from successful operations in Asia Minor, at the head of a substantial force and fleet, procured and supported for him from the wealth and gratitude of his friend and ally Pharnabazus. He was not admitted to Syracuse, so crossed to Himera to smite the common enemy. He sent the unburied mortal remains of the massacred Syracusans of Himera back to Syracuse in a dramatic gesture aimed at reversing his political standing in Syracuse. He was only half successful—the return of the skeletons of the slaughtered countrymen was a moving one—Hermocrates was voted out and exiled, and not readmitted. (Himera was eventually rebuilt as the modern Temini.) Hannibal was again called to the colours and an army even larger than that of 409 was raised in Spain and Italy and Africa, in 406. He landed in the southwest, diverting the Syracusan fleet with a decoy squadron, and marched on Acragas, the richest city in Sicily, and neutral between Carthage and Syracuse. The Acragantines resisted and were besieged, and Hannibal persisted despite harassments on land and sea, and a pestilence, from which Hannibal himself died. His cousin Himilco assumed command, and quieted his uneasy troops whose superstitions had been aroused when lightning struck the tomb of Theron. Himilco completed the causeway that Hannibal had begun, to facilitate an assault on Acragas. The battle see-sawed as a Syracusan relief army blockaded the besiegers but broke up when the Carthaginians seized a fleet bringing food and other supplies to the Syracusans. The Acragantines were almost starving when, in dead of night, they moved, the whole population, swiftly and silently out one of the gates and made their escape. Himilco occupied Acragas, looted it but did not fire or demolish it and adapted it as his quarters, reconstituted as a Carthaginian state.

Under threat of complete domination by Carthage, Syracuse debated fearfully, and it was then that Dionysius, who had been given up for dead in a previous battle, a friend and son-in-law of Hermocrates, arose and gave an extremely inflammatory patriotic speech in the Assembly, which caused him to be fined but widely listened to, and he was elected general. After insidious maneuvering worthy of later Sicilian lore across the coming ages, he became the sole general. He was, like Peisistratus and Themistocles, an Odyssean figure, crafty and devious, brilliant, decisive, and brave: a natural and often inspiring leader as well as a deadly enemy at close quarters. He would build Syracuse into an empire that metropolitan Greeks viewed as a comparable power to Persia in the east, though more benign and noble, as it was at this time, Greek.

Dionysius began this progress by engaging the Carthaginians who threatened the complete subjugation of Sicily. Dionysius took his army to Gela, where Himilco had seized the golden statue of Apollo to Tyre, the source of the original settlers and colonists of Carthage. Dionysius' debut as supreme commander was a complete failure and the civil populations of Gela and Camarina trailed pitifully behind him as they retreated to Syracuse. The whole south coast of Sicily was now in the hands of the Carthaginians and the Syracusan horizon was darker than ever. Dionysius was suspected with some reason of conciliating the Carthaginians, and he did make a treaty with Himilco that gave some credence to that proposition. Mobs attacked Dionysius' home in Syracuse, roughing up his wife, and the supreme general was reduced to burning down one of the gates into Syracuse to return and rescue his wife. His own cavalry were plotting against him. The arrangements Dionysius made gave Acragas and a substantial part of southwest Sicily to Carthage. Gela and Camarina were unoccupied and also unwalled, so subject to general Carthaginian influence. Messana and Leontini were to be independent, and Carthage was to guaranty Dionysius in power in Syracuse: this was almost the opposite result to the one Dionysius had been empowered to achieve when he led the Syracusan army to Gela. As it would soon be clear, Dionysius used the Carthaginian guaranty of his own position to establish his dictatorship in Syracuse but had no intention whatever of honouring the other terms reinstalling Carthage durably in Sicily.

Dionysius built a very large navy and revolutionized weaponry, as Napoleon and Hitler and his generals would do. He commissioned immense catapults that could hurl unheard-of payloads up to three-hundred yards, smashing down the greatest walls. He was the forerunner of Epaminondas and Philip and Alexander of Macedon. He set himself up in the impregnable island fortress of Ortygia, and a completely secure port was built for the navy. Parts of Syracuse adjacent to Ortygia were a vast barracks—the soldiers and sailors were paid and cared for by priority and the whole society was honeycombed with loyalist spies. He was an irreligious bigamist who didn't hesitate to plunder temples, but was not boorish or vulgar, and lived well but soberly and without debauchery or excess. He was generous to slaves, emancipating many, and unpredictable to enemies, sometimes completely forgiving and sometimes mercilessly severe, depending on which policy he thought would serve him best afterwards. He governed constitutionally, even if the democracy was rigged by his supporters to assure that he was reelected every year as Supreme General (strategos autokrator), just as in Athens under Peisistratus the Solonian constitution was studiously observed.

Dionysius first violated the treaty with Carthage, as he had intended even as he negotiated it, when he attacked Herbessus. Both the Carthaginian leaders and Dionysius realized that the independent Sicilian cities were the balance of power in the island between Syracuse and the Carthaginian cities. He took over other cities consecutively and by different stratagems—at Enna he encouraged a local notable to become the tyrant, then incited public discontent and seized the tyrant and handed him over to his domestic opponents asking nothing in return. His former protégé was summarily executed and the state was grateful and deferential to Dionysius. At Herbita, he was unable to seize the city but set up a rival city beside it and gradually infiltrated Herbita. Dionysius prevailed upon enough of these communities to receive, with incentivized spontaneity, the title "Ruler of Sicily," exploiting his advantage over Carthage in Sicily of being the local candidate.

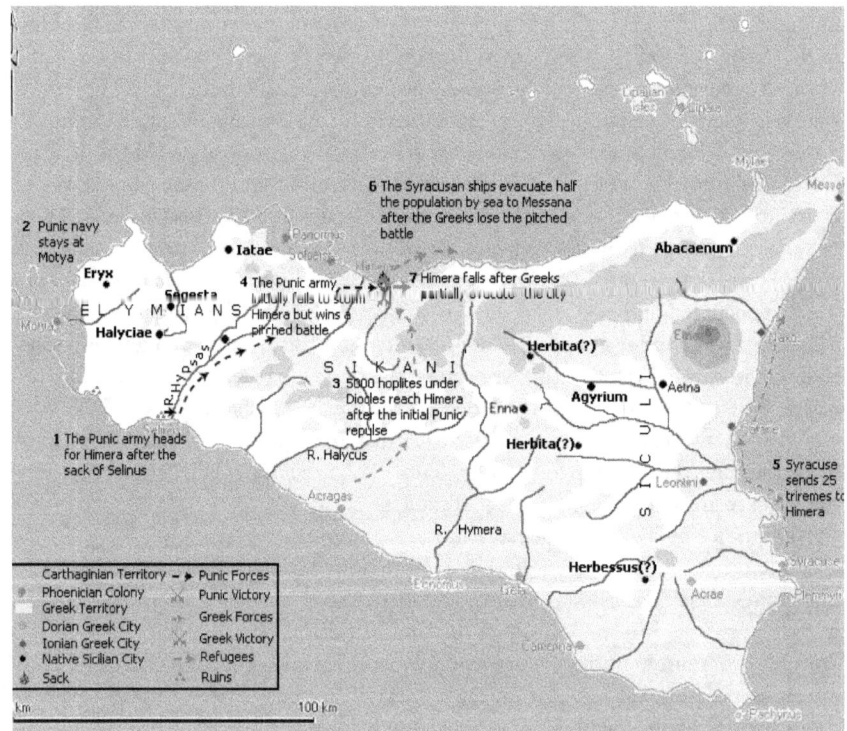

Battle of Himera

Dionysius then conquered some of the smaller centres, starting with Aetna, where the vocal opposition to the Syracusan simply vanished, not, in all probability, voluntarily or painlessly. He was really aiming at Catana and Leontini, and bribed malcontents within Catana to betray the government and then gave the city, under Syracusan suzerainty, to Campanian mercenaries, who culled the population in a very arbitrary manner to assure the prevalence of the faction that had betrayed it, and then infused sufficient Italians to make it Sicily's first really Italian city. The much-admired city of Naxos was completely destroyed and its population largely killed or enslaved. Thus cowed, Leontini, at the approach of Dionysius at the head of his army, meekly submitted, and accepted Syracusan citizenship and Dionysian rule, bloodlessly. He knew that these accumulated violations of the Carthaginian treaty would mean war and based on the lessons of the struggle with Athens, made Syracuse the most fortified and impregnable city in the known world.

Dionysius had been marching around Sicily at the head of an army of eighty-thousand infantry and over three-thousand cavalry. (This was almost half the size of the initial Allied invasion force in Sicily in 1943, at the time the greatest amphibious landing in history, led by the renowned generals Eisenhower, Alexander, Patton and Montgomery.) In the first year of his undeclared war on Carthage in Sicily, he started with places where he might be positively received, and the Greek populations that would greet him preemptively massacred the local Carthaginian minorities in the most brutal manner, even for the times and even by Sicilian standards, which notoriously excelled in this sort of sadistic murder through the subsequent ages.

He moved on to break in his new heavy catapults on Motya, an island city which tore down the causeway before the Syracusan leader fetched up, hoping to confine him to sea-landings at the foot of the town's strong fortifications. He had his naval crews build a mole far larger than the causeway, and besieged a couple of neighbouring towns while he prepared his assault on Motya. Carthage, too, was preparing a rescue effort and sent some ships to harass merchant traffic at sea near Syracuse, but Dionysius was not to be easily diverted. The trusty Himilco arrived at Motya with a large fleet and surprised Dionysius, but he recovered at once, placed archers in his ships, which were beached, and rolled up his siege engines to the shore and hurled projectiles of unprecedented weight at the Carthaginian ships, which had no way of absorbing such damage or replying to it and withdrew. Dionysius put his fleet quickly to sea to give chase, but Himilco wasn't having it. Motya had a small surface area on its island and was built up in places to six or seven floors. Dionysius built towers of equal height and rolled them forward on wheels. Archers on the top exchanged fire with the defenders while on the floor below on the moving towers, archers fired and other ordnance was dumped down on the walls, which were being attacked by the great catapults until an aperture was smashed open and the Syracusan army fought its way in.

The Motyans did not flinch; they resisted fanatically and every inch of ground was defended fiercely. The tall houses were crammed with defenders, and they had to be cleared room by room and floor by floor, and the wooden towers were wheeled inside the walls and made slow progress like lurching monsters as the Syracusans slowly advanced through the city. The Greeks took heavy losses and Dionysius ordered a night assault from the other side to the Greek point of entry. This was successful and Motya was subdued. The Syracusan army set about slaughtering the Motyans without regard to age or sex until Dionysius, who was pretty relaxed about atrocities, said all who sheltered in religious buildings would be spared and focused his army's attention on looting. The able-bodied civilian population was sold into slavery. But the Greek mercenaries serving the Carthaginians were separated out and all were crucified in public squares. Dionysius was not especially cruel by nature but did not hesitate to have recourse to such methods when he thought them justified or potentially useful. He was deterring other Greeks from serving the Carthaginians.

Carthage was now fully aroused, and the redoubtable Himilco was back at the head of an army almost as large as that of Dionysius, though the brother of the Syracusan leader, Leptines, an admiral, managed to sink a number of Himilco's troop transports. At this point, Dionysius opted for a war of maneuver with diplomatic initiatives toward the various Sicilian cities. Himilco reoccupied the ruins of Motya and constructed what would become the great Carthaginian naval base, Marsala. Himilco advanced upon Syracuse itself from the north. An eruption of Mount Aetna required a change of plan and a thorough change of the correlation of forces was effected by Leptines' division of his fleet (one-hundred and eighty warships), in a way that enabled the Carthaginians to inflict a heavy defeat on him. Dionysius, whose conduct had been inexplicably passive, sent messages requesting help from Sparta, Corinth, and Italy. Himilco quartered himself in the sanctuaries of the temples of Zeus and Demeter, further enraging the Syracusans. Though Himilco was now at Dionysius's throat, the Sicilian leader still had a larger army completely intact. The two sides settled in for the winter of 397 and Dionysius learned of a plan of his domestic Syracusan opponents to overthrow him with the connivance of Peloponnesian reinforcements, but upright (at this point) Sparta made clear that it would have nothing to do with such treachery.

Fortune shifted again when plague attacked the Carthaginian army bivouacked in marshy land. Dionysius saw this as his opportunity to attack and told Leptines and another experienced naval commander, Pharax, to attack the Carthaginian fleet, and simultaneously the Syracusan cavalry and mercenary infantry attacked Himilco's secondary camp, but as a feint: on the other side of Syracuse, Dionysius himself led a general attack and the cavalry from the initial attack had by pre-arrangement circled back and struck Himilco's rear. It was a complete success; Dionysius swept right through the Carthaginian encampment as the Syracusans lay about them and special parties set fire to most of the Carthaginian fleet. It was an overwhelming Syracusan victory and a triumph of conception and execution by Dionysius. Dionysius rejected the ambition of his countrymen to kill all the Carthaginians, as he considered some Carthaginian presence in Sicily to be useful, as long as it wasn't hostile nor as formidable in Sicily as Syracuse itself.

Accordingly, Dionysius and Himilco made a secret arrangement whereby Himilco would extract his Carthaginian troops from the mercenaries in his army and would move them by night to the nearby port of Plemmyrium, where he retained forty triremes, and these ships would take the Carthaginian land units out of Sicily. The nearby Corinthian allies of Dionysius asked his authority to attack, but he withheld it until most of the Carthaginians were away and only the rear guard of their fleet was sunk. Himilco returned to disgraced retirement. (If he were a returning Greek commander, he would have been executed at dockside to popular enthusiasm.) Most of the rest of Himilco's army, apart from some Sicilians from cities that Dionysius wished to placate, were sold into slavery. The exception were the Iberian mercenaries who refused to surrender and fought their corner with such ferocious bravery that Dionysius took them into his service.

This battle around Syracuse in 396 B.C. was one of the brilliant military victories of ancient history, more than equal to Epaminondas' success at Leuctra, though not equal to Themistocles' naval triumph at Salamis. But Dionysius was that rarest of talents, a great military commander who also had an extensive grasp of diplomacy and the balance of power between states and was also a cunning dictator of his own country. To some extent, he may be said to have demonstrated some of the genius, in a smaller theatre, of Julius and Octavian Caesar, Richelieu, Napoleon (as long as he listened to Talleyrand), and Bismarck. Dionysius had rolled the Carthaginians back to the southwest corner of Sicily and had no ambition do dislodge them from there, as he apparently considered that a Carthaginian presence in Sicily would be useful to him in keeping his domestic Syracusan political enemies at bay. Carthage was sorely embarrassed by the fiasco at Syracuse and was additionally burdened with uprisings by some of the nearby African tribes.

From 395 to 392, Dionysius busied himself getting control of the Sicel (long-time native Sicilian) towns. He took many of them but a bold winter attack on Tauromenium was not successful, Dionysius, on important occasions, did not hesitate to lead his men personally and on this occasion, he almost perished descending an icy cliff. The Carthaginian War flared up again in 392 when their commander in Sicily, Mago, marched on the Syracusans at Messina, to encounter Dionysius personally, at the head of a larger army; Mago was decisively defeated, and sailed to Carthage to seek much needed reinforcements while Dionysius marched on Rhegium. This operation was interrupted by Mago's return at the head of an enlarged army and the two sides fought it out in the Sicel centre of the island. Dionysius again got the upper hand and the war ended with a treaty in which it was acknowledged that the Sicels were subjects of Syracuse, and Tauromenium, which Carthage had set up for its local allies, was conceded to Syracuse. Dionysius had compelled Carthage to abandon its local allies, poisoning the wells of any alliance between Carthage and any of the different elements of Sicily. He had thus avoided a total humiliation of Carthage and established Syracusan primacy in Sicily, while retaining Carthage, without local allies, as a caution to his own enemies in Syracuse, while establishing Syracuse as preferable to the Carthaginian outsider in the eyes of the other Sicilian states.

Dionysius attacked Rhegium, at the Straits of Messina, as his first step in extending his influence into Italy. His targets were the Greek cities in southern Italy. Rhegium called on the help of the Greek-Italian cities and Dionysius' attack by land and sea failed. He now allied himself with the Lucanians, ostensible barbarians, against his fellow Greeks in Italy. In 389, Dionysius was investing Caulonia when an army of nearly thirty-thousand under a Syracusan exile, Heloris, approached to relieve the siege. Dionysius fell upon Heloris at dawn and Heloris was slain, and his force defeated, but, with his usual political shrewdness, Dionysius released his prisoners and did not hamper the retreat of the defeated army, and the gratitude of the Greek-Italian states who had sent the relief force was such that they withdrew from their alliance with the Syracusan ruler's enemies.

Dionysius captured and destroyed Caulonia and Hipponium and Rhegium sued for peace. This was agreed, but Dionysius had allegedly developed an insatiable hatred of Rhegium because many years before in a gesture of conciliation he had asked for a wife from among the noble daughters of the city and this was refused and instead he was offered the daughter of the municipal hangman. In 388, he picked a dispute with Rhegium, attacked again, and subdued the city after a siege of nearly a year, as they fought bravely under their general, Phyton. Those of the Rhegine adult population who could pay a fine were left alone and the rest were sold into slavery. Phyton, for his gallant resistance, was flogged in front of the Syracusan army, and then drowned with his family, including young children. Syracuse now controlled the Straits of Messina and in 379, Dionysius took the leading Greek city in Italy, Croton, from the Temple of Hera in which city, the Syracusan leader removed the famous dress of the goddess and sold it to Carthage for an immense sum.

He cherished some ambitions to hold the boot of Italy and then up the Adriatic. He set up some communities in Illyria and did a favour to all the Greeks by suppressing Illyrian pirates, who were extremely aggressive. He gained control of the ports that are now Brindisi and Otranto, and thus at his zenith, about 385, had a very extensive empire that stretched from southern Sicily to Illyria and included almost all of the Greeks outside Greece and Asia Minor, traditionally known as Magna Graecia. His prestige was such that when the Gauls surged down the Italian Peninsula and seized most of Rome in 391 B.C., they made contact with the Syracusan leader who was intruding on Roman territory in southern Italy and offered him an alliance. Dionysius entered discussions with them and did engage a substantial number of Cisalpine Gauls as mercenaries. He was developing his thoughts and actions about the Adriatic when war with Carthage erupted again.

Dionysius won the initial main engagement and Mago was killed, but in a second battle, after Dionysius determined that Carthage should be chucked out of Sicily completely, the son of Mago, Carthage's new Sicilian commander, heavily defeated Dionysius and forced him to concede territory. His brother Leptines was killed. Matters stayed like that for ten years until Dionysius saw his chance with a new plague across much of North Africa and a revolt in progress in much of Carthage's empire. Dionysius attacked in the west of Sicily and won the opening engagements, but was again defeated, but not disastrously so. By this time, Syracuse had established itself as a power that could hold its immediate theatre in place but whose ambitions outside Sicily were hazardous.

Dionysius didn't have great ambitions in Greece itself but supported Sparta throughout his reign; as a tyrant he was not overly appreciative of Athens, and seems to have got on unusually well with Lysander, who visited him and must have been awe-struck at the mighty fortress and naval facilities of Syracuse. Once Sparta was an out-and-out tyranny herself, she seems to have developed a greater affinity for the Syracusan leader. The relation of Greece with Syracuse and of Phoenicia with Carthage were both in some ways a little like the relations of Britain and the United States, Syracuse became the most powerful of the Greek states but never became as preeminent in the relationship as the United States did with the U.K. and eventually, they were, unlike Britain and America, subsumed into a larger entity. Carthage overshadowed Phoenicia as comprehensively as Brazil did Portugal but came to a tragic end in the show-down of the central Mediterranean.

Syracuse was much courted. In 393, just twenty years after Syracuse had completely defeated and humbled Athens, the Athenian Assembly passed a resolution of greeting and a decree honouring Dionysius, Leptines, and the other brother, Thearidas, and even the Ruler's brother-in-law, Polyxenus. In 388, Dionysius was going to arrange a large Syracusan presence at the Olympic Games, participating in the chariot races and poems of Dionysius were going to be read. But the delegates were whipped up by an anti-Dionysian speech by the Athenian writer Lysias. (The Greeks were as easy to enflame with oratory as Nineteenth Century Latin Americans.) The Syracusan tents were attacked, and the large delegation was not allowed to make their sacrifices. The Syracusan chariots raced but did not win and the crowd would not allow any poem of Dionysius to be read publicly. It must have been very irritating for the Syracusan leader, but he assisted Sparta in imposing the (Persian) King's Peace in 387-386. Fourteen years later, in 372, Dionysius offered to help Sparta and in 369 he actually sent some soldiers to assist Corinth against Thebes. In 368, the Athenians again passed a flattering motion about Dionysius in the Assembly, and the two states formed an alliance in 367, the year of Dionysius' death. These ever-changing alliances were a striking display of diplomatic cynicism and of the stubborn refusal to learn from even recent history.

Like many worldly absolute rulers, Dionysius fancied himself a patron of the arts and a poet and playwright of stature himself. His plays gained second and third prizes in Athenian drama festivals, as did his poems. That view was not widely shared. The poet Philoxenus was at the court of Dionysius and could not bring himself to tell the ruler that his poems were good and was sent to work in stone quarries for a time. After a while, he was recalled and invited to comment on a recent composition by Dionysius. He gestured to a member of the ruler's guard and said, "Back to the quarries." Dionysius credited him his honesty, frankness, and sense of humour and did not bother him further.[1] Plato visited Dionysius in 389-388 and neither was impressed with the other. Dionysius became sufficiently exasperated that he shipped Plato off to Argina in a Spartan ship, and he was sold into slavery there, but immediately ransomed by a friend from Cyrene and returned to Athens. Syracuse's leading cultural figure was the outstanding military historian Philistus, broadly as distinguished and pioneering as Thucydides and at least as reliable. He was a trusted counselor of the ruler and married the niece of Dionysius, but they had a falling out as Dionysius had not been consulted about the marriage and feared court intrigue and the bridegroom was exiled. After Dionysius died, and after Philistus had presented a rather favourably edited history of the reign of Dionysius, Philistus was invited back to Syracuse, vested with honours and constituted admiral of the fleet, a serious position in such a great maritime power. He was however, defeated in a critical naval engagement a decade later and honourably committed suicide at sea to avoid disgrace and execution from his countrymen when he returned. A play of Dionysius, *The Ransom of Hector*, did gain an Athenian first prize in 367, although there was speculation that the judges were influenced by the fact that Athens and Syracuse were in the midst of critical treaty negotiations. Dionysius' contentment

---

1 CAH VI, p. 133 (J.B. Bury).

was unconfined, however, to the point where he over-indulged in feasting and the consumption of wine, contracted a fever, and died, allegedly from an over-mighty soporific. He was sixty-five (432-367 B.C.).

He was an important historic figure, the most successful of all Greek state-builders and the first to create a national state that extended far beyond the jurisdiction of the city. He was effectively a monarch, though in theory Syracuse was a constitutional republic. (Napoleon's restored empire, between Elba and Waterloo, 1814-1815, was an empire with a Republican constitution.) Dionysius had a constitution liable to amendment almost unilaterally by the ruler. He somewhat presaged Alexander the Great and Julius and Augustus Caesar in several of his techniques and institutions: a military quasi-monarchy maintained by a broadly derived army. He surpassed Pericles as a geostrategist but was distinctly inferior to him as a humanist and enlightened and cultured ruler, and Dionysius was the leading Greek statesman between the death of Pericles in 429 B.C. and the accession of Philip of Macedon in 359 B.C. He taxed his people very heavily and was constantly wary about their fidelity, as they bore the cost of his immense fortifications and large fleet, while most of the fighting and policing was conducted by unpopular and highly paid mercenaries from Spain, Gaul, and Italy. He performed ably in his first war with Carthage and was promoted to high command on undoubted merit, and then enhanced his position by staging a false assassination attempt on himself, then an original gambit, subsequently often repeated (even occasionally by democratic politicians, including subsequent French president Francois Mitterand in 1959, "the Observatory Affair"). By this means, Dionysius had gained a personal bodyguard of six-hundred mercenaries which he managed to raise to a thousand, and then gained by some combination of bribery, intimidation, and genuine leadership qualities a majority of legislators who accorded him dictatorial powers swaddled in republican terminology, in 405. These were only relinquished when he died after thirty-eight years as leader of Syracuse.

He pioneered the elevation of the city to a higher level of extent and influence, straddling between Athens, Thebes and Sparta, and the short-lived Macedonian ascendancy based on military success like the ancient Middle Eastern peoples such as the Hittites and Assyrians, and more aptly, Rome, which would vastly exceed, both in extent and durability, any jurisdiction that had been imagined in the world, apart from India and China. But Rome owed a good deal to Dionysius, including a foretaste of the ancient version of Great Power politics practiced by Dionysius when he negotiated with the leader of the Cisalpine Gauls (Senones, from the Seine near modern Paris), and Brennus, to squeeze Rome between them, like Poland historically, between the Russians and Germans. (The Romans held, under Manlius Capitolinus on the Capitoline Hill, and Brennus was defeated and killed by Marcus Furius Camillus in 387. The Gauls retreated, as did the Syracusans, and Rome was deemed to have had a second birth. It would be eight-hundred years before another foreign army penetrated the City of Rome).

Dionysius also preceded Alexander and the Caesars in effectively conferring upon himself religiously super-human status, as pharaohs had done, thus moving to gather into his hands ecclesiastical authority, a one-sided resolution of the ancient and still conducted competition between secular and spiritual authority. As has been recounted, Dionysius was also a military commander of great ability, originality, and courage, a pioneer in armaments and tactics, though he seems on occasion to have become so ensnared in his diplomatic maneuverings that his focus on military questions flagged, the few occasions when he was soundly beaten on the battlefield. But he always snapped back quickly, or, after allowing his vindictive and violent nature to craft an elaborate vengeance. On balance, Dionysius was an important figure who achieved much from a marginal position and turned a centrifugated insular town into the greatest Mediterranean city for a time. But he was a transitional figure whose career informed even more talented men of somewhat more respectable principles in the construction from greater foundations of much greater empires. He was a prototype but without mass appeal, or great consequentiality which is the reason that he is not renowned in posterity as Philip and Alexander and Julius and Augustus Caesar are.

2. Carthage in Spain

While the Greeks had colonized the Central Mediterranean, especially southern Italy, Sicily and Sardinia, and had pressed on under the Phocaeans to Massilia (Marseilless) and as far as Malaga in Spain, in the Sixth Century B.C., Carthage, the most successful and ambitious of the Phoenician colonies, spread its commercial activities along the North African coast from Libya to Morocco and became steadily more active in Spain. The Greeks and Phoenicians had an approximately equal vocation as seafarers, but the Carthaginians were more commercially enterprising than any early people except, in some respects, the Jews, who have never been a maritime people. The Carthaginians were natural enemies of the Greeks of Magna Graecia and the enemies of one were natural allies of the other. Rome at this time had no maritime interests and was still a Tarquinian kingdom confined to central Italy, but the Carthaginians became natural allies to the Etruscans, who had long resented the descent of the Greeks on the coasts of Italy.

A talented Cathaginian leader, Malchus, went to war against the Greeks in Sicily and Sardinia in the mid-Sixth Century, and the war was continued by a group of successors of the House of Mago. It was fortuitous for the Carthaginians that they were engaging the Phocaeans in the Western Mediterranean at the same time that the Phocaean homeland and other Ionian Greek states were under heavy attack from the Persians. A large naval battle took place in 535 B.C. off Alalia on the west coast of Corsica between the transplanted (twenty years before) Phocaeans and a combined Carthaginian and Etruscan fleet. It was a sort of ancient Jutland, in that the Phocaeans appeared to be narrowly successful tactically, but their fleet was so heavily damaged they evacuated the settlement and withdrew. This was the ebb of the Greek influence in the Western Mediterranean.

What ensued was a primitive world war, in that the known world was engaged, with the Persians, Carthaginians, and Etruscans fighting the Greeks; by this criterion, the Peloponnesian War was also eventually a world war. The barbarian methods of war-making, including, at this time, the Carthaginians, if they were in barbarian company like the Etruscans, were very uncivilized; Phocaean prisoners of war were executed by stoning. Following Alalia, the division of spoils was that the Carthaginians occupied Sardinia and the Etruscans occupied Corsica. The greatest prize in the Western Mediterranean was Andalusia, in Spain, because of its silver mines.

Carthage claimed some status as successor to the Tyrian (Tyre, the great Phoenician city) colony at Gades (Cadez), established in the Ninth Century B.C. After the fall of Tyre in the first half of the Seventh Century, the Tartessians reestablished their independence and flourished under great and durable King Arganthonius, who is generally believed to have ruled from 620 to 540 B.C. This was the view of Herodotus, who also claimed that he lived to the astounding age of one-hundred and twenty; a strain of credulity even by the flamboyant standards of Herodotus. But there is no doubt he was a much-admired king who reigned for many decades. The king maintained friendly relations with the Phocaean Greeks as well as with Carthage. Tartessus was about fifty miles northwest of Gibraltar, where the Guadalquivir River flows into the Atlantic. The original Iberians were Africans up to the Pyrenees along the south and east coasts of Spain, and Celts in the central areas and the north and west.

In the late Sixth Century, copper and tin to make bronze were mined in Iberia (both Portugal and Spain) and exported as far along the Mediterranean as Greece. Arganthonius' Tartessian sailors told of Breton sailors who had gone along the North Sea coasts (Ireland and Britain) in boats made of animal skins. This was history's first reference to the British Isles which would play such an immense role in the development of the world's history after slumbering for another fifteen-hundred years. Ligurians by this time had got to northern France and northern Spain. The traders from Tyre had arrived in about 700 B.C. The origins of the Tartessians are a howling mystery; they could have been Phoenicians or Cretans, or Africans originally, but they were not Celts and by the time of Arganthonius they were a much more sophisticated society than the barbarous Ligurians and Celts. Apart from bronze from nearby quarries, tin was also imported from Britain via Brittany and transshipped down the Mediterranean, and gold and ivory were imported from the west coast of Africa. The Tartessians made splendid works of art from bronze, ivory and precious metals, and produced vases of high artistic merit. Tartessus also manufactured its own tools and wares. The Tartessians also had a considerable literature, of which little trace remains.

Inexplicably, the one important skill to which they gave no attention was military defence, so they were sitting ducks when the Carthaginians, who were more avaricious and domineering than the Tyrians and other Phoenicians, arrived. After the conquest of Sardinia in 535 B.C., the Carthaginians moved on to the Balearic Islands, though they did not at first conquer them; they did occupy Ibiza, and the southern Spanish coast was the logical next step, and only about a day's sail away. Shortly after this, the Carthaginians effectively took control of Tartessus; we know nothing of exactly how and when this occurred, but in the first treaty between Rome and Carthage in 508, Rome concedes Carthage's entire right to the exploitation of Spain. Tartessus was destroyed; Carthage has gained some historical sympathy, because of identification with the often admirable and doughty Phoenicians, Hannibal's valour and brilliance, and its underdog status compared to Rome (Chapter 18).

Carthaginians were ingenious and diligent but they were greedy and merciless; they made no pretense to being on a civilizing mission, and it was not without reason that the Romans, as well as the Greeks, regarded them as barbarians.

Tartessus must have vanished by about 500, because it was shortly after that there occurred two famous voyages of discovery: one of Hanno's innumerable trips down the West African coast, and that of Himilco to the tin-lands of Brittany, if not Britain itself. Carthage imposed a gate on the Pillars of Hercules; foreign ships that had dropped cargoes in Carthaginian ports in Spain could venture as far as the small islands of Paloma and Peregil off the Rock of Gibraltar, and offerings could be made there to the deities of the travelers, but no non-Carthaginian vessel was allowed beyond that point. Carthage would enjoy the fruits and be made complacent by the luxury of monopoly. Not even the Carthaginian allies the Etruscans were allowed through. The enterprising Massiliotes (Marseillais), were barred from the maritime tin trade along the Loire and Seine and Rhône, between Brittany and the Mediterranean. (Marseilless has been a great and flourishing port for more than twenty-five hundred years.)

The Carthage-Rome treaty of 348 replicated almost exactly the words of the 508 treaty; one-hundred and sixty years changed nothing. This illustrates the comparatively stately pace of change in these times—it was as if there were no changes in relations between France and Russia from Louis XVI and Catherine the Great to after World War II and de Gaulle and Stalin, or that the status of relations between Britain and America did not evolve from George III and Benjamin Franklin to George VI and Franklin D. Roosevelt. According to both those treaties, if storms drove a Roman ship into Spanish waters (and Rome was not really a maritime power until the Third Century B.C.), it could only come to port for repairs and stores and thank offerings for its deliverance from the perils of the sea and had to depart within five days. Gades, ten miles south of Tartessus and forty miles northwest of Gibraltar, was the capital of the Carthaginian empire in Spain. Tartessus was soon covered over in sand, as eventually befell many ancient cities (including Carthage).

In these times, the Iberians were really largely Celtiberians, ancient Iberians with some of the traits of Celts who had been pushed over the Pyrenees by even fiercer Celts arriving from the east, all in the very long secular process of fierce, hardened nomadic warrior tribes and peoples from the vastness of Central Asia moving west in pursuit of gentler climes and the resources for more sophisticated societies. We have seen and monitored the process in the Middle East and the Balkans down to Greece and the Aegean, and while it is much less precisely recorded, the same process was unfolding across Central Europe into Germany and France and pushing gentler and earlier-arrived people into Spain, where, after, no doubt, a good deal of skirmishing, they intermingled with the Iberians, and the Spanish and Portuguese eventually resulted. After a pause of nearly two thousand years, they transmitted themselves across Latin America and the far Pacific, to Portuguese India and the Philippines. The Carthaginians only succeeded in reducing the southern tribes; the Celtiberians reigned, and squabbles continued across Iberia unhindered until the arrival of the Romans, and then were only subdued after very determined resistance. The Spanish remained fiercely bellicose throughout their national history and up to the most recent war (the Civil War of 1936-1939 in which between seven-hundred and fifty thousand and one and one half million people perished in a population of twenty-five million). Prior to the arrival of the Romans, the political organization of the Iberians was very primitive. Only a few of them had tribal chiefs that could be called kings, and their regimes were rudimentary, and only in the face of the most serious intrusions from elsewhere did these early Iberians and Celtiberians join in leagues against outsiders or each other. But whether in internecine war or resistance to European intruders, they routinely resisted desperately against sieges, not surrendering until weakened by famine. They endured cannibalism until the defenders became too weak and few in numbers to continue.

As warriors, they were like the North African Berbers, with whom some of the southern tribes and clans had often engaged: they were armed with several iron spears for throwing, a wooden shaft with an iron point, a dagger, and a small, round shield. Their horses were small but fast and sturdy and the Iberians were splendid horsemen. The people were small, but tough. The land was not rich, agriculture was sparse, and there was more grazing than agriculture. Much of the agriculture, such as it was, was conducted by women. Greeks, Carthaginians, and Romans all regarded the Iberians, despite their ferocity, as rather lazy. Religion was a very elemental worship of moon, stars, rivers and mountains. (Spain's rivers and mountains have never been very impressive compared to the great rivers and mountains of Central and Eastern Europe, much less Central Asia, Africa, and the Americas.) Human sacrifice was quite generally practiced, and entrails were deemed useful for divinations. There seems not to have been any priesthood as such, and presumably the secular leader of the Iberian tribes led their peoples in worship also. The bull was, and remains, the most venerated animal in Spain. Xenophobic and war-like though they were, once conquered, if fairly and respectfully treated, the Iberians and Celtiberians were loyal and extremely reliable: Hasdrubal of Carthage, the Romans Scipio, Tiberius Gracchus, and Sertorius would all attest to that.

3. Sicily After Dionysius

On the death of Dionysius I in the spring of 367, his son, Dionysius II, succeeded. True to the nature of the royal house of Syracuse, as Dionysius I lay on his deathbed, his son-in-law Dion, who also happened to be his brother-in-law, tried to get in to the presence of the dying king to advocate the succession of the younger children, with himself as guardian and regent. The dying king's physicians spared Sicily potentially great strife, or more accurately deferred it, by barring Dion from Dionysius' presence; he died unvexed and the succession was uncontested. Sicily had retained its relative isolation from most of the Greek states and observed the rise of Macedonia with approximately as much detachment as the United States in the Twentieth Century at first observed the rise of Germany. Little is known of the reign of Dionysius II, but it lasted ten years, during most of which, Dion schemed to replace him. Dionysius did resolve the war with Carthage at the status quo he inherited, but the exact terms were not immediately negotiated, only a stand-still cease fire. Dion, exiled, removed to Greece, where he became a member of the Platonic

Academy and became a somewhat celebrated figure in Athens. The relationships between Philip and Alexander and Dionysius I and his son could not have been more different. Dionysius I gave his son no part in the affairs of the state and had had no regard for him at all. (It is not clear what he thought of Dion.) Dionysius II, on succeeding his father, was almost thirty and was dissolute and not very industrious, though a skilled carpenter, his hobby. He was regarded by Plato as treacherous and scheming, but Plato may have been influenced in this view by Dion, as well as by his own unsuccessful attempts to mentor Dionysius II at Dion's behest. Dion and Plato had first met on Plato's first visit to Sicily in 389-8, and the two developed a good relationship. Plato's next visit to Sicily, twenty years later, was a little like those of some prominent British writers and intellectuals to the United States in the Nineteenth and early Twentieth Centuries, though Plato was even less impressed with the Sicilians than British intellectuals often were with the Americans, whose energy and conspicuous prosperity, at least, they tended to respect. Plato was enticed to return by Dion's professed belief that Dionysius could be converted from his feckless and rather idle self into a constitutional monarch of a philosophical bent, as had been promoted by Plato as the ideal form of rule. What had possessed Dion to conceive of his brother-in-law-nephew in such a role escapes our comprehension, unless it was an elaborate attempt to flatter and entice Dionysius II to attempt such a metamorphosis in order to democratize the kingship and take effective control from him in a peaceable redistribution of powers.

Plato, in his seventh letter on the subject, explained his preparedness to decamp for a year to Syracuse as required to be consistent with his espoused preference in modes of government. He was well received at the court of Dionysius II who did, indeed, seek to acquire a reputation as a philosophically learned man. When Dion pressed on him the course of democracy and the retirement from the tyranny, the king called back the formerly banished historian Philistus, one of Sicily's renowned intellectuals, who was a defender of tyrannies. Philistus immediately recognized the threat to all those who flourished under the tyranny by the august presence of the illustrious Athenian interloper (Plato), and his tour manager, the ingenious Dion. Philistus started generating rumors and perturbed expressions of concern that Dion was planning to disarm Syracuse, an unthinkable proposal (and not one there is any reason to believe Dion actually entertained), given relations with Carthage, and to some extent Rome. A letter was intercepted from Dion to the government of Carthage urging that he, Dion, be present at any peace conference, as the status quo was agreed but not yet formalized by treaty. On this information, Philistus, now in full Iago role, convinced Dionysius II that Dion was plotting to alter the terms of agreement with Carthage and generally to insinuate himself into the headship of the Syracusan state. Dion was given no opportunity to defend himself and was expelled and exiled. But he retained sufficient influence in Sicily for the king to be prevailed upon to allow him to continue to receive his income and have his personal property shipped to him in Greece. Dion lived comfortably in Athens between 366 and 357.

Dion's high intelligence and gracious manner, his relations with Plato and others, especially Plato's ultimate successor as head of the academy, Speusippus, aroused suspicion with Dionysius, which was fanned by his self-serving courtiers. There is historical disagreement about whether Dion was plotting from the beginning of his exile or only later to overthrow the king and replace him. Plato, though now in his sixties (he was born in 428), remained for a time in Syracuse after the departure of Dion, and tried to prevent a complete breach between the two. Dionysius had no love for Dion but was flattered by the attentions of the renowned philosopher, whose presence at his court endowed the king with considerable prestige (a little like Voltaire in his lengthy stay with Frederick the Great at Sans Souci in Potsdam in the 1760s). Plato's only interest in remaining was to further the fortunes of Dion, for his own merit and as the only method available to Plato to get a trial in a serious jurisdiction of his ideal method of government. Plato even returned in 361, to have one more try on behalf of Dion, but was irritated to find Aristippus well-ensconced in the favor and preferments of Dionysius. Aristippus had been a follower of Socrates and when enticed to Syracuse, he steadily flattered Dionysius' illusions that he (the king) was a serious intellectual, while reinterpreting the Socratic message as essentially one of outright hedonism, a heresy that sorely annoyed Plato. Plato was unable to get Dionysius to consider recalling Dion, and his efforts were counter-productive. Plato's task was not made easier by Speusippus, who had accompanied Plato, whipping up the population while Dion's friend Heracleides attempted to promote a mutiny of mercenaries. Dionysius kept Plato almost as a comfortable prisoner and the ruler of Tarentum, Archytas, had to intervene to secure Plato's return to Athens. Dionysius, steadily incited by misinformation from Dion's enemies, seized his property in Sicily.

What now occurred in the second greatest centre of Magna Graecia, a place that only a few years before had exercised an immense influence in the Mediterranean, having given Athens the most complete and devastating defeat she ever suffered, would be low comical farce if it were not so sanguinary, a drama of descending acts until Sicily, instead of being, as it briefly had been, a power to be reckoned with in the ancient world, became a pawn between Rome and Carthage, on the periphery of Greece and Macedonia. Dion and Plato met at Olympia in 360, and Dion said that events could only be turned by force in Syracuse. Speusippus confirmed to Plato that his public opinion sampling in Sicily revealed that the people were yearning for Dion to take over. Dion took three years scruffing around after mercenaries, and only collected three-thousand by 357, and set to sea with the first half of those, Heracleides following with the rest. Plato seriously considered accompanying him (at the age of 71) because he took this initiative seriously as a trial of his preferred form of aristocratic intellectual government. Dion was relying on mass disaffection to rise up when he landed, and when his mercenaries learned, at sea for the first time what their destination was, they almost mutinied. (They should have followed their initial instincts.)

Dionysius had had intelligence of what was coming and his resident historian-philosopher, Philistus took command of the Syracusan fleet and was on guard for the invaders. Dion won this round, by taking an unusual route, braving heavier weather well offshore and approached Sicily from the southeast, and landed safely at the Carthaginian station of Heraclea Minoa. Dion stopped only briefly and then made for Syracuse and did pick up ten-thousand or more miscellaneous people jubilantly accompanying him on what they took to be their liberation. As he approached Syracuse, the garrisons of mercenaries there defected, on the rumor that their native cities might be attacked, and Dion entered Syracuse unopposed and was acclaimed by delirious masses as "general with full powers." Dionysius was absent at Caulonia, and the message to him from his deputy Timocrates went astray. Dionysius only returned a week later, at which time Timocrates had fled. Dion, like Plato, was not really a democrat, and in fact, they both despised the masses and mobs, and Dion called for the election of twenty generals, half exiles and half resident, to counsel him, and appeared to envision an aristocratic constitution with a Periclean and benignly authoritarian ruler, a role for which he mistakenly considered himself providentially well-suited.

Dionysius still held most of Sicily and the seas around it. Dionysius strengthened his position by building a wall from the inner to the outer harbor and set about building triremes and buying or otherwise rallying them, and by the summer of 356, had sixty vessels. Dion proved to have a fickle, authoritarian, and compulsively meddlesome personality, and was not any more tactically skillful in maneuvering opposite Dionysius than he had been when Dionysius had kept him away from the dying king. Dionysius forged a letter, supposedly from Dion's son to Dion and urging Dion to assume his tyranny at once rather than waste time allowing for it to emerge. This fooled many people when it was made public, as Sicilians were, as they remain, naturally divisive and suspicious. Dionysius tried a surprise attack with his loyal mercenaries, which led to a closely fought action in which Dion distinguished himself by his physical courage. At this point, Heracleides arrived with the last of the three-thousand originally recruited mercenaries, and Heracleides immediately began pandering and posturing to the masses in a way that undercut Dion. Continuing as commander of the loyalist fleet, Heracleides decisively defeated Philistus, who was captured, and scoundrel and poseur though he was, was so discountenanced by his failure as an admiral, committed suicide. His corpse was hideously mutilated by his enemies, in the most barbarous Sicilian manner. Dionysius now tried to throw in the towel on the same basis he had allowed Dion: that Dionysius could live in exile on the income of his Sicilian estates, but Dion was not having it. Dionysius then simply took what he could lay hands on and fled, eluding Heracleides and his fleet. Again, Heracleides, the naval hero, the virtual Sicilian Themistocles of a few weeks before, was now so denigrated in public opinion, he felt that to redeem himself he had to put himself at the head of the demagogic populists and successfully stampeded mass opinion into bullying Dion to agree to radical agrarian reform—the seizure and redistribution of land. This was seen by everyone as weakness and outraged Dion's natural constituency—the relatively enlightened rich. While the Assembly was in full voice and free rein, it abolished further payments to Dion's mercenaries, and sacked his generals and replaced them with popular representatives.

The position of "general with full powers" had not lasted long. Dion, facing a complete fiasco, had to withdraw from Syracuse and decamped to Leontini with his mercenaries. They were welcomed heartily, but as Dion contemplated the fate of his platonic governmental experiment, Dionysius saw what he thought to be his chance and sent a mercenary force back to Syracuse, which achieved complete surprise and landed successfully. Heracleides belatedly sank most of the vessels that had transported Dionysius' mercenaries and the civil population of Syracuse engaged in a mighty municipal orgy of celebration. These raucous festivities had become a complete rout when Dionysius' forces, now stranded, stormed the inner city and, cold sober, massacred thousands of drunken or insensate revelers. It was a horrible bloodbath, to no purpose at all apart from the comprehensive looting and plundering that was conducted. Completely unanticipated, the same contingent of Dionysius' revenge-takers swarmed over Syracuse again on the second night, and this time, with nothing left to loot, they simply murdered whomever they could find.

Finally, the populace rushed the eight miles to where Dion was considering his unpromising options and beseeched his return. He did return, at speed, and his forces, after a brisk struggle, evicted Dionysius' ruffians from the slaughter-strewn Syracuse that awaited them. Although Heracleides had completely betrayed Dion, the returning king pardoned him and reinstated him as naval commander (where, it must be said, he had been competent). Dion felt strong enough to repeal the law on redistribution of land, but this did not entirely placate the landed class that now mistrusted Dion, in whose design they had reposed some hopefulness, and it did enrage the masses sufficiently that Dion felt the need to restore Heracleides to some standing. The incorrigible opportunist (Heracleides) now schemed with two mysterious Spartans, Pharax and Gaesylus, who emerged claiming to represent the Spartan interest in Sicily (which had never previously been expressed). Dion saw the Spartans off all right, and then demobilized Heracleides' triremes and sent Dionysius' son Apollocrates packing, in 355. Apollocrates' mercenaries mutinied and Dion allowed him to quit Sicily, but with empty pockets. Even after all this, Dion had not grasped anything of practical politics and failed durably to conciliate any of the major factions. He had the presence of mind to have Heracleides assassinated, but all the chaos forced the imposition of heavy taxes upon Dion and in 354, one of the associates of the Platonic Academy, Calippus, insinuated himself into Dion's inner circle and arranged for his murder, by strangulation and stabbing, in his home. Calippus had been put up to it by Dionysius, who proved a formidable, if worthless, survivor. Calippus ruled as tyrant with great venality and was overthrown and chased out of Sicily after a little over a year. He imposed himself on Rhegium, but was so wantonly despotic, his own aides impaled him with his sword, allegedly the sword with which he had slain Dion. This was the history of the Platonic form of ideal government, and Plato was witness to the debacle of his ambitious but naïve political dreams. This would be the template for many future intellectual forays into practical politics.

4. Timoleon

In 352, Hipparinus, a half-brother of Dionysius II, managed to seize the apparent headship of the gutted state of Syracuse, but he was displaced after two years, and killed in a drunken brawl. He was replaced by his brother Nysaeus, who careened unsteadily on until 347, when, keeping it still in the family, Dionysius II expelled Nysaeus and regained power ten years after Dion had replaced him and twenty years after he had beaten Dion to the succession to Dionysius I. He had learned nothing of government and continued in Syracuse the repression he had practiced in his most recent exile in Locri, where the angry local population murdered his family in his absence. The desperate and long-wronged survivors of Syracuse (again, twenty years before, rivalled only by Macedonia, Persia, and Carthage as the known world's greatest state) called upon Hicetas, a Syracusan who had removed to nearby Leontini because of the misrule in Syracuse, and he appealed to the mother city, Corinth, as Carthage invaded central Sicily and Italian mercenaries moved in great numbers onto the island, endangering the entire Greek presence in Sicily. The Corinthians received the Syracusan appeal sympathetically and held a fine democratic public assembly to receive nominations to fill the commission to go to Syracuse and bring the stricken city back to life. (It was incredible to imagine that this was the city that had so severely beaten Athens seventy years before.)

Timoleon, was a respected Corinthian citizen who had yet lived under a cloud of suspicion for many years because he had participated in killing his brother, who had abused his position and betrayed a public trust. To some, he was a tyrannicide, an honorable status, but to others, a fratricide, a heinous thing. In these circumstances, he received widespread acclaim as the man for the task, and he sailed with nine triremes for Sicily in 344. Hicetas, now bargaining for his own account, had apparently convinced the Carthaginians that he could front their interests in Syracuse and Timoleon was stopped by a Carthaginian squadron. But Timoleon proposed that they repair to Rhegium and put their views to a public meeting, in the course of which the Corinthian ships slipped out of harbor, Timoleon himself clambering aboard the last one. Timoleon landed at Tauromenium, where the aristocratic constitutional monarch, Andromachus, welcomed him, and dismissed the Carthaginian demand that Timoleon be rebuffed. Dionysius was still in the citadel on the island of Ortygia in Syracuse harbor, with Hicetas ruling the rubble heap of the city and the Carthaginian fleet in the harbor. Timoleon appeared with only a thousand mercenaries; so there were now four contending forces in Syracuse, though an uneasy peace obtained between them.

In the summer of 344, Timoleon and Hicetas both set out to occupy the town of Adranum, after it had split into factions soliciting the assistance of both men. The forces of both arrived simultaneously. Though Hicetas outnumbered Timoleon five to one, Timoleon won the engagement, and he took thousands of prisoners and Hicetas' camp. Timoleon set up his headquarters there and seemed to be endowed with a mystique that served him well in this campaign. This victory brought over several Sicilian towns to favour the Corinthian initiative, and Dionysius, for whom it was all becoming too complicated and unpromising and protracted after twenty-three years of bedlam, bloodletting, and terribly disreputable skullduggery, quit once and for all and departed, universally unlamented—a man who had been the incarnation of squalidly evil disaster for the powerful and prosperous kingdom he inherited. He gave himself up to Timoleon, who, unlike Hicetas, had a ship to evacuate him, and once more Dionysius ran a blockade and escaped to Corinth, penniless and despised, reduced to living like a barfly, from the avails of his undoubted talents as a raconteur, rendering his doubtless heavily ornamented reminiscences of his thoroughly unsuccessful and contemptible but very interesting career. He died in penury in Corinth, the son and heir of a great king, in 343, aged fifty-four. The house of Dionysius, in the compact space of a quarter century of depravity, debauchery, and almost complete failure except for Dion's intellectual dilettantism, would set a trail that the Caesars and the Borgias at their worst would barely approach.

Timoleon had scored this strong victory less than two months after his arrival in Sicily, and picked up extensive stores and munitions, and a thousand mercenaries, and Corinth municipally congratulated itself on entering this arena and sending the expeditionary force leader they did and reinforced him with two-thousand more infantrymen and two-hundred cavalry. Timoleon still had Hicetas to contend with and the Carthaginian dominance of the surrounding sea, but he was progressing quickly. To feed his garrison and maintain morale, he had to bring in a food supply in small fishing craft that evaded the Carthaginian blockade. Hicetas and local allies decided to attack Timoleon's camp at Catana, and while they were away, in the winter of 343, Timoleon surprised their forces at Syracuse and stole a granary full of grain and a great deal of other supplies. Though a smaller force than his combined enemies, he was nimbler, and, for whatever public opinion may have still counted in Syracuse, more popular and respected than his rivals. At this still delicate stage, what Timoleon called his automatic god (Automata, in fact) again came to his aid—this was the fortunate destiny which he announced and prophesied and seemed to onlookers not to be mere flimflam. Mago, the Carthaginian leader in Sicily, with no authorization or explanation, withdrew his men and his fleet and sailed away from Sicily. There has never been any plausible explanation for this. Mago committed suicide on his journey home and his countrymen were so outraged, they convicted him posthumously of cowardice and treason and publicly crucified his withering corpse. The Carthaginians yielded little to the Sicilians in violent savagery. Timoleon was now, in the summer of 343, in clear control of Syracuse, though the rest of Sicily was in a terrible state of disorder.

Even assuming that Plutarch's description of grass growing in such lush quantities on the streets of Syracuse was exaggerated, there was a great task of reconstruction and enticement to return of scattered population before Timoleon would be successful. He made a general invitation to Greeks to join in the resettlement of Syracuse and a formidable sixty-thousand adult males, a great many accompanied by women and children, accepted, including five-thousand from Corinth, which had sponsored the whole initiative generously, in one of the finest hours of that city's frequently brilliant history. Timoleon was absolutely faithful to his promise to banish tyranny and razed the palace and island strongholds of Dionysius to the ground and built law-courts in their place. Timoleon set up a society of laws with a democratic constitution but a somewhat restricted franchise. In 342, Timoleon undertook an unsuccessful campaign against Leontini, but did depose the tyrant Leptines in several northern towns. And banished him to Corinth. He also wrested a few towns away from the Carthaginians in the south of Sicily, but there were clear indications that Carthage was going to attempt a comeback in Sicily, on a more ambitious scale than their somewhat diffident interventions in the last Dionysian era.

A determined invasion followed. In May 341, about seventy-thousand infantry and ten-thousand cavalry, commanded by Hasdrubal and Hamilcar, and including twenty-five hundred Carthaginian citizens of the so-called Sacred Band; two-hundred warships escorted a vast convoy of transports. (It may be remembered that the greatest amphibious operation in history, the Western Allied landings in Normandy, France, on June 6, 1944 A.D., transferred about one-hundred and forty thousand men in one day from Britain to France, in five-thousand ships and a paratroop operation protected by twelve-thousand aircraft. This was just one day, and it was a vigorously resisted invasion, but in the comparative circumstances, the Carthaginian enterprise was as considerable for the Fourth Century B.C.) Most of the Carthaginian forces were Libyans, Spanish, Gauls, and Ligurians. The Carthaginians set out at once after Timoleon, who could only oppose about twelve-thousand men to this prodigious invading force. Timoleon had to suppress a mutiny by some of his mercenaries and sent a thousand of them back to Syracuse under guard and in shame.

The two armies met near Segesta in the southwest of Sicily and Timoleon retained his record of remarkable victories. Carthage had the more heavily armed and less mobile forces, and entered into battle impatiently in a heavy rain that had been in progress for more than a day already. It continued and intensified, the nearby Crimisus River overflowed and assaulted the rear and flank of the Carthaginians, as the Syracusans attacked from higher and less water-logged ground. The Carthaginian army lost the entire Sacred Band, a grievous blow to the ruling families, and over ten-thousand dead in all. Timoleon emerged with a more invincible and virtuous reputation than ever. (The mutinous mercenaries were deported to Italy, where the fierce Bruttians massacred them on arrival.) The Carthaginians repaired to Lilybaeum, where they had landed, protected by their powerful fleet, and regrouped. They opened negotiations with the other tyrants in Sicily. Hicetas, who had briefly supported Timoleon, succumbed to Carthaginian blandishments and did another switch of loyalties. (The Sicilians were as adept at betrayal as the Thracians.)

The Carthaginians returned with a mercenary army (most were veterans of the Segesta debacle) and landed at Messana in the summer of 340. Timoleon attempted harassment and was beaten off twice, but had the pleasure of defeating a raid of Hicetas, pursuing and capturing him, and to the general relief of the entire island of Sicily, summarily executed him as a traitor. Not at all so pardonable was the popular trial by the public of Leontini of Hicetas' wife and children, and the public execution of all of them. This wasn't at Timoleon's urging but it is not clear that he remonstrated at all against it. A less controversial fate awaited the tyrant-scoundrels Mamercus of Catana and Hippo of Messana. Catana surrendered to Timoleon as Mamercus fled to Hippo at Messana. When Timoleon besieged Messana, Hippo tried to escape by sea (leaving his impromptu guest Mamercus behind). The Messanians themselves captured him and were so outraged at his treachery, they made a joyous spectacle of his public execution in the municipal theatre, with even schoolchildren attending the festivity. Mamercus then surrendered to Timoleon, who at least gave him a public trial where he offered a defence, unsuccessfully, and he was publicly crucified. The fluidity and violence of the Sicilian temperament was already legendary and has remained so for over two millennia. Carthage had had enough, and conducted peace talks with Timoleon in 339, and a partition of the island was agreed, along the Halycus River, with Carthage controlling everything on one side, and Syracuse recognized as preeminent, though not in control, of the rest of Sicily, with Greeks free to move from the Carthaginian zone to the Syracusan at will. Timoleon tamed a few minor tyrannies, and then, in 336, retired from public life, but remained in Syracuse, a universally admired statesman and soldier. Not more than a few years after that, but exactly when is unknown, he died and was given an immense state funeral at Syracuse. The proclamation over the pyre, recorded by Plutarch, declared that Syracuse "honors Timoleon for all time with musical, equestrian, and athletic contests, because he defeated the tyrants, conquered the barbarians in war, resettled the greatest of the devastated cities, and restored to the Sicilians their laws."[2] Sicily would, soon enough, reenter the violent phase of its cycle.

In Southern Italy, the barbarous tribes of Bruttians (who had made short work of Timoleon's turncoat mercenaries) and Lucanians steadily attacked the Greek presence in southern Italy. It was mentioned in Section 1 that Dionysius I had joined forces with the Lucanians to defeat the Thurii at Laus in 389—a Greek-Italian alliance. But Dionysius I was not prepared to tolerate Italian aggression against the Greek presence in southern Italy. Obviously, his successors were in no position to intervene there. In 342, Archidamus, the Spartan king, came to Tarentum with a mercenary army mainly derived from the Phocian veterans of the Sacred War (like Timoleon's original mercenaries). He was emulating the mission of succor of his eminent father Agesilaus on behalf of the Greek subjects of the Persian Empire. In 338, on the same day as the fateful Battle of Chaeronea (Chapter 12), Archidamus was decisively defeated and killed at Mandonium by the Lucanians and Messapians.

Through most of the Fourth Century the Macedonian power was rising steadily. Thus did Athens and Sparta, at loggerheads with each other and on far distant fields, each receive its humiliating comeuppance from the new rising forces that would vastly transcend the unneighborly squabbling of the Greek City states, though at Chaeronea it would be the risen Macedonia and its demi-god leader, and at Mandonium, just the rough tribe that festered and agitated on the already extending perimeter of the new force, Rome, already launched on its course to a destiny that would surpass anything the world (except for Alexander) could then imagine, and would maintain its influence, secular and then ecclesiastical, for all of the world's intervening history.

Five years after the demise of the Spartan king, the Tarentines invoked the aid of Alexander of Epirus, brother of Olympias and uncle of Alexander the Great. His ambition was to parallel in the west the astounding exploits of his nephew in the east. He successfully defeated the Messapians and some lesser tribes, and then turned south against the Lucanians, and then had the pleasure of conquering the capital of the nasty Bruttians (Consentia), and held sway over a large part of southern Italy. He had the foresight to make an alliance with Rome, at that time quelling the Samnites. This was a preliminary coming together of the chief in-law of the Macedonian royal family with the precursors of the great Roman Republican generals that culminated with Julius Caesar two-hundred years later. Epirus was over-reaching; however, the Tarentines soon realized they had enlisted not a liberator, but an aspiring conqueror,

---

2 CAH, VI, p. 299 (R. Hackforth).

and turned against Alexander, who made war on those he had come to assist. The Lucanians and Bruttians took advantage of this drastic mission-change of Alexander's and attacked him in great force at Pandosia in 331. Alexander of Epirus fought bravely to the end, worthily of his sister and brother-in-law and nephew, and when he had been completely defeated, he was stabbed in the back by a Lucanian exile serving him, and attempting, presumably, to secure his own safety when captured by his countrymen. Tarentum pluckily continued to recruit assistance in its fight to retain its independence, first from Cleonymus of Sparta, and later from Pyrrhus, but was soon rolled over and gathered in by the great Roman juggernaut as it accelerated out in all directions with a new formula for world domination.

5. Agathocles, Sicily and Carthage

There came at the late date of 321, very surprisingly, the greatest of all Sicilian leaders, more talented even than Dionysius, and more powerful, if less virtuous, than Timoleon: Agathocles. Timoleon appeared to have rescued and stabilized Sicily, when he died in 337 B.C. Sixty thousand settlers from Greece had made good the terrible losses of all the Sicilian wars, the last major exodus of colonists from Greece—many centuries later there would be millions of emigrants, but no colonists. The native Sicels had now been almost completely Hellenized. Timoleon, as was recounted in Section 4, wrought a miracle, but broad-minded Corinthian as he was, he could not cure the Siciliotes (as they were called) of their envious, vengeful, and violent nature. He had formed an alliance of the Greek city states of Sicily and began (with Agyrium) the Roman practice of granting Syracusan citizenship to deserving towns. Timoleon had tried to steer a median course between mob rule and oligarchic self-serving despotism. The self-styled "Six Hundred," a wealthy group of agitators and what would be called today special interests, constituted a powerful force for oligarchic government, led by Heracleides and Sosistratus. They made a preemptive strike against too general a popularization of Syracusan government. They were confounded, outwitted, and defeated by Agathocles.

Agathocles was born in Thermae, a Carthaginian town in Sicily, in 361 B.C. His father allegedly threw him out at birth as an unwanted dependent, to perish in the elements, but he was secretly rescued by his mother and was raised by his maternal uncle. At age seven, he was returned to his father who taught him the craft of pottery. He may have been the most politically successful potter in history. In 343, with his father and elder brother, Antander, he answered Timoleon's call for settlers, and they all moved to Syracuse. Antander worked his way in with the Six Hundred, and was eventually elected general. (He had no military qualifications for such an office.) Agathocles agitated for the same sort of elevation but never penetrated farther up the ranks than chiliarch or captain of one-thousand men. He had been advanced by being the protégé of a wealthy patron, Damas, whose widow he later married. He did gain some distinction in actions against Aetna and Acragas, and gained his promotions in combat service. In about 325, he went on a larger expedition against the Bruttians and again distinguished himself but was denied rightful recognition and promotion by Heracleides and Sosistratus, presumably because they were frightened by his incandescent ambition and indications of leadership skills, as well as military efficacy and courage.

It seems to have been impatience at his unjustly sluggish advance up the ranks, stalling at the rank of chiliarch, that caused him to try his hand at political intrigue. He had been a capable soldier but in Sicilian politics, with its endless maneuvering and chicanery, he would prove a field marshal. Agathocles had the raw courage to attack Sosistratus in the Assembly as the unauthorized dictator he was, and Sosistratus carried a bill against Agathocles and his followers and had him banished. They fled and were pursued by Sosistratus' enforcers. It all rushed to Sosistratus' head, and he allowed Agathocles to frighten him with the spectre of frontal opposition and Sosistratus gained acceptance of a sizeable corps of guardsmen for himself. This was the beginning, unwittingly generated by Agathocles, of the bloodiest civil war of the countless episodes of such conflicts in Sicilian history. Agathocles took refuge in southern Italy and entered the service of Taranto for a time, but they soon suspected his integrity and released him. He then became a pirate and specialized in seizing and looting Syracusan ships. His big chance came in 322 and he seized it: Heracleides and Sosistratus attacked Rhegium with an amphibious force, and Agathocles rounded up a gang of drifters, exiles, scoundrels, and mountebanks like himself, and defeated and humiliated his former tormenters. On the news of the ludicrous failure of their mission, the Assembly, ruthless and vindictive as mobs always are, sacked them as leaders of Syracuse and banished them. Agathocles was recalled and the two deposed leaders pulled all the levers they could reach to aggravate the always susceptible Sicilians to vengeance. They sought allies in the Sicilian communities and refugees of the Western Mediterranean, and made open alliance with Gela, Acragas, and Carthage.

This soon produced mayhem, and soon enough the level of vigorous hostility that has been the vocation of Sicilians from before Dionysius to modern Sicilian politics and some of its more traditional emulators, such as the more famous members of the inter-war Sicilian underground community of Chicago. From Dionysius to Al Capone was twenty-three centuries but not enough time for people to evolve much. This would be "Bellum omnium contra omnes;" total war against everyone, as only the Sicilians can do it. A struggle for control of Syracuse ensued in the Civil War of 321-319 B.C. Again, Agathocles performed with courage and ingenuity. In Gela he led to freedom a column that had made an imprudent raid on the city and had become trapped within it, and was in 319 appointed "general plenipotentiary in command of Sicilian fortifications," an important position he would soon turn to personal account. At the prospect of a possible war with Carthage, the Syracusan government, disheveled and factionalized though it was, recruited another champion from Corinth, hoping for a reprise of the Timoleon magic. Acestorides was the new man, but his methods were generally confined to diplomacy, a skill for which Sicilians have rarely been well-suited. Agathocles was, at Acestorides' insistence, again accused of plotting to take over the government and become a tyrant and was banished. It has been alleged that he narrowly escaped assassination, but only went cross-island about thirty miles to Morgantia, and immediately began assembling an army to attack the revenant Sosistratus and Heracleides. He engineered a blockade of

Syracuse, and the oligarchs were frightened into inviting his return in 317.

He had grown stronger with each twist in his career and now, on swearing fidelity to the constitution (to which no one since Timoleon had paid the slightest attention), was invested as "Strategus and guardian of the peace." Whether he had been planning to become a tyrant before or not, he certainly was now; the accusation was father to the offense. He obtained a commission to put down a scruffy conflict in one of the inland Sicilian cities, and rounded up an army of like-minded adventurers and brigands and unleashed an instant war on the regime. This made no pretense at anything but the naked power grab that it was, though it must be said that while his opponents were prescient to see in him what he could become, they overreacted on the facts. He was unjustly held back in the army and unjustly exiled, certainly on the first occasion and perhaps the second. The political ambiance of Syracuse was extremely intense and violent, and Agathocles aggravated those conditions but certainly was not responsible for their outbreak.

His initial blow was to seize forty of the leading figures among the Six Hundred and summarily execute them. This was a mere sorbet for the sustained street battle that followed; all those political personalities who could not escape over the walls or hide, were slain, or those taken alive were executed at once. He claimed that he was only defending himself from an attempt against him, which was almost certainly at least partly true: there must have been many who would have been consolable if Agathocles had been assassinated. Claiming to be responding to the relatively minor misgivings that were expressed following what had been a ruthless and grossly uncalled for massacre, Agathocles purported to resign his position and withdraw from public life: confident of a popular importuning that he remain, which did occur, but was amplified by his claque of worshipful followers. Unsurprisingly, he consented to do so, in Dionysius' old title of "General Plenipotentiary" and he would remain there for twelve years (316-304).

Agathocles wrote the public relations playbook for an incoming reform administration: he seized and redistributed land, moved around affably and easily among the people, dispensed with his bodyguard of mercenaries (and had un-uniformed local loyalists instead), and had all the airs and self-confidence of a popular leader. He maintained the trappings of constitutional government, including republican coinage without his likeness on it. Heracleides vanished, but the resourceful Sosistratus, bucking for reinstallation as Agathocles' nemesis, rallied about six-thousand of the Syracusans dispossessed and banished by Agathocles and padded around the island seeking the support of other Sicilian cities who did not wish Syracuse governed by so vigorous and assertive a leader as the new "General Plenipotentiary."

He rounded up some support, which was all the pretext Agathocles needed to start attacking and subjugating other Sicilian governments that would give aid and comfort to the new outlaws (and former legitimate, if completely unscrupulous, even by the standards of Sicily, rulers). He struck up the old mantra of Dionysius that Syracuse was not safe so long as the neighboring cities were in the hands of enemies (of his). He began his campaign against these enemies with Messana in 315, but these assaults were unsuccessful, a rocky start to the drive for municipal security. In 314, Messana, Gela, and Acragas, jointly invited a roving Spartan adventurer, Prince Acrotatus, to lead a coalition against Agathocles. Acrotatus arrived from Tarentum (Taranto) in 314 with a small fleet and his own officer corps. Acrotatus did not adequately appreciate the cultural distinctions between Sparta and Sicily and his attempt to impose Spartan disciplinary standards led to a general mutiny, to which he replied by an attempted assassination of Sosistratus, who foiled the plot, roused his followers, and Acrotatus, yesterday's scourge of Agathocles, fled from his command and narrowly escaped being stoned to death. It was a harrowing escape. The three refractory cities, on the heels of this fiasco, made their peace with Agathocles, accepting his nominal suzerainty and retaining their autonomy.

Agathocles observed these terms in the following year, but in 312 successfully attacked Messana, as well as a number of lesser cities. Messana and all the others surrendered, granted liberal terms of submission as long as they handed over political fugitives from Syracuse for summary execution in situ. With Sicily's traditional blasé attitude to death, as if everyone had nine lives, this was not a problematic condition, and Agathocles thus gave all Sicily a thorough house-cleaning of his self-identified enemies. Even Sosistratus found it prudent to depart Sicily at this unpromising point.

Agathocles had cowed Sicilians, no small or bloodless achievement, but he incited the animosity of a more powerful adversary, Carthage. The Punic (Carthaginian) governor in Sicily, Hamilcar, had mediated Sicilian problems for some years, including the return of Agathocles after his second exile, and he made it clear that he had no objection to Agathocles asserting himself on the other towns of Sicily. However, the consolidation of all of Sicily under one ruler was, as in Dionysian times, interpreted by the home government of Carthage to be an unacceptable threat to Carthage's position in Sicily. They were always happy to stoke Sicilian bloodlust against each other, and even enjoyed being a coordinating spectator in it, but they were concerned by any threat to their position in Sicily, and that was what Agathocles now represented. Carthage warned Agathocles of its disquiet after the surrender of Messana in 312, and replaced Hamilcar with another Hamilcar, son of Gisgo, with a more purposeful mandate. Agathocles went to reduce Acragas but found a fleet of sixty Carthaginian vessels ready to assist in the defense of the city and he withdrew. He offered battle to a Carthaginian force that was assembled midway between Gela and Acragas at Monte St. Angelo, but the Carthaginians did not move, and Agathocles knew better than to charge uphill at an entrenched Carthaginian army. It was the last thing Agathocles would have wanted, but he was drawing Rome and Carthage toward each other, to determine which was the leading power of the West, a contest from which, by its leader's impetuosity, Syracuse would exclude itself.

In 311, Carthage sent a large expeditionary force to Sicily. Despite storms that wrecked some of the transporting fleet, Hamilcar Gisgo in the spring of 311 led a combined Carthaginian-Acragan army of forty-five thousand. He returned to Monte St. Angelo (then Mt. Ecnomus), and Agathocles installed himself at Gela, which was astutely maintaining a judicious neutrality. Agathocles stormed the Carthaginian position, though his army was smaller than Hamilcar's and he was attacking a well-prepared position. He charged several times and only then did a hidden cavalry brigade come up from the seacoast and overwhelm Agathocles' flank. His army was routed, the Syracusan cavalry fled, and the Carthaginian cavalry went through and back across the retreating Syracusans, laying about them without mercy. Agathocles suffered a decisive beating and lost over seven-thousand dead (to five-hundred Carthaginians). Yet another siege of Syracuse impended; Agathocles managed to get his harvest in in the summer of 311, but Hamilcar Gisgo had no difficulty flopping all the dependent cities of Syracuse back into the ranks of its enemies in the usual tidal nature of unprincipled fortune and invested Syracuse by land and sea through to 310.

As spring came and the blockade continued, famine loomed and disaster with it. In this desperate condition it must be said that Agathocles, who up to this point had been a routine political trickster and uneven military leader, unimaginably devised a plan of astounding boldness and originality. He conceived of sneaking a force past the naval blockade and invading Africa adjacent to Carthage, which had never had to consider an invasion and had no preparations for it. In order to exact the tax revenues needed, for a purpose he declined to divulge, Agathocles had to resort to summary public executions of tax evaders by ceremonious decapitation, not a civic morale booster, but a fairly good incentive to tax-payers to pay their taxes. He scrabbled together a motley fleet and exploited the approach of a convoy of grain-ships to steal out of harbor. He was overtaken by part of the Carthaginian navy just as he made landfall at Cape Bon, seventy miles from Carthage. He got his men ashore and burned his ships; this was really rolling the dice. The towns on the road to Carthage were completely undefended and the Sicilians (mainly Greek mercenaries, in fact) marched through spectacularly productive wheatfields toward their objective. The initial fear in Carthage was that Hamilcar must have been defeated and his fleet destroyed for the Syracusans to be conducting the only anabasis (suborned invasion) of Greeks in Africa in history. (Pericles' expedition to Egypt was by invitation.) Hamilcar's fleet soon assured the capital that this was a desperation move by Agathocles and a citizens' army of forty-thousand was hastily got together and sent out to repel the invader. Against this, Agathocles only had thirty-five hundred Syracusans and ten-thousand mercenaries.

Agathocles was confident that the Carthaginian defence force would not be remotely as capable as their real army and he was correct. They were brave but disorganized. The best unit, a division led by a real general, Hanno, charged early but was fought to a standstill, and retreated in broken formations after their leader was slain. The other section of the Carthaginian army, led by Bomilcar (a rival of Hanno), began to withdraw when Hanno got into serious problems and was never brought to bear. It was soon consumed in a somewhat unprofessional retreat, and only the fact that it was very close to Carthage prevented Agathocles from shattering this force completely. There was panic in Carthage and human sacrifices to appease Moloch, but the city rallied. Agathocles cut Carthage off from its food supplies, and set up a base for this at Tunis, fourteen miles away. He beat off counterattacks and made contact with Libyans who greeted him as a liberator from the Carthaginian oppressor. At the end of 310, he seemed to have a serious foothold in Africa and had succeeded in forcing Carthage to relax its grip on Syracuse.

Once again, Syracuse had repulsed an apparently invincible besieging power.

This operation by Agathocles has been compared by classicists to Hannibals' surprise attack on Rome a century later when he was hard-pressed at Capua. But it even slightly resembles the sublime movement of United Nations forces bottled up at Pusan at the southern end of the Korean Peninsula, on Inchon in 1950, when ninety-thousand men were disembarked in fifty-seven minutes straight onto the piers by General Douglas MacArthur, and they destroyed the North Korean army completely in ten days. It was not so successful as MacArthur's masterpiece but was from a more desperate position by an infinitely weaker power against a relatively much more formidable adversary. The action raises Agathocles above the level of a run-of-the-mill demagogue, charlatan, and adventurer, to at least the Alcibiades class of adventurer and Dionysian class of Mediterranean dictator.

Agathocles now got the idea that he should turn this raid, which had obliged the Carthaginians to relax their strangle-hold on Syracuse, into a durable presence in Africa; his tactical genius was permutating into poor strategy. He built a naval base at Aspis, twenty miles south of Cape Bon, and offered a joint venture to a former officer of Alexander the Great, Ophellas, who had served Ptolemy I as semi-autonomous viceroy of Cyrene (Cyrenaica, eastern Libya). Ophellas set about recruiting an army of Greek mercenaries about the size of Agathocles' own force in Africa, and they were aiming at the complete overthrow of Carthage. This was not realistic considering the power of Carthage on land and sea when its forces were concentrated; the Syracusan had forgotten the severe beating he had received at Monte Angelo less than two years before, from a serious Carthaginian army.

Even if this project with Ophellas had been successful, it is not clear why he would imagine that Ophellas would be easier to deal with than the Carthaginians. By the spring of 309, Carthage had returned most of its Sicilian army home and it was clearly stronger and closer than any mercenary pantomime horse that Agathocles and Ophellas could patch together. Furthermore, Agathocles' exactions from the Libyans were at least as onerous as the impositions of the Carthaginians and the friendly reception the Syracusan initially received in Libya began to sour. The Libyans began paying tribute to Carthage again, to get rid of Agathocles, and his payment of his mercenaries fell into arears, always a dangerous condition. The Carthaginians lost several engagements to Agathocles, including an attempt to recapture Tunis, but the balance was tilting back in their favour now that they were regaining and defending their homeland.

Ophellas had assembled his force and marched along the Tripoli coast to link up with his ally, but it was immediately clear that this was a very uneasy tandem. The two supposedly co-equal commanders did not like each other, and a rivalry developed at once. Agathocles saw where his original plan was leading and introduced a dramatic change of plan by the application of his customary methods: he murdered Ophellas, and informed his army of mercenaries that he was now the unitary commander. Nasty though it was, it must be admitted that it was another bold step by Agathocles; he advised Ophellas' men that he had reason to anticipate treachery from Ophellas but that he esteemed them, and they could count on his integrity as their new Syracusan comrades and the other lot of Greek mercenaries that he had brought to Africa could attest. In general, mercenaries, people who hire themselves out, have little loyalty and an even greater tendency than most people to believe what it suits them to wish, so they generally took him at his word. They didn't owe much to the deceased man who had recruited them.

Agathocles had doubled the size of his army and it hadn't cost him a drachma, but there is no reason to believe that he had planned such a violent turn when he entered into his arrangement with Ophellas. But unfortunately for him, sorting things out in his own army prevented him from taking full advantage of convulsions in Carthage. Bomilcar, who had withdrawn prematurely before Carthage in 310 when his co-commander Hanno was in difficulties, attempted a coup d'état somewhat like Agathocles' in 316, in Carthage in 309. He met with no popular support and turned his loyal troops loose on Carthage to try to intimidate and butcher his way to power. But an adequate number of soldiers rallied to the legitimate government and Bomilcar was overwhelmed, captured, and after a drumhead court martial was, with some reason for once in these radical ancient denouements, executed on the charge of treason. Carthage now closed ranks against the invader.

The war now resumed but in Africa, as Carthage, under pressure of events, had abandoned its offensive in Sicily altogether. At this point, Agathocles' brilliant African sally had entirely achieved its aim, but he fought on, most likely in pursuit of concessions from Carthage in Sicily that would enable him to dominate the island completely. Agathocles resumed the offensive and occupied all the Carthaginian ports on the north and northeast seacoast of what is now Tunisia, including the port of Bizerte, and he used this position to intercept the vital traffic between Carthage and Sardinia, Sicily, and Spain. He was for a time undisturbed by Carthage, chastened as it was, by defeat and by treason. Carthaginian prospects revived when, in response to disturbing news from home, Agathocles departed Africa in the summer of 308, leaving his son Archagathus in charge. He returned in a far more well-established and accomplished condition than when he had departed Syracuse two years before.

As often happens in the careers of such flamboyant people as Agathocles, fortunes turned suddenly again; Archgathus ordered an expedition to the south led by Eumachus in 307, and this was the opportunity that Carthage had been preparing for, and in any case, the city was running short of food and had to act. A well-organized, disciplined, and professionally commanded army of thirty-thousand in three divisions, came quickly out of the city and attacked Eumachus, who was outmanned. Instead of pulling him back or sending his main force to aid him, Archagathus attacked Carthage, imagining he could clear the board in Africa while his father was tending to the home fires. One of Archagathus' divisions was ambushed and badly mauled, losing eight-thousand dead; and Eumachus was roughly handled. Carthage was again on top of events in North Africa, and Archagathus was in an attenuated and defensive state when his father returned in 307.

He had successfully attracted the aid of the Etrurian navy (presumably currying favour in the hope that Agathocles would help them against the ever-encroaching Romans). With this reinforcement, Agathocles had defeated the Carthaginian navy off Syracuse, and he returned to Africa and was able to take the field with a somewhat polyglot Italian-Greek-African army of over twenty-five thousand, and while he was an erratic and sometimes imprudent commander, he was also brilliant, bold, and resourceful. He was a slightly down-market Alcibiades, but being a Sicilian, was more violent and hot-tempered. He attacked the fortifications at Tunis as soon as he had disembarked, boldly as always, but his luck had fled and the Libyans backed off when the going was toughest, and his Greeks were unwisely deployed and soundly defeated. Agathocles' luck had not deserted him completely, however, and the Carthaginian camp was destroyed by a fire, and a large detachment of Libyans who were deserting Agathocles and were coming over to the Carthaginians in the dead of night, caused an alarm and the Carthaginians attacked them helter-skelter in the darkness. The Libyans, who were trying to defect, defended themselves so fiercely that the Carthaginians, instead of receiving a large advantage in a major defection from the enemy, were badly defeated and the whole army, instead of following up on its victory, withdrew in shambles back into Carthage. Many centuries later, Napoleon would remark that the best generals are the luckiest ones.

But Agathocles' Greeks also had an improvident skirmish with their supposed Libyan allies, and the morale of Agathocles' army was now strained, again a dangerous situation for him, far from home and with a surly army patched together from different nationalities of mercenaries. This was the point at which someone less astutely cynical and sharpened by experience than Agathocles would run the risk of being seized by his own forces and either discreetly executed, or handed over in exchange for a free pass home to the Carthaginians for an even more degrading public execution. The sly Agathocles promptly set himself up as the indispensable person to lead them all to safety, and then stole out in secret and returned to Sicily with the navy he had brought with them, leaving the rag-tag of Greeks and Libyans and Italians in his beaten army behind to sort it out with their unappreciative Carthaginian hosts.

A significant number then signed on with Carthage as mercenaries for this new paymaster. The first act of his abandoned forces was to seize and execute both of Agathocles' sons, with whom he had parted company. It was the particular pleasure of the mutineers to behead Archagathus, who had led them so poorly in battle. The African anabasis (expedition) of Agathocles had begun in glory and ended in shame, but both his arrival and departure were in successful pursuit of his own survival; both were successful in that objective, and Agathocles was not the sort of person who much cared how objectively discreditable his own conduct was, as long as he took care of himself. His conduct was a stark contrast with that of Regulus, who led the first Roman invasion of Africa, fifty years later, who behaved with such courage and integrity he is universally regarded as a hero.

Indeed, this entire episode demonstrated that Carthage did not have either the critical mass or institutional cohesion to win a direct contest with Rome; and Sicily, despite tossing up resourceful scoundrels to lead them from time to time, interspersed with the fortuitously virtuous Timoleon whose like would not be seen again in Sicily, ever, was bound to be squashed between Rome and Carthage. Yet, Agathocles had set out for Africa to defeat Carthage in Sicily and in 306 Carthage agreed to a treaty that rewarded Syracuse with a promise to remain within their old confines in Sicily and to pay a modest indemnity to Syracuse. The days of the first Hamilcar being the arbiter of Sicily were long-gone, and this was Agathocles' achievement. He had also discovered the soft point of the Carthaginian strategic position—its maritime lifeline, and he was not resigned to the correlation of forces that emerged from this war. He built a navy of two-hundred vessels and was preparing to have a return match with Carthage when he died. The lessons Agathocles had learned and taught were not unnoticed by the Romans, who were quickly developing the population, institutions, militarists and statesmen to apply those lessons in making themselves the absolute masters of the central and Western Mediterranean, in Europe, Africa, and the islands between them (and ultimately, and for centuries, from Gibraltar to what is now Pakistan, and from Scotland to Ethiopia).

To return to the departure of Agathocles from besieged Syracuse in 310, Hamilcar Gisgo handed over the bronze bowsprit of Agathocles' flagship, which he had burned, and claimed that his mission had been a disaster and that the General Plenipotentiary was dead. His brother, Antander, was inclined to accept the rather generous terms that Hamilcar offered if Syracuse surrendered, but Erymnon, whom Agathocles had left behind to advise his brother, counseled to wait until confirmation that Hamilcar was not misleading them. The dispatch boat that Agathocles sent back with news of his successful landing clarified matters, and Hamilcar was also repulsed when he attacked Syracuse by land while the inhabitants were celebrating their leader's fine start in Africa. The faint-hearted and questionably loyal Syracusans, who were prominent, were executed or banished, and the city remained in safe Agathoclean hands in his absence. Soon the Carthaginian withdrawals began, and the crisis passed. Hamilcar returned in 309 with a larger force, including a number of Greek mercenaries recruited and led by a second level adventurer named Deinocrates, but this force was suddenly attacked by a flying column of Syracusans who were much more familiar with the territory just west of Syracuse, and in a night attack smashed the Carthaginian force. Hamilcar was captured and executed.

Antander was not as quick to seize the opportunity to regain former dependencies as Agathocles would have been, and Acragasset itself up as a third force on the island, between Syracuse and the Carthaginian section of Sicily. Under their general Xenodicus, they expelled the Carthaginians from Gela, and liberated or successfully wooed a number of other towns, including Camarina and Leontini. It was the success of Xenodicus for Acragasthat brought Agathocles back from Africa in the summer of 308. His absence from Sicily had emboldened Acragas to take the field against Syracuse, and his absence from Africa led, as has just been recounted, to the defeat of his forces commanded by his under-qualified son, Archagathus. This return to Sicily by Agathocles was not very productive either. The loyal Syracusan general Lentines badly defeated Xenodicus, ending that threat, though the scoundrel Deinocrates carried on for his own account and raised a number of the smaller Greek states in Sicily to declare their independence of Syracuse and Carthage, but not to take the offensive. On learning of the African setbacks, Agathocles prepared to depart for that theatre, and in the run-up to his departure he had used his informants to identify a new crop of plotters and troublemakers and had another brisk, robust round of public beheadings allegedly impressing the crowd by employing several formidably accoutered axe-wielding headsmen at once. With this reminder of his penchant for dispatching real and imagined enemies, he returned to Africa for his final, unsuccessful tour.

On his last return from Africa in 307, Agathocles committed the most heinous and inexcusable atrocities of his blood-stained career. He avenged the death of his sons (for whom he latterly had no use at all and he abandoned them to the Carthaginians) by murdering all the relatives of his African soldiers his police could lay hands on, as if Africans were congenitally responsible for the deaths of his sons. And in Segesta, an allied city, he imposed a steep war-tax and when payment was slow, he tortured the wealthy in the most disgusting manner, and sold the poor of Segesta into slavery. At this point he started to lose support to Deinocrates, but once again Agathocles demonstrated his astounding powers of survival. He gulled Deinocrates with the fraud that he was tired of it all and was prepared to surrender everything except his native town of Thermae, and Cephaloedium, but all the while, he was negotiating the peace mentioned above with Carthage. This was consummated and Agathocles passed the word among Deinocrates' followers that he was extending the war for his own profit when peace was available. Nothing is more unreliable than mercenaries being tempted by lucre or a less risky life for undiminished pay, and Deinocrates' force started to disintegrate.

In 305, Agathocles, as he had so often before, took the field and attacked Deinocrates without warning, although he had a larger force than the Syracusan. He caught Deinocrates off guard and his army started to crumble; Deinocrates sued for peace, which was granted on fairly liberal terms, but in accord with his custom, Agathocles seized the division of Deinocrates' army composed of Syracusans, deemed that they had committed treason and executed all of them. Inexplicably, he spared Deinocrates, as he had done once before, and the wandering Greek actually assisted Agathocles in the balance of his term as General Plenipotentiary. Agathocles reduced a number of towns, few of which had the stamina or courage to resist this demonically persevering and severe man. Demonstrating that his morbid love of murdering foes or the merely unfortunate, was spontaneous and reflexive, he conducted an extensive massacre at Leontini, with no pretense of due process or even a legitimate collective grievance. His Syracuse now exceeded even that of Dionysius, and unlike Dionysius, he now proclaimed himself king of Syracuse and settled down to a relatively tranquil fifteen years in that regal title.

His adventures were not over, however. The Italian Greeks (that is Greek settlements and cities in Italy) had traditionally been influenced by the ruler of Epirus, not otherwise a very rich or influential state, except when it had strong leaders, such as Philip of Macedon's brother-in-law, Alexander (of Epirus, uncle of Alexander the Great), and erratic though she was, Olympias, sister of Alexander of Epirus and mother of Alexander the Great. Epirus was essentially Albania, not much richer nor for the most part, better governed than it has been in modern times. This would change when Pyrrhus became king in 297. In the last twenty years of the Fourth Century B.C., as Agathocles flexed Sicily's muscles to the point of strain, in Africa rather than the Italian Peninsula, and Rome expanded in Central Italy, northwards and south, and Greece, Macedonia, and the former Persian Empire and Alexander's extensions to it were convulsed in the struggles of the Diadochi, the Greek communities in Italy were relatively undisturbed (and almost the only part of the known world that was). In 303, the Tarentines (from Taranto) asked for the intervention of Cleonymus the Spartan, but he didn't achieve anything. Agathocles controlled the mainland approaches to the Strait of Messana but had little interest in the rest of Greek Italy. He did use his new navy, conceived for a rematch with Carthage, to seize Corcyra from Cassander, king of Macedonia, but then gave it away as dowery when his daughter Lanassa married King Pyrrhus of Epirus, from whom we will be hearing shortly in this narrative. He had a number of tests of arms with the Bruttians, who, despite their fervent bellicosity, were not drawn into the Samnite Wars. Agathocles generally got the better of them, but indecisively, and lost four-thousand soldiers killed in a night attack near Tarentum in 298. Agathocles wrung a surrender from the Bruttians in 295, when he committed a force of thirty-thousand men against them, but nothing came of it; his interest in Greek Italy was limited and fickle.

Agathocles' heirs had a difficult time. As has been recounted, the sons of his first wife, the widow of Agathocles' patron Damas, were killed by their own men in the war with Carthage. With his second wife, Alcia, he had a son and a daughter, Lanassa, who married Pyrrhus and then Demetrius Poliorcetes. The son, Agathocles II was supposed to succeed his father, and Demetrius guaranteed the succession but Archagathus II, a son of Agathocles' son of the same name, murdered Agathocles II, and Agathocles himself died soon after. There was no real succession and the Sicilian state disintegrated very quickly. Like Dionysius, Agathocles never attempted to set up any workable or durable institutions, except for claiming by sheer force to translate himself from tyrant to king. Once he was no longer there to sustain his power, his monarchy vanished with the speed of unimpeded political gravity, practically without trace. In fairness to Sicily's tyrants, Timoleon had tried to endow the island with political institutions that were civilized and functioned well elsewhere, but Sicily has always been rocky soil for civilized government, as has been steadily noted by sophisticated observers from Polybius and Livy to Leon Feuchtwanger.

Agathocles died of jaw cancer at age seventy-two, in 290 B.C., after twenty-eight years as tyrant and king of Syracuse. He was immediately remembered best for his delight in killing people, usually without any warning, no due process, on rank suspicion or even capricious dislike. His specialty was mass executions in public squares with cowed masses watching as his headsmen in a grand arc with their long axes severed the heads of those Agathocles ordered to be bent over the chopping blocks. The sullen masses watched reflectively as separate carts carried away the decapitated bodies and disconnected heads. In these widespread executions, he prefigured Robespierre's Reign of Terror (1793-4) in the public aspect, and Stalin's Great Terror (1933-8) in the scale of his blood lust. He also enjoyed less ceremonious murders—stabbings, poisonings, and private hangings; and subtler acts of treachery, such as deserting his mercenaries in the face of the enemy, as in Africa with the remnant of Ophellas' army. He did have an inexplicable soft spot for a few individuals, such as Deinocrates, whom he twice spared. He was an indifferent husband and a negligent father and as a ruler had no interest in anything except retention of his own power. Under him, Sicily stalled and went in a sanguinary circle while Carthage grew, and Rome surged forward; thus was Sicily left out of the contest for supremacy in the western and central Mediterranean that was about to unfold. Sicily always reverted to "Bellum omnia contra omnes;" always war against everyone.

But he does excel in one area, as a strategically brilliant general. He was not a good tactician or a thorough or inspiring commander, as he was too impulsive and was often defeated, usually in actions he should not have initiated. But his strategic conceptions, especially in his desperate attack on Carthage, but also in his usurpation of Ophellas' army and in his diplomatic outmaneuvering of Deinocrates where he had been defeated in the field, were brilliant. He showed Rome the way to crush Carthage, and the man who did so, Publius Scipio Africanus the Elder, acknowledged that; he said that Agathocles and Dionysius had been "the world's greatest men of action, who best combined boldness and discretion,"[3] and that Agathocles had shown the strategic key to the conquest of Carthage. Agathocles was a sadistic but successful tyrant, a formidable personality, and, when his survival was most tenuous, a strategic military genius. He was a memorable, if far from admirable, character, but his talent and ingenuity were always at their greatest when his position was most dangerously threatened. In that quality, he equaled some of the very greatest commanders of the future, including Julius Caesar, Frederick the Great, and Napoleon (to none of whom could he otherwise remotely be compared).

---

3 CAH, VII, p. 637 (M. Cary).

CHAPTER TWELVE

PHILIP OF MACEDON, 360-336 B.C.

PHILIP AND DEMOSTHENES

Phillip of Macedon
(Roman copy of original Greek bust)

Demosthenes
(Roman copy of Polyeuctos' bronze original)

1. The Rise of Philip of Macedon

IN 360 B.C., Athens appeared, once again, after another long cycle of bloody fighting all around Greece, to be the leading Greek state. Thebes had been humbled at Mantinea; Sparta was confined within the Peloponnese between and by Messene and Megalopolis, as well as its ancient Argive foe. There were local balances of power in the Greek regions, but only Syracuse, well to the west and with little aptitude to plunge into Greece again, had a position remotely as secure as that of Athens, unthreatened on land and master of the sea, and staring across the Aegean at the crumbling Persian Empire, already on the Ozymandian road. In all this serene horizon, the only fly in the ointment was the inexplicable failure of the Athenian armies against Cotys, king of the Odrysian Thracians. The Athenian interest was led by Iphicrates, despite the fact that he was Cotys' son-in-law, and Charidemus, commanding as mercenary captains. Iphicrates assisted Cotys outside Athenian territory, but when the Thracian set out to attack Athenian cities, Iphicrates withdrew to Lesbos and awaited events. Charidemus, the ultimate unscrupulous mercenary, was unsuccessfully trying to establish a little kingdom of his own in Troad in Asia Minor, Homeric country. He at first made overtures to the new Athenian commander, Cephisodotus, but then transported himself and his army across the Hellespont, and joined Cotys, eventually marrying another of his daughters.

Cotys died in 360 (murdered, naturally, in an obscure quarrel), leaving the scoundrel Charidemus up for bids in Thrace while Athens' relations with Macedonia, especially the ultimate opportunist Perdiccas III, were deteriorating.

The violent death of Cotys opened up the usual rending struggle for the kingship, exacerbated by the youth of his unprepared legitimate heir, Cersobleptes. The two principal contenders, Amadocus a prince, and Berisades, a meritocratic outsider, were shouldering Cersobleptes aside when Miltocythes, an Athenian ally in the region, was betrayed and handed over to Charidemus, who gave him to his Cardian so-called subjects as a bargaining chip, and they murdered his son before Miltocythes' eyes and then drowned (sank) him. The word of this gruesome treachery reached the contending parties, and they joined forces against Charidemus, whose immeasurable odium was almost the only subject all parties could agree upon and divided the kingdom between themselves. Cersobleptes was left with Byzantium, Amphipolis in the west went to Berisades, and the strip between them including the Chersonese went to Amadocus. The same treaty purported to hand Chersonese over to Athens and Chabrias was sent in a single ship to accept the transfer of it, as the Athenians over-confidently stopped funding their local army commander, Athenodorus, who was obliged to demobilize his forces. Obviously, the grasping triumvirs were not going to give Athens anything, and again Athens repudiated the treaty, but not until 357 did they send adequate forces to impose their will on the two scoundrels who had usurped most of Coty's inheritance.

In the meantime, Ataxerxes I had died, bringing in Ataxerxes II (Ochus); Alexander of Pherae, king of Thessaly, was murdered by his wife and brothers-in-law, and Perdiccas III, the Macedonian king, had died of a battle wound or in a plot masterminded by his mother Eurydice—one of the two was the cause of his death but the betting is even between historians on which it was. (The Persian and Thessalian developments and their sequels have already been recorded in Chapter 10.) Perdiccas' son Amyntas was an infant, and the regency was assumed by the deceased king's brother, Philip. He had five powerful rivals for the throne and his prospects did not at first appear promising, but he would be one of the important figures of world history, as prominent as Pericles, though not as affectionately regarded by modern posterity. His rivals were three princes, Archelaus, Arrhidaeus, and Menelaus, Philip's half-brothers; Argaeus, who was the candidate of Athens, and Pausanias, who had been denied the succession when Perdiccas became king by the intervention of Iphicrates in 365.

Philip executed Archelaus; Arrhidaeus and Menelaus fled for their lives; Pausanias bungled his hand by openly accepting the patronage of the Thracians; and Argaeus was immobilized, but not directly attacked, by Philip's skillful diplomacy with Athens, which left the Athenian leaders wondering if they were better off supporting Philip or urging rebellion on Argaeus. Argaeus had promised, if he became king, to give Amphipolis to Athens. Philip withdrew the garrison Perdiccas had placed there, under the nose of Berisades, and wrote to the Athenian government asking for the renewal of the alliance that the father of Philip and Perdiccas, Amyntas, had had with Athens. After this disarmingly friendly action, Athens confined itself to sending an accompanying force with Argaeus to Methone, and from there he inadvisedly pressed on with a small force of volunteers toward the Macedonian capital of Aegae. Philip intercepted and easily defeated him, treated the Athenian prisoners with the utmost consideration and sent them home, well fed and their wounds cared for, in comfortable ships. Argaeus, wounded, was executed and Athens had no more role to play in Macedonian matters. Philip was the prototype of the young monarch underestimated at first, like King Hussein of Jordan (1935-1999), who was assumed to have little chance to retain his throne when he ascended it aged sixteen but ruled with astounding dexterity for forty-seven years and died naturally and was widely mourned. Philip was twenty-two when he became regent (king in fact), and he also set a precedent followed from time to time after by his generous treatment of the Athenian prisoners. (It was by treating Swedish prisoners generously that Napoleon's Marshal Bernadotte would be offered the kingship of Sweden in 1810.)

Philip, as the brother of Perdiccas, had been sent to Thebes as a hostage for the good behavior of Macedonia in its relations with Thebes. He was in the house of the prominent Theban general Pammenes, who was capable and generous, but a pederast who forced himself physically on Philip. This was not especially unusual in these times, and in other respects Philip's stay in Thebes was useful as he got to know and greatly admire his host's most eminent comrades, Epaminondas and Pelopidas. It was from Epaminondas that Philip had his first teaching in generalship and especially his focus on new weapons and flexible battlefield formations. It was also here that Philip developed a high appreciation of Hellenic culture, which was still widely viewed in bellicose Macedonia as somewhat effete and degenerate. He returned to Macedonia after three years, aged nineteen, and was assigned a province to rule and organize, including its military force. As soon as Perdiccas died, after another three years, Philip first appeased the Paeonians to the north under King Agis, and when the king died, he swiftly routed them militarily. As the Illyrian king, Bardylis, in the rough and tumble custom of the times, had invaded Western Macedonia as soon as Perdiccas had died, Philip had to contend with him to protect anything for himself. Bardylis noted that Philip had made short work of Agis' successors and he was known as a military disciple of Epaminondas, the greatest general of the ancient world up to this time, and he offered a stand-still peace. Philip refused to legitimize the Illyrian invasion of Macedonia, and the two armies met near Monastir. Philip's superior tactics won the day, as his cavalry circled around the Illyrian left and attacked that wing of the Illyrian army simultaneously from back and front and rolled up the battlefield. Bardylis had to give back most of what he had taken, and Philip's authority was generally accepted, if tentatively, as all his neighbours and many of his countrymen waited for a misstep.

Philip's chief military innovation at this stage was to train the infantry carefully to execute more imaginative maneuvers than had been customary and arm it with a long pike that enabled the Macedonian infantry to strike the first blow, and to give the infantry more room to maneuver rather than just jamming its ranks to overpower by sheer weight of numbers and density. The infantry were also promoted within the army and no longer belittled as the pedestrian inferiors of the mounted units. The Macedonian army soon assumed a much more professional character than its Greek rivals—citizen armies mustered and demobilized according to political events, where Philip trained his army when it was not in active combat. It was not long before Macedonian muscle-flexing collided with Athenian incumbency. The Euboeans had swiftly tired of heavy-handed Theban suzerainty which had prevailed after the Battle of Leuctra in 371 B.C., and they rose in revolt. As a Theban army approached to smack the Euboeans down, they appealed to Athens, which responded vigorously and promptly mobilized and dispatched a force to capitalize on Euboean discontent with Thebes. Among the volunteers was again Demosthenes, soon to be Philip's most eloquent vocal critic. The Athenians forced the Thebans to withdraw and were very content with this assertion of the eminence of Athens. At this point, in 367, Philip laid siege to the nominally Athenian protectorate of Amphipolis. When Athens required an explanation for Philip's apparent attack on Athenian territory and subjects, he blandly informed the Athenian ambassadors that he would relinquish Amphipolis to Athens as soon as it surrendered. In fact, an arrangement was agreed by which Philip would hand over Amphipolis but would be unmolested in taking over Pydna, a free seaport under Athenian light occupation. As Pydna would not agree to this, they were simply not told about it. (This would become a time-honoured device: as was the case with the revision of Polish and other eastern European borders in 1943-1945, where no one but the U.S., British, and Soviet leaders were aware of what would occur.) Philip overcame brave Amphipolian resistance by betrayal of the town from a suborned internal faction. In a pattern he would replicate, Philip summarily executed his enemies in Amphipolis but treated the general population with considerable kindness. Even now, Philip's assurances were so placatory that Athens declined the beseechings of Olynthus to resist the encroachments of the Macedonians.

Athens was now engaged in combat with some of their ostensible allies, as always happened with Athenian alliances, because of Athens' overweening ambition to dominate and turn alliances into confederacies and then into centralized federations. In this state, Athens declined to agree to the handing over of Pydna, so Philip seized it in a coup de main again assisted by betrayal of the town from within. He did not surrender Amphipolis to Athens as he did so. This was in 356, just three years after Philip's accession, and with the assistance of the Olynthians, who had thrown their lot in with Philip after being shunned by the complacent Athenians, the Macedonian king took over Potidaea. Amphipolis was especially useful to Philip because of the proximity of the Pangaea goldfields. These had first been discovered and publicized by the Athenian demagogue Callistratus, when he was in exile there (Chapter 9), but he fled in advance of Philip and made the grievous tactical error of returning to Athens before the political climate had cooled and he was arrested, tried and executed. The actual mining centre was Crenides, which was technically assigned to Berisades, in the tripartite division of the fiefdom of Cotys (described above in this section). Berisades died in 357, and Philip unceremoniously seized Crenides and the gold-producing property from Berisades' son, Cetriporis, and renamed it Philippi. (It was to be made immortally famous by Marc Antony, Octavian, Brutus, and Cassius, three centuries later, and particularly by William Shakespeare sixteen centuries after that.)

In addition to the gold deposits which Philip began to exploit very efficiently, he also took over extensive forests which endowed him with a much-increased capacity in shipbuilding. The gold and the fleet instantly made Macedonia a great strategic power in southeastern Europe. Philip produced a new gold coinage, as well as a silver one, and circulated a hard currency that quickly came to rival the money of Athens and Persia as the reserve and trading currency of the Eastern Mediterranean. This was a strategic advance so rapid it has rarely been equaled in subsequent times; to some extent Hitler in 1933 to 1938 bears comparison, but Germany and Prussia before it had been a great power for nearly two-hundred years and was only temporarily in a reduced and disarmed state. The Athenians finally partially awakened from their torpor and made an alliance with the three most recent victims of Philip's knockabout aggrandizements: Paeonia, Illyria, and what was left to Cetriporis. But these allies were more a burden than a strength to Athens, and Philip sent Parmenion to punish and subdue the Illyrians, which he did in mid-summer 356. Philip learned of this victory at the same time as he did of the victory of his horse at Olympia, and of the birth of his son Alexander, by his wife Olympias. The tide of events was rolling in for him in a flood, and not so much by chance as from his own mastery of the scene and its opportunities; he was only twenty-seven.

However, Athens had been distracted by the defection from its alliance of Byzantium, Chios, Rhodes, and Cos. The reasons aren't known, but as has been remarked, Athens always had trouble keeping her alliances intact. It is likely that a role was played in these developments by Mausolus, nominally the satrap, but in fact the rather autonomous governor, of Caria and much of Lycia. His capital was at Halicarnassus, and he would eventually give his name to the Mausoleum there, one of the Seven Wonders of the World. He had a large fleet and considered the Ionian Islands to be tempting acquisitions and may have suborned some support from the seceding members of the Athenian alliance. The separatist allies were tangibly encouraged by Mausolus to make war on Athens. Chabrias was sent with a large fleet to suppress this revolt, with troopships carrying mercenary forces under Chares to suppress Chios. Both the fleet and land engagements failed, a severe setback for Athens which poured gasoline on the fire of disintegration, as Mausolus had hoped. Chabrias, a somewhat redoubtable figure and a prominent and often successful general and admiral for 30 years (it was still assumed in ancient Greece that the same skills were needed for both roles), died in the naval engagement and the entire Athenian force withdrew. Sestos revolted from Athens, and a large rebel fleet led by the Chians, did a lot of damage to Athenian loyalist islands Lemnos and Imbros, and were preparing to invade Samos in 356. B.C.

The First Sacred War broke out in 355, as a result of the abuse by Thebes and Thessaly of their control over the Amphictyonic League, ostensibly a religious association that was the governing body for the Delphic Oracle. They charged that their traditional Phocian adversaries were committing the sacrilege of farming some of the land reverently reserved to Apollo around the great shrine. The charge was nonsense and for the Greeks to engage in such almost frivolous internecine bloodletting as Philip built up so powerful a potential challenge—now possibly imminent—to all Greece, as Macedonia had become, is indicative of the indomitable Greek deathwish. A fine was assessed, which the Phocians ignored and in 355 the council voted to seize the Phocian land and donate it to Delphi in honour of Apollo, and the council also voted to collect all outstanding fines, including a large fine it had claimed to levy against Sparta for seizing Cadmea from Thebes in 382. (This was all a little like some of the professed penalties asserted by medieval popes, though they were rarely as dominated by one secular country or faction as the Amphictyonic League now was.)

The Phocians saw the possibility of a fruitful alliance with Sparta against Thebes, and Philomelus of Ledon led an embassy to Sparta proposing a military coalition. The Spartan king, Archadamus, received him positively, but because Sparta had traditionally supported Delphi itself against all comers, the king did not promise overt support, but did undertake to send funds and mercenaries. With mercenaries and one-thousand Phocian volunteers, Philomelus seized the Oracle itself in May 355. Only the intervention of Archadamus prevented a severe treatment of the Delphic defenders. Philomelus seized the high priestess, an unprecedented impudence, and required her to give his future prospects. She confined herself, ingeniously, to saying he could do as he liked, and this coupled with the good omen of an eagle chasing away some of the doves around the Temple, was all the backing he needed to announce that the Oracle had given him a blank endorsement. He cited Homer as the ultimate source for his theory that the Delphic Oracle belonged to Phocis.

This prompted the Locrians to attack the Phocians, but Philomelus defeated them above the Phaedriades Cliffs, and he decimated the Locrian force, at the same time that he sent messages to Athens, Sparta and Thebes promising no military adventure, absolute and verifiable respect for the independence and state of the Temple and its personnel and proposing an alliance around conservation of the integrity of Delphi. Athens and Sparta accepted, though there was vigorous debate in Athens between the advocates of the sanctity of Delphi, and those who were concerned that without Spartan and Athenian assistance, the Phocians could be subdued by the Thebans, who did indeed take up arms and marched against Phocia. Sparta managed to generate a declaration of war on Phocis from the Amphictyonic Council, pretty much now a puppet organization of the Phocians. Philomelus raised a larger army of mercenaries by offering to the cynically mobile ranks of the mercenaries one-hundred and fifty percent of the standard pay-rate. Philomelus mustered a force of five-thousand mercenaries and redefined his brief to defend the Temple of Delphi as a mandate to invade Locria, which he did in the autumn of 355.

Some fighting occurred and the Locrians refused to give up the twenty dead Phocian warriors killed in battle and Philomelus persevered and won a minor victory replete with enough dead to offer to the Locrians in exchange for their own dead decomposing in Locrian hands, as Greek convention required. Philomelus then pillaged the valley adjacent to Delphi and retired to winter quarters at Delphi. The

Boeotians were preparing, though at a very leisurely rate, a massive counter-blow against the Phocians, and Philomelus raised his army to ten-thousand battle-trained mercenaries by raiding and liquidating some of the offerings that had been left at Delphi by the participating countries over the years. Philomelus won a couple of engagements but when suddenly faced by thirteen-thousand Boeotians, he gave battle with the grim determination of an underdog on the north side of Mount Parnassus and fought with great courage and was wounded many times, but at length, saw the complete failure and defeat of the whole enterprise, that had been his gig, and he threw himself over a cliff. His colleague, Onomarchus, assumed command of the defeated army and led it back to Delphi, and the Boeotians, assuming the crisis was over, returned home, not imagining that the Phocians would try to cling to Delphi after the beating they had received.

However, Onomarchus, on regaining Phocia, as one of those who would owe heavy fines if they had to be paid, gave a powerful address to the public assembly of Phocis against giving up and reminding his countrymen of the validity, or at least plausibility of Phocis' claim to the guardianship of the Temple at Delhi. He was narrowly sustained, and redoubled the Phocian effort, seizing all the offerings at the Temple of Delphi and turning the base metals into shields and armour and the precious metal into coinage to pay his volunteers. He also funded his effort by causing the arrest and confiscation of the property of those Phocians who had opposed him. Having thus strengthened and better equipped his force, he invaded Locria again and seized a number of towns and gained control of the Pass at Thermopylae. After several notable victories, he was unable to seize Chaeronea, and returned to Phocis in August 353, victorious overall but having seriously blotted his religious ledger.

The Athenians had meanwhile waited until the summer of 356 to send an adequate relief force to extricate Chares from Chios. The combined fleet then went to Byzantium to intimidate that recently defected state. The Athenian generals, Iphicrates and Timotheus, after they had reached Embatum, concerted a plan with Chares for attacking the Phocian fleet, the land commanders, Iphicrates and Timotheus, were hesitant to take to stormy waters and demurred on the day, and withheld their forces from Chares, who proceeded anyway and was defeated by the rebel forces, though not disastrously so. He preferred charges of treachery against Iphicrates, Timotheus and Menetheus. The public trial took place in 354. The decision went to the defendants, apart from the conviction of Timotheus on a lesser charge. Yet Timotheus departed for Chalcis and never paid his fine and died in Chalcis, adequately comfortably, in 354. Iphicrates was entirely acquitted, and lived on for a while, but was never given another command. Thus did Athens treat two of its most brilliant commanders. Chares was in sole command of the Athenian and allied fleet now, but instead he delivered himself over to the powerful Artabazus, satrap of Hellespontine Phrygia. On intelligence that the new Persian Emperor, Artaxerxes Ochus, was cranking up for massive reprisals against Athens, the Athenian government withdrew Chares and opened negotiations with Persia, resulting in the peace that ended the First Sacred War, and the independence of Chios, Byzantium, Cos, and Rhodes were multilaterally recognized.

There was extensive public debate in Athens. Some orators called for Athens to resume its ancient role of rallying all Greece to smite Persia a mortal blow. Cooler heads prevailed, as they did opposite those advocating disposal of the islands of the Empire and retrenchment to a neo-Spartan isolationism, no longer dependent on Greek mercenaries. Demosthenes, on his way to becoming one of history's most renowned orators, was at this point counseling caution. The Sacred War had already depleted Athens' treasury once more and there was nothing to show for the state's prodigies: Mausolus did not look like a very supportive ally and was snapping off island states as they became available, including Cos and Rhodes. Carian oligarchies were established, apparently cooperating with the pro-Athenian democrats already established. Mausolus' strategies had worked well but he died in 353, and his widow made him immortal by commissioning the Mausoleum, but she was so overcome by grief at her bereavement that she died in two years, as her magnificent mausoleum was under construction.

As may be imagined, as the Greeks were busy with internecine bloodletting, Philip continued to strengthen his position in an ever-heavier arc encircling the north of the Greek world and looming over it like a thundercloud. He must have watched the absurd, compulsive Greek war-making with bemusement. In 354 he encroached upon the Thracian coasts, seizing towns and assisting Cersobleptes in his continuing struggle with Amadocus. This was bringing him into some potential conflict with Athenian interests in Thrace. There was never any rationale for these steady expansions of Philip's Macedonians. He was a Hellenophile culturally and was using an ever-stronger Macedonia for the eventual purpose of uniting Macedonia's broad strategic national vision, as conceived and elaborated by himself and later his son, which grew swiftly out of the petty opportunism of Perdiccas; with the vast cultural eminence of the Greek world. In doing this, he would put the splendid military aptitudes of the Greeks to the united Greco-Macedonian cause, rather than continuing to have them rented out to the quarrels between Persia and her satraps, and between all the Greeks and all the other Greeks, endlessly shifting sides but bleeding and impoverishing Greece uselessly, century after century.

At this point, Artabazus asked the support of Thebes in his revolt against the Persian king, and Thebes, short of money, was materially induced to send Pammenes five-thousand men through Thrace to make common cause with Philip, it was hoped, against Athens. But Philip thought better of it all and withdrew from Thrace, keeping some of his new outposts garrisoned, but unwilling to be drawn into serious combat in such an out of the way place. This discountenanced Cersobleptus who sent emissaries to Athens professing friendship and seeking alliance. Philip focused on reducing Methone, which he did in 353 after a long siege, and after losing an eye in the action. The inhabitants were expelled from the town and scattered. His next target was in Thessaly, where he moved to capitalize on years spent aggravating divisions in Thessaly, which had never really recovered from the tyranny and sequential strife of Alexander of Pherae a decade before. Philip supported the princes of Larissa, Eudicus and Simus, who caused Alexander of Pherae's ostensible surviving successor, Lycophron, to ask Philip for assistance after Onomarchus dispatched his brother, Phaeylus, to Thessaly at the head of seven-thousand men. Philip defeated them on arrival, causing the impetuous Onomarchus, torqued up by his surreptitious pillaging of the Temple of Delphi, to lead his entire army against Philip and his Thessalian allies. He enjoyed a substantial numerical advantage, but that alone would not have prevailed, and Onomarchus scored a considerable feat in defeating Philip twice and forcing his withdrawal from Thrace, in order, as he put it himself, "to butt the harder next time."[1]

So he did. The Macedonian king skillfully roused most of the Thessalians against the sacrilege and impiety of Onomarchus and led a mixed army larger than the Phocian one back into Thessaly. Onomarchus was busy invading Boeotia when advised of this movement in his rear, and withdrew, proceeded against Philip with twenty-thousand men, but was outnumbered. Philip had put on the airs of a zealot and fired up his men, who like many soldiers, were both nationalistically and superstitiously religious, to avenge the desecration of Delphi. Onomarchus' twenty-thousand infantry and five-hundred cavalry were overpowered and cut to pieces by Philip's twenty-five thousand infantry and three-thousand cavalry. The Macedonians and Thessalians cut between units of the Phocian army and drove it into the sea. Few prisoners were taken given the supposed holy nature of the Macedonian mission. Many thousands perished, including Onomarchus, allegedly executed by his own men as their resistance disintegrated, in anger at the defeat that overwhelmed and was about to kill them. The three-thousand Phocian prisoners taken were executed by drowning for reasons of scandalous impiety. This was a cause most of Greece could subscribe to, with varying degrees of hypocrisy. And it certainly did not put Philip in a poor light to appear to be the upholder of Greek religion and especially of the revered cause of Apollo, and of the great shrine of Delphi. Philip retrieved Onomarchus' corpse and publicly crucified it as a measure of religious and cultural chastisement and retribution. These were stern times and hard men engaged, apart from Philip, in fruitless work.

Philip now took Pherae and the whole of Magnesia, established his control of Thessaly and then, in 352, he moved on Thermopylae. The Athenians, finally awakening to the mortal threat at their gates, deployed a substantial force under Nausicles to defend the pass, and Philip was aware of its very formidable defensive advantage, and retired to Macedonia rather than try to erupt into Greece. Philip moved back to Chersonese and engaged Cersobleptes, who appealed yet again to Athens. Athens again was perplexed at the ubiquitous and unceasing ant-like movements of the king of Macedon, and sent forty shiploads of citizen troops, but Philip succumbed to an undiagnosed, but probably a genuine illness, and withdrew with little fighting on either side. But the combination of Macedonia, Byzantium, Amadocus and Perinthus, sufficed to force Cersobleptes to cede some territory and to give his son as a hostage to Philip in assurance of his faithful adherence to the new treaty that had been extracted from him. An epochal struggle between Macedonia and Athens for control of the Chersonese now seemed imminent.

---

1 CAH, VI, p. 220 (A.W. Pickard-Cambridge).

2. The Emergence of Macedonia as the Greatest Power in the Eastern Mediterranean

The principal Athenian leader after Callistratus was banished in 361 (and executed when he returned a few years later), was Aristophon, who returned to then aggressive proselytization of the height of the democracy and whose chief military collaborator was Chares, who was a capable general and cultivated a great popular following, which he had substantially earned. Aristophon demanded war against laggard allies and the punishment of even incompletely successful generals, such as the admirable Timotheus. When his war-making ran the state out of money, he attempted to soak the rich, and in his zeal to expand Athens' influence, forgetting all the lessons of the last century, he forged an alliance with Messene, even though it was almost certain to provoke war with Sparta in 355. As Athens' problems deepened, power started to accumulate in the hands of Eubulus, head of the Theoric Fund. This was a wheeze of Pericles, which distributed money to the people to assist in the celebration of festivals. It was, at best, placation of the masses, and at worst, a slush fund to aid the friends of the regime and buy off recalcitrant segments of opinion. It also carried on Cleophon's innovation of a modest payment to all citizens, as a selective tax rebate that was outright redistribution on no test of merit other than the approbation of the regime of the day. (Cleophon, it will be recalled was the demagogue executed by the oligarchs in 405 B.C.)

As financial conditions became more precarious because of Aristophon's equal-opportunity bellicosity, Eubulus became a prestigious figure of fiscal prudence as well as fecund generosity. By dint of efficient management, Eubulus restored the Athenian fleet to a daunting three-hundred triremes, with excellent docks and yards, and solid fortifications. Athens was thus secure by land and endowed with the naval strength to assure its wheat supply from the Black Sea. He repaired aqueducts and reservoirs and roads and afforded nothing for avoidable wars. Eubulus' administration was intelligent, but it may have failed to glamorize military service, so mercenaries were largely utilized and unintentionally assisted the depredations of Philip as he prepared his direct challenge to Athens and all Greece. For some time, Athenian opinion was divided on the merits of prudent and thrifty administration or going forward to meet the Macedonian challenge as it loomed ever more disconcertingly. Eubulus was successful and supported in making peace with warring so-called allies and in shutting down Chares' expensive activities in Asia Minor, and in averting war with Sparta. But matters were complicated in 352 when Sparta, encouraged by the distraction of Thebes in the Sacred War, moved to encourage all the Greek states to repossess whatever they had lost: back to the status quo ante, to underline the complete futility of decades of internecine war-making and regain effective control of the Peloponnese for Sparta.

Eubulus acquiesced in most of Philip's advances, but it was he who drew the line at Thermopylae and while he declined to assist Cersobleptes, he insisted on the absolute security of the wheat-importation route through the Bosporus. His strategic decisions were intelligent and effective. It was at this point that Demosthenes the orator rose to fame. He had been inspired to study and practice oratory by the astounding speech of defence Callistratus gave at his trial (temporarily) avoiding execution. He was an ungainly man physically, but a fierce Athenian patriot, and led the resistance to Philip against those inclined to see the Macedonian king as an agent of Hellenic unity that Athens could comfortably abide. He supported Eubulus for some years and strongly endorsed his refusal to court armed hostility with Persia. His principal theme was the need for a standing Athenian army of traditional extent, avoiding the recourse to expensive mercenaries of uncertain morale and loyalty in times of adversity. He was not overly concerned with war with Sparta, however, an inconsistency in his general policy of preparing for the strongest possible Greek defence against Macedonia should that become necessary. He developed a rather subtle proposal of using Athenian intervention to maintain the scales in parity on the balance of forces between Sparta and Thebes, and in the east between Cersobleptes and Charidemus. This was sophisticated policy, but somewhat academic in considering the Macedonian threat, and by 352 Demosthenes was calling for Pan-Hellenic preparations to resist Philip, in the high tradition of resistance to Xerxes in olden time.

While these debates were strenuously argued out in Athens, the Sacred War also continued. Despite the absence of Athenian assistance, Sparta took its chance to reassert authority over the Peloponnese and attacked Megalopolis, which was assisted by Argos, Sicyon, and Messene, and awaited further assistance from Thebes. The Spartans had three-thousand Phocian mercenaries, who were probably left unemployed after the decisive and mortal defeat of Onomarchus. Sparta was also assisted by a small detachment from Pherae that Philip had allowed to depart for the purpose. In 351 the Thebans finally sent four-thousand infantry and five-hundred cavalry to assist the Megalopolitans. After some indecisive engagements, everyone went home, but the war resumed and after some minor setbacks, Sparta prevailed, and a truce was signed in which Megalopolis made some concessions but retained its independence.

Phaylus had succeeded Onomarchus and he continued stealing and selling the treasures of Delphi. Even allowing for the corruption and hypocrisy of Greek religion and its personnel, this was a shabby and profoundly offensive activity, and the diminutive Phocians should not have imagined that they would not pay for it, especially given the defeat and death in battle of Philomelus and Onomarchus (particularly if the latter was, in fact, executed by his disaffected ranks before the enemy could slay him). By splashing the proceeds from sale or coinage of the purloined treasures (including minting coins from the blocks of gold donated to memorialize Croesus), Phaylus secured a thousand Spartan mercenaries, two-thousand Achaeans, and five-thousand infantry and four-hundred Athenian cavalry under Nausicles. Lycophron and Peitholaus from Pherae came forward at the head of two-thousand men, and there were smaller contingents from lesser states, all mercenaries contented to be bribed with lucre looted from the Hellenic world's most august and previously inviolable site. Phaylus thus made good, at least numerically, the terrible losses that Onomarchus sustained. In late 352, Phaylus invaded Boeotia with his polyglot army, but was checked three times in the opening weeks, though without crippling losses. But with this unpromising start, Phaylus redirected his soundly whipped army recruited from the avails of rapacious sacrilege, into Locria. There was a general melee, centering on a struggle over the town of Naryx, and including a Locrian raid into Phocis, but Phaylus finally prevailed rather convincingly at Naryx, but then fell ill and died, at least of natural causes, in the early months of 351, the third consecutive Phocian leader to perish among his troops. He was replaced by Phalaecus, the young son of Onomarchus, who had Mnaseus as his guardian. But Mnaseus died in battle and Phalaecus carried on and even captured Chaeronea but was shortly evicted by the Thebans returning from the Peloponnese.

The Sacred War, which scarcely deserved to be so named given the base motives and antics of most of the participants, again went through a lull of inactivity as the Greek states, durably exhausted by these absurd but enervating wars, regrouped. Thebes, militarily strong but strapped financially, asked the fiscal assistance of Artaxerxes, who was happy to oblige, and made over a generous grant, in the hope of continuing the timeless Greek bloodbath to Persia's ultimate benefit (and overlooking Pammenes' late expedition). As was described in Chapter 10, he did succeed in engaging Greek mercenaries in his campaigns against Egypt, Phoenicia, and Cyprus. In 349 and 348, the sacred warriors returned to the game and the Boeotians plundered much of Phocis, but were eventually defeated by the Phocians, and while the Boeotians burned the crops of Phocis in the fields, the Phocians under Phalaecus plundered Boeotia. It was like a war between two animals tearing each other's innards out. Phalaecus and his treasurer Philon exceeded even their immediate forebears in looting Delphi and began excavating in the walls and under the famous oracle. Their rapine was interrupted in 347 by a mighty earthquake that was naturally seen by the pious as an act of divine retribution, specifically of the rage of Apollo.

Incredibly, the Sacred War, even now, did not end. The Olynthians, a Thracian people, had agreed with Philip not to make an alliance with Athens without his concurrence, and naturally became suspicious of Philip's motives and likely next steps, and made confidential overtures to Athens and gave asylum to two of Philip's rivals for the Macedonian throne, Arrhidaeus and Menelaus. Philip warned them "not to invite War and Violence within their borders."[2] By this time, Philip was ramping up provocations against Athens. The climax was finally coming in the long-steeping pressure cooker of Greece and the aggressive ambitions of Macedonia, fortified and amplified by Philip, the most formidable leader in the area since Pericles, and a much less gentle spirit, though far from an uncultured statesman. Philip marched through Olynthia on his way back from Thrace in 350, though without overt acts of hostility. He had largely taken over Epirus, and he raided Lemnos and Imbros, Athenian allies, and took Athenian prisoners there, seized an entire Athenian grain-fleet on its way from the Black Sea, landed a force near Marathon, and seized an Athenian state galley on its way to a religious ceremony at Delos. These were all acts of war. The Macedonian tiger was poised to strike.

The Athenians would certainly not submit passively to such a sequence of affronts, and Charidemus went to the Hellespont on an official mission to recruit mercenaries. A supplementary grain-supply agreement was contracted with the satrap of Orontes. The Athenian general Phocion was then assisting Artaxerxes at the head of

---

2 Ibid., p. 223.

Greek mercenaries in suppressing Cyprus, and Persia was accordingly uninterested in antagonizing Athens. It was at this decisive moment that Demosthenes came to the forefront in demanding that Athens respond to Macedonian provocations and recognize Philip as an ogre and a menace to all Greece. It is disputed whether it was in 350 or 349 that Demosthenes delivered what has been known throughout subsequent history as the First Philippic, a powerful and passionately eloquent call to Athens to resist the Macedonian's encroachments and to bring into being a standing army and navy to assure fully trained personnel ready to act at a moment's notice. He knew that such a force would not be a match in the open field with Philip's entire army, but argued that it could exploit weaknesses, act amphibiously, and defend strongpoints, where if the existing methods of starting to recruit only when a crisis boiled over was adhered to, Athens would always be wrong-footed by so powerful and decisive an adversary as Philip. He particularly insisted that these forces should be citizens and that Athens could not rely for its national life on mercenaries, even if most of the mercenaries happened to be Athenian. The speech was noted and discussed but did not deprive Eubulus of the majority that continued to support him.

Olynthus was back seeking Athenian help in 349 when Philip demanded the release to him of Arrhidaeus and Menelaus, and Demosthens vigorously supported the Olynthians in what has been known as his first Olynthic Oration. He again contrasted the dynamism of Philip with the sluggishness of Eubulus and his followers. It is hard in reading Demosthenes' speeches not to be reminded of the warnings against appeasement of the dictators by Winston Churchill in the 1930's, though it would be unfair to Eubulus to liken him to Neville Chamberlain. Eubulus engaged in no Munich concessions, did not represent himself as the architect of "peace with honour…peace in our time," and he did prepare Athens quite efficiently to bear the burdens of self-defence should this become necessary.

Demosthenes advocated use of the navy against Macedonian ports, tangible and substantial aid to Olynthus, and repurposing of the Theoric distributions from an annual vote-buying exercise to preparations for war. Demosthenes was largely responsible for making an alliance with Olynthus and sending a serious expeditionary force to that state to stiffen its resistance to the Macedonian king. Chares was again in command, but to pay his men, he had to plunder nearby states, which he did with complete disregard for whether they were allies, neutrals, or unsympathetic states. This was not a policy which could create a strong alliance and was nothing like the Pan-Hellenic rallying against Persia under Xerxes. In the Olynthian debates, there was a good deal of comment that Philip was too powerful for Athens to oppose him directly. Demosthenes was not having any of this.

Demosthenes, to facilitate his attempts to rouse his countrymen, claimed great restiveness in the Macedonian dependencies and annexed territories and even factionalism in the Macedonian leadership. This appears to have been exaggerated, if not simply fabricated, but Philip did lead an army to Pherae and then to Thessaly in 349 to expel dissentient forces under Peitholaus. This was a brief diversion from his campaign to subjugate Olynthus and the rest of the Chalcidic League. He burned the town of Stagirus, birthplace of Aristotle, to the ground. (Philip would engage Aristotle as chief tutor to his son, Alexander the Great.) Chares did little to assist Olynthus and was recalled and prosecuted and replaced with Charidemus, who proved even more ineffectual. He made a few excursions while avoiding any concentration of Macedonian forces and then wallowed in the local fleshpots, while his men idled and Philip relentlessly pursued his objectives. All of this at least moved forward the reallocation of the Theoric Fund; after a false start by Apollodorus who was deemed to have passed illegal legislation and was prosecuted and fined, Demosthenes got a technically correct formulation of the same policy back for serious discussion, but by this time Philip had substantially overrun Olynthius, and the Athenian Assembly thought better of the whole business. Despite the Demosthenean oratory, Athens stumbled on irresolutely.

In addition to his talents as a general, Philip was a consummate intriguer and in political terms, seducer, and he had suborned and subverted factions in Euboea over nearly ten years and weakened their attachment to Athens. He undermined Plutarchus, ruler of Eretria, who asked Athens for assistance against the pro-Philip insurrection of Cleitarchus. This was a pincers movement designed to distract and weaken Athens while Philip was overrunning Olynthus. Eubulus favoured assisting Plutarchus as the prospect of losing Euboea and its transition from a buffer zone to a potential invasion corridor for Macedonia into Attica was very disturbing. Demosthenes saw the agitation for what it was and urged that Athenian powers of resistance not be squandered in peripheral areas but concentrated at home where the real danger was. Reinforcements were sent, at a stately pace, given the creaking and improvised Athenian methods of mobilization, despite Demosthenes' best efforts at creating rapid response forces. Phocion commanded them but was subject to the amateurism and fecklessness of Plutarchus, who fled in the face of the enemy at Tamynae, and Phocion barely emerged victorious against Philip's local allies. Phocion managed fairly well, but eventually retired his command in favour of Molossus, who was defeated and captured, and Athens was evicted from Euboea, which was declared independent, except for the town of Carystus. It was an unmitigated fiasco for Athens.

While this debacle was unfolding, Demosthenes was severely physically assaulted at a Dionysiac festival by Meidias, an almost lifelong enemy, and as Demosthenes was a festival official, the assault was doubly illegal as an act of impiety. Demosthenes stated his intent to prosecute and wrote a fierce address of denunciation, but did not deliver it, as the political currents changed and he was reconciled with Eubulus, and lost interest in the incident, from which he entirely recovered. As Demosthenes had predicted, while Athens was fumbling incompetently in Euboea (again, slightly like the British in Norway in April 1940), Philip was mopping up the Chalcidic towns one after the other, usually with the assistance of paid fifth columns within. He professed no fundamental antagonism to Olynthus until he had taken all the surrounding territory and his agents were influential in Olynthus, and then delivered an ultimatum. The Olynthians asked Athens for help, to no discernible effect and tried to give battle, but the Olynthian cavalry was suborned and deserted, and Philip swallowed Olynthus in one snap of Macedon's jaw in August 348. The population was sold into slavery and Arrhidaeus and Menelaus were publicly executed. The more promising of the newly enslaved Olynthians were given by Philip to his friends and officers as slave-servants, along with their property. There were games and feastings of celebration in Macedonia while every community in Olynthus was razed to the ground in a deliberate act of general destruction surpassing anything of its kind in prior Greek history.

Philip, though he was fearless in provoking Athens, and monitored carefully the currents of Athenian opinion between the pre-Churchillian steadfastness of Demosthenes and the quasi-Baldwinian pragmatism of Eubulus, did not want to push Athens into all-out war at this time. Athens was the supreme maritime power and although Macedonia was a distinctly continental power (thus presaging rivalries and conflicts many centuries later between Britain and Spain, France, and Germany), its coasts could be harassed, and Athens behind its fortifications would not be a plum that would fall easily. Philip released a captured Athenian general, Phrynon, and sent a cordial message to Athens also via Ctesiphon, who had been sent to request the repayment of the ransom paid for Phrynon. Philip adopted the same policy of cordial placation of Athens as he had adopted toward Amphipolis and Olynthus before he devoured them.

The Athenian Assembly was discussing a measure to warm up relations with Macedonia when the full horrors of the rape and destruction of Olynthus became known and Eubulus himself moved a superseding motion to seek a Pan-Hellenic alliance of resistance against any further Macedonian depredations. The motion was moved by the rising orator Aeschines, a capable man who had risen from modest work as a schoolmaster and clerk, and now became one of the principal emissaries to rally the Greek states to Eubulus' proposal. They encountered the usual obtuse insularity of the Greek states and particularly the inability of the Spartans to imagine for an instant that they could be in any danger. So limp was the response that Eubulus concluded he had no choice but to make peace with Philip, as he was in conciliatory mood, the wolf in sheep's clothing. Demosthenes was now convinced of the need for peace, even if only to prepare better for war, and he moved for the commendation and reward of Aristodemus, an actor who had been sent to negotiate with Philip, which he did successfully after a good deal of back and forth, in 347.

But the interminable Sacred War (which in its motives and conduct was anything but sacred and was a rather desultory war) continued. The ineffable Phalaecus, a vintage Greek political scoundrel, was accused, doubtless with good reason, by his fellow Phocians, of using the proceeds of some of the Delphic treasures for his own ends. His treasurer, Philon, was tortured to death but revealed the names of accomplices. But Phalaecus retained the support of a large group of mercenaries whom he had also rewarded with the ill-gotten Delphic gains. He set up a base near Thermopylae, and the Thebans, short of manpower as well as judgment, became alarmed and called for the assistance of Philip. Philip was happy to humiliate Thebes but not to assist it, but to show respect for the Delphic Temple of Apollo (though it is doubtful that this was sincere), he sent a token force. A number of the Phocians took refuge in the Temple but died in the accidental fire there (described above). Now the proud Greek states reached out for allies in all directions. The Phocian government of Deinocrates, Callias, and Sophanes asked the aid of Athens and Sparta, and the Boeotians asked the aid of Philip. The Phocians offered Thermopylae in exchange for their assistance, and Athens sent Proxenus to take charge of the encampments around Thermopylae and fitted out a fifty-ship fleet of citizen-soldiers. But Proxenus arrived to find Phalaecus, now a brigand at the head of marauding mercenaries, and not the new Phocian government at Thermopylae. Phalaecus rejected the agreement his successors had made; Athens left their fleet of assistance in port, and the Spartans, who had sent a thousand men were also rebuffed and lost interest. Philip sat by, sphinx-like, awaiting events as the Greeks fumbled and went to and fro almost mindlessly under his stony and covetous gaze.

Parliamentary matters came to a head in Athens in 346, when it was resolved to send ten ambassadors representing Athens and its allies to Philip to try to negotiate durable arrangements with him. It was a high-powered delegation including Philocrates, who had moved and carried this initiative at the Assembly, and Aeschines and Demosthenes. They departed at once and attended upon Philip at Pella, where the Macedonian king received them very courteously, as was his custom. Aeschines, who provided the only account of this mission that we now have, spoke of the Athenian claim to Amphipolis. Chersonese and the troublesome matter of the Phocians was addressed by others, and Demosthenes, who was the wind-up speaker, failed his great opportunity and broke down from nervosity once in the physical presence of the man he had so fervently and eloquently denounced. He was not a great extemporaneous speaker, but he had had the voyage to prepare remarks. It was a terrible let-down to his many admirers, and perhaps even to Philip himself, who rarely felt the need to harangue large audiences. Philip responded warmly and spoke of Chersonese in a conciliatory manner but declined to accept the Athenian argument about Amphipolis. He did promise a splendid and serene arrangement with Athens if that state would make a serious peace and alliance with him. Aeschines, in particular, was impressed with the force of Philip's arguments, as well as with the practicalities of alliance with the man who was now probably the most powerful in the western world, given the decrepitude of Persia.

The issue was vigorously debated in the Assembly and Council when the delegation returned to Athens, Demosthenes now rather ungraciously, given the fiasco of his own performance, said that the Macedonian emissaries should be accorded the normal courtesies but no more. Aeschines was much more enthusiastic, and apparently more representative of the delegation as a whole. In the extensive debates, the allies of Athens asked that the Phocians and Halus be given the opportunity to join the peace within three months. The more expansive faction, led by Philocrates, called not just for peace, but also for alliance with Philip, and that the Phocians and Halus should not be permitted to join the alliance. Philip's emissaries to Athens, Antipater and Parmenion, when questioned directly by the Assembly, acknowledged that their king would not accept the admission of the Phocians and Halus. Indeed, they were so inconsistent and unreliable, it is hard to discern how they elicited so much solicitude from the Athenian leadership.

Aeschines, who, along with Philocrates, seems to have been in direct touch with Philip, assured his colleagues that Philip would be a considerate ally, and was only demurring because of his fidelity to his relationship with Thebes and Thessaly. The debate raged on in the interminable Athenian manner, until Eubulus appended a note of stark realism to proceedings by reminding his fellow legislators that the choice was between acceptance of the Macedonian king's proposal and war, which would consume the festival money, the subject of a powerful addiction, and would involve a military campaign that would be, to say the least, extremely challenging.

It was astonishing that it took so long for the collective intelligence to grasp the obvious and required the principal figure among them to rub their noses in it for the Athenian Assembly to understand the proportions of their dilemma. It was agreed that both sides would keep what they had at time of ratification: the Athenians kept Chersonese except Cardia, and the Macedonians kept Amphipolis. Cersobleptes' effort to join the alliance at this late stage was rejected by Demosthenes as the president for the day (the Assembly rotated the chairmanship daily). In fact, Philip captured Cersobleptes as the Athenian ambassadors were on their way to him with the ratification of his terms. Philip took most of his territory, and left Cersobleptes as a vassal prince, with his son handed over to Philip as a hostage, as Philip had been as a youth. There was an evident chasm between the ambitions of Eubulus and Philocrates and Aeschines for a durable peace with Philip, and Demosthenes and his followers, who agreed that a breathing space was needed but that a fight to the finish, if in stages, was already underway between the civic democracy of Athens and the ravening tyrant of Macedonia.

Demosthenes tried to have the ambassadors get to Philip as soon as possible to give effect to the peace and bring Philip's campaign of aggressive expansion in Thrace to an end. But a special decree was required from the Council, which involved more debating, and Proxenus, Philip's ambassador, departed Athens at once without the Athenian party that Demosthenes had hoped Proxenus would conduct expeditiously to his king. Instead, the Athenians arrived reasonably promptly at Pella, but Philip did not appear until another month had elapsed in the course of which he extracted what he had been seeking from the Thracians. The Athenians were dismayed to find that they had been preceded to Pella by emissaries from a host of other Greek states seeking Philip's favour, including Sparta, Thebes, Euboea, and Phocis, the Thebans and Phocians seeking Philip's assistance against the other. (It is not clear which Phocian faction was present—Phalaecus or Deinocrates.) This activity confirmed that Macedonia was already the greatest power in southeast Europe, and Philip dealt with all these Greeks with his customary suavity and duplicity and distributed generous gifts to the Athenian emissaries.

There was a schism among the Athenian representatives which emerged clearly, as Demosthenes was favourable to Thebes, which would eventually, he thought, be needed in any supreme contest with Macedonia, where the others were partial to the Phocians and regarded Thebes as an old and unscrupulous rival. Aeschines was apparently the chief Athenian spokesman, and he lobbied Philip for the pursuit of a vote by the Amphictyonic Council, and he had in mind a reconstruction of the Delphic Temple and surroundings. Demosthenes, again, seemed not to have been very persuasive, and commended himself for his gracious reception of the Macedonian emissaries to Athens while criticizing his colleagues for being exaggeratedly deferential to Philip. The Macedonian king paid no attention to it, accepted the Peace, but only took the oath until, accompanied by the Athenian ambassadors and at the head of his army, he had reached Pherae, and where his allies also took the oath, rather than, as the Athenian Assembly and Council had decreed—the Athenian representatives traveling between the various capitals and securing the oaths of Philip's allies singly. Demosthenes did succeed in winning from Philip a pledge that all Athenian prisoners in Macedonian custody would be home to celebrate the next Panathenaic festival. The ambassadors returned to Athens on July 7, 346 B.C., but Demosthenes charged his colleagues before the Council with derogation from instructions in not obtaining the oaths of the Macedonian allies individually and not getting more concessions from Philip.

The Council was swayed by this but Aeschines carried the day before the Assembly with his argument that Philip, who had already arrived at Thermopylae on his way to deal with Thebes, would punish the Thebans for their attempt to take over Delphi, and would rebuild Thespiae and Plataea, and a letter from Philip was read publicly, in which he accepted the blame for any apparent shortcomings of the Athenian mission from their instructions, and pledging good faith and conduct. Aeschines won the debate, ascribing his differences with Demosthenes to the fact that "He drinks water and I drink wine." Philocrates' motion of thanks to the Macedonian king for his constructive attitude and demanding that Phocis submit to the decisions of the Amphictyonic League, or face armed conflict with Athens, was adopted. The Assembly also declined Philip's invitation to send an army to join him at Thermopylae, that the two powers could together resolve the Delphic and other issues. This was a serious and almost inexplicable blunder, as it assured that Philip would sort out the affairs of north Greece as he pleased.

Events now moved quickly: the ambassadors conducting the message of Philocrates' resolution to Philip were stopped before they left Attica by the news that the shifty Phalaecus had surrendered to Philip at Themopylae. The Athenians ordered drastic defensive measures as Philip now had the ability to pour into Attica almost unopposed if he wished, but at the same time the ambassadors were told to complete their mission as if the government of Athens was completely serene about these latest developments. Phalaecus was allowed to depart with just eight-thousand mercenaries and he set off for Crete to try his adventurer's hand there, but his luck had run out and he was killed in battle later in 346, generally an unmourned scoundrel, and far from the bravest and most dashing of that type. Such of his mercenaries who survived embarked for Elis and almost all were killed in battle or captured and executed by the winning faction in that conflict, in 344-3. Philip occupied almost all of Phocis in short order and large numbers of Phocians fled to Athens and were well received. Philip finally showed his sterner side and forcefully objected to Athens' disagreement with his actions. He pointed out that Phocis had been excluded from the Peace and that he was well within his rights.

The Phocians were to be judged by the Amphictyonic Council, and it determined that the Phocian towns were to be destroyed and the populations scattered to hamlets of not more than fifty houses each and at least two-hundred yards separating villages. They were ordered to repay the value of the Temple treasures their leaders had pillaged, in annual installments and that until that was done, they could not own horses, and those who fled were subject to seizure anywhere in the Greek world. Thebes occupied some of the Phocian towns and the Boeotian towns that had thrown in their lot with Phocis against Thebes were razed to the ground and their populations were sold into slavery. The Phocians lost their vote in the Amphyctyonic Council and Philip and Delphi took charge of the Temple. The entire Phocian foray into the swaggering politics of the major Greek states had been an unmitigated disaster. It was a mad and corrupt enterprise from the start. Philip was appointed to preside over the next Pythian games, but Athens and Sparta, now sulking and pouting, virtually boycotted the games. Philip then demanded a formal recognition of him by Athens as a member of the Amphictyonic Council. This led to another heated debate in the Assembly. Aeschines pleaded the case for acceptance, and was only sustained when Demosthenes, the foremost of Philip's Athenian enemies, recognized that Athens was in no condition to face off with Philip now, and urged acceptance of the Macedonian demand. Athens had been thoroughly humiliated with no test of arms at all with Macedonia.

At this time, it was clear to everyone that Philip was overwhelmingly the preeminent figure in the Hellenic world and its European fringes. He personified the advantages of autocratic rule and concentration of power in the hands of a single talented individual. Athenian democracy, despite the courage and intermittent eloquence of several of the leading personalities, especially Demosthenes, had been exposed to all as a muddled, ineffectual talking shop, more concerned with the disposition of the festival funds than with the preservation of their civic honour and independence. Demosthenes now entered the most famous and creditable phase of his career with a series of powerful speeches about the need for Athens to revive and assert her selfless martial traditions as in olden time.

Aeschines is not to be despised for his view that at this late stage, Athens was better off acting as a prominent if at least temporarily junior partner to Philip's Macedonia, working with him to suppress pirates and swiftly building their defenses and general capacity to prevail in a future possible war of survival against the suddenly over-powering Macedonian entity. If there is a Demosthenean comparison with Winston Churchill (they were similar only as orators—Demosthenes had none of Churchill's competence as a national war leader), there was also a slight comparison with the evolution of Britain's position and relations with the United States. But this comparison is limited, as the conduct of the United States throughout its alliance with Great Britain, in war and peace, has been exemplary and generous, where Philip of Macedon was crafty, unscrupulous, cynical and at times almost diabolical in his manipulation and betrayal of ostensible allies. He was, however, extremely capable and was moving quickly from success to success. The preposterous and enervating Sacred War was finally over—resolved by an outsider whose only interest in Delphi was as a strategic key to seizing the headship of the entire Hellenic world. The Greece of the city states, of endless war for absurd objectives between thuggish armies and bands of mercenaries was ending. A new, spectacular, and not entirely distinguished era in Greek history was beginning.

3. Macedonian Dominance of the Hellenic World

An unusual feature of Philip's policy was that one of the reasons he wished to be preeminent in the Greek world was that he was in cultural terms, a militant Hellenophile and pan-Hellenist. He wished to strengthen and encourage Greece's cultural supremacy and spread its renown and practice far afield, carried by force of Macedonian arms to territories where it had been of uncertain and fragile influence. His plan was a marriage of his political and military strengths with the cultural exaltation of the puny and bellicosely quarrelsome principal cities of Greece, especially Athens, and to conquer and civilize by stages the adjoining world. It was a vision of remarkable ambition. His sincere respect for the civilization of Greece assured a generally fairly indulgent hegemony, as long as his primacy was acknowledged, and his sponsorship of the Greeks was flattering, even to those who resented his ascendancy and regarded the Macedonians as a rough and indifferent people. In all of this, he somewhat presaged the career paths of the German Catherine the Great of Russia, the Corsican Napoleon as First Consul and Emperor of the French, the Georgian Stalin as Marshal Premier of the U.S.S.R., and the Austrian Hitler, German Fuehrer, though his conduct was not remotely as odious as the last two. Philip appointed Aristotle as tutor to his son Alexander, and his court was packed with Greek cultural figures of renown. He placed colonies of Greeks he had displaced from Thrace and Chalcidia in the interior of Macedonia, to be a reliable frontier force against wild tribes which continued to arrive out of the mists of central Europe and Asia in unpredictable strength and on an irregular timetable.

In 344, he had to carry a campaign to reinforce his frontiers against Illyria, pushing them right to the Adriatic shore, but he sustained a serious wound in his leg. He next imposed himself upon Thessaly and the Thessalians soon realized the wisdom of making Philip archon (ruler) for life, of that country. Isocrates wrote him a famous letter at this point, asking that Athens be treated as generously as Thessaly. This would have been Philip's preference but proud Athens, especially when stirred by the irreconcilable Demosthenes, was not in a placatory mood. Demosthenes had tried to prosecute Aeschines, for taking bribes from Philip during his second embassy to him, but Aeschines put Demosthenes on the defensive by accusing his legal associate Timarchus of immoral practices in his youth. Typically of Greek official pettifogging, such an irrelevant charge was permitted to delay the larger proceedings. Philip tried to improve relations by offering to build a canal in Chersonese, which would provide Athens a defensible eastern frontier, but the Athenian government, fearful of both Philip and Demosthenes, wobbled and straddled. Philip was not prepared to accept any reinflation of the status of Cersobleptes, who in the Macedonian king's opinion, was fortunate to be in place even as Philip's vassal suzerain.

The balance prevailed in the Peloponnese for a couple of years after the Peace of Philocrates between Sparta and its traditional enemies—the Argives, Messenians, and Arcadians of Megalopolis, but Sparta could not control its instinct to become assertive and the other states appealed to Philip. It had taken a great deal of conflict to dilute Greek reticence about seeking the aid of the Persian king in Hellenic affairs, and was at first thought almost treasonable, "medism" was a term of scorn and hate.

There was no such hesitation in asking the intervention of the Macedonians, who were (as they remain at time of writing), quasi-Greek. Philip had been up to his old mischief of subsidizing Fifth Columns (a phrase from the Spanish Civil War of A.D. 1936-1939), in the various Greek states. He encouraged and emboldened them and required Sparta to desist from its high-handed activities and threatened personally to lead his army into the Peloponnese.

This roused the anti-Macedonian party in Athens, led, of course, by Demosthenes. There were many Athenians who preferred Philip to their ancient Spartan foe, so Demosthenes was never able to set himself at the head of united Athenian opinion, as great modern galvanizers of peoples against aggressive neighbours, such as Churchill and Clemenceau, have done. There was a further complication in that Demosthenes was not advocating aid to Sparta against Macedonia, but trying to incite the anti-Spartan Peloponnesian states, Messenia, Arcadia, and Argos, to look to Athens rather than Macedonia as the source of assistance, and he embarked on an extensive speaking tour of the communities in these states to sell his vision. Demosthenes tried to frighten his audiences with references to the fate of Olynthus and other acts of severity by Philip.

Athens and Sparta had naturally drawn closer as the Macedonian proximity loomed and Athens had done precisely nothing before to assist the anti-Spartan states of Peloponnese, and Demosthenes' mission was a delusional resurrection of a fictionalized past in which Athens was any sort of protector of Peloponnesian underdogs and could credibly pose now as a rival to Macedonia in that role. Demosthenes was a minority in this cause in Athens, and Athens was not believable playing any useful role in the Peloponnese. His hosts heard him out politely but invited Philip into the Peloponnese: the fox was invited into the henhouse and lavished with honours and deferences, including a bronze statue of Philip at Megalopolis and a crown for him from the Argives. Demosthenes was thrust back onto a more familiar dais, and proclaimed his Philippics, causing a formal protest by Philip, denying that he had ever failed in a promise he had made to any Peloponnesian state. As his protest was being debated, Demosthenes delivered his second Philippic, accusing Philip of having suborned the support of treasonable Athenians and of befriending the Peloponnesians and Thebans as part of a plan to subjugate Athens. There was undoubtedly some truth to these charges, but making the charges did not in itself make it easier to frustrate the policy Demosthenes imputed to the Macedonian king.

Demosthenes, probably with some justice, accused Philip of pretending to take his distance from Thebes in order to help soften Athenian resistance to his designs. Philip did apparently impede Thebes from exacting specific imposition of peace terms from the Phocians over the pillaging of the Delphic temple of Apollo—this was not the first or last occasion when victorious allies have differed over the collection of post-war reparations. Philip did make the positive gesture of supporting Athens in the administration of the sacred island of Delos, against the wishes of the Delians themselves. Philip was one of the great masters in all history of playing military, diplomatic, and cultural cards with many parties at the same time with brilliant attention to the fine points of ambition, vulnerability, and rivalry between all the other parties. In his dexterity he would presage a number of outstanding modern statesmen, such as Richelieu, Metternich, Palmerston, Disraeli, and Bismarck, and Philip was also a king and a general, though he operated in a smaller and simpler theatre than national leaders in Europe from the Seventeenth to Nineteenth Centuries.

In this phase of maneuvering, Demosthenes got the upper hand in Athens, as Philocrates does appear to have been tangibly induced by Philip, and he fled Athens before his trial could begin and was sentenced to death in absentia. Philip continued his peace offensive, sending Python of Byzantium (an unpromising name for a negotiator) and colleagues from other allies to Athens to express Philip's greetings and regards to Athens. An effort was made to renegotiate the Peace of Philocrates, but Athens insisted on revisions that would restore to them Amphipolis, Potidaea, and Cardia, and the resuscitation of the imperishable object of Athenian solicitude, Cersobleptes. The proposed terms were delivered to Philip in person with great insolence by Hegesippus, whom Philip dismissed with a minimum of diplomatic formality.

When Philip offered to give the Euboean island of Halonnesus, where Athens had allowed pirates to flourish, which Philip had suppressed and evicted, Demosthenes and Hegesippus demanded that Philip acknowledge that he was "giving back" the island. The Athenians were going to ingenious lengths to antagonize their crafty and powerful interlocutor. This was particularly untimely as it coincided with the trial of Aeschines, which Demosthenes had precipitated, and which became an issue of Macedonian influence on Aeschines and treatment of the Phocians (who, especially under Phalaecus, were completely undeserving of Athens' sympathy). Aeschines was a powerful orator also, and had no difficulty proving that many of Demosthenes' charges were outrageous falsehoods. This was no way to build united resistance to the encroachments of Philip. The anti-Macedonian party continued to be the majority in Athens, and abused their position tyrannically at times, such as in the torture and execution of one Antiphon, as a Macedonian spy, on questionable evidence. This was one of the least salubrious episodes in this stage of Demosthenes' career.

All of this was sufficient provocation to Philip to take a series of initiatives around the perimeter of Athens that signaled his abandonment of his attempt to make common cause with Athens in a joint cultural, military, and economic consolidation and expansion of the Hellenic world. He intervened to secure the success of the pro-Macedonian faction in Elis. Philip was narrowly rebuffed in his effort to take control of Megara through a loyal local faction, but his partisans did take control of most of Euboea, after the overthrow of the democrats of Eretria. A good deal of diplomatic jockeying went on all around the Greek world, as Athens detached Chalcis from Thebes, and moved quickly enough to deter Philip from trying to gain control of Ambracia, Leucas, and Naupactus. The future, and not distantly future, battlelines were being drawn.

In 343 B.C. Artaxerxes Ochus sent emissaries to all the principal Greek states including Macedonia, inviting alliance. It will be recalled from Chapter 10 how dilapidated the Great King's realm had become by this time: the revolts of Phoenicia and Cyprus and much of Asia Minor, the appalling siege of Sidon, and two failed efforts to retrieve Egypt. Demosthenes had long advocated avoidance of any connection to anyone in Asia if it did not directly involve Hellenic parties, and there was a consensus for this in Athens, and Sparta and most of the other Greek states declined or ignored the Persian overture. But Thebes, which had been heavily subsidized by Persia in the Sacred War, and Argos did send military contingents to assist in the reconquest of Egypt, which was achieved in 342. Nectanebo II fled to Ethiopia. Almost all conflicts in Asia Minor for many decades had chiefly been contested by Greek mercenaries; the martial patriotic concept of local or national armies was in disuse and ever more flabby elites were essentially taxing or pillaging their jurisdictions to engage the able-bodied unemployed men of Greece to do battle on their behalf. Throughout western history, when matters deteriorated to the engagement of mercenaries as proxies for quarrelling regimes of doubtful popular support, radical change has been in the offing.

Philip apparently did not respond substantively to the Great King and was preparing an invasion of Asia Minor, if he could be confident of both his northern frontiers and the neutrality of the Greek states. Hermeias, the tyrant of Atarneus, a coastal city in Asia Minor, and a close confidant and follower of Aristotle, steeped in the philosophy and acquaintance of Plato, was a protégé of Philip's. But Mentor of Rhodes, whose reconquest of Egypt for Artaxerxes Ochus was outlined in Chapter 10, approached Hermeias pretending to be a potential ally in assisting Philip's designs in Asia Minor, but seized him and sent him in chains to Susa, where the Great King attempted to torture out of him the plans for Philip's much awaited invasion of Asia Minor. Hermeias died gloriously, like the most admired of anti-Nazi resistance leaders in World War II, such as Jean Moulin in 1943, without revealing a word of Philip's plans. Hermeias was tortured to insensibility and then crucified, an act of extraordinary barbarism even by the worst of contemporary standards. Aristotle immortalized him with a shrine at Delphi, an heroic poem, and reserved for himself the right to marry his daughter or niece when they were of age. This ghastly outburst of treachery and wickedness provided a startling illustration of the gulf in civility that separated Greece and Persia. It did not raise the Macedonian king and court's esteem for the Great King of Persia.

For most of 342, Philip was still bolting down his position in Thrace, further demoting the inexhaustibly rebellious Cersobleptes. He put down frontier colonies and made arrangements with the neighbouring Getae tribe that roamed and more or less occupied the territory between Thrace and the Danube. Philip went through the harsh Thracian winter of 342-1 with his troops, non-mercenaries who were motivated in large part by Macedonian national pride and loyalty to their chief who had led them to so many successes and always paid them well and commanded them boldly but not recklessly. As spring came, there was a sharp dispute with Athens over Chersonese; Athens had dispatched a large number of colonists, who had come in abrasive contact with the Cardians, a local Macedonian ally. The Athenian commander in the area, Diopeithes, was supporting the Athenian colonists, but as Athens sent him no support, to avoid mutinies by his mercenaries, he plundered merchant shipping in the northern Aegean and terrorized neighbouring states with shore raids. Cardia requested protection from Philip who sent some land forces to assist Cardia, but Diopeithes, another overly bellicose figure on a long leash who acted with no thought of where his provocations might ramify, invaded Cardian and Persian territory and took Philip's ambassador to Cardia into custody and attempted to ransom him. Philip wrote to the Athenian government and declared his intention to defend Cardia. Another heated public debate took place in the Athenian assembly. Aeschines led the criticism of Diopeithes, asserting the clear illegality and indefensibly aggressive nature of his conduct, while Demosthenes led his defence, claiming that Philip was already at war with Athens and that no one should be chastised for advancing Athens' interests against the Macedonian ogre.

After a considerable public airing of this and related issues, Demosthenes tipped the scales with his Third Philippic, following which, supplies, reinforcements, and money were voted for Diopeithes, Chares was sent north to command the theatre, garrisons were dispatched, and Demosthenes and his more persuasive associates fanned out across Greece rousing Pan-Hellenic opinion behind a coordinated resistance to Macedonia. This time, they had considerable success. Byzantium, disquieted by the relentless progress toward it of Philip and his protégés, responded to a personal oratorical visit from Demosthenes who was, in his best voice, reviving the Athenian alliance after having allowed it to lapse fifteen years before. The independent Thracian towns and cities rallied. Euboea overthrew its tyrants and elevated the pro-Athenian democrats who returned to alliance with Athens, though not to the Athenian League. Chalcis joined in and Demosthenes and Callias now set out to establish a Pan-Hellenic League. Corinth, Megara, Achaea, Acarnania, Ambracia, Leucas and Corcyra came aboard. This was a substantial achievement largely down to Demosthenes and his powerful (if often demagogic) oratory. Very late, someone, was taking a stand against Macedonia. Philip's was a relatively enlightened and culturally ambitious regime, but Athens retained its superior civic virtue, scrupulosity, and respect for integrity among states, though not, as has frequently been noted, without many failings. It was a contest between enlightened but cynical competence and querulous but relatively gentle good intentions. Both sides had proud and brave aptitudes for war.

A congress of the Pan-Hellenic League was organized for 340 at Athens, which avoided war but passed a lot of resolutions that were overtly critical of and hostile to Philip. There were numerous incidents, including the seizure by Callias of a number of Macedonian towns in the Bay of Pagasae, the seizure of Macedonian ships and sale of their crews into slavery, raids on Halonnesus and other places and numerous reprisals and general skirmishing on land and sea. When one Anaxinus appeared in Athens on an errand from Olympias, Demosthenes had him branded a spy, interrogated and then tortured and executed. It was not greatly more distinguished an incident than the wicked capture, torture, and execution of Hermeias of Atarneus by the Persian king. In 340, Demosthenes, who had now revealed himself as a fanatic, as well as a statesman, patriot, and orator of proverbial gifts, was crowned at the Dionysiac festival.

War finally erupted when Philip demanded that Byzantium and Perinthus act faithfully to their alliance with Macedonia and assist Philip in Chersonese. They refused, and in the summer of 340 Philip sent his fleet up the Hellespont, an explicit threat to the Athenian grain supply. Athens sent its fleet to oppose the Macedonian fleet and clear the Hellespont; the Macedonian ships landed a significant force on the Chersonese shore, which advanced in parallel to the Macedonian navy, and prevented shore sorties. Philip laid siege to Perinthus and the Byzantines, with Athenian assistance, came to the aid of Perinthus, as did, more importantly, the Great King. This was partly in response to embassies from Athens and other Greek states, though it is clear from the Fourth Philippic by Demosthenes, that no formal alliance had been established when Persia intervened. After centuries of internecine Greek conflict and many wars with and within the Persian Empire, most of the known world in the west was coming to a complex triangulated conflict involving Athenian, Persian, and Macedonian coalitions.

Athens and Persia focused against the newly risen threat from the north without any great comradely solidarity between themselves. It was general war rippling and bubbling all around. Philip besieged Perinthus for three months, attacking its steep walls day and night. Perinthus descended in sheer cliffs to the sea, and the only overland access was an isthmus of about two-hundred metres in width. The Persians supplied food by sea, and Philip attacked with mines and sappers and siege towers an astonishing one-hundred and twenty feet in height. He finally took part of the outer wall, but the Perinthians retreated upwards to the first row of heavily fortified houses and Philip suddenly abandoned this impractical approach which risked horrifying losses for minimal gains and tried to take Byzantium by surprise.

4. War Between Macedonia and Athens

The casus belli was the seizure by Philip of two-hundred and thirty Athenian merchantmen ferrying grain and money from the Black sea to Athens. While Chares was conferring with the local Persian commander, in a bold coup de main, Philip seized all the ships, and reduced them to timber for his siege-works. He replied to the extremely strenuous Athenian note with a declaration of war. This had taken an absurdly long time and an immense number of reciprocal provocations, when one considers the flimsy pretext on the basis of which Pericles plunged into the Peloponnesian war in 431. The sequence of events leading to this showdown with Macedonia more closely presaged the "border incidents" between the Soviet Union and Japan in the 1930s, which sometimes involved pitched battles of up to ten divisions. The two countries took a total of about fifty-thousand casualties, but it did not lead to outright war, as Japan thought better of it after a thorough defeat by the Russians at Khalkin Gol in 1939, and turned toward the Pacific, while the U.S.S.R. signed the Nazi-Soviet Pact and invaded Poland two days after a cease-fire went into effect with the Japanese.

The Greeks demolished the monument to the Peace of Philocrates, and Demosthenes instituted the strict reforms he had advocated with the cost of war born fairly and citizen forces raised. He was elevated to a special office as war leader. Chares was ordered to relieve Byzantium, but the Byzantines were mistrustful of him, and serious cooperation did not really take hold until the arrival of Cephisophon and Phocion in mid-340, and further reinforcements were sent by Rhodes, Chios, and Cos. Phocion cleared the Hellespont, and the supply of grain to Athens rose and the cost declined. Philip made a mighty nighttime assault on the walls of Byzantium in 339, but surprise was shattered by the barking of watchdogs, the operation was not successful, and Philip elected to withdraw, as he had at Perinthus, not risking even more on the periphery as the war was on Macedonia's western and southern borders.

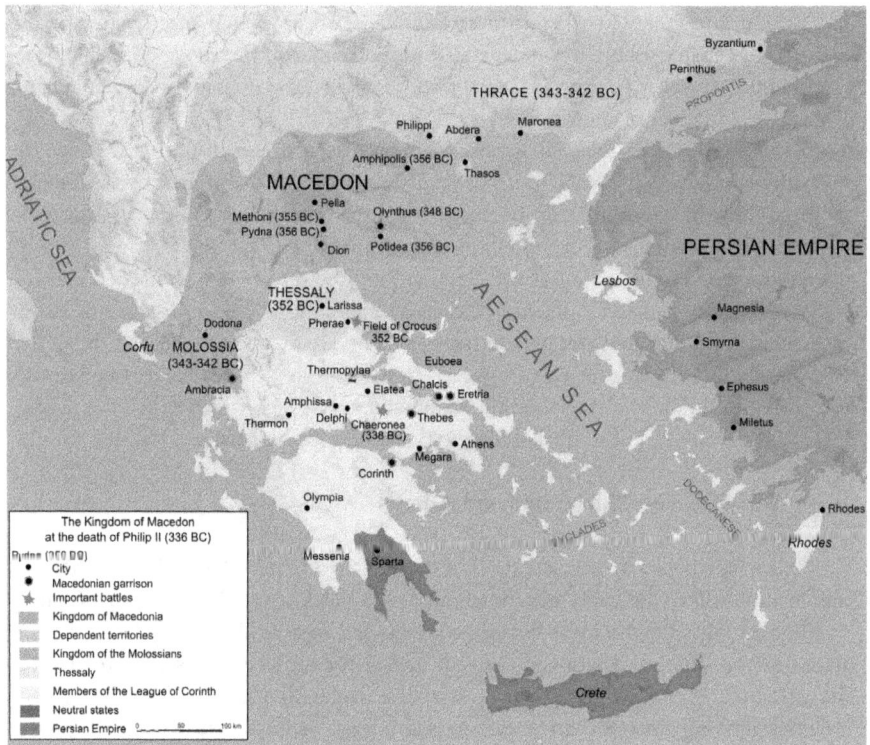

Philip's fleet had been driven into the Black Sea by Phocion and was trapped there. Philip addressed this problem with a ruse by which he sent a message to his general Antipater, advising false movements, which was captured and decoded by the Athenians, as Philip had planned, and caused them to move their fleet in the hope of catching a large Macedonian fleet in a death-trap. The sly Macedonian leader succeeded by this chicanery in extricating his fleet, but he had been defeated in the east and had even greater difficulties in the northeast and north, as he now set out to punish the Scythians and their eighty-nine-year-old king, Ateus, who had refused assistance against Byzantium. Philip defeated the Scythians in a series of engagements and the aged king died gallantly in battle. Philip took huge numbers of slaves and cattle but in his homeward procession was set upon by the savage Balkan Triballi tribe. Philip himself was seriously wounded but he fought his way through, though he lost all that he had plundered from the Scythians and took heavy casualties. It was far from a triumphant return home for the wounded king and his battered army.

On returning to Pella in 339, Philip discovered that a new outburst of Greek squabbling invited his exploitation. The Athenians had opened a new chapel in Delphi and decorated it with some shields that were inscribed as celebrating Athenian victories over Persia and Thebes. The Amphictyonic Council heard a complaint from the Locrians about the insult to Thebes while there was also a complaint from Amphissa about Athens' alleged complicity with the Phocians, who had pillaged and desecrated Delphi. The durable and versatile Athenian delegate, Aeschines yet again, accused the Amphisseans of sacrilege in cultivating about Cirrha, territory dedicated to Apollo. Aeschines was so effective, the Delphic population rose up, marched on Cirrha and destroyed anything the Amphisseans had touched. It was determined to meet at once at Thermopylae, to judge the Amphisseans. Aeschines had undoubtedly spared Athens a new Amphictyonic War, and a war against Thebes threatened, which Demosthenes opposed because he considered Thebes a potential last resort ally against Philip. He persuaded the Council not to be represented at the Thermopylae meeting, and as Thebes also was not present, what was approved was a punitive war against Amphissa. (The Greeks, as we have seen countless times, always had to be at war, preferably with other Greeks.) The expedition sent, under Cottyphus, won a minor victory but the Amphisseans ignored the command to pay a fine, dismiss its political leaders and recall politicians in exile. (This too was typical: an absurd sentence there was no chance of enforcing.) Thus mocked, the Amphictyonic Council invited Philip to conduct a punitive war against Amphissa. Philip may have prompted the invitation and he delightedly accepted it. This was the Amphissean War.

It was also Philip's invitation to move a sizeable army into Greece. Philip marched to Elatea, which was directly between Thebes and Athens (only three days' march from Athens), which indicated that Philip may have become a Trojan Horse in Greece. Demosthenes roused opinion in Athens and carried a resolution authorizing an immediate embassy to Thebes seeking that city's support against Philip. The Macedonian king had also sent emissaries to Thebes and asked them to remain neutral as he dealt with Amphissa (a Theban ally) and to join him in an invasion of Attica. Philip's ambassadors found themselves debating with Demosthenes who got himself appointed Athens' representative to propose alliance between Thebes and Athens and not to allow Philip to divide and conquer Greece. Demosthenes, convinced of the extreme urgency of his succeeding, went to unauthorized lengths to secure Thebes' solidarity with Athens, and offered recognition of Theban supremacy in Boeotia, if necessary, with direct Athenian armed assistance. Athens would command at sea, Thebes on land, and Athens would pick up two thirds of the expenses. Demosthenes prevailed, and Athens accepted his excess of authority, even though several Athenian allies were being put over the side. Both sides tried to round up more allies, but almost all the Peloponnesian states were already allied to both Athens and Macedonia and declared their neutrality in the now imminent struggle. In the circumstances, most such allies were little better than mercenaries anyway, and were apt to quit or even to change sides without notice.

Athens easily approved Demosthenes' longstanding bugbear about redirecting festival funds and revenues to a war-chest, and the improvement of docks at Piraeus, which had begun with the Peace of Philocrates, was again suspended, to focus on immediate tasks. The very capable Lycurgus was brought in as financial director, and troops were sent forward urgently to Boeotia. All the passes between Philip and Athens were occupied, and ten-thousand mercenaries were sent to defend the road to Amphissa and to bar access for Philip to his supporters in the Peloponnese. There was minor skirmishing at the edges of these movements and the Athenians were marginally successful. Demosthenes, now the unambiguously leading figure of Athens and somewhat vindicated by events, was again crowned at the Dionysian Festival in March, 338 B.C.

Philip delayed the start of serious hostilities while he brought up reinforcements from Macedonia and Thessaly, and helped rebuild Phocia as a bulwark against the Thebans getting into Attica while Philip was attacking Athens overland. Philip and his allies on the Amphictyonic Council engineered an eighty per cent reduction of the fine that had been levied on the Phocians for their pilferage, profligacy, and sacrilege, and the method of governing Delphi was changed to give greater secular influence to the Macedonian party, a struggle somewhat prefigurative of secular influences on the Christian Churches in the coming millennia. In a particular breakthrough, Philip was named by the Amphictyonic Council, "Champion of the God of Delphi." It was a matter of considerable prestige. With these preliminaries, Philip again tried his hand at finessing and duping his opponents as he had done to extract his fleet from the Bosporus in 339. This time, he sent a message to Antipater stating he was returning at once to Thrace to put down an uprising there and that Attica could wait; and the courier was sent on a route that was designed to invite capture and was schooled on the histrionics to engage in if captured. The message was captured and Chares and Proxenus, the Athenian and Theban commanders, went to a reduced state of alert and Philip came through one of the passes by night with a large force and severely defeated Proxenus and Chares and easily captured Amphissa.

By this means, Philip was now able to roam at will behind the Athenian and Theban forces holding the other passes to Attica, and he forced the armies opposing him to retreat from their positions of defensive strength and try to stop his advance in the plains of Chaeronea. Philip continued to offer a negotiated peace and was taken seriously by the Theban Boeotarchs and by Phocion in Athens, a respected and experienced statesman. But Demosthenes was at the height of his popularity and rallied an Athenian majority behind the honorable course and the preferable option to giving way to Philip in stages. He shamed the Thebans back into line by asking their permission to evacuate the Athenian forces that had been advanced to the defense of Thebes that they might be available at least for the defense of Athens. The Battle of Chaeronea followed, in August or September, 338. The armies met in open country, each side of thirty to thirty-five thousand men. The Macedonian left was commanded by Philip's eighteen-year-old son Alexander, making his debut and soon to become one of the gigantic figures of world history, surpassing in renown anyone who had lived in the world up to that time. He was anxious to impress his father.

Philip commanded on the right and both men implemented cunning tactics that were very different. Alexander was allotted the more battle-experienced troops and he led them in person with conspicuous courage in fierce combat against the famous "Sacred Band" of the Theban elite guard. On the Macedonian right, Philip fell back and pretended to be in some disorder and at risk of losing direct contact with his centre, drawing the Athenians, led by Chares, forward and onto lower ground. Philip then counter-attacked the left centre of the Athenian line, severing their left, and eviscerated the Athenian left from three sides as Alexander on the Macedonian left forced the Theban right to retreat after the "Sacred Band" in accord with highest traditions going back to Epaminondas, fought to the last man. Alexander then joined his father's encirclement. Over three-thousand Athenian citizens were killed or captured, and the Athenian and Theban armies were shattered. Demosthenes was among those who managed to depart the Athenian force on its far left and escape through the pass to Lebadea. Lysicles, one of the Athenian commanders, as was the Greek custom, was tried on his return to Athens. Stratocles, seems to have died in battle, in the general rout of his forces. Lycurgus prosecuted Lysicles: "The Athenians have been totally defeated in a general engagement. A thousand of our youth have fallen on the field of battle, two thousand have been taken prisoner. The enemy has erected a monument to the total dishonor of Athens; and Greece is now ready to receive the dreadful yoke of slavery. You were the commander on that fatal day and yet you live: you enjoy the sun's light, you appear in our public places, the monument of the disgrace and calamity of your country." That was the entire prosecution as far as is known. Lysicles declined to demur and on Lycurgus' calm assertion that immediate execution was required, the former commander nodded in tacit agreement and proceeded without hesitation to the nearby chopping block, bent over it without guidance or coercion and was cleanly beheaded. His dignity in accepting the just fate in these times for anyone who had led so many to their deaths in a defeated cause was noted but was regarded as the mere performance of a beaten general's duty.[3]

There was no possible doubt who was master in Greece now. And as would be demonstrated often in the future, including by great modern military commanders including Frederick the Great and Napoleon, it was almost impossible to put instant recruits, slave soldiers, or mercenaries up against battle-hardened citizen troops, and a unified army under a competent commander had every advantage over a divided command, even if those who shared command were able enough. (Athens' best general, Phocion, was absent, commanding the navy in the Aegean. The news of the overwhelming defeat was received in Athens with the customary cold and unflapped determination of that oft-threatened city. The walls were reinforced, the entire Attican population was brought within the walls, and all citizens up to age sixty were conscripted. Hypereides, who was in charge in Demosthenes' absence, wished the emancipation of all slaves who volunteered to fight and the naturalization of all foreign male adults in the city, but this was deferred, as illegal, though he won the ensuing trial by imputing the proposed drastic measures to the fate of Athens at Chaeronea. Charidemus, almost as longstanding and outspoken a foe of Philip as Demosthenes, was given command of the defence and Demosthenes returned, and his followers approved all the measures for a defence of Athens to the last extremity.

---

3 Ibid., p. 263.

Philip, as was his lusty Macedonian custom, engaged in a great drunken revel after his victory, and for a day declined even to permit the burial of the enemy dead, but when the well-known Athenian orator, Demades, remonstrated about the honour of warriors and kings, Philip interrupted his orgy, changed his mind entirely on brief reflection, and sent Demades and a group of Athenian prisoners back to Athens offering immediate negotiation of a generous peace. The mood of Athens quickly evolved also from preparation for resistance to the death to a full acceptance of the olive branch the Macedonian king tendered. The peace that was agreed deprived Athens of Chersonese, but restored Oropus in Boeotia, and left Athens otherwise undisturbed, and particularly the important Aegean islands of Lemnos, Imbros, Delos, Scyros, and Samos. The Athenian League was dissolved, and Macedonia and Athens became allies and agreed a joint effort to rid the Eastern Mediterranean and approaches to the Bosporus of all pirates. There was to be complete freedom of trade and navigation, no financial penalty, and Alexander himself conducted the remains of the Athenian dead to Athens for honourable burial. The Athenians, with Demosthenes absent trying to negotiate financing and food supplies for what promised to be a desperate struggle, conferred citizenship on Philip and Alexander and erected a statue to Philip in the principal market square.

Philip had no such philosophical view of the conduct of the Thebans. The leaders of the Macedonian party there were banished or executed. Thebes had betrayed Macedonia, where Athens had been altogether honourable, if antagonistic. An oligarchy of three-hundred, largely composed of individuals Philip knew to be trustworthy, took over the Theban government, a Macedonian force garrisoned the citadel of Thebes, and that city's authority over Boeotia was revoked. The Theban prisoners of war were sold into slavery, and the Thebans were even made to wait for some time before being allowed to bury the decomposed remnants of their battlefield dead.

This was the smart decision in any case, which Philip would presumably have arrived at even if Damades had not appealed to him so eloquently. His main design was on Persia, and he intended to make Macedonia the carrier and agent for transmission of Hellenic culture which flowed chiefly from Athens. He knew from Perinthus and Byzantium how difficult it was to reduce a fortified city that controlled the sea and could assure its grain imports, and Athens would be far more resistant than those cities. The ideal outcome for him was to enlist Athens as his chief ally and associate in the Hellenization of the known world; the states were highly complementary, as long as Philip had control of strategic policy and Athenian sensibilities continued to be massaged.

Demosthenes continued to represent faithfully the animating spirit of unconquerable Athens, and he supervised the original plans for improving fortifications and the harbor at Piraeus, and he delivered the funeral oration for the dead of the late Amphissean War. There was a great deal of litigation in the pettifogging Athenian manner but generally Demosthenes and his astute treasurer Lycurgus enjoyed public respect and support. The regime was not so austere as to prevent the restoration of the popular Theoric distributions (outright vote-buying, even when Demosthenes was the benefactor), and the Dionysiac Theatre was rebuilt on a grand scale. Public honours were heaped on Demosthenes, despite the failure of his noble, if unworldly, policy.

Philip's generosity to Athens was not replicated generally among the Greeks. He planted himself in Northern Greece, with garrisons at Chalcis and Ambracia as well as Thebes. And the Athenian faction in Acarnania was purged. Epirus, Byzantium, Perinthus, and Selymbria all accepted general Macedonian direction and the existing alliances with the Aeolians, Phocians, and Thessalians, became more intimate. In the Peloponnese, Philip installed a garrison at the isthmus near Megara and Corinth and the Arcadian Confederacy was expanded to include Mantinea, and Arcadians, Argives, and Messenians were allocated territory that had previously been in the Spartan sphere. Sparta itself was ignored and isolated and Philip and his local allies looted substantial areas in Laconia. Sparta had abstained from the Amphissean War and did not react at all, officially, to Philip's establishment of himself as the arbiter and quasi-supervisor of the whole Peloponnese.

All this relatively gentle imposition of Macedonian influence on Greece was consummated and formalized in late 338 at a congress Philip convened at Corinth. Sparta alone declined to send delegates, but all the rest of the Greek states joined a League which would be in an offensive and defensive alliance with Macedonia, and all the states would be represented in the League's council, with the size of delegations dependent on the size and strength of the state. The contingents that each would provide to the common forces, whether for offensive or defensive purposes, were agreed in advance, though Athens was fractious, and only the eloquence and good judgment of Phocion prevented an early breach over the size of the naval and cavalry units that Athens would commit.

All the states were mutually supportive, and all guaranteed the frontiers and interests of all. Anyone from any of the states who took up an external interest was subject to banishment and confiscation of assets. There would be no garrisons apart from those already established, and full freedom of the seas. The king of Macedonia would be the supreme military commander, and the Amphictyonic League would be the supreme judicial authority for the entire territory of the league. The long-conceived campaign against Persia was declared to be the chief purpose of the League, and this was a much more constructive and uplifting goal than the endless internecine squabbling of the last two centuries, almost fruitless in substantive political terms as they had been.

The recent murder of Artaxerxes Ochus made the Persian enterprise timelier and more feasible, and at Corinth it was agreed that the generals Attalus and Pharmenion would lead a large Macedonian army into Asia Minor and prepare for the great campaign involving pan-Hellenic forces that was envisioned in the final show-down between Greece and Persia. Philip had shown extraordinary talent, cunning, and breadth of conception in preparing and advancing his plan. It contained military, cultural, and economic elements that made it comprehensive, and the balance between severity, conciliation, and invocation of ancient Greek ambitions in building and organizing his grand alliance was a triumph of grand strategy, as well as mundane politics. Philip emerged from the Congress of Corinth one of the greatest figures of the ancient world, a brilliant statesman, and on balance, with all his trickery and the oriental treachery and debauchery in his court and entourage, for which he would pay the supreme price, he was a very great national and multi-national leader, who laid and executed his plans on a scale and with a sophistication the world had not seen before and would not often see in all the centuries since. The fact that he was about to be eclipsed by his son no more deprived Philip of his historic importance than the greatness of Augustus would obscure or diminish the stature of Julius Caesar. And these were arguably the two greatest pre-planned political successions in major powers in all of history.

Here is where Philip's story ends. He had a stormy marriage with Olympias, mother of Alexander, and had at least six other wives, three of them subsequent to Olympias. Macedonian practice found no fault with polygamy, but it created immense rivalries and jealousies and intrigue in the court and anterooms of the king. At the wedding in 336 of Philip with Cleopatra Eurydice, the niece of his general Attalus (who had just been active in Asia Minor), Attalus proposed a wedding toast in which he expressed the hope that his daughter would bear the king a legitimate heir. This provoked Alexander, twenty, who threw his cup in Attalus' face. Philip jumped up and bared his sword which he was apparently about to wield against his son, but he lost his balance and fell, and Alexander mocked him as someone "who wanted to cross from Europe to Asia and could not make the passage from one sofa to another." Alexander departed and was exiled by his father, and went to Illyria, which he had helped subdue. Olympias had already decamped to her brother's court at Epirus, a person of sufficient influence that Philip did not want to incur his animosity. He made his peace, as he thought, with Alexander of Epirus and with Olympias, and offered his daughter by Olympias, Alexander (the Great's) sister, Cleopatra (absurdly confusing), to Alexander of Epirus: i.e., Philip's daughter would marry the brother of his wife. There was an apparent reconciliation between Philip and his son Alexander, but this was undone by Philip's refusal to condone his son's marriage to the daughter of the satrap of Caria, ostensibly because the girl was beneath the status of a king's son but more likely because of possible political complexity, as well as spite.

The marriage of Philip's daughter Cleopatra to Alexander of Epirus proceeded in July 336, and as the king was entering the open theatre where it was to be celebrated, without escort to emphasize his proximity to his subjects, who were out and celebrating in large numbers, Philip was stabbed and killed by one of his official guards, Pausanias, who was allegedly outraged by an insult from Attalus. It is generally conjectured that Olympias may have had a hand in the matter, but this has never been authenticated. There is no reason to believe the king's son and successor was involved, though it is not impossible. Olympias did order the murder of Attalus' niece's children—her rival Cleopatra's son and daughter. Insight into what the real origin of the murder of the king was had been foreclosed when Pausanias fled but tripped as he mounted his horse that was ready for him and was slain by Perdiccas and Attalus and another who had run after him. Olympias had a diadem of her gratitude placed on the corpse of the assassin, who had been an ardent former lover, and whom Philip should have kept at a distance as a loyalty risk. She also paid for a splendid funeral for Pausanias and he and Philip were burned together in a great national spectacle and Olympias arranged this, evidently with the full concurrence of the new putative king, Alexander. Olympias consecrated Pausanias' dagger used to kill Philip, to Apollo.

Philip of Macedon was only forty-six. He had had an exceptionally full repertoire of talents of persuasion, conciliation, intimidation, subornation, and organization. He was completely ruthless, but always ready to be generous if that suited his interest. He hated some people but could still deal with them if necessary; liked some but could without notice destroy them if that seemed advantageous, and was generally indifferent to people, beneath his considerable charm. He was a capable and thorough general, popular with his men, but not brilliant, and was defeated at times, but always was quite unfazed by defeat. He was a wise and efficient, and even just ruler, except for the incitement or at least toleration of terrible rivalries and hatreds and violence that he did little to discourage in his court and entourage. It soon emerged that his son had even more remarkable qualities and not such conspicuous faults. But he was such a brilliant military commander, he had little need for his father's skills at diplomacy and intrigue, though he may well have possessed them.

Philip's "virtues and vices were directed and proportioned to his great designs of power: his most shining and exalted qualities (were) influenced in a great measure by his ambition. And in even the most exceptionable parts of his conduct was he principally determined by their convenience and expedience. If he was unjust, he was like Caesar, unjust for the sake of empire. If he gloried in the success acquired by his virtues, or his intellectual accomplishments, rather than in that which the force of arms could gain, the reason, which he himself assigned, points out his true principle: 'In the former case, the glory is entirely my own; in the other my generals and soldiers have their share.'"[4]

Philip's principal rival, and the renowned figure whose raison d être was his antipathy to Philip, was of course, Demosthenes. He was a brilliant orator, one of the most powerful and persuasive in all of recorded history, but he was preeminently the incarnation of the heroism and civic qualities and patriotic courage and incorruptibility of the statesman of the Greek city. His contest with Philip was unequal on several levels: Philip was a king, a talented general, and a skilled national strategist and diplomatic tactician. Demosthenes had to rally a democratic following to a difficult course in face of the great temptations posed by appeasing or at least ignoring the rise of Macedonia. Philip was the more powerful statesman, and the representative of the future of larger states and empires and more elaborate strategies to project the power of a state far beyond what a city state could aspire to, but Demosthenes roused Athens to an heroic effort and enabled it to earn a respectable peace with Macedonia when it suited Philip to offer it. Frequently slanderous in his attacks on opponents and a stubborn old donkey often, Demosthenes yet possessed great talents and profound courage and integrity. In modern times, Philip has been portrayed as something of a debauched Richelieu, and Demosthenes, once the Victorian British classical romanticists got hold of him, as a proto-Churchillian hero. Neither was as great as their modern supposed analogues, but they were eminent figures who have endured deservedly. Philip was a striking exemplar of what was

---

4 Thomas Leland, *The Life and Reign of Philip, King of Macedon*, London, 1758, p. 307.

to come, especially of the more talented Roman leaders, and Demosthenes was a brilliant figure from the noble past: ultimately unsuccessful, and somewhat anachronistic, but no less considerable and romantic a figure for that.

CHAPTER THIRTEEN
ALEXANDER THE GREAT, 336-323 B.C.

Alexander the Great
(Battle of Issus mosaic)

Aristotle
(Roman copy of Lysippos' bronze original)

1. The Invasion of Persia

ALEXANDER III, son of King Philip II of Macedon and of Olympias the Epirote princess, assumed the crown of his father at the age of twenty. His parents were substantially Greek and partly Illyrian on the paternal side (Albanian in fact). Philip had invited Aristotle to Pella to be Alexander's tutor when the prince was thirteen. It has been amply noted that Alexander's two greatest formative influences were his tutor, one of history's greatest formulators of moderate logic and reason, and his mother, a careening hellcat, who, if she ever encountered moderation in her own views and conduct, would have excised it. Olympias was very proud and very passionate, and Alexander loved her always and possessed some of her intense emotional qualities, as well as his father's practical genius for organization and sophisticated strategic planning and execution. It is generally agreed that Alexander combined an analytical mind with a passionate nature.

He was not a great sportsman, except for his liking for hunting, and was an avid reader of poetry and of lore. His heroes were Achilles and Heracles, and he kept under his pillow throughout his adolescence and adulthood a copy of the *Iliad* that Aristotle had annotated for him. Aristotle wrote treatises for him on rulership and colonization and gave him a thorough grounding in ethics, metaphysics, scientific technique, medicine, as far as it was known, and philosophy. Throughout his time as king, he was always trying to expand the frontiers of his own and the Hellenic world's knowledge, and took an entourage of geographers, zoologists, botanists, and medical experts with him on his extensive military expeditions. He was lean, fair-skinned and clean-shaven. At sixteen, he had ruled in his father's absence, and at eighteen, as we have seen, he commanded the left flank of the Macedonian army very bravely and effectively at Chaeronea. And he was in the crossfire between his parents, but emotionally on his mother's side. He took Olympias with him into exile after the shambles at Philip's engagement to Cleopatra, but Demaratus of Corinth had been a mediator who effected the return of Alexander and Olympias.

It was the official Macedonian position that the assassination of Philip had been organized and promoted by Persia, whose leaders knew well enough what Philip had in mind for them. There is absolutely no evidence that Alexander was involved, but there is a persistent historic rumour that Olympias, given her relations with Pausanias, the king's murderer, was at least aware of the plot, as well as eminently consolable when it was carried out. But Alexander was the soul of legitimacy: Philip's chief generals, Antipater and Parmenion, immediately professed their loyalty, Alexander rounded up all the plotters who had not made good their escape to Persia and executed them, and cleared accounts with Attalus, who had made the offending toast that provoked the final royal blow-up. Demosthenes had written Attalus in Asia Minor, where he was with Parmenion, proposing making common cause against Alexander. Attalus sent the letter to Alexander and pledged his allegiance, but for a combination of exemplary, vindictive and precautionary motives, Alexander chose not to believe him and had Attalus summarily executed for treasonable correspondence with Athens. Olympias having already arranged the murder of Cleopatra Euridyce's children with Philip, a boy, Caranus, and a girl, Europa, with Alexander's indulgence and probably complicity. Cleopatra Eurydice committed suicide and Olympias withdrew to her native Epirus in 331. She was an epochal personality, and this was far from the end of her story; she maintained a lively correspondence with Alexander throughout the balance of his life, was the regent in Epirus, commanded armies and political factions after Alexander the Great's death and executed Alexander's stepbrother Philip III. When she was defeated, her soldiers refused to surrender the mother of Alexander the Great, but her victorious opponent, Cassander, son of Alexander's general Antipater, arranged for the many relatives in Epirus of people Olympias had had executed or massacred, to stone her to death. Plutarch claimed that she was an orgiastic snake-worshipper. She will reenter this narrative but should be flagged here as one of history's fantastic personalities, and for all, the wife and mother of two of history's greatest kings and conquerors. It will suffice to note that Alexander, despite his youth, needed no schooling in the rough and tumble of Macedonian court politics, and by comparison, sorting the Greek states out was comparatively civilized.

In keeping with the practice of people, including people at the head of states, to believe what they want to believe, Greece considered the League of Corinth and the arrangements with King Philip to have expired with him. Athens rejoiced at Philip's death (though it did not remove or deface the statue of him that Athenians had voluntarily erected). Ambracia expelled the Macedonian garrison, Aetolia recalled the anti-Macedonian politicians whose exile Philip had successfully demanded, Thebes and the Peloponnesians believed they had been given a reprieve, and the anti-Macedonian faction in Thessaly staged a temporarily successful uprising. The Balkan tribes and peoples, whom even Philip had found a handful, were encroaching and skirmishing on the borders. Alexander moved rapidly and started with Greece; by marching his army quickly he went into Ossa and into Thessaly ("Alexander's ladder" as he was climbing quickly in altitude as well as moving large distances), and the opposition in Thessaly collapsed with no armed resistance. Thessaly was a country of horse-breeders and in securing his election for life, as head of the Thessalian League in succession to his father, Alexander secured his supply of cavalry horses, which would water in the Nile, the Caucasus, Tigris, Euphrates and at the gates of India.

Alexander moved swiftly onto the edge of Thebes, which reaffirmed its undertakings to Philip, and the Congress of Corinth elected Alexander to replace his father as commanding general for the anticipated invasion of Asia Minor, and Athens and Ambracia returned to their arrangements with Alexander's father. (It had all been a misunderstanding that inter-state relationships had been altered by Philip's death.) Before resuming matters exactly as Philip had left them, Alexander laid the rod of his military authority on the vulpine tribes of the Balkans. He started with the Triballi, a very war-like people which had been pushed by advancing Celts into what is now northern Bulgaria. Alexander led an army from Amphipolis past Adrianople and in a series of battles drove the Triballi back to the Danube. On the opposite side, the even more belligerent Getae, who have already put in an appearance against Philip, were mustering. Alexander was able to get part of his army across in Byzantine ships and improvised log rafts, and surprised and defeated the Getae, who fought with particular abandon because of their faith in immortality. Alexander defeated the Getae and the Triballi surrendered and produced emissaries from the Celts on the upper Danube. The Celts pledged alliance in a formula that survives in antique Irish documents: "We will keep faith unless the sky fall and crush us, or the earth open and swallow us, or the sea rise and overwhelm us," only the fall of the sky being considered possible.[1]

The next episode on this tour of redressment of the frontiers was in Illyria. Cleitus, the native Illyrian leader, was making common cause with Glaucias, chief of the Taulantini in South Illyria (today, Bosnia and Albania). Alexander's ally from days of exile after the fiasco at Philip's wedding party for Alexander's sister, undertook to restrain the Autariatae of South Serbia, who were also being rebarbative, as Alexander proceeded at the speed only a disciplined army could maintain, to subdue the agitated elements in Illyria. He reached the fortress of Pelion before the Illyrians could concentrate there. After narrowly avoiding encirclement, Alexander severely defeated Cleitus. Greek events required his attention, and he left it there, but the allegation of alliance with the Celts and the sound drubbing he had meted out in his legendary progress between Pelion and Ossa, kept the frontiers quiet for some years. (According to mythology, the centaurs of Pelion tried to enhance their mountains to

---

1 CAH, VI, p. 355 (W.W. Tarn).

attack the Gods, the origin of the expression, "piling Pelion on Ossa.")

The problem that had arisen in Greece was that Philip had died, and the democrats who had been banished from Thebes by Philip had returned and seized power in Thebes, and were violating the peace with Macedonia. Athens, Elis, Aetolia, and Arcadia, were all considering affiliating with Thebes in a general Greek revolt against the Macedonian hegemony. Darius the Great King had given Demosthenes personally the considerable sum of three-hundred talents (about five-hundred million U.S. dollars today), to promote the dissolution of the League of Corinth and generally to destabilize Macedonia's position, which had already incited the fear of bedraggled Persia. Athens had not officially taken the bait, but Demosthenes was giving some of his Persian money to assist Thebes in arming itself. Fearing a combination of Thebes, Athens, Sparta, and Aetolia, Alexander hurried from Pelion to Thebes in fourteen days, an astounding feat (something like Napoleon's progress with his Grande Armee in 1805 from Boulogne to Ulm and Austerlitz). He picked up contingents from Phocis and Boeotia on his route. His sudden return obviously vapourized reports of his demise and gave the wavering Greek states pause. He gave Thebes time to parley and calm matters, but Thebes was determined to fight, a prime illustration of the madness of the bellicose Greeks.

The Thebans stormed out to give battle, but Alexander sent them tumbling back pell-mell and infiltrated the ranks of the retreating force with his own forces, seized the city and completely destroyed it. Everything was razed to the ground except Pindar's house and authentic temples. The Phocians and Plataeans who had joined Alexander's forces exacted a special vengeance for what Thebes had done to them. Some Thebans whom Alexander had reason to think had not urged Theban renunciation of Macedonia, and Macedonia's known friends in the city, were spared. Civilians were not generally massacred, but about eight-thousand Thebans were sold into slavery and the entire territory of Thebes was divided up among Macedonia's Boeotian allies. In theory, this comprehensive suppression of one of Greece's historically principal military states was undertaken by the League of Corinth.

In fact, of course, it was the work of Macedonia and its Phocian and Boeotian allies, considering themselves an itinerant quorum of the league that was unanimous in its course and possessed the force to carry it out without calling on assistance from other league members. Alexander has been much criticized historically for his severity, and it is claimed that he had conscientious problems about his actions. But he was brutally betrayed and there was ample precedent in Greek history for this sort of reprisal. He, like his father, was determined to end the sanguinary and juvenile game of endless, fruitless, pointless internecine conflict. The Philippic and Alexandrine mission was to shape Greece into a unit with autonomous component jurisdictions and lead a Pan-Hellenic and Macedonian military force to the conquest of the known world and the propagation of Hellenic culture and civilization broadly. It was a design of a grandeur worthy of Greece, something the Greeks, even Pericles, had never realistically conceived for themselves. An ambiguous response to Thebes' insolence would have effectively scuttled the credibility of the young Macedonian king to carry out the mighty plan of his father, much less the flourishes and embellishments that Alexander would append to it.

All was now ready to begin the long-awaited and dreaded attack on Persia. Alexander got to his final preparations in 335, recalling Parmenion from Asia Minor. Darius' mercenaries, commanded by Memnon, had defeated Parmenion's successor, but not decisively, and the Macedonians retained control of both sides of the Dardanelles. Darius appears to have interpreted Memnon's perhaps exaggerated account of his victory and Parmenion's recall as an indefinite delay in the project. It has never been clear what Alexander really intended—he had inherited the ambition to invade Persia, and he embraced Isocrates' grand plan of Hellenization. (Isocrates had just died but he had some influence on Philip and Alexander.) There was the theory that Persia should be held responsible for a long catalogue of grievances, starting with its early attacks on Greece and up to its alleged hand in the assassination of Philip (not in itself an event which caused the victim's son to grieve overly—he liked being king, even aged twenty-one). Even Aristotle believed and told his star pupil that it was quite in order to attack barbarians, and to enslave them. Alexander was to prove a much more egalitarian and progressive figure than his illustrious preceptor and armed himself with the ability to enact his ideas on a vast canvas.

Alexander crossed the Dardanelles at the head of thirty-thousand infantry and five-thousand cavalry, leaving Antipater behind with twelve-thousand infantry and fifteen-hundred cavalrymen to secure his communications across the Dardanelles, oversee Thrace, and keep an eye on Greece and Macedonia. His army was composed of twelve-thousand Macedonians, mainly the phalanx of nine-thousand, twelve-thousand Greeks (League hoplites), some mercenaries, Agrianian javelin-throwers, and archers from Crete, and a detachment of Thracians. The core of the cavalry was the Companions, eight territorial squadrons from the Macedonian upper classes, the Thessalian and Thracian horse, four squadrons of Macedonian lancers; there was a battalion of heavy infantry called the Agema, Alexander's personal guard. This army had more advanced and specialized weapons than any other and the different units were deployed with precision to strike a vital point of the enemy, exploit it, and roll it up. Alexander usually led the cavalry personally, but sometimes set himself at the head of other units, depending on his plan of battle. This was still the era when commanders led from at or near the front lines, and no one would be better or more successful at this than Alexander. Hannibal and Julius Caesar, and perhaps Scipio Africanus were his only rivals. Parmenion was his second in command. Alexander's army included a siege-train, engineers for fording rivers, portable siege-towers, wheeled battering rams, sappers, well-diggers, surveyors, a baggage train that conveyed the stores seized at each stage, for distribution at the next. There was a secretarial department, a courier service, royal pages, officer trainees, and some philosophers, literary men, historians and scientists in different specialties. Aristotle himself had retired to Athens, but he sent his nephew, Callisthenes of Olynthus, a skilled philosophical and historical conversationalist. Most important of this intellectual contingent would be Ptolemy of Lagos, who assembled the journal that was kept and edited by the king himself, a serious and generally reliable record of the expedition.

Alexander departed with an almost empty treasury; he was counting on his ability to extract as he progressed what was necessary to pay his army and covering fleet and meet his commitment to Delphi. It added up to three-hundred talents a month and an overall obligation of thirteen-hundred talents to Delphi to be paid in instalments without undue delay. As mentioned above in the gratuity conferred by Darius on Demosthenes, a talent was about fifty kilos or one-hundred and ten pounds of gold, so in current money, Alexander needed five-hundred million U.S. dollars a month just to pay his soldiers and sailors. He was relying on the Great King's land taxes for this, i.e., appropriating the tax for himself, and accomplishing a modest tax reduction in the Greek-speaking areas as he did so, as these had naturally been somewhat overtaxed under the Persian regime. The Persians had plenty of good cavalry, as the rural lords always had a good group of horsemen, but the Persian infantry was vulnerable: either under-armed and under-trained serfs who needed a spear in their backs to risk anything for their commanders, or tribesmen who tended to be fierce and brave but completely undisciplined.

The former Persian technique, which was very effective for a long time: a hail of archery fire followed by a charge of massed cavalry, often from different directions, could not be mounted now after the evolution of the Persian forces and their degeneration into large units of substantially under-armed and poorly trained forces. There was a heavy infantry composed of Greek mercenaries; these were good soldiers, but like all mercenaries, they were not unlimitedly reliable, especially when fighting kinsmen and with competing offers dangled before them. With all this, the Persians could have shaped up a strong fighting force if they had had a single and highly capable leader. Memnon was a capable general and had about twenty-thousand competent soldiers. The main army was of uneven fighting capability and numbered less than fifty-thousand. No Persian commander was remotely of the caliber of Alexander in imaginative tactical conception and exemplary leadership and execution.

Parmenion supervised the crossing of the Dardanelles, but Alexander trod the path of Hercules and landed at Ilium, made his sacrifice in the temple at Athena, took away the sacred shield for his own use and declared Ilium free and democratic and abolished the tribute being paid to Persia. It was a genius stroke on all fronts—the greatest possible appeal to Pan-Hellenic national feeling and the immediate assumption of a quasi-religious as well as folkloric role. He then took the head of his army and marched along the coast past Lampsacus to meet the combined forces of the satraps of Phrygia, Hellespontine Phrygia, Cappadocia, and Lydia. Memnon had advocated retreating and laying waste the country until Darius arrived with the main army. Memnon himself had been assigned to the navy (the Persians no less than the Greeks considered the two commands interchangeable). The satrap of Hellespontine Phrygia (who rejoiced in the name of Arsites), declined to have his satrapy scorched, and there was nothing for it but to give battle fairly early. The four satraps had fewer than twenty-thousand infantry and almost twenty-thousand cavalry and their initial plan was to put their cavalry at the front of their formation with the plan of charging the Greco-Macedonians and trying to kill Alexander, whatever their own casualties. It was already recognized that Alexander was a formidable commander after the way he had wiped out Greek dissent while hammering the disagreeable barbarians in the north and west.

At the Battle of Granicus, Alexander led the right with the Companions, lancers, javelin forces and archers, the phalanx was in the centre and Parmenion led the left with the Thessalian, Thracian, and Greek cavalry. Alexander had some cavalry cross the Granicus River ahead of him and then crossed himself, conspicuous by his royal helmet with white wings on it. The Persians made an immense effort to kill him, and Spithridates, satrap of Lydia almost got within scimitar-range himself but was felled by Cleitus. After the Persians' very brave effort to take down Alexander was rebuffed, and as their point of total concentration, well-selected though it was, did not yield success, the Persian army could not sustain the slaughtering it was taking focusing its whole effort on the person of the Macedonian commander. The entire Greco-Macedonian army crossed the Granicus River and came up behind the Persian army, and killed all but two-thousand Greeks, whom Alexander branded as traitors to the League of Corinth and sent in chains to be forced labour in Macedonia. It was an utterly overwhelming victory. Alexander lost fewer than two-hundred dead and sent three-hundred Persian banners to Athens with a message—from Alexander and the Greeks, except the Spartans. Eight high-ranking Persian notables were killed, and Alexander replaced the local Persian officials with his own appointees. This was one of the storied opening encounters in a great struggle where the first round is one of astonishing apparent ease, like the German victory in France in 1940 or the sinking of *H.M.S. Hood*, the world's most famous warship, in two salvos from *K.M. Bismarck* in May 1941. Granicus had an electrifying impact in Greece—Alexander was accomplishing, apparently effortlessly, what no Greek had ever dared to attempt: attack the Persian Empire directly. He announced that he was establishing democracies as he proceeded, and town after town overthrew the Persian puppet tyrant regimes and greeted the liberator as a fellow-Greek democrat (a considerable liberty with the facts, but his government was in every way an improvement on having the local wheel-horses of the Great King riveted on their backs).

At Miletus, the garrison closed the gates, manned the walls and prepared for a siege. The League fleet of one-hundred and sixty vessels arrived ahead of the Persian navy under Memnon, of four-hundred ships, but the League ships were able to prevent entrance to the port of Miletus. The Persian navy offered battle and Parmenion advised accepting it, but Alexander thought it risky and unnecessary. He said he would defeat the Persian fleet on land and took Miletus with a sudden land assault. He brought into his own army three-hundred Greek mercenaries who managed to escape to an island. The Persian navy retired to Halicarnassus and Alexander sent home and disbanded his navy as he could not afford to pay it. It has been alleged that he had taken a great gamble by leaving himself with no sea power and vulnerable to a severance of communications. But galleys don't function well at night and have limited cruising powers, so the only real threat to his communications would be by land.

Memnon was placed in charge of all Persian forces, and some feared that, as a Greek, he might be able to raise all Greece in revolt against Macedonia, but Alexander correctly reasoned that with the possible exception of Sparta, Persia was less popular and more foreign than Macedonia. He also had about twenty-thousand Greeks in his army who would be potential hostages in the event of disaffection at home. Further, Alexander's promise to defeat the Persian fleet on land was not just a matter of depriving it of bases; his proclamation of democracy shook the Greeks, Cypriots, and Phoenicians among the crews, the majority of the Persian navy's crews, in fact. Alexander judged that "If he secured the coast cities, the fleet would die of dry rot; and it did."[2] Alexander's political judgment was as acute as his military judgment. In this felicitous quality, he was like his father, and was a more original military tactician than Philip.

Alexander moved on into Caria and was greeted by Ada, widow of Idrieus and sister of Mausolus, who had been deposed by her brother Pixodorus. Ada purported to adopt Alexander as her son, vest him with her rightful claims, and handed over her fortress of Alinda. The great obstacle to Alexander's advance was Halicarnassus (where Mausolus' Mausoleum was one of the wonders of the world), and where Memnon had prepared to try to stop the invasion. Alexander brought up his siege train and a fierce struggle ensued. Assaults were generally repulsed, and Memnon was able to burn some of the siege towers, but Alexander persevered and broke through in several places and started through the town in intense combat. Memnon and his deputy commander, Orontopates, were ready for this too, and blew up their magazines in such an immense blast that it covered most of the garrison. Memnon rejoined his fleet and Orontopates retired in fairly good order into nearby forests where it would be impractical for Alexander to pursue them. Alexander lost the chief of his personal guard, Ptolemaeus, but his casualties were sustainable, and he was now the effective governor of the satrapy not just by force of arms, but at the head of autonomous regional opinion as well. Orontopates conducted a virtual guerrilla war for some time, but the satrapy was subdued and pacified by 332, with the assistance of several thousand mercenaries Alexander left behind.

As winter set in, Alexander sent the newly married men of his army on home furlough, left the heavy cavalry and the siege and baggage trains, and the allies with Parmenion in Phrygia, and pressed on in a winter campaign in Lycia and Pisidia. This was his customary military activity in winter—dealing with hill tribes, which were forced into the valleys in winter and easier to mop up as a result of that. It was while conducting this clean-up of the Lycian towns that Alexander learned that Darius had offered one-thousand gold talents (c. US $1.66 billion today), to Lyncestis, Alexander's Thessalian commander along with the crown of Macedonia, if he would kill Alexander. The quantum of the Dane geld or assassination fee the Great King was prepared to peel off to get rid of the young Macedonian king had more than tripled from when it was being handed out to Demosthenes to promote another Greek civil war not three years before. Alexander was not sure what truth there was in this, but sent Amphoterus, the brother of one of his principal phalanx-leaders, Craterus, back with a local guide to Phrygia, to assure that Parmenion removed Lyncestis of command of the Thessalian contingent.

The Macedonian army continued south, most of it right on the coast, though the army had to wade under and past the cliffs of Mount Climax, as the wind turned from north which would have made it impossible to walk beneath the cliffs, to south, which was passable and was seen and represented as a sign of divine favour. He had

---

2 Ibid., p. 363.

now penetrated over four-hundred miles south-southeast from the Dardanelles. He had sliced the western nose off of Persian Asia Minor and now turned north into Pisidia, seizing and razing Sagalassus. He did not conquer eastern Pisidia but claimed to add the western part of that satrapy to the satrapy of Nearchus' new Macedonian satrapy of Lycia and Pamphylia, and he detoured around Pisidia, left the hills and made northeast to Gordium, almost at what is now Ankara, four-hundred miles from the Mediterranean at Phaselis and seven-hundred miles east-southeast from the Dardanelles. Alexander had sliced another chunk of the Persian Empire away.

At this early stage in his career as a military conqueror Alexander was showing the skill at moving around targets and isolating enemy forces in pockets, that would reappear in fast-moving modern campaigns, such as the American advance westwards and northwestwards across the Pacific against Japan, 1942-1945. He was also demonstrating what Napoleon, twenty-two centuries later, described as the equation that military force was mass times speed. With Alexander in Asia, as with Napoleon in Italy, in 1796-7, the mass was thin, but the speed was astonishing. In neither case did the defenders have much idea how to cope with their young assailants (Napoleon was only twenty-seven when he assumed command in Italy), and in Asia Minor, Darius appeared to be trying to recede into his empire, as Russia and China would do when invaded, stretching the invader's communications, and his manpower by forcing him to occupy and control large, populated areas. This wouldn't work in the Persian Empire because Alexander shortly took measures that made him more popular than the Persians, who had not had time to assimilate most of the polyglot empire they had assembled and governed rather despotically. Alexander was both assaulting and undermining Persia and if the Great King did not move soon, the situation could deteriorate quickly. It was time to stop trying to hire an assassin or put Persia's bets on taking advantage of Alexander's combat bravery to kill him.

Celaenae surrendered, by agreeing that it would do so if not relieved in a timely fashion, and Alexander deterred any such relief. At Gordium, he was shown the war-chariot of the founder of the Phrygian monarchy, Gordius. A complicated knot lashed a yoke to a pole protruding from the chariot and the legend was that anyone who untied the knot would rule Asia. It is perhaps the greatest folkloric legend involving Alexander that he sliced the knot cleanly with his sword. The evidence that this actually occurred is thin, but it might have, and in any case, was indicative of his determination and ability to impress whole peoples and current opinion and posterity by simple and dramatic gestures. With spring, the furloughed men returned, bringing three-thousand Macedonian reinforcements as well, and requests from Athens for the return of the Athenian hostages that Alexander had with him as a surety for Athens' conduct while he was in Asia. He replied that he could not do it while the Persian navy was at large, and that Athens should reapply when conditions were less disturbed. This was diplomatic finesse, as an outright refusal would have fanned rebellious activity in Athens and among its allies. The rear area and staging area of Greece and Macedonia had to be settled by a subtle combination of uplifting victories in the field, soothing placation, and the subtle hint of irresistible force. Memnon was quite active with his fleet, but not particularly effectual. He did not want to attack the Greeks because the Persians were trying to encourage the Greeks to join them against the Macedonian interlopers. And he couldn't do much to Alexander, who was correct in seeing that sea power was secondary to the campaign he was waging to shatter the Persian empire into pieces by criss-crossing it and encouraging the subjects, especially the very involuntary peoples under the Great King, to slough off this ancient and corrupt Iranian yoke.

At this point, in 333, Memnon died of natural causes and was succeeded by his nephew, Pharnabazus (son of Artabazus), who brought Mitylene into alliance with Darius, and recovered Lesbos. These were worthwhile enterprises for the Persian side, but they did not really discommode Alexander, though he felt it necessary to reactivate his fleet, which had been gliding at anchor in port and substantially unmanned. At the same time, Darius was finally moving to assemble a maximum strength army of resistance and effectively deprived his navy of most of its manpower and translated it into soldiers. The Persian navy began to break up into smaller units, with many of the ships demobilized. Alexander proceeded eastwards to Angora (Ankara). The Paphlagonians, in whose territory he now was, and which stretched to the Black Sea, were independent of Persia, and asked to be allowed to make an act of formal submission but not otherwise to be imposed upon. This was acceptable to Alexander, who was trying to smash the Persian Empire, not defeat all of its neighbours and constituent parts.

He now turned southeast, for his third sweep of demarcation of forfeited Persian satrapies and dependencies and aimed for Tarsus and the extreme northeast corner of the Mediterranean, almost eight-hundred miles southeast of the Dardanelles and all the way across what is now Asian Turkey. This was obviously a grievous wound to the Persian Empire, and all would be decided fairly soon, depending on whether the Great King could actually repulse the invader. Alexander marched briskly through part of Cappadocia without attacking or purporting to assume the government of it, and armed neutrality and mutual non-intervention prevailed between the Macedonian king and the autonomous Persian dynast of northern Cappadocia.

Alexander raced ahead with his specialists in such matters to take the Cilician Gates, the passage to the Mediterranean about a hundred miles north of Tarsus. The defenders had no expectation of seeing him for at least another week, panicked, and he seized the gates, and his army made the passage—Alexander did not lose a single man in the operation. Advised that the Persians were preparing to raze Tarsus as part of a scorched earth campaign as Alexander got farther and farther from his starting point, he again raced ahead and arrived in time to deliver Tarsus from the unhappy fate that the Great King's officers had been dilatorily preparing for it. Either the strenuous exercise or a hot thermal bath, or both, brought on a fever and Alexander was bed-ridden. The king's physician, his friend Philippus, was about to administer a curative draft when a letter arrived from Parmenion warning that Philippus had been bribed by Darius to poison him. Alexander handed Philippus the letter from Parmenion as he drank the draft. His confidence was well-placed. Philippus drily commented that Alexander would recover quickly and completely if he did as prescribed. The warning was false, though no doubt sincerely transmitted by Parmenion.

Alexander recovered after a few days and sent Parmenion forward to occupy the passes into Syria. Darius was unaware of Alexander's illness and presumed that his stop at Tarsus was due to a determination to stop where he was, having ostensibly lopped off almost a third of the Persian Empire. In fact, Alexander was proceeding south, and Darius set out to interrupt his leisure, or even Alexander's retreat, if that is what it was. The two armies groped toward each other, Darius mistaken about Alexander's intentions and Alexander mistaken about Darius' whereabouts (he thought he was stationary at Sochoi about a hundred miles north of Tripoli in the Levant). Darius moved due east and cut across Alexander's communications, as he was about thirty miles north of Alexander, who had been moving down the Mediterranean shore. Darius had sent his baggage train and support personnel to Damascus and now came upon and massacred Alexander's wounded and sick, and learning where the Macedonian army was, tuned south at Issus to face Alexander, who would have to reopen contact with his far-off base. At this point, Darius had a serious strategic advantage and both commanders knew it. A supreme test of strength was finally at hand, and the Persians realized that even a draw would be a victory for them—Alexander could not retreat south or west; he had to remove Darius from his tracks.

Fantastic stories have arisen, largely made up by Alexander's entourage of the numberless multitude of an army deployed by the Great King. It was impossible for Greeks to judge easily the size of foreign armies that were organized on a different basis to their own. Darius had his home guard and household forces, and the Persian cavalry and archers. His army had perhaps twelve-thousand Greek mercenaries and contingents from other parts of the Empire but was only about ten-thousand more individuals than Alexander's approximately twenty-four thousand infantry and five-thousand cavalry. It served the subsequent Macedonian interest to claim that Darius had put half a million men on the field.

Darius took his position behind the centre, behind his Greek troops. The Persian cavalry was placed on the right as an assault force should it have any chance of turning the Macedonian left and enveloping Alexander's army. Darius placed his archers on the left. The Greek mercenaries in front of Darius had dug in somewhat; all the Persian army had to do was prevent Alexander from retracing his steps. Alexander only believed that Darius was behind him when this was verified by reconnaissance by ship. Alexander assumed his usual formation—he was on the right with the Companions in front of the lancers—a strong massed cavalry, with a further flanking force behind them and ready for a wide encircling or flanking arc. The phalanx, as always, held the Macedonian centre, and behind them were allies and mercenaries. His archers were on the left. Both deployments appeared sensible; everything depended on the quality of the troops and leadership.

Alexander opened what is known as the Battle of Issus by using his deep flanking units to overpower and chase off the Persian light-armed cavalry. This unnerved Darius, who had never really had to deal with a serious adversary in combat and had not had anyone remotely of the caliber of King Philip of Macedon to teach him about war. The Persian right advanced and pushed Parmenion back somewhat but not enough to bare the flank of the phalanx in the Macedonian centre. Alexander sent his massed cavalry forward on the right and once within range of arrows, he charged forward with his closest forces reinforcing and inspiring the charge of his right. The Persian left buckled under the pressure and in order to avoid being encircled and captured, Darius turned his chariot westwards and fled, for all the personnel of both armies to see. But the Persian army stood its ground, and the phalanx was hard-pressed by the Persian right. The Greek mercenaries on both sides, as always with Greeks, were hard fighters and there was not much to choose between them and the Macedonians. Alexander's pressure on the Persian left forced the issue, and with their king having abandoned the field, the Persian army gave way, slowly at first, but then a general, but never disorderly retreat. Darkness came and the Persian army was able to withdraw. Losses were not heavy, under five-hundred for the Macedonians and their allies, and Alexander himself was lightly wounded, and not more than five-thousand for the Persians. But the Greek mercenaries had been poorly served by their commander, and after the engagement had been properly broken off, eight-thousand Greeks under Amyntas marched back to Tripoli and embarked for Egypt. Their next adventure was Amyntas' effort to join in the conquest of Egypt, in which he himself was killed. The rest of his men eventually were repatriated to Greece and fought for Sparta in a later conflict.

Alexander appointed the new head of his royal guard, Balacrus, as satrap of Cilicia. Darius' chariot and bow, and his tent, as well as his mother, wife, and two daughters were all captured. The sumptuous tent was Alexander's first experience of oriental luxury, and he was disturbed by the sound of the four women in Darius' family wailing because they presumed Darius was dead. He sent an officer to assure them that he was not dead and that they were safe and would be treated with the same royal deference they would receive in normal circumstances. Darius' wife was very beautiful, but Alexander never laid eyes on her, though he did eventually marry one of the daughters. He kept his word about the treatment of the women. As Alexander took control of more of the Persian Empire, he installed generals, with some troops to command, as replacement satraps, but cut down their potential to be as autonomous as Persian satraps by leaving finances in the hands of financial superintendents answerable to himself and not to the resident satrap-generals. In the coastal provinces where Alexander's sweep-through had been emphatic, he took over the king's land, and appointed managers for it and added its revenue to his own treasury to help defray the cost of carrying on a far-flung war.

Those provinces or satrapies which had voluntarily deposed tyrants and oligarchies without serious Greco-Macedonian assistance, or had assisted Alexander, were generously rewarded, such as Zelea, Lampsacus, Erythrae, and self-liberated cities became his free and autonomous allies and members of the League of Corinth, thus shifting the balance within that League even further toward the Macedonians. He did not tolerate excessive vengeance on the former governments; rather, he was content to have tyrants and despotic Persian lackeys assassinated or executed but would not abide one faction abusing its position to visit general violence on another and intervened swiftly to stop generalized civil strife. If necessary, he garrisoned towns until confident that factions "be reconciled together," as he decreed in the case of Chios. Tyrants who fled were to be denied sanctuary and when apprehended, tried by the League. Wherever there were boundary disputes between the provinces or satrapies, and there were many, he arbitrated them himself and resolved the disputes. Generally, the Greek communities in Asia Minor became League members and Macedonian allies, and the Persian or other communities were grouped in provinces that were governed by democracies but either financially and militarily administered by Macedonia, or if far from the Mediterranean, such as Bithynia, were left alone as long as they were completely inoffensive to the Greco-Macedonian interest.

There has been a good deal of speculation ever since these times about when Alexander set his sights on smashing the entire Persian Empire. He certainly set out on his expedition confident, partly having imbibed the careful analysis of his father, that at least the Hellenic west and southwest of the Great King's domains could be severed and brought into the League of Corinth, grateful to Macedon for their liberation from the Persians. Both Macedonian kings would have believed that other chunks of the Persian Empire would break off, independent satrapies at the northern and western extremities, and Egypt, which would also be susceptible to alliance with, or at least benign neutrality toward the Macedonian power that facilitated their autonomy. He had essentially accomplished all of that except the formal detachment of Egypt with the Battle of Issus, and the sight of the flight of the Great King might well have broadened Alexander's horizons into a further assault on Persia itself, with his entire train of communications back to Greece fairly secure through territories and peoples which had smarted under Persian rule for three centuries and whose interests and offended sensibilities would be well served if Alexander meted out to proud Persia what it had so contentedly meted out to the whole traditional crossroads of the world and Asia Minor.

The alternative was to follow the advice of Isocrates, who was an intelligent strategist and observer (who had died in 338, lucid to the end, at age ninety-eight), but would not have had reason to believe that the Persian Empire could be folded up so quickly by an invasion not appreciably larger than the principal Greek city states were long accustomed to deploying against each other. And stopping where he was, after emancipating and embracing all the Greek areas of the Persian Empire could not be relied upon as a long-term, imperturbable solution. Persia was too proud and rich to be disabused so swiftly of its declared vocation to rule its neighbors. It was the Pan-Hellenic mission that was the official reason for the initial attack, and this was written up in a manifesto Alexander composed, partly inspired by Isocrates, just before he embarked on this great endeavor.

While pondering these questions, Alexander ignored the discredited Darius and set out after the logical next target: Phoenicia and the destruction of the Persian navy, on his way to the severance of Egypt. He moved south to Marathus, near Tripoli, which surrendered without resistance, and dispatched Parmenion and the Thessalians to take Damascus, which also submitted without audible objection. In this occupation, Alexander gained all of Darius' war-chest and baggage, the end of Alexander's financial austerity, and illustrative of the Persian king's demoralized condition that he appears to have made no effort to salvage this treasure. He captured some of the diplomatic embassies to Darius, but released the Athenians and Thebans, but not the Spartans, as Sparta had been uttering threats against Macedonia again.

Darius wrote Alexander, asking him, "king to king" to release his family and proposing an alliance. There was an implicit acquiescence in Alexander doing pretty much as he wished with the territory he had occupied. Alexander responded by sending the manifesto he had written just before embarking for Asia Minor. Alexander wrote that his purpose was to avenge Xerxes' invasion of Greece, but he also stressed that the current hostilities had begun with Artaxerxes Ochus' invasion of Thrace and assistance to Perinthus against Macedonia. He went on to accuse Persia of suborning the assassination of King Philip, of trying to bribe Sparta into going to war against Alexander while he was engaged with Persia in Asia, and for good measure, he accused Darius of murdering Arses (it was really Bagoas who did it, Chapter 10), and was therefore not the rightful king of Persia. He subscribed himself "King of Asia," and wrote that if Darius wanted anything from him, he would have to petition as a subject. This was evidently designed to keep Darius in the field, as Alexander had made such an easy sweep to this point, he had the light-hearted demeanor of a young and extraordinarily successful man who did not think he could be checked. He at least had the prudence to avoid publicly claiming to be the king of Asia, which would have required that he assert more authority over the independent satraps than he had any practical ability to do at this time, and he knew that Darius was good for another fight, relying on his own Persian forces, defending not their conquests but their homeland. This was presumed to be a more challenging goal than just evicting the Great King from areas where as far as Macedonia and most of the inhabitants were concerned, he had no business.

Alexander moved south from Marathus and Sidon welcomed him heartily. Tyre was more ambiguous; it offered submission in principle but not the occupation of the city. Tyre was an island half a mile offshore and considered itself impregnable given the strength of the naval units there and having withstood the siege of thirteen years by Nebuchadnezzar in the Sixth Century B.C. (Chapter 3). And Tyre's leaders were not convinced that Alexander was at this point a real threat to the status quo. They thought him more of an adventurer than a conqueror, and the Persian era had been good for them. Alexander tested their assertion of submission by asking if he could visit their temple and worship his ancestor, Heracles. The Tyrian leaders replied that they were not accepting any visitors from anywhere, but that there was a suitable shrine to Heracles (Melkart) nearby on the mainland that would be appropriate for his ancestral pieties.

Alexander put preparations for a siege in hand and began filling in an approach from the mainland by a furious land-fill operation. Once the forces accomplishing this work got within range of Tyrian archery, it naturally became more difficult. The water was deeper closer to the island, and winter weather and the harassment of Tyrian war galleys further complicated the landward approach. Alexander brought out two siege towers to the bend of the mole; their outer walls covered with skins that were fire-resistant. The Tyrians were made of sterner stuff than anyone Alexander had yet encountered, and designed a fire-ship, with upraised bows from a weighted stern, and hung out long rods forward from the masts which dangled highly incendiary matter in large pods over the siege-towers when the ship was grounded. The

Tyrians fired the ship and swam back toward Tyre and were picked up in small craft. The burning cargoe fell onto the towers before any preventive action could be taken and set the towers on fire. Tyrian ships filled with archers drove the Macedonians off the mole and then shore parties partially reduced the mole itself. The first round went resoundingly to Tyre. Alexander began the creation of a wider mole but realized that it would be much preferable to be able to mount an attack from the sea.

He went to nearby Sidon and enjoyed a great success raising ships; all the Phoenicians except the Tyrians rallied to him—the Phoenicians had never had unlimited fondness for the Persians and now that all of their home cities were in the comparatively honest and capable and civilized hands of Alexander, they made the logical transition, especially as they were only signing on to attack Tyre, not Persia. This stranded Pharnabazus, the Persian naval commander, in the Aegean. Alexander also drew contingents from Cyprus, Rhodes, Lycia and Cilicia, and amassed two-hundred and twenty vessels of all sizes, a much larger force than Tyre possessed. (He did not ask anything from the original members of the League of Corinth.) Alexander took command of this fleet himself, having loaded the vessels up with his most capable heavy archers (hypaspists), as well as new towers, rams, and catapults. The Tyrian navy declined to come out and join issue, and Alexander launched some towers forward on Sidonian transport ships tied together. The Tyrians had raised their own towers on their walls and created artificial shoals by dropping rocks from the walls. When Alexander sent vessels to sweep for the obstacles, Tyrian swimmers cut their anchor cables. Alexander secured the sweepers with chains—there was a steady escalation of ingenuity, and this got the rocks removed and enabled Alexander to close on Tyre on all sides.

The Tyrians took advantage of the Cypriots having their dinner ashore and sped out of harbor and attacked their anchored vessels. Alexander saw this and put to sea with some Phoenician ships, and captured a couple of the Tyrian vessels, enabling him to partly force the harbor. A general attack was ordered with the full arsenal of floating siege towers and part of the seawall was breached and Alexander exploited this at once with two ships carrying a storming party and bridges. Alexander himself led the hypaspists and the fire from the fleet covered the landing. The bridges were fastened on land and Macedonian troops started flowing into Tyre. The Tyrian lines broke and on confirmation that the Tyrians had barbarously (and unwisely) murdered Macedonian prisoners, a terrible revenge was wrought on Tyre. Eight thousand Tyrian warriors were massacred and most of the women and children were sold into slavery. The Phoenicians saved some Tyrians, and some were able to take refuge in the Temple of Melkart (a relatively inoffensive request by Alexander to pray in which had started this fearful slaughter, and he did pray there at the end of it). Tyre finally fell in July 332 after holding out for seven months. This was one of Alexander's greatest martial feats, combining his ingenuity, indefatigability, physical courage, persuasive talents in winning over the Phoenicians, and his extraordinary gift for improvisation under maximum pressure.

Near the end of the struggle for Tyre, which became a Macedonian fortress after it was finally overrun, Alexander heard from Darius. He offered a ransom of ten-thousand talents for his family (US $17.7 billion), offered the hand of his daugh-

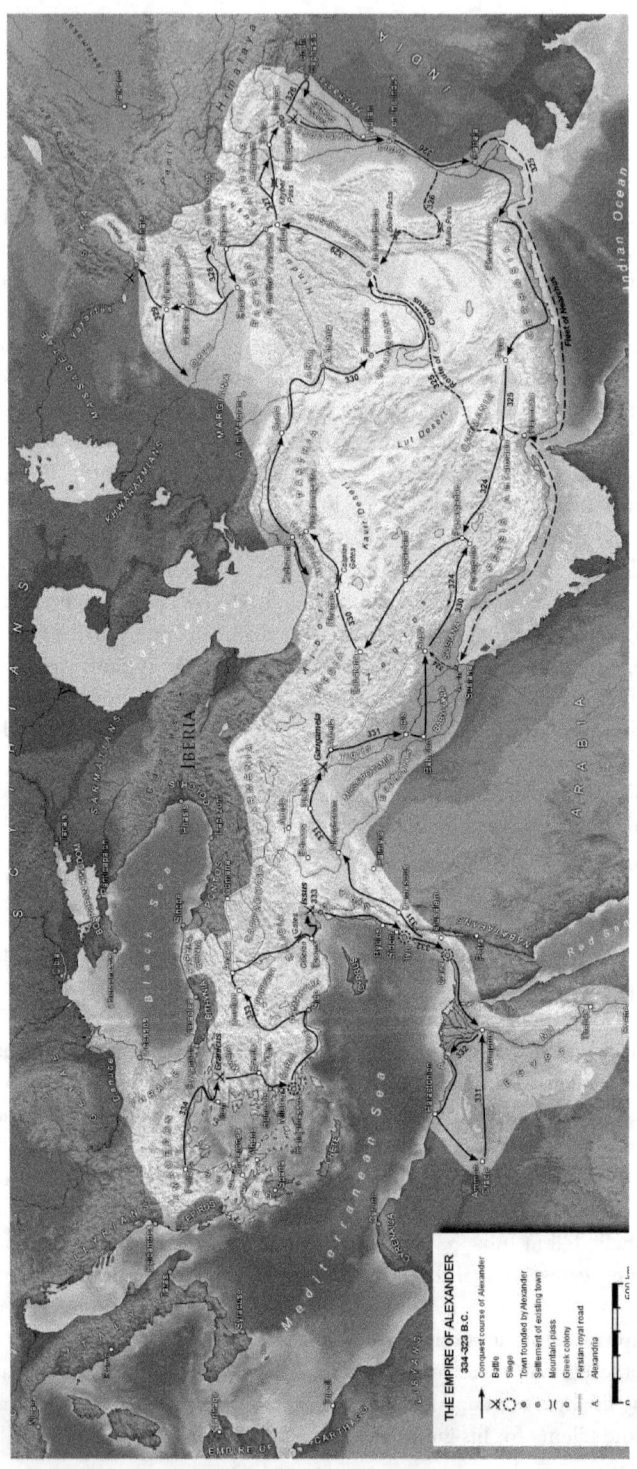

ter as a wife, and conceded his entire empire west of the Euphrates. It is probably apocryphal that Alexander asked Parmenion how he would reply to Darius, and that the exchange followed that Parmenion would accept if he were Alexander, and that he, Alexander, would accept if he were Parmenion, but that as he was Alexander, he would decline to negotiate. In fact, he already had everything Darius was offering other than that he had the formerly Great King's family rather than the offered ransom. With each success, Alexander seemed to be recalibrating where he wished to close the campaign. He installed Parmenion in Damascus to oversee the latest acquisitions of territory and descended the ancient shore route to Gaza and seized that city after a desperate resistance, and he sustained a serious wound. The assertion that he paused to worship in Jerusalem seems to have been a complete fabrication. He proceeded south and entered Egypt without difficulty in November, 332 B.C.

The Persian Satrap rushed forward to proffer the surrender of his jurisdiction to the man who had just practically ignored the Great King's offer of most of his empire (including Egypt) and nearly eighteen billion dollars just to get the four females of his family back and a peace in place while he still had a country he could rule, however radically amputated his realm. Egyptians welcomed the approach and the arrival of Alexander as vengeance, finally, on the Persians who had long been seen not just as interlopers, but as nasty and corrupt overlords who employed Greeks to keep Egypt under the Persian heel, paid them with money wrung from the sweat of Egypt, and demeaned Egypt by lolling and frolicking in its sumptuous places of debauchery. Alexander went up the Nile to Memphis, judiciously worshipped Apis with apparent humility and respect, and was accepted without any apparent demurral as the Pharaoh. The three century Persian interlude, which was neither terribly onerous nor at all distinguished, was over. Alexander returned to the Mediterranean shore and planned out what he intended to be and did become, one of the world's greatest cities, Alexandria. This great project would be pursued by Deinocrates, a visionary sculptor and architect, who wished to turn Mount Athos into an immense bust of Alexander.

Alexander then went out to the west into the desert to the Oracle of Ammon at the oasis of Siwah, with a small number of his followers. This remotely located spiritual centre was equaled only by Delphi and Dodona as a famous Greek oracle. The oracle, as was customary with pharaohs, gave Alexander "dominion over the whole world." Alexander returned to Memphis and reorganized the government of Egypt on sensible lines. He retained any natives in the bureaucracy and appointed two native governors. His tax-collector would collect the taxes through local native tax collectors. He retained Darius' Greek garrisons, though changing commanders, and satisfied himself that they didn't care who paid them and preferred to be employed by a winner. This subtly retained the chief rod on the back of Egypt, but Alexander could not be blamed for their installation. Many of them had been living on granted land for over a generation, and so were permanent residents, domesticated to Egypt but unassimilated. It would come more naturally to them to be employed by the Macedonian king, a student of Aristotle and head of the League of Corinth, than by any Persian. Alexander returned to Tyre in the spring of 331. As the Persian navy had disintegrated, he withdrew his garrisons from Rhodes and Chios, sent Athens back her prisoners as an ex gratia conciliatory gesture. This was tactically astute as Sparta was still sullen and reproachful. Alexander received some ambassadors and reports on local Greek and Macedonian matters, made some administrative dispositions and ordered Parmenion to put bridges across the Euphrates at Thapsacus. Just four years after he crossed the Dardanelles, the Macedonian king was ready for the direct assault on Persia itself, a national sanctum that had not been penetrated for three centuries. (History remains divided and, in any case, uncertain, about whether Alexander had always had an invasion of Persia as a goal, or his horizons broadened as he moved faultlessly from strength to strength.)

2. Alexander the Great II: The Battle of Gaugamela and the Death of Darius III

The Persians made a serious effort to pull a competent army together; they called up a huge number of people and began rigorous training. Their cavalry was fine, but they could no longer raise Greek mercenaries. The best cavalry were armed with shields and spears instead of javelins, and to counter the almost impregnable Macedonian phalanx, they brought back their scythed chariots and trained groups of them to act in unison. The Macedonians had a perfectly trained and experienced army with excellent morale; the Persians could not match it, but they could put a respectable force in the field. The great imbalance was in the commander. Darius was not a stupid man, but he had no natural gift as a battlefield commander and his only appearance in that role had been the rather shaming fiasco at Issus, where, as will be remembered, he placed himself between Alexander and his communications and fled at the first sign of adversity, leaving his mother, wife, and daughters (who should not have been anywhere near a battlefield), behind. Darius might have succeeded if he had been prepared to fight a Fabian action as it became known in the following century when the Roman Quintus Fabius Maximus fell back before Hannibal. Darius stood on his kingly duty, ironically so, given his unseemly flight from Issus, and claimed to be required to stand and fight. If he had been prepared to keep his army intact and to be elusive, Alexander's forces would have been less effusive and would have required more resupply than it was convenient for an invading force of limited numbers to find.

Alexander crossed the Euphrates with Parmenion in July 331, over the bridges at Thapsacus, and continued east and across the Tigris unopposed and then turned south and fetched up at the village of Gaugamela eighteen miles northeast of Mosul, where prisoners and reconnaissance told him Darius awaited him at the head of the Persian army. The Persians had chosen an entirely flat and extensive plain to give a full chance to their scythed chariots. Darius was behind the centre of his line, with a thousand select cavalry of the royal guard. He had units of cavalry interspersed along his line with infantry, with powerful encircling swarms of cavalry on each flank. There were fifteen elephants along the line, which could frighten Alexander's horses, but they tended to frighten the Persian cavalry also, as they were not accustomed to working with them. The Persian scythed chariots were all along the front of the Persian line. It was a formidable army, thoughtfully deployed, but they represented at least ten different areas of present or recent Persian territory, with two-thousand Greek mercenaries in the centre and everything would depend on the Persian ranks holding together and drawing blood in quantities with the scythed chariots. If the Great King himself were irresolute this time, it would be his last battle. On the other hand, if the Persians could even hold the Macedonians with approximately equal casualties, it would partially demystify Alexander and leave him with a convalescing army a thousand miles from the Dardanelles.

Alexander seems to have had perhaps forty-thousand men, including seven-thousand cavalry, an army of about ten-thousand fewer men than Darius deployed, though in fewer and more homogeneous units and well-tested in the fighting of the last four years and for most of them, extensive experience before that. Seeing the cavalry at the Persian flanks, Alexander set up three sides of a square, with the middle section the front-centre and the lines trailing back off each side, to make it practically impossible to turn his flanks. He had mixed cavalry and archers on each side and the phalanx in the centre. He put his best archers, hypapsists, and javelin forces to the front to meet the Persian chariots. Most of the mercenaries were behind the centre with orders to turn about and complete the square if the army were surrounded and to be sure that no one in his army was attacked from the rear. Parmenion and the Thessalians were on the left and Alexander was with the Companions on the right. He gave his men a good dinner and bade them rest through most of the night, while the more nervous Persian command had their men at stations all night. Alexander himself got a good sleep and awakened refreshed on the morning of October 1, 331 B.C.

The Persian cavalry attacked deep on Alexander's right and forced the defenders back, requiring reinforcements; the line was stabilized though with some difficulty. As that part of the battle became less intense, the scythed chariots raced forward on the centre. Alexander had sent the javelin men forward and they seriously disturbed the charging horses and broke up the charge significantly. Alexander had left space for his infantry to part before those chariots that got through, enabling them to come through the line without doing too much damage, and then have to turn at least in right angles as the forces in the interior of Alexander's formation, infantry and cavalry, set upon them from behind or on flanks. All in all, despite a gallant effort, the scythed chariots were assimilated without severe casualties, and having charged once were a generally spent force, as almost all were killed or otherwise deactivated. Alexander put in more reinforcements on his right and then sent in his lancers. To stabilize that side, the commander of the Persian left, Bessus, satrap of Bactria and Sogdiana and the capable leader of fine troops, had to commit all the cavalry he had on the right and the fighting drifted somewhat down the Macedonian line, opening a gap between the Persian centre and left.

Alexander detected this as it started and assembled the Companions whom he had kept out of the action up to now, and ordered his infantry at the hinge of his right-centre to attack into the opening gap and led the Companions himself in immediately behind the infantry. He cracked into the thin section of the Persian line between the centre and left, ordering reserves to follow and cut the Persian army in two. As at Issus, Darius fled, even though the commander of the Persian left, Mazaeus, the competent former satrap of Cilicia was rather getting the better of Parmenion. If Darius had kept his head, he might have won half the battle and Bessus probably could have salvaged part of his army and inflicted casualties fairly equivalent to those he sustained. The Thessalians were in real difficulty on the Macedonian left, and part of the phalanx had to be committed to the left to prevent Mazaeus breaking through and onto the rear of the main Macedonian formations. The left and centre left were too hard-pressed to respond to Alexander's order for a general advance when he charged the opening gap in the Persian centre-right. Astonishingly, Mazaeus split the Macedonian phalanx in half and drove through it, but was unable to direct his forces once they had divided the Macedonian army, and instead of turning and attacking the rear of the right phalanx and starting to roll up behind Alexander himself, which could have at least drawn the battle, his men raced through to seize the baggage and free the prisoners, enabling the Greek mercenaries and other units to regroup and attack Mazaeus' advance guard while they were looting and releasing prisoners as if the battle was over and won. Parmenion sent a message to Alexander asking for help and Alexander departed the right and crossed the battlefield toward his rear-left to assist Parmenion, but he encountered large formations of Persians and Parthians and barred their retreat; very heavy fighting at close quarters ensued, in which the Macedonian king vigorously participated, giving an excellent personal account of himself as always (a striking contrast with his opponent), and sixty of the Companions were lost. The Companions inflicted heavy losses on the units they engaged and when they finally got to Parmenion's assistance, word had spread throughout the Persian army that their king had deserted them, and Mazaeus' cavalry lost their elan and the action was broken off. On the Persian right, Bessus and his men had fought hard and valiantly all day and they retired in good order.

The performance of the Persian ranks was quite distinguished and if Darius had kept his nerve, he would have inflicted sufficient losses on Alexander such that he could not have attacked Darius again soon. No part of the Persian army, after such a day, was much interested in fighting for Darius and against Alexander again. But the day was not over; having prevailed, Alexander set his men on the retreating enemy. Alexander didn't pursue Bessus and his sturdy Bactrians, or Mazaeus and his Armenians, Syrians, and Cappadocians. But he chased the broken-up sections of the army, what survived of the Persian centre and parts of the flanks as long as there was light. Then he rested until midnight and started out again; he reaped the dividend of having let his men rest the previous night, and he finally called off the pursuit after slaying or capturing some thousands more and only stopped when he reached the town of Arbela sixty-two miles distant from the battlefield.

Gaugamela was one of the great battles of world history. For centuries, fantastic tales that in his time Alexander did nothing to discourage, circulated of how Alexander had killed six-hundred thousand Persians at Gaugamela; and even the current Wikipedia estimates forty-thousand Persian dead. The real number was probably not more than twenty-five thousand, but Macedonian losses were not more than about ten per cent of that, and the Persian army was sundered into pieces and Darius and the Achaemenid Dynasty were finished; they had had a long but latterly rather undistinguished inning at the helm of the world's crossroads. Alexander, after resting his army for some days, led part of it to Babylon, where Mazaeus had stopped. Mazaeus deserted a king who had twice deserted him and his army and with no assurance of a civilized reception, he advanced out of Babylon and greeted Alexander in person, "and was received with the honour that was his due."[3] The Babylonians greeted Alexander with great respect and hopefulness, though not without fear, and the Macedonian king again demonstrated how he had already begun to earn the post-nominal attribution of greatness. He reversed all the acts of Xerxes and resurrected all the Babylonian customs and traditions and then named Mazaeus, his gallant battlefield foe of just a few weeks before, the satrap of Babylonia, though he appointed a Macedonian general to command the forces in the satrapy. After what he had been through, Mazaeus was happy enough to retire, he was fifty-four.

Alexander released Darius' family, completely unharmed and unthreatened, at Susa. He named more Persians to high positions, and Amyntas returned from Greece with fresh troops and updated news and assessments. Greece and Macedonia were naturally astonished by the reports of Alexander's victories, which vastly transcended anything in prior recorded history. City states that had squabbled for centuries over tiny and often unyielding acreages and had been threatened for centuries and largely occupied by the feared and despised Persians, could scarcely imagine that this twenty-five-year-old Macedonian had conquered most of the known world east of Greece. Alexander, whose troops were largely hoping to turn homewards, were instead led south and east—it was two-hundred miles south from Arbela to Babylon, and six-hundred miles east-southeast to the Uxii, an Aryan tribe that had been dispersed by the Persians and lived from piracy and brigandage perpetrated against travelers. They were accustomed to collecting some toll of passage even from the Great King latterly, but soon learned that there was a new hand on the empire. Alexander killed those who attacked and drove the rest off and moved on to Persepolis. Here, again contrary to Parmenion's cautious advice, Alexander burned down Xerxes' palace. The legend arose that the dancer Thais appeared and performed at a feast Alexander held and incited him to burn the palace. The utility of this legend was that while Xerxes and all his forces were required to scorch Athens, an Athenian girl could return the gesture in Xerxes' capital. It is a myth, but like the Gordian Knot and a number of apercus, it has persisted through the millennia, testimony to the immense impact Alexander had on the human imagination generally, as well as the legacy of the countries that he influenced.

Alexander remained in Persepolis until the spring of 330, when he happily received the news of the defeat of Sparta in the war it finally unleashed on some of the Greeks who had participated in the League of Corinth. (This will be described in Chapter 15). He moved on to the Median capital of Ecbatana, zig-zagging four-hundred miles back northwest from Persepolis. He settled into the opulent palace of the Median kings, and contemplated his options, enjoying a perspective that in its breadth and possibilities may perhaps never have been equaled in the prospects of any subsequent centuries. The known world then was much smaller than it was even three centuries later in Caesar's time, And Alexander now dominated most of it. He

---

3 Ibid., p. 382.

was no longer Alexander of Macedon, General of the League of Corinth; he was the Great King and was now as much an explorer and discoverer as a conqueror. He had accomplished a phenomenal, an unimaginable odyssey, and it was far from over. He had really only fought four battles—Granicus, Issus, Tyre and Gaugamela, and had not lost much more than ten thousand men. He was twenty-six, moving from the palace of one oriental potentate to the next, and contemplating the organization of peace.

Aristotle had taught him that peace was as difficult to conduct as war, and he knew that simple military conquest was rarely very durable; the Persians had done well to manage it for as long as they had. What Alexander planned was the acculturation of the peoples whose lands he traversed and somewhat occupied to the superior Greek culture and his method of achieving this would be to raise up Hellenic cities at strategic points throughout the parts of the Persian Empire that interested him, and to integrate them into the surrounding territories. He had already demonstrated that he proposed to encourage local self-government and avoid, as much as possible, any notion of despotism imposed from outside. In general, he improved the equity and efficiency of governance in the former Persian Empire, and to the extent Persia was occupied, the occupation was unobtrusive. His long-time adjutant Harpalus had aroused Alexander's annoyance after Issus, but, as was his nature, Alexander forgave him and entrusted to Harpalus the treasury of Alexander's entire government, the presiding officer over all the local financial superintendents, answerable directly and only to Alexander.

Darius had gone from Gaugamela to Ecbatana, and then, with Bessus and his remaining two-thousand Greek mercenaries and some other units, had retired into Bactria in eastern Iran. Alexander was informed that he was gathering reinforcements and pursued him with great speed. He covered the two-hundred miles from Ecbatana to Rei (near the present Teheran), and then on to the Caspian Gates. Here, Alexander received the son of Mazaeus, who told him that Bessus and a few others had deposed Darius and held him prisoner. Alexander, who had made the march from Rei to the Caspian Gates of fifty-two miles without stopping, had been averaging an astounding thirty-six miles a day on this final pursuit of Darius. He broke camp again and with the Companions, lancers, some infantry and only two days rations, made for Bessus' reported camp, but found he had moved east. Alexander kept on his trail and then opted for a short-cut, across desert, but his infantry was exhausted. Alexander had his cavalry dismount and did the same, and placed his foot-weary phalangians on the horses and pressed off into the desert with what he reckoned were adequate water rations. When they came upon a well, Alexander declined the water, but had it rationed among his men. They rode overnight fifty miles and came upon Bessus' camp as he hurriedly departed it. Bessus did not want to rejoin battle, no matter how reduced the number of Alexander's party. Two of Bessus' collaborators, Barsaentes and Satibarzanes, stabbed Darius and left him dying. A Macedonian scout gave the Great King a glass of water, but he died before Alexander arrived. He had Darius' body wrapped in a purple robe and sent to Persepolis for a dignified burial. He may not have been a bad man, but he was a poor ruler, unworthy of the loyalty and bravery of the men who died for him and his dynasty while he deserted them. Had he done his part, he would have salvaged something for the Achaemenid dynasty. As it was, it perished ingloriously with him. Alexander, king of Macedonia, general of the League of Corinth, Pharaoh, was the Great King now.

3. Alexander the Great III: India

At Lindus in 331, Alexander called himself "The Lord of Asia," and the title "king" began to appear on some of his coinage. To shake out the submissions of the loose fringes of the Persian Empire, he moved two-hundred miles farther east from the Caspian to Zadracarta, site of the royal residence of Hyrcania. Here he received the eastern satraps including his father's friend Artabazus, whom he greeted cordially. Those whom he received at this stage he confirmed in their satrapies and other titles, striking the sharp contrast between those whom he treated gently and welcomed when they adhered to him, and those whom he hunted down to the ends of the world when they did not. He continued to flush out and discipline marauding tribes, and they soon retreated into the fastness of Asia. He received further embassies, even at this extremity of the earth, from representatives of previously uncommitted Greek states. The Greeks who had served Darius prior to the Covenant of the League of Corinth he pardoned. He imprisoned the envoys to Persia from the League towns including Athens, as traitors, and accorded the same treatment to the Spartan diplomats—Sparta, as will be recounted in Chapter 15, tried to take advantage of Alexander's absence to make war behind his back in the compulsively bellicose manner of the Greeks, and had been defeated, so he thought it time to make an example of Sparta's sullen insolence.

He had now got so far east that there were no more cities. There were only villages, fortresses and the occasional royal habitation on scrubby plains and hills. Alexander moved toward challenging Bessus in his native Bactria an obscurity five-hundred miles east of the Caspian in what is now Afghanistan. He started on to the east but on learning that Satibarzanes, whom he had confirmed as satrap of Aria, had risen behind him in what is now eastern Iran and killed Alexander's resident general, Anaxippus, he turned south. As usual, he moved like a cat and caught Satibarzanes unprepared and chased him out of his satrapy, which he laid waste in exemplary manner. Satibarzanes joined Bessus and they started to mount a national rebellion against the formidable invader from a far distant land. Barsaentes had risen and Alexander meted out the same treatment to him and when he was betrayed to Alexander, the new Great King executed him to send a message to the like-minded, wherever they might be cowering and scheming. At this time Alexander unearthed what he took as a plot by the son of Parmenion, representing those old Macedonian nobles who had never entirely reconciled themselves to an absolute monarch—even Philip had gone through the motions of some collegiality.

Alexander struck forcefully and executed Parmenion's son Philotas. He was not an old comrade, but his father, though now more or less in involuntary retirement, was a comrade from the start, and this was a wrenching and chilling development that reduced the informality and youthful camaraderie of the king's circle. There were also increased murmurings of impatience for home leave; it had been over five years for most of his army, including himself. The historical notation (by Ptolemy) is that Philotus had a fair trial before the army, as was Macedonian procedure when the king was a party in interest, and the evidence of Philotas' treason was clear and there was no dispute over the sentence. Several other participants in what appears to have been a plotted coup d'état were also tried and executed, but others, including Amyntas, were tried and acquitted, and retained in their positions.

There remained the problem of Parmenion; Alexander believed but did not know, that he was implicated in what had been afoot. He considered it impossible to retain him as director of his communications, and impossible also just to retire him to rattle around as a loose cannon in his rear, so he dispatched messengers on especially fast camels to outrun rumours west, back to the principal generals on the roads back to the Dardanelles requiring that Parmenion be seized and summarily executed with no due process at all. It was a brutal and possibly even an evil deed, but it had the desired effect of cracking the entire vast and diverse class of administrators and military commanders throughout Alexander's realms into a state of galvanized obedience. Ruling over such an immense territory and polyglot population with such a small force required occasional measures of impressive severity. It is still a blot on Alexander's career (a little like the murder of the Duke d'Enghien by Napoleon in 1804). Alexander founded a city, called Propthasia (Anticipation), where the trial and execution of Philotas occurred.

Alexander did not take winter quarters in the winter of 330-329 and continued his pattern in Asia Minor of zig-zagging eastwards dividing the territory into wedges and assigning it to different forms of administration, all on the strength of his immediate force of arms and the mystique of his person. No one imagined the Macedonians were a superior people; their king was superior at rulership in all its aspects to anyone the world had seen before. He continued to dispense liberality and the promise of universal peace and government, interspersed with the savage elimination of someone or a few people, to keep everyone on his toes. He removed three-hundred miles south in Aria, along the eastern edge of the Salt Desert to the Helmund River, where he came upon the Reis tribes, known in Persia as Benefactors, as they had once assisted Cyrus; he exempted them from satrapification in recognition of past services, renewed the expression of gratitude of Persia, confirmed their autonomy even from taxation and moved back northeast to Bactria, still on the trail of Bessus, with the cheers of the Benefactors ringing in his ears. The satraps of Carmania and Gedrosia submitted to him as he approached, but Arachosia was untamed and ungoverned. He arrived at Kandahar (with which the world became refamiliarized by the Canadian army in the Afghanistan war of 2001-2002). He founded towns here and there as he passed, usually named Alexandria and had some soldiers, who became the garrison, and some imported settlers, and a scattering of locals who gravitated toward the new centre; this policy was designed to be the beginning of the tying together of the whole known world. It was a grandiose undertaking, yet one based on some realistic ideas of what was required to give any such ambitious plan a chance of success. The royal Persian capital of Persepolis suffered a bad fire in 330, and it has always been debated whether this was accidental or deliberate Greco-Macedonian revenge for the burning of the Acropolis and much of Athens one-hundred and fifty years before in 480 B.C.

He pressed on four-hundred miles northeast from Kandahar to Kabul, in the heart of Afghanistan and at the edge of Bactria, where Bessus was preparing to resist him with an army of seven-thousand of his regulars supplemented by some thousands of neighbors and northern allies. His men suffered from cold and their rations were sparse and dreary (mule and silphium principally), but their casualties were not great as Alexander led them on an out-of-the-way route into Bactria, He avoided the Hindu Kush, where he had reason to believe that Bessus awaited him, and went through the Khayub Pass, eleven-thousand, six-hundred feet above sea level, before the winter had altogether given way to spring, and Alexander astounded Bessus by descending the mountains on his western flank, causing a precipitate retreat a hundred miles north to Aornos, almost mid-way between Kabul and Tashkent, and close to what is now Uzbekistan. He was now two-thousand miles east of the Dardanelles, ten per cent farther from where he started than Moscow is from Paris.

With this, the Bactrian civic leaders submitted, and Alexander rewarded the doughty and durable Artabazus with this satrapy, as Bessus and his loyalists crossed the Oxus River going north into what are now the bowels of Uzbekistan and was then Sogdiana, the outer northeast limit of any Persian penetration. (It may be remembered that Artabazus, one of the journeyman-satraps and politically agile survivors of the age, had conducted an unsuccessful revolt against Artaxerxes III Ochus and taken refuge with Philip of Macedon, but returned to assist Darius III, and commanded units well in the Battle of Gaugamela, withdrew after Darius, but became effectively neutral when the final revolt against Darius arose in his entourage, and made clear that after the end of the dynasty, he was a supporter of the new world leader, who embraced him as the splendid scoundrel that he was, half cunning and half courage—just what this wild and remote region needed.) Aria had attempted a rising in Alexander's rear while he was plunging northwards into Central Asia, Satibarzanes raised the banner of revolt, incited by Bessus, but was defeated by forces led by Artabazus, and then challenged his leading opponents to single combat, which then occurred with Erigyius, who killed Satibarzanes, snuffing out the insurrection. Alexander did not at once see the distinctly national character of these revolts against him, but soon devised the formula—deference to local symbolism and personnel with strict enforcement by brutal application of force of imperial and universalist suzerainty.

Finally, the elusive Bessus was betrayed to Alexander, who sent Ptolemy to bring him to him in chains. Bessus was put in the pillory and publicly flogged and then his nose and ears were severed, as was customary in unsuccessful rebellions against the Great King. He was sent in chains to Ecbatana and was publicly executed, though there is some dispute about whether he was beheaded, crucified, or drawn and quartered. Whatever the modality, this was his brutal end—a display of savagery that seems excessive and was doubtless intended to be exemplary. Alexander's magnanimity was not unlimited and was not always predictable, as he intended. Alexander pressed on to Samarkand, capital of Sogdiana, but national and tribal revolt in these remote and relatively barbarous areas which had not been disciplined by conquerors before was like wildfire, and a number of his garrisons were overwhelmed and massacred; he summoned the Sogdians to a general meeting (a durbar), and the entire province erupted in revolt which Alexander suppressed, razing to the ground seven different towns, and killing, scattering, or enslaving the populations. He was twice wounded in these frontier engagements.

The Sogdian leader, Spitamenes, took advantage of Alexander's absence in Turkmenistan along the Jaxartes River, almost at Tashkent, two-hundred miles northeast of Samarkand, to erupt in revolt, besieging Samarkand (Maracanda). Alexander could only spare twenty-three hundred Greek mercenaries and sixty Companions to try to deal with Spitamenes while he faced down the Turkomen on the opposite side of the Jaxartes. He built yet another Alexandria, on the banks of the Jaxartes, the outer fortifications in just two weeks, and then used a few of his large catapults to drive the Turkomen back from the far bank of the river, and then crossed on rafts made of reeds, and the horses swam. Once fully across, he threw his heavy cavalry against the enemy; the Turkomen retreated but sent their cavalry around Alexander's flanks in attempted encirclement to cut him off from the river, but he had his archers in place behind his line and ready for such an endeavor; the encirclement was rebuffed and Alexander's whole force charged the Turkomen main body and broke it up and routed it and the new Great King prevailed. He had resolved not to be harassed by "Scythians" as he called all of these Asian barbarians, as Darius had been. His cavalry ran down the Turkomen past nightfall, taking no prisoners, until dysentery or some such indisposition contracted from brackish drinking water weakened him to the point that he had to be carried in an improvised wagon back to his camp.

Unfortunately for Alexander, while he again demonstrated his military genius by instantly adapting to desert warfare even though seriously unwell, Pharnuches and his force sent to quell Spitamenes at Samarkand had been lured into the desert and subjected to similar tactics as the Turkomen had attempted against Alexander. Pharnuches was not a great commander (he was in fact an interpreter in these local tongues, which indicated that Alexander thought the problems might be resolved by negotiation). It was a disaster, and Pharnuches and all his contingent perished. Spitamenes' triumph was brief; Alexander, having smashed the Turkomen and recuperated at Alexandria-the-Farthest, descended on the Sogdians in full array and bent on vengeance.

He made the one-hundred-and-thirty-five-mile journey from Alexandria-the-Farthest to Samarkand in three days and nights, finally realizing the full nature of a national revolt by barbarous "Scythians" and the requirement of extreme severity. He buried Pharnuches and his dead comrades and then completely scorched the rich Polytimetus Valley to assure that Spitamenes could not approach and then took his exhausted eastern army to comfortable winter quarters in Samarkand, while Spitamenes wintered in Bokhara. As spring approached, Alexander arranged for extensive reinforcements from the western satraps and from Europe. In deploying back across the Oxus to subdue Sogdiana, Alexander discovered an open oil spring, history's first recorded oil well.

He divided his reinforced army into five columns that descended more or less in parallel to reconcentrate at Samarkand (Maracanda). He was preventing evasion by recourse to desert maneuver, and retreated southwards across the Oxus, but the savage Massagetae tribe attacked one of Alexander's fortified posts that he had dotted around the area to impede the local guerrilla tactics. Spitamenes then approached Bactria itself, while Alexander was still to the north, and could not engage the garrison Alexander had left, but the person in charge of the sick and wounded of Alexander's army there was less fortunate and Spitamenes massacred them and vanished into the sand. Alexander had reduced half of Sogdiana, but Spitamenes was still saucily Gasconading about, and half the 328 campaigning season had gone by. Alexander had assembled some Bactrian and Sogdian cavalry units, his first Asian forces integrated into his army, the inception of a concept for which he had ambitious plans.

He left these and some other forces with Coenus in charge of Western Sogdiana, anchored in numerous fortified settlements around the territory and himself led highly mobile forces into eastern Sogdiana after the elusive Spitamines, who stealthily reentered the western part of Sogdiana, thinking he would fare better even in fortified Macedonian territory than facing the Great King himself. Coenus soon became aware of his location and was also aware of the tactical response to him and Coenus defeated him decisively. The Massagetes and the Sogdians almost all deserted him, Spitamines' wife sponsored a coup and Spitamines was seized, bound, and executed by decapitation and the not over-grieving widow sent his severed head as a trophy to Alexander, who considered him the most talented opponent he had faced. Alexander subsequently married a daughter of Spitamines, Apama, to Seleucus, one of Alexander's successors, and Apama's son Antiochus I, who succeeded his father as king of the Hellenic Seleucid Empire, reigned peacefully for twenty years until his death from natural causes in his sixties. It was a remarkable evolution in one line in three generations from Spitamines' life and death of utmost savagery to Antiochus' serene and civilized rule and death. Alexander had developed in a couple of days' consideration the anti-guerrilla strategy that would essentially be used successfully by the British in the South African War and the Malayan insurrection more than twenty-two centuries later. If Marcus Crassus, the fellow triumvir of Julius Caesar and Pompeius Magnus, two-hundred and seventy-five years after Alexander, had studied Alexander and his generals' conduct in Afghanistan and Uzbekistan, he would have survived Carrhae, and might have graduated to the Second Triumvirate with Octavian Caesar and Mark Antony (Chapters 20, 26).

An unpleasant and infamous incident occurred in the summer of 328 when, as was his custom, Alexander lingered at dinner in animated conversation lubricated by a sizeable intake of local wine. Alexander did like to drink but was rarely drunk. In these distant areas, there were problems with the quality of drinking water, and increased wine intake was the general remedy adopted by Alexander and his officers. One night of garrison revelry got out of hand and Cleitus, Alexander's governor in Samarkand (hipparch) and a friend of Philotas, uttered a series of remarks suggesting that Alexander had achieved all he had because of Philip's Macedonian army, and he had treated his old comrades with contempt and ingratitude, and the fate of Parmenion and Philotas was mentioned in scathing and accusatory terms. Alexander always had a ferocious temper, and like most such people, this was very accentuated when he was drink-taken. Cleitus extended his arm with clenched fist and said that that was what had saved his life at the Granicus and continued to irritate Alexander until the incident blew up and Alexander seized a sentry's spear. He was restrained by comrades while Cleitus was muscled out of the king's presence, but in a few moments, he raced back into the royal tent and defied Alexander to kill him—provoking Alexander to impale and dismember him.

The king was repentant in the following days and did not eat or emerge from his quarters. After several days, his close comrades, concerned for Alexander and for themselves in carrying on this far-flung enterprise that had erupted out of Macedonia like a mighty jack-in-the-box, satisfied a soothsayer to say that Cleitus had suffered a religious penalty for annoying Dionysius, and the appropriate group of officers passed a resolution: the military judiciary that was competent to judge, held that Cleitus had committed a crime equivalent to treason and had been justly judged and executed. It was a stretch, even Aristotle held that kings are above the law, and as Arrian observed, many kings had committed evil acts, but he was unaware of any other who had repented it.

The task remained of subduing the rest of Sogdiana, ruled in different sections of what is now Kirgizstan and Kazakhstan, by the war-lords, Oxyartes, Chorienes, Catanes, and Austanes, fierce men who had never heard of an invader in what they knew of their tribal history—Alexander had gone well beyond the Persian Empire and was now twenty-five hundred miles east of the Dardanelles in the trackless immensity of the central Eurasian land mass. His men could be forgiven for wondering what strategic purpose they were serving so far from home, and most of them had been absent from home for six years. Only a leader of unheard-of brilliance and charisma could have maintained morale for such a colossal effort. In January 327, at the bottom of the severe Central Asian highland winter, Alexander assaulted Oxyartes' impregnable "Sogdian Rock." Oxyartes was not there, but his family was, so deep was the snow and so elevated the rock, the garrison responded to Alexander's demand for its surrender, that he would never take it unless he could find soldiers who could fly. Always pleasantly challenged by the impossible, Alexander called for volunteers to mount the sheer side of the bastion, with ropes and iron pegs. Three hundred men did volunteer and although thirty of them died in falls from the side of the cliff, many of the others got to the top and looked down on the 'Sogdian Rock' and Alexander had the announcement proclaimed loudly that these were his flying soldiers. The family and guard of Oxyartes were so astounded, they surrendered.

Among those captured was Oxyartes' daughter Roxanne, whom Alexander purported to marry, in an act of political maneuver to pacify the rest of Sogdiana. The father of the bride appeared, beaming, and conducted Alexander and his force to the headquarters of Chorienes at Faisabad, a hundred miles to the east. They made their way via the supposedly untraversable torrent at the foot of Chorienes' fortress, and Alexander had his men fashion a bridge of ladders fastened to rock outcroppings. It was exacting work, but Oxyartes persuaded Chorienes to surrender by representing Alexander as effectively a compassionate superman because of his military prowess and unprecedented powers which he had just demonstrated, and his magnanimity, of which his recently wed daughter was living, blushing proof. (In fact, despite romantic legend, it is not clear that Alexander was attracted to women at all, and not clear what sort of a relationship this was, given their mutual linguistic incomprehension.)

Alexander left it to his capable lieutenant Craterus to subdue Catanes and Austanes east of the Vakhash River and (at the risk of being geographically laborious), over three-thousand miles east of the Dardanelles, the distance from the northern tip of Greenland to Mexico City, and within site of the Himalayas. Alexander returned to Bactria, which he renamed Alexandria (there were now more than a dozen of them, starting with the great project of Alexandria, Egypt) and prepared for his invasion of India. While doing so, the philosopher Callisthenes, one of the intellectuals traveling with Alexander and the professed historian of the expedition, hoping to obtain the king's endorsement of the reconstruction of his native city of Olynthus, raised the question of the possible divinity of Alexander.

In furtherance of this, and acting in effect as Alexander's press agent, he published a biography of Alexander that included some Brobdingnagian whoppers, including the complete invention that the Oracle of Ammon had told Alexander that Philip was not really his father: he was descended from Zeus-Ammon, and that the Oracle of Apollo at Delphi had said he was the son of Zeus, and a number of other such declarations and supportive episodes were improvised to the same end. It has never been clear whether this was spontaneous toadying of an odiously servile nature, or Alexander discreetly commissioned Callisthenes to build his mystique and mystify the susceptible, especially those who might otherwise be tempted to disloyalty. There were more legitimate sources for this view: Isocrates had said to Philip that if he conquered Persia there would be nothing left to aspire to but the status of a god, and Aristotle had said, with Alexander in his thoughts, that when God came, it would be among men and apparently one of them. Alexandrine admirers (and they are overwhelmingly numerous among classical historians), for evident reasons, emphasize that at least this rather tawdry cult only claimed divine descent and did not go the full distance of many other ancient leaders and make an outright claim of deity. Alexander, given the tumult of Philip's private life and the explosively tempestuous and capricious nature of his mother Olympias, was of less than certain paternity, but reaching for Zeus was a bridge too far, even for the man who sliced the Gordian Knot and conquered the rock of Sogdiana.

Alexander himself muddied the waters by adopting, in Persia, the requirement of subjects to prostrate themselves before him, as had been the custom of the Great King. This could be absorbed easily in the former Persian Empire, but Greeks and Macedonians prostrated themselves only to deities. But Alexander, in the guise of uniformity throughout his swiftly magnified domains, purported to require prostration from Greeks and Macedonians as well, and counted on Callisthenes to support this and incorporate it in his campaign of obsequious lionization. But when the time came for the introduction of this improvisation, many Macedonians and Greeks laughed disrespectfully in the presence, even when they complied, and Callisthenes, ever the press agent sensing the shifting wind advised the king to confine Asiatic practices to Asia. Alexander did so but was seriously aggrieved.

This nonsense escalated unpleasantly, and the next step was the pages' conspiracy. One of the royal pages, Hermolaus, preceded Alexander to a royal boar hunt, a terribly pretentious affront to the monarch and the normal punishment was imposed: Hermolaus was soundly whipped in front of the court and deprived of his horse for an indefinite period. While contemplating the austerities of pedestrianism, he concerted a plot among the pages to assassinate the king. This was uncovered and the accomplices were aggressively questioned prior to their automatic execution. They were stoned to death by a representative cross-section of Macedonians, but they all, apparently independently of each other, indicated that they had in considerable measure been incited to contemplate such a terrible act by Callisthenes' talk of the justice of killing tyrants. There was not believable evidence that he was specifically referring to Alexander, but any such sentiment to that audience and after the episode of Hermolaus, was a very dangerous transgression. Alexander was sufficiently irritated by Callisthenes' U-turn on the prostration issue and these further developments that he arrested and imprisoned Callisthenes and ordered his crucifixion.

This ended Alexander's relationship with Aristotle, who considered that he had become a tyrant, and it also stirred a section of the intelligentsia, led by Theophrastus, to take up this charge and leave it to posterity as a blot on the legend of Alexander the Great: that he was a lucky despot, corrupted by power, who succumbed to partly self-inflicted disaster. This negative interpretation is not just or sustainable, but it is there and is argued with something close to the general British view that Napoleon was a monster and the Ciceronian school that Julius Caesar was a public enemy. Only the totalitarian tyrants escape such hostility from their countrymen while they live, but there is no one to defend them for long after their departure (viz. Hitler, Stalin, and Mao, though the extent of their infamies were not fully appreciated while they lived).

In the reorganization of his army at Bactria, and the incorporation of reinforcements as he recycled some of the more battle-weary and home-sick forces back to Greece and Macedonia, Alexander separated the Royal Squadron from the Companions, and placed some noble Persians in it. He enlisted and trained a significant number of Bactrian, Sogdian, Sacaean, and Arachosian cavalry especially, but also infantry, and the army ceased to be Macedonian and was an experiment in the fusion of races in the shared cause of Alexander's apparent invincibility, all in an ostensibly unexceptionable cause: human brotherhood and peace with efficient government, including a level of participatory democracy and an absence of racial discrimination. It was a novel notion of empire though in practice it operated like other empires and Alexander attacked whom he wished. He had a plausible grievance against Persia, but certainly had none with any of the ingredients of India. His chief generals were Craterus, Perdiccas (a cousin), Hephaestion, and Demetrius. He left ten-thousand mercenary infantry and three-thousand cavalry in Bactria. It is difficult to estimate the numbers he led into India, but apparently at least thirty-five thousand soldiers and many thousands of support people, native families, scientists, and assorted experts, traders, and later, local Indian contingents. It was a joint-purpose mission of conquest and discovery. It should be remembered that he had no idea of the existence of all of India, the Ganges, or Hindustan, any more than he knew of China and Siberia. There was no silk Road; there was some trading in spices, fabrics, and precious metals and gems from some mysterious eastern sources, but Alexander hadn't the remotest idea of the scope of the territory or size and sophistication of India as it has been known and defined in modern time. To him, Asia was what Darius I had ruled, and India was the land around the Indus River, and he may have thought, as many Greeks did, that the Indus was the ultimate upper section of the Nile. Artaxerxes III Ochus thought Ethiopia connected Egypt and India. Darius I had occupied and ruled part of Punjab and Sind, but that was one-hundred and fifty years before, and there were not even slightly reliable folkloric descriptions of those territories now. Herodotus had touched on eastern matters, but he was not much read at this time and not especially believed (or always believable). Alexander was setting out to regain the empire of Darius I, levering on his supposedly internationally legally justified assault on Persia to snaffle up and enfold in his multi-racial fraternity of states all that had ever been in contact with the Great King. He intended to explore the "southern sea" (Indian Ocean) and brought with him shipwrights and oarsmen and the nucleus of a navy, from construction to shipboard personnel. It was an astonishingly imaginative and ambitious venture.

Alexander and his extensive train started from Bactria and proceeded across the Hindu Kush through the Kaoshan Pass (fourteen-thousand, three-hundred feet above sea level), to Alexandria in the Caucasus (any route except towards the north would take you to an Alexandria before too long). Finding that city disorganized, he named his new father-in-law, the cliff-dweller Oxyartes, satrap of Paropamisadae (Kabul and Jalalibad) to shape it up. The local tribes greeted Alexander with suitable deference and gave him twenty-five elephants, which he used for transport. Alexander divided his army in two, sending Hephaestion and Perdiccas and the donor of the elephants, Taxiles, with several thousand of his men through the Khyber Pass to the Indus and there to build a bridge of pontoon boats, while he followed the more rugged older route to the north. He tried to move quickly to prevent the fierce local mountain tribes from concentrating, and did defeat them in detail and take many prisoners and a lot of cattle. He was so impressed with the appearance of the mountain cattle; he sent a number of them to Macedonia to be bred there. Alexander was again wounded, though lightly. But he was tempting fate by skirmishing so often with fierce, if primitive, tribal warriors so remote that his reputation for invincibility did not precede him and he was a mere interloper. Eventually his route was blocked by the combined forces of the tribes and a full-scale battle ensued. He broke and scattered his enemies, but it was a good fight.

He proceeded on into Swat, land of the Assaceni, who concentrated before their capital Massaga. They attacked Alexander before he had got close to their capital; Alexander led the Phalanx personally, as always, and pretended to retreat to try to draw them away from the walls of Massaga. They were too prudent for that, and Alexander drove them within their walls. In the first effort to storm through or over part of the wall, Alexander was lightly wounded in the ankle. He brought up his siege train but was unable to breach the walls. Fortunately for Alexander and his expedition, the Assaceni chieftain was killed in one of the periodic drenching showers of arrows, and on this, the Assaceni negotiated terms and their mercenary allies from beyond the Indus left the town and camped not far from Alexander's forces. In the dead of night, the Macedonian-led army descended on them and massacred them to a man. Alexander explained to the Assaceni and to posterity that the mercenaries had come over to him but began preaching mutiny among his troops. There is considerable doubt about the truthfulness of his account; it might have been one of his periodic acts of extreme severity to warn the unwary or inadequately respectful of who it was they were dealing with. He continued to the mountain (he considered it a ridge) of Aornos, allegedly another site that could not be taken, as Heracles (Krishna) was alleged to have tried and failed to dislodge the natives. Alexander sent Ptolemy up one path and himself pursued another. He was stopped on his first try by fierce native resistance on the narrow approach but got a message to Ptolemy coordinating an attack the next day, which was successful. On inspection, Alexander found the ridge unassailable, but there was a rise in the ridge nearby of equal height and he managed to make a trail to its summit and drag his catapults to the summit. The sight of this artillery at point-blank range discouraged the enemy, who had never seen such devices, and they abandoned the ridge, which Alexander and Ptolemy stormed as they withdrew. Alexander marched on to Taxila, the first Indian city he had seen, a renowned university centre and manufacturing town. It did not resist and was a seat of education of the Brahmans. He was presented with eighty-six more elephants. He garrisoned Taxila and appointed Harpalus' brother Philippus as satrap and moved determinedly on to the Hydaspes River at Jhelum (thirty-five hundred miles from the Dardanelles).

Alexander was at war with the Paurava king, Porus, who ruled most of what is today, Kashmir. As the Jhelum River (which flowed into the Indus 200 miles south of the town of Jehlum), started to swell with spring floods, Alexander confronted Porus across the river and made obvious preparations to cross, although he knew it would be impossible, as his cavalry could not come out of the water and meet with Porus' numerous elephants on the other shore. Alexander seems to have had about five-thousand cavalry and twenty-thousand infantry to four-hundred cavalry and perhaps thirty-thousand infantry for Porus. Alexander selected a place eighteen miles up-river, out of sight and with a wooded island in the middle of the river, which made fording it a bit easier. The invader made countless starts and pretended crossings, keeping Porus off-guard and in constant motion, and when he became more wary of responding to false alarms, Alexander crossed at his selected northern site. They were observed early on by Porus' scouts and made their second half of the crossing from the mid-stream island, with great difficulty. Alexander formed up an advance group once on the east bank of the Jehlum and advanced south, defeating and killing Porus' son. Porus himself followed his son with his main army, leaving a smaller force to ensure that Craterus did not cross with a decoy army at the point of original concentration. Porus drew up his forces a little inland from the river to avoid marshy ground, and with two-hundred elephants in his centre with his infantry between and just behind them, including a substantial force of archers with large bows, on each side of the elephants, and cavalry outlying on each flank beyond the infantry. Porus' left, including many of his archers, were on relatively soft ground. His right was ahead of the centre and left, indicating a desire to squash Alexander into the river. Porus had about four-thousand cavalry. Alexander had about five-thousand cavalry, massed entirely on his right, near the river, and his heavy infantry facing Porus' elephants, and light infantry on each flank. Porus saw Alexander's dispositions and moved all his cavalry to his left to face Alexander.

Alexander moved his cavalry forward, but not into range, and moved his horse archers up to pepper the infantry to the left of Porus' elephants and held his infantry until he had settled the test of the cavalry forces. His plan was to send an infantry diversion to his left, drawing Porus' centre to the right, engage the two cavalry forces closely nearer the river, and then have the right side of the Phalanx and supporting light infantry strike behind the enemy cavalry, which would then be surrounded and cut up, enabling Alexander to clear the field while the enemy's elephants were under-utilized and confused in the centre. This plan was, ultimately and by a narrow margin, successful—Porus took the bait on the right, the nearer section of Alexander's right attacked the flank and rear of Porus' left, those who could of the Pauravan forces took refuge behind the elephants and the Macedonian centre advanced against the elephants and the infantry among them. A fierce melee occurred, and many elephants were killed. Craterus had crossed the river and eventually arrived in Porus' rear and there was a general retreat by the Pauravans, after a very brave struggle in which both sides took heavy casualties. Porus finally retired on his great elephant and, when Alexander finally caught up with him, Porus, when asked, said he wished to be "treated like a king," and he was. There is no doubt that this was one of the closest engagements Alexander had fought; his casualties were heavy and his men, including his generals, were shaken by the formidability of massed elephants. Seleucus, when he became a king, ceded a province for an adequate number of elephants to furnish his army with this weapon that had some of the attributes, twenty-two hundred years later, of the tank.

Alexander named a town after his horse, which perished in the battle (Bucephalus). Porus became a valued ally and Alexander mediated the end of the conflict between Porus and Taxiles and increased the size of the kingdoms of both. He left Craterus to complete Bucephala and his other new city of Nicaea and distributed garrisons about and moved east again, across the Chenab and then the Ravi Rivers, and finally the Beas River, through teeming tropical rain that flooded him out of one of his camps. Allegedly, India's first great national leader, Chandraguptra, then a young man, had a brief but satisfactory interview with Alexander at about this time (Chapter 4). Here, he was confronted by a mutiny—in the sense of a refusal to go further. The core of his army had been away for eight years and the territories they entered were becoming steadily more exotic and forbidding and the enemies were becoming fiercer and more aggressive, and the purpose of it was unclear, as they had gone all the way through and beyond the Persian Empire. Half his army was strung out along the lines of communications, and he was using the forces of his late enemy Porus, to garrison his immediate rear area. He had taken a normally sized Greek army and projected it three-thousand miles to the east over the prostrate entirety of the Persian Empire and to within the gates of India, but it was becoming, in all respects, including the danger of a mortal wound of the commander, a tenuous proposition. The men were tired; the rain, and the weather generally, were enervating, and they were unnerved by combat with elephants. Alexander, like Achilles (Chapter 4), waited three days sullenly in his tent, but the will of his army did not change. He consulted the omens and accepted the will of the gods, to the great relief of his men. Reluctantly, but in all of the circumstances with little choice, he consented to return, abandoning the prospect of conquering the whole province of "India," which, of course, was fifty times as extensive as he imagined, and without resolving the question of an eastern ocean. This was his farthest eastward penetration, and he then moved southwest, parallel to the Indus and all the way to the Indian Ocean. His concession to his home-sick soldiers was a compromise—they would be homeward-bound, but not on a direct route between points already in their own or friendly hands.

Alexander handed over everything up to the Beas River to Porus, for whom Alexander's visit, including the bloody combat at Jhelum, had been an immense bonanza, and completed the ships he had set Craterus to building, ultimately the astounding total of eight-hundred vessels, though most of them small launches. He took with him on the ships, his closest comrades: the hypaspists, Agrianians, Cretans, and the Companions, and the rest marched beside the river in three columns, with a large train of women, children, camp-followers and general hangers-on. He began the voyage in July 326 with a ceremony that recalled the departure of the Athenian fleet for the ill-fated exposition to Syracuse nearly ninety years before. From the prow of his ship, Alexander poured potions of wine from a gold cup to Heracles, to Ammon, to the Jehlum, Chenab, and Indus, to Poseidon, Amphitrites, and the Nereids, and to Ocean (a nebulous deity of oceans). Then came the mighty report of his trumpeters, then the shouts to action of thousands of oarsmen as the vast polyglot flotilla and its terrestrial escort started south and homeward.

Just south of where the Jehlum and Ravi had flowed into the Indus, he stopped and turned westwards to attack the Aratta, who were reckoned the fiercest of the tribes in the vast territory he had covered, and were still at war with the new empire, harassing Alexander's garrisons in Gedrosia, Arachosia, and Carmania. He deployed Hephaestion and Ptolemy to be in position to bar their retreat and crossed fifty miles of desert before coming upon an Aratta town; it was completely surprised, and the entire population was slaughtered. Perdiccas did the same with a second town. Alexander was not providing much incentive for the Aratta to do anything but fight to the death. Alexander pursued and resistance stiffened; a town of Brahmans resisted with implacable courage; Alexander himself had to be the first to scale the wall, and jumped down to the citadel and fought the astonished defenders personally with his back to the wall until his embarrassed followers joined him, but Alexander was wounded by a long arrow in the chest. His immediate companions shielded him until his full siege force surged over the walls and slew every man, woman, and child in the town. This time Alexander was wounded seriously; Perdiccas cut the arrow out with his sword, but Alexander fainted several times. He had himself carried into his ship so he could be seen by his men, among whom the dreadful rumor had circulated that he was dead. His enemies the Aratta (Malli and Oxydracae), formally submitted, somewhat intimidated by the newly minted custom of Alexander of massacring his enemies entirely. It was an ugly and hideous campaign; his last was the least distinguished. He was not really ambulatory but made a couple of appearances to satisfy his men that he still lived.

4. Alexander the Great IV: The Return

In July 325, Alexander reached Pattala, on the Indus almost at its entry into the Indian Ocean. Here he began construction of extensive docks and an arsenal, to make a naval base for sea communications via the Persian Gulf with his western Empire. He did a little exploring by sea and sailed out into the Indian Ocean, making offerings to Poseidon and flung his golden cup into the waves. He had already sent Craterus with the elephants, the siege engines, the sick and wounded, the baggage and an adequate infantry covering force home along a secured inland route, which was garrisoned at close intervals the entire way to Asia Minor. Alexander set out for the west in September, 325. First he sailed into the Indian Ocean near Karachi, and waited for 24 days until he caught the monsoon moving west. At the same time, his march homewards along the shore began, with the hypaspists (heavy infantry), Agrianians, archers and seven battalions of the Phalanx. He maintained the fleet from the land, digging wells and killing game to supply the fleet at intervals. This was his farewell to India, and it should be mentioned that even the modest cameo appearance he did make in that already huge country caused the reaction of the Brahman to promote the rise of Chandragupta, who consolidated the northern provinces and became the ruler of northern India. Far from extending Greco-Macedonian influence into India, it raised much of India against unbidden Western influence. The West would not be back with military force for nearly two-thousand years.

He had about fifteen-thousand soldiers with him and perhaps ten-thousand more of assorted people and families in his immediate train. The return, both by land and by sea, was a ragged one, apart from Craterus' comparatively easy progress along the internal route that had been cleared and garrisoned on the way east. When he reached the Tomeros River, only about two-hundred miles in from their starting point, he was obliged to turn inland and wandered, somewhat inadequately guided, for another two-hundred miles in desolate country. It was absurd that the acknowledged head of most of the Western world would be reduced to such an improvident mission. They ate the baggage animals and burned the carts for firewood, marching only at night because of the heat. Stragglers died and the baggage, including The Great King's own, was abandoned or burned. Alexander finally reached the sea at Pasni, a hundred miles west of where he had struck inland, found enough water, and managed to reach a royal residence at Pura, another two-hundred miles west. Rest and food were available here; Alexander had saved his army without serious losses, but the civilians accompanying him suffered very heavy casualties from the elements. He strove on another two-hundred miles to Gulashkird (now officially renamed Alexandria), in Carmania, where he rejoined Craterus.

Nearchus had left Karachi and as the only depot Alexander had left him as stores for the fleet had been broken into and consumed by Alexander's own men, the king feared, with good reason, for his Indian Ocean fleet. The fleet survived for a time on fish and dates and Nearchus was fearful of shore parties because of the dangers of desertion, as they ran out of water at times, as well as food. They came across a school of whales, and in fear charged them in formation to the sound of trumpets and the monarchs of the sea became so alarmed that they dove, to the great relief of the fleet. They also discovered a tribe of hairy fish-eating men, the first outright savages recorded to be discovered by Europeans. They were dressed in fish skins and had huts of bones of stranded whales, and ate only fish, stone-age people with wooden spears and palm-bark fishing nets.

They finally reached the Straits of Hormuz, disembarked and were reunited with Alexander and Craterus near Persepolis (nearly three-hundred miles west of Alexandria-Gulashkird), and in an atmosphere of itinerant celebration that has been somewhat exaggerated in the recounting, continued to the old imperial Persian capital of Susa, where they arrived in the spring of 324. Alexander had come sixteen-hundred miles back from the eastern extremity of his expedition, in northwest India. Alexander's return was timely, as the empire, as could have been predicted, had become a very shaggy and uneven jurisdiction with effectively no central authority in his absence. He discovered that a number of satraps had recruited mercenaries and acknowledged no central authority; some had been very oppressive, and a number had been flagrantly corrupt. Cyrus' tomb had been looted, as several important temples had been. Two thirds of the Persian royal stable of fine horses had been stolen. At Alexander's approach, Harpalus, his old ally who had provided him reading material, had fled to Greece. He later fled to Crete and was eventually executed, or simply murdered, by local authorities or even his own entourage in 323 for his notorious rascality, a learned scoundrel who was at varying times friendly with Aristotle and Demosthenes, as well as Alexander.

Alexander, once he was back in touch and within the traditional Persian Empire, reasserted his authority swiftly and ruthlessly, cracking down especially firmly against those who had tyrannized their populations. He summarily executed the satraps of Persis, Susiana, Carmania, Media, and three generals in Media, including Cleander and Sitalces, who had been entrusted with the execution of Parmenion. The Carmanian and Median pretenders were executed and Aristobulus restored Cyrus' tomb. All mercenaries engaged for the personal service of satraps were ordered to be disbanded and Macedonians were installed in all the vacant satrapies, including those where their predecessors had left office at the stroke of the headsman. Peucestas, an Iranophilic Macedonian, was appointed satrap of Persis and Susiana and the royal Bodyguard; he learned Persian and faithfully instituted Alexander's reforms and pan-imperial ideas and earned great popularity among his adoptive subjects.

Alexander had brought out of the east with him an Indian ascetic, Calanus, a member of a contemplative fraternity of forest-dwellers (Chapter 4, section 1), who had no interest in material things and informed Alexander that his conquests were ephemeral and that he had no more than he, Calanus did. In Susa, he told Alexander that he no longer wished to live, and despite Alexander's persuasive efforts, Calanus persevered, had a pyre built, and as elephants raised a fore-leg in unison and trumpets sounded, he rode up to his pyre, had a stiff drink, uttered a brief prayer, mounted the pyre and lay down on it, and did not flinch at all as the flames approached and incinerated him before the whole army. He allegedly prophesied Alexander's death and said good bye to the generals he had met, but not, at the end, to Alexander; his last words to him were alleged to have been: "We shall meet again at Babylon" (a city of which he had presumably only recently heard).[4] Alexander held a great festivity in Susa to celebrate the union of all his peoples, and married Darius' daughter, Barsine, as Hephaestion married her sister Drypetis. The response of the putative queen, Roxanne, is unrecorded, but although polygamy was the practice among kings throughout the area, she cannot have been delighted. Ten thousand of his soldiers took native wives and Alexander undertook to pay the soldiers' debts, if they would subscribe themselves.

It is indicative of the deterioration in morale that had resulted from the arduous campaigns of the last nine years that many thought this was a ruse of their king to determine who had wasted the state's money without authorization. Alexander, with his usual perceptiveness, detected the problem and changed the format to paying cash in the amounts requested, to all comers from his army, with no names or amounts recorded. However, discontent in the army was harder to deal with in respect of the proposed integration into the army of thirty-thousand native Persians (or from Persian-governed satraps) who had been trained by Macedonians and were part of Alexander's plan for an empire-wide army. This caused understandable frictions that were aggravated by the king's current practice of wearing Persian attire and seeming to pander to his Persian subjects. His brave and loyal soldiers, who had followed him and provided victories to the end of the earth and back, feared that their chief had gone native.

As a measure of security, Alexander decreed the return to their home states of all Greeks except Thebans, hoping to eliminate the floating pool of mercenaries signed up by ambitious satraps and Greek city states whenever Alexander's back was turned. He also hoped that with the return of all the banished Greeks, some greater peace would settle on the Greek states. To placate Greek autonomist feeling he had Antipater, the regent of Macedonia and strategic director (strategos) in Europe, and who was unpopular in Greece because of his frequent imposition of tyrannies in Greece, and past seventy-five years in age, change positions with Craterus, the army commander. The recall of the exiles technically breached the terms of the League of Corinth, as it constituted interference in the internal affairs of the member states, and Alexander had a substantial conflict of interest because he was also the Lord (autocrat) of Asia and the Great King of Greater Persia.

To deal with the breach, he proposed, and the Greek cities accepted the device of deifying Alexander; once he was recognized as a God (to whom the Greeks, like the Persians, had to prostrate themselves), he was exempt from the terms of terrestrial treaties. There is little doubt that while the Greek city states purported to be happy to engage in this act, most were reluctant and resentful, though there is some technical question over whether he was acclaimed as a God or as the son of Zeus, though that was probably a distinction without a difference. Alexander was probably acting more from desire to facilitate efficient government than megalomania, but this is mind-reading with no evidence, and is very hazardous. To Alexander, this

---

4 Ibid., p. 417.

was a political move; to most Greeks, it was an anti-religious move, because it was preposterous and a cheapening of the meaning of deity despite Alexander's great distinction, and to traditionalists like the septuagenarian Antipater, who adhered to the old religion (a clearly declining percentage of people), it was sacrilege. It achieved its administrative aim but was unpopular with everyone. Greek cities had deified living men before, but not all Greece at once in respect of the same man.

Alexander did precipitate a serious crisis when he decreed that all soldiers past normal enlisted age return home with Craterus—on his way to change positions with Antipater. Except for a few of the hypaspists, the whole army rose in revolt and demanded that all be allowed to return home. Alexander performed his usual magic with his men, telling them they were all free to go home and tell of how they had deserted Alexander. He remained in his quarters for two days and then began recruiting a Persian army, whereupon the Macedonian soldiers gathered at his quarters in large numbers and asked that he take pity on them. When he emerged, they cried out that he had made Persians his kinsmen. He replied that he made all of the Macedonian army his kinsmen, and won them over: the revolt collapsed, and the king held a grand banquet of nine-thousand soldiers but seated the Macedonians above the Persians and around him. He prayed for the union of the two peoples and those veterans who wished to, returned with Craterus (ten-thousand men).

In the autumn of 324, his old friend Hephaestion, the vizier (chiliarch) died, which depressed Alexander, as Hephaestion was his closest and most trusted and understanding comrade. He was only thirty-two and Plutarch claims he died from over-eating his breakfast and contracting a severe indisposition and fever; this is medically improbable as a cause of death, though he may well have done what was alleged. Alexander was so upset, he hanged Hephaestion's doctor, and gave his friend an immense royal funeral at Babylon and commissioned a five-story mausoleum designed by the architect of Alexandria (Egypt), Dinocrates. Alexander suppressed his sadness by conducting a successful winter assault on the savage Cossaean tribe in the Lauriston Hills. But the fact that Achilles did not long survive Patroclus weighed heavily upon him as an omen in the tragic lives of great heroes; Alexander was certainly a figure of Homeric proportions, who had every right to make such comparisons.

In the spring of 323 B.C., he returned to Babylon and received embassies from Libyans and Roman tribes (Bruttians and Lucanians), who feared Alexander's vengeance for the death of his uncle, Alexander of Epirus, and the Etruscans had the effrontery to petition Alexander to permit them to conduct their naval piracy at will. He also devoted a lot of attention to his maritime ambitions, sending Heracleides to explore the Hyrcanian Sea, built a huge dock complex for Babylon and improved the state of the Tigris for navigation, and built yet another Alexandria at the mouth of the Tigris. He sent Sidon five-hundred talents for the hire of sailors and colonists to people the east coast of the Persian Gulf. He planned to open up and protect the sea route from Egypt to India by strengthening his navy and had a number of substantial ships built in sections in Phoenicia and rolled overland to Thapsacus and floated on the current down the Euphrates. He himself sailed down the Euphrates, studying how to improve the Babylonian canal system, to improve its capacity for flood and drought control. A legend arose that Alexander's diadem had been blown off and that it had lodged in rushes and that a sailor swam to retrieve it and brought it back dry, on top of his head—the legend held that this was the future King Seleucid. Returning to Babylon, Alexander received petitioners from many of the Greek states seeking innumerable preferments.

5. Alexander the Great V: Death and Assessment

In the midst of preparations for an expedition to Arabia, Alexander was laid low with a heavy fever, aggravated by his exhaustion, and, it has been speculated, his wounds, especially the last one—an arrow that penetrated his chest, in the Battle with the Arrata in 326. He continued discussions with generals and the admiral Nearchus, comrade of the Indian expedition, until his strength failed. He was carried into Nebuchadnezzar's palace and the army insisted on seeing him and his Macedonian comrades filed past him in his bedroom and received faint nods of recognition. He died at sunset on June 13, 323 B.C., not quite thirty-three, after a reign of twelve years and eight months. Calanus had been prophetic in his reference to Babylon. Alexander had a solemn military and religious funeral, but not on a grand scale, and a splendid funerary cart was made for him. Alexander had wished to be buried at the Temple of Ammon at the Siwah Oasis in Egypt, but the funeral train was intercepted en route in 321 by Ptolemy I Soter, in an episode of the rending struggle for power that occurred after Alexander's death. Alexander's remains were redirected it to Alexandria (Egypt), and remained there, though some intimate belongings were conserved elsewhere. Some great Roman leaders of later centuries paid their respects, including Julius and Octavian (Augustus) Caesar and Septimius Severus (a Libyan), but Cleopatra removed some of the gold in his mausoleum and Caligula took some valuable objects as well. The tomb eventually vanished and the whereabouts of Alexander's mortal remains are unknown. Various cults developed in his honour, as may be imagined, and there were rumours, not generally credited, that he was poisoned or that he died as a result of a monstrous drinking bout with his officers. Thus, passed on the King of Macedonia, Supreme Commander (strategic autocrat) of Athens, President of the Hellenic League, Great King of Persia, Pharoah of Egypt and Lord of Asia.

Alexander was a man of superhuman mental and physical energy, and of immense passion, which he generally contained by his formidable self-discipline. He was loyal and principled, usually magnanimous by the standards of the ancient world in his treatment of those whom he defeated or subjugated, though severe for exemplary reasons, and on rare occasions guilty of inexplicable atrocities, such as his massacres of Brahman and Arrata prisoners and civilians, and his execution of Parmenion. It is not clear that he was particularly interested in women, though he ordered his army to be respectful of them in occupied territories, an unprecedented command, and not one much emulated for many subsequent centuries. He had an intense relationship with his fierce and tempestuous mother, with whom he maintained a close correspondence right to his death. Alexander shared the view of Aristotle and Plato that women were not inferior to men and should hold responsible positions. Persistent rumors of his homosexuality seem to have been unfounded. He liked to carouse with his comrades, and some of the Bacchanalian festivities that followed great events were prodigious, but he seems to have had no interest physically in men. (When proffered two handsome young men by a vassal king, he is alleged to have replied: "What evil has he seen in me that he should purchase for me such evil creatures? Tell the dealer to take his wares to hell."[5] Given his power and age and genius; his ego was not conspicuously excessive. In general, Alexander seems to have been thoughtful and generous and while clearly separated by both his position and his aptitudes from his colleagues, he was a staunch and unaffected comrade, joking even about the claim to being a son of Zeus. He was an authentically religious man and was happy to be seen publicly in humble worship of the (apparently) authentic deities.

He had the military genius of instant appreciation of the dangers and opportunities of his position opposite any enemy, and innovative flexibility in use and adaptation of different weapons and formations. He was an inspiring leader, by his unlimited physical courage and great prowess, as by his gift for the dramatic—both noble and histrionic, as required, and where necessary by his oratorical talents. Many Roman emperors were overthrown and murdered by their own troops for much less extreme exertions than Alexander almost effortlessly wrung from his men. He was never defeated and was only on a couple of occasions in a closely contested battle. But it must be said that he fought somewhat uncoordinated Persians armies, indifferently led in the highest command positions, and primitive and remote tribesmen. Though, as we have seen, the Persians were not the numberless hordes of untrained bonzes that posterity long claimed. But successors who are generally grouped with him in the highest category of military genius of conception and execution, such as Hannibal, Julius Caesar, Frederick the Great, and Napoleon, had to win more victories from more formidable enemies. This takes nothing from Alexander's achievement in leading a force that never exceeded fifty-thousand from the Danube to the Indus without a single significant setback in twelve years, twenty-three centuries ago.

As a statesman, Alexander's record is less clear, as he was just settling in to managing his vast domains when he died. He certainly personified an immense accretion of jurisdiction from anything any European, especially any Greek, had conceived, though he was to a considerable extent executing the vision of his father, who saw the vulnerability of the decayed Persian Empire. His principal administrative innovations were separating treasury activities in each conquered satrapy and making the financial officials answerable directly to him, and in standardizing coinage throughout his empire, without interfering with the mint in Athens. There were several satrapies whose leaders professed to be autonomous when Alexander died, though he would certainly have subdued them with his customary thoroughness had he survived just a year longer. He was a visionary, and perhaps even somewhat naïve, in his plan to integrate the Hellenic and Persian worlds; inter-mix administrative and military personnel, and create a Hellenized and culturally ambitious society that would, in matters of local government be rather democratic. The fact that he died before he could submit his plan to a full test does not consign it to failure. It

---

5 Agnes Savill, *Alexander the Great*, Rockliff, London, 1955, p. 211.

was a grand conception and would probably have succeeded at least while he was directing it himself. There is no reason to believe that he seriously wanted to conquer the entirety of Asia, whose extent he could not have imagined, or even the entire Mediterranean area, of which he was well aware. He might eventually have aspired to do that, and certainly could have done it, but that is mere conjecture. It is widely reckoned that it was a terrible frustration for him not to invade the heartland of India, but in that region beyond Persia, on land and on sea he seems to have been more of an explorer than a conqueror. He cannot have imagined that he could easily maintain his authority in the Punjab while meticulously governing everything to the west as far as the Adriatic Sea.

Alexander in some respects presaged several modern phenomena about great leaders. He was the first conqueror to have a genuine idealistic mission as his reason to conquer, and he was the first of the unusual pattern by which a nationality is best roused and led by a person of a nearby and less populous culture, as with Napoleon the Corsican, Stalin the Georgian, and Hitler the Austrian, even, to a slight degree in a cultural sense, Disraeli the ethnic, though not sectarian, Jew.

Alexander entirely earned the distinction of being called "the Great;" the eminent and normally sober classical historian T.R. Glover was only moderately transported by hyperbole when he effused that he was "Alexander the Greatest...the most wonderful man who ever lived."[6] He was one of them, certainly. As a great military commander, wise and innovative ruler, and towering and galvanizing historic personality, he is rivaled in all the annals of world history only by Julius Caesar, Genghis Khan, and Napoleon.[7] And unlike them, his conquests were vastly more than personal aggrandizement; his intention was the cultural elevation and internationalization of all mankind, at least all the peoples that were accessible to him. His plan for pan-Hellenization was a benign civilizing mission, whether its intended beneficiaries saw it as that or not.

Caesar was a Roman expansionist as Genghis Khan was a Mongolian expansionist (albeit of a less sophisticated state than late republican Rome), but Alexander was much more than a Macedonian expansionist; he was preeminently a Pan-Hellenist. Napoleon utilized the exaltation of mind of the French Revolution for a time, but for almost entirely cynical reasons. As a Corsican, he was an egalitarian, but he considered the revolutionary governments to be mob-rule tempered by monstrous licentiousness. He did produce a very democratic and republican constitution for his post-Elba restoration but given that he neglected to do anything of the kind in his previous sixteen years of government, his sincerity is open to question; at the least, his conversion was late in coming. Alexander saw himself as an explorer and a civilizer and an adventurer, and while self-serving, that was not a fantasy. It was perhaps in part the self-indulgence of a younger man who inherited a kingdom already poised to launch his great enterprise. Caesar, Genghis Khan, and Napoleon were put to a good deal more arduous and disillusioning careerism before their greatest

---

6 T. R. Glover, *The Ancient World*, Pelican, London, 1944, p. 216.

7 All will be treated in their turn in this narrative and a reasoned comparison will be made in the appropriate place.

conquests could be undertaken.

Alexander can be distinguished from others, but not denied his almost miraculous life. He was a gigantic and brilliant world-historic personality. There can be no doubt that in his death in Babylon in June 323 B.C., there passed away a glory and a wonder from the earth.

CHAPTER FOURTEEN

THE WARS OF SUCCESSION TO ALEXANDER I: 323 TO 308 B.C.

Coin of King Antigonus   Coin of Cassander (struck 306-297 B.C.)

1. Greece in the Last Years of Alexander—Eumenes and Antigonus

WHEN ALEXANDER departed Europe for Asia in 335, Greece had been thoroughly cowed by the destruction of Thebes. In theory, it was governed by the League of Corinth with Alexander as president, but in fact, Greece had been startled into awakening to the fact that its endless little wars to change the title of a few thousand acres was no longer the means by which states would measure the level of their strength and influence. Alexander gave equal voice to the little states with the large, which the smaller states appreciated. (This was a concept revived in the composition of the United States Senate in 1788 and again by the United Nations at the end of World War II, causing Stalin to say to Churchill and Roosevelt that "The Soviet Union has not taken millions of casualties in order to have a voice in the councils of the world equal to Albania's."[1]) The difficulty the League faced, apart from Alexander's absence, was that the Greeks declined to consider Macedonians to be Greeks, and they all considered that Greece was under foreign domination, a condition Greeks would never accept, in all their subsequent history. Where Jews had only for brief periods been masters of their own state, girt about as they were by larger and often very bellicose nations and tribes, the Greeks long maintained, and eventually recovered their sovereignty, but with a terrible propensity to quarrel among themselves.

Alexander's effort to lift up their hearts with the vision of Hellenizing western Asia did not entirely compensate them for their disconcertion of being under the control of Macedonia, a people the Greeks had regarded as more or less barbarian. Most Greek opinion quietly favoured Persia in the war that Alexander carried into Asia, partially because of the many Greek mercenaries in the Persian army, and

---

1 Conrad Black, *Franklin Delano Roosevelt, Champion of Freedom*; Public Affairs, New York, 2003, p. 1046.

because they knew that Persia, decayed as the empire was, was a much less exacting challenge to Greek sovereignty than the deus ex machina of the Macedonian king. Greek opinion was not conciliated by Antipater, an honest and capable man, but a narrow and unimaginative soldier: the traditional view of the occupied power of the unsubtle and narrow-minded commandant of the occupation—like the French and Italian opinion of crisply uniformed, square-shouldered German occupiers in World War II, until animosity was made more virulent by proscriptions and the imposition of totalitarian Nazism and its genocidal ambitions.

Antipater had no interest in treating the Greeks as free allies, and while he followed Alexander's policies, he had no enthusiasm for them and was no goodwill ambassador within Greece for Alexander's concept of one great Greco-Macedonian brotherhood. He adhered to Alexander's covenant to allow the Greek states self-government, even though he, Antipater, favoured oligarchic government, and was friendly with some of Greece's wealthy citizens. The Macedonian regime was more popular in those parts of Greece that feared the ambitions of one of the principal Greek states, especially in the Peloponnese, where there was ancient and well-founded fear of Sparta. The Macedonian institutions and, if necessary, its army, provided some security against Sparta's will to dominate.

Demosthenes' agitations continued, if somewhat muted, into this new era he had warned against, though he had had no idea of the extent of Macedonian strength, and he held that anything more active than sullen toleration of the League and Covenant was treason not only for Athens, but other Greeks which should be sharing in Athens' wounded national pride. Athens in general had never ceased to feel that she was the premier Greek state, in culture, civilization, and brave leadership in Pan-Hellenic resistance to external threats, and that is certainly the judgment of posterity. In this spirit, there was little sense of resignation in Athens to the status quo, even as years passed, and bulletins came back from the front announcing ever more and greater victories and conquests by their self-imposed but comparatively gentle and benign king. It was to some degree a test of Athens' ability to be just in its appreciation of others—whether they could acknowledge the greatness of the leader of their world. And it must be said that in general, Athens failed that test. Alexander had earned gratitude, and certainly the respect of Athens; Athens could, in the circumstances, hardly fail to respect him, but fell well short of gratitude.

In these early days of the Macedonian ascendancy, there were four parties in Athens: the oligarchs, led by Phocion, an able and principled man but one who, like his followers, and perhaps influenced by their own prosperity, believed (correctly) that the era of the city state was past and that Athens should resign itself to a secondary position made more tolerable by the great regard Alexander had for Athens. The second group was composed of propertied moderates, who had somewhat similar views but were led by Damades, an able but completely unscrupulous man, who recognized realities and was prepared to abuse himself in servility to Antipater but was completely self-seeking and unreliable. Then there was a sullen minority of irreconcilables, the radicals, informally led by Hypereides, who after Chaeronea had advocated arming the slaves and fighting to the last man against Alexander (a course that would, if followed faithfully, have led to the death of every adult male

Athenian). They hated Alexander and the Macedonians and would take up arms any time they felt they had any support in Athens. Finally, was much the largest party, the Democrats, who felt that a second chance must and would come, but not now, and were prepared to bide their time. Demosthenes was their undoubted leader, but for reasons of political opportunism, even he realized that it was time to step aside and, in his place, but in close touch with Demosthenes, Lycurgus led this faction, with apparent moderation and productive inscrutability. Thus, the majority, the last two factions, did not really accept the status quo as durable, but three of the parties, the heavy majority, supported peace, for a combination of reasons: fatigue, avarice, and realistic appreciation of what an uprising against Antipater and Alexander would elicit as a response.

In the twelve years following Chaeronea (338-326), Lycurgus essentially governed Athens, though not without consultation with Antipater representing Alexander the Great, and Phocion, Demades, Demosthenes, and others. Though a student of Plato, Lycurgus was an efficient, humorless, Spartafilic financial administrator, who claimed in muted tones to be a democrat but was in practice generally aligned with the propertied classes and suspicious of public opinion, not only because he judged it immature and volatile by nature, but especially because of the damage too free a rein on opinion could do to relations with the Macedonian king. Though distant and out of sight, Alexander was never out of mind. Lycurgus was that unusual combination of a man very adept with figures who was a formidable orator, at the same level of general eloquence as Demosthenes. His particular bugbear was financial dishonesty, and he was, in matters of finance, a puritanical administrator, and not only in finance. He secured the death penalty for Lysicles, for being defeated at Chaeronea by Philip II and Alexander, hardly a shameful development nor an uncommon one in their time.

His narrow-mindedness notwithstanding, Lycurgus was one of Athens' great builders, and in his frugal administration he created surpluses that permitted him to prepare Athens for the renewed war he expected, and for which he wished to prepare to the utmost. Thus, he built docks, a great magazine-armoury, expanded the fleet to four-hundred and seventeen vessels, including fifty quadriremes and seven quinquiremes. He turned the brick walls to stone, lined with trenches to prevent rams, and largely from public subscriptions, he built the Panathenaic stadium. He remodeled the ephebate—the conscription of young men for military training in their nineteenth and twentieth years. Approximately eight-hundred men per year entered and departed the program, which built military knowledge and intelligence as well as physical fitness.

Lycurgus restored the ceremonial grandeur of Athenian religion, restoring Pericles' ten gold victory statues on the Acropolis, and assuring that religious parades and festivals were properly ornamented. This was a symbolic and traditional gesture, as the young could no longer take the worship of the Olympian gods seriously. Athenian philosophy and scientific research and the compilation of knowledge in the manner pioneered by Aristotle, had made inroads on the old heroic religion, but was insufficient (as science, despite all its advances, has continued to be) to replace it. Just as the known world was proceeding toward organization in larger political units and trade and exploration were spreading the West out in Europe and North Africa and across Asia, religion was beginning to focus on more universal and less multitheistic bases. Lycurgus also passed laws agreeing on official versions of the plays of Aeschylus, Euripides, and Sophocles and requiring that there be no derogation from the official script in any public performance. Of more liberal spirit was his decree that no Athenian could buy as a slave a prisoner of war who was free when captured. This was a great reform in its time that led in the following century to a prohibition against enslaving the nationals of others.

Notwithstanding the preeminence of Macedonia, the flowering of Intellectual Athens, and especially its philosophers, lay ahead, and a number of Greek cities had some of their best days to come, including Sparta, Rhodes, and Megalopolis. The Alexandrine mission to Hellenize the world had lent greater importance than ever to the intellectual powerhouse of Athens. Aristotle was a stranger to Athens and not really a democrat, or even a pretended democrat, and he was drifting away from Alexander in spirit as he was geographically, but he remained the personification of wisdom and science and the fermentation in academic and philosophical thinking in Athens would be strongly encouraged by Alexander and would produce some of Athens' greatest victories as a civic society.

Alexander correctly judged that in his absence, Athens would not go beyond minor demonstrations of independence, such as sending an ambassador to Darius and reprovisioning the Persian fleet at Samos in 334. Sparta, as Alexander suspected, not having so directly tasted the military lash of Alexander's insuperability, was preparing for war and dusting off its dubious Medist (anti-Hellenic treating with the Medes, i.e., Persians) practices of the past, blissfully uncomprehending of the upending and destruction of the ancient balance of power that Philip and Alexander had effected. Sparta's King Agis, undeterred by the current of events, was in negotiation with Persian admirals when news of the decisive victory of Alexander at Issus arrived. Discussions broke off, but the Persians gave Agis ten ships and thirty talents, and he mounted an attack on Cyprus, which Alexander beat off by dispatching Amphoterus with a fleet adequate to defend the island. Agis remained undeterred and accepted eight-thousand mercenaries who had escaped the Macedonian victory at Issus. He attempted to entice Athens. Even Demosthenes wavered briefly, and of course the radicals were ready to take up arms at the drop of a helmet, but cooler heads prevailed in Athens. Antipater was preoccupied with a partial revolt in Thrace, and the radical party leaders orated that Macedonia had violated the Covenant by promoting tyrants in places, though Athens itself had also. Alexander monitored these developments from the Levant and Egypt and had lavished conciliatory deferences on Athens including by sending to the Acropolis the spoils of his victory at Granicus, and it was now that he released the Athenian prisoners taken there. At the same time, he reinforced Amphoterus with one-hundred more ships to protect Cyprus and other Macedonian interests. Athens remained at peace and even Agis was not prepared to undertake war against Alexander the Great on his own. A Spartan army at Chaeronea would have made a difference, but Agis' plan only attracted Elis, Achaea, and part of Arcadia, while Megalopolis, Messene, and Argos remained with Antipater, preventing Agis from molding the Peloponnese to be a solid block to challenge Alexander.

In 331, Agis determined to try his hand and moved at the head of an army of twenty-two thousand and besieged Megalopolis. Antipater tidied things up in Thrace and hurried southwards and met Agis near Megalopolis, right after Alexander's great victory at Gaugamela. It was a hard-fought battle, but Antipater won, and Agis died bravely on the field, ending an absurdly misconceived enterprise by Sparta. Antipater maintained Alexander's conciliatory strategy: he accepted victory on behalf of the League, asked one-hundred and twenty talents of reparations to be paid by Sparta to Megalopolis, asked fifty noble Spartans to be given as hostages to be well cared for by Alexander, and referred judgment on Sparta to the League. Its judgment offended Sparta, proud even in defeat, and Sparta appealed to Alexander in person who moderated the sentence. Antipater sent Alexander the survivors among the eight-thousand mercenaries, and he sent them ultimately to Bactria, where they would again cause trouble eventually.

Though Athens had wisely resisted the Spartan call to arms against Alexander, the debate that ensued was profoundly divisive. Lycurgus prosecuted Leocrates, but he was narrowly acquitted. There were counter-prosecutions, and this was where public opinion sorted itself out—the verdicts in spectacular public cases held to criminalize policy differences, were seen from this distance slightly reminiscent of eventual American presidential impeachment actions. There now came to a head a singly Athenian action: after Chaeronea, Ctesiphon, a prominent legislator, had moved and the Senate had approved a gold crown to be publicly bestowed upon Demosthenes in recognition of the nobility of his service against Philip II. Aeschines sued that the measure was illegal, and the process was suspended when Philip was assassinated.

Aeschines, after the Battle of Megalopolis, revived his action against Ctesiphon, whose defence was naturally conducted by Demosthenes. In the manner of Athenian trials, it quickly became a trial of Demosthenes, and not even that Demosthenes had been imprudently hostile to the Macedonian kings, on the contrary that he had been lacking in thoroughness and efficiency in his early efforts, prior to Chaeronea, to combat the Macedonian influence (as if this had anything legally to do with Ctesiphon's wish to recognize his services). Aeschines leveled his final argument as the charge that Demosthenes failed to recognize the grandeur and generosity of Alexander's policy and should have explicitly either embraced Macedonia or produced a serious alternative rather than just verbosely lament Athens' loss of status. It had some merit, but not as a legal argument. This was sophistry and was irrelevant, and the jury naturally upheld Demosthenes, as it was generally anti-Macedonian.

However, Demosthenes then, in his surpassing argumentativeness, moved the trial (of Ctesiphon, be it remembered) to a new level, with a tremendous panegyric of about twenty-five thousand words which, despite discussions on the personal shortcomings of Aeschines, and even of his mother, and apogees and semi-climaxes of patriotic bathos, makes the case for the noble intention, even when, and perhaps particularly, when it is unsuccessful. "Accursed scribbler! You, to deprive me of the approbation and affection of my countrymen, speak of trophies and battles and ancient deeds, with none of which had this trial the least concern. But I, O you third rate actor! I rose to counsel the state how to maintain her preeminence.!" After preening himself for "going to proper schools" and having a good allowance, he reviled Aeschines "reared in abject poverty...doing the duty of a menial rather than a freeman's son." He reviled Aeschines' mother as some sort of masseuse and accused Aeschines of conducting his "noble orgiasts." It all got pretty well removed from a question of the guilt of Ctesiphon. There were no rules of evidence in these Athenian trials, and everything was determined by the eloquence with which self-righteousness was expressed, and by these criteria, the history of oratory provides few rivals for Demosthenes. In this case, Aeschines failed to obtain even a fifth of the votes of the jurors and went into exile rather than face a heavy fine: he removed to Rhodes where he operated a school of rhetoric, and finally retired to Samos where he died peacefully aged about seventy-five.

Athens was assailed by famine in 333 and five succeeding years, and Demosthenes became the Grain Commissioner, which solicited voluntary contributions to import grain (wheat in fact) at international prices and sell it cheaply to needy Athenians. In 325, after the crisis had passed, Athens sent a strong fleet under Miltiades, a direct descendant of the victor of Marathon, to the Black Sea to establish an Athenian colony that could provide a secure food supply, such as the arrangements of Periclean times more than a century before. Lycurgus was not reelected in 326 and was in failing health; he died that year.

The matter of Harpalus has been referred to from Alexander's perspective. He apparently believed that Alexander would not return from Asia (correct but premature), and he became profligate and corrupt with the treasury whose custody had been confided to him. He comported himself like a king and required those who approached him or his mistress Glycera to prostrate themselves. A false rumour arrived in 325 that Alexander was on his way back to Asia Minor, and Harpalus fled Tarsus and at Demosthenes' instigation, Harpalus was denied admission to the port of Piraeus, though he had a fleet of thirty warships, six-thousand mercenaries, and five-thousand talents (seventy million U.S. dollars today). Harpalus pressed on to Tenaerum and sought asylum. A citizen could make such a claim rightfully and once admitted, he offered his services and resources to Athens if it rose against Alexander. He undertook a campaign of bribery and misinformation, stating that many satrapies had thrown off the yoke of Alexander. As we have seen, several tried to do this but were severely repressed, but this was not known in Greece, possibly not even to Harpalus.

However, a command shortly arrived from Alexander demanding Harpalus' surrender, a step which public opinion in Athens opposed. Amidst great controversy, the now inevitable Demosthenes proposed that Harpalus be detained, and his money impounded. It was conveyed to the Parthenon, but it came to light that the quantum of funds was reduced by three-hundred and fifty talents, presumably in consequence of bribes paid by Harpalus. Demosthenes asked the Areopagus to look into this, while Harpalus escaped his minimum-security detention; he returned to his troops and was, to the convenience of everyone, murdered by his officers, sparing Athens further discord and Harpalus himself a public execution which an aggrieved Alexander could not be counted on to conduct humanely.

It was at this lively moment that Alexander's decrees requiring the repatriation of Greek exiles and the deification of himself be adopted. Athens opposed the return of exiles because it meant that it would have to give Samos back to the Samnians, whom Athens had evicted from their island. But it was a popular decree in many places, and was read at Olympia by Nicanor of Stagirus, Aristotle's son-in law, to twenty-thousand delighted exiles. Demosthenes was present as the head of Athenian religious envoys (he played an astonishing variety of roles in Athenian public life), and he realized that Alexander was being generous. He proposed, and it was enacted, that since Athens could not, because of the Samnian question, agree the return of exiles, there be no impoliteness in its non-adoption, and that the decree of deification be accepted. This was done and Demosthenes squared it with his long-standing opposition to Macedonian influence by agreeing somewhat sarcastically: "Let him be son of Zeus and Poseidon too, if he wishes."[2]

There remained the very difficult question of what proportion of their real property would be restored to returning exiles, and guidance was sought from Alexander on this point. Much of Greece, and certainly Athens, was now in the strange state where many resented and even reviled Alexander, but all Greece, like grumpy children or employees, acknowledged his position as the ultimate authority. The fiasco of Agis' revolt had stayed the doubters who might have imagined that Alexander's rule could be evaded easily. It seems that the usual award was approximately half of its previous value. (Though Athens did not adopt the decree, in practice, most exiles returned to Athens, but Alexander did not agree to Athens' retention of Samnos.)

Considerable controversy arose over the embezzled funds from Harpalus' stolen treasure, and Demosthenes, a suspect as he had supervised the transport of the silver to the Parthenon, asked again for the judgment of the Areopagus. After six months, in early 323, the Areopagus reported without comment, an assessment of amounts against various people: Demosthenes was assessed twenty talents, and among the others liable for various amounts were Demades, leader of the moderate collaborationist faction, Charicles, the son of the oligarchic leader Phocion, Philocles, and the orator Hagnonides. The issue proceeded to trial where Hypereides, the leader of the radical anti-Macedonians would be chief prosecutor, along with Menesaechmus, who had defeated Lycurgus in 326, Pytheas (a yes-man of Antipater) and Stratocles who twenty years later would utterly disgrace himself by his servility to Antigonus' son Demetrius. (Menesaechmus would accomplish the same contemptible feat sooner by his merciless persecution of the heirs of Lycurgus.)

Instead of accepting the conciliatory policy of Alexander, Athens, in its last days as an important political centre, little appreciating the liberality of Alexander's regime compared to what would follow, lurched from one immense, rending public trial to the next, and most of its public men, while swaddling themselves in Homeric lore, were venal and more or less treacherous. Even the relatively ethically upright Demosthenes had frequent and almost self-immobilizing bouts of egomania. Demosthenes' case was heard first, but no record of the proceedings has survived. Hypereides conducted the prosecution, although he and the defendant had been close

---

2 CAH, VI, p. 451 (W.W. Tarn).

allies at the time of Chareonea but had gradually parted company as Demosthenes better appreciated the dangers of antagonizing the all-conquering Macedonian king. Hypereides accused Demosthenes of being pro-Macedonian, the customary drift to the extremes of rebellious movements was repeated—it was a monstrous historical scandal that Demosthenes, who had warned his countrymen of the dangers of Macedonia for forty years, should be so described and that a public court would even partially endorse such scurrility.

As we have often seen, Athenian democracy was an admirable start at popular self-government but was far from the idyllic political science paradise that has been limned and fabricated by its more enthusiastic and imaginative historical sponsors. The jury condemned Demosthenes to a fine of fifty talents, which, as it was well beyond his ability to pay, and he would not ask his wealthy friends to pay for him, caused him to go into voluntary exile in Aegina. Damades was also found guilty but paid the fine and continued to lead his political group. There has been a heated dispute ever since his trial ended over whether Demosthenes was guilty. No evidence of improper use of funds has ever been produced. In all of the circumstances, despite this historian's view of Demosthenes as irrationally attached to an era that was passing, that of constantly warring Greek states, and his failure to recognize either Alexander the Great's liberality of character or the potential for Athens of his vast plan to Hellenize Asia Minor and beyond, he was a much more rigorously honest man than his accusers. Demosthenes showed little interest in material self-enrichment, in the absence of a scrap of probative evidence of his guilt, he deserves an outright acquittal from posterity on these vindictively laid charges.

This trial was followed, after a few months, by the death of Alexander the Great, which news arrived by unconfirmed rumor, officially verified after a couple of weeks. Damades, the orderly collaborationist, spoke nothing but the truth when he asserted that the "whole world will reek of the corpse." Phocion urged restraint, saying if he were dead today, Alexander would still be dead tomorrow, and that it was wise to await events, as no one, with good reason as we now know, had any idea of what would come next. Hypereides wanted war at once and stampeded the legislators and called for the mysterious Leosthenes, apparently the Leosthenes who had been general in 324-3, someone with a good military reputation and proven influence among mercenaries. Eye-witnesses to the fact that the king was dead arrived in Athens in September and despite the best efforts of Phocion (Damades had been sidelined by three capricious prosecutions from Hypereides, which prevented the defendant from participating in debates no matter how spurious the charges), Hypereides, with Leosthenes as the quiet and reassuring military man of strength beside him, carried the vote for war easily. This was Athenian pride, both worthy and arrogant, magnified into suicidal treachery. Even in simple tactical terms, it would have been wise to await events, since it was obvious that some sort of struggle for the succession would occur. Athens could have levered some influence between the factions. As it was, one thing Antipater, Antigonus, Ptolemy, Perdiccas, Polyperchon, Lysimaetus, Cassander, and Seleucid could all agree on was that Athens should be put soundly in her place. Athens continued to be brave, but had also become stupid, and in the process went from being the apple of the eye of the Macedonian king to the prime candidate for exemplary and severe discipline from his otherwise discordant successors. The whole male citizen population beneath the age of forty was mobilized, Leosthenes had already enlisted the eight-thousand Greek mercenaries pushed into unemployment by Alexander's prohibition of the satraps having their own armies, and the government manned two-hundred triremes and forty quadriremes. The Assembly declared the war aims to be the common freedom of all Greek states and the liberation of the cities Antipater was then garrisoning. The Lamian War had begun.

The rising of the Greek mercenaries in Bactria following the death of Alexander may have been part of a general wave of discontent among the Greek mercenaries in Persian service and Leosthenes may have had a hand in it, but this is not substantiated. Athens called for allies, but only Aetolia and Thessaly and a few of the northern states responded. Sparta, so frisky a few years before was content to watch Athens go to the Macedonian woodshed unaccompanied. Aristotle had to leave Athens, and went to Chalcis, where he died the next year, technically homeless though honoured throughout the world. He was sixty-two. Antipater's garrisons in Corinth, Megara, and Euboea could maintain their positions, and Boeotians, enjoying life without Thebes, which Alexander had levelled, regarded the Macedonians as benefactors and remained with Antipater, who, to consolidate his authority in his occupation zone in the Diodochian contest that impended, would have to start by slapping down this revolt of the ungrateful protégés. Antipater had the problem that after his slapping-down of Sparta, replete with the death in combat of King Agis, Macedonia had been depleted of warriors to feed the King's garrisoning and extended penetration of Asia. Antipater had only thirteen-thousand infantry and six-thousand cavalry, and certainly could not suppress Athens with that corporal's guard. He brought Craterus back from Cilicia with ten-thousand men, and asked the aid of Leonnatus, governor of Hellespontine Phrygia, and he collected two-thousand of the excellent Thessalian cavalry.

Leosthenes had shipped his eight-thousand mercenaries to Aetolia and merged them with seven-thousand infantry from that country and seized Thermopylae, inciting Phocis and Locris to rise up and declare solidarity with Athens. Leosthenes won the opening engagements: over the Cadmean garrison of Boeotians and Euboeans, then a landing party from Chalcis was defeated by Phocion, who had rallied to the Athenian cause though he thought the war insane. And Leosthenes defeated Antipater himself and barricaded him into Lamia after the Thessalian cavalry deserted to the Greeks. The solidarity of war brought Demosthenes back to his native city: he had been asked to lobby the Arcadians, who were also being courted by Pytheas on behalf of Antipater. The best Demosthenes could do was obtain Arcadian neutrality, but that caused Athens to ask his return, send a trireme to collect him, pay his fine for him, and accord him a full triumph all along the route from Piraeus to Athens. The siege of Lamia lasted through the winter, but Leosthenes did not have a siege train to force the issue. Antipater offered to negotiate but Leosthenes demanded unconditional surrender, which far exceeded the facts on the ground. This was a mistake as Antipater, at least, would have honoured an agreement made now (though his successors would not have been so civilized).

Unknown to Leosthenes and the Athenians, but probably just reaching Antipater, was the news of the crushing of the Bactrian revolt. Leosthenes was killed in a skirmish and replaced by Antiphilus, who was adequate but not more than that. In 322, Leonnatus crossed the Dardanelles with twenty-thousand mainly Macedonian infantry, but only fifteen-hundred cavalry. Antiphilus abandoned the siege and intercepted and defeated Leonnatus with twenty-two thousand infantry and thirty-five hundred cavalry, and Leonnatus was killed. But Antipater was able to link up with Leonnatus' army, which though defeated and leaderless, was in good order. He did not have sufficient cavalry to have a full-scale engagement and withdrew to Macedonia to regroup and await Craterus' arrival. Hypereides sounded a triumphal note in his funeral oration for Leosthenes: "Athens needed a man, and the man came."

The Hellenic League produced only about eight-thousand Aetolians to assist Athens in this ambitious undertaking. The rest of the member states, less proud than Athens and with less to be proud of, did not want to risk the wrath of any proximate part of the Macedonian Empire, in complete ignorance of what arrangements might have been made for the succession to Alexander. Cleitus commanded the Macedonian fleet, over two-hundred warships after receiving reinforcements from Phoenicia. He met and defeated one Athenian fleet commanded by Euetion off Abydos in the spring of 322; and severely defeated another Athenian fleet, patched together and with slaves thrown in as oarsmen in many cases, but with one-hundred and seventy ships again commanded by Euetion, off Amorgos in July. Cleitus had two-hundred and forty ships and in these two battles he annihilated the Athenian fleet and destroyed Athenian sea-power forever. A noble tradition dating back to Themistocles and indeed to Odysseus, was buried at sea with the navy and seamen of Athens. Cleitus possessed the scepter of the sea and Athens would now have to face Antipater, reinforced by Craterus and others, in a desperate state: Piraeus was blockaded, no forces could be moved by sea. and Antipater could have strangled Athens by blockade and starvation. Instead, he and Craterus invaded Thessaly in August with forty-three thousand infantry and five-thousand cavalry. Antiphilus and Memnon joined battle with them at Crannon with twenty-three-thousand infantry and thirty-five hundred cavalrymen. All knew that this could be Athens' last stand and her soldiers did their duty and held Antipater and Craterus to a narrow but sufficient victory. It was the sixteenth anniversary of Chaeronea, August 2, 322, and Athens had no choice but to seek terms, in little doubt of the general outline of what Antipater would consider acceptable terms, given that he considered the Athenians both treacherous and helpless at his feet. Antipater declined to recognize the Hellenic League and said he would only deal with individual states. Damades was recalled and cleared of past offenses, and, with Phocion and Demetrius of Phalerum, was sent to do their best with Antipater, who had entered Boeotia and was making a stately and irresistible procession toward Athens. Antipater required unconditional surrender, but graciously said that if this distinguished delegation made such a surrender, on their honour, and out of personal respect for Phocion in particular, he would accept that his terms would be carried out and he would not invade Attica.

Although Damades wrote to Perdiccas asking for mercy but received no reply, Phocion submitted after consultations in Athens and Antipater laid down his terms. The Athenian constitution was to be drastically altered and an oligarchy established, and the orators, whom Antipater considered responsible for inciting this insane revolt, handed over. Oropus was to be given back to Boeotia and Samos to the Samnians, and Athens would receive back her exiles. Macedonia would garrison Munychia and Athens would pay the cost of the war, though at Phocion's entreaty, the payment was deferred.

Athens had no choice but to accept and, in the circumstances, was lucky to have got off so lightly. This last Athenian war was even more stupidly conceived than most of the internecine Greek conflicts that preceded it. Aetolia fought on, and Antipater was called to Asia as the succession wrangling began before he could suppress Aetolia. In 321 the Aetolians invaded Thessaly with some success but had to give it up because of the now customary attack in their rear by the predictably bellicose Acarnanians. Polyperchon suppressed the Thessalians; Sparta and Aetolia were the only substantial free Greek cities left.

In Athens, Antipater was honoured by the empowered oligarchs as a benefactor of the city, and the franchise was restricted to those who had two-thousand drachmae, about nine-thousand relatively wealthy people, thirty per cent of the size of the previous electorate. It was proclaimed to be a restoration of Solon's constitution. The jury courts were ended, surpluses would no longer be distributed, many offices were abolished in the interests of economy and efficiency, and rotation by tribe and election by lot ended. The Areopagus had enhanced responsibilities and Antipater offered land in Thrace to those who had been disenfranchised and wished to go into exile. (The more of them that left Athens the better as far as he was concerned.) Demosthenes and Hypereides, and their immediate followers had fled Athens and Damades sentenced them to death in absentia. An unenforceable death sentence with exile was a frequent verdict in Athenian proceedings and it was hoped that this would placate Antipater, but he insisted the sentences be carried out and hunted down the principal exiles so sentenced with his own forces. Hypereides was captured, returned to Athens and executed. Phocion saved the life of Hagnonides, while Demosthenes took refuge in the Temple of Poseidon at Calauria, where Antipater's chief pursuer of such fugitives, Archias, found him and demanded he leave the sanctuary. Demosthenes asked for time to write a letter and took poison that he had put in his pen for such an eventuality. He tried to leave to avoid leaving a corpse in the temple but fell down dead beside the altar, on October 22, 322.

Demosthenes was devious, bitter, and uncharitable, and his strategic judgment was faulty. He had no finesse or notion of compromise. But he was one of history's great and effective public speakers, and throughout his public life of more than forty years he devoted his great talents solely, and with dauntless courage, to the patriotic cause of Athens. He had no idea of tactical maneuver or strategic planning, and little skill at making over differences other than in the over-arching cause of Athens' civic interest as he perceived it. His faith in the city state was ultimately obsolete and doomed, and Demosthenes had no notion of anything grander in scope than what he knew and sought to preserve. But his Athens was a tolerant democracy, even if he was often intolerant and frequently applied his immense oratorical talents to shameful and unscrupulous demagogy. Yet, no one did, or could, doubt his sincere devotion to his cause or his courage or ingenuity and constancy in championing it. In his pursuit of the welfare of Athens as he saw it, and of democracy within Athens, he never wavered, always fought bravely, and ultimately died bravely. Philip and Alexander recognized him as a great and formidable adversary, and he gave to a losing cause an almost superhuman devotion and came surprisingly close to success against heavy odds. His renown has not dimmed these twenty-three centuries since his unjust death, bravely endured, as was customary in these times.

2. Opening skirmishes

Alexander left no plan of succession. His wife Roxanne, daughter of Oxyartes king of Bactria, whom Alexander captured when he took the rock bastion in the king's absence, was expecting a child in approximately four months. Perdiccas, the senior general and acting hipparch (vizier) since the death of Hephaestion, called a council of the generals, which agreed to recommend to the Macedonian army, which had the constitutional authority on the vacancy of the throne with no live direct heir, that they await the birth of Roxanne and the late king's child (there was no suggestion that anyone but Alexander was the father) and if he were a boy, to acknowledge him as king, and the council of generals would determine the regent. Peithon supported this and the others present went along. Meleager, as the senior phalanx-leader, was deputized to take this proposal to the army. He was the only one of the early comrades of Alexander who had not been promoted and he was not a good choice for this role, as he was aggrieved at being short-changed in his career and he presented the proposal to the infantry in a manner that was calculated to assure that they would demand a Macedonian king rather than the unborn child of a savage Bactrian.

Under Meleager's influence, they rejected the nomination of the unborn child of unknowable sex, and surely not knowing what they were getting, chose Arrhidaeus, an illegitimate son of Philip II, half-brother of Alexander, who was an epileptic half-wit. He was renamed Philip III and Meleager, to no one's surprise, was named regent and guardian of the king. The cavalry bucked the infantry and supported the generals' decision. Learning their lesson just in time, the other generals gave the cavalry the proposal instead of Meleager, one of history's all-time aggressively self-serving messengers. Meleager responded to this impasse by attempting to arrange the assassination of Perdiccas. Antipater's Macedonian army and Craterus and his ten-thousand veterans had not so far been consulted. Perdiccas with the cavalry and elephants, left Babylon and blockaded the routes into the city.

A few weeks after the death of Alexander the Great, his vast empire was on the verge of civil war. A compromise was worked out by Eumenes: Philip III and Roxanne's child, if a boy, would be joint-kings and Craterus would be guardian of Philip III. Perdiccas and Leonnatus were to be joint guardians of the new-born co-king (if the baby were a girl, obviously Philip III would be sole king and Craterus guardian and chairman of a state council composed of Macedonian generals. Perdiccas was to be confirmed as vizier and commander of the army in Asia, and Antipater would continue as commander of the Macedonian army in Europe. No regent of the empire was appointed and the whole system was nonsense, as Philip was, in fact, in the hands of Perdiccas and not Craterus. Roxanne gave birth to a healthy boy a few months later and he was named Alexander IV, and proclaimed king by much of the army. The army in Persia was a little like the French army in Algeria in the 1950s, a sufficiently powerful organization to interfere forcefully in the mother country, but not entirely in control of the land where it was stationed. There was no Charles de Gaulle to save the empire and as there was no arrangement between Antipater and Perdiccas, open skirmishing broke out in 321 and continued almost uninterruptedly for twenty years.

It was a bare-faced struggle for power between the generals, few of whom had any aptitude for chicanery of this kind given the previous thirty years of iron-fisted rule by Philip and Alexander. It was essentially a struggle between the territorial dynasts, the more entrenched satraps, and the representatives of centralized rule, generally Alexander's senior collaborators. The protagonists were largely gathered in Babylon and in Alexander's so-called Bodyguard: Perdiccas, Ptolemy, Leonnatus, Peithon, Lysimachus, Aristonous, Peucestas, Seleucus, Eumenes, and Cassander. Antipater was in Macedonia; Craterus was with his veterans in Cilicia with Polyperchon. Antigonus was in his satrapy of Phrygia, and enjoyed the entire support of the senior admiral, Nearchus. This was a varied group as arises in almost any sudden vacancy at the head of an autocratic regime, such as after the deaths of Lenin, Stalin, and Mao Tse-tung, and, no doubt, at many papal conclaves. Perdiccas was a legitimate member of Alexander's house and a capable soldier possessed of the ambition and some of the talent for in-close political maneuver and intrigue of his family, including his ineffably slippery namesake, Perdiccas of Macedon, king from 448 to 413 (Chapter 5).

Ptolemy, who had deep eyes and an aquiline nose, was more gregarious than Perdiccas and was from the start a partitionist, who thought the empire would be ungovernable and had to be rationalized into different components and intended to be the leader of one of them. Leonnatus was ambitious but unmethodical and was not as skilled a political tactician as several of his rivals. Peithon was able and impatiently ambitious, and Lysimachus was also ambitious, but took a long view and moved cautiously. Aristonous would always respond to a call to duty from Alexander's family, while Peucestas, satrap of Persis and Susiana, was popular with the Persians but was without the necessary grasp of the whole extent of the forces contending within the empire to make the necessary alliances to be a faction-head. Seleucus commanded the hypaspist (shield-bearing) heavy infantry; he was a man of great physical strength and while less of a cut-throat than most of the others, he was sage and sensible. Eumenes of Cardia, Alexander's chief secretary and a capable general, was absolutely loyal to the continuity of Alexander as he could best discern it.

Cassander, Antipater's son, was too young to have been through the wars with this group and was thus without any sentiment at all; he was completely ruthless and very astute. Craterus was Alexander's second-in-command and thus the most eminent general, not only in rank but in ability. He was popular and respected and no one's fool at the political arts. His lieutenant, Polyperchon, was a plain and reliable soldier from a noble family, and thus very useful in whatever role Craterus might play. Antipater was a senior figure, very solid and intelligent and rather cynical, and Antigonus, a friend and contemporary, ruled the satrapy of Phrygia and was extremely cunning and subtle and immensely ambitious, for himself and his dashing son Demetrius. It is misleading to bandy about comparisons with modern and evil governments, but there was a slight parallel between Eumenes, Alexander's secretary, and Alexander Poskrebyshev, Stalin's assistant who was suspected and resented by everyone; and between Perdiccas and Stalin's police commissar, Lavrenti Beria. I emphasize the similarity was in their roles and to some extent instincts; Alexander's government was quite distinguished, both in talent and in its moral character, and does not bear comparison with the almost unfathomable odium of the Stalin tyranny.

The natural combinations that arose soon after Alexander's death were between Antigonus and Antipater on one side and Eumenes, whose devotion to Alexander and his mother Olympias was at odds with Antipater, who found Olympias an unimaginable nuisance and menace, with Perdiccas fetching up beside Eumenes. Lysimachus and Cassander had been close school friends (with Alexander, Hephaestion, and Ptolemy, under Aristotle), which gathered Lysimachus into the camp of Antipater, Cassander's father. The plot thickened considerably because of the maneuvering within and around Alexander's family. Perdiccas opened discussions with Olympias, presumably to strengthen his legitimist credentials and to put Antipater on his back foot. Olympias was governing Epirus as regent and quarrelling with Antipater in Macedonia. Alexander's sister, Cleopatra, widow of Alexander of Epirus, sought marriage with Leonnatus, who hoped that this match would land him the kingship of Macedonia. Agitating in a different direction was Adeia Eurydice, only fourteen, betrothed to the incapable Philip. Her father, Amyntas, a son of Perdiccas III, had been executed by Alexander the Great for conspiracy and her mother was the illegitimate daughter of Philip II. Even though she was a second cousin of Alexander the Great on her father's side, and a niece on her mother's, she disliked her relatives and was not in the slightest barred from sinister intrigue by her youth. In the politics of Macedonia, no age was too young for diabolical and deadly scheming.

What will now ensue in this chapter and the next will be an intricate and repetitive recitation of battles, intrigues, alliances and betrayals, that I have to present at least cursorily. It will have its interesting moments, but readers wearied by such sequences can get a summary of the results of it all at the end of section 3 of Chapter 15.

3. The First War of the Diadochi, 322-320

Perdiccas struck the first blow in what would be one of history's most intense and protracted struggles for control of a great jurisdiction by murdering Meleager, who had botched and misplayed his hand as messenger to the army. (This did replicate the early liquidation of Beria after Stalin's death, the only thing, apart from the firing of Poskrebyshev the post-Stalin factions could agree upon.) He then called a meeting of the council of generals to distribute satrapies, a process that naturally entailed intense bargaining. Ptolemy threw in his lot with Perdiccas in exchange for

Egypt. Cleomenes of Naucratis, who had been acting satrap in Egypt and chief tax collector, was retained as Ptolemy's subordinate. Leonnatus took the vacant satrapy in Hellespontine Phrygia, to put himself in post position for the throne of Macedonia with his intended pitching for queen. Antigonus added Lycia and Pamphylia to his satrapy of Phrygia.

Various satrapies in Asia Minor were doled out to second echelon officials and all the eastern satraps, including Porus and and Taxiles in India, were retained. Two of Perdiccas' closest associates had to be rewarded: Peithon was awarded Media, but Perdiccas' father-in-law, Atrapates, who had been the satrap, became the satrap of the new creation of North Media, which included an unconquered area that he named Atrapatene, which evolved linguistically and geographically into Azerbaijan. All pretense to Armenia being a satrapy was abandoned, and its independence was conceded to Orontes, who had been Darius' autonomous satrap. Eumenes was rewarded with the triple satrapy of Cappadocia, Paphlagonia, and Pontus, though this required the military expulsion of Ariarathes, who had governed there since Gaugamela. In Europe, Thrace was taken from Antipater and awarded to Lysimachus. Seleucus accepted to become commander of the Companion cavalry. Harpalus' old treasury office was abolished, and the centralization Alexander had effected by making the treasurers of the satrapies answerable to him was rolled back and these new and empowered senior satraps ran their own treasuries and minted their own coins. Alexander's empire began to crack apart within a few months of the king's death.

The thirteen-thousand Greek mercenaries Alexander had left in Bactria, which were smoldering on the edge of revolt when he died, reverently observed his death by rising in open mutiny and proceeding homewards, drawing in pockets of disaffected Greek mercenaries as they went, totaling up to twenty-thousand infantry and three-thousand cavalry. Craterus supported Antipater in resisting this horde and Perdiccas sent Peithon eastward with thirty-eight hundred Macedonians and an order to furnish them ten-thousand infantry and eight-thousand cavalry from the loyal satrapies. Peithon's order from Perdiccas was to set upon and kill the mutineers, as if they were being court-martialed for desertion. Peithon rather intended to rally them with promises of preferments and send them back to their posts. Promising that they would be called out soon and would be the elite guard of a new political formation. But his own men would hear none of this, ignored Peithon and massacred the retreating and largely unarmed Greeks and plundered any baggage they had. This was a serious problem for the eastern cities of the empire, and Peithon, whose treachery became known, returned to the court of Perdiccas devoid of any use or credibility. He had fumbled his one chance and in this deadly business, one chance is all anyone got, if that.

Perdiccas wished to finish Alexander's work in Asia Minor, though he gave up on his plans for the exploration of Arabia. He ordered Leonnatus and Antigonus to furnish troops for the conquest of Eumenes' Cappadocia. Neither considered that Perdiccas was in any position to command them to do anything; Antigonus ignored the order and Leonnatus invited Eumenes to visit him and asked his support in his proposed marriage of Cleopatra. Eumenes refused and Leonnatus tried but failed to murder Eumenes. Leonnatus was soon killed in the Lamian War, Perdiccas was left with the task of getting an improved position for his ally Eumenes. Perdiccas then invaded Cappadocia himself in 322 with Philip and the main imperial army, captured and hanged Ariarathes, and gave the satrapy of Cappadocia to Eumenes. Moving deftly in the shifting alliances, Perdiccas prevailed upon Alexander's armour-bearer, Neoptolemus, a noble Epirote, to attempt the conquest of Armenia, while he invaded eastern Pisidia, where Balacrus of Cilicia had fought unsuccessfully and died. Perdiccas was successful in a horrible campaign in which his opponents would not be taken alive and the Isaurians ignited their city rather than having it overrun, and perished in the inferno. Perdiccas sent his own brother, Alcetas, to occupy western Pisidia, but Alcetas was playing his own game, and camped with those he was to subjugate and made a warm association and alliance with the wild inhabitants of the area he was to take on behalf of his brother.

Perdiccas had enjoyed a level of success that disquieted Antipater. Antipater had thrown his family into the intense political jockeying, marrying his daughter Eurydice to Ptolemy and his very able daughter Phila to Craterus. He had offered another daughter to Leonnatus, but he had other plans (Cleopatra), and then abruptly perished in the Lamian war (last section of Chapter 14). Seeing the shift of events in Perdiccas' favour, Antipater offered his daughter Nicaea to Perdiccas, while Olympias, not to be left out, urged Perdiccas to marry Cleopatra. Eumenes advised Perdiccas to marry Cleopatra, but he chose Nicaea. The other Eurydice was brought from Macedonia by her mother Cynane, to join Philip and prepare a joint claim to the Macedonian throne. She managed to evade Antipater's intercepting force, as Antipater himself was in Greece. Perdiccas then told Alcetas to stop her, as every faction agreed that the last thing they needed was Eurydice plying her way around the factions at Babylon. Alcetas' men would not raise a hand against Philip's daughter, so Perdiccas attempted to arrange for her murder. But his Macedonians revolted and took Eurydice under their protection.

At this fluid point, Perdiccas miscalculated and purported to compel Antigonus' appearance to face a charge of insubordination. Antigonus instead went to Antipater and Craterus joined them. Antipater believed Antigonus' claim that Perdiccas had murdered Cynane and that he intended to evict Antipater from Macedonia. Craterus considered Perdiccas a usurper, and he and Antipater adjourned their effort to conquer Aetolia and they prepared to invade Asia instead and asked the assistance of Ptolemy, who had assumed control in Egypt uneventfully. In 322, he had added Cyprus to his Egyptian satrapy, on request from the banished Cypriot oligarchs. There was an undignified dispute over the disposition of Alexander's corpse, which was broached in the previous chapter. The splendid bier for him proceeded not to Macedonia, as Perdiccas had wished, on the theory that he who buried Alexander in Macedonia would succeed him as king, but for Egypt.

Ptolemy had fostered the theory that Alexander had wished to be buried at the Temple of Ammon, and directed the funeral procession to Egypt via Damascus, and the late king was interred temporarily at Memphis, pending preparation of a suitably grand mausoleum at Alexandria, Egypt. Ptolemy had now snaffled into his satrapy, which was really an independent principality or even kingdom, a supposedly independent ally, and had snatched the corpse of the late and already profoundly lamented founder of the empire. He knew Perdiccas would have to reply to him and gratefully accepted the alliance of Antipater. Through the winter of 322-321, all sides prepared for the many-sided conflict that would now rage for twenty years and continue intermittently for twenty years after that and would engage the entire military force of the empire, an enervating blood-letting on a grander scale than the Greek city states had ever been able to mount (though they never lacked the taste for such a sanguinary melee). The cavalry employed were mainly Asiatic and the infantry were mercenaries from every part of the empire, all the way to Bactria and India, and all the faction-heads tried to have some Macedonian contingents to be able to profess some authenticity as continuators of Philip and Alexander. The mercenaries did this for a living and didn't really mind, as long as they were paid, though they were always capable of selling out to the enemy for a better offer. The Macedonians tended to stick with the commander they had rallied to, but they disliked the war, preferred to go home, and pressured their leaders to make peace through most of the long duration of the conflict.

Perdiccas joined in alliance with the Aetolians, who were already in armed conflict with Antipater. As he was now directly contending for the grand prize, he shuffled the marital cards and broke off his engagement with Nicaea and sent Eumenes to Cleopatra at Sardes with presents and his proposal. This implicitly included a direct claim for the throne of Macedonia. Antigonus went to Cyprus with part of Antipater's fleet where a number of island kings had already joined with Ptolemy. Perdiccas sent part of his fleet to Cyprus under Aristonaus to try to round up some support, Antigonus landed at Caria and both Asander and Menander of Lydia joined his side and in a lightning raid on Sardes. Antigonus almost bagged Eumenes, who was representing Perdiccas' romantic and dynastic interest with Cleopatra. She warned Eumenes of Antigonus' proximity and enabled him to escape by a hair's breadth. Perdiccas had decided to remain on the defensive opposite Antigonus and Antipater, while dealing with Ptolemy, and to draw his enemies from Asia Minor and Greece toward him, but had distracted Eumenes with his marital mission, when he should have been preparing the defense of their initiative. This was entrusted to Eumenes as a general of demonstrated competence. As Eumenes' army was unprepared, Perdiccas gave him five-thousand Macedonians and promised almost all of Asia Minor if he was successful: the satrapies of Leonnatus, Antigonus, Asander, and Menander-Eumenes was thus entrusted with the task of vesting himself with these satrapies. Eumenes hurried to his own satrapy and raised five-thousand excellent Cappadocian cavalry but was too late getting to the Dardanelles. Antipater, Craterus, and Lysimachus had bribed the troops on guard and crossed the Straits with thirty-two thousand, five hundred men, the majority seasoned Macedonians.

Perdiccas was now scrambling and ordered Neoptolemus from Armenia and Alcetas from Pisidia to join Eumenes, and both had Macedonian contingents. Alcetas refused and Neoptolemus immediately entered into negotiations with Perdiccas' enemies, but was discovered by Eumenes, who defeated him and gained command of his troops as Neoptolemus fled to join Craterus with three-hundred cavalrymen. Eumenes still had a substantial army of about twenty-thousand infantry and five-thousand horse, and his principal generals were the imperishable Pharnabazus (now Eumenes' brother-in-law but on all sides at different times over the previous thirty years), Phoenix, and the eminent historian, Hieronymous of Cardia, the chief chronicler of these events. Antipater divided his forces, taking ten-thousand men to assist Ptolemy while Craterus with twenty-thousand infantry and twenty-eight hundred cavalry was to deal with Eumenes. Antipater's calculation was that Eumenes could not get his men to attack their fellow-Macedonians. Eumenes recognized the problem and held his Macedonian infantry back in defensive posture but attacked on both flanks simultaneously with his Cappadocian cavalry and defeated the enemy's flanks, killing Craterus and Neoptolemus in battle. Though wounded, Eumenes won the surrender of Antipater's Macedonians, but they stole off in the night toward Antipater on the road to Egypt, depriving Eumenes of most of the fruits of his well-fought victory.

As this was in progress, Perdiccas had invaded Egypt, and was in secret accord with Cleomenes of Naucratis, the under-satrap. Ptolemy suspected this arrangement and summarily executed Cleomenes, seizing eight-thousand talents his deputy had embezzled and put away for his own use. Perdiccas was blocked by Ptolemy, who was expecting him, on his first effort to cross the Nile and then both armies tried to outflank each other as they moved in forced marches south on opposite banks, toward Memphis. Here again Perdiccas was unable to cross, and he lost many men drowned in the effort. On this, his Macedonians deserted, leaving Perdiccas acutely vulnerable and far from home. Seleucus, Peithon, and Antigonus, commander of the hypaspists and former phalanx-leader for Alexander, seized Perdiccas in his tent and slew him. The slayers of Perdiccas offered to support Ptolemy for the regency, but he wanted to remain in Egypt and out of the main struggle which he correctly saw would continue for a long time with no predictable outcome. Ptolemy advised that Peithon and Arrhidaeus become joint regents, and they agreed. It was only the day after this was agreed that news arrived of Eumenes' defeat of Craterus and Neoptolemus, which if Perdiccas had known of it, might have caused him to be less impetuous and to retain his stake as a protagonist, or at least his life and a taste of prosperity.

The regents relocated the army and the kings (Philip III [Arrhidaeus] and Alexander IV, a half-wit and a gurgling infant), to Triparadeisus in Syria. Perdiccas, Meleager, and Craterus had been disposed of, but the other leading players were still in place, maneuvering and circling, or, like Ptolemy, watching shiftily from the corners of the Empire. Eurydice was lobbying and agitating for Philip's interest, i.e., her own, and was making headway. Before anything climactic could occur, Antipater and Antigonus arrived, and were now in post-position as the power struggle entered its second phase. Peithon and Arrhidaeus stepped aside and Antipater and Antigonus were declared regents of the Empire by the senior officers of the Macedonian army, still the leading force in the Empire, which was disintegrating each week as satraps withdrew from the divided central influence. Eurydice was not to be seen off that easily. She was advocating the abolition of the regency, encouraged by Attalus, and they managed to persuade the army of Asia, led by the hypaspists (heavy infantry) which had followed Antigenes, to demand immediate satisfaction of the rewards Alexander had promised them when he secured their loyalty on the homeward march. Antipater appeared before the disaffected hypaspists and narrowly escaped being stoned to death. Antigonus and Seleucus facilitated his escape, and he "persuaded Eurydice to keep quiet,"[3] presumably by drawing on what he had learned from his decades of jousting with the fiery and devious Olympias and being fairly explicit about the connection between her political agitation and her physical survival.

Antipater now made the customary redistribution of satrapies: Ptolemy retained Egypt and all to the west of it, which was the first time any Greek cities had been placed in a satrapy, a dangerous step down the trail to fragmentation of the Empire, for the benefit of one of the most slippery operators in this multi-villain cast. Seleucas received Babylon, Arrhidaeus (Eurydice) got Hellespontine Phrygia, Antigones received Susiana, Nicanor (Antigonus' supporter), got Cappadocia, and Peithon got the general command of the eastern satrapies. Philippus moved from Bactria to Parthia, and Bactria was given to Stasnor. His brother Stasander received Caria. Antigonus was entrusted with the task of bringing the extensive royal treasure from Susa to Cilicia, most of the way to Europe, and he was given the politically active Silver Shields (Argyraspids) to help accomplish this. Antigonus also received the command of the royal army in Asia. Menander became Antigonus' second in command and was reinforced with eighty-five hundred seasoned Macedonian infantry and seventy of Alexander's elephants and assigned the task of subduing Eumenes and Alcetas. Antipater also gave his daughter Phila, widow of Craterus, as a wife for Antigonus' son, Demetrius who was only 15, while Phila was probably in her mid-thirties. (It was more successful than most arranged marriages of the time.)

In a considerable outburst of energy to try to get his hand firmly on the helm of the Empire, Antipater also made his own talented son Cassander the chiliarch, commander of the royal Bodyguard and the army's elite units. With this, he withdrew with the balance of the Macedonians and the entire court to Europe. This abandoned Alexander's policy of operating the Empire integrally from its central point in Asia Minor, as a largely Persian Empire which he would Hellenize culturally. He was, as he must have known, converting it back to a Greco-Macedonian empire trying to retain control of the former Persian Empire, from the Hellespont to Armenia and Libya and on to Arabia and Kashmir. It was an impossible arrangement—known Asia and Greece were not going to accept for long to be dependencies of a Macedonia not governed remotely as authoritatively as the empires of Philip II and Alexander the Great had been.

Attalus, Perdiccas' associate, not the original Attalus whom Alexander executed, reduced to somewhat impecunious scrambling in search of shelter, fetched up with Alcetas in Pisidia, and they invaded Caria, successfully, but their fleet was defeated when it attacked Rhodes, and again as it approached Cyprus. They lost everything but Pisidia and were joined there by Docimus, who had been driven out of Babylon by Seleucus. Their position was undermined by Alcetas' refusal to join forces with Eumenes, who was also at loose ends. After defeating Caterus and Neoptolamus, he repaired to Lydia, hoping that Cleopatra would declare in his favour, but she remained absolutely neutral and treated all factions with equivocal respect. Eumenes

---

3 Ibid., p. 469.

had intended to intercept Antipater as he returned to Europe, but Cleopatra prevailed upon him not to compromise her, and he retired to Phrygia where he spent the winter into 320 but had to show considerable ingenuity to keep his army under him, as he had no ability to pay them. He devised a method of retaining their tenuous fidelity by doling out the rights to seize and plunder the fiefdoms within Phrygia, which was supposedly in the domain of Antigonus. His officers did so with enthusiasm, reduced the castles with Eumenes' siege engines and took over Phrygia. It got Eumenes through the winter, ostensibly still at the head of a coherent army.

In the spring of 320, Antigonus invaded Cappadocia with ten-thousand infantry two-thousand cavalry, and thirty elephants. Eumenes had double Antigonus' numbers, but had little authority over his forces, which were now more brigands than soldiers. The two armies met at the Orcynian fields, and Eumenes' army crumbled. Eumenes and Hieronymous fled to the fortress of Nora, and withstood Antigonus' siege for a commendable sixteen months, as Antigonus recovered Cappadocia and Phrygia and evicted Eumenes' usurper-barons. (Hieronymous separated Nora and became a virtual schemer and go-between of fortune.) Antigonus, now at the head of an army of over forty-thousand, defeated Alcetas and captured Attalus and Docimus (the latter proclaiming the grace of conversion to the cause of Antigonus, where he served for seventeen years, before another turn of fortune). Alcetas got away to Termessus where he took stock and committed suicide. Antigonus tried to prevent his burial, but the Termessians insisted. He incorporated Alcetas' forces into his and now had an army approaching sixty-thousand. Eumenes was still barricaded into the fortress at Nora, Antipater's only noteworthy, declared enemy, but with a very small command, a talented general but the only survivor of a defeated faction and in search of freedom of movement and a force of men to restore some influence to him.

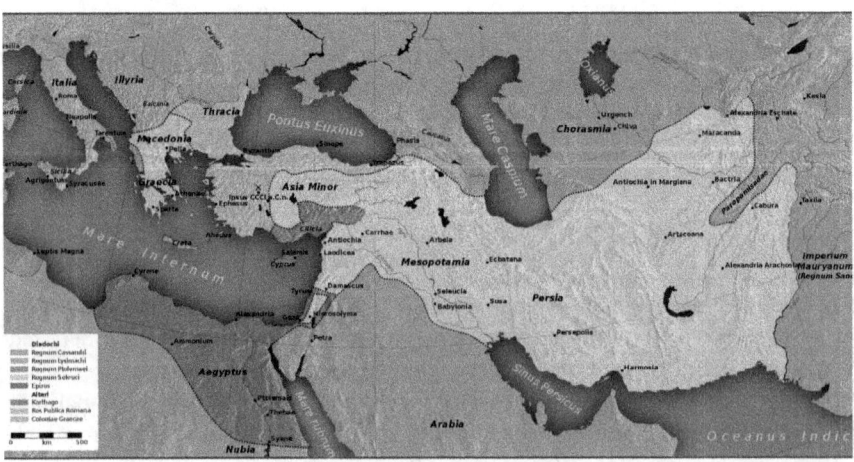

Territories of the Diadochi

4. Second War of the Diadochi 318-315

This is where matters stood when Antipater died in 319, at the age of approximately eighty-one. He was a formidable representative and legitimate continuator of the accomplishments of Philip of Macedon and Alexander the Great and was successfully and believably keeping intact their heritage for Alexander's incapable half-brother and his infant son, though he had effectively reconstituted Alexander's Empire as a Macedonian colonial enterprise that would be impossible to sustain. It was just four years since the death of Alexander and twelve years since the battle of Gaugamela. The brilliant and astounding moment of Alexandrian world unity was passing like a meteor.

The Macedonian army could not be united behind any one successor, and the Greek city states and most of the Asian satraps could not wait to be done with any notion of subordinacy to such a diminutive and culturally undistinguished place as Macedonia, and the vision and power of enactment of Alexander's grand design of a joint Euro-Asian Empire raising up and intensively sharing and reinforcing the genius of Hellenic culture had almost perished with Alexander, and it now departed to the realm of what might have been. Ptolemy and Antigonus took the lead in carving up the Empire. By right of the seniority of Egypt, and of himself among the claimants following the death of Alexander, Ptolemy had already ceased to send on any revenue to the central treasury. He now declared Egypt entirely autonomous and invaded and occupied all of Syria, capturing and evicting the satrap, Laemedon. Antigonus set out to take over the rest of Asia Minor. He seized Lydia from Cleitus, took Ephesus, and even tried to drive Philip III (Arrhidaeus) and the determined Eurydice from Hellespontine Phrygia. These men were just warlords.

Antipater had left the recommendation that Polyperchon succeed him as regent, because of the prestige he had acquired by reconquering Thessaly in 321. Polyperchon had been an ally of Craterus, whose faction had won though he himself had died. His election had been by most of the Macedonian army, but not that part of it that was in Asia (in practice, it was the officers who commanded significant units, not a consultation of the soldiery, but the officers knew their men and could judge whom they would follow). Polyperchon had control of Macedonia and Antipater's army (with sixty-five elephants), and all the fleet that was not under Antigonus, and the residual legitimacy of the Macedonian kingship, a writ that still ran here and there in Asia. He could be relied upon to try to defend what he inherited, but he was not at all as astute as Antipater, let alone Alexander and his father. Nor had he inherited Antipater's good relations with Antigonus, and they were now rivals.

Antigonus prepared for a test of strength with Polyperchon by trying to make peace with Eumenes, still pouring boiling water down the walls on those besieging him at Nora, and sent Hieronymous with a peace offer. Antigonus' peace offer was that Eumenes be entirely free as long as he took an oath to the kings and to Antigonus personally. Eumenes altered this to alliance with Olympias, the kings, and Antigonus, and he asked the Macedonian officers besieging him if they were satisfied with that. They were and Eumenes was free, bound to Antigonus just as the kings' general (a status which Antigonus did not take seriously in any context not helpful to himself).

The first rival Polyperchon had to contend with was Antipater's son Cassander. He had been with Antigonus after the agreement between Antipater and Antigonus, as a goodwill ambassador, but quarreled with Antigonus and returned to Macedonia. He expected to be made regent when his father died and when this did not happen, he returned to Antigonus and asked for his assistance in challenging Polyperchon. Antigonus lent him four-hundred men and thirty-five ships, and Ptolemy threw in with Antigonus and Cassander. Antipater's army had garrisoned many Greek states, where they were not popular, and Polyperchon, pressed by Cassander's insurrection, played this card in making alliances with Greek states that wanted to see the back of Antipater's garrisons. Polyperchon created a very disturbed state of affairs by recalling most Macedonian garrisons from the Greek states and announcing that he was going back to the policy of Philip II and Alexander, and restoring more democratic constitutions, where Antipater had imposed more authoritarian ones. This set the democrats in those states against Pollyperchon's enemies (Cassander), but it also fragmented Macedonian control of Greece and reduced the status of Macedonia from overlord of Greece to alliance, and that only temporarily, with many Greek states. He did not withdraw the Macedonian garrison from Corinth, but all who were deployed by Antipater were required to return to Macedonia in March 318 B.C. Polyperchon continued to give orders as Antipater had. (It was rather gratuitous of Polyperchon to issue a proclamation blaming practically everything that was disputed in the Greek states on Antipater, without whose patronage he, Polyperchon, would be a mere commander of forces as assigned by a higher-up in the Macedonian state.)

Polyperchon's next gambit was to make overtures to Eumenes. He had the royal family of Macedonia send him letters entreating his support against Antigonus. Eumenes was offered the co-regency, or continuation in Asia as commander there for the Macedonian Empire, at the head of the Silver Shields, and in control of what was left in Asia of the royal treasure. Eumenes casuistically concluded that his loyalty oath to Antigonus was without effect when Antigonus was at odds with the kings (again, the incapable Philip III and the three-year old Alexander IV). Eumenes won his brief wrestling match with his conscience as a sworn ally of Antigonus, concluded that was vitiated by Antigonius' status as a traitor to the kings, and accepted the Asian command of the Macedonian forces, and the treasure that went with it. He had his work cut out for him, but it was a considerable uptick from the long siege in the fortress at Nora. Eumenes' decision can be defended, as both Antigonus and Ptolemy were operating for their own accounts and barely paid lip service to the Macedonian crown. Eumenes' ethical problem was with his unilateral amendment of the oath that he took.

Polyperchon committed two mistakes at this point: he neglected to have the Macedonians loyal to him issue a cancellation of the previous death-sentence on Eumenes, and he invited the horrifying harridan Olympias, queen-mother though she was, into Macedonian government. Even Olympias had the intelligence to ask Eumenes his views and he counseled her not to move back to Macedonia and take up the guardianship of the kings. She abided by that but started sending out opinions more or less in the form of instructions that were taken with varying degrees of seriousness by their recipients. The atmosphere quickly became very embittered, as Cassander and his friends, the so-called Peripatetics (because of their unattached view toward the conflicting jurisdictions) blamed Alexander for the execution of Callisthenes, while Olympias replied by fanning the calumny that Antipater, Cassander, and Aristotle had murdered Alexander with poison. Olympias' numerous enemies retorted that she had conspired in the murder of her husband Philip II. (This was more plausible but probably untrue.)

Antigonus immediately sent Menander against Eumenes, who retreated but with the treasure at Kyinda which Polyperchon had given him, he recruited and trained up an army. Ptolemy and Antigonus both tried to bribe over the Silver Shields, the last loyal unit intact of Alexander the Great's. Eumenes steadied them in his service, but they were technically bound by the Macedonian death sentence pronounced on Eumenes in the time of Antipater, which compromised their loyalty to Eumenes. Ever-resourceful, Eumenes improvised the argument that he had had a dream in which Alexander, as the deity he claimed to be, appeared and said he was with them in spirit and approved of Eumenes' enterprise. Eumenes had a royal tent set up and with a golden throne, and set out Alexander's diadem and scepter, and they pretended to meet as equals amongst themselves in the presence of Alexander. Eumenes carried this charade off so convincingly, he held the hard-bitten and unpredictable Silver Shields together with this flimflam for two years, a virtuoso performance before so cynical a group. It did impose on him the requirement of working out his plans collegially, purporting to divine the wishes of the ever-present king, rather than just giving orders as army commanders usually did, but in these exotic circumstances, he had no choice.

In order to open communications with Polyperchon and break down his state of isolation, Eumenes invaded Phoenicia and set about constructing and procuring a fleet to keep him in touch with his ally. The entire former Empire, except for the far eastern part of it, settled into war: Polyperchon (Europe) and Eumenes (Asia) for the royalists, versus Cassander (Europe) and Antigonus (Asia), supported by Ptolemy in Egypt and Syria, trying to decentralize in the hands of the warlords. Given that the royal party was Macedonian, it was natural that Polyperchon should be the leader in the tandem with Eumenes; and as decentralization was bound to come from Asia, it was natural that Antigonus was the royalists' chief adversary. Eumenes had been commissioned by Polyperchon to cause trouble in Antigonus' flank, and Cassander had been sent to Europe by Antigonus to do the same to Polyperchon. These four and Ptolemy, who complacently but vigilantly awaited events, were the semi-finalists in the post-Alexandrine carve-up.

The battle shifts now to sea matters. Antigonus was preeminent in Asia Minor and Egypt was in safe hands with Ptolemy, so he set out for Europe to attack Polyperchon directly. Arrhidaeus (Philip III) held part of Hellespontine Phrygia and threatened Antigonus' ability to cross over to Europe and Polyperchon sent his fleet, under Cleitus, to assist him. Cassander's fleet, under Nicanor, joined with Antigonus' fleet, Nicanor commanding the combined force, and with one-hundred and thirty vessels sought out Cleitus. They met in the Bosporus and Nicanor was badly defeated. But the Byzantines helped Antigonus get some of his men across the straits, and Nicanor had enough vessels (although he lost sixty ships) to get some more across, and at dawn, Antigonus surprised Cleitus' sailors ashore sleeping off their victory and Nicanor captured almost the entire royalist fleet. (It was a repetition of Aegospotami-Lysander's defeat of Conon's Athenians in 405 B.C., ending the Peloponnesian War, Chapter 8.) Cleitus fled by horse, but was apprehended by the forces of Lysimachus, Alexander's former bodyguard, who had sided with Antigonus and Cassander and was governor of Thrace. Cleitus was slain as an enemy it was preferred not to take alive. Antigonus chased Philip III (Arrhidaeus) out of what he still held in Hellespontine Phrygia, but once settled in Europe, Eurydice transferred their allegiance to Cassander, which was preposterous given that Philip III was one of the monarchs the royalists fighting Cassander were trying to uphold.

Antigonus then turned south to consolidate his victory by driving Eumenes out of Phoenicia and permanently separating Polyperchon and Eumenes. Eumenes headed in forced marches to the east and reached Babylonia with fifteen-thousand infantry and twenty-five hundred cavalry. He called upon Seleucus and Peithon to assist the royalists against Antigonus. Peithon declined and Seleucus was cagier, claiming loyalty to the house of Alexander but refusing to be led by an outlaw—his description of Eumenes. Eumenes garrisoned the citadel of Babylon in October 318, and skirmishing began in earnest with those whom he had come east to recruit to his elusive cause. In the spring of 317, Eumenes advanced against Peithon and Seleucus, who flooded his camp by manipulating the Tigris canal and dike system. Eumenes extricated himself with his customary feline agility. Peithon and Seleucus called upon Antigonus for help, and he hurried eastwards. While Eumenes invaded Susiana, Antigonus' satrapy, and was joined by Peucestas and the eastern satraps, with eighteen-thousand, seven-hundred infantry and four-thousand cavalry, Asiatic almost to a man. The Punjabi Eudamus, who had assassinated Porus, brought one-hundred and fourteen of Porus' elephants. Eumenes met Antigonus with a larger army, but still handicapped by the nonsense of exercising his command through virtual seances with the late king. Peucestas was a difficult, conniving, and not altogether reliable comrade. Antigonus crossed the Tigris and occupied Susa (the old capital of the Persian Great Kings) and installed Seleucus as satrap. Eumenes retreated eastward before the advancing Antigonus, but had brought Peucestas fully on board, at least temporarily, and this was a classic early version of enticing the enemy into overreach, as Quintus Fabius Maximus would do with Hannibal, and the Russians and Chinese would do in later times when they faced invaders.

The armies finally clashed at the Koprates, south of the Caspian Sea, and Eumenes soundly defeated Antigonus. Antigonus' forces had suffered badly from the heat and after sustaining a demoralizing defeat, Antigonus determined to withdraw into Media and regroup. He rejected Peithon's advice to pay off the hill-tribes in exchange for unvexed passage, and suffered heavy losses beating off the Cossaeans, who had been troublesome enough for Alexander, although he whipped them badly (as he did almost all adversaries, as will be remembered). Antigonus only saved himself the fate of Perdiccas, a large mutiny and execution either by his own men or the pursuing enemy, by a formidable campaign of profligate gift-giving and solicitude and extravagant promotions and compliments. Eumenes had the inspired strategic notion of crossing to the north of Antigonus, cutting him off from Ptolemy and Asia Minor, mopping up Antigonus' rear while he wallowed in the east swatting bushwhackers and sullen plains populations. His allies from the east did not much like the idea of leaving even a wounded and tired Antigonus vandalizing their satrapies and demurred. Eumenes withdrew to Persis, where Peucestas made a determined attempt to woo Eumenes' officers over to him. Eumenes was too wily and persuasive to lose such a contest, but it was unnerving and treacherous.

In the autumn of 317, Antigonus menaced Persis; Eumenes blocked his path; the armies stared at each other for four days and then moved on parallel lines to Gabiene, where both commanders wished to winter. There was now no real reason based on political choices or nationality in this war. It was entirely a contest between adventurer-generals, and their men had made their bets, though some units were constantly up for competing offers. It had none of the character of a people defending its territory or fighting for a serious cause, other than plunder. The two armies finally came to grips with each other at Paratacene, near Isfahan. Eumenes had thirty-five thousand infantry, about half of them heavily armed, and the three-thousand Siver Shield Macedonians, sixty-one hundred cavalry and Porus' one-hundred and fourteen elephants, to Antigonus' twenty-eight thousand infantry, mainly heavily-armed, including eight-thousand Macedonians, eighty-five hundred cavalry, and sixty-five elephants. Antigonus' Companions were led by his son Demetrius, in his first battle (husband of Antipater's daughter and Craterus' widow, Phila).

The two armies had cavalry on both flanks and the elephants in front of the centre. Eumenes right and centre forced Antigonus' opposing units back but opened up a gap with Eumenes' left; Antigonus only avoided disaster by hurling his cavalry into the gap, requiring Eumenes to call back his expanding offensive on his right to avoid the encirclement and destruction of his left. Both armies reestablished their lines and maneuvered slightly out of range, until midnight, when both rested in place. Antigonus observed the extent of his losses at first light, and he had suffered much more than Eumenes. Antigonus ordered a general retreat, which was entirely orderly and Eumenes did not pursue him. But Eumenes was left to bury all the dead, the traditional lot of the victor. Once again, Eumenes had won and demonstrated his high talent as a resourceful general who handled his units with great skill in even the tightest corners.

The battle was resumed in mid-winter when Antigonus, taking a leaf from Alexander's book and making war in winter, made a nine-days forced march across the desert to take Eumenes by surprise. It was so cold at night; his men defied his orders not to make fires and this gave Eumenes notice of their approach which Antigonus had tried to avoid. Eumenes was able to muster a somewhat smaller army than in the previous autumn. Antigonus now had only twenty-two thousand foot-soldiers, but nine-thousand cavalry, to six-thousand for Eumenes. The fighting was about even when Peucestas abruptly deserted with his men and Antigonus captured Eumenes' camp, complete with many wives, families, and much treasure. But Eumenes saved most of his army and was regrouping for a second day when the Silver Shields, always temperamental, mutinied, seized Eumenes and handed him over to Antigonus.

It was an unspeakably shameful end for the unit that had been the close-in guard for Alexander the Great. Their conduct was so shameful they dishonoured the gigantic and heroic personality who had, militarily, created them.

Antigonus executed Eudamus, for having murdered Porus, which had been a nasty act, but not one that would have troubled Antigonus very plausibly. More barbarous was burning Antigenes at the stake for no apparent or justifiable reason; the other satraps escaped. After some hesitation, and despite the interventions of Demetrius, Antigonus' son and still only eighteen, who acquitted himself well in these battles, and of Alexander's admiral, Nearchus, who both intervened forcefully on Eumenes' behalf, Antigonus invoked the outstanding sentence on Eumenes, which Polyperchon had not formally lifted, and Eumenes was executed, though with as much dignity and respect as that act can comport. He was starved for three days while Antigonus considered it and then the headsman carried out the execution order privately.

Eumenes received a religious ceremony of cremation, and his ashes were collected in a silver urn and eventually delivered to his family. He was forty-six and had been an assistant in executive and military matters to Philip II and Alexander for ten or twelve years, and a combat officer for about twenty years. He was clever and decisive in war as in politics, and lived a somewhat long career for the time, and a very active one always at the edge and entirely by his wits and courage. As a Greek in a Macedonian army, he was always at a disadvantage, and he paid the ultimate penalty for that misfortune. He was a Greek who sincerely grasped and appreciated Alexander's vision. He was one of the ancient world's sadly romantic, and widely admired figures, and one of its great swashbucklers. Antigonus has been almost universally condemned for dealing with Eumenes as he did. "He (Eumenes) had to work amid the perpetual plottings and jealousies of allies who demanded of him victory even while they made victory impossible. Any man's courage might have given way; but for four whole years, through sheer determination and military talent, he had faithfully upheld a losing cause with tools which he knew might at any moment break in his hand," (as they did).[4]

The key point of the Second War of the Diadochi was the failure of Polyperchon to subdue the city of Megalopolis in his siege of that city in 317. Cassander won over many of the Greek cities in consequence of that set-back, and negotiated with Piraeus to ensure it did not revert to Athens. In the circumstances, Athens sued for peace, as it could starve without its port at Piraeus. Cassander was prepared to open Piraeus to the Athenians if Athens proclaimed alliance with Cassander and disenfranchised anyone with less than a thousand drachmae. Cassander would garrison Munychia until the current war ended and nominate an Athenian as governor of Athens itself. In fact, Demetrius of Phalerum, who had approached Cassander for his terms, was the designated governor in January 317. At Cassander's request, Hagnonides was executed for causing the death of Phocion.

In the spring of 317 Cassander invaded Macedonia and drove out Polyperchon, who retreated into the Peloponnese. Cassander captured some of Polyperchon's

---

4 Ibid., p. 480.

elephants, as Polyperchon sent Alexander's son and Alexander IV's mother, Roxanne, to Olympias, in Epirus. Philip III and Eurydice escaped from Polyperchon and joined Cassander. Hard pressed, Polyperchon called on Olympias for help and she invaded Macedonia, delighted to be back in a position of some authority which she rarely had been while Philip ruled—they quarreled so violently—and only by the occasional influence of her letters on Alexander. (Philip had now been dead nearly twenty years, and Alexander seven years.) At this point, Eurydice, exercising her dysfunctional husband Philip III's ostensible authority, claimed to depose Polyperchon, who had been the chief defender of the royal family, abolish the regency, and name Cassander first minister to Philip III. Cassander liked and respected Eurydice and left her in charge of Macedonia with his own brother Nicanor (not the Nicanor who was the son-in-law of Aristotle, whom Cassander had executed in 318 for alleged treachery).

Cassander again invaded Greece and conquered the Thessalians, was held up at Tegea, and drove Polyperchon, who was being hounded and battered from pillar to post, but was an almost Eumenic survivor, and it was at this extremity that he called for the assistance of Olympias. She had responded to the royal family's old champion, and invaded Macedonia. Eurydice led the Macedonian army out to repel Olympias, but the soldiers refused to make war on the mother of Alexander the Great. Eurydice's army defected en masse, and Olympias seized the whole kingdom of Macedonia, whose empire six years before had extended to the edge of the Indian Punjab. Olympias lay about her with the vengeance of a woman who exploded with an entire adult lifetime of inflammatory grievances and hatreds. She executed Nicanor, Cassander's brother, and about a hundred of Cassander's close collaborators, as Cassander himself was absent at war in Greece.

Olympias adopted the now frequent formula for simplifying complex and contentious political disputes by arranging for her quasi-stepson, Philip III, to be executed after a minimalist pseudo-legal proceeding. She then had a sword, cup of hemlock and rope delivered to Eurydice in the cell she had been sharing for a few weeks with her husband, as her choices for the exit from life Olympias now required of her. Eurydice tidied up Philip's physical remains, piously said her prayers, kneeling calmly, including the prayer that Olympias would herself soon have to face the same fate, and with no betrayal of unease, gracefully arranged her own girdle rather than the proffered rope, as the instrument of obedience to Olympias' death warrant, and without comment or apparent unease, stepped into her self-made noose and hanged herself, her arms resignedly at her sides. It was December 25, 317 (years before the first Christmas). "A tribute of admiration may be permitted for the courage with which this girl, left alone at fifteen, "had played her unpromising hand in this desperate game," and made "her throw for Alexander's empire," and on being defeated, "elegantly departed the mortal game in which she had made a spirited effort."[5]

Cassander had broken off the siege of Tegea and returned to Macedonia as quickly as he could spur his army. Blocked by the Aetolians at Thermopylae, on the request of the still active Polyperchon, he returned by rafts with his army to Thessaly, aroused a revolt in Olympias' native Epirus, chased out Aeacides, whom Olym-

---

5 Ibid., p. 481.

pias had left in command, bribed or intimidated the forces of Epirus and Polyperchon's detachments, and hurried on to Macedonia. Olympias' barbarity had made the Macedonians very suggestive of an uprising, and Cassander was by now quite an expert at such activity. Aristonous, Olympias' commander (and, with Cassander, one of Alexander's Bodyguard) was only able to hang onto Amphipolis, so great was Macedonian disaffection with their former queen and queen mother, Olympias fled into Pydna with some elephants, Roxanne, and Alexander IV, and a few lesser royals. Cassander blockaded Pydna, which she had not had time to provision, and Olympia and her diminutive following starved. The elephants were fed sawdust until they expired from malnutrition and were themselves devoured, and Olympias' men resorted to cannibalism, finally on each other. Olympias finally surrendered in the spring of 316 on condition that her own life be spared.

As part of the arrangement, she had Aristonous, who had fought well and somewhat successfully for her, surrender Amphipolis. Cassander procured his assassination, and ignored his own promise to Olympias and put her on trial for her life before the Macedonian army that was present, She did not recognize the court, demanding a trial by the whole army, which was scattered far and wide and fighting for and against many factions within what had been a generally united empire seven years before. Cassander also probably feared the impact a pleading of hers might have on Alexander's soldiers. The army that was present heard the evidence, the absence of any defence, and sentenced Olympias to death. But no Macedonian wanted to be a party to killing Alexander the Great's mother and Philip II's principal wife. After contemplating doing it himself, Cassander recruited relatives of those Olympias had had killed in her brief reign of terror in 317, and they were more than happy to stone her to death. She was haughty, contemptuous, unrepentant and fearless to the very end, as courageous an end as she had inflicted on her quasi-niece Eurydice just a few months before.

Polyperchon was now finished as a major contender, but he persevered in reasonably important and prosperous positions into the Third Century B.C. Cassander, the anti-Alexandrine contender, now controlled Macedonia as thoroughly as Antigonus controlled the Asian Empire and Ptolemy controlled Egypt. These three appeared to be the finalists in the struggle of the Diadochi (Successors). Cassander, Antipater's son, was educated at the Lycaeum by Aristotle, as were Alexander, Hephaestion, Ptolemy, and Lysimachus. He was in Alexander's bodyguard, and it has never been clear why he took against Alexander after the king's death, though the fact that his father passed over him in favour of Polyperchon as regent of Macedonia might have led to a general rejection of the Alexandrine camp, although he was raised within it. Cassander gave Philip and Eurydice a royal funeral and claimed to be the successor of the national kings, Perdiccas III and Philip II.

He married Philp's daughter, Thessalonice, the half-sister of Alexander the Great and Philip III, treated Alexander retroactively as an illegitimate interloper, and took Roxanne and her son Alexander IV into reasonably comfortable, but still unnerving custody. He founded a new capital, Cassandreia, on the foundations of the gutted Potidaea, where he settled the surviving Olynthians (whose city, it may be remembered, Alexander had destroyed and scattered the population). His greatest construction was Salonica, which became, and remains today, the second city of Greece. He entrusted the government of Epirus and the Peloponnese and other Macedonian subordinate areas to generals. He was a cultivated man, had memorized much of Homer, absorbed, presumably, about as much from Aristotle as Alexander did, and was a generous patron of Aristotle's successor, Theophrastus. (Theophrastus held that the gods were only men, always a dangerous concept with egos like Cassander's lurking about in high places.) Cassander's brother, Alexarchus, was insane and believed himself to be the sun, and was indulged in setting up a town on that basis.

5. The Third War of the Diadochi, 314-311

In Asia, Antigonus was supreme after his defeat and execution of Eumenus. He had a battle and loyalty-tested army of sixty-thousand and twenty-five thousand talents in his treasury (U.S. $4.4 billion), and an annual income to his treasury of about eleven-thousand talents (U.S. $1.95 billion). Antigonus' goal was parallel to Cassander's: although he had warm recollections of Alexander the Great, he wanted to rule the Asian section of Alexander's empire in his own right and without reference to Alexander. Symbols of Alexander vanished from the Asian coinage, but in Babylon, Antigonus was still styled as a general acting in the name of the late Macedonian king and his son (he was certainly not considered the present king). He set about eliminating potential rivals: he dismissed Peucestas from the satrapy of Persis (this was another schoolmate from Aristotle's Lycaeum); Peithon had noticed this and was apparently trying to organize a revolt when Antigonus had him assassinated and absorbed his domains. He removed Stasander from Caria and entered Babylon and called for an accounting from Seleucus, who after announcing that he was not answerable to Antigonus or anyone else, quickly discerned where that inquest was headed and with the late Satrap Peithon in mind, fled for his life to Ptolemy, where he lengthily prepared his return to the front rank.

The far eastern satraps were in supportive hands; Bactria and Carmania were not so reliable, but the satraps could not be dispensed with other than by more extensive campaigns than Antigonus wished to undertake at this time, even with his powerful army. Peucestas had betrayed Eumenes at the second Battle of Gabiene in 316, and largely delivered to Antigonus the kingdom he now held, and he departed to join Demetrius. This demonstrated again the fluidity of loyalties, as Demetrius, the talented son of Antigonus, had argued that Eumenes be spared. Yet another Nicanor, satrap of Cappadocia, was placed in charge of the upper satrapies, and Peithon of Sind became satrap of Babylonia. As Antigonus made no pretense to any status in his native Macedonia but wished to uproot any hint of Macedonian hegemony in his swath of Asian satrapies, he started promoting native Asians to high posts in his government, starting with Persians as satraps of Media and Susiana, though he retained control of the garrisons and treasuries himself.

Antigonus was now about sixty-seven. He had served in the campaigns of Perdiccas III and Philip II and then Alexander, and had lost an eye to a catapult bolt, while fighting for Philip. He was a leathery and cunning and ruthless veteran who had been reasonably non-political when serving strong kings but following the death of Alexander he demonstrated a sharp aptitude for the political arts in this deadly game. And appeared to be the big winner, and the big survivor, with about two thirds of what Alexander had left behind.

Seleucus had not taken his disembarkation from his opulent and prestigious sinecure in Babylon in very sportsmanlike fashion, and he spent his time as a fugitive from Antigonus' Asiatic house-cleaning persuading his fellow former intimates of Alexander, Ptolemy (his host in exile), Lysimachus, and Cassander of the great danger posed to them all by the ravening appetite of Antigonus. Seleucus was the convener and promoter of the opposition to Antigonus in what was about to become the Third War of the Diadochi, but he brought nothing to the party at this stage except his persuasive abilities and political skill, and considerable insight into the currents of men and events within Antigonus' Asiatic domain. Cassander controlled Macedonia, much of Greece, Athens, Epirus, and Thessaly, and Lysimachus, though he had a small army, controlled part of Thrace and both banks of the Dardanelles, and therefore the passage between the Black and Mediterranean Seas. Lysimachus had married Cassander's sister, Nicaea, the widow of Perdiccas and those two enjoyed an indissoluble alliance. Ptolemy was impregnable in Egypt and prosperous and had wisely chosen his prize early and avoided all the war-making, but he depended on Greek mercenaries. He had no forces of his own.

The Third War of the Diadochi effectively began with an ultimatum to Antigonus from the coalition of the four notable rivals: Cassander, Ptolemy, Lysimachus, and Seleucus. They demanded a proper sharing of the great trunk of the late empire: recognition of Ptolemy's right to Syria, which he had occupied since 319, restoration of Seleucus in Babylonia, Hellespontine Phrygia for Lysimachus, and Cassander would carve out Cappadocia, Paphhlagonia, and Cilicia. Seleucus must have been a formidable advocate indeed, as there was no chance that Antigonus would acquiesce in being cut off from the Black Sea and inner Asia and cooped up in Asia Minor between his four enemies. It would be like the three partitions of Poland two-thousand years later—Antigonus would just be partitioned out of existence. This was a nervy move against so formidable a man with such a powerful army, from three comparative youngsters, of whom only Cassander had graduated from the contemporary school of hard knocks, and was well-launched by his father, Antipater. Antigonus was a generation older—the others were Alexander's contemporaries and were in their forties.

Cassander, under the quadrumvirate's partition plan, would hold territory stretching Between Ptolemy's Syria and Lysimachus' Thrace, giving him both sides of the Aegean Sea, and to this end he moved forward a substantial force into Cappadocia. Antigonus did not wish to attack Cassander in Macedonia and leave himself vulnerable to a thrust in his rear and flank from Ptolemy, so his strategy was to await Cassander from a defensive position in strength, attack Ptolemy, and arrange harassments of Cassander and Lysimachus in Cappadocia and in the Peloponnese, where his commander was none other than the imperishable Polyperchon, who got his elephants back and conducted operations against Cassander from Corinth. Polyperchon had always resented Cassander's undermining of him after Antipater had favoured Polyperchon over his own son (Cassander), and Antigonus, who did not need much incentive to be annoyed at the quadrumvirate, was especially irritated at Cassander's rank ingratitude for the invaluable assistance Antigonus had given him by eliminating Eumenes and the entire loyalist operation in Asia, without which, Cassander might well have been unable to expel Polyperchon from Macedonia.

Antigonus retained a sizeable mobile reserve to deal, if necessary, with all fronts at once. He started by attacking Ptolemy in Syria in superior strength, and Ptolemy, seeing the force of Antigonus in the open field, garrisoned Tyre for a siege, sent the Phoenician fleet to Alexandria, and retreated in order into Egypt like a turtle withdrawing into his shell. Cassander invaded Arcadia and managed to entice Polyperchon's son to join him against his own father, such was the level of treachery of these Macedonian warlords. In practice, Polyperchon and Alexander did not actually square off-Alexander attacked Antigonus' Peloponnesian general Aristodemus and Polyperchon continued to side with Antigonus against anyone he encountered except his own son. With the Macedonian lieutenants of Alexander the Great disputing control of the Hellenic world the level of chicanery and double-dealing reached new depths of cynicism surpassing even the conduct of the original Greeks and Persians at their lowest levels of treachery.

Antigonus had gained the upper hand in the first round of the Third War of the Diadochi and pressed his advantage by a pair of shrewd escalations of the conflict. He began construction of a sizeable navy in Phoenicia, from ample stock of Lebanese cedar, in order to interdict his enemies in the Aegean and cut Ptolemy off from his allies. At the same time, he played the loyalist and legitimate cards (never mind that he had won a hard-fought victory over the redoubtable Eumenes who was leading the loyalist fight), and that he had uprooted and dispensed with any trace of Macedonian rule in his own domains. He made a 180 degree turn that was artistic even by the standards of these tortuous times and issued a proclamation that listed Cassander's crimes against Alexander's house and demanded the immediate liberation of "Queen Roxanne and King Alexander IV," and declared Cassander a public enemy if he did not release them and raze his revived Thebes and Cassandreia (in place of Olynthus), both cities Alexander had leveled for cause. His proclamation also declared that all Greek cities must be free, without garrisons, self-governing, and that Cassander must obey Antigonus as regent and general of the Macedonian Empire. This was, of course, preposterous coming from the leading disintegrationist of the Empire, but it strongly appealed to all those who revered Alexander, and after eight years of heavy warfare, that meant virtually every Macedonian and a great many others, and it pitched directly to the insuperable will to freedom and self-government of all the Greeks.

With one measure Antigonus was raising a Damaclean sword and with the other he was lighting a fire in dry straw right under Cassander's feet. The revival of Alexander's policy of treating the Greek states as free allies was enormously effective, and he rallied all Greek opinion except for the unrepresentative Cassandreian oligarchies. The tangled alliances had come full circle, as Antigonus, who had raised his standard against the royal family was now its champion, and as a man who did not care a rap for the freedom or welfare of any of the Greeks, he was an admired champion. Greece now tendered to Antigonus, who regarded all Greece with hostility or indifference, a confidence—an appreciation they had largely withheld from Alexander the Great because they regarded him as a foreign conqueror rather than as the greatest champion the Hellenic world had ever had. His proclamation, though it was less sincere, bore a slight tactical resemblance to Abraham Lincoln's Emancipation Proclamation in 1863, in the middle of the Civil War and governing slaves that were not in territory he occupied.

Antigonus needed thirteen months to reduce Tyre, against seven months for Alexander (but Antigonus never pretended to be as great a general as Alexander). His strategic acts and tactical enticement brought Rhodes over to alliance with its fleet and with his new construction, he had by the autumn of 314 a fleet of two-hundred and forty vessels, including the equivalent of super-dreadnoughts, heptiremes—seven men to an oar. His fleet was not at sea quickly enough to prevent Seleucus, the instigator of the war, who was now helping with the accomplishment of his plan (to regain his own satrapy) as commander of Ptolemy's fleet, from bringing some of the Cypriot kings into line with the quadrumvirate, but Antigonus did seize most of the Cyclades. His proffered alliance with the Greeks did not come without a price, as they were expected, as they exercised their freedom, to contribute to the war effort, and they did so. In Greece, Aristodemus, an ingenious commander of Antigonus' bridgehead in Greece, recruited the Aetolians, who had always hated Antipater and did not require over-lengthy argument to entertain the same attitude toward his son (Cassander). Polyperchon's wayward son, Alexander, paid the customary price for trickery on the scale he had practiced and was mysteriously murdered in the summer of 314. No one claimed responsibility for this act and practically all the protagonists including his father could have been so motivated.

Cassander was not to be discouraged easily and successfully carried his war into Glaucias and then Illyria, and he recruited the Acarnanians, but Antigonus' principal strategy of keeping his northern enemies occupied while he pressed Ptolemy was so far successful. In the autumn of 314, Cassander sent a force to Caria, but Antigonus' nephew, Polemaeus, who was his commander in Cappadocia, took his forces along the Ionian coast northwards welcoming the Greek cities into the alliance Antigonus had set up, and he routed Cassander's expeditionary army. Antigonus put his son Demetrius, already a proven talent, in charge of the army at Gaza threatening Ptolemy, and retired inland to winter. He had thoroughly frightened Ptolemy and won the skirmishes that had occurred and he was now ready to attack the main enemy: Macedonia.

Ptolemy had attempted a declaration freeing the Greek states, as Antigonus had, but this was nonsense as Cassander was busily suppressing Greek liberty when he could. Cyrene took Ptolemy literally and revolted against Ptolemy's occupation and he needed most of 313 to quell that uprising. Ptolemy was an astute cynic, but wallowing in the fabled luxury of the Pharaohs behind Greek mercenaries didn't equip him to match swords or wits with such a battle-tested and vehement adversary as Antigonus. Before he made his decisive assault on Europe, Antigonus launched expeditions to harry Cassander and Lysimachus: one thrust supported the Thracian cities on the Black Sea and set up a league and expelled Lysimachus' garrisons. One, under Docimus, former satrap of Babylon, freed Miletus and other Greek cities, and cleared most of Caria, and the third initiative, under another nephew of Antigonus, Telesphorus, attacked Cassander in Greece and freed the whole Peloponnese except Corinth.

The tide of war was now running fairly heavily in Antigonus' favour, and for good measure, Epirus, as if responding to the unquenchable spirit of Alexander's mother Olympias, rose up and expelled Cassander's forces. Cassander made overtures for peace, but Ptolemy, emboldened by the fact that Antigonus was no longer hammering on the gate of Egypt at Gaza, was opposed and Cassander regained his composure and energy and suppressed Epirus by force of arms unsentimentally applied, and he invaded Greece himself and besieged Histiaea in Euboea (which had revolted in response to Antigonus' proclamation. As always, it was not hard to raise the Greeks to war or revolt). Antigonus sent his nephew Polemaeus with fifty-five hundred men to Greece with a fleet and coordinated an attack with the Boeotians on Cassander's stronghold at Chalcis. This was a powerful diversionary attack that brought Cassander hastily over from Boeotia to repulse what he thought was Antigonus' main thrust.

What was really Antigonus' main assault was then attempted: he summoned his fleet north, marched along the Bosporus and sought from his Byzantine friends alliance and a safe passage of the Straits in the autumn of 313. Lysimachus rose to the occasion; he had recovered most of the Thracian cities from which he had been evicted and returned to defend the northern shore of the Dardanelles, looking more formidable than he had the previous year. He bullied Byzantium into strict neutrality. Antigonus had to withdraw, a clear disappointment though not exactly a defeat, but Polemaeus was emerging as one of the stars of this combat as he took Chalcis and left it ungarrisoned, a fact gratefully noted throughout Greece, and cleared the quadrumvirate out of all or most of Euboea, Phocis, Cadmea, Thebes, and Oropus. By the end of 313, Antigonus had clearly had the better of it. His son and nephews had all been outstanding and his advantage in a unitary command against four separate adversaries trying to coordinate their actions had been fully exploited. Cassander had lost most of Greece south of Thessaly and Athens was under threat (and the Athenian civic spirit may be assumed to have been very favourable to Antigonus' proclamation).

Cassander called urgently upon Ptolemy to do something to take the pressure off him. Ptolemy, aware that his own splendid domain on the Nile would be forfeit if Antigonus crushed his fellow quadrumvirs, attacked at Gaza. He had eighteen-thousand infantry and four-thousand cavalry to Demetrius' twelve-thousand, five-hundred infantry, only two-thousand Macedonians, forty-six hundred Asiatic cavalry, and forty-three elephants. Ptolemy had devised a barrier of iron stakes and chains to confound the elephants, and he soundly defeated Demetrius and Alexander the Great's favourite admiral Nearchus. Some of Demetrius' senior officers were killed and eight-thousand mercenaries surrendered. Demetrius was at the head of some cavalry and Ptolemy regained Syria and Phoenicia and gave land in Egypt to the mercenaries who had surrendered to him, moving them permanently out of the hands of Antigonus, though their reliability, as with most mercenaries, was always questionable. Ptolemy had managed a considerable military triumph, as the western flank of Antigonus' empire was now wide open. Seleucus with only a few thousand men, most of them collected en route, led a flying column to Babylon, where he had been a popular satrap and stormed the citadel, and beat off a counterattack of seventeen-thousand men led by Nicanor (the Cappadocian).

This was the beginning of the Seleucid era, a sweet, if rather tentative revenge for Seleucus, even if his allies in the quadrumvirate had not fared so well. Seleucus' forces grew and he proceeded on into Media and Susiana, where Antigonus' satrap had revolted. Antigonus reestablished some of his positions in the balance of 312, recovering Syria and Phoenicia, which Ptolemy did not have the forces to hold faced with Antigonus himself at the head of a sizeable army. Demetrius also redeemed himself by bagging seven-thousand prisoners from Ptolemy's army in one of these actions. On the negative side for Antigonus, he was unable to take advantage in the 312 fighting season of Cassander's entire preoccupation with another revolt in Epirus. Antigonus ordered a number of raids against Ptolemy, but they were neither successful nor serious failures. Demetrius, entrusted with the mission of leading a lightning strike against Babylon to try to capture Seleucus, as Seleucus had retaken Babylon, was successful in retaking the city, but Seleucus was absent in Media.

By 311 it was clear that neither side could defeat the other. They had conducted a general donnybrook that had wrought havoc from the gates of Egypt to Mesopotamia and throughout much of Asia Minor, Greece, Thrace, and Illyria. There was absolutely no point to any of it except the ambitions of individuals who had become significant in the known Western world because of the great man who had promoted them and had died prematurely. At least when Athens fought Sparta or the Greeks fought the Persians, or ancient Egypt or the people of Israel defended themselves, or even the Babylonians invaded their neighbours, there were some questions of ethnic and religious differences and systems of government or levels of cultural sophistication, as there had been in the conquests of Alexander the Great. But this was just naked personal ambition. The only note of reformed government was introduced by Antigonus to complicate the lives of his enemies, not because he cared for democracy or had any intention of practicing it, but out of profound tactical cynicism. It was a squalid war, but peace broke out.

Initially, Antigonus made peace with Cassander and Lysimachus. Ptolemy came along a little later, as was his custom, but Seleucus was excluded. He had done his best and done well as a warrior on land and sea for the war that he incited, but Antigonus was not about to give him back Babylon. However, Seleucus did round up about fifteen-thousand troops from the far eastern satrapies, which were vacant, and some veterans of Eumenes, and settled to the east of Mesopotamia and operated several satrapies there, always planning his return to Babylon. His status was not acknowledged in the peace agreement formally but was a fact that Antigonus was not inclined to try to change. The terms agreed were that Cassander would remain General in Europe until Alexander IV was old enough to rule (he was then only twelve). Lysimachus was to rule in Thrace, Ptolemy in Egypt and Antigonus in Asia, and Seleucus in east Asia (as it then was). All Greek cities were to be free and ungarrisoned. There was no realistic chance that Cassander would allow Alexander

IV to live to maturity—the peace agreement was his death warrant. This was also the formal division of the Empire. It was a fragile agreement and twelve years of slaughter had been required to get to this modest point.

Antigonus also secured a huge public opinion victory in the delivery of the free status of the Greek cities. In his public reflections, he said that he had only been moved to peace by his anxiety for the Greek cities. In sum, Seleucus rose from being a fugitive in Egypt to being the ruler of the eastern extremities of Alexander's conquests—he patched together, at the end of this Third War of the Diadochi, a reward for his having incited the others to war and was the big winner (the modern Iran-Afghanistan-Kashmir). Lysimachus had significantly increased in stature and territory. Antigonus, the intended victim, whom it had been intended to carve up like a Thanksgiving turkey, had held eighty per cent or more of what he had started with, strengthened his hold on much of it, had evicted Ptolemy from Syria and Phoenicia and had become the champion of the Greeks. Ptolemy had lost his possessions in the Near East but was secure in Egypt, and Cassander had been hard-pressed—he had reinforced his position in Macedonia and Epirus, had lost much of Greece, but had strengthened relations with Lysimachus.

Antigonus' capital was at Celaenae, and he had up to Armenia except for Bithynia all of Syria and east to Mesopotamia. It was most of the extent of the Persian Empire of Xerxes, except for Egypt. He had no satraps, only generals, but his government was not overly capricious or severe. Most of the territories he ruled were accustomed to being governed by foreigners and Antigonus was better than most, but there was no cultural or political rationale for his rule, just his ability to maintain and direct a large army and the civilian bureaucracy that ran the state the army maintained. He had a Council of Friends, but its authority was consultative, though Antigonus had sufficient judgment and self-confidence to ask the advice of competent people. Ptolemy was yet another interloper enjoying the grandiose monuments and lascivious pleasures of Egypt, a phenomenon the local population had been accustomed to for fifteen centuries. Seleucus was an Antigonus in the waiting, and Cassander, reduced largely to Macedonia, was at least a Macedonian, and he could play the patriotic card, though not necessarily with much credibility given the rather unscrupulous and supranational nature of his policy on behalf of his native country. Lysimachus was a Macedonian like the others, but Thrace was a closer place in all respects to Macedonia than any place in Asia or Africa was.

Antigonus maintained the client and vassal kings and lords, like the kings in Phoenicia and Mithridates of Cius (whom he executed for treason in 302, but his line continued). He gradually dispossessed and disposed of the Persian landowners and practiced a substantial land reform for the benefit of the local peasantry, which was appreciated. He settled Macedonian soldiers around his territory and maintained Alexander's financial administration and coinage. The Greek cities signed the peace of 311 in their own right, individually. As Cassander dominated most of Greece, he couldn't revitalize the League of Corinth, but recreated sectional leagues. Thus, the Ionian League, the League of Aeolian cities, headquartered at Alexander's Ilium, a League of Islanders, grouping together the Cyclades, centred at Delos, were all established. These leagues weren't really federal arrangements, apart from the setting up of festivals. Not altogether spontaneously, but not directly required by Antigonus, he was worshipped as a god by the islanders. With this feather in his helmet, he conferred upon himself a fluctuating right of interference, but not one that he much abused.

Antigonus founded a number of cities, most importantly Smyrna. He did collect a substantial "contribution" to help deal with accumulated war debts, from all the Greek cities in his alliances. He was a judicial reformer in the Ionian cities, and simplified trade between all the allies, except in the case of grain, which he bought as it was harvested, apart from what the farmers required for their families, and then sold, he claimed at his cost, but no one down to the lowest share-cropper believed that, to his own urban population and to his allies.

The four rulers of Alexander's former empire only gradually crept up to the title of king. First, they founded capitals in their own names; Seleucia on the Tigris, Lysimacheia near Gallipoli; Ptolemy was stuck with Alexandria, but made Ptolemais the capital of Upper Egypt. Antigonus waited until he was the king in 306 before renaming Orontes Antigoneia. They went on with Alexander's coinage until they installed themselves as kings, and then put their own profiles on the same coins. Cassander could hardly fail to recognize how desperately Macedonia needed peace and he set about rebuilding the country's prosperity and social stability with commendable energy. He gained allies in the modern Yugoslavia by defeating the Serbs and moving twenty-thousand of the Paeonians, whom he had assisted to the Thracian frontier to replace his own war casualties. He also mediated a successful reconciliation between Thebes and Plataea and saw several other small states through minor territorial adjustments, and reestablished Thebes as head of the Boeotian League. When Polemaeus, who governed Hellespontine Phrygia, declared his independence of Antigonus, as he had been ungenerously treated, he thought, by his uncle (Antigonus), Cassander recognized him but avoided direct provocation of Antigonus. Cassander's most important and odious initiative was in 309 when, with Alexander IV thirteen-years-old and some agitation for him to be brought forward, Cassander murdered him and his mother, Roxanne, and made no serious effort to disguise the enormity of his act. Given that he had been a school chum of Alexander the Great, had been well taken care of by him, independently of his father Antipater, who was always loyal to Alexander while he lived, this was an utterly evil and wicked act. The other rulers, Lysimachus, Antigonus, and Seleucus, though they had nothing to do with the murders, were also serving in Alexander IV's name and must bear some blame for not only doing nothing to prevent or at least discourage this end but moved with gleeful haste to change the coinage and official styles of address to affirm their own kingship.

Possibly as reciprocity for Cassander's encouragement of Polemaeus' revolt in Hellespontine Phrygia, Antigonus engaged the timeless Polyperchon, now a soldier of fortune who governed Corinth and a few other places, to harass Cassander; he gave him some money to raise a mercenary army and attack Cassander, and with the same ingenuity with which he had set himself up as the protector of Greek liberty, Antigonus also sent a boy (from Pergamon) to Cassander to represent as a pretender to the Macedonian throne. This was young Heracles, supposedly the illegitimate child of Alexander with one of the comely women taken prisoner at Issus. The fact that the years didn't work on the calendar did not prevent the Macedonian population from stirring and agitating for their real king.

Murdering the undisputed child and heir, and widow, of a beloved and worshipped warrior king who was the most awe-inspiring person the world had ever seen at this point (and he remains one of them twenty-three centuries later), is not an image-builder, and Cassander had to pay some price for his sadistic and treacherous effrontery. With Antigonus' money, Polyperchon put together an army of twenty-one thousand and invaded Macedonia in 309, claiming to be restoring the royal house of Philip and Alexander. Cassander's cunning and ethical vacuum where most people even in this rugged peer group might have some scrupulosity, served him effectively; he urgently requested a meeting with Polyperchon and persuaded him that if he succeeded, it would be after a terrible bloodbath, that his false claim (invented, scripted, and live person supplied by Antigonus) was sure to come to light, that even if he won and survived the strife and upheaval he would be a virtual vassal of Antigonus, and offered him the generalship of the Peloponnese and a position of lieutenant governor to Cassander. Doubtless there was a handsome tangible payment as well. Polyperchon accepted, stood down his improvised army and His young Majesty Heracles was quietly murdered, and the royalist cause went with him. Cassander had correctly foreseen that Polyperchon could not admit that he had raised Macedonian opinion on a false claim of royal succession, so it was agreed that poor Heracles died inexplicably of a legitimate illness.

Antigonus didn't become directly involved because he was trying to evict Seleucus from Babylon. Ptolemy, sensing an opportunity to take back some of what he had lost in the Third War of Succession, declared war on Antigonus on behalf of Seleucus and himself. His fleet attacked Cilicia, but was beaten off by Demetrius, his father's commander in Asia Minor. Ptolemy's fleet moved on to Cyprus, where it barricaded King Nicocles, an ally of Antigonus, into the fortress at Paphos, and eventually drove Nicocles and his family to suicide rather than surrender, and Ptolemy regained Cyprus, and his brother, Menelaus, became the governor. He seized some bases from the sea in Asia Minor in 309, but Demetrius defeated him. Antigonus had not succeeded in removing Seleucus from Babylon, and at the end of 309, peace broke out again. Cassander had stabilized his position; Ptolemy had gained Cyprus. Antigonus had the uprising in Hellespontine Phrygia to deal with, and Seleucus was thoroughly unsubdued. What happened next was not a peace, just an armistice.

Ptolemy spent the winter of 309-308 in Cos, siring a son, Ptolemy II as he would become. This was the son of Berenice, not of Ptolemy's other wife, Cassander's sister Eurydice. Relations were cooling between Cassander and Ptolemy, and the demotion of Cassander's sister in Ptolemy's household would contribute to this. Ptolemy also felt that Cassander had deserted him in 311. It was, relatively speaking, a quarrel between thieves, as, in general, Seleucus, Lysimachus, and Antigonus were less prone to abrupt and complete betrayals than Cassander and Ptolemy. At this point, Polemaeus, who had rendered considerable service to his uncle, Antigonus, and been rewarded with the governorship in Hellespontine Phrygia, and then resented his uncle's treatment of him and declared his independence and accepted Cassander's assistance, made a terrible mistake: he defected from Cassander as well and had to flee his province and offered his services to Ptolemy. Someone such as Polyperchon could move back and forth between two parties, but unless it was very carefully prepared or accomplished on a very slow schedule, it was very dangerous to ricochet between three main parties in a continuing conflict. Polemaeus arrived at Ptolemy's headquarters and was unceremoniously executed as worthlessly unreliable: an ingrate to his uncle and a defector from his uncle's chief opponent. As we have often seen, one false step in this company generally led to the radical amputation of the headsman's axe. In Polemaeus' case, it need not have ended like this.

Ptolemy had conceived the ambition of controlling Greece as it drifted away from alliance with Cassander. He now determined to raise his standing in the general affray by marrying the sister of Alexander the Great, Cleopatra. In resume, she was Alexander's only full sibling, and was married off by Philip II to Alexander of Epirus for political reasons, and it was at this sumptuous wedding that Philip II was assassinated. Her husband, Alexander of Epirus died gallantly in Italy fighting for the Greek interest. Leonnatus, as early contender for the succession proposed himself to her for marriage and claimed to have been accepted but died in the Lamian War (first section of this Chapter) en route to Epirus, where Cleopatra was reigning queen in the Epirote custom. Thereafter, her hand was sought by Cassander, Lysimachus, and Antigonus (apart from Seleucus, who could hardly have imagined he could lure her to Afghanistan, this was a complete tour of the contenders). But she was stand-offish, and it was her decision alone. She was semi-imprisoned in Sardes, and tentatively accepted Ptolemy's proposal, a considerable upward socio-dynastic move for him.

However, Antigonus, in the most objectively despicable act of his career, easily surpassing the gratuitous and self-damaging execution of Eumenes, had Cleopatra intercepted and murdered by her court ladies. Aware of how great an atrocity he was committing, he constructed an elaborate fraud that the court entourage had cooked this up themselves and executed them all with some window-dressing of judicial trappings, and gave Cleopatra a grand funeral, professing himself to lead the mourners. Fifteen years after the death of the greatest man in history up to this time, Cassander, a classmate, had murdered the mother, wife, and son of Alexander the Great, and Antigonus, a protégé of Alexander the Great's father and of his, had murdered his sister. In all history there has not been such a macabre and profoundly criminal disposal of the family of a great monarch and military commander. In the contemporary sweepstakes of wickedness, Antigonus moved into second place behind Cassander, though in other and more respectable fields of competition, he was a far superior general and ruler. The end of Alexander the Great's family was a ghastly sequence of heinous crimes that surpassed in fact anything that would be imagined by Shakespeare or Wagner.[6]

Ptolemy soldiered on in his mission without his eminent betrothed. In the spring of 308 he crossed the Aegean and liberated Andros from the garrison Polemaeus

---

6 Probably only the murder of the entire royal family of the last Russian Czar bears comparison, and Nicholas II was not remotely of the stature of Alexander the Great.

had left there (not such a challenging feat as he had already relieved the garrison of its commander), and landed at the isthmus, proclaiming, like General MacArthur walking ashore at Lingayen Gulf in the Philippines in 1944, that he was the champion of Greek freedom. Polyperchon was absent but his daughter, Cratesipolis, handed over Corinth and Sicyon, and Ptolemy garrisoned them in the name of Greece. This was then finally exposed as a farce confected in Ptolemy's sun-raddled mind while basking beside the Nile. Antigonus had established himself as the champion of Greek freedom and had achieved his goals in feats of arms while Ptolemy was in league with the sinister Cassander, who whatever his other trumperies and crimes, never held himself out as any great Hellenophile. Ptolemy's invitation to the Isthmian Games was ignored by all recipients. He had intended to follow it up by claiming to revive the League of Corinth with himself as president, but finally took the hint. Something of a laughingstock of the Eastern Mediterranean, he packed up his cards, embarked his Corinthian garrison for Cyrene, relinquished his status to Polyperchon, a scoundrel but at least not delusional, and established the rejected Berenice's son Magas, as governor of Cyrene in a peace gesture to Cassander.

CHAPTER FIFTEEN

THE WARS OF SUCCESSION TO ALEXANDER II: 308-275 B.C.

SELEUCUS AND PTOLEMY

Bust of Seleucus (Roman bronze)

Bust of Ptolemy I (Greek original)

1. The Fourth War of the Diadochi, 308-301

IT WAS NOW TIME for Antigonus again. It was 308 B.C., he was seventy-six; he had been the victim and respondent in the Third War of the Diadochi, and he would turn the tables and try to reconstitute Alexander's empire in the Fourth War of the Diadochi. It had a symmetricality: Alexander died very prematurely and Antigonus was the great and venerable survivor, and he had a brilliant, charismatic, and altruistic son in Demetrius, who did actually admire Greek culture and believed in Greek Union and its civilizing mission. Demetrius was also, however, extremely vain and even at the age of twenty-nine and by the indulgent standards of the time, was wantonly and unfeasibly licentious. These characteristics need not have been an insurmountable obstacle to his success and were in any case subject to rectification by his father, whom all the world then knew to be capable of severe leadership. Antigonus' plan was that as he could not cross the Dardanelles in the face of Lysimachus, whose alliance with Cassander was as strong as ever, he would try to raise Greece in revolt by enticements and inducements at arm's length, distracting Cassander, while invading Ptolemy's bucolic Nile fastness and giving Ptolemy what Antigonus considered his well-deserved come-uppance. Then, he would proceed to Greece with full control of the sea and invade Macedonia from Greece. He assumed that Lysimachus and Seleucus would then take the hint and get in line without much need for additional persuasion. If Cassander was sinister and evil, Ptolemy was sleazy and hypocritical. Antigonus was hardly immune from criticism himself, but he was a reasonably enlightened ruler and if not unfailingly a man of his word, was not as compulsively treacherous as Cassander, and not as delusionally egocentric as Ptolemy. Antigonus retained some regard, if also some animosity, for Seleucus and Lysimachus.

Athens had been ruled more or less on behalf of Cassander, it was to this that Athens had been reduced, by Demetrius of Phalerum. He presided over an orderly oligarchy, wealth was protected, there was scarcely a hint of any democracy, and the regime was maintained by the Macedonian army. This Demetrius was a learned and intelligent man, and admirer of Aristotle who had made his successor, Theophrastus, leader of the Peripatetics, the virtual official pedagogue of Athens. The city was peaceful and prosperous, and not at all oppressively governed. He was a decent and reasoned ruler who enacted laws that carefully reflected the Aristotelian and Theophrastic theory that all must be treated fairly and all must accept a degree of lawful imposition of norms of conduct. This Demetrius somewhat resembled Solon as author of a society of sensible and evenly enforced, clearly enacted laws.

He lived somewhat opulently and even self-indulgently himself, which relieved his regime of the taint of prudery, but he passed sumptuary laws reducing the extravagance of festivals and public marriages, and regulated the public comportment of people, especially women. He restored the moral authority of the Areopagus, and he implemented a board of seven "guardians of the law" to consolidate and administer statutes. He pleased the poor by ending conscription for military service and satisfied the rich by radically reducing expenses on the army and navy.

The Assembly met and debated freely but was effectively dominated by the guardians of the law and rarely passed decrees. He ruled as general until 309, and then became the archon to govern the reform of festivals and public entertainments. Demetrius faithfully upheld his initial general amnesty and all shadings of political opinion operated and spoke freely, including ultra-democrats such as Demosthenes' nephew Demochares. He conducted a census that enumerated a population of one-hundred and twenty thousand, including twenty-one thousand citizens and ten-thousand metics, and an unstated number of slaves. The most important intellectual event of his time in office was the arrival in Athens of the Cypriot Phoenician Zeno, founder of the school of Stoical philosophy. Demetrius was a proconsul of great integrity, good sense, and enlightenment more so than would have been expected from Cassander.

Antigonus opened his campaign in June 307, when his son, Demetrius sailed at the head of two-hundred and fifty ships to Piraeus and found the booms up, entered the harbor, made the customary proclamation on such occasions that he had come to restore freedom and its constitution to Athens. The garrison of Piraeus retreated to Munychia; Demetrius of Phalerum had no mandate or inclination to make war, and handed Athens over to Antigonus' son Demetrius and under a safe-conduct from Antigonus withdrew to Thebes and then to Egypt where he helped found the Egyptology Museum and advised Ptolemy on legal matters. He lived pleasantly on for another twenty-fie years in Egypt, dying peacefully at age seventy, universally respected by contemporaries and posterity (though Hegel was slightly carried away in claiming that he was worshipped as a god, a conclusion he reached by misreading Plutarch). Demetrius stormed and destroyed Munychia and entered Athens unopposed. The Athenians had had almost no political liberty for fifteen years and responded to this astonishing development by greeting the incoming Demetrius and his father over the water as gods to be worshipped while the Athenian government fell into the hands of the most irresponsible demagogues, in particular Stratocles, a completely unscrupulous and corrupt rabble-rouser.

With the taste of the contemporary left for worshipful adulation of strongmen that persisted into recent and current times, Demetrius and his father (Antigonus) were hailed and worshipped as "savior gods," with their own altars and religious festivals. Gilded statues of them were erected on sacred ground, their portraits were embroidered into the gown of Athena at the Parthenon. Athens determined that only religious envoys could approach Demetrius and Antigonus, and on the place where Demetrius on entering Athens descended from his chariot, an altar was raised to "Demetrius the Descender," and he was beseeched to give oracles. Two new tribes were established and legitimized (if somewhat arbitrarily composed): Antigonus and Demetrius. It was instant deification and somewhat presaged the servility with which the modern left groveled to Stalin and Mao Tse-tung, including eminent beneficiaries of freedom of expression and ideas such as George Bernard Shaw.

The new Demetrius assured that there would be no bloodshed in his revolution and the statutes of Demetrius of Phalerum were retained, though the "guardians of the law" were dismissed. Cassander's principal supporters were banished but not otherwise disturbed. Stratocles was elevated and posed as the continuator of Lycurgus and the office of Superintendent of Administration was established to direct finances with powers similar to those of Lycurgus, and the first occupant of the post was Lycurgus' son Habron. The intellectual tide turned against Theophrastus, who was exiled, and philosophers had to be licensed by the Council and Assembly; but after a year, this law was found to be illegal and Theophrastus and the Peripatetics returned. Epicurus also then came from Lampsacus to Athens and established his school. Lemnos rejoined Athens and Antigonus sent it one-hundred and fifty thousand bushels of grain and the timber to build one-hundred warships. Demetrius ordered all the "free cities" of Greece to join Athens in its agitation to be rid of the Macedonian tyranny (which Antigonus, of course, had helped to impose) and having, as he and his father devoutly hoped, set Athens on a path to a Pan-Hellenic war of distraction against Cassander and Macedonia, Demetrius departed Athens, and in the spring of 306 he sailed for Cyprus with one-hundred and eighteen warships and transports carrying fifteen-thousand, four-hundred soldiers to bring his father's war home to Ptolemy.

Antigonus and Demetrius thought Ptolemy would have to fight to hang onto Cyprus. He also might have had a thought about living down the fiasco of his attempt to rally the Greeks from Corinth as the uninvited guest of Polyperchon's daughter. Antigonus and Demetrius asked the collaboration of Rhodes, but given the value of the trade with Egypt, it stuck to perfect neutrality. Menelaus had had sixty warships and twelve-thousand, eight-hundred infantry for the defence of Cyprus for Ptolemy, and Demetrius landed and defeated him on land and shut his fleet up in Salamis, blocking the harbor exit with only ten ships. As Antigonus and Demetrius had calculated, Ptolemy then sailed for Salamis to relieve Menelaus, with his remaining fleet, one-hundred and forty ships and transports carrying ten-thousand mercenaries. Demetrius had seven heptaremes, the naval equivalent of elephants, and Ptolemy had none, though he outnumbered Demetrius in warships, one-hundred and forty to one-hundred and eight, not counting transports, of which Demetrius had fifty-seven that were armoured. Demetrius had his right close to shore and loaded his left with his heavy ships. Ptolemy engaged all along the line, but Demetrius's large vessels farther out to sea drove in Ptolemy's right and pressed in on Ptolemy's centre and drove the fleet ashore. It was a bone-crushing defeat: Ptolemy lost one-hundred and twenty out of his one-hundred and forty warships, while transports carrying eight-thousand mercenaries were captured, subjected to the blunt suasion of their captor, and professed to change sides, in the manner of defeated mercenaries. Salamis and the sixty ships in it surrendered without further action and Antigonus held the scepter of the sea and he and his successor would hold it for a whole generation. On receipt of the news of Demetrius' victories, Antigonus proclaimed Demetrius and himself to be kings and the pretense of governing in the name of the late king of Macedonia and his now illegitimate and usurpatory heirs was cast aside. The effect of this was to lay down Antigonus' claim to govern the entire domain of Alexander, and he meant to achieve this in practice and he and Demetrius were off to a flying start by inflicting on Ptolemy such a heavy defeat. They claimed to have succeeded on the death of Alexander seventeen years before and acquiesced happily in being declared as and worshipped as gods in the Cyclades and Samos. Ptolemy was bottled up in Egypt, practically without ships and with only Rhodes as his commercial source for timber to replace his fleet. As he could no longer maintain contact with it, he relinquished Corinth to Cassander.

Antigonus struck while the iron was hot and made a decisive move for Ptolemy's jugular, to finish off one of his enemies. He invaded Egypt at the head of an army of eighty-eight thousand with eighty-three elephants, the largest army in Greek history, and the largest commanded by anyone who spoke Greek, in prior history and up to the Twentieth Century A.D. Demetrius commanded the very large fleet that blockaded Egypt on the Mediterranean side. It was November, and foul weather scattered a number of Demetrius' ships.

Even Antigonus, though a very experienced and capable general much admired by his men, had difficulty managing such a large force. They got to the Nile, after demoralizing sandstorms and some shortages of rations, but were not able to cross quickly and it was not possible to bring Demetrius' ships up river to help the crossing. Finally, after Ptolemy had begun energetic seduction by bribery of outer units of Antigonus' army, they retreated to Syria for the winter, undefeated but clearly thoroughly unsuccessful. Ptolemy ponced about pretending that he had routed the treacherous bully Antigonus, declared himself king of the Macedonian Empire as of the death of Alexander, as did Cassander, Lysimachus, and Seleucus also, and Ptolemy instituted the state worship of Alexander the Great (a more credible god than many that Egypt had had in the previous two-thousand years). Egypt was a large and inaccessible country by Middle Eastern standards, with good natural frontiers, and Ptolemy had mounted the sort of defense that many centuries later served genuinely large countries, China and Russia, well. But strategically, Antigonus had sustained a setback.

He compounded it by squandering the year 305, his seventy-sixth year of life, trying to subdue Rhodes. Rhodes supplied Egypt with ship-timber from the Black Sea, but Demetrius had cut off Ptolemy's source of good sailors (Cyprus). Antigonus should not have sent Demetrius with two-hundred warships and one-hundred and seventy transports, carrying the astounding total of forty-thousand troops and crews of thirty-thousand, in disreputable alliance with all the pirates of the Eastern Mediterranean who detested Rhodes as the principal and least corruptible police of the sea, to capture a secondary target while his real and stronger enemies armed themselves to the teeth. Rhodes became the classic doughty little adversary (Belgium in 1914, Finland in 1940). The entire adult male population was mobilized, slaves were emancipated, and two inner walls were built to deepen the defense.

Demetrius attacked the harbor with warships advancing behind a floating ironclad boom, and seized the mole, but two assaults were repulsed, and the Rhodians broke up the boom and took back the mole. Demetrius levelled the ground in an accessible place up to the outer wall and brought in his astonishing and unique Helepolis, "Taker of Cities," an immense armoured tower built in nine stages with mechanically controlled windows through which scores of stone throwers and catapults fired. It was one-hundred and eighty feet tall, required a thousand men to operate it and weighed nearly two-hundred tons. At its base were eight "tortoises," shielding sappers. It was accompanied by four armoured rams one-hundred and eighty feet long and had arms that could be dangled over targets and discharge inflammable or boiling objects on defenders. The Rhodians managed to set fire to the Helepolis, firing twenty-three hundred flaming missiles at it on the last night of this part of the action alone.

Demetrius then tried a silent surprise attack, but this was beaten off, and he settled into a blockade. But faster Rhodian cruisers played havoc with his cumbersome supply ships, and Demetrius could not enforce an airtight blockade, so it was not going to work in any feasible time. Finally, Antigonus, who was never too proud to acknowledge failure, told Demetrius to make peace and an Aetolian mission mediated an agreement, which Antigonus could have had without a fight: Rhodes became an ally of Antigonus except that it would be neutral opposite Egypt because of their commercial relations (which is what Antigonus had wanted to interdict). This was agreed in the spring of 304. If Athens had been a success for Antigonus and Demetrius, and Cyprus and Salamis a smart victory; Egypt had been a disappointment for

Antigonus, and Rhodes had been a sound and humbling defeat at the hands of a secondary power the King of Asia should not have bothered with at all.

There was at least a considerable level of chivalry in this operation. The Rhodians did not destroy, remove, or even desecrate or cover the statues of Antigonus; there were regular exchanges of prisoners, and Demetrius was very careful about historic buildings and works of art as targets for his catapults. Demetrius did manage to loot some outer areas and donated ten per cent of their value to Thebes, while the Rhodians sold the engines of war that Demetrius had left behind to build the only victory monument in history to be proclaimed, as it deserved to be, a wonder of the world: the world-famous Colossus of Rhodes, a statue of the Greek sun-god Helios beside the entrance to the harbor of Rhodes. It was about one-hundred and ten feet high, approximately the height of the Statue of Liberty, which was built of steel components in France twenty-two hundred years later and shipped to the United States for the centenary of the American Revolution in 1876 and erected in New York Harbour.

While this struggle was in progress, Athens had been engaged in the Four Years' War (307-4) against Cassander, who had been distracted by his eviction from Epirus by the formidable Illyrian King Glaucias of the Taulantii (ruled 335-302), who installed the young Pyrrhus as king of Epirus. At first the Athenians did well and defeated Cassander at Elatea when led by Olympiodors, but after the defeat of Antigonus in Egypt, Cassander was able to devote greater forces to taming the Athenians, and invaded Attica and took Salamis, while the inexhaustible Polyperchon, now allied to Cassander again, set about reconquering the Peloponnese. It was partly to assist Athens that Antigonus finally called off his ill-conceived attack on Rhodes, almost a micro-reenactment of the catastrophic Athenian attack on Syracuse more than a century before.

Demetrius arrived with three-hundred and thirty warships and transports to assist Athens and he soon stabilized affairs in Attica. He landed in Cassander's rear at Aulis and defeated him at Thermopylae, freed Euboea and Boeotia, revived the Aetolian alliance and restored to Athens what Cassander had taken from it. It did not redeem the fiasco in Egypt or the debacle at Rhodes, but it did reestablish the point that Antigonus remained the first among the Diadochi, even if he did not possess the ability to suppress the others and occupy the whole extent of the Macedonian Empire. Only Alexander could do that.

Demetrius had commanded admirably, but from this point, his judgment and conduct declined. Athens welcomed him as a deliverer, but he spent the winter in the Parthenon, reminded the Athenians that they rightly considered him a god and that he was Athena's younger brother. He turned the Maiden's Temple into a brothel, and with his notoriously profligate mistress, Lamia, whom he demanded be worshipped as Aphrodite. The better elements among the democrats began to form an opposition to the low demagogue Stratocles, who was just the obsequious mouthpiece of Demetrius' regime of unhinged debauchery and sacrilege. Demetrius began interfering in the government of Athens, which Antigonus had determined not to do, and in 303, Demetrius suppressed a revolt against Stratocles, who took his cue in matters of personal dissolution and corruption from his master. Demetrius exiled

Demosthenes' nephew, the admirable Demochares, and Stratocles caused the servile civic government to adopt a decree that whatever Demetrius commanded was automatically and incontestably for the benefit of the population and to the taste of the gods. In 303, Demetrius had liberated almost all central Greece and moved on the Peloponnese, where Polyperchon had had a good start. Once at campaign, Demetrius recovered his positive powers and drove Cassander's forces out of Corinth, Achaea, and all of Arcadia except Mantinea. He married Pyrrhus' sister, Deidameia, an ingratiating gesture to the locals. He claimed the succession, for Greek purposes, to Alexander the Great, as his wife had once been betrothed to Alexander IV, and he called a Pan-Hellenic conference at the Isthmus and revived the League of Corinth. Thessaly, Sparta, and Messenia were absent, but most of the rest were present. Demetrius was naturally elected general, filling the chair, vacant for twenty years since the death of Alexander the Great, and his and his father Antigonus' likenesses would now be on the coinage. The Corinthians invited him to garrison Corinth (an honour recently confided to Polyperchon on behalf of Ptolemy), and he did so.

The first part of Antigonus' strategy had worked: pushing the Macedonians out of Greece, largely by the actions of the Greeks. Cassander was now under heavy pressure and made peace overtures to Antigonus, who demanded unconditional surrender. As usually happened in Greece, the winning side over-played its hand. This would be Cassander's finest hour. He called on his old ally Lysimachus and it was decided to try to resurrect the quadrumvirate and advise Ptolemy and Seleucus what must be the result for them if Antigonus overran Macedonia: one after the other, they would be eliminated by Antigonus. Ptolemy agreed, but it was difficult to connect with Seleucus because Antigonus blocked all the routes. Ptolemy mastered this by sending dispatch riders on fast camels across the Arabian desert to Jauf, whence they eventually reached Babylon. Seleucus came aboard and they concerted a plan. The original coalition of 315 was resurrected, but not just to partition to themselves chunks of Antigonus' empire; now they were aiming to be rid of the seventy-eight-year-old, one-eyed warlord and king, and his talented but degenerate son with him.

The Fourth War of the Diadochi was unleashed in the spring of 302. Demetrius struck north from Greece into Thessaly with fifty-seven thousand, five-hundred men, eight-thousand Macedonians, fifteen-thousand mercenaries, twenty-five thousand in contingents from the revived League of Corinth, eight-thousand pirates, and just fifteen-hundred cavalry. Cassander had expected some such move and had already concerted a defensive plan with Lysimachus. Lysimachus, with Seleucus, had been the big winner in the thirteen years since 315. While Cassander had been cut back and pressed in Macedonia and lost Greece and Epirus, and Antigonus had added Cyprus but lost the eastern satrapies to Seleucus, but picked up the suzerainty of Greece. Seleucus, who had nothing but grievances and a scheme in 315, had regained Babylon and everything east through and beyond what is today Iran. But Lysimachus had shown almost as much skill as a general as Antigonus at his best possessed, and had quietly almost doubled the population of Thrace, which he ruled efficiently, and without the gratuitous cruelty of Cassander or the decadence of Demetrius.

The plan the other four kings had concerted went into effect when Demetrius moved forward. Cassander took up a strong defensive position on slightly higher ground immediately in front of Demetrius with thirty-one thousand men barring his way in to Macedonia. The two armies eyed each other as Cassander anxiously waited for the first and second parts of the agreed quadrumviral plan to be triggered. On schedule, Lysimachus crossed the Dardanelles just as Seleucus attacked westward with a strong army led by five-hundred elephants. This was an astounding force that Seleucus had acquired from Chandragupta, the great Indian king who built the great Mauryan Empire between 321 and 297 B.C., that spanned the northern half of the Indian sub-continent. As Seleucus moved east to take over the Indian satrapies of Alexander the Great, he found Chandaguptra too militarily formidable to reestablish the old borders and ceded everything east of Kabul in exchange for comprehensive peace and trade and five-hundred camels, and with his eastern border secure, as Cassander's was with Lysimachus, Seleucus asserted himself thoroughly over the Alexandrine satrapies between the Indus in the east and the Tigris in the west, roughly, today, Iraq, Iran, Turkmenistan, Uzbekistan, and half of Afghanistan.

It is not recorded how Lysimachus got his army across the Dardanelles, though corruption of officials at the edge of Antigonus' empire is suspected. Antigonus had placed garrisons in some of the Dardanelles cities and there was considerable resentment of Antigonus' heavy hand. Lampsacus was one that revolted at once, and two of Antigonus' generals Docimus of Phrygia, once a comrade of Perdiccas, and Phoenix of Lydia, once Eumenes' lieutenant, committed treason against Antigonus. It may be assumed that Lysimachus, being nearby, crafty, and patient, had discovered soft points in the Antigonid realm and exploited them.

Antigonus was holding a festival at Antigoneia when he learned of Lysimachus' crossing. Lysimachus' able general Prepalaus conducted a virtual Blitzkrieg along the coast to Ionia, rolling over the Ionian cities in quick succession: "After many years, Antigonus' severities recoiled on his head,"[1] as much of Ionia, including Ephesus, eagerly surrendered, and Phoenix surrendered the former Persian capital of Sardes as soon as Lysimachus' forces were close enough to receive his unconditional submission (at least no public conditions—Phoenix was presumably incentivized). Docimus similarly surrendered Phrygia and its fortresses, treasure houses, and storage centers as soon as Lysimachus crossed his border. Antigonus responded swiftly as he always had and could have been in no doubt of the gravity of the challenge he faced. He sent a flying column to occupy Babylon behind the back of Seleucus, who was proceeding on a more northerly course at the head of his elephants and the rest of his army. Antigonus mobilized his main army and proceeded as quickly as he could against Lysimachus, and he ordered the retreat of Demetrius. He was reorganizing his forces along interior lines and proposing to defeat Lysimachus, Selucus, Cassander, and Ptolemy in sequence. All parties seemed to be agreed that this had to be the end of these terribly destructive wars of the Diadochi. Antigonus almost surrounded Lysimachus at consecutive points, including Heraclea, but the wily Thracian slipped away, twice at night and once in a storm. At Heraclea, which was governed by Dionysius' widow, the Achaemenid (Persian royal house) Amestris, Lysimachus, taking a belt-and-braces approach to his security, married his hostess

---

1 CAH, VI, p. 503 (W.W. Tarn).

Amestris, and was doubly installed.

Demetrius, on his father's request for his return, made a peace with Cassander that effectively left Greece independent of Cassander but secure in Macedonia. Demetrius left Deidameia and part of his fleet at Athens and sailed with Pyrrhus (who had been evicted from Epirus by yet another revolution—it was as if Olympias was still setting the political ambiance of her native land—and Demetrius reoccupied Ephesus and the Dardanelles cities, made an alliance with Byzantium, and finally dominated the straits, but long after Lysimachus had established himself solidly in Asia. Demetrius did intercept Cassander's brother Pleistarchus in the Black Sea, transporting twelve-thousand troops as reinforcements for Lysimachus and drowned about half of them and drove off the others. Demetrius wintered at Ephesus; none of these would-be successors to Alexander the Great was prepared to try to replicate Alexander's practice of braving the elements in the winter and conducting surprise offensives against their enemies. Ptolemy invaded Syria, in the spring of 301, but retired on the false information that Lysimachus had been defeated.

Lysimachus departed Heraclea at the same time, his army now forty-thousand well-tested men, and joined with Seleucus, who ignored Antigonus' capture of Babylon and met Lysimachus in north Phrygia, as Demetrius' main army joined with Antigonus' army at Ipsus. Here one of the decisive battles of ancient history was fought in the late spring of 301 B.C. Antigonus, now eighty-one years old, undefeated in any battle where he commanded in a career of more than fifty years as a general officer, was formidable as always and his son was at the peak of his talents and determination. Facing them were Lysimachus and Seleucus, comrades and contemporaries of Alexander the Great, and clever generals also, in battle as in political maneuver. All knew that the stakes were almost the entire known western world. Antigonus had seventy-thousand infantry, ten-thousand cavalry, and seventy-five elephants; the allies had sixty-four thousand infantry, ten-thousand, five-hundred cavalry, one-hundred and twenty scythe-axle chariots, and four-hundred and eighty elephants. Demetrius opened the battle by leading a full cavalry charge from Antigonus' right that over-powered Seleucus' defending cavalry and started to roll up the alliance's left, but Demetrius became separated from the main body of his father's army and Seleucus moved his elephants into the gap, blocking Demetrius' return and leaving Antigonus with an inferior force to the combined armies of Lysimachus and Seleucus that now invested him, and gradually, in more than four hours of heavy fighting, enveloped Antigonus. He personally led the resistance with his traditional valour and coolness, but the allied archers rained arrows down on the phalanx, and finally, when within range, the javelin forces impaled and killed Antigonus with three direct hits. His last words were allegedly that "Demetrius will save me."

Antigonus did not learn the lesson that many centuries later came easily to Richelieu and Bismarck, of the necessity of not provoking too many states against you; more exalted figures of later ages also failed to see this, especially Napoleon. Frederick the Great hovered on the edge of trespass in this area and the monstrously evil Hitler would vastly transgress, while the equally wicked Stalin would prudently stop short of it. This is the danger of aggression—until it becomes legitimate it is likely to attract great resistance. Antigonus was as legitimate as his peers. When he was facing just Lysimachus, Cassander, and Ptolemy and on the defensive, he held them off. When he attacked them, it was a draw. But when he demanded unconditional surrender from Cassander while ignoring the resurrected Seleucus and was attacked by all four, he was crushed and all trace of him vanished. When there is no ideological, cultural, or ethnic basis to these inter-state quarrels, only the ambitions of leaders playing with the lives of their forces, a slight change of fortune can quickly become a rockslide. Ptolemy and Cassander, at least, could claim some cultural distinctness for their states, as well as comparative geographic inaccessibility. Alexander the Great had built his empire on his genius and his vision of Pan-Hellenic enlightenment and democracy and integrated government, concepts that could lift the spirits of men. When he died, warlords scrambled over his leavings for forty years with no thought to anything but what they could take and hold on to, and murdered the late king's entire family into the bargain, to try to establish some legitimacy for their inadequate selves.

Antigonus had had a remarkable career, stretching back to the early campaigns of Philip II, and other than dying in victory, doubtless departed life as he would have wished, resisting his enemies as he had resisted everything and everyone except the two great kings he had served with prodigious distinction. Antigonus was a very capable general, with Antipater, Eumenes, and Lysimachus and Seleucus and Philip himself, surpassed in the Fourth Century B.C. only by Alexander (who has had very few peers in all of history—Hannibal, Julius Caesar, Napoleon, and only two or three others). Antigonus had been a reasonably enlightened ruler, who governed without great severity but also without more than an old soldier's relative lack of imagination; he maintained everything well enough, but was not a great builder or improver, wasn't much interested in the arts or culture, and was a cynical old campaigner who had no particular vision, unlike Alexander, of what he wanted to make out of his vast jurisdiction. He pretended an interest in Greece but in fact despised them, as most Macedonians did, as effete and pretentious little states that had spent centuries in foolish wars that they fought bravely but not well. He was not overly severe or especially treacherous by his lights, but the completely uncalled for murder of Eumenes permanently darkened his reputation, and the cold-blooded murder of his late chief's widow and legitimate heir, aged fourteen, was a wicked and evil act that has deprived him of much sympathy he might otherwise have earned from posterity by his many decades of always capable and courageous, but rarely brilliant, service. But he was revered by his followers. Lysimachus and Seleucus gave Antigonus a royal funeral with full military honours and a solemn burial appropriate to a great king. Some years later, it is said that a peasant was found to be digging on his farm near where Antigonus had once lived, and when asked what he was doing, said: "I seek Antigonus."[2]

This was the end of the Fourth Diodochian War. Lysimachus and Seleucus carved up all of what Antigonus had ruled, Lysimachus taking western Asia Minor, and the entire south shore of the Black Sea; Seleucus who had promoted the First War of the Diodachi because he had been completely dispossessed, had a vast empire stretching up to the Steppes and east to the Indus, and west to Damascus

---

2 Ibid., p. 504.

and Jerusalem. Ptolemy took part of the Mediterranean littoral north of Damascus and west for three-hundred miles or so. Cassander contented himself with an only slightly expanded Macedonia.

2. The Fifth War of the Diadochi—The Struggle for Macedonia, 298-285

Of the quadrumvirate, Cassander was content with Macedonia, and at least undisturbed in the possession of it, but died of dropsy in 297, aged fifty-eight. His renunciation of Asia at least ended any pretense by Macedonia to influence in Asia, which from the Macedonian perspective, shrunk their national perspective back almost to where it had been in the early years of Philip II; a very thin reward for forty years of almost constant war that had carried its banners to the ends of the earth and left its sons as rulers from Alexandria to Kabul. Lysimachus ostensibly had northern Asia Minor, including Cappadocia, but Pontus and Bithynia were independent kingdoms and a scattering of Asian Greek cities professed loyalty to Demetrius. Pleistarchus held Paphlagonia, and Seleucus was ceded Syria and Mesopotamia, though Tyre and Sidon remained in allegiance to Demetrius. Seleucus remembered that he owed the launch of his project of partition to Ptolemy and made no effort to evict Ptolemy from his occupation of Syria south of Damascus, and of Lebanon. He demolished Antigoneia on the Orontes and built himself a new capital, Antioch, nearby. The mad egotism of the squabbling heirs of Alexander continued, as if in mockery of the dignity and grandeur of the man they were trying to replace.

Demetrius escaped after Ipsus with about nine-thousand men and retired first to Ephesus. He had left his wife, Deidameia, and his personal fortune in Athens, but his friends in power in Athens were overthrown as soon as Antigonus was defeated and killed, and the new Athenian leaders sent emissaries to meet Demetrius in the Cyclades. They brought him his wife and treasure but told him that he could not enter Athenian territory. They did not wish to offend the victors. He retrieved his navy from Athens, but was not allowed to settle in Corinth. Demetrius, apart from the loyalty of a number of Ionian cities, still had the largest fleet, held Cyprus, and was president of the Hellenic League, though what that comported in these changed circumstances was soon revealed to be the leadership of only a few loyal, scattered, states. It was like a sanguinary game of musical chairs: Seleucus, left without a chair by Antigonus, incited the start of the Wars of Succession, and now was comfortably installed on a swath of Asia and Antigonus' son Demetrius was scrambling for a place to sit, much as Seleucus had twenty-five years before.

Demetrius was also rebuffed by Corinth and the Hellenic League collapsed, with most of its states rejecting him. He was largely a king of the sea, which, to retain the status, would require either renting his fleet out to one of the contestants in the next round of the succession struggle, or wholesale recourse to piracy. He did harass a corner of Lysimachus' Thrace, and proved astonishingly astute and persistent in his political manipulations. As he managed to maintain some of the instances and powers of a faction-head, Seleucus, who knew about dispossession, recruited him in alliance in 299.

There had been a febrile round of marital politics. Ptolemy, to strengthen his hand against Seleucus, who was tolerating his occupation of south Syria and Lebanon, approached Cassander and Lysimachus. Cassander's son Alexander married Ptolemy's daughter (with Eurydice) Lysandra; and Lysimachus married Ptolemy's daughter (with Berenice), Arsinoe, and sent his Persian wife Amestris, amicably to set up shop as a sovereign princess at Heraclea on the south shore of the Black Sea. It was at this point that Seleucus, unfazed by having been the chief destroyer of Antigonus and his empire, opened contact with Demetrius, whose fleet and islands and vindictive cunning could be useful against the three other surviving successors, swapping wives around with each other. Not to be left out, Seleucus married Demetrius' daughter Stratonice, and reopened discussions with Ptolemy, the upshot of which was that Seleucus persuaded Ptolemy to betroth his daughter, Ptolemais (with Eurydice), to Demetrius. The lords of the shires of Edwardian England were rigorously monogamous compared to the marital acrobatics of Alexander's heirs. Demetrius sent Pyrrhus, another major personality making his premiere on the stage, as his hostage to Egypt, where Pyrrhus promptly defected and became Ptolemy's most competent general (for a time). Seleucus started courting Demetrius' cities, starting with Miletus, to whose reconstruction Seleucus contributed generously. Demetrius and Seleucus jointly reasserted influence in Ephesus, and Demetrius with Seleucus' support, evicted Pleistarchus from Pamphlagonia.

The new men in Athens were worthy but naïve neutralists, led by Phaedrus and Lachares. They believed, like American inter-war isolationists and Cold War pacifists, that if Athens bothered no one, no one would bother it, and even began to disarm. They went to voluntary military training for young men, with a resulting reduction in annual intake from eight-hundred to thirty.[3] The best guaranty of Athens' safety was Cassander, who intelligently realized that after these decades of prodigious war-making, in which Macedonia had extended its influence vastly beyond anything that could be remotely imagined by such a small state, that Macedonia had to have peace, to rebuild itself physically and demographically, and stabilize popular morale. Cassander was in many ways a wicked man, even by the undemanding ethical standards of these times, but he was extremely capable and clear-headed. He seemed to be well-embarked on a prolonged period of judicious statesmanship when he died, but at least he died of natural causes.

In 296, Seleucus demanded that his beaming father-in-law Demetrius cede him Tyre and Sidon in exchange for Demetrius taking Cilicia, and Demetrius refused, and their relations broke down. Seleucus revived the venerable if inconstant alliance with Ptolemy and Lysimachus, as Antigonus' son had struggled up to be worth dissection by the three—only such projects of joint subjugation of an upstart could keep them away from each other's throats, no matter how many times they shopped their daughters and sisters around between them. While Demetrius tried to seduce or intimidate the Athenian leaders, who had begun quarrelling (being Greeks), and without Cassander to protect them; Ptolemy seized Cyprus, Seleucus occupied Cilicia, and Lysimachus took Ephesus and invaded Miletus, Ionia, and Caria. Demetrius was at first rebuffed at Athens and retired into the Peloponnese. Lachares made himself dictator of Athens, alienating half the population, and causing the demo-

---

3 CAH, VII, p. 78 (W.W. Tarn).

crats, who held Piraeus, to ask Demetrius' assistance. Demetrius was there with the swiftness of a cat and blockaded Athens. Lachares did the customary, stripping the gold once again off Phidias' sacred statue of Athena, and Demetrius had the pleasure of defeating a naval relief expedition made by Ptolemy. He reduced Athens to outright starvation and the city surrendered in 294. Demetrius was back as king at last. He treated his late enemies very gently, and brought in a massive shipment of free grain, but given his circumstances and the nature of the times, he garrisoned Athens and strengthened, extended, and manned the fortifications. After living almost from hand to mouth for seven years, he had a home port for his powerful fleet. The house of Antigonus lived.

He was still following his father's plan of 307—to use Greece as a stepping-stone to the conquest of Macedonia, but as a subject country, not an ally. As always, there was no discernible motive to any of these wars other than the aggrandizement of those who contended for the succession of Alexander, a man with a civilizing and unifying mission. Cassander's elder son, Philip IV, had died of tuberculosis after a reign of just four months. His widow, Thessalonice, a quasi-sister of Alexander the Great and the last of his close relations, arranged through the Macedonian army, which still ruled in Macedonia, to divide the kingdom between her two younger sons, Antipater, and the younger Alexander. Antipater, who had married Lysimachus' daughter Eurydice, and was tacitly supported by his father-in-law, repaid his mother's gracious intervention by murdering Thessalonice and attacking his brother Alexander, who called upon Pyrrhus and Demetrius for help. Pyrrhus arrived first and ensconced Alexander, taking five provinces for himself as a reward. When Demetrius did arrive, having come from the Peloponnese, Alexander accompanied him cordially enough back to the border, where Demetrius had him murdered, claiming he had unearthed a plot of Alexander's to assassinate him (far from impossible as all these participants were always planning to kill each other). At this point, in a truly astonishing come-back, the Macedonian army elected Demetrius king. He had won, it is generally thought, thanks to the support of Antipater's favorite daughter Phila, the position which Philip II, Alexander the Great, Demetrius' father Antigonus, and now Demetrius all considered the indispensable launching place for the conquest of Asia.

Demetrius ruled like an Asiatic despot, completely contemptuous of any democratic or even collegial thought. Macedonia, as Cassander had finally realized, needed peace, and Demetrius, desperate for revenge, wanted war at once, total war, for goals and reasons that found no favor whatever even with the Macedonian army, which had finally more or less rebelled even against Alexander, a rightful king and inspired military commander. Cassander's son, Antipater, and that son's nephew Antipater, and Alexander's widow, Lysandra, all received refuge with Lysimachus, who respected Demetrius' capacities as a general and certainly knew the quality of the Macedonian army. He married his eldest son, Agathocles, to Alexander's widow Lysandra, and he bided his time. Demetrius pursued his objectives by the exactly opposite means: Greece, if united, remained the strongest power in Alexander's former empire, and Demetrius set out to unite enough of Greece by force to enable him to project his newly rebuilt strength back into Asia against his and his father's enemies.

He knew that Sparta, Epirus, and Aetolia, were irreconcilable, but with Macedonia and Athens he set out to get the rest of Greece in line. In 293, he brought Thessaly into the fold, always the most obliging Greek state to the wishes of Macedonia. In Thessaly, Demetrius built the heavily fortified city of Demetrias, on the north side of Pagasae and it steadily enveloped neighboring towns and became a considerable metropolis. (It became famous for a hereditary corps of herbalists who could supposedly cure almost anyone of anything and did so without charge, one of history's first instances of free medical care.)

Demetrius had no difficulty gathering in the Euboean League, and Chalcis. Demetrius became a subject of worship in Euboea, and a month was named after him, heady stuff for someone who fled in brave defeat from the field at Ipsus just eight years before. Demetrius gathered in Boeotia, suppressed a subsequent revolt, but gently, and integrated the ten-thousand Boeotian hoplites into his pan-Hellenic army, and set up the historian Hieronymus as governor, and even promoted the leader of the revolution. He could be a diplomatic and ingenuously fair ruler when he troubled to do so. He gained most of Phocis and Eastern Locris. All this, with Athens, Corinth and Megara gave him a very strong position.

He was no longer leading the Greek democrats, as he had in 302 when trying to take Macedonia from Greece for his father, but he was trying to straddle between the democrats and oligarchs. It was difficult, bridging between terribly fractious and argumentative people. These traditional labels gave way in the stress of the times to the division of pro-Macedonian and nationalist. Given what he might have made of these tergiversations, Demosthenes had passed away prematurely, though if he were still living, he would be in his early nineties. In 292, the normally prudent Lysimachus made the inexplicable mistake of crossing the Danube and attacking the Getae, who soundly defeated and captured him. But their leader, Dromichaetes, saw the advantage of having Lysimachus between him and Demetrius, who was compulsively bellicose, and released Lysimachus, having negotiated (with him as prisoner) an alliance.

While he was captive, Demetrius, true to form, invaded Thrace, and while absent on this mission, Boeotia rose up, allied itself with the Aetolians and Pyrrhus, and the returning oligarchs, in league with Boeotians, attempted a coup d'état in Athens but were frustrated by Phaedrus. Demetrius' son Antigonus managed on his own ability and authority to subdue the Boeotians. Demetrius, having withdrawn from Thrace after the return of Lysimachus, besieged disloyal Thebes, and when he starved it into submission, despite having to beat off an attempt at relief by Pyrrhus, he only executed ten ringleaders and did not otherwise take reprisals, but did install garrisons in Thebes and outlying territory. However, the extensive movement in his rear as soon as he entered Thrace convinced him that no attack on Asia could be conducted in confidence without the neutralization or elimination of Aetolia and Pyrrhus.

Pyrrhus is, apart from the flamboyant and deadly drive-by of the fiery Olympias, almost all that is relevant of the history of Epirus. His was an extraordinary career. He was a relative of Alexander the Great, and had many of his soldierly traits, but unlike Alexander, he had no aptitude for anything except being a soldier. He had no interest in Hellenization or the advancement of learning at all. The entirety of Epirote literature is Pyrrhus' memoirs. He was a dynamic military leader and a dashing public figure, impressive in appearance, gracious in manner, and always popular as a successful and swashbuckling military leader generally is. But he was limited in outlook, cynical, treacherous and had no long-term idea of what he wanted to accomplish. He is now claimed to be an Albanian, and except perhaps for the modern saint, Mother Theresa, is the most famous Albanian in history. In theory, he operated a democratic kingdom and every year pledged allegiance to the people, but this was empty symbolism, as his army controlled everything. Cassander's son, when desperate for Pyrrhus' aid, ceded to him the Macedonian provinces and territories of Parauaea, Tymphaea, Ambracia, Amphilochia, and Acarnania. Pyrrhus also took over Corcyra and a number of other nearby places including part of southern Illyria, cutting Macedonia off from the Adriatic. He made offerings at Dodona, an oracle within his territory, for the sole reason of impressing the Greeks with the idea that he was almost one of them. (For better and worse, he wasn't.)

Aetolia, a courageous and indomitable state, had expanded after Cassander's death, over Western Locris and Delphi and part of Phocis, and Aetolia pursued the policy of supporting the second state in the peninsula against the first, which except when Macedonia was divided, meant opposing Macedonia. This had the consequence of allying Aetolia informally with Pyrrhus against Demetrius, and Demetrius as has been recounted, had concluded that he had to subdue Pyrrhus in order safely to attack across the Straits or the Aegean into Asia. Demetrius rarely needed much reason to attack anyone, but he already had a score to settle with Pyrrhus because of Pyrrhus' thrust into Demetrius' rear when he was engaged in quelling Thebes.

It was a classic quarrel among thieves, and much of ancient conflict was like a natural sequence of disputes between wild animals which keep engaging other wild animals and always end up being crushed and humiliated in a continuing process that never ends, but merely escalates. The law of the jungle is tempered only slightly by diplomacy, and when one party is the strongest, it is eventually dragged down and killed by a coalition of smaller entities. In all that has been recounted from earliest times to those now being described, this pattern was only conspicuously varied by Philip and Alexander the Great, Pericles up to a point, Hammurabi, Nebuchadnezzar, Darius I, David and Solomon, and a few of the pharaohs. And as we have also seen, those who were successful left behind entities of no durability at all, except for a few of the Greeks and Jews.

The Pyrrhus-Demetrius clash, which was bound to occur given their shared treachery and bellicosity, also became entangled in the matrimonial attempts at diplomacy. Pyrrhus, after the death of his famous wife, Antigone, had married the daughter of Agathocles of Syracuse, which is how he got his hands on Corcyra. But he deserted Lanassa and married an Illyrian princess, which caused the jilted Lanassa to decamp to Corcyra and dangle herself before Demetrius for, one assumes, a rich variety of motives. Demetrius took the proposition and apparently wintered with Lanassa one year in Corcyra and became friendly with Agathocles. He planned an isthmian canal at Corinth to simplify his communications. The battlelines were being drawn and Aetolia excluded all Demetrius' jurisdictions from the Pythian games of

290, including Athens. But Demetrius and Demeter were worshipfully welcomed to Athens that summer and staged their own games.

In 289, Demetrius invaded Aetolia, but it is a rather savage country and he wandered around it without doing much damage and he retired, leaving Pantauchus with an army of occupation of Aetolia that was numerically completely unequal to the task. He then invaded Epirus, but Pyrrhus avoided him, entered Aetolia and routed Pantauchus and then returned to Epirus and maneuvered Demetrius back to Macedonia. But when Pyrrhus tried his hand at invading Macedonia, Demetrius bundled him out, and they signed an inconclusive truce, which made no pretense to being a durable settlement, and neither of them could be trusted to honour it for a fortnight anyway.

It was just inconclusive sparring, but at this point, Demetrius made a terrible mistake, of a gravity that in these fierce times of the survival only of the fittest, could not be survived. He put his impatience to repossess his father's estates and reassert his claim to succeed Alexander the Great ahead of his realistic valuation of the strength of his position. He apparently controlled Athens, Macedonia, Thessaly, Boeotia, most of Locris and Phocis, Euboea, Megara, Corinth and Argos, Sicyon, Achaea, Arcadia except for Mantinea, and the Island League. It was an imposing constellation of states, but he only held them through tyrannical garrisoning, and apart from, to a partial extent, Athens and some of the islands, he wasn't popular in any of the places he controlled, and one military reversal could shake the whole precarious, jerry-built hodge-podge of involuntary subjects apart. In theory, it could furnish Demetrius an army of over one-hundred thousand, and he still possessed by some margin the greatest navy in the known world, at over three-hundred warships.

At all times in history, an aggressive attack on a foreign state or people can only be successful if it is either nomadic and the attacker effectively transfers his whole civil population to the territory being occupied, which is the early history of the Middle East, of the settlement of Greece, and ultimately of the attacks on the Western Roman Empire; or by launching an adequately strong military force from a home country that is prepared to sustain and supply the expeditionary force come what may. Demetrius, moved by artificially generated adulation or perhaps just by impatience clouding his judgment, determined to attack into Asia, with Pyrrhus and Lysimachus grinding their teeth and pawing the ground on his flanks. Demetrius had done a remarkable job of patching together a prodigious aggregation of states and peoples after almost being exterminated with his father at Ipsus. But he had not built carefully and was always focused on what he could attack next without consolidating his authority with good government, recruitment of strong internal loyalties, and the other activities that give a country or empire internal cohesion and staying power. For Greater Macedonia as it now was, impetuosity could easily become a mortal danger. Ptolemy, Seleucus, and Lysimachus, had all been around this track before. They had united to crush and kill Demetrius' father, and his son was more imaginative and fanatically motivated, but his judgment was erratic, and he was a less popular leader, of his armed forces and of the civil population.

Demetrius' amassing of reserves in his treasury and an expanded shipbuilding program signaled the other powers what was afoot, and Ptolemy, Lysimachus, and

Seleucus almost reflexively revived their occasional alliance—they had been doing this as necessary for nearly thirty years, and it was natural that they should pick up easy recruits, conspicuously Pyrrhus, who was only a peripheral Albanian scoundrel, but a very capable general and a nasty attack dog. (He bought into the plot, which involved him tearing up his peace agreement with Demetrius for no plausible reason; with him was one of his many fathers-in-law, Audoleon of Paeonia.) Lysimachus was the recruiting sergeant and also, because of his proximity, and harbouring Macedonian royal fugitives in his court, had excellent intelligence about Demetrius' internal problems. After Demetrius had made his deployments, but before he had committed the stroke of aggression, in the spring of 288, Pyrrhus invaded Macedonia from the west and northwest and Lysimachus did the same from the east and northeast.

Demetrius had no idea of what was coming, and his forces were at jumping off points or in garrisons all around Greece. He gathered up the Macedonian forces available and marched to meet Lysimachus. He stopped him before he could take Amphipolis, but when it was learned that Pyrrhus had struck across the western frontier, desertions to Lysimachus began. Demetrius left a restraining force at Amphipolis to try to hold Lysimachus and he raced back with such forces as he could round up, to meet Pyrrhus. But the western Macedonian army, having no particular loyalty to Demetrius such as it had had to Philip, Alexander, Antipater, and even up to a point to Cassander, judged that Demetrius was finished and deserted en bloc to Pyrrhus in September 288.

Amphipolis was betrayed by a fifth column of Thracian agents to Lysimachus and Macedonia was (temporarily) expunged as an independent state. Pyrrhus swallowed most of it and was given some war elephants. Lysimachus took the rest. He, Ptolemy, and Seleucus, all contemporaries of Alexander, had as children seen the rise of Macedon engineered by Philip and they had played a role in it, and they had all ably seconded the mighty triumphs of Alexander, and they had fought their way through the messiest imperial succession in the history of the world and Macedonia was gone, betrayed by its own army, which, undefeated, had conquered the known world.

Demetrius fled to Cassandreia where his wife, the universally admired Phila, daughter of Antipater and daughter-in law of Antigonus, widow of Craterus, mother-in-law of Seleucus, who had gone through all the travails of her husband, on learning the extent of her husband's overwhelming defeat, with few words and no histrionics, and with complete dignity, committed suicide by taking poison. Ptolemy had put to sea and part of his fleet stood off Corinth while part put in at Athens under Olympiodorus and Glaucon and reprovisioned the city. Demetrius fought on, admirable in his indomitability, alone and with very few resources left. He rallied Boeotia by granting autonomy to Thebes and organized a substantial force with which to invest Athens. It was too late for Lysimachus or Pyrrhus to intervene, and Ptolemy's forces had withdrawn, and would not have been sufficient. Demetrius had a substantial following in Athens and when a delegation of intellectuals led by Crates of the Academy asked him to spare "the violet-crowned city" he acceded, and again made peace with Pyrrhus: each would keep what he had, which in the case of

Pyrrhus, meant the majority of Demetrius' former kingdom of Macedonia. Pyrrhus made a public sacrificial offering and advised the citizenry to admit no more kings and departed cordially.

Demetrius did invade Asia, though not in the mighty Alexandrine sweep he had dreamt of and planned. He managed to organize a force of ten to twelve thousand Greek mercenaries and left a small garrison behind at Athens and landed near Miletus, which welcomed him. Here he found Phila's sister, Eurydice (divorced ex-wife of Ptolemy), and Ptolemy's daughter Ptolemais, who had been betrothed to him in 299. They were both now unattached, and they married (It was now 287), and Demetrius remained in Miletus recruiting forces for an attack on Ionia. This came off with some success, late in the year. Sardes was handed over to him, but Ephesus resisted, and at Priene, Demetrius' advance became mingled with a ferocious peasants' uprising, which Demetrius left it to Lysimachus' beleaguered garrison to deal with.

In the spring of 286, Lysimachus' highly regarded son, Agathocles, arrived in Ionia with a strong army. Demetrius judged that his slightly ragged and outnumbered mercenaries could not hold their own with such a force and he retreated east, hoping to move through Armenia and he hoped to raise something farther east or perhaps even make an agreement with Seleucus. Agathocles followed and cut off his communications and supplies. He suffered the same dispiritedness of Greek troops far from home and from the sea as Alexander had, and more so as Alexander was moving from victory to victory. Hunger, plague, exposure, exhaustion, desertions and skirmishing all afflicted his forces as they moved into Seleucus' province of Cilicia. Agathocles shut and manned the passes behind him. Seleucus (his son-in-law, not that these relationships mattered much) at first supplied him, thinking Demetrius might be useful against Lysimachus, with whom he did not doubt a showdown lay ahead. (It was now thirty-eight years since Alexander the Great had died and Seleucus, Lysimachus, Ptolemy, and the deceased Antipater, Antigonus, Perdiccas, and Eumenes, and others had agreed on a peaceful regency.)

Seleucus' senior general, Patrocles, counseled Seleucus not to assist Demetrius, as he could always be dangerous. Patrocles ended the supply of Demetrius, shut the passes behind him and attacked him. Outnumbered, in a foreign land cut off from any assistance, having coped with betrayals by everyone (reciprocating betrayals by him or correctly anticipating them—this was no morality play), after the suicide of his wife; with a rag-tag army, Demetrius, like Napoleon at the Beresina as he left Russia at the end of 1812, reached his highest point of courage and focused intelligence. Whatever the odds, no matter how often assaulted on all sides by superior forces, he set an example of personal heroism and led his forces to victory after victory and was soon gaining strength as astounded and awe-struck mercenaries and foreign conscripts rallied to him. Demetrius appeared to be on the brink of carving out of southeastern Asia Minor a new kingdom, that could be serviced and protected by his fleet. He had become the itinerant terror of Eurasia, battered from country to country, but always rising up and smiting the kaleidoscope of his enemies made of lesser stuff than he.

Just as he appeared to be about to defeat Patrocles and take what he wanted, the physical exertions were too much, and Demetrius collapsed physically. He could not function and almost everyone now deserted him. He struggled from his cot, led the remnant of his forces in a night-attack against Seleucus, but it was rebuffed, and he was repelled. He struck again the next day and despite astronomical odds against him, was pushing Seleucus' forces back when Seleucus himself arrived at the head of his elephant brigade. He inexorably defeated Demetrius' gallant detritus of army and empire and advanced personally, on foot and bare-headed, and asked the final guard of Demetrius not to force them to kill them all. He gave them (and kept) his word that no harm would come to them. Once more, Demetrius escaped, but he was alone, and had no supplies and finally, unable to get to the Mediterranean shore on foot, where he hoped to rejoin his fleet, on the verge of dying from malnutrition, he personally surrendered.

Demetrius was confined, very humanely, in a comfortable house on the Orontes River, but too heavily guarded to have any chance of escape. His son-in-law Seleucus would not release him even though Demetrius' son Antigonus offered treasure, every city he controlled, his fleet, and even his own person for his father's release. It was something of a credit to Demetrius that he was too resourceful and irrepressible and brilliant to be trusted not to fashion yet another attempt to overwhelm the rickety and undistinguished cartel of abrasive and generally unenlightened interests that had ruled so contentiously since Alexander's death. Seleucus could not take the chance, and Demetrius was retired, like a great racehorse, to comfortable pasture but was not to compete again. Demetrius died in 283, aged fifty-four, and his body was transferred with high honours and dignity to his family, and he received a mighty funeral at Corinth, attended by representatives of most of the western world's governments. His ashes were buried in his self-created capital of Demetrias.

Demetrius was too wicked and treacherous to be admirable, but too brave and brilliant and indomitable to be discounted. He lacked consistency and judgment and so was not a great statesman, though he was a very capable general, and a strong and magnetic leader, in war and peace. He had an impressive personality but was never much bothered to do what was necessary to be popular. He was swashbuckling enough to be admired but too unsympathetic and vain to be widely admired. His wife was magnificent and never bolted despite his innumerable infidelities, and his family loved him. Of all Alexander the Great's candidate-successors, he was the most talented and impressive, and not the least scrupulous. He was a brilliant meteor that lit the sky and frightened the world as it passed. Macedonia was reconstituted, as the Pyrrhus-Lysimachus partition was rank opportunism requiring the application of more force than was justified, and the house of Demetrius reigned there for a century, until Rome imposed an order on a scale that not even Alexander the Great had imagined and dispensed with these quarrelling little states.

The Fifth War of the Diadochi was over. The Sixth, naturally, was about to begin.

3. The Sixth War of the Diadochi, Lysimachus and Seleucus, 285-281

Demetrius had not made any durable arrangements for Athens and as soon as it was clear that he would not be back, the nationalist party in Athens prepared to try to oust Antigonus. Lysimachus sent financial assistance and grain was bought and distributed, but Athens, after their mad experiment in pacifist government, had no force of its own and the "violet-crowned" citadel of civilization was going, woven cap in hand to all comers. Young Antigonus played his cards well and once it was clear to Lysimachus that Demetrius was a spent force, he became less indulgent of Pyrrhus, a capable general but at the head of the poor and fractious country of Albania (Epirus). The inevitable occurred—a reconciliation between Pyrrhus and Antigonus. The next, equally inevitable step followed: Lysimachus tore up his treaty with Pyrrhus and invaded Pyrrhus' part of Macedonia. Antigonus sent forces to assist Pyrrhus, leaving his position in Piraeus very vulnerable, though he had some of his father's fleet. Lysimachus had a greater force than Pyrrhus could resist, and he prudently abandoned Macedonia and Thessaly to Lysimachus without a fight. The Macedonian army elected Lysimachus king, which outraged young Antipater, son of Cassander and grandson of the original Antipater, who had been assured he was Lysimachus' candidate for the throne of Macedon. Antipater put his grievances forcefully and personally to Lysimachus, who responded by having his late close friend and ally's son summarily executed. This was a ruthless stroke even for these people. Lysimachus and Cassander, for all their unscrupulosity, were loyal to each other through all political weather. "Aeschylus himself could not have bettered the vengeance which was to be taken by Antipater's furies."[4]

Lysimachus appeared to be invulnerable. He held Thrace, Macedonia, Thessaly, and most of Asia Minor. He had what he had started with after the death of Alexander, plus what Antipater had held, and much of what had then belonged to Antigonus. Ptolemy hadn't moved much and Seleucus had extensive domains, but well back from the centers of events. Lysimachus had moved cautiously and added strength at each stage. If Demetrius had been the hare, Lysimachus had been the tortoise. He had run an efficient government and avoided over-extension and costly adventure. He had extended his sway over much of the Black Sea, massaging, bribing, and over-awing local chiefs, but never over-extending himself. Lysimachus treated the Greek cities as subject states, not allies and the Ionian and Ilian Leagues were managed through generals. The disappearance at last of Demetrius enabled Lysimachus to take back his Ionian cities, except Miletus, where Demetrius' great fleet was inactive and neutral (like the French fleet in Oran in 1940). Demetrius' admiral, Philocles, went over to Ptolemy, taking Tyre and Sidon with him. Ptolemy thus gained control of the Island league and of Delos. Lysimachus secured Lemnos. Imbros, and Samnothrace.

It was now effectively, forty years after the death of Alexander, a division of three: Lysimachus and Ptolemy had engorged themselves; Seleucus had not, but he did regain Cilicia, and all Demetrius' followers and Lysimachus' enemies, flocked to Seleucus, who was Demetrius' landlord. Demetrius still struck terror into the mind

---

4 Ibid., p. 90.

of Lysimachus, who offered Seleucus two-thousand talents to murder Demetrius. Seleucus, to his credit, dismissed "This dirty piece of savagery."[5] Demetrius was able to smuggle out a message, asking all his followers to accept the leadership of his son, Antigonus Gonatas, and to disregard any orders supposedly from him, as they would be forgeries. It was alleged that Demetrius hastened his death by excessive drinking. He undoubtedly found captivity, though comfortable, a depressing environment, a little like the last six years of Napoleon.

The new Antigonus would reestablish the royal house of Macedon and would be something of a philosopher king. He had few of his father's faults and less than his brilliance, but his mother's high character and integrity and was that rarest person—a good man and a good ruler. He was tenacious and loyal and plain-spoken, without vanity, and inspired in his education by Zeno the stoic, and by his tutor, Menedemus, a talented and worldly man. Zeno was a particular inspiration, a man who discerned and elicited a person's soul, above all considerations of war or peace or material or even physical health, a man too shy to lecture, but immensely persuasive in his quiet wisdom. A king could scarcely do better, and Antigonus Gonatas (apparently a youthful nickname meaning knock-kneed) would be well liked and respected by almost everyone. He inherited a fleet and Aetolia, in conformity with its practice of supporting the underdog of its neighbours, allied with Antigonus and Pyrrhus to balance Lysimachus. He was thirty-six when his father died and would be a successful king of Macedonia for a total of thirty-six years and die peacefully at age eighty, in 239.

Lysimachus moved cautiously against Pyrrhus, and invaded Epirus, but was lax in allowing his army to plunder freely, and the rustic Albanians proved very unremitting subjects. Seleucus saw that there must come a showdown between him and Lysimachus, and his respectful transmission to Antigonus of his father's ashes was the opening of a diplomatic campaign of reconciliation with him. Lysimachus trod, diplomatically, the well-worn path to Ptolemy. The cycle of the Diodachi started yet again; the whole world had been through this before, again and again. The long struggle for the heart and attention of the king of Egypt, conducted between his wife Eurydice and her maid of honour and rival, the mistress Berenice, had been won by Berenice, as he divorced Eurydice in 287 and formally married Berenice, and made their son Ptolemy his heir and joint-king. For readers fatigued by the tenebrous complexity of these arrangements, Berenice was the daughter of Antigone of Macedon and the mother-in-law of Pyrrhus, where Eurydice was at the cross-roads of the entire vast Alexandrine entourage: she was the daughter of Antipater, and she was the mother-in-law and sister-in-law (through Phila) of Demetrius, and the mother-in-law of Lysimachus' son Agathocles. Her son Ptolemy, henceforth Ptolemy Keraunos (Thunderbolt) was passed over by Ptolemy I in favour of Berence's son with Ptolemy I, the anti-climactically named Ptolemy II. The inter-marriage, polygamy, and cavalier divorces were so convoluted and malleable, they vastly surpass almost all modern philandering and inter-marriage and make Victorian Europe look like republican meritocracy and Cromwellian puritanism.

The denouement with the young Ptolemies propelled Ptolemy Keraunos to Se-

---

5 Ibid., p. 93.

leucus to seek his support against his half-brother who was one heartbeat ahead of him. Seleucus said he would support him when the kingship of Egypt was open, i.e., when his father was dead; Seleucus did not see the point of alienating the long-incumbent Ptolemy while Lysimachus would be wooing him toward a combination against Seleucus. Full of the impatience of youth and dispossession, Ptolemy Keraunos, the Thunderbolt, sped off to Lysimachus, whose practice it was to give refuge to all pretenders—one never knew when they could be helpful—and his court had a full stable of them from all around the Greek and Middle Eastern world for decades.

Perhaps the wiliest and most clear-headed of all Alexander's professed successors was Ptolemy, who had seized Egypt on the death of Perdiccas and held it for over forty years. He did regain Cyprus after Demetrius was defeated, but had no interest in Greece, Macedonia, or Asia Minor, and was bemused at the overtures he received from Lysimachus and Seleucus. He was a relatively enlightened ruler of Egypt, gentler than his confreres though perhaps at the head of a gentler country. He was interested in the arts, founded the great (new) library at Alexandria and was the patron of the illustrious mathematician Euclid, though he didn't understand all of his formulations. When he asked that they be simplified, Euclid replied: "There is no royal road to geometry, Your Majesty." Ptolemy died peacefully in his kingdom, much admired, in 282, aged eighty-five, the only one of the original Diadochi to die a natural death apart from the original Antipater thirty-seven years before. His dynasty ruled on for a total of nearly three-hundred years until Cleopatra VII, the last and most renowned of his line, famously committed suicide by exposure to an asp, after misplaying her romantic and political cards opposite the invincible Octavian (Augustus) Caesar, in 30 B.C. (as will be recounted in Chapter 28).

Lysimachus covered his bets by marrying his daughter, another Arsinoe, off to Ptolemy II, which caused the Thunderbolt to seek his dynastic fortune in Macedonia. Here he came upon Agathocles (his brother-in-law, of course). Agathocles had his sights set on the Macedonian crown, as Antigonus Gonatas (the Knockneed) and the Thunderbolt did. Lysimachus' court was even more politically intense than Ptolemy's had been; it was closer to the centre of activity, Lysimachus was a more inveterate schemer and swindler than Ptolemy, and the furious competition between Lysimachus' wife Arsinoe and his daughter-in-law Lysandra (the Thunderbolt's sister), continued right under the Thracian king's nose, and much to his entertainment. But inexplicably, Lysimachus now took complete leave of his senses and became so wound up in the dynastic struggles in his court that his mind was poisoned by the Thunderbolt into concluding that his talented son Agathocles had betrayed him. He accused and convicted Agathocles of treason and executed him.

It was recounted eight paragraphs above that Aeschylus could not have conceived of where Lysimachus' murder of the son of his friend Cassander would lead. Now Lysandra, who wins the gold cup of full circuitry of the Diadochi, fled Lysimachus' murderous court for Seleucus and set about stirring up problems for her last father-in-law with the demonic energy of a much-wronged woman. She was, to review, Ptolemy I's daughter, who married Alexander V, Cassander's son who was murdered by Demetrius. She then married Lysimachus' son Agathocles, who has just been murdered by his father. She sought the aid of Seleucus, thus rounding the bases of the Diadochi. The brutality and horror of Lysimachus' murder of his very accomplished son and his friends sent ripples of fear and revulsion through his kingdom. No one was safe, as in the last days of the Reign of Terror in Paris in 1794. Having been manipulated by Ptolemy Keraunos (the Thunderbolt), Lysimachus was now dependent on him. In the bloody confusion, Athens was unable to resist the young Antigonus, who took over its government in 281 and began in a conciliatory and efficient manner as he continued.

In 282, the instability of Lysimachus brought Seleucus out of his fastness east of Babylon, sensing his chance, at the end, now more than forty years since the death of Alexander, to take over the whole empire. Philetaerus, the eunuch from Tios who had helped betray Antigonus I to Lysimachus before Ipsus, struck again and surrendered Pergamum with nine-thousand talents, as governor, a position which had been awarded to him for his betrayal of Antigonus, to Seleucus. (Philataerus may have been the most cunning of all the players in this intense drama—he was the son of Attalus, who had toasted a "legitimate heir" at Philip II's wedding and was executed by Alexander the Great after being implicated by Demosthenes in a letter encouraging revolt, although he gave the letter to Alexander. His grievances antedated those of the Diodachi, and he fatefully asserted seniority—he had been instrumental in the destruction of Antigonus and was now with Lysimachus. He would be rewarded with the kingship of Pergamum and would rule there peacefully for another twenty years, dying in 243 at the age of eighty.) Sardes, once again a treasure house, old capital of the Great King of Persia, surrendered to Seleucus also. Ziboetes of Bithynia rallied to Seleucus.

Lysimachus came south at the head of his army. He was seventy-nine, and Seleucus was seventy-seven, Lysimachus more unsteady on his throne than ever, Seleucus more secure. The sanguinary epic was about to end, and the Furies of Antipater and Agathocles to be heard from. Seleucus won the Battle at Corupedium, Lysimachus was killed by one of Seleucus' javelin-throwers. Lysimachus' dog protected his master's remains from vultures until Seleucus' men gave him a respectful burial. The Thunderbolt was captured. As he (Ptolemy Keraunus) had called upon Seleucus for assistance when he was expelled by Ptolemy I, Selucus received him cordially and not as a prisoner of war. Seleucus appeared to be in charge of the whole empire now, except for Egypt. He was old, but as he had just demonstrated, was physically strong and politically agile. He had succeeded in assembling the coalition for the First War of the Diadochi, artfully carved out a realm for himself in the east, where if whoever ruled Asia Minor attacked him would be vulnerable to an attack in the rear from Ptolemy, Lysimachus, and whoever ruled Macedonia. Seleucus, like Ptolemy and Lysimachus, had made the most of his peripheral position, while war raged, decade after decade in the interior kingdoms of Macedonia-Greece and Asia Minor. Egypt was removed from the equation for a time by the death of Ptolemy; the defeat of Demetrius and the antics of Lysimachus and Pyrrhus had emasculated mother Macedonia; Lysimachus blundered by murdering his son and reducing his court to terrorized schism, a mortal error, for which he paid promptly with his life. Seleucus seemed to have conquered and inherited the world.

The Sixth War of the Diodachi was over but the drama was not quite finished. Seleucus had his mind set on a return to Macedonia after an absence of about fifty years, and moved slowly through Asia Minor, picking up adherences as he went. Miletus came in easily, and Seleucus decreed the customary remittance of his predecessor's taxes. Halicarnassus went over to Ptolemy and Heraclea, Byzantium, Chalcedon, Cius, and Tios formed what they called the Northern League, claiming independence, and were joined by Mithridates of Pontus, a family that would be troublesome to central authority for a long time. Obviously, their independence would depend on how much time and arms Seleucus was prepared to expend in subduing them. Seleucus put first things first and proceeded on toward Europe, crossing the Dardanelles in 280. Having seen off Perdiccas, Antipater, Antigonus, Ptolemy, Lysimachus, Cassander, and Demetrius, he could be forgiven for not paying much attention to the Thunderbolt, a stateless reject in a lesser and more humiliating position than Seleucus himself had been in when he set out to form the coalition that began the First War of the Diodachi in 322. After such a triumph, at the end of such an implacable struggle, he should have been especially careful.

Keraunos (this will be almost the last reference to him as the Thunderbolt), saw that Seleucus was not going to help him gain power in Egypt and intended to take Thrace and Macedonia for himself, and he took advantage of a private moment with the returning champion of the supreme struggle, and stabbed Seleucus to death with one stroke. He died instantly, in victory but with no chance to celebrate it, and Keraunos escaped. He was hailed by Lysimachus' loyalists for having avenged their defeat and the death of their king, and generally tolerated by Lysimachus' opponents in Thrace, because they knew that he would try to preserve Thrace's independence from the Seleucid Empire, which would now be ruled by Seleucus' son Antiochus. Philataerus, the ultimate cynic, his outlook perhaps envenomed by his status as a eunuch, took possession of Seleucus' corpse, and instead of giving it to Antiochus, auctioned it to him. Elegance was rare in the dying stages of this enervating and horrible war.

Keraunos reinforced the Northern League to help keep Antioch at bay. Lysandra and her children, after she had made the grand tour of the components of the Empire, vanished, all of them, without trace. That may not mean foul play, as such would probably have been publicized historically. She may even have returned to Egypt, where she could have lived comfortably. Keraunos further buttressed his position by marrying his daughter off to the ineffable Pyrrhus, who was planning his invasion of Italy. He would be the first of all this cast of characters to encounter the rising might and civic determination of Rome.

Antigonus started for Macedonia by sea, but Keraunos intercepted him with the Thracian and Heraclean fleets and badly defeated him, sending him back to Piraeus well whipped and with a much-reduced fleet. Keraunos then made a change of pace and proposed that Arsinoe marry him and regain the position of queen of Macedonia, and he would adopt Ptolemaeus as his successor. This was Eurydice's son proposing, in the fashion of these things, to Berenice's daughter, but it would certainly knit the world together (apart from Antiochus wandering around in Asia). Arsinoe was seduced by some combination of ambition and Keraunos' charm and admitted her betrothed to Pella. Once inside the gates with an adequate number of his troops, the beaming bridegroom sent the queen of Macedonia off to Samothrace in exile, Keraunos murdered her younger sons, his so-named heir Ptolemaeus escaped to Illyria and Keraunos gave his rejected mother Cassandreia. A few people forgot where they were and with whom they were dealing and the dynastic cards got a drastic shuffle, to the regular beat of royal murders and executions (a distinction without a difference, as there was not the slightest pretense to anything judicial).

In Greece, Areus of Sparta, emboldened by Karaunos' almost effortless defeat of Antigonus, had a rush to the head of ancient Spartan self-importance, as if these were just post-Periclean times of a century earlier and declared himself head of the Peloponnesian League in 281 and with Elis, and most of Arcadia and the Argolid, set out to chase Antigonus out of Athens. Antiochus, starting to play at the top table for the first time (though he had been joint king at Babylon with his father in the east for some years), professed alliance with Areus. Antiochus was half Sogdian, from near the Khyber Pass, as his mother, Apama, daughter of Spitamenes, was one of the king's daughters Alexander had handed off to his generals. For good measure, Antiochus married his stepmother, Stratonice, daughter of Demetrius, patching various dynastic claims together like an ancient Saxe-Coburg-Gotha.

His stepmother bore him five children, including his eldest son Seleucus, whom, in the manner of the Diadochi and their offspring, he executed for treason. In the spring of 278, Argos and Megalopolis expelled Antigonus' garrisons and Areus invaded Boeotia and the tide turned. Areus was not like the heroic leaders of olden Spartan times, and he was decisively beaten by the Aetolians and the Achaeans expelled his garrisons and revived the Aechaean League, but it was still thin gruel for the patient Antigonus. His friends were overthrown in Athens and Demochares, the now comparatively diffident nephew of Demosthenes, moved a posthumous Athenian decree in commemoration of his uncle Calippus, an extreme nationalist, and was elected general. Antigonus was down to Demetrias, Corinth, Piraeus, and a few towns in Achaea and the Argolid. He was still flourishing compared to some of the heirs of the original Diadochi, dead and alive.

Antiochus had to suppress a revolt in Syria, and Ziboetes, the venerable king of Bithynia, who had reigned for forty-eight years, fighting almost incessantly, but alternately, both Lysimachus and Seleucus, threw in with the Northern League and roundly defeated Hermogenes, whom Seleucus had sent to suppress him. This may have been the last hurrah in his tour de force of survival between larger powers, and he died of natural causes in his upper seventies, succeeded by his son Nicomedes, per force, as he had murdered all but one of his brothers and completely subjugated the survivor.

By the autumn of 279 external pressures were prevalent and Antigonus and Antiochus, scions of great Alexandrine generals and governors, signed a genuine peace worthy of the most illustrious and least treacherous, of the traditions they incarnated. Antigonus would marry Antiochus' half-sister, Phila, and the boundary between Thrace and Macedonia was declared to be a permanent and amicable division of their influences. Antiochus would not interfere in Greece or Macedonia, and Antigonus would not intervene in Thrace or Asia. It was the final end of any pretense to put all of the empire of Alexander the Great back together, but it became the principal cornerstone of Hellenic politics. Antigonus reigned successfully for more than thirty years and Antiochus for more than twenty, and unlike their forebears, they would die peacefully on their thrones.

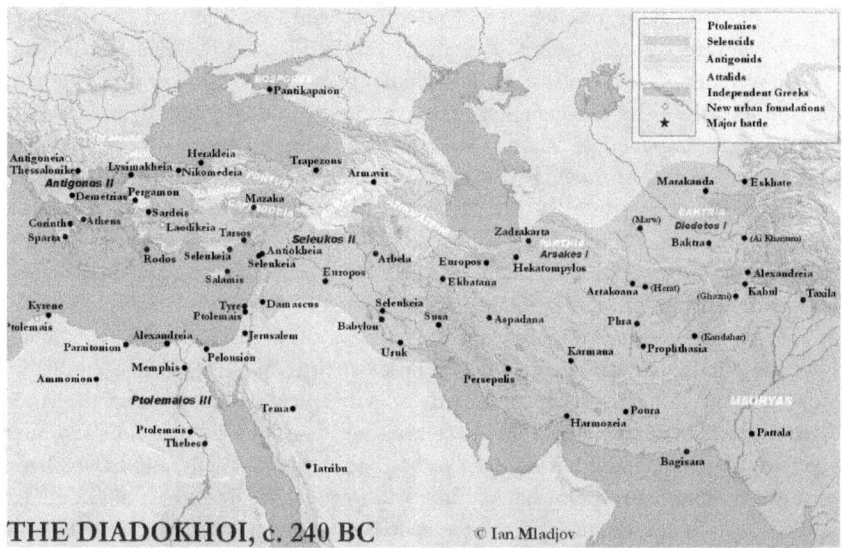

Territories of the Diadochi in 240 B.C.

After forty-four years of almost relentless warfare, in which back-breaking costs and devastations and casualties were inflicted on Macedonia, Greece, Thrace, and Asia Minor, the grandson of Antigonus ruled Greece and Asia Minor, the elder son of Ptolemy ruled Thrace and Asia Minor (for the moment), the younger son of Ptolemy ruled Egypt and Syria, and the son of Seleucus ruled Mesopotamia, Persia, and the approaches to India. There were some smaller autonomous kingdoms, as there had been for centuries, along the northern perimeter and among the Greek islands and to the west, including Pyrrhus' Epirus. There were also, as was about to be discovered, a large and steady migration north of the Alexandrine area from east to west but drawn south toward Thrace and Macedonia by reports of their wealth and sophistication, as Asiatic tribes had been attracted to Mesopotamia and the Eastern Mediterranean. The collapse into merciless and treacherous war for more than forty years and the brutal murder and massacre of the family of Alexander the Great were a terrible desecration of Alexander and all of his goals and talents. It was history's mockery of the immense and benign ambitions of one of the greatest men the world would ever know.

4. The Invasion of the Gauls

Before ushering in the era of Rome, we must deal with an invasion of the Macedonian and Thracian world by the Gauls (and update the Greeks). The Gauls were a large and warlike itinerant people, moving west from the plains of eastern Europe, north of the Black Sea, and now they were drawn toward the evidently relatively advanced and prosperous societies on the Black and Mediterranean Seas. The movement of the Gauls is little known, but they seem to have come after and to the south of the Celts, and generally finding the states in the south Balkans and Italy more difficult to penetrate than the less organized tribes in what are now Germany and France, they kept moving west and were already fairly well organized in what became Gaul, whence they had already invaded Italy and got to Rome (Chapter 16).

The Gauls burst upon Macedonia in 279, completely unsuspected by Keraunos, who was dealing with an attack upon Thrace by Illyrians, torqued up by his half-brother Ptolemaeus. The Gauls were plunderers, but were disposed to settle, as they moved in huge wagon trains and masses of pedestrians, slaves, families, belongings and plunder, led and guarded by substantial numbers of fierce and fairly well-armed if rather undisciplined men. Bolgius entered Macedonia at the Aous Pass; Brennus overran Paeonia, and Cerethrius invaded Thrace. Macedonia's frontier foemen, the Dardanians, having been pressed upon by the Gauls, and having been rebuffed as allies by Keraunos, had gone over to the invaders and served as guides and advance forces. Bolgius offered Keraunos a peaceful passage to the west by his tribes in exchange for an outright bribe, the pre-Alexander practice of the Asian bush-tribes, and Keraunos contemptuously refused with a pompous assertion of his royal prerogatives and armed strength, which would pay no heed to a scruffy gang of bearded nomadic savages, their wenches' whelps and slaves and ragged baggage in tow. They attacked him immediately, before he had any ability to mobilize, defeated him easily and killed him and his meager frontier force, having no interest in prisoners, The Thunderbolt had parlayed his weak hand on quitting Egypt well, if gratuitously ruthlessly, but had lost his sense of self-preservation and did not recognize the danger he was in, even when it was arrayed before him. His exit from the post-lude to the Diadochi era was to have his severed head put on a spear and carried before the Gauls' army as it poured in great numbers into Macedonia, a spectacular exit as far as it was possible to be from what Keraunos would have foreseen, a timeless lesson on the dangers of over-confidence. He was an assassin after all, and the world scarcely noticed as the Thunderbolt crashed into the Earth.

The fortified towns were safe, as the Gauls had no idea how to conduct a siege, but they flooded through the countryside, raping and killing and pillaging. At Cassandreia, which Keraunos had given to his mother Eurydice, the gates and walls kept the Gauls out, but the civic nationalist party staged a popular uprising, Eurydice's mercenaries defected, but she, a good deal more agile in the face of the unexpected than her late son, surrendered the citadel to the mob and was hailed as a liberator. The leader of the revolt, Apollodorus, proclaimed himself a tyrant and seized the property of the upper classes. The Macedonian army, in the post-Keraunos mayhem, elected the late king's brother, Meleager, but soon dismissed him as completely unable, elevated Cassander's nephew, Antipater, but sacked him forty-five days later and elevated Keraunos' capable general, Sosthenes, who declined the crown but accepted the command. Bolgius, after expanding his train with loot, withdrew northwestwards and settled in Serbia.

But Brennus poured into Macedonia via the Iron Gate, as his relatives departed to the west. Sosthenes had had a chance to assemble some forces and put up a serious resistance that prevented Brennus from any contemplation of trying to settle, and somewhat limited the havoc he wrought on the countryside. It was his presence that chiefly motivated Antigonus and Antiochus to make their peace. Brennus seems to have had about thirty-thousand armed (with broadswords) men, but they had no armour, and were only effective at close quarters—they could not cope with archers, javelin-throwers, or cavalry. Brennus came through Thessaly, where the wealthy paid him for not ravaging their estates, and came to Thermopylae, which the Greeks held with twenty-eight thousand trained and well-armed soldiers, from ten or so Greek states, chiefly Aetolians and Boeotians. Brennus quickly saw his men had no chance at close quarters with the Greeks, and he circled round and introduced forces into Aetolia at Malis, and seized, burned, and slaughtered the inhabitants of the little town of Callium. As he had hoped, Brennus provoked the withdrawal of the Aetolians from Thermopylae, and the war settled into the Gauls roaming around marauding, but the Aetolians decimated them with irregular forces of archers picking off the Gauls in ones and twos every time they moved, from trees and behind rocks. Brennus showed tactical skill and formed a flying column that could strike at specific targets, though his forces were suffering steady attrition to no purpose, and he made a terrible mistake when he sent his column to loot Delphi.

The Aetolians made the correct decision to send a small force to do its best at Delphi while surrounding the main body of Brennus' forces, and steadily investing and reducing it with withering archery fire and irregular armed attacks on the entire migrant force, hampered by women and children and baggage. A random group of brave defenders prevented Brennus from taking Delphi, and in the midst of a winter thunderstorm, the priests came down to tell the defenders that Apollo had entered the fight with them, and this passed into the lore of Greece. Brennus broke off for the night, the Defenders were reinforced by Phocians, and at dawn, in a white blizzard (it was January), attacked with a dense shower of arrows, felling Brennus and killing many. The Gauls slew their wounded and carried their leader in retreat but were mercilessly harassed by Greeks whose normal valour was raised to almost superhuman levels of vengeful determination by offended national pride and religious outrage. Brennus eventually committed suicide, the Thessalains and other ostensibly passive Greeks turned on them and most of Brennus' entire invasion force, including large numbers of women and some children, were massacred. The action was a triumph for Aetolia. Delphi thereafter had a festival for the Deliverance of Greece.

There was a further plunge of the Gauls into Asia Minor across the Dardanelles, with the connivance of Mithridates, who cooperated with the Gauls' army from a variety of tribes numbering perhaps thirty-thousand soldiers, using them to pry off parts of the Seleucid kingdom of Antiochus. Mithridates was aiming at Bithynia, Pamphlagonia, Phrygia, and was using these Gauls as his own mercenaries, though they apparently didn't know this. Philitaerus, ingenious in all situations, deflected the Gauls from Pergamum, while Miletus and some other cities paid ransom to avoid invasion. Antiochus came to defend his western frontier but was diverted to Syria in 276 to deal with Ptolemy's invasion. Finally, in 275, having seen off Ptolemy, Antiochus crossed the Taurus and with a force of sixteen elephants in the lead, crushed the Gauls and harried them out of his territory. Defeated and dejected, scared out of their minds by these gigantic beasts they had never heard of, the Gauls recrossed into Europe and joined the westward movement of their people, their next principal encounter with civilized Europe would come in a little over two-hundred years, in an epochal, Alexandrine-scale conquest by Julius Caesar. Antiochus was generally accorded the title of Soter, saviour, as Christian leaders of the next millennium would be celebrated for the often somewhat miraculous salvations of Christianity.

Antigonus had taken advantage of the general confusion and the not unwelcome demise of Keraunos, by invading Macedonia in 278, but Sosthenes drove him back out in 277. While regrouping, Antigonus came in contact with the third large group of invading Gauls, under Cerethrius, who had invaded Thrace. Antigonus squarely defeated them near Lysimacheia and drove them out of Thrace and northwards to join the western trek, an achievement that earned him the gratitude even of Sosthenes, who had not found fighting the Gauls an agreeable pastime, though he had acquitted himself well at it. A detachment of Gauls set up a territory between the Danube and Byzantium, but were reasonably quiescent, though they extracted blackmail from some of the coastal cities for a time. Sosthenes had just died, apparently of natural causes, and there was bedlam in Macedonia, following the various invasions. In the vacuum and the devastation, and in recognition of Antigonus' defeat of the Gauls, he was elected king of Macedonia by what was left of the Macedonian army and was well received by the civil population of most cities, where he was rightly regarded as a moderate and honest ruler. Keraunos had seemed to win and the Antigonids to lose, but these were just semblances.

Antigonus faced rival claims to the throne of Macedonia from the current Antipater, Lysimachus' son Ptolemaeus, and Arrhidaeus, who claimed (almost certainly spuriously) descent from Philip III. Antigonus could not ask the Macedonians to take up arms in an internecine dynastic dispute, and his own men were honourably fatigued, so he emulated Nicomedes and incentivized the Gauls that were around to deal with his challengers, which they did. Ptolemaeus and Antipater fled to Egypt and Antigonus required the Gauls to quit Macedonia, albeit with full pockets. Antigonus employed a similar tactic and engaged pirates to reduce Cassandreia from the sea and expel the Gauls from that city, enabling Eurydice to resume her status. He was master of all Macedonia, a contented state for the first time in many years. He lustily celebrated his marriage to Phila, and calm generally descended on a happier Greece and Asia Minor.

It was pretty much as it had been before Alexander. Antigonus had the kingdom of Philip II, minus Thrace. Antiochus had most of the Achaemenid kingdom after the Great King lost Egypt and India. Ptolemy succeeded Pharaoh, with expanded territory in the Levant and Syria. Macedonia was weaker than under Philip, reduced in size and exhausted by war, and Egypt was much expanded. For some time to come, the Antigonid and Seleucid regimes would cooperate to restrain the influence of Egypt, confirming that of the early claimants to the Alexandrine succession, Ptolemy had been the most durably successful. But the greatest change wrought by the Age of Alexander the Great and the Diadochi was that Egypt, Asia Minor, and Persia were governed by Greeks and to a substantial extent, Alexander's greatest ambition—the Hellenization of the known West, was underway.

It had been a terrible cavalcade of tragedy and comedy, banality, and farce, nobility, cruelty, cowardice, mindless violence, with every permutation of human character, not excluding the periodic interventions of treacherous eunuchs. There was never any point to any of the preceding decades of conflict except the lurid ambition of men whose aptitude for rulership was at best solidly adequate and whose claim to rule was based exclusively on having been of proximate use in service to a mighty conquering genius. Little of Alexander the Great's military genius was continued in his lieutenants, and apart from Ptolemy I and Antigonus II, not much of his interest in good government either. And none of them remotely grasped, or even, so far as is known, approved his plan for homogenizing the imperial bureaucracy and armed forces and Hellenizing and culturally elevating the known world.

In this sense, Alexander the Great had been a sort of Woodrow Wilson, lifting up the spirits of the masses with a vision of peace, culture, and internationalism, or at least a Cromwell, attacking corruption, profligacy, and royal arrogance. This was a more exalted and uplifting vision than the endless municipal squabbling of the Greek city and island states, or the aggregation of conquered peoples of the Persian Empire, or the self-regarding and memorializing lassitude of most of the history of Egypt.

But all of it, having reached a pinnacle of demiurgic brilliance, had been for nothing, except the enhancement, though much less systematically than Alexander had intended, of the Hellenic influence over the whole area. Weakened and confused, civilization, such as it was, and it was still quite vibrant around Athens, plodded on. The world almost audibly cried out for order and peace, preferably with some level of enlightenment, and it was coming, at last. The modest royal house of Macedon had given the western world a taste of what an empire could be, but it was evanescent, apart from the dispersion of a gentle but notable Greek cultural influence.

What already impended, though it would be less dazzled by Greece, would respect the Greek influence, though not its fissiparous politics. And it would establish and maintain a dominion of undreamed of might and extent for seven centuries, which, connecting secular and ecclesiastical matters, has continued for over two-thousand years to our times.

The incomparably long and brilliant day of Rome was dawning.

PART IV

THE RISE OF ROME

FROM ITS ORIGINS TO ROMAN DOMINANCE OF THE MEDITERRANEAN

SEVENTH CENTURY B.C. TO 180 B.C.

CHAPTER SIXTEEN

FROM THE BIRTH OF ROME TO CONTROL OF CENTRAL ITALY ANTIQUITY TO 292 B.C.

ROMULUS AND M. FURIUS CAMILLUS

Romulus & Remus
Fifteenth Century frieze

M. Furius Camillus
Sixteenth Century medal

1. The Latin and Etruscan Origins of Rome and the Roman Kings

THE RISE OF Latin villagers to rulership of the organized Western world and then of the premier ecclesiastical institution in history, establishing Rome as one of the greatest centres in the world for more than two-thousand years, has no close parallel in the history of the world.

In the Neolithic Age, all that is known of the inhabitants of Italy is that they were relatively long-headed people whose practice was invariably to bury the dead. There is evidence of these people in most of Italy, but not in the western central part of the peninsula where Rome now stands. In the Bronze Age came people who lived in dwellings near lakes raised up on piles, and they introduced farming agriculture: wheat, beans, and flax, as well as olives and grapes, and they kept dogs, cats, horses, cows, goats, pigs, donkeys, sheep and poultry. They cremated their dead, and organized their communities behind moats, trenches, and ramparts, in a manner that continued into Roman times and was widely emulated.

By the Twelfth Century B.C., representatives of the Etrurians, the Villanovans (Latian, Tuscan, and Bolognese), appear in the Alban Hills and around where Rome now stands. It was now the Iron Age, and the practices of these people revert from cremation to the Sabine practice of inhumation. With the blending of peoples came the Etruscan era, out of which Rome was founded in the Eighth Century B.C. This was the original Latium, a triangular parcel of about seven-hundred and fifty square miles of fairly rich, somewhat volcanic soil. Rome was founded here on the banks of the Tiber River, about ten miles from the Western Mediterranean Sea. An Alban League of perhaps as many as fifty towns and villages developed, of which Rome gradually emerged as the principal community, which was kept in some unity by an annual festival and religious rites (largely around funerals) on the principal Alban hill. Rome grew on and between the famous seven hills: Quirinal, Viminal, Caelian, Esquiline, Aventine, Palatine, and Capitoline, of which only the last was a sufficiently steep promontory to be useful in defense.

The myths of the founding of Rome are complete fabrications. Virgil originally credited Aeneas with this very noteworthy achievement, but there were gaps of centuries in this version, and Hercules, Evander, and Cacus were all mythologically reported to have been first or early Romans. All this was discarded in favour of the famous collaboration of Romulus and Remus. Another rich profusion of legends arose, with steady retroactive embellishment and magnification as Rome's status in the world became more imposing. In fact, the Greeks came up with Rhomos as the founder of Rome, and the Romans returned the legend to the Greeks, having localized the name to Romulus, whom the Greeks twinned with Remus, and festooned the nascent town with that pair of founders. The lore about being suckled by a wolf and growing into great warriors was the work of Roman fabulists. The Rape of the Sabine Women is another, apparently Greek, innovation, that was conveniently invoked to promote the idea that Romulus constructed and maintained an asylum for virtuous young ladies on the Capitoline Hill, so that Romans could procreate with nubile young women according to civilized rites of conjugality.

Rome appears to have had six or seven kings prior to the establishment of the Roman Republic at the end of the Sixth Century B.C. There are generally agreed to have been six elected kings prior to about 500 B.C., but what the political organization of Rome was prior to that is a howling mystery clouded with a rich overlay of folkloric myth-making. The Rex corresponded to the Celtic Rig and was the chief religious officer of the community, exercising a secular authority because of his perceived talents at interpreting and appealing to divine will. The Pontifex Maximus, a title which of course survives in the papacy, was the principal authority on the state's religion. He was the Rex Sacrarum, who decreed the dates and programs of religious festivals. Here as in other early societies we can note that the instinct of man is to believe in a sacred supreme power responsible for the creation of the world and the direction of its activities and the reward of people and that this seems to have antedated even the organizers of a state. This early government, fairly similar to what we have seen in Egypt and with the Jews and others, was the exact opposite of any notion of separation of church and state.

The kings Numa, Tullius Hostilius, Ancus Marcius, L. Tarquinius Priscus, Servius Tullius, and L. Tarquinius Superbus, are generally conceded to have lived and reigned, and the first three are considered Latin kings and the last three Etruscan kings. Herodotus and the historian Dionysius disagree over whether the admixture of Etrurians that made Latin Rome an Etruscan city was an infusion of new blood from Asia or northern Italy. Herodotus does not believe there was supplementary immigration from outside Italy and Dionysius does. Linguistic evidence (alphabet and vocabulary, as far as it is known) do not legitimize claims of sizeable immigration to Italy apart from southern Greece in the centuries immediately prior to the setting up of the Roman Republic. What distinguished Latium and its immediate vicinity from the rest of Italy was not so much agricultural fertility, which existed but was not unique to the region, but the discovery of iron on Elba and copper at Volterra. The resources generated trade, commerce enriched the trading population, and those riches generated more elevated material and cultural tastes. This was the springboard for the early rise of Rome above its neighbours.

By the beginning of the seventh century, Etrurian commercial strength and demographic growth had fueled Etruscan expansion at least ten miles to the northwest of Rome to Veii, and twenty miles to the east to open the passes to Campania and the south. Throughout this time interaction between Rome and the Etruscans became steadily more intimate, as was shown by Roman adoption of the Etruscan practice of attempting the divination of the wishes of the gods through the examination of the innards of animals. Rome borrowed steadily more from Etruscan architecture and writing, though it is not clear whether there was imitation without a general mixing of populations or if the intimacy of the two neighbours was a forced absorption by the Etruscans rather than arm's-length imitation by the Romans, but the fusion came, and this considerably increased the strength and extent of Rome. Relics of art and sculpture make it clear that Rome was acculturated to the Etruscans in the last three kingships and that those kings were themselves Etruscans.

Servius Tullius was a popular Roman king sandwiched between the two Etruscan Tarquins, of whom, the second, Tarquinius Superbus, was much disliked in Rome. Servius was popular because he was of humble origins, distinguished himself, and married the daughter of Tarquinius Priscus and was popularly acclaimed king on the death of his father-in-law. He is generally thought to have ruled from 575 to 535 B.C., and only ceased to be king when he was murdered by his daughter, Tullia, conniving with her husband, Tarquinius Superbus. There is no doubt that Superbus was always unpopular and tainted by his wicked seizure of the throne and was deposed in an uprising and with him ended the kingdom of Rome. Tarquinius Superbus was king from 535 to 509, a cunning, ruthless, and severe despot who was so reactionary, he accused his opponents of favoring a census in order to publicize the means of the wealthy and arouse the masses.

He may be considered to have presaged the most depraved of the Caesars, the most licentious of the Borgias, the most cynical of those conceived or counseled by Machiavelli, and thus, in his somber and gluttonous way, a pioneer. The champions of the people drove Tarquinius out in 509 B.C. and created the Roman Republic, which, tumultuous though it often was, brought Rome to the forefront of the Western world in the next five centuries. The Republic and the Empire, on an ever-greater stage, would put on display an all-encompassing range of levels of governmental ethics and aptitudes. This may have coincided with the defeat of the

Etruscan advance through Campania by Aristodemus, the tyrant of Cumae in 524 B.C. Tarquinius Superbus was overthrown at a time when the Etruscans were being forced northwards, including at the Battle of Aricia. Rome was never ethnically an Etruscan city, but the evidence that has been unearthed of the cremation and interment of the dead indicates that there was considerable assimilation of Etruscans into Rome as well as a good deal of cultural influence. And there remains speculation that Tarquinius Superbus had forced himself on Rome militarily, though this remains speculative. In this period, Roman construction became almost entirely of stone, and all the subtleties of Etrurian architecture, including wide and elaborate arches, were adopted. The overthrow of Tarquinius Superbus left Rome in control of the Etruscan expansion into the centre and south of Rome. In the regal period, Rome expanded from an extent of about sixty square miles to an area about ten times as large. At the same time, the Romans must be given some credit for devising a system of elected kings, no matter how constrained the size of the electorate and even though the end of the Etruscan and Tarquinian rule was unlikely to have been the Romans' first recourse to change of regime by its violent overthrow. It was also something of a bold stroke to establish a republic at about 500 B.C. (This was, after all, more than twenty-two hundred and fifty years before the revolutionary democratic uprisings in America and France.)

The first major Roman military advance had been by Tullius Hostilius in the destruction of Alba Longa, in the mid-Sixth Century. At the end of the regal period, Rome seems to have controlled about three-hundred and fifty square miles, by some measure the largest of the Latin states (and larger than many Greek states). The first Roman treaty with Carthage, in about 508 B.C. includes Rome's claim of sovereignty for over a hundred miles along the Italian peninsula on the west, with Rome close to the centre of such a line, with an internal penetration of its jurisdiction that might have averaged 20 miles or more, the beginning of a serious expansion, considerably larger than all but a few Greek states, and reminding us that Italy is a larger country than Greece. This was at the time that Philip II was in full array as leader of expansionist Macedonia.

Livy and Cicero attested that Rome was originally organized politically, that the governing body of the early kingdom was composed of three-hundred centurions (in practice, owners of horses, so they rode rather than walked or travelled in ox-carts), and each identified with one of the ancient Roman tribes. These were the Ramenses (named after Romulus—an essentially mythical figure), Titienses (named after Titus Tatius, sometimes reckoned a king and sometimes just a prominent factional leader), and Luceres (whom Cicero represents as named after Lucumo, an ally of Romulus). In Rome's early days, thirty Curiae were also established, which were the basis of an assembly, and from earliest times, when the Roman authorities had public edicts or exhortations or important information to impart, they were loudly read out, on three consecutive days, at the peak hours of the principal public market. This was the convention, but when matters were submitted to a vote, which occurred somewhat irregularly, but early on and often, the conventio became a comitia whose majority vote would determine public policy.

There does not seem to have been any formal constitution and there were doubtless many instances of general insubordination, tyrannical imposition of rules without consultation, repression, corruption, and outright revolt, but from these early times there was a democratic tradition that frequently asserted itself, never died, and continued, century after century, in awkward coexistence with authoritarian tendencies. These contrary currents of what would today be called popular democracy and law and order, persist yet in the mobility of western public opinion, and in sophisticatedly volatile countries such as France, and have been very identifiable in the adjustment and wholesale change of regimes within living memory. Of course, the curia, the only arm of early Roman government of whose existence we are certain, also, remains a familiar word, in the organization of the Roman Church.

The earliest assembly of the Roman people was the comitia curiata, which started with the kings and continued throughout the republic to represent the community in its religious activity. It was summoned to observe the inauguration of kings and to give assent to important private acts. When a king died an interrex was set up by the Senate. This institution, which would become more famous than any Roman term of government except the emperor, grew out of the Council of Elders, which practically every tribe we have observed, develops as its first administrative organ after the chief or ruler or high priest (generally all the same person, initially primitive government required multi-tasking). Senators were members of the patriciate, another concept that was derived initially from the status of heads of families (and even in these early days, the Barberini, in particular, are in evidence, a family whose influence would persist in Rome for two-thousand years. Citizenship belonged to patricians, but was also accorded to plebeian achievers, and as in Athens, the plebeians, the masses, were not difficult to stir up and not easy to appease. Plebeians were citizens, but initially of the lowest rank. Rome had many fewer slaves and a more entitled plebeian class than Athens, a less rigid social structure, with greater meritocratic access to the higher walks of life and standards of elevation. This is undoubtedly one of the reasons why Rome so vastly exceeded the Greek states in making citizenship of their nationality so desirable in the regions where Rome spread its influence. The original Patres, or patricians, principal heads of families, were the original Senate, but its composition naturally evolved into a self-renewing and slowly expanding collection of the meritorious, the politically influential, and the friends of the senatorial faction-heads. In early times, it consisted of one hundred members.

Rome had no priestly caste, another trait that was original and probably reduced civil strife somewhat. Religion was accepted as legitimate and necessary and was controlled in its basic form and rites by magistrates. There were fifteen flamines, who were magistrates but served and organized festivals and sacrifices to the various Roman gods. The flamines abstained from various foods and activities and had special servants who had to be free men who groomed the flamines with a bronze knife for their nails. The flamines stayed away from dead bodies and observed a range of taboos that originated in ancient times, and the distinction of bronze is that it antedated iron, indicating when this religious office took hold. The whole activity had its roots in primitive magic.

There were also the salii, who were dancing priests and custodians of shields that were supposed to have fallen from heaven in ancient times, and they chanted hymns and prayers that were unintelligible to contemporary Romans. There was naturally a good deal of indulgent officialdom going through these ancient rites to maintain continuity and the dignity of the state, but without necessarily attaching a jot of credence to them. This is not unlike a good deal of official ceremony in modern times. These religious officials had no secular authority. The head of the state religion, the Pontifex Maximus, was the paternal overlord of the Vestal Virgins and the head of an ecclesiastical college (eventually two colleges), to prepare and qualify people for religious careers. There were at various times, four, five, nine, and only one of these pontifices maximi. Rome was always possessed of a general notion of ius, meaning not only justice, but what is right, and upright and moral, and the maintenance of this standard was the principal purpose of the religious apparatus, whose senior personnel were, in principle, confined to the patrician families.

In the pre-republican times, the public assembly was the comitia centuriata, where group votes on pressing matters were cast by groups of approximately a hundred participants from the equites—knights, in effect—those with horses. This was the great innovative reform of King Servius Tullius. The assembly was summoned by the blast of a unique trumpet, and it met outside the walls of Rome on the Plain of Mars, and while it was in session, red flags were raised on the Arx and on the Janiculum hill, which were lowered if an enemy approached. It was a military concept and most of the participants in the assembly were active or quickly conscriptable members of the army.

After the equites, not so much cavalry as mounted infantry officers, came five "summonings" of infantry, defined according to the level of their equipment. First came the hoplites with bronze helmet, shield, sabre, spear, and sword, and they tapered down according to the extent they were more lightly equipped. These different levels had differently weighted votes, measured in weights of bronze, and all designed by Servius Tullius to ensure that the least wealthy inhabitants didn't outvote their financial betters. It was a remarkably sophisticated electoral design for the Seventh Century B.C. and superior to contemporary and long-subsequent methods of disenfranchising the poor altogether or countering them with gerrymandered electoral districts or confining them to a relatively impotent legislative body.

It is traditionally believed that Servius Tullius divided Rome into four tribes, named after hills and regions of Rome (Succusant, Esquiline, Palatine, and Hills), and in 495, according to Livy, the number was raised to twenty-one by adding the so-called rustic tribes to represent the outlying areas which Rome had already absorbed. Servius' constitution was deemed by the Romans to be somewhat like that of Solon. The premier military unit was the equites, which seems to have risen in number during the Seventh Century from three-hundred to three-thousand. It was the bodyguard of the king and was commanded by the Tribunus Celerum. This was the beginning of the great office of Roman Tribune, and the holder of the position ranked next to the king. It was the pre-regal office of Tarquinius Priscus and of Servius Tullius and was also held by the founder of the republic, L. Junius Brutus.

2. The Early Roman Republic

The Roman Republic is generally reckoned one of the great formative episodes in the rise of the cause of human liberty, and the birth of Rome as a centre and source of human freedom and the rule of law. Its claim to such distinction is tenuous and in its greatest days, Rome was renowned for the value and pride and accomplishments of Roman citizens and for the mighty power of the Roman state, but its political institutions were unstable and the elaborate forms and formalities of the government of Rome were always subject to modification by senior military commanders and Senate faction-heads. The Empire was the greatest Roman state. As a laboratory for democracy and freedom, Rome's finest hour was the Republic. The creation of republican institutions is generally identified with three men: L. Junius Brutus, Tribunus Celerum and founder of a distinguished family, Valerius Publicola, a renowned patrician champion of the disadvantaged and the working population; and Horatius Pulvillus, who dedicated the temple of Jupiter on the Capitoline Hill (built with forced labor by Tarquinius Superbus).

On the abolition of the monarchy, it was replaced by a dual magistracy of two consuls, to whom were entrusted the imperium of executive authority. The two consuls were elected each year, but there would be a couple of exceptions—a ten-year consulate to effect a codification of laws, and one experiment in a more numerous consulate, and there was provision for suspension of the ordinary system and rule by a dictator in time of emergency. The people would declare the state of emergency and the dictator was nominated by the consuls. The history of Rome in this period remains fuzzy and contested and Livy and Dionysius differ on the date (501 and 498) of the first dictator, and no one has furnished modern historians the name of the first Roman dictator. The position of praetor (leader) was established sometime between the late fifth and mid-fourth centuries, and however and whenever it began, the praetor became a military commander. Rome also established a right of judicial appeal, beyond the traditional recourse to beseeching the mercy of the sovereign.

The Senate was also built up under the Republic, after having been left somewhat depleted by the frequent execution of senators by Tarquinius Superbus. Some combination of Brutus and Valerius Publicola increased the number of senators from one-hundred and sixty-four to three-hundred, where it remained until the time of Sulla, in the First Century B.C. The Republic soon faced the demands of the plebeians for an increased share in government and the solution adopted was to have two assemblies: the populus (propertied citizens) participated in the comitia, and the plebeians, plebs (masses), participated in the concilia. The comitia could, on adoption of a measure, legislate (leges), while the concilia, having adopted a measure, passed resolutions that were expressions of collective opinion, requests for legislation, and were called plebiscita. After about two-hundred years, the Republic narrowed and effectively eliminated the gap between the jurisdictions of the two assemblies, largely in order to facilitate establishing a larger tax base to finance the expansion of Rome's jurisdiction, something all Romans were proud of but the costs of which could not be borne by the wealthy alone.

From time to time throughout this period, the plebeians, always agitating for more authority, would decamp, it was called "secession" and file out of the city, establish themselves in very temporary lodgings in the country and elect their own assembly and officials and pass their own laws. Secessions were recorded in 494, 449, and 287, so they were not frequent, though there may have been others. In 471 the election of tribunes, the chief judges, was transferred from the assembly of the curiae to the assembly of the tribes the comitia tributa. Lesser judicial officers, like lower court judges, were called aedile. They were like small claims judges. The Roman court system became quite complicated and beside the consilium plebis tributum there was created a comitia tributa populi. The frequency with which many of these Roman words entered into the legal and political terminology of the whole western world, and remained there, is a testimony to the originality of Roman legislators.

The main sources of plebeian discontent were a desire for protection from capricious or arbitrary use of the imperium against them, which undoubtedly happened sometimes, to clarify some laws that were sometimes being used against the plebeians in unpredictable and largely unappealable ways, and to gain a share in the exercise of the imperium of government. Similar grievances would be raised by corresponding echelons of the population in many subsequent times and jurisdictions and has not been unknown in contemporary Athens. In response, the plebeians were offered "succor," auxilium, which meant the ability to gain access to the tribune at any time, in symbolic recognition of which their doors were unlocked at all hours. Valerius Publicola, author of the first law of appeal, also legislated a limit on fines that could be imposed, depending on the means of the person being judged. All of these institutions evolved rather flexibly, generally in coordination with the sociological development of the populations they served, and there is a large body of classical historical opinion that gives Rome great credit for the originality and adaptability of its institutions, as they quickly extended their jurisdictions unimaginably beyond the precincts of the original city, unlike their Greek analogues.

The plebeians generally receive the credit for requiring that laws be codified, a movement that began in 462 with a law proposed by a tribune establishing a commission of five to legislate with some precision the imperium of the consuls. This measure was deferred, but in 454 a commission of three was sent to Greece to examine the laws of Solon and other Greek statesmen. They returned two years later and a commission of ten was established and they were installed with an extended mandate to produce a compilation of statutes. The commission reported out but their work was found to be incomplete and a second commission was set up to complete it. The process degenerated somewhat when the second ten were judged by the relevant assemblies to have composed two tables of "unjust laws" (Cicero).

Particular controversy arose over the attempt of the second group to prevent inter-marriage between plebeians and patricians, a proposal that provoked a full secession, the physical withdrawal from Rome of the working and lower middle classes and what amounted to a general strike. Reasonable compromises were worked out after a mass assembly in the Flaminian meadows (future site of the Circus Flaminius), presided over by the Pontifex Maximus, the religious leader then as now. On this as on most other occasions, the Romans were refreshingly free of hidebound rigidities of attitude; there were always some people who addressed these complicated problems in an original way and the results were institutions that were often adapted by successor jurisdictions and their significance ramifies through to contemporary times. The legislative and statutory dispute continued for forty years and is known as the time of the Twelve Tables, and a great deal of wrangling and posturing, but very little violence or severe disruption, was required to produce a consolidation of statutes that was reasonably workable.

The first treaty with Carthage, in approximately 508 B.C., demonstrates that Rome's specialty was politics and strategy, and Carthage's was trade and commerce. Carthage was a Phoenician city—the work of a great maritime nationality, and it projected the Phoenician genius for seafaring and trading. Rome was not a port, and the city's port, Ostia, ten miles southwest, was not a great harbor. The Romans engaged in agricultural processing from the fertile areas around it, but in these early years, were not great traders, or a maritime power at all, and while it eventually became a truism that all roads led to Rome because of its mighty political influence and military power, Rome was not a crossroads city like the great port-cities and trade-route junctions of the Middle East or the maritime cities of Athens. In these respects, it was a little like Sparta, though the temperament of the city and of its public and political vocation could scarcely be more different. Since there was not, at this time, a great deal of manufacturing, compared to the role of secondary industry after the Industrial Revolution, Rome was not as deprived as one might imagine by not being a great trading city.

Early in the days of the Roman kings, if not before, land was divided in somewhat equal portions between public purposes, common-shared land, and a third section for division in parcels between the curiae. This was a bit arbitrary but was generally adhered to for some centuries and was a much more egalitarian division than that which obtained, for example, in France at the beginning of that country's revolution in 1789. There was naturally great and ever-increasing agitation from the plebeians for a distribution of the communal land, and in furtherance of this they frequently withheld their services to the armed forces, which were of increasing importance as Rome expanded. With the growth of Roman territory there was a constant strain between the rights of newly absorbed populations, and the claims of landless Romans to a share of the spoils in the city's growth. A prominent figure in Rome's early republican history, the consul Cassius Vecellinus, was the first proposer, in 486, of a comprehensive agrarian reform law. It was not adopted but versions of it were the subject of intense discussion for decades.

According to Livy,[1] in 467 the customary demands of the plebeian population for land were channeled off to colonization—the establishment of Roman communities, in this case at Antium. This became a method for allowing steam to escape from the demographic pressure-cooker of Rome and it combined relief on the domestic front with the need to have Romans living among and assimilating or at least monitoring local populations as Rome ambitiously extended its authority, at first landwards within Italy. What called itself the Latin League, in which Rome was already the leading member, opened up colonies in southern and central Italy, and

---

[1] Livy, *History of Rome*, III, 1, 5; cf. Dionysius of Halicarnassus, Fragments of Antiquarian Rome. IX, p. 59.

Rome did not at first move citizens outside Roman territory, but extended the territory before transplanting the citizens. This is how the port of Ostia was incorporated into Rome. Apart from the usual discontents of people with modest incomes, Rome had to import grain to feed its population, and not being a manufacturing or trading economy, it had no obvious way to earn the foreign reserves to pay for food. Rome expanded into Pometia, forty miles southeast of Rome, and also seems to have received assistance from Sicily, in one of its better phases, in exchange for political favors.

At the time of the agitation over the Ten and Twelve Tables, another focal point of public discontent was over the baneful amount of debt that abounded. According to Tacitus,[2] the decemvirs of the Twelve Tables enacted a statute that forbade interest rates above eight per cent per month. There is some doubt about whether the forbidden threshold of usury was not lower than that rate, and whether the law was not adopted a century later, in 357 B.C. But something along these lines was adopted. Of more grave concern than the permissible quantum of interest was the remedy for creditors, which included the ultimate right not just to extract work from the debtor, but to seize his person and sell him into slavery. In theory, for what it was worth, there was apparently a right to possess the corpse of a debtor, though not to put him to death, though in these times, a corpse had little commercial value.

In summary, Rome in the early Fifth Century B.C., a century after the start of the Republic, was an expanding but simple place that yet gave few indications of the mighty power and influence it would soon acquire and would yield through the balance of history to contemporary times. It was an agricultural possessing community, a fore-runner of many less historic places, such as Fresno, California, It lived from the soil, including good timber-lands, and was frequently at war, as much in defence of itself as from aggressive ambition, and when war kept men from their agricultural and forestry work, Rome went short of food and its political system registered acute discontent, and the pressures of the poor upon the rich threatened the internal stability of Rome. But the result of this agitation was not so much open violence, or a seizure of the property of the rich and its redistribution, but the rise of talented people who were of modest socioeconomic beginnings. King Servius Tullius had been their model, and this openness to meritocracy was to prove Rome's greatest asset. In this, it was the progenitor of the United States and Canada and Australia, which had the added benefit of immense natural resources and relative isolation from dangerous neighbors. Rome would have to be led by its great men to possession of resources and then organize its neighbors into a protective commonwealth against covetous and belligerent distant neighbors. For now, what was important and would be fruitful was the practice of the plebeians steadily demanding a fair share of what riches there were in early Rome.

The progress of the plebeians was first formalized in 449 B.C. when it was enacted that ten tribunes would be chosen who would be the guardians of the liberties of the citizens, and after each year they would replace themselves, failing which they would be burned at the stake (astonishing severity for such eminent members of the community); and it was established one consul would represent the patriciate and

---

2 Tacitus, *Annals*, vi, 16, p. 3.

one the plebeians, each year. (There is some debate about the dates of these reforms, ranging from 449 to 339 B.C. but whenever they occurred, they were comparatively advanced in democratic and egalitarian terms, considering that dictatorships ruled most of the Great Powers as late as the Second World War.) The authors of these reforms were Horatio and Valerius, and they also gave to plebiscita the force of leges, and restored the right of appeal to almost all litigants, which the decimvirs had suspended. These measures greatly strengthened the meritocratic aspects of the Roman system which, as will soon be clear, was to be the greatest and most unique source of its strength and allure. Rome's early genius was political.

Map of Ancient Rome

The entire Fifth Century B.C. saw Rome advance a little beyond Latium, and then be pushed back, finally subdue Veii, just ten miles northwest, and make further advances in most directions, and then be pushed back again almost to where the century began, by the pressures of the Gauls who had spilled across central Europe and even before they poured into Thrace (Chapter 14), thrust down into Italy as they occupied most of France. Early in the new (Fifth) century, Spurius Cassius Vecellinus fought the Battle of Lake Regillus with those Latin states that objected to Rome's dominance of Latium, and Cassius apparently won rather narrowly, and concluded the treaty that established Rome's local primacy, the Foedus Cassianum. The main terms of the treaty are found in Dionysius[3] and were that there would be permanent peace between Rome and Latin states (the Latin League), neither would encourage aggression on the other, and in the event of aggression by a third party, there would

---

3 Livy. II, 33, p. 9.

be solidarity of all against the outsider. Civil lawsuits between the jurisdictions would be adjudicated within ten days in the place and manner of the state where the action arose. It was a pretty thorough burying of the hatchet and was generally adhered to, unlike the contemporaneous peaces in Greece that almost never lasted long.

Both Rome and the Latin League were menaced by the Etruscans to the north and northeast and by the Volsci and Aequi and Hernici in the Alban Hills east of Rome and the Lepini Mountains and across the Trerus River fifty miles southeast of Rome. Rome and the Latin League agreed to invite the Hernici into their alliance, to make it a tripartite alliance, and this gave Rome and the Latin league a buffer zone separating them from the Volsci and Aequians. There was an informal division of tasks, as the Latins and Hernici fended off the Volsci and Aequians while Rome held off the Etruscans. There were in the first half of the Fifth Century intermittent differences and skirmishes with the Sabines, the Oscan-speaking tribe north and east of Latium and north to Umbria. In general, Sabine advances came between the Tiber and Anio Rivers (from the northeast), the Aequians attacked between the Anio and Praeneste (from the southeast), and Volsci from between the Alban Hills and the sea (from the south). The Volsci were driven by famine to come west from the Appenines near Lake Fucine; they were motivated by hunger and not imperialism.

The chief cultural remnant of the Volscian Wars is the legend of Coriolanus, amplified by Shakespeare but wildly questionable history from the lore of the Second Century B.C. on. He existed and took a side in the Volscian Wars, and almost everything else is rank, though elegantly formulated, invention. More substantial is the record of L. Quinctius Cincinnatus, who was twice dictator starting in 462. He was drafted by the public and retired as soon as the emergency of the invasion by the Aequi was beaten off. He was popular with the plebeians although he opposed the liberalities proposed for them in the controversy over the decemvirs. Cincinnatus may have returned as late as 439 in another emergency, and seems to have been a distinguished public Roman for fifty years and lived into his eighties, and he seems always to have been victorious.

The Sabines were driven onto the frontiers of Latium by the aggression of the Aequi, but their attacks on Rome were not very determined nor difficult to repel. The most noteworthy events in Rome's history with that people are the arrival in 505 B.C. of Attius Clausus (later known as Appius Claudius, founder of the Claudian line in Rome), who preferred peace to war, emigrated with his followers to Rome and was admitted to the patriciate and became a leader in Roman government and his entire following was granted citizenship. The other contemporary episode that is significant in Roman history is the strange matter of Appius Herdonius, who in 460, somehow infiltrated Roman territory with an army of twenty-five hundred, composed in part, it was alleged, by renegade slaves and hoodlums, and in a startling coup de main, seized the Capitoline Hill, like the Hyksos in Egypt in 1650 B.C. (Chapter 2) and the Persians in Sardes in 498 (Chapter 6).

After about ten days of angry ultimatums, the Roman army stormed the Capitoline, Appius Herdonius was slain, and all his followers who were captured alive, about two-thousand, were publicly and crisply executed, the officers with comparative formality and distinction, the soldiery with mechanical swiftness and impersonality as they were bent over the headsmen's blocks and decapitated. The Sabines won a modest victory over the Romans in 450, but were defeated by them in 449, and there were few conflicts with them after that. The Aequi were finally defeated once and for all in 431 on the Algidus Mountains thirty miles southeast of Rome. This reversal also had a discouraging effect on the Volscians.

For the first half of the Fifth Century B.C. the Romans had intermittent problems holding both banks of the Tiber; The Veiians (people of Veii ten miles north of Rome) were a substantial problem in the 470's, and actually besieged Rome itself in 477, but Rome recovered and a peace of forty years was agreed in 474. Rome finally got the upper hand in its region in the last third of the Fifth Century, after the victory of A. Cornelius Cossus over the Fidenae in 435, which had revolted under Veiian incitement, and the defeat of the Aequi on Agidus in 431. These actions broke the back of Rome's local enemies and hereafter for the balance of the century and centuries to come, Rome was generally on the offensive. In 418, Rome conquered Labici, just fifteen miles southeast but the gateway to Tusculum, and for the next twenty-five years the Romans moved steadily south and pushed the Aequi back and into insignificance. Rome steadily defeated the Volsci through the same period, capturing Ferentium forty miles southeast of Rome in 431. Velitrae, south of Algidus, was occupied and garrisoned in 404.

By 393, Rome had cleared sixty miles southeast along the coast, to Tarracina. When Rome captured and absorbed Veii ten miles north but on the Cremera River, Rome had taken more than a bridgehead across the Tiber, and began its expansion northward. None could imagine how far Rome would move up, and beyond, Italy. Veii fell to Rome in 396, after the nearby Alban Lake had risen to alarming levels. Legend holds that Rome sent a mission to Delphi to seek an explanation—the oracle said that Veii, under siege by the Romans, would not fall to Rome until Rome made an outlet for the lake. The Roman commander, Camillus, did so and in the process dug an underground gallery under the Veiian walls and the town fell to permanent Roman occupation. This story's veracity is extremely suspect, but it was one of many ancient legends that had a self-reinforcing life of its own, and the mission to Delphi undoubtedly occurred and was celebrated by a generous gift, the tithe of the pillage of the town, which remained until rifled by Onomarchus one-hundred and fifty years later (Chapter 10).

By the early Fourth Century B.C., when the Gauls descended the Italian Peninsula in strength, Rome had effectively caused the dissolution of the Latin League and was unchallenged in west central Italy, ruling about one-hundred miles from Monte Cimini in the north to Tarracina in the south, with an average depth inland of about twenty-five miles. This was shortly after the death of Pericles, and Rome had already gained the notice of the known world, having grown in a century from a small city at the centre of a hundred or so square miles of territory it governed, an average Greek city state, to twenty-five hundred square miles and a strong civic tradition and comparatively sophisticated political and legal institutions. It was still far from being a power in the world, and was not interesting culturally, but was certainly a state to watch.

But in her domestic arrangements, Rome was still trying to set up stable and flexible institutions. The plebeians were not satisfied with the settlement of 449 B.C., and they were in full and vigorous competition to take over the government. In 448, their leaders managed to wrest the privilege of leaving to the people the right to determine who should have a triumph. In 445, the tribune Caius Canuleius proposed the abolition of the illegality of marriage between a patrician and plebeian (which was clearly a measure that was both unjust and was bound to be impossible as well as undesirable to sustain). He also proposed to permit the elevation to the consulate of plebeians. Valerius and Horatius, who had been the intended beneficiaries of triumphs three years before spoke up for the plebeians, and a compromise was adopted: the marriage ban was abolished and three additional officials with the powers of consuls would be elected and plebeians would be eligible holders of this position, but the consulate would be reserved to the patricians. The plebeians responded with remarkable generosity in electing three patricians as the first holders of this new office, military tribunes.

At about the same time, the Romans were formalizing public administration by setting up the censorship, which meant the creation of officials who were not only in charge of taking the census, but a range of other mundane or routine administrative tasks which the consuls and military tribunes would not have time to attend to, given the frequency and intensity of combat on Rome's ever-expanding borders. Even the census was more than a computation of the population as it also involved estimating property values, and the ability of individuals to endure taxation and also their eligibility for military service, including service in the cavalry as equites. Each censor was allocated to the tribe among which he resided and he assessed people liable for payment of what was called the tribute, should the military condition of Rome require. At times, the tribute was considered a loan from those upon whom it was imposed and at other times it was a loan refundable to the tribute-payer when the conditions of war and public finance permitted. The censor would automatically become a member of the Assembly and had considerable power to set people's taxes according to his determination of their means. This was evidently a system open to extensive corruption. Gradually a code of conduct for censors was built up to curb and regulate their use of what were called infamia, the withdrawal of various civic rights. The adjudication of such matters was by praetors (a title that extended to civil magistrates and military commanders). The censors also had, subject to appeal, the ability to determine who was eligible for election as senators and determined contracts involving state property—such as the exploitation of mines and fisheries. Quaestors were first-instance judges, and were popularly elected starting in 447 B.C. and in 421 a total of four were elected, three to be plebeians.

3. The Gallic Invasion, Disaster and Recovery

The further development of the Roman state awaited the crisis of the Gallic Wars. Romans and Gauls met for the first time at Clusium in Etruria in 391 B.C., the inevitable result of the Gauls pressing southwards into Italy as the Romans moved north through Etruria. The Gauls had poured through the Alpine passes and attacked the Etruscans in the late Fifth Century B.C., and it was the Gallic advance tribe, the Insubres, who led the way south and founded Milan. Before very long, Gallic tribes had occupied the whole of Italy north of the Po River, except around what is now Venice. New waves of Gauls and Celts continued to pass through and press south. The Etruscans resisted bravely and tenaciously and their capital, Felsina, appears to have been captured amid great slaughter in the middle of the Fourth Century B.C. The Etruscans were vulnerable because they were themselves conquerors of the territory, and their Ligurian and Umbrian subjects, though fairly civilly governed, owed the Etruscans no loyalty, and the Etruscans were constantly undermined by the diffidence and at times hostility of the normally rather passive majority of the territory they ruled. It must be inferred from archaeological and other evidence that the Etruscans had also become rather complacent occupiers and overlords, though they fought valiantly when they finally realized that they were not just being pushed back but were no match for the fiercely ambitious invaders who were quasi-nomadic warriors. This is the pattern we have seen often, in the area between Egypt and Persia, and in the invasion of Greece by the Aeolians, Ionians, and Dorians, and ultimately by the Macedonians. The Etruscans were initially good warriors, and their civilization was much advanced on the Italian tribes whose territory they occupied, but they had become rather sufficient. The Gauls were an Iron Age people whose only agriculture was stock-breeding and herding, but on discovering Italian agriculture, they took it up and quickly became very productive cultivators. And as they overran the Etruscans, they rather quickly adopted other comparative sophistications of the Etruscans. They were thus partially softened by exposure to more settled society by the time they encountered the Romans at the northern limit of the Roman expansion, about eighty miles north of Rome.

According to Diodorus, the Gallic leader Brennus arrived at Clusium at the head of thirty-thousand warriors, and Clusium was deserted by the Etruscan League, which had in any case been demoralized and enervated by the onset and advance of the Gauls and would happily dodge further confrontation with them, and Clusium appealed to Rome, whose leaders immediately saw the danger the Gauls presented to them. They responded by sending mediators rather than forces. But the mediators took the side of Clusium and one of them even slew a Gallic chief, causing the Gauls to demand reparations and when this demand was declined, none too politely, the Gauls marched on Rome. The Roman army was a citizen force that was dedicated and valiant but not professionally trained except for the permanent officers, and the fortifications of Rome, as it had pushed out in all directions, had been reduced to unconnected forts, as Rome was in no danger from its near neighbours throughout the Fifth Century which had just ended. The Gauls swept like a tornado down the Tiber Valley and terrorized the countryside with their swarms of cavalry, barbarous disregard for civilians and blood-curdling war-cries. According to Livy, the Roman consul M. Popillius warned the citizens: "We are not facing a Latin or Sabine foe who will become our ally when defeated; we have drawn our swords against wild beasts, whose blood we must shed or spill our own."[4]

The Romans were able to mobilize about forty-thousand men, rather fewer than the size the swollen Gallic horde. The two forces met at Allia near Veii on July 18,

---

4 Livy, VII, p. 24.

391, and the Gauls broke up the Roman field army, though it retreated in more or less orderly fashion, part to Veii and part to Rome. As Rome was not a walled city, it could not be defended against such a host, the population retreated up the various hills and what was still immediately available of the army manned the fortifications of the Capitoline Hill. Livy and Polybius differ in some respects, and both were assembling their facts on the basis of conflicting lore, but there is no doubt the Gauls burned much of the city. They stormed the Capitol repeatedly, day and night, but were beaten off and laid siege to it. After seven months, the Romans negotiated their safe withdrawal, and the Gauls, who had finally taken heavy casualties and were much troubled by pestilence and short rations, also withdrew, harassed by semi-organized bands of armed stragglers and individual military units who had got out of the path of the Gauls between Clusium and Rome. Considerable revisionism was subsequently engaged in by Roman historians, to the effect that Rome had not really been defeated and had inflicted intolerable losses on the Gauls, but these are exaggerated. Though weakened and frustrated by a bitter seven-month siege, the Gauls retired intact and with all they had plundered and accumulated. But the Roman leadership had also remained intact, the defenders of the Capitoline had certainly maintained the honour of Rome, and the legendary fabulists had enough to work with and were made more believable by the swift and immense recovery of Rome.

But for the time being, Rome was devastated and its neighbours, with whom it had with great difficulty and over a long time subdued, saw their chance of revenge. The Volscians went to war against Rome at once, smarting from Rome's conquest of them, the Etruscan League, so passive and helpless opposite the Gauls, also went to war, and the Latins and Henrici, who had been reliable for a whole century, also went into open revolt. Rome, in a severely distressed condition, was at grave risk of complete annihilation and appointed as dictator with practically unlimited powers, the fortuitously chosen M. Furius Camillus. He had been the conqueror of southern Etruria and for the next 25 years he personified the Roman recovery, one of the most brilliant periods of its accomplishment in all Roman history. He had already been military tribune three times, censor and dictator, and in the reconstruction after the visitation of the Gauls, he would again be military tribune three times, four times dictator, and on several occasions the interrex.

Camillus began with an immediate and drastic reform of the army, which was transformed in a few months of rigorous training into a serious professional force with excellent weapons and a sophisticated tactical handbook and a strictly enforced merit system of promotion. The army had had a timocratic (land-owning) class arrangement, which had been adequate to motivate the officers sufficiently in incremental expansions of Roman territory in the Fifth Century but required renovation in this new era of larger armies against more formidable enemies. Rome had bought off the Gauls, but blackmailers generally return for more, and there was her territory to restore, stamping out all the desertions and uprisings around Rome, whatever the Gauls did. There were two principal components of military reform: first was changing the organization from socio-economic to age-based, and arranging the infantry in three sections; advance, principal, and tertiary. The youngest men were placed forward, the more mature in the larger second rank, and the more elderly on the tertiary line, the reserve in fact. The light infantry continued to be drawn from the census.

The second major reform was to replace the phalanx with somewhat smaller concentrations that enabled greater flexibility in exploiting opportunities as well as in defense. Armaments were also improved: an iron helmet replaced a leather cap, the shields were trimmed with bronze, the stake was strengthened with a metal shaft, and the javelin force was enlarged and more flexibly trained. Two techniques were adopted for strengthening Rome's position in the areas it had acquired and lost and immediately set about reconquering: Roman colonies were planted among them to provide loyal clusters and depots among the occupied and to increase both vigilance and the absorption of the economic and even patriotic interests of local elements, and even more importantly, Rome now began the process that in the next several centuries would spread throughout the known world of granting citizenship of Rome to large numbers of quiescent conquered people. This last policy was adopted first with Tusculum in 381. It led, more or less directly, to the dissolution of the Latin League in favour of expanding Rome in 338 B.C.

For forty years the Gauls returned to harass Rome, meeting ever stiffer resistance and reprisals, but initially, Rome's previous local suzerainties, waffled irresolutely between Rome and the Gauls, until Rome had successfully imparted the lesson of loyalty, by a combination of incentives and retribution. Rome itself was fortified, as a priority. The rampart of Servius Tullius was restored, the Capitoline Hill's fortifications made impregnable, and then the Palatine Hill, and Tullius' wall, seven miles round, eventually enclosed the whole city and provided storehouses so commodious, a very long siege could be endured if necessary. The collapse against the Gauls had been not only military but political and this side of affairs was comprehensively addressed also. C. Licinius Stolo and L. Sextius (the first plebeian consul in 375) were elected joint tribunes in 376 and over the next decade struggled with the internecine political division of Rome and eventually produced, in 367, the Licinian Law, which provided that at least one of the two consuls would have to be a plebeian, and restricted the admissible extent of individual land-holdings, and provided for the granting to plebeians of allotments of land in conquered or reconquered territories. These measures produced relative stability, as the remodeled Roman army started to regain territory where Rome could justify seizing some of the conquered land for its own under-privileged, complementing the colonization program and bringing home to formerly disaffected areas the dangers of betrayal of Rome. These measures were adopted in Rome with extreme difficulty and a great deal of counter-legislation back and forth and were finally secured by Manlius Capitolinus, the hero of the Capitoline resistance in 391, and an in-law of Camillus, and the close collaboration of these two with Licinius and Sextius was necessary to secure adoption.

Lubricated by land grants and colonization as Rome regained and grew beyond its former extent gradually allowed a placatory balance between the patricians and plebeians and a reasonable upward access for the successful plebeians. Rome was developing political institutions that by the mid-Fourth Century B.C., contemporary with the rise of Philip of Macedon, were considerably more sophisticated and democratic than anything in all but a very few Greek cities. And the method of colonization with granting of citizenship, if Greeks had thought of it, might have extricated the Greeks from centuries of internecine backbiting before the Macedonian kings swept the whole squabbling League of Greek states away.

The forty years of wars of succession that enervated all Greece, Persia, Asia Minor and Egypt, would be a time spent by Rome in accelerated preparation to assume the leading role in the Western world, in almost direct succession to the superannuated and downtrodden Egyptians, decadent Persians, enervated Greeks and fragmented Macedonians, having advanced the techniques of government, administration, and national expansion to levels of sophistication the previous empires had not imagined, and only the Greeks (including Alexander the Great), had much thought about. As was recorded in Chapter 13, if Alexander had lived, it is possible that he might have implemented in practical ways his visionary ideas for a Pan-Hellenic confederacy encompassing all the territory he subdued. With his untimely death, any such effort had to await the Romans nearly two centuries of prodigious bloodshed later.

Polybius and Livy disagree on the frequency and dates of the ensuing Gallic wars, until Rome finally drove the Gauls completely out of Central Italy for two-thousand years in 346 or 345 B.C. Between 387 and 357, there seems to have been a good deal of skirmishing, but not general war, and all the while the Romans were extending their own jurisdiction and reinforcing it by the transplantation of the masses of Rome and formal colonization and the enticement or outright subornation of influential and susceptible locals to the growing prestigious allure of Roman citizenship. A little like the Greeks in Asia Minor, the Gauls, numerous and naturally bellicose, became the mercenaries of choice in Italy and a little beyond, and were prepared to fight for and against anyone for about two-hundred years until Rome asserted its authority.

The Gauls came in bands and tribes innumerable times in the thirty years following the attack on Rome in 391, interested only in plunder, but soon learned to give Rome a pass as there were easier pickings elsewhere in Italy. Strabo and others claim that the Gauls were relatively absent from the edges of Rome for thirty years because of disputes among their own tribes and continuous warring with the Umbrians and Etruscans. Certainly, the Gauls had little unity, organization, discipline or collective goals; they were just a fierce mass of marauders, as we have seen, overrunning almost everywhere for a time, like the Hyksos and Assyrians, until they are beaten off or assimilated or some combination of the two. But the Gauls were not above having a stab at the diplomatic chicanery of advanced states. As was mentioned in Chapter 11, Brennus had negotiated a mutual assistance pact with the cunning and treacherous Dionysius of Syracuse at the height of his powers, which involved Sicilian maritime assistance and Gallic diversionary attacks if Dionysius sought to exploit Rome's discomfort by advancing up the mainland of Italy.

In 361, a Gallic army approached Rome and was met by a well-organized Roman army led by the unfeasibly named dictator T. Quinctius Poenus (a Latin Dickens couldn't have made that one up). They faced each other from opposite sides of a bridge on the Anio, three miles north of Rome, and the issue was resolved by a hand-to-hand battle between a selected Gaul and the Roman T. Manlius Torquatus. Manlius defeated and killed the Gaul, and the Gauls passed round Rome and attacked Campania. At this stage, Rome was quiescent in raids of that kind as the Roman strategy was that the more the Gauls disturbed others in Italy the less they would object to the comparatively gentle and civilizing yoke of the Romans. In 360 (Livy), or 357 (Polybius), there was another Gallic invasion and according to Polybius the Gauls stopped at Alba and the Romans did not attack them. According to Polybius the new Roman dictator, Q. Servilius Ahala met and defeated the Gauls and they retired. The Roman historians agree that two years later the Gauls attacked again, through Latium to Pedum about twenty-five miles east of Rome, and the new dictator, L. Sulpicius Peticus, a distinguished general, though he wished to let the Gauls mill about and exhaust themselves, was beseeched by his soldiers to lead them into battle. He did so and decisively defeated the Gauls, who were by now starting to understand that attacking Rome might not be very productive or enjoyable.

But eight years later, the Gauls were back and were defeated but not destroyed by the Roman army commanded by the consul, Popillius Laenas. They took refuge in the Alban mountains but were flushed out by the severe weather and lack of food the next year, fought an inconclusive engagement, but were then decisively defeated by Camillus' son L. Furius Camillus, who waited for the Gauls hidden in the Pontine marshes in 349. (The elder Camillus died in 365, aged eighty-one, one of Rome's all-time greatest heroes, a soldier and statesman of the first rank in the darkest times. Livy called him "the second father of Rome, after Romulus.") It was at the beginning of this battle that in the Gallic custom, a Gallic Goliath challenged any Roman to a single combat, and M. Valerius Corvus insisted on taking up the challenge, The legend has been partially translated into history that a large raven alit on Corvus' helmet and repeatedly flew in the Gauls' face enabling Corvus to slay his adversary. The battle ensued and the Roman victory was confirmed. The Gauls did not challenge Rome again, and signed a peace with them in 332-1, for thirty years. Henceforth, as between Gaul and Rome, Rome would be on the offensive for the next seven-hundred years, and would, under its greatest leader, begin the transformation of Gauls into Frenchmen.

While intermittently coping with the Gauls, Rome was faced with the self-appointed task of reasserting itself over its formerly cowed neighbours. These, following the compass, were pursued in four different directions: restoring Roman authority in southern Etruria to the north, defeating the Aequi and Hernici in the east, subduing and recouping the territory of the Volsci in the south, and reconstruction and expansion of Roman preeminence in Latium. In Southern Etruria, two of the principal towns, Sutrium and Nepete (about forty miles north of Rome) had stood by Rome. Veii had already been taken and Fidenae, just five miles from Rome, which had embraced a separatist movement barely in advance of the Gauls, was taught a vivid example: the civilian population was undisturbed, other than by an influx of permanent Romans, but the town was sacked down to its foundations by the Roman army. In 389, Camillus defeated and killed many in an Etruscan army that had attacked loyal Sutrium. Full victory in the north came swiftly and easily. In 387, southern Etruria was annexed outright. This aroused the beleaguered Etruscans and in 386, they briefly captured Nepete, betrayed by the collaborationist party within, as we have often seen in the Levant and Asia Minor. Camillus and his co-military tribune, P. Valerius, chased them out and the treasonous inhabitants in Nepete were identified and executed by public decapitation by the Roman lictors and Roman colonies were established in both towns. These examples were also noted.

In 359, the Tarquinians (Etruscans), fifty miles northwest of Rome, invaded Roman territory and laid waste to some agricultural areas, and the following year, defeated a Roman consul, C. Fabius Ambustus, and massacred three-hundred Roman soldiers whom they had captured. In 357, the Tarquinii made an alliance with Falerii, a city twenty-five miles east of Tarquinii, and they brought the whole Etruscan league into a general attack on Rome. The Roman dictator, C. Marcus Rutilus, counterattacked and defeated the Etruscans and expelled them from Roman territory, though their army retired intact. In 356, Sulpicius Peticus, in his third consulate, pursued the Etruscan army into and through Etruria, burning considerable expanses of territory. No quarter was given by either side and prisoners were usually executed as soon as they had been interrogated, on both sides. In 353, Caere, just twenty miles west of Rome and a long-standing ally, threatened to bolt but backed down on stern Roman warnings, supplemented by a new offensive that thoroughly defeated Tarquinii and Falerii: all three were granted long-term peace agreements (one-hundred years for Caere and forty years for the others—Rome took such things more seriously than Periclean Athens and the Spartans and Persians did).

On the eastern front, Camillus attacked and crushed the Aequi at Bola in 389, and the Hernici in 386, and the dictator A. Cornelius Cossus, repeated the decisive defeat of the Hernici in 385. The Aequi and Hernici remained quiet for over twenty years, and well out of the way on their foothills and mountains, but in 362 Rome determined to subdue them completely, the Gauls being fairly quiet at this point. The consul L. Genucius was taken by surprise and killed, but in 361, the now familiar consuls, C. Sulpicius Peticus and C. Licinius Stolo, defeated them and captured Ferentinum, forty miles east-southeast of Rome, and the following year, the Hernici were again routed by the consul M. Fabius Ambustus, and two years later by the consul C. Plautius Proculus, and the Hernici gave up and sued for peace, which was agreed, with serious penalty clauses for their abrasiveness and treachery. A putative alliance was negotiated.

The Volsci were the most difficult of all (apart from the Gauls, of course). A virtual war of extermination broke out and was escalated, especially with the chief hostile cities, Antium, Satricum, and Velitrae (a Latin colony) all in an arc about forty miles southeast of Rome. In 389 they had been roundly defeated by Camillus at Markion, but they regrouped and made common cause with the Hernici and Latins and were again beaten by Camillus as military tribune and surrendered to him in large numbers before Satricum. Camillus was called away to deal with the the Etrurians. (He was for a time like Frederick the Great in the Seven Years' War 1756-1763 A.D., dashing from one frontier to the next fighting invaders on three sides.) The dictator Cossus, on the heels of his rout of the Hernici in 385, smashed the Volsci, but they were back in 382 and with their Praenestian allies actually captured Satricum, though it was vigorously defended and had a Roman colony of two-thousand citizens. In 381, the irreplaceable Camillus, military tribune for the sixth time, badly defeated the Volsci, but the Volsci retreated and regrouped and in 379 surprised and defeated two Roman military tribunes who were not equal to the task, C. and P. Manlius. A disaster was narrowly avoided.

In 378, Rome launched a pincers attack into Volsci territory using Sp. Furius and M. Horatius (military tribunes) in the west along the coast, through mountain passes from the east by Q. Servilius and L. Geganius. They destroyed everything, homes, towns, crops, and cattle were herded away or driven off. All trees were felled, bridges and aqueducts torn down or burned down where possible. But in 377, the Volsci again attacked Satricum, but the Romans under P. Valerius and L. Aemilius, smashed the Volsci army and scattered it with much slaughter. A twenty year informal standstill cease-fire ensued, in which Rome continued to strengthen its hand in the other theatres, but in 358, Rome annexed the Pontine plains immediately adjacent to the Volsci capital of Antium, on the coast sixty miles southeast of Rome. This cut the Praenestians off from the Mediterranean and facilitated the eventual Roman conquest of Campania. (The nearby Pontine marshes, where armies of all sides hid at times, were pestilential ground, and were only drained and made fertile by Benito Mussolini in the 1920s A.D.) The Volsci weren't quite finished. They attacked Rome in 348 and a war continued for ten years, without prolonged lapses, but finally, in 338, Rome captured the Volsci capital at Antium and Rome was able to demand and receive the complete submission of the Volsci people. It had been a very nasty war, but its end was as final as the war had been long and fierce.

The struggle to reestablish Rome's premier position in Latium continued for thirty-five years. These towns revolted in two cycles. In 386 and 385, the principal Latin cities, Tibur and Praeneste and Velitrae sought to establish their independence. Tusculum and Norba and a number of the other southern cities remained loyal to Rome, but the uprisings that did occur, assisted by the Aequi, Hernici, and Volsci, were very troublesome and Camillus and Cossus, the dictator in 385, put them down firmly but not durably. After the surrender of the Antiates at the end of these engagements, the Latins withdrew toward their places of origin but not because they were resigned to resumption of the Roman yoke.

The second phase of this Roman restoration was a much less spirited revolt by Tibur, Praeneste, and Velitrae and lesser states, but was made dangerous by their recruitment of the Gauls as mercenaries. But, as the Romans knew, mercenaries were unreliable, always subject to taking a higher offer, and were expensive. The Latins soon discovered that the Gauls they had engaged were capable of turning on them and sacking some of the towns that were paying them to fight the Romans, especially after they were defeated in 360 B.C. by the Roman dictator Q. Servilius Ahala, referred to above. In 358, Latium generally had been so drained by war and beaten down by the Romans and taxed and betrayed by the Gauls, that they accepted the old Treaty of Spurius Cassius of 493 B.C. with substantial revisions detailing Rome's preeminence and right to require the adherence of the old Latin League to join in Rome's military requirements and initiatives. Rome was head of the Latin League and all the cities and towns were forced into the League by 354, the accepted date of Rome's return to its position prior to the Gallic invasion, with significant enhancements earned by its ultimate heavy defeat of the Gauls, who had swept down northern and central Italy like a tornado. Rome was back to its previous largest extent of over twenty-five hundred square miles and had developed an appetite for more.

Gaul had not been just a barbaric tempest; as was mentioned in Chapter 14, and earlier in this chapter, Brennus had connived with Dionysius of Syracuse. Manlius Capitolinus and Furius Camillus, by their strenuous response to the Gauls, prevented that unholy alliance from effecting the carve-up that was probably envisioned. Yet the Gauls had rendered Rome some service, inadvertently. It was their military pressure on the Etruscans that enabled Rome in the early Fourth Century to conquer Veii and southern Etruria. And the Gauls were the principal agent of the magnificent reassertion of the nascent Roman vocation for conquest and government, the radical reform and improvement of the Roman army and extensive reform of the Roman state, that made it institutionally stronger than any other government in prior Western history. The Gauls also, whether as invaders or inconstant mercenaries, helped mobilize Pan-Italian sentiment behind the strongest central Italian city. This was the beginning of the concept of Italian unity, which would prevail for seven-hundred and fifty years, and then be revived again after a lapse of nearly fifteen-hundred years. In 354, Rome concluded her treaty with the Samnites, opening the era of her great expansion in Italy, and six years later, in 348, she signed her second treaty with Carthage (after a lapse of one-hundred and sixty years), opening up formally her Mediterranean ambitions, an entirely new endeavour for a city that was not on the sea and had had no maritime tradition or interests at all.

The revived trajectory of Roman military fortunes was conducted roughly parallel to the maturation of the state. In 385, Manlius Capitolinus, hero of the Gallic reduction of Rome, attempted a coup d'état on behalf of the plebeians whose champion he affected to be. He was imprisoned then released, but on a second coup attempt was executed by being thrown from the Tarpeian Rock in 384. The stormy passage of the Licinian Law redistributing land and assuring a plebeian consul sponsored by Licinius Stolo and L. Sextius, as was mentioned above, was achieved in the midst of the military recovery. Between 360 and 340 B.C., the plebeian consuls, changing every year, were confined to four individuals. The patrician consuls in the same period were largely confined to the Manlius and Fabius families. There was back-sliding, as there were as many as six years when there were no plebeian consuls in this period, though the victorious general C. Marcius Rutilus, was the first plebeian dictator in 356 B.C. A mutiny of Roman soldiers, in 342 in Campania, was blamed on usurious lending and was addressed by a law prohibiting extortionate interest rates. There were various laws assuring joint occupancy of the consulate, the censorship, and other offices, through the middle and late-Fourth Century. It seems that never after 342, were both consuls patricians, but it was not until 215 that both were plebeian. This all somewhat prefigured the struggle between the nobles and commoners in England and other countries many centuries later, and replicated to some degree, through similar agitation in Athens in the previous two centuries. Publius Philo, a frequent mid-Fourth Century holder of high offices, was in 327 granted prorogatio imperii, by which he continued as consul in consecutive years to deal with a military emergency. This was typical of Roman practicality, and this became more frequent than not, as time went by. The Romans were a good deal less hide-bound and combative over subtle political refinements than the Athenians.

One of Rome's most important statesmen in this era was Appius Claudius Caecus (340-273), who was censor from 312 to 308, consul in 307 and 296, interrex three times, and a prominent figure in Roman public life for forty years (though Livy claims that he retreated to his home for a time, professing to be blind, to avoid his critics). He is especially well remembered because he commissioned the great highway to Capua (still the Appian Way), and Rome's first aqueduct, bringing pure spring water eight miles from the Arnio River. He was a plebeian and a champion of inscribing the sons of freed slaves on the senatorial role. In his time the tug of war between the patriciate and the plebeians was still very agitated and around the turn into the Third Century B.C., two important reforms were gained by the plebeians. They carried, with the approval of Appius, the right of plebeians to appeal a capital sentence to the whole people, and contrary to Appius' wishes, the priestly colleges of Pontifices and Augurs were opened to the plebeians. The office of aedile was created at the same time as that of tribunes of the people, in 494, and they were a sort of deputy consul, between quaestors (inspectors) and praetors (judges), who managed public property and festivals. In 446, they were given authority to enforce Senate decrees and in 367, curile aediles were established, who were also magistrates. In the Fourth and Third Centuries B.C., there were intermittent measures to relieve the magistrates of their administrative tasks so they could concentrate on judicial matters and mediation. Commissioners were established for various functions, including allotment of property in conquered territory, establishment of colonies, and naval or maritime disputes—the start of admiralty law.

Intermittently between 450 and 300, there were serious food shortages in Rome that naturally caused great anxiety and public outrage. One Sp. Maelius, around 440, had privately accumulated food which he allegedly released in support of a drive for confirmation as dictator, and he was slain "in the public interest" by the general whose feats have been mentioned, C. Servilius Ahala. By the end of the Fifth Century, the allocation of conquered land to Roman plebeians had substantially relieved the problem of famine. Nothing in the activities of Licinius Stolo and Lucius Sextius was more controversial than their decree of limitations to the extent of land anyone could own in Rome. The stability of the food supply was also assisted by the ambitious colonization schemes that followed the eastern offensive of 423, after the refounding of Antium in 338, and following Rome's absorption of much of Umbria in 293 and succeeding years. Rome's growth, like that of any modern metropolis, was in a series of lurches where expansion and consolidation followed each other and the emphasis on agricultural production and the infrastructure to assure movement of people and goods and secure the water supply were somewhat in arrears of practical requirements.

Legislation about debt was another burning issue, especially with the plebeians, and was subject to a good deal of political posturing. The maximum annual rate of interest seems to have been fixed in 357 at a rather predatory one-hundred percent, but was cut in half in 347, and the debtors were granted three years to pay. Usury was outlawed, though the definition of it varied from time to time. The greatest victory of the plebeians in these matters was the virtual abolition of the nexum, by which a defaulting borrower could be subject to personal servitude to the creditor, which seems to have occurred in 313. By the turn into the new century in 300 B.C., the distress of the plebeians had been substantially relieved and the relative prosperity that followed conquest of neighbors became a popular policy. The Romans became more efficient at it and had the ability to govern better than the regimes they overthrew and to suborn the susceptible leaders of the societies they overran and occupied with the privilege of Roman citizenship and office, as well as a more civilized and orderly civic life and the protection against invasion by others. They inculcated a wider nationalism, something the Greeks had never managed, though Alexander the Great was certainly aiming at it. The small tenants, sharecroppers, and indebted had all received some redress. Tensions remained but had been alleviated—the only issue that had been absolutely resolved was the right of (relatively wealthy) plebeians to hold the offices of state. It will be remembered that even at this late date, Sparta was still overwhelmingly a city of slaves.

The consequences of the cumulative changes in the Roman state brought forward a ruling elite that after about 340 B.C. was much enlarged by meritorious plebeians. As Rome adopted the vocation of expanding and governing, it became practically impossible, even if there was a strenuous ambition for it, to confine the leadership to the patricians. Colonization and allotment of conquered land benefited the plebeians and as they became wealthier, their motivation to participate fully in the rise of Rome grew with their aptitude to do so. The Senate of Rome gradually but fairly swiftly evolved into a legislative chamber that faithfully reflected a striving and talented people where all classes had a chance to reach the summit of Roman life. Throughout its formative centuries, Rome kept grafting new offices and statutes onto its state, confident that flexibility and practicality would blend laws and institutions in practice and serious abuses that arose would be dealt with as required. This confident adaptability served Rome much better than the rigidity of most Greek governments, which prevented them from adapting to sociological changes and tended to freeze the societies of the diminutive Greek states, with little vocation for anything except endless war for small prizes. Alexander the Great showed the world how to break out of those confinements, geographic and psychological, but did not live to put a successor regime durably in place. We saw in Chapters 14 and 15 what a sanguinary fiasco was the effort to maintain his empire. Rome approached it from a different perspective, without the intellectual vivacity of Athens, but building steadily on its merited success, not carried to the ends of the world by a single, perishable and irreplaceable genius. And in Rome there was never anything like the compulsive civic envy that caused the Greeks to torment and punish their most successful leaders.

4. The Roman Conquest of Central Italy

The historical evidence for the rise of Rome to dominance in Central Italy is scantily and not very believably chronicled, Livy being the greatest source but often an unreliable one. In the early Fifth Century B.C. the most formidable peoples in all Italy were the Etruscans and the Greeks. Rome and the Latins had freed themselves from Etruscan influence. If the Greeks of Sicily had been capable of unified action, they could have asserted themselves over southern Italy, and had nothing to fear from Carthage at this stage, and if they had been able to forge an alliance with the principal powers of Magna Graecia, they would have been a great force. As we have seen, Sicily virtually committed suicide and was only rescued from itself by the courageous and generous Timoleon (Chapter 11). In the second half of the Fifth Century, the Italians asserted themselves in their peninsula and pushed the Greeks and Etruscans back. There was a good deal of migration in Italy because of the over-population of mountainous areas.

This jostling about of populations toing and froing made the Roman task of expansion easier. The Etruscans and Picentes held the territory to the north, until the arrival of the Gauls, and to the south were the Sabellians, or Oscans. Dionysius of Syracuse, in addition to making a miniature Nazi-Soviet Pact with Brennus the Gaul against Rome, effectively traded control of all Sicily for abandonment of his Sicilian countrymen on the mainland of Italy. The Sabellians of the south Apennines formed a loose confederation which Rome called the Samnites. The Lucanians and Oscans and a few neighbouring lesser tribes, living on sparse foothill terrain and relatively primitive, held the south of Italy. Rome and the Samnites made an alliance in 354 B.C. in which they affirmed non-aggression and respect for the allies of each other. But as the threat of the Gauls receded, it was inevitable that they would become rivals in Campania, the rich province southeast of Rome. In 340, the Romans and Samnites together inflicted a stinging defeat on the Latins at Trifanum. This was finished off with a number of fine victories of Camillus and others and seems to have been the last cooperative effort between the Romans and the Samnites.

Rome, in a good tactical gesture to advance its expansion, handed out citizenship to a number of Italian towns including Lanuvium, Aricia, and Pedum, and Tusculan noble, L. Fulvius, became a Roman consul in 322. Rome made its next leap southward by granting citizenship to the towns along the southwestern coast from Fundi forty miles from Rome, to Cumae, fifty miles further and only ten miles from Naples. These advances enabled Rome to convert alliance with Campania almost to suzerainty. Campania nestled in politically close to Rome and without formally annexing Campania, Rome tucked it under its wing without any overt act or condescension and a de facto condition of semi-dependence resulted. Campania was a place of colourful decoration, lively minstrelsy and skilled craftsmen, and the mutual adherence was profitable to both in many ways. Rome gave Campania the security of an alliance without smothering its local autonomy; it was an agile and subtle takeover. At this point, Rome was clearly making a bid for domination of Central Italy. It continued to pick off target cities at intervals, and without violence, by the suddenness of their takeovers and usually the connivance of locals.

Naples (Neapolis) was a Greek city, and the municipal political factions were divided between pro-Roman and pro-Samnite groups, and the Samnite allies succeeded in having a Samnite garrison invited into the city after nearby Cumae had come under Roman protection. This led to deteriorated relations between Neapolis and Capua, which latter city asked for Roman assistance. Q. Publilius Philo, an able soldier-diplomat, surrounded landward Neapolis, which was sustained through the winter of 327-326 only by sea, and Publilius intrigued with the pro-Roman faction inside the city, which eventually wrested control from Rome's opponents, more or less peacefully. The result of this jockeying was another substantial accretion of the Roman orbit in Italy, but relations with the Samnites were now becoming very tenuous. The Samnites were hill people who lived in smaller towns and had an army well-adapted to their territory: they fought in smaller bands than phalanxes and carried a short stabbing sword and a long, throwing spear. The Samnite foot-soldiers were mobile but steadfast, altogether a formidable adversary, and a state that was so decentralized it could not be defeated by taking its capital, though in Campania, they were city-dwellers. Rome could clearly occupy Samnium but whether it could control and suppress it was another matter. They were tenacious and independent people and it would not be possible to plant enough colonists among them to dilute their patriotic zeal; rather, any colonists would be put at serious risk. The Romans had the benefit of their experiences with the Aequi and Hernici and Volsci, but with the Samnites, they would draw on all their experience and the patience they had shown with the Etruscans and Gauls.

The First Samnite War had been a rather limited series of skirmishes in 343-341, that it is generally agreed Rome won but not decisively and not at great cost to either side. The Great Samnite War began badly for Rome. Rome had to recruit allies in Apulia, and in 321 had both its armies for the campaign at Calatia, about ten miles northeast of Neapolis, and they imprudently allowed themselves to be ambushed by the Samnites in the narrow valley between Saticula and Caudium. The consuls, T. Verturius and Sp. Postumius, were starved into surrender. To secure peace, the Roman Senate had to agree to vacate a number of towns near Samnium, and the captured army passed beneath a symbolic yoke of spears publicly, and six-hundred Roman knights were detained pending senate approval. This was another grievous blow to Roman prestige, but the more astute bystanders had come to realize that Rome could be humiliated as it was most notably by the Gauls, but it was Rome's habit to claw its way back. The section of posterity which has elevated the Samnite bushwhackers into the last brave custodians of the integrity and virtue of native local Italy have reproached them for not finishing Rome off, but as was shortly demonstrated, this was vastly beyond their capacities. On the other hand, Roman historical mythmaking was soon hard at work downplaying the humiliating fiasco of the two incompetent consuls, and condensing the minor setback of 321 with Rome's later victories. The Samnites occupied Fregellae, fifty miles north of Neapolis as part of the Caudine Peace that reigned for five years after the initial debacle.

Despite this setback, Rome now extended over a thousand square miles, and after its military leaders had studied the mountain warfare methods of the Samnites, devised new, more flexible formations and adopted the pilum (the Samnite javelin). Capua and Cumae had seen the return of the badly beaten Roman army from Caudium, two legions humbled, and were henceforth wobbly allies. Rome sent prefects to the two cities in 318, who advised the local worthies that Rome, in its habitual manner, had learned the lessons of the Caudine fiasco and were soon going to put matters right. Despite these warnings, the League of Nuceria, south of Capua, declared itself an ally of the Samnites, in one of the ancient world's more seriously untimely strategic realignments. The Romans replaced the two political incompetents who were responsible for Caudium with their two most accomplished generals, Lucius Papirius Cursor and Q. Publilius Philo, between them at the head of five Roman and Campanian legions. Papirius guarded the establishment of a colony of three-thousand at Lucera and suppressed its rebellion to stabilize Apulia, and Publilius besieged Saticula. These two towns were seventy miles apart and the Samnites sent an army between the two Romans and threatened Campania. The dictator, and talented general, Q. Fabius Rullianus, rushed against the advancing Samnites with an army of reservists. Fabius was defeated, though narrowly, and lost his cavalry commander. At this point, in the accustomed manner, Rome's less respectful allies started to peel off, but the Latins held firm and Papirius reduced Satricum and assured Rome's security. The Romans reestablished themselves in the south, starting with the outright massacre of almost the entire population of the Aurunci, and the installation of a Latin colony at Suessa. Satricum rebelled and was reconquered and the ringleaders of the insurrection were publicly executed in the main civic square, an instructive spectacle. In 313, Fregellae was recaptured, as was Calatia in the following year, and it succumbed with the grace of conversion to the merits of the Roman alliance. Papirius Cursor liberated the Roman hostages and forced seven-thousand Samnite soldiers to pass under his yoke at Lucera.

Strategic colonies were established at Saticula and Pontia, to protect Campania. Rome set up a colony at Ostia and finally built a small navy, which disembarked a shore party in 310, to harass and discomfit Pompeii. It was in this period that Rome distinctly developed its plan to take over all of southern and central Italy, which would make it one of the world's great states, however the bitter fighting of the wars of Macedonian succession worked out, and they were now into their second decade. The Etruscans and beyond them the Gauls lurked to the north, and the Umbrians, Sabines, and remnants of the Aequi to the northeast. There were a lot of less numerous states to the east, that generally cooperated with Rome, and allowed Roman legions to pass unhindered through their territory and on to Apulia, but these tribes were somewhat related to the Samnites, and most identified with the Samnites as exurban hill-dwellers. As Rome grew stronger, the Etrurians to the northwest also became uneasy; all Rome's neighbours noted and were to varying degrees disconcerted by the steady accretion of Roman territory and by Rome's welling vocation for expansion and domination. It need hardly be recorded that their apprehensions of Rome's appetite were abundantly prophetic, though over time, Italy would uniformly benefit from it.

The Etruscans had reached a state of considerable dissolution, accelerated by the relative quiescence of the Gauls, who were themselves settling into the natural comforts of northern Italy, and the Etruscans set themselves the task of stirring up the Etrurians against the Romans. Rome had honeycombed all the communities of central and northern Italy with their agents and received regular advice of any unfriendly movements and actions. As Etrurian news became more ominous, Rome elevated a dictator in 311 and sent the consul Aemilius Barbula to relieve the town of Sutrium, which the Etrurians had invested. The Romans slapped down the Etruscan troublemakers smartly in 310. While they were besieging Sutrium, the consul Quintus Fabius marched through Monte Cimini and administered an almost effortless beating to the unprepossessing and listless force the Etruscans mustered against him. This produced the usual repercussions in many of the Etruscan towns: just as a Roman defeat (or that of any other state) brought to power the faction that opposed that state, Rome's easy victories nearby elevated the pro-Roman factions in a number of Etruscan and Etrurian cities. Given how much easier it was for Rome to spread her mantle to the north than to skirmish fiercely with the Samnites, it is little wonder that putting the Etruscans in their place was a pleasing diversion for the legions of Rome, and it provided greater accretions of wealth and influence for less effort and sacrifice.

In 311, the consul Junius Bubulcus extricated himself with difficulty from another ambush in northern Samnium and in 310, the Consul C. Marcius Rutilus won a narrow hard-fought victory in western Samnium. The illustrious L. Papirius Cursor was made dictator to defeat the Samnites, which he did at Longula in 310, and Fabius was recalled to deal with a Samnite move in the country of the Marsi to the southeast of Rome. He fended them off, but the unworldly and slightly barbarous Samnites were preternaturally resistant to the usually successful Roman combination of military repression and political and economic blandishments. The consul Lucius Volumnius (the first plebeian consul) made headway against the Samnites in northern Apulia in 307, but it was hard slogging.

The Hernici started up in revolt again in 306, prompted by the Samnites and Aequi; there was a good deal of reasoning that if the surrounding states and tribes didn't unite against Rome now, Rome would crush them all sequentially. There was no counter-argument except to agree that Rome would prevail anyway so get on board early. The Latin communities, such as Aletrium, Ferentinum, and Verulae, all required revisitation from Marcius Rutilus. In 305, the Samnites joined forces with those Hernici who were still up in arms, as well as a significant number of still disaffected Aequi and several years of hard fighting ensued. One Roman consul, Tiberius Minucius Augurinus, was killed in battle at Bola by the Samnites, but his replacement, Fulvius Curvus, won a substantial victory there and completed the subjugation of the Aequi. With the fall of Arpinum, the Hernici ceased to exist as a force of organized resistance. In 304 the Samnites accepted a peace that left them with their frontiers little changed, but Rome now held all the locations, which they proceeded to garrison and fortify, that enabled them to bottle Samnium up, prevent the Samnites from any worthwhile contact with Rome's northern enemies, and facilitated Rome's consolidation of central Italy. Though Rome had got the better of the combat with Samnium, its victory was strategic: Samnium was isolated. It tried to attract the Greeks to their assistance, but the Greeks were, as always, squabbling among themselves, had been deflated by the Macedonians and didn't want to take on the Romans, against whom they had no grievance, any more than they had any reason to feel affectionately toward the Samnites, who were a bristling porcupine to all comers. The hour of Pyrrhus had not yet struck. The Samnites' former allies in Central Italy had either been crushed or both intimidated and seduced by the Romans, whose overlordship had its compensations.

Rome turned again toward the north, where the Gauls had withdrawn or settled reasonably peaceably, and the Etruscans wanted no part of challenging the risen Rome; but there were new Celtic groups and tribes that kept streaming down the Adriatic coast of Italy, and Rome, representing the general Italian interest, wanted to keep them out. Rome set out to occupy Umbria or bind it to Rome in order to close any access to outsiders in significant number to take this route to central Italy or to the reignition of the smoldering Samnite menace. Rome seized Nequinum, which was garrisoned and repopulated as the colony of Narnia; it stands at the point where the Roman road that would be the Via Flaminia crosses the River Nar. In 299, a new threat arrived with new Gauls of the still-marauding variety, thrusting into Etruria, where the locals ushered them south to assault the Romans, with some of the Etruscan cities joining them. They were rebuffed and retired back into Etruria where the different elements busied themselves in internecine squabbling. (Etruria was the Mediterranean littoral of northern Italy while the Etruscans were a people that included about half of Etruria but other territory to the east and northeast of Italy.) At the same time, Samnium, hoping that Rome was completely distracted in the north, attacked Lucania, but the consul Cornelius Scipio Barbatus reached Lucania via southwestern Samnium in forced marches and required renewed loyalty from the Lucanians and evicted the Samnites, while his consular colleague, Cnaeus Fulvius invaded northern Samnium and routed an army hastily improvised for a defense. He occupied the old capital of the Samnite League, Bovianum Vetus. Both consuls had earned and received official triumphs in Rome.

Rome now saw the chance to crush Samnium once and for all and elevated as consuls for 297 its two ablest current generals, Quintus Fabius Rullianus and Publius Decius Mus. This was the Third Samnian War and they attacked Samnium on a broad front and laid waste the country, wintering there and preventing the people or their herds from coming down onto the more temperate plains. The Samnites devised a desperation plan of attacking around Rome in the west and joining with the aggressive New Gauls (Celts), who, the Samnites had reason to believe, would be attacking Rome from Etruria in the north. Quintus Fabius and Publius Decius both received intelligence reports that such might be afoot and moved quickly north to meet the Gauls, preferably before the Samnites could arrive by their circuitous route. Once again, Rome was being put to a severe test, and this was the time of truth for the new Roman army.

A great battle occurred in 295 near Sentinum, where the Romans fought to keep the Gauls and Samnites out of their territory. Outnumbered, Publius Decius' army started to give way, and he invoked the Roman traditions with an ecclesiastical condemnation of Rome's enemies to the diabolical underworld and personally led a charge to the death against the enemy. He perished but turned the tide of battle, which Quintus Fabius, commanding the other flank, confirmed and after continued heavy fighting, he split the Gauls from the Samnites, the former retreating northward, while the Samnites retreated east and south toward their homes, harassed and badgered much of the way by units of Fabius' army. It was a decisive victory; the Romans and their allies had about forty-thousand soldiers and the enemy probably somewhat more. The Romans and allies suffered nearly nine-thousand dead, nearly a quarter of their men, but the enemy lost about twenty-five thousand dead and eight-thousand prisoners. Again, the Samnites have been widely seen by historians as the doughty underdogs fighting for the civic virtues of decentralized Italy against the bully of the Italian peninsula. This is a somewhat outrageous caricature. At Sentinum, Rome represented civilization and its enemies were barbarians. Rome rendered great service unifying Italy and emancipating its regions from bellicose and unworldly tribal warfare and carrying a civilizing mission to the ends of the known world. The time would come when Rome was obsolete and corrupt, but that was many centuries later and long after it had delivered Italy (and Gaul), from the bestialities of tribalism.

The Romans had not quite finished with the Samnites and after regrouping and shuffling senior personnel, set out in 293 to deliver the coup de grace to this implacably resistant enemy. Lucius Papirius II, son of Papirius Cursor I, and Sp. Carvilius were the consuls and commanded in this mopping-up operation, as it was conceived. Carvilius invaded Samnium striking east and seized Amiternum, about sixty miles northeast of Rome across the Peninsula, and then wheeled south-southeast and laid waste to Samnium for eighty miles and appeared at Comimium, which he seized, and then carried on another one-hundred and thirty miles to Velia, tearing up and burning Samnium as he went. Velia is sixty miles southeast down the Mediterranean coast from Neapolis (Naples). Papirius met the main Samnian army near Aquilonia. Samnite bands pledged to fight to the death, and many did, but after a very long day of charges and hand-to-hand combat, the much-diminished Samnites attempted to disengage and retire, and Papirius set his whole army on their backs, running down and killing a great number. This was the end of Samnium as a serious rival or even nuisance to Rome. Papirius and Carvilius received great triumphs in Rome. In 292, the Romans rounded out their victories by sending the general Curius with a substantial army into Sabine territory and proclaiming all Sabine adult men Roman citizens, sine suffragio (without the right to vote in Roman elections). Within a generation, this right too was accorded, and the Sabines were full-fledged Romans, while retaining some autonomy in local government. Rome had become one of the powers of the world, with Greece, Macedonia, Egypt, and Asia Minor, the latter four moving into the third decade of the post-Alexandrian war over the spoils of his conquests and the corpse of the Persian Empire. It was not a lightning advance like Alexander's nor an endless tag-team match of wars between kindred states as Greece had pursued. The Romans learned from their victories and their defeats and were prudent and natural strategists, not attempting to add more than they could digest or engaging in insane over-reach, like the Athenian attack on Syracuse or even the Greek attempts to take over Egypt. Rome moved steadily, taking and digesting what it could, with pauses for absorptive purposes at stages. They easily led the other Italian states, much less the Gauls, in quality of institutions and of government. It was gradual, inexorable conquest by a people that paced its expansion well and adapted its institutions with ingenuity. The Senate had performed admirably and deserved to retain control of the government. Rome's administration was tolerant, reasonably democratic, and relatively consistent and civilized. Rome had come a long way, but its rise had only begun.

CHAPTER SEVENTEEN

THE PYRRHIC WARS, THE ROMAN FEDERATION THE ROMAN RIVALRY WITH CARTHAGE THE FIRST PUNIC WAR – 292 TO 240 B.C.

PYRRHUS, GAIUS DUILIUS, AND HIERO

Bust of Pyrrhus

Coin depicting Hiero

1. Pyrrhus and Roman Expansion over Central Italy

AT THE END OF the Third Samnite War in 290 B.C., Rome had separated her rivals and potential enemies of north and south Italy by occupying Sabine and neighbouring territory and stretching across the Italian Peninsula with extensive coastlines on the Mediterranean and Adriatic. The question when a country had enemies on both sides was whether the centre was strong enough to be a point of strength based on interior lines, as it was for Prussia in the Eighteenth Century, or one of weakness, as it was for Germany in the Twentieth Century (once the United States stepped onto the scales in the West). It would soon be clear that Rome was now too strong for all the rest of Italy to contain, especially as Greece was exhausted, the detritus of the Persian and Macedonian Empires were also exhausted and at each other's throats, Sicily, as we have seen, was a self-recirculating bloodbath, and Carthage had no finesse diplomatically and was overly preoccupied with merely commercial matters. Rome was able to expand at will and did so in digestible increments, entirely unlike the magnificent but evanescent lightning bolt of Alexander the Great, but also unlike the endless internecine squabbling of the Greeks.

The Greek tragedy was that with their very advanced Athenian culture and relatively sophisticated political institutions, they never developed the ability to federate seriously and spread their culture and institutions beyond colonization in Asia Minor and Italy and Sicily, which ultimately proved temporary. They had to await the great Macedonian kings Philip and Alexander to do that, and they were only able to set up the initial framework and all the talent of their entourage was squandered in fighting each other. It was a false start toward a higher civilization than the western world had known. And it soon became evident that the logical and much the most promising engine for this was Rome. Its culture was not as distinguished as that of Athens, but it was considerable (and imitative of Greece in some respects), and it possessed and retained the genius of organization and a strategic grasp of what was attainable, something that had eluded even Pericles. The most capable Roman leaders over about four centuries realized roughly what Rome could aspire to do and did it, in a manner that in modern times was possessed by a few statesmen of different countries, especially Elizabeth I, Richelieu, Peter the Great, Frederick the Great, Catherine the Great, William Pitt, elder and younger, Metternich, Bismarck, in his evil way Stalin, de Gaulle, and a number of American and Chinese leaders who had the advantage of very large countries comparatively little menaced by neighboring nations, apart from in China's case, and only briefly, Japan.

The advantageous position of Rome that had been built up in the preceding century was demonstrated in 285 B.C. when the Gauls, one-hundred and six years after they besieged the Capitoline Hill, burst over the Apennines for the sixth time seeking both land and treasure. They were led, as they had been a century before, by the Senones of the Ager Gallicus. In 284, the consul Caecilius Metellus, who had gone forth to the rescue of Arretium, which the Gauls were besieging, was defeated and slain in a battle that cost the Romans thirteen-thousand casualties and the majority of their military tribunes, as well as the consul. As was the long-established custom, the more reluctant and recent additions to the Roman jurisdiction began fidgeting and sending feelers to the Gauls (whom they should have known by now were as dangerous as allies as they were as enemies). The Samnites, Lucanians, Etruscans of Vulci and Volsinii all repudiated their treaties with Rome. The consul elevated to replace Metellus, Manius Curius, sent emissaries to the Senones chiefs to suggest an exchange of prisoners, and Rome's emissaries were brutally murdered. A reconstructed and expanded Roman army marched into the Ager Gallicus, obliging the Senones to retire to defend their homes, and Manius badly defeated the Senones, pursued them as they retreated, expelled them completely from Roman territory and administered the worst defeat the Gauls had ever sustained. A garrison colony was established at a strategic point on the new frontier, to the north of the previous one.

The neighbouring Gallic tribe, the Boii, instead of grasping the moral of the Senones' debacle, that attacking Rome was becoming a steadily less promising activity, took this as their opportunity to take the lead among the southern Gallic tribes and attacked south to make contact with the Etruscan cities that were in revolt. The consul for 283, Corneius Dolabella, led an army swiftly against them and shattered the Gauls and Etruscans at Lake Vadimo. The Boii tried it again in 282 and were again badly defeated and sued for peace. Rome was happy to agree as it had proved its point and was mopping up recalcitrance in Etruria and along the Po Valley. The Senones were so badly whipped, they were not encountered again by the Romans for more than two-hundred years, when Julius Caesar overran them in Gaul (around the present city of Sens). The Etruscan cities of Vulci and Vosinii held out for two years, as the Romans were content to starve them out; they surrendered, and the Romans reduced their territory and they were admitted to the Roman Federation.

The Etruscans had failed because of disunity and a degree of decadence. The Campanians were united but isolated and were gradually overpowered rather gently and subsumed by the Romans. The Greeks in Italy had relied on Greek mercenaries, a strategy that had no chance of ultimately resisting Roman strength. The Romans trained and motivated their own armies and used the gift of citizenship as the currency for bribes to the more talented and motivated people in the surrounding territories; success reinforced itself and accelerated the growth of Rome. The pressures of tribes in Central and Eastern Europe impinged on Greece and Italy and Gaul itself, and the Romans gradually built a defensive firewall along the Apennines.

The Lucanians posed a particular puzzle because they had been Roman allies, but inexplicably defected. They had been intermittently skirmishing for a hundred years with the Greek settlements to the south of Magna Graecia, and Rome carried on its now traditional policy of allying itself with the other enemies of those with whom they were currently in dispute. This involved befriending Thurii, Rhegium, Hipponium, Locri, Croton, and Caulonia, all of which had been somewhat enervated by the depredations of their neighbours and particularly the attacks of Dionysius, who made their conquest the object of his unimaginative and unsuccessful Greek policy. The Bruttians and Lucanians, as was often the case with barbarians, were more fierce than these colonial Greeks, who loathed them for their crudeness and belligerency. Nothing could be more natural than that they would look to Rome for protection, especially as Rome had a good reputation with the Greek-Italian cities of Neapolis and Massilia.

The most vigorous of these cities was the prosperous commercial port of Tarentum, which had established a protectorate over a number of Greek-Italian towns including Heraclea, but Tarentum followed the now almost obsolete method of engaging mercenaries to fight its battles. Archidamus of Sparta had come as the paid defender of Tarentum, but was defeated and killed by the barbarians in 338 B.C. Then came Alexander of Epirus, who defeated the Bruttians and Lucanians and restored Heraclea and other towns to Tarentum. He even negotiated a spheres-of-influence agreement with Rome, the first contact Rome officially had with the Macedonian leadership. (Alexander, again, was the brother of Olympias and uncle of Alexander the Great.) But his ambitions exceeded what Tarentum was prepared to concede him, and he removed his headquarters to Thurii, where he was insufficiently strong to resist the attack of the Lucanians, against whom, as has been recorded, he died fighting in 330 B.C.

The Tarentines held off the Lucanians and Bruttians on their own for about twenty-five years, and then, hard-pressed, asked for the aid of the Spartan Cleonymus, who like those who preceded him, arrived in 303 imagining that he would set up a kingdom of his own, which is not what the Tarentines had in mind. Quarrels began swiftly, the Greeks deserted him, and the barbarians drove him out. Livy alleges, and it is quite likely, that as Lucania had assisted Rome against the Samnites, Rome assisted the Lucanians in seeing off Cleonymus. The Tarentines were fatally slow learners and next asked the aid of Agathocles. The least familiarity with his career would have left them in no doubt he would be the most treacherous and rapacious and ruthless "ally" of all. It was in 296 that he seized the city of Croton from his supposed friends, but for the advancement of his own interests and not the Tarentines, he defeated and imposed peace on the Bruttians.

A decade after the departure of Agathocles, the Bruttians and Lucanians were back at the gates of Thurii and Hipponium. It was obvious to everyone except the governors of Tarentum that this farce could not go on indefinitely, and that either Tarentum would select its protector, who would insist on taking over Tarentum with reasonable benignity or the barbarians would finally overwhelm it and the blood would really flow. The Thurii, who had had the Lucanians and Bruttians in their midst and experienced their impertinences more directly than had the Tarentines, and whom Rome had befriended, got ahead of Tarentum and asked the protection of Rome in 282. Fabricius, the Roman consul in 282, answered the call, to the annoyance of the Tarentines, who still imagined themselves competent protectors of the nearby Greek-Italian cities.

In Rome, it was the newly fully enfranchised plebeians (287) who led, as the patrician senators were unenthused about too much adventurism. Rome relieved Thurii, and shortly after, a Roman naval squadron of ten ships anchored just off the breakwater of Tarentum. This was Rome's first attempt at gunboat diplomacy; it wasn't hugely successful, as the Tarentines sunk four of the Roman ships, and then marched to Thurii and demanded the withdrawal of Roman forces. Rome withdrew but demanded reparations from Tarentum, which were refused, and Rome's ambassadors were insulted. The Senate had proceeded cautiously and had not at first raised the ante, but Rome was finally concentrating on the possibilities in the far south of Italy, now that its defensive frontier in the north was fairly secure.

2. Pyrrhus at Large

Even the Senate had had enough and the consul for 281, Aemelius Barbula, who was operating in south Samnium in 281, was ordered to march on Tarentum and press Rome's demands. The Tarentines, trying the old card-trick again, had now asked for the aid of Pyrrhus, the new king of Epirus, but on the arrival of the Roman army, the Tarentine government asked one of their pro-Roman officials to placate Rome. This was in progress with Barbula at the walls of the city when the first three-thousand of Pyrrhus' soldiers arrived in response to the entreaties of the immediately preceding Tarentine regime. The Tarentine politician Cineas carried out a counter-revolution, a coup d'état and Tarentum declared war on Rome. This was an absurd start to the conflict, that would rank with many other nonsensical accidents that would lead to wars, including the War of Jenkins' Ear and the War of 1812.

Thus, there entered on the scene one of the more memorable and talented, and well-remembered characters of the ancient world, whom we have already seen, King Pyrrhus of Epirus, a cousin of Alexander the Great and son-in-law of Agathocles. He was an inspiring leader and gifted military tactician, but was impulsive and reckless and rather provincial; he had no idea what he was getting into in Italy. He had already twice lost and twice won his own throne and had even been the king of Macedonia for a few weeks. Whatever was loose within sailing distance of what is now Albania, Pyrrhus would try to pocket. The Tarentines must have known how unreliable his promises of disinterested assistance were likely to be and could not have imagined that he would be more reliable than some of the frightful scoundrels who had preceded him. Now Rome was the alternative, not the Lucanians and Bruttians, and this game was ending.

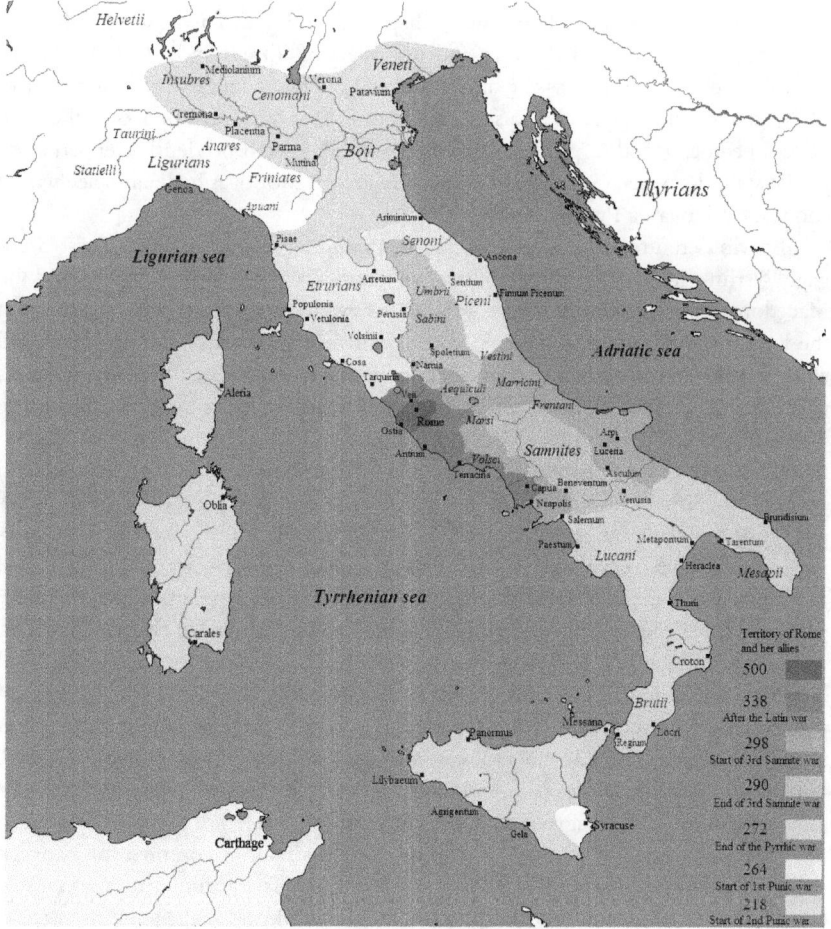

Roman conquest of Italy

Consul Aemilius Barbula, having laid waste the Tarentine countryside but spared the property of the friends of Rome, and having no authorization to attack

Tarentum itself, withdrew and returned to keep the grumpy Samnites in check, just before Pyrrhus' forces arrived. This was in 280: Pyrrhus had a well-trained army of twenty-five thousand, including three-thousand cavalry and two-thousand archers. He also brought twenty elephants, animals Rome had not yet encountered in combat, for he knew that it was Rome that he would soon be fighting. Pyrrhus immediately took unto himself considerable authority within Tarentum and purported to conscript the able-bodied males of the city. They were horrified at this prospect, assuming that fighting was the task of Pyrrhus, and they stayed away from his recruiting offices. So, he closed the gymnasia and theatres and places of entertainment and started press-ganging the slovenly Tarentine male young men into his drill halls. While these preparations were afoot, the new Roman consul, Valerius Laevinus, marched through central Lucania and left Roman garrisons in the Greek towns that had supported Rome, including Thurii, Rhegium, and Locri. The jig was up, this was a war between Rome and Pyrrhus, and the rulers of Tarentum had fumbled away even their civic authority, as the ambitious and energetic and over-bearing relative of Alexander and Agathocles was preparing to fight it out with Rome over the state he had been engaged to protect from the barbarians (who prudently stepped aside to allow the Romans, Greeks, and Albanians to sort it out). A general melee would soon be underway, a Pyrrhic melee at that.

Laevinus returned from threatening the Samnites and crossed the Siris to engage Pyrrhus. It would be the first direct encounter between Roman legions and the Macedonian phalanx. Both armies were about twenty-five thousand strong, though the Romans were only two legions, about eight-thousand men, plus auxiliaries and allies. The Romans had a thinner and longer line that could attack the Epirate flanks if the assault from the Pyrrhic phalanx could be held in the centre. Instead of using his elephants like modern tanks to cut holes here and there in the line preceding infantry and even cavalry penetration, Pyrrhus deployed his elephants on the flanks to frighten the Roman cavalry, so that his own cavalry could envelop the Roman flanks as his great phalanx over-powered the Roman centre. Hannibal, who will be appearing soon in this narrative and was the first general in the ancient world to be a rival as a military commander to Alexander the Great, used his elephants in the same way at the Battle of the Trebbia, the only occasion when he employed elephants in Italy.

Hannibal regarded Pyrrhus as his preceptor in tactical matters, and considered him an outstanding if uneven general, an opinion that was widely held. Pyrrhus' plan was broadly successful; the Romans finally had to quit the field in retreat, but it was not at all a rout. Laevinus took seven-thousand dead and seriously wounded, but Pyrrhus lost over four-thousand, and for him replacements were less plentiful and farther away. The disgruntled Tarentines were certainly not going to step up to the mark. It was at this point that Pyrrhus made his famous comment of concern at having another victory over the Romans like this: the Pyrrhic victory where the casualties were so great it was almost a defeat. The battle did shake loose the weaker and less spontaneous Roman allies; Croton swore allegiance to Pyrrhus and Locri dismissed its Roman garrison. Rhegium seemed about to bolt, when the undisciplined Campanian garrison revolted and massacred a swath of Rhegium's leading citizens; Rome later inflicted a severe retribution on the Campanians to retain their reputation for integrity and fair governance among the Greek communities of Italy.

With this hard-fought victory behind him, Pyrrhus made a lightning dash for Rome, under the misapprehension that the balance of Rome's so-called allies would react as Croton had, or at least play for their own account as the Campanians had, however savagely and imprudently. (Hannibal would make the same mistake sixty years later.) The Samnites did not rally to Pyrrhus, and Capua and Neapolis would not open their gates to him. The other consul, Coruncanius quickly settled matters in Etruria and with the Vulci and Volsinii and returned in time to man the walls of Rome. The citizens were called up, including, for the first time, the unpropertied classes, but all rallied to the colours and Rome was ready to defend herself. This revealed the weak point in Pyrrhus' nature: he was brilliant at the sudden and imaginative stroke, but quickly discouraged by tests of endurance and hard slogging. He saw that Italy was not rising against Rome and grasped how seriously he lacked the force necessary to take Rome, or even to maraud in Italy given the surliness of the provinces and the considerable hold Rome had over them.

When just forty miles from Rome, but meeting well-organized skirmishing parties, he turned south and sent Cineas to Rome with offers of peace. Cineas bore rich gifts in the oriental manner—this was new to Rome and while they accepted the gifts stiffly but politely, they thought it was a crude attempt at bribery. Pyrrhus' terms were that Rome should make peace also with Tarentum, give freedom and autonomy to all the Greeks in Italy, and vacate Samnium and Lucania and the land of the Bruttians, the dauntless ally of all of whom Pyrrhus now pretended to be. He didn't presume to ask concessions from Rome herself and promised the return of all prisoners. There was a peace faction in the Senate, and the question of whether to entertain serious discussions was being closely debated when the venerable Appius Claudius, now in his sixties, took the floor and harangued his colleagues as dishonourable and pusillanimous for considering negotiations involving distinct concessions to a foreign invader while he was still at loose and undefeated in Italy. This steadied the ranks and firmed up a majority for knocking the invader around a bit before considering peace with him. Fabricius was sent to decline Pyrrhus' terms but to offer to pay ransom for their prisoners. Pyrrhus needed peace not gold, but he learned quickly the nature and susceptibilities of the relatively incorruptible and certainly brave Romans. He replied that he did not accept the terms, sought no gold, but would give back the prisoners gratis, as a gesture of his goodwill, but that they would have to return to his gentle keeping if negotiations did not take place within a reasonable time and in good faith, in which case the return of the prisoners was left as a matter of Rome's honesty and honour.

Rome trained new armies and in 279 elected as consuls P. Sulpicius and P. Decius Mus, son of the consul who had perished bravely at Sentinum. The war continued. Rome fielded an army of about forty-thousand including four Roman legions, and Pyrrhus had managed to obtain reinforcements to achieve about an equal size. He turned back toward Rome, but along the Adriatic coast, avoiding the easily roused Campanians, who seemed generally somewhat loyal to Rome. Pyrrhus hoped to liberate Samnium and seriously fluster the Latin towns east and southeast of Rome. The armies met on wooded territory near Asculum, east of Venusia. The terrain was not favourable to elephants, cavalry, or a dense phalanx. The armies fought all day without victory for either side. Early the next morning the king seized the river fords and moved to territory better suited to his tactics, and for action by the phalanx and by elephants. Battle was resumed and the phalanx pushed the Romans back, but they retreated in orderly recession to their armed camp and beat off further attacks. Again, the Romans had taken losses of about six-thousand, including the consul Decius, who died in combat as his father had, but Pyrrhus suffered nearly four-thousand dead and was wounded himself, though not seriously. He won but gained nothing from it except increased impatience—another Pyrrhic victory.

By this time, Pyrrhus had learned that the Celts who were always active north of Macedonia, had gleaned the throne of Macedonia and were threatening his own borders in Epirus. It was obvious that he wasn't going to get anything from the Romans, whose armies could, at best, be forced to vacate the field, but intact and after inflicting heavy casualties. He had come to regret ever having embarked on this mission and now received an invitation from some Sicilian towns who asked him to come and help them against the Carthaginians, who since the death of Agathocles, sought to conquer the whole island. The Romans correctly surmised from the fact that Pyrrhus made no effort to follow up on his ostensible victory and instead retired to Tarentum, that he might be prepared to offer more acceptable terms than he had in 279. Fabricius returned in 278 and met Pyrrhus at Tarentum, and seemed to have reached agreement, subject to Senate approval, on peace with a full exchange of prisoners and no money transfers, but with the independence of Tarentum assured. While the Senate was deliberating, and even though Appius Claudius' terms had been met and Pyrrhus would happily depart Italy; Mago, the Carthaginian admiral, had arrived in Rome to urge Rome not to free Pyrrhus to depart Italy, and to keep him engaged for a few more months. Mago revealed as little as he could, but Rome was well aware of the ebb and flow of Carthage's effort to seize all Sicily and of its present blockade of Syracuse (which was going a good deal better than the catastrophic Athenian effort at the same object of one-hundred and thirty-five years earlier). The agreement gave Rome precisely what it needed, a good payment of silver to pay and keep happy the southern Italians, and the undertaking that if either Rome or Carthage was engaged in war with Pyrrhus, the other party will assist against Pyrrhus and Carthage shall provide all the naval transport and support, though each party will pay its own men. Mago came to Ostium with his fleet of one-hundred and twenty vessels, and Carthage was an infinitely greater sea power than Rome at this time and would provide its fleet for any assistance against Pyrrhus Rome wished. This practically guaranteed Rome's ability to expel Pyrrhus from Italy at modest cost, and Rome didn't care who ruled Sicily. Provision seems to have been made for further incentivization of Rome in assisting Carthage in Sicily, but on unspecified terms. Both sides negotiated skillfully, and both had reason to be pleased with their achievement. Pyrrhus, whether he realized it at once, was now very much on his back foot, and could not move his army out of Italy easily without encountering the mortal danger of the Carthaginian fleet.

Mago sailed back to blockade Syracuse harbor, dropping off five-hundred. Roman legionaries on the way at Rhegium, where they tried to overwhelm the Campanian rebels who had massacred the leading citizens (who were about to secede from the Roman alliance). The rebels survived this attempted suppression, narrowly beating off the Roman anti-insurrection squad, but this so incensed Rome that it would return the next year and finally subdue the revolt with prodigious severity. In 278, Fabricius and Aemilius Papus were the consuls, and they marched south and into Tarantene territory, but Pyrrhus was absorbed in Sicilian matters and did not stir. The Romans did not want to besiege Tarantum until the Carthaginian fleet was available to blockade it. But an Epirote defector who gained an audience with Fabricius and promised to murder Pyrrhus with poison if Fabricius greased his palm with an adequate quantity of silver, was dismissed and Fabricius sent the message to Pyrrhus. This was the traditional morality of the still prominent Roman rustic aristocracy: solid, high-minded and unworldly. The Roman consuls won back many of the defected and wavering cities: including Heraclea, which hereafter enjoyed a status of independent ally to Rome, and Croton and Locri. All the territory of Samnium and Lucania that Rome had lost (though it was not extensive), it regained.

Pyrrhus went to Sicily in 278. Sosistratus was now the tyrant of Acragas, and was at war with the Syracusan tyrant Thoenon, and was besieging him on the island of Ortygia in Syracuse harbour. With Mago's arrival, Sosistratus and Thoenon hastily composed their differences and joined in resistance to the outsider. They offered their fealty to the inevitable Pyrrhus, who had learned a lot about Sicily and come to covet it as a result of having married Agathocles' daughter Lanassa. He was almost certainly generally aware of the accord between Rome and Carthage, so this was a natural alliance for Pyrrhus as well as a stepping-stone to hegemony in Sicily, and, given Pyrrhus' mercurial nature, perhaps Carthage as well. He left strong garrisons in Tarentum and some of the other Greek Italiate cities and sailed with ten-thousand troops to Catana, having sent Cineas ahead with requirements for written commitments to acceptance of his overlordship, which were accepted and signed. Pyrrhus was greeted as a liberator in Sicily and his army quickly grew as he picked up contingent forces as he processed toward Syracuse overland. Pyrrhus was acclaimed at Acragas, Selinus, Heraclea, and Segesta, reducing the Carthaginians to Lilybaeum. The Carthaginians, recognizing that they were under grave threat and that Pyrrhus had eluded and foiled Mago, offered him all Sicily if they could keep Lilybaeum. He was tempted but shamed by the Greek Sicilians to finish the job and expel Carthage from Sicily.

Pyrrhus rose to the call for further combat as the Roman Senate had when Appius Claudius had attacked them for slacking in considering Pyrrhus' peace terms two years before. Pyrrhus besieged Lilybaeum for two months and twice stormed it unsuccessfully. The volatile Sicilians who had accused him of slacking for not finishing Carthage off, soon resented his exactions and knowing how formidable Carthage was, they were unenthused about his extravagant dream to conquer Carthage. There were rumblings of mutiny in the Sicilian ranks, and Sositratus, once the rival of Agathocles, abruptly pulled out of the alliance that had saved him from Carthage and repaired to Acragas. The Carthaginians were emboldened to send reinforcements and to try to turn the tide in Syracuse. Pyrrhus feared that Thoenon would bolt from his alliance with him too, so the king had Thoenon murdered, a fate he visited upon a number of dodgy Sicilians. Such campaigns in Sicily, or among expatriate Sicilians, merely whipped up more violence, an activity Sicilians profess not to enjoy, but can rarely resist, in any context.

There were many requests of aid from Carthage by Sicilians wanting to be rid of Pyrrhus, whom they had recruited to fight the Carthaginians for them, and whom they now requested the aid of Carthage in helping them to evict. By 275, Pyrrhus had had enough and sailed back to Epirus, washing his hands of the whole business. He went back to Italy, but the Carthaginian fleet, in loyalty to its treaty with Rome, intercepted him and sank half his fleet. Pyrrhus had fully maintained the record of Sicilians in enticing outsiders onto their island and then dispensing with them after bitter and dangerous disappointments. Pyrrhus set out to regain lost territory in Italy and took Locri by trickery and robbed the Temple of Persephone, which was considered a grievous sacrilege and theft throughout the Greek world, not the sort of sentiments to which Pyrrhus had been in the habit of paying much attention. However, he was so bedeviled in Italy, he eventually made some restoration, as he attributed his misfortunes there to his scandalous profanation at Persephone. He regained Croton from the Campanians who had taken it two years before.

This foray came to an end when Pyrrhus stole north and tried to take advantage of the distance between the two Roman armies, one commanded by Manius Curius Dentatus (so named because he was born with teeth already emerged), and the other under Lucius Cornelius Lentulus. Both were seasoned commanders and Curius was at Beneventum watching the roads between Samnium and Rome, and Lentulus was in Lucania watching the central Italian road. These were logical deployments for the interception of the Epirate king who was likely to appear suddenly anywhere. Pyrrhus thought to take Curius' army by surprise by night marching but arrived a little after daybreak enabling Curius to move his army into battle formation quickly. This time the Romans had the advantage of size and they had had a night's sleep. Pyrrhus put up his usual determined struggle, but the Romans were becoming accustomed to his tactics, and Curius narrowly won a battle of about five hours, during most of which Lentulus' army was hastening to the rear of Pyrrhus to finish with this unbidden visitor once and for all.

Curius captured a couple of his elephants and Pyrrhus abruptly, but skillfully withdrew and regained Tarentum at speed, narrowly escaping the trap the Roman consuls had hoped would destroy him. The effect of the action was practically the same, as Pyrrhus embarked the battle-scarred remnant of his initial force, eight-thousand infantry and five-hundred cavalry, less than a third of the force with which he answered the call of Tarentum six years before. He left a small garrison at Tarentum, commanded by Milo and Pyrrhus' son Helenus, implying the king would be back. He returned to Epirus and the eastern Greek world, his prestige much diminished. He had been the most interesting and talented soldier-king since Alexander the Great and had certainly not discouraged speculation that he would replicate the feats of the Macedonian. (Even Alexander himself would not have made of the Romans the short work he did of the Persians, Egyptians, and the eastern satraps, but he would not have lurched from target to target and squandered his forces as Pyrrhus did.)

In light of these events, Pyrrhus returned, another Eastern king, like the survivors of the Great Wars of the Diadochi, which had finally ended, but with a more modest kingdom. But for the first time, the Hellenic world finally took note of the rising power in the West. Rome had been vaguely known but had generally been assumed to have been a rather pedestrian Italian farmer state, tenacious of its own territory and gradually spreading both up and down Italy, but not a state that was likely ever to be relevant to the Greek mainland or Asia Minor. This was reasonable as, at this time, Rome had no ambition to be an influence in the East. But the methodical way that it built and held its jurisdiction: conquering, suborning the leading figures, governing with comparative civility and integrity and conferring benefits of good government, security against more dangerous and primitive enemies and drawing the leading local figures into the governance of Rome, was unlike anything the western world had seen before. It grew steadily, but there was no logical necessary end to such expansion.

Rome built the world's best roads and aqueducts and was beginning to become a naval power; it could pursue the formula for gradual expansion a long way. Rome had already cured Italy of the terminal Greek malaise of municipalization, and though less cerebral than Greece, it was beginning to develop a culture, substantially influenced by the Greeks, but was above all, a practical nation. No one, including the most trenchant and lyrical Hellenophiles could say any such thing about the Greeks. Ptolemy Philadelphus, the leading monarch in the east after the terrible shakedown of the Alexandrian succession, sent emissaries to Rome to begin a cordial diplomatic exchange. Rome was happy to reciprocate, and what would be one of the most famous international relationships in all history was under way and wending toward the fateful climax two-hundred and fifty years later of Cleopatra and the last Ptolemys with Julius and Octavian (Augustus) Caesar. Rome was a world power, and after four-hundred years, it was just warming up.

3. The Roman Federation

Rome moved into its increasingly important role cautiously, as always, and determined that the Roman Federation must be consolidated, supposedly to assure a more rapid reaction and effective defense should the dread Pyrrhus return. (Nothing within the gift of any person or regime could induce him to do so). Rome broke up the Samnite League, which had revived in the Pyrrhic troubles and was a serious and sinister nuisance and cut a strip along the Calor River dividing Samnium and large Roman colonies were placed at strategic locations including Beneventum, near the site of the battle (which had been called Malventum before but was renamed in recognition of Rome's victory there). Parts were trimmed off Samnium and Lucania, colonies installed, and the process began of seducing, suborning, or repressing the leading figures and winning over the population with the durable policy of sensible government and external peace, and the rising prosperity of what was one of the world's greatest powers and becoming more prosperous every month.

Croton and Locri, both of which had had a rough war, were reintegrated into the Roman Federation, where they would remain. Croton had bolted to Pyrrhus, then was seized by Rome under Rufinus, then the Campanian rebels seized and plundered it, then they were evicted by the returning Pyrrhus, and he was driven out by the Romans. Since the Crotonians had shown no great partiality for any of those regimes, they were not accorded much consideration in return, and the Campanians in particular felt that regime change required the summary execution of a broad swath of leading worthies; it was an action-packed five years, and Croton was doubtless grateful for the prolonged Roman peace that followed. Locri was favoured as a free territory, i.e., its population was not liable for conscription to Roman military service.

Rome confiscated half of the Bruttians' forest-land, mainly for ship-building purposes, an activity in which Rome would become steadily more ambitious. In 272, Rome finally got to the sole of the Boot of Italy and laid siege to Tarentum, which had been a rather outrageously awkward component of Italian and Magna Graecia politics for centuries, bringing in mercenaries and then taking against them. The consul Papirius Cursor the Younger was entrusted with this mission. As usual, Tarentum was itself divided, the Pyrrhic garrison was still there and did not want any part of fighting it out with the Romans, while the civic leaders wanted resistance, but, as was their custom, wished others to provide it for them. The Epirotes made their deal with Rome and escaped the city with well-filled pockets and retired homewards.

Taranto vanished as an independent country after a prolonged turn in that role based altogether on the imaginative rascality of the city's rulers. The association of the Tarentine leaders with Pyrrhus was never more than a union of convenience of thieves that inevitably ended as such arrangements almost always do. Tarentum, like Locri, would be spared conscription and was not deemed to have been taken by force (as Pyrrhus' corporal's guard had somewhat treacherously surrendered it), but the city was not autonomous and Rome was sufficiently suspicious to take a number of hostages, who were very well treated in Rome, including by Rome's first respectably talented tragedian, Livius Andronicus. Taranto would stand Rome and ultimately Italy in good stead as a fine harbor—it would be the chief naval anchorage of many regimes, including the modern unified Italy up to the present time (and was the scene of a famous British raid by torpedo bombers in 1940). There ended finally, in 270, the painful episode of the Campanian occupation of Rhegium, when the consul Cornelius Blasio stormed it and in savage fighting, killed most of the Campanians, and sent three-hundred Campanian survivors to Rome in chains, where they were publicly scourged and then executed, to the general approval of Magna Graecia.

Rome also took advantage of this relatively tranquil time to shore up and strengthen the north of Italy. Many colonies were established with large garrisons, but without the customary right of Romans to return or of local people to marry Romans. The Senate and government of Rome were concerned to end excessive migration into the city of Rome, and to strengthen the northern frontier of Roman Italy. An elderly person could still remember a grandparent describing the terrible havoc wrought by Brennus and others when the Gauls besieged the Capitoline Hill and destroyed most of the city in 391. Rome also moved whole populations, reasonably humanely but in a very arbitrary manner, to scatter them, reducing the danger of revolt and accelerating assimilation, and getting more refractory and susceptible communities away from any likely inflammatory contact with an invading enemy.

Rome won a number of triumphantly celebrated victories over Celts, Gauls, and Umbrians in northern Italy in the mid-Third Century B.C. By this time, Rome effectively ruled or dominated almost all of mainland Italy southeast of what are now Genoa and Bologna. A number of anomalies occurred, such as among the Etruscan Volsinii, who had been freed from slavery to join the army and fight the Romans (unsuccessfully), and had persisted as a civic bloc, inter-married with their former owners. They exercised their numbers to gain control of the democratic civic machinery and somewhat lorded it over their former masters, or at least their descendants. The Romans helped them sort it out, but homogenizing Italy was a challenging task (that is not complete even at time of writing).

This was a very large jurisdiction by the standards of the times, and Latin was steadily expanding as the uniform language of the whole population, as Roman laws and their administration also spread throughout most of Italy. Local dignitaries such as magistrates automatically became Roman citizens. Most inhabitants of the Roman Federation could become Roman citizens by assuming a high local office that comported an oath of loyalty to Rome, or by becoming residents of Rome itself, though, as has been mentioned, this was somewhat restricted, especially in the north, where Roman security required large numbers of able-bodied adult males to deter and repel the barbarous forces north of the Po River. The Federation was bound together by a complicated welter of different treaties and arrangements that Rome had made over centuries with all the tribes and towns in central and southern Italy. In this method of organization, it was a little like British India (India, Pakistan, Bangladesh, Sri Lanka, Myanmar, Nepal, Bhutan), where the East India Company owned stretches of territory, British treaties with individual maharajahs and other notables, and colonial establishments were all bound together in a very complicated thicket of arrangements.

It must be said that Rome was a very liberal governing power. It never tried to abolish local customs or languages, enforce conformity with Rome other than in important laws and their administration, and in coinage, or impose any form of segregation. The advantages of peace and a common language and jurisdiction, in the absence of cultural oppression, soon drained most secessionist sentiment away. In northern frontier areas, Rome settled large numbers of reliable Romans and reserved the right to take and enforce extraordinary powers to stamp out the temptation to desert to an invader at his approach. We have already seen how little there was of this in Italy opposite Pyrrhus, compared to other places such as Sicily and most of Persia, and many of the newer or lesser Greek states, which, led by generally strictly virtuous Sparta, had treated with the Great King to outflank local rivalries. Rome would create an immense loyalty to and respect for its citizenship. In 268, Rome also produced the denarius, a sixth of an ounce of silver, and it was emulated or taken over exactly throughout the Roman Federation, and when there was not a serious war in progress, the money supply was managed conscientiously and there was very little inflation.

Rome was also relatively democratic. In Rome itself, after a long but almost entirely peaceful tug-of-war, it was finally agreed in 287 that a public assembly of citizens could overrule the Senate. This did not often happen and in general the Senate tended to represent popular opinion fairly faithfully anyway, but this was far from oriental despotism; it wasn't Periclean Athens either, though it was less elitist. (This was the so-called Hortensian Law, after a journeyman politician of that name.) Similar methods of generating and responding to public opinion existed throughout the Roman Federation. These democratic flourishes notwithstanding, Rome continued through the Third Century B.C. to be essentially an aristocracy. The Senate was dominated by the great families but with a heavy admixture of the meritocratic achievers and an increasing participation by senators from outside Rome. Like most Roman institutions, it had the character of an adaptable instrument of government which would bend to the correlation of forces within society. In the famous incident of the punishment of the Campanian rebels who had massacred the leading citizens of Rhegium, and clung to their tyranny for several years, the decision to transport the rebels in chains to Rome to be publicly whipped and then publicly beheaded was determined by public forum, the plebeian assembly, but on the advice of the Senate. Despite the Hortensian Law, the plebeian assembly was more of a method of letting off steam than a regular quasi-referendary method of legislation.

Rome's system of government was certainly imperfect, but for its time and compared to governance elsewhere, it managed efficiently to conduct Rome from a nondescript village to one of the great powers of the known world in a couple of centuries and would continue to adapt and respond to reforming needs. The weakness was already in the executive process, and this would be aggravated with time. Two equal consuls who spent most of their time commanding armies and other than in an emergency served only for a year, was clearly an inadequate level of authority for the executive, and too much power for the legislative. In the coming two centuries, the Senate would cling too long to its factionalized authority to name the executive, would be too attached to the interests of the privileged classes and would become vulnerable to the power of army commanders. There would not be a system for the formation of a non-political officer corps, and methods of organization and payment of the army would soon assure that the legions transferred their allegiance from anyone in Rome to the army commanders. But for now, Roman democracy spread in Italy and deepened responsively to society's needs throughout the Roman Federation.

4. The Struggle for Supremacy Between Rome and Carthage - The First Punic War

The Pyrrhic War had brought the two rising states of the Western Mediterranean, Rome and Carthage, into closer contact, and closer to direct rivalry. The original leading western and central Mediterranean state, Sicily, because of its inability to govern itself and its vulnerability to Greek and Carthaginian intervention, after a final bloody and flamboyant elevation of Agathocles, had disintegrated into a potentially contested area between Rome and Carthage. Though they were geographically not far apart, these states had had relatively little to do with each other. Carthage was a Phoenician colony originally and retained some colonial affinities to what remained of Phoenicia. Rome, as we have also seen, arose from land migration into Italy, and was still not an important maritime power. Rome had been an agrarian state that became a civilizing-expansionist land power that had now come to dominate the entire Italian peninsula, relatively defensible along its northern, mountainous frontier, and large but manageable all the way to its southern extremity. Rome showed aptitudes for government and demographic and cultural homogenization and with its expansion, Rome grew into a more complex economy—manufactures, enhanced trading, including the beginnings of maritime trading, and the beginnings of base and precious metal extraction. Carthage was a maritime state of traders, operating trading posts throughout the Western Mediterranean and on the Atlantic shore of North Africa and Iberia. Carthage had developed silver mining in Spain and was extremely commercially industrious. It was more adventurous and materialistic than Rome, and Carthage was a larger and richer city than Rome, but its critical mass was smaller: it was a string of trading towns out from Carthage, including Sardinia and Sicily, and mining and trading colonies in Spain. It had a great deal more difficulty dealing militarily with Pyrrhus than Rome did, and Pyrrhus, always slave to his ambitions, quickly saw that Rome was unconquerable, Sicily a push-over, and Carthage potentially very vulnerable (as his father-in-law Agathocles had shown). But he couldn't fight the Sicilians and Carthaginians at once, given that his only excuse for being west of Greece and Epirus was to save the Tarentines, who were soon scheming to be done with him (and whom the detritus of his garrison eventually happily betrayed to the Romans).

Carthage had never had a king, largely because it began as a colony and when it emancipated itself, by becoming larger and richer than Phoenicia, and unthreatened where its mother country was constantly being swept over by the great land powers of the Middle East and constantly challenged at sea by the Greeks. Its governmental system bore some resemblance to Rome's and had been admired by Aristotle for its aristocratic aspect and its relative stability. It was not very democratic: "Pure democracy, for some reason, never found favour among Semitic peoples"[1] (until the successful launch of the State of Israel). Yet there was a powerful tension within the Carthaginian state between the agrarian elements, the rich landowners, who sought ever greater arable territories, and the commercial interests who wished to monopolize the excellent Carthaginian navy for the enhancement and protection of their activities.

Nor was Carthage as open to consulting the plebeian masses as Rome was. The senior figures of government were two magistrates, judges, with powers not unlike Roman consuls and also selected annually, but not selected for their assumed or demonstrated talent at commanding armies or navies. The magistrates had to be men of property. However, Carthage had the advantage of a system that placed selected individuals in command of armies for prolonged periods, rather than the helter-skelter Roman practice of changing commands every year or eighteen months. This tended to assure better generals and admirals in Carthage than in Rome, though

---

1 CAH, VII, p. 666 (T. Frank).

not unfailingly so. The legislature was the Council, of about three-hundred, with an inner committee of thirty. Matters were referred to a popular assembly only if the Council was unable to reach a decision. This was the only valve for the release of popular impatience or anger., and the recourse to emergency powers in war, like the elevation of a Roman dictator, was a sensible arrangement and not one subject to frequent changes of personnel as Rome was.

Where Rome had a clear advantage was in the method it devised for expanding gradually and in what would in modern colonial times be called a civilizing mission, where the absorbed groups were generally left autonomous, given access to influential positions in the Roman government, and treated as equals of Rome, though sometimes after a brief transitional period, as long as they were quiescent. Carthage had no institutional interest in taking over and appending to itself other populations; it only expanded for commercial or agricultural reasons. Rome set up a federation, where many powers were reasonably decentralized, and unlike the Athenian and Corinthian Leagues, and lesser versions of them in the Hellenic and Macedonian spheres, there was no exaction of tribute or institutionalization of the inferiority of the adherent jurisdictions. Carthage commandeered troop contingents from the Phoenician colonies and from the nomadic tribes of North Africa, and extorted annual tribute from all peoples where it possessed the practical force to do so. Carthage required the nomadic tribes of Africa to forfeit from twenty-five to fifty per cent of their annual crops to Carthage, and they weren't providing these people any service in return, unlike the sophisticated government of Rome and its military alliance system which sprang instantly to the defence of any part of the Roman Federation.

This was not a realistic plan for Carthage to encourage a spirit of reciprocal loyalty and voluntarism. Agathocles and Pyrrhus (and Hannibal) discovered how uninterested many of the Italian towns were to calls to rebellion against Rome, compared to towns and tribes in Sicily and North Africa. The explanation is not hard to find. It seems that Carthage had a revenue about twenty times as great as Athens earned from her league at its height, and Carthage had more money than Rome did to support a military campaign against a powerful foe—and Carthage had never been at war with so formidable an adversary as Rome—always before she was dealing with little states or primitive peoples, or mercurial adventurers like Agathocles and Pyrrhus. What was afoot now was entirely different. Rome and Carthage were about to conduct a contest between a federation whose members were autonomous in local matters and were kept together by a shared political system that worked well and commanded general loyalty, and a wealthy city that had no real allies and used its money to pay mercenaries or conscripted often somewhat disaffected subjects to fight for her. It would be an epic contest (in three stages), and one of the most famous wars in all history.

Like most great wars, the Punic Wars began somewhat obscurely and improbably, for factors settling on the Mamertines (Sons of Mars), a fierce mercenary group that had been recruited by Agathocles in his wars, from Campania and Bruttium and which seized the Sicilian city of Messana (Messina), after the death of Agathocles in 289. They quickly transformed an industrious city of trade and routine commerce into a base for unbridled piracy on land and sea, and in some ways presaged the failed states of very modern times that became illegitimate staging areas for ambitious criminal activities, such as terrorism, though the Mamertines made no claim to any ideology or beliefs; theirs was a gangster state. The immediate successors to Agathocles (to whom, in their way, the Mamertines had been loyal on the "takes one to know one" formula), were incapable of quashing the Mamertines, and Pyrrhus in his brief and inglorious sojourn on the island never got round to dealing with them (though he could certainly have done so if he had given them his undivided attention for even a few months).

Pyrrhus departed in 276 and the capable Hiero, was chosen Strategus of Syracuse, by the highly malleable electoral system of Syracuse—he was left in charge of the forces Pyrrhus left behind and had the most military muscle in the city. Hiero claimed descent from Hiero I, a successful Fifth Century Sicilian king, and was the son-in-law of Leptines, the reasonably successful military commander who was the most important post-Agathoclean Syracusan. Hiero wished to be tyrant for life like Dionysius and Agathocles, though his methods were more respectable (but they were still eminently Sicilian and recourse to violence was always a ready option). He proclaimed himself tyrant in 270, aged thirty-eight, and would maintain his position for the astonishing total of fifty-five years, dying of natural causes aged ninety-three.

Hiero refused to recognize the legitimacy of the Mamertines, who were a general international nuisance. It is impossible to blame the Carthaginians for not tolerating the antics of the Mamertines. Hiero showed early his talents and cunning as a Sicilian leader, as he rightly judged the Mamertines less dangerous to his plans for Syracuse than Carthage. He accordingly marched out to do battle with the approaching Mamertines in 270, but deliberately put his most unruly and questionably loyal forces to the forefront, and the Mamertines crushed them effortlessly. Hiero then retired in perfect order back into Syracuse, shorn of the elements of his army of most potential danger to him, and drilled his forces very thoroughly, in a manner worthy of Agathocles and Pyrrhus.

He shaped up his forces and municipal administration, and finally, when all was ready, he sallied forth at the head of a properly trained and equipped army, captured towns on the way to Messina, and completely defeated and almost destroyed the Mamertines on the Longanus River in 265. He moved on to Messina, but the Carthaginians, under Hannibal the admiral, wanted control of all of Sicily, and disembarked a Punic (Carthaginian, from an ancient contraction of the Latin word for Phoenician) garrison, which saved the Mamertines. Hiero did not wish to engage Carthage at this stage and did not press the attack on Messina. He returned triumphant to Syracuse and was elevated by the manipulable local political machinery to be king, beginning his reign of fifty years.

The Mamertines certainly did not want to lose their independence and debated among themselves what to do with the Carthaginians who were welcome among them as defenders against Hiero but not in any other capacity. Hiero had destroyed their army, so the Mamertines had to accept durably the protection of the Carthaginians, try to make their peace with Hiero, or invite the protection of the Romans. Sicily was probably no longer capable of defending itself against both the Romans and the Carthaginians, and the Mamertines were certainly not strong enough to retain their independence opposite all three powers; it was time for everyone to choose allies. The Mamertines sought the assistance of Rome, presumably as the most distant, probably the strongest, and in Sicilian matters the most disinterested potential ally. The Romans discussed the Sicilian question extensively in the Senate.

There was a considerable reservoir of good will in Rome for Hiero; he had been helpful in the suppression of the Campanian rebels at Rhegium, and he had fought the Carthaginians, whom Rome now recognized as their rival, in Sicily, and had been much offended by Carthage's descent upon Messina in aid of a wretched gang of brigands and desperadoes. The Romans saw the escalated rivalry with Carthage and were in no mood to accelerate or aggravate it, but they did not want Carthage taking over Sicily any more than Carthage wanted Hiero to take over Sicily. No one had any use or sympathy with the Mamertines, but they were the focal point of the interests of the three main powers of the region at the time.

Rome had already felt obliged to concede Carthage a trading monopoly in North Africa, Spain, and Sardinia, and was not prepared to do so with Sicily. Any such development, while it would not hinder Rome itself particularly, would cause the southern Italian cities like Tarentum to seek Rome's assistance in breaking the Carthaginian commercial monopoly, failing which, such cities would come under great pressure to make similar arrangements with Carthage as she already enjoyed in Spain and Sardinia. This would be an intolerable intrusion in Italy from the Roman perspective. No Roman senator considered the Mamertines a respectable beneficiary of Rome's assistance, but if the alternative was, as it appeared to be, that Carthage would control Messina and gain a hammerlock on all Sicily, and continue to the Italian seaboard, it was better to move now, and tighten relations with Hiero also. The Mamertines had no more claim to legitimacy than the Campanians at Rhegium had had, but the Mamertines had been in Messina for twenty-five years, starting in times when Rome had no interests south of Neapolis. Now they were faced with having to sail around Sicily to get from Neapolis to Tarentum.

The senators knew that when Rome responded to a similar call for assistance from Thurii, it led to a prolonged, and at times tense, war with Pyrrhus. Rome did not need land, as there was plenty for distribution in Etruria and Ager Gallicus, where the army had pushed back Gauls, Celts, and lesser barbarians; it did not need food, as Roman Italy already produced a surplus of wheat, and all crops (including grapes). The old aristocracy didn't like the expansion of Rome as it led to a wider and more democratic and polyglot electorate, but they were proud Romans who would not back down to foreigners. As happens with all growing nations, as their interests become more varied, valuable, and extensive, the requirements of defending their interests grow also. Carthage was very rich and could probably hire mercenaries for longer than Rome's newly recruited allies could be relied upon to stay the course. And while Rome had only a trivial coastal naval force and no maritime tradition, Carthage had one-hundred and twenty quinqueremes that constantly patrolled the Western Mediterranean like sea cats.

But for all the arguments and reticences over intervening at Messina, as a practical matter, Rome had to act to prevent Carthage from taking over Messina, though not to confer any more durability on the presence there of the Mamertines. All these related issues were publicly debated in the Roman Senate, and the Carthaginian, and Syracusan governments, as well as the Mamertines were well aware of the opinion of the Roman government. Rome was not ready for all-out war with a great sea-power, and the decision thrust upon the Roman Senate by the infestation of cut-throats and scoundrels in Messina was in fact the choice between becoming a great imperial power, building a first class navy, and almost certainly engaging in a serious and prolonged war which would bring to the fore a great wave of new generals and admirals who would earn great popularity from the newly enfranchised plebeians (in the Hortensian Law); and ceding Sicily to Carthage.

Rome had to accept a sharp and potentially demeaning limit on its ambitions or come forward out of central Italy and bid to become the greatest power in the western world. No one familiar with the rustic pride and rigid ethical standards of the Roman state as it had developed and extended itself over semi-voluntary adherent neighbours, could doubt its vocation to rise not only above its attainments in the five hundred years of its existence, but in its natural destiny to teach the world lessons in empire and governance that no one in the West except Alexander the Great had dared to imagine possible. A giant step in world history was about to be made, in, as often has happened, a most improbable place.

Though there is some argument about it, Rome seems not to have broken any treaties in an alliance with Messina, and the public assembly, the plebeians, approved the formation of an alliance with Messina, after public discussion that it must be said was more extensive and perhaps more substantive than current public airings of great strategic issues in advanced democracies. The Senate, under the Hortensian Law, was left to implement the policy. Since the Mamertines had requested the alliance, and Carthage had gone to the aid of the Mamertines also, there was not technically a direct collision between Rome and Carthage, just a difference of motives. Carthage did not want Hiero taking control of Messina, and Rome didn't want Carthage taking control of Messina, and so the gang of thugs and scoundrels in power in Messina enjoyed the momentary legitimacy of the intersection of greater powers. The Senate had to send a consul to Messina with adequate force to be a credible bearer of the policy to be followed by the Roman state and this delicate and difficult task was entrusted to Appius Claudius, younger cousin of the famous censor who had secured approval of the continuation of the war against Pyrrhus. As it was going to take some time to mobilize two legions and march four-hundred miles to Rhegium and there to embark for Messina, Appius designated another relative, the military tribune, Cadius Caudex, to sail to Messina at once with a small expeditionary force. The Carthaginians took it upon themselves to try to block the entry of the Roman ships into the port of Messina, but were unsuccessful, though they did board and capture a couple of Roman ships. These were returned however, as the Punic (Carthaginian) commander had orders to avoid open conflict with Rome, but he informed the Romans that Carthage considered these to be closed waters.

Claudius did not respond to this warning, and the Mamertines were so emboldened by the arrival of even a small number of Romans that they bade the Carthaginian garrison to depart. As they had come on invitation and he did not have contrary orders, the Punic commandant of the garrison, Hanno, a relatively junior officer, withdrew. He was rewarded for his prudence and scrupulous adherence to the limits of his orders by being summarily court-martialed and executed for betraying the state's interest. Carthage immediately dispatched an army to Sicily under the command of another Hanno, son of Hannibal the admiral (Carthage suffered from an extreme paucity of names for its prominent personages). Hanno landed at Lilybaeum, marched to Acragas, and then contracted an alliance with Hiero. This must have been more of a preliminary cease-fire for Hiero, as he would certainly not want to become too intimate with Carthage, given the now notorious Punic desire to take the whole island. Hiero and Hanno marched on parallel routes to Messina, where Appius Claudius had arrived with his two legions. The Punic naval commander, despite the exemplary treatment of the late (first) Hanno, had no orders to go to war with Rome and he did not impede their landing. Hiero and the surviving Hanno (henceforth the only one unless specified otherwise), were in separate camps several miles apart, and Appius opened separate negotiations with both, rightly suspecting that any joint effort between Carthage and Syracuse was a very fragile enterprise.

Appius Claudius made especially friendly overtures to Hiero, claiming Rome's desire for friendship, which was reasonably sincere—Rome was happy with an inoffensive regime in Sicily, but not with a Punic one that would close the ports and infringe on Roman waters. Neither negotiation was successful, so Claudius attacked Hiero first, believing him to be the weaker of the two armies. The attack on Hiero was not entirely successful, but the Syracusan got a good foretaste of what fighting with Roman legions was like, and he suspected his ally (who was in fact his feared enemy) had deliberately allowed the Romans through the blockade, and had not rushed to his assistance when he was attacked, though what he might have imagined the Punic motive to be in allowing the Romans to land has escaped the comprehension of historians. Hiero was sufficiently shaken by his encounter with the Romans and the passivity of the Carthaginians that he withdrew and returned to Syracuse. He would be happy to have the Romans and Carthaginians fight it out for the honour of subduing the Mamertines. Claudius attacked Hanno and inflicted considerable damage on him. Hanno withdrew also and retreated to more defensible territory. Claudius seized a fort at Echetla, near Leontini and the eastern boundary of the Carthaginian section of Sicily. He marched on to Syracuse, to try to extract an alliance from Hiero, who just barricaded himself into his fortress city and did not respond to the Romans. A siege was out of the question with the harbor open. With this, Appius Claudius returned to Messina, left his forces there for his successor and returned to Rome. Despite his undoubted military success in Sicily, besting both armies and keeping Messina out of the hands of Carthage, he was coolly received for not having brought back peace with victory. Instead, Rome now faced more war to preserve its modest victory in Sicily. Instead of a peace making Italy more secure, there was now the prospect of war with both Carthage and Sicily, though Sicily would presumably be easy to detach. As for Carthage, the Senate can scarcely have imagined that that was not a very live possibility given that Claudius had carried out his orders to get the Carthaginians out of Messina.

There was a change in public mood and in 263, Rome elected people with no relationship to the Claudians as consuls: Manius Otacilius, a plebeian of Samnite ancestry, and Manius Valerius, who arrived in 263 with four legions and a large contingent of allies, a combined army of about forty-thousand. Given the Carthaginian supremacy at sea and what must have been their awareness that Rome was likely to send reinforcements, the consuls seem to have slipped through the Punic blockade fairly effortlessly. Their remit from the Senate and people was to gain recognition of Rome's assurance of the independence of Messina. The first priority was to get relations with Hiero straightened away. The Romans were not going to war to prevent Carthage from taking over Sicily without at least the benign neutrality of the principal Sicilian. Since Rome still officially hoped that this would not be a prolonged war, it had not ordered a large construction of warships.

Valerius and Otacilius marched quickly into Syracusan territory and seized the fort of Hadranum under Mount Aetna. This show of determination by a large and battle-hardened army was, as usual in Sicily, sufficient to shake loose a virtual blizzard of expressions of municipal submission. The Roman consuls knew how reliable was the grace of these instant conversions, but they were intended to shake Hiero and they succeeded. They marched directly on Syracuse and invested it, though a siege continued to be nonsensical as long as the port was open. But the Romans had calculated correctly that the Syracusan population would be eminently unenthused about taking up arms as part of an effort led by their Punic enemies, whom everyone in Sicily knew had the ambition of turning Sicily into a Carthaginian customs house. A fifteen-year peace was quickly concluded by which an indemnity of one-hundred talents (about two million dollars) would be paid by Syracuse and Hiero would be recognized by Rome as king of Syracuse and most of the territory he controlled prior to the arrival of the Roman legions—a radius from Syracuse along each coast and inland for about thirty miles. It was understood that Sicilian grain would be available to Rome if needed. Nothing was said of naval warfare as the Romans still hoped to avoid that, but why they imagined that Carthage would just roll over at this point remains a mystery (though it would have been better for Carthage if it had).

Roman opinion was generally pleased with this result, cheaply gained, and Rome enjoyed a good reputation for not exacting tribute and for leaving various free cities within her sphere virtually unaffected by the Roman domination of most of Italy. Rome also kept its legions, as occupying forces, under tighter control than did other warring powers and most mercenaries were conspicuously rapacious, as money was their only object in being soldiers in the first place. Valerius was given a triumph in Rome, assumedly an act of hopefulness that the war was already winding down. One feature of the peace was that Rome began to emulate the painting of large heroic murals of its victories, which Hiero had shown Valerius and Otacilius in Syracuse. The Senate withdrew half of Rome's forces from Sicily, since it was only now facing one enemy there, but thought better of that when intelligence advised that Carthage was recruiting large mercenary forces among Celts and Ligurians. The consuls for that year were Lucius Postumius and Quintus Mamilius, a once obscure plebeian, and they led replenished armies of over forty-thousand men in Sicily in the summer of 262. The consuls arrived in June and began to besiege the Carthaginian army in Agrigentum, a seaport in southern Sicily. They took in the harvest but Carthage could supply the city by sea. The defenders were led by yet another Hannibal, though still a generation away from the most famous one. The besiegers expected that heavy reinforcements would arrive in the course of their siege, which was meant to lead to an assault, given Carthaginian ability to supply Agrigentum by sea. In preparation, they dug a triple-trench line of contravallation, should the besiegers themselves be besieged. Hannibal and his forces were suffering from famine when another Hanno arrived in November with fifty-thousand infantry and six-thousand cavalry and sixty elephants. This would seem an overwhelming force, but they were a wild rout of mercenaries scraped hastily together and with no interest in anything except plunder. Hanno at least managed to stop Roman supplies so they too were reduced to low rations. Eventually, Hiero ran the blockade successfully and kept the Romans fed while they besieged the walled city on one side and held the mass of undisciplined mercenaries at bay on the other.

After two months of the double-siege, Hanno concluded that he had to attempt to relieve the city and attacked the Roman trenches. The Legionaries and their well-trained allies defeated Hanno's unruly mob of rudimentarily trained and dubiously motivated hooligans and smashed the mercenary army killing or capturing about twenty-five thousand men and driving Hanno back to Heraclea. The unsuccessful commander escaped with his life, but was stripped of his rank, fined, and publicly censored by the annoyed Punic government. The Romans had however, sustained substantial casualties themselves, to the extent that they could not prevent Hannibal from escaping around Roman lines with his hard-pressed siege-defence force, and he fled on foot, leaving Agrigentum without defenders and the city gates wide open. It was not a proud feat of Carthaginian arms, as the Romans entered the defenceless city and pillaged anything of the slightest value. There was no massacre of the civil population, but it was sold, nearly fifty-thousand souls, into slavery. This had ample precedent in Sicily, but it had been the custom to distinguish between Greek and other populations. The Romans made no such distinction and their treatment of the people of Agrigentum startled the world. It doubtless comported an element of terror for the fickle polity of Sicily, but as acts of severity generally do, it hardened resistance as much as it deterred it.

The war escalated. Carthage made no overtures for peace and Hanno was replaced by Hamilcar and started preparing a new and better army. Rome would have been happy to settle, but as Carthage evinced no such interest, it accelerated its war preparations and the Senate announced the goal of taking over all Sicily. Rome was taking the great step of becoming an imperial power: simply taking over states because it was more powerful and could govern them better. Of course there was an element of this in Rome's expansion in Italy, but it was also a response to the aggressions of Gauls, Etrurians, Umbrians, Etruscans, Samnites, Hernici, Lucanians and the rest, and as soon as feasible, Rome enfolded these peoples in a federation almost of equals. It was the most benign expansion of any of the states and peoples that we have traced, and Rome was much less convinced of the virtue of war and combat than even the most sophisticated Greek states had been.

Its interest in Sicily began with not wishing Carthage to take it over. Carthage could have divided it with Rome, but tried instead to expel Rome. Rome defeated

Carthage and a carve up in Sicily could still have been done, but when Carthage returned to the warpath, they opened up a fight to the finish. Rome wanted all Sicily but could only take it after administering a severe defeat to Carthage, demoting it from a peer-state to a lesser state. As it turned out, Rome had a formidable aptitude to conquer and consolidate and rule. Rome was an empire on the rise, an imperial government. Carthage was a commercial plutocracy, a nation of traders and sea commerce. It was altogether dependent for its security on mercenaries hired from its profit. Rome was a people born and self-groomed to conquer and rule. It was an uneven match, prolonged and made more suspenseful by Carthage's possession within its ranks of one of the greatest generals in all history, and the first of comparable ability to Alexander the Great.

There was no progress in 261, and the Carthaginian navy marauded the Italian coast. The Senate finally recognized that to win this war it would have to remove Carthage's maritime advantage. They were skilled sailors, but were very vulnerable if seriously challenged by sea, in this respect, somewhat like modern England, but unlike pre-Twentieth-Century England, there was no balance of power Carthage could manipulate. Once Carthage had antagonized Rome, there was no other power they could stir up to prevent Rome from acquiring great sea power. France could never decide whether it wished to cross the Rhine or the English Channel, and so never crossed either, except for the Napoleonic excursion into Central Europe. Carthage had no ability to force Rome to fight on more than one front. It made a catastrophic strategic miscalculation in provoking Rome when it could have coexisted with it, and in doing so, it enticed Rome out of Italy and set it on the road to the conquest of the world.

The Mediterranean is too calm most of the time to depend altogether on sails, and naval engagements, before the existence of serious naval artillery, were by out-maneuvering and ramming the enemy. For these purposes, triremes were insufficiently large and fast, and the Roman Senate ordered one-hundred quinqueremes and twenty triremes to be delivered in two months, and thirty-thousand rowers were identified and trained. The Romans also got from Hiero, long cranes that would drop marine skirmishing parties on the decks of enemy ships and fit grappling hooks to bring the ships together. Rome, with astounding boldness, set about to become the greatest naval power in the world in a few months. Hardy, jaunty Italian peasants were lifted from the vineyards and transformed into mariners. In the spring of 260, the consul Cornelius Scipio sailed south with his new fleet, and the other consul, Gaius Duilius, was in charge of land operations.

Scipio sailed from Messina with twelve ships to receive the fealty of the city of Lipara but was overwhelmed there by the Punic fleet and carried off to Carthage as a prisoner. This left Duilius in charge of the whole expeditionary forces, land and sea, a combined force of perhaps eighty-thousand. Duilius boldly sailed to intercept the main Carthaginian fleet that was operating against the coast around Mylae, ten miles west of Messina. Hannibal, the (inevitable) Punic admiral, was slightly bemused at the approach of this force, manned by landlubbers, which he outnumbered by thirty quinqueremes. But Duilius steered straight into the enemy fleet and deployed the cranes ("ravens" they were called, "corvus"), quickly seized and boarded many Carthaginian ships and over-powered the crews, and captured or sunk about fifty Punic ships, forcing the rest to flee. It was one of the stunning naval victories of world history, an inspiring debut for the Roman Navy.

The Carthaginians regrouped and upgraded their tactics, and in 259 the new consuls, Aquilius Florus and Lucius Cornelius Scipio, brother of the unfortunate prisoner of Lipara hereafter known as Scipio Asina—donkey), sailed for Corsica and Sardinia but failed to join issue with the reinforced enemy. But in 258, the consul Sulpicius engaged Hannibal and defeated him comprehensively, forcing the Carthaginian to ground his ships. His men saved the Carthaginian state the disciplinary problem of punishment: they were so disgusted by their leader that they seized and bound and crucified him, one of history's more dramatic mutinies. On land, the Punic general Hamilcar was doing better, and Carthage won its first land battle with Rome at Thermae, about eighty miles west of Messina. The situation was tightly contested, and the consul Aquilius Florus remained through the winter and in 258 he and the new consul Atilius Calatinus pushed Hamilcar back into Panormus (Palermo). They stormed Mytistratus, a thick-walled fortress that had held out for seven months after the fall of Agrigentum. The Romans smashed the walls apart with heavy catapults and sold the population into slavery. Carthage was now confined to the western sixth of Sicily, behind a line running approximately from Heraclea in the south to Palermo in the north.

In 257, a Roman army of fifty-thousand was required to keep Hamilcar within his confined limits. The Roman navy had been astoundingly successful but had not been able to land a large enough amphibious force to challenge for control of Sardinia. There wasn't much movement in Sicily, but the consul Atilius Regulus seized the island of Melita south of Sicily, and sacked and razed it. Returning to Sicily, he encountered and defeated the Carthaginian fleet off Tyndaris, a few miles west of Mylae, He sank eighteen Carthaginian ships. Regulus returned to Rome and received a great triumph, though not a triumph as immense as Gaius Duilius' in 259, who was so uproariously celebrated he was granted a torchbearer and flautist to accompany him at all times. Rome's sudden emergence as a great naval power is without any precedent or sequel in the history of war. The Germans caught on quickly in the late Nineteenth Century, but they only had one battle, at Jutland, where they sank more ships than they lost, but retired into port and never came out again except to surrender. The Russians built a fine navy quickly after the Cuban Missile Crisis, but never seriously challenged the United States for the scepter of the seas and their navy was divided up among the Soviet republics and grew old.

The Romans, eight years into the First Punic War, decided to try to force the issue by attacking Carthage in Africa, forcing its retreat from Sicily, the Agathoclean strategy on a grand scale. In the summer of 256, Rome launched an immense assault on Africa, led by two-hundred and fifty quinqueremes escorting about eighty transports, which carried fifteen-thousand infantry and five-hundred cavalry, and food for a whole campaign season. The warships were about one-hundred and fifty feet long and thirty feet wide, and each carried three-hundred oarsmen on its five decks, plus one-hundred and twenty marines. The commanders were L. Manlius Vulso and M. Atilius Regulus (succeeding his cousin, C.A. Regulus, of the preceding year). The

Roman fleet met a large Carthaginian fleet off Cape Ecnomus on the south-central coast of Sicily. The Romans formed up as a triangular wedge with the transports in the centre and a line of battleships a line across the base of the triangle. The Roman fleet drove through the thin Punic line, which was just one ship deep. The Carthaginians were more maneuverable, but the Romans again deployed their "ravens" and grappled in many Carthaginian ships, the marines killed off the crews or rendered them servile, and half the Carthaginian fleet fled and the rest the Roman fleet pressed up against the Sicilian coast. They captured fifty Carthaginian ships and sunk thirty and lost twenty-four, among which there were no transports. The Romans paused near the site of the action, repaired their ships and the captured vessels, and resumed their assault on Africa with a fleet of three-hundred and fifty-five ships, to one-hundred and seventy Carthaginian, which had retired to home waters to face the invaders there.

The Romans disembarked their troops at Aspis (Clupea), three to four days march from Carthage fifty miles to the west. Carthage was well-fortified, and the Roman expeditionary force was not sufficiently numerous to imagine storming the Punic capital. It is not clear that the Roman government had thought this strategy through, as they could not leave one-hundred thousand men (counting prisoners) in what is now Tunisia, so the main force was ordered back, leaving Regulus with fifteen-thousand men and five-hundred cavalry and forty ships in case of emergency evacuation, and the balance returned to Rome, to come back in the spring. It has never been clear what Regulus was supposed to do over the winter, other than interdict Carthage's commerce with Numidia, where the Punic upper classes had developed lush estates that the Numidian tribes would like to take back.

Carthage itself had a small land area and depended heavily on its trading posts all about the western and central Mediterranean, especially in Spain, and the many coastal states from which it exacted tribute. Regulus could certainly cause havoc in Numidia, but he was in some danger of being crushed by a larger Carthaginian force, unless he could embark quickly and elude the Carthaginian fleet. But Rome had carried the war right to the environs of Carthage and was bound to be back in 255 in great strength. Regulus invested the rich town of Adys, where many of the wealthy Carthaginians homes were located; and incredibly, Carthage, which enjoyed a great land and sea numerical advantage over Regulus, sent their forces into the hills around Adys to relieve the town and Regulus moved rapidly around the wooded areas pouncing on Carthaginian detachments at will until the Carthaginian army finally retired to its capital and Regulus took winter quarters at Tunis, not ten miles away.

Regulus became too bold; he did nothing to incite and join forces with the Numidian rebels, and invited Carthage to discuss peace but proposed outrageously one-sided terms and demanded a complete cession of Carthaginian sovereignty and its assumption of a status more subordinate than that of Tarentum. This was the problem of the Roman system that left consuls in military commands out of reach of the Senate and endowed with diplomatic powers as well; some could manage it all and most could not. If Regulus had whipped up the Numidian rebellion and really squeezed Carthage's food supply and then offered "a peace of the brave" (a phrase from Charles de Gaulle trying to resolve the Algerian War twenty-two centuries later) in which no one is embarrassed but Rome keeps most of Sicily and has access to Sardinia, a durable peace might have been agreed. But if Carthage had not been so greedy in trying to take all Sicily from under the nose of Rome, Carthage would not have had to give up anything and it could have been a long time before Rome really came out of Italy with drawn swords and took the trouble to become a great naval power. Carthage completely underestimated Rome, especially at sea, but now Rome, and not just Regulus, was underestimating Carthage. Rome was the greater power, but Carthage would not give way without a fight that would shake Rome to its foundations.

At this point, the wheel of fortune turned again. Carthage had engaged a talented Spartan, Xanthippus, to shape up its mercenaries, and he trained them well and inspired them as a leader of strength and solicitude for his men. He led the main Punic army out of Carthage and onto the Plains of the Bagradas, formed up in solid Greek phalanxes with one hundred elephants in front and four-thousand cavalry on the flanks. Regulus had no idea of flexible tactics, and massed his men in front of the elephants, which trampled and terrorized them (instead of keeping his ranks thin to enable the elephants to pass through with minimal damage). The elephants smashed the Roman centre and the Punic cavalry attacked from both sides and the rear and the Roman force was decimated and decisively beaten. Only two-thousand Roman soldiers escaped to Aspis. Regulus and five-hundred of his men were captured, and about twelve-thousand Romans were killed in one of the most incompetent deployments of an army in Roman history. Regulus, as he was to prove, was very brave, but no better a military tactician than he was a diplomatic strategist.

The tide of fortune had not come all the way in for Carthage. The Roman survivors of the rout by Xanthippus held out at Aspis but did not dare to embark for fear of the Punic navy. In Rome, preparations were ready to dispatch a fleet of three-hundred and fifty vessels to blockade Carthage while Regulus attacked by land. (Where the Roman strategists imagined that Regulus' force of a little over fifteen-thousand had the manpower to invest Carthage remains a mystery.) It is perhaps excessive to lament the absence of tactical sense in the field commander when the grand strategists of Rome had been propelled by their instant success as a maritime power into a fantasyland. The news of Regulus' disaster arrived before the Roman navy sailed, but it sailed anyway, with the mission of destroying the Carthaginian navy and rescuing the remnant of Regulus' shore party. The consuls of 254 were Aemilius Paullus and Servius Fulvius and they commanded this great armada. They found the Carthaginian fleet off the northeast promontory of Tunisia (Hermaean Point) and soundly defeated it, taking twenty-four ships and their crews. It was considered as great a victory in Rome as Gaius Duilius' inaugural triumph of the Roman navy. They collected and returned the survivors of Regulus' battered force. Off Camarina, however, on Sicily's south coast, a terrible cyclonic storm overtook them and inflicted what may yet be the greatest maritime disaster in all history: two-hundred and eighty-four of three-hundred and sixty-four ships were destroyed and twenty-five thousand marines and seventy-thousand sailors (rowers) were drowned; as all these were free men, about fifteen per cent of Italy's able-bodied adult males perished. Carthage's luck could not improve on this, but Rome, unshakeable in its purposes and moral confidence, declared an emergency tax increase that in the circumstances was not significantly resisted, recruited eighty-thousand sailors and began training them before the two-hundred new quinqueremes that were ordered were completed and handed over in three months. Rome itself had only three-hundred thousand citizens (free adult males), though the Federation may have supplied some of the replacements. The consuls who had been returning for triumphs for their great naval victory were not blamed for the natural calamity and were retained in command of the new navy, it being assumed that they had acquired a formidable education in seamanship. Carthage eventually became aware of its good fortune but needed most of its army to suppress the Numidians. The commander in Sicily, Carthalo, was reinforced by elephants but not many men, and essentially held his position, apart from seizing the unlucky city of Agrigentum and burning it to the ground. While the former consuls stayed with the navy, overall command resided with the two new consuls, Atilius Calatinus and Cornelius Asina (the resuscitated donkey), attacked the Carthaginian headquarters in Sicily at Panormus (Palermo) constantly by land and sea, and overran it. Any inhabitants who could produce two-hundred drachmas were allowed to redeem themselves at that price, and the thirteen-thousand who could not were removed as captives, but in humane conditions. This treatment impressed a number of Sicilian cities that had been held in check by Carthage taking hostages from them. Apparently, many of them were among the thirteen-thousand people Rome bagged at Palermo, and a number of cities in Sicily, including Tyndaris and Petra. They evicted the Punic garrisons and joined the Roman side in Sicily that continued to hold all but the far southwest of the island.

However, Carthaginian luck had not yet run out. The new consuls for 253, Servilius and Sepronius, set out to invade Africa again, but in unfamiliar waters, a number hit shoals and the mission returned to Italy, and another terrible storm at Cape Palinurus, near Naples, wrecked one-hundred and fifty ships, though with heavy but significantly less loss of life than at the Camarina disaster. Here matters settled for two years; Rome was master of the seas at the inter-naval level, but was perplexed by the misfortunes of meteorology and had sustained terrible human losses. It was decided to proceed slowly on land and grind Carthage down but nothing could be done in Sicily, where the Roman soldiers were afraid of the Carthaginian elephants, and the navy was not prepared to blockade Sicilian ports because of unpredictable weather. Yet this policy of attrition did take its toll on Carthage, and the tides of fortune finally shifted. In 250, Hasdrubal took the offensive in Sicily and approached Palermo; the resident consul, awaiting the arrival of his annual replacement, Caecilius Metellus, responded very carefully and came out of the city walls, but just to entrench himself near the walls. This tepid response finally provoked Hasdrubal to attack the entrenched troops, which confused the elephants as they became disoriented in the trenches and obstacles and killed a number of their own men. Metellus struck hard on Hasdrubal's flank and Hasdrubal's army disintegrated. Rome captured sixty elephants and their Indian minders (mahouts), and they were shipped back to Rome. Hasdrubal's army was run down by the Roman cavalry and almost completely destroyed, and the elephants, apart from the fact that Rome now had a good contingent of them, had been demystified in the eyes of the Roman soldiers.

Hasdrubal returned for condemnation and summary execution, which he accepted with dignity as the fate he deserved and was replaced in Sicily by Adherbal.

The new consuls for 250 were C. Atilius and Manlius Vulso, both experienced generals. They set their sites on Lilybaeum, the main Carthaginian port in Sicily, at the far-western point of the island. They brought a new fleet of two-hundred and forty warships, that had been built at deliberate speed, manned and trained, and with four legions and a large detachment of marines, the consuls deployed a combined force of over one-hundred thousand well-trained soldiers and sailors. The city was defended by ten-thousand Gallic mercenaries and ten-thousand Africans. At Drepana ten miles north, Adherbal had a fleet that could not challenge the Roman fleet but was skillful and useful at blockade-running. The Romans applied all their siege talents, sinking ships filled with rocks at the harbor entrance, building towers that rained down hellfire and rocks on the walls and the city, digging under the walls, but the Carthaginians kept building new walls in the interior, as the perimeter shrank, and Lilybaeum held out until the end of the war after eight more years. The Romans did not take heavy losses but did tie up a large fleet and land force.

The new consuls of 249, P. Claudius Pulcher and L. Junius Pullus arrived with orders to act decisively to try to win the war. In their haste to try a lightning naval attack on Adherbal at Drepana, their ships fouled each other; nearly a hundred ships were lost, but they were so close to shore the loss of man-power was a grievous, but far from unprecedented, twenty-thousand. Claudius was recalled and forced to pay a fine of twelve-thousand denarii, a heavy hit for an old soldier. His colleague Junius had an even more difficult time. He was entrusted with the conveyance of supplies to Lilybaeum as food could not be requisitioned locally without dangerously embittering relations. Apart from armed combat, Rome and Carthage were to some extent competing for the goodwill of the Sicilians, which could be determining in the close-fought war in Sicily. Not knowing of his colleague's dreadful fiasco at Drepana, Junius sent part of his supply fleet of eight-hundred transports ahead, with the rest and the supporting escort of one-hundred and twenty warships following. Adherbal sent Carthalo with the whole Carthaginian fleet out to intercept them. Carthalo was a very capable admiral, and he forced the initial force to anchor offshore in difficult waters and with rising gales, and then attacked the second division and forced it also into the rocky shore as Carthage again forged a solid alliance with the elements which thoughtfully smashed the entire Roman convoy. The losses seem to have approached another hundred thousand men, a staggering and mystifying total, and Rome again was deprived of its entire navy, carefully built, trained, and manned. Junius reached Lilybaeum with two ships and the Roman army in Sicily had to put together an emergency land convoy to deliver in carts and by mule-back bare rations for the siege force.

Junius gamely marched on Drepana with half the Lilybaeum siege force to try to recoup his honour, and by this means Rome at least managed to cut the two main Sicilian ports off from the rest of Sicily. However, his luck (and judgment) did not improve, and he was captured by a Punic night attack party and when returned in a prisoner of war exchange, committed suicide to avoid condemnation. A dictator was named in Rome to take this very difficult and star-crossed enterprise in hand.

Rome was in difficult straits, nearly bankrupt and morally exhausted. The census showed that in twenty years the population (of adult free males) had shrunk by fifty-thousand, seventeen per cent, instead of rising by twenty per cent as would normally have been expected. These terrible tempests were more devastating than a plague and roused a good deal of superstitious defeatism. Rome had lost five-hundred warships and a thousand transports, and casualty rates of oarsmen sitting on protected sea-borne wooden benches were much higher than among the Roman legions. There were real concerns about trying to recruit allied sailors for the Roman navy, which swept the seas of the Carthaginians when they met but was singled out for exemplary destruction by the tempestuous perils of the deep. It was in all respects a state of anomalous and puzzling disconcertion. The stand-pat consuls of 252, C. Aurelius and P. Servilius, were returned for 248; Rome would regroup and build her strength, but in the Senate, the debates were vigorous but affirmed the view of Appius Claudius in previous times of crisis, that Rome only negotiated after victories. So, it was to be.

Carthage reciprocated with a policy of relative passivity also. While the savage maritime weather had saved it from probable defeat and humiliation, it had not won anything and even Regulus had demonstrated its weaknesses in its African habitat, inept though he was at exploiting them. The most distinguished of the many Hanno's was in charge and he devoted considerable time to slapping down the Numidians. Carthage sent a mission to Rome to negotiate a prisoner exchange, and if possible, begin general peace negotiations. Here is where, according to Sempronius Tuditanus, hugely amplified by Horace's stirring ode, Regulus distinguished himself and graduated from the asinine company of Claudius to an heroic status that causes modern nations to name engines of war after him (e.g., the American Regulus missile). Regulus was sent on the mission to Rome but refused to advocate acceptance as it would demoralize the Roman army and returned honourably with the ambassadors and died in captivity of "neglect" which assumedly means famine and not torture. But it enflamed Roman opinion and he did become and has remained an inspirational figure, not a great commander but a sublime patriot and tower of courage and integrity. He earned no less. On learning of her husband's death, the widow of Regulus murdered the Carthaginian hostage, Bodostar; she was not prosecuted.

As well as buttressing Roman pride and morale, Regulus was also the harbinger of better diplomatic news. On the expiry of the friendship treaty with Hiero, which the Syracusan king had scrupulously honoured, and had paid the entire indemnity, it was permanently renewed as a treaty of equals. Syracuse paid nothing and its many favours, especially the unlimited use of its great port were recognized, and Rome expressed its gratitude that the king was a resolute ally in the most difficult times. Rome had also been good for Syracuse; Hiero now had unchallenged control of the most prosperous quarter of Sicily and had already taken his place as the successor to Timoleon in the heritage of Syracusan benignity in government, and enlightened rule; the two being the flip-side of the iron-fisted and endlessly duplicitous Sicilian dictators Dionysius and Agathocles. This was the first flowering of the Pax Romana.

In 247 Carthage elevated a more energetic commander, Hamilcar Barca, a daring and imaginative young general. Considerable though his talents were, he would be overshadowed by his son, the great Hannibal, as Philip of Macedon was overshadowed by Alexander the Great; the distinction of their progeny took nothing from their own qualities. Hamilcar declined to squander his forces on the besieging armies at the two Sicilian ports and attempted a series of coastal raids on Italy itself, starting with an ambitious attack on Locri, which was foiled by the Romans, who refused to be distracted by such amphibious pin-pricks. They maintained and pressed their stranglehold on Sicily and did not rush to build a huge navy again, they had been so victimized by inclemencies. They did subsidize privateers, who attacked Hippo (Bizerte), and departed with their ships low in the water with the volume of their plunder. The war was now one of attrition in which the Romans squeezed the Carthaginians in Sicily and drained the Carthaginian treasury that was paying for large numbers of mercenaries, whether they were gainfully employed or not. In 244, Hamilcar tried to besiege the besiegers at Drepana, but was not entirely successful—the siege continued and Hamilcar's initiative didn't really achieve anything.

The Romans concluded that Hamilcar was too talented to send a consul elevated for a year against him and turned again to a naval solution. There was no money left in the Roman treasury and taxes could not be raised without potentially dangerous aggravations of the populace. Rome, not for the first or last time, decided upon a novel method for financing a supreme effort. The Senate composed in substantial part by the wealthiest men in the Republic and Federation, imposed what amounted to a voluntary refundable wealth tax on its wealthiest citizens, to pay for a new fleet, which tax would be refunded in the event of victory. A fleet of two-hundred warships, lighter and faster than earlier quinqueremes, in the hope that if necessary, it could outrun the weather, and more than five-hundred transport vessels were constructed. Once more, hearty crews were recruited.

Finally, in the summer of 242, this new fleet sailed, under the command of Lutatius Catulus, to Drepana. The Romans were astounded to discover that the Carthaginian fleet was not only not there, it had not really been manned—the Carthaginians assumed the weather had banished the Romans from the sea and they could economize by not hiring a mercenary navy when there was not going to be an adversary. There is no evidence that Punic intelligence picked up the Roman naval construction. The Carthaginian fleet finally arrived, but was badly undermanned with new and unskilled recruits. Finally, in March 241, Hanno was sent with the whole Carthaginian fleet and a large convoy of transports to engage the Roman navy and resupply Hamilcar's forces, which had lived for several years on emergency rations. Catulus awaited Hanno at the Aegates islands just off the westernmost coast of Sicily. The winds were picking up but this time they did not interfere with the correlation of forces and Catulus fairly smashed the Punic fleet capturing seventy ships and sinking fifty, and no supplies got through to Hamilcar whose forces were now starving and unable to get through another year, which would be required to rebuild the Carthaginian navy. Hanno escaped personally and sailed dejectedly home in no doubt of his fate, nor that it was deserved, and he turned himself over for prompt public crucifixion.

The simple but brave tribes of southwestern Spain were, next to the Africans, the principal mercenaries of the Carthaginian commercial state. They were strong, bellicose, the products of a simple society, and saw no indignity or anything in the slightest unseemly in deriving their welfare from the gold and silver from territory they populated but which the Carthaginians exploited, and from which they paid the tribes a small portion to fight Carthage's battles for it. These were the Indigetes, Gymnetes, and Celts, and further to the northwest the Cilbiceni and Mastieni. Ultimately, these kinds of regimes always break down, when the principles of territoriality and tribalism and nationalism assert themselves within, as with the long and painful decolonization of most of the Americas, Africa, and South Asia; and this sort of economic structure is also vulnerable to strong excluded powers. Carthage may have kept the Spanish tribes in line, though the history of its operations in Spain is too sketchily known to be sure of that, but they were no more going to be able to keep the Romans away indefinitely than the Sixteenth and Seventeenth and Eighteenth Century Spanish could keep the British away from their rich Latin American colonies.

Gold, silver, copper, and iron all abounded in Andalusia (north of the Guadalquivir River and the city of Seville), two-hundred miles north of Gibraltar. The valleys were rich in grain and wine and oils and the coastal fisheries were abundant; Carthage had happened upon a treasure trove operated by a singularly un-warlike people (Tartessians), and they mined it for all they could, as long as they could, but the vulnerabilities of the arrangement were clear. Alexander the Great allegedly contemplated liberating Spain from the yoke of Carthage, and could certainly have done so, had he focused on it.[2] The Carthaginians must have had some inkling of their vulnerability to be so extremely restrictive in the enforcement of a policy more isolationist and monopolistic than they objectively could permanently enforce, especially as they employed the natives of the exploited area to protect their exploitation and paid them a small share of the riches the natives could have enjoyed themselves if they had evicted the Carthaginians and capitalized on their own natural resources. It was an early case of the potential and problems of occupying rich territory by force or at least with an insufficient level of consent from the indigenous population and at risk of the arrangement being overturned by powerful and envious onlookers, as well as by the discontent of the local population.

Some variant of these vulnerabilities occurred when between 264 and 242, the status of Carthage as a combatant had been profoundly undermined by the attack of the Massiliotes (Marseillais) on the Carthaginians' Empire in Spain. The Marseillais could be assumed to have some familiarity with the dynamics of the Carthaginian position in Spain, as they were themselves a part native, part foreign, Mediterranean trading state. It can also be assumed that Rome incentivized and encouraged them to incite Iberian unrest and assist it, and that Carthage, while at grips with Rome, could not deal with it.

Rome had discovered Carthage's Achilles' Heel. The mineral wealth of Andalusia (the Sierra Morena), was the principal source of revenue for Carthage, as well as a well-spring of mercenaries, and while the Carthaginian navy kept the Romans away (and their navy as we have seen, was in no position to depart the principal combat area anyway), they had no ability to resist the Massiliote amphibious onslaught

---

2 CAH, VII, p. 780.

which overwhelmed the threadbare Carthaginian garrison, and incited the Andalusian tribes to seize control of their own resources. This led to acute Carthaginian pay shortages, including the partial demobilization of the Carthaginian navy, and an outright revolt by the mercenaries who controlled Sardinia for Carthage.

In the circumstances, Carthage did well to get the peace it did and to cut its permanent losses to just Sicily. In its deteriorated condition, Carthage became a recipient of Roman solicitude and even assistance, as weakened allies were unthreatening. As soon as peace was concluded, Carthage's first order of business was sending all the forces it had to regain Carthaginian Spain and then to revive the flow of money to mercenaries and the whole structure of its administration. The Romans, though it took them some time to do it, found and struck the weak point of the whole Carthaginian political and economic system. This would have necessitated the return of the Barcid party to quell the mercenaries and then to retrieve Carthage's position in Spain, for although the mining areas and their out-ports were in revolt, the Carthaginians had kept other navies out of the area, and they ended the war with Rome (temporarily) and shaped up their empire, with (unbecoming but doubtless necessary) severity, just in time.

Rome had won, though both combatants were drained; the Carthaginian government gave Hamilcar plenary powers to make the best peace he could, and Rome gave Catulus wide latitude in the negotiations. After protracted but civilized discussion, a peace was agreed subject to ratification by the Roman people. Rome and Carthage would declare a state of friendship between themselves, and Carthage would evacuate Sicily entirely, all prisoners would be handed over, and Carthage would pay twenty-two hundred talents over twenty equal annual instalments (387 million U.S. dollars in total). Neither party would attack the other, impose contributions or conscript soldiers or sailors in the defined sphere of the other, nor form alliances with the ally of the other. In this way, Rome received back the funds it could pay back to the wealthy senators who had personally financed this final naval construction and offensive. Carthage could afford the burden from its rich trading relationships, to which it was now able to return. The two famished Carthaginian garrisons in Lilybaeum and Drepana would surrender but would be repatriated.

Such was the state of opinion in Rome that the public rejected these terms as too gentle, and ten commissioners were sent to tighten the terms. They extracted an additional thousand talents (176 million dollars) in cash up front (again quite affordable to Carthage now at peace, and it was agreed that the Lipari Islands just north of eastern Sicily would belong to Rome, and that no Punic warships would enter Italian waters and that Carthage would not recruit mercenaries in Italy. These terms were ratified, and the First Punic War ended. It had been long and difficult but only because of the terrible setbacks Rome suffered at sea from cyclonic storms. The amazing feat was that Rome started a navy from scratch and demonstrated again and again that she had the world's greatest navy, if not one that was unsinkable for the most severe forces of nature. Without the nasty weather, Rome would have thrashed Carthage decisively within a few years. This fact was not lost on the parties or the world. Rome had instantly become the world's greatest naval power and had added the great island of Sicily to its domains, although Hiero continued as an autonomous king but cozily within the Roman orbit.

Fundamentally, the war demonstrated the superiority of Rome's greater manpower over Carthage's greater wealth that would buy the services of mercenaries less motivated than Roman citizens and allies, and the superiority of the Roman system of soliciting recruits from autonomous allies over the Carthaginian system of extracting onerous tribute from reluctant parties like the Numidians. Rome had a greater population, a better political system, reliable allies, a greater navy, and henceforth, the strategic ability to cut Carthage off from her sources of funds and mercenaries by her greater maritime strength. The most dramatic element of the First Punic War, apart from the terrifying Mediterranean storms (which would undoubtedly have been less catastrophic if Roman captains had been more experienced), was the ease and swiftness with which Rome defeated and humbled what had been for over a century the world's greatest navy. The primary fact of this war of twenty-four years was that the Romans won six of seven engagements at sea, one-sidedly, and that they won every single engagement on land other than on the plains before Carthage, and that defeat was due to the incompetent tactics of Regulus, who miraculously redeemed himself by his epic courage and selflessness.[3]

The war was won by the property-owning citizenry of Rome and the Roman Federation; there were no significant numbers of Roman desertions, unlike the Carthaginian mercenaries. The Italians were the best soldiers, because their own interests and national pride were involved, and the Roman federal government was stronger than that of Carthage for the same reason-it was participatory and based on a common federal interest, not conscription or subornation. Most importantly of all, Rome had begun by intervening to prevent the complete takeover of Sicily by Carthage and ended by Rome effectively swallowing Sicily; in this act, Rome departed the confines of Italy and blooded itself in empire, an intoxicant against which it was likely to be steadily more resistless. Henceforth, Rome would generally be extending the bounds of its empire, not a semi-voluntary federation. And Rome was already worldlier; almost an entire generation of Roman citizens was processed through the armed forces in Sicily and Africa and at sea, and the literature and arts responded with foreign themes and began a more serious scouring of what could be gleaned from the Greeks and replicated or embellished in more ambitious Latin writing, art, and oratory. Rome was less puritanical, less rigid, like Americans, Canadians, and Australians and even British returning home after the Great Wars of the Twentieth Century.

Rome was already the greatest power in the known world, and it had just begun. It would retain this status for nearly seven centuries.

---

3 Diodorus Siculus, *Fragments of Books,* pp. xxii-xxiv.

CHAPTER EIGHTEEN

THE SUPREME STRUGGLE FOR THE MEDITERRANEAN THE SECOND PUNIC WAR, 240-201 B.C.

HANNIBAL AND PUBLIUS SCIPIO AFRICANUS

Bust of Hannibal
(Found in Capua)

Statue of Quintus Fabius Maximus
(Eighteenth Century)

1. Roman-Carthaginian Relations After the First Punic War; Sardinia, Corsica, and Sicily

AFTER THE FIRST PUNIC WAR, relations between the late enemies were cordial. Carthage was in a desperate struggle with her mercenaries who were in revolt at their arrears of pay and other grievances. Carthage had rejected the leadership of the Barcid party (broadly those named Hamilcar or Hannibal, as opposed to those named Hanno). Hanno favoured expanded efforts in Africa, especially Numidia, and was wary of dependence on the sea lanes after Carthage had been so decisively defeated by Rome, an instant maritime power. This accorded with Rome's strategic interest, and it was helpful to anti-Barcid Carthage. Hanno represented the landed nobility rather than the commercial classes and there was profound division in Carthage, aggravated by the repudiation of all promises

Hamilcar had made to his forces (with full authorization) during the war with Rome. What was called the "Truceless War" ensued with the African tribes, especially the Numidians. The Roman Senate forbade sale of grain or any commerce with the Carthaginian rebels, and did send grain to Carthage with the value of it to be paid later at Carthage's convenience, and rounded up the Punic prisoners who had been scattered in Italy, many as slaves, and returned them, gratis, to Carthage, and even permitted Carthage to recruit mercenaries in Italy, waiving a clause of the 241 treaty. When the Punic mercenaries revolted in Sardinia, Rome declined to assist them and when Utica defected from Carthage and joined the African revolt and accepted the sovereignty of Rome, Rome declined to accept its adherence.

But Hanno badly mismanaged the war and by 239, a reconciliation had been effected between the two factions, and Hamilcar was back as joint and senior commander. In 239, Carthage attempted to regain Sardinia, but the mercenaries again revolted, slew the Carthaginian officers and repulsed Carthage. But in 238, the native Sardinians attacked the governing former mercenaries and invited Rome to take over Sardinia, and this time, the Senate, concerned at the revival of Hamilcar and his faction, accepted. Rome explained this derogation from the 241 treaty with evasive sophistries about having fulfilled the 241 treaty to the letter by declining initially to take over Sardinia, thus vacating the future application of the treaty in that respect. Even Polybius, normally rather protective of Rome's actions, condemned its conduct here.

Rome prepared an army of occupation, and Carthage prepared to send a fleet of interception, and Rome declared war and declined arbitration. Carthage, in the circumstances, could not fight another war with Rome so soon and sued for peace, which was granted with the unconditional surrender of Sardinia to Rome. Rome had pursued the correct strategy in befriending anti-Barcid Carthage, and accurately foresaw where matters with Hamilcar would lead. But its violations of the primitive canons of international law placed it squarely as a cynical expansionist power. This did not, as it emerged, retard Rome's progress, and the community of nations at the time attached little real premium to good behaviour, but nor could the Roman Senate and leadership, military and civilian, have had any idea of the proportions of the struggle they were entering. The First Punic War was a mere sorbet, enervating though it was, compared to what would come next.

As Carthage geared up for a rematch under Hamilcar and his brilliant son, Hannibal the Great as he would become, the Romans imposed themselves on Sardinia and Corsica. Carthage had just occupied the ports, left the locals to govern themselves, and bought and exported whatever of value the island populations sold them—a straight commercial arrangement. Rome set out to rule at least as formally as it did in Sicily, though presumably amenable to arrangements like those with Hiero, if suitably enlightened local officials came to the fore. What resulted was five years of exacting war to suppress the local tribes, who had no idea why the Romans were so interested in their islands. Rome took serious casualties, but successive consuls were victorious from 235 to 231, and the islands eventually submitted, none of the local chiefs had earned preferential treatment, and in 227, Rome elected a praetor each to deal with Sicily and with Sardinia and Corsica together. Rome consolidated Corsica and Sardinia into a single province.

Rome had settled quickly into the government of Sicily. Lutatius Catulus remained in Sicily after his naval victory at the Aegates Islands in 241, assisted by his brother, who was consul. He disarmed the Punic garrisons in Sicily and established the system that the Sicilians would govern themselves except that they would pay a tax to Rome of ten per cent of all they produced, with variances for cities that had made specific arrangements with Rome. This standardization was an exacting process, gently absorbing the tortuosity of the ever-mobile currents of Sicilian politics. The principal exemption was for the kingdom of Hiero, and a number of cities that had rallied to Rome in timely fashion had been promised immunities and Rome honoured these promises in every case. Rome did not have the civil service to collect such an elaborate tax and did not trust any method of renting the right to collect taxes, which would undoubtedly lead to embezzlement and extortion, and it being Sicily, soon enough to violence. Lutatius wisely adopted exactly the method employed by Hiero. Magistrates were responsible for an annual census, based on acreages and quantities of seed grain acquired, and all relevant documents were open to public view and kept by the magistrates.

Cities were encouraged to acquire from Rome the right to collect their own tax to prevent abuses by outsiders. As the tax was paid in crops, it rose and fell with the harvests and accurately reflected the ability to pay, from year to year. Ten per cent was not an onerous tax in Sicily at this time. Dionysius, Agathocles, and the Carthaginians had all taken more, and collected their taxes with considerable determination. A number of cities set up their own coinage and there was general satisfaction across Sicily that the struggle between Carthage and the Syracusan kings, which had moved back and forth across Sicily for two-hundred years pulling the red-hot rake of war, was over, and there were no recorded problems with seriously corrupt officials for over a century, though unscrupulous Romans or locals who bribed Romans for their non-interference arose eventually. In almost all Sicilian cities, there was local rule by the popular assembly, a system to which Rome itself was dedicated at this time. There was a problem of over-cultivation, as Rome sought the Sicilian harvests to placate its own urban masses, and the soil had to be rested and restored in the time of Augustus, two-hundred years after these events.

The restoration of peace was the occasion for settling accounts in Italy and sorting out administrative anomalies that had arisen. The only member of the Roman Federation which had refused to pay the heavy war taxes was Falerii, advantageously placed on high cliffs, but in 241 both Roman consuls marched on the city, subdued it, and required the population to rebuild their city on flat plains where it could not instantly become a redoubt. There was a partial equalization of the voting sections of the centuriate, and artisans and the bourgeoisies were granted rights fairly comparable to the wealthiest class in the Assembly. The propertied classes retained their advantage over the proletarian tenants and squatters.

2. The Carthaginian Reconquest of Spain and the Rise of Hannibal

Carthage did not take this latest humiliation in Sardinia passively. In 237 Hamilcar landed at Gades in Spain with a force whose mission was the reconquest of the economically useful parts of Spain, to reopen the conduit of money that would enable Carthage to revitalize and transfuse its withered state. This was undoubtedly the correct strategy, not Hanno's lateral immersion in the comparatively unremitting and fiercely resistant land of Numidia. He was accompanied by his nine-year-old son Hannibal, whom he made swear eternal hatred of Rome on the night before their arrival. The Carthaginian presence had been reduced to a few other Phoenician towns, including Malaga. He first faced the Tartessians' Celtic or Celtiberian mercenaries (as the Tartessians had still not acquired much taste for war) numbering some tens of thousands and led by Istolatius and Indortes. Hamilcar overcame them, and allegedly put the mercenary leaders to death with great cruelty but successfully persuaded the mercenaries to transfer their allegiance. Carthage was experienced at recruiting mercenaries and precisely these Iberians had furnished them vital fighting forces for over a century before the Roman-backed Masiliote overthrow of the Carthaginian position in Spain. After successfully regaining the area from Gades east to Gibraltar and Malaga and conducting extensive and successful campaigns in the interior to repossess the Sierra Morena and reactivate this vital spigot of cash for the Carthaginian cause, Hamilcar attacked to the east about three-hundred miles, past Cape Palos to Cape Nao. Near Cape Palos, he built a fortification at Alicante. The centre of the Spanish operation was later moved to the new city of New Carthage, the modern Cartagena, just west of Cape Palos.

It was now early 228, and while Hamilcar was besieging the town of Ilici ten miles southwest of Alicante, he drowned in one of the seasonally swollen rivers in the area. He had regained the rich mining areas that were his primary target and he died undefeated, moderately successful in Sicily, fully successful in Spain, champion of the return of his (Barcid) family to power in Carthage. And while conditions required that he be somewhat discreet about it, he was a burning Carthaginian patriot and considered his campaign in Spain to be a prelude to a war of revenge against Rome. Hamilcar thought that Rome showed no moderation in challenging Carthage's position in Sardinia after the peace and that it was an untrustworthy and dull race and government.

Certainly, Rome did not have the flamboyance of Carthage, nor, at the best of times, its wealth. But, as we have seen, Rome was built on a more solid foundation, and ultimately, no state dependent on mercenaries could prevail against such a determined adversary. Rome was at the strategic centre of the Mediterranean and possessed the whole extensive and well-populated perimeter of Italy. Carthage was a spider's web of colonies and outposts, with vulnerable points, as was highlighted by the ease with which the Romans built a navy, manned it with Italian farmers, and smashed the Carthaginian naval supremacy again and again, before the Roman captains had learned enough to deal with high Mediterranean seas. Apart from anything else, Rome had a greater strategic insight than Carthage. It took some time, but it finally severed Carthage's economic windpipe in the First Punic War. It was impetuous to imagine that Rome would not learn as much and as quickly about how to conduct a rematch. But this was the Barcid family mission, and the fulfilment of it now rested with the eighteen-year-old Hannibal; he would soon prove to be a mighty and brilliant warrior, almost equal to the immense task his father and countrymen set him. Hamilcar was approximately fifty-three when he died, nineteen years a general. He was also the father-in-law of Hasdrubal, and both of them, and Hannibal, demonstrated the comparative superiority of avoiding the Roman habit of considering that every elected consul knew how to command an army or navy, and that it was wise to change them every year. It maintained the power of the Senate, and discouraged, for a time, military encroachments on government, but it needlessly complicated the winning of wars. Hasdrubal followed Hamilcar in command and conducted a war of revenge on the Orissi, with whom Hamilcar was at grips in the siege of Ilici and the nearby area; he razed all the Orissi towns and extended Carthage's Spanish empire north and west beyond the Guadiana, so it occupied and governed about a quarter of all Spain. Hasdrubal was also a skilled diplomat; he married a daughter of an Iberian prince, and extended Carthage's domains farther east. This enabled him to raise the size of his army to fifty-thousand infantry and six-thousand cavalry. This would have been one of the reasons why Rome sent an embassy in 226 asking that Hasdrubal not cross the Ebro, which is only about a hundred miles south of the Pyrenees and indicates how extensive the reconstructed Spanish empire of Carthage had become. Rome was contending with another outburst of Gallic bellicosity in northern Italy and was as placatory as she was with Carthage because she did not want to stoke up hostilities with a renascent and vindictive Carthage while manning the barricades on her northern frontier against the always aggressive Gauls. It is generally believed, though there is no proof of it, that Rome secured a promise from Carthage not to make common cause with the Gauls, and in return, Rome abandoned her sponsorship of the Masiliotes (Marseillais), whose last three towns on the Spanish coast were taken by Hasdrubal; there was nothing Masillia could do about it now.

Hasdrubal the Fair, as he was known, to distinguish him from his brother-in-law, Hasdrubal Barca, Hannibal's brother, was assassinated by a slave of the Celtic King Tagus in 221, to settle a score over an injustice to his family that he considered Hasdrubal to have been responsible for; and after much fanfare, his command was assumed by his brother in law, Hannibal, who was now 25. He spent the winter at New Carthage and in 220 attacked the Carpetani and Olcades tribes east of Toledo and defeated them, gaining Carthaginian control of the valley of the Tagus River all the way to its mouth (where Lisbon now is). In 219, Hannibal found a casus belli in the quarrel of the inhabitants of Saguntum (about 20 miles north of Valencia) and the Tartessians, and he exercised the obligation of Carthage to support the Tartessians. This somewhat antagonized Rome. Saguntum asked Rome for help and Rome asked Carthage to desist from besieging Saguntum. Carthage replied that the Ebro Treaty with Rome gave Carthage a free hand up to the Ebro and what happened to the west of the Ebro was none of Rome's business. As this was correct, Rome did not come to Saguntum's assistance during the eight-month siege, but had signaled its concern. When Hannibal took the city by storm in the autumn of 219, Rome declared war on Carthage unless Hannibal was handed over to them, a preposterous demand, and the Second Punic War began. It would get underway in earnest in 218, when Hannibal set off for Italy in one of the most famous campaigns in all history.

3. Rome, Northern Italy, and the Gauls

As the Roman Senate decided to seize Sardinia, it further addicted its formerly semi-pastoral and relatively unacquisitive nature to the possibilities of outright conquest. For the first time, there are reports of skirmishes north of the Arno River with Ligurian tribes. These mountainous tribes were not well organized politically, but they held all the territory from the Upper Savoy Alps through the Apennines, and the whole of the Italian Mediterranean coast beyond the Arno. The Etruscans had formerly held this territory, but they had been unable, in the Third Century B.C., to protect it from the encroachments of the Ligurians and the Romans had been too preoccupied with Carthage to assist the Etruscans, who had become members of the Roman Federation, and the Ligurians advanced forcefully. Pisa became a Ligurian city and they were on both banks of the Arno. As the First Punic War wore on, the Romans continued to strengthen their population numerically and in terms of political integration, by granting citizenship to many classes of Italians who had been subject peoples or slaves, and eventually, practically all Italians became eligible for such elevation except, for a considerable time, Sardinians, who were deemed primitive and suitable only for agricultural menial labour. The elevation of the others was accelerated by the requirements of free manpower to deal with Carthage and its mercenaries. Part of this extension of Roman citizenship and the progressive demographic invigoration and expansion of Rome was the granting of land seized from Gauls to Roman citizens, including Roman citizens of relatively recent date. In 232, Gaius Flaminius carried a motion, the famous Lex Flaminius, as tribune in the plebeian assembly that distributed formerly Gallic land to Roman citizens of modest means in small lots. The Senate opposed the measure unsuccessfully, saying it would lead to the "demoralization of the Roman people." But the real concern, which proved well-founded, was that it incited the fear of the Gauls in northern Italy that they were being set up for attack as soon as the Romans had dealt with the Punic menace. These lands were taken from Roman landlords who enjoyed their revenue from them and were supposed to be shared equitably with Rome's allies, but Flaminius ignored those considerations. The policy of Flaminius was sensible, and it carried; his contemporary and historic enemies have claimed that he invited reprisals from the Gauls, who rightfully felt threatened, although the Gauls did not register their disapproval and formally remonstrate with Rome about it for another seven years.

Historians have generally been critical of Flaminius for provoking the Gauls, but that is because most of the contemporary writers were of the senatorial party and subscribed to the view that Flaminius was taking democratization too far, and pushing into needless wars when Rome's hands were full dealing with Carthage. Flaminius also supported a measure, the Claudian plebiscite, a few years later, and was the only senator to support it, banning senators and their sons from owning sizeable sea-going ships. (Julius Caesar would reenact this measure, nearly two-hundred years later.) In general, Roman legislators would continue to over-value landed property for its extent, and not take into account its agricultural yield. Out of this complex state of affairs, the Ligurian tribes and the Gauls continued to look upon this northern emphasis as a provocation. However affronted they may have felt, Rome was growing stronger every year, especially as it became clear that it had won the current Punic War, and as it drew to its excruciating close, the northern neighbours of Rome were right to consider the northern projection of the Roman population as an ill wind that would do them no good.

These were the origins of the new Gallic threat. In 236 some of the southern Gallic chiefs asked trans-Alpine assistance from kindred Gallic tribes in attacking the Romans preemptively, but nothing much resulted, after Rome sent an army of observation north to deter aggression. Roman concerns by this time were aggravated by reports of Hamilcar, after the Truceless War (237), having not only reasserted Carthage's position in southern Spain, but marched northeast through southern Spain, defeating the local tribes, loading his baggage trains with spoils, and recruiting fighting men of fierce Spain, men ready to risk all for their worthy conqueror. Rome sent emissaries to confer with Hamilcar in 231, after Massilia complained very insistently to Rome that the Carthaginians were cutting off their commerce with Spain and with the Atlantic. Hamilcar assured his Roman visitors that he was only accumulating what would be necessary to pay the Roman indemnity from the late Punic War. The Romans then made their alliance with Saguntum. Hamilcar died in 229 and was succeeded by his brother-in-law, Hasdrubal, who resumed the inexorable Carthaginian advance toward Massilia and Italy as was described in section 2, above.

In 226, Rome heard of the Gallic recruitment of allies in trans-Alpine Italy and prepared for war in the north. At the same time, the expressions of alarm from Massilia at the approach toward the Ebro of Hasdrubal, caused the Roman embassy to Carthage's leader in Spain, as has been mentioned, and to Hasdrubal's assurance that a Carthaginian army would not cross the Ebro (which was Massilia's gateway to Atlantic trading ports in northern Spain and western Gaul). This enabled Rome, with a little breathing space from Carthage, to deal with any problems in the north. The strongest tribes that were flexing their muscles in the north were the Taurani (around what is now Turin), the Insubres (in Piedmont and Lombardy), the Cenomani between the Po and Lake Garda, and the Boii between Bologna and Piacenza, south of the Po. The Cenomani had already signed peace agreements with Rome and would abide by them. The Venetians were neither Celtic nor Latin, but claimed kinship and friendship with Rome, and pledged non-interference, and honoured their pledge. Sometime in the mid-220's, the Boii, Insubres, Taurini, and Lingones formed a Celtic League with the explicit purpose of attacking Rome. The Celtic League did their best to recruit allies just to the north of the Roman Federation borders and regaled the target of their importunity of the "easy" fall of Rome against the Gauls in the early days of the Republic (it was anything but easy and didn't entirely fall), and promised astounding rewards of Roman land and treasure to their allies. An army of fifty-thousand infantry and twenty-thousand cavalry sprang into existence, and another in the long sequence of marches on Rome got underway in 225.

Rome and its adjacent allies were thoroughly alarmed, and the Roman Federation members responded very purposefully to the call to arms, and produced one-hundred and seventy-five thousand men, among Umbrians, Etruscans, Sabines, Latins, Samnites, Lucanians, Messapians, Apulians, the Sabellic tribes, and even the

Venetians and Cenomani. These numbers indicate that the total adult male population of the Roman Federation was about two and a half million. A considerable agglomeration in the time. Rome sent both consuls north, each leading four legions totaling twenty-thousand, eight-hundred infantry and twelve-hundred cavalry, as well as thirty-thousand allied infantry and fifteen-hundred horse. It started badly for Rome, as the Gauls defied expectations of an attack around Ariminum and instead attacked through high passes north of Bologna and marched to Clusium. Both Roman armies closed in behind them and the second wave of Gauls rushed southward on the track of the two Roman armies. The Gauls thought better of trying to emulate Brenner's overtouted phased assault on Rome in 376, and moved west to get away from the large Roman armies in pursuit and chivvied their wagon-trails of loot north along coastal roads. Roman intelligence gathering and signalling were very effective, and the Roman army under the consul L. Aemilius Papus, stayed right behind the Gauls in hot pursuit, and Consul Atilius, coming from Sardinia and marching from Pisa to Rome came upon the invaders and the two Roman armies fell upon the main Gallic force almost simultaneously. The Gauls formed in two lines, back-to-back to fight their encirclers to the death.

Aemilius Papus took personal charge of the cavalry and defeated the Gallic cavalry, who, as always, fought gallantly. Aemilius died in the battle but defeated his Gallic enemy and drove off the enemy cavalry. The Celts fought bravely in a prolonged resistance, but the Romans pressed them without respite and determined to destroy the enemy completely. The invading host took forty-thousand dead and the remaining ten-thousand were taken prisoner; the army was completely annihilated, apart from about half the cavalry, that made good its escape. One of the Gallic chiefs, King Consolitanus, was slain in combat and the other committed suicide as the battle reached its climax. The Romans had suffered almost half as many casualties, but no prisoners, and went north quickly and counter-plundered the homeland of the Boii, in addition to retrieving much of what the defeated enemy had looted from Rome's allies. Rome was well-pleased with its victories but had determined to crush completely the possibility of Gallic invasions and large raiding expeditions whenever they thought Rome might be too heavily engaged to deal with an incursion. Rome was determined to subjugate, destroy, or drive off in irreversible flight these nasty and cutthroat tribes that had never ceased to be a threat.

The 223 consuls were Gaius Flaminius and Furius Philus. Flaminius, who was unpopular with the Senate for his prior distribution of land adjacent to the Gauls to Roman citizens of modest incomes, set himself at the head of the principal expedition and to get to grips with the enemy as quickly as possible, moved north of the Cenomani, crossed the Po, burned his bridges behind him to assure that his army would fight to the death against the defending force, which, at fifty-thousand infantry, was as large an army as that of Flaminius. The two armies met at Bergamo, and Flaminius personally led his forces to a crushing victory. He destroyed the Insubre army, and only after the victory, read the orders from his enemies in the Senate demanding his return. He remained long enough to require the enemy to send peace emissaries to Rome and then retired and handed over his command to the next consul. The Senate disliked him, but had to grant him and his consular colleague

Furius Philus, each a triumph. They had earned them, though Flaminius' derring-do in burning his own line of retreat was unjustifiably impetuous.

The Senate refused to listen to any of the peace overtures that the Insubres had been bullied by Flaminius into making, and demanded unconditional surrender, but the Gauls would require more diligent persuasion. The new consuls for 222, Claudius Marcellus and Gnaeus Cornelius Scipio, invaded Insubrian territory. The Gauls had been reinforced by thirty-thousand Gaesati from the Rhône Valley. The Romans besieged Acerrae, north of Piacenza, and the Insubres besieged Clastidium, where Rome had stored supplies for the campaign. Marcellus marched in haste to relieve the siege. The Insubrian commander, the chief Virdumaras, challenged Marcellus to a duel—single combat war. Marcellus, though the Roman army had outgrown this sort of risky bravura, and he was over forty-five, accepted, broke past the Insubrian's shield and knocked him off his horse and then threw himself on him and slew him. He then defeated the enemy army and put it to flight and both consuls descended upon what was and remains the principal northern Italian city, Mediolanum (Milan). The Insubrians surrendered unconditionally. Marcellus' heroic performance became the first Roman stage-play on this theme. Cisalpine Gaul was now quite thoroughly conquered (barring being stirred up by an intruder, i.e., Hannibal). Only the far northeast beyond Venice was left to be dealt with, and the Senate in 221 sent the consuls for that year forward at the head of another large army, and their terms were accepted without serious dispute. (The Romans made exception for the local pirates, with some of whom, leading Roman capitalists were in open concert; capital has its rights.)

Rome had now extended itself to the full natural boundaries of Italy, a very large state by the standards of these ancient times, and almost the extent of the united Italy that emerged from the Risorgimento of 1871. The colonies of Placentia and Cremona were set up in 218 as guardians of the Po Valley with three-thousand citizen-soldiers in each. There were a large number of disgruntled Illyrian barbarians within the new Roman perimeter, and the Romans did not at first fortify the passes through the Alps, but they were in much better position to deter or respond to trans-Alpine hostility than in the previous history of Rome, throughout which, swarms of bloodthirsty and avaricious Barbarians surged down the Italian peninsula with no warning. Throughout 219, the able Roman consuls for the year, Aemilius Paulus and Livius Salinator, were busy on the upper Adriatic coast of Italy suppressing an Illyrian uprising. Had they not been thus preoccupied, they would have been available to take their armies to Spain, reinforce Massilia, and possibly settle matters with Hannibal there, without his getting loose in Italy. Though so great was Hannibal's ability, it is more likely that the Romans would only have slowed his advance and made his expeditionary force a smaller one by the time it crossed the Alps. Hannibal does seem to have risked the invasion he did in part because of the Illyrian distraction.

Up to this point, there has been no evidence of a Roman grand strategy; unlike the United States of America two-thousand years later, it grew as the natural principal town in its region, expanded not according to a manifest destiny, but to the logical accessible limits and occupied its peninsula for largely defensive reasons, and then, like the United States after its Civil War, its foreign policy was mainly to avoid being disturbed or threatened. But then, unlike the United States, it gradually came to treat any threat as a necessity to completely defeat and even expunge the challenger, and the extension of Roman influence may have been for punitive, or defensive, or acquisitive motives, but as time elapsed, the Roman Senate and ruling parties had little difficulty convincing themselves that some over-arching interest justified the extension of Rome's fiat over far-flung populations where Rome was not welcome. Unlike Carthage, Rome was not at all a mercantilist or commerce-seeking state, though the eventual extent of its empire certainly cultivated an interest in these matters as well. Up to this time and beyond, it was a regular occurrence for Rome to consider, with some reason that it had been provoked by another state and to respond effectively; this generally required it to strike hard and not withdraw very far. The Gallic raid of 225, after so many previous raids in the previous four centuries, seems to have resolved almost unanimous Roman opinion to secure Italy's natural frontiers and keep the Gauls out. Thus, in almost spontaneous or reactive increments did a sturdy, but not apparently predestined market town grow into a mighty and, for the times, globe-girdling empire. There was no governing consensus in matters of empire, nor any dominating personality who reigned for a whole generation. Rome was still the collective wisdom of its governing interests, mobile in their opinions and incentives and always still available to appeals to the civic and national or federal interest, but not seeking ambitious defined goals of foreign adventure and expansion.

Governmentally, Rome remained the quasi-democracy of the Hortensian Law of 287, but the plebeians really did not have any powers except the election of the tribunes and plebeian aediles, and the rarely invoked right of the plebeian assembly to determine policy. In 223 the plebeian assembly overruled the Senate and ordered a triumph for Flaminius (and he had certainly earned it in his defeat of the Insubrians). The only plebeian plebiscite we hear of after that was that of Metilius, which determined the momentous issue of the detergents to be used in cleaning industrial tiles (controversial because of their astringent qualities). It voted in elections, but rarely parted company with the Senate. The occupation of Sardinia and of the northern bank of the Arno and of the Po Valley were treated as administrative acts in which there was no need to consult the plebeian assembly, and in 218 the plebeians agreed entirely with the reasoning of the Senate to declare war on Carthage, on the theory that it was a compulsively belligerent rival state that had to be stopped. The Senate gradually curtailed the civil powers of the consuls, though they retained untrammeled powers in matters of war, once that condition had been declared or was being waged by an adversary. The urban praetor and praetor peregrinus (an office created in 242), by their ability to revise the praetor's edict, effectively largely removed legislators from both civil and criminal law, though in general, praetors paid close attention when the Senate in particular expressed itself strongly in a certain direction.

The censors retained essentially the broad powers they had held since Appius Claudius, a local official so powerful he was a precursor of such modern figures as Baron Georges-Eugene Haussmann of Paris (1853-1870), mayor of Paris and future prime minister and president of France Jacques Chirac (mayor 1977-1995), and New

York City's great source of municipal authority, Robert Moses, from 1924 to 1980. Democracy was served in practice by the fact that plebeians could be elected to all these posts, as Flaminius, despite the hostility of the Senate, was elected censor in 220. It seems that the Ovinian law was interpreted as meaning that only magistrates or former magistrates could be elected senators, and it is noteworthy that there is no record of censors abusing their considerable powers. The Romans were far from saintly and had not made a self-regarding cult of public service as the Athenians had, but their system seems to have been operated by reasonably public-spirited men and to have possessed the flexibility to allow it to reform itself as opinion and practicality required. In this it more closely resembled modern British institutions than those of the United States which adopted much of the vocabulary and symbolism of the Roman Republic, which it claimed in some measure to resurrect.

In practice, the Senate largely governed the Roman federation. All the members as magistrates had experience of judicial and administrative functions. They were all prominent citizens with some personal following and were people of means who had the time to give to their important functions. There was a fairly notable level of public duty, noblesse oblige, and distaste for down-market pecuniary self-service. The Senate adjudicated between allies and determined when Rome was at war, either as initiator or respondent. The majority of senators were solid, patriotic, honest and rather unimaginative, but formidable in courage, tenacity, and devotion to Rome. Such were Quintus Fabius Maximus Cunctator, who would soon be dueling with Hannibal, and Marcellus, hero of Clastidium: courageous, dauntless, but with no thought for strategy in war or in politics. Such a ruling class guided Rome with integrity and built on its strengths but had no personal ambition beyond traditional and almost passive service to Rome, and no plan or strategy to determine what could be done, in their own careers or in the destiny of Rome. Rome was in a civic era. The time was not far off when demagogy and the arts of the strongman on horseback would be asserted and often appreciated. But for now, it was a polity of articulate lawyers and competent but unexciting gentlemen. Again, a comparison with England between Cromwell and Victoria somewhat commends itself (with the conspicuous exceptions of Walpole, Fox, and the Pitts). As it ambled toward the Second Punic War, Rome was increasingly an aristocracy, though certainly not, as Gaius Flaminius demonstrated, a repressive or impenetrable patriciate.

4. Hannibal's Invasion of Italy

The Romans did not at first have any idea of the scale of threat renewed hostilities posed to them. Though the First Punic War had been lengthy, Rome had been delayed by improvident storms that destroyed its new navy; it won, as was recounted in Chapter 17, almost all its encounters with the Carthaginians, and was confirmed in the superiority of its citizen forces over Carthaginian mercenaries, and in their robust but conventional nationalism over the cupidity of Carthage's commercially ambitious rulers. Hannibal was only twenty-nine when the Second Punic War broke out, and though his father and brothers and brother-in-law were all talented commanders, the world, specifically Rome and Carthage itself, knew nothing of the immense talent as a grand strategist, tactician, and inspiring battlefield commander, of Hannibal. He was embarking on this extraordinarily daring campaign at almost the same age as Alexander had been when he invaded India, after his conquest of Persia and Egypt, and as Napoleon when he evicted Austria from Italy at the head of a ragged and almost untrained army of revolutionary zealots and plunderers. Hannibal and Alexander inherited their positions and Napoleon gained his through revolution, but all three were in their late twenties and had the genius of strategic originality and the unshakeable ambition of youth. All three are universally acknowledged to be among the very greatest military commanders in all history. Rome had no inkling that it was about to be assaulted, almost to its walls, by such a demiurge.

Carthage's deep desire for revenge has been mentioned, and it was enflamed by Rome's seizure of Sardinia, under no claimed colour of right, in 237. It was just naked exploitation of the transitory vulnerability of a former foe, and Rome raised Carthage's war indemnity by a further twelve-hundred talents, well over a billion dollars in contemporary figures. It was in 231 that Hamilcar, Hannibal's father, assured Roman emissaries that he was only repossessing Carthage's control of Spanish gold and silver mining in order to pay Rome its (unilaterally increased) indemnity. Two years later, Hasdrubal succeeded Hamilcar and more by diplomacy than force of arms he expanded the Carthaginian position in Spain until the Romans, faced by a strenuous test of strength with the Gauls around the Po Valley, recounted above in this chapter, sent emissaries again to the Carthaginian commander in Spain and negotiated that he would not cross the Ebro River northwards or eastwards toward Rome's ally Massilia (Marseilless). Rome, for its part, promised not to cross the Ebro in the other direction, nor to disturb Carthage's exploitation and enjoyment of Spanish precious metals resources.

However, Rome was already, anomalously, the declared protector of the otherwise unimportant town of Saguntum. Both sides respected the status of Saguntum and the terms of the treaty generally, but in 221, after Rome had repulsed and suppressed the Gallic threat, it caused a party to come to office in Saguntum that was overtly hostile to Carthage. It used this regime as a position from which Rome began to incite unrest and factional strife in Carthaginian Spain. This was clearly a violation of the treaty, but it seems that the intent of the Roman Senate was not another war, just another instance of bullying Carthage, as in Sardinia.

Hannibal succeeded Hasdrubal in 222, but Rome had no reason to attach much importance to that fact and in 220, their emissaries visited Hannibal and Carthage itself and asked for full respect for Saguntum despite their presumptuous unilateral redefinition of the Ebro treaty in Rome's favour. Neither Hannibal nor the Carthaginian government accepted the Roman claims on behalf of Saguntum, though they declined politely. The elements of direct conflict continued, Saguntum escalated its provocations and in 219, Hannibal laid siege to Saguntum from March until November when it surrendered. All through 219, the Roman consuls and the regular army were preoccupied in Illyria, as Rome eased its way along the northern end and down the eastern side of the Adriatic, now slowly expanding in all directions. It was in some disagreements with Macedonia and was prudently wary of conflict in more than one theatre. Rome was still a young country assimilating much of its newly acquired population and alert to the dangers of becoming too aggressive. The senators had seen what had happened to Pyrrhus and others (including Pericles) who became more belligerent than they had the resources and manpower to sustain. There was extensive debate in the Roman Senate and among the political leadership generally over how to respond to Carthage. There was considerable opposition to another war with a formidable, if, as the Romans believed, distinctly inferior adversary.

Eventually, as was usually the case with rising powers, and often even decaying regimes, pride, prestige, and the requirements of state self-respect asserted themselves and emissaries were sent to Carthage to demand that Carthage desist, relinquish Saguntum, and hand over the impudent young Hannibal. They left the Carthaginians in no doubt that the consequence of refusal would be war. In vain did the Carthaginians remonstrate that Saguntum was not on the list of Roman allies that was appended to the peace of 241, which Carthage had pledged not to disturb, and that Saguntum had behaved with gratuitous insolence toward Carthage. Nor was it expressly safeguarded in the Ebro treaty.

This was a little like the start of the Peloponnesian War, with the insignificant nonsense over Corcyra, the First Punic War (Chapter 17) and the Mamertine pirates, and even the start of the First World War, where an assassination in which none of the Great Powers was implicated, aggregated up into cross-declarations of war so that in a few weeks almost all Europe was in total war—whole populations called to the colours in a four-year hecatomb in which sixteen million Europeans died. Saguntum had provoked Carthage with Roman approval, but instead of, as far as is known, Carthage asking Rome through diplomatic channels to cause Saguntum's provocations to abate, it besieged and seized a town it knew to be under Roman protection. Though neither side actively wished war, war came. Rome had little notion of nor interest in the revanchist spirit of Carthage or the extent of its resentments, and Carthage, including Hannibal, underestimated Rome's steady determination. It was the classic set of circumstances for a very destructive war: both sides underrated the other, as in the U.S. Civil War.

There is no evidence, and the principal historians of this time, Polybius and Livy, don't claim to have any, that Rome actively sought to wrest Iberia from Carthage. What is available of the debates that went on indicate a general satisfaction with having taken effective control of Sicily and Sardinia and pressed northward to Italy's natural borders. It was the Roman habit to digest these new populations, not just attack over them and appoint the governors, in the ephemeral manner of Alexander. There was enough legitimacy to the Roman position to give its historians and contemporary orators enough to righteously swaddle themselves in, and Carthage was a little reckless, provoked, and, in the circumstances, impetuous. But Rome was the principal aggressor in this war. Suggestions that were made in the aftermath of the war that Hannibal had deliberately driven Carthage into war without authority are unfounded. Rome must have believed that it could deal with Carthage more quickly in a renewed war and could do so before Philip V of Macedon got clear of his conflict with Sparta and the Aetolians and was able to smite Rome in Illyria. Rome knew its demand for the physical surrender of Hannibal would be rejected as outrageous, and Hannibal calculated that Rome had no idea of the gravity of the threat that he could quickly produce within Italy itself. Rome left only one legion in northern Italy and its consuls for 218 were ordered to open campaigns in Spain itself and in Africa, exploiting Rome's new status as a great sea power, as Hannibal began his mortally dangerous lightning strike at Italy itself.

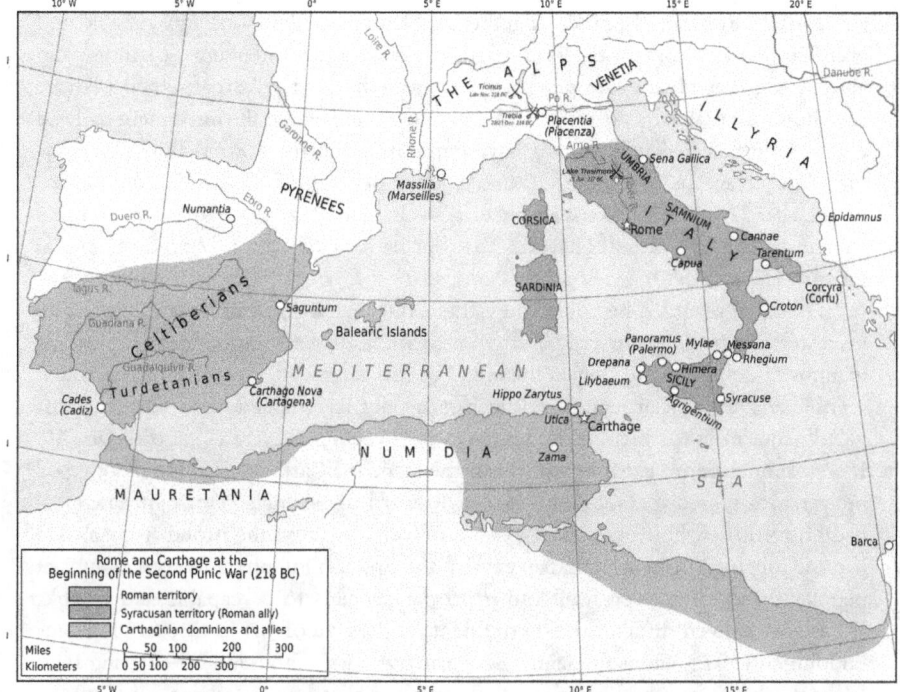

The consuls for 218, P. Cornelius Scipio and Tiberius Sempronius Longus, each had the usual consular forces of two legions each plus allies. Scipio had eight-thousand legionaries, fourteen-thousand allied infantry, six-hundred Roman cavalry and sixteen-hundred allied horse and a fleet of sixty ships. Sempronius had an additional two-thousand allied infantry and two-hundred allied cavalry, and one-hundred and sixty quinqueremes. The Senate's plan was for Scipio to sail to Massilia and from there to invade northern Spain. Sempronius was sent to Sicily from which point he was to invade Africa at the most vulnerable point. The experiences in Africa of Agathocles and even Regulus (at first) were enough to satisfy Rome that Carthage was vulnerable near its capital; it never seems to have entered the minds of the Roman high command that the same might be possible for Rome. Their complacency is amply demonstrated by the fact that Rome had only mobilized five legions from the very extensive manpower that could have been recruited easily in Italy, without the costly and risky recourse to mercenaries on which Carthage continued to rely. On the other side, Hannibal was an avid student of both Alexander the Great and Pyrrhus, and the Carthaginian leadership had noted how close Pyrrhus had come to wringing an advantageous peace from Rome after he won two battles in Italy in 279 and 278, and thought that Rome could be shaken profoundly within its peninsula. Carthage had not noticed, though it should have been obvious to its diplomats and Carthaginian observers of Italian affairs, that Rome had whipped up great pan-Italian enthusiasm for repulsing the Gauls, and there was no reason to imagine it could not do the same against Carthage. Nor had Carthaginian observers noticed how successfully Rome had knitted together the Roman Federation with capable and even-handed government that had helped generate a substantial unity of outlook in all Italy; Carthage had never practised similar methods of governance and we have seen how vulnerable its positions in Africa and Spain were to the incitement of local revolt. One factor that historians have much noted in the Second Punic War was the great advantage of mobility Rome enjoyed because of her sudden dominance of the sea. This point was especially effectively made by the great American naval strategist, Admiral Alfred Thayer Mahan in his seminal work, *The Influence of Sea Power on History* (1890).

Hannibal assumed he could rouse the badly beaten and smarting Gauls to one more try at cracking into Italy and counted on adding to the critical mass of his manpower deployable to Italy in this way. For this campaign, Hannibal had recruited a noble and tested Carthaginian officer corps and had trained his forces and provided generously for them as he prepared his expeditionary force all through 219. It was a much more capable army than the standard Carthaginian hodgepodge of mercenaries tossed together and thrown forward for a single campaign. Hannibal had imbued his whole army with a sense of vengeance on the proud Romans. He had the much-respected Numidian cavalry and Spanish infantry and even as subject peoples these forces were well-known to the Romans to be capable and reliable. It has always been difficult to be confident of the size of his forces, and Polybius undoubtedly exaggerates in claiming his army was fifty-thousand on entering Italy. It seems that it was perhaps forty-thousand and that he was relying on Gauls to make good his losses on his route of march. Carthage retained a defensive force of twenty-thousand men in Africa to protect Carthage itself, and Hasdrubal and Hanno seem to have had about twenty-five thousand men and thirty elephants to protect Carthage's position in Spain.

The view of Roman historians, especially Polybius, was that Hannibal's actions were an ingenious and heroic desperation play to reverse the inexorable rise of Rome and its domination of the central and Western Mediterranean, but there is no evidence that Hannibal or the other leading figures in Carthage thought it unrealistically risky. They were right to fear the inexorable aggrandizement of Rome, and Rome was chiefly responsible for this war, as has been described. It was now or never to retrieve Carthage's position as the major commercial power in the central Mediterranean, secure in her Spanish gold and silver mining wealth and in her domination of central North Africa, which, in this era, was a good deal more prosperous than it has been in modern times.

Hannibal set out from Nova Carthago in May 218. He left his departure a bit late to allow for swelling and flooding of the Spanish rivers to subside and make his northern movement more rapid and more complete a surprise for the Roman government, which had taken no precautions against such an aggressive enterprise. Like other immensely ambitious overland invasions, such as Napoleon's and Hitler's invasions of Russia (1812 and 1941), it began late, and it took Hannibal five full months to get to the Po. Whatever element of surprise he sought was forfeited in the fierce resistance of Rome's Massilian allies, reinforced by the Gallic tribes that were loyal to Massilia. At least he didn't have to contend with Scipio's legions, which had been redirected to stamp out an insurrection of the Insubres and Boii.

It is generally assumed that Hannibal's agents had set this tinder alight, but their timing was optimistic, as it took until August to get to the Rhône, north of Massilia. Hannibal's army had been given to expect a fairly brisk and unencumbered progress to Italy. Getting through the passes in the Pyrenees was a challenge, as the Massilians chose to contest his approach with countless ambushes and skirmishes that were endlessly enervating for the Carthaginians. Scipio was thus enabled to take command of two new legions and arrived at Massilia as Hannibal passed to the north of the city. Scipio and his senatorial colleagues still apparently had no idea of the grandeur of Hannibal's strategic conception, and Scipio only sent a cavalry observation force to see what Hannibal was doing.

Hannibal found the farther shore of the Rhône crowded with the war-like Massilians and their allies and demonstrated for the first of many times his tactical ingenuity. He judged that crossing in the face of such opposition could be very hazardous and costly and sent a cavalry force under Hanno twenty-five miles north with local guides. They were able to cross while Hannibal ostentatiously prepared to force a crossing in face of the enemy. Hanno rode back down the east bank of the Rhône but somewhat inland, fell upon the enemies' camps and sacked and burned them. On learning that Hannibal had forces in their rear and had burned or stolen all their supplies and captured, killed, or scattered all support ranks, the Gauls fled backwards from the Rhône and Hannibal crossed, elephants and all, with no casualties. Scipio arrived three days later and inflicted a minor defeat on a Numidian rearguard but was dismayed to see that Hannibal had struck his camp and got across the Rhône.

Hannibal's campaign in Italy is one of the most famous and admired in world history. It ranks with Alexander's mighty sweep across Asia Minor to India, Caesar's campaign in Gaul, Napoleon's campaign in Italy and his Austerlitz campaign, Grant and Sherman's campaigns to end the U.S. Civil War, and the German Campaign in France in 1940, the Soviet resistance to Germany, and the American-led final campaigns of Eisenhower in Western Europe and of Nimitz and MacArthur in the Pacific. Alone among all of these, it was not ultimately successful.

It has never been clear which passes Hannibal had used to enter Italy, but presumably the western ones. He paid dearly for being so late getting his army to the Alps, particularly in taking so long to get from the Ebro to the Rhône. It was early September when he started through the Alps and there had been a heavy snowfall, which made the descent very difficult for his transport and elephants and assisted the hostile Allobroges tribe, a Roman ally, in inflicting serious casualties on the Carthaginian army. Hannibal descended onto the plains of northern Italy probably with no more than twenty-thousand infantry and six-thousand cavalry. He invested the town of the Taurini (the modern Turin), which had not very formidable fortifications, and breached them and seized the town after three days, The Taurini, being enemies of the Insubres, were friendly with the Romans and therefore hostile to Rome's enemies. To make an example of them and incentivize the onlooking Gauls to place their hopes in him, Hannibal massacred the Taurini men of war-making age that he captured. This action was, as was intended, noticed by everyone in and near the theatres of operations of the second Punic War.

Publius Scipio gave an indication that, though he had arrived three days late at the Rhône, he was a daring and imaginative opponent, whom Hannibal would underestimate at his peril. Scipio had continued with the original plan and sent his two legions to invade Spain and cut Carthage off again from the chief source of its money and cut Hannibal and his army off from any communications to anything, as Rome ruled the waves, the Massilians would interdict the normal lines, and Spain would be unavailable to any Carthaginian purposes. Scipio himself arrived in Italy by ship ahead of Hannibal and took command of the two legions the Senate had designated for the defence of the north of Italy. It was a bold strategic choice by Scipio, but the correct choice; Rome would be able to raise more manpower throughout Italy to expel Hannibal and he would be unable to get any reinforcements beyond whatever Gauls were prepared to commit to give it another try. Sempronius mustered twenty-six thousand troops at Lilybaeum in Sicily, ready for the attack on Africa. King Hiero, now ninety years old, held absolutely unswerving in his alliance with Rome and was much admired by Rome for his solidity and logistical assistance. The Roman navy again got the better of the smaller Carthaginian navy and repelled raids designed to harass Sempronius en route. In revenge he seized Malta and its Carthaginian garrison. Matters seemed to be unfolding, at least in this sector, as in the First Punic War, until Sempronius was suddenly ordered to return to Italy. This recall order was received by Sempronius just as he was about to embark for Africa, and as Hannibal set upon the Taurini. The forces Scipio had taken over in the Po Valley were deemed adequate to deal with the Gauls, not with Hannibal, and especially not with Hannibal reinforced by a substantial number of Gauls. Scipio had about twenty-thousand infantry and two-thousand cavalry and accepted the task of trying to make Hannibal's life in Italy difficult. Sempronius got his men by ship to the Straits of Messina, and they quick-marched north, making the seven-hundred miles to central Italy in about seven weeks from their initial turn-around. Scipio encountered Hannibal's cavalry advancing ahead of the Carthaginian army, near Lomello. Scipio only had a light reconnaissance force and did not want to engage Hannibal's massed cavalry, but the Numidian horse overhauled him, and a desperate action was conducted by the Romans, in which Scipio was lightly wounded and only escaped by the heroic assistance of his son, who thus enters history. Scipio regained his army on the north side of the Po and got it all across the river and a pontoon party was destroying the bridges behind the Romans when Hannibal's swift and aggressive cavalry arrived and captured some of his bridge battalion. They were now near Placentia.

Scipio realized that he had to get back from the Po and away from Hannibal's direct route of march, as he would need reinforcements to resist such a powerful and cunning enemy. The proportions of Hannibal's threat were now well-appreciated; the confidence of the Roman leadership had not been badly shaken, but they had been relieved of their earlier complacency. Scipio had taken fairly light losses and now moved about twenty miles west to Stradella, just south of the Po, where he could, if necessary, retire into the hills south of the Po, giving him some protection against Hannibal's powerful and numerous cavalry. Hannibal gave chase to Scipio and approached him from Tortona thirty miles east-southeast of Stradella. Scipio wisely declined to give battle, and this was all his Gallic allies needed to switch sides, vindicating Hannibal's aggressive strategy and severity with the Taurini. The Gauls, murdered their immediate Roman commanders and stole across to Hannibal in the night. Scipio retreated briskly behind the Trebbia south of Placentia. It was at this point that Sempronius arrived with his army and assumed command of the entire force of four legions. Scipio had resupplied and morally reinvigorated his battered frontier force and had done well keeping it intact to this point.

Contrary to all advice, Sempronius determined to attack Hannibal, who had raised his army, with Gallic reinforcements and the recovery of some of his lightly wounded, to about thirty-eight thousand infantry and four-thousand cavalry. Sempronius might have had as many infantry and fewer cavalry. "On a December morning, breakfastless, the legionaries waded waist-high across the icy stream to fight with their backs to the river on ground chosen by the enemy."[1] Hannibal had arranged an ambush and as his elephants and cavalry attacked the Roman flanks, and the Celts and Gauls swarmed against Sempronius' centre, Hannibal's brother (Hanno) and cousin Mago led a charge into the Roman rear. It was a perfect destruction of the enemy except that the Roman centre, attacked on all sides, surged forward and part of it overcame the Celts and about ten-thousand Romans broke through and were able to escape down river and back across the Po near Placentia. It was a debacle in which the Romans lost at least twenty-thousand killed and captured, to much smaller losses for Hannibal, and almost entirely among the Celts. This defeat rallied many more Celts and Gauls to Hannibal. Scipio bore no responsibility for this fiasco and was dispatched to Spain to rejoin and lead his army. The winter weather made more serious offensive action by Hannibal in Italy impractical, and Rome set about coming to grips with a much more formidable threat than it had imagined it was facing.

The Roman people had too much respect for the Roman legions and the army generally to be satisfied with the bland reassurances of the Senate with a clearly formidable adversary apparently immoveable and at least somewhat victorious in the Italian peninsula. For 217 they chose as consuls Gnaeus Servilius Geminus and their old anti-favourite, Gaius Flaminius, who had won the war with the Insubres six years before. He had since raised his popularity by, as censor, beginning the great trans-peninsular road to Ariminum, and passing the Lex Claudia, which barred maritime commerce to senators, a popular move with Rome's rising merchant class that grew with the territory and influence of Rome and was covetous of everything Carthage possessed. There were dangers, in a national emergency, in elevating a general for reasons of his appeal to a class or a public sentiment rather than his clear military talents. The Insubrians were a fierce and primitive tribe not large enough to endanger Rome itself. Only when Darius faced Alexander the Great more than

---

1 CAH, VIII, p. 42 (B.L. Hallward).

a century before, had a major power faced anything as dangerous as Rome when it contemplated Hannibal at the head of forty-thousand trained soldiers in northern Italy, having just smashed four Roman legions. A politicized military is always dangerous, especially when political talents are assumed to be transferable to the military arts. The contrary, as with Julius Caesar and Napoleon, at least assures fine generalship; some individuals, such as Washington, Eisenhower, and de Gaulle, excel at both. But neither as a general nor as a politician was Flaminius remotely comparable to such exceptional leaders.

In addition to the Senate's intense dislike of Flaminius, the ambiance was made more febrile by a pandemic of public superstition, including a general belief that an entire hostile navy had appeared in the sky over Rome, and an ox apparently climbed to the third floor of a building. These and other unusual happenings were recorded by Livy from the pontifical records. (Times of national danger do sometimes provoke astonishing fantasies, such as the claim, to which even General George C. Marshall attached some credence, that a hostile air flight of over fifteen aircraft had overflown Los Angeles about ten days after the attack on Pearl Harbor in December 1941.[2]) Rome had spent the winter bulking up and preparing an army of about one-hundred thousand in eleven legions, two under Scipio in Spain, four to meet Hannibal in the field, and two in reserve to conduct a thoroughly prepared defence of Rome should that be necessary. There were two legions in Sicily and one in Sardinia, that were busy enough where they were, but could be sent on as planned to attack Carthage and its environs, or be recalled as Sempronius had been (though presumably with more sober rules of engagement). It was a thorough and well thought out plan to deal with a very serious threat. The question was whether Flaminius was the right person to execute the plan. The Senate had determined not to meet Hannibal in the Po Valley, where the Gauls could be a serious negative factor and the Numidian cavalry would have ample room for their encircling movements. The military colonies of Cremona and Placentia were fully stocked and well defended and left to their own devices, it being reasoned (correctly) that Hannibal did not have proper siege engines with him and would not waste the time required on a military side-show given that the outcome of the struggle between Rome and Carthage was fully underway and approaching its supreme climax. The defense of Rome and the Roman Federation would be conducted in central Italy, close to supplies and reserves and in an area populated by proven and tested allies of Rome.

Hannibal had moved to Bologna and had concentrated on raising the Po Valley in revolt against Rome, with very indifferent results. The Romans took the chance of dividing their northern forces in two separated by the spine of the Apennines. Flaminius was at Arretium, sixty miles south of Bologna, to block the southern pass out of the Po Valley and toward Rome. The other army was to the east at Ariminum on the Adriatic to prevent a Carthaginian sweep south on the eastern side of Italy. This separation of armies had worked well with the Gauls, but the Roman strategists seem still not to have fully grasped what they were dealing with. Hannibal, as soon as his scouts told him the snow had cleared in the Apennines, set out to the southwest toward Pistoia and through the passes about thirty and forty miles northwest and

---

2 Conrad Black, *Franklin Delano Roosevelt: Champion of Freedom*, Public Affairs, New York, p. 721.

west of Flaminius at Arretium. There were terrible vicissitudes with the weather and the flooding of the Arno above Florence and Hannibal himself, traveling on an elephant, suffered an influenza so severe that it permanently damaged his sight in one eye. The melting snow created extensive semi-frozen marshes that were very exacting to cross and left Hannibal and his army in an enervated condition from which, however, they recovered very quickly and before Flaminius realized that the invader had moved past him in the west.

Hannibal ostentatiously marched past Flaminius, exposing his left flank, should Flaminius be as lacking in judgment as Sempronius. He was not, showing he was not as rash and mindlessly belligerent as his critics claimed; he reoriented his forces but allowed Hannibal to pass to the south, which Hannibal did, foraging liberally off the rich Tuscan countryside, not a practice that facilitated his incitement of anti-Roman sentiment among the populace. Hannibal now set a subtler trap, assumed that Servilius must be hurrying west from Ariminum and Hannibal boldly turned due east, leaving Flaminius still on his left staring at him as the Carthaginians moved away from Rome and toward the eastern Roman army. He placed himself between the two Roman armies, a hazardous position if he were not moving quickly and purposefully, although his army was almost as large as their combined strength, better trained, and, as was about to become even clearer, better generaled. Hannibal had carefully researched central Italy topographically and he built a very strong defensive position beside Lake Trasimene. A clearing about five miles wide and a mile deep was just to the north of the lake and Hannibal held the right end of the plain and all the north side in the hills, where his Gauls and cavalry were placed, partly hidden and somewhat inaccessible in the foothills. Flaminius would have to run the gauntlet between the lake and the foothills to get to the main Carthaginian army. Hannibal held the central hills with his Spanish and African troops; the main body of infantry was at the eastern end of the cul-de-sac, and his Balearic, Gallic, and Numidian light cavalry were in the western foothills ready to descend and tighten the string on the neck of the cul-de-sac if Flaminius took the bait and entered it.

Incredibly, Flaminius did: his whole army marched into the trap, with the lake on its right and the foothills on its left, and only when the entire Roman army was inside the trap did Hannibal order that the cul-de-sac be closed behind the Romans and that they be attacked from all landward sides at once.

It was over before it began and was one of the great and decisive victories of history. The Roman legionaries fought bravely for three hours, and Flaminius himself was killed in single combat by a Gaul; he died valiantly. The Roman vanguard of six-thousand fought through the Carthaginian infantry at the far end of the entrapment but were pursued and surrounded by Hannibal's cavalry and given an honorable but unambiguous surrender. Hannibal sustained light casualties, and among his Gauls mainly. A Roman army of two legions had been obliterated. This time there was no disguising the defeat from the public, especially as the popular darling Flaminius whom the plebeians had elevated, was responsible for it. The praetor solemnly advised a large public gathering: "We have been defeated in a great battle." So they had, but at Lake Trasimene as at the Trebbia, the Roman commanders had given battle in impossible circumstances. Though Hannibal was obviously a brilliant field commander, so far, apart from a little skirmishing with Scipio, he had won because of the utter foolishness of Sempronius in seeking impossible conditions for a battle, and from the recklessness of Flaminius in being drawn into a trap that a more mature military intuition and more thorough reconnaissance would have caused him to avoid.

Hannibal made a tremendous display of releasing all the prisoners he had taken that were allies of Rome and proclaimed, for the whole Italian peninsula to hear that "My quarrel is with Rome alone." It didn't immediately shake too many people loose, but it was clearly destabilizing. Meanwhile, he was closely following, from spies and reconnaissance, the approach of Servilius. Hannibal's plan had never been to try to take Rome, which he knew to be beyond his capabilities; it would be another siege of Syracuse. He proposed to force Rome to make a reasonable peace that recognized Carthage's historic position by demonstrating his ability to march at will through Italy, raising subject peoples in revolt and defying Roman attempts to defeat or expel him. It was the playbook of Agathocles, but in Italy. There were two basic problems with the long-term strategy: Rome could do the same to Carthage while its greatest general and principal army were absent in Italy: it could and was already attacking Carthage at its financial source in Spain and was ready with short notice to attack Carthage and neighbouring areas in Africa. Second, Hannibal would have to assume that no Roman army could ever hold its own against him, despite Rome's relatively great reserves of manpower, and as he roamed about Italy living off the land, since the Roman navy would assure that he received no supplies or reinforcements directly, he would inevitably incur the dislike of those Italian provinces he was trying to raise in revolt against Rome.

These factors began to emerge in the aftermath of Lake Trasimene: Hannibal roamed down the eastern side of the Italian peninsula, as Servilius was ordered to avoid the Carthaginian leader, but no one answered his call to revolt and fortified cities such as Luceria and Arpi closed their gates to him. Hannibal's military analysis and execution had been incidences of genius, but his political miscalculation was serious and inexplicable. Carthage assumed that Italy was seething with resentment that they could inflame, as Agathocles and the Romans had stirred revolt in Numidia and Spain. Hannibal and the other Carthaginian leaders should have realized, especially after the First Punic War, that just as Rome was not dependent on mercenaries, neither was its Federation an exploitive occupation. Carthage had a better system than Rome of selecting professional military commanders and giving them reasonable terms to carry out objectives, unlike the Romans elevating politicians one year at a time. But Rome left more to popular vote with a broadened electorate, and had expanded rather generously, extending citizenship liberally and promoting the able men of newly acquired territories meritocratically and rallying them to Rome as a centre of good government, collective security, shared values, and rising prosperity as the Roman world itself expanded. Hannibal must, within six months of his great victory at Lake Trasimene, have begun to appreciate that Carthage was a city assaulting a much larger political entity than itself and counting on paying soldiers to defeat in their homelands people who did not wish a Carthaginian invasion; Carthage's mercenaries' whose enthusiasm to fight would diminish precipitously as soon as the Romans seized the wellsprings of Carthage's money, as Scipio was in the act of doing in Spain.

5. Hannibal and Fabius

Following the Lake Trasimene disaster, Rome, as was its well-established custom, appointed a dictator, but in a novel way. Servilius, the surviving consul, was cut off from Rome by Hannibal's army and though he was not in immediate danger, he could not be directed from Rome. A tried and experienced, distinguished, cautious leader, Quintus Fabius Maximus, was elected dictator by the centuriated assembly, a restricted but still pan-Roman electorate. Fabius had been consul in 233 and 228 and dictator without powers of decree in 221, and on this occasion, the deputy leader, the magister equitum, was not left to the dictator to choose, but was also elected: Minucius Rufus. This was a partial gesture to the popular classes, as Fabius was a patrician. Rufus had been consul in 221, and was also respected and experienced, but the appointment of a dictator with a semi-autonomous vice-dictator invited discord. Fabius raised two new legions (and according to Polybius put in train the recruitment of two more, but this is uncertain[3]), and he logically marched (ironically) along the Via Flaminia and met Servilius at Ocriculum forty miles north of Rome and absorbed his two legions into his army. Fabius turned south into Apulia and declined battle at Vibnium when Hannibal offered it. Hannibal then struck south into Samnium (which Rome had so painstakingly subdued a century before) and Campania, to provoke a major battle or demonstrate the weakness of Rome to its allies. In the meantime, he sacked and razed Beneventum, an act which turned the admirable post-Trasimene posture of war against Rome and benign neutrality toward the rest of Italy into an assault on Rome and all who cooperated with Rome. Hannibal carried wholesale destruction into Campania; he was now unambiguously at war with practically all of Italy, and was without communications with Carthage, a dangerous and powerful but lonely and not unlimited force rattling around within Italy. The American Admiral Mahan's comments on the importance of sea power were now very clear.[4] Hannibal had to infuriate the local population to survive, could not assault Rome itself, and had no exit. Rome was a vast Trasimene battle-site, he was in the cul-de-sac of the Italian Peninsula, but there was no believable exit strategy except continuous victory ad infinitum until Rome lost its nerve, if it ever would. (He was a little like Napoleon at Moscow in 1812—the weather would not become as severe, but at least Napoleon could fight his way out, it was unlikely that Hannibal could.)

Hannibal's ransacking of Campania, apart from feeding and enriching his army and intimidating the people of Italy, was designed to shame Fabius into giving battle, and it is not surprising that Roman opinion, public and senatorial, was deeply taxed by the dictator's passivity. Hannibal was destroying the richest part of Italy which in

---

3   Polybius iii, 88, 7.
4   Alfred Thayer Mahan, *The Influence of Sea Power Upon History*, New York, Little Brown, 1890. The Roman naval advantage over Carthage was the principal illustration of the author's thesis.

Roman lore had been contended over by gods.[5] Fabius was called "cunctator" the delayer, but it was the correct strategy. His army was barely larger than Hannibal's in infantry, much inferior in cavalry, and though Fabius was skillful and Roman legions were always brave and competent, Hannibal was clearly one of the greatest commanders in history and his army was steeped in the battle honors of triumph. Prolonged inaction, however, was damaging to Roman morale and prestige, and eventually, it seemed that Hannibal was offering battle in the confines of one of the passes out of Campania. Hannibal had incurred great resentment in his plundering and all the Campanian cities, and the surrounding rural populations had taken shelter within its towns, so he had to return to Apulia for winter.

His army was now encumbered with a heavy train of plunder and stolen cattle, and so could not move with its commander's customary agility. Hannibal managed his escape to the north with another of his ingenious improvisations. Fabius had placed Minucius at the western pass and he oversaw the others from foothills. Hannibal lighted pieces of kindling attached to the horns of bullocks in the night and launched two-thousand of them up the foothills, which Roman sentries assumed was an attack and deployed accordingly. Fabius suspected something, as there was no reason why the Carthaginians would illuminate a night attack, but he remained in his camp as he mistrusted the approaching sea of lights as a distraction. He was correct in that supposition, but didn't move, and Hannibal made his way through the pass to Apulia without casualties (though the Franconians did get much of their cattle back to their scorched fields).

Fabius was recalled for consultation, so great was public disappointment that Hannibal appeared to have escaped serious challenge after visiting grievous damage on Franconia and Campania and unprecedented insolences on Rome. Officially, Fabius was returning for religious observances. Hannibal set up the small town of Gerunium, twenty miles from the Adriatic and one-hundred and fifty miles east of Rome. Minucius assumed a more active role, pursuing Hannibal and camped near Larinum, about half-way between Gerunium and the sea. He harassed Hannibal's foraging parties, which Hannibal refused to take off their winter preparations, and this enabled Minucius to attack the foraging parties in some strength and inflict on Hannibal the first serious casualties he had sustained since he crossed the Alps into Italy. Victory-starved Rome embraced this as a real victory (as Hannibal may have hoped), and although Fabius tried to placate opinion by nominating the venerable Senator Atilius Regulus as consul to replace Flaminius, the people weren't having it and by popular direct action, named Minucius co-dictator with Fabius and with equal powers, thus vitiating the whole purpose and advantage of dictatorship.

Fabius joined Minucius Rufus where he was, near Larinum, and the Roman army remained divided in two and with two near-by camps. Hannibal followed this Roman dissension, which he had avidly tried to sow, with keen interest. The ground between Hannibal's camp and that of Minucius was unsuitable for cavalry and Hannibal calculated that he might be able to entice Minucius, whom he suspected was drinking his own bathwater over his supposed victory against Hannibal's foraging party, into an impetuous attack. Under cover of night, he deployed a large force in ravines and

---

5 Polybius iii, 91.

woods around a modest hill, where he sent a large and not very mobile foraging party in the morning. As he had hoped, once again the Roman commander took the bait and Minucius attacked the foragers with most of his army, which was immediately engulfed on three sides and at once in danger of another annihilation. Fabius, though not, so far as we know, consulted, saw what was happening and rushed to the aid of his colleague, sparing him and Rome another disastrous destruction of two legions. Minucius was whipped soundly but was extracted intact and with most of his army. At this point, Fabius' term as dictator ended, and Minucius with him, and Servilius and Atilius Regulus succeeded as commanders at Gerunium. Fabius had restored his reputation and Minucius graciously acknowledged his debt to his nominal co-dictator.

6. Cannae

The new consuls were L. Aemilius Paullus, who had done well in Illyria three years before, when Hannibal was plodding between the Ebro and the Alps (the Illyrian campaign will be summarized later in this chapter), and the wealthy merchant C. Terrentius Varro, an able politician but without qualifications as a military commander. Varro was a bizarre, even a perverse, popular choice with Fabius and Scipio available and one of the greatest military geniuses in world history loose in Italy ravaging the countryside and thumbing his nose at Rome. The result was by now somewhat predictable, but perhaps Aemilius could measure up to the task. As Hannibal would have been informed by his spies and agents, Rome was clamouring for a serious show-down, a pitched battle, and he again engaged in his preferred tactic of choosing his place to fight and exploiting the enemy frustrations that he had incited to entice the enemy there. He moved east and south to Cannae, near the Adriatic and two-hundred miles east southeast of Rome. The Roman army was composed in part of veterans of the Trebia and Gerunium and was reinforced to a total of almost fifty-thousand troops. Hannibal had only about thirty-five thousand, only nineteen-thousand veterans and the balance Celts, who were unreliable and whom the Romans regarded rather contemptuously. There was, as always, no doubt of the valour of the Roman legions. The question mark was the quality of Roman command decisions opposite so formidable an opponent, and the defect in the Roman plan was again cavalry. Rome had bulked up to six-thousand, but Hannibal had ten-thousand battle-tested and faster than the Romans.

The Roman army marched the eighty miles from Gerunium to Cannae, beat off Numidian cavalry attacks without great difficulty, and encamped about three miles from Hannibal. Hannibal again deployed his sharp apprehension of Roman psychology and applied his tactical skills accordingly. When the Roman army had encamped near him, he then decamped across the Aufidus River, as if he were ill at ease in the presence of a large Roman army thirsting for revenge and was scrambling somewhat. In fact, this was the ground he had chosen from the start. It was August 2, 216 B.C., and the little town of Cannae was about to be lodged in military history forever, like Austerlitz, or Waterloo, or Gettysburg.

The two armies crossed the river and took up positions with their flanks on the

Aufidus, and the modest plain that Hannibal had carefully selected on the other side. Both sides were spoiling for the fight, the Romans for vengeance and the Carthaginians to continue the habit of crushing the Roman army. The Romans had their citizen cavalry near the river, their massed centre of Legionaries, and on the outer flank, the Roman left, were the main bulk of their cavalry, including that of their allies. Hannibal's army was in a crescent, with the centre advanced, Gauls strengthened by Spaniards. On each side, but back from the centre, were African infantry; farther back on the left, beside the river, were Gallic and Spanish cavalry, and on the Carthaginian right, well back, were massed the dreaded Numidian cavalry. The African troops were now entirely equipped with Roman shields and spears captured in previous victories, and the Spanish were distinctive in short linen tunics bordered in purple stripes. The Romans opened with their anticipated offensive in the centre and pushed the Gauls backwards until Hannibal's convex line became concave. Hannibal, with his young brother Mago were behind the centre. This was the decisive moment—if the Romans broke through the centre and cut up Hannibal's army into three or more parts, they would win, but as Hannibal had planned, the Roman flanks were now thinned and vulnerable. Hannibal had organized the retreat of his centre so that it was a sort of funnel for the Romans, squeezing their centre into a narrower formation. The African infantry now attacked the flanks of the Roman centre, further squeezing it and obliging it to fight on its flanks as well as the centre; the Spanish and Gallic cavalry easily overcame the less numerous and experienced Roman cavalry by the river and thrust into the right flank and rear of the Roman centre, and a contingent of the Spanish cavalry charged on and struck the Roman cavalry to the left of the Roman line as the massed Numidian cavalry swarmed into it. Some of the Roman cavalry was driven off and pursued, and for the most part run down and killed and the Roman army was completely surrounded and was steadily reduced by slaughter on all sides.

The Roman army might yet have salvaged a significant number of men if, as at the Trebbia, they had managed to break through the Carthaginian centre, but the Gauls fought better than anticipated and the Spanish and African flank infantry attacks and the disorder caused by the cavalry assault on the rear of the Roman army prevented this. In the terrible melee, about two-thousand of the fifty-two thousand Romans and their allies escaped. Aemilius died in hand-to-hand combat and Varro, who should never have been near a battlefield, made good his escape on horse. The Carthaginians lost perhaps sixty-seven hundred men, four-thousand of them Gauls. Cannae is rivaled in the entire history of warfare only by Napoleon's greatest victory, Austerlitz (December 1, 1805), as the most perfect tactical annihilation of an opposing army at minimal cost to the victor. Hannibal had now eliminated eight Roman legions, not just defeated them, but practically wiped them out. It was an astonishing performance, and this time, the Roman Federation was visibly shaken. Hannibal ignored advice to make a race for Rome; "In five days we shall dine on the Capitol," said Maharbal. Hannibal declined, as he knew he had no chance of capturing Rome and would just dissipate the impact of his victory.

Instead, Hannibal made a stately progress through Samnium and Campania, and sent Mago with a smaller force into Lucania and Bruttium. Finally, parts of the

Federation started to peel off. Arpi (Apulia), Salapia, Aecae, Herdonea and Compsa all came over to Hannibal, and most of the Samnite mountain tribes that Rome had suppressed with such difficulty, happily revolted, delighted, a century late, to see proud Rome humbled and beaten. In Lucania and Bruttium, all but the Greek cities joined the revolt. Most worryingly for Rome, Capua, then the second city in all Italy, revolted in the autumn of 216. Rome had become commercially dependent on the export of the work of Campanian artisans, and the local population of Capua much resented what was widely considered the obsequious adherence to Rome of the local patriciate, who were showered with favours for their grace of conversion, in the Roman manner. A number of smaller Campanian towns followed, but once again, the rot stopped and the Roman Federation generally held, even after this horrible debacle of Roman arms. Latium, Umbria, Sicily, still under the brilliant leadership of Hiero after forty-five years, was unshakable and Hiero publicly saluted Rome and emphasized his continued solidarity at the age of ninety-one.

And there was some good news. The Scipios, as will be recounted, had done well in Spain, and the strategic position of Carthage, with Hannibal stranded, however productively, with the main Carthaginian army in Italy, was unsteady. Rome dominated the seas completely and no part of Rome's problem had been any failing in the courage and competence of its legionaries. The problem was the politically selected commanders, and Rome had good generals. It was time for the leaders of the Roman state to reach for their best commanders, as Lincoln did in sending Grant and Sherman against Lee and Johnston, and Churchill did in sending Montgomery against Rommel. Rome had not lost, but it could not stand any more unmitigated humiliations. As the time passed, Carthage was running out of men and money, despite its small numbers of casualties and Hannibal's ability up to this point to live off Rome's client states.

7. Roman Recovery

Grim as the news was for Rome in Italy, it was much better in Spain, and this helped mitigate to some extent the gloom of the Senate and the Roman political class, which, apart from the nomination to their positions of Scipio and Fabius, had made such a horrible mess of the second Punic War. Spain was difficult for Carthage to defend, cut off as it was by the Massilians on land and by the Roman navy from any resupply of men or even information. It was a bold move for Scipio to order from the Rhône where he had just missed Hannibal passing east that the invasion of Spain proceed, and he initially delegated the command there to his brother Gnaeus. The two assigned legions were landed at Emporium, the principal trading city of northern Spain and an outpost of Massilia, whose commerce had been negatively affected by the Carthaginian advance to the Ebro and was as staunch an ally as Hiero's Syracuse. Gnaeus began by marching south to Tarraco (Tarragona), where Hanno was hoarding Hannibal's baggage train with eleven-thousand troops and some local supporters. Gnaeus Scipio, with the two Roman legions he commanded, crushed the Carthaginians and captured Hanno and all his stores and equipment. Hanno had been taken completely by surprise because of the speed of the Romans, taking full advantage of their capacity for naval transport. Hasdrubal arrived more than a week later from Nova Carthago and captured a few Roman sailors on shore leave but could not challenge Scipio and withdrew across the Ebro.

In the summer of 217, as his brother rampaged around Italy, Hasdrubal executed a combined land and sea attack against Tarraco, bringing forty ships into the mouth of the Ebro and setting up a camp nearby.

Gnaeus Scipio attacked at once with a slightly smaller naval force, bolstered by Greek contingents, close inshore, and destroyed six and captured twenty-five of the Carthaginian ships, another signal Roman victory. This shattered whatever confidence, as well as much of the fleet, that Carthage possessed, and hereafter, thoroughly intimidated, it confined itself to modest raids (like the German navy in the World Wars of the twentieth century). The performance of Carthage's navy in the Second Punic War was an even greater fiasco than it had been in the first. After Hannibal's great victory at Lake Trasimene, a fleet of seventy vessels sailed from Carthage to Pisa hoping to add encouragement to their military commander but were chased off by a fleet of one-hundred and twenty vessels under Servilius. The Carthaginians, understandably, but without much dignity, fled precipitously.

In the autumn of 217, both Scipios led their two legions south across the Ebro as far as Saguntum, but did not assault any of the Carthaginian fortress towns. At this point, a stasis had settled on Spain, where the Romans had reimposed the Ebro line and hemmed in the Carthaginians, who could not export anything in quantity from the gold and silver mines they exploited in Spain but remained in their third of the Iberian Peninsula. The Romans had also undermined the standing that Carthage had enjoyed among the Spanish tribes. In 215, uplifted by the news from Italy, and strengthened by a reinforcement of four-thousand infantry and one-thousand cavalry, as well as a relief garrison for Nova Carthago which successfully ran the Roman blockade, Hasdrubal attacked the Scipios. Both sides had armies of about twenty-five thousand and they met at Dertosa, just north of the Ebro.

Hasdrubal had deployed his forces as Hannibal did, with a protruding centre that was designed to give way under the usual Roman attack of massed infantry, while the best Spanish and African troops and the Numidian cavalry made up the flanks that were to snap closed behind the Romans, as happened at Trasimene and Cannae. The battle started as planned, but where the Romans had managed finally to breach the Carthaginian centre and ten-thousand of their legionaries got through (though they were forced to surrender later when overtaken by the Numidian cavalry), at Dertosa, the Roman legionaries tore the centre out of the Carthaginian army before the flanks could close. The entire Spanish-Carthaginian force was overwhelmed and almost entirely killed or captured. The Carthaginian equivalent of two legions were destroyed, regaining, in effect, half of what Rome lost at Cannae. Had the result been entirely different, the victorious Carthaginian army in Spain could have reinforced Hannibal. As it was, Carthage's position in Spain was very tenuous and vulnerable, and Roman morale, at a dark time, was appreciably raised by the distant victory (as Britain's was by El Alamein in November 1942, after years of defeat of the British army in France, Greece, Malaya and Egypt).

Hannibal's brother Mago had the pleasure of announcing to the Carthaginian

Senate the proportions of the victory at Cannae, before a pile of golden rings from the Roman knights (equites) that were killed in the battle. There was no question of the scale of the triumph, but it was already clear that the Roman Federation, though shaken, was not about to disintegrate. It was a year before the decisive Roman victory in Spain, but Hannibal was now rattling around in Italy annoying the population by living off it with increasing rapine and the Romans could not be counted upon always to put up such inept army commanders as those whom Hannibal had so completely defeated. The war had gone well but it wasn't easy to see how Carthage could bring it to the desired conclusion. Hannibal devised a new strategy. He would remain in Italy, prying off what he could from the Roman Federation, especially the Greek states in Italy which resented being Latinized, and threatening Rome itself, while the Carthaginian government would undertake to secure Spain, expel Rome from Sicily and Sardinia, and entice the active collaboration of the king of Macedonia, aggrieved by being shouldered out of Illyria (in the campaign that will be described in Chapter 19). It was an ambitious plan, but it counted on continued Roman failure, which had not been the pattern of Roman history, including in the First Punic War. It would be doubly hard to implement, given Roman control of the sea, as Carthage's ambition was to box Rome into Italy.

Hannibal needed reinforcements to keep his army at full strength and garrison any towns that he took over. It was intended to send him twelve-thousand infantry, fifteen hundred cavalry, and twenty elephants, but as the news came in from Spain in the summer of 215, these forces were diverted there, ultimately to replace the Carthaginian army that the Scipios annihilated. Carthage did succeed in landing a modest support force at Locri in the late summer of 215, while Hasdrubal the Bald was sent to Sardinia to join forces with the local population that deeply resented the heavy-handed Roman governance, quite unlike the Carthaginian style of conducting commerce from the seaports and leaving the rest of the islanders alone. The Roman governor, Quintus Mucius, was ill and disliked the Sardinians, a sentiment that was richly requited. Rome had a legion in Sardinia, and it was believed that with a smaller force and the help of the locals this alternate Hasdrubal could shake Sardinia off the Roman tree.

Fortune did not accompany the mission: it was blown well off course by stormy weather and made port in the Balearic Islands. While the mission was being reorganized, Rome sent T. Manlius Torquatus with another legion to reinforce its Sardinian garrison and replace Mucius. Torquatus knew Sardinia well from having campaigned there as consul twenty years before and gave the rebels a good cuffing and placated the civil population while the allegedly bald Hasdrubal was still wallowing toward Sardinia. The Carthaginians landed and linked up with the remaining insurgents, but Torquatus attacked them at once with both legions, smashed the Carthaginian expeditionary force and took Hasdrubal and a number of other Punic nobles prisoner. The insurgent leader, Hampsicoras, committed suicide. At about the same time, following the debacle in Spain, much of the Carthaginian force there had to be sent to Numidia to quell a revolt by the Numidian chief, Syphax.

Hannibal's new strategy was off to a rocky start: a year had passed since Cannae and nothing had moved in Italy, where Hannibal was a generally unwelcome visitor. The Spanish position was very parlous and the Sardinian expedition had been a disaster. Between Spain and Sardinia, Rome had destroyed the equivalent in the Carthaginian army of three of the eight Roman legions Carthage had eliminated. Carthage had done better on the diplomatic front. The Macedonian king, Philip V, sent envoys to Hannibal proposing alliance. Polybius reproduced the text of the agreement that was concluded: Macedonia would attack Rome in Illyria and Carthage would make the return of Illyria, Corcyra and Pharos to Macedonia a condition of any peace it made with Rome. Both parties would reinforce each other. They also pledged to conclude a defensive alliance after the end of the present war. It seemed a distinct setback to Rome, as the Macedonians would need to be resisted in Illyria, and it also played into the next piece of Hannibal's strategy, which was to promote anti-Roman sentiment among the Greeks of Sicily, where the great Hiero II had finally died, aged ninety-one.

Sicily was the next theatre of this wide-ranging war. Hiero's eldest son, Gelo, who was a Carthaginian sympathizer, narrowly predeceased his father, and the heir was the late king's fifteen-year-old grandson Hieronymus. There was a regency cabinet appointed in Hiero's will composed of fifteen men, led by Hiero's sons-in-law, Adranodorus and Zoippus. Adranodorus soon announced that the young king was competent to rule and resigned, and the regency cabinet dissolved and thereafter only the new king's uncles (Adranodorus and Zoippus) and one Thraso, a Roman loyalist, had access to the king. The other two cooked up a false charge of plotting against the life of the king by Thraso and had him executed, and the sons-in-law opened negotiations with Hannibal, seeking to rid Sicily of Rome.

Hannibal sent two seasoned diplomatic negotiators, Hippocrates and Epicydes, to Syracuse and they negotiated a treaty with the new rulers there. When Roman envoys arrived to renew the long-standing treaty, they were dismissed. The treaty was finalized with Carthage, and it recognized Syracuse as hegemon of all Sicily. Of course, it could decide later, if it was successful against Rome, whether to honor that agreement, but it immediately aroused resentment in other parts of Sicily, of a bitterness and violence only Sicilians can achieve. Syracuse organized forces to attack Roman garrisons when Hieronymus, after one of history's short and undistinguished reigns, was conveniently (for Rome) assassinated in Leontini by disloyal soldiers. (It may be surmised that Rome had a hand in this, but nothing has ever come to light to confirm this.)

The regicide party got the upper hand in Syracuse. The Roman legions on Sicily were the somewhat replenished remnants of the legions decimated at Cannae, and only numbered the normal strength of one legion, but Rome, for whom events had taken an uptick in Italy (as will be described in a few pages), sent a new legion under Marcus Claudius Marcellus, five times consul, and particularly famous for having killed the Gallic chief Viridomarus in single combat at the Battle of Clastidium in 222. He was conducted to Sicily by a fleet of a hundred vessels commanded by the praetor Appius Claudius Pulcher. In the tumult in Syracuse, Adranodorus was murdered, along with all the women in the royal family. It had taken only a year for the august serenity of Hiero's long and prosperous reign to give way to torrential Sicilian blood-letting. However, Rome missed its chance, as there was a revulsion, even in

Sicily, at the slaughter of the royal women, and in the Syracusan elections, the two Carthaginian envoys, Hippocrates and Epicydes, who as far as is known, had not sought any position for themselves, were elected generals.

This naturally escalated matters in uniquely Sicilian ways. Hippocrates was at once dispatched at the head of four-thousand men to protect Leontini from a feared Roman attack. There was escalating skirmishing between the Greek and Roman areas adjacent to Leontini and then Hippocrates massacred the soldiers in a Roman outpost. The Roman government through its representatives in Sicily (Marcellus), demanded the expulsion of Hippocrates and Epicydes. Hippocrates and Epicydes then, despite their election as Syracusan generals, got fully into alignment with Sicilian patterns of conduct in tempestuous times and declared themselves the government of Leontini, on no authority whatever and declared the city's independence of Syracuse.

In the spring of 213, Marcellus stormed Leontini, and the Romans sacked it to ruins and conducted numerous summary and exemplary executions as they did so. After peremptory interrogation with some recourse to torture, they extracted two-thousand alleged Carthaginian sympathizers, publicly flogged them severely and then for the further delectation of the civil population, brusquely fed them to a score of headsmen for decapitation. The two Carthaginian envoys/Syracusan generals managed to escape the Romans and were very enthusiastically received by the approaching Syracusan army of eight-thousand sent to save Leontini from the Romans. On the news of the Roman methods in Leontini, the army returned in a forced march to Syracuse, Hippocrates and Epicydes, now swimming like fish in the raging sea of Sicilian politics, were confirmed as generals of Syracuse and a terrible massacre of thousands of Roman sympathizers in Syracuse was conducted with no pretense to judicial or even interrogatory formalities. "Finally the brilliant and indefatigable machinations of these two Carthaginian agents had their reward. Syracuse, the capital of Western Hellenism, had abandoned the cause of Rome for Carthage."[6]

The Romans furiously responded with an assault by Marcellus and Appius from land and sea, but the Syracusan ramparts, made impregnable by Dionysius and reinforced by the genius of Archimedes, with swinging arms that were extended over the approaches to the walls and dropped great weights of stone and flaming oil on those trying to scale the walls, beat off the Romans, who then, once more in its contentious history, laid siege to Syracuse. News of Sicilian developments stirred Carthage to a fever of patriotism and an army of twenty-five thousand infantry and three-thousand cavalry and twelve elephants under the command of Himilco landed at Heraclea and moved on to take the island's second city, Agrigentum. Marcellus was too heavily engaged at Syracuse to do much, but he still held an important section of Sicily and had the satisfaction of badly decimating a Syracusan force dispatched under Hippocrates to assist Himilco. Once again, the wily Carthaginian, escaped personally. Rome sent another legion in reinforcement, bringing the Roman expeditionary force in Sicily to four legions. Himilco and Hippocrates were frustrated in their attempt to ambush the arriving legion and 213 ended with the contending forces about evenly divided.

---

6 CAH, VIII, p. 65 (B. L. Hallward).

It must be said that after six years of war, Hannibal in particular had accomplished a considerable work of reassertion of Carthage in carrying the war very successfully to Italy, putting the Roman hold on Sicily gravely in doubt, while holding, with great difficulty, the majority of its Spanish territory. Sardinia alone had been a failed operation, and little was committed to it. But Carthage was extremely strained, and Rome was still gathering strength. This is where things stood as 212, the decisive year in the Sicilian campaign, opened.

Marcellus conducted the siege of Syracuse with great skill. In the early spring of 212, he seized parts of Epipolae on the north side of Syracuse, by exploiting the drunkenness of the defenders on the festival of Artemis. (This would be a time-honoured version of opportunism. George Washington did the same in crossing the Rapahannock River on the day after Christmas, 1776, and Sam Houston did the same at San Jacinto in 1845 against the Mexicans. The North Vietnamese Tet offensive of 1968 was on Vietnam's greatest holiday, and the Egyptians launched the Yom Kippur War against Israel in 1973.) Marcellus sent in a scaling party over the lowest section of the wall, and they admitted the Roman army which thoroughly sacked a sizeable part of Syracuse, and then, inexplicably, the Greek governor of Dionysius' mighty fortress of Euryalus surrendered it to the Romans, and Epicydes was in an unstable position in a main section of the city. He and Himilco attempted counterattacks, but Marcellus beat them off. The Carthaginian admiral Bomilcar managed to raise Syracusan morale by injecting ninety ships past the Roman embargo and right into the inner harbour of Syracuse, and withdrew most of them again, also successfully. The marshes of the Anapus, which had caused such terrible problems to the Athenians in their disastrous siege of 415-413 now returned to haunt the defenders, and a plague broke out. The Romans too were affected, but not too seriously, as they were on higher ground and their army was more aware of the exigencies of sanitation. From this point, Rome had the steadily stronger hand in Sicily and Marcellus forced his advantage with professional thoroughness.

Carthage made its last big attempt to turn the tide of war in Sicily in the spring of 211, when Bomilcar returned with one-hundred and thirty vessels escorting a large transport fleet, but a Roman fleet of one-hundred ships intercepted him and Bomilcar, in choppy weather, was imbued with the defeatism the Carthaginian fleet had taken on in the First Punic War, not the cunning revanchist defiance of Hannibal. He sent the transports back to Africa and fled with his warships to Tarentum; Bomilcar almost completely escaped, but this desertion unhinged the Syracusan defenders. Epicydes had sailed out to meet Bomilcar and couldn't or in any case, did not return to Syracuse, and went instead to Agrigentum to try to organize an overland relief force. Carthage sent an army relief force under Hanno, and Hannibal sent his best cavalry commander, Muttines, but resistance in Syracuse itself snapped.

New generals were elected to replace Epicydes but were immediately assassinated and a Spanish mercenary commander was induced (presumably bribed) to admit the Roman army to Ortygia, and it flooded into the city and the siege prevailed after two-and-a-half years. Marcellus seized the official treasury but in the Roman custom then abandoned Syracuse to the avaricious and sexual appetites of his army. Considerable treasure was destroyed by ignorant soldiers, though most was carried off for the benefit of Rome. Archimedes was slain by a Roman private as he contemplated scientific problems drawn in the sand. It was an uncivilized treatment of one of the Mediterranean world's great cities.

Syracuse would never fully rise again, having been seduced by the losing side, and after losing its sense of self-government and strategic survival when it buried its nonagenarian leader Hiero II. In broadly strategic terms, it was a win-double for Rome: it was disappointing that Syracuse flipped against it, but it was the provocation to smash a potential rivalry once and for all, as it scored a heavy blow against its current mortal adversary. A powerful city that is an ally can become an important enemy; when it is reduced to rubble populated by quaking survivors, the alliance has withered but the potential rivalry has evaporated. It was now a matter of time before Rome flung Carthage out of Sicily once and for all.

Matters moved swiftly; Marcellus caught up with the small Carthaginian army on the Himeras River; the Numidian cavalry conveniently deserted, and Marcellus killed or captured most of the enemy force, but some escaped into Agrigentum. It was too late in the season to mount a siege, and Marcellus returned in triumph to Rome and there was an uplifting public display of the treasure looted from the erstwhile Syracusan ally. The praetor M. Cornelius Cethegus replaced him and tidied up a few areas over the winter. The consul, M. Valerius Laevinus, arrived in the early spring with reinforcements, although Rome now possessed an overwhelming superiority of numbers. Laevinus exploited the differences between Hanno and Muttines (defeated generals frequently fall out with each other), and a faction within Agrigentum betrayed the defence and Laevinus stamped out Carthaginian resistance almost effortlessly. It had been a close contest, but Carthage had had bad luck with the plague, and the untimely death of Himilco, and its other commanders, especially Hanno, who was incompetent, and the fearful Bomilcar, were unequal to their tasks.

8. Spain and Italy

The Roman victory in Sicily was diluted somewhat by reversals in Spain. As was mentioned, the revolt of the Numidian leader Syphax had forced the recall from Spain of Hasdrubal from 214 to 212, dealing with this urgent problem close to home, and the Scipios were able to take Saguntum, a city which changed hands like a barometer of the war in Iberia, and penetrated well into the centre of Spain, taking about a third of Carthage's traditional position in Iberia. Having defeated Syphax, by the end of 212, Hasdrubal made peace with him when he managed to reestablish himself with the aid of the king of the Mauretanians in Morocco. Carthage had stabilized its Numidian position and extracted itself from desert politics and sent three new armies to or back to Spain to shore up what had become a critical condition. Hasdrubal took his men, with some replenishment, back, and Hannibal's capable brother Mago led another army (in which the 26-year-old Numidian chief Massinissa commanded the cavalry), and just to confuse historians, Hasdrubal of Gisgo arrived at the head of another army. The Scipios had become so entrenched, they were able to strengthen their forces with perhaps ten-thousand Celtiberian troops.

Given the lengthy absence from Spain of a serious Carthaginian army, the Scipios had separated their forces and grown accustomed to a relatively uncontested time; they were abruptly awakened by the returning Carthaginians. The Spanish recruits, unceremoniously deserted en masse back to their former Carthaginian allies and masters and the two Scipios were separated and soon surrounded by the three Spanish armies with a much larger combined force. Publius Scipio made a reasonable gamble in a desperate situation and stole off under cover of night to attack a native force of seventy-five hundred Suessitani led by their chief Indibilis, that was on its way to join forces with Mago. It was worth a try, but it failed: Mago arrived and the Roman force was almost wiped out. Publius Scipio died in battle, and Gnaeus was similarly overwhelmed by the armies of the two Hasdrubals and Mago in his rear. The skeleton force that Scipio had left behind at his camp under Tiberius Fonteius gathered together a relatively few survivors and managed to recross the Ebro; the detritus of the formerly victorious Roman armies elected L. Marcius Septimus as their commander and he managed to retain the loyalty of the tribes to the north of the Ebro, but all the gains of the Scipios south of the Ebro had been lost with the Scipios. Carthage's losses of personnel in Sicily had been matched by Rome's in Spain, but Carthage was hiring mercenaries, and paying them with difficulty from contested Spanish sources. Rome recruited new armies (and new Scipios).

Reviewing the ledger of the war, Hannibal had virtually obliterated eight Roman legions at the Trebia, Lake Trasimene, and Cannae, Carthage had lost the equivalent of two legions in Spain, one in Sardinia, and two in Sicily, but Rome had lost most of two more legions in the renewed action in Spain: Rome had lost most of ten legions to about half those losses for Carthage. However, the opposition of Macedon had not seriously inconvenienced Rome, and the war was developing more favourably for Rome in Italy after the unimaginable debacle at Cannae. Rome had responded with formidable determination and sangfroid to the series of Hannibal's great victories. The historian Quintus Fabius Pictor (the last name means "painter" because his grandfather was the first known Roman artistic painter), was sent on a mission to the Oracle at Delphi to seek guidance after Cannae; the democrats ceased their agitation and united with the Senate and suspended their practice of elevating populist rabble rousers such as Flaminius to the consulate. The survivors of Cannae, strengthened somewhat with recruits, were sent to Sicily, as has been recorded, and the Sicilian legions, untainted with crushing defeat, replaced them in Italy and two new legions were recruited and trained up and joined the two legions from Sicily and the two that were on the Po. This conferred manpower equivalence with Hannibal on the Romans, though they could not at this point remotely claim parity in quality of high command.

The emergency measure of the purchase of the liberty of slaves who were willing to serve in new legions was enacted by the dictator M. Junius Pera and his major equites, T. Sempronius Gracchus. At the same time, very energetic efforts were deployed to recruit fresh legions in Umbria, Etruria, and the Sabine country, and while more than a year was needed for the results to be tangible, this also was successful. In response to public superstition, a Gallic man and woman, and a Greek couple were buried alive under the Forum Boarium as human sacrifices. Prisoners would no longer be ransomed and Hannibal's customary offer to redeem his prisoners was declined, though the prisoners continued to be treated reasonably. But Roman fortunes in Italy did not turn in 215. In late 215, the consul L. Postumius commander of the two legions in Cisalpine Gaul, defending the approaches to Italy, was almost overwhelmed by Gauls in revolt, and it took almost a year for adequate reinforcements to be sent there. Faced with a mortal crisis, Rome responded with cool determination and total war; no Latin city had revolted and most of the fortress cities around Italy remained loyal to Rome and could not be overcome by Hannibal. He had to shore up his few Italian allies and could not be everywhere at once.

Quintus Fabius Maximus was back as consul and presiding strategist. Wherever Hannibal was not, the growing Roman legions stamped out revolts, moving around Italy and avoiding Hannibal himself, as the Allies of the Sixth Coalition avoided Napoleon in 1813 and 1814, except for the Battle of Leipzig, where they had a heavy numerical advantage. Hannibal's army gradually shrank in size from skirmishes and desertions, while Rome drew upon the demographic mass of Italy. From 215 to 212, it bulked up the Roman army to an unheard of (since Persia) force of two-hundred thousand men in twenty-five legions: sixteen in Italy, two each on the Po, at Rome, in Etruria, Apulia, and Lucania, and six in Campania. There were four in Sicily, two in Sardinia, and the balance in or on the way to Spain. The Carthaginians had steadied their position in Spain and Numidia, been defeated in Sardinia and Sicily, failed to wring much that was useful from Macedonia, and by 215 it had been three years since Hannibal had won a serious battle and Rome now had one-hundred and thirty thousand men under arms in Italy, approximately three times the size of his army. He could not count on any more Roman impetuosity of the kind he had so lethally exploited in his three great early victories.

Rome also had a fleet of two-hundred vessels that ruled the waves and doubled the war-tax in 214 and increased it again the next year. Rome's older allies were faithful, but hard put upon, and Hannibal did terrible damage to the richest rural areas of Italy as he ravaged the countryside, partly to feed his soldiers but partly to try to sow defeatism and desertion among Rome's allies. In 215, Tiberius Sempronius Gracchus, who had shown great talent as a cavalry commander, was elected consul.

Postumius had been killed in Gaul and Claudius Marcellus was nominated to replace him, but the Senate objected to having two plebeian consuls, despite Marcellus' exemplary performance in Sicily, and he stood aside in statesmanlike fashion, and the now considerably revered Quintus Fabius Maximus was elected. Marcellus and Fabius were both elected in the following year. Marcellus was a consul five times, as was Fabius, who was also dictator twice and censor once. These two valiant and determined men, one a patrician and the other a plebeian, personified probably more than anyone the indefatigable and unwavering courage and determination of the Roman state, people and Federation, which carried Rome through the immense crisis of the Second Punic War.

In the winter of 215-214, Hannibal stayed at Capua and made a mighty effort to cajole and negotiate the adherence of some of the Campanian towns, but without success. He had managed to take the fortress of Casilinum, one of the gateways to Samnium, in 215, but Marcellus kept him out of Nola, where Hannibal had had extensive discussions with the local democratic faction. There were now six Roman legions hovering around him at all times, but always eluding him when he offered battle. The tide of battle in Italy started to turn in 214. Hannibal intensified his campaign in Campania and summoned Hanno to join him from the south, but Tiberius Gracchus sortied out of Beneventum and intercepted and severely defeated Hanno. With this, Hannibal marched swiftly to the south to attack Heracles and Tarentum, but the Roman fleet resupplied the towns and lent them manpower with which Hannibal was repulsed and he retired back to Apulia for the winter.

In 213, with rising hopes, Rome elected Fabius' son consul to command one army and Gracchus again to command the other army; and each army now comprised four legions and there were plenty of reinforcements around. The young Fabius was able to retake Arpi, though there has been much speculation that Hannibal had left it as a decoy as he again surged south to Tarentum, and took advantage of discontent at Rome where some rebellious Tarentines had been thrown from the Tarpeian Rock in exemplary punishment, and the recalcitrant elements in Tarentum opened a gate for Hannibal at night and he seized the town but not the fortress. Despite all they had been through with Hannibal, some of the local Roman commanders were over-confident, and the Greek cities of Magna Graecia, following the apostasy of Syracuse (and in spite of the disaster that ensued), forgot the benefits of the Pax Romana and rose up against Rome. Hannibal exploited Greek discontent, representing Carthage as a fellow-Aegean state because of its Phoenician parentage and a natural ally of the Greeks against the Roman usurper. Rome retained the great citadel-fortress of Tarentum which denied Hannibal much use of the great harbour, although Hannibal did concoct a system of rollers for moving ships between the sea and the harbour over the isthmus. However, 213 did not go well for Rome in Illyria, where Philip V defeated Rome's allies and the Sicilian revolt became so serious that Marcellus was, as we have seen, dispatched there.

Roman popular impatience surfaced again and neither Fabius was elected consul in 212. Quintus Flavius Flaccus, who had been consul twice before, was elected along with Appius Claudius Pulcher, whom we have seen as praetor in Sicily. Except for Gracchus, all the commands in Italy were shaken up. The Romans again pounced on the unfortunate Hanno as he rounded up supplies for Hannibal in Campania. Flaccus took the Carthaginian camp by surprise and seized an immense quantity of supplies, and the Romans besieged Capua. However, this produced Hannibal, his dread self, to preserve his control of Capua, but he faced the full application of the Fabian system: Rome had picked the countryside of Campania clean and deposited everything within the walls of the fortified towns and Hannibal could not maintain his army in Campania for more than a week without running out of food. He withdrew to the south and the Romans completely sealed off Capua for a long siege. The Romans did suffer a reverse when Tiberius Gracchus was surprised and killed by Numidian cavalry near Beneventum, according to one account, while swimming. His funeral at Rome was a scene of prodigious public and official lamentation. His two legions of redeemed slaves were disbanded, as the Roman army was now awash with manpower, and the weight of sixteen legions in Italy, removing or destroying what could be of use to Hannibal and harassing and baiting him at every turn. The consuls for 211 were Gnaeus Fulvius Centumalus and P. Sulpicius Galba, and

Rome recovered most of the disaffected cities of Samnium and Apulia, and Capua was reduced to a desperate condition by the leak-proof siege which was imposed throughout the year.

Hannibal, though now largely confined to south Italy by the concentration of fourteen legions in central Italy, steadily squeezing and shrinking his zone of operations, would not concede Capua without a final effort to save it for his forces of discontented Roman subjects. He moved by forced marches, leaving his baggage train behind, and descended upon the besiegers of Capua from a little-used pass in the Campanian hills. The Romans had provided for an attack on their siege lines and drove Hannibal off. The Carthaginian commander, as cunning and resourceful at improvisation as always, abruptly broke off and suddenly and by a roundabout route fetched up three miles from the heavily defended walls of Rome itself. There had not been an army at the gates of Rome since the Gauls got to Allia in 390 under Brennus, nearly one-hundred and eighty years before—the time that elapsed between the Battle of the Plains of Abraham in 1759 and the Fall of France to the Nazis in 1940.

There was some alarm in the city, and Polybius claims that some of Rome's women cleaned the steps of the main temples with their hair to appease the gods, but there were four legions in the city and plenty of supplies of all essentials. Fabius spoke for the Senate and advised against any move to call for reinforcements, and Hannibal abruptly departed, after a small skirmish with the Consul Galba, and returned to Bruttium. He was finally running out of options and Fabius' emphasis of the greater strength of the defensive side had been successful. Capua was abandoned to its fate and soon surrendered. Rome executed thirty prominent nobles and imprisoned the Capuan senators that were not beheaded and confiscated a good deal of their property, but the general population was undisturbed. Capua would be governed by a prefect elected by and in Rome. It was not a severe municipal punishment and the fall of Capua had an immense impact on the war in Italy and beyond. The fall of Syracuse to Marcellus was announced shortly after and only then the news came of the defeat and death of the Scipios in Spain, and by this time Rome could send a substantial army to Spain to ensure that Roman fortunes in that country were not crushed, as Rome won Sicily and gained the upper hand in Italy at last. Rome also negotiated an alliance with the Aetolian league against Macedonia.

Marcellus and Valerius Laevinus were elected consuls in 210. The army was reduced from twenty-five to twenty-one legions, but composed of the best and most seasoned troops, and Gaius Claudius Nero, who had commanded a legion in the siege of Capua, was sent to Spain with two good legions. In Italy, the Roman army continued to press and harass Hannibal and only offered battle on unfavourable terrain and when possessed of much superior force. Marcellus commanded opposite Hannibal, and though he did not possess Hannibal's innovative and tactical genius, he was far too competent to make the horrible blunders that endangered the Roman Republic in the first years of Hannibal's invasion of Italy. He was like Wellington opposite Napoleon or Montgomery opposite Rommel, or even Grant opposite Lee—not as original but very solid and competent and able to prevail with a stronger army and keep the pressure on his opponent. Gnaeus Fulvius was relatively inexperienced militarily and allowed himself to be trapped by Hannibal near Herdonea and Hannibal had the pleasure of again giving the Romans a good thrashing and painful lesson. Fulvius, most of his officers, and several thousand men were killed, but there was not a rout and Marcellus closed up and more than held his own against Hannibal himself at Venusia. The Roman garrison in Tarentum was hard-pressed for a time, as the Tarentines, freakishly, managed to drive off a supply convoy from Sicily. The call for new soldiers in the autumn of 210 was resisted by twelve of the thirty Latin colonies in Italy, which indicated that war weariness was setting in even though Hannibal, his threat much reduced and his mystique somewhat eroded, was still alive and dangerous and moving about in southern Italy.

In 209, progress resumed. Hannibal marched into Apulia, but was met by Marcellus and the two maneuvered without any loss of position or advantage by Marcellus. At the same time, Quintus Fulvius Flaccus, a new consul, marched from Rome through Hirpinia and Lucania and regained a number of towns. The other consul, again Fabius, marched on Tarentum and with thirty quinqueremes sent by Laevinus, he imposed a siege by land and sea. Hannibal hurried from Bruttium, where Marcellus was at the head of a large army, but he arrived too late to save Tarentum, which returned to Roman hands. Fabius enabled his soldiers to express the pent-up rage and tension of Rome and they sacked Tarentum thoroughly, although such severity was generally only engaged in when it was necessary to break a siege by storming over the walls, and there had been no such resistance here. Fabius sold thirty-thousand of the civil population into slavery. Hannibal, though boxed in and deprived of victory, was unquenchable and required Rome to retain an enormous army and for it to stay on its toes nine months of the year. War fatigue was making inroads and there was some sentiment to seek a peace now that this could be done on fully respectable terms. By a narrow margin, the party that wanted, after such a prolonged and desperate struggle, to press on for a decisive and humiliating defeat of Carthage prevailed, and in the Roman tradition of luck crowning mighty and long-unyielding effort, a commander of genius emerged to win the war.

9. Publius Scipio and Roman Victory in Spain

Through 210, Nero, in command north of the Ebro, practiced Fabian tactics where appropriate, to avoid direct encounters of main force units, but blocking any large advance of reinforcements for Hannibal across the Ebro and toward Italy. Again, Carthage paid a heavy price for the inferiority of her naval forces: there was no reliable way to reinforce Hannibal, who was now somewhat beleaguered and could only maintain a position in southern Italy by his extraordinary tactical dexterity and highly trained army; although many were mercenaries, they had unshakeable faith in their commander. He had earned it, but the strategic correlation of forces was shifting unfavorably. Carthage was recruiting Celtiberian mercenaries in large numbers with a view to attacking across the Ebro and through southern Gaul to Italy, and the Roman Senate acted with great boldness, the more surprising given its lengthy addiction to extreme caution. It was as if the whole Roman Federation struggled to relieve itself of an imminent mortal threat, considered a reasonably positive peace of attrition that would confirm possession of Sicily and Sardinia, and then suddenly determined to try to finish the war at once and in total victory. To this end, it appointed the younger Publius Scipio, who had rescued his father and saved his life at Placentia in 218 and was only twenty-five and had only been an aedile, as commander in Spain at the head of a reinforced army of four legions. The Scipios were popular and respected and though the new commander's father and uncle had been defeated and killed by the enemy, they had been victorious, died bravely, and Lucius Marcus and Claudius Nero had been able to conduct a successful defence with the remnants of their army. There was great rejoicing in Rome at this appointment. The tired Rome of Fabius had done its long-drawn work of attrition and vigilance. All sensed that the time had come for decisive strokes. So it had, and the Senate's intuition was inspired.

Scipio landed at Emporium near the end of 210 and prepared for the extremely daring blow of capture of the Carthaginian capital in Spain, Nova Carthago. He was a very dynamic and confident young commander, sincerely and fervently religious with a sort of mystical sense of mission that presaged such holy fighters as Joan of Arc and lent him an uplifting spirituality and eloquence that could inspire his men. He claimed that Poseidon himself, god of war, had appeared to him in a dream to commend a plan of attack. His plan of attack was brilliant. The three Carthaginian armies were wintering at considerable distance from each other; Hasdrubal Gisgo was near the mouth of the Tagus, the present day Lisbon (illogically, as far from the Romans as it was possible to be), Mago near Gibraltar (again an inexplicable location), and Hasdrubal Barca in central Spain, ten days march from Nova Carthago. The situation of Nova Carthago was enviably strong, on an isthmus within an inlet and the walls of the city were on steep rocky slopes. Scipio appeared as a complete surprise, by forced marches, and blocked the isthmus while the Roman fleet blocked the access to the inlet where the isthmus was located. The next day Scipio launched an attack with scaling ladders from the isthmus, and when the entire garrison was preoccupied with this attack, he sent another large detachment, with local fishermen as guides, wading through shallow marshes and penetrated an under-defended portion of the north wall, swept the defenders off the ramparts, threw open the isthmus gate and the Roman army seized the capital and citadel of Carthaginian Spain in one full day's action. It was a thunderclap. Immense quantities of stores and treasure were seized, as well as the hostages that secured the loyalty of antagonistic tribes. The battered Roman army in Spain was instantly reconstructed psychologically, the Carthaginians were steeped in gloom, and the Celtiberian natives took note of the change of fortunes.

Scipio returned to Tarraco, introduced the Spanish sword—a cut and thrust weapon rather than the traditional Roman stabbing sword, and devoted himself to diplomacy to win over the Spanish tribes whose hostages he had found in Nova Carthago and sent to Rome. Indibilis, the surest barometer of the state of the conflict in Spain, again came over to Rome, with some others, Edetani, Ilergeti, and Mandonius. The Carthaginian commanders just pretended nothing had happened and remained where they were, overseeing the Tagus, Anas, and Baetis valleys. They had not done anything to strengthen their empire in Spain or ingratiate themselves with the Spanish tribes, and unlike Rome as its influence spread through Italy, they built nothing, conferred no honours or dignity or trust on the local chiefs, and knew that only force of arms maintained their position in Spain, which funded the Carthaginian state, especially in wartime. The Spanish empire of Carthage was effectively a house of cards, and the Romans now had a charismatic and bold commander at the head of four well-trained and highly motivated legions. Hasdrubal Barca was still raising an army to send to Italy, precarious though his position in Spain had become.

In the early spring of 208, Scipio marched south quickly toward Hasdrubal (Barca), hoping for a decisive battle. Hasdrubal withdrew to a very strong defensive position at Baecula, where he expected to be joined by the Carthaginian army at Gades (Cadiz). Scipio's army was about thirty-five thousand first class troops, to about twenty-five thousand for Hasdrubal and as always, Scipio had devised a clever strategy of attacking frontally on a wide, thin front while his main forces attacked up-hill on both flanks. The Roman army gained on both flanks and Hasdrubal prudently retired in good order, with his entire baggage and treasure train. He was effectively retreating toward reinforcements and was probably justified in not wanting to risk Spain on a battle with Scipio at the head of a larger army. But Hasdrubal skillfully executed a tactical change and determined to march to Italy to gamble on the main theatre, leaving still two armies in Spain that might have hoped for reinforcements from Carthage and a chance at keeping Scipio out of the gold and silver mining areas, which were also the richest recruiting grounds. He evaded Scipio, who was assuming his task was to defend Spain, and Hasdrubal marched north and across the Pyrenees with the Atlantic on his left at the modern Biarritz and proceeded across Gaul toward Italy.

In early 207, Carthage did indeed send the well-travelled (but rarely successful) Hanno to Spain with a reinforcement army, Hanno joined Mago in central Spain where Hanno was busily training Celtiberian recruits when Selano, whom Scipio had dispatched for the purpose, prorupted upon him with ten-thousand men and five-hundred cavalry and captured Hanno (not to be confused with the oft-defeated Hanno, son of Admiral Bomilcar, who also suffered many reversals at the hands of the Romans), though Mago and the main force made off successfully to join Hasdrubal Gisgo near Gades, where Scipio shortly arrived with the main army. Both sides recognized that a battle could not be avoided and that the future of Carthaginian Spain would depend upon it. Hasdrubal Gisgo and Mago could not retreat from where they now were and retain anything in Spain, nor any credibility for Carthage's recruiting efforts in that country, which had furnished tens of thousands of first-class Spanish soldiers for Carthaginian service over many decades, as well as funding the Carthaginian paymaster. Rome now had one hand at the Carthaginian fiscal jugular in Spain, and another grasping after Hannibal himself in Italy.

Gisgo and Mago gathered all Carthage's forces in Spain, an army of about fifty-thousand, to meet Scipio, who had about forty-thousand. As the Romans fortified their camp, Mago sent a cavalry attack against them, but Scipio, expecting such a move, had stationed a large contingent of his own cavalry concealed in a nearby wood, and it fell in behind the attackers and drove them off with considerable loss. For several days there were deployments in full battle formation late in the day when a battle would not realistically occur. Scipio on these occasions had his Roman legions in the centre facing Gisgo's elephants and African forces, and Rome's Spanish allies on both wings. After some days of this routine, Scipio roused his army early, had it take its breakfast before sunrise and deploy with the Spanish thinly in a recessed centre, and the Roman legions on the flanks and well forward, and he launched his cavalry against the Carthaginians scouts and outposts, forcing Hasdrubal Gisgo and Mago to send their men out unfed into the positions they had trained in for the previous several days. They deployed into a battle in progress and intensifying and the Roman legions on the wings steadily squeezed the Carthaginians and its centre was never able, because of the encroaching attacks on its flanks, to mount a heavy attack against the Roman centre. Scipio had adapted Hannibal's own tactics, and Carthage's Spanish levies were no match for the experienced Roman legions bearing down on them from both sides.

Had Scipio's timing slipped, and the Carthaginian centre been enabled to attack straight ahead at the softer Roman centre of new Spanish recruits, disaster might have resulted for Rome. But moving as swiftly as he did, Scipio rolled up the Carthaginian army, and forced it to break up and retreat. Scipio did not have the massed cavalry that would have been necessary to run down the retreating army and surround and annihilate it, but it was a decisive victory and he stayed on his enemy's trail as it withdrew. The Spaniards in the Punic army put up a very respectable fight but were ultimately crushed and broken up and scattered by the Roman legions, and the Africans and their Carthaginian officers retired more or less in order, but after heavy casualties. Hasdrubal Gisgo and Mago tried to make a stand in their somewhat fortified camp, but Scipio overwhelmed the defense and the Carthaginians resumed their retreat to the sea, harassed all the way in the rear and flanks. Hasdrubal Gisgo and Mago and a corporal's guard departed Spain by ship, escaping by a hair's breadth, but practically the entire remainder of the army was rounded up by Scipio. All were treated humanely as legitimate soldiers of a respected enemy. Thus ended the Carthaginian era in Spain, with Hannibal's relatives scrambling onto a ship which rowed at ramming speed for deep water and home. The greatest source of wealth of Carthage, whose gold and silver mines had financed the entire Carthaginian enterprise since it outgrew its status as a Phoenician colony and became a power in the central and Western Mediterranean two centuries before, passed into the now unshakeable hands of Rome.

Scipio sent his brother Lucius to reduce the Carthaginian fortress town of Orangis and then to carry the welcome news to Rome. There were many Carthaginian-held towns in Spain, but no field army between them and little coordination. This was a mopping-up operation conducted throughout 206. The Segura Valley was a lengthy battle, and the Romans were unphilosophical at the end of it; the captured enemy were massacred for punitive and exemplary reasons. Astapa surrendered, but only after a heroic finale in which the Carthaginian warriors and their acculturated comrades immolated their wives and children in a sort of prevenient suttee, and then charged out en masse and fought to the death to the last man. The Romans closed in on Gades, where Mago had landed and taken over. Attempts were made to entice a fifth column to arise within it, given the evident hopelessness of the

Carthaginian cause in Spain, but Mago snuffed out any trace of it. A Roman naval expedition eventually had to retire, and Rome was distracted by the incorrigible Indibilis who had again revolted (somewhat resembling in his unreliability Perdiccas the Epirate—Chapter 14). The problem was amplified by the indisposition of Scipio, whom, it was feared, had contracted a dangerous disease, but in fact recovered quite quickly from severe influenza. Scipio quickly made good arrears of pay, moving around amongst all the disgruntled groups, placatory here and reproachful there, and for good measure, rounding up the most outspoken and antagonistic ringleaders and summarily executing them in front of their erstwhile supporters.

The struggle in Spain entered its final act as the Romans tightened their grip on Gades. Mago, who had remained there, emulated the greater generals of the war, his brother Hannibal and his nemesistic opponent Scipio, and launched a surprise assault to recover Nova Carthago. The Romans were too strong and well-organized and repulsed him. He was barred from returning to Gades because he had treacherously murdered the chief native citizen and the city fathers were contemplating a negotiated surrender to Rome, as Carthage's day in Spain had clearly passed (making Indibilis' treachery the more surprising). Mago went on to Minorca, where the capital, Mahón, is still named after him. Scipio did agree to the handing over of Gades and granted it status as a free city, and it enjoyed many centuries of prosperity in that state. Massinissa, who had made his mark as a Numidian divisional military chief under Mago, requested to meet Scipio and they had a very productive and historic talk. Massinissa rallied unequivocally to Rome and was welcomed into its upper military and political ranks. He would be an even more durable and as positive an influence in North Africa than Hiero II had been in Syracuse. Massinissa would be a mighty ally of Rome, who would transform Numidia into the proverbial breadbasket of Europe and would be a universally admired king throughout his reign of more than fifty years. His meeting with Scipio would prove a major historic encounter that would influence the ancient world and serve Roman interests mightily.

The Roman conquest of Spain was complete in 206. Scipio's four-year campaign ranks as one of the most successful in all military history. It was the supreme strategic stroke: he amputated the source of Carthage's money (the gold mines alone are estimated to have produced the modern equivalent of about five billion U.S. dollars a year), and the principal source of its best infantrymen as well (the Numidians provided the Carthaginian cavalry). The campaign was splendidly conceived and executed by Scipio, and after founding the first Roman colony in Spain, Italica, and leaving his lieutenants, Marcius and Silanus in charge of the Roman legions and garrisons there, he returned to Rome in 205, to stand for and be (unanimously) elected consul. Publius Cornelius Scipio was thirty-one, and the supreme showdown between the two greatest generals in history up to that time, apart from and perhaps approximately as talented as Alexander the Great, was about to take place.

10. The Last Phase of the Second Punic War in Italy

While the campaign in Spain unfolded satisfactorily and then miraculously well for Rome, it remained sluggish in Italy, where Hannibal's genius was undiminished despite being contained and notwithstanding the passage of ten years marching about Italy. Marcellus was, in 208, for the fifth time, elected consul, in the hope that he would carry the battle more successfully to Hannibal. Elected with him was T. Qinctius Crispinus, who had served as one of Marcellus' officers in the outstandingly successful operations around Syracuse. Marcellus and Crispinus with four legions and many auxiliaries and reinforcements, found themselves at close quarters with Hannibal near Venusium, and Marcellus was trying to place Roman forces in an adequately advantageous position to offer a decisive battle to their imperishably cunning and resourceful enemy. But Hannibal pounced on both consuls when they were unwisely with a relatively small reconnaissance force and Crispinus was seriously wounded, and Marcellus was killed. Hannibal accorded him a very grand and respectful funeral with full military honours. He was greatly lamented in Rome. Posidonius referred to Marcellus and Fabius as, respectively, the "sword and the shield of Rome." For the balance of 208, fear of Hannibal, restored to almost neurotic heights, prevented Rome from anything very ambitious in Italy. Rome had been conducting a siege at Locri, and Hannibal concluded a good operational year, though another indecisive one, by proceeding to Locri in forced marches, catching the Roman besiegers by surprise and bundling them unceremoniously into an emergency evacuation fleet, relieving the siege.

Elsewhere, the war was going almost as well as in Spain for Rome. Philip of Macedonia had had the upper hand over Rome's ally, Attalus of Pergamum, but Carthage had not been able to provide promised naval support and Philip had not much inconvenienced Rome. Hannibal, it would be recalled, had regarded this as a diversionary and pincers challenge to Rome, but it had been ineffectual. And Valerius Laevinus, always a reliable admiral, had soundly defeated the Punic navy, with one-hundred quinqueremes to Carthage's eighty-three, capturing eighteen ships in the summer of 208, and effectively shutting down Carthage's well-intimidated navy in port. But the news in late 208, that Hasdrubal Barca had departed Spain and was traversing Gaul to infuse another Carthaginian army, albeit of only about twenty-thousand men, into Italy, caused an uneasy winter 208-7 in Rome. For 207, the consuls elected were Claudius Nero, a solid veteran of Capua and Spain, and Marcus Livius Salinator. He had distinguished himself in the Illyrian campaign of 219. The number of active legions was raised again to twenty-three—fifteen in Italy, four in Spain and two each in Sicily and Sardinia.

Hasdrubal crossed the Alps in the early spring of 207 without difficulty, given alliances Carthage had with Gauls on both sides of the Alps. He descended to the Po Valley and recruited about ten-thousand Celts and Gauls to strengthen his army. He moved cautiously south to the northern end of the Via Flaminia and found his way blocked by the combined armies of the praetor Porcius, and the consul Livius, at Sena Gallica. Hannibal had struck his camp in Bruttium and tried to maneuver north to meet Hasdrubal in central Italy, but was harassed and challenged by Flaccus and Nero, but not with the impetuosity of earlier times, and the Romans also threatened Hannibal's communication point with Carthage at Locri, so Hannibal thought better of striking off toward central Italy. On intercepting a message from Hasdrubal to Hannibal indicating Hasdrubal's intention to plunge into Umbria and try to rejoin

Hannibal there, Nero took the bold and clever move of detaching six-thousand elite infantry and one-thousand cavalry and leading them swiftly north along the Adriatic coast to join Livius and Porcius. He also urged the Senate to move the Capuan legion to Rome and release the two legions in Rome for service in the north. He thus quickly assembled a solid veteran army of forty-thousand to greet Hasdrubal when he descended from the Apennines onto, as he presumably imagined, the broad boulevard of the Via Flaminia.

He started down the Via Flaminia and moved up the Metaurus Valley at night, while Nero fell in behind, beside, and in front of him. Hasdrubal's Gauls were relatively undisciplined and had indifferent field formation, and the Roman cavalry was harassing his flank. With daylight, he formed up his army to meet the enemy squarely. Hasdrubal wisely found a position where a steep ridge protected his left wing and he placed his Gauls there. The battle commenced fairly evenly, but Nero deftly moved his right, which was masked off by the ridge that Hasdrubal had anchored his left against, and got his right behind the Roman lines to his far left flank and around the Carthaginian army out of sight and then struck Hasdrubal's army suddenly and full-force in the rear. The Carthaginian elephants panicked in the melee, further disturbed by distracting trumpeting by the Romans which caused the elephants to run amok among Carthaginian ranks and many of them had to be put down by their minders, with a hard mallet-stroke on a chisel behind either ear. Nero supervised the complete encirclement of the invading army and ordered an air-tight closing from all sides; every single enemy soldier was to be killed or captured, but prisoners would be taken and not killed. Hasdrubal led his men gallantly in increasingly hopeless combat and then rushed into direct combat with Roman infantrymen and was quickly slain, as he had wished. Livy wrote that he "fell fighting—a death worthy of Hamilcar's son and Hannibal's brother."[7] It was a complete and overwhelming victory, the total destruction of a Carthaginian army of thirty-thousand, a great turning point like Vicksburg (1863) or Stalingrad (1943). The news was received with immense and prolonged public rejoicing in Rome. Hannibal, on learning of the fate of his brother and his army, retired to Bruttium, in a comparatively subdued mood. This redeemed Cannae.

For 206, Rome elected L. Veturius Philo and Q. Caecilius Metellus as consuls. They were cautious men and such was their regard for Hannibal, they did not attack him, even though they had a total of thirteen legions in Italy and not more than two would be needed to keep the Gauls away (and the Gauls had just lost ten-thousand men in Hasdrubal's suicide mission and were none too frisky at this point). All was in waiting for the return of Scipio.

Came now the man predestined to end Hannibal's unconquerability. With his acute strategic judgment, Scipio detected that Hannibal's presence in Italy was now a Roman advantage. Rome held the Carthaginian treasury (Spain) and held the Mediterranean. It had more than adequate forces to keep Hannibal on his toes in Italy while attacking Carthage directly. Scipio planned to build on his relations with Massinissa in Numidia and carry the battle to Carthage with Hannibal unable to intervene without abandoning his army in Italy, where, given numerical superiority,

---

7 CAH, VIII, p. 95 (B. L. Hallward).

the Romans had generals such as Claudius Nero who could certainly defeat the Carthaginian army if Hannibal wasn't in command. (It was slightly like General Bernard L. Montgomery defeating the German Afrika Korps at El Alamein while German Field Marshal Erwin Rommel was home on sick leave.)

Scipio did not hold an office that entitled him to a triumph, which augmented public gratitude and determination to confer the consular office on him. Elected with him was Licinius Crassus, who, because he was Pontifex Maximus (again chief high priest of the college of pontiffs), could not leave Italy. This left Scipio as the consul in charge of military operations, as he had taken the extraordinary step of revealing to the public, and therefore the enemy, his strategy—to attack directly against Carthage and take advantage of the presence, bottled up ineffectually in Italy, of the one Carthaginian who had any chance of saving Carthage from an adequately large and trained Roman army commanded by Scipio. Divisions quickly developed between public and senatorial opinion. Rome was not as envious and backbiting a society as Greece, but there was much envy in the Senate over the swift rise of Scipio, and it was aggravated by the traditional rivalry between the Cornelian (Scipio) and Claudian families. These reservations about a young and charismatic hero were amplified by a natural sense of their own comparative impotence—Scipio was a deus ex machina who had suddenly changed the whole correlation of forces, and these reticences congealed easily around the accustomed caution in any contest where Hannibal was on the other side. The Carthaginian leader had completely mesmerized the Roman public and especially its leaders.

Fabius and Flaccus opposed Scipio's policy in the Senate. Their rationale was that there should be peace in Italy before carrying war to Africa. But Scipio saw not only the strategic advantage in striking at Carthage while Hannibal was grappling with a numerically superior group of Roman legions in Italy; he saw that if Hannibal were forced out of Italy, evacuating his army or losing it at the expense of an approximately equal number of Romans (as no sane person could imagine Hannibal losing his army without inflicting terrible casualties on his opponent), it would then be very difficult to persuade Rome—the people, never mind the Senate—of the wisdom of invading North Africa with Hannibal waiting on the shore to repulse the invaders. Scipio had the strategic argument and he bolstered and sold it with the insuperable emotional argument that it was time to mete out to Carthage what it had meted out to Italy, to avenge the sacred dead, and so forth, always a powerful argument, especially in these earlier times when war was commonplace, and blood was high much of the time. In fairness, Hannibal had had no colour of right in invading Italy, and while he was a comparatively civilized commander, the Roman Federation had a just and formidable grievance with Hannibal's presence around and among them these thirteen years.

As so often happens with political meddling in military matters, Scipio was authorized to enact his plan but not really accorded the ability to do it. In this way, the skeptics, in the event of failure, could claim that it was as they had foretold. Scipio was authorized to move his headquarters to Sicily and go on from there to Africa whenever he pleased. But he was given no additional forces beyond the two legions in Sicily, which though replenished, were still living down the disgrace of Cannae (though the legions had behaved exemplarily and the entire fault for the catastrophe resided with the commanders). Scipio would have to appeal for volunteers to strengthen his expeditionary force, thus testing the strength of the hold his magnetic personality and military victories had given him over the public imagination. The people of Umbria and Etruria, who had never yielded to Hannibal's threats and blandishments to desert Rome and had not enjoyed his exploitation of them, furnished timber and equipment for a fleet of thirty ships to transmit an invasion force, and seven-thousand volunteers flocked to the cause at once.

As he was readying this initiative and training up his invasion army, Scipio unearthed a possibility for seizing Locri from the Carthaginians, which would seriously isolate Hannibal from Carthage. A dissident faction within the town, as usually arises when the occupying power is not doing well, wanted to evict the Carthaginians and strike a blow for Italy. Hannibal had been a civilized occupier, but all such regimes are onerous for the local occupants. Some prominent Locrians were the ringleaders, in league with artisans whom the Romans had returned as hostages for ransom and were in fact Roman agents. They caused the betrayal of one of the two prominent citadels that the town lay between, and although Locri was outside his Sicilian and African zone of occupation, Scipio provided both land and naval forces to assist and the citadel fell, compromising the Carthaginian position in the town. Hannibal came quickly, hoping to find Roman forces in action that he could surprise and assault, but the civil population had rallied to Rome and Scipio's forces offered determined resistance from their position of strength in the liberated citadel, and four Roman legions under Metellus and Crassus closed in on him cautiously. Hannibal was forced to abandon the town, the other citadel fell, and he was stranded in Italy with no obvious exit, seriously outnumbered with Scipio in Sicily cranking up to invade North Africa and besiege or even storm Carthage itself. The whole strategic game had turned in a few cleverly applied and cleanly executed strategic strokes by Scipio: Nova Carthago and the subsequent offensives in Spain, preparing the African invasion force and exploiting discontent in Locri. The strategic condition of Carthage was suddenly very serious.

Scipio left as governor of the Greek-Italian state of Locri his force commander Quintus Pleminius. It was alleged that Pleminius had helped himself generously to plunder in Locri, and as was the Roman custom, Scipio was not over-brimming with sympathy for the formerly revolted state. It was alleged that Pleminius ransacked the temple of Persephone, which even Hannibal had left alone. Scipio needed funds, of which his enemies in the Senate, incredibly in the circumstances, were starving him, and a Senate commission investigated and after moralistic noises and a rap on the knuckles for Pleminius, contented themselves with joining the popular and ever-victorious Scipio for a crisp military review. Behind the scenes, like dogs fighting under a blanket, Roman factions were at odds with each other, with the mortal enemy still at large in Italy. (The shabby treatment of Scipio, even at this stage, prefigures the political setbacks, immediately after leading their countries to victory, of David Lloyd George and Georges Clemenceau after World War I and of Winston Churchill and, to a degree, Charles de Gaulle, after World War II.)

There were a variety of diversionary actions in the build-up to Scipio's long-promised invasion of North Africa. In Spain the pro-consuls Cornelius Lentulus and Manlius Acidinus commanded an occupation force of just two legions but had no difficulty suppressing a revolt north of the Ebro. For once, Indibilis couldn't resist and was killed in action. Less fortunate was his often-rebarbative colleague, Mandonius, who was seized and bound by his followers and handed over for execution by the Romans in exchange for slightly merciful terms, as Roman patience was wearing thin with these inconstant Celtiberians. Also, in the summer of 205 B.C., Mago made a bold move by launching a sea-borne invasion of Liguria from the Balearic Islands where he had fetched up after being evicted from Gades and barred from Nova Carthago. He captured Genoa and with thirty warships and fourteen-hundred men tried to enflame the Po Valley, but the southern Gauls were still smarting from the ten thousand dead they had taken in the flame-out of Hasdrubal at the Metaurus. The Carthaginians managed to reinforce him with another six-thousand men, some elephants and eight-hundred cavalry, but the Romans had six legions, under Valerius Laevinus (as reliable on land as he was at sea), and Livius Salinator guarding northern Italy, and Mago was in no condition to engage such a powerful combined force. Mago festered uselessly for two years. Carthage was unable to get any supplies to Hannibal and the Roman Gnaeus Octavius captured or destroyed eighty transports of a one-hundred-transport resupply fleet in stormy seas off Sardinia in late 205. The supposed diversionary operations in Greece, which had not really disturbed the Romans, ended with the Peace of Phoenice in 205. Rome was poised to bring the Second Punic War to a satisfactory end at last.

11. The Last Battles, Zama

Scipio had dispatched his personal diplomat, Laelius, to North Africa to test the waters. He found Syphax, who had oscillated between supporting Rome and Carthage to be obstinately anti-Rome. His revolt after Cannae had assisted the elder Scipios in the initial foray into Spain, but his alliance with Carthage had been cemented by his marriage with Hasdrubal Gisgo's comely daughter, Sophonisba. Syphax ruled most of Numidia, what is today Algeria, between the Ampsaga and Muluchat Rivers. But between him and Carthage were the Massyli, now led by the young Massinissa, a Roman ally. Laelius wisely made an alliance with him that would prove as durable and even more valuable than that with Hiero II of Syracuse.

In the spring of 204, Scipio embarked from Lilybaeum, and had forty quinqueremes escorting a large number of transports that carried his army of about twenty-five thousand. They landed at Utica, about ten miles northwest of Carthage. The Carthaginian navy had almost ceased to exist and there was no fear of any interference. This was adjacent to Massyli territory and Massinissa met Scipio with his cavalry (and henceforth, he would provide most of the Roman cavalry for a very long time). Syphax was already en route at the head of a large force to join Hasdrubal Gisgo (his father-in-law). An advance reconnaissance detachment under Hasdrubal's son Hanno was lured into an ambush by Massinissa and annihilated. Scipio pressed a siege of Utica by land and sea. Utica resisted the siege and the approach of Hasdrubal and Syphax leading large armies required Scipio to abandon the siege and retreat into a pre-selected rocky peninsula about two miles from Utica, where he could protect his position and be supplied by sea. Scipio's position was precarious, and he didn't have the forces to challenge seriously for control of much of the North African shore or to threaten Carthage. So he had to attract reinforcements from the Senate to appear that he was doing better than he was and that they must fly to the aid of his impending victory.

Syphax, with Hasdrubal's complete concurrence, put himself forward as a mediator during the winter and proposed that Hannibal and his army and Scipio both return home peacefully (and Mago's near Genoa as well), and that peace then break out along the actual lines. That is, having lost Sicily and Sardinia in the First Punic War, Carthage would be sheared and shed of Spain in the Second Punic war, a swiftly shrinking empire, but not an unreasonable offer. Scipio strung out negotiations in order to get a clearer picture of Carthaginian dispositions. A little like Metternich dickering and stalling with Napoleon in 1813 and 1814, Scipio was not bargaining in good faith and had no real interest in peace. Scipio sent his field officers as messengers and aides, so they could estimate professionally the extent of the armies of Syphax and Hasdrubal Gisgo and the topography of their dispositions. This was invaluable intelligence. In the spring of 203, despite his inferior position and numbers, Scipio ostentatiously readied his siege engines, and he occupied highlands closer to Utica, which had been the launching point for his unsuccessful siege the previous year. (There was no great importance to Utica; it just happened to be a town near where Scipio landed and very close to Carthage.)

As his excuse for his sleazy diplomatic fakery, Scipio claimed that the Senate was opposed despite his advocacy of acceptance of the proposals by Syphax. When he delivered this message, it was a spring afternoon and he had already planned an attack for that night by Laelius and Massinissa with half the army; the target was Syphax's camp, which was built up but entirely constructed of highly flammable thatched reed, with no use of timber or a solid building material such as earth or clay. Laelius and Massinissa were equipped with torches and flaming arrows and they suddenly charged the Masaesylian camp in the dead middle of the night and ignited an immediate conflagration. Scipio was ready with the other half of his army to attack the Carthaginians. Syphax barely escaped personally and there was a panic-stricken retreat from the blazing camp with Massinissa's cavalry charging through and killing the fleeing Masaesylians in great numbers. Hasdrubal Gisgo tried to hold his ground, but was forced to withdraw from Utica, leaving Scipio free to renew his siege (though the purpose of doing so was never clear apart from symbolism). It was a great victory, but Scipio's conduct was extremely dishonorable. It was only marginally less outrageous than a sneak attack initiating hostilities, as Germany made on the Soviet Union in 1941, or Japan did against the United States a few months later. Here, at least the powers had been at war for many years and the Roman leader had invaded Carthaginian territory, but it was still an act of bad faith to pass in a few hours from fraudulent negotiations conducted mainly for reconnaissance and sedative purposes, to a savage incendiary attack in the middle of the night. Though highly unethical, it was immensely successful, and Scipio had a triumph again to report to his generally ungrateful political leaders in Rome, who saw each enhancement of

Scipio's success and popularity as an ever-greater threat to themselves. In fact, they were ahead of their time. Publius Scipio was a loyal and traditional republican who would be unjustly suspected by the Senate. In the next one-hundred and fifty years, outright political generals would dominate the Roman Republic and deliver it to Octavian (Augustus) Caesar to transform it into an empire.

The Carthaginians strove to regroup. About four-thousand Celtiberian mercenaries arrived, and Syphax set about reorganizing his shaken survivors and gathering a new army. Scipio recognized that more important than his siege of Utica was to strike Hasdrubal hard and in open battle before he could fully regroup and reinvigorate his forces. He proceeded in forced marches over four days to the reorganization camp Hasdrubal and Syphax had set up seventy-five miles south of Utica on the Bagradas River, with just one legion and all his cavalry. In what is known to history as the Battle of the Great Plains, Hasdrubal stood and fought. Laelius and the Italian cavalry faced Hasdrubal, and Massinissa faced Syphax in a blood match of ancient desert tribal rivalry. In the centre, Scipio and his legionaries, some of them veterans of Cannae fifteen years before, faced the Celtiberian mercenaries. They were polyglot armies hastily assembled, but uniformly determined and courageous. All units fought it out to the end—there was no panic or defection. Scipio again showed that his tactical skill yielded little, if anything, to Hannibal, whose battles he had studied as closely as Hannibal had studied those of Alexander. For the first time in Roman history, its army was victorious because of the cavalry. Massinissa charged Syphax's Massylians irresistibly and under Laelius the Roman horse charged the Carthaginians under Hasdrubal. Scipio ensured that his legionaries fully engaged the Celtiberians, so they were unable to assist the flanks as they were crushed in on each side. The Spanish fought almost to the last man. Syphax retreated into his extensive domain, pursued by Massinissa, and they fought again near Cirte, the eastern capital of the Massylians about two-hundred miles west of Carthage. Massinissa was completely victorious. Syphax was captured and sent to Rome as a prisoner. He died the next year at Tivoli, apparently of natural causes. The modern Tunisian city of Sfax is named after him, and Massinissa married his widow, Hasdrubal Gisgo's daughter Sophonisba, whom Scipio distrusted. Two years later, when Scipio required Sophinisba to appear in his triumphal parade, she asked Massinissa for a lethal potion to avoid the humiliation of such an appearance and Massinissa provided it. Sophinisba attracted universal admiration. Massinissa now ruled everything between Carthage and Mauretania, what is today Algeria, then an immensely rich country, led by an unshakeable Roman ally.

The position of Carthage was now desperate. Rome had taken Sicily, Sardinia, Spain, and Numidia and despite early command incompetence in the Second Punic War, had conceived and executed a masterly strategy: becoming a maritime power and inciting revolt in Spain and Sicily; returning to war with the seizure of Sardinia, and patiently wearing down Hannibal while he was invincible; seizing Spain and then turning Hannibal's position in Italy into the Roman advantage of his being unable to defend Carthage when Rome finally was able to assault it. Now, the Carthaginians feverishly tried to reinforce their city, which had never seen the campfires of a serious invader, and Hannibal was recalled from Italy. The entire Italian campaign of nearly fifteen years, despite its brilliant successes, had failed in the end and was no longer affordable. Scipio captured Tunis, just fifteen miles from Carthage. The Carthaginians tried a lightning attack by their small navy against Scipio's ships near Utica, but Scipio saw the Carthaginians leave port in the distance and hurried to his landing area and formed a barricade of the harbor-of transport ships, to protect his fleet which was immobile because of the heavy siege engines that had not yet been disembarked. It was another illustration of Scipio's alertness that even in this hour of great victory he was vigilant and thorough.

Mago had finally steeled himself to cross the Po and found himself facing seven Roman legions that almost surrounded him and took Genoa in his rear. He was forced to give battle and did so with great valour. His army held its ground; mainly Spanish and African veterans, but they could not withstand the Roman infantry. Once again Carthage's cavalry defeated the Roman flanks and enabled Mago to regain the shore and disembark with his force, after substantial casualties, more or less intact. Mago himself, a brave and imaginative fighter who had been assigned many rude tasks, had sustained a wound in the battle and died on shipboard. Like Hannibal's other brother, Hamilcar Barca, he was a good commander and a very brave man. By this time, Hannibal was confined to the boot of Italy, outnumbered three to one by experienced Roman legions whose commanders were yet fearful of battle with Hannibal other than on favorable terms, which his agility never permitted to occur. After the fall of Spain, he knew there was no chance of shaking Roman control in Italy and was merely providing a bargaining chip in peace negotiations and, he hoped, preventing Rome from sending a large army to Africa against Carthage. But Scipio had managed such an assault, with a small army despite the factional envy and pusillanimity of many of Rome's political leaders, and had exploited the incompetence of the generals entrusted, in the absence of Hannibal and Mago, with the defence of the home country. Throughout these fifteen years, even as he was crowded and the local populations defected and saw that Rome was the winning side, Hannibal never had to deal with direct insurrection by civilians, and his own troops, Spanish and African mercenaries as most of them were, never wavered, even in the smallest number or in the slightest degree, in their loyalty to and confidence in him as commander. He had kept his casualties low, and although there was an effort to pretend that he had been bested in a skirmish near Croton, he was, in fact undefeated, though he was almost always outnumbered, and was after all, an invader whose presence was fundamentally unwelcome. Hannibal sadly answered the order to return, with his diminished army, having established and confirmed himself, by universal agreement, as one of the greatest generals in history, a rank he has retained these twenty-two hundred years.

As Hannibal returned with his army, now reduced by the privations it had suffered, to about fifteen-thousand men, only half Carthaginians, peace negotiations were under way, Carthage accepted and the Roman Senate ratified these terms offered by Scipio: Carthage would remain independent and intact, but would recognize Massinissa as king of all Numidia and would not extend in the east beyond her colonies in Libya (as far as Leptis Magna), but would respect the independence of Cyrenaica and other tribes to the east toward Egypt. She would renounce any interest in Italy (including Sicily and Sardinia), Gaul, and Spain, would reduce her fleet to not more than twenty vessels, and would pay an indemnity of five-thousand talents (approximately nine billion U.S. dollars today). Carthage was rather resigned to this, but Hannibal's return changed public morale and obviously affected the correlation of forces—Syphax and Gisgo were one thing, but the undefeated man of Cannae something else, and when Mago's army, bearing the honoured corpse of Mago arrived in Carthage shortly after, Carthage's pride reasserted itself and the peace party was thrown out. The determining incident was when a Roman supply convoy of two-hundred ships was driven ashore by a storm and the hungry populace appropriated its contents, Scipio demanded restitution, which was rejected, and Rome and Carthage were at war yet again.

Massinissa was absent in western Numidia, bundling up his kingdom and fighting Syphax's son, Vermina, when Scipio's message asking his urgent return arrived. Scipio proceeded along the Bagradas River valley destroying anything of any value to Carthage. Hannibal waited at Hadrumetum, about fifty miles southeast of Carthage, hoping for some Numidian cavalry himself. Massinissa did arrive, with four-thousand cavalry and six-thousand infantry, and a renegade Numidian prince, Tychaeus, joined Hannibal with about two-thousand cavalry. Each army numbered about forty-thousand but for the first time in his career, Hannibal had inferior numbers of cavalry. The two armies met at Zama, forty miles southwest of Carthage, to determine the outcome of these long and horrible wars, on October 19, 202 B.C., Hannibal had to attempt the reverse of Cannae, and win the battle in the centre. He massed his eighty elephants there with his late brother's Ligurian, Mauretanian, Gallic, and Balearic veterans, solid troops, and behind them were the Carthaginian citizen troops and disparate Africans, upon whom Hannibal placed little reliance, and in the rear, like Napoleon's Imperial Guard two-thousand years later, were Hannibal and his long-serving veterans, men who would fight to the death with unlimited bravery against any odds. Hannibal intended to hold them in reserve and commit them when needed, he hoped to make a decisive blow. Scipio deployed his army in stages, with plenty of space to enable the elephants to come through and enabling lines to re-form behind them. He had Laelius on his left and Massinissa on his right, each in charge of roughly half the cavalry, intending them to close on the enemy's flanks as at the Battle of the Great Plains.

The elephants were soon unmanageable and were not an asset to Hannibal and they frightened and distracted his outnumbered cavalry. Scipio's cavalry, having four times as many horse as Hannibal's, easily cleared away the Carthaginian cavalry and were able to close in on the enemy infantry. The Roman legions in the centre gradually forced Mago's old army backwards, but in hard and close fighting. As Hannibal had feared, the rag-tag of draftees behind Mago's old army panicked backwards and tried to flee as it became clear that they would have to engage in direct combat with Roman legions. They fled even when Hannibal's own corps made a point of killing them if they attempted a head-long retreat past them. After about two hours, the centre of the battlefield had the Roman legions from Cannae on one side and Hannibal's veterans also from as far back as Cannae, facing each other, with their commanders behind them. This was the final battle. In a remarkable show of discipline, Scipio had his men stop and form distinct rows; Hannibal had hoped they would charge forward irregularly and that his men could wreak havoc with them. Instead, the Romans advanced steadily and waited for the cavalry to close on both flanks. Hannibal's veterans fought to the end and died in large numbers in a lost cause. Hannibal stayed in personal command until very late on and made his escape miraculously and returned to Hadrumetum, but his army had been almost completely destroyed. The war was over, and Carthage had no bargaining position left. Polybius accurately wrote that he had done all anyone could to salvage a victory. It was Hannibal's only defeat.

It would be hard to make the case that Publius Scipio was as great a general as Hannibal; his strategic imagination may have been as great as Hannibal's, but his tactical gifts were perhaps not quite as unfailingly original. But Scipio was a great general, and the perfect general for the task. He used Rome's superior forces wisely and forced each issue on his own terms and timetable and won at every stage. There is some comparison here too, between them and the match-up of Grant and Lee and of Wellington and Napoleon, including Scipio's and Wellington's successes in Spain. Scipio, known henceforth and deservedly as Scipio Africanus, was a Hellenic scholar, though not a Hellenizer like Alexander, and Rome was a much different and greater culture than Macedonia (which was essentially a down-market adjunct to Greece). But Scipio had a concept of Roman greatness, despite his duplicity and chicanery at times, that was much worldlier than the contemporary Roman political leaders possessed. And unlike the political generals in Rome's future, such as Julius Caesar, Marius, Sulla, and Pompey, he was a legitimist, and was never tempted by what in the modern world has been called Bonapartism.

Just as Napoleon should have stayed in Elba or moved to the United States until Europe settled down, Hannibal should have let the original Carthaginian Peace proceed, and left it to its authors to bear the responsibility for it. Something could have been done by Carthage as a reliable ally of Rome, a little like Hiero's Syracuse only stronger and more prestigious. Hannibal was a great general and a magnetic personality, but not a great statesman, Scipio was a great general if not a military genius like Hannibal, and a considerable statesman. Hannibal lived on and rendered great service to his stricken country, though his subsequent career was an anti-climax. His achievement in launching and maintaining such a stern challenge against a fundamentally much stronger country is a testament to his brilliant qualities. Carthage had been a Phoenician trading people that coerced Spaniards into mining precious metals and furnishing mercenaries for them that were paid with proceeds of what they themselves mined on their own (Spanish) territory.

It was always a vulnerable operation when in competition with Rome, a solid mixed economy with a population that expanded in response to better Roman government and the gradual assimilation of contiguous populations. Carthage was a rickety, commercially based levitation. Its naval mastery was quickly revealed as a scam. All this just elevated Hannibal's astounding achievement in mounting such a prolonged threat to Rome's very existence. That Scipio saw the grand strategy to end the challenge and possessed the tactical skill, militarily and in the slippery ground of Roman politics, to assert Rome's advantage and defeat Hannibal, proves his greatness also. Each achieved prodigies for his country. Rome, as the larger and greater power, was victorious because it had the leadership it needed at each stage: Gaius Duilius and Lucretius Catulus, when great admirals were needed for a new navy; Fabius, when a patient and evasive general and calm leader was needed; Marcellus, when a solid man of war was needed; and Scipio, when the time had finally come to resolve the issue. All came in their methodical turns and Hannibal tested the Rome they built to the last extremity. It was a great achievement to have done so, and a great achievement of Scipio to have prevailed over so formidable and implacable an adversary.

Scipio had won but it was the Roman people, including almost all its federated allies, and even the Roman Senate, that had persevered through the greatest adversity, badly defeated at times, but never demoralized and always of unshakeable collective will. The people of almost all Italy remained in solidarity, astounding even Hannibal by their indefectible loyalty to Rome. "Polybius pauses after Cannae to note, with the natural wonder and admiration of a Greek that Romans were more dangerous in defeat than in victory…It is indeed a spectacle full of grandeur—the triumph of the Roman character in this supreme ordeal, and inevitably the mind turns to contrast with it the tragic picture drawn by Thucydides of the progressive demoralization of the Athenian character in the stress of (Pelopnnesian) war and of the utter failure of the Athenian democracy to direct the war which it had provoked."[8]

12. Peace in the West

Scipio sacked the Carthaginian camp and easily defeated Syphax's son Vermina, when he eventually arrived. Scipio marched to the coast and prepared to invest Carthage. Hannibal used all his influence to persuade his townsmen to accept any peace they could get; there was nothing to be gained from having Scipio raze Carthage to the ground and sell the population into slavery after more definitively disposing of the city elders. His counsels prevailed and the terms that were agreed during a three-month cease-fire, were to pay for all damage to the ship-wrecked convoy whose looting caused the resumption of war with provisions and enhanced pay for the Roman army throughout the cease-fire. The Libyan tribes were to become independent and allied to Rome. Massinissa was to take everything to which he had any historic claim; Carthage handed over all her elephants and all but ten of her warships, and a hundred hostages were to be selected by Rome and sent there and ten-thousand talents were to be paid over fifty years (eight billion modern U.S. dollars). Carthage would become a client state of Rome, would make no wars outside Africa and those in Africa only with Rome's agreement; Carthage would have no security against her African neighbours, not all of which were over-brimming with affection for Carthage.

It was one of history's epic contests, like the Napoleonic and American Civil Wars, which has never ceased to fascinate posterity. Rome was enervated by the great struggle but would obviously recover quickly and was now incomparably the greatest power in the known (Western) world. The quarrelsome Greeks and despotic remnants of Alexander's empire could not imagine that Rome would have no

---

8 CAH, VIII, p. 109 (B. L. Hallward).

eastward ambitions. The Western Mediterranean was now tidily arranged, if war-ravaged. In the east, all the consequences of the endless trivial bellicosity of the Macedonians, Persians, and, for all their commendable culture, the Greeks, had created almost uninterrupted chaos for a century. Alexander had shown how a great empire could be swiftly put together. Rome had shown that a great empire could be built steadily and maintained over generations. In a phrase that would be coined and made famous two-thousand years later, the Greeks and Persians had forgotten nothing and learned nothing. They would soon pay for it; their time was passing.

The Roman Hortensian Law of 287 B.C. had raised the prospect of democracy, but progress was deferred to deal with the emergencies of the Pyrrhic and First Punic wars, when dictators or at least small delegations of senators had to be granted sweeping powers. The redistribution of public land to the dispossessed in 232 and the Lex Claudia barring senators from maritime commerce in 218 were remarkable advances for popular democratic government. The defeats of Flaminius and Terentius Varro sullied the prestige and credibility of popular government, and the progress toward democracy was arrested. Between 233 and 133 B.C., there were two-hundred consulships, and one-hundred and fifty-nine were held by twenty-six noble families, and fully one-hundred by just ten families. Rome became an elected oligarchy based on the great prestige the Roman Senate had earned in the Second Punic War after the populists were replaced by the able combination of Fabius and Marcellus (consuls seven times between 215 and 208). War always favours the executive, especially if the war is successful. The censorship and tribunates had diminished authority. There were more military praetors and alternations of command were largely suspended; Publius Scipio Africanus was effectively supreme commander from 210 to 201. To cope with financial pressures, taxation was doubled and, as has been recorded, the wealthiest citizens were prevailed upon to make generous loans to the state. The basic bronze coin was halved in size to one ounce and silver coinage was also devalued. In production of armaments after Cannae, the Senate traded the cost of weapons and military apparatus for exemptions from conscription and other deferments and future tax-forgivenesses. Here again, Roman government showed remarkable ingenuity. But the Senate became more aristocratic in composition, and more interested in military and diplomatic affairs, and less preoccupied with fiscal administration. Individual, non-recurring arrangements were worked out that invited a certain amount of corruption; war profiteering is a timeless discreditable activity. At the same time, public religion, invoked in spikes of fervour, became more superstitious, irrational, and prone to dubious claims of visions and revelations, and more susceptible to the interventions of charlatans.

Most importantly, Hannibal's raising of an alliance with Macedonia, as well as his purported emancipation of Greek cities in Italy and Sicily, although none of it caused Rome excessive inconvenience, naturally attracted the interest of the Senate in punishing Macedonia for its impertinences. Rome succeeded seamlessly, though with a more sophisticated provincial organization, to Carthage in Spain, assumed its suzerain sponsorship of Massinissa and other African chiefs, effectively took over Liguria, and tightened arrangements with Massilia, the overland route to Spain. Rome effectively ruled everything on the Mediterranean west of the heel of Italy and Carthage, and it had been provoked to punish the country that seventy years before, under Alexander the Great, had ruled everything to the south as far as Egypt and to the east as far as India.

Philip V had opened the door of the Hellenic world to Rome by ineffectively allying himself with Carthage. Now that that door had been opened, Rome, on the heels of its mighty and crushing victory over its long-time rival, could be expected to enter Greek affairs, sword in hand. Tired Greece and the deracinated satrapies of the formerly Great King could not be expected to put up even a trivial opposition compared to the demiurgic challenge Hannibal had mounted. For much of the ancient world, worn down by endless, mindless, purposeless bloodletting, submission to Rome would be a relief. We saw, and certainly the Romans did, that in the Wars of the Diadochi, the Greeks, Macedonians, and Persians had lost practically all capacity for responsible self-government. Rome, growing swiftly into its aptitude to rule, would not find it too much of a challenge to convince itself of the benignity of its mission to relieve these ancient states of the onerous burden of independent self-government.

CHAPTER NINETEEN

ROME TURNS TO THE EAST—THE TEMPTATION OF THE FORMER MACEDONIAN EMPIRE

PHILIP V OF MACEDON, ANTIOCHUS III, PTOLEMY IV
253-215 B.C.

Phillip V's tetradrachm
(struck c. 220-211 B.C.)

Bust tentatively identified as Scipio Africanus

1. Rome, Illyria, and Macedon

THERE HAVE BEEN some references to the Illyrian campaign; in the interregnum between the First and Second Punic Wars, Rome began to pay some official attention to the Greek world, as it had extended its suzerainty over a substantial part of Magna Graecia, in southern and Adriatic Italy and in Sicily. The Roman Senate accorded official recognition to and exchanged diplomatic missions with Athens and Corinth in 228, though the principal Greek city states and Rome had been aware of each other and had had extensive unofficial contacts for two centuries or more. Neither the Greeks nor the Romans were in any hurry to get to know each other better. Rome was an authentically introverted country until it became entangled with Carthage and flourished as a Mediterranean trading power. It was Roman commercial interests and the need to protect them that caused the opening of official relations. The learned classes of Rome had long given considerable study to classical Greek literature, Homer and the other ancient poets, whose epics bore little resemblance, in content or form, to contemporary Greece, diminished as it had been by centuries of squabbling and blood-letting, culminating in the prolonged hecatomb that followed the death of Alexander the Great.

The initial interventions of Rome with Greece over commercial matters were occasioned by piracy in the Adriatic, which the Greeks considered a sinister and dangerous area for maritime activity. The expression "sail the Adriatic" was a Greek description of a dangerous enterprise. The eastern coast of the Adriatic had intricate inlets and caves and currents and required comprehensive exploration to have any idea of how to find the lairs of the pirates who from earliest times feasted on the peaceful Italian commerce on the western side of the Adriatic. The pirates developed the famous lembi, single deck vessels that were lightly constructed and very swift, which the Dalmatian and Illyrian pirates built and maneuvered with great skill. They carried about fifty men apart from the oarsmen and rammed their targets, seized what they wished from the ships they boarded after ramming, and then disengaged and sped away. Dionysius aspired to substantial commerce in the Adriatic and with his customary thoroughness, assaulted the pirates and severely restricted them, and provided naval protection for convoys of his transports, but the pirates knew to lay low when the Syracusans were about and scratched together what they could take from other states' ships. Under Philip and Alexander, Cassander, Agathocles, and Demetrius, and again in the time of Pyrrhus, the Illyrian pirates were bottled up in the central and northern Adriatic and didn't much venture into Macedonian, Epirate, and Greek waters, though they continued to terrorize Italian shipping.

In about 253, the Illyrians, with the help of Egypt, seized Corinth and effectively set themselves up as a brazen pirate state in that historic city. Once settled here, the pirates expanded into the Ionian Sea, and went as far and took as much as they could get away with. The various Illyrian and northern coastal groups were tribal kingdoms and had their own limited civilizations, but by the time they set up in Corinth, the pirates had been largely concentrated under the Taulantini king, Glaucias, and the Ardiaens, who had been pushed south and then into the sea by the Celtic migration. A substantial Illyrian state developed in the latter half of the third century B.C. and while there were individual privateers, Illyria was a veritable pirate kingdom, devoted altogether, and even somewhat self-righteously, to the piracy industry, as if it were a legitimate form of adding value to goods and services by seizing goods on the high seas and selling them on as if Illyria were a rightful and industrious owner of what it fenced to the comparatively civilized states of the Mediterranean. Illyria reached the summit of its buccaneering days between 240 and 229 under King Agron and the regency of his widow, Queen Teuta. They took full advantage of the destruction of the Greek fleets in the pandemonium of the time in Greece. Demetrius II, son of Antigonus Gonatas, was so preoccupied fighting with the Aetolians, Achaeans, and Dardanians, in the desperate Balkan manner, the enemy of his enemies was his friend and Demetrius II forged an informal and rankly opportunistic alliance with Agron.

In 231, Demetrius turned to Agron to save Acarnania, which the Aetolians were besieging and trying to press-gang into their League. This was a perfect demonstration of the pitiful state to which the Greek states had descended after the last ninety years of almost indiscriminate armed conflict since the death of Alexander. Acarnania was saved by the dispatch of one-hundred lembi carrying five-thousand fierce Illyrian warriors, who sharply defeated the Aetolians and put Demetrius well into their debt. Agron celebrated his victory to Bacchanalian excess and died, and his widow Teuta carried on and escalated her husband's growth strategy. It was by her aggressive and avaricious agency that Rome was drawn into the Greek vacuum. The Illyrian regent-queen was not satisfied with ravaging the western Greek states and started to poach on the commerce of Rome. Astonishingly, the Roman Senate was rather slow to respond though the Illyrians were seriously interdicting the extensive Roman commerce out of Brundisium and with the Greek states and trading stations. There were also allegedly some shore parties that seriously disturbed some of the southeastern Italian seaside towns and farming communities. In 230, Teuta defeated the Epirotes, who received the desperately sought assistance of the Aetolians and Achaeans, but then withdrew from that arrangement and effectively paid ransom to Teuta for her toleration of their maritime commerce. Teuta would have been greedier, but she had to bring back her five-thousand marines to deal with rebellious tribes.

Where Teuta went too far and the game changed was when her freebooters took it upon themselves to execute some Italian merchants in Phoenice. (This was like the origin of British foreign secretary Viscount Palmerston's Don Pacifico Affair of A.D. 1850, when he blockaded the Greek coast after the home of a British subject in Athens was burned down in an anti-Semitic riot. Palmerston told the House of Commons that Britain must adopt the rule of Rome, that "Civis Britannicus sum" is a condition to be proud of and defended.) The Roman Senate, which had been uncharacteristically quiescent in the rise of piracy against Roman commerce, demanded reparations and a promise of better behaviour. Teuta haughtily dismissed the Roman emissaries, saying she had no power over privateers. The Roman diplomat, Lucius Coruncanius, replied "Rome will find the means of compelling a reform of Illyrian laws," and she dismissed the delegation with a severe rebuke. Then pirates gave chase to the Roman vessel returning the emissaries, and overhauled and boarded it and killed Coruncanius. This naturally inflamed Roman outrage and while the Senate was considering the appropriate response, Teuta, who really had the bit in her teeth, took advantage of the death of Demetrius II after his defeat by the Dardanians, and laid siege to Corcyra, blandly assuming that the Romans would do nothing in this action-packed Mediterranean summer of 230 B.C. The Corcyreans appealed to the Aetolians and Achaeans but the Achaean fleet of only ten vessels was intercepted by the Illyrians who sank or captured half the ships, causing Corcyra to throw in the towel. Teuta, conducting what she apparently considered to be an unstoppable victory lap around the Ionian Sea, then invested Dyrrhachium. It was at this point that Rome finally intervened. The two consuls, Fulvius Centumalus and Lucius Postumius Albinus, were dispatched with a fleet of two-hundred full-sized warships and transports carrying twenty-thousand Roman legionaries and two-thousand cavalry. Centumalus arrived at Corcyra too late to relieve the blockade, but the city revolted and the commander of the Illyrian garrison, who had had a dispute with the queen, eagerly surrendered the town and his garrison to Rome, and Centumalus sailed on to Apollonia, arriving at the same time as Postumius Albinus with his army. The Apollonians surrendered at the appearance of the Roman armada, and Postumius only disembarked the horses to give them a run. The Roman force accepted the profession of fealty of Apollonia, a replication of that of the Corcyreans, and the military promenade, which had begun as an anticipated amphibious action against a somewhat serious adversary, proceeded to Dyrrhachium. The Illyrian lembi fled, leaving some of their marines behind. The Romans sank a few straggling lembi and received the now customary prostrations of submission and fealty from the town and sailed on to Issa, which Teuta was besieging. The Illyrians fled as the Roman armada appeared on the horizon and the Issaeans jubilantly surrendered. A pandemic of thanksgiving was sweeping the Ionian, that the new great power of Italy would deliver Greeks from the horror of centuries of almost constant warfare. The Romans sailed on north to Pharos and their legions finally did encounter some resistance at Noutria, though they subdued it.

Teuta fled up the Adriatic with her immediate entourage. The consuls considered that they had carried out their mission, and in the autumn of 229, Postumius returned to Rome with most of the ships and men, leaving Fulvius to winter in Illyria with forty ships, by far the largest naval force in the waters. Teuta finally sued for terms in the spring of 228. She conceded everything the Romans had taken, accepted to pay a war indemnity over a period of years (effectively incentivizing lesser piracy in the northern Adriatic as this was her only source of revenue). Teuta promised that she would never send more than two lembi at a time south of Lissus, and those unarmed, securing Hellenic waters and the crossing between Italy and Greece, the purpose of Rome's intervention. It had been an improbable leitmotif to the struggle between Rome and Carthage. Almost a pantomime war, but Rome had planted itself on the edge of the Hellenic world. It is hard not to question the sanity of the Illyrian queen-regent for embarking so cavalierly on the provocation of the world's most powerful state. She had had her moment in history.

Demetrius Pharos (not to be confused with the Macedonian Demetrius) was now Rome's ally and he received back his hereditary capital of Pharos and some nearby islands and was set up in an autonomous state which he ruled in the name of Rome as suzerain power. His task was to monitor Illyrian affairs and keep them away from Roman commerce and interests. Rome itself maintained Corcyra, Apollonia, Dyrrhachium, and Issa; it was easing itself into Greece, having already effectively taken over Magna Graecia. Rome established itself between Illyria and its ostensible Greek allies, the Epirotes and the Acarnanians, and bottling Illyria up in the central and northern Adriatic. Having entered the Greek world, tentatively and by a side entrance, and acquired Greek protectorates, Rome was not explicitly seeking, but was almost certain to receive overtures from the ever-fractious Greek factions in constant abrasive fermentation, as even the Great King, the erstwhile common enemy, had received ultimately from Sparta, which had remained piously aloof from such profane "medism" for centuries of virtuous insularity.

It is not clear at this early date that Rome was also deliberately blocking Macedonia's progress as well as Illyria's. Macedonia had been enfeebled by the latest melee of internecine Greco-Macedonian war-making and was chastened at its inability to defend its Illyrian ally, and to be hemmed in on the west by Rome, as Pyrrhus had done fifty years before. The Romans rounded out their military tour de force with a diplomatic sequel, not only the exchange of embassies with Athens and Corinth, in both of which cities they were cordially received, but with Achaea and Aetolia, principal Greek confederacies which, though they lamented their weakness and need for a military bail-out from Rome, were no less content to have received it. Corinth and even Rome were invited to the Isthmian games. They were still regarded as barbarians by the Greeks, including the Macedonians, whom the ethnically unambiguous Greeks did not accept as altogether civilized either, but at least as a related people. In fraternizing with and being benefactors of the Achaeans and Aetolians and Corinthians, Rome was playing the anti-Macedonian card in Greek affairs, though the initial extent to which this was intentional is not clear.

Antigonus Doson, who inherited the kingship of Macedonia when Demetrius II (Aetolicus) died fighting the Dardanians in 229, as Demetrius' cousin, and regent of the child king Philip V (and strengthened his position by marrying the queen-mother), proved himself a very agile diplomatic expansionist, slightly reminiscent of Philip II (Alexander's father). With all the complicated family inter-connections, Antigonus Doson was related to the Ptolemies as well as the Antigonids. Within eight years, while giving no offense to Rome, Antigonus Doson had built up a formidable naval base in Corinth, had reconstructed the Hellenic League, had reduced the Achaeans to a junior ally, intimidated the Aetolians despite their friendship with Rome, and had crushed Cleomenes of Sparta and thoroughly humiliated legendarily invincible Sparta. (Cleomenes eventually had to flee Sparta to escape the opprobrium of his countrymen and found refuge in Egypt, where he committed suicide to avoid execution after an unsuccessful attempt to incite a revolt. He was a very talented leader, but such a bold adventurer that he could not survive a serious defeat and was so aggressively ambitious, he was bound to have one eventually.) The resurrected Hellenic League placed Macedonia at the head of much of Greece, as the Hellenic League was a league of leagues: the Acarnanian, Achaean, Boeotian, Epirote, and Euboean leagues, and non-Aetolian Phocis, as well as Megara, Magnesia, and most of Locris.

It was as Antigonus reconstituted a powerful Macedonia that the Second Punic War approached. Rome negotiated the Ebro agreement to deal with the renewed threat of the Gauls, and was generally too preoccupied with Carthage and the Gallic and Celtic tribes to pay much attention to Greece or Macedonia. Only an extreme level of distraction could have enabled Demetrius Pharos to metamorphose politically as he did while under the nose of the Romans. He had gone from being an ally of Agron and Teuta to the caretaker of Rome's Adriatic interests, and unnoticed by the Romans, moved on to become an active senior figure in Illyrian affairs after Teuta's brief and disastrous interlude. He became co-leader of the Illyrians with Agron's cousin Scerdilaidas, a partner-enabler and even commander of the gangster pirate-state. Demetrus Pharos was a compulsive gambler of unreliable judgment—

he had the boldness of Cleomenes, but nothing like the integrity or stature, or generally acute appreciation of risk-reward ratios, and, of course, not a great state to lead.

When Antigonus Dosun died in 220, his stepson Philip V became king at age seventeen. There were immediately great pressures on the young king; the Achaeans sought his aid against Aetolians, and Sparta's Peloponnesian rivals sought his alliance against Sparta. In this fraught atmosphere, as Rome subdued the Gauls but noted the war-preparations of Hasdrubal and Hannibal in Spain, Demetrius Pharos, as if drinking from the same cup of self-destructive insouciance as the late Queen Teuta, seized several Roman Adriatic towns by amphibious assault, including the important regional town of Dimale, with Scerdilaidas, who then proceeded inland, rented his savage soldiery out to the Aetolians and threw himself into the pillage of Arcadia. Demetrius was even more incautious, compounding his assault on the Roman interests he had been engaged to protect and sailed a full war fleet of ninety lembi through the agreed line of restriction and prowled around the Aegean, robbing and extorting the Cyclades until chased off by the Rhodians, traditional protectors of the Aegean. He was incorrigibly directed by the mind of a pirate, a usurper and a thief.

On his return, using the superior speed of the lembi to stay just ahead of the Rhodian avengers, Demetrius Pharos stopped at the Macedonian port of Cenchreae in the Peloponnese, and Philip had evacuated his fleet by winch and rail across the isthmus, eluding the Rhodians, and Demetrius Pharos assisted Philip in harassing the Aetolians returning from Arcadia. Philip was not only at war with the Aetolians, but the Cleomenists regained office in Sparta and prepared for the resumption of war against Macedon. Philip could be of no assistance to his Pharian colleague, who had managed, despite the example immediately before him and from which he had benefited, of the unhappy Teuta, to antagonize Rome with no possible helper in absorbing whatever punishment Rome chose to mete out to him. It had substantially repulsed the Gauls, and while tensions with Carthage were rising and Rome occupied Saguntum in Spain, a technical casus belli, Carthage would not require the commitment of the Roman navy, which would not, in any case, need long to put the insolent Pharian pirate and ingrate in his place. In 219, both consuls, Aemilius Paullus and Livius Salinator, almost exactly ten years after Fulvius Contumalus and Postumius Albinus had performed a similar task, set out with similarly strong naval and ground forces to deal with Demetrius. The Illyrian chief hid his lembi in the caves and up the rivers of the Adriatic and concentrated his forces behind walls, such as had inflicted some inconvenience on the Romans at Noutria almost ten years before. He defended his fortified capital of Pharos, which Rome had given back to him, with six-thousand of his best men. The Romans aimed to swat this fly before the main event began with Carthage. It was another exquisitely planned and executed Roman operation.

The Romans disembarked their two legions at Apollonia and Dyrrhachium, which had remained loyal to Rome, and advanced in quick march on Dimale. Aemilius commanded land operation and stormed the town and seized it after a week. This was, as was the Roman calculation, sufficient to resolve any ambiguities in the minds of the neighbouring tribes and towns: all professed welcome and fealty to

Rome, an even more fiercely competitive race to surrender to Rome occurred than had happened ten years before. The consuls then advanced upon Pharos, which was ready to face a prolonged siege, but that was not what Aemilius had in mind. He disembarked most of his army silently in dead of night in a heavily wooded and remote part of the island, where they remained hidden, and a few hours later appeared at the island's harbour with just twenty of his ships and started disembarking a virtual skeleton force. This, as was intended, drew Demetrius out and he was supervising a vigorous attempt at repulse of the Roman force when the main invading army materialized behind him. It was a perfect trap, and the Illyrian garrison was slaughtered; it broke and those few who could, fled. They were led in this activity by their leader; Demetrius had kept two fast lembi suitably provisioned and with some bullion for general purposes, in case of need of a swift departure, and he got away in an even closer call than he had had the year before from the ships of Rhodes. The inveterate scoundrel was finished as any kind of a ruler but was welcomed by Philip V and exercised a malign Mephistophelean influence on the young king for four more years, until he was killed attempting to take Messene in 214. He was an outrageous character even by the most slipshod standards of the ancient world, but he had the charm and panache of the bold and consistent brigand and mountebank, unashamed of what he was and rarely pretending to be otherwise.

2. War Between Rome and Macedonia

(This section is another thicket of Balken treachery and complexity, and readers who simply can't endure it, or don't chose to, can just read the last few paragraphs of this section.)

Philip V had got off to a pretty good start and moved with great swiftness and agility against the Aetolians. If the Romans had retained even a small naval squadron in the Adriatic to assist Macedonia's and Illyria's enemies, it would have reduced Philip's amphibious mobility, as Roman naval dominance of the Western Mediterranean required Carthage to do everything overland from Spain, past the large trap of Massilian obstruction. But the Carthaginian danger, especially after Rome got a good look at Hannibal, consumed its attention. Philip's great objective, in which he was warmly and deviously encouraged by Demetrius while he lasted, festering and whispering in Philip's ear, was to evict Rome from Illyria. To this end, Philip conducted a lengthy courtship with Hannibal and his government. Philip was at the Nemean games in July 217, when a courier apprised him of the Roman disaster at Lake Trasimene, and he negotiated the Peace of Naupactus with the Aetolians, who were relieved to be able to end the war honourably. The Egyptians, to whose languid tropical affairs we shall return at the end of this chapter, mediated the peace, but it was effectively dictated, as is usually the case, by the military facts, which were heavily in Philip's favor. Demetrius was an enthusiastic champion of war against Rome and Philip prepared determinedly to launch it.

Distracted though it was, Rome managed to sponsor a quarrel among thieves and induced Scerdilaidas to break ranks with Demetrius and attack Macedonia by land with no notice or the slightest pretext. He compounded the element of surprise by marching through Roman territory (presumably with permission). It was an unwise move for Rome, as Philip, with the Aetolians at peace, had no difficulty cuffing Scerdilaidas and his land-bound pirates about, and annexed a substantial share of Illyria to Macedon. There seems little doubt that Hannibal's early victories, and especially the overwhelming rout at Cannae, whetted Philip's imagination with dreams of a trans-Adriatic assault, in which he could claim some credit for a decisive Carthaginian victory and join in a defeat of Rome so complete that he would have the entire eastern shore of the Adriatic tucked permanently into Macedonia. Despite these exultant ambitions, his initial foray against Apollonia in a hundred lembi was cancelled and the whole operation abandoned in unseemly haste at the report of the approach of the Roman navy. In fact, only ten quinquiremes arrived (on Scerdilaidas' warning), though they would have destroyed any number of lembi they could reach. Thus ended the Macedonian campaign of 216, and the Second Punic War would never be as favorable for Rome's enemies again. In 215, Philip sent Xenophanes, an Athenian, to Hannibal to propose alliance. Matters had settled down in Italy and it was clear that Rome was not quitting the war anytime soon, so instead of flying to the aid of victory (as Mussolini did, in Charles de Gaulle's words, in going to war to support Germany against France and Britain in 1940[1]), Philip's assistance could be very influential, and as has been recorded in Chapter 17, Hannibal set great store by it.

The terms of the treaty were negotiated by Hannibal as if he were the head of the Carthaginian government—he was, in fact, a military plenipotentiary, with a blank cheque from the state he served (unlike the Duke of Wellington in 1815 or General Douglas MacArthur in 1951). There was no role for Philip in Italy, but he was to have all he wanted in Illyria and Dalmatia; it was an inoffensive alliance while the Second Punic War was in progress, and a defensive alliance thereafter. Philip didn't think he was taking much of a gamble, but if Roman indifference to Greece condemned it to misjudge Greek affairs for a time, Greco-Macedonian underestimation of Rome was just as great and would prove far more costly. Even more oblivious to the war in Italy and its protagonists was the Achaean leader, Aratus; he "was egotism itself."[2] He considered that he owed no more to Philip for having saved Achaea from the Aetolians than Demetrius Pharos felt he owed Rome for having reinstalled him on Pharos (which he was even now planning to repossess). At least Demetrius had the excuse of being a pirate and swindler as his avowed vocation; Aratus pretended to be a king.

The first disagreement Aratus and Philip had was in Messene, where Philip, although he had been consulted as an arbiter, had helped provoke a democratic revolt against the local oligarchs (these struggles between the people and the oligarchs were the systole and diastole of Greek history for centuries). He condoned the massacre of the Messenian magistrates and about two-hundred patrician leaders (optimates). Aratus rushed in person to Messene and had a furious argument with Philip, claiming Messene for Achaea. Demetrius, as was his custom, counseled Philip to hold fast and famously said that with Messene and Acrocorinth, Philip would "hold

---

1 Charles de Gaulle, *Compete War Memoirs*, Simon and Schuster, New York, 1959, p. 865.
2 CAH, VIII, p. 120. (Maurice Holleaux).

the bull (the Peloponnese) by both horns."[3] Polybius and others claim that from this point on, Philip became a nasty and ruthless despot under the saturnine influence of Demetrius Pharos, having been an amiable and accomplished monarch up to now.

Philip and Hannibal had hoped to keep their treaty a secret, but Xenophanes and his delegation were captured by the Romans on their way back from Italy and the always reliable warhorse Marcus Valerius Laevinus, at this point the naval commander at Tarentum, was ordered by the Senate to patrol in the southern and central Adriatic with fifty warships carrying troops. He was empowered to cross to Illyria and smash up Philip's lembi and anything else, if he chose. The revised version of the treaty between Hannibal and Philip is assumed to have included a clause of Macedonian ground forces being injected into Italy as reinforcements for Hannibal, who by 214, was running out of troops, as Rome soldiered on, gaining strength slowly and frustrating Hannibal's efforts to gain a timely victory. The consideration for such a Macedonian expeditionary force was provision by Carthage of a heavy naval escort, as Laevinus would dispatch Philip's lembi to the depths in double-quick time.

In the circumstances, and with Rome carrying the war to Spain under the original Scipios (Scipio Africanus' father and uncle), Carthage was in no position to send even a dispatch boat to the Adriatic, so the perfervidly negotiated alliance was inchoate. In 214, Philip struck quickly with one-hundred and twenty lembi carrying troops to seize Apollonia, but Laevinus (who for twenty-five years in various senior roles was always rushing to the rescue like a U.S. Civil War cavalry general) arrived while the issue at Apollonia was in doubt, disembarked forces that turned the tide and forced Philip into a humiliating overland retreat to Macedonia after burning all his lembi. Laevinus retained control of the Illyrian ports and Philip was unable to dislodge him. Philip was out of his depth trying to play in the same league as Hannibal and Quintus Fabius, and as time would demonstrate, his antagonization of Rome would be almost as conspicuous a strategic blunder as Carthage's challenge to Rome, and a much less militarily distinguished one. It remains a mystery what Hannibal thought he was getting with Philip as an ally, since there was no chance the Carthaginian navy was going to be in any position to convoy Macedonian troops across the Adriatic.

Philip's conduct became steadily more bizarre; he again assaulted Messene, which had been a friendly state, again without success, and this time he lost Demetrius Pharos as a casualty of battle in the process. That might have been expected at least to raise the moral quality of the king's judgment, but instead, he completed the embitterment of Aratus, king of Achaea, by seducing his daughter-in-law, Polycrateia of Argos. Aratus died, apparently of heart failure caused by rage against Philip's peccadillo, and Polycrateia decamped to Philip and was probably the mother of his son Perseus. He did better in 213 when he returned to Illyria and took back Dimale and other towns, but not Apollonia and Dyrrhachium. He battered the ineffable Scerdilaidas about and seized Lissus, reemerging on the Adriatic shore again, in late 213. In 212 there were naval stirrings in Carthage, but it was directed entirely toward the unsuccessful effort to save Syracuse from the Romans. Laevinus, getting

---

3 Ibid., p. 121.

ahead of events, determined to play the logical card against Philip and capitalize on the longstanding Greek animosity to Macedonia. It was hard, both in practical and objective terms, to object to Alexander the Great, and few Greeks audibly did. Demosthenes could not abide Alexander's father, Philip II; it is a challenge to imagine in what frightful strictures he would have phrased his Demosthenean Philippics against the current Macedonian king. Laevinus, on Rome's behalf, negotiated an offensive alliance with the Aetolian leaders and contributed a Roman squadron to conduct direct war on Philip. With Aratus dead and his son mad, and Messene allied to Aetolia, the Aetolian leaders, Dorimachus and Scopus, raised an alliance uniting all of the non-Achaean Peloponnese.

There were positive developments in Asia Minor, a theatre that will be revisited and updated as soon as the Illyrian developments contemporaneous with the Second Punic War are completed. In a word, the Seleucid king, Antiochus, crushed a rebellion and the rebel leader, Achaeus, was betrayed and seized in the Acropolis at Sardes and Antiochus had him publicly scourged, mutilated, beheaded, and then crucified in an ass's skin. This thorough debriefing of dissentient sentiment enabled Antiochus and his ally Attalus of Pergamum, to pursue normal ambitions: Antiochus invaded Armenia, but Attalus wished to assist his Greek allies against Philip V.

The versatile Laevinus tried his hand at military diplomacy in late 212, commanding the first Roman fleet to drop anchor in a Greek port, when he visited Aetolia and gave his hosts a stirring speech on solidarity and the need to discourage aggression. He negotiated for Rome's account an alliance with Aetolia, which Elis, Messene, Sparta, and Pergamum (which had a considerable navy) as well as Scerdilaidus were all invited to join; the object was to make war victoriously on Macedonia. Rome would receive the plunder from any conquests, but Aetolia would annex conquered land, where it would sack to "ground, roof, and walls" to Rome's benefit. It was a very well-crafted alliance, as it gave Aetolia a free hand as far north as Corcyra, invited the allies to demarcate their own winnings, enabled Rome to withdraw part of Laevinus' squadron to home waters, and in taking the fruit of plunder, made it a profitable war for Rome that defrayed some of the immense expense incurred in the war with Carthage. There was reticence in the Senate about adopting an eastern policy and being distracted with Hannibal still prowling around the Italian countryside, and the treaty wasn't ratified for two years. But as it took effect immediately, that was unimportant.

In fact, because of the nature of the Rome-Aetolia agreement, Rome was not really at war with Macedonia in practice, as Aetolia attacked first Acarnania, a proximate adversary that Aetolia could subdue, and looted for the benefit of Rome. This was the first effective Roman contact with Greece-Aetolia pillaging certain Greek states against which Rome had no grievance at all, but for Rome's material benefit as recipients of the fruit of Aetolian rapine. Philip admirably attempted to defend his allies, even though Aetolia was not actually making war on Macedonia but on its allies. It was a war of shadow-boxing, Laevinus seized Zacynthus (except for the Acropolis) from Philip and a couple of centres from Acarnania and handed them over to Aetolia. The Acarnanians packed off their women and children and elderly to safety in Epirus and vowed to defend their country to the last man against Aetolia, but with Philip in Aetolia, that proved not to be necessary. The years 211 and 210 passed with little naval activity except the odd coastal raid from the Romans, and a bit of feinting and skirmishing. In 210, Philip did get something going on land and captured Echinus. Aetolia wasn't accomplishing much, but the allies had rallied, including Sparta, now governed by Machanidas as guardian for Lycurgus' minor son Pelops. But Sparta was interested in defeating Achaea, which was a militarily incompetent state; Sparta was not much concerned with Macedonia. Pergamon also prepared to join the fray, buying the naval base Aegina, from the Romans. There was now the prospect of the Pergamenes from Asia Minor, as well as the Romans from the west milling about in the traditional intra-Hellenic non-stop war-making of the Greeks. The Romans not only sponsored Aetolia's rapacity on their behalf; from time to time they intervened, mainly to encourage Aetolia to do the necessary to prevent Philip from attacking Rome itself. Greeks were startled by Rome's severity; they had not been acquainted for some generations with the Roman practice of selling civil populations into slavery.

Rhodes, Chios, and even Egypt attempted to promote peace between Aetolia and Macedonia; war disturbed the commerce of Rhodes and Chios, and Egypt, under Philopator, concerned by the assertiveness of Antiochus, was seeking a Macedonian alliance against him. This scruffy contest, recklessly undertaken by Philip at the behest of Hannibal, was threatening to become a vast conflagration involving almost all the governments of the known world. In the spring of 210, Philip received an appeal from the hard-pressed Achaeans, who were being attacked by Machanidas of Sparta in the south and Aetolia in the north. The Aetolians, with some Roman and Pergamene reinforcements, were driven back into Lamia by Philip, and the Aetolians, discouraged by their indifferent performance in this widening and unsatisfactory war, contemplated peace and discussions began at Aegium.

An armistice was agreed, but on hearing of this, the Roman naval commander, Sulpicius Galba (who had replaced Marcus Valerius Laevinus, who had gone to Sicily replacing Marcellus who was now consul) arrived at Naupactus with his fleet while Attalus of Pergamum landed nearby with thirty-five ships. These suddenly tangible and active allies emboldened the Aetolians, who, with a Roman prod at their back, offered impossible conditions to Philip and the war was on again. Another disappointment for Philip was that a Punic squadron heaved to off Corcyra, but would not stay or go any farther, and returned to home waters (fearing, assumedly, interception by the Romans). Nor had the small number of ships promised by the Bithynians materialized. Philip at least enjoyed political success in Achaea and in Argos; he mingled well with the public and was much admired, though that sort of popular favour roused the envy and hostility of the upper classes, which were always fearful of political manipulation for bad purposes at their expense, and always susceptible to fits of complete xenophobia.

Sulpicius wintered 209-208 at Aegina to discuss strategy with Attalus. The Pergamene king was planning on taking over islands in the Aegean and in eastern Greece, so the naval war, where he and the Roman admiral had the waters to themselves, shifted their activities from the Ionian to the Aegean, and in the summer of 208 they sailed a joint fleet of sixty ships along the eastern Greek shore, landing shore parties here and there. Again, Philip distinguished himself by the assistance he gave his Greek allies, stationing himself and part of his army at Demetrias in Magnesia, and using an elaborate system of beacons on hill-tops to advise of the movement of the enemy fleet and moving swiftly to repulse them at any landing point. His vigilance and aggressive response was generally successful and much appreciated, especially by the most vulnerable allies, Boeotia, Euboea, and Phocis. Attalus was busy looting Opus, in Locris, when Philip unexpectedly arrived after a forced march and chased Attalus to his ships, which departed in confusion and ignominy. This was Attalus' farewell to Greece, as Pergamum, doubtless at Philips' behest, had been invaded by Prusias, king of Bithynia. Philip was just settling into giving a serious fright to the Aetolians, when the Achaeans beseeched his assistance against Machanidas and the Spartans. He came promptly and the Spartans withdrew at his approach. On his return, he was again distracted by a Dardanian sally against northern Macedonia. With this, winter descended and 207 came, and Sulpicius seized and sacked Dyme on the northwest coast of Achaea, and deported the inhabitants, but then withdrew and watched the Illyrian coast. Rome had achieved what it had wanted and had got through more than a decade of the Second Punic War without any serious threat from Macedonia.

What started as a Roman-Macedonian war and became a Roman-Hellenic war, metamorphosed into a Macedonian-Hellenic war, but it was suddenly transformed by the instant evolution of Achaea from the weakling of the principal Greek states into a formidable warrior nation and Macedonian ally by its leader, Philipoemen. He had served under Antigonus and as a condottiere in Crete and was installed as hipparch and then general in his native Achaea and set about readying his army to see to the defence of the country without endlessly imploring the assistance of the Macedonian king. He meticulously trained, rearmed, and inspired his army and drilled it in precise and sophisticated field maneuvres, and he astounded Machanidas by intercepting him as he was marching to take Mantinea. Both armies were of about fifteen-thousand men, the Achaeans perhaps a little more numerous. Philopoemen had chosen his ground carefully and hurled his phalanx on the astounded Spartans, who had not been accustomed to serious backtalk from the Achaeans, as the Spartans were drawn into a wide ditch that separated them from their opponents. The battle was not easily broken off as the Achaeans persisted and eventually Philopoemen himself killed the Spartan commander Machanidas in single combat like Marcellus over Viridomarus at Clusidium in 222 B.C. (Chapter 18), and the Achaeans swarmed the retreating Spartans and killed or captured almost ten-thousand of them. It was a stupendous rout and Philopoemen followed up by ransacking Laconia without a peep from mighty Sparta. It was like a parable of the uprising of the meek against the overbearing.

The self-emancipation of Achaea freed Philip to focus on Aetolia and he again demonstrated how much better a general he was than an architect of foreign policy. He traded the island of Zacynthus to the king of Athamania to grant him secret free passage through his territory so he could strike the Aetolians with great force. They were awaiting Philip and his army well to the east of where he erupted into their country. The neutrals returned in force, their ranks swollen by Byzantium and Mitylene. Thrasycrates of Rhodes played the old Greek race card, that had been echoing against the Great King and then Philip II of Macedon and now the Roman "barbarians" who were the real enemy, not the ultra-civilized, compulsively blood-letting Greeks, who must compose their differences whenever an outsider engages them in the activity they constantly engaged in amongst themselves for five-hundred years. Aetolia, inexplicably, had faith in their Roman ally, but Rome was now into the end game against Carthage and didn't really care what happened in Greece, or would deal with it when the principal crisis was resolved. Aetolia was forced by Philip to make a very one-sided and expensive peace, thoroughly disillusioned by their desertion by Rome.

Rome, for its part, never forgave Aetolia for making a separate peace, though Rome was the cause of it. Rome had its own integrity. It was not one of many states jumbled together in a peninsula at the water's edge of a continent as Greece was; an array of towns and cities separated by hills and mountains, stubborn, impractical, and essentially convinced that the manly conduct of war was a state of nature and a good thing in itself, though accompanied by other legitimate goals and activities, cultural, commercial, agricultural, and hedonistic. Rome had interests, recognized no peers, considered war a necessary means to gain security, to expand the state by the assimilation of other peoples into the Roman federation and government.

Rome was never a member of any league and rarely of a multilateral alliance. It was a phenomenon—a town, then a city, with a countryside that grew steadily, organically, ingesting peoples and transforming them into Romans. Rome valued courage and cunning, but everything was a means to the end of the expanding greatness of Rome. It was about to assert its absolute mastery over the Western Mediterranean including, most of North Africa west of Egypt, almost all of Italy, much of Spain and most of southern Gaul. As far as Rome was concerned, it was still at war with Macedonia, and would deal with Macedonia in the sequence that was convenient to it. It would not be drawn into the squalid mayhem of the puling and squalling little Greek states and did not consider the disparagement of Rome by them as barbarians to be entirely unflattering or, by Rome's reckoning of the aggregation of factors that made up the strength of a country, even relevant.

Rome was Rome, and all other states and peoples were inferior, if not racially, by virtue of their diminutive size, indifferent ambition, or political or strategic incompetence. Rome respected Hellenic culture, but culture was no substitute for wealth, power, and authority. It was not as crude as Nazi leader Hermann Goering's famous comment: "When I hear someone speak about culture, I reach for my revolver." Rome was not remotely a Nazi-like state, nor anti-intellectual, but fine verses and lyrical music were no substitute for a pacifying authority. But nor was it a particularly imperialistic state. It grew in Italy out of self-protection, and it found that Italians were relatively easily assimilable when integrated into the government of what became the Roman Federation before it simply became Rome. It gained Sicily after a long war which started because it did not want all Sicily occupied and governed by Carthage. It took Sardinia as an afterthought, as Disraeli scooped up Cyprus at the Congress of Berlin in 1878. It took Spain to deprive Carthage of its source of money, and enjoyed the appropriation of that wealth, and it gained allied protectorates in southern Gaul and North Africa to protect its communications with Spain, deny these areas to Carthage, and as a source of good soldiery to supplement its own legions and mariners. There was no plan to be "a universal emperor" like Napoleon, or dominate the world by fiat, as Germany at one point aspired to do, or by an ideological regime of universal application, as Soviet Russia espoused. Rome grew in digestible increments-each stage protected the preceding ones, in pursuit of natural and manageable frontiers. These were finally arrived at and were held, effectively, for nearly five-hundred years, and in the east for another thousand years. Rome didn't set out to achieve this; it just happened in phases that seemed logical at each stage and were successful and durable.

As Aetolia left the war, and as the second Punic War was finally proceeding very satisfactorily, the Roman Senate in 205 sent the latest Adriatic naval commander, P. Sempronius Tuditanus, with thirty-five quinqueremes and ten-thousand infantry and a thousand cavalry to Illyria and he tried to rouse Aetolia to reenter the war. The Aetolians had learned their lesson and saw that Rome was prepared to fight Macedon to the last Aetolian and declined to be remobilized. Sempronius exercised the other side of his mandate and entered into peace negotiations directly with Philip V. They met at Phoenice and easily reached agreement. Rome recovered the little it had lost, Macedonia took what it wanted from everyone else, and the peace was deemed to bind the allies of both sides, though the only allies Rome had left were Attalus and Pleuratus, the sidekick of the finally (and none too soon) deceased Scerdilaidas. The Senate and the people, all tribes in a public vote, ratified the peace in 204 and Sempronius was elevated to the consulate.

3. Egypt, Greece, and Syria, From the Wars of the Diadochi to the End of the Second Punic War

(Readers who can't bear any more of the dynastic complexity and treachery of the Near East may safely ignore the balance of this Chapter and just read the last paragraphs of each section. The Greek and Middle Eastern states continued to degenerate, conveniently, as Rome contemplated the East.)

Returning briefly to the end of the sanguinary forty years of war between Alexander the Great's principal collaborators, what had been his empire shed some satrapies at the edges and for the rest was still divided between four important powers; the Seleucid empire from the eastern edge of what is now Turkey (Anatolia) east through what is now Iran; Ptolemaic Egypt, which also controlled what are now Syria, Jordan, Lebanon, Israel, and Palestine; the Antigonist regime in what is now Asian Turkey and including some of Syria; and Macedonia, which more or less controlled most of Greece and parts of what are now Albania, Bulgaria, and parts of the former Yugoslavia. The Greco-Macedonian component was obviously apt to split apart at any time; nothing but the imposition of forces was keeping the Seleucid empire together, as had been the case with the Persian kings. Egypt possessed some integrality, as well as being relatively difficult to invade (because of the Red Sea), but it was an occupying power in the Levant. At the beginning of the period, the Egypt of Ptolemy sought an Aegean Empire—the islands, and the coasts of Asia Minor and southern Greece itself. Macedonia was naturally a threat to that. Egypt masqueraded as the champion of Greek autonomy against the Macedonians, and prowled around the Aegean with their large navy, intimidating the relatively landbound Macedonians and encouraged Greek uprisings against Macedon. Their naval strength was such that they could generally have their way in the Aegean islands.

Seleucus I and Ptolemy I had always got on well, and as was described in Chapter 14, Ptolemy had given Seleucus asylum, and they had generally been allied throughout the prolonged convulsions of succession and emerged cordially from them. Egypt was not disturbed for sixty years in its possession of Tyre, the terminal point of the great commercial routes from India and the East and from Byzantium Egypt, Africa and Arabia. The coalition treaty against Antigonus in 303 had assigned all Syria to Ptolemy, but conditional on his helping in the fight of the coalition against Antigonus. Ptolemy made no such contribution, so Seleucus assumed Syria at the end of that war. So long as Seleucus I and Ptolemy I were there, the natural abrasions between their kingdoms were settled peacefully, After the death of Seleucus I, Ptolemy II became somewhat aggressive toward his successor, Antiochus I, giving some Seleucid land to Miletus, and recognizing Keraunus and not Antiochus as king of part of Macedonia. In 276, Ptolemy invaded Syria and took Damascus. The complicated conflict was starting up again, after the briefest respite. Antiochus evicted Ptolemy from Damascus after a few months. One of Antiochus' principal sources of soldiers at this time was Gallic mercenaries.

Antiochus saw them off also, employing a new shipment of elephants from Bactria to do so. Antiochus had more problems with Ptolemy's sister, Arsinoe (2), widow of both Lysimachus and Keraunus. This led to a state of sinister confusion that could have instructed the Byzantines: Ptolemy dismissed his wife, Arsinoe (1), for conspiring against him, and married the other Arsinoe (2) and adopted her son by Lysimachus, Ptolemaeus, and she adopted his eldest son by the other Arsinoe (1), who became Ptolemy III. In adopting the son of Lysimachus (Ptolemaeus), Ptolemy was picking up the legitimist claims of Lysimachus' son to Ionia. Ptolemy's marriage to his sister was scandalous even in these times of frequently exotic and preposterous marital arrangements, but Arsinoe 2 was a fierce and authoritarian woman, had her likeness placed on the coinage with that of her brother/husband, and the royal pair claimed to be the terrestrial replication of the alleged marriage of Zeus and Hera.

There was a good deal of ineffectual skirmishing in Cyrenaica, where Ptolemy's half-brother, Magas, had married the daughter of Antiochus and threw in with his father-in-law over his father. Ptolemy held Magas at bay, and did gather in some Ionian islands and part of Syria was regained, though not Damascus. Egypt flourished and the exotic duo on Pharaoh's throne were popular and much celebrated, a dual monarchy as Ferdinand and Isabella in Fifteenth Century Spain, and William and Mary in Seventeenth Century Britain would be (though they were not siblings and the circumstances and beliefs and conduct of the arch-Catholic Spanish monarchs and the arch-Protestant Anglo-Dutch dual Monarchs were radically different to the lascivious and incestuous Egyptians, yet William and Mary cheerfully overthrew and evicted Mary's father, King James II).

Pyrrhus died in 272, strengthening the hand of Antigonus, who had been facing a wavering alliance of Macedon and Egypt. Joint monarch Arsinoe, as the former queen of Macedonia, wanted that throne for Ptolemaeus, and the Egyptian royals and Antigonus conducted an intense contest through their sponsored factions in Greek politics. Egypt supported the Greek nationalists who continued the Demosthenean traditions in opposing Macedonia. Antigonus, unlike Ptolemy and Arsinoe, had no dynastic designs on Macedonia, and supported the pro-Macedonian faction in Egypt. Greece, which was relatively uniform in its political views now that it was again overshadowed by Macedonia, and Seleucid Asia, and Egypt, which were all meddling in her affairs. Rome and Carthage had to be on good terms with either Macedonia or Egypt, as their navies controlled the access to Greece's grain (wheat) supply, whether from Africa or the Black Sea. Egypt sent a high-level mission to Athens in 271, and met with the city elders, including the philosopher Zeno, and in 267, their constant intriguing secured the victory of the nationalist anti-Macedonians in Athens, led by Glaucon and Chremonides. Egypt had already secured the alliance of Sparta and its allies, Elis, and Achaea.

Later in 267, Chremonides successfully moved a declaration of war against the Seleucid Empire, invoking past alliance between Athens and Sparta and claiming again to lead the liberation of Hellas against a tyrant from outside, as against Xerxes in olden time. This argument was naturally very eloquently presented, and carried the vote, but it ignored the fact that far from emancipating Hellas, they were going to subordinate it to Egypt. The modern Pharaoh may have been preferable to the Great King, but Ptolemy and Antigonus and the Seleucids were all essentially Macedonians, and not presentable as personifications of liberated Greece.

The Athenian-Spartan alliance came back to life in what was known as the Chremonidean War, but Argos and Elis were allies of Antigonus and Boeotia and Aetolia were neutrals friendly to Antigonus. Antigonus invaded Attica in 266, and Egypt confined itself to posting its fleet, commanded by the Macedonian Patroclus, off Cape Sunium, but didn't really do anything. Areus, the Spartan king, led the Greeks and he and Antigonus were approaching each other near the isthmus when Antigonus' Gallic mercenaries mutinied and turned on their commander-paymaster. Antigonus won a signal victory over his own mercenaries but did not engage Areus and retired. Both returned in 265, and Antigonus completely defeated Areus and killed him in action, in a day-long and closely fought battle near Corinth; Antigonus' son Halcyoneus, also fell in the battle.

Ptolemy was not an astute military strategist, unlike his last wife and sister. He allowed Antigonus to dispatch his enemies sequentially, while his navy sailed about as if in a naval review, unchallenged but not intervening. Antigonus delegated the command against Alexander of Epirus, who was eventually defeated after he had overrun Pyrrhus' former possessions in Illyria, and Antigonus supervised the defeat and siege of Athens in 263-262. Athens resisted gallantly, as always, but was reduced to starvation and surrender, and ceased to be an important and autonomous political capital. It had declared war, been let down by its ally who had induced the war, and it was ground underfoot by its enemy. The venerable poet Philemon, who remembered Demosthenes, revealed, just before he died, near the end of the siege of Athens, that the Muse appeared and said she declined to witness the fall of Athens. Centuries of gallant war and often advanced politics had come to this sad end.

What is known as the War of Eumenes quickly followed the Chremonidean War and is named after Eumenes I, ruler of Pergamon. He shook off the suzerainty of the Seleucids to set up Pergamon as an independent state in what is now northern Syria. The importance of this obscure conflict is that Egypt as a maritime power needed pitch to provide the caulking between boards in its ships and Pergamon became a supplier, as Syria and the Troad near the Bosporus, were the only two sources, and Seleucus or Antioch could effectively determine the price and availability of pitch. This followed the wars in Spain between Rome, Carthage, and the Celtiberians, as the second instance of the ancient world going to war over strategic resources, though there were other wars where timber (also for ships) and precious metals were involved, as well as strategic harbours and trade routes. Most wars we have seen up to now in this narrative have been simple matters of conquest for the avails of conquest, or manly struggle for the retention of Hellenic virtue. But as states became more politically sophisticated, strategic resources started to figure more prominently in the ambitions of governments. Eumenes defeated Antiochus near Sardes in 262, and at about the same time the Persian king Ariarathes had established an independent regime in Seleucid Cappadocia, while Egypt had wrested

Miletus and Ephesus, in Caria on the Aegean coast of Anatolia (Asia Minor), from the Seleucids. Antiochus I died in 261, after a reign of twenty years. He was a distinguished Hellenizing ruler, who generally kept the polyglot realm of his father Seleucus together despite endless disturbances and rebellions. He was a great builder of cities and generally less treacherous than the Ptolemies and the majority of the Antigonids. He was succeeded by his younger son (having dismissed the elder son as co-regent, and probably executed him), as Antiochus II.

The Second Syrian War, whose exact beginnings are unknown, was the result of the large scores both Antiochus and Antigonus had to settle with Ptolemy. Antigonus realized that he had to have a navy to protect his Aegean shore and carry the war back to Egypt, which possessed an immense fleet-approximately three-hundred ships, many of them even larger than quinqueremes. This was a larger navy than Antigonus could possibly build, but he had his naval base at Corinth and emulated Corinthian naval architecture, which was also followed by Syracuse, and ultimately Rome. The emphasis was on size and hull-strength, not speed, and the ships carried marines and grappling equipment and would close on and grapple-in adversaries and then board them and kill the crews and capture or burn the enemy vessels.

In contrast, Egypt, like Athens and Phoenicia, had lighter and faster ships which fought the enemy with hails of arrows and by ramming the opposing ships side-on at speed. Egyptian oarsmen could not resist Macedonian marines once they were aboard, and in this way, an Antigonid or Macedonian ship could deal with more than its number of Athenian or Egyptian adversaries. It was a little like Twentieth Century capital ship construction, in which the British and Japanese emphasized speed and were generally less heavily armoured than American or German Battleships, which was demonstrated in the vulnerability of swift but thinly armoured British battlecruisers at Jutland in 1916 and in the famous exchange in which the German *Bismarck* quickly blew up and sank the British battlecruiser *Hood* in 1941; and the success of the American battleships *South Dakota* and *Washington* and other units against the Japanese battlecruisers *Kirishima* and *Hieii* in the Solomon Islands in 1942.

The Asian part of the Second Syrian War apparently began when Ptolemaeus, in the family tradition, revolted against his adoptive brother Ptolemy, who had been knocked about by Antigonus, and staked his claim as Lysimachus' son, as he reasoned that he now had a stronger claim from that angle than an Egyptian one, for any part of Asia Minor and Thrace. He was quickly assassinated by Thracians, probably with the complicity of Antiochus, who regained Ephesus and went on to throw the tyrant Timarchus out of Miletus, took Samos, and evicted Egypt from Ionia altogether. He then expelled Egypt completely from Cilicia and Pamphylia, reestablishing his father's borders. Egypt retained her position in Caria. Eumenes was unable to assist Ptolemy as he had his own problems to deal with: some of his relatives, as well as many of his mercenaries mutinied. He managed these crises but had no ability to help his ally. Antiochus even threatened Byzantium, but Heraclea rallied to the Byzantines and Antiochus, having made his demonstration, withdrew. He had settled scores with Ptolemy. All that is known about the war in Greece is that Antigonus suppressed a revolt in Athens and executed the historian Philochorus for treason. The Athenian nationalist war party here disappears and does not surface again. Antigonus did see an opportunity in Cyrenaica, where Magas had died in 259 and leaving as heiress the fourteen-year-old Berenice. Magas betrothed her on his deathbed to Ptolemy III, and the queen mother, Antiochus' sister Apama, who was the head of the Cyrenaican nationalists, to gain independence, offered the throne instead to Antigonus' (and her own) half-brother, Demetrius the Fair. At some point in the mid-250's, after a great deal of intrigue, and a public affair between Demetrius and Berenice's mother Apama (i.e., between Antigonus' half-brother and Antiochus' sister), Demetrius was assassinated with the complicity of Berenice, but in the early 240's, Ptolemaic Egypt regained control of Cyrenaica. The decisive event of this war was the naval Battle of Cos in 258, in which Antigonus himself commanded his new heavy fleet and fully vindicated his naval construction strategy (as the Germans and Americans did theirs' in World Wars I and II) by decisively defeating the more numerous but lighter Egyptian fleet. Ptolemy made peace in 255, having lost considerable ground to both Antigonus and Antiochus. Antigonus' success was widely memorialized, most successfully by the winged victory of Samothrace, now best known as the hood ornament of the Rolls-Royce automobile.

4. The Third Syrian War and War of the Brothers

In 252, Ptolemy helped to incite the revolt of Alexander of Corinth, who expelled Antigonus from his fine and strategic harbour at Corinth. There was also some contest about who controlled the prestigious island of Delos, and both Antigonus and Ptolemy established the new showcase of competitive excellence: a vase festival. This was added to the games that had been held since and before the Olympics and were approximately culturally equivalent, as the vase festival allowed for the display of the most artistic pottery and ceramics, a sign, perhaps, of the progress of civilization, and certainly a less laddish and brawny field of rivalry. Ptolemy secured a formidable diplomatic victory with a dynastic stroke. Antiochus had married his cousin Laodice, daughter of Achaeus, a younger brother of Antiochus I, who bore him two sons and two daughters, but whom he found somewhat dominating and insubordinate. Ptolemy persuaded Antiochus to dismiss Laodice (in the memorable tradition of Ptolemy and Arsinoe) and marry Ptolemy's daughter (another) Berenice. Ptolemy promised a Croesian dowry, on the understanding that the entire and united kingdom would ultimately go to this Berenice's son, the grandson of both present kings. The marriage occurred in 252, and a son was born of it the following year. It was a genius stroke, and Antiochus had prefigured Napoleon dispensing with the popular and flamboyant Josephine to take a Habsburg queen of child-bearing potential. Ptolemy's plans were frustrated by the deaths of Alexander of Corinth which enabled Antigonus to recover that city, and of Antiochus in 247, and Ptolemy himself died in 246. His eldest son became Ptolemy III and married the Cyrenaican Berenice (who had a sweet revenge on her relatives).

A battle naturally erupted between the rival queens. Laodice fought for her son, and was supported by her brother, Alexander, who was the general in Lydia and proclaimed his nephew King Seleucus II. Berenice was supported in Antioch and Egyptian forces from Syria and Cyprus intervened to assist her. But after intense intrigue and some far-flung skirmishing, traditional methods were resorted to and the Laodicean faction infiltrated Berenice's court in Antioch and murdered Berenice and her son. Berenice's entourage managed to conceal her death and Ptolemy, ostensibly as a friendly relative of the legitimate royal house soon arrived at the head of an army, in parade mode, and went through Syria and east toward Bactria, all in legitimist solidarity. He made a ceremonious circuit and returned to Egypt, subsequently claiming to have conquered all of the Seleucid Empire, one of history's more ambitious fabrications. By the end of his promenade, The Laodiceans had unearthed the fact of Berenice's death and her son Seleucus II, stepbrother of the murdered son, though young, was very capable and quickly recruited an army and a fleet. He married his sisters to King Mithridates of Pontus, and King Ariaratheres of Cappadocia (the new self-nominated Persian king), assuring himself of their alliance. In 244 he crossed the Taurus mountains and descended into Syria and the Egyptian domain, not represented by any living and legitimate Egyptian claim, collapsed like a punctured balloon. After some hard fighting around Damascus, most of the status quo ante was restored. The late King Ptolemy had squandered an immense dowry.

Seleucus lost his fleet in a storm and the alliance of Antiochus II with Egypt in 253 put a permanent end to the long cooperation between the Antigonids and Seleucids. In 246 and 245 Antigonus enjoyed the revenge of regaining Corinth and defeated the Egyptian fleet off Andros and took back much of the Cyclades. Antigonus was now seventy-five and celebrated his latest recovery of fortune, in one of the most durable and tortuous careers in all of Middle Eastern history, with a veritable World Cup of vase festivals at Delos. He died in 239 of natural causes, aged eighty, and after a total of thirty-eight years as king of Macedonia. It will be remembered that Antigonus I was defeated by the joint forces of Ptolemy, Seleucus, and Lysimachus at Ipsos in 301, the Battle of Leipzig of ancient times, as a coalition victory over the leading contender for the succession to Alexander the Great. Antigonus died on the field, aged eighty-one and undefeated up to that day, and his son Demetrius escaped with nine-thousand men and eventually swashbuckled his way back to the throne of a diminished Macedonia, but was squeezed out by Lysimachus on the Thracian side and Pyrrhus in Epirus in the west. Demetrius fled across Asia Minor and eventually surrendered to Seleucus, who maintained him comfortably under house arrest in the interior of Syria. Antigonus II was a dutiful son and tried to ransom his father unsuccessfully. He was in all respects more moderate than Demetrius. When he asked his father why he was wasting troops on hopeless siege assaults against Thebes, Demetrius replied, as his son would never have done: "We don't have to find rations for the dead."[4]

Antigonus II asserted his claim to the Macedonian throne, emphasizing his mother, Phila, daughter of Antipater the initial regent following the death of Alexander the Great, rather than the tempestuous Demetrius who never craved or received mass popularity. Antigonus governed part of Macedonia, though contested by Pyrrhus, and joined in the repulse of the great Gallic invasion by Brennus in 279, at Thermopylae, and after the death of Pyrrhus in 272, Antigonus was the more or

---

4 Nicholas Lempière and Frank Walbank, *A History of Macedonia: 336-167 B.C.* Oxford University Press. 1988, p. 221.

less uncontested king of Macedonia. He was not an especially successful general, but was cautious and thorough, a just and well-liked ruler, and a patron of the arts and a friend of Zeno and other philosophers. He was almost a Metternichian figure, patiently constructing alliances and maintaining himself over a swirling variety of interacting peoples through successive tumultuous decades. Where his father had been a ruthless, brilliant but erratic egomaniac, Antigonus II was a well-rounded ruler, skilled in diplomacy and administration and a considerable strategist who had realized the great lesson of Alexander and the Diadochi: unless one could rule by insuperable military genius at the service of a great ideal—racial homogenization in a Hellenized civilization in the case of Alexander—government had to maintain a reasonable degree of public contentment for its judiciousness and facilitation of prosperity and cultural attainments, or all the dynastic legitimacy conceivable would be insufficient to assure its incumbency. Antigonus II had seen at close hand (he was eighteen at Ipsos) that conquering peoples could only be sustained if the right combination of intimidation and benevolence could be applied to deter revolt and incite contentment. This was still a slightly radical notion of governance.

The Third Syrian War ended by a peace agreement in 241, after a few more towns changed hands back and forth at the edges between the Ptolemaic and Seleucid empires. (It was now eighty-two years since the death of Alexander the Great.) Ptolemy III had a somewhat stronger position in the northern and eastern Aegean than Ptolemy II had had, but Egypt had lost naval supremacy in the Aegean to Macedonia. Neither Antiochus II nor his son Seleucus II, had been able to disentangle themselves from Asia Minor long enough to give any attention to the east. Under Diodotus, Antiochus' general in the great satrapy of Bactria and Sogdia, it became effectively autonomous about 250. The struggle with the surrounding nomads never stopped for long and was better organized and commanded locally than from Antioch. Examination of the coinage of the jurisdiction indicates that it took Diodotus II until about 227 to inform his subjects and fellow-Seleucids that he was a king and not a Seleucid colonial official, though this was a confirmation of a long-standing fact at this point. Arsaces, king of Parthia, established an independent kingdom in what is now northeast Iran, and effectively cut Bactria and Sogdia off from the rest of the Seleucid Empire.

The War of the Brothers began shortly after the Third Syrian War ended. In the midst of Seleucus II's struggle with Ptolemy, Seleucus signed over northern Asia Minor to his brother Antiochus, presumably under extreme duress of combat with Egypt compounded by family revolt. Once he had negotiated peace with Ptolemy, Seleucus attempted to regain what he had given away to Antiochus. The history of this conflict is quite fuzzy and there are many imputations of actions to Laodice, who was alive and presumably active, but her role is not certain—her benignity should not be assumed and she is generally thought to have favoured her second son (the Hawk) over her first. She was an astute and ambitious woman, but she could not have just manipulated the supposedly crowned heads who were contending for supremacy in the latest of countless rounds of war in what is now Anatolian Turkey and the Levant.

Diligent readers still trying to keep track of all these wars and conspiracies and dynastic contortions should remember that in the action-packed year of 246 B.C., Ptolemy II died in January and Antiochus II then returned to Laodice at Ephesus where she had been residing after she was shuffled out to allow Antiochus II to marry Berenice, daughter of Ptolemy II, who produced the heir to the combined Ptolemaic-Seleucid Empire, also named Antiochus. In 246, this heir, little Antiochus, was six years old. Antiochus II died in July 246, possibly having been murdered by an unphilosophical Laodice, though this is not certain, and for good measure Laodice did have Berenice the daughter of Ptolemy II and widow of Antiochus II, seized and executed and her heir, the young Antiochus, murdered. At this point, Ptolemy III went to war against the Seleucid Empire to avenge his sister, Berenice. After a good deal of milling about, he did have the pleasure of capturing Laodice and settled accounts promptly: without histrionics or sadism, he had her bound and silently witnessed her beheading and had her buried with dignity as a queen. As noble ladies of the time customarily did, Laodice, once captured, submitted expressionlessly to what she had no doubt would be her fate, giving no hint of remorse or even wistfulness. In these times, an inordinate number of leading people ended their lives in battle, execution, assassination, or suicide (like most members of Lenin's Politburo under Stalin and all the leaders of the Third Reich). Seleucus II was already at war with his brother Antiochus the Hawk to take back from him Northern Asia Minor, which he had given him. The entire region descended, yet again, into general combat. Small states, such as Caria, declared their independence as the larger ones struggled, all with each, on numerous fronts, and ambitious medium-sized states strove for an advantage. In this last group was Pergamon, now ruled by Attalus, who was the nephew of Eumenes (who died in 241) and also of Laodice.

The wild card in the equation, not that one was required, was that the Gauls were still rampaging where they could. Generally, they united all the fragments of the old Alexandrian Empire against them, as Persia had once united Greece, and the Gauls made no pretense to anything except murder and pillage—they had no interest in settling or governing; they were unregenerate murderers, arsonists, and robbers, but brave and resourceful. No one could have imagined that their descendants would be exemplars of la douce France. (History's first important Brennus was the Gallic leader who took all Rome except for the Capitoline Hill in 391 and was then repelled by Manlius Capitolinus and Marcus Furius Cornelius. The second Brennus (not apparently related) was repulsed at Thermopylae in 279 by the Aetolians, Antigonus II and others, and these Gauls still in northern Asia Minor were a leftover community still active east of Byzantium.) Antiochus the Hawk made an alliance with these Gauls to try to hang onto what he had been given by Seleucus II when he had been in the thick of the fight with Ptolemy II, and this was widely seen by all the factions as treachery beyond what even this free-wheeling political culture could tolerate.

This was where Attalus of Pergamum made his play. With the customary hypocrisy of degenerated states and cultures, most of the governments in Asia Minor were paying Dane Geld to the Gauls who were hovering above them at the entrance to the Black Sea, periodically ravaging northern Cappadocia and Phrygia to remind the Hellenized locals of their methods and aptitudes. Attalus, with great fanfare, announced that Pergamum would not pay anything to the Gauls and effectively invited the Gauls to come to try to extract it from him, thus immediately becoming the hero of all Asia Minor, the Hellenic champion. The Gallic tribes set upon Attalus and were defeated beneath the walls of Pergamon. They had invoked their alliance with Antiochus II who did commit the grievous offense of facilitating the invasion of Asia Minor by these wild and destructive barbarians against a Hellenic state. Once thrown back from Pergamon, the Gauls turned on Antiochus and murdered his father-in-law, Ziaelas. Attalus assumed the kingship of Pergamon and systematically defeated Antiochus in Hellespontine Phrygia in 230, and the next year in Lydia and Caria, hurling Antiochus back from the Mediterranean and crowding him eastward and to the north. Attalus governed most of Seleucid Asia Minor by 228, and carefully represented his victory, not as an internecine victory over the Seleucids, but as an Hellenic victory over the vilest genus of barbarians. (Remember that at this point, the Hellenic world was still purporting to regard the Romans as barbarians, though admittedly of the most advanced kind—they were certainly united in their aversion to the Gauls.)

While Attalus was hammering the unloved Antiochus II, Seleucus II was trying to retrieve Parthia from Arsaces II. Antiochus II tried a comeback, linking with his aunt, Stratonice, the divorced wife of Demetrius II, son of Antigonus II, and attacked Seleucus while he was preoccupied in the east. Seleucus had to depart the contest with Parthia and return to the west; he defeated Antiochus and suppressed the revolt Stratonice had raised in semi-official circles in Antioch itself and executed Stratonice for treason and abuse of his hospitality and regained everything Antiochus had overrun. Fortunately, for Attalus, Seleucus II died in the summer of 226, in a riding accident, before he could put Pergamon in its place. Antiochus was now without any semblance of a domain, and fell into the hands of unsympathetic Gauls, who recognized him as an unfaithful ex-ally and a corrupt (and illegitimate, though that would not have bothered the Gauls) king and he was summarily executed, virtually as a miscreant.

Seleucus II was followed by Seleucus III, who sent his uncle, Andromachus to recover Asia Minor from Attalus, but Attalus defeated him several times and captured Andromachus and sent him into exile in Egypt. Seleucus took matters in hand himself in 223 but was assassinated in Phrygia by some of his own officers. Seleucus' cousin (and Andromachus' son), Achaeus, succeeded Seleucus III as commander in Asia Minor and executed the rebellious officers and launched a strenuous and well-organized offensive that pushed Attalus back into the original frontiers of Pergamon by 220. Thus ended the so-called War of the Brothers.

5. Antiochus III and the Fourth Syrian War

Antiochus III was to prove again the luck of the dynastic lottery, made even more unpredictable by the frequent violent deaths of rulers and their close relatives. In these times and for many centuries, except for the greatest monarchic talents, such as Alexander and Augustus, all heads that wore crowns rested uneasily on their shoulders, always aware of how easily royal heads could suddenly be forcibly surrendered to the executioner's axe. The new king, though he was only eighteen at his accession in 223 and was overshadowed by his loyal cousin Achaeus and by the grand vizier Carian Hermeias, was to prove an outstanding monarch, ultimately revered as "the Great" and in the oriental manner, "the Great King." He delegated the effort to regain the east and govern what was left of it to the generals Molon and Alexander, and left Achaeus in charge of the Asia Minor he had regained for the Seleucid house. Within a year, following the example of Diodotus in Bactria-Sogdia but on an accelerated schedule, Molon was in revolt and trying to set up his own kingdom across Media, Persia, Parthia, and Hyrcania, and purported to be resurrecting Babylonia. In the autumn of 222, Molon set up at Ctesiphon and sported a diadem as king of Babylonia. Antiochus received divided counsel and was menaced in the west by Egypt. His capable general Epigenes said Antiochus would have to go in person to defeat this threat and Hermeias, the vizier, was concerned about him leaving Syria with Egypt coveting it. Antiochus sent Xenoetas to deal with Molon, but Molon ambushed and severely defeated him and advanced to take Chaldaea, but was stopped at Susa. Antiochus now came in person at the head of a considerable army, and as much of Molon's army was composed of Greco-Macednian soldiers who had some loyalty to the Seleucids, mutinies occurred and Molon thought it best to give battle at once, on the the theory that the tocsin of combat would steady the troops. But Antiochus appeared in person at the head of his army, recognizable to the other army, and one entire wing of Molon's army abruptly deserted and Antiochus led his whole army against Molon, who committed suicide with his brother to avoid death by torture, the customary sentence for treason in the Seleucid kingdom.

It was a great victory for Antiochus, who made a considerable public spectacle of redundantly but symbolically crucifying Molon's corpse but was generally lenient. He restrained Hermeias from wholesale tortures and executions among the numerous suspected disloyalists in Seleucia, but for good measure, as Hermeias had taken advantage of Antiochus' absence in the east to arrange the murder of his rival Epigenes, Antiochus arranged the private detention and immediate execution of the grand vizier. Getting in step with official policy, a group of militant women then brutally murdered Hermeias' wife and family. The assassination of Epigenes had caused a revolt in Cyrrhestice, and when even the admirable Achaeas thought Antiochus might be a long time in the east, he went there and joined the rebellion. Antiochus entrusted Media to Diogenes and returned to Syria. The late Hermeias had been right about the dangers of going to the east, but the late Epigenes had been right that only Antiochus himself could end the usurpation by Molon. Achaeas soon learned that the mystique of the Seleucid crown that had undermined Molon's revolt was effective in Cyrrhestice also, and before it was certain that Achaeas was in fact leading a revolt, he took the opportunity to purport to carry out his intended mission by suppressing a Pisidian tribe en route, that was, in fact, not being particularly obstreperous. Antiochus, who clearly had a natural talent for the extreme deviousness and trickery of an ambulatory Middle Eastern court, pretended not to realize that Achaeas had attempted an uprising, and led his main army against Egypt in Syria, confident that though a Putschist was in command of his home army, Achaeas had learned the lesson just in time, and thus was spared the fate of Molon.

It was the apogee of Near Eastern treachery. A disloyal general who knew his troops would not follow him into open revolt was as good a guardian of the palace and its environs as an ultra-loyalist.

For Antiochus, the times continued to be fortuitous, as Ptolemy III became sedentary and his kingdom decayed in his inertia over the last twenty years of his reign, which ended with his natural death in 221. There had been general peace since the agreement ending the Third Syrian War in 241, apart from Ptolemy's leisurely stroll in Asia Minor in 236 to find, capture, and behead Laodice. His most strenuous activity in the last quarter century had been the pantomime "conquest-tour" of the realm of Antiochus in 246. As Antiochus III prepared to evict Egypt from Syria, Egypt seemed to have neither the army nor the leadership to resist him. Ptolemy III had not supported his Spartan ally Cleomenes, a man of great distinction, and maintained Egypt's record as an unreliable ally. Its land army, which had always been mercenaries, had almost withered away, as the other powers were warring with or within each other.

Ptolemy IV, Philopator, was lazy and debauched. He was not cruel nor necessarily stupid and seems to have pondered the propagation of a universal and unifying religion, putting together elements of different faiths and even compromising with Judaic monotheism, but he didn't do anything about it. He favoured the arts and his father had engaged the eminent Eratosthenes as his tutor. Philopator built an immense warship and a magnificent houseboat for excursions on the Nile, but he was negligent and decadent. Ptolemy Philopator left government to his chief minister, Sosibius, who was odious but cunning and brave. In service to his master, he had murdered the mother of the king, Berenice of Cyrenaica, and his uncle Lysimachus, and his brother, Magas. He murdered the wives and families of Cleomenes, who had all been given asylum by the king after Ptolemy III had conspicuously failed to assist them. But he served Egypt when Antiochus III assumed that Philopator's indolence would make Egypt's position in Syria and Palestine and the Levant easy pickings.

In 219, Antiochus attacked Seleucia in Pieria, only ten miles from Antioch, and induced Theodotus, who had resisted tenaciously at Gerrha on the Persian Gulf the year before, to hand over Tyre, Acre, and forty ships, as he felt under-recognized by the Egyptian government. Antiochus proceeded along the Eastern Mediterranean shore but allowed himself to be misled by carefully planted rumours generated by Sosibius to the effect that Pelusium, at the eastern side of the Nile Estuary, was an impregnable fortress bulging with well-trained troops, a preposterous canard. Antiochus accepted a four-month truce and put his army in winter quarters, and prepared to receive negotiators who would hand over Palestine. Sosibius and Agathocles, the brother of the king's mistress Agathoclea, determined to build an army, since Egypt did not have one. They recruited the best mercenaries that could be had in Greece and Macedonia, and to fill up his numbers, Sosibius recruited twenty-thousand Egyptians, though most of them were probably Berbers, desert warriors with some martial aptitudes. The peaceable masses of Egypt had not had weapons in their hands or faced an armed adversary in ninety years; they defended Gaza in 312 but were none too war-like even then. Greek officers trained up these forces as quickly as they could in a large secret camp near Alexandria, and Sosibius strung things along further by sending a negotiating team to Seleucia who waffled and pettifogged and finally said they had no authority. The normally intuitively astute Antiochus finally realized he had been played and summoned his army in the spring of 218. But he continued to concentrate on southern Syria, presumably oblivious of the lengths Sosibius and Agathocles were going to in the conjuration of a real opponent for the Seleucid king.

The intelligent strategic move would have been to move early on Egypt as everything that could be conquered in Syria and Palestine could be wrung from a successful assault on the Nile Delta and Alexandria, but Antiochus, though he can't have continued to believe in Sosibius' military Potemkin Village, must have assumed that his advances would demoralize Egypt and he was in any case only seeking Egypt's territory in Asia, nothing from Egypt itself. Ptolemy's chief general, the Aetolian Nicolaus, a competent soldier, tried to bar the way to Antiochus down the coastal road before Sidon, and the fleet Sosibius had resurrected simultaneously engaged the Seleucid fleet. The admirals were Diognetus for Antiochus and Perigenes for Ptolemy IV Philipator. Both were Greeks and the fighting was hard and brave by land and by sea but Antiochus prevailed. The Egyptians retired in order (there were few Egyptians among them) and Antiochus struck inland and went round Sidon. He took Galilee and Samaria and some cities beyond the Jordan and Arab tribes rallied to him. He took Philadelphia by severing the water supply, and retired to Ptolemais, just south of Tyre for the winter. The stately pace continued.

Finally, in the spring of 217, Antiochus advanced to Raphia, a border point fifteen miles south of Gaza, with his army of sixty-two thousand infantry, six-thousand cavalry and one-hundred and two Indian elephants. His phalanx, of twenty-thousand Greco-Macedonian settlers, and his ten-thousand well-trained hypaspists were very solid. The Egyptians had fifty-thousand foot, five-thousand horse, and seventy-three African elephants (larger than their Indian relatives). The Egyptian phalanx had five-thousand Greeks and Sosibius' twenty-thousand Egyptian recruits. Sosibius himself, a civil servant and courtier who must have been in his fifties, led the phalanx, with Andromachus of Aspendus (no relation, as far as is known, to Achaeas' son Andromachus). Ptolemy had six-thousand hypaspists, half of them Libyans, and accompanied by his sister Arsinoe (whom he was about to marry in the bizarre Egyptian manner), personally commanded the left wing. The two great armies met on June 22, 217, the Egyptians confidently moving inland rather than having their left flank secured on the Mediterranean shore. As the Seleucid army approached with battle flags flying, the glamorous young Arsinoe rode across the front line of the Egyptian army urging her brother/fiancé's troops to stand firm.

The Egyptian cavalry on the right defeated Antiochus' left and drove it back, but on Ptolemy's left, his elephants gave way through lack of mobility and the Indian elephants trampled down the Egyptian and Libyan hypaspists and broke the line. Antiochus led into the gap that had formed in the Egyptian line and drove hard to exploit the opportunity. Ptolemy, showing admirable sangfroid and tactical insight, broke loose from the rout around him and rode to the centre, which had not been engaged in either army, and the two great phalanxes, with their flanks swept away in opposite directions, then engaged in a pitched battle: forty-five thousand men in intense combat, no quarter asked or given. Fighting for their king in person (a greater contrast with Darius V at Issus and Gaugamela could hardly be found). Ptolemy led his men in person and the twenty-thousand Egyptians had been well-drilled and slowly carried the day over the five-thousand fewer Greco-Macedonians of the Seleucid phalanx. The Egyptian phalanx gradually prevailed and the Seleucid centre gave way and retreated. Ptolemy didn't have enough cavalry to set on the backs of the Seleucids, who half withdrew/half fled. Antiochus rode back to his defeated army and helped get it in order, but he had been soundly defeated and lost fourteen-thousand dead and four-thousand prisoners, to only about three-thousand Egyptian and allied dead. Ptolemy IV and Arsinoe, and the otherwise egregious Sosibius, had a glorious day. Antiochus conducted the retreat to Raphia, where his army still numbered fifty-thousand and could still fight, but their king went quickly to Antioch, fearful of how this calamitous news might alter Achaeas' game-plan. But Achaeas did not yield to temptation at once. A ceasefire was agreed and in peace discussions, Antiochus, who had wasted two years occupying Syria and Palestine, had to yield much of it back: southern Syria, Palestine, and Phoenicia reverted. Sosibius went to Antioch to sign the peace. Andromachus was rewarded with the governorship of Syria and Ptolemy distributed three-hundred thousand gold pieces to his army. Antiochus appeared to be finished but was already determined to resume his mission of a resurrected Empire of Darius or Alexander.

Ptolemy IV had a genuine triumph in south Syria and then with his new bride, returned to his lascivious pleasures in palatial carnal hedonism in Alexandria. Antiochus had had a sobering lesson, a humiliating come-uppance in fact, and he learned from it. Achaeas would, like Antiochus in the late campaign, move too late, and finally strike his royal master in the back the following year. Antiochus had stabilized his army and the politics of his capital by then, and defeated Achaeas and executed him in the normal denouement of such events; once Achaeas was finally in open revolt, one of the cousins was going to forfeit his head. Antiochus would spend the next twenty years methodically reconstructing his empire in the north and east (with the incomparable military advice of the great Hannibal), and then again finally evict Egypt from Syria and Palestine. His reign was a long era of gradual reconstitution of the great Seleucid Empire, with generally prudent campaigns on the frontiers and competent and judicious autocratic government within. He and his almost exact contemporary Philip V of Macedon would cross swords a number of times, and Rome, as will be described in the next chapter, in finally getting around to Philip, would adopt the natural position of defenders of the Greeks, most of whom would stifle their condescension to the barbarians on the Tiber, and accept Rome's leadership as more enlightened and in any case more powerfully imposed and evenly directed than the previous alternatives provided by Persia and Macedon (other than by the generally absent Alexander the Great).

From the events described in this chapter, two historic points emerged: the Egyptians won the Battle of Raphia: the Egyptians held when their Greek instructors broke, and the Egyptian phalanx defeated the Seleucid Greco-Macedonian phalanx in hand-to-hand combat. Henceforth, Ptolemy IV Philopator was referred to in Egyptian as an Egyptian, and described officially in terminology retrieved from the days of the Pharaohs. The Macedonian Ptolemaic dynasty, under the great grandson of Ptolemy I who had snatched it from the legacy of Alexander the Great, revived long dormant Egyptian nationalism. This was the beginning of the decline of Greek prestige in the east, a process that would be quickly accelerated once Rome was drawn into the equation. Greece had given the world the polis, an advanced notion of civic government, though Rome and Carthage and some lesser centres developed their own models of it. The Greek cities had aggregated themselves to leagues but could never agree on anything for long.

The other remarkable development was that Rome was absolutely supreme in the central and Western Mediterranean and was operating on a scale the known western world had not seen before: it raised its own armies, genuinely extended its nationality to people usually happy to have it, and governed competently with some recognition of individual rights, an advantage to those who lived under it. Instead of plunging into other countries and subjugating them for the sheer love of conquest and plunder, or as a lethal and almost uninterrupted escalation to armed combat of the Olympic Games, as the Greeks had been doing for centuries, Rome responded defensively to the Gauls, the Carthaginians, and were about to respond in the same spirit to Macedonia. Their rule became so vast not because they set out to govern the known world, but because it was better government than the Mediterranean world had had from others, except for parts of Greece at their most enlightened, and the security of Rome always required friendlier neighbours and stronger frontiers. Rome had brought the concept of a country and the nature of governance to a new level. Carthage had been reduced to a dependent city; the Gauls and Celtiberians had been roughly handled or seduced; the Massilians and Numidians were subordinate allies; the Greeks couldn't defend themselves; and Macedonia, Asia Minor, Egypt and Asia as far as the gates of India were misbegotten peoples unsteadily ruled by elements that were descendants, fugitives, or excrescences of Alexander's magnificent but evanescent empire. Rome was the future, and the western world would not have long to wait for it.

CHAPTER TWENTY

THE TRIUMPH OF ROME IN THE EAST, 215 - 155 B.C.
❦
FLAMININUS, PHILIP V, AND ANTIOCHUS THE GREAT

Titus Quinctius Flamininus, gold coin

Bust of Antiochus the Great

1. Rome at the End of the Second Punic War

THERE WAS STILL no consensus in Rome for a full expansion to the East, as had occurred in consequence of the wars with Carthage in Africa, Spain, southern Gaul, Sicily, and Sardinia. Nor at this point were the leaders of the Roman state particularly enthused at the prospect of a permanent occupation of Greece in the same measure that the Greeks now looked with belated concern and largely misplaced condescension on Rome as outsized, muscular, and imperious. Rome, after a gentlemanly doffing of the laurel to Hellenic culture and bravery, essentially considered Greece a cul-de-sac of squabbling and pretentious little states. Egypt was potentially more interesting, but it was in the hands of a capable leader with whom Rome had no quarrel. The once vast Persian Empire fragmented by Alexander the Great and ruptured into quarrelsome components in the long struggle between his heirs, was at the end of the Punic Wars of almost no interest at all to Rome. Of all of history's great empires, none was more haphazardly constructed through most of its development than Rome's.

Rome was somewhat enervated after the great struggle with Carthage and was busy incorporating most of Spain and part of the North African littoral (modern Tunisia) into its domains; it was only drawn further to the east, as it had already been by the current Philip of Macedon, when a rambunctious local leader disturbed Rome's composure. Antiochus, unsubdued by his reverse at the hands of Ptolemy IV, resumed his determination to reconstitute the entire Seleucid Empire at its height, and he started with Armenia, marching on the capital Arsamosata, where the young King Xerxes did not resist him and was generously treated, including being betrothed to the sister of Antiochus, Antiochis. Xerxes thus passed from being a rebellious governor to a submissive foe to a grateful brother-in-law. With the Caucasus in order, Antiochus plunged eastwards into Hyrcania, Media, and Bactria. He sailed down the Euphrates in 211 and rifled the Temple of Anaitis at Ecbatana of four-thousand talents to finance his great expedition to the east (always a perilous method of financing aggressive war, given the ease with which sectarian sensibility metamorphoses into extreme bellicosity). He essentially followed the route of Alexander the Great. He was hard put to it to dispose of the fierce mountain and salt plains tribes but beat them off, and where necessary, reduced forces in his path by siege. At Tauranga, despite valiant efforts, he was unable to save the local Greek population of several thousand, which was massacred, a fate he shortly imposed on those responsible.

He marched against Bactria in 208 and after two years of hard fighting, the Bactrian King Euthydemus warned him that if they became more debilitated, they would both be vulnerable to the barbarians to the north, and reminded Antiochus that Bactria had from Alexander's time more than a century before, been regarded as an "Hellenic" barrier against the cloven-footed masses of Central Asia. Antiochus found this argument persuasive, agreed a "perpetual alliance," accepted the cession of the Bactrian king's elephants and married off one of his daughters, in absentia, to Euthydemus' son Demetrius. (Readers will recall that the Bactrian royal house had had Alexander the Great himself in the family for a time.) Antiochus pressed on across the Hindu Kush and into India, in fact the Kabul Valley, where he parleyed with the Hindu prince and celebrated the revival of the relationship the Seleucids had had with Chandragupta. With the gift from his host of a number of splendid elephants and a substantial quantity of precious gems and metals, Antiochus returned by a more southerly route toward Syria, proclaiming the glory of his triumph throughout his route of march.

In 204, after an absence of six years, the population and the diplomatic representatives of other countries were thoroughly impressed by the one-hundred and fifty elephants he had acquired and the great loot and tribute that he took or received in his eastern campaign. He then more or less conferred upon himself the traditional title of Great King, and has generally been known as Antiochus the Great, not undeservedly, given his prudence, moderation, and general success. He became the victim of the apprehensions of the Greeks and Egyptians that he really was another Alexander the Great, at least in his own ambitions, and could be assumed to have equivalent territorial and avocational appetites. In fact, he was a cautious man highly ambitious within his carefully calculated sense of what was possible. He became the victim of his own success in that he had no such ambitions as Alexander (nor his aptitudes), and need not have been looked upon with such suspicion as he was in Greece and in Egypt (and before long, in Rome).

Antiochus was determined to redeem his defeat at Raphia in 217 at the hands of Ptolemy (Philopator as he was known) and Sosibius. But as he returned to his capital it was Philip's successful settlement of his conflict with Rome that concerned him. Philip and Antiochus were exact contemporaries and had ascended their thrones almost simultaneously. It became clear that Antiochus' ambition was to redeem his losses to Egypt in 217, which Philip was determined to try to prevent: substantially the same calculus of the comparative strength of Macedonia, Egypt, and Asia Minor that operated throughout the lengthy and profound wars of succession following the death of Alexander the Great. Philip moved to block Antiochus, beginning with an encroachment in the Aegean, the occupation of islands under the protection of the forces of Rhodes although it technically was subject to Egypt. Philip was officially one of the protectors of Delos and had arranged to have conferred upon him a special status as guardian of the Aegean. He sought to dominate that sea and the straits to the Black Sea.

Philip had been severely disappointed when he had been drawn westward toward the Adriatic and his alliance with Carthage, which he had relied upon to counter the Romans, had proved worthless (and he was worthless to the Carthaginians). The irrational adherence to the Roman alliance of the Aetolians and the unexpected animosity of Pergamon had forced Philip to conduct an underdog battle with Rome for nine years. He felt with some reason that he had rendered great service to Greece and been betrayed by his beneficiaries. In general, his diplomacy, which had been offered in good faith, had been rejected or betrayed. He had seen the strength and courage of Rome, recognized it as an adversary, but he despised virtually everybody active in the Greek peninsula, Aegean, Egypt, Asia Minor, and the eastern reaches of Alexander's old Empire. In the wrath of his comparative isolation, Philip became a severe tyrant, executing summarily anyone in his entourage who expressed a word of disagreement. His likeness appeared on the coinage, and effigies of him popped up all over his kingdom. As he had demonstrated in his patronage of Demetrius of Pharos, he liked scoundrels and now engaged two of the most notorious contemporary examples of the type; Dicaearchus, an Aetolian, and the Tarantene architect Heracleides, who had been exiled from his country for high treason and was destined to be Philip's chief admiral.

Philip's opening gambit was to try to eliminate the ability of Rhodes to exercise its generally appreciated role as chief defender of the Aegean against pirates. He sent his newly recruited Heracleides to try to burn, after surreptitious advances, the fleet of Rhodes in harbor. Heracleides went to Rhodes and began febrile conspiratorial discussions with local natives of Crete who resented Rhodes' domination of their island. He managed to burn thirteen triremes and escape by a hair's breadth. As there was no hard evidence against him, Rhodes did not break relations with Philip, but henceforth regarded him with extreme suspicion. While Heracleides was carrying out his mission at Rhodes, Dicaearchus, while inciting the nationalist resentment of Cretan patriots, was also plundering other islands and ships and by this crude method produced enough money for Philip to build forty cataphracts (ships with a closed hull to protect the rowers). The conduct of Macedonian policy by these two outrageous reprobates assured the escalation of tensions throughout the area.

Two of Antiochus' old adversaries now entered the fray. Scopas and Dorimachus, having been previously deposed as the leaders of Aetolia, as economic difficulties might make conditions ripe for their return, now proposed the total cancellation of debt, usually a popular move. But the leader of the capitalist party of Aetolia, Alexander Isios, whom Polybius cites as the wealthiest man in Greece, defeated the two mountebanks and chased them out of Aetolia. Scopas, though a political low life on all fours with Heracleides and Dicearchus, was a respected general and he went to Alexandria offering his assistance to Sosibius, perhaps the most treacherous schemer of them all, who was happy to take it. Always an astute opportunist, Sosibius had been planning on developing an alliance with Philip to keep Antiochus at bay, and Scopas fitted into his plans despite Philip's antagonism to him. Antiochus was now prowling around Asia Minor extending his influence, if need be by force. Storm clouds were rising throughout 203, and Philip and Antiochus were contemplating each other with increasing suspicion when the news arrived that Ptolemy IV Philopator, Egypt's king, and Queen Arsinoe, had been murdered. Officially, Egypt's ruler was now a seven-year-old child. The egregious Sosibius, now maneuvering with even more than his customary tortuosity, remained at the head of Egypt's uneasy state.

He and Agathocles (not related to the Sicilian leader) had organized the murder of the king, and shortly after, his wife (and sister), Arsinoe, and forged a will of Ptolemy Philopator making themselves the guardians of the infant king. Having murdered the rest of Philopator's family: Lysimachus (uncle), Magas (brother), Berenice (mother), and Cleomenes (ally, whom Sosibius drove to suicide), it was in the normal order of things that Sosibius would himself be summarily executed by Agathocles, when he was of no further use to him. Agathocles was, if this were possible, even more unscrupulous than Sosibius and with a greater pedigree. Sosibius was seized, murdered and his corpse disposed of with no notice or publicity; he just ceased to exist, as if he had never existed, in the manner of liquidation and repression of twentieth century totalitarians, such as Stalin. The regency was Agathocles, Oenanthe and Agathocleia, who had the care of the child-king, Ptolemy V. As the French classicist Maurice Holleaux remarked, "The Regency could not have been in baser hands."[1]

According to Polybius, Agathocles, having, as he thought, assured his own position, retired to his customary life of frivolous debauchery. But he did recognize the danger posed by both Philip and Antiochus. He had given Scopas the resources to raise mercenaries in Greece and an emissary was sent to Antiochus to remind him of the desirability of honoring treaties. He even sent Ptolemy of Megalopolis to Rome to announce officially the accession of the new King, and to request placatory Roman intervention with Antiochus. Given the shabby Egyptian interference in the Macedonian war, he was not optimistic that Rome would assist him. He pinned more hopes on his dispatch of the recently inelegantly departed Sosibius' son, Ptolemy, to Philip proposing the engagement of Philip's daughter to Ptolemy V, and a defensive alliance against Antiochus which Agathocles was prepared to sweeten with treasure and territorial concessions. Considering Agathocles' lascivious and normally treacherous passivity, it was an ambitious plan.

---

1 CAH, VIII, p. 149 (Maurice Holleaux).

Antiochus could be assumed to guess something of what was afoot and acted preemptively by sending a plenipotentiary to Philip and proposing that they divide the spoils of Egypt. Antiochus proposed that he take lower Syria, Cyprus, Cilicia, and Lycia, while Philip could help himself to all Egyptian interests in the Aegean and along its coast, in Thrace and adjacent areas, and Cyrenaica (which had proved almost impossible for outsiders to administer). The problems with such a proposal were obvious to Philip; he and Antiochus would thereafter have an extensive common intersection of their spheres of influence and would be natural rivals in carving up the carcass of Egypt itself. But Philip purported to accept Antiochus's proposal and at the same time he warmly welcomed Sosibius' son Ptolemy and hosted him graciously at his court for approximately a year, representing himself as the ultimate protector of Egypt against the designs of the Seleucid leader.

This did not deter him for a moment from agreeing with Antiochus in early 202 their partition of Egypt's Asian and Mediterranean interests in what history has never ceased to regard as a thoroughly disgraceful agreement—more shameful than the Nazi Soviet pact of 1939 because neither Philip nor Antiochus had the slightest intention of honoring any part of what they had just agreed. Philip immediately set about taking over much more than had been conceded to him, including Lysimacheia, Chalcedon, Perinthus, Cius, sacking much of what he occupied and selling much of the population into slavery, although the agreement did not consign any of these places to Philip. The Greek world, downtrodden as it now was, objected vocally but rather impotently. Antiochus, though he was in no position to become moralistic about it, was seriously annoyed, but the first response to Philip was from the still formidable island of Rhodes, which had great power and influence in the Aegean and many allies, and a long record of comparatively principled interstate behaviour. The capable Theophiliscus was elected navarch of Rhodes, a peace-loving nation that nonetheless declared war on Philip, bringing in its allies led by Byzantium. It was the summer of 202. Antiochus was quietly occupying southern Syria and encroaching upon Egypt. Rhodes had no grievance with him.

In the spring of 201 the designs of Philip and Antiochus were assisted by the abrupt general revolt in Egypt, the highlight of which was the seizure and brutal murder of Agathocles, Agathocleia, and their entire corrupt clique, again a feat that they had frequently visited upon others. The leader of this coup, Tlepolemus, took charge of Ptolemy V, who was being handed physically around like the Infant of Prague. He started out with considerable support but soon proved to be inefficient, extravagant and dangerously unpopular. His pretense of government was carried on before a backdrop of native rebellion that raged from Nubia to the Nile Delta, actions in which many mercenaries had joined, having been enticed by Scopas to come to the defense of Egypt. With Egypt so distracted, Antiochus had no difficulty occupying as far as Gaza, but there he met very stiff resistance. At the same time, Philip subdued much of the Aegean, though he generally honored the Egyptian-occupied islands until he got to Samos, which he had to blockade and storm. In this action he captured fifty-three cataphracts and a lot of lighter craft, a solid victory which yet had the effect of arousing Attalus of Pergamon to join with Rhodes, and Philip shortly found himself faced with a very substantial joint fleet in opposition to him.

Philip was cruising along the Ionian coast imposing himself upon locals, when Theophiliscus and Attalus arrived with a somewhat larger fleet. Philip and the Macedonians acquitted themselves with distinction as always, but superior Rhodian seamanship forced the Macedonians back in one side of the action. On the other, Philip repulsed the Pergomene attack led by Attalus, ran Attalus into shore, seized his flagship, and chased him inland. Attalus escaped but Theophiliscus died bravely in action. The battle was a draw, but Philip lost almost half his ships, far more than were destroyed among his opponents. Philip broke off the sea action and attacked Attalus overland but was repulsed at the gates of Pergamon, though he managed a good deal of rich plunder outside that city. Philip then attacked southern Caria and captured a number of towns. In the autumn of 201, Philip prepared to sail back to Macedonia but found himself blockaded once again by a joint Pergamene and Rhodian fleet. Antiochus assisted in the reinforcement of the towns separating Philip from Macedonia, to make a landward return more difficult, and the Macedonian king was reduced to a very harrowing winter raiding for rations in neighboring towns and, as he put it, leading "the life of a wolf."[2]

There was, at last, in the late summer of 201, nothing for it but to appeal to Rome, which all knew to be the greatest power in the West. Pergamene and Rhodian envoys appeared at the Roman Senate. Even though Rome was exhausted, with fighting personnel enjoying a well-earned rest after the long battle with Carthage, and with a depleted treasury, it still responded positively to the Pergomene and Macedonian appeal. The apparent reason for this is that the Romans sagely judged that Philip could be a dangerous threat and that it was time to deal with him now while his fleet was blockaded in Caria. It was indicative of the unsentimental clarity of the Roman collective leadership that the elders of the Senate all concluded at once that, although they had no grievance whatever with Philip, they had been warned about Antiochus, had seen Philip in action, saw the potential danger to themselves and acted decisively and presumptively rather than defensively. Philip was not only blockaded and separated from his home country, he was none too popular where he had been foraging for the last six months.

More sinister in Roman eyes was Antiochus, whose measure they had not taken, but whose reputation as a great Eastern King disquieted the Senators with the lore of Xerxes and Alexander himself. The news that Philip and Antiochus were cooperating was particularly disturbing to the Romans. As the now governing authority of the central and Western Mediterranean, they could scarcely imagine that if Philip and Antiochus were cooperating, their cooperation would not soon be at the expense of Rome itself. The leading senators quickly devised a subtle plan: they would attack Philip in Greece and drive him out of Greece, establishing themselves as heroes to the fractious Greeks, who were certainly full of a Demosthenean hostility to the Macedonians. In doing this they would sever at the elbow the arm that Antiochus might otherwise raise against Rome. Rome, in a football expression of more than two-thousand years later, would get its retaliation in first. It was the sign of a virile and growing nation that it would contemplate taking such drastic mea-

---

2 Ibid., p. 155.

sures with no notice at all. It is also likely that Rome wished to punish Philip for his alliance with Carthage even though nothing came of it, and it would certainly be a prestigious thing to become protector of the Hellenic states from which Rome had received so much gratuitous condescension. Rome's aggressive response where it was scarcely involved suited Rome's security concerns and certainly did not imply a late-blooming filial affection for the Hellenic world.

Further finesse had to be displayed by the Roman senators in producing a state of war with Macedonia when Philip had given no recent offence and Rome and the Roman populace were tired of war and had absolutely no problem with Macedonia. It would be necessary to devise some grounds for an ultimatum that could not become self-damagingly absurd or Roman opinion would revolt, but it would have to be severe enough that there was no chance of Philip accepting it. As Polybius described it, "Philip was to grant to Attalus, for injuries caused to him, reparations to be fixed by arbitrators; if he complied, he might consider himself at peace with Rome, but if he refused, the consequences would be the reverse."[3] Obviously, Philip could not possibly accept such a preposterous ultimatum. What their ultimatum in fact stated was "the Pergamene fleet, together with the Rhodian, had attacked the Macedonian fleet at Chios, therefore the successor of Alexander must humiliate himself for the parvenu King of Pergamon." In addition, the Romans took it upon themselves to forbid Philip from making war on any Greek state. This would redouble the outrage they were hurling in the face of the king of Macedonia, but it would make every Roman legionnaire a hero to the fundamentally ungrateful population of Greece. This was a complete reversal of Rome's recognition of Philip's sovereignty over much of Greece in 204, and now they were claiming, contrary to their treaty, virtually to destroy the authority that Philip exercised in Greece. It became an illusion that he was unable to uphold by force because of the Roman prohibition, and in addition the Romans implicitly declared to be unjustified all the wars that Philip or his predecessors had waged against the Greeks and all the results of the victories that they had won. They were seeking the destruction of everything that Macedonia had achieved in expanding its borders since Philip II. In demanding what Philip could not possibly concede, the Roman Senate drove Philip to extreme action and earned a great deal of popularity with the Greeks. In the spring of 200, Rome sent three legates to deliver its ultimatum to Philip and to ensure pro-Roman agitation increased and reinforced Attalus and the Rhodians in the fact of Roman support, and also, if possible, to get the temper of the Syrian and Egyptian courts. Rome wished to know more about Antiochus' intentions.

In March 200, Philip, by a cunning maneuver executed against a complacent blockading force, escaped with his fleet and returned to Macedonia with Attallus and the Rhodians in hot pursuit. The Athenians had foolishly put to death two Acarnanian agitators who had broken into the Eleusinian Mysteries in one of the temples. Acarnania asked Philip for troops to join with them in their planned invasion of Attica. Athens could not possibly resist Philip in support of a smaller state and appealed to all Greece and indeed to almost anyone except Rome for assistance. Rome's senatorial legates were already embarked on their mission. They were C.

---

3 Polybius, xvi, 1.

Claudius Nero, P. Sempronius Tuditanus, and M. Aemilius Lepidus, and they were making a virtual traveling salesmen's tour of Greece and had made their pitch at Epirus, Aetolia, Achaea, and a number of other places where they paid no attention at all to whatever alliances their hosts might have had with other states. After the rough handling that many Greeks had received from the Romans in recent memory, it is little wonder that the prospect of a Roman return in strength roused little local enthusiasm.

The notion of Rome as a Panhellenic defender aroused considerable incredulity among the Greeks. At Piraeus they were joined by Attalus, and the climate was much more favorable there to an alliance with Rome against Macedonia than it had been in the early stages of the legates' visit. Hearing the persuasive arguments of Attalus and then the visiting Rhodians, seconding what the Roman legates had to say, quickly brought the Athenian assembly around and it happily declared war on Philip. Rome hastily built its goodwill with the Athenians by telling Nicanor, the commander of the Macedonian auxiliaries who had thrown their weight around in Acarnania, that he should desist from his pillaging of the suburbs of Athens or face the wrath of Rome. He retreated and Rome's power was warmly appreciated by the Athenians for the first time. Unfortunately for Rome, Athens at this time was penniless and did not have the means of raising money that Rome herself had, so her support was essentially a moral boost and a matter of prestige. The Roman envoys had an excellent visit to Rhodes while Philip, unable to dispute the open seas with Rome, moved to strengthen his overland communications in Thrace and the Hellespont, and the eastern shore of the Dardanelles. Attalus and the Rhodians responded at first rather lethargically.

By this time, the Romans had become annoyed, as opposed to just tactically imperious, at the failure of Philip to respond to their ultimatum. The consul Sulpicius presented an act of war alleging that Philip had attacked the enemies of the Roman people, which of course was false, since Attalus, who was not officially an ally at all, had initiated the hostilities with Philip. It took a couple of months of argument before Sulpicius received his war vote. Lepidus, the youngest of the legates, was entrusted with the task of communicating the declaration of war to Philip. To ensure that the Macedonian king had no possible honorable method of retreat from the war foisted upon him, he was further forbidden to occupy any Egyptian dependencies and was commanded to make reparations to both Attalus and to Rhodes. When Lepidus caught up with Philip and presented his escalated ultimatum, Philip pointed out that the Rhodians had attacked him, and Lepidus became unacceptably obnoxious to the king whose guest he was. Philip with cool aplomb excused him because of his "youth and inexperience, as well as being a very handsome young man and, above all, a Roman. If it please the Romans to violate the treaty between us we will defend ourselves with the help of the gods."[4]

As Lepidus departed, Philip was advised that Sulpicius had invaded Illyria with two legions, about twenty-five thousand men. Philip hurried back to Macedonia to deal with this new crisis, as the Roman legates continued on to the court of Antiochus and attempted to persuade him to declare his neutrality in the war that had just

---

4 Version of Polybius, CAH, VIII, p. 165 (M. Holleaux).

broken out between Macedonia and Rome. After their outrageous insolence to the king of Macedonia they demonstrated extreme deference to the so-called King of Asia. This meeting occurred shortly after the redoubtable Scopas had pushed Antiochus back from Gaza, but at the Battle of Panion Antiochus had avenged Raphia, and driven Scopas with ten-thousand men inside the walls of Sidon, which Antiochus was besieging by land and sea as his Roman visitors arrived. While claiming to be offering mediation, the Roman legates were in fact attempting to encourage continued war between Antiochus and Egypt to distract the Syrian king. The legates assured Antiochus of the Senate's goodwill and Antiochus was extravagant in his expressions of friendship and respect for Rome and proposed an immediate exchange of ambassadors.

If Rome was happy to have Antiochus enmeshed in war with Egypt, it feared the Seleucid king coming to the assistance of the king of Macedonia, his nominal associate in the territorial division of the Near East. And the Romans' pleasure at Antiochus' state of war with Egypt was considerably exceeded by the delight Antiochus felt that his ostensible partner, but in fact principal rival, would now have the pleasure of trying to repel the attacks of the greatest power in the world. The Roman Senate continued to worry about the possibility of simultaneous war with Antiochus and Philip, and Antiochus undoubtedly enjoyed keeping Rome in a state of uncertainty even though the last thing on earth that he wished was a direct conflict with Rome. The legates stopped in Alexandria to advise the Egyptians that their attempted mediation failed because of the obstinacy of the Seleucid king. They returned to Rome leaving the outmatched Egyptians on their own to deal with a powerful invader who was himself delighted at the prospect of Rome putting the king of Macedonia in his place. This was a mission that Rome had undertaken on dubious pretexts in order to assure that they did not have to face the combined aggression of Philip and Antiochus; it was a military and diplomatic minuet with an ever-shrinking number of participants.

Carthage after Zama was in a sorry condition. The city and its walls and self-government were retained, but it had no possessions such as Sicily, Sardinia and Corsica, nor its Spanish wealth, and was being constantly harassed by Massinissa, Rome's protégé whom Rome encouraged to keep Carthage on its toes. Its navy was shattered, and Carthage was reduced to being an obsequious ally of Rome. The difficulties of Carthage's fallen condition were aggravated by the shortsightedness and avarice of its rulers. The greatest immediate problem was paying Rome the indemnity that it required, and instead of facing up to this task, the city's oligarchic rulers attempted to inflict the chief burden upon the penurious lower classes of Carthage while sparing themselves. They imposed such heavy taxes on the poor that the installments on the indemnity paid to Rome were rejected by the Roman quaestors as being composed of diluted and inferior silver. After several years of these odious exactions, which were further tainted by extensive official embezzlement, the population became rebellious and demanded the return to high office of the one trusted person in the beleaguered country, Hannibal. Under the pressure of public discontent and fiscal embarrassment, Hannibal was invited to take office as Sufete, or Prime Minister in 196. Like great generals in other countries who assumed great office at least somewhat by popular demand, from Caesar to Washington and Napoleon and de Gaulle, Hannibal had little respect for the politicians or the oligarchy, especially when they were essentially the same people.

Hannibal prepared his political campaign with the same insight and meticulousness that he had prepared his military campaigns. He was determined to ensure that Rome had no complaint with Carthage. The financial officials were dragging their heels and Hannibal summoned one of them who rejected his instructions, being confident that he would be in the Court of One-Hundred and Four (judges) that was the supreme governing and judicial body of Carthage the next year. Hannibal had him arrested and when he received substantial support in the Court of One Hundred and Four, Hannibal defended his position with such vigor that the matter was referred, as the Constitution required, to a popular assembly, where Hannibal put his views with great eloquence and was heavily sustained. Hannibal then conducted such a thorough investigation into the financial arrangements of the repayment of the indemnity that he was able to announce after purging many officials and seizing a good deal of treasure improperly siphoned out of the public accounts, that by the imposition of honest government the special tax upon the lower income groups was abolished. This naturally brought him great additional popularity. He translated this popular acclaim into support for annual elections of the Court of One-Hundred and Four, a radical reform that was immensely popular but forfeited permanently for Hannibal the goodwill of the city's most influential people.

Carthage and its commerce now recovered quickly, but his opponents agitated and finally repaired to the only place that could challenge Hannibal's influence and popularity: Rome itself. Here the influence of Scipio Africanus and his friends, in the highest traditions of chivalry between great military commanders, resisted Roman suppression or harassment of Hannibal or any cooperation with his domestic enemies. But after over a year of this pressure in Rome, legates were finally sent by a combination of factions in the Senate to look into affairs in Carthage; they were advised by Hannibal's enemies not publicly to acknowledge that they were investigating the great general but rather to state that they were looking into the alleged aggressions of their protégé Massinissa, and they did that. Hannibal recognized that he was ultimately going to be overthrown in Carthage by the oligarchs propped up by the now irresistible Romans and was convinced that the Romans would demand he be given to Rome. Ever the master of stealthy tactics, he put on a considerable masquerade of normalcy in early 195, but after a few preparations, he stole away one evening. In twenty-four hours, using a relay of horses, he fled one-hundred and fifty miles east where a ship was awaiting him and conveyed him to Tyre and to Antioch. There evidently was some truth to the allegations that he had been consorting with the Syrian king and the moment his flight from Carthage was known, the Roman legates, Gnaeus Servilius, M. Claudius Marcellus, and Quintus Terentius Culleo, set out their accusations against Hannibal conniving with Antiochus. There was a parallel in the expedient but principled departure of Hannibal from Carthage, the city which he loved and served with greater distinction than anyone in its history but where he was severely undermined and betrayed, and the retirement of Scipio to Liternum, where he audibly denounced the ingratitude and corruption of the

Roman Patriciate and Senate. We have seen in Greece also the tendency to trivialize or cut down those who have rendered the greatest and most popular service, from Themistocles to Pericles and beyond.

2. War With Macedonia

Sulpicius and his lieutenant, Apustius, arrived at the Macedonian border before the defenders were ready for them and destroyed several towns, and a squadron dispatched to Piraeus to protect Athens surprised and did heavy damage to one of Philip's forts nearby. Philip went hurriedly there with reinforcements but the Romans having moved on, he launched two fierce but unsuccessful attacks on Athens and then ravaged the countryside of Attica for the fifth time in less than a year. He destroyed everything, even smashing stones so they could not contribute to reconstruction. Greek hatred of the Macedonians attained a summit that would have made Demosthenes seem like a groveling appeaser. Philip called upon Achaea and his other nominal allies for solidarity, but they were all terrified at the prospect of war with Rome and sat on their hands. Showing the current of events, a number of the barbaric neighbours offered to assist the Romans, but Rome's initial judgment was that since its proclaimed mission was the protection of Greek civilization, such a coalition would be implausible. However, the rest of the Greek states were waiting to see how the struggle went before they committed themselves.

Sulpicius now reversed course, irritated by the opportunistic neutrality of the other Greeks apart from Athens, and concerted a pincers strategy with the Dardanian leader Bato, and the outright barbarians Pleuratus and Amynander. These would attack Macedonia from the north and south while Sulpicius invaded from the west, and the Roman, Pergemene, and Rhodian fleets, approximately one-hundred vessels combined, would concentrate at Cassandreia and Chalcidice and eliminate those Macedonian strongholds. Philip had an army of only about twenty-thousand and two-thousand cavalry but all of them were battle-hardened loyalist Macedonians and close allies, and he awaited his enemies in the center of his country, able to respond in any direction. Sulpicius entered his territory first and Philip inflicted a minor defeat on him at Ottolobus, near the center of his kingdom on the Erigon. Philip then conducted a skillful quasi-Fabian defense harassing and nipping at the Romans but never offering a pitched battle. Sulpicius, after great effort, managed to force his way through the pass at Banitza and into lower Macedonia but as winter was approaching, he found it difficult to feed his army, was concerned about being cut off from his base and contented himself with ransacking a couple of regions on his way out of Macedonia to Illyria. After five months he had returned to his starting position.

The Roman withdrawal saved Philip as he had had to recall troops from the North which permitted the Dardanians to enter his territory unmolested. And after Ottolobus, the Aetolians suddenly attacked Thessaly, making serious inroads. But with the Romans away and in winter quarters in Illyria, Philip quickly chased out these invaders. The Roman-led coalition was more successful by sea; the Macedonian fleet declined to give battle and the coalition seized a number of coastal towns though they were decisively defeated in their attempt to invest Cassandreia. Philip realized that to maintain his prestige and his position he would have to change his turtle-like campaign from the middle of Macedonia and move forward to defend his frontiers against the Romans he correctly calculated would return in the spring and unite with the Aetolians to launch a joint attack upon him.

Sulpicius, a grave Roman soldier of the old school who had not endeared himself to the Greeks in previous campaigns there, retired and was replaced in 198 by the twenty-nine-year-old T. Quinctius Flamininus, a fervent Hellenophile with extravagant dreams of establishing a popular protectorate over a grateful Greece on behalf of an enhanced and admired Rome. It is illustrative of the mystique and eminence of Greek civilization that the most learned and ambitious of young Roman politicians would seek as the highest attainable honor assuming the protection and attending to the needs of Greece. Other formerly preeminent peoples pass more-or-less without notice under the yoke of those who succeed them, but the permeation of surrounding peoples with the strength of Greek culture made Greece for a long time the supreme prize coveted by neighboring powers. It is little wonder that Twentieth Century British classically educated leaders, in particular Harold Macmillan, imagined that there was some comparison to be made between the relations of Greece and Rome and those of Britain and the United States. The parallel was stretched and Rome's infatuation with Greece did not endure indefinitely but even after Greece had reverted to being squares on the chessboard between greater powers, it maintained a great magnetic intellectual and spiritual attraction for its neighbors.

The new consul was well suited to his role, a suave diplomat exquisitely learned in Greek and Greek culture and perfectly capable of flattering the considerable vanity of his hosts. It was never clear how sincerely dedicated a philhellene he really was, but he certainly acted the part well. There were large anti-Macedonian factions throughout Greece, and he quickly rallied them to the cause which he represented as nothing less than Roman expulsion of Macedonia from all of Greece and the reestablishment of the Hellenic areas as a peaceful and prosperous protectorate of its great and admiring Roman friend. The worldly Greeks, though deeply flattered and profoundly pleased, generally knew better than to invest unlimited confidence in cultural idealism and fair play as the entire motivation of such an extensive Roman military enterprise. Flamininus had brought eight-thousand fresh troops with him and the authorities of Epirus arranged a meeting between the new consul, shortly after his arrival, and the Macedonian king on the banks of the Aous. Flamininus required Philip's abandonment of all of his Greek possessions, including those that he inherited, but beyond that professed no designs on Macedonia. He was addressing himself as much to the Greeks as to Philip, assuming his target audience would vastly prefer Roman occupation to Macedonian; so haughty a people as the ancient Greeks tends to be unequivocally disdainful of all foreigners. Despite the fripperies and posturing, what was afoot was a straight contest of force as the rising power of Rome cast its gaze inevitably to the east.

Philip indignantly terminated the discussions with Flamininus, who quickly managed to take Philip's frontier defenses from the rear and forced his retirement into Thessaly with the loss of two-thousand Macedonian soldiers and a large train of supplies. Flamininus invaded Thessaly from the north, while the Aetolians struck from the south and Amynander invaded from the west. There was a general melee in much of Thessaly all summer, but most of the Macedonian strong points held and in October Flamininus repaired towards the Corinthian Gulf to remain in contact with his sources of resupply. The Allied fleets arrived almost simultaneously. Flamininus now put practically irresistible pressure on Achaea, offering to recover Corinth for the Achaeans in exchange for their participation in the war against Macedonia. The Achaeans had to choose between Rome as an ally or as an enemy. The Romans were ardently supported by Athens but only after three days of stormy debate did the Council of Demiurges by a narrow margin accept Roman terms. The allies then attacked Corinth on the supposition that the inhabitants would be happy enough to be rid of the Macedonians. Instead, they fought side-by-side with their occupiers and forced the retreat of the besiegers. Philip not only kept Corinth but added Argos which seceded from Achaea at the height of the battle for Corinth.

Though Philip had survived in Corinth, he had retreated in Thessaly and much of it was lost, and most of Euboea, Locris, and Phocis had been taken in other actions by Flamininus. The Hellenic League was cracking up under Roman pressure and Philip was short of supplies and of men, despite calling in many distant garrisons to strengthen the defense of the Macedonian homeland. In a pattern that was becoming familiar, Roman power was overwhelming and Philip requested a peace conference under no illusions about the severity of the terms that he was likely to receive. It met in November at Nicaea in Locris. Rome demanded all of Illyria, restoration of the three Syrian towns taken from Ptolemy, and as in the initial demand, the evacuation of the Greeks. In addition, Rome's allies had to be reckoned with: Attalus demanded reparations; Rhodes demanded the abandonment of all Philip's conquests in Asia and in the Hellespont; the Achaeans demanded Corinth and Argos; and the Aetolians the cities wrested from their league. Philip was prepared to concede everything except the last of his Hellenic territories and in particular the fortress towns of Demetrias, Chalcis, and Acrocorinth. Flamininus, despite his youth and Hellenophilia, was an agile and unscrupulous negotiator, and represented himself to Philip as well disposed and struggling with the extreme demands of the Senate. But the Senate promoted him to proconsul and rejected Philip's terms and the conference broke up without an agreement.

Philip now was plunged into a desperate and practically hopeless last stand. To appease the treacherous Nabis of Sparta, he handed Argos to him in exchange for an alliance and was then betrayed by Nabis, who switched sides to the Romans after taking over Argos and contributed six-hundred mercenaries from Crete to the Roman army. Flamininus had now raised the entire Peloponnese against Philip, and then broke up the alliance between Philip and Boeotia, by massively intimidating that state, slipping two-thousand mercenaries into Thebes behind him, when he went to confer with the Boeotian leaders there, and they threatened to pillage the city. Flamininus in two years had almost completely separated Macedonia from Greece. It was an admirably and ingeniously executed and very thorough dismemberment of Philip's position. In what was for Rome a sideshow, one of the greatest figures of the east, a peer of Antiochus, had been sliced down to a pitiful and precarious position; with just a few local alliances and a not overly imposing number of mercenaries, Rome had effectively made itself master of Greece. It was an artful exercise of the techniques available to a Great Power and was well noted throughout the parts of the known world that Rome did not already control.

Naturally, Antiochus watched with undoubted pleasure the relatively effortless Roman reduction of his rival, the Macedonian king, to a state of desperation, but he could not be complacent about what the Romans might choose to do next. While Philip was being put soundly in his place, Antiochus invaded the Asian territories of Egypt. After defeating Scopas at Panion, Antiochus starved him into surrendering at Sidon in 199, but the resourceful and imperishable Scopas raised another sixty-five hundred mercenaries in Aetolia and deployed them in the Sinai for the defense of the Egyptian homeland. Antiochus rightly judged that he could strengthen himself more quickly and efficiently opposite the Romans by trying to repossess the former Seleucid possessions in Asia Minor and Thrace, which had been stolen by Ptolemy or Philip. He sent placatory messages to Rome (which was not now in the habit of taking such overtures very seriously), and in the spring of 197 his sons Antiochus and Seleucus and the generals Ardys and Mithridates advanced along the Cilician coast while Antiochus himself commanded a total of three-hundred vessels moving offshore parallel to his army. He was in the midst of besieging Coracesium by land and sea when a Rhodian embassy, incited by Flamininus, arrived.

The Romans and their allies were concerned, though it is not obvious why, that Antiochus was coming to assist the stricken and threadbare Philip. The Rhodians, who could deploy the Allied fleets of Rome and Pergamon, as they had been functioning quite successfully as a unit, gently demanded that Antiochus' expansion in the Eastern Mediterranean go no further, and they also sought some assurance that their interests in the nominally Egyptian parts of Asia Minor that Antiochus was about to devour be respected. It was at this point that the news of Philip's complete defeat arrived and on the Seleucid king's assurance that Rhodes had nothing to fear and that he would abide by the innumerable limitations requested, an agreement to share the spoils of the defeated powers, Egypt and Macedonia, was amicably agreed.

Philip made a final stand with recruits drafted from the age of sixteen and every available able-bodied man, totaling about twenty-six thousand, near Cynoscaphalae. A prolonged, close-run dual battle occurred: the Roman commander, narrowly defeated in the first part of the engagement raced through open country several miles, took personal command of the second half of his army led by a number of elephants, and it crashed into the rear of Philip's apparently victorious army and completely smashed it. As M. Holleaux, implying a reference familiar to his countrymen, wrote, "Cynoscephalae was the Jena of Macedon."[5] (The Prussian king in 1806, Frederick William III, drew with Napoleon's able Marshal Louis Nicolas Davout at Auerstadt and was then defeated by Napoleon at Jena.) The Prussian king was in less extreme straits than Philip, who rallied those he could, after losing thirteen-thousand men, and retired into the bowels of Macedonia, beset on all sides. The Corinthians were defeated by the Achaeans, the Romans violently assaulted and overwhelmed the Acarnanians, and the Dardanians struck Philip overland in the back, in the accus-

---

5   CAH, VIII, p. 175 (M. Holleaux).

tomed manner of the Balkans, one of the fiercest theatres of war in the world, into current times, but the tenacious Macedonian king defeated them at Stobi.

At this point, the esteemed Flamininus was happy to receive Philip's latest and most fervent peace overtures. He was concerned that Antiochus could form an extremely advantageous alliance with Philip and quickly rally the Macedonian remnants and drag Rome into a much more prolonged and complicated war than Flamininus had any mandate to provoke or conduct. He also wished to formalize his victory before the Roman consuls for the succeeding year were installed. Flamininus was also exasperated by the Aetolians, who seized more of the spoils of Macedonia than they had earned on the battlefields and were demanding that Rome continue the war at its own cost to the benefit of themselves. It was also time for Flamininus to dispense with the fiction that Rome and Greece were allies of equal strength; the Greeks remained divided and quarrelsome, and the Romans' objective was not the revival of Greek glory and autonomy but the imposition, gently or otherwise, of Roman overlordship over all Greece. All loyalties were ephemeral, and the correlation of forces had fluctuated to the point where the Roman proconsul could achieve more by recognizing and cooperating with a chastened Philip and making an equitable demarcation of spheres of influence with Antiochus than by indulging the unrealistic ambitions of the Greek states. With the approval of the Senate, he made peace with Philip on acceptance of his original conditions: that Philip abandon everything outside of Macedonia itself. Philip had no choice but to accept; he would live to fight another day. In these circumstances, his mere survival was a considerable achievement.

Flamininus also judged that it was time to send all the Greeks a message by giving the greedy Aetolians a sharp slapping down and he denied them the fruit of the victories in Thessaly by asserting that Rome had conquered that territory and announced with Roman self-confidence with which the world was becoming familiar, that the alliance that they had formed had in fact implicitly dissolved nine years earlier. Flamininus in a considerable feat of improvisation, advised the Greeks that Rome would resuscitate Macedonia to serve as a buffer state between Greece and the barbarians. According to Polybius,[6] this argument, which was scarcely plausible to begin with, suffered reduced credibility when it was taken up by the principal barbarian neighbors themselves, the Illyrian's, Thracians, and Dardanians. This turn of events was a shock to Rome's local allies, also including the son of Attalus, and a new Pergamene King, Eumenes, who on hearing of these events, succumbed to an apoplectic stroke at Thebes in February 197 and died. Philip said that in completing the details of what was emerging as a more generous peace than he had feared, he would submit his case to the determination of the Roman Senate and abide by its verdict. Flamininus granted him a four-month armistice with the handing over of a cash deposit and a number of hostages, including Philip's son Demetrius. The other parties, including the Aetolians, all then agreed to send representatives to Rome to plead their cases before the Senate and to accept its determination of the peace terms. It was a stunning accomplishment for Flamininus—he had arrived in Macedonia with a small force and with modest loss of Roman lives, he was now the mas-

---

6 Polybius, xviii, 37, 9.

ter of southeastern Europe with all of the contending parties obediently submitting to Rome's authority.

Antiochus took advantage of the final stage of Philip's humiliation by repossessing the former positions of the Great King in Asia Minor and Thrace. He busily reasserted himself over the Egyptian, Pergamene, Macedonian, and Greek cities in Asia Minor. Antiochus continued to placate the Rhodians and ceded to them Halicarnassus, Samos, and a number of other strategic locations, and he also treated the Pergamenes and the autonomous towns of Asia Minor respectfully. The only two substantial towns that resisted Antiochus were Smyrna and Lampsacus, and having nowhere else to turn, they made entreaties to Rome. The Lampsacans even purported to have discovered an ancient blood relationship with Rome, and also with the Massiliotes (Marseillais), Rome's model subordinate allies. They sent representatives to Massilia to request sponsorship for them in Rome. Rome had been invited to defend the European Greeks against the Macedonians and were now invited to defend the Anatolian Greeks against the Seleucids. It was an historic moment: Rome had arrived at last at the gates of Asia. There were only two great powers in the known world; one was a carefully and lengthily developed system with a homogeneous core, and the other was a talented royal parvenu set atop a pile of ethnic fragments. It was an uneven match.

By 197 B.C., the desire of Flamininus to end the Macedonian War was shared by all of the Roman policymakers. They had won a decisive victory at little cost, effectively eliminated Philip, and had even Antiochus III joining the threatened city states of Asia Minor in petitioning Rome for its approval. But there was a full-scale revolt in progress in Spain as well as a good deal of commotion in Cisalpine Gaul, and these were areas of much more central strategic interest to Rome than Greece was. The Macedonian peace was approved by an overwhelming popular vote, and the Romans then added some clauses for their own pleasure without consulting the Greeks and nominated ten commissioners who along with Flamininus (their chairman), had a mandate to "settle Hellenic affairs."[7] Flamininus' command had again been prolonged, to the consternation of Claudius Marcellus, who aspired to succeed him while a war that had already been won was not yet ended, so he could add some easy victories to his own column.

The Romans were not distracted by the torrent of messages of goodwill that they received from Antiochus or those who would resist him in Asia Minor. They had enjoyed an astounding success, protecting the interests of the Greeks against the king of Macedonia and it was now appropriate for them to take the interests of the Egyptian king and the remaining city states of Asia Minor against Antiochus. In the interests of containing this latest Middle Eastern hegemon, Rome interpreted its Philhellenic interest as including the partially Greek autonomous city states of Smyrna and Lampsacus, which had appealed to Rome and furnished a convenient way to begin the process of picking a fight with Antiochus and trimming him down to size as they had Philip. And although they had neglected Ptolemy V for several years, they suddenly resumed the mediation activities he had asked them to take opposite Antiochus and sent the legate L. Cornelius Lentulus to relaunch the mediation and

---

7   CAH, VIII, p. 180 (M. Holleaux).

lobby Antiochus on behalf of the Egyptians. The envoys sent by Smyrna and Lampsacus were received in Rome with great popular enthusiasm and official deference.

Polybius gives this summary of the decree Rome issued to conclude the peace dictated to Philip: "All Greeks in Europe and Asia were to be free and governed by their own laws. All Greeks subject to Philip were to be handed over to Rome. Philip was to withdraw garrisons from all Greek places, and Philip was to surrender to Rome all his navy except five ships and to pay a heavy fine to Rome, half at once and the rest in ten annual instalments." It was the final signification of an utterly crushing defeat, but in sparing Philip any constraint on his army, the Roman leaders in the Senate, on the advice of Flamininus, were leaving him with the ability to join the imminent assault on Antiochus, and in the process, the ability to build up his empire again though not at the expense of the Greeks, and to assist Rome in creating a correlation of forces between comparable but not overly strong local powers that would balance each other off without threatening Rome itself. In establishing itself as Protector of the Hellenes, Rome included Asia Minor, awarding itself a license to evict Antiochus from much of Asia Minor, and had already recruited and incentivized the well-chastened Philip of Macedon to do a good deal of the heavy lifting that would be involved. With the brief and limited exception of Persia, Rome was the first government in the history of the West to have the mentality and the strategic confidence and sense of self-protection of a Great Power. Rome's performance of this role would run for over six-hundred years and in its posterity, it would have many emulators.

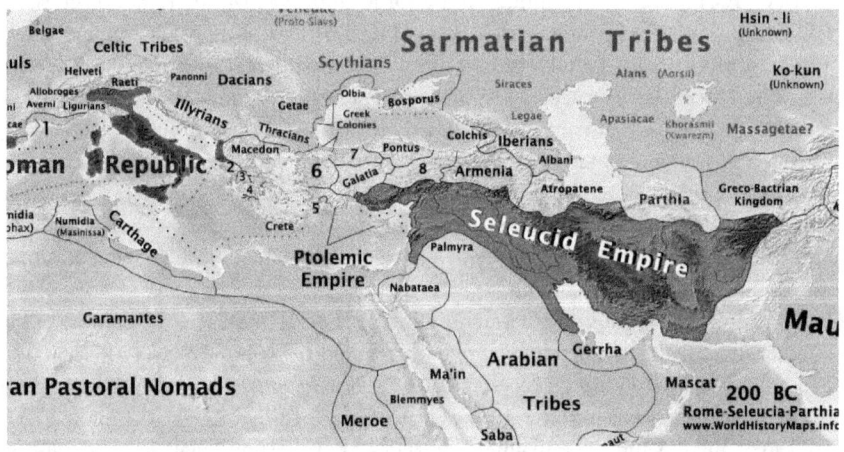

Rough borders in the Mediterranean and Western Asia in 200 BC

3. Rome and Antiochus

Rome did not have long to enjoy its role as champion of the Greeks, because the same fractiousness that had afflicted the entire history of the Greek city states swiftly returned in rank ingratitude and even some rediscovered affection for the former Macedonian tormentors. Flamininus agreed to the return to Boeotia of volunteers who had served in the Macedonian army led by Brachyllas. It was meant to be a conciliatory gesture by Rome, but on the return of Brachyllas and his men, it was immediately clear that the hearts of the Boeotians were with those who served Philip and not with their ostensible Roman protectors. The Roman faction in Boeotia, with the approval of Flamininus, arranged the assassination of Brachyllas but instead of silencing the Boeotian masses, in the unchanging and inimitable Greek custom, it stirred them to mass rage and the visibly pro-Roman faction of Boeotians fled for their lives, apart from those who could not move quickly enough and were seized, and over five-hundred were executed. Flamininus was only dissuaded from invading Boeotia and dealing with it with the proverbial severe efficiency that only Roman armies when invited by their commanders to sack, rape, and enslave at their pleasure, could display. Only the desperate intervention of the Athenians and Achaeans persuaded the Roman leader to overlook the Boeotian impudences.

When the commissioners released their decree, there was much discontent throughout Greece that a Macedonian conqueror had simply been replaced by a Roman one. Though irritated and disappointed, Flamininus did his best to salvage the public relations front at the Isthmian Festival in June and July 196. The herald opening the games proclaimed: "The Roman Senate and the consul Titus Quinctius Flamininus, having overcome King Philip and the Macedonians, leave free without garrisons or tribute and governed by their ancestral laws the Corinthians, Phocians, Locrians, Euboeans, Achaeans, Magnesians, Thessalians, and Perrhaebians." This assertion was greeted with hysterical jubilation and Flamininus was almost crushed by masses of newly converted and reassured Greek admirers.

Flamininus resorted to the well-tried formula of evicting everyone else from Greece, assuring the Greeks their rights, but not renouncing Rome's ultimate authority, the price to the Greeks of relying on a foreign power, no matter how well disposed, to assure their rights. In such circumstances, the Greeks were free, but not entirely independent. Flamininus and his commissioners delivered some Greeks who had been hostile to Rome into the hands of other Greeks who had been favorable to Rome; they "settled Hellenic affairs" and determined who would govern. In all of the circumstances, Greece was well treated indeed, but they were having a problem that continued for two-thousand years of reconciling their objective weakness in numbers, coordination and resources with Greece's national self-perception of superiority and greatness. It was a human shortcoming: they were in many ways superior, and they were undoubtedly great, but they had never succeeded in turning their city states or leagues of states into a Greek national state capable of resisting a more powerful neighbor. They managed it, through prodigious and legendary courage and ingenuity against the Persians, who were not tactically skillful invaders and from another continent, and Macedonia was the first neighbor to overrun them and the Romans the second; many would follow. Greek history has often been magnificent and often tragic but it is the glory and the tragedy of the small people and such a justly self-regarding nationality does not accustom itself easily to subordination, even to a very powerful government at the head of an immense state bringing with it a distinguished culture. Such was the correlation of roles between Greece and Rome in the Second Century B.C.

In 196, Antiochus crossed the Hellespont and took over the whole Chersonese and Lysimacheia. The latter had been completely destroyed by the Thracians and Antiochus undertook to rebuild it and sought the return of the scattered population. He fought off barbarians and sent messages of reassurance and friendly intent to the Romans, but they were not believed. Antiochus wanted no part of war with Rome and he was only regaining the last of the lost areas of the Seleucid Empire at its height. But that did not satisfy Rome, whose leaders felt they knew expansionist rivals when they saw them approach. The Great King as he was now styled, sent a strong delegation to the Isthmian games, led by the distinguished historian and poet ,. They bore very respectful greetings to Flamininus and his commissioners but were frostily received. The Roman position was repeated that the autonomous cities of Asia were inviolable, and Antiochus was asked to vacate the towns that had been held by Ptolemy and Philip, and to remove himself from Europe. The Romans also proposed to send a delegation of the commissioners to meet with Antiochus. Ever fearful that Antiochus would entice Philip into alliance, the Romans pressured Philip for an alliance with them. Having barely survived as the king of anything, Philip accepted the Roman offer and determined to try to rebuild his position as a Roman ally. In any case, he was at this point more annoyed at Antiochus's seizure of Philip 's Asiatic possessions than he was at the Romans. The commissioner Gnaeus Cornelius negotiated the treaty with Philip and then undertook the even more challenging task of trying to restrain the Aetolians from breaking with Rome and prevailed upon them to refer their claims to the Roman Senate where, he promised, they would receive "full justice."

In October of 196, L. Cornelius Lentulus, who had been named by Rome as mediator between Antiochus and Ptolemy went to Thrace where three of the commissioners joined him and the party proceeded to Lysimacheia for extensive discussions with Antiochus himself. After a courteous beginning the discussions quickly became difficult. Lentulus agued that it would be "ridiculous"[8] if the fruit of the Roman defeat of Philip were to be appropriated by Antiochus. He stressed the concern the Roman Senate felt at the presence in Europe of an Asiatic monarch with such extensive military and naval forces and asked how Antiochus could imagine that Rome did not feel threatened. Antiochus replied forcefully that the Roman claims of solicitude for Asiatic towns were bizarre and, in effect, that nothing that happened in Asia was any business of Rome's. He rhetorically asked his Roman guests if they thought he, Antiochus, was attempting to meddle in the affairs of Italy. And he emphasized that he had only crossed into Europe to recover the Chersonese and the coastal towns of Thrace as the rightful heritage of Seleucid Nicator. In the most astute element of his reply, he assured the Romans that they need not alter and scruple about his relations with Ptolemy, as those relations were being settled amicably and he had arranged with the de facto regent, the Acarnanian Aristomenes not only on peace terms that surrendered Egypt's Syrian, Asiatic, and Thracian dependencies to Antiochus, but it was also agreed that Ptolemy V would marry Antiochus' daughter Cleopatra. With these revelations, the Romans looked somewhat foolish pledging to

---

8 Ibid., p. 186.

protect Antiochus' allies and about-to-be in-laws from the Seleucid leader. Antiochus would accept Rhodian, but not Roman, mediation.

Lentulus retreated and went back to the issue of autonomous cities, bringing in the representatives of Lampsacus and Smyrna who spoke strongly in favor of their Roman association. Rumors that proved to be false of the death of Ptolemy caused the conference to end as Antiochus hurried to Alexandria hoping that he might take that crown for himself, but he learned en route that the rumour was false, the product of an abortive insurrection by Scopas and the Aetolians. It was at this point that Scopas' energetic career as a scoundrel and political double-dealer came to an abrupt end under the axe of Ptolemy's headsman, Aristomenes, as he had Scopas' severed head placed on a pike in a large public square, and determined that Ptolemy had come of age, although he was only thirteen or fourteen. Aristomenes and his allies also managed to suppress the revolt that was in progress on the lower Nile and several other towns in Egypt. Again, after the brilliant triumph of Flamininus in Greece, the Romans appeared awkward and inept at raising the so-called Egyptian question with Antiochus, after Antochus had resolved such questions. The Great King's pledge of no more that he aspired to in Europe was entirely believable, as the small part of Thrace that he had taken over had indeed belonged to Seleucid at the height of its power, and in these circumstances, whatever his misgivings, the possibilities of Philip sloughing off the Roman alliance and joining against Rome were practically zero. In the early summer of 195, Antiochus returned to Thrace, sent greetings to Flamininus, and proposed negotiations of a treaty between the two powers. But Rome was so offended at what it took to be his rebuff of Rome's imperious notions of its own interests in Asia Minor and Egypt that the Romans did not answer; the commissioners then departed and Flamininus said that any such discussions would have to be conducted by the dispatch of adequately empowered representatives by Antiochus to Rome itself.

Flamininus settled on a consolation program of chastising Nabis, the treacherous King of Sparta. The Romans had informally allied themselves with Nabis when he was useful, but now that Philip had been put in his place, Nabis was a lingering irritant. He was aspersed as the "Tyrant," as Sparta continued to be almost a communist dictatorship with an eighty to ninety percent slave population. It was a pariah among the Greek cities, and furnished Rome a convenient method to complete their sojourn in Greece victoriously. Nabis' piracy, in association with Crete, had terrorized all Greek shipping, and Nabis occasionally attacked even Roman merchant vessels. Flamininus was given a full mandate from Rome to deal with Nabis and he summoned all the Greek states to send representatives to meet with him at Corinth in May 195. He put the Nabis issue in a way bound to appeal to his guests by asking if Argos, which Nabis had occupied, should be liberated. Apart from the always grumpy Aetolians, all the Greek states voted to support the liberation of Argos. It was agreed to send a combined Greco-Roman mission to liberate Argos, but it was left in the air what would be done with Nabis. Most of the Greeks wanted to destroy him and the Achaeans wanted to take over Sparta, but Flamininus was wary of upsetting the internal balance of power within Greece and was more interested in slapping Nabis down than firing the starting gun in another intra-Hellenic battle for control of Sparta.

All Greece except the Aetolians, as well as Philip, contributed forces to accompany the Romans to subdue Nabis and evict Sparta from Argos. The armies, under Aristaenus, were repulsed from the walls of Argos and the anticipated revolt within did not materialize. Sparta itself could not be assaulted and the armies contented themselves with the destruction of the countryside of Laconia. Most of the combat was conducted at sea. Flamininus prevailed in asserting more moderate conditions than his Greek allies and was entrusted to negotiate peace himself after Nabis had been bottled up behind walls, having got the worst of it, by land and by sea. Nabis rejected the terms as excessively harsh and was supported by the unruly but ferocious mob of his followers. Flamininus was determined not to impose a lengthy siege and instead brought his sailors ashore and added them to the armies, bringing the total number of warriors up to fifty-thousand, and hurled them up the walls of Sparta. The city would have fallen if Nabis' brother-in-law and stepbrother, the Argive noble Pythagoras (unrelated to the Sixth Century B.C. mathematician), had not lit strategically located fires which finally repelled the assailants. But Nabis had reached the last extremity and another assault would destroy him, so he sued for peace and promised the Romans good and unexceptionable conduct. Argos had finally expelled Nabis' garrison from Lacedomonia, and Nabis surrendered it, along with Argolis, to Flamininus. Nabis also gave up his pirate stations in Crete, the Laconian coastal towns, almost his entire navy, and his right to rebuild his navy or army. He would pay five-hundred talents and hand over a number of hostages including his son Armenas. Flamininus came to Argos in September and replicated the festivities at Corinth, with the herald again proclaiming Rome the liberator of Argos. The Roman Senate ratified this peace in 194; Nabis had been completely humiliated and neutered, but his tyranny remained intact, those he had exiled could not return, and he just festered, in the now antiquarian serf-state of Sparta, tolerated by the Romans.

It was as the Spartan war was ending that beleaguered Carthage was heard from again. Hannibal's austere and absolutely honest financial administration had strengthened the government of Carthage but alienated many of his fellow citizens, who denounced him to Rome and incited the suspicion that was not difficult to inflame, that Hannibal was plotting with Antiochus. If there were any chance of a war with the Seleucid king, the last person in history the Romans would wish to face again on the battlefield was Hannibal, and it was Ephesus where Hannibal fetched up when he fled Carthage in the summer of 195, to await the return of Antiochus. The Romans were so uneasy at this prospect that they recalled Scipio Africanus to the consulate. But he advocated retention of Greece as a consular province. Flamininus, almost always an astute strategic judge of eastern affairs, warned the Senate that such a course would alienate the Greeks and make collaboration with Antiochus tempting to them, whereas conserving Greek liberties would make that group of states a much more redoubtable bulwark against any European ambitions that Antiochus might have.

Flamininus remained another winter in Greece, "settling" matters and then presided over a second Panhellenic conference at Corinth, which he concluded by announcing a complete withdrawal of Rome from Greece as had been promised. He became an immense hero in Greece and went from garrison to garrison withdrawing them and finally returned to Rome in late 194 bringing with him one-hundred and fourteen gold crowns given him by Greek cities and two-thousand Roman and Italian prisoners sold into slavery by Hannibal. He was a profoundly admired and even beloved and worshipped figure in Greece and returned to Rome a very successful proconsul aged just thirty-four years. He had had a brilliant tour in Greece, but given the fluidity of the situation and the temperament of the Greeks, it was not as durable as had been hoped.

The Romans had scarcely departed Greek shores when the status of Rome's relations with Greece began to become uncertain. Flamininus had made a serious error in so needlessly mistreating and even deceiving the Aetolians; they had been badly treated twice by Rome and had been denied any concessions at all in the great Roman victory, when and if the gesture had been made, it might have gone a considerable distance to quieting the anger of that indomitable and ferocious people. And while Greece's freedom had been restored and the Romans had departed, they took with them a great deal of treasure and they left behind an extent of devastation indicative of the Roman concept of almost total war, that the Greeks considered to be uncivilized. Indeed, the Greeks were incapable of regarding the Romans as other than barbarians, though they had to admit that they were relatively cultured and certainly very powerful and well-organized barbarians. But the stubborn and unshakable Greek ethos of superiority and a civilizing mission made it impossible for them not to resent Rome's power and even perversely, Rome's generosity. As Rome had not set up new frontiers with the restrictions on the diplomatic liberty of many states, including those in obligatory and somewhat restrictive alliances with Rome itself, almost all Greece was to some extent dependent upon Rome, a condition which naturally rankled with such a proud and fractious people.

Flamininus assumed some level of loyalty from the Greeks thereafter, if not from gratitude, at least from fear of what revenge provocations might produce. Most of the Greeks were neither loyal nor grateful; many resented not only the demarcations Rome had decreed among the Greek states, but most Greeks also implicitly considered that Rome should regard it as an honor to be of service to Greece. The peace that Rome imposed was all too reminiscent to them of the King's Peace imposed for a time by the Persians, though they were hardly comparable. The Persians never really roamed throughout Greece, never sorted out problems between the Greek cities, and did not remotely possess the gift for administration and political organization that Rome had developed, and Italy was across the Adriatic; the Persians were Orientals.

The one area where the Romans did have a significant level of reliable support was with most so-called Optimates, the wealthy and the governing class who disliked revolution and populism and all forms of despotism and who had powerfully assisted the Romans against Philip and incurred Roman gratitude. Flamininus was perhaps overly influenced by the "cross-grained temper of the Greek notable,"[9] which, though useful, also helped to antagonize the Greek masses, left miserable and destitute by the war Rome had conducted among them. To the Hellenic masses the

---

9 Ibid., p. 197.

Roman peace merely enabled their own oligarchic masters to persecute them more freely. To such angry and distracted people, it was not difficult to portray the great Syrian king as a genuine and semi-serious benefactor of the Eastern Mediterranean, and not a barbaric interloper from the primitive East. People, and whole peoples, tend to believe what they want to believe. This was a particularly powerful instinct among the headstrong Greeks, and in subscribing to it they would pile new disappointments upon themselves. Greece was not in itself strong enough to be either a major protagonist or to provide the balance of power between Rome and Antiochus; but it was, unfortunately, important and obstinate enough to be a powder keg.

4. The Contest between Rome and Antiochus in Greece

Some sort of showdown between Rome and Syria, as Antiochus' kingdom was officially known in Rome, was now practically inevitable. As Roman frontiers extended, they kept bumping into potentially resistant states, which because of their imperious notions of Rome's security, caused the Romans invariably to decide that the power of their new neighbours to resist Rome's wishes had to be preemptively reduced. This policy would be pursued until Rome's ultimate frontiers were along natural lines, rivers and mountains and deserts, beyond which were relatively primitive and often nomadic peoples. This policy was bound to lead to problems eventually, but it was generally successful for more than five-hundred years until the accumulation of barbarians on the frontiers was so great and so volatile, and the populations under the Roman umbrella had become so fractious and the whole imperial structure in varying degrees so decadent, it collapsed under pressure from within and outside. Even then, temporal Rome would continue from Constantinople for nearly a thousand years and spiritual Rome remains after two-thousand years. In the extent and longevity of its significance, by the early Second Century B.C., Rome had already attained a status that the Western world had never imagined to be possible. This, in its early days, was the comparative colossus into a rivalry with which Antiochus imprudently entered.

By mid-195 B.C., there were no formal relations between Rome and Antiochus, though the Great King had organized the rest of his relationships very methodically. He had reoccupied the former Seleucid territories in Thrace, had an alliance with King Ariarathes IV of Cappadocia, his son-in-law, and in 193 his daughter Cleopatra married Ptolemy V of Egypt, strengthening that alliance. He had nurtured excellent relations with the Eastern Greeks especially around Byzantium by defending them against the barbarians and had arranged a respectful peace with the Eastern Gauls in the Balkans, and if inspired military strategy had to be devised and executed, the greatest general in recorded history, along with Alexander the Great (and possibly Scipio Africanus) was at hand to serve him (Hannibal).

The point of initial dispute was the two cities in Asia Minor, Lampsacus and Smyrna, which declined to pledge allegiance to Antiochus, encouraged by Eumenes, who had rejected the Syrian king's customary tactic of conciliation by declining to marry one of Antiochus's numerous daughters. Antiochus made a direct overture in 193 to the Roman Senate and proposed a treaty of friendship, it being understood that his own sovereignty over Asia and Thrace would be part of the agreement. Antiochus had mistakenly concluded that Rome's inactivity in their relationship implied lethargy, but in fact Rome was preoccupied suppressing uprisings in Spain and Cisalpine Gaul. Rome was also not in a hurry to engage with Hannibal again, especially when he would be at the head of greater forces than he had commanded in Carthage. They proposed to the Syrian envoys a treaty based on Antiochus' renunciation either of Thrace or of the autonomous cities of Asia, though they must have realized that neither would be acceptable to Antiochus and nor at that time was there any reason why he should consider them acceptable. Flamininus had established his position as Rome's authority on the Hellenic area as chairman of the itinerant senatorial commission and he made it clear both to the Syrian diplomats and the representatives of the autonomous cities themselves that Rome would no longer profess to be actually protecting them if the Great King agreed to withdraw from Thrace. The Romans sent envoys back to Antiochus via Pergamon, where Eumenes agitated against any accommodation of the Syrian king, who was distracted by other matters including the premature death of his eldest son, and the negotiations dragged on inconclusively. They ended very unsatisfactorily when, as previously at Lysimacheia, Rome produced representatives of the autonomous cities who spoke insolently to Antiochus who had received them graciously at Ephesus. The diplomatic minuet had ended, and the two Great Powers of the Eastern Mediterranean were on the brink of hostilities.

Antiochus was urged by his advisors, including Hannibal, to go to war. Hannibal claimed that with ten-thousand infantryman and a thousand cavalry and one-hundred warships (the entire Syrian Navy in fact), he could go to Carthage and raise it against Rome and then land yet again in southern Italy. This seemed a reasonable plan to Antiochus as it would have set Hannibal nipping at Rome's heels, and he did underrate an attempt by a collaborator of Hannibal's to generate a revolution in Carthage in 193. But the scheme as a whole was nonsense: Rome would have crushed Hannibal and not more than two legions would have been needed to dispose of an army of ten-thousand even with so distinguished a commander, and the Romans would hold Antiochus responsible. Clearly the great Carthaginian fugitive was transported by his family's hatred of Rome to the point of a considerable loss of strategic judgment. Antiochus did not wish war with Rome and was preoccupied suppressing rebellious tribes and factions in Lydia and Phrygia. He had rapidly reassembled the former Empire created first by the force of Persia, and then by the lightning conquest by Alexander, and more or less maintained in the wars that followed Alexander's death by the Seleucids. This was a fragile arrangement compared to the source of Roman strength which had been gradually built and spread for several hundred years.

Instead of pursuing a madcap Carthaginian excursion, Antiochus settled on the much more easily mobilized hostility to Rome of the long-wronged Aetolians, smarting under Rome's claimed protection, amplified by Attalus' just resentment of Rome's bad faith in the late Greek wars. Antiochus made himself popular in Greece by graciously receiving the missionaries of many of the Greek states and implicitly holding himself out as an alternative protector to Rome and one not at all disposed to interfere in internal Hellenic affairs. The Greeks, as always in politics, more headstrong than cunning, subscribed to this fairy tale and accepted Antiochus' representations with unjustified credulity. He considered that in stoking Aetolia and arousing what the Romans still did not understand was residual Greek resentment of Roman overlordship, he was merely responding to Rome's unreasonable attempts to meddle in Asia Minor. He believed that Greece and Aetolia would furnish him a buffer state adequate to keep Rome out of his kingdom in the now likely event of war. There is little doubt that he hoped for a withdrawal of Roman claims in Asia Minor without recourse to armed hostilities. His opinions and ambitions were reasonable; he just didn't understand how the Roman leaders thought, though by now, Philip, in particular, could have told him.

The Aetolians, burning with recriminations against Rome, clamoured for revenge, and while one party in Aetolia had seen the Roman armies in action and did not want to risk war with Rome, another led by Thoas of Trichonium pandered to public sentiment and espoused the concept of the Great King that portrayed him as a benign liberator of Greece from Roman influence and a man committed to autonomous leadership of the Greek states. Generally, and especially in heartfelt political causes, the judgment of people is influenced by their ambitions and hopes; there was nothing to justify the thought that Antiochus had any great desire to set Aetolia at the head of the Hellenic world. While he was confident of the sustainability of his position, he had to do what he wanted in Thrace and Asia Minor, and it was up to the Romans to dislodge him if they chose to try. He wished to avoid war with Rome and recognized that any such conflict could be very hazardous.

Thoas and his Aetolians were aggrieved hotheads. Appeals were made to Philip, but he had been cut down so drastically by the Romans he could not be induced back into the field against them unless there was a drastic change in the correlation of forces. No one had come to his assistance when he was being taken to the woodshed by Flamininus, but Philip did incite rebellion in those parts of his kingdom that Flamininus had given the Achaeans to govern, and by this method he took back several towns.

The Achaeans went to war at once against the Aetolians led by Philipoemen, a talented general, and successfully agitated the Romans. Nabis too, had a hand in the anti-Roman movement, not having absorbed his comeuppance in sportsmanlike spirit. The Romans sent the praetor, A. Atilius Serranus in 192 with twenty-five quinqueremes, and two legions were prepared for intervention, but Flamininus, who always exaggerated his influence on and standing with the Greeks, arrived in the Peloponnese in person to conduct a diplomatic offensive. Before Atilius could arrive, Philipoemen and his Achaeans had been defeated by Nabis at sea but routed him at the land battle of Mount Barbosthenes, chased him back within the walls of Sparta and laid waste to the much downtrodden Laconia. Atilius repossessed the coastal towns for the Romans and Flamininus imposed a peace on the Achaeans and Nabis and embarked on a tour of most of the Greek states attempting to inspire calm and conciliate the always tempestuous factions of the Hellenic world. He had some success in raising Rome's prestige, if not its popularity, but the returning Roman commander saw many signs of incipient bellicosity. The Greek peace of which he was so proud was obviously very fragile. At Demetrias, he had a public altercation with the general Eurylochus and prevailed upon the city to drive their leader into exile.

Thoas had visited Antiochus in 192 and used the latest Roman intervention in Greece as a pretext to argue that the Great King should assert himself to discourage a Roman reimposition of their influence in Greece. Antiochus sent Menippus, his former ambassador to Rome, back with Thoas and had him advise the Aetolian leaders privately that the Great King would be sending formidable military forces soon and that he would make his immense wealth available to those Greeks who would deter a Roman return. Menippus told the Aetolian assembly that Antiochus was ready to join with the Aetolians "in resurrecting Greece, standing by its own strength, independent of the caprice of others."[10] Flamininus and his legates were present for this session and warned the Greeks not to pursue this course; he was supported strenuously by the Athenians but not heeded. The Greeks had managed to make themselves the jam in the sandwich between the two great powers: Rome was inciting the ambitions of the Greeks of Asia minor while Antiochus fanned the hopes and resentments of the European Greek states.

Antiochus had said nothing of war and was at this point merely trying to deter the Romans; the effect of his words and actions was exactly the opposite: the Romans always expected him to advance in Greece and to threaten Italy by approaching through Greece. The Romans were also concerned with a strong rumour that was reported that Antiochus intended to invade Sicily and the Romans dispatched a fleet of seventy quinqueremes to protect Sicily and the adjacent Italian seaboard and deployed an army in southern Italy and Sicily to repel invaders. Another army of thirty-thousand men was assembled at Bruttium, and with considerable additional reserves, Rome was signaling that it was not prepared to tolerate any advance by Antiochus into Greece. In order to try to accelerate the Great King's involvement in Greece and entry into war with Rome, the Aetolians attacked Demetrias, Chalcis, and Sparta. Nabis was to be got rid of once and for all and his treasure rifled. The operation against Chalcis was a fiasco but in Sparta by rank treachery and pretense to sending him reinforcements, the Aetolians were able to seize Nabis and murder him and temporarily become rulers of Sparta. However, the ancient spirit of that indomitable and austere city asserted itself within a few days and the Aetolian occupiers were massacred to a man. Philipoeman then occupied Sparta and unilaterally admitted it to the Achaean League. Aetolia had managed to humiliate itself. It did, however, have a success at Demetrias, and Eurylochus was brought back, and his opponents were conveniently murdered by the Aetolians. Flamininus, still in Greece, watched all this in public silence, but noted that there was still no sign of Antiochus or his forces.

He was still suppressing Lampsacus and Smyrna but finally late in 192 came from the Hellespont with ten-thousand infantry, five-hundred horse, six elephants, a fleet of one-hundred vessels, as well as two-hundred transports, and was accompanied by Hannibal, whose planned action against Carthage had been rolled into this theatre instead. The diminutive size of Antiochus' expeditionary force disappointed

---

10 Ibid., p. 206.

the Aetolians who were anticipating a vast army, and Antiochus was with difficulty elected commander of what was not yet remotely an army that might expunge Roman influence in Greece. The Great King was limited by his own prudence and ambiguity. He did not wish war with Rome; he only wished to retain what he already had and he squandered the fervent early adoration of the Greek masses by padding around the Peloponnese explaining with no great confidentiality to the many governments that he visited that they should make peace with Rome, knowledgeable of the fact that his presence gave them a stronger hand to play, but not encouraging the war parties in the Greek states. His entire tour was unsuccessful and was further hampered by Flamininus stirring up the wealthy classes ("Optimates") in the Greek cities who governed more or less in the Roman interest and with Roman support. He thus undermined the credibility of the Seleucid assault upon Rome's position in Greece. He had little difficulty in driving a wedge between the Achaeans and Aetolians, ancient and natural rivals. Antiochus was even denied entry to several of the Greek states, including Boeotia and Chalcis.

His tactics had been disastrous: too provocative not to arouse Rome to a mighty retaliatory stroke, but too diffident to enlist the passionate support of nationalist Greece; an armed presence in Greece sufficient to arouse Rome but not to persuade Greece he was serious, and completely inadequate to deal with the Roman blow when it came. He had spent too long wheedling and bribing and marrying offspring into the municipal politics of congeries of sleazily governed little states. He had never dealt with a Great Power before and would not have an opportunity to do so again.

Antiochus now changed his tactics and seized Chalcis and Demetrias by force. This brought him into armed conflict with Pergamon and Achaea, both allies of Rome that Rome would protect and avenge. Much more seriously, his forces killed nearly five-hundred Romans at the sacred shrine of Delium, ignoring the universally respected sanctity of that place and splashing Roman blood around with no colour of right, temporal or spiritual. This made Antiochus the aggressor through a mindless and useless provocation and sacrilege that had an effect on Roman attitudes that virtually presaged American reaction to the attack on Pearl Harbor twenty-one hundred and thirty-three years later. Flamininus, in Corinth, publicly called God and man to witness the Seleucid aggression. The Boeotians and Chalcidions now rallied to Antiochus, but not to the point of sending him any reinforcements, and his expeditionary force was not large enough to occupy more than a couple of towns.

The Romans hastily cobbled back together their implausible alliance with Philip and sent a detachment along with a Macedonian army into Thessaly where Antiochus had attempted to subdue a number of towns. Flamininus, in another considerable triumph, convinced Philip that he stood to gain by retrieving lost territory now being occupied by the Seleucid leader. Philip was intensely jealous of the rise in Antiochus' fortunes in comparison to the heavy setbacks he had endured, and he took the bait. Once again, Flamininus demonstrated that as long as he was not laboring under illusions of being an honorary Hellene liberator, he was a cunning and effective Roman proconsul, both as a soldier and as a diplomat. Antiochus had not reinforced his contingent in Greece, but had been diplomatically energetic, even marrying a Chalcidian woman. He made one foray against Acarnania in 191 but the arrival of a Roman armada prompted him to retreat in caution.

He had lost his opportunity: the Greeks were disillusioned and divided and quarrelsome as always. In modern urban gang parlance, Antiochus had brought a knife to a gunfight. The Romans had prepared carefully both diplomatically and militarily and were about to strike the Great King who was still wallowing in Greece with only about ten-thousand soldiers. His only objective strength was the military genius of Hannibal which he ignored and to whom he entrusted no forces appropriate to Hannibal's talents, and whom, having recruited, he was alleged to regard with envy. He had spent too long sorting out scruffy little states and alternately flourishing sticks and carrots. Rome, he had apparently not noticed, though he had had ample opportunity to appreciate it, was a political force unlike any other. His enlightenment was now close at hand, and he would never recover from it.

5. Renewed War in Greece

The Romans dawdled for several months after declaring war in November 192, but the following February they landed twenty-thousand infantry, two-thousand cavalry, and fifteen elephants at Apollonia under the consul M. Acilius Glabrio, a friend and comrade of Scipio Africanus. Acilius marched inland and joined King Philip in Thessaly in reconquering the state from which they had evicted the Macedonian monarch six years before. Their combined forces easily drove the Syrians and their local allies out of Thessaly and pushed them back to the famous pass at Thermopylae. The Romans and Macedonians tried to force the pass and were taking heavy casualties without success when the force of two-thousand led by Marcus Porcius Cato, which had picked its way along a steep trail, prorupted onto the Syrian rear and caused the panic of Antiochus' army. The Great King escaped with only five-hundred men and left Greece from Chalcis and returned to Ephesus, his initiative a complete and humiliating fiasco. He had completely misjudged the spirit of Rome and imagined that the Romans would be quiescent. To continue the analogy with the Pacific War of 1941-1945 raised in the reference to Pearl Harbor, he imagined, as did the Japanese, that their opponent would simply retreat and accept the setback they had suffered. (Like General Douglas MacArthur leaving Corregidor in 1942, Antiochus brought his new Greek wife with him.) If he had not squandered his first months in Greece and so disappointed the hopes of the Greeks who welcomed him, he could have mobilized a very formidable pan-Grecian army to resist the return of the inevitable Flamininus, who though highly competent, would not have been a match for Hannibal. The Romans too, were remiss in sending too small an army initially to Greece, but Antiochus obligingly did not punish them for it.

Antiochus possessed a much greater navy than the Romans and so was not in danger in Asia Minor, and he still had the cranky Aetolians as an ally. Thoas and Nicander went to Ephesus and beseeched Antiochus not to abandon Aetolia. He effusively promised that he would not and with his spirited encouragement Aetolia remained in a state of war with Rome, requiring the maintenance of a substantial Roman army in Greece. Attacked by both the Romans and Macedonians, Aetolia gradually gave way, but encouraged by the Great King, it fought between shrinking frontiers with habitual Greek heroism. While Acilius conducted an extensive siege of Naupactus, Philip took back Demetrias, Magnesium, and Antron, and a number of other cities he had been forced by the Romans to disgorge and was reestablishing himself in northern Greece. Acilius had none of the diplomatic suavity or Hellenophilia of the now reverently recollected Flamininus, who had returned to Greece to try to resurrect his delusional happy Commonwealth of grateful Greeks. Flamininus settled down the Aechaeans, who were feasting on the beleaguered Aetolians, and then prevailed upon Acilius to suspend his assault on Aetolia by pointing out that having taught them a lesson, it was better to leave them reduced but intact than hand the whole state back to Philip who was subsuming it from the north. He secured peace for Aetolia, and they consented to seek a resolution of their many grievances by the now almost automatic pilgrimage to the Roman Senate.

Having set out to remove Antiochus from Europe, the Romans were not content to stop among the squabbling Greeks. They reinforced their navy with the intention of removing the Great King from the European side of the Hellespont. Praetor C. Livius Salinator crossed the Aegean with over one-hundred vessels in the summer of 191 and joined with about fifty other vessels of the Greek allies, especially the Rhodians, who had no grievance against Antiochus but knew the Romans well enough to be confident who was going to win the current contest. Eumenes joined the Romans with about fifty Pergamene vessels, and the Syrian admiral, Polyxenidas, gave battle to Livius Salinator although he was outnumbered, just before the Rhodians could join forces with the Romans. This engagement took place off Cape Corycus, and the skilled Roman use of grappling hooks enabled them to sink or capture twenty-three of the larger Syrian vessels and Polyxenidas retired to Ephesus. The Rhodian fleet joined Livius the next day; the Syrians declined combat and both fleets retired to winter quarters, Livius in Pergamon, the Rhodians at home. This victory caused many of the rest of the Greek states of Asia minor to throw in with the Romans, but Antiochus was far from finished. The Roman Senate demanded such humiliating terms from Aetolia that it refused, assuring the resumption of war in the spring of 190. This was good news for Antiochus who spent the winter building his forces.

Given the success of Acilius, and the presence of Hannibal—again in the ranks of Rome's enemies—the Romans entrusted the consulate in 192 to the incompetent brother of Publius Scipio Africanus, who was not eligible to be the consul and general as he had held that position in 194. But he was asked to accompany his brother and effectively take command of a Roman army whose objective was to evict Antiochus from the European Hellespont. Scipio wanted to fight in Asia as he had fought in Africa and not in Greece and he prevailed upon Acilius to stop besieging Aetolian towns and persuaded the Aetolians that if they returned to Rome, they would get somewhat more generous terms from the Senate than they had the previous year. The Scipios pressed on with about fourteen-thousand men to join forces in Thessaly with Philip and continue on to the Hellespont. Antiochus was busily building ships and recruiting sailors and had Hannibal raise a fleet in Phoenicia, Carthage's mother country, to join Polyxenidas at Ephesus, while his son, Seleucus, had a third fleet that harassed the Pergamene coast. He also organized for privateers and other pirates to roam the Aegean searching for Roman supply convoys. Livius and Eumenes were trying to force open the Dardanelles but with no more success than the British and French would enjoy in the same exercise in 1915 A.D. Polyxenidas surprised and almost destroyed the Rhodian fleet at Samos, while a revolt broke out against the Romans in Phocaea and several neighbouring cities.

L. Aemilius Regillus relieved Livius at the end of his term in April 189. His initial efforts to relieve the Rhodians in their activities in Asia Minor were not successful and Seleucus and Antiochus invaded Pergamon in the absence of Eumenes. But Aetolia started agitating for peace and Antiochus put out feelers in May; Rhodes was agreeable, but Pergamon was not and Antiochus still did not understand the proud (and ruthlessly cynical) Roman mentality. The war continued. Eumenes secured Pergamon but the combined Allied fleets were unable to suppress the revolt in Phocaea. The tide of fortune turned when the Rhodian fleet, though outnumbered, demonstrated its seamanship and defeated Hannibal, who was trying his hand as an admiral for the first time. (It would be almost another century before the Mediterranean countries recognized that the skills and training required to command on land and sea were different.) The Phoenician fleet was badly roughed up and withdrew and would not be battle-worthy again for several months. At this point, Antiochus risked a decisive action and told Polyxenidas to engage Regillus. The two fleets met again near Corycus. Once again, the legendary Rhodian sailors turned the match for the Roman allies and Polyxenidas, though he almost took the Romans by surprise at the outset, was outmaneuvered by the Rhodians and lost forty-two ships on the day, a decisive defeat that required him to return to Ephesus. The Syrians were no longer able to contend for mastery of Hellespont waters and the Scipios hastened on their mission to evict the Great King from Europe.

Scipio proceeded at a brisk pace through Macedonia and Thrace, picking up a couple of thousand volunteers, and Antiochus prudently withdrew from the great fortress of Lysimacheia, which could not be held without sea access, but imprudently left a great quantity of stores behind. The Roman and allied forces crossed into Asia without opposition, though in a quaint manifestation of the Roman state religion, Publius Scipio, as a Salian priest, had to remain in Europe for a month. When he did cross the Hellespont, he was greeted by an emissary of the Great King, who with his navy shattered, and many parts of Asia Minor already shifting beneath his feet and only Ariarathes of Cappadocia remaining in alliance, sued for peace. His envoy offered permanent abandonment of Europe (which had already occurred) as well as Lampsacus, Smyrna, and some other Greek towns in Asia Minor, and half of Rome's war costs. But Rome, once stirred, was so powerful it did not have to listen so attentively to the counsels of prudence that were finally guiding Antiochus. Scipio responded, on his own authority, but with a practically open mandate from the Senate, that it wanted all Asia Minor up to the Taurus Mountains and all the cost of the war. When the envoy offered return without ransom of Scipio's son, who had been captured, and a handsome personal tangible incentive for Scipio himself, the conqueror of Hannibal was indignant. This was the last sort of approach to make to Rome at this point in its development, when civic virtue still flourished, especially with a man of such distinction as Scipio. This was an impulse that was completely incomprehensible in any part of the Middle East.[11]

Antiochus (mistakenly) calculated that defeat would be no more expensive than acceptance of these terms and would probably be less humiliating. He had assembled an army of seventy-thousand to only about thirty-thousand in Scipio's army, though Scipio proceeded into Asia Minor with his customary confidence, emboldened by the knowledge that Antiochus's army was a polyglot force, composed of many ethnicities of varying military aptitudes and fidelity to their commander. The Great King took relatively high ground near Magnesia and awaited his visitors. The Romans proceeded along the coast and then turned inland through Pergamon after being joined by Eumenes with a substantial contingent. Publius Scipio was unwell and remained on the shore to recuperate. Antiochus, always diplomatic and cool-headed, learning of his indisposition, released his son as a hostage and had him conveyed to his father's bedside. In return, Scipio gently advised Antiochus not to continue with the war. Without Publius Scipio, the Roman military command was considerably less confident and talented, and allowed themselves to be maneuvered by Antiochus onto a broad plain where the Syrian king had already constructed a fortified camp.

The two armies clashed on a rainy morning in January 189 and although he was over fifty, Antiochus led his cavalry on the right wing personally and overcame the Roman left and threatened his enemy's rear. But the Romans had massed almost all their cavalry on their own right: nearly three-thousand horse, and with Eumenes commanding on this flank, drove back the scythed-wheeled chariots that faced them, which threw the Syrian left into confusion and then attacked the overcrowded and confused Syrian left with all his force and broke it up. Then the Roman center attacked the great Syrian phalanx of sixteen-thousand men thirty-two ranks deep. As Eumenes pressed on into its flank the Roman center was ably commanded by Cn. Domitius Ahenobarbus, in place of Publius Scipio. He poured a teeming rain of darts and arrows down upon the Syrian phalanx and its twenty-two elephants broke formation and rampaged among the Syrian ranks as Eumenes pressed in from the left. The Romans and Pergamenes maintained their attack on both sides with great determination and the Great King's formations collapsed. His camp was overrun, though bravely defended, and as a disciplined army, the Romans did not stop to pillage or to rest but set out in hot pursuit of the retreating enemy. Antiochus escaped but lost, according to contemporary accounts, more than fifty-thousand men. He was now a king with no army, and a badly gored kingdom, facing a victorious and formidable enemy that had suffered only minor losses.

The conflict was effectively over as Antiochus fled from outpost to outpost and much of Western Asia Minor opened its gates as the Romans approached. Even Ephesus, where Polyxenidas was at anchor in what remained of the navy, welcomed the Romans who declared that this was all they sought and that they had no interest in continuing the conflict. Neither did Antiochus; Rome had made its point and the

---

11 A similar event occurred in the Vietnam War in 1972 when the North Vietnamese offered the return of John McCain, a prisoner of war who was the son of a distinguished admiral. The prisoner himself, a future presidential candidate, adamantly declined unless all his comrades were treated equally.

whole known world had witnessed it. It was one of Rome's greatest victories to date and was certainly not entirely earned, other than opportunistically, but their luck had been extraordinary. The chronically bellicose Aetolians had made peace at a convenient time rather than continuing to mire Rome in a remote and nasty war. And Philip of Macedonia, an unscrupulous and even treacherous ruler even by the contemporary Balkan standards, was apparently overawed by Publius Scipio Africanus when they met and was entirely faithful to the Roman alliance, a novel and unforeseeable fidelity to his word. Peace terms were easily agreed: Antiochus renounced any position in Europe and adjacent Asia Minor and agreed to a war indemnity of fifteen-thousand talents over twelve years. Antiochus agreed to hand over Rome's enemies, including Hannibal and Thoas, but chivalrously saw to it that Hannibal escaped. The great Carthaginian captain's hatred of Rome had driven him a long way from home. "Within ten years the gods in their kindness granted to Rome this double boon, that Antiochus did nothing to prevent her from crushing Philip, and that Philip did his best to help her to crush Antiochus."[12] (Cunning Roman strategic diplomacy had something to do with it also. It wasn't just dumb luck.)

It was assumed that as in Greece, Rome would not persist in the occupation of all that it had conquered in Thrace and Asia Minor but would determine who governed the different cities and provinces. Every conceivable claimant descended upon Rome in 189 to beseech the favour of the Roman Senate. This sort of swarming of ambitious smaller states would become a periodic rite of postwar diplomacy as when Vietnamese communist Ho Chi Minh and a host of other native leaders in colonial territories arrived in Paris in 1919 after World War I to lobby Woodrow Wilson, Georges Clemenceau, and David Lloyd George for their independence.

Before these matters could be peacefully determined in Rome, the always bellicose Aetolians attacked Philip and attempted to seize back lost territory. This was proceeding well until the decisive action of Magnesium, which caused the Aetolians, in despair, to send yet another emissary to Rome seeking the peace that they had themselves violated. While this mission was underway, Rome determined to make a clean sweep of these fluctuations and sent the consul M. Fulvius Nobilior to Apollonia with the troops that had been held in reserve for several years at Bruttium. It had been determined to put Aetolia firmly in its place, which was not going to be an exalted one. The Aetolians proved as resourceful at diplomatic intrigue as they were determined as warriors, and although they were attacked by Philip, the Achaeans, and the Illyrians, they resisted so heroically that Fulvius allowed himself to be persuaded by the moderating advice of Athens and Rhodes and made a relatively generous peace with the Aetolians, though there were some territorial sacrifices. Aetolia was however, in the Roman manner, press-ganged into an involuntary alliance couched in the promise to "respect the Empire and the majesty of the Roman people and to fight their enemies as their own."[13] Aetolia had begun its relations with Rome as its first Greek ally, and though it was still intact and the largest state in central Greece, its pugnacity and underestimation of the Romans had cost it dearly.

Rome's ambitions were not yet entirely sated, and it now turned upon the pirates

---

12 Ibid., p. 225.
13 Ibid., p. 227.

who had been such a nuisance for so long. They liberated many Roman and Italian prisoners held by pirates on Crete and abruptly attacked the Galatians for having supplied mercenaries to Antiochus and for frequently raiding the Hellenic coast and towns. The general Manlius, with Eumenes' brothers Attalus and Athenaeus, marched from Ephesus through Caria and Pisidia, Pamphilia, Phrygia, and Galatia, extorting obscene quantities of treasure at every point in the route of march as the price of buying "Roman friendship," the absence of which, it was made clear, would lead at once to the complete sack and pillage of each centre and very rough treatment of their populations. The Romans were not bearers of anything analogous to the civilizing mission of the Greeks, and especially the grand plan of Hellenization devised and partly implemented by Alexander the Great.

The Galatians, composed of three different peoples, resisted fiercely, as Rome had made no secret that their punishment would be severe for supporting Antiochus and ravaging the Hellenic Greek shores. Manlius recovered immense loot that the Galatians and barbarians had seized and the proceeds of having sold more than forty-thousand of their military and civilian population into slavery. The whole region noted Rome's punitive efficiency but was also grateful that the avaricious barbarians had finally been virtually ground to powder by a comparatively civilized nation. The Roman Senate tightened the terms on Antiochus. He could not engage in war in Europe or the Aegean, and while he could repel attacks from the west, he was not to take territory nor make alliances with the aggressors. He had to give up and could not replace his elephants and his fleet except two ships which were bound to stay out of any waters remotely close to Rome and its allies. Eumenes was given almost everything in Europe that had been taken from Antiochus. Rome set another example by being generously loyal to its faithful ally, the Pergamene king Eumenes; he was allowed to repossess virtually everything that his antecedents had held at the height of Pergamon's influence.

Manlius established himself at Apamea with his commissioners just as Flamininus had done at Corinth in 194. Antiochus faithfully complied with the conditions of the peace and had already handed over naval vessels and the required twenty-five hundred talents and had become an unofficial "friend" of Rome. Ariarathes, now Eumenes' father-in-law, paid his indemnity; and the Galatians complied. The challenge was in what was called Cistauric Asia, which was Asia Minor consisting of approximately two thirds of what is now Asiatic Turkey, and bounded by the Taurus Mountains, which begin at about the midpoint of the southern coastline of Asiatic Turkey and proceed east northeast from there, preserving in these times, the eastern half of that coastline and all of the Levant and the Middle East beyond Turkey for the (significantly diminished) Great King. All of the Greek cities which were independent before the war were confirmed in that status; all of those formerly subject to Antiochus, but who had faithfully served Rome during the war, gained their complete freedom. The others generally were deemed to be within the orbit of Eumenes, with certain exceptions for individual reasons, including Ilium, Chios, Smyrna, Miletus, Phocaea, and Mylasa.

The next category was the formerly Seleucid lands. Rhodes received most of Caria though the commission did not specify whether the Lycians were allies or subjects of Rhodes, thus generating lengthy conflict. Eumenes had had an excellent war; he gained Thracian Chersonese, Lysimacheia, the pro-Pontus coast, and in Asia he became the largest state in Anatolia. But the Greek towns largely interrupted his access to the Aegean, and he was soon engaged in a dispute with Syria over a Pamphylian corridor to Telmessus, an enclave on Rhodian coastal territory. The Roman Senate granted Eumenes most of what he sought. The shaggy edges and unresolved disputes left by the commissioners under Manlius' chairmanship at Apamea presaged the bitter and durable quarrels generated by the arbitrary settlements at Vienna in 1815, Versailles in 1919, and Teheran and Yalta in 1943 and 1945, not to mention the many European partitions of Africa.

The Romans, having established themselves as protectors of the arrangements that they had imposed, emulated their formula in Greece of completely withdrawing. It would prove a much more intelligent tactic than attempting simply to assimilate all of the territories involved into the Roman empire and committing themselves to endless internal struggle and guerrilla skirmishing and the forced admission to the cadres of Roman leadership of numbers of ultimately hostile foreigners. But it also assured that they would be repeatedly called upon to return and reimpose settlements on the regions where they had intervened. They had left Antiochus undisturbed in the territories he had taken from Ptolemy, and with what the passage of a little time would show to be an open invitation to reassert Seleucid influence where it had been lost, as long as that did not discommode Roman interests or Rome's genuine allies. (Ptolemy had conceded some of these places to Antiochus and Rome saw no reason to be a more vigorous defender of Egypt than its king was.)

Eumenes and some of the other Greeks constituted a plausible buffer between the turbulent forces of Asia and the central and Western Mediterranean heartland of Rome. Eumenes was involuntarily replicating the role of Massinissa opposite Carthage forty years before. Proud Rhodes emerged expanded and fortified and effectively revived the League of the Islands in the Aegean. Rome astutely did not impose formal friendship or alliance but achieved just as much with a full alignment of interests between the two governments. Time would show, here as in Greece, that having protégés, though not as onerous as having dependent allies, brings its complications. Manlius returned to Rome in 187, as Fulvius did from Greece, neither leaving a single Roman soldier, administrator, or overseer behind. All the states with which Rome had been in contact or in conflict were, in their self-government, free, except temporarily for Aetolia.

After departing Antiochus, Hannibal took refuge with Prusias of Bithynia, who was sporadically at war with Eumenes II of Pergamon. Hannibal won several naval battles, on one occasion hurling pots of venomous snakes by catapult onto his opponents' decks, an innovative phase in the earliest stages of naval artillery and of chemical warfare. He also defeated Eumenes in several armed clashes ashore. To the end, Zama was his only defeat on land and his record as a naval commander was quite successful also.

Eumenes asked Roman intercession and once again, Rome demanded that Hannibal be handed over. Prusias could not refuse, and Hannibal had nowhere else to go. Accounts differ, but it seems that Prusias provided painless poison for him. It was approximately 185, and Hannibal was about sixty-five. In the eight-hundred years between Brennus in 391 B.C. and Attila in 415 A.D., no one terrified Rome militarily except Hannibal. (Cleopatra would frighten Rome politically.) Unfortunately, Hannibal's entire magnificent career was sustained by his hatred for Rome, which was reciprocated by Rome's obsession with him as an impossible nemesis.

Hannibal's military genius and the drama of his astonishing career have never ceased to fascinate the world. He ranks with Alexander and Julius and Augustus Caesar as a gigantic historic figure of the ancient world.

It was a genuine shock to Roman statesmen that Greece was ready to prostrate itself at the feet of Antiochus if the Romans had not defeated him at Thermopylae. Flamininus, as has been described, was an astute and very successful manager of Rome's interest in Greece, and he was worshiped as a "saviour" in Chalcis. But he was mistaken in imagining that Greece could be charmed, maneuvered, or coerced into loyalty to any outside power. All Rome desired from the countries to the east of it was not to be threatened or bothered. But having once imposed itself on Greece and Asia Minor to prevent the materialization of threats and having established relationships with countries to keep a cordon sanitaire between them and Rome, calls for assistance and intervention became unavoidable. Philip of Macedon in particular, having taken his terrible defeat at the hands of Rome in a sportsmanlike fashion and been an invaluable ally opposite Antiochus, was certain to encroach again on Greece in a way that compromised the settlement that Flamininus had made. Before this could happen, the ambitions of Achaea threatened the peace. They had made themselves the leaders of the Peloponnesian League, but in Sparta, where Philipoemen had dealt successfully with the pro-Achaean party in 192, the ancient patriotic spirit of Sparta was asserting itself. There were repeated revolts against the regime dominated by outsiders and the inevitable return of exiles, especially the followers of Nabis, assured increased agitation.

There were large numbers of obstreperous Spartan exiles in the coastal towns that had been assigned to Achaea by Flamininus, and both their presence and Sparta's artificial isolation from the sea steadily aggravated political conditions in Sparta. There was a Spartan attempt to liberate exiles in the coastal town of Las, and Philipoemen, without even notifying Fulvius, demanded the surrender of those who had launched the attack. At this ultimatum thirty pro-Achaean Spartans were murdered, Sparta voted secession from Achaea, and sent a delegation to Fulvius proposing direct arrangements with Rome. The Spartans were prepared to pledge subordinacy to Rome, whom they could scarcely fail to respect as powerful outsiders, but they were no longer prepared to accept an inferior status to Achaea. Philipoemen declared war on Sparta, but the approaching winter season did not allow him to proceed, and Fulvius required that the issue be referred to the Roman Senate rather than resolved by armed combat.

The Senate was well disposed to both claimants and its judgment produced an ambiguous response which Philipoemen exploited by occupying Laconia and bringing in crowds of exiles, and seizing the leading secessionists, at least eighty of whom were massacred or executed after drum-head trials. Philipoemen was not remotely satisfied and fell on Sparta and dismantled her walls and expelled all mercenaries and enfranchised Helots. He also took over the institutions of Lycurgus and ordered the immediate return of all exiles. The anti-Achaean leaders were exiled or executed. A prolonged and bitter dispute was assured that would ultimately require the abandonment of the policy upon which Rome had heartily congratulated itself, of sorting out adjoining regions, adjudicating their internecine disputes, and imagining that they could then leave them in peace and harmony, not to mention gratitude, to mother Rome. This policy was more sophisticated and successful than the outright occupation of foreign territory, yet it ultimately failed, from trying to present overlordship administered by collaborators as the respected conduct of sovereign states.

The technique of defeating troublesome neighbors, selecting junior allies among them, and leaving them to manage the territories around them, while vastly superior to the simple brutal conquest of neighbors for no plausible reason, which had been the modus operandi of almost all previous states that expanded beyond their own initial borders, still involved the permanent vigilance, adjudication, and occasional intervention of Rome as the monitor state. But it was a much less constant drain on Rome's resources (and indeed initially was the source of an immense creation of Rome's resources) than the rapacity of Rome's armies when imposed on its uncooperative neighbors and indeed all states within its range which were not fully submissive. The development of this policy was somewhat accidental: Rome would not have attacked across the Adriatic in 229 if it had not been provoked by Teuta. It would not have entered Greece in 214 if it had not felt it necessary to counter the alliance between Philip and Antiochus.

It is a great strategic irony of this time that Rome intervened in Greece because it felt threatened by an alliance between Philip and Antiochus. The alliance was merely a preliminary division of spoils, a temporary accommodation between natural rivals, again, almost a forerunner of the Nazi-Soviet pact. It did not imply any substantial community of view between the two kings, and Rome had plenty of evidence available to it of a natural and probably irrepressible conflict between them. Rome's brilliantly executed defeats of Philip and Antiochus established Rome as the undisputed master of the known world. No state or country or regime we have reviewed in the preceding chapters remotely possessed the strategic sophistication that Rome demonstrated in this sequence of actions, and on other prior and subsequent occasions.

But if Rome had just been vigilant and maintained deterrent strength, it could have concentrated on Western and Central Europe and ultimately been a stronger power based on what eventually became the supreme source of political strength in the world: Germany, France, Britain, and northern Italy. That would ultimately have been a more formidable empire than one based on the Mediterranean, most of the shoreline of which is less wealthy, inhabited by less diligent and organized populations than the subsequent great nation states of Europe, and is more vulnerable to the barbaric hordes of Asia. After the initial rapine, Rome gained little from the Eastern Mediterranean. For the time being, they had favored Pergamon and Rhodes, which could insulate them from what lay beyond, but the complexities of the south Balkans and Middle East would require immensely greater effort and sacrifice for much less strategic reward than would the territories that eventually became France,

Germany, and Britain. Julius Caesar would partly correct that misjudgment, but the fact that Germany never came substantially under Roman influence would unfavorably alter the entire future of Rome, and of all Western Civilization itself for two-thousand years.

6. The Deaths of Antiochus, Philopoemen, and Philip V and the Decline and Fall of Macedonia

The next phase of Rome's on-again, off-again relationship with the Eastern Mediterranean would be a reversion to Macedonia. Antiochus, who had succeeded Philip as the chief threat on Rome's eastern flank had not only been soundly put in his place, but in 187, he died in Elymais while trying to seize the treasure of one of that city's temples. It was an inglorious and premature end to someone whose reassertion of the hereditary Seleucid position had earned him the style Antiochus the Great but had not reduced his vulnerability to the ire of Rome once it was provoked, even in its imagination and inadvertently. At first Rome was well satisfied with both Philip and Antiochus cut down, Armenia and Sophene independent, and Bithynia, Pontus, and Cappadocia somewhat raised in stature. From such a melange of states with plenty of friction between themselves, no threat to Rome seemed likely to arise anytime soon, and Pergamon and Rhodes were happy and friendly states rewarded for their support of Rome.

Egypt was in no position to cause trouble and would continue to be chiefly preoccupied with the depredations of Syria, as was now a well-entrenched tradition. Greece was, as usual, more complicated. The Aetolians, considering their insolence, got off relatively lightly. The Achaean League now claimed to include the entire Peloponnese, but Sparta was constantly simmering with revolt, and it was all made more complicated for Rome by the abrasions between Flamininus who was always hovering over Rome's Greek policy and Philopoemen (the Achaean leader) who thoroughly disliked and mistrusted him. Sparta's status was still in ferment when Philopoemen, engaged in successfully suppressing the secession from the Achaean League of the Messenians, was captured in a skirmish when his horse threw him. In deference to his stature, the Messenians allowed him to take poison, rather than simply executing him. They returned his ashes respectfully. Polybius carried the urn of his ashes and eulogized him as "The last Greek." He wrote later that "Greece ceased to bear good men." This was in 183, in the twilight of Greece's autonomous days.

The relations between Rome and both the Aetolian and Achaean Leagues were influenced by the extent to which those groups of Greek states feared the revival of the Macedonian appetite to control Greece, a condition that had existed for nearly two-hundred years since the rise of the original Philip of Macedon. Rome only wished not to be threatened or bothered by any of it. Philip had dutifully retained Roman goodwill by a high level of cooperation and his son Demetrius, who had been hostage in Rome and very well treated, was released to return to his father. As almost always with Rome's allies, fickle and unreliable as they usually were, Philip felt that he had been under-compensated for his extensive assistance in the campaign against Antiochus. Polybius believed that from this point on, Philip was determined to return to war with Rome when he could get favorable circumstances, but this remains conjecture after more than two-thousand years. He did move forcefully to shape up his diminished kingdom, by reopening closed mines, imposing increased tariffs, and admitting a good deal of immigration to do the more unskilled work in an economic buildup of strained and condensed Macedonia. Thessalians and others of Philip's neighbors petitioned Rome to keep Philip in his place, and Rome, as was customary, sent three commissioners to investigate.

The commissioners met in Tempe and received, as usual, a large number of petitioners. Practically every Greek state complained about every other Greek state and many factions within many Greek states complained about the other factions. Roman officials were by now long-practiced in dealing with such fragmented little jurisdictions, and such activities could only serve to increase their impatience. The principal subject was the status of the king of Macedonia and the initial comments to the commissioners were reasonably diplomatic, but the tenor of proceedings gradually degenerated and the traditional Greek suspicion of and hostility to powerful neighbors reasserted themselves. Rome had promised to Philip any place which had joined the Aetolian adversaries voluntarily, but the Aetolians made it difficult to determine if this condition had been met, which threw the status of many places into confusion and dispute. Philip was able to give a strong and logical response to most of the complaints and did so reasonably good-naturedly. But the Macedonian king could not resist disparaging comments about freedom from those who had little experience of it and comparing his accusers to recently emancipated slaves. He said: "My sun has not altogether set,"[14] which not only alarmed the Greeks, but made the Romans edgy also.

The commissioners determined that the Macedonians should withdraw from all places which were doubtful by the criterion established of voluntary appearance to Rome's enemies, and an arbitration system was established for resolving further questions between Macedonia and its neighbors. They also declared that Macedonia should observe its ancient borders, which if strictly followed was a judgment that would require considerable movements of population and alterations of frontiers. While it probably was not intended to cause any such problems, it convinced Philip that Rome had reverted to a policy of animosity and was inciting the appetites of his snappish Greek neighbors to start the ball rolling. They then removed to Thessalonica to deal with the questions about Aenus and Maronea, which Rome considered to be more important. Eumenes' position was that he could tolerate those cities being free, but that if they were deemed to be prizes of war, they belonged to Pergamon rather than to Macedonia. Philip's position was that since the commissioners had given Chersonese and Lysimacheia to Pergamon he was entitled to Aenus and Maronea.

When advised that Eumenes had made a greater contribution to Roman victory over Antiochus than Philip had, Philip responded that if he had sided with Antiochus, Pergamon would have been occupied and that Pergamon had no choice and he had exercised his free choice in Rome's favor. He made a powerful argument concluding that he had behaved as a friend and an ally to Rome despite past differences

---

14 Livy, xxxix, 26, 9.

and it was neither sensible nor ethical for Rome now to treat him as an enemy. The Roman commissioners found that persuasive, but the Maroneans complained that Macedonia was already occupying them and that the notion that their city was free was a fraud. With this, the commissioners recognized the limits of their authority and referred the Maronea and Aenus question to the Senate of Rome. A new commission was sent out led by Appius Claudius to ascertain the state of affairs. The Senate had decided that the two cities should be genuinely free, and Claudius was to find out if that was the case or if the complaints of the townspeople that the Macedonians were in fact governing and oppressing Maronea were accurate. This toing and froing caused Philip once again to temper his judgment. He was determined to punish his opponents in the city and ordered his local officer in command, Onomastus, to arrange through his agent in Maronea, Casander, to admit to the town by night a band of hired Thracians who conducted a massacre of Philip's designated enemies. Philip had often demonstrated before his faith in terrorizing populations to assure their docility or punish them for lacking docility. But this time he seriously misjudged matters in imagining that Rome would tolerate such an outrage. Claudius demanded that Onomastus should go to Rome for examination there by the Senate. Philip declared that the massacre was conducted by locals against locals and that he had nothing to do with it and he claimed that Onomastus was not in the district at the time. He finally allowed Casander to embark for Rome, but he died en route, and it has never been possible to determine whether suggestions that Philip poisoned him in order to avoid embarrassment in Rome were true or not.

The idea finally dawned on Philip that he was risking a great deal in antagonizing the Romans and he sent his son Demetrius, who had impressed the Romans when he was their hostage, back to Rome to try to put relations on a more positive footing. In 184, the Roman Senate was in practically open session receiving petitions from, according to Polybius, every regime at or near a frontier with Macedonia, all complaining of Philip's bad faith or oppressive conduct. Eumenes' brother, Athenaeus, was among the plaintiffs, and naturally received a respectful hearing. On request, Demetrius read a paper from his father which stated that he had done all that was required of him, and to the extent that there were any shortcomings, they were the fault of others, and that he did not accept the justice of all the decisions to which his compliance was demanded. The Senate responded most graciously to Demetrius and said that envoys would be sent to reassure Philip of Rome's gratitude for his fidelity to their alliance. True to the fluidity of fortunes and the instability chronic to almost all courts at that time, Demetrius's success was resented by those who thought he was attempting to leapfrog into the succession to his father as the Roman candidate for the throne of Macedonia. This was not a suspicion from which Philip himself was immune. In particular, Philip's elder son, Perseus, of whose legitimate birth there was some question, was disturbed by Demetrius' emergence as a rival favored by all those who wished to placate Rome.

Again, Philip's nature, essentially that of a barbarian, got the better of him. If he was being closed off from the Thracian coast, he would strike inland and he invaded Thrace, and annexed territory and set up a new town named after his elder son. As matters became perturbed around the court and factionalism developed between the heirs, Philip became more restive and ordered the arrest of all the relatives of the many people whom he had executed. In one clean move, Philip launched an exploratory expedition into the Balkans, but it achieved nothing, aroused some local tribes, and incited Roman suspicions about Philip's motives. The whole ambience of the Macedonian court was now so sinister that Perseus was believed by his father when he advanced the tale that Demetrius was planning to dispose of both of them and seize the throne in the Roman interest and supported this with a letter from Flamininus to Demetrius, that eventually proved to be a forgery. The beleaguered King had Demetrius poisoned and suffocated in a classic royal tragedy. He was then heavily oppressed by guilt at his filiacide, and died in 179, ostensibly of distress but otherwise natural causes, aged fifty-nine. Whatever anyone thought of the complicated and tragic events that led to this point, there was no alternative except Perseus, and he ascended the throne, but in a poisoned atmosphere.

Perseus began by requesting the renewal of the alliance with Rome, which was immediately agreed to, but relations between the two powers were not improved by the death of Philip, though he was certainly not someone who enjoyed much goodwill among those influential in the Roman government. Perseus also opened his reign with several conciliatory and generous acts that were well appreciated by his subjects. He released prisoners, recalled exiles, gave a good many of his father's opponents back their property, and was generally placatory in his opening contacts with neighboring states. He repelled an attack from a Thracian tribe, and married Laodice, the daughter of Seleucus IV of Syria, married off his sister to Prusias, King of Bithynia, and made a highly publicized pilgrimage to Delphi in 174. It was a good start.

Eumenes journeyed to Rome in 172 to inveigh against Perseus, whom he claimed was intelligent, physically strong and aggressive, cunning, ambitious, and a war-lover, who had been sent by his father on many missions of acquisitive war-making. The Romans received him as a valued and respected ally and heard him out politely. But Eumenes appeared to be motivated by envy and none of it had anything to do with Rome. His hosts responded more positively when he reminded them that the Illyrian chief Artetaurus had been murdered, presumably on Perseus' instructions, and had been given refuge in Macedonia. He recounted an extensive list of grievances based on Perseus' tacit or even relatively overt support for the enemies of Pergamon and claimed that Perseus had a history of attempting to patch together anti-Roman intrigues with Carthage and others. There was a great deal of tittle-tattle and straws in the wind: Perseus had no business assisting Byzantium against its Thracian enemies, had been more successful than his father in gaining influence in Greece, and had almost persuaded the Achaean League to accept undue Macedonian influence and physical presence in its territory. Eumenes claimed that Perseus had murdered Greeks on their way to Rome and had fomented rebellions in various Greek states friendly to Rome and had inscribed unacceptable ambitions in sacred places in Delphi and Delos.

The Romans were hardly able to complain about Perseus favoring factions in different Greek states, as they notoriously did the same themselves. But Eumenes did succeed in persuading the Roman policymakers to regard Perseus as the head of a regional faction that was at the least insufficiently respectful of Rome and possibly unfriendly to her. Eumenes was cleverer than his local contemporaries and seeing how well-served he would be by aligning his interests with the Roman interest, he was an uncommonly persuasive courtier and agitator. It was not difficult for him, and in any case not entirely untrue, to convince the Romans that his unpopularity with many of the Greek states was due to his dogged adherence to his alliance with Rome. He had a terminally lucky break shortly after he departed Rome, when he was on his way to perform a sacrifice to Apollo and was struck down and almost killed by a rock rolled down the hillside. It was generally assumed he was dead or inevitably about to die as he clung to life by a thread as his brother, Attalus, laid claim to the succession and announced a marriage which Eumenes would not possibly have sanctioned. However, to his brother's astonishment the Pergamene king recovered and blamed the attack upon him on Perseus. Polybius and Livy believe that he was guilty,[15] but this was never established. There is no rational reason why he would have done such a thing and it is more likely that someone else did it, attempting to promote a war which would eventually drag Rome into the lists against Macedonia. Polybius considers that this incident was the real beginning of the war between Perseus and Rome that followed.

The surrounding powers were almost all well-disposed to Rome, including Ariarathes of Cappadocia, and the current Ptolemy, and young Antiochus IV, as well as Prusius of Bithynia, even though he was Perseus' brother-in-law. There was considerable alarm in the Eastern Mediterranean at long last about the rise of Rome, and its military and diplomatic prowess had been demonstrated so often it was finally recognized as a potentially dominant force along the entire Mediterranean littoral. Perseus, however, given the fear in which Rome was held, was unlikely to be able to generate any underdog sentiment for himself that could be translated into military solidarity against Rome.

The Achaean League was entirely pro-Roman, but the Boeotian League was divided and broke up, and the Thracian states were also divided. Rhodes was favorable to Rome as always but declined to be more than a well-disposed neutral in any hostilities. Perseus informed Roman envoys that he would not renew the friendship treaty that Rome had had with his father but would propose another one in due course. Quintus Marcius Philippus had been an envoy to Macedonia and was friendly with King Philip V and was invited by Perseus to return to Macedonia to see if they could not resolve things between them as old friends, reconstruct relations between their countries. Marcius saw clearly enough that reconciliation was not possible but conducted himself with great suavity and returned to Rome and assured the senators that he had bought six months peace in which Rome could catch up with Macedonian preparations for war. There were still at this late date a few Roman senators who considered this ruse incompatible with the honour of Rome, but the cynical majority in what was now the principal organ of government for the greatest power in the known world had already adapted to the customary tactics of a state in Rome's exalted position and Marcius was commended by his colleagues.

Rome finally declared war in 171, having assured itself of a significant contin-

---

15 Polybius, xx, 18; xxvii, 6. Livy, xlii, 15.

gent of opportunistic allies, led as always in these times by Eumenes of Pergamon. The consul Licinius led two legions and some auxiliaries totaling thirteen or fourteen thousand men; all in, the Macedonians had an army of forty-three thousand including four-thousand cavalry and Rome and its allies only about thirty-eight thousand. The Romans themselves were generally battle-hardened veterans who volunteered but as usual in these alliances, the quality of the allied forces varied considerably. Perseus moved quickly, took the pass at Tempe, and after light skirmishing failed to induce the main Roman army to give battle, Perseus brought his full army forward and an action involving about twelve-thousand men on each side took place at Calicinus. Perseus shook the Roman side with a mass cavalry attack, but the Roman position was stabilized by its experienced reserves. Perseus declined to use his phalanx which should come forward on its own initiative and the Romans withdrew intact across an adjoining river to a place of greater security.

It was clear that Perseus' strength in cavalry could induce an action if he wished but he was not headstrong and knew that Rome had an almost infinitely greater capacity for war-making than he did. He sent a peace messenger offering a modest indemnity and withdrawal from all places that his father had agreed to give up. It was a clever move, as it offered Rome a perfectly reasonable peace without a distinct humiliation. But everyone in authority in Rome now understood that it was essential that the Romans never accept anything less than victory if it wished to maintain its deterrent strength and general mystique, and the terms were rejected. Perseus continued to offer terms, but Rome did not accept them, and after one further skirmish the fighting season ended, and the armies took winter quarters. The Macedonians were disappointed that the king had not made more of having got somewhat the better of the fighting, and the Roman leaders recognized that they would have to insert more forces to be confident of victory against a strong and clever chief fighting on his own frontier. The Roman commanders cannot be faulted except for Admiral C. Lucretius Gallus, who had overwhelming sea superiority but did not use it to impede Perseus' communications, especially with Thessaly. He was also judged to have been unacceptably brusque with Rome's allies and was removed and fined.

The balance of the year and the ensuing year of 170 did not yield any significant events except an ill-considered Roman attempt to invade Thessaly that was repulsed by Perseus. The Macedonian king demonstrated his nonchalance by taking the opportunity to discipline a few of the neighboring northern tribes that had imagined he might be distracted by war with so formidable an adversary as Rome. The consul for 169 was the respected statesman Quintus Marcius Philippus who arrived with reinforcements and insisted on coordinating operations with the navy. He moved so quickly and arrived on the Macedonian coast unexpectedly, that Perseus feared that his advanced forces had been routed rather than bypassed and withdrew his garrisons to a tighter perimeter, abandoning the Tempe pass. Philipus had taken a heavy gamble and it had worked, but his maritime colleague failed to supply him adequately and he felt it prudent partially to retrace his steps, and Perseus sent his garrisons forward again. The first two years had been something of a minuet.

The consul for 168, L. Aemilius Paullus, sent a commission in advance to inquire into the state of Rome's and its allies' forces, as there was some agitation from the allies for a more determined effort or an end of it. There was likely to be new belligerency in Illyria and the condition of the fleet was dire, with illness, inadequate clothing and irregular pay. This finally galvanized Rome into shaping up its forces on land and sea and sending substantial reinforcements and experienced military tribunes, and not the flabby politicians who cluttered the Roman army at inactive times. Rome had the complacency to arm itself lethargically but had now crossed the threshold into the determined state that always emerged when the pride and dignity of the Republic were engaged. Paullus sacrificed at Delphi and proceeded on to take up his command.

Perseus had made the serious tactical error of not exploiting the time in which he was better prepared for war than was Rome, and that time was ending. Perseus attempted to detach Rhodes and Pergamon from their affection for Rome and made overtures to Antiochus IV and his navy became more active. Paullus devised the bold plan of immobilizing the Roman and Allied fleets and conspicuously gathering and reprovisioning them correctly while a force of almost ten-thousand commanded by Scipio Nasica was gathered there but was surreptitiously moved in a series of stealthy night marches well to the north of the Roman position. At the same time, Perseus, distracted by a variety of attacks and developments again withdrew northwards and Paullus concentrated his forces. The Battle of Pydna occurred on June 22, 168. The Macedonians attacked with their entire phalanx and Rome's ally, the Paelignians courageously absorbed this tremendous attack and fought a tenacious and brave retreat in good order while the main bulk of the Roman army turned the flank of the Macedonians and because of the terrain and their pre-positioning, Paullus' main force smashed the Macedonian army which retreated in some confusion after taking, it was alleged, nearly twenty-thousand casualties, half of its total force and a high multiple of Roman losses. Perseus fled to Pella and then to Amphipolis and finally to Samothrace. His star had set and like the latter Persian kings, his support had evaporated. Peace overtures to Rome received a curt demand for unconditional surrender. Perseus accordingly surrendered and was treated courteously by Paullus. He had to serve in the victorious general's triumphant parade and was thereafter imprisoned at Alba in rather shabby conditions, though it is alleged that Paullus objected to these. He lived very unhappily for only another two years, and his elder son did not long survive. The younger son of Perseus, King of Macedonia became a magistrate's clerk in Italy. The war and the Macedonian dynasty were over.

No Macedonian city resisted the advance of Paullus, and he occupied much of Macedonia peacefully and without subsequent looting or repression. Some cities that had reneged on previous professions of alliance with Rome were punished but none severely, and the Macedonian navy passively delivered itself to Rome, and was graciously received; it had not been defeated and had no cause for shame—it had no bases to operate from nor any sources of pay or supply. Paullus' entire campaign after the decisive encounter at Pydna was over in fifteen days.

At that time the entire campaign in Illyria had also been successfully completed. Genthius, the Illyrian leader, had not taken on board that the Romans would now act with a good deal less lethargy than heretofore and was suddenly overwhelmed by Appius with the consular army of thirty-thousand. The king, the royal family, and the leading chiefs and officials were all bagged in one sweep and this campaign ended within a month of its beginning. Less straightforward was Anicius and Paullus' campaign in Epirus in 168 and 167. Paullus occupied seventy cities and enslaved one-hundred and fifty thousand people. No reason for this has come down to posterity. He was not often an abnormally severe commander, so it may be safely judged that there was some provocation. Both Livy and Plutarch allege that the orders for such a draconian action came from the Senate, which was presumably aggrieved by some treachery, which would not in itself be a surprising development. The historians also suggest that the Roman soldiers involved had felt themselves somewhat shortchanged of loot and made amends.

As was now the Roman custom, senatorial commissioners acting with the victorious Roman commanders were empowered to settle the affairs of Macedonia and Illyria. The formula that had previously served in the region was resurrected, that all of the jurisdictions involved were to be free and Macedonia was to be divided into four regions and Illyria into three. Rome would require only half the tribute previously paid to the various kings and a profit-sharing system for Macedonia was devised for its rich gold, silver, copper, and iron mines so that the whole Macedonian population could profit from them, though the gold and silver production was reduced to avoid excessive mistreatment of the mine-workers. Paullus conducted an extensive tour of Greece which almost replicated the passages of Flamininus, as Paullus and his sons were authentic Phil-Hellenists, and they spoke Greek well and were knowledgeable of its culture.

Paullus made a point of contrasting with the visits of Perseus in 174, when he had made a good impression personally but also made the Greeks uneasy by the very large military force that accompanied him. Paullus had only a small entourage. The announcement of the decision of Paullus and the commissioners at Amphipolis was well received, but the Romans miscalculated in thinking that Macedonia would be grateful for a confederal arrangement. They were happy to be considered Greeks rather than barbarians, and even though there remains serious tribal strife within Macedonia, greater Macedonian nationalism militated against any dilution of central authority by the Macedonian government. Macedonians valued nationalism above liberty, despite having aspired to Greek status, an ambition for which they had chiefly the Greek world Hellenizing mission of Alexander the Great to thank. Ultimately, Macedonia wished to be sufficiently strong and authoritatively governed to be preeminent among Greeks. They were glad to be spared Roman occupation but were not then or ever (up to the present) particularly uplifted by the notion of personal liberty.

The installation of republics which had previously been monarchies, as always, had its complications. There were many factions and the Romans moved to exclude from public life most of those who had dominated in the different cities and states that they were now reconstructing. Within a decade, the Republican status of Macedonia was already coming under internal pressure: gold and silver production was expanded in 158 in order to alleviate economic discontent. Paullus' son, the talented general Scipio Aemilianus, because of the popularity in Macedonia of his father as a generous opponent (like Douglas MacArthur and Dwight D. Eisenhower in post-

World War II Japan and Germany), was spontaneously invited by the Macedonians to come and mediate their internecine differences in 152. For the fertile republican soil of Macedonia, a series of pretenders arose starting with Andriscus, who claimed to be a son of Perseus. He made little headway at first in Macedonia and tried his hand in Syria where he was arrested by Demetrius and sent to Rome. The Romans, convinced and slightly evangelical republicans as they were, had trouble taking anyone who aspired to be a king seriously, and he was released.

Various people professed to recognize and identify him as the true King, and he raised his flag on Macedonia and won the adherence of a large share of the population and former royal officials. He defeated republican rivals in battles in 149 and briefly ruled all of Macedonia. The Thessalians became alarmed and sent urgent requests to the Achaeans and Romans. As usual, Roman incredulity at the conduct of the Greeks caused a slow and gradually escalated response; first, Scipio Nasica was sent to mediate, but he was rebuffed. Then Juventius Thalna was sent with a legion, but he was defeated and killed in battle which stirred Rome to send Quintus Caecilius Metellus at the head of a sizeable Army in 148. He defeated Andriscus and chased him into Thrace, which he tried to use as a point of infiltration, but was again defeated and captured, returned in chains to Rome where he walked with bowed head in Metellus' triumph. At the terminal point of the parade, he gamely mounted a scaffold and the festivity concluded with the axe-man's severance of his head, which was held up for the approval of the large crowd before it dispersed. Public decapitations were always a popular entertainment in Rome. There were successor claimants to the throne of Macedon, but they did not have as much impact as Andriscus.

These experiences in Macedonia caused the Romans to embark upon a momentous new course: though the four divisions of Macedonia were geographically and ethnically legitimate, a single Macedonia was reestablished under a Roman governor, a magistrate who would be responsible for the administration of Macedonia, Illyria, and Epirus, though the local and municipal institutions were left intact. This proved to be a successful regime for some time and the competition developed between what the Romans called freedom which in practice meant much of the time the freedom of protectorate states to squabble with each other and irritate Rome, and a Roman governor ruling with as light a hand as possible and through local officials. The success of this new regime was assisted by the construction of a highway from the Adriatic coast to Thessalonica, which greatly reduced artificial barriers and expedited trade and travel. There were milestones at every point along its five-hundred and thirty-five-mile length. The defeat of Genthius in Illyria extended Roman control of the Adriatic coast on the east side to the Narenta River. The Dalmatians to the north continued to observe without enthusiasm the approach of Romans and Greeks and harassed colonists and skirmished generally until in 157 the Romans intervened, motivated also, according to Polybius,[16] by a desire to assure that the Roman population did not become complacent or too combat-averse, if the need arose. Rome accused the Dalmatians of disrespectful treatment of Roman envoys and the consul Gaius Marcius Figulus was sent to put that to rights. After an initial reverse, he laid waste a vast territory and besieged the Dalmatian capital, Delminium.

---

16 Polybius, xxxiv, 12.

Scipio Nasica succeeded him and completed the siege, ending this war and earning a triumph for himself in 155. There was now only a small part of the Adriatic coast that was not Roman government territory, and this would be dealt with at the next local provocation.

Rome was now growing automatically, organically.

PART V

THE CRISIS OF THE ROMAN REPUBLIC

CHAPTER TWENTY-ONE

DIGESTING AN EMPIRE, STRENGTHENING FRONTIERS, AND THE THIRD PUNIC WAR, 155-140 B.C.
CATO AND MASSINISSA

Bust of Marcus Porcius Cato

Massinissa of Numidia

1. The Eastern States

ROME'S DECISIVE victories over the Seleucid and Macedonian empires, long the two leading powers of the Eastern Mediterranean, had suitably impressed the surrounding governments. This era had for some time been characterized by endless envoys and petitions dispatched to the Roman Senate to enlist Rome's assistance and the reciprocal travel of Roman commissioners to determine how to rationalize the complexities of Greece and the Near East. But very few of these states had troubled to inform themselves at all thoroughly of the vagaries of Roman politics and the subtleties of official Roman decision-making and the art of influencing it from the outside. It was naturally assumed that it was Rome's ambition to extend its influence as far and as quickly as it could, as that is all that the Eastern Mediterranean had ever seen before, other than from a few eccentric Greek city states such as Sparta. Since Rome had made its power conspicuously clear, almost all ambitious Near Eastern and South European leaders of any stature made the trek to Rome early and often, laying out their ambitions and the grounds for them.

The standard response of the Roman senators canvassed was to assure the petitioners that if the facts were as stated, the claimant's request seemed reasonable. In general, it must be said that Rome grew into this role as arbiter of the known world with maturity and usually tried to determine issues placed before it justly. Rome was not always entirely disinterested, but in the absence of a vital Roman interest, if acted on the belief that the prestige of Rome would be best served by a fairly motivated attempt to be equitable. The endless request of such resolutions of local conflict by the Roman Senate naturally imparted a notion of incomparable world prestige and self-regard to the ruling class of Rome.

Dealing with these rulers from the farthest to the nearest, Eumenes' enemies in Pontus (King Pharnaces), comes first and he was little interested in what Rome thought of anything, though he maintained civil diplomatic relations. Ariarathes IV, king of Cappadocia, though he had sided with Antiochus, made his peace with Manlius with a payment of three-hundred talents, and remained loyal to Rome thereafter. Rome tended to favour Cappadocia, even when it was embroiled with another state, though a smaller one, that was also friendly to Rome. Galatea was a rival of Pergamon and accordingly only flexed its muscles in a manner offensive to Pergamon when King Eumenes was in one of his rare discordances of view with his Roman ally, as immediately after the Battle of Pydna, which concertinaed the Macedonians.

Bithynia was ruled throughout this time by Prusias I and II. Prusias I objected to the expansion of Pergamon that Rome had authorized during the war against Antiochus, and he attacked Pergamon with the illustrious and timeless Hannibal as commander of his navy, a role he had grown into and exercised quite victoriously. It was perhaps the presence of the great Carthaginian that provoked Roman intervention, and Flamininus was sent to Pergamon as emissary to end the war satisfactorily and require the handing over of Hannibal. Prusias was sufficiently intimidated that he did not feel he could resist and, as was mentioned in Chapter 5, he ensured that Hannibal had the means of a painless suicide. It was a sad end to a great career but only undignified in the sense that Hannibal's talents were deployed exclusively to serve powers which meant nothing to Carthage and which, unlike Carthage, had no capacity to worry the Romans seriously. Nothing in his career after the Punic Wars did anything but reinforce his military reputation. Hannibal Barca has never flagged in universal regard as one of history's greatest military commanders and adventurers.

In Egypt, the king now was Ptolemy Epiphanes, who forfeited Roman support by his negotiations with Antiochus, and the Egyptian throne was periodically weakened by nationalist uprisings. Ptolemy unwisely alienated Rome by attempting to establish an alliance with the Achaean League just as the last nationalist uprisings were being crushed between 185 and 183. Rome was apparently slowly organizing a thoroughly persuasive disincentive to Egypt to imagine that it had any vocation to meddle in Greek affairs when Ptolemy Epiphanes died and was replaced by the child Ptolemy Philometor, for whom the Seleucid Queen Mother Cleopatra ruled, but not for long. When the Queen Mother died, the regents were the barbarian and servile Eulaeus and Lenaeus, who were looked down upon in the ruling circles of Egypt.

Rome was in the midst of the third Macedonian War and did nothing to deter the joint regents from attempting to recover part of Syria. But Antiochus quickly defeated them and invaded Egypt. Ptolemy, under the Mephistophelean advice of the scoundrel regents, was prepared to accept a Syrian protectorate over all Egypt which would have brought the entire Hellenistic East under Antiochus. The Alexandrian civic leaders not only dissented, they proclaimed the new King Ptolemy Euergetes, Physcon, brother of Philometor. Philometor agreed to a shared authority with his brother rather than to accept the hegemony of the king of Syria and Antiochus prepared to invade the whole of Egypt in 168. At this point Rome did intervene and demanded that Antiochus withdraw from Egypt, which he did. It was another convincing affirmation of Rome's authority (and the irresponsibility of most other contemporary governments in the region).

Egypt lumbered perilously on for five years with two kings but Ptolemy Physcon, elevated by a popular uprising, had more support and was constantly scheming against his brother. In 164 Philometor was forced to flee Alexandria and Rome felt obliged to act. The Senate, without being specifically invited to do so, purported to decree that Ptolemy Philometor should rule Egypt and Cyprus while his brother ruled Cyrenaica. When Ptolemy Physcon claimed Cyprus the Senate in 162 declared in his favour, but Philometor did not accept this, and Rome did not immediately take action. In 154, Physcon accused his brother of attempting to assassinate him and on this unsupported charge alone, instructed their allies in the Eastern Mediterranean to install him in Cyprus. The allies did nothing and Philometor took his brother prisoner, treated him gently, and left him as the ruler of Cyrenaica. With this, Rome, impressed, withdrew its support from Physcon. Philometor was being powerfully supported in Rome by Cato, and Roman opinion turned generally when, after reconquering parts of Syria for Egypt, he declined the Seleucid crown which would have united those two large sections of the old Alexandrian Empire. That end was the possible outcome of Egyptian and Syrian affairs that Rome feared most. Well satisfied with Ptolemy Philometor, Rome withdrew Egypt from its emergency watch and relations between the two states continued serenely for the time being.

Rome carefully monitored the transition from Antiochus the Great to Seleucus to Antiochus Epiphanes to an infant King and his corrupt minister Lysias, at which time Rome sponsored some guerrilla activity to reduce the state of Syria's armed forces (burning ships and poisoning some elephants). This helped produce a revolt which was led by Seleucus' son Demetrius, who had been detained in Rome, escaped and returned to Syria; he led a popular revolt against Lysias. Rome increased its espionage effort in the 160's and gave extensive moral support to the pretender Alexander Balas. Relations between Rome and the Greek world were correct but uneasy; neither trusted the other and Rome's armed vigilance somewhat stifled the spontaneity and confidence of the Greeks and their culture. Rome was not overawed by Greek culture and had long tired of its endless quarrelling and conflict.

Roman opinion had soured on Eumenes after it was reliably reported that even after all Rome had done for him, he hedged his bets with Perseus as the Macedonian war approached. He sent his brother Attalus, to Rome in 167 to ask for help against the Galatians as well as to offer congratulations on the great Roman victory, the Romans expressed their dissatisfaction with Eumenes, and when he requested to be allowed to address the Senate to explain his conduct and answer criticism, the Senate, swaddling itself in Republican virtue (and hypocrisy), quickly passed a resolution that no king would be received in Rome. (King Prusias of Bithynia had scarcely left Rome after what amounted to a state visit.) Eumenes died in 159 and his relations with Rome had still not been fully restored, but Rome well knew his heir Attalus II and immediately made it clear from the beginning of his reign that he had Rome's support. Squabbling continued, however, and Attalus encouraged Prusias' son Nicomedes to revolt, hoping the fact that Nicomedes had resided in Rome for some years and had powerful friends there, would cause Rome to be more supportive of Pergamon.

Rome moved too slowly and finally sent three commissioners, the gout-ridden Marcus Licinius, A. Mancinus, who had allegedly not fully recovered from the effects of a tile falling upon his head, and Lucius Malleolus, according to Polybius: "The stupidest man in Rome." This moved Cato to tell the Senate that before such a commission arrived at any decision Prusius would be dead, Nicomedes would be elderly and that a commission could not move quickly or achieve anything when it had "neither feet, head, nor intelligence."[1] Cato proved prophetic as Prusius died, Nicomedes replaced him and there was no need or justification for anyone to do anything more. Good relations followed between Bithynia and Pergamon.

Not so easily resolved were Rome's relations with Rhodes, which were absurdly complicated. Rhodes deserved to be rewarded for its support of Rome against Antiochus with most of Caria and Lycia in Asia Minor except the port of Telmessus reserved for Pergamon. But the status of the Lycians was left ambiguous as between being allies or subjects of Rhodes, and in order to resolve that issue by ensuring that the Lycians understood they were subjects of Rhodes, force was applied, causing the Roman Senate to determine in 177 the Lycians were friends and allies of Rhodes but not subjects. This did not grant the Lycians total independence, but it was unsatisfactory to the Rhodians also. Perseus sent emissaries to Rhodes in 171 asking for mediation with Rome though the Rhodians also requested that nothing in the exchange be possibly construed as Rhodian hostility to Rome. Subsequent Roman requests for naval assistance were promptly met and even exceeded. Rhodian opinion was irritated when the Macedonians captured a Rhodian quinquereme, but the Romans alleviated that tension by approving the importation from Sicily to Rhodes of one-hundred and fifty thousand bushels of grain. In 168, Perseus persuaded Rhodes to send envoys to Rome to urge the end of the Roman war with Macedonia. They arrived after the news of the crushing Roman victory at Pydna had been received and attempted to change their request to a message of congratulation. This did not placate the Romans, who pointed out that Rhodes had done nothing about Syrian actions in Greece for two years without a Rhodian complaint. The proposal was tendered in the Senate to declare war on Rhodes, but this was rejected on the recommendation of Cato, who famously said that "Rome could not lament being

---

1 Polybius xxxvi, 14.

more feared than loved."[2]

Rhodes was rattled enough by the froideur of newly risen Rome that it departed Rhodian tradition and requested an alliance with Rome. This was only agreed after two years. As this was being signed, Rhodes faced a revolt from some of its subjects in Caria, which they easily suppressed, but Rome took the opportunity to repeat their now tiresome litany about Caria and Lycia being friends and allies and not subjects of Rhodes. This meant also the abandonment of Caunus and Stratoniceia, which would produce a heavy income loss, aggravated by the transference of Delos to Athens. Lumbered with what was perceived in the Eastern Mediterranean and Asia Minor as a softened relationship with Rome, those disinclined to be governed by Rome and by Rhodes made themselves heard. In 155 the island of Crete was entirely united in defense of piracy against Rhodes, which was generally assigned the responsibility for dealing with piracy in the Eastern Mediterranean. The loss of credibility that Rhodes suffered in the visible cooling of her relations with Rome coupled to the sharp reduction in the permitted naval strength of the Seleucids, encouraged the rise of Cilician piracy. Rome's subtle cat and mouse game with lesser states now required her to deal with pirates herself. Calibrating and maintaining a balance of the correlation of forces in the regions bordering the expanding Roman world was bound to be tiresome but failing to do the necessary to maintain that objective ultimately imposed upon Rome the onerous burden of doing it directly. The Pax Romana was designed to be a rewarding trade relationship in the practically uncontested leadership of a large block of reasonably like-minded states. By observing a few niceties Rome could masquerade as the first among equals while in fact running the entire group. Now it was coming perilously close to conscripting itself to do the heavy lifting it had been in the habit of underpaying formerly vanquished parties to do.

Rome had entered Greek affairs with a high respect, if not a profound veneration of the Greek states' cultural eminence, their civic and political values, which to a substantial degree Rome had emulated, their seniority to Rome as a distinguished and influential civilization, and their unfailing courage in defense of advanced European civilization. Rome was also bound to admire Greece's remarkable maritime aptitudes that had propelled the spread of trade and the comparatively advanced civilization of Mediterranean Europe into Asia Minor, North Africa, and throughout and beyond the Mediterranean. A generation as the Protector of the Greek states naturally eroded Rome's impartiality toward the squabbling jurisdictions whose freedom it guaranteed, and inclined the Roman government to be more appreciative of those Greek states which were more compliant to Roman wishes (that were not onerous). These states were more respectful of and even grateful for Rome's role as an equitable suzerain. However admirable the Greeks were and remain, they have always strained the patience of all those with whom they have dealt, themselves first and most of all. The Romans found them magnificent in their way but also tiresome as only they could be, and as Roman responsibilities and ambitions slowly expanded, Rome's interest in endlessly moderating the fermentation of the Greek states steadily declined.

---

2   CAH, VIII, p. 289 (P.V.M. Benecke).

It was inevitable that some of those Greeks most apparently responsive to Roman wishes were unscrupulous scoundrels who sacrificed panhellenic patriotism in the interests of securing preferments from the Roman overlords. Many Greeks naturally reacted against the antics of excessive collaborators and could not resist assisting those forces opposed to Rome, including the very Macedonia from whose unappreciated domination Rome had liberated the Greeks. The Greek state the Romans admired most and which was coincidentally also the most cooperative was Athens. Appropriately, the greatest cultural center in the world, the most politically advanced civic jurisdiction in the world, and if such a distinction may be fairly made, the bravest of all the brave Greeks in the defense of that civilization, seemed to appreciate best the mighty role in the world that Rome was assuming, and the comparative gentleness and benignity of the moderate discipline it placed on fractious Greece. There had been some good feeling in Athens towards Antiochus, but no official manifestation of it during his unhappy war with Rome; and Athens had been unshakable and generous in its offers of military collaboration in Rome's conflict with Perseus.

Alas, even a cordial relationship with Athens had its complexities. Athens claimed the city of Oropus as a tributary state under somewhat ambiguous aspects of the previous Roman settlement of Greece. Oropus accused Athens of an illegal use and threat of force and the Roman Senate appointed the Sicyonians to arbitrate. Athens did not accept the authority of this comparative upstart state to play any such role, and the Sicyonians, with evident relish, ordered Athens to pay a colossal fine of five-hundred talents. Athens then sent to Rome to argue their position, in an elegant and ingenious tactical improvisation, the heads of three of their most illustrious schools of philosophy, Carneades, Diogenes, and Critolaus. This was a completely extra-legal proceeding; it was a little like the current government of France sending the three most eminent members of the French Academy to dispute a tariff assessment before the European Commission in Brussels, if Brussels was forearmed with all the authority of the other member states of the European Union. It dazzled the Roman Senate and academic community and Roman society, and although they considered that technically Athens was wrongfooted legally, the Senate acknowledged the complaint of Oropus, but reduced the penalty by four-fifths to one-hundred talents. Unfortunately, Athens being Athens, rejected this finding as excessive. A suspension of hostility was arranged between Athens and Oropus, but not on any basis that had a chance of lasting very long. Oropus appealed to the Achaean League claiming that the Athenian garrison in their city was behaving abusively, and the League decided against Athens and resorted to force against the offending Athenian garrison in Oropus, putting the Roman cat squarely among the Greek pigeons.

The Romans had been somewhat ambivalent about whether they favoured these Greek Leagues as instruments of conciliation between their member states or regarded them with suspicion as organizations intended to increase the power of the constituent states to object to Roman policy. Like all the Greek quarrels, the Romans found their internal deliberations squalid and tedious. As has been recounted, the principal figure in the latter Achaean League was Philipoemen, who had supported

Rome against both Macedonia and Antiochus and gained Roman favour thereby. He respected Rome but did not wish its influence on Greece to stifle his own ability to lead the Greeks; the formula he devised was to assert the League interest gradually within Greece on a legally arguable basis which, given past services, he was confident would be approved when submitted for ratification to the Roman Senate.

This formula functioned well enough for a time, but started to come unstuck in 185, when the former consul and dictator, Q. Caecilius Metellus was returning from Macedonia and Philipoemen and his colleagues debated with the eminent Roman on Greek issues and rejected his request that the assembly of the Achaean League be convened. Rome went over the head of the League and constituted a commission of three including Flamininus and Metellus, as their leading Greek experts, to consider the legitimacy or otherwise of Philipoemen's crowning ambition-to confirm Sparta's entire adherence to the Achaean League.

In 183, when Messenia sought to secede from the Achaean League, Q. Marcius Philippus, another Greek hand who had just returned from there, advised the Senate that if Rome did not assist in suppressing the secession, that movement might gain strength and oblige the League to be more cooperative. Rome accordingly declined to help suppress Messenia and warned the League that its conduct could provoke the secession of Sparta, Corinth, and Argos as well. The League easily suppressed Messenia but had to live with the paradox of Philipoemen: he was a greater soldier than he was a statesman, and in building Achaean strength on the imposition of military gradualism within Greece with a tacit sanction from Rome, he gradually stirred Roman concerns that what was intended was a greater degree of autonomy than Rome could happily tolerate. His talents as a general and in Hellenic diplomatic maneuver were greater than his ability to placate the Roman overlord. Rome was somewhat complacent but not at all naïve, and it viewed the gradual rise of the Achaean League with mounting disquietude.

In Sparta, the league had to intervene against the demagogue Chaeron, who appeared to be a rabble-rouser successor to Nabis. The Roman Senate diplomatically determined that the only exiles allowed to return were those who were not deemed to be militant opponents of the Achaean League. This was a conciliatory gesture, but Rome soon determined that it had been too indulgent, and a debate began between the League and the Senate about which movement would be permitted to return to Sparta. The customary representations were made to the Senate but Callicrates of Leontium unwisely advised the Senators that if Rome had strong views on any subject involving constituent states of the Achaean League, it would do better to enforce them rigorously in order to stamp out the temptation to secure or dilute Senate decisions and play for patriotic and nationalist enthusiasm in the Greek states. This was widely seen in the League states as dishonorable advice and the betrayal of the Greeks to Rome. Roman policy evolved slowly and the Senate had come to look upon almost all petitioners with considerable skepticism. But from this point on, Rome tended to apply the test of a willing execution of Senate decrees as the principal criterion for assessing the performance of the Greek governments and Callicrates was cited as an admirable example to be followed. The Romans applied the same standards to the Aetolians, Epirotes, Athenians, Boeotians, and Acarnanians.

Callicrates now became leader of a movement throughout the Achaean League, to play upon the fear of Roman intervention as a guide to policy. It was heroic and somewhat antithetical to the irrepressible Greek political temperament, but it found prudent favour for about a decade. No party in the Achaean League wanted any part of the proffered Macedonian alliance and Perseus' overtures were rebuffed. When Appius Claudius asked the league for five-thousand soldiers to assist him in Epirus, the Achaeans, on the advice of Marcius Philippus, declined to do anything for Rome unless it was requested by the Senate. In seeking to pretend to be a serious autonomous power when the Achaean League was really only a circumscribed satellite of Rome, it helped propel Rome into becoming an ever more authoritarian suzerain trying to masquerade as a conqueror without the bother of actually conquering and occupying.

After the Macedonian War the Romans sent commissioners to Achaea to determine what the league had actually done and they decided that all the Achaean generals since the beginning of the Macedonian war were unsuitable and rounded up a thousand people from a list supplied by Callicrates, and sent them in custody to Italy, supposedly for ultimate trial, which in fact never occurred. Requests for their release continued for over a decade; survivors were finally allowed to return in 151, after Cato publicly declared that they were too elderly to do any harm to Rome. Callicrates died in 149 on his way to Rome to petition the Senate yet again. His fellow petitioner, Diaeus, carried on and was of a much more independent frame of mind. He aggressively challenged the Senate's authority, which caused Rome to incite secessionist activity in other Achaean states besides Sparta. Achaea and Sparta appeared to be close to a resolution of their differences in the summer of 147 until the arrival of a Roman commission led by L. Aurelius Orestes, who announced to an assembly of the league at Corinth that Rome had determined that not only Sparta but also Corinth, Argos, Orchomenus, and Heraclea were all henceforth detached from the league. This provoked spontaneous anger in which various Spartan delegates were roughed up, and the Romans present, unaccustomed to anything except servile deference, were rather liberally insulted.

Rome was inscrutable and Critolaus was elected General and Achaea rejected the Roman Senate's demand for the punishment of those responsible for the disorder at the assembly in Corinth. Secretly the Senate ordered Metellus to advance upon Greece from Macedonia and Attalus was invited to contribute forces to an impending Roman disciplinary expedition or move against Greece. By early 146, it was clear that there was widespread sympathy in Greece for the Achaeans. Critolaus responded to Roman overtures with the assertion that the Achaeans sought friendship with Rome, not submission to it. The consul Lucius Mummius was given an army of thirty-thousand and a fleet and a mandate to knock the Greeks down a peg. Neither Mummius nor those who commissioned him retained any of the previous Roman sentimental or cultural veneration of the Greeks. It was a straight question of giving an unruly nationality of upstarts, quibblers, and ingrates a good thrashing. Critolaus was not a talented tactician and impetuously besieged Heraclea, dividing his forces.

Metellus saw the opportunity that opened and attacked Critolaus in the rear and the flank at Scarpheia in Locris. Critolaus died fighting and his army was routed as were the reinforcements rushing to its assistance. Boeotia was now wide open to Roman invasion. The Achaeans responded resolutely; Diaeus became the general and barred the Corinthian isthmus to the Roman army, which had to stop as the Roman fleet was still under construction and had not been fully deployed. Mummius arrived and assumed command of a combined army. Diaeus took the bait which was offered and came forward to engage the superior Roman forces: he was overwhelmingly defeated, Corinth opened its gates and surrendered, most of its population having fled, and the Romans sacked the city severely. Diaeus honorably committed suicide, and all Achaean resistance collapsed.

They had insanely overplayed their hand and the whole escapade was a mad enterprise. Democratically chosen regimes which had encouraged resistance to Rome were overthrown by angry mobs and the Greek states engaged in widespread trumped-up trials and public executions of their recent former civic leaders. The Achaean, Boeotian, Euboean, Phocian, and Locrian leagues were dissolved. Corinth was singled out: after being sacked down to its basements, all its worthwhile accumulated treasures were transported to Rome for permanent display or sale and the city was burned to ashes. Greece finally learned the lesson that insolent disobedience towards Rome was mortally hazardous, and the lesson, as had been intended by those who imparted it, did not go unnoticed throughout the region.

In fairness to Rome, at least it gave a gentler option a very good try. When it finally responded to the endless Greek mischief conceived and carried out with the ingenuity of fiendish children, Rome's anger was legitimate. But subduing the Greeks as severely as they did, was regrettable and ultimately counterproductive. The historian Polybius distinguished himself by urging moderation on the Roman commissioners and by declining to accept any consideration for the good advice and public support he'd given to Rome and for his efforts to make the drastic transition that occurred as smooth as possible. The Romans declared the Achaean War to be over in 140, and thanks in some measure to Polybius, they imposed a more generous peace than the fierce antics of Mummius would have inspired anyone to expect.[3]

2. Rome and Spain

By 205 B.C., thanks to Scipio Africanus, both as a general and a politically agile governor, Rome controlled those parts of Spain that interested it. These were the provinces of Nearer and Further Spain, still governed at that point by private individuals with the title of proconsul but in large measure trading for their own account. Spain attracted Rome initially, as has been mentioned, in the Punic Wars, to deprive Carthage of the gold and silver that it extracted from Spain and used to engage its mercenary armies and navy. Once the rivalry turned to war, the Romans quickly realized that Spain was Carthage's Achilles' heel and they struck there with irresistible force and captured the mining centre, New Carthage, in 209. The Romans quickly discovered that northern and central Spain also contained considerable min-

---

[3] I would be remiss not to mention my gratitude to my grade eleven history teacher, Angus Scott, for first interesting me, in 1960, in Mummius, an unusual and little-noted general.

ing resources and as part of their civilizing mission the Romans easily determined that this wealth should not be left to the barbaric Spanish tribes alone. They soon came to value not only the precious metals of Spain, but its value as a source of grain and other crops, and of warriors also. Unlike Carthage, Rome comprehensively subsumed territories into itself, dispersed Roman citizenship to the eminent local loyalists, provided improved security and roads and increased commercial trade, and imposed usually, lower taxes than the locals were accustomed to and conscripted the young men to the Roman armed forces, as needed, but paid them well. The Romans gradually reduced the Spanish tribes, dividing them, absorbing some of their number, driving some completely out of the Iberian Peninsula, and steadily reducing their numbers and significance as distinct entities. Within a few years, vast quantities of grain were being exported from Spain to Rome.

As usually happened with populations the Romans had taken over, a revolt arose in 197, led by the usually rather tranquil if uneuphoniously named Turdetanians, who took advantage of the preoccupation of Rome in the Gallic and Macedonian Wars and managed to raise all the western half of the Further Spanish province. The revolts spread to the eastern Spanish provinces almost at once. The following year, the Romans did gain the upper hand in Further Spain, but the condition of Nearer Spain became so dire that the redoubtable Cato, now the consul, was dispatched with a regular army which expanded the Roman force in Spain to approximately fifty-thousand men. Cato enjoyed considerable success as he marched all the way across Spain and back, winning a number of engagements and diplomatically as well as with grants of money, winning over a number of the Spanish tribes in 190. Aemilius Paullus, later victorious over Perseus, suffered defeat against the Lusitanians before reasserting himself. Cato's march provoked the Celtiberians, the most formidable of all the Spanish warrior tribes, and war broke out between the Romans and the Celtiberians; it would continue intermittently for sixty years.

The eminent consul and statesman Tiberius Gracchus, father of the tribunes whose careers will arise in the next chapter (and who have resonated throughout subsequent history), managed to conciliate a number of the tribes while strengthening Rome's position in Spain through the late Third Century B.C., and in 179, he did negotiate a truce with the Celtiberians, which endured until 153 B.C. The Celtiberian War, when renewed, lasted from 153 to 151 and resumed from 143 to 133; at the same time, the nearby Lusitanians initiated a revolt by plundering Roman territory and the ensuing war frequently overlapped the Celtiberian revolt, and continued without interruption until 138, with the death of their leader, Veriathus. The Lusitanians, led by Punicus, were victorious several times against a series of praetors, spread their revolt to neighbors, and invaded the Roman western Spanish province and sacked much of it.

Punicus was killed by a Roman stone-slinger and was succeeded by Caeserus, his deputy, who administered a severe defeat on the young Mummius, who would go on to destroy Corinth. The Romans lost nine-thousand dead in this bitter engagement and Caesarus was able to rouse the Celtiberians back to war, though the Romans were able to win their temporary abstention with a treaty of concession. The rampaging Lusitania invaded the district of Algarve, now in Portugal, and crossed the

Straits of Gibraltar into what is now Morocco until Mummius drove them back.

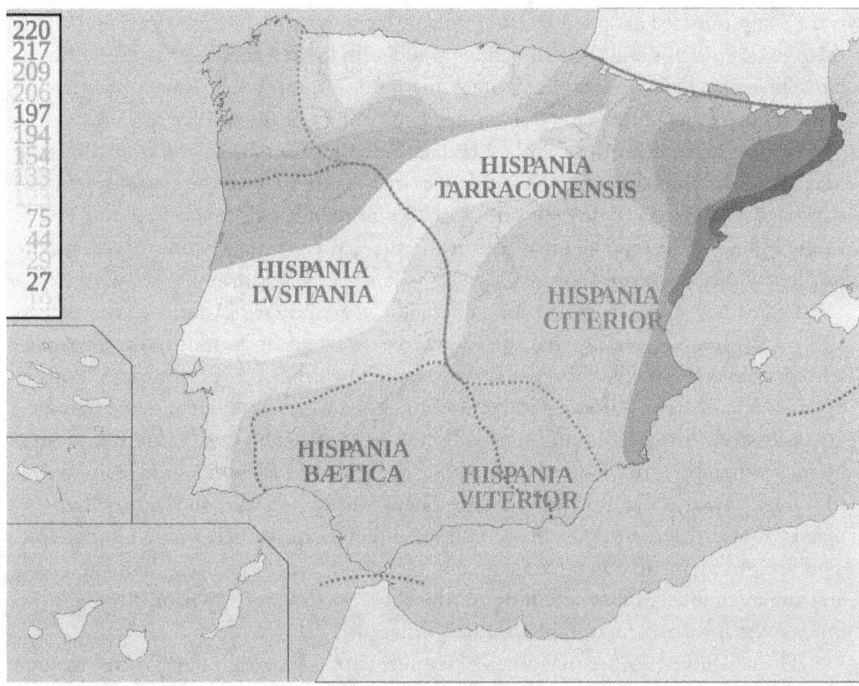

Roman conquest of Spain 220-19 B.C.

This soon led to one of the most undistinguished chapters in the history of Roman expansion: the successor to Mummius, Marcus Atilius, was somewhat successful and the Lusitanians made peace, but abandoned it without notice as soon as Atilius had retired into winter quarters. He was replaced by Galba, whom the Lusitanians defeated in 151 killing seven-thousand Romans. Lucullus, the governor of Nearer Spain, assisted Galba, who persuaded the Lusitanians to make peace in exchange for land. They surrendered their weapons and divided into smaller groups to facilitate settlement on their new land grants, at which point Galba massacred virtually all of them. Galba retained most of what he had seized for himself, to the disconcertion of his forces. When he returned to Rome, he was tried, and violently denounced in the Senate by the eighty-five-year-old Cato, who had left his command in Spain just five years before, having, as always, conducted himself with impeccable distinction. Galba made no attempt to defend his conduct, but rather called his family before the Tribune and pleaded necessity, accompanied by systematic bribery of the tribune's court, and he was acquitted (and elected consul in 144).

The Lusitanians were not finished yet; about ten-thousand survivors and other able-bodied men gathered together and re-invaded Further Spain. They were surrounded by the praetor Vetilius and were once more contemplating surrender, when Viriathus, an ingenious soldier and a bold tactician, called them to their duty. He was chosen leader and managed a concentrated breakthrough at one point in the Roman perimeter and used his knowledge of the terrain to depart the road along which they were being pursued at speed by the Romans, lay in wait in nearby woods and attack them in both flanks and the rear suddenly and with great ferocity at the Sierra Rhonda, killing four-thousand Romans, including Vetilius himself. Viriathus now gave the Romans the most convincing lesson they had yet had in the warlike qualities of the Spaniards. He marched through La Mancha, defeated Plautius, killing four-thousand more Romans and laid waste the whole area in 146. He crossed the Guadarrama and advanced to Segovia, defeating one Roman commander after another, and in 145 Rome again had to send a consular army of two legions under Fabius Maximus, the brother of Scipio Aemilianus.

Fabius had some successes for a couple of years but in 143 and 142 was defeated by Viriathus so soundly that the Celtiberians saw an opportunity for vengeance and reentered the conflict against Rome. Rome's position was extremely perilous in Spain as Viriathus had aroused all the mountainous tribes in revolt and he attempted unsuccessfully to make common cause with the Gauls, who were none too pleased by the Roman presence among them either (and this was a century before the arrival of Julius Caesar). The Spanish and the Gauls were both wild and almost unorganized tribes and serious coordination between their commanders proved impossible. The remote Spaniards were considerably more rambunctious even than the Gauls and organizing them into anything of the slightest military sophistication was too much even for a great natural leader like Viriathus.

The adoptive brother of Fabius Maximus, Fabius Maximus Servilianus, was the Roman commander in 141 and was serially defeated by Viriathus, but as usually happened with these native people, they tired of war and pressured their leader to make a generous peace with Rome. The Lusitanian leader thus allowed the Roman consul to withdraw in order, and the Roman Senate dutifully ratified the treaty, though both parties knew that this was a charade, and that war could break out again at any time with no warning, by either side. Similar conduct occurred in the Celtiberian War in Nearer Spain, where Pompeius, the Roman commander, had concluded a peace with the Celtiberians. These are savage wars even by the standards of the time. The next Roman commander was Servilius Caepio, who was not overly successful on the battlefield but outdid even Galba in treachery. He gave large bribes to three of Viriathus' supposedly intimate friends to poison him. The war ended. Viriathus was irreplaceable, a brilliant tactician and strategist and inspiring leader with a mystical quality that imposed a common determination on the otherwise fractious and unmanageable Lusitanians. He was the forerunner for Sertorius, the renegade Roman general in Iberia seventy years later. Viriathus' achievement in almost always winning and maintaining a coherent army in the field for eight years qualifies him as one of the outstanding military commanders of the ancient world.

The next outburst of the Celtiberian War was between 153 and 151. The nearby tribe of the Belli, with whom Rome had signed a semi-serious alliance, had set about building a great fortress at Segeda, which the Romans considered threatening and demanded that construction cease, and when this was ignored, Rome declared war, immediately fomenting a widespread conflict with many very bellicose tribes. Praetors were quickly replaced with consuls commanding at least two legions, which had occurred only once before in Spain, in 195. The consul Nobilior marched to attack Segeda at the beginning of 152, and the inhabitants fled, seeking refuge with the Arevaci, and rousing other tribes as they did so. Nobilior marched on to Numantia but was intercepted and crushingly defeated with the loss of six-thousand men, but he inflicted heavy casualties also, including the death of the Arevaci general, Karos. They were unable to complete their victory and Nobilior built up a formidable camp on top of the mountain Gran Atalaya, four miles from Numantia. Nobilior sustained a few more lesser defeats and then went to winter quarters, which Polybius tells us were nightmarishly cold and under-supplied. Nobilior was replaced by the much more experienced general, Marcellus, another Roman soldier-statesman who well knew how to placate and incentivize peace even as he waged war. He was followed by Lucullus, who was accompanied by the principal personality in the balance of the war, Scipio Aemilianus, a worthy bearer of his great name.

Lucullus departed westwards to Further Spain with some of the army looting and massacring as he went to the aid of Galba, who as we have seen was already engaged in similar activities. The scandalous and murderous activities of these two men caused the establishment of a permanent court to deal with unauthorized extortion from foreigners in 149. The standstill remained for eight years, until Lusitania rose up; the war broke out again in 143 and the consul entrusted with it was the experienced and capable Metellus, who would deal effectively with the Macedonian revolt (Chapter 20 above). He pacified the area around Numantia, but his term ended before he could subdue that fortified town itself. He was succeeded by the generally incompetent Pompeius, who attempted to storm Numantia, unsuccessfully, even though he had four times as many men as there were defenders, and his army had been well-trained by his predecessor. He had a few other lesser campaigns, but they were all failures. But he did follow the traditional Roman practice in the region when a test of arms was unsuccessful and bribed the Numantian leaders into ending the war, a privilege for which they were paid thirty talents. When his successor, Popillius Laenas, arrived in 139, Pompeius declared the treaty null as it had not yet been ratified, and took the Numantian silver given in consideration for a peace treaty, mainly for himself, thus earning a dishonored place in Rome's Spanish history beside Lucullus and Galba.

Popillius too was unsuccessful but was a virtual Hannibal compared to his successor, Mancinus, the author of perhaps the most disgraceful episode in the entire history of the Roman army. He suffered a series of defeats in 137 while approaching the Ebro and surrendered with twenty-thousand men to between four-thousand and eight-thousand Spaniards. There was not the slightest excuse for such a shameful and cowardly act. The Numantians agreed to a treaty on the word of Tiberius Gracchus, the future Tribune, on the basis of his father's great prestige in Spain and in Rome. But under Scipio's influence, the treaty was not agreed by the Senate and in 135 Scipio himself was by general public demand, sent to Spain to eliminate this tumor and restore the honor of Rome, both from the treachery and the cowardice of previous commanders, and from the fierce insubordination of much of Iberia. This breach between the Gracchi and the Scipios, almost equally illustrious families closely related (the talented daughter of Publius Scipio Africanus, Cornelia, was married to Tiberius Gracchus), would have an immense destructive influence on Roman politics for the next seventy-five years.

Scipio now had an army of about sixty-thousand, but forty-thousand were Spanish auxiliaries and the Romans were very demoralized after the degrading leadership they had had. Scipio trained up his men as best he could but knew that they were not disciplined enough to take Numantia by storm, so he invested the town, built a perimeter around it with a system of signals that was able to bring reinforcements to any sector that was under attack swiftly. The besieged Numantians made many courageous efforts to break the encirclement without success although their leader Rectugenos, did get through but was unable to stir up any support from neighbouring tribes. The besieged population was reduced to cannibalism and then suicide and only a relative handful, starving, survived. Scipio burned the town to the ground and the war ended. He became Scipio Numantinus.

These wars had been very enervating for the Romans, causing the deaths of many thousands of their soldiers and severe division in Roman opinion. It performed a role in Roman and international politics slightly like that of the war of 1812 or the Vietnam War for the United States and the American Revolutionary War and the South African war for Great Britain, and the Algerian War for France. In all those wars, as with Spain for Rome, there was large public dissent from the moral and strategic implications of the wars. Tiberius Gracchus, the rising reform leader in Rome, advocated a substantial increase in the agricultural population both by settlement and by the intake of new groups of citizens, in order to raise the number of people that Rome could send to its various wars. Because of silver in Spain and Macedonia, a Roman campaign in either place could substantially pay for itself. The waving of the rule that consuls could not serve more than once in every decade and could serve for only one year and the setting up of a standing army all, in hindsight have been seen as indicative of the coming of an Emperor in place of the beleaguered Republic. Scipio returned to Rome almost as able to have seized power as Caesar would be eighty-four years later, but he had no such interest.

The Romans hereafter had undisturbed possession of Spain and took full advantage of the gold and silver mines. In the ensuing years, Rome sometimes sold some of the mines to private interests and took them back. Polybius records that forty-thousand slaves worked at the silver mines of New Carthage alone. The financial oppression of the Iberians was extremely severe and led to further revolts in 98 and in the 70's under Sertorius and in Augustus' times. The Roman treatment of the Spanish was barbarous, and it was counterproductive. The elder Gracchus and Scipio Numantinus achieved more by their firm but clement policy than those who ruled Spain in Rome's name by sword and lash. Augustus, more than a century later, would institute a more generous form of administration.

Rome did contribute importantly to the public works of Iberia, In particular the road from the Pyrenees to Gibraltar, about a thousand kilometres. There were also many other fine public works and finally some manifestations of Roman civil society. But in Spain more than in Italy, Gaul, or Greece, the Romans were slow to add a mission to civilize and construct to the most odious exploitation and plunder which initially attracted them to Spain. In general, and starting in about another two centuries, Rome would do better in Spain in a religious than a political capacity. It may also be said that Carthage and Rome in their exploitation of Spanish gold and silver, educated the Spanish on how to extract the resources from primitive societies with a minimum concern for the rights and dignity of the inhabitants, and the Spanish emulated the Romans and Carthaginians when their turn came to plunder Latin America fifteen-hundred years later.

3. The Final Destruction of Carthage

In general, the government of Carthage had adhered scrupulously to the undertakings that it signed at the catastrophic end of the Second Punic War. The independent revolt in northern Italy was disavowed by Carthage and in the Roman wars against Macedonia and Syria. Carthage provided naval and military assistance to Rome and offered more but was curtly declined. Carthage even sent to Greece supplementary shipments of grain to support the Roman armies in the East. Against these efforts to adjust to the new correlation of forces in the central Mediterranean were the schemings of Rome's African ally Massinissa. At the close of the Hannibalic war, Massinissa was thirty-seven and a tall and extremely vigorous and energetic man. He would continue in this state into his nineties and when he was eighty-six, one of his innumerable wives presented him with his forty-fourth son. He set himself the goal of uniting the Numidian tribes and turning them into a coherent kingdom. He had spent his youth in Carthage and was therefore a more metropolitan figure than his fellow Numidians, and he had married the daughter of Hasdrubal and assimilated some of the attitudes of the leading family of a serious power.

His goal of taming his barbarous tribes required him recruiting them to the occupation of stationary agriculture as he stretched his empire, as he hoped, with Roman sponsorship, from Morocco to Egypt. In the Second Punic War, with Roman help, Massinissa had defeated the empire of Syphax and other independent princes whom he reduced to vassals. He also gained extensive Carthaginian territory with the blessing of the Romans and had the advantage of being able to offer greater security as Rome was friendly to him, and reduced taxation. He was a man of such force that even at the age of ninety, he mounted his horse without assistance and rode bareback. He established his sons as proconsuls governing in his name and taming the barbarous tribes as the extent of his kingdom expanded.

The peace dictated by Scipio after Zama confined Carthage almost to its original charter which is approximately the upper one third of modern northern Tunisia. In the ensuing fifty years, Massinissa seized all Carthage's leavings, as well as infiltrating part of its rightful territory. Carthage was prevented from responding effectively to these depredations as under its treaty with Rome it could not undertake even a defensive war without Roman authorization. In these circumstances, as the Roman statesmen presumably foresaw, such an aggressive neighbour as Massinissa was certain eventually to provoke Carthage to war whatever its treaty obligations. Starting in 160, the Carthaginian officer Carthalo began plundering expeditions into the territory that Massinissa had illicitly occupied that was part of Carthage itself.

These raids were reciprocated and Massinissa added to the territory that he was already occupying in Carthage, causing the dispatch of commissioners from Rome led by the imperishable Cato in 153 (he was eighty-one). The Carthaginians were reluctant to be completely submissive in these circumstances, which rekindled Cato's ancient hatred of them. He judged Carthage uncooperative and began his famous rhetorical campaign; he sounded his final tocsin, concluding each public comment: "Delenda est Carthago,"[4] like a 1930's Nazi shouting "Heil Hitler!" at the end of every conversation.

Cato, 234-149, was a farm-owner and soldier who rallied to Rome's military needs again and again, and returned, like Cincinnatus, to his farm, where he dressed and behaved like his farm workers, and ate with them and had the same meals. He was an outright plebeian, but of solid and sturdy patriotic stock. Having achieved considerable military success, he came to Rome, and though regarded at first as a parvenu and even a yokel, though a brave and outspoken one, he climbed the official ladder meritocratically: military tribune (214), quaestor (204), aedile (199), praetor (198), consul (195), censor (184). He was always vigilantly defending ancient Roman customs and virtues and resisting Hellenic cultural and social influences, which he considered effeminate and decadent. He was on the staff of Quintus Fabius Maximus in the Second Punic War and was instrumental in the defeat (and death) of Hasdrubal at the Battle of the Metaurus (207).

Rome was at this time evolving from the rustic, ancient virtue that Cato epitomized, and had absorbed a good deal of rational and artistic Greek culture, with some of the sumptuousness and even debauchery of the Orient. Cato was the powerful leader of the traditionalists. Marcellus, Scipio, and Flamininus are exemplars of the partially Hellenized Romans. As praetor in 199 Cato restored the long-lapsed Plebeian games, and as praetor in Sardinia the following year, he outlawed usury in Sardinia. In 215 he helped pass the Oppian Law which strictly limited the quantity of precious metals women could have, to promote the war effort, and restrained the conduct of women generally. There were large feminist demonstrations and various harassments of males, from which modern suffragettes and feminists could have learned much. After the defeat of Hannibal, the law was repealed over Cato's objections, shortly before he embarked for Spain. As has been described, he was successful in Spain, through severity and integrity and bold command, as he was at Thermopylae in 191 against Antiochus.

In 181, he supported the Lex Orchi, which would limit the number of people at a private entertainment, and in 169 he supported the Lex Voconia, which purported to limit the quantity of wealth any citizen could have. It was after he visited a rebuilt and flourishing Carthage in 157 that he became convinced that Carthage was recovering so well that it must be destroyed in the Roman national interest, which is what caused him henceforth to begin and conclude all public remarks "Delenda est Carthago." Cato was the formidable head of a traditionalist faction of twenty-five or thirty percent of Roman citizens though there were inconsistencies in his position that he never addressed. In fact, his military severity was sometimes oppressive, his attacks on rivals were frequently unjust and excessive, and he had no rightful

---

4 "Carthage must be destroyed."

purpose calling for the destruction of Carthage because it had recovered well from its defeat at the hands of the Romans. And his opposition to Rome's rising cultural standards and its expansion as a jurisdiction were essentially humbug, xenophobia, and philistinism.

By mid-century, divisions had arisen in Carthage between those who wished to make common cause with Massinissa, who would not be so overwhelming an ally as Rome, and those who wished to avoid any provocation of Rome for fear of where it might lead. Cato was not immediately successful in his campaign and in 152, Scipio Nasica conducted a commission that ordered Massinissa to withdraw from some of his usurpations. Carthage expelled the pro-Massinissa faction from within its walls and banished it from its territory. When Carthage refused to receive these exiles back as Massinissa sent them, they were attacked by the general Hamilcar, and some were killed. There was now a sort of a no-man's land between Carthage and the Numidians where these unfortunate double-expulsees festered.

In these circumstances, Massinissa considered that he had been the victim of a Carthaginian attack and in 150 they squared off west of Carthage each side having built its army to over sixty-thousand men. Carthage had received about six-thousand defecting Numidian cavalry, led by two of the teeming mass of Massinissa's sons, Agasis and Soubas. Scipio Aemilianus arrived from Spain on a defense procurement visit to acquire elephants, the day before the two sides clashed. The battle between the two armies lasted all day and produced a slight advantage for the Numidian king. (Scipio watched from the height of a nearby mountain and said he felt like the mythological observations of Zeus at Ida or Poseidon at Samothrace.) The Carthaginians asked Scipio to mediate, and he proposed extremely reasonable terms. But they refused to hand over the Numidians who deserted to them, and Scipio withdrew and returned to Spain. Massinissa surrounded the Carthaginian army, and they were unable to reconnect to their supplies and gradually succumbed to disease and hunger. After killing their animals and resorting even to cannibalism they marched out and surrendered, each wearing only a single brief garment. Quarrels died hard in the Numidian desert, and Massinissa's son Gulussa took it upon himself to massacre the wretched column of the defeated army almost to a man. Massinissa was confirmed in his latest territorial acquests.

As Carthage, even in responding to the outrageous provocations of the Numidian leader, was violating the Zama treaty which required Rome's consent for Carthage to go to war, it had furnished the militants, led by Cato, with an excuse for the resumption of war. Cato once famously held up a fig in the Senate which he said had been picked in Carthage three days before. The danger now was not a Carthaginian return to war, it was an over-mighty Numidian king taking over Carthage and challenging Rome's position in the central Mediterranean. Rome mobilized four legions, and Carthage realized its error and condemned the authors of the war to death, including Hasdrubal, who escaped however and rallied twenty-thousand men in rebellion against the beleaguered government of Carthage. Roman envoys arrived and demanded to know why the authors of the war against Massinissa had not been deposed and executed before the war and were purposefully vague when asked what Rome's terms would be for peace. Rome responded to insistent Carthaginian emissaries with studied vagueness until, after extensive activity in Utica by Roman agents, Utica defected from Carthage and promised Rome all support it could give as the consuls for 149 were chosen. These were M. Manilius and L. Marcius Censorinus, who crossed to Utica at the head of approximately eighty-thousand soldiers and with more than one-hundred and fifty warships.

Carthage saw that its lot was hopeless and sent five plenipotentiary representatives to Rome offering unconditional surrender. What was now unfolding was one of the most prodigious humiliations of an important state in all the history of the world, and it would shortly be succeeded by one of the most shameful outrages ever committed by any Great Power in history against another country. Rome purported to grant Carthage "freedom and the enjoyment of their laws; and more over all their territory and the possession of their other property public and private,"[5] provided Carthage sent three-hundred noble hostages to Rome and pledged obedience to whatever commands the consuls would give. The consuls were in Utica and required that Carthage surrender all her arms and engines of war, orders that were immediately complied with, despite protestations that that would leave Carthage defenseless against Hasdrubal and his twenty-thousand rebels. Many thousands of weapons, including two-thousand catapults, were surrendered and the consuls then demanded a deputation of thirty of the most important citizens of Carthage to attend upon the Roman Senate to hear its final demands.

Only at this point were the people of Carthage, whose only offense was protecting themselves from the aggressions of Massinissa, informed that they must leave their city which would then be completely obliterated. The displaced population could settle where it wished as long as no one was within ten miles of the sea. Carthage had been finessed into disarming before receiving its death sentence. Carthage itself would no longer have any strategic significance and its population would be completely at the mercy of Massinissa and others. Banno, one of the envoys, made a powerful plea for mercy but the Senate coldly declined to alter its terms. The envoys returned to Carthage and pressed through the dense crowds of urgently curious citizens to deliver their grim message to the Carthaginian Senate.

The massed crowds hearing cries of dismay and horror from within the Senate broke into the building, seizing the envoys and summarily stoned them to death along with many others who had proposed submission to Rome. Violent chaos engulfed the city with the mothers of the hostages sent to Rome inciting further violence on those responsible for this final descent of a great city. Slaves were freed, the gates were closed, Hasdrubal was recalled to take command with a grandson of Massinissa and the entire city worked at a furious pace to produce new weapons. Carthaginian women of all social classes offered their hair to make strings for catapults and bows. Hasdrubal energetically gained the loyalty of the Libyan tribes and brought prodigious supplies of food into the city in preparation for a final siege. Manilius and Censorinus were in no hurry as they assumed that Carthage was disarmed and would be unable to contemplate resistance after its current tantrum had run its course. Massinissa, Rome's great ally, seeing that the Romans were denying him his long-held objective of taking over a vital and viable Carthage, ceased to be a reliable

---

5   Polybius, xxxvi, 4.

ally (in so far as he had ever been one).

The fortifications of Carthage were extremely powerful—the main walls were forty-five feet high and thirty feet thick-and Hasdrubal stirred up the surrounding tribes to harass the Romans as they commenced the siege. Hasdrubal also managed repeatedly to break the siege. Carthage could only be approached in two places, neither advantageous. The collection of timber for siege engines required a foray of some distance by Censorinus, where his forces were ambushed causing the loss of over five-hundred men. A combined attack was made at both susceptible points. One was beaten off but the other succeeded in slightly breaching the walls before the Romans were repulsed. Carthage conducted emergency repairs overnight with the efforts of thousands of men and in the morning the Romans were again rebuffed, with substantial losses. There was no alternative but a prolonged and complete blockade, but Rome suffered further attrition from unhealthy conditions in the marshes near the sea entrance, and Censorinus had to retire.

Manilius' position was heavily attacked one night, and only stabilized by the quick actions of Scipio Aemilianus. Manilius maintained the siege through the winter into 148 and launched expeditions into the interior to deal with Hasdrubal, which were unsuccessful, and the second one almost led to a complete disaster. Once again, the consul was saved by the agility and courage of Scipio Aemilianus. At this point, Massinissa died, aged approximately ninety-two, and his kingdom was divided among the many sons, who had different mothers and a conspicuous absence of fraternal affection. Massinissa left it to Scipio Aemilianus, explicitly in his will, to sort out his kingdom and legacy, and Scipio availed himself of his fiduciary role to persuade Phameas, the head of Hasdrubal's cavalry, to desert.

The year 148 went surprisingly well for the Carthaginians considering how desperate their position had been a year before. The new Roman consuls were Calpurnius Piso commanding the army and Lucius Mancinus commanding the navy. They continued attacking the smaller towns around Carthage to try to cut off any supplies into the besieged city. It did not even achieve that objective and dispersed the land forces amongst secondary targets when one of the towns besieged voluntarily surrendered long before conditions required such a thing, the Romans barbarously sacked the town, which was incitement to all the other towns to fight to the end if necessary. Scipio had persuaded Massinissa's most soldierly son, Gulussa, to contribute forces to the destruction of Carthage, but at this stage a substantial part of his cavalry deserted to the Carthaginians. The besieged city was more than holding its own and was now in contact with the pretender Andriscus, who was discomfiting the Romans in Macedonia. Carthage's most immediate problem was internal divisions—the commander of the city garrison was killed in a melee in the Carthaginian Senate after an allegation was made against him of treachery. The new consuls were not making any more headway than the first pair. Rome was becoming impatient over the sluggish pace of the campaign that was supposed to be little more than a surrender after a show of strength. Massinissa had divided his kingdom chiefly between his three legitimate sons, and all the others had more remote fiefdoms, but there was no central direction and the Numidians had no interest in helping Rome if their own objective of governing the entire African coast from Egypt to Morocco was not going to be advanced.

In the Roman Senate, where there was great impatience, Cato moved the appointment of Scipio as supreme commander, and formalities were overridden in the intricate procedures of the Senate. Dissenting parties and the People's Tribune proposed and passed a measure that specially qualified Scipio's elevation from candidate for curule aedile to full consul. Another Tribune's bill on behalf of the people was required to assure that the other consul, C. Linius Drusus was not sent to Carthage and that that mission was entrusted to Scipio. On the day of his arrival Scipio was able to disperse a Carthaginian attack group that had surrounded Manilius' siege team. He settled in and carefully trained Manilius' discarded and disgruntled army.

The Carthaginians prepared for the supreme climax; Hasdrubal was recalled from the interior, where he had been merrily harassing Roman outposts, and the whole population girded its loins. Carthage would fight to the last able-bodied adult and sent that message by mutilating and murdering Roman prisoners on the walls of the city and hanging them on the outer walls to show that they expected no prisoners to be taken on either side.

There was no point in compromise. Scipio retreated and tore down Hasdrubal's fort near the harbor as Hasdrubal was not conducting the Carthaginian defense itself. A Carthaginian fleet of fifty ships, built since the collapse of the spurious peace negotiations and unknown to the Romans, had been constructed. It sailed out to the edge of the harbor and engaged in a prolonged action with the Roman fleet, which after about six hours of intense fighting the Romans won. Scipio now secured the surrender of virtually all of the small city states around Carthage and treated them all gently. Still the siege continued, and Hasdrubal shrunk his perimeter and ordered the dockyards and magazines to be blown up. Finally, Roman persistence pierced the walls in a couple of places and six days of intense hand-to-hand fighting ensued, as the Romans gradually took over the city, street by street, house by house, in fierce combat. Approximately fifty-thousand inhabitants, including many women and children, survived and were sold into slavery. Salt was sown on the furrows of previously rich agricultural land around Carthage. The fortifications and docks and anything ostensibly permanent was destroyed by carefully managed inflammation and by using the locals as slave labor to dismantle the entire elaborate complex. Scipio allegedly wept at the site of the destruction of Carthage, some of Massinissa's sons were given the use of a few properties but for the most part the entire area was divided up among pieces of land granted to Romans and Utica became the capital of the new Roman province of Asia. This would have offended Massinissa, but it barely distracted his heirs from their comprehensive squabbling and snarling at each other. The war was over, and Carthage had ceased to exist.

4. The Conquest of Cisalpine Gaul and Liguria

Hannibal had stirred up a great deal of anti-Roman mischief in northern Italy, and as soon as Roman armies were dispatched to Greece in 200, the Insubrians attacked Piacenza and razed it before the Roman praetor, Furius, commander of a northern frontier army, could relieve it. He did arrive in time to save Cremona and defeated the Insubrians and stabilized the northern front, but the Cisalpine Gauls and northern Italian tribes remained hostile and resentful of Rome's success in the rest of Italy as well as in Spain, Africa, Greece, Macedonia and Asia Minor. It was now confidentially agreed Roman state policy to subjugate or expel those in the north until Rome held the natural mountain frontiers and passes of entry to Italy, as soon as their hands were free from the Greek intervention.

When Flamininus had quelled the Greek problems in 197, Cornelius Cethegus came north, rallied the Cenomani, and routed the Insubrians near Mantua, and the following year Claudius Marcellus, son of the victor of Clastidium, shattered the Insubrians at Lake Como. They capitulated and signed a treaty that included a clause that they would never be eligible for Roman citizenship. Large numbers of Italians steadily moved north and settled near what is now Milan, and eventually all traces of Celtic civilization had vanished. The Boii, who lived south of the Po between Piacenza and Ariminum were officially still in revolt and skirmished with the Romans from time to time through the 190's. Finally, in 191, Scipio Nasica appeared in force and crushed the barbarians and evicted them from their main city, Bologna. The Boii gradually withdrew across the Alps and into Bohemia over the next fifty years. The Romans established the town of Aquileia in 181 and moved adequate forces right up to the main passes through the Carnic and Julian Alps. In the next few years, the Romans also defeated the Istrians in the northeast and assured the occupation and the peopling of all of northern Italy right up to the Alps and down to the Mediterranean and the Adriatic.

Dealing with the insurrections and disorders that Hannibal had provoked in northern Italy brought the Romans into rather abrasive contact with the Ligurians, who occupy the Apennines and their foothills from north of Florence all the way to Savoy in what is now France. Roman armies skirmished with the Ligurians for some years and there was particular squabbling over who would control the great port of Genoa. The Romans built a complicated network of military roads around northern Italy so they could deploy their forces rapidly against invaders through the passes or along the coastal roads. The Romans moved thousands of people into colonies all around northern Italy and over the next century practically eliminated the foreign presence, by removal or assimilation. This campaign was effectively over by 180 though the Ligurians continued to harass Rome's allies in Massilia and Antipolis (Marseilless and Antibes). There were also uprisings generated by the Ligurians in Sardinia and Corsica, but these were famously subdued by Tiberius Sempronius Gracchus.

There remained an immense amount of reconstructive work to do throughout southern Italy after the Punic Wars. What had occurred there presaged in some measure both the Thirty Years' War of the Seventeenth Century and the Russo-German war of 1941 to 1945: hostile armies went back-and-forth over the same territory taking and retaking the same cities and mistreating the populations. Frequently whole populations were sold into slavery by both sides. Taranto, which we recall as having regarded itself as an independent state virtually on the scale of Rome or Athens, remained relatively serene and self-important in its independence long after Pyrrhus' sojourn there. This doughty imposture ended in 209 when the Roman army sacked the lower town and sold thirty-thousand people into slavery and confiscated much of the city's land. When Hannibal finally departed, he took thousands of people with him and slew twenty-thousand who refused to go. After this immolation in war between Great Powers, Taranto remained an independent city but not one of any significance.

Rome's population fluctuated between six-hundred and seventy-five thousand in 234 B.C. to over a million in 125 B.C., depending on farm conditions and the numbers of young men sent on Rome's many wars. Another factor was the drift around the Roman world of huge numbers of slaves that had been hurled into bondage by one side or the other in the Hannibalic Wars. The Greek towns in southern Italy were virtually demolished, and large numbers of Greeks, dislocated in South Italy and in Asia Minor were, both as slaves and as freed men, much seen in Roman and southern Italy and the Roman elders still looked with suspicion upon the importation of Greek culture and social norms as particularly odious.

They legislatively oppressed Bacchic clubs and associations of slaves or of slaves and freed men, both of which were regarded by the Roman Senate and authorities as particularly vulnerable to relatively easy agitation and in all cases subversive. Rome took it upon itself even to suppress these societies in allied cities. (We have seen Rome's high-handed version of an alliance.) Rome was more confident about dealing with large numbers of slaves in the Greek cities because their numbers were proportionately smaller, but slave uprisings had occurred from time to time and the Romans preferred, if possible, to prevent them preveniently.

Roman law was further extended throughout Italy and beyond by the tendency to rationalize Roman and non-Roman law by the adoption of the Roman version. One such case was the passage by the Senate of Tiberius Gracchus' Sempronian plebiscite in 193, extending Rome's laws (long advanced by Cato) against usury to most of Italy and foreigners in Italy, as they were being used by Roman moneylenders to subvert Roman law. It revealed a preparedness of the Roman Senate to override unilaterally the treaties by which it had extended its general authority over many parts of Italy. It was only logical that Rome would cease to be just a city state as the Greek city states had been and would extend its jurisdiction and become, in modern terms, a country on its way to becoming an empire. The so-called Latin cities had the right that their citizens could become Roman citizens if they moved to Rome, a privilege not granted to other cities. These were the growing pains of what had been a modest market town, becoming a colossal metropolis at the centre of the known world, and Rome managed it relatively well. It was a stark contrast to the stunted and temporary growth of one Greek city state after another advancing and retreating over centuries. But it must be said that as Rome's authority grew it effectively transformed its allies into subjects and was enabled to do this by the ravages of the Punic Wars across most of Italy, but not in Rome itself.

In the first two thirds of the Second Century B.C., Rome had continued the methodical expansion of its influence. It had destroyed its ancient foes and was a greater power than ever, a model of efficient empire-building from which the Greeks could have learned a great deal. But it had become in some ways almost a gangster-state, not ethically much more elevated than Persia, Babylon, or even Assyria, though with much more substantial and popularly based institutions. The great and near-great families wrestled in the Senate for the scepter of Roman preeminence in the Western world. But in destroying Carthage, for no remotely valid reason and with barbarously excessive force, and Corinth in the same year, on a colossal pillaging operation though with less barbarity than at Carthage, Rome lost much of its own virtue. This was especially true as the chief advocate of this gratuitous, draconian onslaught was Cato, the senior sponsor of traditional Roman values, an austere, and supposedly selfless man of inflexible principle, who was revealed in the wreckage of Carthage as a bigot, a savage, and a hypocrite.

Rome had an aptitude to govern and to organize, and had a long succession of capable leaders, though with dangerous gaps between them. But the Roman system was breaking down: there was great urban unrest, and large numbers of dispossessed people flowed all around Italy, angry and excitable, especially by demagogues. Rome tried to govern all of this through the quarrelling factions in the Senate, as if it were still almost a group of aldermen. Rome had grown logically and sensibly, unlike any previous empire. And for all its corruption, it retained some important democratic aspects and a genuine legislature and semi-plausible judiciary in the tribunes. But after Spain, came the stigma of gratuitous belligerence and mistreatment of the civil population of another country while in search of wealth, which then poured into Rome, as did the spoils of the East, and infected the ruling classes of Rome and adjacent Italy.

Carthage had always been vulnerable: it depended on mercenaries, was a trading city, and paid its mercenaries by extracting the precious metals of Spain. It should never have blundered into war with such a dangerous adversary as Rome, which conscripted and paid its own sons and could not be subdued even with Hannibal spending a decade moving around Italy beneath Rome's walls. Rome was beginning to be the world's great ogre, as well as its greatest power, and was beginning to shed the moral, if not the military respect in which it had long been held. Rome would now enter upon a succession of tumultuous events caused by the inability of the Senate and the complicated arrangements with the related states to deal efficiently with such a large and varied jurisdiction. Roman institutions commanded declining respect, and their place was filled by men. Some of them were constructive statesmen, some more or less talented adventurers and military commanders, some companionable or insidious nonentities. This historic sequence began with one more mighty effort at legislative reform under the talented populist heirs of Tiberius Gracchus. And it led in less than a century, through the renowned ascendancies of Marius, Sulla, and Pompey, to the earth-shaking and world-shaping careers of Julius and Octavian (Augustus) Caesar, and for centuries beyond.

CHAPTER TWENTY-TWO

THE PEOPLE AND THE GENERALS
※
THE TRAGEDY OF THE GRACCHI AND THE RISE OF GAIUS MARIUS—140-100 B.C.

The Gracchus Brothers, Tiberius and Gaius
sculpted by Eugene Guillaume, Nineteenth Century

1. The Roman Republic in the 130s B.C.

WE HAVE SEEN HOW Rome slowly asserted itself in central Italy, and expanded gradually in the Italian peninsula, and really didn't venture much into the wider world until it was impetuously challenged by Carthage. It took over Sardinia and Sicily to get Carthage out of them and seized much of Spain to deny Carthage the wealth it needed to pay its mercenaries to conduct war against Rome. Rome only developed a navy to defend itself against Carthage and it only went to Greece to meet the challenge of Macedonia. It became active in Asia Minor to prevent a threat from Seleucid Syria. These wars brought Rome immense wealth, but even with that, the attachment of Rome, led by Cato the elder, to its historic virtues of quasi-agrarianism and civic duty were taken seriously though they were becoming subjects of nostalgia. The elder Cato was a constant proponent of these virtues and rendered great service to the state, returning always to his modest farm. But even he, as has been recounted, became infected with the imperialist bug and demanded a sadistic and unjustified destruction of Carthage after it had ceased to be anything but a reliable junior ally of Rome.

This relatively rapid transformation of Rome from an inland agrarian market city to the most powerful political center in the known world with interests that it aggressively and preemptively defended and promoted from one end of the Mediterranean to the other assured a tremendous influx of wealth into Rome. Tens of thousands of young Romans also became a good deal worldlier as they served tours of duty in the war zones around the Mediterranean. Hannibal's decade of milling around all Italy inciting and incentivizing hostility to Rome shook millions of people loose from their own native areas and ultimately promoted a massive accretion of the size of the Roman population.

The arrival of very large numbers of impecunious rural people in Rome transformed that city into an immense metropolis, a role for which the municipal government was not at all prepared. The wealth of empire flooded very unevenly into the city and the combination of the sudden development of an unprecedentedly powerful city influencing the whole known world, inundated with the plunder of the East and the gold and silver of Spain, challenged Roman statesmanship. The Roman leaders, as we have seen, managed the expansion capably and defended the ever-larger range of Rome's strategic and security interests with a generally high level of skill. Fabius, the leading Scipios, Flamininus, Marcellus, Paulus, and many others were highly competent generals and proconsuls.

But within Rome, the pretense of the Senate with its factions and dominated still by the ancient families of Rome, the government of the city and its environs all came under great strain. An oligarchic clique still governed, though Rome had a complex constitution and the people, if they could be organized to express themselves, had great power. There were only factions in the Senate and in popular assemblies, not parties. Individuals or individual policies would attract support, but this was very changeable.

There were infinite opportunities and temptations to seek popularity from sections or even all of the voting public. Rome, as we have seen, was organized on what was known as the cursus, the course or game, meaning the ladder of political office. At each stage there was a public election by a more or less broad electorate. There was a good deal of guidance from leading senators, but also a respectable facsimile of elections of aediles (who supervised public buildings and festivities and assured the food supply of Rome), quaestors (in charge of fiscal affairs), praetors (generals for specific purposes or magistrates in charge of various government departments and activities), consuls (the chief ministers and commanding generals), tribunes (judges with a right of intervention in state proceedings), and censors, who were ex-consuls and had extensive rights of prosecutory intervention in various state activities. It had evolved a good deal as a system from when it only managed the affairs of a city of twenty-thousand and its immediate outskirts.

It was, by modern standards, rudimentary government. There was no welfare system nor any state education system. There were periodic dispositions of money usually related either to natural calamities, national bonanzas, or most frequently, the political ambitions of those in a position to make such dispositions. The collecting of tax was largely privatized, or, in times of great need, entrusted to the army. One area of government where Rome was a world pioneer was law. There was no department of justice as such; there were compilers of legislation and a rudimentary police force which when necessary was supplemented by the armed forces. It was a rule that was never violated until Lucius Sulla called the Senate's bluff and occupied Rome with his army in 87 B.C., that no one bore arms within the walls of Rome. The army was not above the restoration of order when that was required but did not have recourse to deadly weapons within Rome itself. There were no public prosecutions; crimes had to be alleged like civil lawsuits and convictions had to be won from juries or public votes of observers, depending upon the case, and all depended on the forensic powers of the barristers. It was here that Marcus Tullius Cicero made his reputation as Rome's greatest orator. This recourse to a court system, primitive though it was, was much more advanced and even in its way equitable than anything in Athens, and indeed this was one area where even the Athenians did not look down their noses at Rome.

As part of the homage that Rome paid to the masses, which in the minds of the noblest senators was merely a placebo, the Roman people technically had the power to vote for magistrates to enact laws and to authorize Rome to go to war. But the Roman Constitution was very imprecise, and the Senate had a great variety of quasi-mystical methods for taking almost any authority it wished upon itself. But there were competitive elections and while there was undoubtedly a great deal of electoral fraud at the heart of it, there was some honest expression of public will, even if that will had been shaped by bribery and molded by colossal disinformation and assisted by widespread intimidation.

We have seen at every stage of Roman development the fluctuation of the internal political forces within that city as it grew, culminating in the acquiescence in the joint authority of the plebeians, accepted in 287 B.C. Political stability within the city was always dependent upon the numbers of unemployed, the adequacy of the food supply, and the extent of the right to vote. The status of citizens and the accompanying voting right were at times liberally dispersed in outer areas but elections themselves took place in Rome and it was often an insurmountable inconvenience to a great many non-Roman resident citizens to vote. This was the Senate's solution to the battle between the aristocrats and comparative democrats: the franchise was broadened but the ability to exercise it was not.

Physically, Rome had grown in a completely disorganized way and as officials were elected for one-year terms as part of the general desire to prevent dictatorship, much less monarchy; there was never any time or reason to plan anything. From time to time in periods of great prosperity, ambitious leaders built monuments and boulevards. The public works aspect of Roman government was handled with great vision and the aqueducts that brought fresh water right into the city from many miles outside were in their time one of the engineering marvels of the world, as were the roads leading to and from the city. But within Rome there was terrible overcrowding, inadequate roads and lanes for pedestrians and in many places, inadequate sanitation with a danger even for well-to-do people of encountering ordure either underfoot or jettisoned from windows above, carelessly, and only occasionally with malice. Rome was not remotely as pleasing aesthetically as Athens and the other leading Greek cities. She gradually became a city of monuments and great boulevards in the Augustan and subsequent eras, but republican Rome was a sprawling, helter-skelter, polyglot city with great energy but little charm and not much of interest aesthetically.

By the time of Tiberius and Gaius Gracchus starting in the 130s, Rome was ready for some elements of a revolution. The city was too successful and its leaders too confident and astute to provoke a revolution as in France or Russia that overthrew the ruling classes. But there was tremendous agitation and residual desire to address the problems of overpopulation, unemployment, inequitable distribution of wealth, all the grievances of outlying regions that had lost their former capacity for self-rule. The whole ambience was further complicated by the steady importation of influences from Greece and the Middle East and Spain and Africa, from all of which Rome had long been largely or wholly insulated. Added to this was the costly war in Spain which in casualties and money was very prolonged. Of course, it was not a conscript Roman army and there was never any question about what the objective was: Rome was enriching itself with Spanish gold and silver and no altruists in Rome are recorded in opposition to that, though there were horrors about reports of the severity of the operation of the mines and treatment of the slave labor in the mining process. There were no such simple and plausible explanations for what the United States was doing in Vietnam, but with the Spanish war many Romans were exasperated by the taxation and constant loss of Roman life, largely because of the incompetence of most of its generals there as we have seen. Romans were not much more patient and reserved than they are now and the Spanish War made much of the Roman public impatient and angry.

2. The Gracchi

It is time to introduce the Gracchi. Tiberius Gracchus was married to the brilliant daughter of Scipio Africanus, Cornelia, and was himself a great figure of the Roman state as a holder of its highest offices and as a military commander. The fusion of these families concentrated great power and prestige between them but also led to a boiling over of corrosive infighting between them that afflicted other families and elements of the public. Scipio Africanus, as has been recounted, not only won the Punic Wars but returned almost like Cincinnatus in the hour of need by defeating Antiochus the Great at Magnesia in 190. Scipio Africanus' brother, Lucius Scipio Asiaticus, somewhat overshadowed Africanus after his own Asian victories, but Roman opinion, especially in the Senate, was deeply suspicious of the rise of these great and popular generals with loyal armies and in the case of the Scipios, concerns were aggravated when Africanus' generous settlement with Antiochus was overturned and Rome's putative allies, in particular Eumenes, king of Pergamon, became more powerful than Rome found convenient. The backbiting against the Scipios became intense and shook the Roman world. The attack upon them was most strongly led by the eighty-five-year-old Cato who for decades had warned of the evils of the pursuit of wealth and Empire and the intended corruption of ancient Roman virtues that would result. It was at this point that Africanus' son-in-law, Tiberius Gracchus stepped to the first rank of Roman affairs.

Cato, always the enemy of anything that he thought was undermining traditional Roman virtues, and suspicious of those who had grown popular and rich fighting aggressive rather than defensive wars, fanned claims that various of the Scipios had been corrupt in the campaign against Antiochus. Lucius Scipio was thrown in jail for taking bribes from Antiochus, but in the absence of evidence, the second Tiberius Gracchus, nephew of the accused, exercised his right as tribune, to order the release of the accused. Scipio Africanus himself was accused of taking bribes and exceeding his authority. He interrupted the pseudo-judicial proceedings to announce that as it was the anniversary of his victory over Hannibal at Zama, he would lead the people to the Capitol to give thanks to Jupiter. Africanus again withdrew to his country estate.

There was another attempt to recall him for trial on similar charges and it was again Tiberius Gracchus who stopped that initiative, asking the Senate if there was no level of service to the state that could ensure a man a peaceful old age, and the indictment of Scipio Africanus was abandoned. Polybius, Livy, Plutarch, and Cicero all ranked Scipio Africanus as one of the greatest generals and public servants in Rome's history. From this distance, it is astonishing that there was anyone to contest that, no matter how driven by envy and rivalry. Such contentions only illustrate that Rome was almost as envious as Greece and tended to inflict equivalent levels of ingratitude upon those who would render the greatest service.

The first Tiberius Gracchus, founder of the family as a great force in Rome, was a hero in the disaster at Cannae and a successful leader of the patched-together force of twenty-four thousand armed boys and slaves that modestly defeated Hannibal in a side-action in 215. He continued with an army of slaves victoriously and then liberated them all. Reelected consul in 213, he was betrayed into an ambush by Hannibal and fought so bravely right to his own death in close action that Hannibal gave him a hero's funeral and returned his corpse with honors to Rome. His nephew, the second Tiberius Gracchus married Cornelia Scipio, who was much younger than her husband and bore the two famous brothers, Tiberius and Gaius Gracchus, leaders of Rome's early populist democratic movement. This Tiberius Gracchus, father of the two populist politicians, was a diplomat sent to deal with Philip of Macedon and then, in 180, he was dispatched to northern Spain. He arranged a cease-fire and then after receiving reinforcements when the cease-fire expired, he fought with great success in the Spanish mountains and concluded a peace that would last for twenty-five years. He carried out land reform for the benefit of the Spanish peasants and the tribute Rome collected was a reduction of the tax already being paid. He was elected consul in 177 and spent most of his term successfully crushing a revolt in Sardinia. As in Spain he conquered and ruled with great magnanimity and was immensely popular. When Perseus set out to regain the kingdom of his father, Antiochus initiated hostilities, and again, as has been recounted, it went badly for Rome at first. Gracchus was reelected censor in 169 and expanded and sternly enforced conscription to organize an invincible army to resolve the eastern problems.

He and his fellow consul P. Licinius Crassus, also reformed the practice of giving building contracts to friends of the regime with practically no cost control on them. The developers' allies among the knights managed to put Gracchus' and Crassus on trial but they were narrowly acquitted. Gracchus was instrumental in rolling back the franchise among free slaves to ensure that they did not cast a majority of the votes in any election. It was at this point that Aemilius Paullus defeated the Syrians at Pydna in 167 and he returned a triumphant hero to Rome. Three thousand men were required to carry the coined silver and two-hundred and fifty wagons to bear the statues and other works of art looted from the palace of Perseus in Paullus' triumph parade. In 165, Tiberius Gracchus led the embassy to the east that settled arrangements with the kings of Pergamon, Syria, and others. He went on from there to subdue another revolt in Corsica. Gracchus made a further successful embassy to the east after Syria had murdered the Roman ambassador Octavius, who was widely mourned. A few years later his sons Tiberius and Gaius were born in, 163 and 154 and their father died within the five or so years following the birth of Gaius Gracchus. Cicero, in particular, memorialized Tiberius Gracchus as a gigantic real and symbolic figure of the Golden age of the Roman Senate. He deserved that praise, but it is doubtful that the Senate did by this time.

The next Tiberius Gracchus, and the most famous, was born in 163, and elected to the College of Augurs at sixteen, when he began his obligatory ten years' service in the Roman army, necessary to become a political candidate. In 146, he was the first man to scale the walls of Carthage, then under its final assault from the Romans. He was serving on the staff of the commander, his brother-in-law, Scipio Aemilianus. This Scipio was the son of Aemilius Paullus, the victor of Pydna, and Scipio Africanus was his uncle, having married his aunt, Aemilia Paullus, Cornelia Gracchus was his cousin, and to make the bonds between these great and conquering noble Roman families even tighter, Scipio Aemilianus married Sempronia, sister of the young Tiberius and Gaius Bracchus. Scipio Aemilianus' great service after Pydna was in Spain, where, as has been recounted, he brought that long and terrible conflict to a brutal but temporary end, until Viriathus arose and plunged Spain back into war.

Tiberius Gracchus came back from Carthage a hero and stood for aedile, but the people were so agitated by war in Spain, Africa, and Greece and Asia, that they elevated him at once to consul, in defiance of the age of qualification (Gracchus was only seventeen in 146), but the Senate graciously suspended the law for a year. Cato again railed against the evils of empire and treasure-seeking. Rome had destroyed Corinth under Mummius in 146, and the same year, Carthage, too, was destroyed for no particular reason except the ravings of Cato, and in response to Cato's own endlessly repeated imperative exhortation: "Delenda est Carthago." Yet, Cato denounced Roman degeneracy, exemplified by "pretty boys being sold for more than farms, and a jar of caviar for more than a ploughman."[1]

Plundering Asia had yielded enough to pay off the entire Roman debt and to suspend taxation. It is little wonder that short rich wars were popular. From the

---

1 Keith Richardson, *Daggers in the Forum*, Book Club Associates, London, 1976, p. 31.

same source, roads were built connecting the burgeoning empire and Rome itself, with an adult, free, male population of several hundred thousand out of a total population approaching a million, was made a splendid city in its formal areas and best neighbourhoods. Rome was wrestling with itself, as Cato's laws were passed punishing bribery and restraining spending on banquets and other Oriental habits. Greek philosophers fetched up in Rome but were periodically expelled for leading their students into too much theorizing. When the censor in 154 decided to build the city's first permanent theatre, the Senate took it down on a motion of Scipio Nasica, but even he is celebrated in the sack of Carthage by throwing captured deserters and fugitive slaves to savage beasts. Rome had also begun to abuse its powers as the arbiter of the known world: it frequently extorted money from neutral states, gratuitously attacked peaceful neighboring tribes, and was capable of selling whole city states into slavery, generating abrasions even with allies such as Rhodes and Pergamon.

Former Roman standards of civilization plunged in Spain; we have seen the atrocities of Galba and Mancinus, who were almost ready to surrender twenty-thousand Romans to four-thousand Spaniards and sued for peace. As the young consul Tiberius Gracchus, now twenty-five, because of his reputation as a warrior and the venerated memory of his father, was the only Roman the Spanish would deal with, and he managed to secure the safe retirement of the entire Roman army though all their equipment was given up; Tiberius returned to Rome, as he thought, in triumph. In fact, he was denounced for dishonoring Rome and making any arrangement to save such a wretched defeated army, and the treaty that he had negotiated was rejected. Tiberius Gracchus himself barely escaped prosecution and he correctly saw the hand of Scipio Aemilianus, still absent in Carthage, in his humiliation.

The antagonism between these two intimate and formerly mutually affectionate families reached a summit when, as was recounted in the previous chapter, with a mandate and an instruction to end the war in Spain satisfactorily, Scipio Aemilianus was again elected consul in 134 and sent back to Spain where he did achieve the destruction of Numantia. Tiberius Gracchus considered that he had been betrayed: he had given his oath to Spanish tribes engaging his honor and that of his family and this had been repudiated and treated as worthless by Scipio and the other leading Romans. He cast his lot with the people and became that most dangerous of politicians—a wealthy and well-connected rabble-rouser. In 133 he was elected Tribune of the people with, as far as he was concerned, a mandate for a virtual revolution.

The dispute between the Gracchi and the Scipio families, the defection of the Gracchi from the traditional methods and orientation of Senatorial government, and the move to greater popular involvement in the government of the ever-expanding Roman world were going to put great stresses on the ramshackle Roman Republic. It had been created for a small city and was now stretching throughout Italy and around the Mediterranean and well into the Near East, the Balkans, and across the Alps. Whatever disrupted Rome now affected the whole known world. The Gracchi would be the first of five personal movements that would shake and alter Rome profoundly in the next one-hundred and fifty years, the twilight of the Roman Republic and one of the decisive periods in world history.

The Gracchi ultimately and for their own reasons, raised the question of the legitimacy of authority over all Italy and far beyond vested in the unchecked hands of the Roman Senate. Despite much controversy, the Senate, on balance, was fairly judicious in the treatment of Italy. Even visiting kings routinely addressed the Senators as 'Divinities' and 'Saviors,' and senators often treated even the locally deified kings of Asia Minor like messenger boys. The Roman Senate sometimes forgot that their old Italian allies were reconciled powers (not downtrodden and conquered people), and reconciliation became very difficult at times. This is not surprising, but Rome was still a model of egalitarianism compared to "purple-crowned Athens," which for all its democratic credentials, couldn't stop, as we have seen (Chapter 7), trying to turn a federation into an outright colonial overlordship.

3. Tiberius Gracchus

The tribunate of Tiberius Gracchus II opened a new era in which one of Rome's most prominent families became identified with radical reform in favor of the disadvantaged and at the expense of the authority of the Senate, and particularly of the other great families so long and heavily represented in the Senate. Rome was able to turn for a time from the military requirements of the protection and advancement of its interests outside Italy to the focus on attempted reform of its domestic politics and institutions. Rome thus was the first Western jurisdiction to grapple with the problems of fusing the polis of a city state with the Empire that it had acquired and was governing, not as temporarily occupied territories, or even as dynastic prizes of war and aggression as in the acquests of the great King of Persia and his successors, but rather as territories that had been conquered in essentially defensive wars and where Rome remained more or less at the wish of the populations that it governed more efficiently and equitably than had the regimes that Rome replaced.

The whole question of reform was inextricably tied up with the patchwork of arrangements by which Rome ruled Italy. Many parts of Italy were former small states with whom Rome had resolved disputes by victory in armed conflict in those jurisdictions. However reluctantly and however frequently some of them periodically took up arms to try to throw off the yoke of Roman rule, ultimately, they had to accept whatever Rome gave them. But many other cities and provinces in Italy were former allies which officially retained a substantial degree of autonomy. Roman citizenship had been used as a reward for cooperative local officials, and had at times been generalized in areas of Italy that had earned Roman goodwill. The economic basis of the country had also evolved over several centuries from small farmers towards medium or large farmers with a corresponding migration of relatively unskilled labor to the metropolis of Rome itself.

The economic potential of the newly acquired precious metal and base metal mining resources of Spain and Macedonia and the loot removed from Asia Minor greatly enhanced commercial activity in Rome and built a finance, investment and entrepreneurial industry that was a new phenomenon in the known world. This new wealth enabled Rome, between 187 and 167 B.C., to abolish one of the previous pillars of the state's revenue collection apparatus, which was known as the attribute: tax plans imposed on territories ruled by or closely affiliated with Rome. The new wealth of empire enabled landowners to enlarge their estates and the large numbers of what amounted to slave labor acquired in successful foreign conflict enabled the landowners to increase the profitability of agriculture by exploiting that labor. This amplified the problem of displacing free but poor Romans and Italians from the land they had worked either as small farms or as tenant farmers or as outright agrarian employees of the rich landowners. An idle, steadily more discontented and volatile urban proletariat was created in Rome and other Italian cities, and it grew quickly.

Roman elections had been by the centuriate assembly, in which, prior to 241, the knights, effectively a patriciate, possessed a majority of the votes along with a number of categories of wealthy individuals. But artisans, farmers, and other groups were also represented. The extraordinarily complicated voting system was made more intricate by completely obsolescent tribal divisions across the voting groups, as well as by the requirement of physical presentation in Rome to exercise voting rights. It seems that the five classes of voters were divided tribally into thirty-five separate groups and each of these was divided between juniors and seniors. The seniors were forty-five years old and above and though they were generally in a minority they were assured of having as great a total weight as the juniors. It was determined in advance by the administrators of the elections how many votes would be necessary for a majority and the first group to vote was drawn by lots among the knights and well-to-do sections. Then it proceeded in a sequence that generally followed the socio-economic importance downwards into society. It need hardly be emphasized that such a complicated voting system was subject to an extraordinary amount of skullduggery.

In 241 B.C., censors exercised their power to enroll voters by simplifying and somewhat democratizing the process. Officially, the centurion assembly, presided over by the consuls, was of equal weight to the plebeian assembly presided over by the tribunes, but in practice the centuries had more influence. It was in its way an extraordinarily ingenious system as there was some level of representation for all adult men except the slaves and it was so amorphous that much of the agitation that occurred in more modern political societies for expansion of the franchise as in the British Reform Acts in the Nineteenth Century were mitigated, or even avoided altogether. Starting in the last third of the Third Century B.C., plebeian consuls became quite frequent occurrences. In all of this, it must be said that Rome showed remarkable adaptability, even if, as is often the case throughout history, apparent liberalizations by governing elites are in significant measure a mirage.

What brought the problem to a head in the time of Tiberius Gracchus was that the number of freed men displaced by more efficient agriculture and the use of slave labor on the large rural estates made the plebeian electorate within Rome itself larger than it had ever been and more likely to vote at elections than had been practical when the same people or their fathers were more widely dispersed in Italy prior to these rural economic changes and the demographic upheavals caused by Hannibal's invasion of Italy. Gracchus' proposed measures would distribute state-owned land to these freed men, which would both alleviate their economic distress and restore a more stable and prosperous majority in the electoral process in Rome.

Tiberius Gracchus, as tribune, in 133 introduced a measure that would distribute an expanse of state land to unemployed urban dwellers. It was acknowledged that this would reduce agricultural efficiency and production, but it was argued that it would alleviate a great deal of human misery, make Rome and other urban centers in Italy more liveable, would broaden the base of recruitment for the Roman army (soldiers had to be citizens) and the rural slave population utilized by the large landowners would be sold out of the country. Rome had no audible objections to slaves, especially foreign slaves, but did not want Italy threatened by their numbers. Slavery had already become a substantial problem and when Tiberius Gracchus became a tribune, Sicily was already occupied by a consular army that was chiefly occupied running down renegade bands of marauding slaves and suppressing slave resistance and dealing with slave herdsmen, who, as they were mounted, possessed an enhanced capacity for disruption of society, and frequently roamed the countryside in mounted gangs spreading lawlessness all around Sicily. A formidable inspirer of the rebel slaves, Eunus, arose, and although he was not personally a practitioner of violence, he inspired the emergence of an army of twenty-thousand slaves, which occasionally massacred free landowners, but generally behaved in a relatively civil manner unless they felt themselves provoked. They seized a substantial part of rural Sicily and a number of towns. A Roman army of eight-thousand was defeated by a substantially larger slave force in 135, and it was not until 133 when Consul L. Calpurnius Piso turned the tide, and in 132 his successor, P. Rupilius, besieged and starved the slaves at Tauromenium and restored Sicily to comparative tranquility. Eunus was captured, but treated generously, and this conflict, known as the First Servile War, was raging in much of Sicily when the Gracchus tribunate began.

The Sicilian violence would have been a spur to Gracchus and his plan was based on the Ager publicus populi Romani, land which Rome seized from other areas in Italy as they came under Roman authority and government. This was the property that was used for the setting up of Roman colonies around Italy, and it was on the less valuable sections of this land that Gracchus proposed to settle large numbers of the urban poor.

Tiberius Gracchus, having been the first Roman to scale the Carthaginian walls, was generously commended for his heroism. He became a quaestor and in 137 served under Mancino in Spain. It will be recalled that it was his intervention that saved the Roman army after Mancino surrendered; and that the good relations between the Gracchus and Scipio families ended when Scipio prevented ratification of the Spanish treaty that Gracchus had negotiated, because he preferred the sacrifice of the defeated army in Spain to the dishonor of Rome concluding a war with a treaty that effectively acknowledged its defeat.

Gracchus presented his Lex Sempronia Agraria, which expropriated state land in parcels which had exceeded a certain minimum that was permitted to be retained by its incumbent occupants, and then it was to be dispersed to the urban poor in small allotments. To prevent opportunistic speculation, those awarded land could not sell it for at least twelve years. Gracchus designed the law to be as gentle as possible on the large landowners and to be administered with civility and consideration for those whom it inconvenienced. But it was, nonetheless, violently opposed by the possessores, as the great landowners were called, and they had a great traditional influence in the Senate.

When the measure reached the Concilium Plebis, it was vetoed by a tribune, Marcus Octavius, a well-regarded young man with whom Gracchus was friendly, acting within the rights of the tribunate. Faced with this challenge, Gracchus amended his bill; though the details have not come down to us we can only surmise from Plutarch that he did not make concessions to Octavius in his amendment. Tiberius referred his measure to the Senate, in no optimism that it would smile upon it, but to justify taking more drastic measures with the popular assembly. When the Senate balked, he resorted to the only means left to him to gain adoption of his agrarian law and exercised a plebiscitum by which Octavius was legally removed by the Concilium Plebis as a tribune and the way was cleared for the enactment of the Gracchus measure.

There was immense controversy at the time, and has been amongst historians ever since, over Tiberius Gracchus' actions. Plutarch and Cicero claimed from their fundamentally anti-democratic perspectives, democratic poseurs though they both were, that Gracchus suddenly became a megalomaniacal despot and tried to impose his will upon a hostile Rome. This is nonsense and one need only examine the conduct of many of the prominent succeeding Roman leaders to discover what megalomaniacal despotism looks like. The technical position of Gracchus' enemies was that if Octavius' tribunal veto could be overturned by removing him, then there would be no defense in the future against the actions of more dangerous demagogues than Gracchus. But there was no defense against the actions of such people anyway, and Tiberius and Caius Gracchus were Rome's first serious democrats, and it must be added that, fatefully, they were also the last. They deserve admiration, but it must also be said of Tiberius that it was impetuous to whet the appetite of the Roman masses with a vision of their own potential political supremacy, and in seizing upon a method to enact the plebeian will over the wishes of the traditional governing, or at least predominating, elements of the Roman polis, he was moving onto very dangerous ground, for himself and for Rome.

The Senate attempted to delay the distribution of allotments to the beneficiaries by starving the agricultural commission of funds. Tiberius evaded this action by the good fortune of the fact that Attalus III, King of Pergamon, had died and left the Roman people as the heir to his kingdom. This is a unique event in world history, and certainly confirmed the wisdom of successive Roman leaders in favouring Eumenes and his family in the enhancement of the Pergamene interest. It provided the Roman treasury an immense windfall, which solved the question of funding the Gracchus land transfers. But so deteriorated were the relations between Tiberius Gracchus and his followers and the leaders of the traditional bloc in the Senate that Gracchus raised the ante.

He introduced a bill before the Concilium Plebis allocating some of the wealth to help settle the allottees and announced that the disposition of this windfall from Pergamon was not the Senate's business, and that he, Tiberius Gracchus would put before the Concilium Plebis his proposals for the application of those funds. This was a bold stroke and a drastic escalation of the dispute between the plebeian and patrician assemblies, effectively telling the Senate that the plebeian assembly could govern in a very important matter without consulting it. It was one thing to push these important reforms through in the assembly of those who mainly stood to gain by them; it was something else altogether to tell the Senate, which had effectively governed Rome for over three-hundred years, that its jurisdiction had been sharply curtailed effectively by the executive decision of a young tribune, albeit the scion of distinguished families.

Tiberius had substantially removed the tribunician veto on the popular assembly when he had deposed Octavius. Emancipating the plebeian house from the need of consulting with the Senate even in a foreign matter, was a drastic change of jurisdiction effected on the authority of Tiberius himself, though he was doubtless supported by a popular majority, when that body could be convened in relatively full numbers.

By the summer of 133 B.C., it was already time to consider candidates for the tribunate in the coming year and it soon became evident that Tiberius considered that as his principal legislation had not been fully enacted, it would be appropriate for him to break the long-standing custom and seek a second consecutive term. To elaborate on the argument for this ambition, which could be fairly expected to cause further alarm in the Senate and elsewhere that Tiberius aspired to an undemocratic and even autocratic status, he brought forth a program for a second term that included reduction of the period for conscripted military service, increased rights to challenge decisions of Senate appointed judicial commissions, and the composition of financial courts' juries to be changed from senators exclusively to equal numbers of senators and knights. This program was never made explicit by Tiberius (though it was pursued by his brother Gaius twelve years later), but the fact that it was rumoured that these were Tiberius' intentions only amplified the concerns of all those who imputed to him the ambition of unlimited personal authority.

It was clear enough by now that the collegiality of Roman government even within the Senate, the many mechanisms in place to ensure against continuous exercise of authority by any individual, and the intermittent but unending friction between the patrician and plebeian assemblies, representing as they did quite different economic goals and public policy objectives, assured that the government of Rome would be a complicated and inefficient operation. The Republic was founded on the fear of royal tyranny and Rome was built on an almost aldermanic system appropriate to municipal government, but which required all the fecundity of Roman improvisation and political ingenuity to provide effective government for what was now the principal jurisdiction in the Western world. What was obviously needed was some method of elevating an individual to a leading role in the government for a durable period, but without disenfranchising the representatives of a wide range of Roman society. Approximately a century later, Octavian Caesar would devise this method, the principate, and supplemented it with the Augustan dignity of an Emperor. Structurally, this would prove an adequate method of organization, though its actual success depended altogether on the political and executive skills of the Emperor, most of them were not equal to the challenge and would die violently. But at least the apparatus would work if the personnel vested with the responsibility for operating it knew how to do so.

Tiberius Gracchus' talents, the sincerity of his objectives, and the need for something like what he was advocating to take place have never been seriously disputed but his project ended in tears because of his tactical failings in recognizing the correlation of forces within the Roman state. The party of senatorial continuity which guided the Republic with astonishing success for so long was more entrenched than he thought and was readier than he imagined, and than their frequently torpid conduct would indicate, to resort to violence to repress what they considered to be sedition, despite its popular democratic base.

When election day came, the Senate met in the Temple of Fides and the presiding consul Publius M. Scaevola, an eminent and respected barrister, was publicly asked by the Pontifex Maximus—the unelected life appointment as chief religious leader of Rome, Publius Scipio Nasica, cousin of the tribune, to save the state from the threat that the tribune presented to it. He went so far as explicitly to ask the consul to destroy the tyrant. To this Scaevola correctly replied that he would do nothing illegal, but he would prevent any illegality from being validated. He was not convinced even by the powerful case that Tiberius then made to a right to reelection. Scaevola ruled that if he as consul purported to elect Tiberius to a second consecutive term, it would be illegitimate, but he counseled against any recourse to force to prevent it. But at that, Nasica in a peculiar interpretation of his high religious responsibilities, declared that the consul was himself betraying the state by allowing this illegal reelection of the tribune to occur and invited the large majority of opponents of the reelection of Tiberius present to take matters into their own hands. Tiberius Gracchus was clubbed to death with the leg of a chair and over three-hundred of his supporters were savagely murdered without the flimsiest pretense to any form of due process. It was the first such recourse to bloodshed in the public square of Rome since the overthrow of the Tarquin monarchy in 495 B.C.

The consensus of Roman historians, including Plutarch and Cicero, was that Tiberius Gracchus was a capable and admirable man who had been transported to megalomania and sociopathy by the adulation of the unwashed masses of Rome. This is not a just or sustainable description. The goals he sought were admirable; the practical measures that he wished to impose were reasonable, but his political tactics aroused a much greater state of alarm than he could resist. Especially with his family's long and distinguished background in service to the state and his own remarkable career, youthful though he was, and with his brilliance and universally admired mother Cornelia, daughter of Scipio Africanus advising him, he should have proceeded more cautiously. His death was a terrible tragedy both personally and for Rome. The popular masses were bitterly disappointed; the principal immediate beneficiaries were the most reactionary elements of the Senate, and the Senate as a whole certainly did not secure to itself as it had hoped, the restoration of its serene and unchallengeable authority.

The era of the Gracchi was only half over, and the wiser members of the Senate party should have realized that if they did not now compromise with the elements that Tiberius Gracchus respectably and responsibly championed, those same forces, the unquestionable heavy majority of Romans and a far more popular political option amongst Rome's allies and (colonized or otherwise) occupied territories than the Senate, would ultimately be led by men much less respectful of constitutional niceties and the preferments of the old families of Rome than the Gracchi. This civilized solicitude for the broad public interest from a great patrician family was not widely perceived for what it was: the last chance for the patrician classes to earn and retain the confidence and the respect of the people of Rome.

This was the very first example of altruistic and demonstrably talented members of the governing class attempting by sensible and equitable reforms to recruit the loyalty of the working and agrarian and lower middle classes to the legitimacy of a system led by a hereditary meritocracy. It was, to some degree, the earliest precursor of such great modern families of statesmen as the Churchills and Roosevelts. If these interests could not be harnessed together in a way that adequately served the legitimate ambitions of all Romans, the Senate was making itself a hostage to demagogues who would inevitably not be the mellifluous orators who moved men by their eloquence alone, but articulate and crafty generals pandering to public tastes and supplementing their call on the affections of the majority with the iron fist of Roman legions loyal to them and not to the state.

For twenty-five hundred years, evidences of the Roman government, even the municipal government of Rome today, have born the imprint SPQR: for the Senate and People of Rome, implying a unity of the Senate and the people. The Gracchi offered that unity as a natural integration. If their option for social and institutional reform did not fare better, now that it had passed violently from Tiberius Gracchus to his even more talented brother Gaius Gracchus, authoritarian leaders would take command of the state and govern the people by some combination of competence and the imposition of force, and consult the Senate as much and as little as pleased them. Rome had improvised and adapted and compromised its way through centuries to maintain the authority of a few senators. That game was up: they had now to share authority with those below or lose it altogether to those outside. And if Rome was to be governed by unaccountable dictators and emperors, succession would not be in annual elections but in military coups d'état and occasional assassinations. Rome, and the entire political civilization of the West were at an early but critical turning point.

The oligarchs had won, for the time being, and they had been so shaken by the onslaught of democratic reform that they had faced that they were careful not to repeal the agrarian law but only to apply it with an obstructive and pedantic tardiness. Their real counteroffensive was in the classification of Gracchi's proposed reforms of abolishing veto of a single tribune, submitting provincial financial questions to popular decision, and to elect popular tribunes annually—the active championship of any or all of these was designated as a capital crime. While Tiberius Gracchus' most powerful friends such as P. Licinius Crassus and Appius Claudius, and Scaevola were left alone, those who had adhered to the cause of the reforms imputed to Tiberius, but not including the Agrarian Law, were retroactively guilty of capital offenses. Those who were able to flee were banished but the rest, scores of them, were executed after precooked trials, except for Blossius, who fled to Asia but eventually committed suicide.

The Agrarian Law itself was mired in bureaucratic pettifogging and prevarication and eventually was simply ineffectual, though Gracchus' brother, Gaius, became a commissioner, and for the first time, in 131, there were two plebeian consuls. Scipio Nasica had somewhat disgraced the position of Pontifex Maximus by his own ecclesiastical assault upon Tiberius Gracchus and was now something of an embarrassment to a Senate more conscious than ever of its own dignity. He was sent to Asia for an indefinite period on a commission of investigation. The Senate had thus severely repulsed this democratic challenge. It had the collective intelligence not to be completely reactionary and to make some tokenistic gestures to the reform movement. But in fact, it stunted the organic evolution of Roman government in the middle of its progress from municipal to imperial scale. What would prove to be the last chance for a reasonable democratization of Roman government for a century was personified by Gaius Gracchus, who was already sizing up the possibilities for a resumption of what his brother had begun.

Gaius' fellow land commissioners were Marcus Fulvius Flaccus and C. Papirius Carbo, an unscrupulous political maneuverer but also a powerful public speaker. The commission was gradually worn down over the next decade in endless disputes over the legality of appropriating and allocating land from Rome's allies in Italy, who insisted that they retained much more legal authority over their public lands than the Constitution and activity of the land commission would indicate. The agrarian commission proved to be an unbearable irritant to many of the other cities and regions of Italy, now mangled up with Rome in what was broadly called an alliance. Each former autonomous city or regional state had made its own treaty of substantial submission to Rome as the jurisdiction of Rome was expanded over centuries. It was not a uniform Confederation of defined powers at different levels of government like modern states such as the United States and Canada. The different entities retained more or less authority but there was substantial resentment in virtually all of them about the extent to which Rome taxed and conscripted within those formerly autonomous states to serve purposes that were generally considered to be Roman and not Italian. The Roman empire was built mainly on the efforts of its soldiers and taxpayers from elsewhere in Italy than Rome, which was overwhelmingly the principal beneficiary of its empire. The last thing that they wished was for a substantial part of the patrimony of their formerly autonomous states to be expropriated for distribution to the relocated Roman proletariat. Considerable agitation resulted.

Large official parties from around Italy arrived in Rome to protest agrarian reform and the shaggy structure of Roman government in Italy generally. The censuses appear to report that the agrarian commission accomplished the settlement of approximately seventy-five thousand adult males in the reallocated property between 136 and 115, a significant achievement but far from the massive reduction of the penurious Roman masses that had been planned. It appears that Scipio Aemilianus, probably now Rome's most distinguished citizen, intervened to direct a large part of the relocation of the poor and unemployed of Rome from Italy to Africa, where Rome could expropriate what it wished and largely ignore any complaints from the local tribes. Massinissa's dream of the trans-North African state had been shattered and there was plenty of room for colonization.

Scipio had returned from his success in Spain in 134 and enjoyed immense popularity, but after diluting the activities of the agricultural commission and redirecting its beneficiaries from Italy to Africa, he became an extremely contentious figure and died mysteriously at home in 129, while preparing a reply to a denunciation from Fulvius Flaccus in the Senate. The cause of death has never been known and while foul play has been suspected, there was insufficient evidence to rebut the assumption that under pressure of events he had suffered a coronary in his sleep. He was fifty-six and was unhappily married to the sister of the Gracchi, Sempronia, who was an uncharged suspect in his death.

By this time, the agitation over the Agrarian Law had blended with a movement to extend Roman citizenship throughout Italy. This was generally regarded as an equitable reform by its advocates in Rome but was dismissed by some of the aggrieved in the provinces as a tokenistic placebo, where much local autonomous sentiment remained. Flaccus, when a consul in 125, proposed to enfranchise those of the allies who wished to become Roman citizens and to grant to those in Italy who did not have the right to appeal to the popular assembly against what they might consider abuses of the authority of Roman magistrates. The measure was stalled because the notion that the person could responsibly be a citizen of two coextensive jurisdictions had not penetrated the Roman or Italian imagination. It was thought that if someone was a citizen of both Naples and Rome, he would really only be a Roman and Naples would retain no authority for itself. The idea, commonplace now for many centuries, that a person could have certain rights as a citizen of the city and as a citizen of a state or province and as a citizen of a federal state, had not taken hold. This was a constitutional breakthrough, one of many, for which we have Rome to thank. Flaccus was induced to defer his reform and accept military command in Gaul. Again, the oligarchy had staved off reform, but the powers advocating change were growing ever stronger.

The city of Fregellae rose in what was almost a state of revolt, and the inert mass of Senate and elite opinion that held justly to the status quo was quickly disabused of its complacency. Rome was facing a possible violent disaffection of practically all of Italy and as with the threat posed by Tiberius Gracchus, it responded vigorously. Rome did not then have a professional army and it would not have been able to deal with uprisings in more than one or two other Italian centers at a time. The Roman army invested Fregellae and internal dissidents admitted the besiegers and the city was seized. Rome permitted the entire population to depart and destroyed the venerable city of Fregellae completely and the following year the colony of Fabricaria was founded in its place. This thoroughly deterred comparable activity by other parts of Italy without being so barbarous as to cause a revulsion throughout the Italian peninsula. It was another close call, and the matter was certainly not durably resolved. It was in this fraught atmosphere that Gaius Gracchus was elected tribune in 124.

4. Gaius Gracchus

Gaius Gracchus, who had been biding his time carefully, and preparing for a rematch between the forces of reform and of senatorial and oligarchic reaction, was elected Tribune in December 124 B.C. His first task was to reform and stabilize relations with the so-called Latins, the Italian cities and provinces and seaboard nations that were tied to Rome with a quilt-work of connections, generally depending upon the circumstances with which they rallied to the Roman interest. There were the standard resentments of decentralized jurisdictions at the overbearing nature of the higher government and there were particular objections to excessive taxation and conscription for Rome's interest out of all proportion to the interests of those states called to sacrifice for it, and there were also questions of voting participation in Roman affairs, the overlap of laws and confusion of jurisdictions, and various regional rivalries and preferments.

Gaius began with a comprehensive measure to standardize and reform relations between Rome and the related jurisdictions in Italy. He set out to address concerns about tax conscription and the extent to which the Roman Senate could legislate beyond the borders of Rome and its most proximate areas. The opponents of the Gracchi had seen this threat coming and in 123 elevated to the leadership of the opposition the tribune M. Livius Drusus. He was a skilled tactician who offered alternative measures to everything that Gaius put before the Concilium Plebis (popular assembly). Like his brother, Gaius Gracchus knew that he could not carry the Senate and conducted his effort to enact reforms entirely in the People's forum, where he presented a measure for the extension of the franchise to all of the Latins as defined and many other Italians. The history of the time has not come down to us in adequate detail to be overly precise, but it appears that one of the key measures proposed by Drusus was to end the ability of Roman officers to flog Italian recruits in the Roman legions and navy. Drusus preyed upon the reluctance of Romans to part with their preferments and suggested that that would be adequate to placate restless Italy, counting on the desire of people, especially Romans to believe what they want to believe.

Apart from his bill to broaden the franchise, Gaius also proposed to appoint a substantial number of new senators and to revoke the eligibility of senators to sit on juries. He was thus proposing a vast expansion of the electorate for the lower house and a partial packing of the upper house with people whom he would have confident reason to believe would be more amenable to his reforms than the incumbent senators. Gaius started out with an expanded franchise for the Latins only and a modest dilution of the Senate. But once he saw the nature and effectiveness of Drusus' tactics, it is generally felt by Plutarch and other Roman historians that in order to secure passage of his reforms he made the more comprehensive proposal to broaden the franchise and further proposed an increased number of senators. He pitched this proposal directly to the discontented masses and alienated most senators who might have been disposed to support him. In the heat of the early stages of Gaius' reform campaign, he introduced a measure confirming that it had always been constitutionally possible in Rome for the popular assembly to depose a tribune as his brother Tiberius had done with the Tribune Octavius, and to establish that anyone so barred could not hold high office again. This was contrary to the advice of his universally esteemed mother Cornelia, and he withdrew the measure but had given notice of ambitions that the oligarchic families and other prominent senators could not fail to regard as a direct threat to their continued influence. They had long used friendly tribunes to stop the bad things from happening in the popular assembly. That Gaius would contemplate such a measure was taken as a serious escalation of the political crisis especially as he moved to drive out the consul Popillius Laenas, who had presided over the hanging court that ordered the execution of a large number of Tiberius Gracchus' followers in 133. Eventually, Popilius was driven into exile.

Gaius did gain general adherence to the view that the Roman state had a high obligation to assure a plentiful food supply. Prices of the basic foodstuffs fluctuated quite widely according to harvesting conditions and political interruptions in places from which Rome imported food. He built great granaries beneath the Aventine Hill and stored huge quantities of grain in them to counter speculative manipulation in the grain market and assure that no Roman died of famine.

Gaius Gracchus succeeded in being elected to a second consecutive annual term as tribune. This was the point where his brother Tiberius had failed and been murdered and scores of his principal followers were also murdered either summarily or by execution after drumhead trials. Gaius managed this step without apparently great difficulty. It was feared by his enemies that he was seeking to be consul but instead supported Gaius Fannius, a Scipionic Roman Whig who proved to be of no use to him at all. Gaius Gracchus was generally reckoned to be considerably more talented than his very capable brother, and possibly even than his very distinguished father; Cicero is among those who reckoned him the greatest Roman orator of all, not excluding himself, an astonishing act of modesty by Cicero.

Gaius' reforms came in four groups: provision for the surplus population of Rome which had been his brother's chief objective, reforms to the administration of justice, his continuing efforts to improve and strengthen relations with states and cities of Italy, and some miscellaneous measures. In this last group was a law which banned the enlistment of youth in the Army beneath the age of seventeen and required the state to supply its soldiers. This permitted Rome's armies and navy to be broadened beyond well-to-do citizens and vastly expanded the potential pool for the military requirements of its ever-growing sphere of influence and interests. It was an important move toward a broadly based professional army. Another measure required that the Senate declare in advance what provinces would be assigned to consuls prior to rather than after their election. It was the custom that an incumbent consul received the government of a province but the allotments of the provinces had become a scandalous matter of patronage conducted by the leading senators to assure that recipients would remember the interests of those who had so endowed them, and a democracy would be served because the Senate's assignment of provinces was subject to confirmation by the local populations, though in practice this was usually not difficult to arrange. This has been held by historians to be a contest between "the incompetence and venality of the many and the possible dishonesty of the few," and it remains difficult to judge which was preferable.

Another of his measures was the privatization of the collection of income tax which traditionally in outlying provinces was a share of agricultural production. In this way the revenue to Rome would fluctuate with the value of the harvest and was thus something of a progressive income tax. But it was very complicated to calculate and collect and in selling the right to collect tax, Gaius correctly calculated that he would make the process more efficient, but he apparently gave little thought to the influence that would shortly be exercised by the new class of wealthy and powerful man thus created. The rights to collect the taxes of Pergamon which it will be recalled was bequeathed by Attalus III to Rome, would prove to be a lucrative position for which there was fierce competition.

There were a good many measures promoting new colonies and expanding upon Tiberius's policy of settling the surplus Roman population elsewhere in Italy where they would not only be upholders of Rome and be gone from the capital, for their activities in large and unruly numbers were frequently disruptive, but most of these colonies were commercially successful as well as sociologically: they became useful sources of revenue and the settlers ceased to be a charge on Roman welfare. The focus of these colonies was shifting from agriculture to commercial ventures as Rome itself had evolved from an agricultural market town to a far-flung and diverse Empire.

It was at this point that Gaius Gracchus added to the Senate, as people eligible to serve as jurors, six-hundred wealthy individuals, who it was assumed would be less susceptible to bribes than were some of the less well-to-do senators. And it was at this point in his program that Gaius offered citizenship to all adult Latins, an ethnic and geographic definition. This was, of course, a large addition to the Roman citizenry but a very wise measure of democratization and strengthening of the core of what was now an empire that stretched from the Atlantic Ocean in what is now Portugal to what is now the Western side of Anatolian Turkey. Such an expansion of the franchise was bound to affront the traditional Roman reluctance to share the spoils both in status and in tangible rewards of the rise of their city. Here the conservative elements of the Senate, who had reacted to Gaius with watchful passivity up to this point, decided that it was time to oppose him and brought forth the talented M. Livius Drusus.

Drusus countered Gracchus' proposed law establishing colonies from the poor people of Rome by proposing six times as large a program and a more generous regime for those who participated in it. Drusus' objective was to shake the loyalty to the Gracchi in the Concilium Plebis, by simply outbidding Gracchus for their support. Gaius Gracchus replied by claiming that it was his intention vastly to expand his program and he seized upon a recent plague of locusts and consequent disease in the province of Africa near Carthage and Utica which had laid waste to that rich agricultural area. An initial colony of six-thousand people was planned for a short distance away from the pitiful remains of the great city that Tiberius Gracchus had helped to lay low. He further offered this and other relocations of the poor not in place of the proposal of Drusus but as supplements to it. There was audible concern in Roman governing circles about becoming too ambitious with colonization: Phocae, Corinth, Miletus, and Tyre, had all been surpassed by the towns they founded: Massilia (Marseilless), Syracuse, Byzantium, and Carthage. But Gaius Gracchus prevailed; Drusus was not opposing his bill and vice versa, and the measures proposed by both men were adopted. They were just fencing at this point.

Gracchus then raised the ante with a law which excluded senators from juries altogether. They were to be replaced by non-senatorial people of some wealth; this was a direct transfer from the traditionally most powerful faction in Roman political life to a rising rival faction. In the process it might likely eliminate a good deal of corrupt practice as a number of senators certainly blotted their ledgers with incentivized questionable verdicts, but there was no guarantee that the parvenus of the new commercial Rome would be more circumspect. It was, in any case, an outright declaration of war on the most powerful incumbent political faction. This reform effectively made the judges of the criminal law partisan officials subject to electoral rebuke, and while it was more democratic than leaving these functions with the Senate, it almost certainly reduced the quality of the law courts.

On extension of the franchise and the perquisites of citizenship among Rome's allies and affiliated states in Italy, Gracchus was pushed into attempting to get his entire proposed reforms through in one omnibus bill, because the challenge from Drusus had convinced him that he was unlikely to be able to get a third consecutive term as tribune. The original plan had been to proceed in stages and offer the equivalent of the status of a Roman to all those with a Latin name, indicating an adequate level of assimilation to Rome. But in these circumstances Gaius Gracchus apparently made the same proposal to all Italians. This too was bound to be a difficult pill for the Senate to swallow, attached as it was to the management of Rome and to Rome being of a manageable size. The consul Fannius, who had been elected on the recommendation of Gracchus, led the opposition to this measure specifically by gaining adoption of a ban on any non-Roman coming within five miles of the city while the bill was being adopted. Fannius proposed this in the name of clean government and avoidance of votes of the ineligible, but it essentially doomed the prospect of success for Gaius' expanded franchise bill, at least for the time being.

Gaius Gracchus now placed his bets on an ambitious colonization scheme near Carthage and spent a great deal of time there. The new town was to be named Junonia and caused his opponents immediately to set about an insidious campaign to debunk the entire project. Tales were circulated in Rome of the worksite having been attacked by winds of unheard of strength and attacked by wolves to the point that superstitious Romans believed it was a God-forsaken project. He was also accused of putting his Italian protégés into Junonia ahead of rightful Romans. These are political techniques that in a slightly more sophisticated way are familiar in modern democracies, but Romans were religiously primitive and relatively superstitious.

When reelection time came round in 122, Gaius Gracchus was dependent on the poor to win; all the more prosperous and influential classes were now arrayed against him. Some of this was Gaius' impatient honesty, but much of the blame for the choppy reception given Gracchus' sensible reforms was due to the self-serving reaction of leading members of the Senate, swaddling themselves in impersonation of the austere virtue of Roman lore, the spirit of Cincinnatus. Tactically, Drusus had attracted a substantial percentage of the proletariat, splitting Gracchus' electoral base. Gracchus moved from his comfortable home on the Palatine Hill to the poor Velabrum neighborhood and demolished a building that prevented the poor from being able to see a much-anticipated gladiatorial combat. But all his strenuous electioneering did not suffice and his term as Tribune came to an end at the end of 122 B.C. The results of the consular elections were also unfavorable: the honourable Quintus Fabius Maximus Allobrogicus, and the scoundrel Lucius Opimius, now remembered for the outstanding vintage of 121. He was elected on the basis of his reputation for the severity with which he had participated in the repression of the rebels of the city of Fregellae in 124; the leaders of the Senate felt that he could be relied upon to restore order should pro-Gracchan agitation make that necessary. In this, at least, their judgment was correct.

Entering the year 121, Gaius Gracchus retained a large following and was much feared but his only official position was on the agrarian commission where the majority were not enthusiastic promoters of its objectives. Gaius became concerned about the level of public agitation and formed a bodyguard to assure that he did not suffer the fate of his brother. Shortly afterwards, in a drunken public fracas, a consular crier, reader of public pronouncements, Antullius, was killed by one of Gracchus' followers. His corpse became an iconic item of political agitation and was carried in a parade past the door of the Senate House. This had the desired effect of alarming the senators who, ignoring the terrible precedent of Scipio Nasica and Tiberius Gracchus, for the first time in Roman history, adopted the ultimate sanction, the resolution Senatus Consultum Ultimum, which gave the magistrates what amounted to a blank cheque to "defend the state and to see that it suffered no harm."

This was all the encouragement Opimius needed, and he called the senators and knights (equites) to arms, as there was no regular police force in Rome. This naturally incited the fears of Gracchus and his collaborators that they were about to be arrested even though they had done nothing illegal and Gracchus himself had nothing to do with the death of Antullius. Grachus' loyal colleague, Fulvius Flaccus called for revolt, but Gracchus declined this and counseled avoidance of provocation. But when Opimius summoned both of them to appear in the Senate, Gracchus concluded, almost certainly correctly, that it was the consul's intention to act on the ultimate authority granted by the Senate and to find Flaccus and himself guilty of capital crimes and execute them with a minimum of legal formality.

While he was contemplating his alternatives, Flaccus and his followers seized the Aventine and gave Opimius and the Senate all the justification they needed to suppress an insurrection. There were some negotiations, with Flaccus' son conveying messages back and forth, and Gracchus made some conciliatory proposals but both he and Flaccus declined to give themselves over to the mercies of Opimius and the Senate. Opimius martialed all the forces he had mobilized, stormed the Aventine, routed Flaccus' motley group of malcontents and Gracchus' hugely outnumbered bodyguard. Flaccus was slain and his son, who had been nothing but a go-between, was put to death, though given his choice of method of execution. Gracchus prayed at the temple of Diana allegedly asking vengeance on Rome, and then fled across the Tiber with a few followers. He was greeted cheerfully by the populous but not offered shelter when he asked for it. Before he could be captured, he committed suicide with the aid of his faithful slave Philocrates.

Because Opimius had offered the weight of Gracchus' head in gold, he was decapitated, and Septimuleius extracted his brains and inserted molten lead, raising the weight to 17 pounds, but was quickly discovered and received no reward. The corpses of the Gracchans were thrown into the Tiber, and Gaius Gracchus' devoted widow, Licinius Crassus, was forbidden to indicate she was in mourning and her dower and other possessions were seized. Cornelia, the mother of the Gracchi and daughter of Scipio Africanus, built splendid tombs for both of them at the places of their deaths, and within a few years, they had become legendary icons of the disadvantaged, whose condition substantially deteriorated after the Gracchan era had passed. Plutarch, uncontradicted, claims Opimius massacred three-thousand Gracchan sympathizers. Gaius Gracchus was thirty-three.

Roman posterity closed up, led by Cicero, behind the theory that the Gracchi were initially good and very talented men who had been swayed by the adulation of the riffraff of Rome and became cynical demagogues who tried to unhinge Roman government. It was held that they had tried to sabotage the interests of the meritocratic leaders of Rome and deliver the state over to the caprices of unruly and impressionable mobs. They clearly undertook more than they were able to deliver and lacked the tactical skill necessary to get such a comprehensive program of reform adopted. This would have required a larger number of collaborators of stature, as it would not be possible, as Tiberius discovered, to count on reelection to consecutive terms. They made a mistake attempting to do all of it themselves and at once, but the charges against them of being unprincipled or of having been seduced by the popularity of the masses have never been convincing.

They failed, but the greater failure was Rome's. This was the last best chance for the renovation of Roman institutions, of the Senate, the Concilium Plebis, the tribunate, the consulate, and the judiciary. The Roman aristocracy and the talented young men whom the flexibility of the system permitted to join them, had closed the route to the peaceful or at least civilized adaptation by Rome to its ever-enlarging status. With a regime now so dedicated to the possession and retention of far-flung interests, it would ultimately be impossible for those claiming a right to govern to do so within the narrow confines of Rome's institutions, despite the penetration of the ruling class by plebeians, though plebeians who had accepted the system they had entered from below.

Soon the power would reside with the generals. Up to a point, the Senate could try to play the generals off against each other, but as Roman generals were politicians before they were generals, they would soon see through that and combine against it. As the army commanders had authority over what their soldiers could pillage and keep for themselves and could be assumed to have the political influence to require that their men be treated generously for their services to the state, it was likely that the day was not far off when victorious generals would exploit the fact that their soldiers' primary loyalty was to them and not to the unrepresentative government in Rome.

A court of inquiry in 120 cleared Opimius of any wrongdoing in the death of the three-thousand Gracchans. This was a foregone conclusion and an expression of the collective Roman upper-class view most effectively propagated by the likes of Cicero that the Gracchi were rogue scions of great families who though motivated by good intentions, inexplicably turned illegally upon the system they were bound to uphold. This is a self-whitewash by the Roman establishment. Equally inaccurate is the claim of modern revolutionary movements that the Gracchi were some sort of a precursor to them. They aimed at a reform of the system to make it stronger, not its overthrow. They were attempting to address the real and dangerous grievances of the vast population of displaced poor and of the majority of inhabitants of the Italian peninsula, who felt that they were being unfairly used by Rome. They were trying to change problems that had to be addressed. It is not entirely the fault of the Gracchi that they were unable to liberalize the so-called Roman "democracy," from which nothing less than the menace of the Social War (conducted by Julius Caesar sixty-five years later) was required to extract concessions.

With its brutal rejection and destruction of the Gracchi, the traditional Roman system of government by the Senate, and particular factions within the Senate, had seemed to triumph over its greatest challenge. But as is often the case in such matters, in rejecting the authors of a reform program that would have preserved most of the rights and privileges of the Senate, they were forcing an eventual confrontation with people much less well disposed to themselves. The loquacious and self-satisfied Senate and patriciate would be practically resistless against the successors to the Gracchi, other than by recourse to the evil of assassination. By treating the Gracchi as they did, the leaders of Rome were foregoing the path of gradual and relatively continuous institutional renovation that would be followed by the most successful modern states, especially the British, Americans, and their emulators. Tiberius and Gaius Gracchus are generally considered to be the world's first seriously democratic reformers.

Plutarch reckoned that Tiberius and Gaius were similar in their bravery, self-discipline, generosity, eloquence, grandeur of spirit, valor, sense of justice, care and industry in office, and self-control in private life. But Tiberius was gentle and composed and Gaius was earnest and vehement. The Gracchi slightly presaged the Kennedys of the American Twentieth Century, though they had a noble and civic, as opposed to a brief and commercial, family background. They were all excellent men in talent and in nature, extremely patriotic, and they died tragically and prematurely for their country; but the Kennedys did not die at the hands of the system in which they held high office, rather as victims of insane extremists who profited from the relative accessibility to its leaders provided by the exigencies of American democracy. The Kennedy Brothers were mourned by the whole nation and also by the contemporary American political class, roughly the people comparable to those who murdered the Gracchi.

The greatest importance of the Gracchi was not specifically intended by them as far as is known: the concept that the tribune could be removed by will of the people and that the tribune could be elected to successive terms. These principles were not accepted by the Senate, but Tiberius did have Octavius removed and when Gaius sought reelection, even though he was not successful, his right to be reelected was conceded. The implications of the ability of the proletariat holding the head of the Roman government answerable not especially to the Senate but absolutely to a majority of the lower classes was a concept that the anti-Gracchi forces of the day would have been better to accommodate up to a point than to try to extirpate. The Gracchi gambled and they lost; Rome eagerly took the gamble to squash their movement and to murder them, but the Romans that did so, in almost equal measure to the Gracchi themselves, and much less historically lamented than they, lost everything. The era of the generals was almost at hand.

5. Frontier Wars and the Origins of Gaius Marius

In the aftermath of the death of Gaius Gracchus, the Senate was again the undisputed master of Rome, but the allies of the Gracchi were not persecuted and ostracized as they had been after the murder of Tiberius Gracchus. Opimius, as has been mentioned, was acquitted of the death of Gaius Gracchus and others but only after a sensational and tumultuous trial. Gaius' old ally, Gaius Carbo, managed to gain election as consul in 120 but in the following year was charged with an unknown offense and prosecuted by the great orator Lucius Crassus. The allegations were so strenuously advanced that Carbo while awaiting the verdict, committed suicide by swallowing Spanish flies.

It was at this point that the first of a line of political generals leading directly to Augustus Caesar came to general notice. Gaius Marius was in some ways the precursor of a great swath of political generals over twenty centuries: all those who translated the support of the soldiery and in most cases the personal loyalty of a substantial section of the Army into the highest political office. People as varied as Napoleon, Juan Peron, Charles de Gaulle, Augusto Pinochet, and Indonesia's General Suharto and many others could in some measure be considered heirs of Marius.

He was from a small town in Arpinum and had gained recognition as a junior officer under Scipio Aemilianus in Spain. After the death of Scipio, he became a protégé of the Metellus family and became a tribune, a position he held contemporaneously with Lucius Metellus in 118. For the next thirty years, he alternated between being principally a military commander and principally a politician. It was to become a combination fateful and ultimately prevalent in Roman history. As tribune, Marius put through many popular reforms, but was much more than a mere demagogue. His voting reforms so scandalized the Senate he was summoned to be cross-examined by the senators; he faced the challenge ably and a stormy debate ensued, in which his former patron Metellus defected and Marius announced to the Senate in his tribunal capacity the arrest of Lucius Metellus, whereupon the Senate opposition collapsed and Marius returned to the seething masses of Rome a great hero.

He did successfully resist a move to repeal Gaius Gracchus' Lex Frumentaria in a way that was deemed likely to reduce the cost of wheat and bread. This was perhaps why he failed in his attempt to be elected aedile, but won a praetorship narrowly in 115. He did not excel in this office and the greater political office at the time was the consul. Aemilius Scaurus, was also a soldier of humble origins but unlike Marius, owed the success of his career almost entirely to his colleagues in the Senate. He married a daughter of Metellus Delmaticus, who subsequently was the wife of the dictator Lucius Sulla, Marius' greatest rival. Delmaticus became the most influential figure in the Senate.

The state of the relocated people under the Gracchan agricultural statutes was stabilized as the land board was abolished in 119 and perpetual tenancy was assured, though they were to pay a modest rent that Tiberius Gracchus had suppressed, though the revenue was to be dedicated to a good and popular end. And in 111, the rent was cancelled and in the Italian re-allocations of public land and the colonial initiatives in Africa and Greece, the status of all beneficiaries was strengthened: ownership was confirmed, tenancies made permanent, and colonies enlarged and treated as if they were in Italy itself. Marcus Livius Drusus, when consul in 112, also put through some upgrades and preferments for Latin and Italian holders of public lands. To some extent there was Gracchus policy without the Gracchi (the forerunner of such hybrid concepts as Gaullism without de Gaulle and Trumpism without Trump). Henceforth, the beneficiaries of land distributions would be soldiers rather than the Roman unemployed, because of Marius' reforms, and would be farther from Rome than the Gracchan allotments because the Roman common lands had been almost entirely distributed except the Campanian domain. Because Marius was no toady to the Senate he's not been particularly popularly remembered apart from Sallust, to whom we are much indebted for knowledge of the career of Marius. Scaurus was in office for a series of reforms castigating the morals of Romans, especially the upper classes, a righteous fervour that gripped the city intermittently for many centuries (and not without considerable justification). The great scandal in 114 B.C. was alleged licence among the Vestal Virgins. Three were accused and after immense controversy, only one was convicted by the Pontifex Maximus. Rome became particularly sensitive on questions of public pecuniary ethics; the most frequent complainant on these matters was the flamboyant barrister Lucius Cassius Longinus, familiar still because of his constant repetition of the question: "Cui bono?—Who profits from this?"

At the same time, a large number of Romans were driven to transports of religious fervour and these were among the leading champions of human sacrifices in the forum before huge audiences. In 111 BC for three days, it was alleged the sky rained milk and that a large part of the city was destroyed by fire. This cannot be substantiated either, but there was clearly a considerable moral laxity and appropriate climate of moral reproachfulness. This public desire for purgation reached its apogee in an astounding act of barbarity as two Gauls and two Greeks were put to death in the forum to expiate the sins of the Romans. This became one of the great spectacles of Rome, but fortunately, in 97 the Senate and Popular Assembly agreed that this pseudo-religious and macabre homicidal lunacy had to stop.

We have seen that Attalus III left the kingdom of Pergamon to the Roman people in his will, and that this greatly assisted Tiberius Gracchus in distributing land. Before the will of the late king was formally recognized by his Roman beneficiary, but after it had been published, the government and Pergamon moved quickly to give land and other benefits to the poor classes of Pergamese and the mercenaries who had served Pergamon and settled in that country. In 133, the Roman Senate adopted a decree entrenching all the acts of the kings of Pergamon up to the day before the death of Attalus III. Early in 132, a commission of five was sent from

Rome to make arrangements with Pergamon giving effect to the late king's will (and among the members was the scoundrel Scipio Nasica, who had been bundled out of Rome to escape prosecution).

As Nasica and the other commissioners arrived in Pergamon, an astute revolutionary, Aristonicus, allegedly the product of a dalliance between King Eumenes II and an Ephesian concubine, arose to lead the aggrieved. Aristonicus set out to rouse local resentment against the announced Roman government and also to convince the lower income classes of Pergamon that it was high time they received a fair share of their kingdom's wealth rather than being handed off in destitution to an unwanted foreign Imperial occupying power—the traditional pitches to national and socio-economic discontent. He anticipated the adherence of the Greeks of Asia but was somewhat disappointed in this hope. He managed to put together a fleet but it was decisively defeated by the Ephesians off Cyme and Aristonicus was thereafter obliged to retreat into the interior of Asia Minor and rely for support on the discontented serfs, claiming the Romans would be even more oppressive than the local landlords they had known. A paradisiacal tone was adopted and under the influence of Blossius of Cumae, who was visiting from Italy, the new putative state was christened "City of the Sun," after the Blessed Isle in the romance of Lambulus.

The commission sent from Rome in 132 which included Nasica could only help organize and coordinate those local elements already disposed to take up the Roman side. These were principally Mithridates V, Euergetes of Pontus, Nicomedes II of Bithynia, Pylaemenes of Paphlagonia, and Ariarathes V of Cappadocia. These men held their own kingdoms and territories and assisted in some neighboring ones but it was soon clear that a Roman army would have to be introduced into the theatre to quell uprisings, stabilize borders, and decide which local potentates to favor with the gift of provinces that they could suppress as conduits of barbarians into Roman government territory. The Romans naturally kept the best territories for themselves.

In 131, Crassus Mucianus arrived at the head of an army but after an unsuccessful attempt to besiege Aristonicus at Leucae; he was captured by the Thracians in the early 130's and died from an unknown but almost certainly unnatural and probably nasty cause. Crassus was immediately succeeded by Marcus Perperna, consul in 130. He severely defeated Aristonicus and then besieged him in Stratoniceia and forced his surrender. The defeated and captured Aristonicus, in chains, along with a great accumulation of Attalid treasure was shipped off to Rome. Perperna died in Pergamon apparently of natural causes in 129. He was followed by the Roman consul for 129, Aquilius. Aquilius was accompanied by ten senatorial commissioners, and they carved up territory according to the customary Roman colonial model of taking all that was useful and promising territory for Rome and leaving the less favored and more remote frontier areas for the more promising locals, and particularly those who had rendered conspicuous service to Rome itself.

Mithridates (Pontus) and Nicomedia (Bithynia), vied with each other for control of eastern Asia Minor, and Rome put it up for bids between these two valued local allies; Mithridates won, and Nicomedes was disgruntled. Aquilius conducted a traditional auction for greater Phrygia from Lydia up to the borders of Galatia, and Mithridates' was again the winning bid. Aquilius returned to Rome in triumph in 126 after this rather cynical resolution of eastern questions but was so widely accused of corruption that he was charged and tried but acquitted, to considerable popular annoyance. Because of the squabbling between Mithridates and Nicomedes, Rome finally opted to keep all of Phrygia for itself. It would require garrisoning, but it was an intelligent decision and a satisfactory outcome for Rome, as most campaigns in this prolonged era of Roman expansion, were.

For the last third of the Second Century B.C., Rome was almost constantly in campaigns all along its frontiers to make them more defensible and improve communications between the now far-flung units of what Rome considered its permanent patrimony. It linked through ambitious roads and ports the Thracian Chersonese, Macedonia, Illyria, and the Alps in order finally to accord security to the northern Italian plains, and in Dalmatia well into the interior of what for most of the Twentieth Century was Yugoslavia. Gallic tribes had moved into the Balkans north of the Alps and southwards below the Saba River and the governor of Macedonia, Sextus Pompeius, was killed fighting the Scordisci tribe in 119 B.C. and the consul of that year, Lucius Metellus resurrected the Roman position in the Balkans in 117 B.C. when he returned in triumph to Rome and was thereafter referred to as Metellus Delmaticus.

M. Aemilius Scaurus moved east from the Alps in 115 and imposed Roman control on the headwaters of the Saba but the Scordisci were back in the following year and defeated Gaius Cato and advanced as far as northern Greece, where the sinister Cimbrians were already roaming and probing aggressively. In 112, C. Metellus Caprarius and the versatile M. Livius Drusus, suppressed the southwestern Balkans and Drusus finally gave the Scordisci a well-earned comeuppance, and advanced to the banks of the Danube in what is now Romania. In the last years of the Second Century B.C., the plebeian T. Didius, praetorian governor of Macedonia, was so successful in extending Roman jurisdiction to naturally defensible mountain and river frontiers, that he was elevated to the consulship in 98 and peace prevailed in the area for the next twenty years.

Rome's western frontiers were also unstable in this period. The Gauls now largely grouped around the Arverni tribe and possibly pressed from Teutonic invaders in the Northeast, attacked Rome's old ally Massilia (Marseilless), requiring a forceful Roman military intervention in the middle of the Second Century B.C. Thirty years later, the revival of that pressure came when the Roman Senate, influenced by the increasing power of the commercial classes of Rome and seeking a distraction from Gracchan agitation for reform, sent a large force under Fulvius Flaccus, Gaius Gracchus' closest ally in 125. He cleared the Gauls back from the coast separating northern Italy from Massilia and was accorded a triumph in 123, just a year before the final eruption of Gracchan political turmoil. However, Sextius Calvinus was obliged to return a couple of years later and carry on a prolonged offensive against the southern Gauls, concluding with the capture of the capital of that tribe on a plateau a couple of miles northeast of what is now Aix-en-Provence. He built a large fort called Aquae Sextiae between Massilia and northwestern Italy and left behind sufficient forces to begin the creation of a Roman province in southern France.

What followed was a preliminary to Julius Caesar's war of conquest in Gaul sixty years later. Rome's incursions offended the incipient nationalism of the Gauls and the Arverni took up arms under King Bituitus, an alliance with the Allobroges, who marched on the Roman positions but were decisively defeated in 121 by Domitius on the banks of the Rhône near Avignon. The Allobroges allegedly lost twenty-thousand dead and three-thousand prisoners. Determined to subdue the Arverni as well, Rome sent Quintus Fabius Maximus, consul in 121, and he decisively defeated Bituitus near Valence. While Fabius returned to triumph in Rome, Domitius received protestations of fidelity and submission from numerous Gallic tribes and clans and set up government in a territory stretching from Geneva to the Pyrenees. Domitian negotiated alliances with some of the neighboring tribes, led by the Aedui, who had supported Rome in the preceding struggle with the Arverni and Allabroges. Massilia was awarded responsibility for maintaining this corridor between Spain and Italy which the Gauls feared, not without reason, would be the launching point for a Roman assault upon the entire country between the Rhine, the channel between Gaul and Britain, the Atlantic, and the Pyrenees. A colony was established in Transalpine Gaul at Narbo Martius, despite extensive opposition in the Senate. The prolonged controversy was somewhat reminiscent of the recent debate over the Gracchan colony of Junonia (Carthage). The new project was championed by the rising orator Lucius Crassus and that it was successful indicates the growing power of the commercial interests in pushing Rome's influence throughout the Mediterranean for pecuniary rather than cultural or simply imperialistic reasons.

As the European frontiers were stabilized, new problems arose on the southern shore of the Mediterranean. Rome had richly rewarded Massinissa's Kingdom of Numidia for his support against Carthage, and as has been reported, his realm extended from Mauretania to Cyrenaica when he died at the age of ninety in 148 B.C. His kingdom was divided, effectively by decree of Scipio Aemilianus between his three legitimate sons, Micipsa, Gulussa, and Mastanabal. The last two died within a couple of years and Micipsa ruled the whole territory that had been built up and governed by his father. Micipsa sheltered a son of Mastanabal, Jugurtha, whom Massinissa had not recognized as a legitimate heir because his mother was a concubine. He was a forceful and intelligent personality and much respected, and a rivalry developed between him and the two sons of Micipsa, Adherbal, and Hiempsal. Micipsa sent him as commander of the contingent he dispatched to assist the Romans in the siege and reduction of Numantia (Spain). The historian Sallust claims he was motivated by a desire that he would advance the family interest by bravely dying in Spain and spare Micipsa the adjudication of the competing interests between him and his natural sons. In fact, he distinguished himself and returned to Numidia a hero, and a protege of Scipio and Micipsa adopted him, intensifying the rivalry that already existed with his two step-brother-cousins.

Micipsa died in 118 and in 117 Jugurtha arranged the murder of Hiempsal, and the kingdom was riven between the followers of Jugurtha and the adherents of Adherbal. Jugurtha militarily defeated Adherbal, who fled to Rome to plead for the patronage of his father's ally. Jugurtha sent his own envoys to Rome and the Roman Senate, as had now long been general practice around most of the Mediterranean, was called upon to adjudicate between the competing interests. Jugurtha had learned at Numantia how efficacious bribes to selected Roman senators could be and deployed that knowledge effectively. The Senate had no ability to select the more believable of the diametrically opposed arguments, and the scoundrel Opimius was appointed head of a delegation of ten to conduct a tour of inspection in Numidia in 116. Jugurtha became impatient with this and attacked Adherbal under the noses of the Roman commissioners and routed him, having first attempted to provoke a retaliatory attack by Adherbal.

Adherbal barricaded himself into the city of Cirta, where a large delegation of Italian traders helped him to resist the siege Jugurtha immediately imposed. Adherbal smuggled out a note for the Roman Senate and it aroused considerable sympathy, and a new group of emissaries was sent immediately, led by Scaurus, the former consul. They met with Jugurtha, but not Adherbal and returned impotently to Rome. Jugurtha tightened the screws on Cirta and the Italians within opened the gates on the assumption that they would be spared. They miscalculated, and so did Jugurtha. He summarily executed Adherbal, but slaughtered the Italians while he was at it, despite the fact that they had admitted him to the city. This aroused immense outrage in Rome, as the murder of its citizens abroad always did. In 112, a tribune named Gaius Memmius led the war party, which swept the Senate and Consul Lucius Calpurnius Bestia was sent to Numidia at the head of a substantial army to bring Jugurtha to heel. He belatedly sent emissaries to Rome, but they were expelled from Rome without being heard, even unofficially. As soon as Bestia's force had crossed into Numidia a peace was signed, in which Jugurtha paid off Rome with thirty elephants, large herds of cattle and horses and a modest amount of cash. Bestia's well known venality is the most likely reason for this, but it does not explain the concurrence of Scaurus, who accompanied Bestia. Memmius thundered against Jugurtha in the Senate. Cassius Longinus, a praetor, was commissioned to bring Jugurtha to Rome to answer the allegations against him. He did arrive, but when interrogation of him began, Tribune Gaius Baebius intervened and stopped proceedings and Jugurtha returned to Numidia.

But he committed another error of aggression like his massacre of the Italians at Cirta, when he commissioned the assassination of Massiva, Gulussa's son and Jugurtha's cousin, who was living in Rome and was induced by Spurius Albinus, consul in 110, to claim to be the rightful king of Numidia. He had entrusted this task to one of his courtiers, Bomilcar, but the assassin bungled the task and was captured and sang like a canary flying backwards, inculpating Bomilcar and Jugurtha. Jugurtha bailed Bomilcar and they slipped out of Italy. Rome went to war.

Most of Jugurtha's defensive forces were in the central massif, in what is now Algeria, but well back from the Mediterranean. Rome's heavily armed legions were at a disadvantage in this very hot and in the spring, extremely rainy, country. Albinus returned to Rome for the elections in 110, leaving his less capable brother, Aulus, in charge. In the autumn of 110, he was taken by surprise in his camp late at night. Their lives were spared but they were flung out of Numidia with little deference. But when the Romans pursued some of Jugurtha's men well to the West, and then Jugurtha successfully stormed the camp of the main Roman army in Numidia in the dead of night, the Numidian king forced a peace in which the Romans had to withdraw from Numidia within ten days.

This treaty was a fantastic disgrace and Rome was roused to real anger; and a special court was established to judge offenses in the Jugurthine conflict. Scaurus was on the bench of this court of war offenses and Opimius, Bestia, and Albinus were among those charged with various counts of negligence and general misconduct. The court admonished the whole Roman state that collaboration to assist Jugurtha would be regarded essentially as treason. It was generally recognized that the problems of Jugurtha were soon to be evoked to the Roman army to address, and any assistance to Jugurtha of any Roman would be judged criminally, regardless of the age of the party litigated against. Jugurtha's aggression had startled Rome, as it had served him well. But he had now gone too far and had roused a mighty giant against himself. As often happened in these times, Rome was slow to anger, but once at war, required a decisive and prestigious outcome.

6. The Jugurthine War and the Rise of Gaius Marius

In 110, Spurius Albinus returned to Africa with the goal of restoring his family's reputation after the damage done to it by his brother's inadequate performance. He found the army withdrawn and demoralized and incapable in its current condition of avenging Rome against Jugurtha and he dejectedly returned. The consuls for 109 were Marcus Junius Silanus and Quintus Caecilius Metellus, brother of Metellus Delmaticus, nephew of the great Metellus Macedonicus, who was given command of the mission to put Jugurtha in his place once and for all. So great was his reputation for integrity and his influence in the Senate that there were no fears of the frequent corruption of Roman consular adventurers at the head of Roman armies abroad, and many parts of Italy and Roman allies voluntarily furnished contingents for his mission. His chief adjutants would be P. Rutilius Rufus and the now rising star Gaius Marius of the Roman army. Jugurtha made a desultory effort to negotiate as Metellus brought in reinforcements and snapped his legions into fighting trim.

By the summer of 109, Metellus was ready and moved westwards into Numidia and fought a lengthy battle with Jugurtha near Cirta. The Romans were victorious and smashed up Jugurtha's army, but at the expense of substantial casualties and the Numidian king withdrew in good order and able to replenish his ranks. This induced a change in Metellus' strategy to lightning assaults on populated centres, separating Jugurtha from most of his people. Metellus garrisoned a number of cities and towns before the two armies took winter quarters. Metellus attempted to negotiate through the treacherous Bomilcar, hoping to bankroll an assassination or coup d'état. Jugurtha prevented that but was in all respects on the defensive within his own kingdom.

The campaign resumed in 108, with a Numidian uprising in the town of Vaga, in which every Italian in the town, military and civilian, was massacred except the commander, Turpilius Silanus. Metellus set out to avenge this outrage, captured the town, executed the suspect Turpilius Silanus, and Bomilcar attempted to overthrow Jugurtha, probably incentivized by Metellus, and was executed with his co-conspirators. If Jugurtha's nerves had not been rattled by this experience, he was certainly shaken when the Roman legions decisively defeated him and he fled into Thala, and then departed in haste just before Metellus closed a siege around their city. After about a month it fell and yielded up a great store of precious metals. Jugurtha vanished into the interior of his country to create a new army and enter into contact with King Bocchus of Mauretania, Jugurtha's father-in-law. They marched jointly on Metellus at Cirta, but the Roman commander did not offer battle, and Jugurtha and Bocchus did not have the troop-strength to enforce a siege by full encirclement.

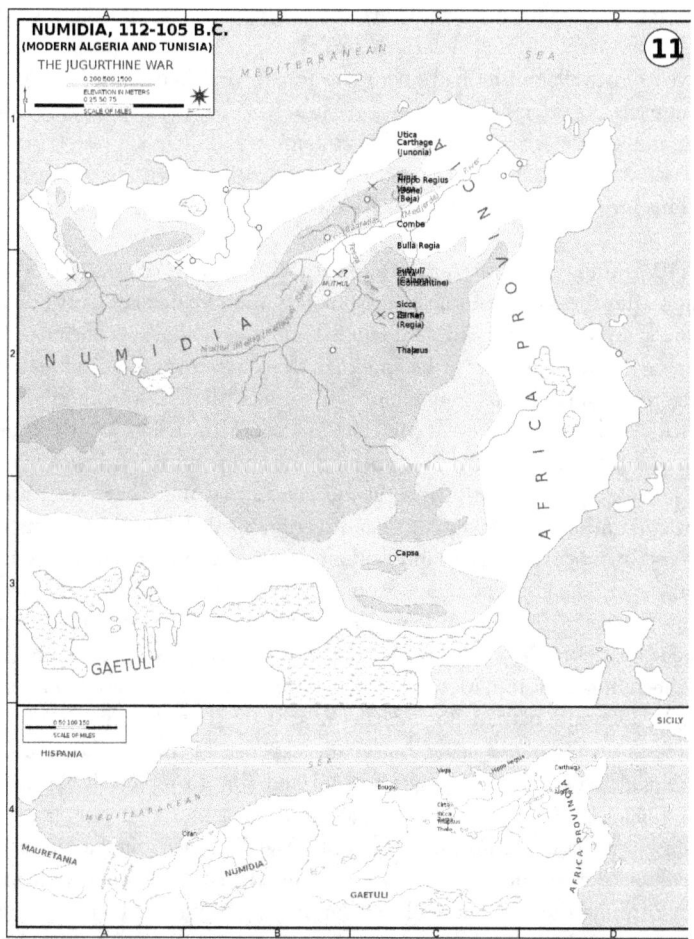

There was division in the Roman camp, as Marius, already a prominent Roman politician, had been conducting his own propaganda operation with self-serving leaks and scoops made to cooperative agents who saturated the political community of Rome with tales of Marius' impatience with Metellus and agitation for a more aggressive campaign which he held would have Jugurtha in custody in chains within a few days. Marius managed to arrange leave to return to Rome to seek the consulate and was duly elected—he had convinced the Roman electorate that his benefactor's caution had prolonged the war, exploiting the ambition of the commercial class to return to exploitation of the Numidian market. Metellus returned to Rome and was hailed as a conqueror and given a triumph, but Marius had raised hopes for greater and swifter success. Marius' press releases and grandstanding somewhat put down a precedent for a great deal of emulation over the following twenty centuries, including, up to a point, Field Marshal Garnet Wolseley, and Douglas MacArthur, George S. Patton, Irwin Rommel, and Bernard Montgomery of World War II. Marius' greatest innovation, and it would prove to be extremely important, was attracting and recruiting reinforcements from citizens of very modest means. He departed from the long Roman habit of having only soldiers of middle and upper class backgrounds who were essentially able to afford to lend themselves in the Roman services to the state for a campaign. Marius implied a share of the spoils for his forces and it was inevitable that if he were successful, the loyalty of his soldiers would in many cases be to him rather than to Rome, which was represented by the colonial governor of many of the Italian cities from whence his expanded army was created.

When Marius was appointed, Bocchus peeled off from his alliance with Jugurtha and returned to Mauretania. Marius struck at Capsa, in the south of Numidia, sacked it, to the gratification of his soldiers, and to intimidate Jugurtha's Gaetullian allies—he had tentatively talked Bocchus into joining him, and Marius did not want any such desert conjuration to succeed again. Marius continued to occupy the towns in eastern Numidia and effectively forced Jugurtha entirely out of the Eastern half of his kingdom. Marius took home leave for some months to fortify his position in Rome but in 106, he returned to a point five-hundred miles west of where he had departed Numidia and drove a wedge between the remaining Western section of Jugurtha's kingdom and his now very tepid ally King Bocchus, of Mauretania. He thus isolated Jugurtha and cautioned Bocchus, and was reinforced by a powerful cavalry unit led by another figure who would rise to great prominence in Rome, Lucius Cornelius Sulla, quaestor in 107 B.C. Broadly speaking, Sulla would have a relationship with Marius somewhat as Marius had had with Metellus; but the breakup and rivalry with Sulla would be much more aggravated and ultimately sanguinary than Marius' parting of the ways with Metellus.

As Marius was retiring towards Cirta in late 107 to take winter quarters on the Mediterranean where he could easily be supplied, he learned of an attack near Cirta and hurried to repel Jugurtha. Two heavy battles ensued a few days apart; the first was particularly closely fought and barely won by Marius but in the second, after a full day of combat Marius succeeded in retiring to an elevated point, moving his forces in the night and descending with great concentration in the morning and shattering Jugurtha's army. Four days later the emissaries of the Mauretanian king arrived and he left it to Sulla, who had greatly distinguished himself in the recent fighting, to negotiate while Marius himself led a mopping up operation to the south. Bocchus requested that he might be granted an interview with the government in Rome and after exhaustive consultation with the Senate by Marius, this liaison was granted.

The Senate pardoned and excused Bocchus on condition that he performed certain acts of friendship to expiate his past misconduct. Bocchus asked that Sulla visit him that they might work things out and this was agreed although it required the Roman general to embark upon a hazardous mission including an accidental encounter with the sullen Jugurtha himself. The price Sulla extracted was that Bocchus should attract Jugurtha to visit him and then seize him and deliver Jugurtha to the Romans. In all of the circumstances the Mauretanian king did not require excessive persuasion and the fallen King of Numidia was treacherously betrayed to Rome and was the star attraction in the mighty triumph given to Marius in 105. Jugurtha was not subjected to a public execution but at the end of the parade was led in chains to the Tullianum prison where he was shortly and discreetly executed. In the long history of Rome's unsuccessful enemies, few had miscalculated more completely than the late King of Numidia. Though Metellus and Sulla had both greatly contributed to it, Marius was the principal architect of a complete victory in North Africa. Rome followed its usual policy, other than in extremely prosperous areas, and divided conquered territories into numerous petty fiefdoms and principalities over which it claimed general suzerainty but retired to allow locals to govern themselves while maintaining nearby vigilant forces to prevent improvident things from occurring. The new King of Numidia was Gauda, a son of Mastanabal and half-brother of Jugurtha. Bocchus emerged well from his treachery and had an expanded kingdom and was an official national friend and ally of Rome.

The significance of the Jugurthine War vastly exceeded the subjugation of Numidia. It was remarkable that Rome continued the war long after it could easily have been ended satisfactorily. Rome still had nightmares about a challenge from a powerful African state such as Jugurtha was trying to build up, elaborating on what Massinissa had done, even though Carthage had been eliminated as a rival a century before. Numidia, surprisingly when viewed from the modern condition of North Africa, possessed the potential to be a very rich area and access to it was strongly desired by the steadily more influential Roman commercial class. They were regarded as vulgar arrivistes by the ancient senatorial families, but as in all other places and times (except for a time, Sparta), money was influential.

The greatest significance of the Jugurthine War was Marius' military reform. It decisively changed the nature of the political organization of Rome and all that Rome ruled and influenced. The Roman army was not a standing force; as emergencies approached, the government called for volunteers and relied on a citizen-militia, composed mainly of somewhat prosperous people whose careers motivated them to seek the earliest possible end to the emergencies that generated the call to the colours to which they responded. Most of the volunteers acquired their own weapons and equipment. Practically all the soldiers were from the five classes of the centuriate, while the so-called proletariat did not meet the criteria. It was an army of vested interest stakeholders. At times, in emergencies, the proletariat was taken into the army by exception and the standards of the classes of the centuriate were lowered somewhat; Marius, at the outset, professed only to be attracting people who had already been declared eligible.

It is difficult to judge to what extent Marius realized the impact of what he did. The more frequently encountered view is that he needed more manpower and did the logical thing and facilitated the recruitment of people of modest or irregular means, who could be counted on to agitate for maintenance of force strength because, unlike the citizen militia of the centuriate, they needed military employment to alleviate their under-employment and often penury. This author believes that the political ambition and astuteness of Gaius Marius was already too well known and had been too often demonstrated for him not to imagine that generals could by this means generate large forces more loyal to their commander as long as he believably claimed to be pursuing the Roman national interest, than to alternative persons or institutions claiming to speak for the Roman people and state, conferring the ultimately unanswerable advantage in whatever rivalry was underway. In any case, this was what occurred, and war was almost continuous for the next seventy-five years, until it was ended by Julius and Octavian (Augustus) Caesar. The Senate had failed too frequently to impress its strength and legitimacy on the public, and power gradually passed to the most successful and politically astute military commanders. As in many other countries that dissolved in factional strife, and over many centuries, the victorious faction had to sell itself as wronged, preferable for some ideological, ethnic, or opportunistic reason, better led, as well as likely to be successful, and altogether deserving of support.

The Senate had demonstrated an incorrigible incapacity to reform or to satisfy the demands of a large share of the Roman population in its brutal rejection of the Gracchi, who despite the malicious propaganda even of reputable commentators such as Cicero, essentially wished to preserve the old Rome of which they were exemplars, by making it more worthy of the loyalty of the disadvantaged masses. It was to protect Roman political civilization from the mountebanks and demagogues that the immoveable senatorial reactionaries accused the Gracchi themselves of having become, that Tiberius and Gaius Gracchus sought to reform Rome's political system. When this endeavour was smashed, it was likely that the disaffected masses would look outside the existing political system for the reforms they sought. Because the consuls were the generals, the more talented ones were bound to amass great popularity.

It is not really conceivable to this historian that Gaius Marius, who was a politician first and a soldier second, though very capable in both roles, did not realize that in opening the army to the masses who would need soldiering as an occupation and would be dependent on the commander to pay them, enrich them with plunder, lead them successfully but with care to spare casualties, and get them pensions; he was arming the victorious general, i.e., Marius himself, with irresistible political power in the Republic. He may not have foreseen the eventual clash between commanders that would beleaguer the Roman world for decades, and he may not have been looking much beyond his own interest, as well as the need for more soldiers to deal with more adversaries in more places than when Rome was smaller and less involved all around the Mediterranean. Thus did the evolution of the Republic's institutions, which had proceeded more or less adequately for several centuries, enter a new phase, which profoundly shook the known world, and has engrossed posterity for twenty centuries.

The end of the Jugurthine War was a timely denouement, because on October 6, 105, for the first of many times in the ensuing two-thousand years, a Teutonic invasion of Gaul starting with the defeat of two Roman armies, threatened Italy, and the whole central Roman Confederation of states and territories. Marius was elected consul for the second time for 104 as even his political enemies acclaimed him as the designated Savior of Rome's position from the Teutonic hordes.

By the time Marius returned from Africa, Germanic tribes had thickened and been active along much of Rome's northern borders and in Gaul. The Teutons and Cimbri, who seem to have originated in Denmark and northern Germany, largely departed their home territory, where they were relatively advanced, with large towns and extensive agriculture, in search of more clement weather, richer agriculture, and treasure and adventure. They recognized the formidability of Roman frontiers but probed them and advanced through what is now Belgium and into northern Gaul. They were apparently under some pressure from fierce but less sophisticated tribes in the east but seem mainly to have been motivated by their conviction that those to the south and southwest of them enjoyed a better standard of living.

They were repulsed by the Boii in Bohemia and then by the Scordisci around what is today Belgrade, and then moved westwards and stopped in Carinthia facing the Roman garrison. Rome had undertaken the protection of the Taurisci during Scaurus' operations there described earlier in this chapter and in order to forestall and deter a German assault, the consul for 113, Gnaeus Carbo was sent northwards with a large army and the Cimbri, fearing another defeat, withdrew. However, Carbo had delusions of imminent glory, set out after them and the Cimbri rounded on him inflicting the defeat that was only less than annihilation by the miraculous intervention of a thunderstorm. This occurred between the present Klagenfurt and Ljubljana; Carbo returned to Rome, was prosecuted for his incompetence and negligence and was poisoned either by himself or his jailers. He had squandered Rome's reputation along the Danube and the Alps for invincibility and had dangerously whetted the appetites of the Germanic tribes, not to mention that he lost an entire army. The Cimbri continued to wander however and in 110 B.C., crossed the Rhine and entered Gaul.

Marcus Junius Silanus, consul in 109, had been sent to Gaul to reinforce the Roman position in the last of the tribes with which it was allied. The Germanic visitors presented a forceful demand for territory where they could settle and Silanus informed them that their request would be sent to the Roman government; naturally it was refused. Silanus, like Carbo, had delusions of Roman grandeur and of his own invincibility as a great captain and sortied to attack the Germanic tribes. He was decisively defeated, a terrible humiliation for Rome in Gaul that set many Gallic tribes contemplating whether the hour of their own liberation had struck. Rome hurriedly sent another army under the consul Lucius Cassius Longinus. He was not markedly better suited to his task than Carbo or Silanus had been: after clearing some of the invaders from near what is now Toulouse, he proceeded down the Garonne Valley and was crushingly defeated and personally killed in battle along with the former consul Lucius Piso.

Total annihilation was only avoided when the senior surviving officer, Gaius Popillius Laenas, surrendered half the baggage and agreed that the survivors would pass beneath the yoke. For this the lives of Roman soldiers were spared. It was an immense disgrace which virtually obliterated the prestige of Rome in Gaul. The victor in this battle was the chief of the Tigurini, Divicus, who continued as a Gallic eminence for more than forty years and would encounter Julius Caesar (unsuccessfully).

The next Roman commander in Gaul, Quintus Servilius Caepio, who had some military experience, started well and easily recaptured Toulouse. He treated those who had betrayed Rome with appropriate severity: he sacked the temples of the local tribes and shipped back to Rome as much as fifteen-thousand talents of gold and silver. Unfortunately, this convoy was interrupted on its way to Massilia for transport on to Rome, and its precious cargo was seized and never recovered. There was eventually considerable speculation that Caepio had stolen it himself. This was never substantiated and because he had had a modest military success, he was retained in Gaul and joined by another army commanded by another consul Gnaeus Mallius Maximus. Mallius, like Marius, was a Novus Homo, an upstart, and the lack of rapport between him and Caepius prevented their cooperating. The Germans marched south down the Roman road with Mallius retreating before them on the east bank and Caepius on the west. Mallius successfully demanded that his colleague cross the river, but they stayed in separate camps enabling the Germans to deal with each in turn and in detail and such was their tactical ineptitude that with their backs to the river both armies were practically completely destroyed at Arausio on October 6, 105 B.C. The barbarians killed an estimated eighty-thousand Romans and their allies. There was nothing left of Roman prestige in Gaul; it retained no allies in Gaul, and there were now no defense forces left in Gaul and the road to Rome was open.

Rome had on this occasion exceeded its general practice of rising slowly to the need for war-making and beginning awkwardly without an immediate and energetic reply to the succession of disasters. Rome would be inviting barbarian invasion. (The surviving commanders were prosecuted; Silanus and Mallius were acquitted, but Caepio suffered confiscation of property and exile and died, dishonored, in Smyrna.) Rome had improved on the Greek and Carthaginian practice of executing defeated commanders without trial and banishing even victorious ones.

7. The Mortal German Threat and the Triumph of Marius

The other consul besides Mallius in 105 was P. Rutilius Rufus, who responded energetically to this cascade of disasters and effectively conducted a drive for volunteers throughout Italy, emphasizing that all Italy was now in danger and all past disputes within the Peninsula had to be set aside in the common defense. Fortuitously this was just as the Jugurthine War ended and on New Year's Day 104 B.C., Marius, already elected to his second consulate, enjoyed a brilliant triumph in Rome celebrating also his appointment as supreme commander of Roman armies for the stabilization of Gaul and the defense of Italy. Very late, but not too late, Rome had found the right man and elevated him to the right position. He would be slightly outnumbered by the Germans but always made up for this with the extreme efficiency with which he deployed his men. He trained his army intensively and all through the summer of 104, Rome reasserted its authority within its transalpine province and Sulla replicated his African success and captured one of the rebellious tribal leaders.

Marius improved the equipment of his army and made certain modifications that especially enabled his troops to take advantage of the fact that the invaders carried shields but not armor. He also divided the army into cohorts, which proved a more mobile and effective unit size than the phalanxes and squares that had generally been in use. Marius was reelected consul in 103 but the enemy was still shy and he spent much of the year building a canal that enabled Mediterranean traffic to come up the Rhône. This was in its time one of the engineering marvels of Europe.

As there was unlikely to be any combat in late 103, Marius returned to Rome and with the help of his friend the demagogic tribune Saturninus, he was elected consul for the fourth time. Saturninus was Marius' bridge to the Roman masses but was so disreputable and unscrupulous, he alienated much of the Senate. When news reached Rome of the move of the Cimbri, Marius hastened back to his military headquarters. The Germanic-affiliated tribes had adopted an extraordinarily complicated and ambitious plan: they would leave their train under guard of six-thousand men on the Meuse; they assumed that Gaul was in hand and the Teutons were to advance past Geneva and down the west coast road of Italy; the Cimbri were to come through the Brenner Pass and erupt into Lombardy, and the Tigurini (from Toulouse) were to make their way behind their allies and then attack at Aquileia over the Julian Alps. Marius and his able adjutants operated on interior lines with highly trained and motivated forces.

Marius set up his camp on the Rhône and when the Teutons arrived he refused to give battle, so they eventually simply advanced down the river leaving the Roman commander and the main body of his forces directly in their rear, an unimaginable miscalculation in a civilized army. Marius then struck camp and moved down the other side of the Rhône stealthily and swiftly and surprised the vanguard force of thrity-thousand Teutons, who attacked piecemeal and uphill in a disorderly charge and were almost literally massacred by the disciplined Roman legions under Marius' direct command. They killed approximately all the thirty-thousand Teutons in one day to minor casualties to themselves. Marius was then able to send a force of approximately three-thousand, undetected, around behind where enemy reinforcements would arrive, two days after the first battle. Marius engaged the main Teutonic army with the advantages of position, training, and armament, against superior numbers. At the appropriate moment the contingent sent to the rear of the enemy suddenly struck it in the back and the Teutonic offensive collapsed in a terrible bloodbath. All of Rome's almost paralytic and on this occasion well-founded fear of invasion, and that of all Italy, vanished, and Roman prestige skyrocketed once again. All of the ancient estimates of Teutonic killed and prisoners taken in these actions were of at least one-hundred thousand men. This was one of the most gigantic and brilliant victories in the history of classical warfare and ranked in conception and execution with the greatest triumphs of Alexander the Great and Hannibal.

The Cimbri came through the Brenner where Quintus Lutatius Catulus awaited them. He moved his forces into a narrow pass at Trento, but his officers remonstrated with him that this would be impossible to operate to advantage, and they retired to the south of the Po River, abandoning Transpadane Gaul. Marius arrived after obliterating the Teutons to take command in this theatre, retaining Catulus as a colleague and at Campi Rudii near Vercellae, the Cimbri were overwhelmingly defeated and suffered over sixty-five thousand casualties; all survivors were captured: it was a complete destruction of the invader. Witnessing the annihilation of their Teutonic and Cimbran allies, the Tigurini quietly folded their tents and withdrew toward distant Toulouse, understandably reluctant to try the issue with Marius at the summit of his career. All Italy heaved an immense cry of relief and gratitude. After such terrible defeats, Marius' overwhelming victories had the character of a miraculous deliverance: he was hailed in a gigantic triumph as the third founder of Rome after Romulus and Camillus (who repulsed the Gauls in 390 and in the 360s B.C. [Chapter 16]).

It was a multiple victory for Marius: while Metellus began the reduction of Jugurtha, Marius sealed the fate of a new Carthage or even an extended Massinissan challenge. He restored Roman suzerainty in North Africa so that it would be unassailable for a long time. He moved directly into Gaul and single-handedly put down an incipient revolt in Gaul and single-handedly crushed the apparently invincible Teutons. And then he was the principal architect of the complete defeat of the Cimbri. Northern Italy would not see such skillful generalship again for nineteen centuries, when the twenty-seven-year-old Napoleon would maneuver an army of untrained ragamuffins with such skill that he bundled the Habsburg Holy Roman Empire right out of Italy after seven-hundred years there.

The Germanic tribes, exploiting the lore of the Gallic assaults of the Fourth Century B.C., even unto the Capitoline Hill, and of Hannibal in the late Third Century, had struck cold terror into all Italy. But in retrospect, once the Roman legions were led by a first-class general, it was an uneven match despite the Germanic preponderance in numbers. Aquae Sextiae, like Salamis, was the supreme crisis of the invasions. Vercellae was a sequel, like Plataea (Chapter 6). The Germanic tribes had beaten the Celts of Gaul, who had been driven off the Danube and had shown themselves not to be a match for the Belgic tribes and had failed to penetrate the Pyrenees. Thus, Rome had routed the best soldiers that the barbaric areas of Europe had to offer. Marius had also promoted the thought in Gallic minds that the Romans might, if the choice had to be made, be preferable to the Germans.

The Gauls were a much less formidable opponent for the Germanic invaders than the Great Power that had risen so quickly to dominate central Italy, had completely destroyed Carthage, almost effortlessly reduced all Greece and Macedonia to client-states, humbled Antiochus the Great, and imposed itself not just militarily but by administrative and diplomatic skill as well upon much of the Mediterranean littoral. With the passage of just a little time, it would become clear that the significance of the Cimbri and the Teutons, in their first of many appearances in the great Roman chronicle, was not their ability to imperil Rome. It was their provocation of the elevation to paramountcy of a common soldier who had become a fine army commander and a talented military and political adventurer.

Marius was a "new man" who became somewhat well-to-do and joined the rich with a luxurious villa on the Bay of Naples, the Cote d'Azur or Palm Beach or Newport of its time, where there were heated swimming pools and the cultivation of oysters and other succulent shellfish, and prodigiously opulent homes. Marius was a soldier-politician, not a soldier statesman like Alexander the Great or Julius Caesar, or Napoleon, or even Wellington and MacArthur. He was much more than a mere demagogue and stager of coups d'état in the officers' club like Juan Peron. He was perhaps more of a Franco or Tito, though a much more accomplished battlefield commander but not a long-serving dictator. He was not a Washington either, who founded a country, or a de Gaulle, who reconstructed one. But he saved Rome at the end of the Second Century B.C; he modernized the army, and he played a decisive role in the last phase of the Republic. He would have many emulators over many centuries.

CHAPTER TWENTY-THREE

THE SOCIAL AND MITHRIDATIC WARS
THE RISE AND DICTATORSHIP OF LUCIUS CORNELIUS SULLA, 115 B.C. TO 78 B.C.

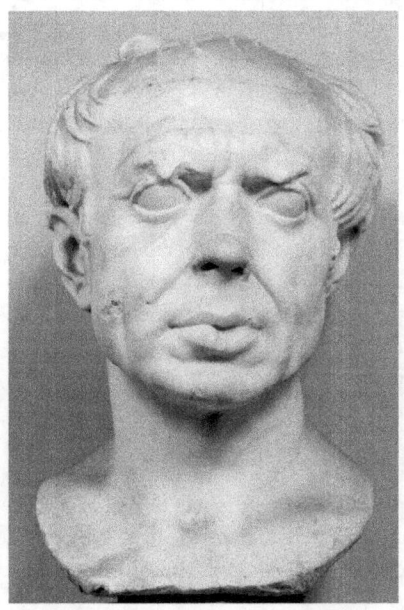

Bust of the "so-called" Marius
(original First Century B.C. artwork)

Bust of the "so-called" Sulla
(copy from the time of Augustus)

1. The Legacy of the Gracchi and Social Wars

THIS PERIOD OF forty years after the end of the episode of the Gracchi was one in which the Republic struggled to regain authority over commanders of large armies in distant theaters; attempted to cope with demagogues espousing similar goals to the Gracchi but with, as should have been foreseen, much less scruple or patriotic self-control; the rise of Marius, as we have seen, the first soldier politician and forerunner of so many more; and the agitation for enfranchisement of all of the Italians.

As the Senate tried to regroup and lead Rome out of the Gracchan era, the only judicial remedy to abuses of office was the arcane procedure of perduellio, essentially hostility to the state, which was difficult to prove: it had to be conducted in a complicated procedure beginning with the centuries, small groups of somewhat eminent citizens. The Mamilian Commission, set up in 114 to look into the scandal of the Vestal Virgins, did facilitate the prosecution of a few allegedly corrupt officials. But, as in many other respects, the Republic lacked the institutions and procedures that were needed to govern a much more extensive and sophisticated jurisdiction than the one for which it was established. By dealing as brutally as it did with the Gracchi, and then by failing to endow itself with a modernized constitution, the Republic became increasingly vulnerable to internal dissension. The election of Marius as consul in 108 raised a prominent storm signal that the popular majority could easily be seduced by a national military hero and requite his achievements by elevating him to an office above the patriciate. The failure of the old families and the great figures of the Senate was not just in their brutal repulse and murder of the Gracchi, but in their failure to provide for and obviate much more sinister manifestations of the same, generally reasonable, grievances that Tiberius and Gaius Gracchus tried to resolve within the existing Republican system.

In 106, the Senate revoked one of the Gracchan reforms and reconstituted criminal juries as composed of knights and senators sitting together. The proletariat responded in 104 by approving Tribune Gaius Servilius Glaucia's measure approving the prosecution of people who wrongfully received money even if they had not been instrumental in the act by which it was received. It can easily be imagined what abusive torment of the wealthy was facilitated by that measure. In 104 another Tribune, Gnaeus Domitius, put through a measure that effectively transferred to the popular assembly the approval of all priestly appointments. They had formerly been entirely within the gift of the Pontifex Maximus. (A few years later, when Domitius was himself elected Pontifex Maximus, he prevailed upon the dictator Lucius Sulla to repeal his own measure, but in 63, Julius Caesar would reaffirm it. Obviously, the popular election of priests was a radically irreligious concept, an outrageous profanation.)

In approximately 110, Lucius Apuleius Saturninus, of praetorian background, became a quaestor and was placed in charge of Ostia and its port, with the task of regularizing the arrival and distribution of Rome's supplementary grain (wheat) supply. A shortage occurred for which Saturninus was blamed, scapegoated in fact, and removed, infusing him with a violent hatred of the Senate and a determination to avenge himself. He returned as a tribune in 100 B.C., and he decreed an artificially low price for the sale of wheat to the Roman masses, a popular gesture with most of the public but a clear affront to the Senate and especially to its wealthiest members. The public assembly was broken up by force, but Saturninus proceeded on the basis of his bill anyway, although it was apparently not adopted.

Saturninus was a corrupt political maneuverer with only the most superficial resemblances to the principled and conscientious Gracchi whom he pretended to be emulating. He next attached himself to Marius' war chariot, ensuring land grants and other preferments for Marius' returning soldiers. Another of Saturninus' wheezes was to support the candidacy as an illegitimate son of Tiberius Gracchus of the obscure hustler Lucius Equitius. Sempronia, sister of the tribune and widow of Scipio Aemilianus, vehemently denied under oath that Equitius could possibly be the relation that he claimed to be, and Equitius was rejected. But he retained considerable credibility in the popular classes and Saturninus had him as a campaign helper and rewarded him with election to the tribunate in 100. However, Lucius Equitius was murdered on his first day in office.

Saturninus and Glaucia had achieved a status that the Senate was afraid to challenge. Though few at the time apparently reflected upon this, they would have been infinitely better off had they acquiesced in the reforms of the Gracchi. In 102, the consuls were the distinguished cousins Metellus Numidicus and Metellus Caprarius. Metellus Caprarius secured the expulsion of Glaucia and Saturninus from the Senate and was attacked by a mob and chased into hiding on the Capitoline Hill. Caprarius undid his ill-considered initiative, and an uneasy peace was restored. But the Republic was very fragile.

In 101, Saturninus publicly rebuked emissaries from King Mithridates Eupator, who were allegedly bearing extensive quantities of gold with which to bribe Roman senators as necessary. The emissaries objected to the Senate at their treatment and the elders in the Senate were pleased to arraign Saturninus on charges of severe misconduct. His conviction was likely until he whistled out his mob from the slums of Rome; the court was intimidated and Saturninus was released, his popularity in good standing. In 100, with Marius successfully returned from campaigns, an explicit alliance was formed between Saturninus and Glaucia and the great general, who was elected consul for the unheard of sixth time.

This coalition prevailed in the election but neither Marius nor his rabble-rousing associates had much idea of what to do with the government they now controlled. Marius, like the younger Africanus, though he was supported by the Roman masses, had little regard for their populist judgment, and though he was willing, like a true popularis, to use the people for his own ends, knew the danger of handing over government to the rabble, even a rabble largely composed of the veterans of his own armies.

They had no difficulty collaborating in land distribution schemes for the benefit of Marius' soldiers and the more noteworthy and demonstrative followers of Glaucia and Saturninus. The bias toward distribution of land to Marius' veterans stirred up hostility between these staunch, brave, and well- disciplined men and the idle but excitable masses of Rome's destitute, and at the same time friction continued to grow between Rome and the Italians.

In legislative terms, the reign of these three was a fiasco. Saturninus determined that senators were forced to swear to abide by all laws that were enacted, under pain of exile and heavy fines. On voting day, the now traditional methods of obstruction were produced: dissenting tribunes and unfavorable omens, but the veterans chased off the dissidents and this sham measure became law. It was Marius' task to ask the fathers for their oath and Metellus Numidicus declared so vehemently that he would refuse that the meeting ended ineffectually. Four days later Marius returned to the task and said that he would take the oath himself and commanded the Senators to recognize that once the mob had returned to their homes there would be no difficulty passing a measure repealing the one that had just been adopted. Even for Roman political generals this was a stark display of cynicism, but it was successful.

This whole episode ended badly. Saturninus was elected with the imposter Gracchus as tribunes and Glaucia became a candidate for consul. He seemed to be headed to election, especially after he murdered his most serious challenger Gaius Memmius, who was well regarded for his service in elevating Marius to be the general that saved the Republic in the Jugurthine Wars in 112. His murder completed the alienation of Marius from Saturninus and Glaucia and the Senate once again overcame its reservations about Marius to call upon him to restore order. Marius' veterans smashed the mobs and bundled them back into the poorer areas around the Aventine Hill. Glaucia and Saturninus were barricaded into the Capitoline Hill. Marius cut off their water supply and they surrendered to try and spare themselves from the mob. Marius detained them in the Senate house but on the last day of the term of the old tribunes, the mob climbed the roof, tore off the tiles and stoned the detainees to death. It was not an entirely unsuitable end to such brutal scoundrels as Glaucia and Saturninus. One of the assailants, Gaiaus Rabirius, was finally charged with perduellia for his part in this stoning thirty-seven years later.

Marius returned to his troops in Asia, entirely voluntarily, yielding the Senate an opportunity to regroup and attempt to rise to the task of governance one more time. And Marius would be back as well, disgusted both with the inveterate demagogues and the deracinated, casuistical, abstainers among the older classes and factions, including Cato. These issues were just kicked forward, not really tackled.

With the abomination, as the Senate regarded Saturninus, and his accomplices disposed of, the Senate had an opportunity to distinguish itself in a renascence of a responsible civic government. Metellus Numidicus triumphantly returned and led the customary outburst of vindictive prosecution of the former regime. Publius Furius, an unscrupulous demagogue who had opposed the recall of Numidicus, was put on trial in the midst of which the mob chased off the small and under-motivated court security unit and it literally tore the defendant's limbs off him, as well as his head. Apuleius Decianus was found guilty for lamenting the manner of the death of Saturninus. Sextus Titius, a former tribune, was condemned in large part because he had a bust of Saturninus in his house. These were the customary results of retributive Roman justice, and after they were carried out, the Senate took advantage of its opportunity to redeem its severely tattered reputation as at least a potential organ of good government. Relatively unknown people were elevated as consuls and the worst initiatives of the previous regime were repealed.

Lucius Crassus, the noted orator, and the Pontifex Maximus, and Domitius Ahenobarbus, were entrusted with the census of 92 B.C., and although they disagreed on many points, one matter where they were in accord was in the suppression of the Latin teachers of rhetoric. It may be recalled that those who taught this subject in Greek were suppressed seventy years before, because of the agitating influence they were deemed to exercise on Rome's young men; this same misdirection was deemed to be the result of Latin instructors and rhetoric, and the consequence of this new suppression was to bring back the study of Greek oratory.

The brief period of benign senatorial rule ended abruptly in 95 B.C. with the promulgation of the Lex Licinia Mucia, which expelled non-Romans from Rome. The Italians, as they were known, did not bother Rome while it was heavily engaged in the Jugurthine, Gallic, and German wars as the Italians did not want to undermine Rome's ability to defend them. But with the end of those wars, increasing numbers of Italians crowded into Rome and began to challenge the local members for control of the Concilium Plebis, the Popular Assembly. This was an insane enterprise, as the Italians had been patiently awaiting the end of Rome's great wars in order to press for what the Gracchi had promised them—equal rights with Romans. Only a delusionally complacent group of inbred political leaders could imagine that the vast expanse of what Rome now ruled could or would consent to be governed by a distant, single city. It was among the Italian allies that most of Rome's still viable armies had been settled after their campaigns and when heavy fighting was needed these troops would be called upon. How the Senate imagined that it could exercise such authority while treating the inhabitants of the areas where the Roman veterans lived as disposable cannon-fodder (taking an expression from fifteen centuries later) is another of the many instances that there will be in this narrative, of the self-destructive collective vanity to which isolated governing cliques usually degenerate.

The status of the Senate was further compromised when one of the most distinguished Romans of the time, Publius Rutilius, had been such a conscientious and honest governor of Asia, especially in punishing the rapacity of the Roman commercial class that attempted to plunder his province, that he was tried for "illegal exactions" in 92. He insisted on defending himself and not availing himself of the talents of the most flamboyant barristers of the time and the court was apparently moved by agitators paid by the complainants. Rutilius was accordingly convicted, completely unjustly, and his property was seized and as it was insufficient to retire the fine assessed against him, he retired to Smyrna, to bask in the gratitude and admiration of those who appreciate capable and honest governance. This was clearly not the way to keep a great empire functioning well.

2. The Social War

Rome was still rippling over the implications of these developments when M. Livius Drusus was elected tribune at the end of 92 B.C. He was the son of the challenger to Gaius Gracchus and would adopt the father-in-law of Augustus Caesar. Drusus had an ambitious program that began with revival of the colonial settlement schemes of his father and included more generous distribution of free bread and a partial debasement of the coinage to afford a more generous treasury. He set out to reinstate senators as jurors. This move outraged the public without adequately placating the senators and Drusus was starting to see his position unravel when he was assassinated by an unknown person. This was a miniature reenactment of the Gracchan tragedies. Drusus was attempting to remedy essentially the same problems and he suffered the same fate. With his failure, the anger and impatience of the Italian provinces and allies boiled over and the Social Wars began.

Preparations for war apparently began among disenchanted Italians after their expulsion from Rome in 95. Drusus warned the consuls of 91, Caesar and Philippus, that he had heard of a plot to assassinate them when celebrating a festival on the Alban Mount; this caused the Senate to dispatch emissaries throughout Italy to seek reassurance of their friendly attitude. All sides took this as indicative of the rising danger. Q. Pompaedius Silo, leader of the Marsi and a friend of Drusus, was found marching on Rome at the head of ten-thousand armed men but was persuaded to withdraw. This too was belatedly seen in Rome as evidence of the state of alarm and impatience in Italy. Because Gaius Servilius, on a reconnaissance mission in Picenum, was informed of the exchange of prewar Allied hostages between Asculum and another city, and Asculum's authorities became aware of this, every Roman in that city was massacred. The Italian states knew that they had now gone too far: it was war.

The Picentines, Marsi, Paeligni, Vestini, Marucini, Frentani, Samnites, and Herpini formed a league that purported to secede from Rome. The revolt spread through the high country of northern Italy, and then into Central and Southern Italy as well. These were known as the Marsic Wars. The war spread quickly as Lucania, Apulia, and southern Campania joined the revolt, but Etruria, Umbria, Calabria, and Bruttium abstained. Tight relations between the Roman and other Italian leading families played a benign role in the continued adherence of several of the Italian provinces to the Roman alliance.

The League headquarters were established at Corfinium, renamed Italia, for this honour, in the central Apennines; the League was structured on its original cantonal arrangements, Pompaedius Silo was put up as the commander, and Papius Mutilus as Samnite commander. The Italian armies were considered to be comprised of excellent fighting stock, especially Sabellian and Oscan dalesmen. They began producing their own coinage.

The Romans were taken completely by surprise by the revolt, but they rallied forces from Cisalpine Gaul, Spain, Sicily, and Numidia with ample rations. The Roman peace protester, Caius Vettienus, was so hostile to the war that he cut the fingers off his left hand to gain discharge from conscription for it. The war unfolded into theaters, from Picenum into the mountains in the north and in southern Italy around Samnium. P. Rutilius Lupus, consul in 90, commanded for Rome in the north against Pompaedius Silo, with five eminent legates immediately under him: Marius, Gnaeus Pompeius Strabo (father of Pompey the Great), Q. Servilius Caepio (son of the Caepio who had been defeated at Arausio), C. Perperna, and M. Claudius Marcellus. These were the best generals Rome had.

The Italians naturally suffered from a divided command. They spent much of their energies trying to reduce stubbornly manned Roman fortresses in their midst and had no concerted plan for an attack on Rome or any vital Roman installation. Rome responded with its customary self-confidence and the sophisticated road network in Italy served it better than its scattered opponents. Pompeius Strabo was a large landowner in Picenum and so was the Roman commander to avenge the massacre at Asculum. Strabo was initially driven back and forced to take refuge in Firmum, but he was relieved by forces from Cisalpine Gaul led by Sulpicius, and returned to the siege of Asculum, where Strabo was again successful. Pompeius was rewarded for this by election as consul in 89.

Around Fucine Lake in the northeast, matters fared less well for the Romans. Perperna was badly defeated and was dismissed from his command. Rutilius Lupus himself was badly defeated and killed in action with Vettius Scato in the Tolenus Valley. The still formidable Marius, who was down the valley, saw from the bodies carried past in the stream of the Tolenus that the battle was in progress before he had been advised of it, crossed the river hastily, advanced and captured Scato's camp and supplies, and forced the retreat the following day after attacking successfully and inflicting heavy casualties.

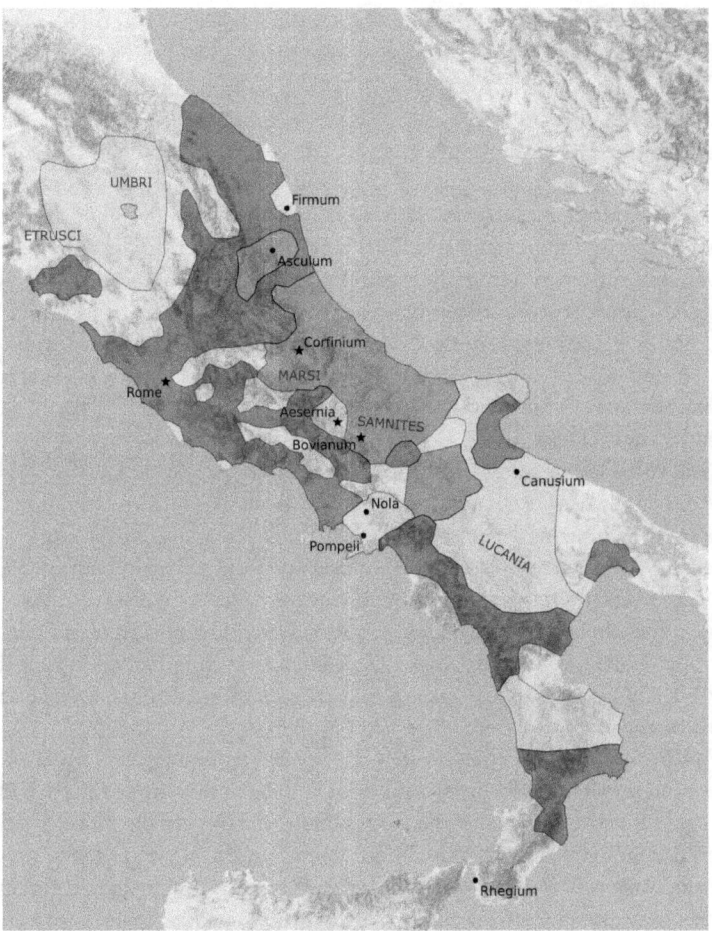

Social Wars: Roman territory darkest grey, with the territory of the initial insurgents in dark grey. Territory in light grey were groups that later joined the insurgents.

It was then the practice in Rome to display the bodies of its officers slain in defending the city but in this case, the dead body of the consul Rutilius Lupus demoralized the Romans, and it was decreed that henceforth the dead should be buried where they fell. Because Q. Servilius Caepio had also been successful, Rutilius' command was divided between him and Marius.

However, Servilius Caepio was lured into an ambush by Pompadeius Silo and his Marsi and Vestini, and his force was annihilated and Caepio himself was killed. With this, Marius, long Rome's greatest general, who had delivered the city from the menace of its enemies often before, over many years, took sole command in the north. He soon smashed the Marsi and Marrucini, and after they had been put to flight, his talented adjutant, Sulla, now becoming a rival, slaughtered the retreating enemy.

The other consul besides Rutilius Lupus, L. Julius Caesar (no known relation to Gaius Julius Caesar, who at this point was ten years old), was in charge of the southern front, and initially focused on the strategically important town of Aesernia, which the rebels tried to seize. Caesar was at first badly defeated by the peripatetic Vettius Scato. Caesar and Sulla tried to relieve Aesernia without success. After driving out the slaves and living off dogs and other animals, the garrison, under M. Claudius Marcellus, surrendered. The Samnite army, under C. Papius Mutilus, invaded southern Campania in an effort to cut Rome off from the south and deny it access to its most prosperous and agriculturally rich province. Mutilus did well for a time and laid siege to Accerae but was decisively defeated by Caesar. Mutilus did incite enough desertions from the Numidians that that entire unit had to be demobilized. Rome was so hungry for victories that Caesar was hailed as imperator in the Roman population, which had been dressed in mourning or military togas, and now returned to normal civilian dress. After losing more ground in Lucania and Apulia, with Caesar having departed for Rome, Vidacilius did make serious inroads in the South and did cut Rome off altogether by land from its southern operations.

Rome was now hard pressed though it stabilized things in the north and recovered slightly in spite of strenuous but unsuccessful efforts to extend the revolt to Etruria and Umbria. Shortly prior to leaving office as consul L. Julius Caesar discerned that the time was right for compromise and adopted the Lex Julia which offered full Roman citizenship to all Latins and all the communities in Italy that did not revolt. This law was quickly followed by the Lex Plautia Papiria, which effectively granted citizenship to anyone who asked for it anywhere in Italy.

This proved to be a cunning and a decisive blow: Rome gained population, the provinces in revolt lost population and the revolt lost momentum: since its objective was to gain Roman citizenship, the longer the rebels fought, the more difficult and the less desirable their victory would become given the strain on the entity whose citizenship they were seeking to attain. In 89, Pompeius Strabo and L. Porcius Cato were the consuls and Cato succeeded Marius as commander against the Marsi. Lucius Sulla assumed the command of L. Julius Caesar. Cato advanced to the Fucine Lake, but was defeated and killed there, joining Rutilius Lupus as the second consul killed in action in these operations.

The fighting reached its climax in the battle for Asculum which festered and raged all through 89 as both sides poured in what manpower they could afford: at its height there may have been seventy-five thousand Romans against sixty-thousand Italians. The Romans prevailed, although the Marsi seem to have got as far as a mountain pass where Strabo caught up with them and killed virtually all of them. The gallant Vidacilius fought his way back into his native Asculum, but eventually conditions became so dire, as the population wished to surrender but the rebel army did not, he had himself burned alive, incinerated, in one of the city's major temples.

The Romans wrought a fearful vengeance: all rebel officers and civic leaders were severely whipped and then publicly decapitated. The rest of the population were permitted to leave, though destitute. Slaves were sold at auction, though it has been alleged that Strabo did not remit the auction proceeds.

Strabo did enfranchise thirty Spanish cavalrymen, a significant innovation, and on his staff were Lepidus, consul in 78, Catiline, and Strabo's son, just seventeen, subsequently Pompeius Magnus. One of the prisoners who marched in the triumphant parade of Strabo was P. Ventidius, who was eventually promoted by Julius Caesar, and then made consul by Mark Antony, and would enjoy a great triumph of his own 51 years after being marched as a prisoner in this triumph, after he defeated the Parthians in 38 B.C. The Paeligni turned on their leader, P. Vettius Scato, and would have torn him limb from limb had his slave not, at Scato's demand, killed him first.

Resistance continued in Campania, where Sulla was in command and seized this as the opportunity to rival Marius as Rome's premier general, and one more trusted by the Senate. The Roman fleet mutinied in the Bay of Naples and the commander, Postumius Albinus, was martyred by his sailors. Sulla handled the mutiny with consummate skill: he said that he would permit the mutineers to expiate their crime by conspicuous gallantry in action. Shortly after Sulla met the rebel leader Cluentius, reinforced by Gallic deserters from Roman armies. Sulla won an overwhelming victory. With his skill and his fortunes both at their peak, Sulla pressed on; he ended a siege at Aeclanum by torching the city and then by forced marches and a little-used access, surprised the Samnite commander Papius Mutilus and drove him and the fragments of his army back to Aesernia. Sulla seized the Samnite capital, Bovianum Vetus, and returned to Rome to stand as consul.

In Apulia, the Roman general Gaius Cosconius had an unbroken series of victories as the Social Wars had turned into a mopping up operation. Q. Pompaedius Silo, irrepressible, mustered an army of thirty-thousand infantry and a thousand cavalry, including twenty-thousand recently liberated slaves, made a gallant last stand, but his luck deserted him, and he perished with most of his army.

It was the end of an odd war, in which one side was fighting for the privilege of becoming citizens of the other side. In that sense it was successful but in succeeding, the Italians merely achieved what the Romans should have given them long before, and the effect was to make Rome stronger than ever: instantly a much larger and more populous and contented country. It had also demonstrated again the failure of the Senate—they finally conceded what they at the least, by acquiescing in the murders of the Gracchi and the young Drusus, tried to prevent, and again, they relied on the senior generals to protect Rome, without much apparent thought to where this would lead. Only the arrogance of the old Roman Senate families could have maintained the aerated self-importance that what was little more than a haughty municipal council could rule the known world. Rome loomed over that world with ever greater dominance, but its political system was not functioning well and was in almost constant need of shoring up by the army, an arrangement that was bound to lead to direct military intervention in the government eventually.

3. The Rivalry Between Sulla and Marius

The consuls for 88 were Lucius Cornelius Sulla, Marius' former deputy commander and his only rival as the leading Roman general of the time, and Quintus Pompeius Rufus, a much less significant person whose only call on high office was in achieving the invitation to Metellus Numidicus to return from exile, when Pompeius Rufus was tribune.

Sulla had served distinguishedly in the wars in Africa, Gaul, Asia, and Italy and had gained the eastern command for the intended settling of accounts with Mithridates, king of Pontus (most of what is now Asiatic Turkey), who had massacred eighty-thousand Romans and Greeks in Asia Minor. Sulla was interested in taking to the field as soon as possible. Rufus was rather inert and unenterprising as consul, but the legislative initiative thus devolved upon the eloquent tribune P. Sulpicius Rufus, generally reckoned to be the greatest orator of the time, along with C. Aurelius Cotta, both of them students of Licinius Crassus, along with Gaius Gracchus and Cicero, allegedly the greatest Roman orator of all time. Cotta was a second cousin of Gaius Julius Caesar and he and Sulpicius, progressive products of the oligarchic class, had considerable influence on the young Caesar.

Sulpicius was to prove an important and controversial legislator. He prevailed upon the Senate to reverse the assignment of the Asiatic command from Sulla to Marius. Marius was nineteen years older than Sulla, nearly seventy and he remained Rome's premier general, it's greatest general since Scipio Africanus. Sulpicius' reasoning was that Marius deployed immense popularity with the people, and with the new men—the parvenus and entrepreneurs; he had earned the gratitude of the Senate and was at the head of a large number of active and retired legionaries. Sulpicius was motivated to do this in order to strengthen his hand in bringing in one of the most important legislative initiatives in the history of the Roman Republic: instead of allowing the Italians to vote in Roman elections in only seven or eight different tribal categories, that the freed men, emancipated former slaves, were to be spread across all thirty-five tribes. Thus they would break the gerrymander put in place by the Senate which at the end of the Social Wars conceded the Italians the right to vote but focused their vote on the election of only about one sixth of elected officials, thus preserving the government of Rome as a sort of rotten borough for genuine Romans.

With some difficulty, Sulpicius got this measure through and it revolutionized Roman government: the citizenship of Rome was really the citizenship of Italy and Italy was no longer Roman territory: Rome was the capital of Italy; the city state was over. In the process, a mighty struggle between the great personalities of Marius and Sulla ensued. The initial battle was between Sulpicius and Sulla. Sulla and his fellow consul Pompeius Rufus purported to assume absolute powers of government at the expense of the tribunate. There was a clash in the forum in which the tribune's bodyguard of nearly four-thousand knights prevailed, though Pompeius Rufus' son was killed. Sulla was forced to take refuge briefly in the home of Marius, who despite their rivalry and what Marius considered to be Sulla's contemptible behavior as an ingrate and a protégé in revolt, did not (for the time being) wish Sulla dead.

Sulla made his escape to the nearby camp of his army at Nola, but when Sulpicius sent messengers to recall Sulla's army northwards to accept the command of Marius, they were firmly under Sulla's influence, and he was among them. The tribunes' messengers were stoned to death. This was the first time that a Roman army was in open revolt against Rome. Since Sulla's army was loyal to him, and Marius' army had been demobilized, Marius' only possible defense in Rome was the mobilization of slaves with the promise of emancipation, not an offer that rallied more than a few skirmishers, and Marius hastily vacated Rome. Sulla seized the capital and supplemented the legalism of the consulate with the de facto powers of a military despot. He intimidated the Senate into declaring Marius, Sulpicius, and a number of their prominent collaborators to be outside the law, enemies of the Roman people who could be murdered with impunity and whose property was automatically forfeit to the Roman government. Sulpicius was murdered but Marius escaped to Africa. He still had one chapter left in his extraordinarily long and eventful political and military career.

Sulla was still determined to leave as soon as possible for his Asian command and in order to try to secure his position while he was absent, he declared that the popular assembly could adopt no laws without the prior approval of the Senate, that the Senate would prevail over any complaints from the tribunes, and he doubled the size of the Senate from three-hundred to six-hundred. It is not at all clear that he succeeded in appointing three-hundred new senators before he left, and in any case he must have had some idea that in taking such drastic and hasty measures and then departing for the East he was leaving the back door of Rome open to a familiar caller: Marius was alive and well in Africa and awaiting just such an opportunity.

Sulla hastily arranged for the election of the successor consuls. One, Gnaeus Octavius, was a reliable supporter, but the other, Lucius Cornelius Cinna, was a known supporter of Marius, and so Sulla required him to swear a "mighty oath" of loyalty to Sulla personally and to his cause. Sulla was, if anything, reassured by the murder of his colleague Pompeius Rufus, whose loyalty he mistrusted. On this macabre note, Sulla departed with his army to deal with Mithridates. He must have had more than an inkling that Cinna would return to his Marian loyalties and that Marius might return to Rome. But Sulla was confident that when he himself returned to Rome it would be as the unquestioned head of the victorious main army of what was now in name only the Roman Republic. It was scarcely a Republic, and it was no longer Roman.

4. The Mithridatic Empire

Asia Minor, where Sulla was about to arrive at the head of a powerful Roman army, had traditionally been divided between western Anatolia, facing Greece across the Aegean and happily importing and imposing Greek culture on western Anatolia; and the eastern interior stretching between the land-locked Black Sea and through Cappadocia which was once occupied by the Hittites and then the Phrygians and then Persia and towards the Tigris and Euphrates. This part of Asia Minor had been relatively little influenced by the Greeks and drew its inspiration from Oriental monarchs, from the Armenians to the Parthians and Persians. Pontus was Western and Central Cappadocia were chiefly preoccupied in coveting and conquering the rich mining areas of Asia Minor which produced large quantities of iron, copper, and silver. Most progress in the early Iron Age, at least in the Western world, was in Pontic Cappadocia, which had supplied metals to all of the Near East and across the Black Sea, and Dardanelles and Aegean to the Greeks and Macedonians. It had attracted Greek colonization and trans-shipment ports around the Black Sea. Mineral resources had long been sent west as Hellenic influence increased in Asia Minor, even before Alexander the Great.

But eastern Pontus remained, even under the Persians, Seleucids, and Antiochus, essentially divided into states of Oriental inspiration. The political structure had not much evolved in the fifteen centuries since the Hittites ruled there. Our chief authority on all this is the historian Strabo. They were decentralized kingdoms, with royal residences scattered around, and much of life unfolded in and around a small number of gigantic temples, and the Mithridatic Citadel in the capital of Amasia. A special permission from the superintendent of the Citadel, who was usually a eunuch, was required for anyone to enter, and here were the royal palace, the king's altar, the tombs of the fathers of the dynasty, and the shrine to the Greco-Persian deity Zeus Stratios. The great temples had thousands of sacred serfs, of both sexes including temple prostitutes who were revered physically as well as financially. The high priests were subject to the kings, and the kings were themselves often regarded as deities. These were not very metropolitan arrangements and would not have competed successfully even with the highly superstitious, not infrequently corrupt polytheism of Rome and Greece, much less the infinitely more potent religious concepts that had been fostered by the Jews somewhat mysteriously and whose messianic arrival was now not far off.

The Mithridatic dynasty began its rule in Pontus in 302 B.C. and was a branch of the highest Persian nobility. The early Mithridates and Ariobarzanes were referred to earlier in this narrative and Mithridates' son of the same name were in the camp of Antigonus in the great wars of succession following the death of Alexander the Great in the Fourth Century. Antigonus rightly became suspicious of these religious cliques and was about to seize and execute them when, warned by the prince Demetrius, they fled. The elder Mithridates died in flight but the younger, Ipsos Mithridates, set up a kingdom for himself in Paphlagonia on the southern shore of the Black Sea and successfully defended it even against Seleucus I. The Mithridatic dynasty steadily built Pontus up alongside Bithynia, Pergamon, and Cappadocia, along the northern fringe of the Seleucid Empire, and all of these states aspired to the distinction of having Greek subjects and all attempted to encroach upon Anatolia from the north with competing levels of success. Pontus grew steadily from the early Third Century B.C. Mithridates III married Laodice, sister of Seleucus II, and daughter of Antiochus II, and his own daughter married Antiochus III. The son of Mithridates III, Pharnaces I, accelerated the rise of Pontus starting in 183 when the helter-skelter competition with Pergamon and Bithynia to seize the remains of the Seleucid dynasty was at its height. Pharnaces' brother and successor, Philopator, appeared in Rome in 167, and he and his nephew, Euergetes, applied the precedents in succeeding decades of allying themselves closely with Rome against Carthage.

Euergetes played his hand carefully, participated successfully in the war against Aristonicus and wrestled control of Phrygia and Galatia away from Bithynia. He also installed his son-in-law Ariarathes as king of Cappadocia. The Mithridatic house was esteemed in elevating the Greek in the towns that they occupied and using their superior skill in military organization. The royal house itself became Hellenized and became a primarily Greek-speaking family, like Frederick and Catherine the Great speaking French two-thousand years later, and the British royal family speaking German among themselves from the arrival of the Hanoverians in 1714 to the 1770's and then intermittently until the death of Prince Albert in 1861.

What gradually developed was a Pontic Greek dynasty that riveted itself on its cohesive Oriental subjects and ruled them relatively benignly. The Black Sea coast was Greek, and the hinterland was Oriental. Euergetes was a brilliant monarch, but was assassinated by his courtiers in 120 B.C. This was not unwelcome to Rome, which might even conceivably have incentivized the murderers, as Rome had already begun to look with concern at the steady rise of Pontus in the East. From the Tiber, it was all tiresomely reminiscent of the rise of Macedonia and Syria under Antiochus. Rome assisted the neighbors of Pontus in trimming that kingdom back to the size that it had had before the time of Aristonicus.

The next expansion of Pontus was across the Black Sea to Crimea, where a Greco-Scythian state had arisen and prospered on commercial trade from all shores of the Black Sea through the Dardanelles to Greece and even Italy. The trade in grain became enormously profitable, serving Asia Minor, Greece, Macedonia, Italy, Carthage, and Massinissa's Numidians. Belligerent tribes from the interior north of the Black Sea encroached dangerously upon the Crimea and in their distress, Chersonese and the Bosporan states of Crimea appealed to Pontus for assistance. An army was dispatched to the rescue under Diophantus, which routed the disarmed nations and Scythians and occupied their capital and subjugated them. He returned in triumph across the Black Sea to Pontus, was invited back again after a couple of years near the end of the Second Century B.C., and with an army of only six-thousand again soundly defeated fifty-thousand of the enemy. He conducted a mopping up operation but became incautious and moved around his new territory with insufficient security. He was almost killed in a surprise revolt but repaired to Nessus and again defeated his enemies and sent the leader of the revolt, Saumacus, back to Pontus in chains to what was unlikely to have been a gentle demise. The clearly very capable Diophantus then disappeared from history.

Pontus was also expanding to the northeast, which, like the Crimea, was beyond the reach or influence of Rome. It converted lower Armenia from suzerainties into integrated territories. Mithridates VI was buoyed up by his successes to attempt to take the headship of the group of neighboring states: Cappadocia, Galatea, Paphlagonia and Bithynia all of them virtually Roman vassal states despite their pretensions to the contrary. Mithridates succumbed to the addiction that possessed some of the rulers of neighboring states who preceded him: to reestablish a great state in Asia

Minor that could take Alexander's Hellenic vocation and crowd Rome out of the Eastern Mediterranean. The Roman government, as we have seen, and whatever its internal disruptions, was ever vigilant toward just such an endeavour.

Cappadocia was the strongest of these states having, under Ariarathes, been most successful in clinging to Rome and mopping up much of what was left in the shambles of the Empire of Antiochus the Great. Ariarathes maintained an excellent alliance with Pergamon and was a very successful ruler, but following his death, his wife Nysa, murdered five of her sons to maintain her power but was outwitted by her sixth son who was himself then murdered by Gordius, a protégé of Eupator. After a further round of court murders, Laodice, the sister of Eupator, governed in the name of her son Ariarathes VII Philometor. All this familial bloodletting naturally reduced standards of governance and Cappadocia may have been surpassed by Bithynia as the most sophisticated and powerful of the neighbors, having been carefully built up over many years by the Greco-Thracian dynasty of Nicomedes and others.

In the last year of the Second Century B.C., Mithridates VI toured his kingdom and parts of its neighbors incognito to make a strategic assessment of the possibilities. He assessed the vulnerabilities of his neighbors and found himself resistless against the temptation to lead the challenge against Rome. The receptivity of the Athenians and the macabre debacle at the court of Cappadocia whetted his appetite. In his absence, his wife and sister had confected a plot to murder him, and it seems to have motivated Mithridates to aspire to greater things. He began by forging an informal alliance with Nicomedes of Bithynia. This was instantly a powerful combination and attracted Rome's concern at once.

They quickly seized Paphlagonia and Galatia and divided them between themselves by prearrangement. But at this point the partnership broke down as Nicomedes suddenly occupied Cappadocia with a lightning strike by his own army and persuaded Laodice, the mother of Ariarathes VII to marry him, establishing himself as king of Cappadocia as well as Bithynia, having engorged himself of half of Pamphlagonia and Galatia. Eupator was rightly discountenanced and invaded Cappadocia and reestablished Ariarathes VII back on his throne. Marius was then in Asia and is widely thought to have contributed to the breakdown of this tandem. And Ariarathes began constructing an anti-Mithridatic coalition, starting with Nicomedes. However, Mithridates amassed sufficient influence at the Cappadocian court that he was able to bankroll the murder of Ariarathes and then shattered the Cappadocian army. He put one of his sons on the throne, a precarious arrangement that only lasted a few years, but Mithridates was able to assert himself finally and established the Pontic interest in Cappadocia.

The tangled plot entered a new phase when Nicomedes appealed to the Romans and the Senate ordered the two kings to restore independence to Paphlagonia and Cappadocia. The Cappadocians elected a new king (Ariobarzanes), but Mithridates, undaunted, tried a new trick. Tigranes, King of Armenia, at the Pontic king's behest, married Eupator's daughter Cleopatra and in 93 B.C., invaded Cappadocia and expelled their king Ariobarzanes, and appointed the emeritus assassin Gordius, close ally of Mithridates as ruler of Cappadocia.

This was more than Rome could endure and it was at this point that Sulla made his premier appearance in the region; he was sent with the task of restoring Ariobarzanes to the Cappadocian throne in 92. Sulla met with the Parthian envoy and the Cappadocian king on the banks of the Euphrates and Sulla prevailed. This convinced Mithridates that to achieve anything of his goal he would have to enter into direct conflict with Rome, though he must have known from recent history how hazardous a course it was that he was choosing.

We have just followed the syncopations and upheavals of the organization of Roman government through the Gracchi, the senior and elder Drusus, the Social Wars and the rise of the generals, first Marius and then Sulla, and have seen the gradual breakdown of the authority and capacity to govern of the Roman Senate. But even in the most contentious times, it was always possible to rally a consensus for the sacred risen entity of Rome, a city and a concept, however tarnished and divided, however corrupted and cynical and swayed by superstition and demagogy, millions of people now bore it a fervent and inborn allegiance that in time of need could be rallied. Mithridates was about to assault the most powerful government ever devised by Western man from a distance and with a ramshackle state, cobbled together by force and bribery, dependent exclusively upon himself for direction and subject at all times to the crosscurrents of Oriental conspiracy and treachery. And his opening challenge was to defeat Lucius Sulla, already one of the very greatest generals in history.

Mithridates began by driving the Roman choice as successor to Nicomedes' Bithynia, his son of the same name from his throne, replacing him with his brother Socrates; and with Tigranes of Armenia again driving Ariobarzanes out of Cappadocia and replacing him with Mithridates' own son, Ariarathes IX, who was only eight years old, and was placed under the regency of the ineffable Gordius, who had followed a long trajectory from murdering Ariarathes VI on Mithridates' instruction in 116 to standing as regent for Ariarathes IX in 91.

Ariobarzanes did not take his latest disembarkation in a very sportsmanlike fashion and appealed to Rome which was already emerging from the worst of the Social Wars. Unruffled in what it took to be its authority, the Senate gave Gaius Cassius, governor of Asia, a commission to restore Nicomedes to the Bithynian throne and imperiously ordered Mithridates to cooperate. The Pontic king cooperated only to the extent of executing Socrates whom he had himself a few months earlier placed on the Bithynian throne. Mithridates now adopted a more submissive tone, disappointed that the Social Wars of Rome had not more severely disrupted his rival. He acquiesced in the return of Ariobarzanes, and to keep his Roman masters content, Nicomedes staged a raid on the Paphlagonian ports to produce enough pillage to satisfy the Roman commissioners who had restored him to his inherited throne. Mithridates sent an envoy, Pelopidas, to ask Rome to desist but was bluntly rebuffed and Rome prepared for war with Pontus at last.

There was only one Roman legion in the area and Rome was thus compelled to rely upon its erratic and frequently undermotivated Asiatic allies. Cassius advanced into Cappadocia and Nicomedes II did the same but was decisively defeated by Mithridates' chief generals Archelaus and Neoptolemus, while the leader of Roman reserves, Aquilius, was heavily defeated and only narrowly escaped personally into Pergamon. Cassius retired southwards and evacuated by sea, to Rhodes. His comrade, Oppius was less fortunate, reaching Laodicea with a force of mercenaries and light cavalry, he started to resist a siege, but was seized and handed over to Mithridates, who detained him but did not harm him. Aquilius fared worst—he became ill at Mytilene, while trying to make his way from Pergamon to Rhodes, was captured by Mithridates' forces who paraded him around his kingdom bound to an ass and hand-cuffed, or to a giant Bastarnian horseman, who whipped him along, until Mithridates ultimately imposed the chastisement of pouring molten gold down his throat, to punish Roman greed.

Mithridates left others to wrap things up and proceeded south into Hellenic Asia Minor. In general, after news of Roman defeats were reliably received, the Asia Minor towns did not resist him. But as he got closer to the Mediterranean coast, he encountered considerable resistance. Caria, Lycia, and Pamphylia resisted strenuously. Ephesus also resisted for a time, but once in the presence of the Pontic king himself apparently at the head of superior forces, it quietly opened the gates and submitted. Mithridates played to perfection the role of preserver of Asia. He was generous to cities that received him happily and canceled debts and conferred five years of immunity from taxation throughout the province.

This was sensible enough, but it was at this point that Mithridates took complete leave of his senses and ordered the simultaneous massacre of all Romans and Italians in Asia Minor. The Ephesians, Pergamese, and other cities acquiesced, and Roman and Italian refugees were butchered, it is rumored in the number of eighty-thousand. A provocation on this scale assured a war to the death with Rome; Mithridates must undoubtedly have understood this, and it is indicative of the colossal megalomania that can grip the mind of such a person and there have been many subsequent emulators, to imagine himself capable of winning such a contest.

It went well for a time, and as we have seen, the Romans tended at the outset of such campaigns to be overconfident; so they were again. Even a Roman fleet disappeared, leaving Mithridates master of the Eastern seas as well. The inhabitants of Cos handed over to Mithridates the son of Ptolemy Alexander king of Egypt who had been sent to the island by his grandmother Cleopatra along with an extensive shipment of treasures as well as eight-hundred talents of temple money deposited in the island by the Jews of Asia.

Mithridates attacked Rhodes, which had remained faithful to its alliance with Rome, but he had waited too late in the season for siege and was forced to try to assault the island fortress. He produced an immense seaborne siege tower known as the sambuca, which rested on two ships tied together and could be extended to an altitude taller than the city wall. As this ingenious device was being prepared for the assault, its great weight overbore the craft on which it was placed, and it plunged into the sea. The assault on Rhodes was abandoned, but up to this point, as in other conflicts in this area, Rome had been underprepared and had been sharply defeated in the initial skirmishing.

Undismayed by this sideshow, Mithridates had already carried his war across the Aegean and into Greece. Here the Roman governor of Macedonia, Gaius Sentius, had been busy with incursions from Thrace, and there is reason to believe that these attacks were coordinated with Mithridates. There had been overtures to the Pontic king from disaffected Greeks including an Athenian delegation that objected to the aristocratic regime foisted upon Athens by Rome. The principal Mithridatic fifth column leader appears to have been a peripatetic philosopher of humble origins, Aristion, who made himself a personal publicity agent for Mithridates' enlightenment and benignity. This too conformed with the Greek, and especially the Athenian predilection, to imagine that surrounding areas were led by those who wished to expel foreign influences from Greece for the sole pleasure of allowing Greeks to pass from century to century unencumbered by the tedium of aggressive neighbours, the better to enlighten the world. Many had thought the same of Antiochus and even some of the Macedonians, and initially and with some reason, Flamininus and the Romans (until Mummius disabused them). The Greeks should never have allowed subsequent episodes to cloud the lessons of their experiences with the Great Kings of Persia.

Aristion won over Athenian opinion and was elected hoplite general. Little remained of the Periclean spirit in Athens and Aristion seized and executed most of the leaders of the aristocratic party, including some that had to be extradited from Attica, and confiscated their property. Athens was now militarily insignificant and an effort to seize the island of Delos was a complete fiasco, but Piraeus did provide Mithridates an excellent port of entry from which he swiftly commenced his effort to overrun all of Greece under the noses of the Romans.

He effortlessly occupied the Cyclades and expelled the Romans from Delos. However, Sentius' legate, Quntus Bruttius Sura, was able to repulse the invaders from the coast of Thessaly and seized the island that they were using to store their plunder. He went on to occupy most of Boeotia, which Archelaus had won for Mithridates, and he forced Archelaus to fall back into Attica.

5. Sulla's Campaign in the East

It was at this point that the balance shifted with the arrival of the advance guard of Sulla's army in Boeotia, under his quaestor, Lucius Lucullus. Sulla arrived with five legions and cavalry, and such was his prestige he had no difficulty raising reinforcements and provisions and the Boeotian population, despite their previous wavering, quickly returned to their Roman allegiance. Sulla defeated Archelaus and Aristion and drove them back into Athens and Piraeus.

Sulla was himself engaged in a high-stakes gamble for, as we have seen, he had scarcely departed the shores of Italy before his former chief and now bitter rival and equally distinguished commander, General Gaius Marius, had seized control of Rome. Though Marius would not wish to be responsible for the failure of the defense of Rome's Greek and Asian interests, he would happily incur Sulla's own failure. In place of the reinforcements and supplies he might normally expect, Sulla was required to impose himself heavily on the Greek states, which could be notoriously resistant to such exactions. Archelaus dominated the adjacent waters and could supply Piraeus as necessary, while Sulla was required to maintain communications through Boeotia by strengthening his forces there and diverting a subsequently arrived legion under Lucius Hortensius to Thessaly. Sulla funded these operations by the outright seizure of the treasures belonging to the Greek shrines of Epidaurus, Olympia, and Delphi. He sent Lucullus out to raise a fleet with some of the proceeds of these impious expropriations, which did not strengthen Greek goodwill towards their Roman overlords. Aristion held Athens while Archelaus held Piraeus. Sulla smashed the walls protecting the road to Piraeus and isolated Athens, which would be starved out eventually, but Piraeus was too well-fortified to be stormed by land and a siege was impossible without a fleet, so Sulla awaited Lucullus' acquisition of one with what had been pillaged from the Greek religious shrines, as Marius was not about to send him any naval support. Sulla was as much campaigning to recapture Rome as to expel Mithridates from Greece; it was a question of sequence.

Sulla had agents within Piraeus and thus defeated any attempted sorties by Archelaus, but was unable to break the fortress, but after a full winter, conditions in Athens had become desperate. Sulla, though a handsome man, had a ruddy complexion that produced white spots when he was angry. Messengers he sent to Athens' gates to invite surrender were serenaded with rude songs about Sulla's face that Aristion had composed, along with insults directed at Sulla's wife, with lewd sexual references and gestures. Aristion had completely lost his popularity in Athens, having led the city astray about its best political options and abused his position as siege governor. By the spring of 86, the proud Athenians had been reduced to cannibalism and Sulla, learning from informants the weakest point in the city's walls and after beating back a final attempted relief operation by Archelaus, smashed into Athens, whose population was now too enfeebled and demoralized to carry on. Sulla tolerated a medium level sacking and executions for cause but in deference to the glorious history of the city, forbade its destruction. He said he "would spare the living out of respect for the dead."[1] Aristion retreated to the Acropolis where he finally surrendered after running out of water. Sulla had moved on to his final attack on Piraeus and left it to Gaius Curio to receive Aristion's surrender and execute him, by the administration of poison, to the relief of the downtrodden populace of Athens. Sulla gradually forced Archelaus out of Piraeus to a fortified point at Munychia, which was impregnable but useless as a port and so was evacuated by Archelaus. He might have been able to hold if Ariarathes had advanced more diligently from Thessaly instead of attempting to build himself a functioning kingdom before seeing to the war where he was anxiously awaited by his father's generals. Ariarathes died of natural causes and was replaced by Archelaus who resumed his invasion of Greece, this time from the north via Thermopylae.

Sulla concentrated his forces with Hortensius, but he only had about sixteen-thousand, five-hundred men, counting fifteen-hundred cavalry, although they were crack, combat-proven Roman legionaries led, by an undefeated commander. He was still outnumbered about three to one and the Boeotian countryside would lend itself to Archelaus' cavalry, and he was certainly a competent general, though his forces suffered the usual problem of disparate units that didn't interact well and were of uneven quality, as usually came out to fight Rome in the area. A complicated

---

1 Tom Holland, *Rubicon*, Doubleday, New York, 2003, p. 79.

battle of maneuver with both commanders moving swiftly from flank to flank between Chaeronea and Mt. Thurium led finally to a close but decisive victory for the Romans that turned into a rout on retreat. Archelaus escaped with only ten-thousand of the forty-five thousand men he opened the battle with and Sulla, having extracted such a brilliant victory from so challenging a position, may be excused for reporting home that he had suffered only fourteen casualties, a considerable improvement on the facts. Sulla mopped up Pontic auxiliaries and foraging parties and surrendered half of their territory to the gods whose treasuries Sulla had already rifled at the start of the war, and whose terrestrial representative for his generous bequest to the deities of the Theban lands, he now claimed to be.

Sulla had won a great victory, but his task was far from over. Archelaus shortly returned via Euboea at the head of a new army, increased, according to Plutarch and others to between seventy and eighty-thousand men. He reentered Boeotia and approached the plain of Orchomenus. Sulla was again outnumbered though he had a substantially larger force than the previous encounter and was again in unfriendly territory. He was preparing the plain with trenches and ditches and the planting of spikes to restrict the movement of the Pontic chariots and cavalry and facilitate his pushing them against and into the large, adjoining Copais Marsh, when Archelaus opened his attack. Another intense and confused action took place but the devices that Sulla had installed to frighten and misdirect the Pontic cavalry were successful and they turned back on the phalanx behind them, and Sulla was able to strike heavily in both flanks and drive the entire Pontic army headlong into its camp which he then surrounded with a ditch and besieged. Archelaus left fifteen-thousand dead on the battlefield on the first day and on the second day his attempt to break out of his camp enabled the Romans to take it by storm, run down fleeing units and drive the remnants into the marshes. Archelaus had two days in the swamp and effected his escape in a small boat to Chalcis. He attempted to rally the remnants of the Mithridatic army but the Pontic invasion of Greece was over. Sulla had scored a stunning victory just as Flaccus, nominated commander to replace Sulla for the succeeding year approached to enjoy the fruits of his triumph.

The recent fortunes of battle had naturally caused some shuffling of affiliations and affections in Greece and in Asia Minor. The Galatians rose in revolt after Mithridates seized their leading men at a banquet and murdered them. The fleeing survivors raised a rebellion throughout the kingdom and expelled the Mithridatic satrap and his garrisons. Mithridates narrowly suppressed a revolt on the island of Chios but Ephesus rose against him and executed his local commander. Smyrna and a number of other cities of Asia Minor followed. Mithridates now had the good judgment to blend severity with magnanimity and canceled a lot of debt, freed slaves and generously granted citizenship. Conspiracies and distressing rumors abounded, however, and Mithridates also conducted a reign of terror against those whom he suspected of being well-disposed to Rome. It is reckoned that more than sixteen-hundred Pergamese were summarily put to death on this account.

After the Battle of Orchomenus, Sulla destroyed several Boeotian ports to prevent their use by returning Pontic forces and marched northwards to Thessaly to await the arrival of Flaccus. He had no intention of responding to recall notices from Rome until it suited him, and he took winter quarters. Flaccus arrived with two legions, but he was militarily incompetent, and his soldiers quickly indicated their preference to be commanded by Sulla. Flaccus' legate, Gaius Flavius Fimbria, was a more able man than his commander and marched most of their legions off towards the Bosporus. After some hard fighting, they did expel the remaining Pontic forces from Europe.

A completely ludicrous sequence of events ensued that was quite un-Roman. Fimbria gave his men unlimited freedom to plunder and when the aggrieved inhabitants on the route of march appealed to Flaccus, who ordered restitution, Fimbria counseled disobedience. Flaccus ordered that the troops not enter Byzantium, given the outrages that might be committed, but Fimbria exploited Flaccus' absence to countermand those orders and a considerable melee ensued. After further disputes between the two men, Flaccus purported to dismiss Fimbria and replace him with "a certain (Minucius) Thermus."[2] Fimbria declined to be so cavalierly dispensed with and raised a mutiny that swept the ranks and he chased his ostensible former commander across Asia Minor to Chalcedon and Nicomedeia and captured and executed him (and then decapitated him and hurled his severed head into the sea in a macabre public ceremony). The Senate expressed its official disapproval of this rather astonishing level of insubordination but confirmed Fimbria in his command. Fimbria gave no early sign of disobedience to Sulla who disdained Flaccus and was indifferent to this unorthodox shuffling of subordinates. But Fimbria was a Marius supporter, hostile to Sulla, who would only use his services while he needed them.

Mithridates ordered Archelaus to enter into peace discussions with Sulla and a meeting was arranged at Aulis in northern Boeotia. Archelaus offered peace on the basis of the status quo and Pontic provision of a fleet and reinforcements to assist Sulla in retaking Rome. The Roman commander brushed aside this insulting overture and suggested instead that Archelaus defect to him with his fleet, attach himself to Sulla's fortunes and desert his doomed and vainglorious master. The two had a good laugh and got down to serious discussions. Archelaus surrendered his fleet to Sulla; prisoners and escaped slaves were returned, and Mithridates was to retire from all conquered territory including Paphlagonia and pay Rome an indemnity of two-thousand talents, for which he would once more be recognized as a friend and ally of Rome. Archelaus so feared Mithridates' response to his treaty-making that he was anxious to retain Sulla's goodwill. He had on balance given a good account of himself in his unsuccessful resistance to Sulla, who regarded him as a substantial and capable military leader. While awaiting the Pontic king's response, Archelaus was Sulla's guest and was extremely well treated, including when he came down with an illness. While waiting upon Mithridates, Sulla spent the summer of 85 clearing the northern Thracian tribes away from the Macedonian border which they had been harassing.

Mithridates was in no position to resist Sulla's offer. He had heavily taxed his subjects to pay for the catastrophic campaigns against Sulla and now the brutal but capable Fimbria was carrying the battle to him in Asia Minor very effectively. Fimbria surprised the king's son at the head of a substantial army in Bithynia and

---

2 CAH, IX, p. 256 (M. Rostovtzeff and H.A. Ormerod).

shattered yet another Pontic force, driving the younger Mithridates to join his father at Pergamon. Fimbria drove the pair to Pitane on the coast and summoned Lucullus, who had finally assembled a fleet for Sulla, to support his entrapment of the Pontic Royals. Lucullus judged the order so insolent that he declined to cooperate. After some toing and froing, Mithridates finally concluded that he had no choice but to accept Sulla's terms which he did in person when they met at Dardanus in the Troad in August, 85 B.C. Sulla's henchmen thought he had made a rather soft peace, but he reasoned that Fimbria was capable of defecting to the Pontic king and prolonging hostilities.

Fimbria was taking no orders from Sulla and plundered Phrygia for his own account. Sulla began to invest Fimbria's camp and many of his troops deserted, Sulla being in all respects a more estimable commander and the more promising magnet militarily and politically, to opportunistic Roman soldiers of fortune. Some of Fimbria's men even assisted Sulla in completing the encirclement of Fimbria's camp. Characteristically, Fimbria attempted to arrange Sulla's assassination and that failing, sought an interview with him, which was declined. He fled to Pergamon, his legions almost entirely rallied to Sulla and Gaius Flavius Fimbria, a talented but very sinister man, just twenty-nine, followed the well-trawled career path to suicide, assisted by a slave.

Sulla restored Nicomedes and Ariobarzanes to their kingdoms, rewarded allies, especially Rhodes, and plundered hostile areas ruthlessly, restoring many to slavery, and rewarding his legionaries (including the Fimbrians) handsomely, no doubt with an eye to the main prize in Rome. Arrangements with Mithridates were flimsy and the Pontic king was completely unreliable, not even inspiring Sulla's confidence that he learned the lesson from the terrible drubbing he had received. These Middle Eastern potentates tended not to be quick learners even when put smartly in their place by Roman arms and generals. In 84, leaving Urena in charge with the two Fimbrian legions, Sulla embarked from Ephesus, collected his army in Greece and returned to raise his standard on the Capitoline Hill. He brought with him much treasure as well as the long concealed treatises of Aristotle, an intellectual collection of permanent historic value.

Sulla's expedition to Greece and Asia Minor must be counted with the greatest victories of Publius Scipio Africanus, Gaius Marius, and the great Roman generals who swiftly followed, Gnaeus Pompeius Magnus and even, almost, Gaius Julius Caesar. He had taken immense chances on behalf of Rome, showed consistent genius as strategist, battlefield tactician, inspirer of his troops, diplomatic maneuverer, and even, though heavy-handed, talented administrator of conquered territory. He did his full patriotic duty by remaining longer than he needed to and achieving more than was ever expected of his mission, and returned to Rome meritocratically elevated by his own exertions alone to a very exalted status.

6. The Death of Marius and Sulla's Return

Rome in his absence had endured a time as sordid as Sulla's mission was glorious. Lucius Cornelius Cinna was ostensibly in charge as senior consul when Sulla departed and he quickly took up the Sulpician program of advancing the interests of the Italians and the freed men, which generated violence around Rome and caused large numbers of Italians to enter the city and assert themselves against the traditional Romans who had never acquiesced in the Gracchan reforms. The Roman traditionalists rallied behind the other consul, Gnaeus Octavius, and the struggle for mastery in the streets and squares of Rome where the rule of mobs contested when the expected Tribunician veto was announced. A pitched battle took place in the Forum itself, but Octavius personally led his forces and after Cinna's now customary appeal in such hard-pressed circumstances to the slaves, whom he would emancipate in exchange for their soldiery, he was chased out of the city.

This was only the opening round as neither Cinna nor Octavius had an army and victory would go to the party which first assembled one. Mobs were fine for beating up civilians and terrorizing opponents' families in their homes but in these times as ever after, they could not hold their own with genuine soldiers for more than a few minutes. Sulla was soon declared by the Senate to be deprived of his citizenship and an enemy of the state, ending his consulship. The Senate eccentrically named Lucius Cornelius Merula to replace him, but as he was the high priest of the temple of Jupiter (Flamen Dialis), he was forbidden by his office to be in the presence of either a corpse or an army, which made him completely useless in these circumstances. It was clearly the Senate's intention to make Octavius the sole consul.

Cinna was able to recruit the army of Appius Claudius Pulcher in Campania presumably with promises of the fruits of power and the gratification of enfranchisement and he marched on Rome in a manner already familiar and which would be intermittently repeated for many centuries. It was at this point that the inevitable Marius saw his chance again and landed in Etruria and proclaimed his devotion to the Sulpician program. He and Cinna, soon allies again, advanced upon Rome from North and South, practically unopposed. (Marius, in any case, still well remembered how to command an army and could have brushed aside anyone who stood in his path, with Sulla absent.) Cinna had a much larger army than Marius, but it was essentially a political force and Cinna divided it into three sections and Rome was invested from four incoming roads at once.

Octavius and Merula persuaded Pompeius Strabo to join them, but their forces were completely inadequate. Marius seized the port of Ostia, gaining control of the grain supply, but he was effectively blocked for a time at Janiculum by Octavius and was about to relaunch his assault when resistance gave way, undermined by defeatism, infiltration of Rome by the followers of Cinna and Marius, and the disease that often afflicts crowded and besieged cities. Strabo, the only defender capable of commanding armed men, died of some disease. Octavius sued for peace but the best he could get from Cinna was that he would be "as merciful as circumstances allowed."[3] Marius did not even promise that; nor did he give that. Merula was deposed as high priest, a position offered to Marius' fourteen-year-old nephew Julius Caesar, an offer that was subsequently withdrawn. This was the first cameo public appearance of the greatest of all Romans and it was indicative of his precocity and promise that he was championed for this role when still a boy.

---

3 CAH, IX, p. 264 (Hugh Last).

Cinna was now the unopposed consul again and his first act was to remove officially the outlawry of Marius. He accepted the consulship for the unheard-of seventh time. But it was a sorry ending to a brilliant career. Marius spent his time and energy exacting vengeance on all those many whom he felt had betrayed him over his long career. Five days of horrible carnage mark this last return of Marius. Octavius was publicly slaughtered along with the distinguished orator Marcus Antonius. Marius' fellow consul in 102, Quintus Catulus, and Merula, received the dignity of a prosecution but had the good sense to commit suicide before their fast-track, pre-ordered trials could occur; Catullus suffocated himself in charcoal smoke and Merula bled to death in the temple of Jupiter. Numerous senators were decapitated, and their heads were displayed from the rostrum of the Senate, but the less prominent senatorial victims were simply abandoned as carrion, their terrified supporters afraid to bury them. This was the final act of Marius as a statesman. Even Cinna, as cynical and vicious as almost any Roman politician, was disgusted and after five days he ordered his troops to kill Marius' bloodthirsty slaves. The old general was sated, and a semblance of administration returned as the carnage subsided.

Sulla was declared an outlaw and his previous legislation was repealed. Everybody knew that this was a cowardly gesture, but Marius, having taken leave of his senses in a St. Vitus' Dance of evil violence, had ceased to be a serious contender for the headship of the state. All knew that Sulla would return and that the only person who might have had the military ability and political strength to stop him was now mad, completely unserviceable, and on the brink of death. Marius did at last, die peacefully on January 13, 86 B.C., aged seventy-one.

He had taught Sulla a good deal about war-making and was, as has been recorded, the principal architect of the professional Roman army, and the first of the Roman generals to organize and lead military formations capable of dictating the political course of the state whose primary loyalty and practice was to their commander and not to Rome. These were not wholly admirable innovations, but they were inevitable, and the Army reforms in particular were absolutely necessary for Rome to achieve the mastery of the world that it did and to retain it for more than four centuries. And where Sulla had suppressed Rome's enemies in the east, Marius had saved Rome herself in some of the most perilous moments in her history. Both were great men, and gruesome and monstrous though the final chapter of Marius' career was, it was fortunate that the two former comrades did not have a final crossing of swords. All now knew that the future of Rome awaited the return of the conqueror from the East.

The new consul was Lucius Valerius Flaccus, whom we have already seen floundering between Sulla, Fimbria, and Mithridates, and whose pitiful and humiliating demise has already been recounted. He had been consul and censor but was a very limited statesman and a completely incompetent general, as has been noted. The state of Roman government was naturally in complete shambles and the measure adopted to address the fiscal crisis was the stark devaluation of the currency by seventy-five percent. This was very unpopular and Flaccus was packed off to his catastrophic mission to the east. His record of failure would be unbroken to the miserable end.

Cinna and his colleague Gnaeus Carbo did make a substantial contribution to Roman government by finalizing the enfranchisement of the Italians: all free inhabitants of Italy became equal members of a single state. Nearly fifty years after Tiberius Gracchus had begun this mighty effort that was so obviously necessary, it was accomplished. In thus reforming itself, the Roman Republic almost completed a metamorphosis simultaneously of renewal and exhaustion. It shed the husk of abusive municipalism, but it had sacrificed the dignity of the Republic to the iron rod of the generals and, more contemptibly, to the rapacity and corruption of demagogues who intermittently ruled through the thuggery of lawless and depraved hooligans. The state of Italy had risen but the Republic of Rome was in extremis.

At the end of 85, Sulla sent a letter to the Senate announcing his intention to return and recounting with no great or necessary modesty his services to Rome and his misgivings at the treatment he had received. (His property had been confiscated and his family fled for their lives to Greece.) Some began to prepare resistance, but the Senate, naturally shaken by its many reverses and failures and the savagery visited upon it by Marius, purported to wish to mediate between the interests of Sulla and Cinna. It had all really gone too far by now for this; naïve in its insolence, the Senate promised Sulla safety if he returned, as if he had any intention or requirement to do so as a private citizen rather than at the head of his army. Cinna and Carbo prepared to try to resist, and while their true state of mind is not known, such gritty realists must have had some concept of the improbability of the mission thrust upon them. Sulla, peerless and impeccable, set at the head of a great and battle-proven army whose absolute loyalty he had earned, was just across the Adriatic. His time had come.

Cinna and Carbo determined to try to resist Sulla by crossing to Greece and attempting to prevent his reaching Italy. After part of the intendant contingents had sailed, rioting broke out amongst the second group waiting to embark and Cinna was killed in the fracas. Carbo was happy to reign as a sole consul and scrapped Cinna's ambitious plan. He recalled the forces that had been sent and prepared to await Sulla's invasion of Italy. The Senate rejected Carbo's hare-brained scheme of taking hostages from the civil population as an assurance of their loyalty, but it did broaden a grant of citizenship as an encouragement to defend the regime against the returning general.

Sulla eventually replied to the Senate's offer of mediation and safety. He said that he would never be reconciled with his enemies but would not resent it if the Senate spared their lives, and he offered to protect the Senate and all those who had taken refuge with him. He thus informed the ostensible authorities that his army would not be disbanded and that he would become the military dictator over Rome and all Italy unless there was someone who could defeat his intentions by force.

On July 6, 83 B.C., the always superstitious Romans were profoundly disturbed when the Temple of Jupiter was destroyed by fire, including its statue. Carbo awarded himself the command of Cisalpine Gaul, though he remained in northern Italy; this was hardly a statement of confidence by the defending authorities. The new consuls, Lucius Scipio Asiaticus and Gaius Norbanus, were respectable Marians, but were clearly unequal to the task of organizing a defense against Sulla.

Sulla landed at Brundisium in the spring of 83 at the head of his army of forty-thousand legionaries, all of whom had sworn an oath that they would stay with their general and be prepared to organize Italy and assure its security. Sulla made the point that he was a patriotic Roman who accepted the entire community of Italian citizenship, that he would chastise his enemies but uphold the Roman state. Carbo attempted to pretend that Sulla would roll back the rights of the Italians, but Sulla made it clear he accepted the Italian settlement entirely and was pledged to the maintenance of it. He met with the consul Scipio Asiaticus and assured him of the safety of the Senate and of the Constitution. At the beginning of 82, Sulla proclaimed a treaty binding himself to maintain the rights of the Italians, and with this, the tumultuous transformation of the Italian peninsula was finally accomplished.

Sulla marched northward to Rome, receiving the adherences of prominent Italians and Romans as he progressed. Quintus Caecilius Metellus Pius was confirmed as proconsul in Liguria; Marcus Licinius Crassus was confirmed in Africa and Lucius Philippus was sent by Sulla to secure the government of Sardinia. Marcus Lucullus confirmed his adherence and ultimately even more important than the others, the young Gnaeus Pompeius, son of Pompeius Strabo and just twenty-three, raised three legions and led them to Sulla where he was most warmly received. So formidable was the field formation of Sulla's army and so spontaneous the widespread move to acclaim the returning general, consul Scipio Asiaticus' army deserted their nominal commander in the midst of amicable negotiations with Sulla and joined Sulla's swelling ranks.

The forces of resistance regrouped again; the new consuls were Gnaeus Papirius Carbo and Gaius Marius, son of the late general. They raised forces in Etruria and Cisalpine Gaul and exploited the semi-independence of the Samnites and Etrurians and attempted combat, but their front of resistance collapsed and Sulla's influence extended up the Peninsula. Finally, in 82 Sulla determined to seize Rome. The young Marius resisted in Campania but after a gallant fight, was overwhelmed. Sulla entered Rome unopposed, although the young Marius, emulating the worst traits of his father, had several opponents seized and executed including Lucius Domitius, a former consul, and Quintus Mucius Scaevola, Pontifex Maximus. What remained was essentially a mopping-up operation, although there was hard and close fighting beneath the very walls of Rome at the Colline Gate. It degenerated into massacres and approximately four-thousand Samnite captives were killed, and the city's gates were only opened after Sulla had the severed heads of some of his more prominent enemies thrown over the walls as an incentive to cooperation. The young Marius attempted to escape through an underground drain passage but was captured and committed suicide and most of his loyal party was summarily executed.

Sulla approved the pillage of disaffected parts of the city. All Italy was now resigned to its conqueror, but Sulla's wrath was thoroughly stirred and was not ready to subside. As Marius had avenged the violent death of Sulpicius with his vicious proscriptions, and his son had slaughtered his father's resurgent enemies around and among the senators, the massacre of the Marian leaders and Samnite prisoners was equally horrible and more protracted: Sulla ordered the summary execution of everyone who in any capacity had aided his opponents and he assaulted the equestrian orders with particular savagery, generously rewarding the more bloodthirsty of his executioners. The families of murdered opponents, while generally permitted to survive, were permanently excluded from office and deprived of property, though Sulla emancipated their slaves. Though Marius has historically been more severely criticized for his vengeance, it cannot be said that Sulla's was any more merciful.

The posthumous end of the once brilliant relationship between Marius and Sulla was especially gruesome. The General's ashes were disinterred and scattered, and his monuments were overthrown. This was inexcusable treatment of the man who had been acclaimed "the third founder of Rome" for saving it from the Teutonic and Gallic hordes less than twenty years before, when he had recreated the Roman army after others had led it to disgraceful defeat and killed or captured more than two-hundred thousand invaders in two mighty battles of national salvation.

Marius' well-regarded adoptive nephew, Marius Gratidianus, twice praetor, was dissected live in a revolting public offering. These and similar atrocities were replicated in towns across Italy. Many communities in Etruria and Samnium were put to fire and sword and left in smoking ruins. "This reign of terror was never forgotten by the Romans. Whenever it seemed possible that some commander with a victorious army at his back might seize the government, there arose the fear that the horrors which had followed the Colline Gate might be repeated. Few of the letters of Cicero written early in 49 B.C. fail to testify how deeply the terror of the Sullanum regnum had bitten into the imagination of his fellow citizens."[4]

7. The Dictatorship, Retirement, and Assessment of Sulla

After this bloodbath, following several episodes scarcely less sanguinary, it is a very radical school of historiography that can believably claim that the Republic meaningfully survived. Sulla was now the master of Italy and was not slow to assert himself in the rest of the Roman world. Spain, Sicily, and Africa had received large numbers of fugitives from Sulla's terrible vengeance. Sicily and Africa, the chief sources of Rome's grain, were a strategic priority that Sulla assigned to the young Pompey; his performance had been so impressive he was entirely excused for his brief flirtation with Cinna. The first of the great Marius' ashes had scarcely been rifled and scattered by his successor when the next in succession stepped forward to stake his claim as the coming warlord. Pompey cleared Sicily easily and he put Carbo to death on the island of Pantellaria after an excruciating trial, earning from some the description "the young carnivore." Pompey moved on to Africa, bringing one-hundred and twenty warships and eight-hundred transports carrying six legions to Utica. He flattened his opponents, executed the king of Numidia, installed a new regime and returned after a totally successful and dazzling campaign of only forty days. The successor to Marius and Sulla could not be doubted. Sulla was slightly concerned by the triumph of his protégé and commanded Pompey to disband all but one of his legions, a measure that led to considerable agitation for revolt among his officers.

Having seen at first hand the consequences of Sulla's vengeance, Pompey com-

---

4 CAH, IX, p. 277 (R. Gardner).

plied with orders but in sufficiently dilatory manner that Sulla felt moved to concede Pompey a triumph, which Rome witnessed with appropriate respect on March 12, 79. The imperator Pompey was twenty-seven. (His only quasi-visible contemporary rival, Julius Caesar, Marius' nephew and Cinna's son-in-law, was in the wrong camp and reasoned that he should distance himself from the high priesthood and make his way in the army, clearly now the path to power. He served with distinction in the east under the "certain Thermus." Sulla purported to see in him "many Mariuses" but did not pursue or prosecute him. Caesar spent so much time seeking an alliance with Nicomedes on behalf of Thermus, it was alleged that he had a homosexual liaison with the king of Bithynia, an apparently malicious falsehood that he never entirely lived down despite his coming decades of almost frenetic womanizing.) It was Sulla's hour; Pompey and Caesar were the coming men.

A war of renewed subjugation loomed in Spain, but fundamentally the Roman and Italian jurisdictions were now stable but war-ravaged, traumatized, and in many places destitute. A vast task of physical and institutional reconstruction awaited. Despite his terrible savagery, Sulla was just the man for this task. He was not only an efficient soldier and a cunning diplomat and politician. He was an administrator of remarkable talent. The Gracchi had demonstrated that politics alone could not rule Rome. Marius had perhaps demonstrated that a political general could rule Rome but not necessarily be a durable and effective governor. Sulla had played the roles that he needed to play—conqueror and vindictive dictator—but unlike Marius he had well-developed ideas on how government should be conducted and he now had an unlimited mandate and ability to enact them.

The two principal problems that Sulla had to grapple with administratively were the application of the general suffrage of all Italy to the governance of the entire state, and the integration into a functioning system of government of the professional army and warlordism that Marius had originated and Sulla inherited. The system of providing pensions, generally land grants, for veterans would have to be taken from the military commanders and shouldered by the state itself if the loyalty of the army were to be transmitted back to the national entity from the commanding generals, and some pan-Italian form of popular consultation had to be devised to make the state squarely reliant on national consensus and not just self-interested Roman factions.

Sulla removed to the country outside Rome and allowed that to redesign the state's institutions a dictatorship was required. The two consuls, Carbo and the younger Marius, had been murdered. Since he had the ability to confer such jurisdiction on himself, and the whole population was prostrate with the after-effects of political chaos, there was no vigorous debate on the issue. Sulla supported the nomination of L. Valerius Flaccus, Princeps of the Senate, as interrex. There was no precedent for a dictatorship other than by a consul or for more than a year at a time, but Sulla wished to discard both precedents. Flaccus asked the popular Committee to make Sulla "legal and constitutional dictator" to serve at his own pleasure, and then resigned himself. The closest precedent was the Decemvirate of 449 B.C., which provided open-ended rule by decree but with the ability to end it by popular vote eventually. (A four-century reach into the past was a pretty threadbare connection to representative democracy and constitutional legitimacy; to all intents and purposes, Sulla was starting from scratch.)

Sulla had eliminated one-hundred and five senators, mainly killing them, but recognized the Senate had to be revived and raised the membership by three-hundred, earning considerable praise for the inclusion of a full variety of opinions and constituencies. He also ended the censors' right to add senators and conferred this right on the less exalted quaestors. In the colleges of pontiffs and augurs also, Sulla promoted new blood and variety and was a legitimate reformer. The principal restraint on democracy that Sulla retained was the requirement that bills had to be moved in the assembly by magistrates, and Sulla did not revolutionize that group. But like many dictators, he curtailed the previous governing elites in favour of broader exposure for the general public. Sulla decreed that consuls had to be at least forty-two years old, praetors thirty-nine, and quaestors thirty. He moved to prevent a Marius of the future perennially holding the consulship by resurrecting the ten-year gap between consular terms. Sulla tried to weaken the tribunate by making it illegal for any holder of it to accept any other office. (This rule was revoked by Pompey and Crassus in 70 B.C., but the tribunes lost their ability to introduce legislation.)

If Sulla could successfully protect the Senate from the magistrates and tribunes, he was less effective at insulating legislation and government from the generals. He instituted the practice of consuls and praetors moving on to provincial governorships after their terms, while generals were not usually the consuls after Sulla's time. There weren't absolute prohibitions, but it was accepted that state policy required provision for veterans, so the legions of retired commanders did not become, in fact, their private armies awaiting mobilization at an opportune political time. Sulla urged the change of provincial governors promptly also, preferably yearly, to prevent the encrustation of their personal sovereignty as a counterweight to central authority during their provincial incumbency. At this time there were ten governorships: two Spains, two Gauls, Asia, Macedonia, Africa, Cilicia, Sicily, and Sardinia and Corsica together. Sulla further strengthened the central government by defining as treason any unauthorized armed departure from a province by its governor, and any unauthorized act of war against a third party. He also showed considerable enlightenment as a professional soldier in defining any gubernatorial disobedience of the Senate as a crime. Sulla thus strengthened the Senate and got off to a good start by packing it with prosperous and successful meritocratic people from all around Italy.

Sulla expanded and strengthened the administration of the courts by increasing the ranks of the praetorship and defining their tasks just as he fed the Senate from the ranks of the quaestors. He founded new courts and ended the practice of public assemblies hearing all cases, which had become a ludicrous circus. He established specialized courts and an appellate system; these were among his most valuable and long-lasting reforms.

His very first order of administrative business was to regain control of the finances of the chronically mismanaged Roman government. He imposed a special tax on the whole Roman world, not even exempting states which had been granted immunity, and raised substantial further resources by the outright sale of political privileges. He stopped the public sale of grain for the Roman population and imposed economies both on the government and on citizens, legislating puritanically against private extravagance. He purported to limit expenditure on food, the cost of funerals, and masqueraded as a champion of sumptuary legislation which, in practice, then and always, was almost entirely delusional.

Sulla continued the punishment of communities and individuals who had opposed him and one city, Voltaterrae, was besieged until 80 B.C. when the dictator in person subdued it. All recalcitrant communities lost their citizenship. Peace settled so determinedly upon the Roman world, Sulla was able to demobilize twenty-three legions which required him to provide allotments of land for over one-hundred thousand men. Settling them all caused considerable dislocation, and of course not all of them took to rural life. Many longed for war and its plunder and the large contingent of retirees from Sulla's army were, if anything, more of a menace than a reinforcement of the social stability of Italy and the provinces.

The dictator took the consulship, also in 80 B.C., with his colleague Metellus Pius, a respected individual, but Sulla saw that he was stifling the spontaneity of Roman government and felt that he had accomplished what he had sought, and he retired. He was no less selfless in retiring than Cincinnatus (or Washington) and he retired from a dictatorship. Sulla laid down his dictatorial powers with no fear of recriminations against him and retired to his country home in Campania. Here he died in 78 B.C., aged sixty, and received an immense funeral; the majority of Romans undoubtedly honored his memory. Ultimately, his reputation depends upon his administrative reforms more than his talents as a general though they were, of course, great. At detailed administration, he was one of the ablest leaders Rome would ever have, in the same category as Augustus, and he did more original thinking on the Constitution of Rome than any previous Roman statesman.

He has been blamed for failure to abolish the popular assembly completely, but this is surely an unfair criticism since it was a pillar of the Roman ethos that always remained in some measure a popular state. And he has been blamed for not entirely suppressing the tribune who always retained the potential to be a grandstanding prosecutor who could distract the whole Roman world. But abolishing offices and governmental structures for which there was tradition and demand is difficult and is not always advisable. The fact that Sulla's reforms did not prove to be permanent, or durably adequate, takes nothing from the astuteness of their conception and the substantial success that they enjoyed. (His greatest oversight was in not extending the consular term to two years.)

Sulla was a handsome and convivial man, a swashbuckling hedonist in his youth, jovial and companionable and throughout his life always loyal to his friends; he was a cynic but understood that too much cynicism could be dangerous in a Rome that never lost its emotional attachment to ancient virtue. He never hesitated for an instant to take measures of the most extreme severity, convinced from his rugged experience that nothing else could assure survival or even make it likely. "Like a man whose supreme conviction is that death comes soon or late to all, he never allowed the lives of a few hundred of his opponents to stand in the way of his considered policy. Yet for all the forbidding savagery of his methods, he inspired unyielding loyalty in vast numbers of supporters. Indeed his epitaph, which he is said to have composed himself… proclaimed to posterity that 'Man had never known a truer friend or a more remorseless enemy.'"[5]

Where Marius founded the professional and the politicized army and saved the nation from its enemies, Sulla, though he was approximately equally competent as a general, won less important victories but was much superior as a statesman. Both rank among the greatest leaders in a thousand years of continuous Roman history.

---

5 Plutarch, Sulla, 38, 4.

CHAPTER TWENTY-FOUR

WAR IN SPAIN

THE RISE OF GNAEUS POMPEIUS MAGNUS AND MARCUS TULLIUS CICERO, 78-62 B.C.

Bust of Gnaeus Pompey the Great

Bust of Marcus Tullius Cicero

1. Sertorius

THE DEATH OF SULLA found Rome financially solid, with capable senior officers of the state and provincial governors in place and only under particular threat in Spain. But there was instantly no overriding authority in the state. Even though he had retired, Sulla was the authority, and his death left a vacuum which in politics as in physics is quickly filled.

In 79, Marcus Lepidus, a corrupt adventurer, was elected consul standing against the Sullan tradition and promising a less regimented society. The other consul was Quintus Lutatius Catulus a principled oligarch at the opposite pole to Lepidus. They rapidly fell out, ostensibly on the issue of Lepidus' wish to revive the tribune, but in fact, over philosophical and jurisdictional differences. There was periodic friction in the provinces where dislocated loyalists took against settled veterans of Sulla's army. These rugged men generally knew well how to take care of themselves.

Lepidus thought he saw his moment and marched on Rome with his army demanding a second consecutive consulate (which Sulla had decreed to be illegal), and the restoration of the tribunate. The Senate called upon the young Pompey to defend Rome against the renegade consul. Catulus defeated Lepidus who retired to Etruria. Junius Brutus, his lieutenant, was besieged in Mutina by Pompey and after extensive negotiations was brutally murdered by his still young opponent. Lepidus washed up in Sardinia and it is not clear whether his early death was natural, violent, or induced by the egregious conduct of his slatternly wife.

The misadventure of Lepidus revealed an alarming degree of discontent in Italy: it showed the Senate behaving with that anxious energy which is the mark of feeble governments, and above all it provided Pompey with another stepping-stone in his unprecedentedly swift advance to the position of first citizen of Rome. The death of Sulla had also brought the return to Rome of Julius Caesar, the rivalry of Pompey, and Caesar would be the central Roman story for the next thirty years.

There had been comparative peace in Spain after the burning of Numantia and the defeat of the revolt of the Lusitanians and the Celtiberians (Chapter 21), though, as would long continue, the Spanish were restive and never hard to stir to rebellion against foreign occupation. There was a good deal of bloodshed through the 90's but the Roman governors Didius and Licinius (consuls in 98 and 97), suppressed the uprisings in the usual heavy-handed Roman manner. Whole towns were razed to the ground and entire populations transported or scattered. The massacre of unarmed Celtiberians was a particularly disgusting incident. The Romans and the Spanish seemed to bring out the worst in each other for centuries (even, eventually, in papal affairs).

At this point there emerged one of the unique personalities of the time, Quintus Sertorius, a Sabine born in Nursia in 123. He served under Marius against the northern barbarians and as a military tribune under Didius in the Celtiberian War, where he became an expert on guerrilla warfare and became intimately acquainted with the Spanish. He was quaestor in Cisalpine Gaul in the Marsic War and became a popular military hero but was rejected as a candidate for the tribunate by the intervention of Sulla who did not wish a soldier unsympathetic to himself in such a position. He suffered the misfortune of being branded a Marion by Sulla although he was in fact mistrustful of Marius. Instead of retaining him in Rome as the only person who might have successfully resisted Sulla, he was dispatched to Spain to deal with a new round of perturbations. Starting in 81, he organized Spain against Sulla and to a large degree went native with the Celtiberians. Sulla dispatched two legions under Gaius Annius Luscus; they chased Sertorius to Mauretania. At this point the Lusitanians recruited him to lead yet another revolt from Rome and he took over a force of nearly five-thousand at Tarifa in 80 and defeated the governor of Further Spain, who rejoiced in the name of Lucius Fufidius. His renown and his army grew and from 79 to 72 he successfully conducted a combination open war and guerrilla resistance and was undefeated in any engagement. Quintus Caecilius Metellus Pius attempted an offensive against him in 79 but Sertorius kept him at bay while his lieutenant Hirtuleius defeated and killed the governor of Nearer Spain, Domitius Calvinus, on the Tagus River. A war of maneuver ensued in which Sertorius' territory spread considerably across the center of Spain and by the end of 77, he was the master of much of Iberia. He contemplated a possible intervention in Italian affairs as Rome's hold on Spain was now reduced to New Carthage and the Ebro, albeit the principal gold-producing regions. Sertorius established a capital at Osca and created a Senate of three-hundred and set up a school for the children of Celtiberian chiefs. At this point, at the end of 77, he managed to rally the remains of the army of the dead Lepidus from Sardinia and his forces exceeded thirty-thousand. By this time, the Roman authorities were fearful of the replication of the attack of Hannibal on Italy from Spain and commanded by a soldier, Sertorius, of not incomparable ability. With Sulla dead, it was in these serious circumstances that the Roman Senate swallowed their distaste for the precocious Pompey and invested him with the authority and the resources to extirpate the Spanish apostasy.

Pompey fought his way into Spain and across the Ebro but was badly beaten by Sertorius at Valentia and then lost an entire legion in ambush. "The pupil of Sulla had indeed been taught a severe lesson."[1] Metellus somewhat retrieved the Roman position by defeating Hirtuleius at Italica, and Pompey had a modest success on the upper Ebro. Sertorius even made a distant alliance with Mithridates, from whom he received three-thousand talents and forty ships. Fortunes turned in 75 when Metellus again defeated Hirtuleius at Segovia and Pompey fared better on the plane of Valentia. Though outnumbered, Pompey fought Sertorius to a draw in the lower Sucro Valley, though Pompey needed Metellus to make it a victory on the second day. "If that old woman did not come up I would have thrashed the youngster and sent him back to Rome," said Sertorius,[2] apparently with some justification. Metellus withdrew but Pompey continued to harass Sertorius and try to bring him to battle again. Metellus and Pompey demanded reinforcements from Rome which in addition to the Spanish problems was being severely harassed by pirates and was suffering food shortages from the failure of the Gallic harvest. Pompey rattled nerves in Rome with a message that concluded: "I warn you that unless you come to the rescue I shall be unable to prevent your armies from marching back to Italy and bringing with them the whole Spanish war."[3] the consul Lucius Lucullus was, in any case, concerned that if Pompey returned his Asiatic command could be endangered, and it was agreed to send two additional legions and a substantial amount of money to reinforce Pompey and Metellus in Spain.

The Romans altered their tactics and abandoned the struggle in the plain of Valentia, where they were also tormented by pirates' shore parties and settlements and focused on hammering the Celtiberians and on siege warfare. Even with this they were hard put to it: Sertorius forced Pompey to give up the siege of Pallantia and defeated the combined Roman armies at Calagurris with the loss of three-thousand men at the end of 74. In 73, Metellus substantially withdrew and Pompey conducted a war which became a struggle of attrition. Spain had put up a valiant resistance but

---

1 Plutarch, Sertorius, 18.
2 Ibid., 19.
3 Sallust. History, II, 98.

Rome kept pouring in resources and wearing down the enemy on his own territory. Sertorius grew old with disappointment and struggle and was outmaneuvered by the evil Perperna whom he had imported with the remnants of Lepidus' army from Sardinia. At what he judged to be the right moment, Perperna murdered his chief in 72, somewhat replicating the tragic fate of Viriathus (Chapter 21). Pompey then crushed Perperna, whose talents were confined to scheming and treachery. The Spanish fought to the physical finish—the siege of Calagurris only ended after the garrison devoured the bodies of the women and children. Pompey and Metellus returned to Rome in 71 and Pompey erected a monument to himself and the capture of 876 towns.

The renowned German historian Theodor Mommsen only lightly exaggerates with the reflection: "So ended one of the greatest men, if not the very greatest man that Rome had hitherto produced—a man who under more fortunate circumstances would perhaps have become the regenerator of his country." In addition to being a master of guerrilla warfare, Sertorius seemed to have possessed much of the talent as a commander of Hannibal as well as the genius for military organization of his old chief Marius, and the originality and talent for military surprise of Caesar. But he did not have either the political good fortune or sure instincts of the other great Roman commanders of his time, Marius, Sulla, Pompey, and Caesar. All were in exile at times but played for the main chance until it came. He could have made his peace at the latest after the death of Sulla and a brilliant future could have been reserved to him. Such a talent should not have been squandered in a losing enterprise. Ultimately, it was Sertorius' misjudgment that caused him to be "hunted as a rebel, with a price on his head; he was loyal to any Rome except the Rome of Sulla."[4] But that was the only Rome there was and it was fairly won by Sulla. Sertorius died like Colonel Kurtz (Marlon Brando) in the film *Apocalypse Now*, deranged in the wilderness, a casualty of the wrong side in the wrong war.

2. Caesar, Crassus, Pompey, Cicero and the War of the Gladiators

The quietly returning Caesar gained popularity by prosecuting Gnaeus Dolabella for corrupt practices in Macedonia and acted for Greek plaintiffs against an agent of Sulla. These were popular positions, and Caesar prefigured future political prosecutors, or at least accusers, from Cromwell and Robespierre to Thomas E. Dewy and Rudolph Giuliani. This was the focus of the first post-Spanish War controversy— the status of tribunes, which had been curtailed by Sulla. Gaius Aurelius Cotta, scion of a distinguished reform-oligarch, Whig family, a cousin of Julius Caesar's mother, facilitated the suspension of the prohibition on tribunes from seeking other offices. Cotta soon thought better of this, and so did the Senate, but the advance of the tribunes passed. The 70's were very difficult and politically tense; in addition to the perilous struggle in Spain, Mithridates bore constant watching in Asia; Macedonia was unsettled, and soon came the uprising of the slaves. All these military operations put even Sulla's reformed treasury under extreme pressure, and grain shortages almost produced general rioting in 75. Though strained, the Sullan constitution held

---

4 CAH, IX, p. 326 (Hugh Last).

through the difficult decade of the 70's.

Rome's state of belligerency reached its climax with the Servile Wars, or War of the Gladiators in 73 B.C. There had been repeated acts of slavish revolt on a small scale for centuries, but the slave population of Rome and of Italy was a distinct minority and was generally not severely mistreated as had usually been the case in Greece. A special case was the gladiators whose destiny was to kill each other or be killed by beasts in public entertainments. The more capable of them enjoyed a prolonged survival but they were all essentially doomed to a terrible and undignified death eventually. Seventy-four gladiators in a camp at Capua broke out and seizing whatever weapons they could, retired to the summit of Mount Vesuvius and rallied recruits. The Servile Wars of Sicily had been fought by slaves against Italians and this was a European gladiators' uprising: Gauls, Thracians, Teutons and Italians.

The leader was the Thracian Spartacus aided by two Gauls, Crixus and Oenomaus. In an astonishing comment reminiscent of Mommsen's lionization of Sertorius, Karl Marx called Spartacus "the finest fellow that the whole of ancient history has to show, a great general (no Garibaldi), a noble character and a true representative of the ancient proletariat." To this, Caesar's biographer Christian Meier responded: "This is of course, nonsense. In reality Spartacus seems to have been a robber chief on the grand scale; we have no evidence that his abilities and intentions went beyond this. His task was impossibly difficult—to lead a large motley undisciplined host that had no land, no military bases, no proper weapons, and no common objectives beyond plunder and rapine, in such a way that it could assert itself against Rome. This meant living and surviving as an excessively large robber band-somewhere, somehow. For a long time. Spartacus performed this task with bravura."[5]

Spartacus was a capable tactician and he benefited from having extraordinarily determined and capable warriors and from the official Roman underestimation of the difficulties that he could cause. Spartacus started from Vesuvius to the south and defeated the force led by Gaius Claudius Glabera, praetor. This attracted a flood of recruits so that both Spartacus and Crixus commanded separate armies. Spartacus moved north to break out of Italy and disperse his men to their freedom, but Crixus was too attached to the joys of brigandage in the south and kept his army plundering there which doomed him to eventual failure. In 72, Romans dispatched the two consuls, Lucius Gellius Publicola and Gnaeus Lentulus Clodianus, each with an army to suppress the slaves. Gellius caught up with Crixus near Monte Gargano and destroyed him and all of his force, but Gellius and Lentulus together had no success against Spartacus, who kept moving north, defeated both consuls separately in quick succession near Picenum; and both were dismissed by the Senate. Spartacus continued north and defeated a Roman army at Mutina (Modena) in the Po Valley, commanded by Gaius Cassius, proconsul of Cisalpine Gaul. and the whole of northern Italy was open. He could have crossed the Alps to freedom, but at this point, Spartacus too succumbed to the delusion of invincibility.

---

5 Christian Meier, *Caesar*, Basic Books, New York, 1982, p. 119. The film *Spartacus* (1960) took serious historic liberties and swaddled the story in a fictitious romance, but Laurence Olivier as Crassus, Kirk Douglas as Spartacus, John Gavin as Julius Caesar, Charles Laughton as Sempronius Gracchus, and Peter Ustinov as Lentulus Baratus memorably portrayed the characters and the general ambience of late Republican Rome.

Spartacus turned south and went all the way to Bruttium, apparently contemplating an embarkation for Sicily where he could revive the slave cause and dream of governing an independent island country. As was its custom, Rome finally responded comprehensively to the threat and sent out the praetor Marcus Licinius Crassus, at the head of eight legions with the mission of bringing Spartacus to battle and defeating and crushing his revolt before he could cross the Straits to Sicily, where he could become a durable nuisance. Crassus was cautious but imposed iron discipline on his own forces, which included the units battered in previous encounters with Spartacus. He tried to barricade Spartacus into the toe of Italy with a wall thirty-seven miles long behind which he hoped he would starve the slaves. It was an insane concept as even eight legions could not hold such a line in adequate depth to prevent breakage at a precise point, which Spartacus easily managed.

The Death of Spartacus by Hermann Vogel, 1882

At this point, Pompey returned from Spain and the popular masses agitated for his deployment against Spartacus. The Senate was resistless against such a sensible policy and Pompey departed with his Spanish veterans to "cooperate" with Crassus. Obviously, the prospects of the gladiators had darkened suddenly, and this trend was reinforced by the unexpected arrival of Lucullus with his victorious army from the Black Sea, forcing Spartacus swiftly northward, trying to retrace his steps of the previous year. Two Gaul gladiators, Castus and Cannicus, leading factions of their own, split from Spartacus' main column and imagined they could remain in the south. This and the unbidden approach of Pompey galvanized Crassus into action and in a complicated battle fought among the mountains between Paestum and Venusia he destroyed the forces of both gladiators and pursued Spartacus to the south and caught and overwhelmed him; Spartacus died in single combat in the battle, perishing valiantly as he doubtless would have had he persisted as a professional gladiator. He tried to reach Crassus but was cut down. Crassus rounded up the scattered surviving slaves and gladiators and lined the Appian Way from Capua to Rome with six-thousand crucified prisoners. The customary Roman timetable had been followed: tentative beginnings suddenly turning to overwhelming force and crushing victory. Slave discontent did not surface in Italy with any significance again for a long time. Crassus received some credit for his gruesome victory. Next to his support of Sulla's forced occupation of Rome, it was the finest hour in his uneven military career. (He was the greatest financier in Roman history.)

Spartacus' political significance was not great though he has been romanticized in modern times as a crusader for social justice, an absurd contention, as has been mentioned—like Stalin's pretense that his career as a bank-robber made him something of a Robin Hood. The chief political consequence of the Servile War was Crassus' resentment of Pompey's effort to seize the credit for the victory. Pompey returned heavy-laden with justly earned honors from Spain but made no significant contribution to the defeat of Spartacus (though he would certainly have defeated him had he had the chance). Crassus' resentment of Pompey would be a factor in the developing rivalry between Pompey and Caesar.

Gaius Julius Caesar was now twenty-nine. His was a second-echelon noble family and his aunt (Julia) married Gaius Marius. Caesar was evidently a brilliant young man, which is why he was put forward as Pontifex Maximus at age fourteen, when Marius returned to office for the last time. Caesar was close enough to the highest Roman circles to know the personnel and how the system worked but his family was not so successful that he was altogether of it, and he always combined in his cunning and precise calculations of self-interest the perspectives of both an insider and outsider: the insight of the first and the ambition of the second. Caesar knew how to flatter the pretentions of the Senate, and how to exploit its venality, factionalism, and frequent cowardice. Julius Caesar came to embody almost all talents: he was physically strong and athletic, and from all accounts, most authoritatively Cleopatra, an unsurpassable swordsman throughout his adult life.

He sought education and became and has always been regarded as a brilliant author with exact vocabulary and precise phraseology. His memoirs of the Gallic and Civil Wars have been revered as classics without interruption since they were written more than two-thousand years ago. He studied oratory at Rhodes and was acknowledged even by Cicero to be a brilliant public speaker. His campaigns do not, in decades of warfare, often against daunting odds, contain a single serious defeat. Some of his victories were stunning in their originality and improvisation. He generally ranks with Alexander the Great and Hannibal as the greatest classical military commander, and with them is put in the company of the very greatest later and modern commanders such as Genghis Khan (or his chief lieutenant, Subutai), Frederick the Great, and Napoleon. Jacob Burckhardt and Theodor Mommsen regarded him as "perhaps the most gifted of all mortals."⁶ His name came to symbolize natural state authority as in the adaptations Kaiser and Czar. He ultimately defeated everybody but did not take on more than he could accomplish as Alexander did and did not antagonize all others against him as Napoleon did. In the end, like Lincoln, he was vulnerable only to assassins. And although he would not live to reshape the Roman state or to leave a clear indication of how he wished to do that, he did clearly make the most brilliant selection of a successor of any great ruler in all of history. His grand-nephew and adoptive son and heir, Octavian (Augustus) Caesar would rule jointly and singly for fifty-eight years with incomparable virtuosity and success, seventy-two years in supreme office between the two great Caesars.

Julius Caesar was somewhat vain and stylish, often wearing a raffish toga, and he spent much of his political life in debt, from buying public favour with vast entertainments and banquets and circuses and other unscrupulous but routine political horse-trading and chicanery. His swagger offended many but there was always enough reason to attach credence to his self-regard that he was never reviled as a fop or a poseur; his talent was never doubted, and his sinister capacity for vengeance could never be ignored.

Sulla was instantly suspicious of him, both as a nephew of Marius and son-in-law of Cinna and he demanded that Caesar jettison his wife, Cinna's daughter Cornelia. Caesar declined and felt obliged to leave Rome while Sulla ruled there. (He eventually married Sulla's granddaughter.) He departed shortly after his successful prosecution of Dollabella, which made his reputation as a great Roman orator. Caesar studied rhetoric under the celebrated Apollonios Molon in Rhodes who had previously taught Cicero. On his voyage there he was captured by pirates six miles south of Miletus. They demanded a ransom of twenty talents and he rebuked them for not knowing who he was and offered fifty. He was in captivity for approximately forty days and behaved with aristocratic self-confidence, demanding quiet when he wished to sleep and composing and reading poems to his captors, while jocularly assuring them that he would execute them all in due course. Once his liberty had been acquired, he hired a few vessels at Miletus and pursued and captured the pirates who had captured him. He confiscated what they had plundered and when the governor of Asia hesitated to prosecute them, he had them strangled and then crucified. Episodes like this spread Caesar's legend quickly.

Pompey was six years older, and had a more influential father (though Pompeius Strabo was a widely distrusted scoundrel), and had a considerable head start on Caesar with a brilliant military career. With the end of the War of the Gladiators and the 70s, it was time for new leadership. Pompey was the inevitable man, but Caesar would not be far behind him.

Pompey returned to Rome amid widespread insistence that he be elevated to the consulate despite being six years beneath the age the Sullan Constitution stipulated (forty-two). Pompey took post at the gates of Rome with his legions and as an insurance policy on political events declared that he would support the return of the political tribune, a popular stance with the masses of Rome and Italy. Predictably, the Senate overcame its humbug and discovered that the bar to Pompey's election

---

6 Meier, Ibid., p. 17.

as consul was surmountable. The Senate capitulated and Pompey maintained his understanding with Crassus, who was elected consul with him in 70 B.C. With this development, the Sullan reforms had essentially failed: the senior army commander took over the headship of the government, resting on the loyalty to his own person of his legions, contrary to Sulla's chief constitutional objective. And the tribunes were free to terrorize the state as they wished and were indebted to Pompey for the restoration of their powers and in most cases their personal elections. Rome was almost back to a dictatorship, though Pompey, a young and exceedingly assertive man, was not as tested and respected in the challenges of military and political life as the previous dictator, Sulla, or his precursor, Marius, had been.

One issue that really did engage the interest of Pompey and Crassus was the poor quality of juries. Sulla's replacement of popular assemblies by juries staffed by senators did not produce improvement in the quality of verdicts and sentencing: the old families and the oligarchs were just as dishonest jurors as the bourgeoisie and the rabble. The whole Roman concept of citizenship, though it contained a husky notion of national pride and honor and the favor of deities when Rome was under foreign attack, did not much comport onerous requirements of civic duty such as taxpaying or jury service that became matters of considerable honor in more modern Western government.

Hostility and suspicion towards the Senate were widespread as, despite Sulla's best efforts and the warnings provided by the increasing presence and influence of powerful political generals, the Senate remained fractious and cynical and had failed in the reforming mission that Sulla's constitution had given it. The next controversy involving the integrity of the Senate arose from the return as governor of Sicily of Verres, who was universally condemned for corruption on a stupefying scale, and yet was defended by the great orator Hortensius, and other worthies including P. Cornelius Scipio, eventually Pompey's father-in-law. Verres was ultimately condemned after a brilliant prosecutorial performance by Cicero, establishing himself as the leading figure in the Roman courts for many years, and a political force in Rome. Finally, and chiefly because of the efforts of Lucius Aurelius Cotta, a cousin of Caesar's, juries were to be derived from three groups of relatively moneyed citizens, a compromise that did not wholly appease the popular masses but gave them the satisfaction of ripping this function back from the Senate, which rankled with the Senate but not as severely as giving it to mass popular vote would have done. The fact remained that the generals were no longer necessarily subordinate to the civil authorities. No one was really governing Rome other than when a military dictator asserted himself. The road was open to civil war.

Pompey and Crassus disbanded their armies and retired quietly after serving their consular terms. The replacements, Gaius Calpurnius Piso and Marcus Acilius Glabrio, were only elevated after an immense amount of semi-public bribery. And at the same time, two energetic popular tribunes of the crowd-pleasing kind, Gaius Cornelius and A. Gabinius, were elevated. They did accomplish significant reforms, and these contributed to the impression that the Senate's influence continued to decline. The Lex Cornelia forbade the determination of cases otherwise than by the criteria that had prevailed when magistrates entered upon their offices. Cornelius also managed adoption of a statute severely condemning bribery in elections; it is generally thought to have been somewhat useful.

In 68, the thirty-two-year-old Caesar departed Rome for Further Spain to assume his quaestorship. Just prior to leaving, he had spoken at the funerals of his wife Cornelia, Cinna's daughter whom he had refused to divorce when asked to by Sulla, and his aunt Julia, widow of Gaius Marius. Caesar spoke elegantly, implicitly highlighting his Marian (i.e., populist) connections, mentioned the legend that his and his late aunt's ancestry had been half royal and half divine. These comments were appropriate and not overly noticed at the time, but historians have often wondered if these references indicated Caesar's view that the Republic simply could not succeed and that some sort of monarchy would need to be put in its place.

3. Suppressing the Pirates

The problem of piracy had become so intense that it intruded upon Rome's commerce and was affecting the grain supply unfavorably and producing politically unpopular price increases. This was another military area where Rome had been patient too long and then responded by half measures, and a tremendous tide of public opinion quickly arose to the effect that the black-market activities in commodities of interest to Rome had to be stopped. Gabinius had six-thousand talents voted, which would be a considerable strain on the treasury, for a fleet of two-hundred sail, and an almost open-ended number of men and a staff of fifteen legates to support an admiral who was not identified other than that it had to be an ex-consul. This, as was certainly intended, was sufficient to satisfy the masses of Rome that Pompey was to be given this command. The debate was vigorous, replete with death threats and threats to fire the tribune as Tiberius Gracchus had done to Marcus Octavius in 133. As Rome warmed to the task and envisioned expansion of the required fleet to five-hundred ships and one-hundred and twenty thousand men, the appointment was conferred upon Pompey with practically unlimited powers of execution.

The pirates had taken hold of Cilicia and flourished because Rhodes and Egypt had declined, and Rome had severely limited Antiochus after the Battle of Magnesia—his navy could only contain ten vessels and could not sail west of Cape Sarpodonium. Similar restraints were applied to Mithridates, who was happy enough to make alliances with the pirates anyway; they rose like a monster and terrorized all of the Eastern Mediterranean. One explanation for Rome's lassitude was the extreme efficiency of the pirates at operating their slave market; next to Roman tax-farmers who enslaved provincial farm tenants, the pirates were the chief slaveowners and traffickers of the ancient world. One punitive mission was launched by Marcus Antonius in 102, and was deemed a success but was not a durable solution. They became so brazen, the privates sacked the temple of Samothrace while Sulla himself was on the island, and extended their cruises the whole length of the Mediterranean, enacting the cooperative alliance with Sertorius in 81 B.C.

While the pirate threat steadily expanded, Mithridates was attempting to reconstruct his empire that Sulla had left in shambles. He withdrew his son Mithridates Philopator as regent of Cholcis and executed him as a conciliatory gesture and prepared an expedition to attack the Bosporus. Sulla's successor, Murena, invaded Cappadocia on the grounds that Mithridates failed his treaty obligations there. The Pontic king appealed to the Roman Senate who upheld him, but Murena continued his offensive and Mithridates decisively defeated him, propelling the Roman army back into Phrygia.

With the death of Sulla in 78, Mithridates had made a formal alliance with the Cilician pirates and incited his son-in-law Tigranes, king of Armenia, to occupy Cappadocia. The Pontic king was also stirring up the Thracian tribes against the Roman garrisons in Macedonia. The Roman general Lucius Lucullus settled upon a plan to attack Mithridates through Phrygia. The campaign eventually settled on a siege of the city of Cyzicus, where Lucullus eventually prevailed, and annihilated approximately half of Mithridates' army, as the king took hurriedly to the sea to save himself. Mithridates was abandoned by all of his allies and was in a desperate condition but responded with heroism and determination. He conducted a war of maneuver against Lucullus in Pontus and withstood a siege at Amisus. In the next phase, however, he was overwhelmed by the Romans and only escaped capture by scattering some treasure from his retreating baggage train; for once the well-disciplined Romans paused to plunder even when their orders were to ride up the backs of the retreating enemy.

Lucullus, who was striking in every direction sequentially to complete the destruction of Mithridates, was generally victorious but never seemed able to close the campaign. His next gambit was the invasion of Armenia. He scored a brilliant victory over the combined forces of Mithridates and Tigranes at Lake Van, but the road to the Armenian capital of Artaxata was too treacherous; the weather in the foothills had become too cold. Lucullus' soldiers, like Rome, were tired of endless fighting with no conclusion and his men refused to continue. Lucullus was honorably superseded; the Romans retreated unvexed from Armenia, uncertain as they left, as they had been at the beginning, about what they were doing.

Pompey began his campaign against the pirates in 66 and he cleared practically all of the pirates of the Mediterranean within three months. It was an astounding achievement that deservedly won him the profound gratitude and admiration of all of Italy. It also demonstrated Pompey's extraordinary organizational and administrative talents. He never had anything remotely like a maritime command before and had no particular knowledge of maritime navigation, and the pirates were as good and dauntless sailors as the gladiators had been rebels. Pompey applied his customary principles of land war, divided the Mediterranean into thirteen zones and organized a force of two-hundred and seventy vessels and twenty legions. He focused first on the routes followed by the food supply and quickly accomplished a sharp increase in supply and welcome declines in the cost of grain in the domestic market. The pirates were even in infestations on the western Italian coast, so insolent had they become, but this made many of their more daring footholds vulnerable. Pompey interdicted pirate movement between the different zones, blockaded the pirates in their bays and coves, disembarked his legionaries, and they went through the pirate camps killing able-bodied men with abandon, looting everything that was valuable and burning everything else to ashes. Over four-hundred towns had to be cleared. Pompey obliterated the pirates in the western and central Mediterranean, defeated the pirate fleet at Coracesium and then besieged the pirates in their Cilician fortress, but they soon recognized that their plight was impossible against so relentless and powerful a foe. It was a campaign of genius, completed by a peace of equal brilliance: Pompey dealt gently with all those whom he felt had become pirates by default caused by economic hardship, and not from any vocation or ambition for brigandage. He treated these people with some solicitude and resettled many among the pirate-ravaged areas where they could constructively rebuild their lives.

When he returned to Rome in 66 he was the outstanding candidate to take the post-Lucullan command in the Mithridatic Wars which were about to resume. Sulla had not had time to complete his destruction of Mithridates, although he had roundly defeated him. The civil strife in Rome had become so severe that Sulla had no choice but to dictate a peace that his arms had won, in the knowledge that he would not be staying to enforce it. Pompey was the Grand Admiral, and it was proposed to add to his command of the Mediterranean, complete authority in Asia also, to enable him to finish the job that Sulla had so ably begun. This was almost as great a weight of authority as had been given to Marius to stop the Cimbri attack on Rome, and to Sulla as dictator. Cicero and Caesar both spoke in favor of this measure while the Senate traditionalists led by Hortensius and Catulus objected.

4. Pompey's Campaign in Asia Minor

Pompey took up his command as governor of Cilicia and Bithynia and commander of operations against the kings of Pontus and Armenia, while remaining grand admiral of the Roman fleet. It was a prodigious commission. He moved his headquarters to Halys, met with Lucullus in a session that began with compliments but ended in vituperation. This began a public relations campaign of vilification between the two men: Pompey dismissed Lucullus as a human tragedy whose victories were stage operations of no consequence, and Lucullus described Pompey as a carrion bird come to feast on the kill of others. It was a one-sided contest as Pompey had the legitimate command and the adherence of his forces and Lucullus was soon banished and silenced. Pompey gave him an escort of sixteen-hundred to assure his safe return back to Italy.

His first endeavor was a diplomatic mission to the Parthian king Phraates, to divide and conquer among his objectives. Mithridates and Tigranes, as well as Pompey were offering Phraates Western Mesopotamia as an inducement to join them against the other. Lucullus had made the same offer unsuccessfully, but it was undoubtedly the mighty prestige of Pompey and his immensely expanded force that persuaded the Parthian king to throw in with the Roman grand admiral and generalissimo. Phraates may also have been influenced by a son of the Armenian king who had "fled to the Parthian court because his father was unconscionably slow in dying and dangerously quick in sending undutiful sons before him."[7]

Phraates immobilized Tigranes and Mithridates was left to face Pompey alone. Pompey gathered together most of Lucullus' force and other remnants and loyalists

---

7 CAH, IX, p. 377 (H.A. Ormerod).

in Asia Minor and shaped it up quickly into an army of over fifty-thousand. Against this Mithridates had approximately thirty-thousand plus two-thousand cavalry and only about a third of these, mainly Italian fugitives and old Pontic veterans of unquestionable loyalty, were in first class fighting form. The Pontic king was an unenviable underdog. In the summer of 66, Pompey advanced from Galatia into Pontus. Though Mithridates shrewdly retreated along the Lycus River Valley and harassed Pompey as he had Lucullus with cavalry raids, skirmishes and miscellaneous guerrilla activities. Pompey had underestimated the strength of his opponent's cavalry, and recognizing his error, attempted to disengage towards lower Armenia in order to cut Mithridates off from Tigranes and to threaten the treasure that he had piled up in the region he was approaching. Mithridates was again too agile for that and barred Pompey's passage by occupying the fortress of Dasteira. He resumed his guerrilla activities, but his cavalry, repeating their mistake of 72 against Lucullus, became impetuous and Pompey trapped and almost destroyed them in an ambush. Reinforced by his reserve army, Pompey surrounded Dasteira and after a siege of forty-five days, Mithridates deceived the Roman night watches with false flares and evacuated all of his army except the wounded. Because he had saved his baggage train, his columns moved slowly, and Pompey was able to outpace him on a parallel route toward Armenia and then pounced in the middle of the night on the Pontic camp and decimated Mithridates' army. The Pontic king, elusive and resourceful as always, made his escape. But he had very little left to fight with; he was in exile from his kingdom and once again put himself at the mercy of Tigranes, which proved not to be ample.

Tigranes had effectively repulsed Phraates and had the pleasure of defeating his ne'er-do-well turncoat son, who determined to join Mithridates, but when he found out that Mithridates had been routed and was approaching his father with cupped hands, the young Tigranes tried to join Pompey. It was an almost ludicrous west Asian roundel of unscrupulosity and treachery. It was little wonder that the Romans looked with such disdain on almost all of them. We have seen a great deal of the ethical imperfections of Roman generals and statesmen, but in comparison with the East, they were pillars of virtue and integrity. Tigranes (senior) answered Mithridates' beseechings for assistance by offering a reward for his capture, dead or alive. The itinerant, homeless king made a hasty course correction and secured himself a port on the Black Sea in Colchis, where he tried to begin the collection of loyalists, malcontents, and adventurers, with whom he could try to regroup. Pompey ordered a blockade of Black Sea ports but did not strenuously enforce it as the Mithridatic threat had almost vaporized. Pompey did respond to the invitation of the younger Tigranes, who was showing promise as an oriental schemer, and crossed the Euphrates and journeyed towards the Armenian capital of Artaxata. Here the Armenian king came in panic to his capital and preemptively surrendered to Pompey. The Armenian wars ended without another arrow being shot.

The campaign of 66 closed on an obscure note when a nasty band of itinerant Albanians descended upon Pompey's winter camp in the shelter of Mount Caucasus. As the Roman forces were divided in three clearings, the attacking chief, Oroezes, thought the Romans could be taken unawares. Pompey was much too experienced a general to do without adequate sentries and lookouts in a distant land and it was not in the cards that Rome's greatest current leader, heavy with the honors of victory earned from the Ebro River over land and sea to the Euphrates River, would be overcome in his camp by a riffraff of marauding Albanians. Oroezes was beaten off without difficulty and sent fleeing for his life into the Caucasian winter.

The presence of Albanian forces in Armenia, no matter how unprepossessing their formations, was, it must be said, a considerable feat of nomadic adventurism, and Pompey did not leave it here. In the spring of 65, Pompey bluffed his way through what is now Georgia by a show of force that overawed King Artoces, and proceeded to the Black Sea coast, meeting up with a part of his vast fleet. He searched along the coast for a time for Mithridates but left him to the navy and devoted the balance of the year to the systematic conquest of the mysterious Albanians on the Caspian borderland. Like many conquerors who arrived approximately at this point, Pompey developed a fascination for opening relations across the Caspian to the Far East, a preoccupation that Seleucus I had also had. Returning to Armenia, he enticed the Albanians like a cat luring a mouse and staged a miniature Battle of Cannae, encircling the impetuous King Oroezes, and receiving his submission. It was suggested that Pompey at this point was attempting to impress Rome with the humbling of kings of unheard-of peoples bearing unpronounceable names. He concluded the year by capturing Mithridates' treasure castles in Armenia Minor and was mindful of the lesson of Lucullus not to exhaust his men, far from home who did not share their commander's fascination with exotic tribes and bands.

Pompey now looked upon Phraates, who courted him, as a doubtful ally and quasi-enemy but did mediate a peace between him and Tigranes. He sent his lieutenant, Gabinius, to conquer Damascus. In the spring of 64, Pompey went to Amisus on the Pontic coast and auditioned client kings and provisional rulers and started to prepare his general settlement of Asia Minor. This activity was interrupted by the reappearance of the imperishable Mithridates, who slipped past the Romans on the Black Sea to make war on his own son Machares, who had made peace with Lucullus in 70 and became the ruler of the Mithridatic towns in Russia. Mithridates won the allegiance of the native chieftains from his renown of decades of fluctuating survival and attacked and cornered his son and drove him to suicide—the Pontic royal house had even less regard for what might be called family values than most of the contemporary neighboring dynasties.

Mithridates now asked Pompey's acceptance of him as king of Pontus but a vassal of Rome, but Pompey, doubtless reflecting Roman opinion, was not going down this route again as Sulla had done with his hasty Peace of Dardanus in 85. The king rejected Pompey's demand for personal submission. In what was now a grand tour of the Middle East, Pompey proceeded to Syria, which outside the walls of Damascus was a chaotic place governed if at all by robber-bands. The ancient land of Syria was in a labyrinth of murderous confusion. Antiochus XIII, Asiaticus, whom Lucullus had accepted to be the ruler, had been kidnapped by Samsideramus, Sheikh of Emesa. But no one really had any authority except the arriving Romans. It was no better in Palestine, where the Maccabaeans were divided among themselves but quarreling with the Nabatean ruler Aratus III, who was besieging Jerusalem. Pompey and his lieutenants resolved these disputes in favor of Aristobulus II, the

Maccabaean contender whom they judged the most likely to be malleable to Roman desires, and they established him in control in Jerusalem.

5. Pompey, the Jews, and Egypt

This was the Romans' first serious contact with the Jews, and as all the world knows, it would become one of the most important relationships in world history, and would lead to the most momentous religious events ever recorded. Nearly five-hundred years after Babylon snuffed out the old Davidic Jewish kingdom, in the vortex between the weakening of the Seleucids and the arrival of the Romans, Israel was again independent and without a Gentile overseer, under the Hasmonaean Dynasty. The Hasmonaean high priest became the Jewish king, but with a growing estrangement between the royal house and the more religious section of the people which had helped elevate it. Aristobulus, the Roman protégé, conquered Galilee, which was largely a heathen population, the ancestors of Jesus Christ, and they were forced to be circumcised and become Jews by Aristobulus. He was succeeded by his brother Jannaeus (103-76), who combined the kingship and office of high priest and was the first Levite, as opposed to Davidic, king of Jerusalem. Jannaeus expanded across the Jordan, but was sharply rebuffed by the Nabataean king, Obodas I. The war was escalated by the insurgent Jews' recruitment of Demetrius III Eukairos, one of the princely Seleucid faction-heads and they defeated Jannaeus, until a large number of Jews rallied to Jannaeus rather than entrust their destinies to the great-great-great nephew of Antiochus Epiphane. Jannaeus beat down the Jewish rebels and had "eight-hundred of them crucified in rows where he could watch their dying agonies from the terrace of his palace in Jerusalem while he caroused with the women of his harem."[8]

Jannaeus was succeeded by his wife, Queen Salome Alexandra, apparently a religious sentimentalist, who elevated the Pharisees. With the death of Salome in 67, war broke out between the brothers, and Aristobulus prevailed, but an extraordinary contender arose, Antipater, who would dominate the Jewish state for twenty-four years. With the arrival of the Romans in 65, they immediately assumed decisive influence. Pompey himself arrived in Damascus in 63 and in Jerusalem a few months later and defeated the priestly aristocracy that clung to the Temple.

Pompey took the Temple of Jerusalem by storm after three months, and profanely entered it, but did no damage to it. The first Roman over the walls was Faustus Sulla, son of the dictator (who had always regarded Pompey as a talented egomaniac of unbalanced judgment—he considered Caesar more intelligent and ultimately more dangerous but did not live long enough to have any need to worry about either of them). Aristobulus, who blew his opportunity to be the Roman protégé, was packed off to Rome to be a trophy in Pompey's next triumph. This was the end of the Hasmonean dynasty and Hyrcanus was left as the nominal ruler of a reduced realm with the title of ethnarch as well as high priest. But the Roman proconsul of Syria would govern.

Between 63 and 55, the Romans had to subdue three rebellions, and the real

---

8 Ibid., p. 400 (E.R. Bevan).

director of the Jewish state was the Idumean Antipater, whose principal policy was to secure the favor of the ruler of the Roman world. This was complicated following 63 given the rivalry between Pompey, Caesar, and Crassus; Antipater's natural tendency was to rally to Pompey, whom he knew, but he was suitably cautious and took every opportunity to placate all of the contenders for the scepter of Rome. Antipater was poisoned by a domestic rival in 44, before it was clear who would emerge from the thunder clouds over Rome.

Antipater's son, Herod, had been governor of Galilee where he had contended with the local leader, Hezekiah. Herod regarded him as a brigand and suppressed and killed him, which to the people of Judea was a grievous crime. The governor of Syria, Sextus Caesar, Julius Caesar's cousin, summoned Herod to the Sanhedrin but as Herod had himself accompanied by a substantial armed guard, the occasion was an anti-climax. Sextus Caesar liked Herod and became his patron and for the balance of the first century, politics in Israel revolved around the rivalry between Rome and Parthia. Herod knew where his interest lay and in 40 B.C., he would make a virtual secular pilgrimage to Rome and succeeded in having himself proclaimed by the Senate: "the king of the Jews."

Herod would prove an astute and ruthless ruler who ground down those beneath them in the same measure that he venerated the undercarriage of his Roman sponsors above. He was an ethnic Edomite, a circumcised Jew by his professed religion, and more or less of a pagan in his religious practice; he was ideally equipped to manage the kaleidoscope of loyalties and hostilities and the cross-currents of ever-swirling events that made his native country so unimaginably complicated to govern successfully (traits it has substantially retained but harnessed and mastered successfully at last in the Twentieth Century).

As Pompey continued his grand tour of the Middle East, like a dustman sweeping up the debris of past kingdoms and empires, he came to the fringes of ancient Egypt. The Ptolemaic dynasty, after the death of Ptolemy VI Philomotor in 145 B.C., had gradually crumbled into a decadent regime where hideous strangulations, poisonings, and stabbings degraded any pretense of government from the fleshpots infested by the dynastic imposters of one branch and another of the collective Ptolemaic hedonocracy. Eunuchs, dwarfs, and mad women and deranged adolescents surged through the royal residences which subsisted with little real relationship to the condition of the bored, oppressed, and hostile masses of Egypt. Philomotor's son was rejected by the Alexandrian party which favored his brother Ptolemy Eurgetes II, nicknamed Physcon (meaning "Puffing Billy").

Physcon returned from Cyreneaica and occupied Alexandria without opposition, and reached an apparent settlement with Philipometor's sister, Cleopatra II, who agreed to marry another brother in exchange for retrieving a share of the throne of Egypt. As part of the bargain, she paid no attention when her husband dispensed with her child by her previous marriage. But she did become rather shirty when Physcon repudiated her in favor of her daughter by Philomotor, Cleopatra III. Cleopatra II appealed to the Alexandrians' human instincts and an apparently spontaneous wave of mob opinion rejected their former favorite Physcon, who was monstrously corpulent as his nickname implies. Physcon was able to beat down the rioters in almost constant civic combat for a year from 130 to 131 but was finally banished to Cyprus and Cleopatra ruled Alexandria. As a gesture of husbandly reproof, Physcon murdered their only child and sent his estranged wife the body with the limbs torn apart according to rules laid down for villains in Greek mythology and arranged for this grim token to arrive as a birthday present.

Astonishingly, in 129, he managed to return to Egypt and was apparently somewhat reconciled with the queen. But the reconciliation did not extend to the populace, and while they cohabited in the palaces of Alexandria, a protracted civil war raged across Egypt. This ferment eventually exhausted the country and in 118 an Act of Grace was issued in the name of the King, Queen Cleopatra the sister, and Queen Cleopatra the wife. This manifesto ambitiously demanded the end of the extortions and oppressions that had been crushing Egypt throughout these terrible disturbances.

This widespread civil chaos caused the area of Egypt under cultivation to recede badly from its former extent and the peasantry, who detested their Greek masters but could not remove them by rebellion, displayed great ingenuity of passive resistance and conducted an almost century-long work-to-rule in refusing to take up leases or do more than feed themselves from their masters' agriculture. Egyptian commerce was to some extent compensated by increased trade through the Red Sea and across the Indian Ocean. In 120 B.C., even the lethargic Physcon engaged a Greek adventurer, Eudoxus of Cyzicus, to explore the route from Aden to India with, as his pilot, a Hindu who promised to show him the secret of the monsoon, which he said could be manipulated to provide propulsion. Cleopatra III equipped a second expedition by the same captain, and he brought back from both cruises a rich cargo of spices and precious stones.

Ptolemy Physcon died peacefully in 116 B.C., leaving Cleopatra III as heir. He was ludicrous but also in his way a fantastic historical character. (The Egyptian King Farouk of the 1940's comes to mind.) Cleopatra selected her younger child as successor to the throne, but the Alexandrian mob thought otherwise and bestowed the crown upon Ptolemy VIII popularly known as Lathyrus, "Chick-Pea." They eventually had a falling out and the mobs were persuaded to expel Lathyrus. His brother was retrieved from Cyprus to reign as Ptolemy IX Alexander I, but skirmishing between them continued for many years. Cleopatra IV tried to compensate for her disembarkation from Egypt by marrying the Seleucid pretender Antiochus IX Cyzicenus. But he was routed by Antiochus VIII, who seized Cleopatra and had her hacked to pieces on the altar of Apollo at Daphne, where she had fled for sanctuary. "This sacrilege casts the fierce light upon the curse that was working itself out among the Ptolemies in mutual murder, for the ex-Queen's executioner was her own sister Cleopatra Tryphaena, the wife of the victorious Antiochus VIII. Nemesis claimed her next victim the following year, when Tryphaena fell into the hands of Cyzicenus and was immolated to join her murdered kinswoman."[9] Egypt was becoming completely unfeasible, and Pompey may have wondered how long it would be before he or one of his countrymen might find it necessary to stop this insane and degrading bloodbath. Rome was no paragon of impeccable civic government

---

9 CAH, IX, pp. 386-387 (H.A. Ormerod and M. Cary).

but retained some sense of official dignity.

After the death of Cleopatra III in 101, Ptolemy Alexander I became ruler of Egypt, but the mobs of Alexandria took against him and particularly resented his corpulence, which surpassed even that of his father (Physcon). He was driven from his throne in 89 B.C. in a military coup and although he recaptured Alexandria with Syrian mercenary forces, he despoiled the tomb of Alexander the Great in order to pay off his mercenaries and the Alexandrian mobs chased him out again. He was finally defeated in a naval battle in 88 and died making a final attempt to return. Each Alexandrian rebellion put further burdens on the people and embittered all the factions of the city and each wave of violence gave way to the next with increasing frequency and ferocity. Thebes (Egypt) was destroyed in 85 B.C. in another civil war.

Lathyrus died in 80 B.C. and was succeeded by popular concurrence in Alexandria by his daughter Berenice. She seemed to forget her stepson, who had been sent by his grandmother to the island of Cos to escape Alexandrian factionalism, had been taken up by Mithridates for a time, but subsequently escaped to the camp of Sulla, who almost adopted him, and he lived with the dictator in Rome for a time. Shortly after the death of Lathyrus, he arrived in Alexandria with a warrant from Sulla which no one in Egypt dared to dispute. The protégé of the Roman dictator was proclaimed Ptolemy X Alexander II and by taking his stepmother, Berenice, as his queen he resolved dynastic problems, but only for one day. The day after their blessed event he murdered his queen and sixteen days later, the city mob lynched the Ptolemy, oblivious to what Sulla's reaction might be. The Alexandrians put up the illegitimate son of Lathyrus, Auletes, but as he was the successor to Sulla's candidate, what became known as an "Egyptian Question" arose in Roman politics and hovered over Egypt. Throughout the 70's and 60's the absurd and horrible minuet of Ptolemaic court plots and coups continued. Ptolemy X purported to will Egypt to Rome as Pergamon had done and Crassus proposed its annexation but the Senate, probably disgusted by the spectacle of Egyptian dysfunctionalism, declined. Ptolemy Auletes, realizing that he was the focal point of such "Egyptian Question" as remained in Rome, generously offered Pompey the use of eight-thousand cavalrymen in Palestine. But Pompey remained aloof from the Egyptian quagmire and prepared his settlement for Asia Minor in 63 and 62. Egypt would have one more final flash of immortality, due to the mighty allure of the ultimate Cleopatra, and the dalliances on the Nile of Caesar and his chief lieutenant.

6. Pompey's Asian Settlement

As Pompey marched towards Petra, he finally received the news of the death of Mithridates. He had managed to raise a new fleet and an army of nearly forty-thousand in Russia, recruited from among the Balkan peoples, and planned to march up the Danube and across the Carnic Alps and into Italy, a concept reminiscent of Hannibal and anticipating Attila. That he would imagine such an expedition was illustrative of his imperishable ambition and his indomitable determination. But this force of purpose ultimately exhausted the loyalty of his subjects, who were terribly overtaxed and over-conscripted and practically none of whom had the least interest in invading Italy. In early 63, a revolt erupted against him in the Crimea which Mithridates subdued with his customary severity. He pardoned his discontented son Pharnaces, who had inspired the revolt and Pharnaces ungratefully responded by raising a second revolt that drove his father into the citadel of Panticipaeum. Pharnaces declined any compromise and Mithridates murdered his remaining children and his harem and after attempting to commit suicide by poison but finding it unable to overcome his resistance to it, he secured his own death from one of his Celtic bodyguards.

The Mithridatic Wars only ended when Mithridates was dead; he had been an implacable enemy, but a hopeless one. He built up a good aggregation of territories and allies that he dominated but like many local chiefs before him, he was transported by sheer delusion to imagine that he could challenge mighty Rome. He only gained a reprieve because of Sulla's need to return to protect his domestic political position and should not have returned to war against Rome. But he kept taking up arms after each fresh defeat until finally Pompey didn't have to bother with him anymore and he came to a pitiful and suicidal end in a remote corner of Europe. "In his last hopeless struggle against Pompey, Mithridates displayed a stubborn pluck like that of a wounded boar returning again and again to the charge. But success against the Roman Republic required either a military genius or a prophet and leader of a holy war…Mithridates knew how to buy servants but not how to win friends. As a father and husband, he out-Heroded Herod; in his political dealings he stooped to assassination whether by his own poniard or by the mass attack of headhunters. He was neither of east nor west and his Greek allies were bound to him only by dislike of Rome. He was a capable leader of guerrillas, but not a good general. He won skirmishes but lost battles. In a trial of strength with Rome's new professional army led by three of its ablest generals, he protracted the conflict but achieved no more than to delay a defeat that was certain."[10]

Pompey had been authorized to decree a settlement of Asia Minor as he wished and without the customary reference to a committee of the Senate. He enlarged Bithynia and Cilicia, annexed the island of Crete to Rome and incorporated Syria to assist its population against coastal raiders. Rome directly took over the whole seaboard of Near Asia except for Lycia, Cyzica, and Pontic Heraclea. But where military and strategic requirements did not require annexation, Pompey adhered to the traditional Roman policy of leaving these territories in a state of dependence but entrusted with the administration of their own affairs. He confirmed Pharnaces in his Russian possessions, a reward perhaps for finally ridding the world of Mithridates, and he gave the Galatia Chieftain Deiotarus an expanded territory, and the vaguely romantic King of Albania became a Roman vassal. Various petty dynasties and principalities received a semi-autonomous recognition. Ariobarzanes of Cappadocia and Antiochus of Commagene were confirmed in their positions and given pieces of Mesopotamia as reward for good behavior. He departed from the Seleucid policy of secularization and left the great Temple domains of Asia Minor under ecclesiastical administration. He made the son of Sulla's talented adversary, Archelaus, the high priest of the Pontic sanctuary of Ma. Beyond the Euphrates he somewhat

---

10 Ibid., p. 392 (H.A. Ormerod, M. Cary).

shortchanged Phraates of Parthia, which was already likely to be Rome's next rival in the region as its expansion continued. Pompey proclaimed special charters for the new or enlarged provinces, erected a large number of towns, and promoted urban life throughout Asia Minor. He maintained the liberties of the older cities and granted autonomy to the new ones. In general, all of these jurisdictions were required to pay taxes to Rome and only a few of the long-time tax immune allies such as Rhodes and Cyzica maintained that status. Pompey imposed a reasonable cap on the rapacity of the tax-farmers and retained the Roman practice of tax collection by privatized publicans.

At his great returning triumph in Rome in September 61, Pompey displayed placards which declared that he had conquered fifteen hundred and thirty-eight cities and a population of twelve million, one-hundred and seventy-eight thousand people and that he had carried the standards of Rome to the Sea of Azov and to the Red Sea. Pompey had retained discipline in his forces, almost entirely preventing plunder and sacking, and never lost control of his forces as Lucullus, and even to a degree, Sulla did. There was considerable truth to Lucullus' charge that he had done the heavy work and Pompey reaped the benefit, and with augmented forces at that.

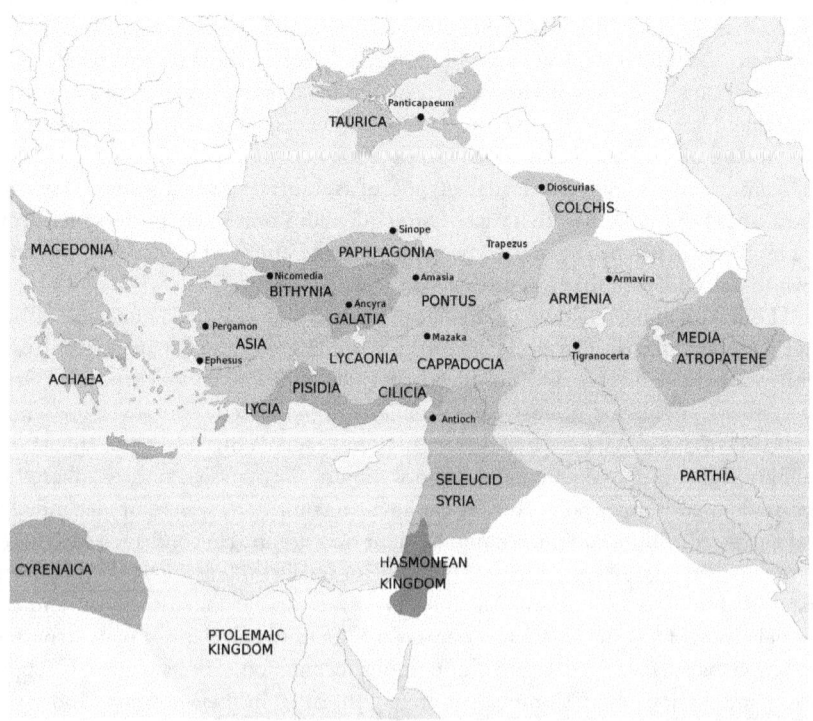

The Middle East, Greece and Asia Minor, 89 BC.

But if Pompey's command in the East was not as great a military challenge as Sulla had faced there or as had Metellus, Pompey's administrative arrangement was a masterpiece of jurisdictional planning and statesmanship. This campaign brought Rome the greatest accretion of wealth that it achieved from any of its foreign wars: after a very generous distribution of bounty among his soldiers he still had the modern equivalent of perhaps ten billion U.S. dollars to contribute to the Roman treasury, and he increased Rome's revenue from tribute-paying territories by seventy-five percent. In return for the taxes that he levied, the people of the near East enjoyed peace and prosperity such as had not reigned in Asia Minor since the fall of the Persian Empire. He cleared the seas of pirates, rescued Syria from anarchy, and almost entirely banished war from Asia Minor for generations. He did create flashpoints for future possible conflict with Parthia but if it came, it would be a war that Rome would enter upon from a position of great strength. And although it is not clear that he sought to do this, in promoting urban life in the Near East, Pompey gave new impetus to Hellenic civilization, laid the groundwork for a major economic renaissance, partially integrated the governance of the region and thus in considerable measure resumed the work of Alexander the Great after a lapse of two-hundred and fifty years.

Of all Rome's wars, only Caesar's immensely celebrated and brilliantly executed conquest of Gaul would rival and even surpass Pompey's success in Asia Minor. These two great events in almost direct succession to each other would raise the might of Rome to a level that could scarcely have been imagined even fifty years before.

7. Political Developments in Rome in Pompey's Absence: The Catilinarian Conspiracies

Pompey returned to Rome in 61 after an absence of five years. His prodigious accomplishments for the state had been gratefully noticed, but Rome had been seething with political intrigue and activity throughout his service in the Eastern Mediterranean and Asia Minor. While Pompey held the political destiny of Rome, in keeping with age-old habit, the envious senators schemed and harassed his followers. A pro-Pompey tribune, Gaius Cornelius, who would criticize the corruption of some senators and praetors, was accused of the ludicrous offense of "contempt of the government." Pompey's supporters in his absence were numerous and they did not respond passively; there were frequent outbursts of mob violence at public political meetings, and special police had to be enrolled to maintain security in the courts.

The lengthy and complicated sequence of Catilinarian conspiracies followed the consular elections of 65. The ostensible winners of the election, P. Autronius Paetus and P. Cornelius Sulla (a nephew of the dictator), had led the polls but been disqualified by being judged guilty of bribery. A third candidate, L. Sergius Catilina, was prevented from standing for election. Catiline, as he is generally known, was the continuing heir of a patrician family that had fallen on evil days, and he was intent on reviving it. He was much admired as a senior officer of Sulla in the Civil Wars and was a swashbuckling leader and comrade.

But he also attracted much criticism for his extravagance and a reckless disregard for human life, both of opponents and his own men. He was one of Sulla's principal agents in the proscriptions, in which he acquired a reputation for bloodlust and mindless violence and was suspected of disposing of a few relatives and personal enemies in the name of the dictator. He was elected praetor in 68 and pro-praetor of Africa in 67. But on his return in 66 he was accused of and tried for extortion. It was on this basis that he was not allowed to proceed with his candidacy for the consulate. This was an arbitrary decision of the incumbent consul, Volcacius Tullus. From here, events precipitated themselves.

The three disqualified candidates agreed on a plot to murder the two elected consuls, to elevate Paetus and Sulla in their place, who would then support the election of Catiline as consul in 64. The plan was to assault the targeted victims on the first day of 65 when the new consuls would be at the Senate house on the Capitol, and to seize the fasces on behalf of the deprived candidates. It was also agreed that a number of other joint enemies would be murdered without any due process, including Volcacius and his circle. A number of other conspirators joined them, most conspicuously Gnaeus Calpurnius Piso. Sulla was the person who bankrolled this mad scheme, and it shortly emerged that insofar as there were any brains behind it, they belonged to Catiline. It was preposterous to imagine that the Senate would acquiesce in any such assault upon it, or that it lacked the generals and political leaders adequate to see off such a disreputable enterprise. On New Year's Eve, Catiline was conspicuous in some of his preparations and the Senate empowered the two consuls-elect to assemble a bodyguard and on the day of the intended coup they deterred the attack. The consuls served their terms.

An investigation was launched but was quickly suspended when a tribune raised objections. Further, the unqualified Piso was appointed by the Senate to be the governor of Nearer Spain apparently and according to the historian Sallust, under pressure from Marcus Crassus. Crassus was the wealthiest man in Rome and probably its most feverish political schemer; he was constantly recruiting amongst Rome's numerous community of compromised politicians and undoubtedly had bought the service of a sizable number of senators and lesser political figures. He had much to fear from Pompey's return, especially if it resembled in the slightest degree the hecatombs produced by Marius and Sulla when they returned to Rome.

It seems that the appointment of Piso was pressed by Crassus to give himself substantial influence over the gold and silver resources of Spain, so vital to the financing of the more ambitious endeavors of the Roman government. With that said, there is no reason to believe that Crassus approved of the original Catalinarian conspiracy: it was amateurism and mere assassination with no prospect of success. He appears to have intervened only after the fact to patronize the conspirators and recruit them to more intelligent plans. He had miscalculated, however, in sending to the turbulent and challenging jurisdiction of Spain so rank an incompetent as Piso. The new governor deeply offended the Spaniards, historically infinitely sensitive and violently resentful, and local Spanish interests lost no time in taking the measure of Piso and they murdered him after only a few months of frolicking in his lofty position.

Crassus was already focusing on the most absorbent of all political quagmires, late Ptolemaic Egypt, where Crassus professed to take Ptolemy Alexander II's bequest of Egypt to the Roman people seriously (Section 5 of this chapter). Crassus had a friendly tribune bring before the Concilium Plebis a motion to accept the bequest. The principal favorable arguments were the great treasures of the house of Ptolemy and the security that would be provided by Egypt's grain supply. There were senatorial objections on the grounds of the traditional and well justified Roman policy of steering clear of Egypt, but the chief architect of the rejection of Crassus' proposal was Cicero. It is a considerable affirmation of his oratorical powers that he carried his case before a large popular assembly, which might have been thought susceptible to influence by reference both to the treasure and cheap grain that Egypt would provide. Cicero had adopted the role of being in effect a representative of Pompey's interest in absentia in this period. It is hazardous to speculate on Cicero's motives, but he likely considered Pompey to be the emerging principal Roman statesman of the next decade and one who was a good deal more scrupulous than Crassus and from the standpoint of respect for the Senate and the Republic, more reliable than Caesar.

Crassus, who had been elected censor for the year 65, now proposed immediate full citizenship for the population of Transpadane Gaul. That jurisdiction was now the chief recruiting ground for the Roman armies but still languished in the status of being a Latin affiliate of Rome and not a province. Crassus did not immediately attain his objective of enfranchising that semi-province but his effort to do so was well appreciated there. This was the tactic employed by Carbo in the Civil War against Sulla when he enfranchised the Samnites. It seems that the grateful Transpadanes sent a delegation of armed men to assist Crassus' designs; as in 64, the Senate felt it necessary to expel all Transpadanes from residency in Rome. This was accomplished by a tribunician law that made all non-citizens liable to eviction. It offended a great many people and was an unwise political gambit by the Senate.

The duel between Cicero, who now fancied himself the defender and watchdog of the Republic, and Crassus continued into the consular elections of 64. There were three serious candidates, and one of these was Catiline, who had been acquitted of the charge of extortion in Africa (though he was undoubtedly guilty). His defense, astonishingly, had been energetically and effectively conducted by the consul Manlius Torquatas, whom he had conspired to murder. Torquatas gave a stirring defense of Catiline's character, and he was assisted by the prosecutor P. Clodius' allowing some notorious supporters of Catiline to be impaneled as jurors. Once confirmed as a candidate, Catiline bribed on an historic scale, running himself heavily into debt. There can be little doubt that the paymaster was Rome's premier plutocrat, Crassus. The historical betting has been that Crassus' principal motive at this point was to set up a coalition of deterrence against a return by Pompey to Rome that would in any way replicate the occupation of the city and the imposition of a personal dictatorship, for which the return of Sulla was a vivid and recent precedent.

Catiline and Crassus recruited as a consular running mate the ne'er-do-well Gaius Antonius, son of the famous orator Marcus Antonius, but someone whose career had been devoted to "pilfering and profligacy."[11] What made this election particular-

---

11 Ibid., p. 483 (M. Cary).

ly remarkable was the presence as the chief competing candidate of Marcus Tullius Cicero, evidently the most distinguished claimant to the honor. He was still young and genial and full of optimism and had attracted a great deal of admiration and respect in Rome. Though somewhat scheming in the manner of an academic dilettante, he was a man of integrity as well as great talent. He would eventually be out of his political league contending with Julius and Octavian Caesar and their enemies and with great faction heads of Roman public life such as Cato the younger, Brutus, even Mark Antony, and certainly Pompey. By any reasonable measure, Cicero was more than a match for a violent scoundrel like Catiline, but Catiline supported by Crassus represented a threat that Cicero was not especially well-equipped to meet.

Cicero had offered himself as counsel to Catiline's trial, presumably as a cautionary tactical political maneuver, but Catiline had contemptuously rejected the overtures of this son of a country worthy presuming to assist a member of the (decayed) patriciate. But Catiline misplayed his hand as a candidate and Cicero was able to incite fears that another conspiracy might be afoot. His witty condescensions to Catiline's capacity and tendencies to violence were appreciated by the voters and resonated in the Senate. Cicero won the election, followed at a distance by Antonius; it was a respectable but humiliating third place for Catiline.

As soon as Cicero took his place as consul, he was embroiled in an extensive controversy over a comprehensive land bill presented by P. Servilius Rullus, who was reviving the old measure of Tiberius Gracchus but with a vast expansion of land appropriation and reallocation throughout the entire Roman-governed jurisdiction, including affiliated and unoccupied states such as Egypt. While on its face, like all of these land reform measures, it had the attractions of equity, resettlement, and the satisfaction of legitimate and long pent-up ambitions, it also contained measures so arbitrary and authoritarian that they rightly excited the wariness of conservative and even moderate elements in the Roman political community. In fact, Rullus appears to have been fronting yet another scheme for the fecund Crassus. As Rome's leading real estate owner, developer, speculator (and operator of his own arson service and fire department), Crassus seems to have changed course from obstructing Pompey and began lining up a vast allotment and settlement scheme for Pompey's veterans to smooth an alliance with the returning hero who was now expected in Rome within the next year or so. Cicero attacked his measure, as he historically attacked the Gracchan schemes, somewhat reflexively and with exaggerated ridicule, dwelling on tiny points and magnifying them absurdly. For good measure, he effectively bribed Gaius Antonius, who was supposed to sit on the board of allocation for the administration of the land reform scheme. Cicero offered Antonius a proconsular province and faithful to the ethos of his preceptors, Atonius defected from Catiline. Time had now run out for Crassus' maneuvering in anticipation of Pompey's return. There was nothing for it but to wait for the returning conqueror to play his hand.

It was now, finally, the turn of Gaius Julius Caesar. Though, as has been remarked, Caesar was a powerful orator, he was not always effective in the law courts, although he did win a number of cases. His talents were better and more rewardingly deployed whipping up electoral audiences and constituencies, not excluding the raw-boned rabble of the streets of Rome and the slums of the Aventine. His efforts were complemented by a great talent as a showman: he regularly staged gladiatorial games and beast hunts during his aedileship (65). Building on this steady accumulation of popular and influential support, Caesar launched a carefully calculated electoral assault in 63 and 62 to set himself up in a strong position for Pompey's return. The death of Metellus Pius created a vacancy in the chief pontificate, on its face an unlikely target for the ambitions of Caesar, who was not known to be a pious or in his romantic life a remotely circumspect man. This position had been, naturally, a preserve of the elders, but Caesar directed one of his lieutenants, Titus Labienus, to present a measure in the Concilium Plebis which transferred the choice of Pontifex Maximus to an electoral College of seventeen tribes by lot. In fact, Caesar was effectively enabled to rig the election and he staked his own last cent on his campaign. It is said that on election day morning he told his mother not to expect him back unless he won, as he would not be able to face either her or his creditors. As would often prove the case in his career, the luck of the fearless but cunning gambler did not desert him. He defeated two previous consuls and set about refreshing his office as one of moral authority and influence. It undoubtedly assisted him in his successful campaign for a praetorship the following year, which comported the right to a provincial governorship and a high military command. He was making his move at last. (He was only thirty-seven, six years younger than Pompey.)

In the mid-60's, Caesar made an alliance of convenience with Crassus, in order to service the immense debts he was piling up as he courted public opinion with his circuses and festivities and general largesse. Unlike the run of Roman politicians that Crassus manipulated as far as their serviceability allowed, much less the Catilinarian lower varieties, Caesar was a very respectable candidate as an ally of Crassus, sufficiently formidable and endowed with his own ambition to join him in a powerful counterweight to Pompey. Financing Caesar's activities was a far more sensible investment for Crassus than all his nonsense with Catiline and Piso and the political cesspool of Egypt.

Caesar does seem to have collaborated with Catiline in 64, having stayed well clear of him in the initial plot. He favored some elements of allotment reform and definitely supported the enfranchisement of the Transpadanes for whom he would prove a durable and efficient champion. In other areas, Caesar's political judgment was much superior to that of Crassus: he had supported sensible, moderate rule through the early 60's and was careful at all times to avoid any disparagement or harassment of Pompey, of whom he always spoke respectfully. There is no reason to believe that he approved of any of Crassus' schemes, but was only using, indeed manipulating, the political financier's vocation for intrigue and factional sponsorship to build up his own career as quickly as he could before Pompey returned from the East to reassert his influence. Caesar frequently in these times reflected critically on the vindictiveness of Sulla and other victorious generals in recent conflicts. While these retroactive reflections were not particularly influential, they do reveal that Caesar, compared to most of his rivals and immediate precursors, was a man of conciliation who possessed the maturity of judgment and the self-confidence to stay well clear of acts of excessive severity. In the end, his moderation would prove a vulnerability. In 64, Caesar was appointed chairman of the court for the trial of murders and attempted to prosecute two of Sulla's executioners. This was a mistake in that the accused benefited from an indemnity and it unnecessarily stirred up controversy and the animosity of the Sullan party. It led to a counter-charge against Catiline whom Caesar was, in cooperation with Crassus, assisting at the time. It was for Caesar an unusually maladroit imbroglio, but he eluded it through a series of delays and lateral moves.

Less innocuous and less explicable was a political trial Caesar generated in 63 against Senator Gaius Rabirius for having participated in the killing of Marius' disreputable ally in 100 B.C., Saturninus. Caesar's sense of the dramatic caused him to be carried away to the point of alleging an ancient act of high treason which he wished to be tried before the Concilium Plebis, and he requested that the judges be drawn by lots. They turned out to be his distant cousin Lucius Caesar and himself, whereupon Caesar condemned Rabirius and in accord with an archaic criminal provision required that the defendant be tied to a cross and suspended from a barren tree. This farcical and outrageous proceeding was quashed by Cicero on his consular authority. Caesar then relaunched the case before the Consilium Plebis on minor charges to which he added a murder indictment. Cicero then returned to the issue as defense counsel and purported to construe it as an affront to the consul in the year of the alleged offense, the man whose cause Caesar was attempting to uphold, the late Gaius Marius. Caesar then arranged for the red flag on the Janicular Hill to be lowered, which in ancient times meant the warning of an attack on the city, an absurd dramatic flourish which signaled the end of this ludicrous proceeding, "that throughout had smacked of comic opera. Whatever lesson Caesar intended to convey by the prosecution of Rabirius was lost in the strangeness of its mis-en-scène."[12] These episodes revealed the gimcrack and cheesy aspects of Caesar's political antics, traits that were less frequently manifest as his status rose and he transitioned from political office-seeker to provincial governor and combat general and beyond.

Caesar also caused a tribune to bring a bill for the reinstatement of the status and property of the children of Sulla's victims. This was thrown out by Cicero who claimed that Sulla's laws must be accepted or declined altogether, and it was not until fourteen years later that Caesar was able to secure justice for these victims. While the initiative was not a success it did again reveal Caesar's wish to bind up the wounds of these terribly divisive years in Roman political life.

With his defeat in the election of 64, Catiline lost the support of Crassus, who now had to make his peace with Caesar and lock arms and attempt to withstand the force of Pompey when he returned. But Catiline was determined to seek the consulship again, and not having the resources for such an extravagant campaign as on the previous occasion, he ran as the candidate of a clean slate promising the cancellation of all debt, one of the oldest and shabbiest demagogic tricks of all. This was apparently a pitch to the rural poor as their welfare was ground down by the tides of movement over Italy and the acquisition by Rome of access to cheap grain abroad. No class of the population had been more laboriously plundered and exploited, but relatively few of them voted in Roman elections as they were poor and scattered outside the city. The real target was a somewhat threadbare nobility, who despised

---

12 Ibid., p. 490.

money and had little aptitude at the accumulation or even conservation of it and yet could be very influential wire-pullers in rotten boroughs at election time, and despite their airs and graces, few of them scrupled over acceptance of such an enticement.

Once again, Cicero was the chief enemy. He had many of the creditor class among his clients and supporters and his cause was assisted by a financial panic which caused a sharp tightening of credit. Catiline's frequent boastfulness made it easy for his opponents to raise once again the alarm of a potential coup d'état. Cicero's tactics were successful and Catiline was defeated again. Instead of cooling Catiline's ambitions or causing him to become more conventional and respectable in his pursuit of them, this further defeat drove him to more dangerous extremes. Catiline's immediate aim was to create a vacancy in the consulship that he could fill, though there were undoubtedly many scores to be settled as well. He prepared for an outright insurrection. He gathered approximately sixteen disgruntled senators, engaged Lucius Manlius, one of Sulla's ex-officers, to raise disgruntled colonists and he arranged for a march on Rome from Praeneste, twenty miles away, on October 28, 63 B.C. While Catiline observed more than his usual discretion, some of his confederates did not and rumors spread. Crassus, who had abandoned Catiline, arrived at Cicero's house at midnight in mid-October and deluged him with a packet of incriminating letters from Catiline. Cicero summoned the Senate and announced the date of the intended murders, yet the Senate was content to instruct Cicero to make further inquiries. Cicero shortly conveyed that Manlius and his gladiators were en route and the Senate proclaimed a state of emergency and delegated all powers of defense to the consul.

Cicero forced the gladiators to withdraw to Capua, mobilized the militias and commissioned the praetor Metellus Celer to raise new levies. In the absence of irrefutable evidence against him, Cicero would not take the chance of arresting Catiline and the anticipated date of the coup passed with nothing occurring. Catiline finally got down to trying to organize a coup against Rome on the night of November 6-7, 63. He started fires in different parts of Rome and called out the slaves that would collude and he also, ironically, attempted to stir up a general revolt of farmworkers throughout Italy. Cicero learned of an attempt to force open his house and remove him from it and had the opportunity to deploy adequate security to prevent success of the Catalinarians in Rome. Catiline left Rome on November 9, a fact which Cicero revealed to a large and enthusiastic public audience. Delays caused his partisans in Rome to wonder if they should try and carry out a coup anyway and they determined to call out the slaves and attempt to take over the city on December 17. But by their own amateurish indiscretions they gave the plot away, ruined Catiline's final hope, and put themselves, bound and noosed, on the gibbet to be executed for treason.

In November, Catiline's chief lieutenant in this flickering plot, Lentulus, tried to bring over a tribe of Gauls to the impending coup attempt. But they informed upon the conspirators, who were overpowered and captured with massive incriminating documentation. Because most of those detained were senators, they were allowed to reside in the private homes of prominent Romans pending their trials. Cicero had all the burgesses of Rome sworn as special constables and had the official areas of

Rome swarming with reliable security. Practically all of Roman opinion supported Cicero and condemned Catiline. Catiline now determined to flee Italy into Gaul, but Metellus Celer, who had pacified central Italy, closed the Alpine passes of Pistorius and Bononia. Antonius was now leading the search for the fugitive (his former champion), and with Manlius and a handful of followers Catiline was found at bay near Pistorius. In the battle that followed in January 62, Antonius was the first casualty. Catiline fought to the end and died bravely, one of history's more storied villains though because of the times and the personalities amongst whom he moved, not because of any Satanic distinction of his own personality or intelligence.

A professional informer named Lucius Tarquinius mysteriously attempted to implicate Crassus in the final Catiline conspiracy, but he had no evidence and no credibility, and his attempt was completely unsuccessful. The Ciceronian magic also started to wear off, as he soon began implying that Caesar had supported the Catilinarian conspiracies, but Caesar faced him down and ridiculed his complete lack of evidence. Throughout the year 62, defendants were tried. Antonius was exiled and Sulla was defended successfully by Cicero. However, in respect of those who really were guilty, Cicero suddenly and uncharacteristically determined that the prisoners against whom there was a strong case should be summarily executed. Using his magisterial authority, he secured the adoption of a decree of Senatus Consultum Ultimum, and although this should not have occurred in place of due process, once the accused were disarmed and incarcerated and the Republic was not in danger, most senators supported Cicero's motion.

At this point, Caesar made a powerful intervention casting doubts on the legality of Cicero's proposal and recommending that the plotters should be interned for life. Though he began as the sole advocate of such a course, so powerful were his arguments that Cicero's support seriously eroded, and he was unable to reply effectively to Caesar's arguments. The matter was only settled when Marcus Cato, a tribune-elect, delivered a fierce moralistic address worthy of the tradition of his great-grandfather, apart from his full and defamatory insinuations that Caesar was complicit with Catiline. The clinching argument made by Cicero, and reinforced by Cato, was that prompt measures would have a wholesome moral effect. The accused were executed at once.

The most important development in this final phase was the antagonism between Caesar and Cato, which soon escalated to a place of high importance in the politics of Rome. Caesar was now the advocate of constitutional propriety and Cato of rough justice. Caesar's general championship of conciliatory measures and avoidance of severity was both statesmanlike and politically effective. Caesar came through this crisis well and impressed all factions. The golden rise of Cicero had been blunted, and a few days after the end of these proceedings the tribune Q. Metellus Nepo began a rhetorical campaign against what he regarded as Cicero's illegal conduct and in 62 he introduced into the Concilium Plebis a bill inviting Pompey to rescue the Constitution from what he described as Cicero's "autocracy." Caesar supported this measure, presumably in revenge for Cicero's defamation of him as a Catilinarian sympathizer, and Cato, true again to the family tradition of incompetent, impulsive political misjudgment, attacked both Caesar and Pompey, who between them, now commanded almost all of Roman opinion.

With this, the hothead Metellus Nepo called for mob violence as a public protest against Cicero, and the Senate suspended civil government and then escalated to another Senatus Consultus Ultimum under which Metellus would certainly have been singled out for murder in the manner of Gaius Gracchus or lynched in the manner of Saturninus (Chapter 8). Caesar had disregarded much of the wrath of the debate and in one of the outstanding episodes of his career he publicly dissuaded Metellus from recourse to extremes. It was theater; Metellus' attack upon Cicero was designed to assist in securing for Pompey a commission to save Roman society from his domestic enemies (indicating that Pompey did not attach much value to Cicero's support). It was an attempted preparation of a virtual Sullan dictatorship (though it is not clear that this was Pompey's objective). Caesar suavely deescalated the crisis.

Pompey's return was now imminent; the real issue would be whether he would disband his army and reintegrate himself into the traditional power structure of Roman politics or follow the Sullan tradition of attempting to impose a dictatorship upon Rome. Cato had sought a tribunate in order to shut down Metellus. Caesar, much more clear-sighted and imaginative, thundered his opposition to Cicero and Cato while proffering an alliance with Pompey and reaching behind to lock arms with Crassus, that they might present Pompey a sufficient obstacle to a Sullan solution; and that some community of supreme interest between Pompey, Caesar, and Crassus might emerge to stabilize the Roman world and satisfy the ambitions of all three of its chief protagonists.

Pompey had rendered mighty service and enjoyed great prestige. But he was even more unproven in politics than Caesar was in war. In Rome those who conquered were envied as much as they were admired, and in setting himself at the head of those who wished to withhold absolute power from Pompey, while holding himself out as Pompey's chief natural ally, Julius Caesar eased himself into the critical strategic position. The issue would become whether Pompey could master Roman politics as well and as swiftly as Caesar could acquire and lead a great Roman army. Both were necessary to govern more or less independently of the Senate. Sulla was the only leader who had done this.

Rome ruled, though its leadership was divided. It would now spend nearly three quarters of a century under the sway of the two men who, along with Alexander the Great, would be the most formidable leaders in the western world prior to modern times: Julius and Octavian (Augustus) Caesar. The importance of these events would be immortalized by William Shakespeare.

CHAPTER TWENTY-FIVE

THE FIRST TRIUMVIRATE, CAESAR IN GAUL, CRASSUS IN PARTHIA

❧

CROSSING THE RUBICON, 62-48 B.C.

Marble head of Marcus Licinius Crassus

Vercingétorix Memorial in Alesia

1. Cicero's Moment and Pompey's Return

CICERO WAS STILL much honored for his coolheaded success in dealing with the Catalinarian conspiracy. There were widespread petitions of support and thanks to him and he proclaimed the Concordia, the agreement of all good men, on moderation and respect for Roman institutions. Having had to turn as a single-minded leader preserving the forces of legitimacy against Catiline, Cicero now would try his hand at conducting Pompey back into support of senatorial government. Cicero wasn't an adequately competent politician to realize clearly all the reforms that urgently needed to be enacted by Rome to refresh the ranks of the Senate, insulate the city better against rioters and assassins, and reduce the economic parasitism that Rome was responsible for inflicting on some of the provinces. This serene coalition of people of goodwill was, as might have been expected, a dream of Cicero's, and it frayed quickly.

A couple of ludicrous incidents were its undoing. In December 62, a young patrician, P. Clodius, entered the Regia, the official residence of the Pontifex Maximus, trans-dressing as a female and intruded upon archaic worship whose rights were forbidden to men. The Senate embarked most soberly on an investigation of the scandal establishing a special court and allowed the jurors to be drawn by lots from the ordinary panels which enabled Clodius' patron, the inevitable Crassus, to bribe the jurors in the normal way. Better known and more damaging to the credibility of the political arrangements was the reputational loss to the chief pontiff himself. On the rumor that Caesar's third wife, Pompera a daughter of the consul of 88 B.C., had been the object of Clodius' intrusion, he divorced her, though he declined to give evidence against Clodius. When asked why he had acted as he did, he famously replied that "Caesar's wife must be above suspicion." Given his extraordinarily well-known and flagrant womanizing, the whole proceeding which had begun solemnly descended into low farce.

The other incident, at the end of 61, was of the company of tax collectors' attempt to buy the right to collect the taxes in the province of Asia. It was discovered that the head of the bid had petitioned for a rebate. Crassus was the financial interest behind them but his influence in the Senate was ineffectual against resistance of Marcus Cato, who pettifogged and filibustered the proposal to an end.

Pompey would not be returning to an august political scene in Rome with the entire state arrayed in its dignity and on its best behaviour. But to the immense relief of almost everyone, he disbanded his army when he landed at Brundisium in December 62, and proceeded to Rome escorted by a small guard. In Rome he went almost directly to the Senate and addressed them with great humility and in earnest. He confirmed in all respects his acceptance of the regime as it had evolved and pressed just two entirely reasonable requests, for one who had rendered such prodigious service to Rome. Pompey sought the confirmation of his settlement of the East and the normal arrangements to settle approximately forty-thousand of his veterans with suitable land and arrangements.

Cicero stepped back into the role of Pompey's advocate and fancied himself something of a counselor to Pompey, although where Cicero imagined that he had acquired the standing to be such a source of tactical political advice eludes the imagination. More surprising is the failure of the Senate to grasp its opportunity: for five years it fretted about Pompey's return. When it came, none of the fears of the Senate that Pompey would like to lead the masses in Roman politics as Marius had done or impose a military dictatorship that would disregard the Senate completely as Sulla had done, proved justified. As so often since the murder of the Gracchi, the Senate again completely overplayed its hand.

Pompey had even suggested marrying into Cato's family, but Cato, always mistrustful of victorious generals, would not hear of it. It was now appreciated that Pompey had never been as politically ambitious as Marius or Sulla or Caesar; he was a general, but he liked applause more than power as long as he was adequately respectfully treated. He could have been the perfect collaborator for the Senate and Cicero could have been useful in coordinating a gentle Pompey on leadership in cooperation with the noble families and keeping Caesar at bay, though this would not under any circumstances have been easy, and Cicero was not the man to do it. The Senate dithered and havered and a tribune favorable to Pompey, Lucius Flavius, introduced a land purchase scheme at the Concilium Plebis. This was an inexcusable humiliation to inflict upon Pompey and the Senate would soon pay for it. They were effectively inviting him to recall his troops to the colors and teach the Senate a lesson, but from some combination of fatigue after a long and distant campaign and what observers identified as an increasing tendency to indecision, as well as the desire to be admired rather than to actually rule, Pompey did nothing. But he did have, and had certainly earned, an immense triumph.

However, the senators compounded their errors by insulting Caesar as well. Caesar returned from a pro-praetorship in Further Spain in 60, having been a very successful administrator of the province, pacifying it and setting up its finances on a solid foundation and also having shown great skill as a general in extending Roman rule through what is now Portugal. He earned a triumph and was off to a much better start establishing a military reputation than Pompey was establishing a political one. As Cicero said when Caesar returned for his triumph, "The wind is now blowing full into Caesar's sails."[1] Caesar returned to Rome determined to become a consul as well as a proconsul with a considerably expanded military command. To receive a triumph, he could not set foot in the city until the day of it, which would have prevented him standing for election as consul. The Senate declined to give him a dispensation, so he deferred the triumph, was easily elected though lumbered with M. Calpurnius Bibulus, an insidious opponent, as fellow consul. Bibulus was elevated to this position by a concerted campaign of bribery in which even the unctuous Cato had participated. To complete the Senate's provocations of Caesar, instead of offering him a serious governorship, it offered what was called a jurisdiction of silvae callesque (forests and cow-droppings).

2. The First Triumvirate and Caesar's Consulship

The Senate evidently imagined, with the colossal insolence that habitually infected it, that it could simply slap Rome's two most popular public figures, who were also its greatest military commanders, in the face before the whole world and continue to amuse itself in its authority which was insouciantly imagined to be unchallengeable. Their action opened the final chapter in the overthrow of the Roman Republic. Caesar immediately entered into negotiations with Pompey with a view to establishing their own authority. Needless to add, the conduct of the Senate towards Pompey had made him highly suggestible. Caesar also invited Cicero to join them, presumably imagining that he was better inside the tent than out and that such influence as he might have with Pompey could be useful, but Cicero virtuously declined as the whole scheme smacked of anti-parliamentarianism, and he had (mercifully)

---

1 CAH, IX, p. 512 (M. Cary).

no delusions about his ability to stir the masses or lead an army. Crassus joined eagerly when asked, happy to be free of Pompey's hostility and to be recognized formally as one of the three most powerful men in Rome.

Caesar proved an extremely energetic and effective consul. He pushed through an agrarian bill that not only found the land for Pompey's soldiers but alleviated over-population in Rome. Since it was effectively a gift to scores of thousands of citizens, it didn't do Caesar's popularity any harm either. The senatorial opposition generated three tribune's vetoes and consul Bibulus announced that he would "watch the skies," meaning he was prepared to adjourn any legislative activity for superstitious reasons. Caesar responded by mobilizing Pompey's veterans himself and deployed them to expel his political enemies from the Forum, a rowdy process that began with Bibulus receiving a basket of excrement over his head and ended with having his fasces broken.

This was the first notice or inkling the senators had that Caesar and Pompey and Crassus were cooperating—it came as a thunderclap, and they finally realized that they had over-played their hand. Bibulus convened the Senate the next day at his house and asked for a decree such as was issued against the laws of Saturninus and Drusus the Younger. But the Senate had been intimidated and finally understood that it was not dealing with such people as Saturninus and Drusus. Bibulus remained in his house issuing grumpy notices and directives to passers-by.

Julius Caesar now ruled Rome. A second land act had to be passed to provide a greater pool of land for settlement, and Caesar moved briskly on to have his legislative assistant, the tribune P. Vatinius package up a confirmation of Pompey's eastern settlements. Lucullus objected, but Caesar summoned him and threatened indictment for his apparently heavy embezzlement, causing Lucullus allegedly to kneel and beg Caesar to believe that no such thing happened.[2] Vatinius put through measures that sorted out the Asiatic tax rental, to Crassus' liking, and getting rid of most of Caesar's indebtedness to Crassus also.

The Senate was now entirely docile and instead of awarding him a province of trees and cow-flaps, they awarded Caesar Cisalpine Gaul, Illyrica, and shortly after, Transalpine Gaul as well, all good provinces-breeding grounds for armies, which is what Caesar coveted. The provinces came for five years, an unusually long term; it is not improbable that the Senate was now minded to give him plenty of rope to hang himself, since they had no other tactic to get him out of the way now. They still had no reason to believe that he would immediately become Rome's greatest general, surpassing Scipio Africanus, Marius, Sulla, and Pompey.

Caesar was unambiguously the chief executive, as convener of the Triumvirate and principal consul. (Bibulus had become a completely nonsensical figure.) He was largely focused on political details to coordinate the shared interest of the triumvirs and assure their invulnerability to legislative snipers and sappers such as Cato. He saw the opportunity Cicero was chasing, and Cicero naturally felt that to some degree, Caesar had kidnapped Pompey from what Cicero imagined would be his tutelage of him. Caesar's principal institutional reform after his agrarian law was a consolidation of extortion statutes which put as much of a rod as Rome could on

---

2 Ibid., p. 518.

the back of corrupt provincial governors, who were always a burdensome problem.

The enemies of the triumvirs were very active pamphleteers and often sharp epigrammatists. Crassus, rapacious, insidious, and unscrupulous, was always vulnerable. Pompey, who for the last decade had been an almost apolitical national hero resolving one immense foreign problem after another, a chronic seeker of applause and unfamiliar with the popular political arena, was thin-skinned and vulnerable and was occasionally maneuvered into embarrassed apologies for Caesar's high-handedness in directing the triumvirs' business. Even Caesar himself was once provoked in the Senate to depart his customary icy demeanor and threatened senators with imprecise vengeance, and his public addresses to the Roman rabble were sufficiently inflammatory to incite fears of how far he might go deploying both the mobs and the legitimate armed force available to him, if provoked.

There was a farcical denunciation of a proposed assassination of Pompey, allegedly by Scribonius Curio, who cleared himself and implicated the shadowy political faction-agent Lucius Vettius. Vettius attempted to implicate Marcus Brutus, but Caesar would not have this—it was generally believed that his notorious liaison with Brutus' mother operated in favor of the accused. Caesar and Vatinius did cross-examine Vettius publicly in the forum where he "produced from his conjurer's bag a catalog of fresh culprits, including Lucullus and, by implication, Cicero."[3] His charges were so fantastic that the entire enterprise collapsed in multi-partisan mirth, and most of the initial resentment against the coup of the triumvirs subsided.

The new regime was vulnerable, however. What Caesar did was not strictly legal, and especially after he retired as consul, was subject to being revoked. One tribune, Lucius Antistis, prepared a personal impeachment against Caesar which the target was able to stop before it was launched. But Pompey was not only showing signs of embarrassment, but also of resentment at occupying a secondary role despite his eminence, although Caesar had undercut both his animus and his ability to act on his misgivings, as the benefactor of Pompey's legionaries and as the legitimator of his eastern settlement.

3. Caesar and Clodius

To strengthen his position and armor himself against a legislative or tribunician harassment, Caesar elevated Publius Clodius, a much more ferocious tribune than Vatinius, as chief defender of the regime. Clodius was completely unprincipled and almost unlimitedly audacious and had already therefore been of considerable service both to Crassus and to Caesar. Caesar managed to arrange Clodius' transition from being a designated patrician to a plebeian, exercising his powers both as consul and Pontifex Maximus, and facilitating his election as tribune in 58. Once again, as with the setting up of the Triumvirate itself, Clodius' attachment to Caesar was a well-kept secret. To deepen the disguise, Clodius pretended to solicit the post of ambassador to the king of Armenia, and Caesar pretended to be aggrieved at its refusal, which he had in fact himself arranged.

Clodius got off to a flying start as Caesar's chief Tribune. On January 3, 58 B.C.,

---

3 Ibid., p. 521.

he put forward four laws, one prohibiting censors from expelling senators other than after extended due process, which was self-serving as well as placatory to the Senate. A second measure revoked the ability of magistrates to obstruct legislation on the antediluvian excuse of "watching the heavens" a right henceforth confined to augurs and tribunes. The third measure of outright vote-buying on behalf of his patron abolished payment for public grain. This was in fact an escalation of the battle for public popularity with Cato, who in 62 had sent a monthly ration of wheat to three-hundred and twenty thousand applicants at less than half the normal price, justified, as such hypocrisy usually was, by the Catos, with invocation of the overarching national interest. This was really irresponsible public policy as it squandered more than half of the new revenues that accrued from Pompey's conquests in the East and effectively accomplished the pauperization of the Roman masses. The last of these early measures permitted unlimited numbers of political clubs to be formed; these had been sharply restricted after many of them had been put together amongst the drifters in the population and set up to participate in riots fomented by factions. Clodius practically assured the regime of the monopoly of these hooligans.

After a brief interregnum, Clodius returned to the charge, directly attacking both Cato and Cicero. After declining Caesar's invitation to join the Triumvirate, Cicero had left active politics and returned to the practice of law and to writing, although not without a final attempt to reestablish (if he had ever really had any) his influence upon Pompey, whom, he felt, "had tied himself to Caesar's chariot wheels."[4] In April of 59, Cicero had publicly accused Caesar and his associates of illegalities, which caused Caesar to try to placate Cicero with a place on the land commission, on his proconsular staff in Gaul or almost any foreign mission Cicero might wish. Caesar correctly assumed that Cicero would decline, and he prepared grounds for exile. For this, Caesar revived Cicero's hasty execution of the Catilinarians, which the Senate had declared to be morally justified, but not legal (typically mealy-mouthed senatorial casuistry).

Cicero had prosecuted Clodius unsuccessfully, and defeated his first attempt to become tribune, and it was naturally with the greatest zeal that Clodius presented in March 58 his law which "debarred from fire and water," i.e., outlawed "anyone who had condemned a Roman citizen without trial." There was no mystery about the identity of the target of this measure, and Cicero's oratorical self-confidence gave way at once to fervent entreaties to both Caesar and Pompey, and solicitations of support from the new consuls, Pompey's lieutenant A. Gabinius, and a father-in-law of Caesar's previous wife, L. Calpurnius Piso. Cicero should not be blamed for recognizing the danger that he was in, but it clearly came as a stark lesson to him of the correlation of forces in Roman public life between sophisticated eloquence, and the combination of mass public support reinforced by a large contingent of armed men and access to extensive quantities of money.

Cicero did receive widespread expressions of sympathy, delegations of support from around Italy, and the Senate invited all citizens to dress in mourning. One tribune, Lucius Ninnius, announced that he would veto the bill. Caesar handled the affair deftly; Clodius promised Gabinius on Caesar's behalf a good province follow-

---

4 Ibid., p. 524-5.

ing his consulship and Gabinius forbade the wearing of mourning. Clodius deployed his private army and gave Cicero's demonstrators a good cuffing about; and Caesar himself, while supporting his tribune, asserted that Cicero was guilty, but as he had with the Catilinarians, made a plea for mercy. Pompey, again showing his lack of aptitude for the kind of political maneuvering that was required, withdrew from Rome and did not respond to Cicero's appeals. So much for Cicero's avuncular guidance of Pompey. At the Senate, Lucullus urged resistance, but even Cato advised surrender. On the eve of Clodius' bill, Cicero departed Rome in self-imposed exile and a few days later this was made compulsory, though probably not legally valid, by an act which forbade Cicero to be within five-hundred miles of Italy. He would remain in exile for fifteen months.

Cato was a more complicated problem for Caesar, but one he managed successfully. Cato had very carefully avoided any possible charge of illegal conduct and so Caesar and Clodius settled upon a foreign mission for their opponent. Ptolemy Auletes had been deposited by family members on Cyprus with the title of King, although Egypt's authority to make any such arrangement was unclear. Given the prevailing military facts in the Eastern Mediterranean, Clodius drew up a bill which declared Cyprus to be a Roman province, and as this might prove somewhat contentious, the redoubtable Cato was nominated to lead a military and administrative mission to Cyprus that would dispossess the king and assert Rome's authority. This was a perfectly legal move in Rome, and Rome was not in a position where it had to pay much attention to its status in international law. Cato would remain for three years and would be an extremely efficient and inflexibly honest governor who returned and made an accounting to the last penny. If his "bailiff's errand" was faultlessly executed, at least, as Cicero wrote, Caesar and Clodius had "plucked out his tongue."[5]

With these measures and the departure of Cicero and Cato, it only remained for Clodius to distribute the rewards for the facilitators of his somewhat outrageous regime. Gabinius became governor of Syria and Piso of Macedonia. Clodius himself became an outright vendor of offices and privileges, the most egregious being his sale of the hastily carved out kingdom of a part of Galatia (and the devil take Rome's so-called ally, Galatian King Deiotarus), and the generous acquisition of its throne by Brogitarus, chieftain of the Trocmi. (He was no more kingly than the wandering Albanian Oroezes—this was shameless oriental jobbery of the first order.)

The only danger to the Triumvirate now was internal friction, and Pompey was evidently very uneasy at the ceremonial role he was now playing in the government run in every material respect by Caesar. He let it be known that he wished to be recalled to the Senate, and Caesar left it to Clodius, who had well established that he was equal to the rudest tasks, to deal with Pompey. This was in itself something of a comedown for the great general-that he would be seen to by such a preposterous scoundrel. As Pompey's veterans had now all been settled contentedly and well away from Rome, and Clodius was at the head of the large and almost united cohort of heavily armed and trained rioters within Rome, Clodius amused himself with little ambushes of Pompey.

The son of Armenian King Tigranes, whom Pompey had lodged comfort-

---

5 Cicero, Pro Sestio, 28, 60.

ably in the house of the praetor Flavius, was released by Clodius' gang, who overwhelmed Flavius' security unit. This was something of an affront to Pompey, the sponsor of the agreement to detain young Tigranes. Clodius' next provocation was against his former colleague Gabinius, a Pompey loyalist. Gabinius had responded to Pompey's call for assistance and Clodius' thugs broke his fasces. In August 58, Clodius introduced an armed slave into the Senate (a seriously outrageous act) and let it be known that his purpose was to murder Pompey. His real purpose was to frighten the general, a man whom it was supposedly not possible to frighten, but he was successful, and Pompey spent the rest of the year within his house, like Bibulus, except that he spared Rome the torrent of Bibulus' absurd public notices and accusations. It was yet another humiliation for Gnaeus Pompeius Magnus. On June 1, the tribune Ninnius, in Clodius' absence, obtained the consent of the Senate to Pompey's return, but he was frightened off the presentation of such a measure in the Concilium Plebis. Eight tribunes proposed a measure for Pompey's return but on reflection watered it down so thoroughly that it was useless.

Finally, after a year of Clodius' nonsense, Pompey devised an efficient method of counterattack. He assisted the independent tribune T. Annius Milo to organize a street gang and then made a general appeal to the Italians to take Cicero's cause and pass resolutions on his behalf in their municipal assemblies or in Rome. Pompey personally visited a large gathering of his veterans at Capua, and they rallied to him with enthusiasm. Stirring up the Italians was Pompey's first clever political initiative and indicated that while he was not a quick study, he could not be presumed to be made politically of sawdust either, a General Boulanger.[6] A large number of Pompey's supporters made the traditional march on Rome and gave every sign of being ready for a showdown with Clodius in the Forum.

Pompey felt impelled by Clodius' provocations and the banishment of Cicero to seek to dig himself out from the place where Caesar had parked him. In consequence, he declined the advice of some supporters to divorce Julia, Caesar's daughter and set out his stall again before the Senate. Pompey had seen enough of the insolence and hostility of the Senate, and he preferred to try to reason with Caesar. He wished to secure Cicero's return as he had again come to recognize his potential utility, especially as he was now again at odds with Crassus who though nothing like as well-regarded a public personality as Pompey or Caesar, was extremely wealthy and hyperactive in all spheres of Roman political intrigue. Caesar proposed that Cicero be allowed to return but with a guarantee of good conduct by him from his brother Quintus and Pompey regarded that as reasonable and accepted the condition. Under the pressure of Clodius' mobs attacking the street forces of Pompey's ally Milo, Pompey suddenly exploded in the Senate and said Crassus was planning to murder him, an allegation that delighted the senators with the possibility that the usurpers of the Triumvirate might be at each other's throats.

In January 56, Cicero's case was brought before the Senate, but Clodius stopped that by using a band of gladiators borrowed from his brother to intimidate Cicero's followers. As this was occurring there was a pitched battle in the Forum between

---

6 Georges Ernest Boulanger, 1837-1891, a dashing French political general, who was indecisive in crises and his support crumbled.

Clodius' thugs and those of Milo which resulted in such extensive bloodshed that a thorough washing down was necessary and the sewers were choked with corpses. Soon after, Clodius' ruffians attacked Sestis who only escaped by feigning death. Finally, in July, Pompey imported enough stalwarts from Italy to reinforce Milos' bands that reasonable liberty of speech became possible again at public occasions. On the motion of Lentulus Spinther, the Senate approved the recall of Cicero by a vote of 416 to Clodius alone. The great orator, a popular favorite in the circumstances, returned to general acclamation on October 9, 56. It was a victory for Pompey no less than for Cicero. This was the end of Clodius as a political force. He kept his gangs together for a time and specialized in burning down the homes of his opponents, but barely escaped with his life from a couple encounters and his active career as a force in Rome ended with a sequence of ludicrous lawsuits between him and Milo, almost all of them interrupted by gross abuses of judicial procedure conducted by the hooligans of both litigants.

Three days after his return to Rome, Cicero led in a senatorial debate on the crisis that had arisen swiftly of widespread famine. A raging mob was threatening the Senate with extreme violence. Cicero had the inspired idea of recommending that Pompey be appointed a dictator for food collection and distribution and the consuls gained adoption of a law conferring such widespread powers upon him. The old fire and crisp administrative energy instantly returned, and Pompey delighted the public with his dictum: "We have to sail; we do not have to live," as he made winter voyages to Sicily, Sardinia, and Africa and returned literally bringing in the sheaves. The famine itself did not especially embarrass Caesar since he was exercising no such responsibility. But it became a matter of contention as to whether speculators close to Pompey and Cicero had generated the crisis in order to put Pompey forward to resolve it.

4. Disagreements in the Triumvirate

The famine controversy was complicated by a measure proposed by Gaius Messius in the Senate which would have given Pompey authority to raise an army and override all provincial governors. It was a preposterous measure assured of rejection by forces supportive of the other triumvirs, but it raised the question in all minds as to whether this was Pompey's ambition and whether he was preparing a direct challenge to Caesar's control of most of the levers of power and office in Rome. Another plot line was the sudden arrival of Ptolemy Auletes in Rome, fleeing his angry subjects in Alexandria who resented their king's taxation, which, he said, was required to pay off his debt to the triumvirs. Ptolemy's local Alexandrine opponents also arrived in Rome but were dispatched by a combination of bribes and swordstrokes; their leader, Dio, was first bribed and when this proved insufficient, he was stabbed to death; Ptolemy won the argument by default. The versatile consul Lentulus Spinther was sent in 56 to force Ptolemy Auletes back on his throne. This initiative was interrupted by a flash of lightning which struck the statue of Jupiter on the Alban Mount at the beginning of 56. The custodians of the Sibylline Books then purported to discover an Oracle that forbade the restoration of an Egyptian king by armed force and the Senate determined that Roman intervention in Egypt must be by diplomacy alone. There was a good deal of posturing and dithering as Cicero upheld Spinther and others proposed Pompey and Crassus make overtures on his behalf. The Senate shelved the whole question sine die.

Rome's strategic development was superior and its organizational and military talents, supported by remarkable sophistication of infrastructure-roads and aqueducts especially, were much more highly organized than its politics, which were acutely unstable and poorly demarcated between legislative, judicial, and executive competences; and its religious institutions and practices were somewhat absurd and frequently seen to be so.

The Egyptian debate raised but did not answer the question about Pompey's ambitions, but it prompted the appearance of a serious setback for Pompey, since the itinerant claimant to the Egyptian throne had counted on his effective support and did not receive it. This affair also revived the dispute between Pompey and Crassus. This would be a fissure in the Triumvirate but one of some assistance to Caesar as he was on better terms with his two associates than they were with each other.

Caesar was by now generally absent from Rome recruiting an army in his new provinces for reasons that the Senate could only guess at uneasily. Cicero, still no great judge of political men and events, determined to try to foment the disintegration of the Triumvirate and in March 56 launched in the Senate a powerful attack on Clodius and Vatinius that was clearly really directed at their master, Caesar. Next, Cicero reopened Caesar's Campania law of land distribution, attacking Caesar's interests and protecting Pompey's in order to separate their interests and provoke discord between them. Lucius for Domitius Ahenobarbus, who was standing as a consular candidate for 55, declared that he would, if elected, deprive Caesar of his provinces.

This was a frontal assault on the chief leader of the state; Cicero was obviously behind it and his objective was to draw Pompey out in opposition to both Caesar and Crassus and rally the Senate to cautious, qualified support of Pompey as a disinterested patriotic soldier better and more morally qualified to be first among a number of equals (obviously led by Cicero), and to emancipate Rome from the sleazy financier and intriguer Crassus, and the cold-blooded demagogue and political adventurer Caesar. Caesar had by this time begun his ambitious activities in Gaul and was at Ravenna, well advised of Roman developments, a week away, and at the head of the only powerful army in Italy.

There has been much speculation about whether Caesar at this point seriously considered attacking Crassus and Pompey as disloyal and attempting to replicate Sulla's imposition of a military dictatorship on Rome. The general historical betting is that Caesar had not at this stage contemplated such a unilateral authoritarian course and there might have been some concerns about Pompey's ability to raise a popular muster throughout Italy against such a radical prospect. In any case, he invited Pompey and Crassus to join him in a conference to compose differences. Crassus came at once, but Pompey kept the others waiting until Caesar crossed the Apennines to the obscure town of Luca, bringing Crassus with him. The meeting occurred on April 15, 56. There were approximately one-hundred and twenty senators and two-hundred lictors present at the little town, but the conference was between the three principals alone. Pompey sent a courteous request to Cicero to postpone his motion on the subject of Caesar's land law and Cicero at once recognized that he had been defeated and abandoned his motion. Caesar took Cicero's brother Quintus on to his military staff and the triumvirs required Cicero to place his services at the indefinite disposal of the three principals. Both Pompey and Caesar formulated their requests deferentially and Cicero submitted to the inevitable somewhat graciously. He was henceforth and for a time a spokesman for the Triumvirs, a somewhat astounding turn of events. Cicero gradually worked his way up this new ladder as a conciliator supporting Caesar's request for an extension of his term in Gaul and defended both Vatinius and Gabinius in the law courts. He even was invited to attempt some mediation here and there between Caesar and Pompey.

Domitius Ahenobarbus did not go so quietly. It had been agreed at Luca that Pompey and Crassus should stand as consular candidates to ensure Domitius' defeat, but the incumbent consul Gnaeus Lentulus Marcelinus claimed that the names had been given in late. Pompey and Crassus responded by suborning the tribune to veto the elections for the rest of Marcelinus' consulship. In January 55, they were finally admitted to the polls and Caesar delegated a strong detachment of his furloughed soldiers to canvass aggressively on behalf of Pompey and Crassus, exhibiting what was called "forcible persuasiveness." For good measure, Pompey misused his authority as an augur to impede the praetorship candidacy of Cato. One day during this time, Pompey returned home with blood on his toga and so shocked Julia (Caesar's much-loved daughter) that she miscarried. Caesar's daughter proved a good and loyal wife of Pompey and as Caesar had great affection for her, Julia was a considerable reinforcement of the stability of the Triumvirate right up to her premature death in 54.

The Triumvirate was reinforced, and Caesar was able to pursue his mighty project in Gaul. Pompey had emerged from obscurity and Crassus had repaired his relations with him. Pompey could play the premier role in Rome for a time, uneasy all the while over what Caesar might bring back with him from Gaul, and when. Everything would now depend on Caesar's attempt to become a great commander and add the immense fruit of Gaul to the Roman tree. If he succeeded, all would be his; if he failed, the repercussions would be deafening and unsurvivable. Julius Caesar remained the bold, determined, and fortunate gambler.

5. Caesar's Gallic Wars

Julius Caesar launched his conquest of Gaul, one of the most famous and consequential military campaigns in all of history, in 58 B.C. He was the governor of Transpadane and Cisalpine Gaul and in addition to the legions entrusted to him to govern those provinces, he was in charge of a fecund recruiting ground for soldiers of fortune whom he could incorporate into Roman legions. The Celtic Gauls in the southeast had been conquered and annexed by the Romans in 121 B.C. and the Rhine Teutonic tribes were advancing steadily southwards pushing the northern Celts ahead of them. They had been further impoverished and diminished by the invasion of the Cimbri and the Teutons, though the Celts had the undoubted pleasure of watching the Cimbri descending into Italy to be eviscerated and overwhelmingly defeated by Marius in 101. The Celts tended to confederate into larger units, but they were fragmented between the nobles and the Gallic hierarchy, the Druids. The free farmers and artisans had been pauperized and reduced virtually to slaves, and the military organization of the Gauls was largely influenced by their social strata. The Gauls were warlike and brave but had given no thought to military strategy or tactics. Their only method was to assemble as many people as possible and charge the enemy as soon as possible. This was clearly going to lead to real problems defending themselves against Roman legions.

Transalpine Gaul had risen in revolt in 77 B.C., encouraged by the successes of Sertorius in Spain. Pompey crushed the rebels on his march toward Spain and the new governor, Marcus Fonteius, pacified the province but taxation became so severe to finance the war in Spain that much of the population was indebted to Roman moneylenders. The principal states of Central Gaul were the Aedui and the Arverni. The Romans had helped the Aedui to become the more important of these rivals. They fared less well against the Sequani, who now took the impetuous step of inviting foreign assistance from Ariovistus, leader of the Germans beyond the Rhine. He was assured he would be rewarded with the plane of upper Alsace and arrived in the mid 60s to claim what he now regarded as his birthright. The Aedui appealed to Rome, which replied with suave messages to other Gauls to assist their Gallic brethren. As has often been the case since, the Gauls were in no hurry to go to war with the Teutons and nothing was achieved by this softest of Roman endorsements.

In 59, Ariovistus secured recognition of his position in Gaul and went to Rome bearing gifts; in a shrewdly executed operation, Ariovistus was formally recognized by the Senate as a king and friend of the Roman people. A strong historical tradition remains that Caesar was behind this campaign with the foresight to have Ariovistus as a (co-)conqueror of Gaul. Caesar had four legions in Gaul to begin with, and remained in his Alpine province for several months waiting to see if he needed to support his henchman Clodius in Rome. When it seemed that he would not have to do so, he went swiftly northward to deal with a threat from the Helvetii who were mustering opposite Geneva. It was the spring of 58.

The immigration of the Helvetii was an immense and heavily regimented operation which included women and children. The entire population including four other tribes and totaling three-hundred and sixty-eight thousand people were to move into Gaul ahead of the advancing Teutons. To assure that there were no stragglers, all buildings and grain stocks were destroyed except the rations taken for the journey. There were approximately ninety-thousand able-bodied potential soldiers in the huge migration. The ambition was to move all the way across Gaul—taking one's distance from aggressive Germans even in these primitive times. Because the Sequani were blocking their way, the Helvetii asked the Romans for permission to go through the Transalpine provinces. When Caesar arrived in Geneva, he said he would need some time to consider their request and he used that time to levy new forces and to fortify the left bank of the Rhône below Lake Geneva. Only then did he refuse to allow the Helvetii to enter his provinces. Sporadic attempts to cross were made anyway but were repulsed easily.

The Aeduan leader, Dumnorix, persuaded the Sequani to allow the Helvetii to pass through their territory anyway, but Caesar was determined to pursue the traditional Roman policy of preventing the growth of any strong independent power near any Roman frontier, and he judged that the Helvetii in Western Gaul would be a threat to his plans. He brought up three legions from Aquileia and two new legions which he had just formed from his provinces and crossed the Rhône in the Jura. The pro-Roman party among the Aedui, who were now in the ascendant, conveniently appealed to Caesar for protection against the Helvetians, most of whom were now in their territory. Caesar moved promptly in a night march and defeated the unsuspecting Helvetians, and he deflected them north and west in pursuit of their ultimate destination. Caesar followed them at a distance of a few miles in country that was unsuitable for attack and because he considered his cavalry, led by Dumnorix, to be unreliable.

Caesar decided to reprovision his army at the Aeduan capital of Bibracte, but the Helvetians suddenly and inexplicably developed a thirst for battle with Caesar. He drew up his legions, which had no difficulty repelling the first assault but two of the fiercer accompanying tribes, the Boii and the Tulingi, attacked Caesar's right and a dual battle continued all day and into the evening. In the struggle that ensued, the Helvetian main body, now reduced to about one-hundred and thirty thousand fled to the east. The Roman army was too fatigued to pursue it but Caesar acquired such prestige by this victory he was able to persuade the Gauls to deny all supplies to the fugitives, who were thus forced to surrender. A section of the Helvetians tried to escape to the Rhine but was captured and sold into slavery. The rest, in keeping with Caesar's normal custom, were treated gently and at the request of the Aedui, the Boii were allowed to settle in Aeduan territory. Most of the central Gallic states now sent emissaries to congratulate Caesar on his victory. The Aeduan Diviciacus revealed to Caesar the greedy ambitions of Ariovistus and complained of his oppression of the Gauls and urged Caesar to help protect Gaul from the danger of continued German immigration.

Caesar promptly recognized both the Teutonic danger and the opportunity to extend his authority in Gaul by leading the defense against the intruders from across the Rhine. Caesar entered into negotiations with Ariovistus, probably without optimism, but given the friendly status that the Roman Senate had conferred upon him, it was important to expose him for dishonest negotiations. When Ariovistus refused to meet him, Caesar obtained a decree of the Senate authorizing an ultimatum to the Germans to leave the Aedui in peace and to retire beyond the Rhine.

When these demands were contemptuously rejected and Caesar was advised that a new horde of Germans was about to cross the Rhine, he took the offensive with his usual haste and occupied what is now Besancon, but his army momentarily wavered at the prospect of a pitched battle with a huge army of Germans. For a time, mutiny threatened, but Caesar at once summoned his officers and rebuked them for their cowardice. If the rest would not follow him, he said, he would carry on with the Tenth Legion only as he could rely on its constancy. This was the last time Caesar's men would waver in their loyalty to him throughout all the hardships of the campaigns to come. The Army moved by a circuitous route to the Belfort gap and upper Alsace, where Ariovistus and his people were complacently encamped. The German chief now consented to the meeting that he had refused with the Roman triumvir. Caesar opened by repeating his ultimatum, to which Ariovistus boastfully replied that he had entered central Gaul before the Romans and intended to remain. He knew that if he killed Caesar the noble Roman senators would be pleased but if Caesar would leave him free to do as he wished, Ariovistus would reward him. Caesar strenuously declined this condescending proposal and said that because of their victory over the Arverni in 121, Rome had established an exclusive claim to the sovereignty of Gaul against any other foreign power.

After the failure of this meeting, the two armies maneuvered for some days. Seeking favorable ground for battle to resolve the issues with Ariovistus, Caesar eventually found one one near Cernay, where the Germans had greater numbers and their initial charge shook the Romans. But Caesar set his reserves on the German right under the command of Publius Crassus, son of the triumvir, and he turned the battle. Caesar ordered his whole army forward on the back of the Germans who fled to the Rhine fifteen miles to the east. The Roman cavalry slew thousands of the enemy and Ariovistus himself barely escaped and died a few weeks later.

The Swabian host which had arrived on the right bank of the Rhine withdrew. It was clear that if Caesar ceased to guard the entry to Gaul, the Germans would be back, but he had established himself in the eyes of the Gauls as the indispensable defender of their country. Caesar recognized that the best method of conquering Gaul was precisely to defend against the Germans and incur Gallic dependence upon him. In order to guard the Rhine, he would have to defeat the Belgic Confederacy in the north, and he fixed the winter quarters of his army at Besancon, which alarmed the Belgians, and they spent the winter preparing for war. Caesar raised two new legions in Cisalpine Gaul and in the early spring of 57, he led his army of eight legions to the north. The tribe of the Remi (from around Rheims) volunteered their submission and played in the north a supportive role to the Romans similar to that of the Aedui in central Gaul.

The Belgic army duly appeared, though the number given to it by Caesar himself of two-hundred and ninety-six thousand is almost certainly exaggerated. Like most Gallic armies, the Belgians were large and fierce but poorly organized and co-ordinated and were constantly having difficulties supplying their ranks with rations and weapons. Caesar devised an ingenious plan to occupy a strong defensive position near Berry-au-Bac, to diverge by sending Diviciacus and the Aedui to ravage the land of the Bellovaci around Beauvais. The Belgic army floundered back-and-forth ineffectually and soon ran out of supplies. The Bellovaci dispersed to their homes and those that attempted an orthodox retreat were intercepted and surrendered. Many were intimidated by the appearance of the Roman siege engines.

Four of the northern tribes, led by the Nervii, who had planted high hedgerows throughout their territory to obstruct hostile cavalry operations and confuse invaders, determined to resist the Romans. Late on one day, as the Roman army was fortifying a camp for the evening above the Sambre, the Nervii suddenly attacked with great determination and took the Romans by surprise. Only Caesar's extraordinary energy and courageous personal example prevented a catastrophe; but by his intervention he rallied the section of his forces that had been surrounded, until the rest of his army came to the rescue of their commander. It was a total Roman victory but with significant casualties from the Nervii, who fought bravely and to the last man. Caesar next attacked the Atuatuci, who resisted with courage but then offered to surrender but instead treacherously attacked the Romans in the dead of night. Caesar again rallied a successful response and ultimately captured the entire Atuatuci force, fifty-three thousand men, and sold them all into slavery giving notice to all Gaul of how he responded to bad faith.

Publius Crassus took a legion to Normandy and Brittany, which submitted without struggle or argument and gave hostages. Thus, after less than two years, all Gaul from the Garonne to the Rhine, except for part of the very far north, was under Roman control. An attempt was made to open the great St. Bernard pass which would have eased communication with Italy, but the force sent was insufficiently numerous to achieve its objective. Everywhere else, Roman arms had been entirely victorious, and the greatness of Caesar's achievement was recognized by a fifteen-day official Thanksgiving in Rome. Matters were not as tranquil as they seemed, however. The Gauls had been mystified and grateful for protection from the Germans and astounded by the rapidity of Caesar's movements, and almost hypnotized by his combination of military thrusts and diplomatic initiatives. But they were too proud and too aggressive to accept so quickly this lightning subjugation of their country in the guise of protection from their ancient Teutonic enemy.

6. Britain and the First and Second Revolts of the Gauls

In the late summer of 57, Caesar sent Publius Crassus across the Channel from Brittany to explore southern Britannia. This disturbed the Veneti, who lived in Brittany and considered relations between Gaul and Britannia to be a monopoly of their own. They renounced their submission to Rome and arrested some Roman officers, hoping to exchange them for hostages they had given to Caesar when they accepted Roman overlordship. This was enough to raise much of the northwest of Gaul in revolt and they were joined by the far northern tribes the Morini and Menapi, which had not submitted, and the Belgians became restless as well.

This sequence of unrest spread across the Rhine and the various Teutons appeared to be mustering for a further invasion to complement the upheaval that was teeming in northern Gaul. It was to this cluster of problems that Caesar hastened back from his meeting at Luca with Pompey and Crassus in the spring of 56. He began by sending twelve cohorts and a cavalry detachment under the recently returned Crassus on an invasion of Aquitania that was completely unprovoked and which he justified by expressing the suspicion that those tribes might momentarily join the revolt. It was a completely successful expedition and many of the tribes in southwestern Gaul submitted. Labienus, Caesar's most talented lieutenant along with Crassus, managed to maintain order in the northeast by moving substantial units of cavalry constantly around the restless area. The German invasion was deferred and Quintus Sabinus, another competent junior commander, crushed the rebellion in Normandy with the heavy-handed imposition of three legions.

Caesar conducted operations against the Veneti personally and realized that in order to prevail he would have to destroy their maritime supremacy, which would require the creation of a Roman Atlantic fleet. In the winter of 57-56 ships were constructed on the Loire and the new fleet was manned by sailors from coastal towns in western Gaul. Decimus Brutus was made the admiral of the combined fleet and Roman legionaries served as marines. The new fleet was late and confounded by contrary winds. The Veneti, when attacked, simply moved to their next cove or bay and continued the resistance. It was late summer when the Roman fleet finally got to grips with the two-hundred and twenty Veneti ships that sailed out to meet it. This was the first of several historic naval engagements over many centuries in Quiberon Bay and the first fought by Roman vessels in the Atlantic.

The Veneti had sailing ships and the Romans had galleys and the Veneti vessels were too large and thickly built of oak for the Roman galleys to ram them effectively. The greater height of the Veneti ships made boarding difficult and javelin fire ineffectual, but the Romans had foreseen this and when the two fleets were at close quarters, the Romans had devised long sickles with which they cut the ropes that fastened the enemy sails, an action which reduced the Veneti ships to immobilized hulks vulnerable to Roman marine boarding parties. Once the Veneti saw their difficulties, they attempted to flee but were becalmed and most of their vessels were captured. It was another overwhelming victory that conferred naval supremacy in the Bay of Biscay and the channel on the Romans in their first foray, and the maritime tribes in Brittany thought better of their dissent.

But Caesar was not in a merciful mood and on the pretext that the officers of his that the Veneti had arrested were ambassadors and that the action was a breach of international law worthy of severe punishment, the Veneti chief senators were executed, and the balance of the population sold holus-bolus into slavery. Caesar clearly intended deterrence, but subsequent events indicate that his effect was more generally one of increased resentment and rebellion. The Morini and the Menapii continued in hostility and in the late summer Caesar attacked the Morini, but they retreated into their forests and adopted guerrilla tactics until Caesar was obliged to defer their subjugation until the following year.

Caesar's position in Gaul came under threat in the winter 56-55 when the entire population of the Usipetes and Tencteri tribes, which had been driven from their homes by the Swabians and had wandered listlessly around Germany for several years, crossed the lower Rhine near Xanten, driving the Menapii before them. Caesar estimated the population of these two aggressive tribes at 430,000 and their presence on the Gallic side of the Rhine was intolerable and threatening to his position. The anti-Roman elements of the Gallic population were already soliciting the support of these newly arrived malcontents against the Roman occupier. Caesar convened a council of the Gallic chiefs and secured the aid of most of them for the coming campaign. He declined the request of the Usipetes and Tencteri to remain in Gaul, but he offered to obtain land for them on the right bank of the Rhine. He moved his entire army up to within a few miles of the invaders' main position near Liège.

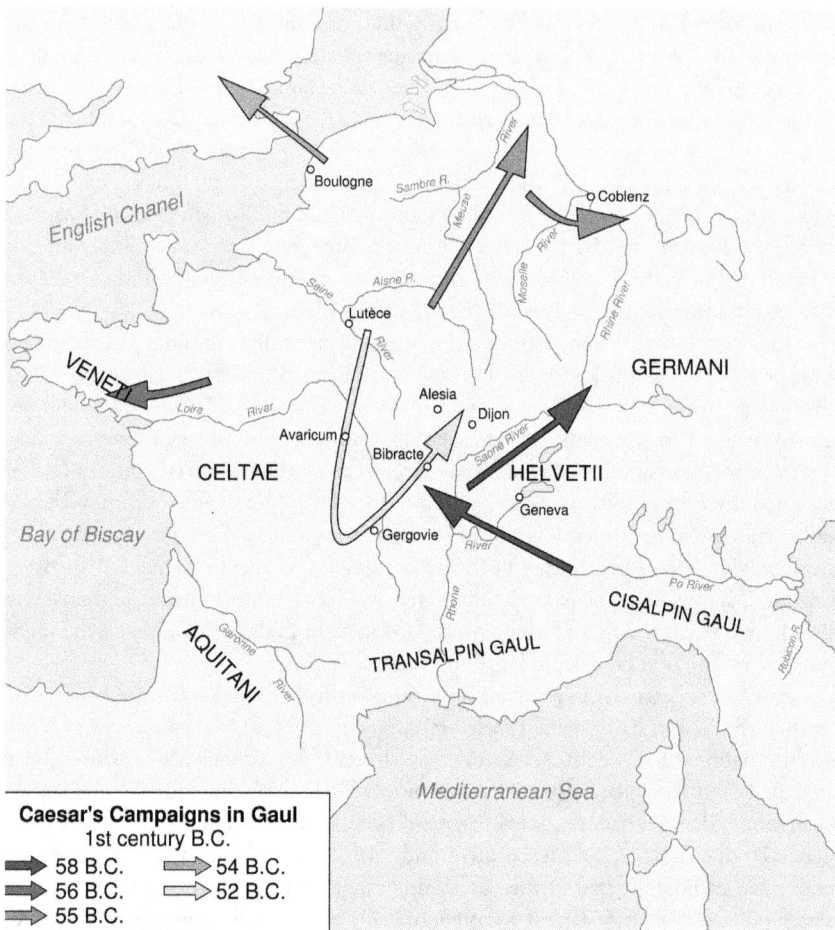

Caesar's Campaigns in Gaul
1st century B.C.
- 58 B.C.
- 56 B.C.
- 55 B.C.
- 54 B.C.
- 52 B.C.

Units of the two armies collided and the Germans routed the Romans' Gallic allies. Caesar arrested the German chiefs when they came to see him the next day to explain what had happened, and then he attacked the German force which, leaderless, was taken by surprise, and little resisted the Roman onslaught. Those who escaped drowned in large numbers in the Rhine and the barbarians were almost completely annihilated. This deliberate massacre is generally recognized as the most disgraceful of Caesar's actions and the worst example of the atrocities which were often perpetrated in collisions between civilized and barbarian races. Caesar attempted to excuse it by the peril that threatened the Romans, but there really was no such excuse. However, Cato's proposal to surrender Caesar to the Germans in retribution was mere political antipathy and was disregarded even by Caesar's critics in Rome.

Caesar now determined to secure the Rhine frontier by demonstration of Roman strength on the right bank, thus to remind the Germans that interference by them west of the river could provoke severe retaliation. Accustomed as the Germans were to trying to intimidate the Gauls, they had already learned that the same sort of activity directed against the Romans could be extremely hazardous. The Roman army built a bridge on piles across the Rhine just below Koblenz, which was an undoubted monument of Roman engineering skill that the Germans could not fail to notice. The Romans ravaged the territory of the Sugambri and offered battle to the Sugambrians, who were not tempted and retired into the legendary forests of Germany. Caesar had made his point and was not to be drawn into the pre-Wagnerian mists of German forest land. After nearly three weeks he recrossed the Rhine, removing the bridge by which he had traversed it.

Following the sortie into Germany, Caesar's plan for the campaign season of 55 was a reconnaissance mission to Britain. His expressed reason for undertaking this was to prevent British meddling on behalf of restive elements in Gaul, but this was almost a complete fiction, especially as the Roman fleet now controlled the English Channel. There was no military or strategic argument in favor of the mission other than Caesar's sense that it would strike the Roman imagination favorably and redound to the benefit of his reputation as a military adventurer. He claimed to have reliable information of the great natural wealth of Britain but that was almost certainly an outright fabrication. There was a fair amount of traffic between Belgic tribes and Britain and northern Gaul and some relationships between the Gallic and Britannic chiefs, in particular Commius, whom Caesar had elevated to the status of King of the Atrebates tribe, around Arras. Commius was sent on a mission to Britain by Caesar to urge submission to Rome, but he was unsuccessful and was imprisoned. Caesar departed Boulogne with an army of two legions on August 25, 55 and anchored off Dover. He landed at Walmer and defeated a fierce assault from British cavalry and war chariots. The Kentish tribes then released Commius and offered to submit but changed their minds when Caesar's ships suffered severe storm damage several days later. His cavalry were on board vessels that were wind-driven back towards Gaul, and without cavalry Caesar did not dare to advance inland. The Britons tried to take advantage of Caesar's discomfort but he decisively defeated their attempt to overrun his beachhead and the Kentish chiefs professed to submit again. Caesar felt that he could claim victory and withdraw and did so.

Clearly a more convincing demonstration of Roman power was required and over the winter Caesar ordered the construction of six-hundred new transports. Roman opinion settled on this widely publicized project with great interest, and it was being prepared at the same time as Crassus' great expedition against Parthia. The British expedition remained questionable and impetuous however, given the insecurity of Caesar's position in Gaul. In order to prevent severe problems in Gaul while he was in Britain, Caesar took most of the Gallic chiefs with him, supposedly as allies but in fact as hostages. When his old dissident adversary, the Aeduan Dumnorix fled the Roman camp he was pursued and killed protesting to the very end of his life against the violation of Aeduan independence.

The departure was delayed until July 54, and what was styled an army of conquest of five legions and two-thousand Gallic cavalry landed near Sandown on the Kentish coast unopposed. The British had not expected the attack, nor unified their forces against it, and Caesar hoped to crush their tribal warrior bands piecemeal. He started inland within a few hours of his arrival and defeated the Kentish forces on the plain of Canterbury. For once, Caesar's extraordinary fighting rapidity did not serve him as he had left his fleet at anchor instead of hauling it on shore, and in the night after his initial victory a great storm destroyed forty ships. This required Caesar to repair back to the coast and secure his communications to Gaul, strenuous work which left only two months of the campaigning season and provided the Britons a valuable respite during which they finally combined to repulse the invader and chose as their leader the king of a region north of the Thames, Cassivelaunus. He had recently taken over the Trinovantes of Essex, which drove Mandubracius, the son of their former ruler, to seek refuge with Caesar. The Britons still used war chariots, which were generally not very effective against the Romans and after some initial setbacks the British retreated gradually and with frequent recourse to guerrilla warfare: the countryside was denuded of cattle and men, and the Roman advance was constantly checked by specially selected and skilled charioteers.

When Caesar reached the lower Thames, Mandubracius brought the Trinovantes over to Rome, an example followed by several other tribes. Caesar attacked Cassivelaunus' headquarters and captured a great many cattle, but not many prisoners, and the Britons countered with an attack on the Roman beachhead, hoping to force Caesar to retreat, but his shore parties beat the Britons off easily. This induced Cassivalaunus to negotiate with Caesar, which was providential news, as he had just learned of acute instabilities in Gaul and wished to quit Britain as soon as respectably possible. It was agreed that Caesar would retain the captives taken by the Romans in Britain and that Mandubracius and the Trinovantes would be undisturbed. They could represent the Roman interest in Britain and with this fig-leaf of partial success, the Roman army returned posthaste to Kent and sailed at once for Gaul on approximately September 20, 54 B.C. The British expedition has, for obvious reasons, always held some romantic interest for the English-speaking world, but it did not really fire the Roman imagination, had few useful sequels, and though Caesar's critics have judged it a failure, it could be argued to have been a very modest success, but very much a side-show. Developments in Gaul relieved the British of the need to pay the promised tribute, though they did respect the status of Mandubracius, as Caesar's proxy.

As Caesar had been warned, shortly after his return to Gaul, the second revolt erupted. The former gratitude at Rome's defense of Gaul against the Germans evolved into acute resentment of the cost of maintaining a large Roman army and at the same time tolerating the aggressive avarice of Caesar and his officers. Every rapacious adventurer in Rome and all Italy had attached himself to Caesar's army in Gaul in pursuit of plunder, following, it must be said, the example of the commander himself. Caesar had long eliminated his time as a debt-ridden politician; he was flush when he arrived in Gaul, and he was very rich after a few years ensconced there. It was becoming harder to exploit inter-tribal quarrels as the grievance of alien oppression gradually elicited a pan-Gallic attitude of resistance. The central Gallic tribes were for the most part not yet ready to join in such an uprising.

But the revolt came when the Carnutes around Orleans assassinated the king who had been imposed upon them by Caesar. There quickly followed the revolt of the Eburones on the Meuse, incited by Indutiomarus and by their co-king Ambiorix. He attacked the Roman winter camp at Atuatuca and when that was unsuccessful opened negotiations with Sabinus and offered him and his men safe passage to the nearest Roman camp. Against the strenuous advice of Lucius Cotta, his second-in-command, Sabinus accepted this offer, and his fifteen cohorts departed their fortified camp. Ambiorix had placed his Eburones in perfect position to ambush the itinerant Romans at each end of a valley two miles from their camp and when he thought them fully enclosed, he attacked. Cotta rallied them and fought hard but was unable to get to grips with the Eburones, who reigned arrows down upon the Romans. After seven hours, Sabinus, again against Cotta's advice, sought a meeting with Ambiorix, who disarmed and murdered the Roman commander and his escort. Barbarians now stormed the Romans in massed attack and Cotta and most of his men were killed. Some committed suicide and only a few survivors escaped through the woods to advise Labienus of the disaster that had occurred.

Ambiorix went south immediately and induced the Nervii to join his uprising and attack the nearby legion, which was commanded by Quintus Cicero, the younger brother of the great orator and former consul. Cicero refused to pay any attention to the offers of the enemy and valiantly beat off their attacks. His messages to Caesar seeking help were intercepted until a Gallic slave of a pro-Roman Nervian chief reached Caesar at Samarobriva (Amiens). He had been blissfully unaware of the disaster rolling up parts of his forces. Caesar quickly organized a relief force of seven-thousand men and proceeded in forced marches north to the relief of Cicero. An advanced messenger was able to give Cicero notice of Caesar's approach by attaching his message to a javelin and hurling it over the ramparts from a great distance. It was only discovered after two days and soon approaching clouds of dust heartened Cicero's besieged garrison. The besiegers turned to resist Caesar, but he slaughtered them with little regard for the niceties of war and congratulated the valiant garrison. Cicero's brother did almost as well for Caesar in Gaul as did the son of Crassus.

The heavy defeat at Atuatuca, due to Gallic treachery and Sabinus' astonishing stupidity, had shattered the spell of Roman invincibility throughout Gaul. Caesar had to admit that every state except the Aedui and the Remi was in the condition of shaken loyalty. There were sounds and signs of unrest throughout Gaul. Caesar wintered in Gaul for the first time and moved busily around the country vigilantly preventing any spread of the revolt in the central states while Labienus stamped out incipient discontent in the Northeast. Indutiomarus had raised a new army among the Treveri and was attended by a huge swarm of desperados from all over Gaul. He wasted his time in shows of strength around the camp of Labienus, who was too experienced a soldier to be impressed. Labienus had organized the neighboring Gallic states to send a large cavalry force which he managed to introduce into his camp at night, unknown to the enemy. The following afternoon they suddenly stormed out of the Roman camp against the Treveri and routed them completely, trampling hundreds under the horses' hooves. Labienus had offered a reward for Indutiomarus and the Roman cavalry ran him down and killed him, thus removing the most influential Gallic leader in central Gaul.

Over the winter, Caesar replaced the cohorts lost at Atatuaca with three fresh legions, including one borrowed from Pompey, raising Caesar's army to ten legions. With this force, he compelled the Nervii to submit. He rallied the Senones and Carnutes in the spring of 53 with an overwhelming display of force and finally subdued the Menapii in the far north. The reliable warhorse Labienus again gave the Treveri a good beating. Ambiorix and his Eburones were now thoroughly isolated, but before dealing with them once and for all, Caesar made another demonstration against the Germans. It was reminiscent of the original crossing of the Rhine two years before: the Swabians again retired into the Teutonic Forest. Caesar would have wished to pummel the Germans, but he was not prepared to go on a wild goose chase into the heavily forested bowels of Central Europe. This time he left his bridge intact with a fort and a garrison of twelve cohorts and marched against the Eburones with a mighty vengeance. They retreated and scattered without serious resistance, and he razed their country to the ground, destroying all crops and killing almost all able-bodied men that he found. The Roman cavalry searched far and wide for Ambiorix himself but without success.

At the end of the summer, he held an inquiry into the causes of the revolt by the Senones and Carnutes, at which Acco, the leader of the anti-Roman faction of the Senones, was condemned to be scourged and beheaded and other patriots who had fled were formally outlawed. In these proceedings, Gaul was for the first time treated as a conquered province and its inhabitants as Roman subjects. It was again a misjudgment: the central Gallic chieftains were deeply offended and not at all intimidated, and as soon as Caesar departed Gaul and made his way through the Alps to update his status in Rome, the Gallic leadership began planning for a new and comprehensive national uprising.

7. Vercingetorix and The Third Gallic Revolt

What became known as the Great Gallic Revolt of 52 B.C. was almost confined to the states of central Gaul. Aquitania abstained and the Belgic tribes did not move until it was very late. Commius, now a leader of the anti-Roman party, had promised to rally the support of the Belgic tribes, but Labienus, in charge of Roman forces in Gaul in the absence of Caesar in Rome, learned of his plan and almost succeeded in having Commius assassinated. He was seriously wounded and incapacitated for several months and there was no one else to bring the Belgic tribes into the revolt. The Gallic plotters were also encouraged by reports of disorder in Rome following the death of Clodius (murdered by Milo in rampant street violence). The Gallic patriots determined to rise before Caesar's return and turned to a young and galvanizing leader of the Arvernians, Vercingetorix, and the Carnutes volunteered to be the first of the Gallic tribes to rise in revolt.

The revolt got off to a good start: the Carnutes massacred the Roman officials in Orleans and Vercingetorix overthrew the oligarchic government of his own Arvernian state. Most of the tribes between the Loire the Garonne rallied as well as the maritime tribes of the Northwest and the Bituriges, around Bruges. A second force under Lucterius roused the Ruteni and Nitiobriges and prepared to invade the Roman province of Narbo. The Sinones had intercepted many of Labienus' supply trains and he was very slow countering the uprising.

As soon as he was able to quit Rome, Caesar went to Narbo and organized a chain of frontier posts which Lucterius was unable to penetrate. Ignoring six feet of snow in the passes, Caesar plunged through the Cevennes mountains creating a diversion in Arvernian territory. In a remarkably vigorous and difficult march, the Roman forces quickly arrived in the Auvergene, putting it to fire and sword. This wrong-footed Vercingetorix who was forced to reverse course while Caesar hurried through the Aeduan territory, picked up his two legions among the Lingones, and regained the headship of his united army in Gaul. He had moved with his usual decisive effectiveness to take the initiative, but it was too early in the season to be able to conduct a campaign reliably and the revolt cost too much of his cavalry, which he now, somewhat daringly, replaced with German mercenaries. Vercingetorix forced him to move by besieging Gorgobina, a town of the Boii who had settled among the Aedui in 58. Caesar could not abandon it without irreparable damage to his position and strategic credibility and so marched to relieve it by a circuitous route on which he captured the Cenabum and sacked it thoroughly to avenge the massacre of Roman citizens there at the beginning of the revolt. This forced Vercingetorix to abandon his siege of Gorgobina and Caesar proceeded south towards Avaricum.

Vercingetorix wished Avaricum evacuated as the Romans had shown their ability to overwhelm any Gallic fortress, and the Gallic leader had resolved upon tactics of guerrilla warfare and harassment of Roman supply trains, desolation of the country and forced expulsion of the Romans by a policy of starvation and scorched earth. This inflicted great hardships on the Gallic civil population and there was strenuous opposition to the destruction of Avaricum and Vercingetorix was obliged to yield and set up a powerful nearby camp from which his cavalry intercepted Roman supplies. The town was bravely defended but Caesar commanding his veterans prevailed over all difficulties, constructed an immense siege-mound, and stormed the town by surprise attack. Everyone within, men, women, and children were mercilessly slaughtered. It had become a very hard war, but Caesar had never had any conceptual problems with that kind of combat. The Romans found extensive supplies in Avaricum, which enabled Caesar to move to the next phase of suppressing the revolt.

Vercingetorix proved to be an uplifting and popular military leader and his harangues of his countrymen raised their spirits to fierce and mortal levels of belligerency. He brought forth thousands of cavalry and archery recruits and redoubled efforts to rally states that had not yet joined the revolt, particularly the Aedui. With the arrival of spring, Caesar sent Labienus with four legions against the Senones and Parisii, while he took the remaining six legions to attack the Arverni. Caesar and Vercingetorix met at the fortified town of Gergovia, fifty miles south of Gorgobina. Gergovia was nine-hundred feet above the surrounding plateaus and Caesar saw that it would be impossible to take it by storm. He believed a blockade would be possible, but Vercingetorix retained some nearby forts and the area that would be required to be besieged was too great for an investing force of only six legions.

Caesar was considering withdrawing when he thought he detected an opportunity to take some of the Gallic outer forts. He cunningly induced his opponent to concentrate forces in an inopportune place and then personally led his main force up another slope while the Aeduan infantry ascended by another route. Three Gallic camps were surrounded and captured, and then contrary to their orders, at least according to Caesar's subsequent account of the battle, his men pressed on to the wall of Gergovia itself. Vercingetorix soon came to the rescue and the Romans mistook the abrupt emergence of their Aedui allies as enemy reinforcements, and for once Roman soldiers lost their composure and were driven off the hill with the loss of seven-hundred men, including forty-six centurions. It was the first defeat Caesar had ever sustained and the effect on the entire population of Gaul was electrifying. The Aedui thought they could dessert at last and seized Caesar's depot at Nevers, a few miles north of Gorgobina, taking stores, reserve horses, and liberating Gallic hostages. Vercingetorix made a spirited effort to cut off Caesar's retreat across the Loire, but Caesar got across the river and rejoined Labienus, who had partially stabilized the Roman position in Gaul with a decisive victory over the northern insurgents on the left bank of the Seine opposite Lutetia, what is now the Ile de la Cite in Paris.

Caesar and his army rested for several weeks among the Lingones and Remi, who had remained loyal, and were reinforced by cavalry and light armed infantry from the German tribes across the Rhine, which were apparently happy to make common cause with the Roman leader whom they much respected, against the Gauls whom they despised and whom they generally believed they would already be dominating if it were not for the Roman intervention. The Aedui at this point attempted to remove Vercingetorix and take control of the Gallic armies, but a general council at Bibracte confirmed the Arvernian leader in command. He increased cavalry to fifteen-thousand and tried to promote a revolt in the Roman Province but this was foiled by the firm opposition of the Allobroges. When Caesar marched towards the Province, Vercingetorix launched his cavalry against the Roman column hoping to seize its baggage. The Romans were surprised but their valiant German cavalry defeated the Gauls at Dijon and Vercingetorix was compelled to retire northwest to Alesia with his infantry. Caesar hotly pursued, and on his arrival at Alesia again defeated the Gallic cavalry. Vercingetorix saw that he would have to endure a siege and sent his cavalry to summon a general levy to assist him. Alesia stands on Mont Auxois, is almost isolated, and here one of the most famous battles in the history of the Western world would now occur.

Eventually, the relieving army, which Caesar estimated at two-hundred and fifty thousand infantry and eight-thousand cavalry appeared and encamped on the hills to the west of Alesia. The Gallic command was not unified, and time was wasted in a cavalry and archery attack and then on a night attack on Caesar's lines, and both failed. There followed an attack by sixty-thousand men under Vercingetorix's cousin and although Vercingetorix and his besieged army supported them as best they could from within their positions, the rest of the relieving army was not helpful and Caesar was able to concentrate most of his men in the sectors where the enemy had broken through. Caesar's position was astonishingly difficult as he entirely surrounded Vercingetorix and was himself surrounded by the relieving force and was therefore conducting a double front: his men virtually back-to-back for 360 degrees for miles, retaining a besieged enemy and resisting a besieging enemy.

Caesar was continually visible to all in the crimson cloak of a Roman combat general, encouraging his men and defying the efforts of Gallic archers to cut him down. Eventually the Roman cavalry whom Caesar had requested struck Vercingetorix's army in the rear and smashed it. The huge Gallic Army dispersed and on the next day Vercingetorix surrendered to the Romans to save the lives of his men. According to Plutarch,[7] Vercingetorix approached Caesar alone mounted in his finest armor, rode once around his tribunal, dismounted, took off his armor in silence, and sat down in submission at the feet of his conqueror. He was retained in civilized captivity for six years and was finally led through the streets of Rome in Caesar's mighty triumph and then put to death by garotte before the huge crowd.

He had earned and has received the permanent renown usually assured to the heroic leaders of great popular and national struggles for independence. If he had been successful at Alesia, he would not have been able to unify Gaul and his defeat may have spared him the bitterness of the German hero Arminius, who liberated his country from the Romans but was a victim to the envious ingratitude of his own people, the heroic leader's traditional cup of hemlock. Or he might have suffered the endless postwar frustrations and disappointments of a Simon Bolívar. Julius Caesar's victory against overwhelming odds in an unceasing double-battle against a fierce if somewhat primitive enemy was an epic victory that established him beyond any question as one of history's great conquerors and commanders.

Despite Caesar's bone-crushing victory at Alesia, some of the Gallic patriots fought on. There were thousands of homeless and desperate men in Gaul who were warriors and brigands by vocation and while they could not form up in battle against Roman legions, many maintained troublesome guerrilla activity for some time. Some hoped to continue until Caesar's command ended, and then to raise the standards of independence again. Caesar had to end the revolt quickly, as he had now been largely absent from Rome for eight years. He remained through the winter of 52-51 and reimposed Roman government in central Gaul, the Aedui and Arverni having submitted in exchange for the restoration of their many thousands of fighting sons captured at Alesia. The Bellovaci and the Belgic tribes gave it one more try, led by the able Correus, courageously seconded by the indefatigable Commius. Caesar concentrated seven legions in this area but did not make much progress until Correus was killed in an ambush. The Bellovaci resistance abruptly collapsed, proving again the importance of a strong military leader.

A Celtic army had been operating south of the Loire, but Caesar dispatched a force adequate to defeat it. However, two-thousand men fled south under Lucterius and Drappes and occupied the Puy d'Issolu near the north bank of the Dordogne. The rebel leaders collected supplies for a siege and were intercepted on the return; Drappes was captured and committed suicide by starvation. The resourceful Lucterius escaped but was finally surrendered to the Romans by the Arvernian chief. Yet the garrison held out and the Roman blockade could not for a time suppress it until Caesar arrived in person and saw that the only method of throttling it was to deprive it of water. Finally, he had to mine a spring just outside the wall of the besieged town

---

[7] Plutarch, Caesar, 27

and divert its course. The valiant Gauls staged desperate but unsuccessful sorties before concluding that their gods had deserted them, and they surrendered. This was a garrison largely composed of desperadoes who had committed atrocities against the Romans and were a menace to the civil population. Caesar ordered their hands to be cut off as the ultimate warning to like-minded elements scattered about Gaul. It remained a hard war to the end. It was August, 51 B.C.

Caesar visited Aquitania in the summer and then moved from region to region restoring peace with a subtle and finely tuned combination of firmness and clemency. Even Commius, who had been conducting guerrilla warfare against Roman convoys around Arras, agreed to honorable terms with the Romans. But he thought better of his submission and in 50 he escaped to Britain, where he established a kingdom south of the Thames, "and the last defender of Gallic independence ended his days as a free and powerful ruler in the land which as Caesar's agent he had once tried to enslave to Rome."[8] He would be the first of many prominent French exiles who would take refuge, voluntarily or otherwise, under the British, including both Napoleons, Louis XVIII, Charles X, Louis Philippe, Victor Hugo, and Charles de Gaulle.

Caesar's victory was complete, astonishing, and an event of permanent importance to the world. He had arrived in Gaul with only brief and secondary experience of military command in Spain and with no authorization whatsoever he took unto himself in his confected position of chief triumvir, indifferently supported by his colleagues and without genuine legitimate authority, the task of invading, subjugating and reducing to provincial status a vast and turbulent land of tribes and races as large and more complicated than Italy itself. Against great odds and while having at all times to stay in close touch with the ever-mobile currents of opinion and faction in Rome and elsewhere in the Roman world, by his own genius, determination, and force of personality alone he conquered and tamed and brought under Rome's authority a great and rich swath of people and territory.

And he took the Gauls, mercilessly belittled in Rome as savages with stinking trousers attempting to climb unworthily into togas, and more than anyone else, transformed them into that most magnificent and sublime of all European countries, la douce France. He was fortunate, as it turned out, that Vercingetorix had launched and so powerfully led the third great revolt. So proud and bellicose a people as the Gauls would not otherwise have resigned themselves to Roman subjugation. They only did so because they had not only been defeated; they had been defeated by so great a man, the emissary of so great a government, that they recognized spontaneously that the submission was honorable as well as preferable to continued hopeless resistance against a power so indefatigable and intelligent.

Caesar's deft alternation of conciliation with firmness and occasionally carefully selected ventures into brutal severity and open-armed magnanimity, created a faultless rhythm of administration that never yielded an advantage, never lost the initiative, and responded almost miraculously to a long sequence of deadly challenges. Gaul was tranquil for fifty years. With this campaign, unanticipated in Rome and executed with such breathtaking success, Caesar leap-frogged Pompey as Rome's

---

8 CAH, IX, p. 572 (C. Hignett).

greatest general, built Rome's largest army and fired it with an indefectible loyalty to himself, amassed an immense fortune that greatly strengthened his hand in the maneuvering to come, and effectively created a mighty provincial personal fiefdom on the border of Italy. With surpassing skill, he aligned his own interests with those of Rome. He showed himself a cruel man at times, something that was never said of Pompey (though it was of Marius and Sulla), and while this was not attractive, it was all the same effective for the accomplishment of his vast ambitions.

It must also be said that in taking it upon himself to conquer Gaul, Caesar undoubtedly spared Gaul the much more terrible fate of being subsumed by the Teutons. If the French have been able as they have these two-thousand years to hold their own against the Germans, so great a treasure as France is to civilization, that is not only a good thing in itself, but a providential development for the French and for all who would otherwise have been overrun by the Germans. Gaul received the benefits of Roman civilization, the Latin language, and the Pax Romana. Caesar had departed Rome its premier politician; he returned to it the greatest Roman, the successor to Alexander the Great, the heir and continuator of Romulus himself.

8. Rome After Luca and Crassus and the Parthian Disaster

In Rome, the law courts were not functioning particularly well and so Cicero was not so much in them and he busied himself plying between Pompey and senatorial factions and trying to find some method of reestablishing the Republic. It was going to be very difficult since practically all the power resided in Rome's two greatest generals, and what was left over was in the hands of its wealthiest man, Marcus Crassus, who aspired to become a combat theatre general like the other triumvirs and was preparing his expeditionary force to punish the Parthians. (Cicero should have taken Caesar's offer to make it a quadrumvirate—he could have led the whole Senate and not just been a scheming shuttlecock careening between the hard men who had the power.)

Cato returned from Cyprus, where he had behaved more circumspectly in all things than a saint and was more popular than ever. He was determined to make a final stand for honest government, opposition to military showmanship and intimidation, and plain and fearless integrity. In this hour of the warlords and of Clodius and Milo's street gangs, and of Crassus' corrupt wheezes, an honest and dutiful servant of the state like Cato and even a silver-tongued man of culture and the law, schemer, gossip, and poseur though he was at times, Cicero, resonated well with those who are naturally wary of masters of the battlefield and of the now well-trodden route of march to Rome like Pompey and Caesar. At least for a time, Pompey and Crassus were determined to make the regime work, and neither of them fancied a dispute with Caesar. The stone theater that Pompey built from some of his winnings in Asia went up and its opening in 55 was the scene of the grandiose and macabre slaughter of five-hundred lions and the chase of seventeen elephants. Cicero was disgusted.

Caesar wanted to return to Rome and become consul again; Pompey wanted to retain his influence in Rome by managing its food supply while maintaining an army in Spain of comparable size to Caesar's in Gaul. Crassus was preparing to complete

Pompey's work against the Parthians and was hoping to prove that he too was a talented general. (Crassus was an authentic general, and a moderately successful one, but with no claim to exceptional military talent, as his eminent fellow Triumvirs had certainly earned.) Cicero made up with Crassus just before he departed for Parthia. There was a lot of scenario-gazing and wistful romantic daydreaming among the leading Roman figures but in Caesar's absence the greatest star turn was being produced by Cato—it was at this point that he declared that Rome had been disgraced by Caesar's treatment of the Usipetes and Tencteri and that he should be ordered to surrender to his victims. "Rome had not conquered the world by punishing successful generals," and this was an idea that never took hold. (Cato didn't suggest how it would be enforced on Caesar, set as he was at the head of ten invincible legions entirely loyal to him.[9] Cato's integrity was so respected, the four candidates for the consulship each deposited five-hundred thousand sesterces which would be forfeited if they resorted to illegal behavior, and they left Cato to judge it alone and without appeal. Notwithstanding Cato's morality play, heavy election bribery drove the rate of interest on borrowed money from four to eight percent.

The conference at Luca seems not only to have arranged that Pompey and Crassus would be the consuls for 55, but also approved Crassus' mission to conquer Parthia as proconsul in Syria. Crassus was now sixty years old and smarted at his inferior prestige to his two co-triumvirs. It has been widely alleged that his proposed mission to Parthia was not only intended to confer upon him the laurels of the conquering general, but also to feed his insatiable avarice with control of the silk trade with the Orient. The Tribune Law of 55 gave the consuls the power to recruit troops in Italy and in the provinces; Pompey and Caesar had so conscripted for themselves that most of the prime youth of Italy was enlisted under arms with one or the other. For his mission to Parthia, Crassus had to employ press gangs to round up second rate fighting material.

When he departed Rome on the ides of November 55, the attending crowd was so hostile to Crassus that Pompey had to throw the cloak of his popularity over him and getting through the crowds was difficult. In Rome, Crassus was always a crooked and ruthless businessman and a completely unscrupulous and shameless political schemer with none of the integrity, mass appeal, heroism, or patriotism of Caesar and Pompey. However, as the type—the cunning and vastly rich cynic and wire-puller, political boss and sophisticated financier—he was as formidable an exemplar as Caesar the conqueror and demagogue and Pompey the irresistibly efficient man for all military seasons.

He made most of his great fortune buying up the estates of those whom Sulla had proscribed which did not make him popular, but he was very astute and relentlessly ambitious. He amassed a fortune that would today be about fifteen billion dollars. As he passed out of the city, Crassus noted an ancient ritual in which solemn curses were delivered against him, an event that was generally regarded as a very poor omen. He embarked at Brindisi and in the spring of 54, took over Syria and the troops there.

In July 54, Caesar's beloved daughter Julia, Pompey's wife, died in childbirth.

---

9 Ibid., p. 620 (F.E. Adcock).

The people carried her body to the Campus Martius and gave her a mighty funeral; to the masses of Rome, she was more than Pompey's wife and Caesar's daughter; she was the link between the two dynasties, the strongest possible bond and the greatest assurance of cordial relations between Rome's two masters.

Within Parthia a civil war was in progress, which augured well for the success of Crassus' mission. He had seven legions in Syria and their quota of cavalry and light armed infantry. His legates were Octavius, Vargunteius, and his son Publius Crassus, conqueror of Aquitania whom Caesar had sent to him with a thousand picked Gallic horse. Gaius Cassius Longinus was the quaestor. Crassus had been principal commander against Sparticus and a senior commander under Sulla in Greece and in defending this attack on Rome, he was adequately brave, very obstinate, ordinarily competent and very conventional. His general attitude was that if he brought the legions in contact with the enemy, they would manage themselves. His men had no great devotion to him, and he did not understand how to win their devotion. But he had moments of great solidity and determination under Sulla, but as an independent commander, he tended to be over-confident.

Crassus' chief opponent would be Surenas, a tall man in his late twenties with elaborate apparel and a painted face, a peculiar military commander but a fearless man of great imagination, precisely the sort of person that the complacent and corrupt Roman political boss and avaricious speculative plunger and promoter would have difficulty understanding. Surenas had created a unique private core of ten-thousand horse-archers, as large a force of that kind that he thought he could maintain and coordinate. They trained constantly and were accompanied by one-thousand Arabian camels, one for each ten archers, which carried an immense reserve of arrows. As far as is known, this was the first time in history that there was a trained professional force entirely dependent on long-range weapons and furnished while fully mobile with enough ammunition for a protracted battle. Crassus had no idea of the existence of such a force, and he committed the fatal initial mistake of failing to conduct an adequate intelligence canvas, as this unit was famous in the area and much of Syria was already familiar with it. During the winter of 54-53, Crassus recruited some Syrian cavalry, but didn't train them very strenuously and true to his natural proclivities, spent his time plundering the temples at Bambyce and Jerusalem.

Eventually the Syrian Civil War was resolved in favor of the elderly Orodes over the younger current Mithridates, and in the early spring of 53, Orodes sent an emissary to Crassus to inquire if he was leading a war on behalf of Rome or, notorious as Crassus' cupidity was, conducting personal brigandage with Roman and mercenary forces. The Syrian king's emissary allowed that if it was a personal matter they could resolve matters easily—Orodes was full of years and did not wish a life and death struggle with a Roman consul who was merely garnishing his own treasure box. Crassus replied that he would give his answer at Seleucia, and the Parthian ambassador held out his hand and said: "Hair will grow on my palm, Crassus, before you see Seleucia."[10] the Armenian king, Artavasdes (son of the durable and crafty Tigranes), also called on Crassus and offered him the Armenian cavalry in support of his operation if he would invade Parthia through Armenia. Crassus naturally declined this

---

10 Ibid., p. 607 (W.W. Tarn).

as it would have been a more distant route with, to say the least, an uncertain ally. He seems to have continued to believe, however, that the Armenian king would still fulfill his obligations to Rome, and there is evidence that Orodes also believed this.

Orodes' plan was that as Parthia was threatened with war on both fronts, he would conduct the main offensive against Armenia himself while Mesopotamia's defense was entrusted to Surenas against Crassus, and to this end, Orodes assigned a thousand mailed knights to reinforce Surenas, whose orders were to keep Crassus busy and as best he could, out of Mesopotamia. Surenas deployed his forces along the Belik River on the western border of Mesopotamia and the Euphrates to the southeast, where the Parthian and Arab roads to Babylonia intersected. Crassus, with no imagination whatever, crossed the Euphrates at its westernmost point at Zeugma, getting approximately thirty-two thousand men across his own pontoons in the middle of a sandstorm. The Syrian mercenaries under Abgar and Alchaudonius closed up behind and Crassus pressed on eastwards arriving at midday on May 6, 53 on the Belik River, between Carrhae and Ichnae. Crassus' officers advised him to reconnoiter but the Roman commander was convinced that the enemy was fleeing before him, and he was determined to catch him. His men could eat a hasty meal in their ranks amidst much grumbling and had started southward when sentries advised that the Parthians were upon them. The entire mercenary force at this most inconvenient moment deserted, Abgar leaving with the parting question of whether Crassus thought that he was engaged on "a route-march through Campania."[11]

Crassus formed up his troops in a square with one side on the Belik River and Cassius and Publius Crassus commanded the left and right. About a thousand cavalry were left outside the square and free to maneuver. The Roman formations were still taking their positions when the Parthians appeared over rising ground under their silken banners and announced by deafening kettledrums. Their mailed lancers charged once to hem the Romans in as tightly as possible and then retired behind the archers who hailed arrows down on the Romans. A legionarie's shield could stop an arrow but Surenas' well practiced battlefield tactics had the front rows of archers firing parallel to the ground at their targets and the rows behind arcing their fire upwards, so it came down almost vertically upon the targets, and the Romans were unable to protect themselves adequately against such fire. Heavy casualties began to mount. The Romans assumed, on the basis of their inadequate experience, that this teeming assault of arrows could not continue indefinitely and that then they would have a chance for a counterstroke. We may imagine how demoralizing it was for them to see, as it was in plain sight, the camels bringing up practically unlimited reserves of arrows.

Crassus' greatest immediate concern, however, was that although he outnumbered his enemy by more than three to one, they were threatening to turn his right flank and his square was still not formed. He ordered his son to charge and give him room to complete. Publius Crassus did so, Parthians fled, and his eight cohorts tore after them whooping of victory. A dust cloud enshrouded the next phase of proceedings as Crassus completed the square. But once Publius had been drawn away from the main body of his father's force, the heavy Parthian cavalry rode down the

---

11 Ibid., p. 609.

light-armed Gauls that Caesar had sent with Publius Crassus from Aquitania. They fought for their lives with the unlimited bravery of Gallic and Roman warriors but were ultimately resistless against such heavily armed and armored cavalry. A few escaped and told Crassus of his son's predicament and he moved quickly forward to his support but was met by an on-coming Parthian flying squadron bearing the severed head of Publius Crassus on a lance in front of them.

At this ultimate crisis of his life, Marcus Crassus conducted himself with the dignity of a Roman consul and general. He rode along his ranks, ignoring the incoming fire, saying that the sorrow was his alone and that they must all stand and fight on for Rome. The legions did so until the dark prevented the Parthians from being able to fire accurately. At this point, Crassus seems to have been somewhat incapacitated; Octavius and Cassius ordered a retreat, abandoned four-thousand wounded to their enemies but by dawn almost all of the remaining thirty-thousand men of Crassus's army were within the walls of Carrhae. This would provide shelter from Surenas' fire, but there were not provisions to sustain the army for more than a few days and there was no relief column within reach. Surenas was able to find and destroy four cohorts under Vargunteius that had departed the main body and were wandering about aimlessly. Surenas was hoping to take Crassus alive and deliver him like a trussed-up partridge to Orodes, an unimaginable humiliation to Rome and to the co-triumvir of Caesar and Pompey.

Crassus gambled on a night retreat to the town of Sinnaca, which was in the foothills of the Armenian mountains, country inhospitable to Surenas' cavalry. This was the last chance, and it was a sensible tactical decision, but Crassus paid for his lack of thorough preparation and chose as his advisor for this escape the undeclared leader of the pro-Parthian party within Carrhae, Andromachus, who led the Romans astray and wasted the night. They not only had to face the dreaded Surenas again, but the fiasco of the wasted night brought the rare curse of indiscipline into a Roman army. Cassius had impatiently deserted his general in the middle of the night and with five-hundred cavalry made it back to Syria, claiming that he was saving Roman soldiers rather than running for his life. (This explanation was doubtful but was officially accepted.)

The most distinguished performance was that of the legate Octavius, who kept five-thousand men together and reached Sinnaca at dawn. He waited for Crassus, who eventually appeared on a low foothill two miles distant with only four remaining cohorts and swarmed from behind by the enemy. Octavius went to his aid, but at this point, the diabolically perceptive Surenas, fearing that his quarry could escape, came forward with outstretched hand and unstrung bow and addressed the dazed Roman troops in the presence of their commander. He declared that he had demonstrated that Parthia could fight and wished now to show that it could also forgive, and invited Crassus to covenant with him that they should go home in peace.

Severely shaken by the dreadful struggle of the last few days, Crassus, still the cunning chancer, detected Surenas' treachery and effectively replied to his own troops as if he were having a debate with the enemy commander. He warned his men of Surenas' true intentions and urged them to fight their way into Sinnaca as Octavius approached to assist. Now came the final horrible shame: Crassus' ravaged, blood-stained ranks turned upon him and reviled and threatened him. If their commander could not face Surenas unarmed, they would not take the hail of arrows again. Crushed in sequel by a painted, mounted, serpent of Oriental trickery and then by his own mutineers, Crassus went forward alone and on foot to meet Surenas. He allegedly asked Octavius via a messenger to report to Rome that he was deceived by the enemy and not betrayed by his own soldiers, a valiant and undeserved consideration for the reputation of his sullen forces. Surenas brought up a horse for Crassus and said that the treaty must be signed on the bank of the Euphrates, gratuitously adding: "You Romans some times forget your treaties." Octavius and some other officers had come forward to join their commander and they all assumed that Surenas intended to seize Crassus. A scuffle ensued and the Roman officers were all slain; Marcus Crassus died in combat with the courage and dignity of his rank. One of history's legendarily unscrupulous and grasping men, he died with honor, attempting to avenge Rome against a barbarian enemy, a brave and talented man if an uneven general.

Crassus was the author of one of the greatest disasters ever sustained by Roman arms. Of his forty-four thousand men, counting those in garrisons, only ten-thousand reached Syria and were formed into two legions by Cassius for the defense of that province. Ten thousand prisoners also survived. Surenas, whose capability as a military leader cannot be disputed, did not attract history's salutation with a mockery of a Roman triumph at Seleuceia, in which a prisoner who resembled Crassus was frog-marched along in women's clothes and was heckled as "Imperator." Surenas sent Crassus' severed head and hand to Orodes, who was at the Armenian capital, Artaxata. Once invaded, King Artavasdes deserted the Roman alliance and confirmed his solidarity with Orodes by giving his sister in marriage to Orodes' son, Pacorus. According to Plutarch, the wedding feast included a bowdlerized version of Euripides' *Bacchae*, with the addition of a final scene in which the head of Crassus is flung about, and his murder is cited as an honor.

The haughty Surenas had cackled too loudly and too soon: Orodes executed him, wary of his ambition and overconfident intelligence. The Parthians under Pacorus invaded Syria in 51, but the military success of Surenas proved difficult to replicate. The Parthians were impotent before the walls of Antioch, and when they attacked Antigoneia, Cassius had the pleasure of defeating them and chasing them out of Syria. The proconsul of Syria, Bibulus, now hardly recognizable as the poltroon who was Caesar's co-consul of 59, by suborning Parthian officials, made Pacorus a suspect in the eyes of Orodes, and he was recalled.

While they coarsely celebrated, the Parthians had assured themselves of a dreadful vengeance. Rome had just completely subdued vast Gaul and was led by two great generals at the head of an incomparable army. Civil strife in the Roman world would grant the Parthians a respite, but no one in the known world could possibly imagine that Rome would leave relations with insolent little Parthia on this basis. Crassus was largely unlamented, and his removal didn't much alter the political correlation of forces in Rome. Rome remembered Carrhae; its revenge would not be swift, but it would be inexorable.

9. The Descent to Civil War

Following the elections of 55 B.C., the Triumvirate seemed completely secure and relatively united, and traditionalist Republicans despaired of the concept of liberty as they had known it. Cicero, in his letters, counseled endurance of the regime and celebration at least of internal peace and stability. There was no question of the competence of the triumvirs and as long as they remained united, Rome would be strong and effectively administered. The principal dissident was Cato, who was determined to resist the coalition by all legal means. Most of the senators could live with the preeminence of Pompey while the commercial classes and knights thought the consulship of Crassus at least made the world safe for the plutocrats. The Roman mobs could be whipped up by Clodius, and Clodius did what Caesar told him to do. Government by Pompey and Crassus, following Luca, was actually somewhat progressive. Laws were adopted to discourage and punish bribery in elections and Crassus even sponsored a law discouraging the employment of political clubs in the interests of candidates for public office.

Cicero spent from 54 to 51 writing his constitutional books, *Of the Republic* and *Of the Laws*. These were scholarly and idealistic works that indicated the sort of republican government that Cicero hoped would someday be restored to Rome with a balance between the nobility, the oligarchy, and the people. These ruminations and writings were at some variance with the run-up to consulate elections in 52 which led to a pitched continuous street battle between the forces of Cicero's ally, the hot-blooded Samnite T. Annius Milo, and Caesar's hitman and street fixer Clodius. Cicero lent his sophisticated tongue to this bare-knuckled struggle out of fear that Clodius, if elected praetor would resume his vendetta against him. January 18, 52, Milo's gang succeeded in killing Clodius on the Appian Way. The resulting riots made the elections impossible. Clodius' followers burned the Senate house to the ground, saying it was a pyre for the body of their leader. The disruptions of Roman life became so severe that all eyes turned to Pompey for the restoration of order. The Senate called upon him and the tribunes and the interrex to save the state. Pompey raised troops from his traditional ranks and prepared to enter the city. Bibulus returned to the fore with a proposal that instead of being a dictator, like Sulla, Pompey be elected consul without a colleague, and he accepted this compromise that still left him almost dictatorial powers. Pompey brought forth laws that made political bribery extremely difficult and shortened trials, in preparation for the trial of Milo.

Cicero conducted Milo's defense with something less than his customary articulation, distracted by the demonstrators and rioters, and when Clodius' followers disrupted proceedings around the courts at the end of the trial, Pompey's soldiers restored order promptly. Milo was convicted by 38 of the 51 judges and went into exile at Massilia (Marseilless), where he lived on comfortably, married to the daughter of Sulla, until he was induced to return to the provocation of violence in 48 and was killed when struck by a stone thrown by an opposing faction. Cicero was more successful defending some of Milo's lieutenants.

These times were the summit of Pompey's career. The Senate knew that he was gentler and more respectful of them, and less prone to commanding and manipulating the Roman mobs than Caesar was. It was accidentally an excellent division of labor: Caesar was even more effective than Pompey at the reduction and absorption of non-Roman territory, and Pompey was a much more respectful traditionalist and gentler wielder of the rod of state than Caesar was. Pompey added to his credentials as the Senate's favorite leader by associating with himself in his consulate his father-in-law, Metellus Scipio. Pompey could be relied upon to defeat Rome's enemies and also to resist the temptation to overthrow the Senate completely. He had no great gift for stirring the Roman masses and while his vanity caused him to seek endless commendation and public gratitude, he earned that gratitude and was generally more a seeker of the approval of the leading figures of the Senate than he was indifferent or hostile to them as Caesar was. Pompey's problem was that he could never be sure whether he was Caesar's comrade who would share power with him, or Caesar's rival who could only maintain himself by conspiring with Caesar's enemies. He was very late facing up to that decision and Caesar knew his dilemma and mired him in it. In the end, Pompey would make the wrong choice.

As the war in Gaul and the ten years since Caesar's consulship in 59 also neared its end, which would permit him to seek election as consul again, there was great suspense in official circles about whether Pompey and the leaders of the Senate would attempt to squeeze Caesar legally. There was not only the bar on his seeking reelection as consul within ten years, there was the fact that he had never received any authority whatsoever to undertake the conquest of Gaul or his incursions in Britain and across the Rhine. There was no shortage of senators, especially of the Cato variety, that wished to recall Caesar from Gaul, cancel his provincial governorships, prevent him seeking the consulship, and despite the mighty acquest he had made for Rome, punish him for his acts excessive to his authority. Pompey was constantly being importuned by members of that party that would take refuge in the less threatening figure of Pompey to preserve the Republic against a man whose usurpatory instincts were intuited, suspected, assumed, and then railed against, though, as we have seen, Caesar was comparatively moderate about pressing his claims on future office.

Caesar had been voted a law permitting him to seek election as consul in absentia. This measure was revoked, but Pompey alleged forgetfulness and reinserted it in the law, a special recognition of Caesar's status. It has been speculated ever since that Pompey's forgetfulness came after Gergovia and his reparation of it after Alesia, though this is conjecture. It was indicative of the extent to which much of the Senate had become a silly, chronically fearful hotbed of gossips and ninnies, too far removed from being men of action to have any idea how a man of action acted, and able only to think of petty legislative and regulatory ambushes and mousetraps; and endlessly approaching Pompey to be the sword for the resurrection of their prerogatives. There was a natural legitimacy about the great noble families of Rome. Many were now in threadbare circumstances, and many had few current members of any great merit. Yet together they were continuity; they were the history of Rome from Romulus to the present. They were like great Roman trees that had long been there, had sheltered the city, but were no longer relevant to anything except memories.

Pompey was increasingly reluctant to make Caesar's way back to power in Rome easier, but he was also reluctant to be disloyal to his old ally and father-in-law. Like everyone else, Pompey was somewhat afraid of Caesar, but being Pompey, he was less afraid of him than anyone else was, except Cato, who knew no fear, and in his spartan austerity forced himself to affront fate to demonstrate his courage to himself and the world. Fundamentally everybody except Caesar's followers wanted him out of his big provinces straddling between Italy and Gaul and heavily populated with soldierly young men. But they would have preferred him there to resuming his consulship. The Senators didn't want to be threatened by Caesar and generally knew that if they passed individual specific laws and regulations hostile to Caesar, that they had no capacity to prevent Caesar from marching on Rome and throwing them all into the Tiber (headless or otherwise). It was to arm themselves with the potential to resist that they wooed Pompey, but Pompey as a great general knew better than anyone what Caesar could do. He was a plain-spoken and relatively guileless, though vain, man, but he saw he was being flattered and courted by people who wanted to use him, and he saw how unequal in merit and talent were Caesar and his enemies. Pompey did not want to test the issue of ultimate authority with Caesar, but he would prefer that Caesar conformed to rules that somewhat confined him. Since Caesar was unlikely to subscribe to that regime voluntarily, Pompey was naturally tempted to associate himself somewhat with senatorial pettifogging to restrain Caesar.

It was a delicate dance. No one had Caesar's confidence, and no one now had his power: neither such a large and capable army, nor the ability to seize Rome and govern as he wished. The senators tried to convince Pompey that they could create Caesar's illegalities and Pompey could enforce the law. They and Pompey wanted to believe it, but what assurance could anyone, including Pompey, have that he could stop Caesar, who since Alesia, when he appeared to be doomed, had, and wore casually, an impenetrable aura of invincibility?

What gradually emerged was a consensus among all those trying to set up a coalition to contain Caesar's power that Pompey could take a position that would cause Caesar to choose between remaining in Gaul in his transalpine provinces and forego returning as consul and retiring from his governorships and return to Rome as consul without his army. Caesar's position was that this must be offered in a way that assured there was no gap between his retirement from his provinces and his election in absentia as consul, so there would be no window for him to be prosecuted for his supposed illegalities—incumbent consuls and provincial governors were immune from such prosecutions. Caesar wished the Constitution stretched for him as it had been for Pompey and for the same reason in the case of both men: conspicuous service to the Roman state, acclaim none could say they had not earned.

Caesar's senatorial enemies insouciantly refused to make this concession to Caesar and Pompey, though he would not renege on commitments to Caesar, was willing to see his plan for a second consulship frustrated by his parliamentary enemies. The anti-Caesar party had emboldened itself to an extreme failure of judgment. Caesar had already prepared tribunician obstruction that, as we have seen, at intervals since the Gracchi, could always be invoked to immobilize the official process. He attracted to his service a formerly hostile tribune, Marcus Scribonius Curio. Beyond that, Caesar had the masses of Rome, and behind that an insuperable and fiercely loyal army. For two-thousand years, the world has wondered what these men were thinking. The consuls for 50 were Claudius Marcellus, who although married to Caesar's grand-niece Octavia, was an opponent, and his colleague Lucius Emilius Polis, less decided and not incorruptible. Cicero was still in his rusticated status as proconsul and solicitor, anxiously looking forward to returning to Rome in July 50. His letters reveal that he still thought the situation could be stabilized if Pompey stood firm.

Curio prevented any determination of Caesar's ability to maintain his governorships until his consular election, and by the spring of 50 it was clear that either Curio would maintain his veto or if adequate pressure were put on him, Caesar would defend him and Pompey and the Senate would have to decide whether to insist that Caesar leave his provinces, whatever the tribunate thought of it. Curio stood his ground and while Pompey pretended to be acting fairly, it was clear that he intended to prevent Caesar from retaining his army and provinces until his election as consul. It was a self-escalating confrontation that was certain to reach a condition of extreme civic danger if neither side compromised.

Curio's tribuneship expired on December 9, 50, and Caesar advanced Mark Antony as his replacement and put forward Sulpicius Galba as consul and delivered what amounted to a large rotten-borough vote in favor of both from Cisalpine Gaul. The sudden death of the great orator Hortensius caused a vacancy in the College of Augurs and Antony determined to be a candidate for that also. Caesar's aristocratic enemies put forward Lucius Domitius Ahenobarbus as his opponent. At the same time, conditions in Syria were deteriorating under the pressure of those who had disposed of Crassus' expedition (except for Suranus of course), and the Senate voted the dispatch of one legion each from the forces of Caesar and Pompey as reinforcements. Pompey elected to send legions he had loaned to Caesar, which was his right and Caesar thus lost two of his legions though he could replace them with recruits from his provinces on short notice if needed. (The Parthian invasion of Syria did not occur, and the two legions remained in winter quarters in Campania. They were loyal to Caesar and now close to Rome.)

The 50 elections were held in July and Antony was successful in both of his elections, but Galba was defeated; the new consuls elected were Lucius Lentulus and Gaius Marsalis, both enemies of Caesar. Pompey had clearly not assisted Caesar's candidate Galba and Caesar made what amounted to a political tour of Cisalpine Gaul scattering largesse in politically fruitful dispensations and then returned to Gaul to review his legions and extract from them a pledge of loyalty to their commander even, if necessary, against the Roman state in arms. He disposed the legions in a way that was not provocative but the whole Roman world was becoming very jittery. In Rome, Curio had maintained his veto and the consul Marcellus had failed to produce a vote of moral pressure against him. Pompey was wavering and found the political pressure almost unendurable; he had to withdraw in May to Campania and convalesced from anxious nervosity until the summer. The consul-elect, Lentulus, was suspected (unjustly) of succumbing to Caesar's blandishments. The atmosphere was febrile.

Curio, and it is not known if this was his idea or Caesar's, devised a new method for turning up the pressure by repeatedly calling for the Senate to invite both Caesar and Pompey to disband their armies. This attracted the support of the majority who opposed civil war under any circumstances, but it also put Pompey on the horns of a dilemma if the armies of both duovirs were disbanded. Caesar could still control Rome through his leadership of the popular classes. Pompey could not bring himself to make such concession and no such step was taken. Caesar had technically retired as governor of his provinces on November 19, 49, but the practice was that the governor continued until his replacement arrived and Curio followed by Antony were prepared to veto any nomination of a replacement, so nothing changed, except that the pressure kept rising.

The Roman Republic was being slowly strangled by a chain of circumstances: with his governorship expired, Caesar's right to be a candidate in absentia could not prevent the Senate from appointing his successor as governor and that successor from assuming command of Caesar's army. The impediment to that lay in the tribune's exercise of his constitutional veto, but once Caesar's term was over the tribunes' mission of obstruction was in a grey zone of constitutional law and was not necessarily a legal challenge to the Constitution, though it was a practical obstacle. Caesar could not claim that the national interest of the Republic required that he remain in command in Gaul and the Republic could allege injury from the failure to appoint new governors, though Caesar's provinces could hardly be claimed to be lacking proper administration as long as he was directing them, whatever the technicalities of his incumbency. On equitable analysis, Caesar could be pardoned for being unwilling to give up a military command until he had become a consul designate, because his fear that his enemies in Rome would attack him through the window of any gap between his governorships and consular term, illegitimately and with no recognition of the immense services he had rendered the Republic, was justified. And that justified fear justified the actions of Caesar's tribune also. Nor could Caesar's enemies claim that his retention of command of his army threatened the safety of the state: he had made no threats. And his enemies did not dare to conjure the vision of war, not only because of its fearful implications but because gnawing at the bowels of all of them was the dreadful knowledge that they had no power to resist the man that they were almost reflexively and with terror in their hearts, tormenting and provoking.

By this intricate confluence of events, all depended on Pompey who could, if his resolution held, plausibly hold his own with Caesar on the battlefield if it came to that. And Pompey, as we have seen, had gradually arrayed himself, first very tentatively and then with subtle explicitness, in the ranks of Caesar's enemies. Two years before Pompey was asked "What if Caesar wishes to be consul and to retain his army?" He replied: "What if my son raises a stick to strike me?"[12] It was not a satisfactory answer. Now he had gradually committed himself against Caesar and if he stood aside, as he recognized, he would seem to Caesar "willing to wound but afraid to strike," and to Caesar's enemies it would appear that Pompey the Great was

---

12 Ibid., p. 630 (F.E. Adcock).

Caesar's lackey.[13] Caesar, one of history's most decisive men, also knew how to wait, and in waiting he had shattered the nerves of his rivals.

On December 1, 50, Curio sponsored a Senate vote of 372 to 22 that both generals should lay down their commands. The vote was denounced as a surrender to Caesar and was vetoed. It was effectively acknowledged that if the future of the Republic were referred to its citizens, Caesar would win. The only alternative to civic consultation was a clash of arms and while a general of Pompey's great ability could not be discounted, by that test, Caesar's prestige was considerably greater and he had by now demonstrated that he was the master of the great game of rulership, composed of its various political, military, pecuniary and public relations elements, where Pompey was a participant serving with distinction and seeking honors, but not motivated as his rival was, all the time and in every thought and action, to be master of the world. On December 2, the consul Marcellus asked Pompey to take command of the Republic's forces in Italy and Pompey accepted the commission. The Roman Republic was entering its supreme crisis.

Caesar returned to Cisalpine Gaul. It seems that the long-reliable Labienus, possibly envious of the rise of Antony, was in conversation with Caesar's enemies. (He was from the same province as Pompey and had known him for decades.) Grave though the situation was, Caesar still hoped to avoid civil war. He was prepared to retain Cisalpine Gaul and Illyrica and only two legions and he sent his lieutenant, Hirtius, to negotiate with Pompey's father-in-law, Metellus Scipio. Hirtius reached Rome on December 6 and only then learned that Pompey had been entrusted with the command to protect Italy against invasion and assumed that negotiations would now be impossible. He departed Rome without seeing Metellus. This convinced Pompey that peace was impossible; events quickened again. Caesar ordered his legions to concentrate on the border of Italy. Curio went to Ravenna and received from Caesar an ultimatum which he sent back to Rome for delivery to the consuls before the meeting of the Senate on January 1. The proposal was Curio's previous one of both generals disbanding their armies with an ultimatum: the offer had to be accepted in its entirety.

The Senate was asked to give effect to something it had overwhelmingly approved only a month before. The consuls would not allow a vote on the precise offer and instead conducted a debate on the general situation—the ultimate political response: when the political fate of the known world hung in the balance and a decision had to be made, the last Senate of the old Roman Republic fell to waffling and bloviation. Pompey was now the only member of the Caesar-resistance capable of sounding a note of realism and he advised the Senate that it must stand firm or forfeit his services. After another couple of hours of syncopated cacophony, Metellus Scipio put the fatal motion: Caesar must lay down his command by a fixed date and if he did not he would be regarded as a public enemy.

The Senate was telling Caesar he had to release his army without assuring him that he could immediately achieve election as consul, and so they were also telling him that he would be subject to prosecution for high crimes against the state, although those crimes consisted of the greatest single accretion of wealth, power,

---

13 Ibid., p. 635.

and security to the Roman world in all of its history—the conquest of Gaul. Having behaved evasively, deviously, and inconsistently for years, and having squandered its best options and undoubted opportunities to negotiate many reasonable compromises, the ostensibly legal Senate, riven with faction, enfeebled by pusillanimity and corruption, now demanded the self-abasing surrender of a man who was intellectually incapable of contemplating surrender and upon whom it was objectively impossible to impose surrender.

Caesar had given his answer with his announcement that he would only lay down his command if Pompey did also and this was repeated when the new tribune, Antony, interposed his veto, prevented the resolution from taking effect after a large majority had voted for it, and repeated Caesar's conditions. Pompey exercised his command by mobilizing more troops and Antony and the tribune Quintus Cassius were warned that if they did not leave the Senate, they might not escape violence. This was itself illegal; they departed Rome but not without the constitutional battle cry that the suicidal decision of the Senate had given them: the rights of the tribunes had been usurped. The Senate continued its macabre death plunge and acted as though Caesar was Catiline; it empowered the consuls, proconsuls, praetors, and tribunes to protect the state against the common enemy. Of all of them, only Pompey retained a serviceable connection with the realities of the correlation of forces and the flow of events, and they made him very uneasy. Caesar had already moved his crack 13th Legion to Ravenna. On the night of January 10, 49 B.C., he ordered it to cross the Rubicon, the modest river that separates Cisalpine Gaul from Roman Italy.

Fifty years of almost constant war in the times of Marius and Sulla and Pompey and Caesar were coming to their climax. The mighty power that had conquered most of the known world had now to resolve the strife within itself. Rome ruled the world but unless Pompey, who for all his talents, had never shown either the firmness of judgment or artfulness of maneuver for political rulership, could miraculously re-create the Republic, the Mediterranean world was about to come under the swaggering but inspired dictatorship of Gaius Julius Caesar. He dined quietly with his staff and then rode across the Rubicon himself into world-historical lore and renown, after concluding: "The die is cast."

PART VI

THE TRIUMPH OF JULIUS AND OCTAVIAN CAESAR

CHAPTER TWENTY-SIX

CAESAR, POMPEY, AND THE CIVIL WAR, 48-46 B.C.

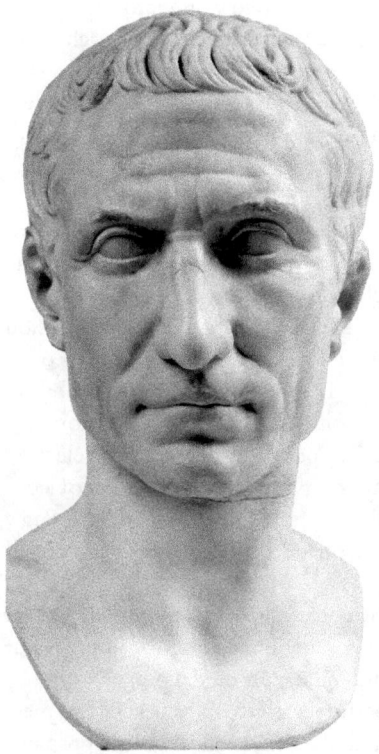

Bust of Gaius Julius Caesar

Bust of Pompey the Great,
(Augustean copy of original)

1. The Civil War in Italy and Spain

CAESAR'S LEGIONS IN Gaul were in winter quarters, and while the province was calm it would have been impractical to denude it of its garrison and in any case, as usual when Caesar determined to strike, he would strike at once. He invaded Italy and began a forced march on Rome with only the Thirteenth Legion, having judged that it would be riskier to take the time to assemble a larger force and permit his political opponents to strengthen Rome's defenses than it was to attempt immediately to seize the Capitol, where he anticipated an enthusiastic welcome. The Senate was inexplicably reluctant to declare a state of war and could not levy forces until it had done so, though it did have the ability to transfer divisions from Spain. At this point no one would have expected much dynamism or military savoir faire from the Senate, but Pompey might have been expected, having cast his lot against Caesar, to take what preparations he could. He did declare that he had ten legions ready to take the field, but Caesar knew this to be false, as most of them were in Spain, many weeks away from Italy. Pompey had been joined by Labienus, who apparently advised that Caesar's legions would not follow him into war against Rome itself. (Both men, as has been mentioned, and their families, knew each other from Picenus.)

The hesitancies of some of the factions in the anti-Caesar resistance surfaced, revealing again the frailties of a coalition. Pompey had been given the authority to command his forces, but not to decide when he was at war. Cicero was working for peace and Pompey, seeing the difficulties of mobilization in the absence of a consensus to act, half-heartedly tried to open negotiations. He sent Caesar a private message which, according to the recipient, was just an appeal to subordinate thoughts of Pompey's opposition to the public good and not to think ill of him. Caesar's description of the message cannot be entirely trusted but his conclusion that it was an attempt to gain time is probably accurate. Caesar replied with his offer to disband his army if Pompey would also, and if Pompey would end the mobilization and assume his command in Spain, Caesar promised to hand over his provinces to his chosen successor and to present himself in person in the consular election for 48, even waiving the right granted to him at Pompey's recommendation of connecting his governorships directly to his consular election. Caesar was still offering a compromise and made it clear that he would accept and act on Pompey's agreement as a Roman officer and old friend and former in-law.

Pompey came back with the promise of the consulship and a triumph if Caesar would withdraw to his province and disband his army but wrote that until Caesar pledged to abide by his own offer, the mobilization must proceed. Pompey would be prepared to go to Spain but no date for his departure was given. He declined to meet Caesar at this point and conditions were so fluid, the Senate and Pompey probably did not trust Caesar's word and the Senate itself was unsure of Pompey and particularly of what he might do if left alone with Caesar for more than a few minutes. Caesar did not consider Pompey to be adequately independent of the scheming and deluded leaders of the Senate to be reliable and believed that the Senate as a collective entity was almost completely dishonest.

The descent into war continued and had begun six weeks before Caesar crossed the Rubicon. Caesar seized Pisaurum and Fanum, on the coast road giving him control of the north end of the Via Flaminia, while Marc Antony, in-country with five cohorts, occupied Arretium on the Via Cassio by December 11, and Curio held Ancona and with four cohorts marched south and occupied Iguvium. In all of these places the townspeople welcomed Caesar's forces with enthusiasm. Caesar's forces kept moving south on almost all the main roads as he watched from Ravenna. His ant-like movements were greeted with continual defections and spontaneous adherences from his opponents to Caesar's forces; from the intelligence he was receiving, crossing the Rubicon was not quite the high-risk adventure that has been portrayed to history. We are entitled to wonder what possessed a man of Pompey's competence to accept such a commission as he did from the dithering and corrupt talking shop of the Senate. And Pompey's misjudgments were not as grievous as those of the lesser Caesar-resisters: Asculum was held by Lentulus Spinther with ten cohorts, but his men declined to face Caesar's veterans and after about ten days much of this force melted into Caesar's hands; he had picked up a whole legion of new recruits and his officers were busy recycling Pompey's deserters into Caesar's ranks even before he entered Italy.

At this point, Pompey had moved from Campania to Apulia with fourteen cohorts from the two legions that he had withdrawn in the Parthian alarm the year before. In the light of Caesar's approach and his thickening ranks, Pompey concluded that not only Rome but all of Italy would have to be abandoned. Pompey moved his loyal forces to Canusium and Brundisium and called for all loyal Republicans to join him there. He was hoping for thirty more cohorts and with all of it, he could have made an army capable of resisting Caesar to some plausible extent. Pompey called for Lucius Domitius Ahenobarbus to join him with all of his forces, but at this point Ahenobarbus suddenly became the latest Caesar-resisting commander to take leave of his senses: determined that he was not only a soldier by vocation but a talented and courageous one, he determined to hold his ground and believed that his destiny was to stop the advance of Caesar. Pompey warned him that that was very problematic (December 27), but Ahenobarbus would not hear of it and continued to meditate, in apparent confidence that he could either stop Caesar or delay him with an orderly retreat towards Pompey's embarkation ports. But his entire garrison abruptly surrendered under him, pitch-forking Ahenobarbus into the hands of Caesar's lieutenants as a prisoner. Caesar permitted Ahenobarbus, Spinther, and the other senior ranks to depart unvexed but had the pleasure of enrolling eighteen new cohorts into his army as well as other units which had just surrendered and which he sent to take possession of Sicily and secure Rome's food supply. Caesar was joined by the Eighth Legion and twenty-two cohorts of new recruits, a force that would have overpowered even Pompey's embarking armies had they met.

With the rest of his swelling army, Caesar resumed the march directly against Pompey. With all of those units that had rallied to him, Pompey and the contingent of senators began departing Brundisium to cross the Adriatic on January 12, only two days after Caesar had crossed the Rubicon. Caesar was a man with broken promises of Luca ringing in his ears and made twenty miles a day and arrived at Brundisium before Pompey had departed Italy. Caesar again invited Pompey to meet him and was again declined. He arrived at the port city to block Pompey's departure on January 25, but Pompey's military skill was undiminished, and he executed a crisp escape responding to Caesar with correct protocol: he could not meet him without the presence of the consuls. In two months, Caesar had taken all Italy, with minimal casualties, devastation, or inconvenience to the civil population. There was now no hope of an early peace. Caesar moved on Rome and Pompey would not see Italy again.

Caesar continued a full peace offensive even as he occupied all Italy. He corresponded with aristocrats and practiced a level of clemency that is almost unheard of in the history of civil wars. Yet Cicero and others persisted in regarding him as a

Catiline or an avenging Sulla. There is no reason to doubt Caesar's sincerity at this point and there is no reason either on his record up to now or after, to believe that he was at heart anything but a sensible reformer. He now had no reason to doubt his ability to prevail, and every reason to seek peace and stability as swiftly and with as little further violence as possible.

The effort at the time, led by Cicero, and echoed through the ages and particularly by many British historians, driven perhaps by their long and satisfactory experience of parliamentary niceties, to portray Caesar as a rabid proto-Bonapartist if not a wanton despot or even an antique totalitarian, is not sustained by any significant evidence available to us to evaluate his methods and his nature. He was a Roman patriot who wanted Rome to remain faithful to its highest traditions and to rule the world in an equitable and efficient manner.

Pompey having eluded him, Caesar marched on Rome on January 27. Even before he arrived, the praetor Lucius Roscius had proposed and passed a bill that conferred the full Roman franchise on the population of Cisalpine Gaul as having come into effect on January 19 and confirmed all grants of citizenship which Caesar had made as governor and completed the enfranchisement of all of Italy. That province had served Caesar well and he was right to reward it handsomely.

In order to maintain his proconsular status, Caesar could not enter Rome until he was elected consul, and so he attempted to convene a meeting of the Senate immediately outside the walls whose gates had been opened to him. He stopped on his way to Rome to confer with Cicero formally but was unable to persuade him to attend. Those senators with whom he met outside Rome's walls declined to take peace proposals to Pompey. Caesar no longer had any conceivable fears of the actions of the Senate, whose most antagonistic members had departed, and which was now a mouse squiggling beneath the paw of the feline.

In order to pay for what was now going to be a somewhat far-flung civil war, Caesar focused on the treasure in the Aerarium, which the consuls had neglected to remove. The now malleable Senate voted that he could draw from it but the tribune Metellus vetoed the proposal and moved to secure the treasure by interposing his own person on site. Caesar was not going to be confounded in war with the peacetime bias for statutory consistency; he told Metellus that it would be a trivial matter to put him to death if Metellus provoked him, and he had smiths enter and remove fifteen-thousand bars of gold, thirty-thousand bars of silver and thirty million sesterces. Such a sum was certainly worth the indignity of modifying his views on tribunician inviolability. Caesar appointed Marcus Aemilius Lepidus as prefect of the city and Mark Antony, although he remained a tribune, was placed in charge of the Italian Peninsula as a military command and took overall charge of training large numbers of people for war. Two squadrons of galleys were launched to form a patrol of the Adriatic and Tyrrhenian Seas; Antony's brother Gaius was sent as legate to Illyrica to deter the tribes from belligerency, and a new Marcus Crassus replaced Labienus in Cisalpine Gaul. After two weeks under Rome's walls, Caesar departed in pursuit of Pompey.

As a practical matter, it was already difficult to see any outcome of the Civil War except a victory for Caesar. He had already chased Pompey out of Italy and with his control of Italy and Gaul, he was able to separate Pompey from his forces in Spain. The only legions Pompey had that were adequately trained were the two he took from Caesar in the Parthian scare, and though these men were well-trained, there was no reason to be confident that they would be prepared to fight their former commander. There was already a lot of squabbling in the anti-Caesar camp: Cicero blamed Pompey for excessive optimism about mobilizing Italy, but his attempts to masquerade as a military strategist and upbraid Pompey for leaving Italy, and for not going to Spain were the nonsense of a disappointed schemer. It would be impossible for Pompey to have got his Spanish legions through Gaul to Italy as Hannibal had done and trying to bring them by sea would have been mortally dangerous. Pompey could get resources and some mercenaries in the east, and his only chance was to lure Caesar there and defeat him. Transport to the east was constrained and Caesar might not have a cavalry advantage. In general, Italian and Gallic forces were better trained and more reliable and responsive than those of the east, Caesar developed a naval edge as engagements now tended to be won by boarding parties, at which the grim Roman legions, even on uncertain sea-legs, were superior to Pompey's nimble Greeks and Asians. (But these would be lost in the victories of Pompey's superior admirals—he had learned a good deal about naval warfare cleaning out the Mediterranean pirates in 66.) Pompey also had better senior officers than Caesar (such as Labienus), but Caesar had better centurions and middle officers. And he had himself—Pompey was efficient and capable, but neither as indomitable as Caesar nor possessed of such a spontaneous genius of improvisation or the swashbuckling panache to fire up his men to heights of combat at the climax of mortal battle. A few weeks into the conflict, Caesar had the main units of the Roman world, the best recruiting ground, most of the forces and all of the momentum, and he was Julius Caesar. He respected Pompey, but Pompey feared Caesar.

Caesar had to be careful of what Pompey might be able to do supported by the Numidian king, Juba, and as has been mentioned, he sent Curio to assure the Roman food supply in Sicily, a mission that was extended to include Sardinia. He decided also to reduce Pompey's greatest ultimate potential source of strength in Spain, which he could do overland while Pompey was scrambling to patch his forces together in the east. Eliminating this force in his rear would permit Caesar, if necessary, to use all of the legions that could be raised in Gaul and Italy to subdue Pompey in the east. Caesar deployed six legions from Gaul and three from Italy which were applied to the siege of Massilia under Gaius Trebonius. Caesar himself, with the other six legions and nine-hundred cavalry, proceeded across the Pyrenees. The Pompeian army had seven legions, three under Afranius in Nearer Spain, two under Petreius in central Spain, and two under Varro in the West. Afranius and Petreius were tough and capable generals. Pompey's commander in the West, Varro, was an intellectual and it has never been clear what he was doing at the head of two legions in a civil war for control of the whole Roman world. Pompey's forces were attempting to avoid defeat and generally to evade the enemy and Caesar's were seeking an early and relatively bloodless victory.

The battle for Spain began at the Spanish town of Ilerda, a well-situated hilltop semi-fortress above intersecting rivers with a strategically valuable stone bridge. Caesar would not be sending his forces in an uphill attack in which his seven-thousand cavalry could not participate. The goal of Caesar's initial skirmishing, to get a position beside the town from which he could attack it, was unsuccessful, and the spring water levels in the surrounding rivers rose ominously. After Afranius was forced out of his little redoubt in Caesar's next enfilade, and he attempted to retreat forty miles to the south to the Rio Ebro, Caesar harassed his retreat comprehensively setting his cavalry on Afranius' flanks night and day while Caesar's infantry ran down the Pompeians from the rear. Caesar's tactics cut Afranius' army off from their supplies and he and Petreius, with no food or water, were obliged to capitulate after about ten days. Caesar's objective of eliminating these two legions with minor casualties himself was achieved. As he was dealing with Romans, Caesar treated them generously. And his deputy commander in Spain, Fabius, was able to confound and outmaneuver the academic civilian Varro after a few more weeks. It was the completely successful and swift campaign Caesar had hoped. On his route of march home, he found Trebonius' struggle to subdue Marseilless had reached its climax. Caesar constructed a mighty siege engine and with this the Massilliotes surrendered. For over two-hundred years Massillia (Marseilless) had flourished as a Roman ally. Since it knew Pompey, because of his service in Spain, better than they knew Caesar, because his operations in Gaul were to the north, they made the mistake of siding with Pompey in this conflict. Caesar determined that because of the past loyalty of the city, it should be undisturbed, but he deprived it of most of its territory and dependencies and robbed it of its formerly considerable political and strategic influence.

2. The Civil War in Africa and on the Adriatic Coast

After Curio's successful expeditions to Sicily and Sardinia, he over-confidently set out to subdue Africa with only two legions, facing the Pompeian commander. P. Attius Varus, with three legions and the pledge of support of the Numidian king, Juba. He captured an important baggage train shortly after his arrival, and then won a naval victory which included a large convoy of supplies. His troops somewhat prematurely hailed him as an imperator, and Curio advanced upon Utica and defeated an advance force from Juba. His army was already coming down with illnesses that may have been caused by a deliberate poisoning of the water supply. Curio made a stirring effort to rally his army and then attacked Varus before Juba could join him. Varus emerged from Utica, hoping to provoke a mutiny in Curio's ranks; when that did not occur, he retired back into the town. Curio began a siege but gave it up at the Numidian king's approach, installed himself on the coast and called over the two legions that he had mistakenly left out of his original plan of attack.

He might have rebounded to victory but was duped by a false retreat from Juba, and attacking at night, found himself facing the king's entire army. He was drawn forward and up to higher ground into a skillfully laid trap. Curio personally ignored an opportunity to escape and died with his legions bravely but in total and catastrophic defeat. Fragments of his army were elsewhere, and in their haste to withdraw from Africa they capsized some of the ships they had over-loaded; the departure of others was blocked, and many surrendered and were massacred by

Juba, a cunning and ruthless African despot. Curio, it will be recalled, was elected an anti-Caesar tribune, but was persuaded by an immense bribe to change sides. He served Caesar well as a tribune and initially well as a general, a young and very capable, but headstrong and unstable man, with the dangerous combination of much more bravery than judgment. For the party of Caesar this was an untimely and severe defeat and it left Africa as a point of potential shelter for the Pompeians if the campaign that would now soon be opened in the east by Caesar required them to fight on elsewhere.

Pompey enjoyed a further success at sea. His admirals, Marcus Octavius and Lucius Scribonius defeated Caesar's Admiral Dolabella, in the Adriatic, and Dolabella was unable to withdraw Caesar's forces from the island of Curicta; some managed to escape in two large rafts, but a third of the Gallic auxiliaries were trapped by the enemy, and after a heroic fight against vastly superior numbers, the Gauls killed themselves rather than surrender. To complete this terrible rout, another fifteen cohorts of Caesar's forces who had been unwisely deployed in Illyrica were surrounded and forced to surrender and substantial numbers of them defected to Pompey, albeit with questionable spontaneity and conviction. Others of Caesar's inept naval commanders managed to lose an additional forty ships, rendering Caesar's pursuit of Pompey into Greece and the Balkans an extremely hazardous business. Caesar's forces did, at least, retain control of Illyrica, and continued to protect northeastern Italy.

After the end of the campaign in Spain, those of Pompey's legionaries who were not domiciled in Spain were conducted by Caesar's forces to Transalpine Gaul, where they were released and free to disperse as they wished. Caesar's own four legions awaited him at Placentia—disappointment that the loot that they had expected was not forthcoming had provoked them to rumblings of mutiny. The ringleaders of the discontent were in the Ninth Legion, and they hoped to be authorized by Caesar to enrich themselves at the expense of the civil population. Advised of the problem, Caesar hastened to Placentia, organized a march-past of his men and let it be known he would decimate the Ninth Legion as mutineers.[1] The Army tribunes pleaded for their men and he, as he had no doubt intended to do, confined the execution to twelve rebellious officers. The effect on his men created by this incident propelled them on the march to Brundisium for a campaign in which they would show their heroic devotion to their commander and bring great honor to themselves.

Caesar still had to pay some attention to Roman politics. He did not bother the existing consuls since they could no longer exercise their powers, but he was determined to secure his own election as consul in 48, which would legitimize previous activities of his which had been called into question. The absence of the consuls prevented him from organizing his election and he attempted to have the praetor, Lepidus, conduct the election but was unsuccessful in gaining passage of this measure due to absences of quorums of necessary levels of officialdom in the administrative chaos of Rome in the midst of civil war. In the circumstances, Caesar

---

[1] It was customary when loyalty was wavering to "decimate" a legion, which meant identifying ten percent of its men who were the most vocal of the malcontents, and executing them, to deter and encourage the others.

prevailed upon Lepidus to create a dictatorship and insert him in it. It appears to have followed the precedent of Sulla and to have conferred upon Caesar wide powers including the competence to conduct elections and celebrate festivals. His belief was that the greater the powers, the more his abdication from them would impress his countrymen, and this was a step he intended to take as soon as he had himself returned as consul. As might be expected, his elevation as dictator finally lifted him above the pettifogging and harassments of layers of officialdom.

In order to loosen up the economic conditions prevailing in Rome, and particularly a scarcity of money and the prevalence of deflation, Caesar revived commercial borrowing and lending by requiring debtors to surrender property but at prewar values. This enabled most of those in debt to acquit their obligations at slightly artificially inflated values, but Caesar also discounted debt, which was appreciated by the debtors and endured by the lenders as preferable to debt cancellation, the only realistic alternative. Commercial conditions improved markedly and Caesar became something of a hero to Rome's ever more powerful and ingenious financial community. His measures also included forbidding the hoarding of more than sixty-thousand sesterces in cash. Caesar was careful not to admit slaves to the benefit of any of this, as they were always regarded with apprehension and particularly in such tense times as these. Even in these times, Caesar managed another much-appreciated gesture in reinstating in their civil rights the descendants of those whom Sulla had proscribed. While he was at it, he did the same for the benefit of those who had been condemned under Pompey's laws, even though those laws were comparatively gentle and un contentious in their application. Under his dictatorial arrangement, Caesar was indeed elected consul for the succeeding year, 48, alongside a respectable but docile aristocrat, Paulus Servilius. Caesar himself appointed the provincial governors to succeed him including Decimus Brutus to Transalpine Gaul and Lepidus in Nearer Spain.

As Caesar prepared to try to force the sea with Pompey across the Adriatic, Pompey had coopered together an army of nine legions. Two of these had been previously lent to Caesar, three had been formed from the Italian levies which escaped with Pompey from Brundisium, one came from Cilicia, the combination of two weak legions that Cicero had found there to his surprise: time-expired soldiers who had retired to Crete and a detritus of forces left by the consul Lentulus. Pompey had drafted some Greeks, as well as the troops captured from Gaius Antonius. Metellus Scipio was approaching from Syria with two more legions and Pompey was busily training up three others. He also had three-thousand archers, twelve-hundred slingers, and seven-thousand cavalry including eleven-hundred excellent Galatians. He had built up forty-nine great stores of food and munitions. The mercilessly imperishable Bibulus was now Pompey's grand admiral and commanded a fleet of three-hundred vessels. These numbers vindicate Pompey's judgment in retiring across the Adriatic and show that he was steadily building a competent fighting force that might be expected to give an excellent account of itself if he were allowed the time to bring it to full combat-readiness. Caesar now had twelve legions, though several of them were under-strength. He clearly had to rise above the fiasco in Africa and attack as quickly as possible, before Pompey turned Greece, the lower Balkans, and even Asia Minor, as well as Africa, into a schismatic redoubt.

Caesar's legions would win a pitched battle with Pompey's and so he would seek such a battle, but Pompey would be much too astute to permit one. But before that issue could even be tested, the heavy challenge lay upon Caesar to get his forces across the Adriatic in the teeth of Pompey's naval superiority. Caesar only had transport for twenty-thousand men and attempting to move his army in successive groups not only risked both of them at sea but risked the first group if it were able to land, as it would be heavily outnumbered by Pompey's army prior to the arrival of the second half of Caesar's army. Caesar went to Brundisium to prepare his plan of attack. On learning of his arrival there, Pompey moved his army westwards from Macedonia toward the coast where he might expect Caesar to land. On this point Caesar's luck as well as his strategic insights fortified him. He managed to get seven legions into his ships and committed them to a northerly wind that carried them around the southern end of the Adriatic, evading Pompey's sea patrols. But for his second wave, fortune flickered again as many of his transports were destroyed at sea and the still fulminating Bibulus (it had been over a decade now) blockaded the rest in Brundisium. For the moment, Caesar would have to try to take his target, the key transit port of Dyrrhachium, with the forces that he had already got across.

On landing, he sent his prisoner, Vibullius Rufus, to Pompey with peace proposals. Pompey was much closer than Caesar had imagined and by mighty exertions Pompey, while ignoring Caesar's message, got his army to Dyrrhachium, determined to strangle him there or throw him into the sea. Caesar threw himself on the port with seven legions, but they were not sufficient to force an early capitulation and he took up a position in the foothills south of the town and Pompey with his forces now composed and slightly rested, faced him on the opposite side of the Apsus River. At this time, Pompey had the upper hand: a larger army, a better position, and assured supply lines, where Caesar was relying on supplies from across the Adriatic, and his naval forces were inferior to those of his opponent. It was the classic struggle between Pompey's astute professional calculation of the correlation of forces and Caesar's immeasurable talent at conjuring unimagined methods of countering them.

Ever happy to have recourse to diplomacy when war was not going as well as it might, Caesar attempted to exploit the contacts between the two armies as they foraged and fraternized somewhat, but this came to nothing. In his impatience, Caesar tried to cross back to Italy in order to bring his remaining legions over himself, but he was not successful. Bibulus died full of hate of Caesar to the end, but of natural causes. Pompey appointed L. Scribonius Libo, a capable man and feasible personality, to succeed him, blockading Brundisium from an island off the harbor mouth. However, Mark Antony, a resourceful soldier who had replaced Labienus, was equal to the challenge. The season of winter storms was easing and in good weather it would be almost impossible for the balance of Caesar's army to cross. But near the end of February, Antony exploited a southerly wind and slipped away with four legions, eight-hundred cavalry and some slingers, and glided into shore under the eyes of both Caesar and Pompey. Pompey's galleys almost caught the incoming transports, but a freshening breeze brought them in at Nymphaeum.

Pompey broke camp and marched at once to try to liquidate Antony's force before it could join Caesar. A few hours later Caesar marched to Antony before he came face-to-face with Pompey and when Caesar approached from the other side Pompey recognized that fortune had turned another quarter and that he was in danger of being overwhelmed by the combined enemy. The two parts of Caesar's army joined together and cautiously followed Pompey. Caesar offered battle, which, as he expected, was sensibly refused. Caesar was ready with a back-up plan and moved at once against Dyrrhachium. When Pompey learned of this development, he rushed to the port city but underrated the discipline and marching speed of his enemy's legions and Caesar arrived at the targeted city ahead of its defender. Pompey occupied the high ground of Petra, six miles below the town, a position that made a normal siege impossible. Pompey had a greater number of fortress builders and utilized them to contain Caesar's beachhead, and Caesar enacted a counter-operation to imprison an army superior in numbers to his own. This attempt was much criticized eighteen centuries later by a general who could be argued to be an even greater military genius than Caesar: Napoleon, but he was writing in a time when trench warfare was not much practiced. It was an imaginative idea of Caesar's, but it did not succeed. Caesar had to detach some units to other areas and his men suffered from inferior rations that were little available where they were. Pompey did not have the same problem of provisioning his men but he began to run short of fodder for his horses, imperiling the one land arm that he possessed that was superior to his opponents. As the season warmed, both sides knew pestilence would not be far behind.

Pompey's next gambit was a series of offers made to Caesar to betray to him the seizure of Dyrrhachium itself. Caesar did take the bait on one of these and barely escaped with his life. There was a second round of this type of espionage when two Gallic notables defected to Pompey, bringing precise information about the disposition of Caesar's forces at a particular point guarded by the quaestor Marcellinus, who was ill. There was a vulnerable point adjacent to Antony's Ninth Legion and Caesar and his headquarters were close by. Pompey threw six legions and boatloads of lightly armed troops at the weak point. The attack succeeded for a time, but Antony held it up and Caesar shortly arrived with reserves adequate to repulse the initiative. Caesar struck with thirty-three cohorts and Pompey brought up reinforcements and the lines swayed back and forth for some time. Astonishingly, there was some panic in Roman ranks, and only Caesar's ability to reorganize his men in a labyrinth of trenches and fortifications while under heavy fire resurrected the situation. Labienus, who had often served Caesar so brilliantly, but was now a complete apostate, now took charge of dealing with the prisoners captured from Caesar's legions. He shouted in their faces the question of whether it was the habit of veteran soldiers to run away and then he executed them, a shameful act of barbarism that Pompey should not have tolerated, and that when it became known, filled Caesar and his whole army with a terrible resolve.

The fact that Pompey's troops had at last seen the backs of some of Caesar's veterans was an immense encouragement to them. "In their newly won confidence, the nobles ceased to fear the one thing they had still to be wary of—the genius commanding an army that had a defeat to avenge. Pompey, on the other hand, lacked the fiery energy needed to drive home his success. "Method, calculation and dexterity had done their work, and to these he still trusted. His troops, as will be seen, were partly out of hand: whereas, shaken as were his opponents, they were still veterans. With consummate skill, Caesar withdrew them from the lines and concentrated them at a point a few miles to the south. There he addressed them with the pregnant message "balancing courage and reason" and promising victory if they would behave as Romans.[2] Pompey was encamped opposite him, but in the night Caesar's army slipped away and Pompey's cavalry could not stop or seriously threaten it.

The climax had come and the struggle between these two illustrious leaders for supreme power in the known world would be determined at the next full clash of arms.

3. The Decisive Battle: Pharsalus

The Pompeian forces had tucked themselves into the belief that they had won a tremendous victory at Dyrrhachium and had demystified the legend of Caesar. They had indeed reduced some of Caesar's men to a battle-unworthy state of irresolution, but they had only prevailed by a narrow margin and in the entirety of the encounters and maneuvering, Caesar had held his own—the two armies naturally required a few weeks to regroup and prepare for the next phase of the Civil War. Metellus Scipio had conferred upon himself the dignity of Imperator for a series of reverses he had suffered on his difficult march of two legions and a cavalry force from Syria, where disappointments were compensated for by rapine and plunder. There was a good deal of maneuvering in Macedonia, where Caesar's commanders, Domitius Calvinus and Cassius in Thessaly tried to catch Metellus without success. The commotion and toing and froing in Macedonia and Thessaly drew both Caesar and Pompey toward each other in Macedonia.

At a recent council of war, Afranius, his performance in Spain not having conferred upon him any role as a grand strategist, urged Pompey to invade Italy, leaving Caesar in Greece, and to return like Sulla and conquer Rome. This was rejected as it would abandon the entire east to Caesar and Caesar's loyalists in Gaul would prevent an early return to Spain. Caesar's popularity in Italy would not vanish overnight, and it would be difficult for Pompey to ingratiate himself with Italy given the exactions that he would be making to pay for a war in which most Italians favored his opponent. Pompey believed that he now had momentum and having gathered forces from Asia Minor thought it was now his chance to defeat Caesar. If he could destroy his army Pompey would win.

Caesar was engaged in a morale-building exercise with his own forces and treated them in Thessaly with loot, wine, fiery speech, and along with the occasional small massacre of obdurate locals, many demonstrations of Caesar's famous clemency. The grain was ripening around them and the meagre rations of the previous winter faded from memory. By the end of July 48, the two armies were only a few miles apart in Thessaly. Caesar offered battle several times, but as was his custom, Pompey declined. He had taken position on somewhat higher ground than Caesar

---

2 CAH, IX, p. 662 (F.E. Adcock).

and so could not be forced to battle other than by his enemy charging him uphill, too imprudent an initiative for so capable a general as Caesar.

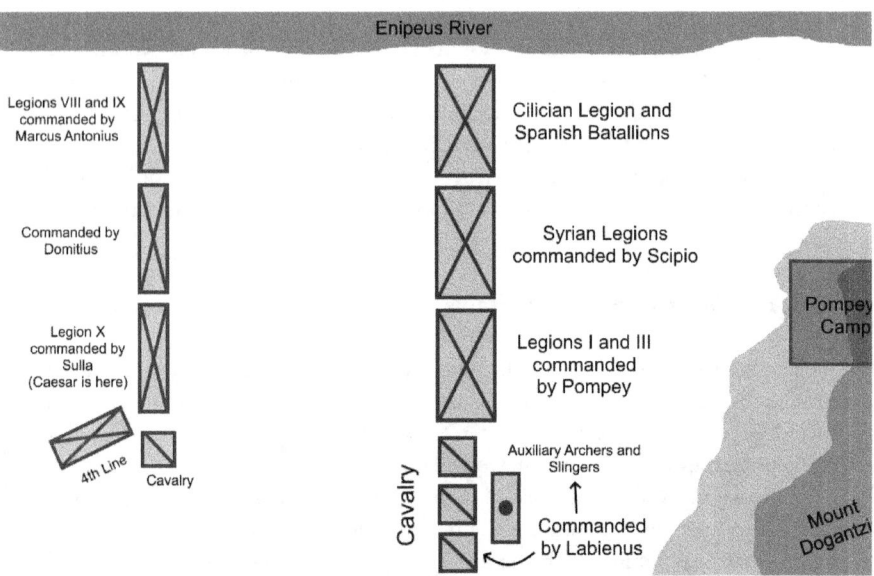

The positioning of troops at the Battle of Pharsalus.

Caesar eventually started to move off, to try to attract Pompey into a close quarters war of maneuver where he might be able to produce an advantageous position. But as he did so, Pompey's army formed up below the plateau where it had been camped signaling that he was ready to determine the issue. Caesar repositioned his army with great precision, indicating extensive forethought. History has puzzled over Pompey's motive in proceeding to a decisive battle at this time, and it is generally assumed that he wanted to strike while the legend of the Dyrrhachium action was vivid in the mind of his army as a great victory (which it wasn't—it was a drawn engagement although Caesar failed to take the important gateway port away from Pompey, and retreated but with no great loss of life). Labienus seems to have been the champion of the theory that the forces of Caesar had waffled and broken and that his cavalry could win a direct contest between the two armies. The senatorial hangers on at Pompey's headquarters would undoubtedly have been agitating for battle, but Pompey knew the soldiers too well and the venality of politicians too extensively also, to be influenced by that.

Pompey seemed to have thirty-six thousand infantry and seven-thousand cavalry to only approximately twenty-four thousand Roman infantry and one-thousand cavalry. The Roman legions of Caesar were substantially better and more reliable troops than Pompey's infantry but Pompey followed the advice of Labienus and placed his faith in his cavalry to stampede the opposing army and more than make up for the imbalance between the competence and motivation of the infantry forces of the two armies.

Pompey ordered his infantry to stand in place so that the Cesarean legions would arrive in front of them out of breath and in poor formation. While his infantry stood fast, Pompey would have his cavalry strike the enemy flank and rear, after sweeping away Caesar's thousand cavalry. Once this was done, Pompey was confident that cavalry harassments of Caesar's legions would more than compensate for their superior fighting qualities over his infantry, largely from Syria. Pompey should have known that Caesar would foresee the problems that he intended to exploit, and he did withdraw eight cohorts from his normal reserve and formed them into a separate unit placed obliquely behind the line and ready to use their pilas as stabbing spears to divert the Pompeian horse and then fall upon the flank of Pompey's army. Caesar also instructed his infantry not to arrive breathless, face-to-face with Pompey's infantry, but rather to pause halfway towards them and ensure that they retained adequate energy to engage and contain the enemy front.

The battle unfolded precisely as Caesar had foreseen. Pompey's cavalry swept away the Caesarean horse but were stopped cold by the eight cohorts stabbing the Pompeian horse and riders with their long deadly pila (heavy spears). Pompey's cavalry scattered, Caesar's reserve struck his flank and Caesar's legions, chastened by Dyrrhachium and not over-strained by their approach, forced the Pompeians back and the retreat gradually became disorderly. Caesar set his general reserve on the wavering Pompeian center, and it crumbled, broke, and fled. Pompey retired to his tent when he saw the defeat and flight of his cavalry, resignedly, and then removed his general's insignia, found a horse, and fled, almost alone, as Caesar's legionaries swarmed into his camp. Caesar led the pursuit of Pompey's infantry along the ridges to the north of the battlefield and before dusk, had caught up with and surrounded them. Through the night, Pompey's forces all surrendered to Caesar's tireless legions. They had fought well and had no cause for embarrassment, and Caesar ordered that they be received as brave men and neither taunted nor denied the rations of Roman soldiers. More than sixty percent of Pompey's army surrendered and most of the rest were killed or wounded. It was a complete annihilation and only a few stragglers remained.

Pompey's forces did much better in a series of naval engagements, but in light of the proportions of the debacle at Pharsalus, there was little point or consequence to their success. There were combined naval and tribal threats against Illyricum, and Gabinius, a somewhat egregious adventurer, met his end there from an epidemic having in this last action of his life been somewhat ineffectual. Eventually another flamboyant support person from Caesar's entourage, Vatinius, undaunted by Cicero's frequent diatribes against him, won a picturesque naval battle that chased off the naval opposition at Illyricum and he returned in triumph to Rome.

After the debacle at Pharsalus, Pompey escaped by sea to Amphipolis, then Mitylene, where he was reunited with his wife. He could choose between Egypt and Asia as his next destination, though the outlook was unpromising. Julius Caesar was a much less vindictive opponent than the Romans were to Hannibal or even than the former comrades Marius and Sulla had been toward each other. But it was not entirely clear if Caesar could continue to tolerate Pompey, especially if he were the focal point of opposition, and the balance of fortune tipped so decisively, that Pompey had no reliable friends left, and would have to be careful that those proffering assistance were not Caesar's agents.

Africa at first seemed more promising, as he could rally his fleet, gradually assemble some remnants of an army, and probably make an arrangement with King Juba. But Juba was both an insolent and a treacherous ally and making a deal with him would not necessarily prove a durable or mutually fulfilling exercise. Egypt it was. Three years before, Ptolemy Auletes (Chapter 24) had died leaving as his successors his eldest daughter Cleopatra and his elder son (Ptolemy), who was only nine or ten. He entrusted them to the protection of the Roman people, but the real guardians, if such a ring of swindlers and murderers could be so described, were the tutor Pothinus, the rhetoric teacher Theodotus, and the half-breed soldier, Achillas. Beyond this was what was known as an "army of occupation" left by Gabinius, which was clinging to the furniture of the royal palaces and was protected by a riffraff of mercenaries. Many of these had once served Pompey, but in these circumstances that did not assure continuity of their kindly disposition to him.

In a few months preceding these events, Cleopatra had been driven out of the country by another uprising in Alexandria promoted by the minders of her younger brother. With the determination and enterprise which the world was about to learn about and would forever remember, she had raised an army which was now facing off against another army at Pelusium that was nominally supportive of her brother. At such a time, the arrival of Pompey, who knew nothing of these events, was untimely. "Dead men do not bite," said Theodotus. It was September 28, 48, the thirteenth anniversary of his reentry of Rome in triumph over the pirates and Mithridates.

As Pompey stepped ashore from the small launch sent out for him, and in plain sight of his wife, Gnaeus Pompeius Magnus was stabbed in the back by the lowlife Achillas and two Roman officers. His death disgusted the whole world; he was universally judged unworthy of such a miserable end. He was an inept and tortuous politician who did not have the energy or determination to rule but did have the vanity to wish that others did not rule. Yet he believed in good government and served the Roman state with immense distinction and success for thirty years. He handled great tasks no matter how rude and difficult with consummate skill and courage, but was incapable of seeking power normally, and when responding to a competitive instinct to deny power to others, was maladroit. "An excellent organizer, a skillful tactician, a wary yet bold strategist, he was in the field no unworthy opponent of Caesar himself. Yet at Dyrrhachium, Caesar had been the last soldier in his army to be defeated: at Pharsalus, Pompey was the first. Herein lay the difference between them, not in technical skill or judgment or resource, but in that Pompey lacked that fusing together of spirit and intellect that marks off genius from talent."[3] If Pompey had sided with Caesar when he crossed the Rubicon, instead of listening to the false moralists like Cato and Cicero, he could have been the ceremonious first duovir, while Caesar governed the resurrected Republic. Pompey takes his place beside Marius and Sulla as one of Rome's greatest public men and generals, forcibly

---

3 Ibid., p. 669.

behind Caesar, but a more civilized person and abler administrator than Marius or Sulla, though with lesser political talent and not called upon to save Rome in a very dark hour as Marius was, and did.

4. Caesar and Cleopatra in Egypt

Three days after the murder of Pompey, Caesar arrived in Egypt at Alexandria. He decreed the remission of some taxation to Egypt and put his name to a few commendable reforms. Almost any official measure that was not excessively authoritarian or confiscatory taxation was a positive departure from the preceding two-hundred years of Egyptian history. His motive in coming to Egypt was apparently to head off Pompey of whose death he only learned when he was greeted by Theodotus with Pompey's embalmed head and signet ring in his hands. Though Caesar was personally revolted and officially affronted by the barbarous end of his great countryman (and former cordial son-in-law), his mood was at least ameliorated by the convenient permanent disappearance of his rival. He need have no immediate qualms about eliminating any persisting Pompeian dissidence. Seasonal winds confined him to Alexandria, a city which he apparently found mysterious, exotic, and agreeable and one from whose generous Alexandrine layout and opulent public buildings he felt Rome had much to learn and emulate. He intended to collect the money owed to the triumvirs, i.e., himself alone, in respect of the restoration of Auletes.

Caesar advised in his account of the Civil War that when he arrived in Egypt he was "in the mood to trust to the prestige of Pharsalus,"[4] and with the confidence of a Roman magistrate he landed preceded by his own victories and announced as a consul, he would decide the fate of the Egyptian throne in the name of the Republic. The Alexandrians had been playing their game of making and remaking what passed for the Egyptian government for a long time and were too steeped in the decadent presumption of the Egyptian court to be brought to attention by the arrival among them of the world's most powerful man. The king had come to Alexandria at Caesar's request. Since Caesar had only a very small contingent with him and was stranded in Alexandria by unfavorable winds, he was, despite his now insuperable position, very vulnerable. Caesar had sent for reinforcements, though he could not be confident that they would arrive promptly.

The mundane course of Egyptian affairs was suddenly transformed into one of history's most famous dalliances. When Cleopatra determined to be heard, Caesar was prepared to judge the merits of contending factions, and she contrived to have herself delivered wrapped in a rug to Caesar's attention. It is generally said, in a good but not entirely accurate play on his comment on his five days in Syria shortly after, "She came, she saw, and she conquered" (and coarser versions such as: "He saw, he came, and she conquered"). More accurately, her timing was perfect as there could be no more gratifying relaxant after the intense strain of the great struggle that he had just successfully concluded than for Caesar to plunge into an intense and exotic romance with one of the most legendarily captivating women in all of history. No

---

4 Ibid., p. 670.

one familiar either with Caesar's enjoyment of sex and romance, or his recognition of the potential of the submission of Cleopatra to add to the overpowering aura of his personality in Italy, could be surprised that he once again ignored the perils of his military position in pursuit of an altogether different form of gratification.

Caesar could have been in no doubt about what Cleopatra wanted from him, and given that at fifty-two he was thirty years her senior, even he cannot have imagined in straight physical terms that he would have been surpassingly desirable to the Egyptian queen. But that was irrelevant because for a variety of reasons she could be had and for obvious reasons he wished to have her. Such was his confidence in himself and his destiny, he set aside the easy course of attempting a swift exit despite unfavorable sailing conditions and determined to remain at his pleasure. Incidental to proceedings was his summary determination, based on esoteric factors, that she had the better side of the successoral argument to the throne of Egypt. Yet as if it were a mere parlor game, rather than a matter of life and death, as almost all politics within the palace at Alexandria were, Caesar was determined to establish her on her throne although the short and tightly confined war that that would incur taxed his genius as much as most of the great conflicts and dramas of his astounding career.

Caesar took over the great lighthouse and burned the Alexandrian fleet of seventy-two ships. Unfortunately, the conflagration seems to have consumed some warehouses of books that were to be placed in Alexandria's world-famous library. Caesar had opened his way to the sea and now controlled access to the harbor with his own fleet of thirty-four ships, despite indifferent or hostile wind conditions. With unusual industriousness, the Egyptians had set about building a new fleet on the side of the harbor that Caesar did not control. As was always the case of the court in Alexandria, the plot thickened continuously: Cleopatra's younger sister Arsinoe escaped from the palace and declared her candidacy as queen, associating herself with the self-elevated general, Pompey's chief assassin, Achillas.

Caesar intercepted messages from Pothinus to Achillas urging Arsinoe's consort to stand by the king against Cleopatra, to which Caesar responded by executing Pothinus at once and displaying his head on a pike in the Oriental manner. In a parallel move, Arsinoe had her champion Achillas murdered and replaced him with her own teacher Ganymedes. His chief contribution to what was now the seemingly normal proportions of an Alexandrian palace struggle, was to raise seawater in the pipes supplying the palace so that it could spoil the drinking water coming into the palace on conduits from outside the city. This rattled the nerves of Caesar's embattled legionaries until he told them to dig wells which after a couple of days produced a reliable source of fresh water. The day after the resolution of the water problem a fleet of transports arrived bringing the thirty-seventh legion from Syria. Caesar had ordered Domitius overland to Egypt and though he was detained dealing with Pharnaces in Syria, Domitius sent two legions to support Caesar and Alexandria.

Caesar was by now warming to all aspects of the Alexandrian problem and had sent messages to the ports of the Levant demanding ships and to Malchus, king of the Nabataeans for cavalry. He had also commissioned the prominent adventurer Mithridates of Pergamon to raise such troops as he could in Cilicia and Syria and march to Egypt. Mithridates quickly rounded up an interesting group of soldiers of fortune, admirers of Caesar, and haters of Pompey or of Egypt, and they proceeded to answer Caesar's call. The most interesting of these was Idumaean Antipater, who had only flipped sides on hearing of Pharsalus. Caesar managed to bring in the transports that had been driven beyond Alexandria by the nasty winds, relying on his Rhodian allies to defeat Ganymedes, the versatile tutor, who was now Arsinoe's admiral and who put up a good and ingenious fight.

Caesar's allies crowded Ganymedes into the harbor and here the legionaries formed boarding parties and had every advantage. Ganymedes took refuge in the Heptastadium, a large waterfront building that contained a vast arsenal of defense weapons. Caesar determined to attack and to take over this building, but the Alexandrians fought well, his own forces were impetuous and retreated prematurely, and the whole operation was a fiasco. Caesar himself swam for his life and four-hundred of his legionaries drowned. It was incredible that at the summit of his career, Julius Caesar, because of his infatuation not just with the personality and physical charms of Cleopatra, but with the role of seducer of the mysterious Queen of the Nile, was now in some personal danger in what apart from its exotic aspects was a squalid and labyrinthine tail of Egyptian bum-squat street-fighting and decadent Ptolemaic palace treachery.

The population of Alexandria was tiring of this combat raging amongst them and Caesar exploited their fatigue. In general, they disliked foreigners, but they were afraid of Caesar and were becoming skeptical that they had the ability to drive him out. In these circumstances a pretense of conciliation began to arise. A large delegation requested that Ptolemy be allowed to leave the palace, which he fervently wished to do as he hated both Cleopatra and Caesar, as well as Arsinoe, and feared all of them. Ptolemy and Caesar met and it has been clear ever since that neither of them believed one word the other said, in each case with good reason. Caesar played the amateur of Egyptian affairs pretending naïvely to agree that the king would depart and work for peace. When it was agreed that he would leave, Ptolemy allegedly burst into tears, ostensibly from nostalgia at leaving his palace but as Caesar said to his entourage, undoubtedly they were tears of joy at the prospect of continuing his treacherous struggle without having to do so under the same roof as his sister and other enemies.

Rome's ally, Mithridates of Pergamon arrived on the frontier and took Pelusium after a hard day's fighting and marched down the Eastern branch of the Nile, avoiding the complex of streams and canals in the Delta. Ptolemy proved a surprisingly adept military commander and moved his forces down the Canopic Nile hoping to defeat Mithridates before Caesar could arrive to assist him. But Caesar moved with his usual speed and efficiency, changed the course of his ships immediately after nightfall, got as close as he could to Mithridates and joined him by forced march just before Ptolemy could arrive. Caesar's German cavalry (a nationality that would not put in an appearance in Egypt again until led by Field Marshal Irwin Rommel nineteen-hundred and ninety years later) were instrumental in defeating the Alexandrian advanced units, but the king's main force held for a time until Caesar detected a weak point, sent in one of his experienced officers, Carfelenus, with three cohorts and they suddenly broke into the rear of the king's position, the Alexandrians broke down the wall of their camp to escape by water, and Ptolemy was killed in the flight and shambles of his forces.

On receipt of this news, Alexandria greeted the returning Caesar as a hero—the whole population came forward like supplicants bearing before them the images of their gods, "who having failed to bring victory were now mobilized to secure forgiveness for their worshippers."[5] The debt was paid to the surviving Triumvir. Caesar had done it again but at terrible risk for little evident purpose other than the undoubted macho satisfaction when it became known to the world that he had impregnated the temptress Cleopatra on his first night of opportunity. He and Cleopatra spent the next two months largely on an opulent state barge on the Nile enjoying the queen's company and seeing the sights of Egypt. The officers and men of his diminutive army were given a blank cheque from their commander and from the host population in the legendary fleshpots of Egypt, and from all accounts, they maxed it out. Julius Caesar gave new depth and definition to the concept of the conquering hero.

5. Cleaning up Asia and Africa

It was over a year since Caesar had departed Rome in pursuit of Pompey, and there was now pressing business in his absence; his desire for respite was understandable but he could not direct the affairs of the known world from a floating bed of enchantment on the Nile. Many of his Italian followers were disappointed by his absence and in particular by his distribution of preferments and rewards. The most evidently aggrieved was Caelius, who had been rewarded for his service in Spain with a praetorship and had set it to thwart the administration of Caesar's new law of debt. Not satisfied by legal obstructions, he resorted to rioting until Caesar's consular colleague, Servilius, invoked the Senate to terminate his activities in Rome. Caelius then became a full-time malcontent and after an unsuccessful attempt to raise mayhem in Campania, he joined the inveterate T. Annius Milo in the south of Italy. Milo had returned from Marseilless because his talents at rioting and civil insurrection were requested in the absence of the dictator, and he indiscreetly (and falsely), let it be known that he was acting under orders from Pompey, while Caelius claimed that he was in fact on his way to join Caesar. Both men misjudged the times: they were very expendable. Milo resorted to violence at Cosa and Caelius tried bribery at Thurii, and Caelius was arrested and executed, and Milo was killed in the factional mob violence.

About a month after Pharsalus, Mark Antony returned with four legions and advised the political community that Caesar wished to be confirmed as dictator on the original terms, that he, Antony was to be Master of the Horse, effectively the chief military enforcer of the regime, a role to which he was well suited, both by his fighting qualities and his loyalty to Caesar (the contrast in this respect between his predecessor, Labienus, and himself could hardly be greater). Antony had to maintain order, at which he would prove competent for a time, and to keep Caesar's veterans in good humor until the dictator returned, and at this, Antony was also proficient,

---

5 Ibid., p. 674.

being, after all, foremost among his veterans. He was also enjoined by Caesar to be clement towards Pompey's supporters without permitting any liberties or substantive concessions to former enemies. Antony managed well, but his efficiency was diminished by his compulsive drinking and his habit of wenching like a rutting panther.

Cicero's dissolute son-in-law, Dolabella, tried to exploit the unextinguished rights of the tribunate by legislating against his own creditors. His colleague, Trebellius, prevented this, and the Senate, suddenly rendered docile after all these centuries of bloated institutional self-importance, adopted resolutions that new laws should not be proposed until Caesar had returned and, to assure against disorder, Mark Antony might keep troops within the city. Tribunician grievances simmered and bubbled until, in 47, Mark Antony arrived at the Forum at the head of an entire battalion and prevented Dolabella's proposals from being adopted. As the year 47 went by, Marc Antony was having considerable difficulty dissuading his own legionaries from extracting their deserts from the territory that they policed. Antony also had to be concerned about Pompeians who might consider a sudden stroke from Africa against Italy or against the provinces which fed Rome.

In Caesar's absence, all manner of plots were bound to be hatched, though the dictator undoubtedly calculated that he had more leeway than usual before he had to worry about being struck in the back, a nightmare with which he had lived throughout the Triumvirate decade and for many years prior to it. Caesar believed that he had to clean up Syria and Asia Minor, which had, even more than usually, become a catchment for petty tyrants and bloodthirsty adventurers, and North Africa where Jupiter and pharaoh commanded substantial armies and were receiving Pompeian fugitives in significant numbers. Ariobarzanes of Cappadocia and Deiotaris of Galatia and Lesser Armenia had assisted Pompey and they were not reliable, but after Pharsalus, they advised Caesar of their wish to buy into his good will by generous payments of tribute. Pharnaces, son of Mithridates Eupator, was yet another Asiatic dreamer who imagined that he could antagonize Rome indefinitely and become a local hero with impunity. Pharnaces set out to overrun Cappadocia and Lesser Armenia. Caesar sent Gnaeus Domitius Calvinus with three legions to deal with him, but as has been mentioned, two of those were sent on posthaste to Egypt to assist Caesar in his Alexandrian man-trap. This left Domitius undermanned to deal with Pharnaces, who succumbed to the Asiatic fever of withdrawal from and provocation of Rome.

He was no longer prepared to evacuate lesser Armenia. Domitius gathered together what he could, including the excellent Thirty-Sixth Legion and advanced to Nicopolis, ignoring both the gifts of and attempted ambush by Pharnaces. Domitius risked battle but it was not successful, only the steadiness of the thirty-sixth division kept it fairly even. With the advent of winter, Domitius went to quarters and Pharnaces went around Pontus plundering the province and amusing himself with the public castration of Roman youths. In March 47, as the campaign season for Asia Minor was opening, Caesar sailed from Alexandria. For Cleopatra and her new child, he left behind three legions and took only the sixth legion with him but would soon add the forces of Mithridates and Domitius' second legion. The Jews had generally supported Caesar in Rome and Jerusalem, and Caesar rewarded them. He restored Jerusalem to its status as a capital, rebuilt its walls, and reconnected it to its port at Joppa, and reinstated Hyrcanus as high priest and promoted Antipator to be administrator of Judea. All this won for Caesar the solid support of the Jewish Diaspora. He proceeded from Jerusalem to Antioch and left the province in the charge of Sextus Caesar and sailed on from Seleucia to Tarsus, where he received the factions of Cilicia, and met with Gaius Cassius, who, after defecting from Crassus at Carrhae, had sided with Pompey. With his usual magnanimity, in this case gravely misplaced, Caesar pardoned Cassius.

Moving briskly, he went north in forced marches to Mazaca and then to the borders of Pontus where he joined with the Thirty-Sixth Legion, the Pontic Legion and a cavalry legion provided by Deiotarus, and moved against Pharnaces, who was falling under the Oriental delusion of invincibility and a predestined status to repulse and humiliate Rome. There were exchanges of messages in which Caesar implied that he was in a hurry to leave Asia Minor, but in fact, he advanced his camp closer to that of Pharnaces until they were suddenly only about a mile apart. Pharnaces suddenly was seized of the vision of attacking and defeating the great Caesar and sent out his scythed chariots. They were driven off by soldiers wielding the pila, and Caesar set his legionaries on Pharnaces' more excitable soldiers. The sixth legion cracked open the king's line and Pharnaces' camp was stormed and overwhelmed, the king fled in defeat. It was here that Caesar world-famously summed up this five-day campaign: "I came, I saw, I conquered." ("veni, vidi, vici") Pharnaces sought refuge with the rebel governor in the Bosporus, Asander, who received him warmly and put him to death at once. Caesar granted the kingdom to Mithridates of Pergamon, but in attempting to establish himself on his throne he was defeated in skirmishing and killed. Caesar left it to Domitius to sort out the remaining absurd complexities of the area and embarked for Italy, returning to Rome in mid-July.

As Caesar had not been in Rome since he departed it in pursuit of Pompey, there had naturally been a good deal of political agitation and some disorder in and around Rome as all parties and factions and interests uneasily awaited Caesar's return and the resumption of his dictatorship. A serious mutiny among the legions in Campania had broken out and the historian Sallust, who was also politically involved, was sent with promises of a pay supplement to the disaffected, but was stoned almost to death and barely escaped. Another March on Rome was organized, and the malcontents bivouacked in the Campus Martius. Fortunately, it was at this time that Caesar suddenly returned, and he addressed the grumbling men with his customary authority and effect, appealing to their dignity as Roman legionaries and promising reasonable rewards, but also threatening that if they did not do as asked, they would not share in his triumph, and he concluded by haranguing them on the rights and duties of Roman citizens. As such occasions always were, he was very effective, and the men rallied strongly. Where eleven years before, the Tenth Legion was the most solid and he said that he would march against Ariovistus with it alone, it was now the center of the mutiny, and he said that he would retain all the legions except the Tenth, whereupon it returned to his service. All the legions were told to prepare for the Africa campaign, at the satisfactory end of which, it was assured, the men would be generously rewarded and discharged.

Caesar reproached both Antony and Dolabella but did not otherwise punish them, given the difficult conditions that they had had to manage. Caesar imposed further debt reform that was generally satisfactory both to the lenders and the borrowers and restored the commercial public's confidence that Rome's treasury was in responsible hands. Pompeians were pardoned in large numbers for their professions of submission and Caesar rewarded his loyalists handsomely. Calenus and Vatinius were elected consuls for the balance of 47 and additional praetors and other officeholders were named and the Senate, far beneath its normal strength, received a large number of equites and even centurions who had served Caesar reliably. Caesar himself retained the dictatorship and was in addition elected consul for 46. With this he departed for Africa at the end of September to deal with Juba and the remaining Pompeians once and for all.

Most of the Pompeian fugitives from Pharsalus, as well as Cato with fifteen cohorts, the formidable apostate Labienus with Gallic and German cavalry, Afranius and Petreius who had tried to defend Spain, Faustus Sulla and Pompey's sons Sextus and Gnaeus and Quntus Caecilius Metellus Pius Scipio, a large group of able and highly motivated men all leading seasoned soldiers and in opposition to the dictator gathered with the egregious but formidable King Juba of the Numidians. The King had over thirty-thousand men and he had more than sixty elephants. His ally Massinissa also possessed an army and the Pompeians probably numbered thirty-five thousand by the time Caesar arrived. They had retained most of Pompey's strength of naval forces and so constituted a threat to Italy that justified Caesar's view that he had to lance this boil at once.

Caesar sent ten legions to Africa and could rely on the Mauretanian kings, Bocchus and Bogrud, who were accompanied by the Roman adventurer Publius Sittius, who fled his creditors and proved a talented military adventurer in Africa. The Mauretanians could draw off about half the strength of Caesar's opponents and his own forces would have been only somewhat smaller than the balance of the Pompeian-Juba coalition. Caesar landed in Leptis and moved inland to occupy a plateau at Ruspina as he hastened the embarkation from Sicily of his remaining forces.

Labienus attacked but Caesar improvised a defense in which his cohorts faced alternately in each direction which beat off the attackers from both sides. Caesar was only strong enough to attack when the balance of his army finally arrived. He had ten legions, five of them solid veterans, and thought that he could win a pitched battle with the enemy, all other things being equal. Caesar's next gambit was to move farther south into open country seeking a war of maneuver, having tried his hand at naval warfare and producing an indecisive result. Ten weeks after departing Ruspina, Caesar fired his camp and marched southeast hoping to entice the enemy to general engagement, but Scipio, the enemy commander, would not oblige. None of this toing and froing produced a serious engagement and Caesar returned to Aggar after roaming about seeking an engagement for four months.

Another fresh enforcement of troops, four-thousand legionaries and fourteen hundred cavalry and archers and slingers arrived from Sicily and convinced Caesar this was the time for decisive action. He knew that to draw the enemy into an engagement that they mistakenly thought they had a good chance of winning would require considerable ingenuity, a quality in which he was never found lacking. It is widely believed that it was now, at the Battle of Thapsus, that Caesar's military genius reached its highest point. Thapsus was favorable to Caesar but was held by a powerful enemy garrison and by a night march Caesar reached the eastern of the two isthmuses which stretched across a wide lagoon to the city. This gave Scipio an unfavorable series of options: he could try to circumscribe the area of Caesar's supplies, almost a siege, which would overly extend his forces, or he might try to pin Caesar in by holding both ends of land abutting the two isthmuses until Caesar's army was starving. This would require the separation of his forces which in the presence of so talented a commander as Caesar was always dangerous. Scipio did this, leaving Juba and Afranius at the end of one isthmus while he took the other. Scipio thought that the positions he and Juba were holding were sufficiently narrow, they could contain Caesar even if he moved almost all his army to break open just one isthmus and staged a holding action on the other. It was a fatal miscalculation.

Caesar's enemy lay with one flank on the lagoon and the other with the temptation to advance to the narrowest part of the isthmus. Leaving two legions to prevent a sortie from the city, Caesar advanced with his remaining forces against Scipio, sending his ships on ahead for a demonstration and (false) threat of an amphibious action in the enemy's rear, while Scipio's army was busily entrenching its position to bottle Caesar up in the eastern isthmus. Caesar had forces that were specially trained to deal with elephants and deployed them appropriately; he waited for the two wings of his army to be aligned and as each corps came into line, he addressed it in terms of confident victory. Putting the Tenth Legion first, at the sound of a trumpet it forced its way past Scipio's force and pressed it against the lagoon. The other legions moved forward swiftly, one by one and turned to attack the enemy. The special anti-elephant forces panicked the elephants on the enemy left and drove them back toward Scipio's camp. With the left wing broken, Scipio's army could not hope to hold its position, and his army broke in very close quarters and fled back into its own camp.

Caesar set two experienced legions on Scipio's rear, and they ran down the enemy and completely shattered the defeated Pompeian army. Caesar's own command had headed off another group of fugitives which surrendered and asked for mercy. Caesar attempted to restrain his men but the long wait for the rewards of victory, the months of squatting, maneuvering in the arid Numidian desert, and this intense battle had filled them with hatred for these over-persistent rebels and despite Caesar's efforts his legionaries killed the surrendering forces practically to the last man. For Caesar to have thought of a maneuver that would lure his enemy into a position he believed to be one of strength, but which Caesar foresaw that he could exploit and use to defeat Scipio, and then execute a complicated plan to perfection, was a remarkable feat of arms, and ranks with Alesia as his most brilliant battle.

In three weeks all Roman Africa was in his hands. Caesar marched on Juba, who was already in flight at the news of the decisive defeat of Scipio and Juba's chief general Saburra. The king himself reached his capital Zama, where he had taken the precaution of preparing an immense pyre on which, if he were defeated, he proposed to immolate his wealth, subjects, family and self successively, seeing everyone else into the flames before torching himself, an infernal enactment of the sea captain going down last with his ship. "In this high act the people of Zama were unwilling to play their part and closed the gates against him."[6] Juba and Petreius jointly committed suicide. Massinissa vanished and his son Arabion escaped to Spain. Caesar set up most of Juba's kingdom as the new province of Africa Nova and Bocchus of Mauretania and Publius Sittius took the rest.

Gnaeus and Sextus Pompeius, Labienus, and Attius Varus removed to Spain; it was the last stop in the known world. Sittius captured Faustus Sulla and Attius Varus and handed them over to Caesar. Faustus (twin of Fausta), the dictator's son and Pompey's son-in-law, first over the temple wall at Jerusalem, and Varo were executed. Mind-reading at this distance is dodgy, but it is difficult to think that Caesar was not motivated by a final spirit of vengeance against the two great generals who had interceded in Roman history between his patron and uncle, Gaius Marius and himself—Sulla had banished Caesar and Pompey had betrayed him. By his lights and given his unlimited authority, Caesar was magnanimous, but he was neither saintly nor, when he determined against civility, was he in the slightest sentimental. Scipio stabbed himself to death on his ship, having been overtaken by Sittius.

Only Cato remained, in Utica. He reinforced the city as best he could as Caesar approached, but then, when he saw it was hopeless, he sought to spare the inhabitants, and then stabbed himself in his innards, finally pulling out his own intestines to finish this gruesome but indisputably brave deed, an inflexible and stoical Roman to the end, incorruptible certainly, other than to the extent that his somewhat unworldly and impractical and histrionic moral dogmatism was afflicted by a taint of the nihilistic, since it had no possibility of recruiting more than passive curiosity and respect—no significant body of emulators. The younger Cato has been a popular historical favorite, especially among British historians, because of his absolute financial honesty and devotion to traditional, patriotic, agrarian Roman values, his opposition to commercial avarice and political opportunism and self-seeking, and his avoidance of the shortcomings of his great grandfather, who has, deservedly, been unforgiven for his sadistic insistence on the destruction of Carthage for no remotely morally acceptable reason.

It has often been held that Cato gained a moral victory over Caesar by killing himself and not allowing Caesar to spare his life. This puts the competition between the two men on a plane that is completely esoteric: Cato's opposition to Caesar was based on fidelity to a Republic that did not exist and to the extent it ever had existed, did not deserve such terminal fidelity. Caesar ran a more intelligent and successful government than any previous regime of the Roman Republic and he achieved more for Rome, whether it was really still a Republic or a transitional system, than anyone else in its prior history with the sole possible exceptions of Romulus, Camillus, and Marius, founder and military saviors. Cato was in some respects an impressive man, his courage and his probity and his patriotism were almost superhuman, but he was not, could not be, and never seriously pretended that he was a candidate to lead the mighty Roman state with all its dependencies and affiliations as it had arisen in his

---

6 Ibid., p. 688.

time. He was no rival to Caesar in talent, natural authority, or historical significance.

He attempted to undermine Caesar's moral authority by stridently advancing a counsel of moral perfection which had no possible applicability in the politics and government of contemporary Rome. He acted out a morality play of unwavering courage. But if he committed suicide in order to seize the moral high ground against Caesar, the motivation was unworthy of the act and failed in its objective thereby. If he took his own life merely to deny Caesar the ability to spare his life, it was a narrow-minded decision more spiteful than heroic. Of all this galaxy of personalities, Cato, distantly followed by Cicero, did put up some sort of symbolic moral or intellectual opposition to Caesar's astounding sequence of military, political, and literary triumphs. But they were secondary players, and in the end, Caesar's death was greatly more tragic, more noble, and infinitely more significant in every respect than Cato's, much less Cicero's.

Yet, the legend has persisted: "Vastly superior as Caesar was to Cato in intellectual power and breadth of vision, he saw in him a man before whom his genius was rebuked, as was Macbeth's by Banquo; and knowing that Cato was more dangerous dead than living, he pursued him, alone of his opponents, with rancor and calumny until he himself perished, the victim of the ideas for which Cato had died."[7] In the opinion of this author, that widely held view is mistaken. Cato attempted to achieve such a status, it was a lofty ambition, and he sacrificed everything for it, but it was an unsuccessful attempt to deny an immense historical status that rightfully belonged to a greater man.

There followed Caesar's long-awaited and unprecedentedly mighty triumph which was spread over four several-day periods, for Gaul, for Egypt, for Pontus, and for Africa. The procession passed endlessly toward the Capitol, senators, magistrates, trumpeters, floats piled with massive spoils and plunder, pictures, including of the deaths of Scipio, Petreius, and Cato, to show that they were enemies of Rome. (Pompey of whom that could hardly be claimed, and whose death he disapproved, was not depicted.) Prisoners were paraded: Arsinoe, Princess of Egypt, Juba, son of the Numidian king, and Vercingetorix, who was garrotted at the end of it, as Caesar had little mercy for barbarians. Finally came Caesar himself and then his great legions singing ribald songs about their partially bald-headed yet frenetically womanizing general. Wagons rolled by loaded down to the axles with golden crowns and exotic treasure. Every legionary received five-thousand denarii, ten-thousand for every centurion, and even one-hundred denarii for every one of the hundreds of thousands of spectators. There was still colossal treasure left from Caesar's many years of conquest and at the end of the last day, Rome dispersed from twenty-two thousand tables piled high with rich food and good wine, a feast for every Roman. Jubilation was unconfined.

The dictator was escorted to his house by elephants, his late daughter, Pompey's wife, was commemorated in shows and plays; there was a mimic naval action, a battle between prisoners of war and criminals and a hunt of four-hundred lions and of giraffes. A Julia Basilica and a Forum Julium which were eventually completed by the dictator's chosen successor were solemnly dedicated along with a Temple of Venus

---

7 Ibid., p. 689.

Genetrix. There were a couple of discordant notes: Caesar's chariot broke down in front of Lucullus's temple of Fortune, and some of his old veterans became drunk and disorderly complaining that some of the money lavished on this mighty extravaganza should have been given to them. At this, the dictator, on this day of all days, lost patience and seized a ringleader and personally led him to be executed as if in an act of military sacrifice to complement the otherwise uncircumscribed festivities. According to Dio, two other rowdies were, in an act of religious improvisation, sacrificed by the priest of Mars in the Campus.

To maintain his sense of piety and proportion, Caesar had on each day ascended the steps of Jupiter's Temple on his knees to lay his laurels on the altar of the God. "The awnings which protected the people were of the silk which had begun to come from the East to be the standard luxury of Rome under the Empire. In such a setting of the old and the new, of open triumph and inward resentment, the Civil War ended."[8]

Rome was not quite finished with internecine strife.

---

8 Ibid., p. 690

CHAPTER TWENTY-SEVEN

GAIUS JULIUS CAESAR: DICTATORSHIP, ASSASSINATION, VENGEANCE, AND SUCCESSION, 46-37 B.C.

THE IDES OF MARCH AND PHILIPPI

Julius Caesar, the Tusculum portrait

Marble bust of Brutus Massimo

1. The Dictatorship

CAESAR'S DELAY IN returning to Rome and the disorders in his absence incited increased fears that he would not entirely restore the Republic. Cicero engaged in a great deal of soul-searching and general correspondence trying to convince himself of the benignity of the regime of the returning Caesar, having struck out with his faith in Pompey. He had to acknowledge his clemency as well as the proportions of his victory and persuaded himself and some others that Caesar would be essentially a protector of the traditional Republic, rather than an enforcer of a new and less democratic republic as Sulla had been. It is not clear how much encouragement Cicero had from Caesar in this view, but he did conclude that Caesar should press a program of comprehensive social and economic reform. There were limits to what Caesar was prepared to do to create a commonwealth of lesser men; he accepted Cicero as his equal in political thought and writing but he was no man of action. Cicero's difficulty in imagining or recommending the conduct of the conquering heroes, like the hesitancies of Pompey and the stoic ideals of Cato, impressed Caesar negatively in that the ancient tradition that Rome was greater than its greatest man was not a view to which Caesar adhered. He had become as Cicero described him: "a portent of incredible speed, application, and insight."[1]

As 46 ended, it was clear that Caesar was in no hurry to resurrect the Republic and he departed for Spain to deal with the last rebels there, leaving his consular colleague and magister equitum (master of cavalry), Lepidus in charge. Nothing better or more depressingly illustrated the incomparable power of Caesar than the extent to which the state went to sleep in his absence. It soon became clear that Caesar had no intention of standing aside, but nor would he govern ineffectually or without ambition. He quickly granted the Transpadene Gauls and other non-citizens in that area the full franchise that he had intended twenty years before, the completion of the work of the Social War. He continued the restoration of political exiles and his amelioration of the status of debtors and lessees. He put through a number of measures to enhance the efficiency of administration and to adjust the calendar to comply more exactly with temporal and seasonal facts. Less successful was his faith in sumptuary laws, which, like Plato and Sulla, he believed were worthwhile and enforceable. He deregulated or prohibited wearing pearls and purple, riding in litters and burial under sepulchral monuments. The sale of various comestibles was subjected to regulation or prohibition. Lictors and soldiers guarded markets and even invaded private dining rooms until Caesar departed for Spain and Roman society returned to self-indulgent practices which traditional Roman sentiment accepted with no great embarrassment or regret.

Caesar also had considerable success in reducing the influence and containing the presence of the rowdy rabble that filled much of the city of Rome. In southern Italy, there were bands of rough herdsmen on the great estates among whom Pompey had raised cavalry troops and Milo had collected his insurgents. Where these bands were slaves, they could easily be encouraged to revolt but it was not possible to destroy the only practical method of ranching without striking at private property in a way that Caesar wished to avoid. He legislated that at least one third of the rough shepherds and herdsmen of southern Italy should be recruited among men of free birth. Caesar was always mindful of having a reservoir of strong and adaptable manhood to fill the ranks of his armies in time of need. He reimposed light customs duties that had been abandoned in 60 B.C. with modest economically stimulative consequences. Caesar incentivized large families, as he considered a declining birthrate to be a sign of degeneracy. He tightened laws against murder and affronts to the state but encouraged former governors and other provincial officials to remain in the provinces that they helped administer in furtherance of better provincial government. Substantial improvements in the distribution of grain

---

1 CAH., IX, p. 694 (F.E. Adcock).

and the maintenance of roads and public buildings were legislated. Caesar also had the vision to drain the Pontine Marshes and the Fucine Lake in order to increase the arable acreage of Italy, projects continued intermittently to the time of Mussolini. He lay down a new road across the Apennines to the Adriatic, deepened the harbor at Ostia so that it replicated the role of Piraeus for Athens. The site of the artificial lake for his naval battle at his first triumph became the site for a great Temple of Mars. Vast public libraries directed by Varro, a new theater to stand on the Tarpeian rock, and a codification of the civil law were all projects that were taken in hand and laid down. All were completed by his successors. All of these works of Caesar's have usually been positively compared to those of Sulla who generally regarded Caesar as an enemy, and Caesar considered that Sulla's ruthless exploitation of his victory was unworthy and counterproductive, and that he had been foolish and irresponsible to abdicate (though he was personally somewhat relieved when he did).

Since Caesar departed Spain after his victory at Ilerd, his Roman successors in those provinces had destroyed the goodwill of Rome in Spain and made it extremely vulnerable to the temptations of Pompey's sons when they were chased out of Africa. After his success in Africa, Caesar sent some contingents under Quintus Pedius and Quintus Fabius, but they were unable to stop the spread of the revolt and by late 46, Gnaeus Pompeius commanded thirteen defected or locally recruited legions. Most of them were competent and brave and he had six-thousand cavalry and Labienus with him. Caesar had no lieutenant capable of subduing the Spanish provinces, so he set out to do it himself, arriving at the Spanish front in December 46. He had eight legions, four composed of veterans and eight-thousand cavalry as well as a substantial number of auxiliary forces. As four of his legions were battle-tested and he himself could not be rivaled by Pompey's son or anyone else except to some extent Labienus, Caesar was confident of winning a showdown battle with the young Pompey.

After some maneuvering, he set up a battle at Munda, in southern Spain on March 17, 45. Pompey had slightly more favorable ground. It was a day-long battle and courage was equal on both sides. Finally, at what he saw as the decisive moment, Caesar put himself at the head of the fray as he had done against the Nervii thirteen years before and led his intrepid if temperamental Tenth Legion in a turn of the enemy left and now came the Mauretanian cavalry and a mighty sweep of the enemy's flank and rear. Labienus saw the threat and drew back forces to counter it but this was mistaken by the Spaniards as the beginning of flight and even Gnaeus Pompeius cracked; the rebel army failed and Caesar made no effort to spare them casualties: his entire army, cavalry and infantry, hunted down the enemy all night and utterly destroyed Pompey's army. Labienus and Varus both died bravely in action and Caesar ordered a funeral with full honors for both. Gnaeus Pompeius fled but was chased down and after three weeks, his severed head was brought to his palace and displayed to the public. His brother Sextus Pompeius found refuge among the Lacetani, who revered his father and he lived on for some years conducting sporadic guerrilla operations and will reappear. Caesar was looking for money for his wars and land for his veterans and for once he showed no clemency. He deemed it a rebellion rather than a war, which relieved him of responsibility for humanitarian considerations and like all the wars in Spain from earliest times to the great Civil War of the 1930's it was fought savagely.

This would prove to be Caesar's last combat. He did not specialize in a branch of war as Alexander did with cavalry, Pompey's grasp of amphibious warfare, Marius and his design of weapons and new formations, some of the maneuvers of Sulla, and Napoleon's use of artillery. The key to Caesar's success was his genius: he took in the formations and the terrain, advanced where he thought appropriate, awaited events, always confident that as the climax approached he would see the way to victory and so he always did. He had two minor reversals in Gaul and the Pompeians claimed a victory at Dyrrhachium though it was more of a draw, but apart from that he always won and when the stakes were at their highest, he won more brilliantly than otherwise: the greater the pressure, the more original his responses and the more flawless his execution. He ranks with Alexander and Hannibal as the greatest of the ancient generals and at approximately the same level of permanent military prestige as the very greatest of modern generals, including Napoleon. And he takes leave of most great commanders in that his political insights and diplomatic talents were of almost as great a level of mastery as his genius as a field and theater commander, and his talents as a historical chronicler and wordsmith, a writer and orator, were also exceptional.

Caesar set out with great energy and thoroughness to find land for all of his retired veterans, and also to resettle hundreds of thousands of the indolent and frequently destructive masses of the tenements of Rome itself. In these efforts he was substantially successful and taking care of his veterans helped to ensure his succession and resettling a significant part of the Roman underclass as well as large groups of wandering and generally somewhat sinister semi-rural Italians, making Italy and especially Rome safer and more smoothly functioning, and removed from the Roman political equation a frequently highly inflammatory and unmanageable urban proletariat (over eighty-thousand people, according to Suetonius). Caesar continued the colony of Gaius Gracchus at Junonia near Carthage and he developed a plan for the complete reconstruction of both Carthage and Corinth, and the cutting of a canal through the isthmus at Corinth. Here, as in many other areas, Caesar showed himself an imaginative and monumental creator of works, a liberal statesman, even if his desire to rebuild Carthage was influenced by his intense detestation of the family of Cato. He settled large numbers of citizen soldiers in northern Italy dealing with three problems at once: making restless veterans happy, settling down urban mobs, and putting many thousands of rugged veteran legionaries in northern Italy where they could be quickly marshaled and deployed against an invader.

Caesar made war support war, and he confiscated the estates of avowed Pompeians as long as that did not make a complete shambles of his general policy of clemency. He imposed enormous fines on recalcitrant African communities and confiscated the land of cities that had sided with his enemies in Spain. He was a grandiose builder in Rome which generally pleased the vanity of the Romans as long as Caesar could pay for it from his foreign conquests, which he did and as a further tangible gesture towards political stability he doubled the pay of the legionaries much of it to some extent retroactively.

It is not clear how far Cleopatra remained in Caesar's life; he put her statue in his temple to Venus Genetrix and built her a small pavilion on his property in Rome. Caesar was certainly planning a campaign against Parthia, not only to punish that country for the treacherous death of Caesar's old financial backer and co-triumvir Marcus Crassus, but also to push the borders of the Roman interest in Asia Minor out to the natural frontiers of the Caucasus Mountains and the Tigris and Euphrates. There was skirmishing and intrigue in Syria in 45, and Ceasar's young cousin Sextus Caesar, whom he had left in charge in Syria, was murdered in a coup fomented by a follower of Pompey, Quintus Caecilius Bassus. Caesar ordered three more legions to Syria in 44 to stabilize that province and start preparations for a Parthian campaign. He also sent Vatinius with three legions to pacify the northern and eastern edges of Illyrica. He carefully distributed thirty-five legions around the Roman frontiers and ensured that no governor or local commander had more troops under his command than could be easily outnumbered by the central Roman government, and that no military or civilian governor stayed in place for so long that local loyalties crossed over to him.

There has always been a great deal of speculation about Julius Caesar's view of his continuing role at the head of the Roman state including frequent suggestions that he could be tempted to assume the role of a monarch. There is no evidence whatever that he considered anything of the kind or aspired to it, and indeed had he aspired to it, he could easily have conferred it upon himself. On the one occasion when it was publicly suggested by Mark Antony, Julius Caesar strenuously declined any such suggestion. There is no evidence that he believed in hereditary monarchical rulership and all the evidence is that he believed in the radical reform of the Republic from his position as an ultimately long-serving dictator, somewhat like Sulla but clement, imaginative, and untempted by the prospects of retirement. Nor did Caesar have the slightest interest in the Hellenic monarchy; he was familiar enough with the Greeks, and a respecter of Greek culture and civilization, but did not consider it necessarily superior to that of the Romans and in fact thought its utility confined to the creation, as Alexander and others had foreseen, of a trans-national elite culture of civilization in Asia Minor, Egypt, and to the east, a sort of Mandarinate, but absolutely nothing to displace the Latin language as the language of the world and the Roman Republic as modified by him as the preferable props and anchors of the mighty and ever-expanding Roman state.

As Pontifex Maximus, he was a reasonably diligent guardian of the state religion. And he certainly demonstrated superstitions and religious proclivities that implied that he gave that religion more than mere lip service, though he was in no sense pious and as far as can be deduced, neither fervent nor particularly convinced of the efficacy of the complicated schedule of indulgences and extravagant conclusions derived from minor and dubiously relevant events. But in these latter years, there was a continuous reference to Caesar as a partial or outright deity. As uncertainty persisted over his political plans, increased honors were heaped upon him including terming out his dictatorship and proclaiming him to be dictator for life, with no evidence that he sought these honours other than the fact that he did not decline them. The motives in attributing a quasi-deified status to Julius Caesar seemed to have been a combination of trying to elicit his ultimate ambitions, seeking his goodwill whatever those ambitions were, and building resentment and suspicion against him because the very excess was sure to incite envy and the hostility of usurpation. As Florus put it: "they decked him with fillets like a victim to the sacrifice."[2] It is not clear to what extent he was regarded as a deity while he lived but the Romans seem to have developed a special status of particularly inspiring people that retained them in the human fraternity while enhancing and enlightening them with at least moderately superhuman aptitudes for leadership, courage, intelligence, and felicity. No fair-minded judge could withhold such distinction from Gaius Julius Caesar. There is no evidence that he sought any more than that or looked upon those who would push more upon him with anything more forthcoming than bemused indifference.

On the Ides of September 45, Caesar had made up a will which was deposited with the Vestal Virgins. Prior to the Civil War, Pompey, his son-in-law, was his heir. The new will named Octavius, grandson of his younger sister Julia, as heir to three quarters of his estate. Other relatives ranked next and eventually came to Decimus Brutus and Mark Antony. At the end of the will Octavius was adopted as Caesar's son. No mention is made of his son with Cleopatra, and he remained married to Calpurnia with apparently continuing hope that she might bear him a son. Caesar had undoubtedly seen good prospects for Octavius whom he kept close to him in the Spanish campaign and in his triumph, Octavius followed closely behind Caesar's chariot and was made a patrician and a member of the pontifical College. Octavius was sent to pursue his studies at Apollonia until the time would come for him to begin his military apprenticeship, presumably in the coming Dacian and Parthian campaigns. Octavius was going to be master of the horse for the remainder of the year 44, succeeding Lepidus. From all of this it is clear that Caesar had high hopes for Octavius, considered him his ablest possible heir and in the event of anything befalling him Octavius would be launched with every advantage to succeed to Caesar's offices. That he foresaw what an immensely talented and successful leader Augustus Octavian Caesar would become is not clear, but he did see him as the most promising successor available who should prevail despite the claims of Mark Antony and Lepidus should the succession to Caesar suddenly open up.

Readers are respectfully advised to ignore all intricate historical mind-reading by Suetonius and others trying to make a case for Caesar's claim to royal or divine status, or his preference for constitutional offices such as the tribune, or to make something out of the exact designation of himself on Roman coinage. All manner of theories can be elaborated but none of them holds water and there's no evidence that Caesar ever considered a royal option, much less the claptrap about divinity, though he certainly considered himself endowed with a greater aptitude to rule than anyone else that he knew of, with customary acknowledgment of the extraordinary gifts of Alexander.

Caesar did intend to refill the Senate and add to it respected and loyal representatives of all Italy and ultimately of other parts of the Roman world. And after resettling the rabble in Rome around the Roman provinces, which they would help develop and romanize while removing themselves from the turbulent political equa-

---

2 Suetonius. Divus Julius, 42, 1.

tions of the streets of Rome, he would stabilize the equal powers of the popular assembly with those of the Senate. And at the summit of it, Gaius Julius Caesar, dictator, would rule. He would not meddle constantly nor weaken his powers by their excessive imposition. He would be clement, and he would be moderate but when he wished to assert himself, he would do so at once and without argument or dissent. The entire vast collection of fragments and impressions, intuitions and allegations, can be ransacked as they have been but they will not produce, after these thousands of years, any more evidence than we have long had that Caesar would rebalance the Senate with the popular assembly, reform the laws and their administration, broaden the electorate and the base of government, strengthen the Republic in every way, and above all strengthen it by his presence as dictator for as long as he wished followed by at least the intermittent dictatorship of his grandnephew and adopted son Octavius Caesar.

It could be claimed that Caesar's position was merely the logical round-up of the precedents set by the three principal soldier-statesmen who had preceded him. Marius rolled up a succession of seven consulships, and Sulla became dictator while retaining the consulship, and Pompey became a sole consul while delegating entire responsibility for a single imperium or event. After his Spanish campaign, the Senate offered him a right to nominate the holders of the great offices of state, but he contented himself with recommending people to the Senate from time to time. Illustrative of Caesar's refusal to take these matters too seriously was his nomination on the last day of the year 45, when the consul Quintus Fabius died and Caesar named a consul for the last hours of the year, causing a tremendous flood of bitter reproach from Cicero who accused Caesar of bringing the Senate and the consulship into disrepute as positions of ridicule. There is no evidence that Caesar intended any such thing but there seems to be reason to think that he didn't think much about the Senate at all. It was galling for exceptional men like Cicero and even more the silence of great aristocratic houses with centuries of patriotic background to fester in Caesar's anterooms or address their concerns to the new men who buzzed around Caesar's presence in these years. Caesar was generally very polite and respectful but there were occasional incidents such as when the Patres filed in to announce to him in early 44 a new grant of honor and he failed to stand at their approach. But this was the depth to which these matters had descended: the supposedly great men of the Senate contemplated assassination over trivial matters of protocol. Caesar should have had some more emollient advisers to deal with the hyper-sensitive, but failure to do so is scarcely a capital offense. John Wilkes Booth and Lee Harvey Oswald, in their lunacy and wickedness, were more substantially motivated than Brutus and Cassius.

2. The Ides of March

Where the breach seemed to open up between Caesar and the traditionalists was in the increasing evidence that Caesar, as he allegedly said, considered that: "The Republic has become a form without substance." He had been dictator but abdicated on becoming consul for 48; he was made dictator again after Pharsalus and was slow to surrender it and then his friends conferred the office for ten years. Only three of the years had passed when his friends voted in the Senate that he should be dictator for life. They did him a bad turn, perhaps deliberately and perhaps not, but he compounded it when, as his coins illustrate, he accepted that offer. This vast deposit of powers for life in the hands of Caesar in the absence of an emergency caused any constitutionalist to regard Caesar, however great his services and his ability, as a tyrant. It was inevitable that many people in the Senate and other government circles would see Caesar's dictatorship as the end of traditional government, and yet all that was needed to restore that government was to remove the dictator, as he showed no disposition to remove himself. Gradually, and in keeping with the well-known human habit of believing what one wishes to believe, those offended or threatened by the vast powers of Julius Caesar came to see themselves as defenders of a governmental system of everybody associated with the anti-tyrannical storied history of Republican Rome. And gradually they saw the removal of the one human obstacle to the restoration of that grossly over-romanticized era and entity as a deliberate and benign act. Caesar's enemies grew in numbers, righteousness, and in delusional notions of the just and beneficial act they were contemplating, while Caesar, who was fearless always, even facing desperate odds against his mere physical survival, could not take seriously, even if he was dimly aware of, the schoolboys' scheming and ludicrous moralizing over the brutal and cowardly murder of the greatest and most talented leader, with a doffing of the laurel to Alexander the Great alone, that the Mediterranean world had ever known.

We cannot know to what extent Caesar realized that he was in some danger. Presumably, had he known, he would have taken greater precautions, but he was so unwaveringly courageous he might have considered precautions cowardly. It was revealing when he said, of his practice of clemency, "I wish for nothing more than that I should be like myself and they (his opponents), themselves." He may have found it difficult to realize how blind those envious of him could be in not seeing the services he might yet render to the Roman state. Whatever his thoughts, he had granted a general amnesty though obviously defeat still rankled with his ungrateful enemies. The Senate had voted him sacrosanct, and the senators had bound themselves by an oath to protect him. He dismissed the Spanish horsemen that had been his military bodyguard and he moved freely about the city in apparent confidence and security. "If he was to be treated as a tyrant, he would not suffer the tyrant's punishment to live in fear."[3]

It is impossible to guess when the actual plotting against Caesar began but it must certainly have been underway throughout the hectic early weeks of 44 as Caesar prepared to depart for the Parthian expedition. People like Trebonius and Decimus Brutus owed a great deal to Caesar yet plotted his death. The decision of the conspirators not to attack Antony was probably an effort to use him to silence Caesar's following by elevating him into a post-Caesar junta of joint leadership. But no such proposal ever materialized. To kill anyone except the tyrant turned a sacrifice into an assassination—there's no evidence that any of them gave a moment's thought to the eighteen-year-old Octavius Caesar.

There has been a good deal of speculation that Caesar was about to stage a

---

3 CAH, IX, p. 735 (F.E. Adcock).

coup to make himself king just before he departed for Parthia. But this must be nonsense; as Napoleon, a thoroughly qualified judge of these matters, would point out, the eve of a prolonged departure to a distant place "is not the moment to subvert the Constitution."[4] There was a series of incidents: a diadem was placed on the statue of Caesar and was removed by the tribunes. As the dictator was returning on January 26, 44 B.C. from celebrating the Latin festival, the cry "Rex!" was raised, and Caesar replied: "I am not Rex but Caesar,"[5] which did not assuage opinion. Romans believed that the king's role usurped the rights of the people; the notion of constitutional monarchy had not arisen.

The Death of Caesar by Vincenzo Camuccini, 1804-5

When these tribunes claimed that their freedom of action had been infringed, Caesar had them removed. Three weeks later, Antony offered Caesar a diadem which he ostentatiously refused before dedicating it to Jupiter Capitolinus, the only king of the Roman people. In the last days suspicion arose because of a priestly finding that the Sibylline books revealed that if Parthia was to be conquered, it would be by a Roman King. Caesar thus came under pressure to cancel his expedition to Parthia which was out of the question. But this absurd incident rippled around Rome inciting further dark suspicions. Caesar's patience with this homicidal hysteria was formidable and indeed excessive. His solution to the Sibylline problem was that, if necessary, he would invade Parthia as a king of one of Rome's Asian provinces but would return to Rome the dictator of the Republic. This led to further febrile anxiety that Caesar planned to move the capital of the Roman world to Alexandria or Ilium.

---

4 Ibid., p. 736.
5 Ibid.

Caesar was not entirely blameless in the horrible tragedy that was about to occur. He could easily have divided the conspirators and satisfied most of them that what he planned to do was reform and strengthen the Republic and not much interfere in the normal workings of the state. And he should have arrested a couple of the conspirators and shaken the plot down, and he should certainly have retained his full security unit. That he did not do any of these things indicates he was prepared for another test of wills, for that is what he considered most conflict to be and he was right to believe that he normally would win such a test. But he should not have submitted himself or Rome to such a roll of the dice.

Caesar attended the Senate on March 15, 44, was approached by sixty of his colleagues all with daggers hidden under their togas and they mercilessly assaulted and stabbed him to death. He allegedly uttered the famous "Et tu Brute?" (to a man he had endlessly helped, forgiven, and befriended), and gathered part of his cloak over his head "that he might die decorously. And great Caesar fell," at the foot of the statue to Pompey. (It is not clear he reproached Brutus, and if he did, it was probably in Greek: "Kai Su Teknon" ("Even you, Young man?") Suetonius, one-hundred and fifty years later, contradicted the rumour of this utterance, and Shakespeare changed it to Latin for the convenience of his Sixteenth Century English audiences.)

> No man has ever been so determined to impose his will on others and no man has been so gifted by nature for the achievement of his purpose. Alexander alone in antiquity rivals Caesar in the range and speed of his exploits. it was inevitable that he should be compared with Alexander because of his victories and because of his death cut off as he was in the plenitude of his power as was Alexander in the midst of his days. Yet the likeness between them belongs to rhetoric rather than to history... The Greek ideas of Alexander were new ideas, the ideas of the unity of mankind. Caesar was a Roman aristocrat, steeped in the Roman tradition of reasonable, calculated, but inflexible domination, the belief in power, rather than conquest in the extension of Rome to the Romanized, in steady progress but in continuity of policy."[6]

This is the standard summary of Julius Caesar by British historians. The Germans rarely draw conclusions from their learned ancient chronicles, and the French tend to be more generous. To the British there was some grievous limitation in the civic virtue of Caesar, some transgression in his vast ambitions causing them to fall short of the pursuit of an ideal of government. It was as if he had let down Dr. Arnold's side in a cricket match. The British historians have been seduced by the rubbish of the noble Republic, which had been attempting to commit suicide since it squandered its armies fifty years before and left all Italy defenseless against the Cimbri and Teutons and cast itself at the feet of seven-fold Consul, General Gaius Marius, as the first of the four military saviours (Sulla, Pompey, Caesar).[7] Having

---

[6] Ibid., p. 739.

[7] Even here there was an element of continuity and political legitimacy, as Caesar was the nephew of Marius, the great grandson-in-law of Sulla (via his second wife Pompeia), and the father-in-law of Pompey, as well as the great uncle and adoptive father of Octavian: one-hundred and twenty years of Roman government.

bought into and largely confected the myth of the virtuous republic, British historians, including Gibbon, consigned Caesar to mere Bonapartism, conflating their customary libels of Napoleon into the contemporary equation.

Shakespeare himself, the sublime playwright and Bard of Avon, propagated some of this and also Plutarch's nonsense about Caesar's madness, but Shakespeare was a dramatist, not a historian. The simple facts are: Caesar vastly expanded the Roman world, stabilized its institutions and was in the act of reforming them, and his clemency and even-tempered self-confidence were rewarded with the most gratuitously brutal assassination in the history of the world apart from the murder of Jesus Christ. His enemies were not worthy continuators of a great tradition; they were a wretched gang of self-deluded back-stabbers and cowards, who panicked into treason and murder out of nervosity at proximity to such greatness as the inscrutable Caesar. And Alexander the Great's Hellenizing vision was indeed magnificent, but it failed almost completely and led to a fifty-year tri-continental bloodbath (Chapters 14 and 15). Caesar's Rome grew and spread and ruled for nearly five-hundred years more.

Caesar's murderers represented a Republic that had never existed and when the dim facsimile of it which they and their immediate forebears had fumbled out of existence was retrieved, they treacherously murdered the redeemer lest he succeed in the objective—the creation of a mighty functioning republic, whose absence, they claimed, justified their treachery. Cassius, who had betrayed Crassus at Carrhae, and deserted Caesar for Pompey and been pardoned, ran from the Senate holding up two bloody daggers and shouting to a crowd attending a nearby sporting festivity that they had murdered the tyrant. He expected popular acclaim. Cicero, who knew of the plot but kept some distance from it, wrote with self-gratification of Caesar's murder as if anyone could conceive that such a monstrous crime could be a constructive event in the history of a serious Republic.

The murderers momentarily imagined that Cassius had caught the public mood and that they would be hailed as liberators. Caesar's corpse was removed with dignity by his followers. It was clear from the beginning that the masses of Rome despised the murderers. In leaving Mark Antony and Lepidus untouched they had ensured the swift rise of a party of vengeance. The deserts of the assassins would be swift and terrible; they may barely have had time for some nostalgia for Caesar's clemency.

Gaius Julius Caesar's greatest triumph was yet to come. Octavius Caesar returned from Apollonia and it was revealed that he was Caesar's heir; he would complete Caesar's work. He was the man to end the Civil and Social Wars, to reform the Republic and enfold it in an Empire, to launch the great Roman enterprise upward to new heights, to synthesize peoples and regimes somewhat as Alexander had hoped, and not just to avenge Caesar but to put that mighty name over the whole earth and water of the known world in unchallenged and momentarily tranquil glory. For nearly sixty years, Octavius Augustus Caesar would rule benignly and successfully, in the most masterly and seamless succession in the history of government. As after the return from Spain and Caesar's immense triumph, in which he allowed Octavius to share, the prolonged triumph of Augustus would very much be Julius Caesar's supreme victory also.

3. Avenging Caesar

The Ides of March in Rome ended in fear and rumour. Antony barricaded himself into his house with his closest legionaries; Lepidus crossed the Tiber to his country house which he could better defend, and even the murderers were forced to group in comparative strength for the night at the Capitol, as the public mood was already hostile to them. Everyone awaited their next move, but they had none. They naïvely expected that with the sudden violent removal of the greatest figure in the history of Rome they would have the bumbling little talking shop of a Republic back unvexed. Brutus consulted Cicero who was clearly the senior figure of the party of constitutional government. He advocated a general amnesty, which was a sensible course, but in discussion with the murderers, an unsatisfactory compromise was reached. Caesar's will should be confirmed, and a state funeral given to him and the Caesareans invited the conspirators to dine with them and reopen relations. It was a surreal pantomime, awaiting the outbreak of vindictive violence, as the vacuum that had been created collapsed.

Antony was calling the tune for the party of Caesar as he was considerably more eminent than Lepidus and Octavian (as he was now known) would not yet have learned of the death of his adoptive father and would require a couple of weeks to return from Apollonia. His succession to Caesar would only be revealed in a couple of weeks, and it came as a bitter shock to Mark Antony—he had imagined and had perhaps been encouraged by Caesar to believe that he was the dictator's heir. He scarcely knew and had little regard for the young Octavian, though he was obviously an intelligent youth, but he had no choice but to accommodate Caesar's adopted son and chosen successor. The Caesarean party was technically on the defensive and could not afford any internecine strife, but it was relatively easy for Antony, Octavian, and Lepidus to concert policy at the outset: they had to get rid of the assassins, reassert the authority of the party of Caesar, divide the spoils, and make it up from there as they went along. Antony had the loyalty of most of the army and Octavian had the loyalty of Caesar's family and his nonmilitary entourage. Lepidus, master of the horse, could at least provide security in Rome. Caesar's murderers had only the palsied and now criminal Senate to support them. It was an unequal match even before it began.

As the conspirators had no plan and no unity of view, the initiative passed at once to Mark Antony. He was a tough and competent soldier who had replaced Labienus as Caesar's principal lieutenant. He was not a tactical or strategic genius like Caesar, but a good top soldier who commanded the loyalty of his men and who had generally learned too much to be easily bested on or around the battlefield. After the death of Pompey, he had probably been Rome's second greatest general and rode beside Caesar back from Spain. In light of the newly created vacancy, his status as Rome's greatest soldier brought vast power within his reach. Mark Antony had spent most of his early manhood in legendary debauchery, but as conditions evolved, his behavior sobered significantly. In any case, his late chief was no pillar of restrained sexuality, though Caesar had never personally been renowned for excessive drinking or sexual exhibitionism. Antony was a swashbuckling and purposeful man of action and a powerful orator. He saw at once that his time had come; he did not hesitate.

Mark Antony was thirty-nine when Caesar died (aged fifty-five). He moved quickly to neutralize the murderers and remove them from proximity to power while assuring unity in Caesarean ranks and satisfying the extreme eagerness of the Senate to justify its action and inaction with the restoration of a semblance of constitutionality. Caesar's widow, Calpurnia, had given Mark Antony all Caesar's papers, from which he fashioned elements of his political tactics. He revealed from Caesar's will the great benefactions that Caesar had conferred on the Roman people. Nothing could have been better calculated by the late dictator to raise his popularity at the end of his life than the income that he passed on to his fellow Romans accompanied as they were by vast grants of money and valuables which he had earned abroad at the head of Rome's armies. Caesar's enemies were, perforce, silent.

On March 20, a great and elaborate funeral procession escorted the body of the dictator into the Forum with all the grandeur of a Roman state funeral. Antony had arranged the ceremony so the vast concourse of the people, many who would normally be described as part of the Roman mob, but at least initially in their best apparel and behavior, listened to the formidable recital of the honors the Senate had heaped upon Caesar and of the oath that the Senate had taken to protect him. Throughout the proceedings, the whole crowd saw the tattered and bloodstained toga in which he had been murdered and there was extensive interruption and heckling in admiration of the deceased leader and hostility to his murderers.

Shakespeare's version of Antony's funeral oration is taken from Plutarch, who seems to have got it largely from preserved letters of Cicero and it may be considered reasonably accurate. Antony dwelt at first with apparent sincerity and gradually more mockingly on Brutus' stature as an honorable man and incited the mob's curiosity about the generosity of Caesar's will, which he ultimately revealed (seventy-five drachmas for every Roman citizen). By the time he had finished, after no more than ten minutes, Antony had the crowd screaming of treason and vengeance. It was one of the most effective political speeches in all history and there is no reason to believe that Shakespeare's mastery of prose embellished much upon the original. At the end of his remarks Antony held up the torn and bloody toga and delivered his indictment that the conspirators were no more than murderers and common criminals. The crowd shouted for the blood of the assassins and the hands of the professional mourners raised up by prearrangement a wax image of Caesar in which every one of his 23 stab-wounds had been faithfully reproduced. Someone shouted a line from Pacuvius: "Pardoned I these men that they should murder me?"[8] This could not have been spontaneous, but it was unanswerable.

A brief debate about where the cremation should take place was cut short when someone set fire to the bier where it rested and the crowd started piling on benches and stalls, the mourners threw on robes, the veterans-weapons, women jewelry, and the Jews of Rome, specially favored by Caesar who came out in strength to mourn him, wailed their haunting Kadesh lamentations. Some of the crowd snatched brands out of the fire and rushed to burn the homes of the assassins while others searched them out in person. All had already fled and the only casualty was Gaius

---

[8] Alan Roberts, *Mark Antony*, Malvern, London, 1988, p. 105.

Helvius Cinna, the poet who came personally to honor Caesar and whom the mob mistook for Cinna the assassin, and tore him limb from limb in the street. The home of a Pompeian senator was burned to the ground and Antony and the magistrates had some difficulty preventing a general conflagration which could have made the whole of central Rome a mighty pyre for the late dictator.

Antony emerged from this world historic event as the master of the unfolding drama: he had turned Roman opinion decisively against Caesar's murderers and much strengthened his hand as consul. He held the loyalty of the army and was in undisputed control of Rome, including his ability to whip up and also to contain the rage of the Roman mobs. Antony secured Lepidus' loyalty by giving him the office of Pontifex Maximus which was made vacant by Caesar's murder. Antony was also very politic, correctly consulting all the ostensible authorities at every stage and showing an open and fair mind to all factions. He proposed the abolition of the office of dictator, and this was unanimously agreed and brought Antony considerable support from the Senate, which was beginning to realize how heavily it depended for the repossession of any of its authority, upon him.

At the beginning of April, Trebonius left Rome to take up his position as governor of Asia and Decimus Brutus slipped away to Cisalpine Gaul. Cleopatra, who had been in Rome, left shortly after Caesar's death. Brutus and Cassius were praetors but were nonetheless intimidated by general hostility and Brutus requested and received from Antony agreement to ignore the requirement that the urban praetor not be absent for more than ten days; they removed to Antium.

Antony with a lengthening beard of mourning for the late dictator, went to Campania to supervise the establishment of large settlements for Caesar's veterans. He had effectively banished the conspirators without completely alienating them because of their awareness of how dependent upon his goodwill they now were. He had conciliated most of the Senate as the best possible option for leadership of Rome imaginable to the Senate in its present condition. He had solidified the loyalty of Caesar's legions and his large following within Rome.

His smooth glide-path to substantial succession to Caesar was only suddenly derailed in late May with the return to Rome of Octavian. He had declined the offer of the governor of Apollonia to send a large escort for him. Octavian shared his thoughts with Marcus Agrippa and Salvidienus Rufus, his intimate collaborators, and came quietly and by a circuitous route as a private citizen in order better to judge the prevailing mood. He landed at the small port of Lupa and on April 21 was staying with his mother and stepfather, Lucius Marcius Philippus, who lived next to Cicero in the country at Puteoli. He had been acclaimed along his route by the soldiers and veterans but in the cities and towns had been welcomed politely but without great enthusiasm. His mother, the redoubtable Atia, and Philippus advised not to accept the adoption or to take Caesar's name, and to avoid a feud with the leading senatorial families in Rome, as well as a rivalry with Mark Antony.

Octavian was made of sterner stuff and came on to Rome in early May. With Antony still in Campania, he prevailed upon the tribune Lucius Antonius, to call a meeting of the people where he announced that he would accept the adoption. On May 12 the postponed spring games witnessed his attempt to have the golden throne awarded to Caesar by the Senate and the golden diadem which Antony had tried to crown him with set up in Caesar's honor in the place that he would have occupied.

Two tribunes refused to allow this. These were the early days of the cult of Caesar and given his testamentary status, Octavian had the inside track. In the circumstances, Mark Antony returned to Rome. Octavian made a courtesy call upon him as consul and the leading Caesarean and gently reminded him that he, Octavian was the principal heir to Caesar's private fortune which at the moment was in Antony's hands and which Octavian now required to pay Caesar's legacy to the citizens of Rome.

Antony effectively repeated the warning of Octavian's parents against taking Caesar's name, which did some lasting damage to their relations. Octavian felt that he was not being taken seriously and that as Caesar's heir he had been rebuffed by Caesar's principal lieutenant. It was a terrible mistake by Antony, though an understandable one. Octavian's high intelligence, keen look-out for his self-interest, and self-regard as the worthy heir of the greatest of all Romans could be easily deduced in conversation; superficially he was a callow and not entirely physically developed youth opposite a battle-hardened military commander and dashing and daring political general. From the start, Octavian emphasized the need to be hard on the conspirators: as long as the issue was Caesar's murder, Octavian could put his legitimacy as Caesar's heir up against the loyalty of many of Caesar's soldiers to his chief lieutenant whom he had passed over as his heir. A delicate and dangerous political minuet ensued; this would prove a field in which Octavian could more than compensate for the preference of the majority, but far from all, of Caesar's legionaries for Mark Antony as the dictator's successor.

Octavian was a frequently sickly youth and his mother, Atia, devoted herself altogether to securing for him an excellent education and ministering to his medical needs. When he returned to Rome he responded to those who gave him, for whatever reason, the same advice as his mother and step-father to decline Caesar's name and inheritance, the reply: "I cannot think myself unworthy of that name of which Caesar had thought me worthy."[9] From the start he played his hand with sublime craft.

British historians, in their manner of evaluating the history of great states like a cricket match, distinguish between the uneven scrupulosity of Octavian's early years, and his universally admired career as emperor, oblivious to his ability to refine his techniques as his position became more (literally) august.

> The image of the murdered dictator was ever present to his mind; to avenge his death and then to complete his work became the secret object of his life. In the pursuit of that object, he was to meet many obstacles. His ill health he overcame by the sheer courage of a will that refused to give in; against enemies or against those who (as he considered) would not further or misunderstood his adoptive father's plans, he was to struggle for some fifteen years, sometimes openly and in strength, sometimes with the weapon of weakness, deceit, but always with one over-mastering motive and with the clear consciousness of work

---

9 Appian, *The Civil Wars*, III, 13, pp. 46-7; CAH, X, p. 7 (M.P. Charlesworth).

reserved for him. And that consciousness came to him early, a consolation in perplexity (as to many another great man): in mid-July when against opposition and backed only by a few he was celebrating the Ludi Victoriae Caesaris, a comet appeared in the heavens: the populace took it as a proof of Caesar's final reception among the gods, and he naturally encouraged this belief; but with an inner joy he recognized it as a sign for himself and knew his manifest destiny.[10]

Octavian sent agents to retrieve the funds Caesar had deposited in Asia for the Parthian War and in mid-April he met with Cicero, who "despite his mistrust, was as always easily flattered and in any case had the intelligence to be impressed by Octavian's modesty and perceptions. 'He is completely devoted to me,' Cicero wrote to Atticus, and he predicted 'a terrible fracas between him and Antony.'"[11] When allowed to address the people, Octavian made an excellent impression, emphasizing his birthright and expressing himself frankly about the assassins. He met with Antony in the garden of Pompey and placed his claim before him asking for his help. Antony patronized him and treated him with contempt.

This deeply offended Octavian but was also a very serious tactical error by Mark Antony. Antony hastened to strengthen his position against this unsuspected rival. On June 3, the resolution of the popular assembly was passed giving him command for five years in Cisalpine and Transalpine Gaul and he was able to maintain his Macedonian legions as well. To get rid of Brutus and Cassius, senators were induced two days later to have them take charge of the grain supply from Asia and from Sicily and they would eventually be assigned appropriate provinces. Antony also passed a new agrarian law distributing all the available land in Italy to veterans and poor citizens. He also set the rough but capable P. Ventidius Bassus raising recruits for him should he need them. By these measures he had, he thought, strengthened his position sufficiently to deal with any threat from the young Octavian.

Their relations started to come dangerously apart. It was reported that Octavian sought to be a tribune and that Antony declared that he would do anything to stop such an illegality. In October Antony imprisoned and executed some of his own bodyguard on the grounds that they had been improperly influenced—it was immediately assumed that he was alleging Octavian had tried to bribe some of his own security unit to assassinate Antony. It is more likely that Antony fabricated the whole business than that Octavian did anything of the kind, but we will never know. The episode would not have achieved wonders for the morale of Antony's inner military circle. Antony went to Brundisium to meet the legions that he had recalled from Macedonia, and which would occupy the provinces granted to him in the plebiscite of June 3.

Octavian responded to this escalation by leaving Rome on a visit to his father's veterans (as his relationship with Julius Caesar was now styled), and dispatched agents to Brundisium to challenge the returning Antony over why the murderers had not been more harshly treated. Antony was so hard-pressed by Octavian's planted questioners at Brundisium that he felt compelled to execute the more assertive of

---

10 Pliny, *Natural History*, II, p. 93; CAH, X, p. 8 (M.P. Charlesworth).
11 CAH, X, p. 10 (M.P. Charlesworth).

the questioners and cried poverty in explaining the differences between the allocations Octavian had made from the estate of his adoptive father and what he himself had the means to distribute. The Macedonian legions were wooed by speeches and propaganda leaflets, as Caesar's heir and Caesar's chief lieutenant were already almost at war, testing for the moment the aphorism that the pen is mightier than the sword. Antony did manage to rally his men to march on Ariminium while he himself advanced on Rome with the Allaudae Legion, as Octavian had returned to Rome with three-thousand loyal veterans raised without authorization and he was openly invading Rome against Antony. Octavian was in constant touch with Cicero, who, as always in moments of great drama, hesitated.

Octavian again left Rome, destined for Arretium, but he was raising an army wherever he went. In mid-November Antony returned to Rome with the intention of having the Senate declare Octavian a public enemy. Before he could do this, two legions defected from his camp to that of Octavian and Antony hurriedly summoned the Senate to meet on November 28 to redistribute provinces among his supporters. Antony departed Rome to remove Decimus Brutus as governor of Cisalpine Gaul. Brutus declined and barricaded himself into Mutina to stand siege. Antony's departure from Rome in evident discomfort motivated Cicero to emerge from his retirement, return to Rome and deliver to the Senate on 20 December his Third Philippic. In this and his following speech he urged war against Antony and support for Decimus Brutus. He had nothing but praise for Octavian Caesar who "by his own initiative and exertions raised forces and freed Rome from the domination of Antony; all honor to him and his gallant legions."[12] Cicero seemed to be coveting his old position as political counselor to a leading general. He had clearly thrown in his lot against Antony and was scattering praise around a number of candidates with an unbecoming neutrality: Brutus, Cassius, Octavian.

On New Year's Day 43 B.C., the Senate gathered under the presidency of the new consuls to consider the situation. The senators were not disposed to take the drastic step of declaring Antony a public enemy and a motion put forward by Fufius Calenus was adopted that an embassy should be sent to Antony requiring him to withdraw and submit to the wishes of the Senate and People of Rome. Cicero considered this inadequate and asked for honors to be conferred on Lepidus for bringing Sextus Pompeius over, and on Octavian, of whom he declared: "I know the inmost secrets of his heart. Providence itself intervened to produce this divine young man who had delivered them from the tyranny of Antony."[13] The great Cicero had been completely snowed by a man a third his age. The Senate decreed that Octavian should be given the rank of senator and should, together with the two consuls, join in command as pro-praetors of the force that was to be dispatched against Antony. Antony sent back his response to the embassy that had been made to him; he showed no sense of submission and had counterclaims to advance. The Senatus Consultum Ultimum was formally passed. Antony could still rely on his supporters in Rome to protract proceedings, but his position was becoming tenuous.

By early spring, Decimus Brutus was running short of rations in Mutina and

---

12 Ibid., p. 13.
13 Ibid., p. 14.

was awaiting the arrival of Pansa and Hirtius to assist in lifting the siege. Octavian also placed his newly formed Legion close to these events while carefully disguising what role he might wish to play. Antony ambushed Pansa, who was seriously wounded, and his troops were victorious, but they then unexpectedly encountered Hirtius, who defeated them, a significant blow to Mark Antony's military prestige, as he was effectively trying to represent himself as Caesar's heir as a battlefield commander. As this action proceeded, Octavian successfully defended the Republican camp, showing considerable personal bravery; both Hirtius and Octavian were (a bit over-hastily by traditional Roman standards) declared to be Imperators (April 15, 43 B.C.). Six days later, Antony offered battle and Brutus came aggressively out of Mutina while Octavian and Hirtius attacked Antony's camp and caused such consternation in his rear area that he was obliged to withdraw. With this, Antony, who had clearly got the worst of these engagements, reestablished his talents as a general by leading several legions into Gaul to join forces with Lepidus and with Vintidius Bassus and three legions he raised in Italy. It was a difficult march through the Alps in springtime and Antony was much harassed but showed his steady judgment even at the head of some skittish and hastily assembled forces. When he arrived at Forum Julii, he was now able to assemble a serious army in a strong place. Octavian's luck, which must have been dispiriting and worrisome to Mark Antony, had reasserted itself. Hirtius was mortally wounded, Pansa died from his earlier injury, and Octavian effectively inherited an entire army.

On news of Antony's arrival at the head of expanded forces in Cisalpine Gaul, but before hearing of Octavian's parallel accretion of forces, the Senate impetuously declared Antony a public enemy. This was another demonstration of their complete tactical incompetence; they could easily have killed Antony while they were killing his leader and instead, they incited his ambition to succeed Caesar although they should have perceived that in doing so his first step would be to attack them as a wretched gang of murderers. The Senate had cast its lot against Mark Antony and in favor of his opponents indiscriminately, but a year after Caesar's murder, the twenty-year-old Octavius was now the front-running contender to pick up all the pieces of the immense jurisdiction his adoptive father had ruled. The Senate now became eccentrically insouciant in playing the limited hand left it: Brutus and Cassius were confirmed in their provinces and given authority over governors in the East. Sextus Pompeius was recalled from Marseilless and put in charge of the entire fleet and defense of the coast of all Italy. Decimus Brutus was actually given a triumph (for accepting liberation from his siege by the deceased Pansa and Hirtius, and by Octavius). Octavius himself was denied the ovatio that Cicero had proposed, and the Senate purported to transfer his forces and those of the consuls to the command of Decimus Brutus. A commission of ten was appointed to distribute bounties to the troops of Octavius, a commission from which Octavius was excluded. Marcus Brutus wrote to Atticus that there was "a risk that the boy might become difficult to hold in check." He also wrote that Cicero's enthusiasm for him was a mistake.[14] (Brutus had not hitherto been known for understatement.)

Again, Octavius showed his cool and even suave judgment: he offered a con-

---

14 Cicero, *Ad Brutus*, I, 17.

ciliatory hand to Mark Antony, who could scarcely reject it, declined to hand over his legions to Decimus, indignantly refused to serve, along with all his forces, under Marcus Brutus whom, as the Senate was well aware, Octavius regarded with a plenitude of justification as a treacherously dishonorable assassin of the greatest man in Roman history and Octavius' adoptive father. How the Senate could have arrived at such an insane and unenforceable order escapes the historian's imagination even after more than two-thousand years. The Senate had placed all its bets on Lepidus and his seven legions, although Lepidus was known to be loyal to Mark Antony while not at all hostile to Octavius. Antony's and Lepidus' soldiers commingled happily and in short order the two men reaffirmed their alliance and Lepidus sent the Senate a letter of resignation. The Senate naturally declared Lepidus a public enemy, and Cicero's letters to Brutus reveal that he finally realized he had been duped all the way round, though he still did not regret his approval of the murder of Caesar.

Octavius and Mark Antony were now of reasonably equal political strength and influence, though Octavius moved more deftly, had a greater support now among both the masses of Rome and Caesar's armies, had actually performed more distinguishedly in the skirmishing and maneuvering than had Mark Antony, although Octavius had had no military experience at all, apart from accompanying Caesar for part of the last Spanish campaign. Octavius judged that it was now time for him to act and in July, a party of his centurions entered the Senate house and demanded the consulship for, as he would now be styled, Gaius Julius Caesar Octavianus, but generally Caesar, a magic name then and in all subsequent history—it is not easily discernible from this distance, but the acceptance of his change of name brought a flood of automatic legitimacy and respect. He had eight good legions behind him and the support of most of the masses of Rome, a finely played hand in the sixteen months since the death of the dictator. The Senate, incompetent to the very end, offered a praetorship to which Octavius replied by marching on Rome, now a somewhat routine event for large, angry, well-trained military formations, against all of which the Senate in its loquacious nudity and guilt was resistless. The Senate capitulated and the offer was made. Octavius Caesar assured himself of the safety of his mother and sisters and paid the promised bounties to his troops and then respectfully waited at the city gates until elections were over, in the traditional manner. On August 19, Octavius and his uncle Quintus Pedius were elected consuls. Caesar rammed through a sentence of outlawry upon all assassins after reform of trial had occurred, kicking the Senators back into line in a renunciation of their former bloody handed leaders, which had the added benefit of putting the new Caesar at the head of all of the avenging Caesareans. With this, Caesar, his army now grown to eleven legions, departed Rome for the north while the Senate was persuaded to revoke the decrees against Antony and Lepidus. Another round in the drama of the succession to Julius Caesar had been concluded with his adopted son showing again an extraordinary mastery of the deadly and intricate game in which he was engaged.

As republicanism crumbled in Italy, it swiftly failed in the western Roman jurisdictions as well. The dangers of a civil conflict between Decimus Brutus and the Republican outpost in Cisalpine Gaul and the surrounding Caesareans evaporated when Asinius Pollio arrived from Spain with two legions which he delivered to Antony and Plancus, from whom the Republic expected some support, and they defected as well. This left Decimus with no military support and he was apprehended in flight to Aquileia by a Gallic chief who on behalf of Antony and Caesar thoughtfully ended his absurd imposture by summary execution. Again, whoever was apparently doing the thinking for the Senate must have been mad to imagine that Lepidus, Julius Caesar's leader of cavalry, would support the assassins, and they should have known they were placing an impossible burden upon Decimus Brutus, who was completely out of his depth in competition with Octavius Caesar and Mark Antony.

The Republic did manage rather better in the East. Syria at the beginning of 44 was held by a Pompeian general, Caecilius Bassus, and Caesar had sent Marcus Crispus and Staius Murcus to remove him and had assigned the province of Asia to Trebonius (who repaid his confidence by joining the assassins). At the end of 44, Dolabella left Rome to take up the government of Syria, and on his way through Asia, encountered and killed Trebonius. But Cassius, also bound for Syria, outstripped him traveling by sea and won over not only the forces of Bassus, but also of the Caesarean Murcus, and snaffled up four other legions which Cleopatra had sent from Egypt to assist Dolabella. As always, loyalties became more cynically fluid the farther one progressed towards the Orient. Cassius over-matched Dolabella with twelve legions and drove him to suicide. Cassius received urgent appeals from Marcus Brutus to meet at Smyrna. In theory these two men were assuring the Roman grain supply, but the desperation of the Republic banished that task to lesser hands. Having announced a punitive expedition against Cleopatra, Cassius renounced such an absurd moralistic escapade and after extorting seven-hundred talents from the Jews, enslaving a number of towns, and setting up petty tyrannies in some of the Syrian cities, he marched off to meet Brutus.

Brutus had had a good passage to the east. He was warmly received in Athens and many idealistic young men rallied to him. Cicero and Valerius Messella Corvinus and Q. Horatius Flaccus enlisted under him in a freshet of Hellenistic Republican enthusiasm. Vatinius' Illyrian legions rallied to Brutus and induced the surrender of Gaius Antonius, to whom the Senate had assigned Macedonia on November 28 and which it had ordered him to surrender on December 20. Brutus was continually in touch with Cicero and was conciliatory in comparison to Cicero's militancy. Brutus did not wish to drive Antony into complete animosity (though how he imagined that Antony was not already in that condition is inexplicable). He spared the life of Antony's brother Gaius, though later he did put him to death in reprisal for proscriptions. Brutus cautions Cicero against excessive faith in Octavius and it is again impossible to understand how Cicero did not by now realize what a mortal danger to his ever-fluctuating political preferences the young Caesar now posed.

Brutus took heart briefly from events at Mutina, and he received a number of adherents from Asia Minor and also the support of several Thracian tribes. The ultimate battle lines were taking shape and by the end of 43, Brutus and Cassius were at Smyrna, at the head of a new fleet and substantially expanded numbers of legionaries. The Caesareans consolidated their ranks as well.

4. The Second Triumvirate, Proscription, and Philippi

When Octavius departed Rome in the autumn of 43, his clear intention was to make an opportunistic pact with Antony and Lepidus. Whatever their differences, they were Caesareans, and the first object of all of them was to dispose of Caesar's assassins and establish Caesarean control over the ghost of the Roman Republic which had sickened and died for at least the last sixty years, amid many colossal strategic blunders culminating in one of history's most monstrously evil acts of violence.

Caesar, Antony, and Lepidus met at Bononia after extraordinary security precautions, and in the presence of their senior comrades, and within sight of their soldiery, on a small island in the Lavinius River. What emerged was a triple dictatorship that somewhat replicated the first Triumvirate of 60 B.C. The earlier arrangement was a secret and extra-legal arrangement, this would be a triple dictatorship, and the Senate was to confirm their status as Triumvirs of the Republic for over five years, to December 38, a term that would exceed that of magistrates and governors, whom the triumvirs would appoint. The correlation of forces reflected continued primacy of Mark Antony: he would be governor of Cisalpine and Transalpine Gaul, Julius Caesar's old positions, and Lepidus would be at the head of Gaul and Spain. Octavius would have Africa, Sicily, and Sardinia, leaving Mark Antony in effective oversight of Italy, but Lepidus was given control of the government of Italy as a neutral gesture between the two other protagonists, who were expected and authorized to deal with the Republicans in Asia. Holding the central Mediterranean provinces, Caesar had most of Rome's naval forces. To deal with the demands of veterans, allotments of land were agreed from eighteen of the richest Italian towns, including Capua, Beneventum, Reghium, Vibo, Cremona, and Venusia. To build an insuperable war-chest to see off the assassins and their sympathizers completely and bring peace to the whole Roman world, in place of Caesar's clemency which had backfired, the three triumvirs embraced "Sullan" methods: all opposition would be uprooted and resources to finish the pacification of Roman territory and punish treason would be obtained by proscription of the disloyal—a bounty for the delivery of the murderers' faction, dead or alive. With this, Caesar resigned his consulship in favor of Antony's legate, Ventidius Bassus, and would receive Antony's stepdaughter, Claudia, as his wife.

Asinius Pollio was left to supervise the distribution of lands to veterans and the triumvirs marched together on Rome where the tribunician law gave them the powers they required. Though a proscription list was published with a preamble of civic justification and one-hundred and thirty names, an earlier list with no fineries or civilities at all had been circulated. They were terribly fraught days in Rome as people fled and hid. The consul Pedius, uncle of Octavius, tried to discourage panic but died of exhaustion. Those who had a bounty on their heads were mercilessly slain, and some of the property of the most wealthy was not left to their heirs but rifled by the representatives of the triumvirs. There were some loyal wives and family and slaves who risked everything to hide the hunted, sometimes successfully. The majority of the proscribed were the last detritus of the old aristocratic order, who had supported Pompey in the Senate and among these was Pompey's surviving son Sextus, who took possession of some towns in Sicily and though proscribed himself made a great effort by the dispatch of ships and men to rescue as many of the unfortunate fugitives and bring them safely out of Italy as he could. The number of those murdered appears to have been about three-hundred senators and two-thousand knights. Even in these times and even in retribution for the terrible crime of the murder of Julius Caesar, and even in the interests of ending the Civil War, it is impossible to justify such a horrible act as the proscriptions of the Second Triumvirate.

Cicero was among the first victims. He had finally given up his long held political ambitions and retired to the country in August. When news of his proscription came, he considered fleeing but was restrained by the winter and his own indecision. Soldiers arrived, his slaves were ready to fight, but he forbade them. Life was no longer of interest, and he faced his executioner with exemplary Roman courage:

> There can be few whose character has been more bitterly impugned or more warmly defended, and fate ironically ordained that his own matchless power of expression as exemplified in his letters should survive as the most relentless witness against him. His native horror of bloodshed and of 'Sullan' cruelty, his legal training, and his humanism as a scholar all gave him a traditionalist standpoint making him an admirer of a stable Constitution where life could be lived in peace and reasonableness, and of this he saw a pattern in the times of Scipio Aemilianus before the Gracchi disturbed the state. It was his particular misfortune to be thrust into an age when all the arts of peace were powerless against brute ambition which left no choice to a reasoning and sensitive nature save that between two evils... In an age of apathy and corruption he could sympathize with the needs of the provincials and strive for better government. In his treatises his insights so gauged the trend of politics that, as Nepos remarks, "He foretold even the things which are coming to pass now.[15]

Yet, it is not as consul or statesman that he vindicates his claim to fame, but by the influence that these speeches and writings exerted after him, so that, in the generous phrase of Julius Caesar, "He advanced the boundaries of the Latin genius and fashioned Latin into an enduring and universal speech."[16] Though he was aware of the mob against Caasar, he took no hand in it. There was no excuse for murdering such a man and the act shames all three of the triumvirs beyond any act of any member of the original Triumvirate.

On January 1, 42, the Senate, twenty-two months after it jubilantly hosted the assassination of Julius Caesar, proclaimed him a God, and the triumvirs imposed the recognition of his acts on magistrates and senators. Octavian Caesar was official Divi filius, the divine son.

The triumvirs had forty-three legions to deal with Brutus, Cassius, and the rest. This would be overkill unless Antony had lost everything he had ever known about

---

15 Pliny, *Natural History*, VII, p. 117; CAH, X, p. 22 (M.P. Charlesworth).
16 Ibid.

war-making. Lepidus retained three legions to maintain order in Italy (obviously, the opposition was credited with no disruptive ability). Eight legions were sent as a vanguard under Decidius Saxa and Norbanus Flaccus. And the other large force was transported across the Adriatic over the summer. They certainly had adequate manpower, but there were other problems. The proscriptions, appropriately perhaps for such an unjustifiably ferocious act of oppression, had not only brought hatred down upon the triumvirs but failed to provide adequate funds for the campaign. The supplementary revenue property tax was imposed, which was strenuously resisted and expensive to collect, as it involved using the three legions that had been left behind for Lepidus to maintain order as tax collectors. In early 42, Sextus Pompeius gained control of much of Octavian's province of Sicily but he seemed to lack the initiative to join the Republican admirals Staius Murcus and Domitius Ahenobarbus in assaulting the transport of the triumviral forces. The Caesarean forces landed at Dyrrhachium, where Octavian became ill and had to be left behind, while Mark Antony thundered along the Via Egnatia connecting toward the enemy about two-hundred miles east, eighteen miles beyond Thessalonica, almost at the frontier of Thrace.

The Republicans had prepared deliberately also. Both sides knew that this was the showdown. Brutus had forced the cities of Lycia to contribute; Xanthos refused in its pride and when besieged by the legions, rather than surrender, men and women destroyed their city and committed suicide. Other cities so approached were more forthcoming. Cassius simply robbed places that he occupied to gain the money to pay his forces: Tarsus was fined fifteen hundred talents; the Rhodians eight-thousand; ten years tribute was imposed on many cities in Asia.

Brutus and Cassius reached the Hellespont in September commanding nineteen legions whose loyalty was strengthened by a profit-sharing agreement. They hoped for a deferral of combat through the winter during which their dominance of the sea could potentially force the triumvirs to proceed back toward the Adriatic, overland. Republicans had the better ground and only a slightly smaller force. But the Caesareans had the best general of the time in Antony, and Octavian, having substantially overcome his illness was now in the Caesarean camp the continuing semi-divine heir of Caesar himself. The triumvirs were Rome and they were legitimacy and they had the best commander. The Republicans were assassins and representatives of a much amputated and decapitated Senate.

The Republican camp was to the west of Philippi on both sides of the via Egnatia and a large marsh was to the south defending against out-flanking. Antony saw the only way to bustle Republicans out of their waiting tactics of anticipating the winter was to get through this barrier and he started building a causeway across it. When Cassius did the same in reverse, Antony simultaneously attacked here and at Cassius' camp; his confident and energetic belligerency carried both movements forward and Cassius' troops were pushed back, and Octavian's troops broke into his camp and plundered it. Brutus had rushed his own troops into battle virtually without orders, but they stormed the camp of Octavian. Cassius was unaware of this movement and committed suicide. He was a more competent officer than Brutus who now had Cassius' body removed, and he moved into his camp himself to continue the depressing policy of completing the action. The Caesareans bombarded the Republican camp with scathing leaflets and vocally mocked their opponents. This was more than Brutus could take and he came out to face the enemy on October 23, 42.

Octavian's forces bore most of the battle and gradually drove the Republicans back and Antony led his reserves in and accelerated the advance and pursued the retreating enemy with ruthless professionalism into the night. Octavian lasted as long as he physically could, a brave personal effort, and handed over his command temporarily to Norbanus. The Republicans were completely destroyed as a fighting force; some of the leaders committed suicide; some scrambled aboard the fleet; a few were pardoned and some simply vanished. With the encouragement of Mark Antony and Octavian, the troops of the line were invited to reenlist with the Caesarean generals, and most did so.

Brutus fled with some loyalists but eventually, on seeing how hopeless was his cause, "crying out, like some ancient Hildebrand, upon that righteousness which he had followed so unswervingly and which had at last left him destitute, he fell upon his sword. So passed away "the noblest Roman of them all," according to Antony [a preposterous assertion]. Brutus was the last representative of the aristocratic tradition, and with him died the Republican spirit, "for henceforward men fought for a leader" (as they had for the past sixty years when the Republic squandered its armies and threw itself at the feet of victorious generals whose soldiers followed the stars of their commanders). "He is one of the most famous figures in antiquity, yet the theme seems fictitious, the figure suffered strange distortions. To the oppressed and revolutionaries he has been the ideal combination of patriot and philosopher, his name one 'before which tyrants tremble'; modern critics, emphasizing his dourness of manner, his bluntness of speech, and that superior expression which Cicero noted, heap scorn on virtue that could pray on provincials and kill a benefactor for the sake of principle… Brutus was a more ordinary man—what held admiration in antiquity was his steadfast adherence to a creed [however narrow], and his intense earnestness of purpose. But firmness of character and loyalty to an ideal, however admirable in themselves, are no sufficient guides through changing political conditions unless based upon an equipment of intellect [and here Brutus was not impressive]. His was a creed of negative principles, lacking any trace of constructive policy to meet the needs of the time, ineffectual against those who fought for a person and a memory."[17] This was the end of the Republic Rome had once, and for a long time, known.

5. The Division of Spoils Between the Victorious Triumvirs

Mark Antony emerged as the principal triumvir. Lepidus was rumored to be in negotiation with Sextus Pompeius and was effectively suspended pending review. While Antony won the battles, Octavian was plucky, and none could doubt that his relationship with Caesar made his presence particularly valuable. In the new division, Antony took all Gaul and had the task of settling the East and of finding the resources to execute Caesar's plan of attacking Parthia. Octavian received Spain,

---

17 CAH, X, p. 25 (M.P. Charlesworth).

Sardinia and Africa, the last conditional on his handing it to Lepidus, if he was cleared of the suspicion that hung over him. Only eleven legions were to be retained on active service of the twenty-one that had been at or near Philippi. The legions to the West would be left intact. Both principal triumvirs were committed to finding suitable land or other occupations for all those who had served. Octavian had the responsibility of dealing with Sextus Pompeius and was the principal supervisor of all distribution of land to veterans. This would evidently become a function of immense significance should relations between Octavian and Antony deteriorate.

Six of their legions were sent to Macedonia to deal with the renegades and Antony took two legions with him to Asia while Octavian took three legions and four-thousand horse back to Italy. There were eleven legions in Gaul and thirteen in Cisalpine Gaul. These were all ostensibly under Antony's command, but he was going to have trouble maintaining close touch with them if he became heavily engaged in the East. The two principal triumvirs parted cordially enough, though Octavian was still unwell and was sometimes carried in a litter. Once returned to Rome, Octavian showed Antony's representatives his copy of the written compact that had been signed. This was not questioned, and Octavian confidently sent six legions to Spain and left two in Sardinia. Sextus Pompeius was a substantial threat and Sicily was constantly gathering the proscribed, renegade slaves and the detritus of previous losing factions including his father's. Murcus had eighty ships and was prowling the central Mediterranean quite fearlessly. There was a great deal of disorder, and all manner of dissidents, pirates, and scoundrels were dispossessing honest landowners. The great poet Virgil only maintained his property by the grace of some powerful and appreciative landowners. By early in the new year, after a very difficult passage to Brundisium, Octavian's physical condition was recovering well, and his political position was of such strength he was able to follow his instinct and his preceptor's example and emancipate a number of the proscribed. He naturally did this with considerable political insight.

Antony and his friends soon realized what a dangerous mistake they had made in leaving to Octavian the entire management and distribution of property to veterans. Octavian took particular interest in this and layered in ancillary benefits and consideration for the retiring legionaries. Mark Antony's brother, Lucius Antonius, consul in 42, claimed to be a Republican and Fulvia, Antony's wife, was eventually persuaded to join Lucius in fierce opposition to Octavian and the outright harassment of Octavian's legions in Mauretania and Spain began in earnest. Antony, absent in Asia Minor, had nothing to do with this as his brother and wife began committing acts of war against his fellow triumvir. Octavian was naturally left to wonder if Antony was so removed from the operation as was pretended. As always until he was ready to deliver a decisive blow, Octavian moved cautiously. To prevent further reinforcement of subversives, he recalled Rufus and his six legions from Spain and placated Lepidus who was still theoretically a coequal triumvir, with a couple of legions in charge of Rome (in which role he proved completely incompetent).

Eventually, Antony's brother had himself barricaded into Perusia, where Fulvia was able to help attempt unsuccessfully to breakout on New Year's Eve. Lucius Antonius surrendered in February 40, and Octavian accepted all his excuses as he did not wish a showdown with Mark Antony at this point. Lucius was released and his soldiers were pardoned, and Octavian's close friend and associate Agrippa brought two of Plancus' legions into Octavian's camp; the Divi Filius made no effort to impede the escape of Fulvia and Plancus. Octavian authorized the complete destruction of Perusia; his soldiers plundered it before burning; the ordinary citizens were allowed to leave peacefully but the Republican senators and other opposition members that were hiding there received no mercy. Particularly curious was an attempted slave insurrection in Campania led by the fierce Republican Tiberius Claudius Nero. Octavian's legions crushed it easily and the insurrectionist fled to Sicily with his wife Livia and his son Tiberius: the woman was to be Octavian's wife and he chose the boy to be his successor. The new regime was not off to a very happy start, and Octavian won this round decisively, and probably before Antony had a clear idea of what was happening and what was at stake.

As it was not clear how cordial Antony would be when he returned from the East, Octavian had to deal with Sextus and Lepidus, either of whom could tip the balance against him. The fortuitous death of Calenus, commander in Gaul, enabled Octavian to take temporary control of the eleven legions in that province and he gave them to his loyal colleague Salvidienus Rufus and in a conciliatory gesture made Lucius Antonius governor of Spain. In a further esteemed political gambit, he rejected the allegations against Lepidus and presented him with two African provinces and six legions which he borrowed from Antony's Gallic Army. And the talented Sextus stamped out what disorder remained in Africa and gave Lepidus his four legions as well. In the circumstances, though he engaged in a little amateurish scheming, Lepidus was content with his sinecure.

Sextus Pompeius remained and was a clear problem. Although Octavian was married to Antony's step-daughter, Octavian had now married Scribonia, aunt of the wife of Sextus. This may seem like a remote connection, but in Rome at this time it was close enough. It was also an original Octavian scheme; in such a mighty clash of arms and intrigues to try to link himself to the surviving son of Caesar's greatest rival by a marriage that would send a relative of his present co-triumvir packing. Sextus was almost demiurgically treacherous (much unlike his father), and was already in communication with Antony and offering his services to him. Mark Antony would be back in Italy soon, though Asia Minor was still contested. The prestige of the victor of Philippi was deservedly great. Octavius was naturally curious to learn his chief associate's state of mind.

The apparent division between Antony and Octavius was deceiving: Antony had primacy in Italy but in fact he was in Asia and Octavian was in Italy and it was soon obvious that although Octavian paid all official deference to his senior partner, he was taking thorough control of Italy for himself. And while there was supposed to be some level of collegiality in determining the distribution of land to veterans, as this had been ascribed to Octavian, he exercised that authority personally and generously, and profitably to his status and reputation.

Where Octavian had within him a divine fire to gather up and exercise the status of Julius Caesar, Antony wished to be respected and to live well, to take orders from no one, but was far less than fanatical in the extent of his ambitions. He was periodically stirred to greater things by Fulvia and eventually by Cleopatra, but left to himself, he had reached the fullness of his ambitions. Antony landed at Ephesus, where he was welcomed as the new Dionysus. He was worshiped as a god as Asians tended to do with visiting Roman governors, generally for reasons having little to do with theology. He distributed favors to the states that had been helpful: Athens, Rhodes, Lycia, Tarsus. Since he was there to quiet the area but also to raise the money to conduct the Parthian war of punishment, he was constantly vectoring his message. Local orators despaired at him trying to collect what Cassius had exacted all over again, and he modified his requests. He met and was impressed by Herod in Bithynia. Antony moved very slowly and cautiously with the client states Galatia and Cappadocia, which in return for their ostensible independence guarded the frontiers well. Antony tried not to get drawn too far into the desperate complexities of the palace politics of these places; he elevated Castor to succeed his grandfather Deiotarus in Galatia and Ariathares X in Cappadocia.

Obviously, Rome's principal client monarch was the incomparable Cleopatra VII, who was now twenty-nine. Our chief source for her now is Plutarch, who became more complementary once he got his hands on the diaries of her physician. She was apparently half Macedonian and half Egyptian and while not beautiful, she was extremely interesting and seductive looking, tireless, fearless, always active, highly educated, multilingual, and commercially esteemed (something of a precursor of the Empress Josephine). "Brought up at a corrupt court, she knew no conventions and few scruples; she was her own law. But she was to be a loyal wife to Antony though certainly she did not love him. Perhaps she never loved any man; her two love affairs were undertaken quite deliberately with the same purpose as all her actions for the keynote of her character was not sex at all, but ambition… The essence of her nature was the combination of the charm of a woman with the brain of a man, both remorselessly bent to the pursuit of that one object, power."[18] She was an astute and even somewhat popular ruler of Egypt, other than with the partisans of her rival Princess Arsinoe. There is evidence that she was a progressive ruler in matters of agriculture and that Egypt's grain harvest rose with her and that she did not oppress the landlords and tenant-farmers with excessive taxation.

Having returned to Alexandria on the murder of Caesar, she patiently awaited the issue of subsequent events. Antony confirmed the two principal dynasts, Ptolemaeus of Chalcis and Lamblichus of Emesa, and chased off some petty tyrants. The Jews sought the removal of Herod, but after consulting the high priest, Hyrcanus, Antony made Herod and his brother, Phasael, tetrarchs; and when it was Antony who came to the east, Cleopatra's ambition was to get him to Alexandria. She answered his summons to Cilicia and fed his vanity by inducing him to succeed Caesar as lover of the Egyptian queen. The Ptolemies were well practiced in dynastic murder: Cleopatra had seen her father murder her elder sister, herself a murderess, and Antony was happy to execute Cleopatra's sister Arsinoe, before following Cleopatra to Alexandria. Cleopatra seduced Antony's pursuit of her to Alexandria where he was lured back into his youth and became the leader of some gilded young men who called themselves "The Inimitables." And she became his good comrade in

---

18 Ibid., p. 35.

hunting and fishing, in statesmanship and in nightlife, and he liberated her as a client monarch and endowed her with the full authority of the Queen of Egypt. It was not too unruly, but it was easily portrayed in Rome as a monstrous indignity for the first triumvir to be so disporting himself.

Historians have remained divided on the question of whether Antony deliberately absented himself while Fulvia and Lucius were testing Octavian, to see how it would play out, while he retained, to use a modern expression, plausible deniability. The alternative is that he was simply too preoccupied, not so much with Cleopatra and pleasures as with preparing revenge for the Parthians, and let matters in Italy take shape as they would since that responsibility had effectively been delegated to Octavian in any case.

After making some further dispositions in Asia Minor, Antony crossed to Greece and met up with his wife Fulvia who had fled there after she and Lucius had been forced to surrender and Octavian had given Lucius a governorship in Spain. Fulvia had been a loyal and devoted wife for Antony, had fervently upheld his part in the great disputes in which he had been engaged and felt with some reason that she had been effectively thrown over and embarrassed and forsaken for Cleopatra, and that he had responded to her efforts on his behalf by reproaching her because she had been unable to prevent Octavian from stealing Antony's legions in Gaul, usurping the role of benefactor to the veterans, and effectively filling the vacuum in Italy that Antony had himself created.

He felt that she had unnecessarily clouded relations with Octavian while he was trying to arrange an important endeavor for the whole Roman world in the East. Fulvia withered and died, apparently of natural causes but nature at its most depressing. Because of what he considered to be Octavian's aggression in Gaul, Mark Antony was prepared to go to full Civil War with Octavian, but he was also prepared to reach a compromise if one could be had. Another of these astounding ancient survivors, Domitius Ahenobarbus, had got hold of most of Illyricum and let it be known he was prepared to make common cause with Mark Antony and Sextus Pompeius. The correlation of forces had shifted sharply again, and Octavian now appeared to be the principal triumvir but he was making nothing but placatory noises in all directions. It was agreed to meet at Brundisium and Plancus, Domitius Ahenobarbus, and Mark Antony went together to meet the young Caesar.

Antony and Octavian met warily. Antony suspected Octavian of trying to steal Gaul from him with all of its legions, and of deliberately putting him in a bad light in his conflict with Fulvia and trying to seduce his own brother away from him. Octavian suspected Antony of promoting the entire diversion of Fulvia and Lucius and now making common cause with outlaws, Ahenobarbus and Sextus. Antony took the first conciliatory step by sending Sextus to Sicily and Ahenobarbus to be governor of Bithynia and Antony chose Pollio and Octavian chose Maecenas to represent them in negotiations. The tempo of events was decided by the legions who had fought together under Caesar and forbade their leaders to fall out now: it was an apparently spontaneous and a gallant collective gesture.

A fresh partition was agreed: Lepidus would retain Africa and the rest of the Roman world would be divided into Antony taking all of the East and Octavian all of the West and they were to have equal recruiting rights in Italy. Like Julius Caesar, they nominated consuls for some years ahead and once embarked upon reconciliation, the two rivals bound themselves together with hoops of steel: Octavian gave his own sister, Octavia, to Antony in marriage and Antony put Manius to death for provoking the Perusine War and he informed Octavian that his supposedly dear collaborator Salvidienus Rufus, whom he had made governor of Gaul, had considered revolt. Octavian had Rufus summoned to Rome, accused before the Senate, convicted and executed, and he gave Antony the remaining five divisions of his army in Gaul, which he had snaffled up, and confirmed Lucius as governor of Spain. This was the Pact of Brindisi (Brundisium) of October 40. It was greeted with tremendous enthusiasm by soldiers and civilians alike throughout the Roman world; such was now the terrible dread of Civil War. Virgil wrote his Fourth *Eclogue* in celebration of the event.

The celebration was interrupted by Sextus Pompeius, who felt that he had been treacherously treated by Antony and set his pirate fleet on Rome's grain supplies. This quickly raised the price of bread in Rome and as always, in such times, public opinion became seriously agitated. Heavy rioting broke out at the popular fair in November, that could only be suppressed by the army. A concordat was achieved off Misenum in the spring of 39. The preparations for the meeting were absurd: Sextus remained on his ship while Octavian and Marc Anthony set up their camps on shore. Two rafts were placed on piles driven into shallow water, close enough so participants did not have to shout at each other, but too far for an assailant to jump between them. This was at the insistence of Sextus, because of his mistrust of the others, but he was the only participant who would have dreamt of such treachery as he was determined to prevent. In return for concessions by Sextus: it was agreed to give him a substantial command for the duration of the Triumvirate—Octavian gave him Corsica, Sardinia, and Sicily (most of which he had already occupied). Antony threw in the Peloponnese as well as a cash settlement for his confiscated property. Sextus would stop harassing the grain supply and stop receiving runaways or furtively planting garrisons, one of his nastier tricks as they shortly became extremely destructive. Finally, astonishingly, for someone whose father had been overwhelmingly defeated and murdered and whose brother's head had been virtually treated like a football, Sextus Pompeius was to become an augur and at a not indefinitely remote future date a consul of Rome. (It was odd to see the Peloponnese thrown in like a bauble in the Roman leaders' negotiation with a pirate: the setting for most of the glories of Athens and Sparta.)

Octavian and Antony traveled together to Rome, a triumphant progress sanctified by the endless cheers of the Roman streets and the steady escalation in mutual flattery between the principal triumvirs, which reached a crescendo when Antony consented to be designated priest of the deified Julius Caesar. Octavian replaced Salvidinius Rufus with Agrippa, his most trusted lifelong friend and Gnaeus Domitius Calvinus an almost Cato-like stern traditionalist was sent to Spain to deal with an insurrection of the Cerretani. Still looming over everything was the impending Parthian invasion. For once, Italy was without war or even rumor of war.

6. The Parthian Invasion

It was extraordinary that at this late stage in the immense struggle for control of the Roman state, Parthians should intrude. A nasty, bellicose, fearless band of warriors, they had thought nothing of treacherously murdering a Roman triumvir and like a number of other groups in the East that popped up and surged forward because of some new type of weaponry or military formation, they quickly assumed that they were in perfect position to batter and humble proud Rome and lay claim to much of what Rome had spent the last three centuries cautiously but thoroughly amalgamating and administering. Quintus Labienus, son of Caesar's talented chief lieutenant, who had defected to Pompey, had been left at the court of Orodes, King of Parthia, after Cassius had called upon him for assistance. After Philippi, Labienus was stranded in Parthia and in the winter from 41, with only two other disaffected legions in Syria and Antony in Alexandria, Labienus persuaded Orodes' very intelligent son Pacorus that a conquest of Asia Minor was possible. Labienus and Pacorus entered Roman Syria early in 40. Decidius Saxa, the governor of Syria, was defeated by Labienus and Pacorus, and Cassius' old forces defected to Labienus. Saxa held out in Apames for a time, but was forced out and retired to Cilicia where he was killed. As with Antioch and Mithridates, who had travelled the same roads, dreaming the same incensed fantasies about chasing Rome out of Asia Minor, and possibly out of Greece and Macedonia as well, Labienus and Pacorus exploited Antony's failure to reorganize the client kings properly. Arearathes of Cappadiolid and Antiochus were pro-Parthian, while Castoria of Galatia made no attempt to stop Labienus who moved quickly westward recruiting men from the Taurus tribes. The Roman state structure in Asia Minor, which neither Sulla nor Pompey, nor Julius Caesar had had time to organize thoroughly, crumbled again almost completely. Only Stratoniceia and Aphrodisia held on successfully for Rome. Labienus, a late Roman general, put "the Parthian Imperator" outrageously on his coins. Pacorus took all Syria except for Tyre.

The Hasmonaean Antigonus (Mattathias), son of Aristobulus and pretender to the throne of Judaea, offered Pacorus a thousand talents and five-hundred women—from the families of his political enemies, to make him king. The Jews hated the rule of the Idumaeans and welcomed Antigonus, and a Parthian force entered Jerusalem and seated him on the throne. Antigonus severed the ears of the high priest, Hyrcanus, which disqualified him from continuing in his position, and gave him to Pacorus who took him out of Syria to Parthia where Orodes generously received him and gave him a residence in Babylonia. Antigonus ingeniously struck bilingual coins: "King Antigonus" in Greek and in Hebrew "Mattathias the High Priest, Commonwealth of the Jews." (The next such initiative will be the unsuccessful proposal in France in 1848 A.D. to have the Republican tricouleur on one side of the flag and the Lily of the Bourbons and Orleans dynasties on the other.)

Herod and Phasael resisted the Parthians until Phasael was captured by the Parthians and committed suicide, whereupon Herod collected the threatened women including Hyrcanus' daughter Alexandra and her daughter, the beautiful Mariamne, Herod's betrothed, and fought on at the great fortress of Masada. Herod left his brother Joseph to hold that fort which he did successfully, and after being denied any assistance by Mattathius of Nabataea, Herod took the road to Egypt. Cleopatra favored him as an impressive young man struggling to uphold Antony's interests, and she gave him a ship with which to seek out Antony and ask his assistance. Antony agreed to help him and interested Octavian in the project as he remembered Antipater's services to Caesar. A compliant Senate recognized Herod as King of Judea. This first break with the Roman custom that new client king must be chosen from the old one's family was made by Antony and Octavian jointly. Herod would remain loyal to Antony and from that day he returned to Palestine, raised mercenaries, and attacked Antigonus. Some of this, and not just the names, were reminiscent of the wars of the Diodochi, following the death of Alexander the Great one-hundred and eighty years before.

Antony, after the peace of Brindisi, had six legions from Macedonia, seven under Pollio, four under Ventidius, two from Domitius and five formally under Calenus: his thirty-six legions were now down to twenty-four. He was certainly not over-manned for the government of the whole East and the conquest of Parthia, although this demonstrated that he was not seeking sole power in the Roman world. Antony also had ten-thousand cavalry, mainly Gauls and Spaniards and undoubtedly further contingents from Ventidius and Pollio. His first priority was the Illyrians, who had invaded Macedonia in 40 and been expelled by Censorinus. Antony gave Pollio eleven legions and sent him to subdue Macedonia. Pollio reduced the Parthenia, retook Sulinee, and celebrated his triumph on October 25, 39. Antony divided Pollio's army: four legions would be in Epirus and seven to deal with Macedonia and Illyria. He gave his other eleven legions to Ventidius with a strong force of cavalry and slingers and sent them against the Parthians. He himself was needed in Italy. He had his hands full on every front.

Antony or Ventidius discovered that the sling with leaden bullets had a greater range than Parthian archery, but they did not know that Parthian tactics had evolved and it was not the archers who defeated Crassus whom they would meet. Carrhae had been won by the common man trained and led by the quasi-genius, Surenus, who had enraged the Parthian nobility; they were now going to show the Romans what they could do. Antony appointed Plancus, a thoroughly competent officer, governor of the province of Asia.

We learn from Sallust of Ventidius' successes; he landed in Asia in early 39 and surprised Labienus, who evacuated Caria, fled to Cilicia, and fortified a camp on the Taurus slopes, and summoned the Parthians. Ventidius camped on rising ground and waited for his legions who arrived just before his opponents. The Parthians, more cocky even than usual, evacuated Syria and instead of joining Labienus, they attacked Ventidius on their own, pressing uphill against his strongly positioned legions who threw them back down the hill and discovered, to Ventidius' great happiness, that they could unleash their slingers on the Parthians rear and penetrate their armor. Ventidius then attacked Labienus' camp, driving him off. Labienus was hunted down and killed. The Parthians tried to hold the Amanic Gates, but the Romans forced the pass; the defenders fled across the Euphrates and Ventidius had cleared Roman Asia as quickly as it had been overrun. Antony took the title of Imperator for the second time for the victories of Ventidius and Pollio and Ventidius marched through Syria to confer upon himself the pleasure of dethroning Antigonus. But Antigonus gave him a large bribe and Ventidius obligingly went into winter quarters with his army strung out from Judea to Cappadocia, a hazardous position should Artavasdes of Armenia, Parthia's ally, enter the war.

Early in 38, Pacorus assembled a large force and brought every cataphract Parthia had to support it. Then Ventidius let it be known that he was afraid Pacorus might cross the Euphrates, which caused Pacorus to detour to the north, entering Cyrrhestice. The Parthian cavalry charged Ventidius' camp again uphill and were soundly defeated; Pacorus was killed although the main body of his army escaped across the Euphrates.

Ventidius gained great popularity in Rome, for he was deemed to have avenged Carrhae, and the death of Pacorus was a heavy blow to Parthia as he was highly regarded as a general and as a ruler of moderation, softening and making more equitable the heavy hand of Orodes. But Pacorus' defeat also made clear to the Parthians that they could not rely upon cataphracts against a Roman army, and they changed tactics radically to prevent another debacle on such a scale. The Parthian invasion of Syria had been a disaster, but Rome had only begun to settle accounts with the Parthians.

Octavia proved to be one of the most admired women of the ancient world; she tolerated Antony's infidelities and her brother's manipulations. She stayed loyal to Antony as long as that was possible and when it was no longer possible, she took care of his waifs and foundlings as if they were her own. Some of the most distinguished philosophers of the time were among her friends and as she demonstrated on various occasions when her husband's and brother's interests were not aligned, she was a talented statesman. Antony remained in Italy until after the birth of Octavia's daughter, the elder Antonia in September 39, and then he and Octavia went to Athens for the next two years where he kept his headquarters. Labienus had gained the assistance of the Taurus peoples and Antony selected his client monarchs, Amyntas from Galatia, former secretary of Deiotarus and Polemo of Laodicea and put them in authority over the tribes. Antony strengthened Tarcondimotus a dynast in Amanus. Cleon the chief of the brigands, who had defied Labienus, was confirmed as head of Mysian Olympus, and the resourceful Aphrodisias was liberated and granted immunity from taxation-and a most favored nation status, which seems never to have been accorded by Rome before. Antony raised his fleet to three-hundred ships; he was not going to be weaker than Sextus, whatever happened. Marriage with Octavia had virtually made Antony over: he dressed simply, went with his wife to philosophers' lectures in the public festivals and served as minister of education (gymnasiarch). He did however fit quite easily into the Oriental tendency to elevate Hellenistic kings as gods, and proclaimed himself a new Dionysus, the God who conquered Asia.

Octavian was having trouble with Sextus and asked Antony to meet him at Brindisi, Antony came on the agreed day, but Octavian did not, and Antony who was always vulnerable to perceived snubs was angry at what he considered an insult that embarrassed him in front of the whole Roman world. He left a message for

Octavian to keep his agreements and returned to Athens. But Pacorus' second invasion deferred the conquest of Armenia. Some fugitive Parthians had taken refuge with Antiochus of Commagene, and Ventidius marched on Somosata. Antiochus, in imitation of Antigonus, offered him a thousand talents to wait, and the siege made no progress. The second scandal created an impossible state of affairs and Antony was forced to supersede him and take command in person. Samosata surrendered to him, and he removed Antiochus, who was not heard of again, and made his brother Mithridates the king and took the title of Imperator for the third time really for Gindarus. He sent Ventidius to Italy for the well-earned triumph which the people voted him and of which he was too generous to deprive him in spite of his misdeeds. Ventidius had his triumph on November 27, 37 and he, too, was never heard of again.

Herod went to lobby Antony at Samosata which Antony was besieging and as soon as it had surrendered Antony put Sosius in command with strict orders to deal with Antigonus. Sosius sent Herod ahead with two legions, a rare instance of a foreigner commanding Roman troops. Herod defeated Antigonus at Jericho and besieged Jerusalem. When Sosius arrived, the siege was energetically pressed by the entire Roman army. Jerusalem held out bravely but fell in July 37. Herod prevented the desecration of the temple and ransomed the town from pillage, saying that he wanted a kingdom not a desert. Antigonus surrendered to Sosius who took him to Antony. Herod, who had married Mariamne, the last Hasmonaean princess, began his long reign as king of Judea. Sosius commemorated his success by issuing a coin with the figures of Antigonus and of Judea as a captive woman. But there was an uprising of Jews and at once, notwithstanding his numismatic status, Antony executed Antigonus in early 37, lest he become a rallying point for the disaffected. After taking Samosata, Antony returned to Athens and again spent the winter with Octavia; he was still not able to deal with Armenia as Octavian, after his disaster at Cape Scyllaeum (Chapter 13) where he lost half his fleet to a heavy storm, sent Maecenas to see Antony with an urgent request for naval assistance.

Antony's star was rising again as three of his generals had recently been granted triumphs and Sosius' was yet to come, while Octavian's campaign against Sextus in 38 had been a failure. Antony stood loyally by his colleague and in the spring of 37 sailed to Tarentum with Octavia and his whole fleet only to find that Octavian had built a new fleet during the winter and now intimated that he no longer required his help. Relations became so strained that Octavia was required to prevent a complete breakdown between her husband and her brother. Octavia prevented war by producing instead the Treaty of Tarentum under which Antony handed over to Octavian two complete squadrons, one-hundred and twenty ships against Octavian's promise of four legions which Antony perhaps claimed only because he was short of money and wished to get rid of the upkeep of the ships.

The treaty itself was only an uneasy truce, though Octavia showed great professional suavity in getting it approved at all. The legions were never given and when in the autumn of 37, Antony quit Italy for Greece, he had already reconsidered his position: he had been loyal to all agreements with Octavian but did not believe that Octavian had been loyal to him. From his standpoint, he had been shut out of

Brindisi in 40, Italy was common ground but he had been excluded from it, Octavian called him to a conference and had never appeared and Octavian had asked for and then not needed his help, and for two years Antony had been prevented from beginning the conquest of Parthia because his treaty right of recruiting in Italy was a dead letter, and now Octavian had his ships and he didn't have his legions.

Antony had become convinced that further cooperation with Octavian was impossible, and this was reinforced by a personal motive: he was tired of Octavia; he could not live on her level—his was a nature which no woman could hold unless she was something of a devil, like Cleopatra. His mind, reacting from Octavia's virtues, had contact with a very different woman and memory and Cleopatra loomed in his romanticized recollections as more desirable even than reality, more fulfilling than the imagination could grasp; he fell in (unrequited) love with her during and perhaps because of his absence from her. He sent Octavia back to Italy with her approaching confinement and his imminent Parthian campaign as the excuses, and summoned Cleopatra to meet him at Antioch. She came and he married her on arrival. He had fired his bridge with Octavian and profoundly offended Rome.

This was Antony's downfall in a contest with Octavian: he was more appetite than strategy, a rougher and coarser version of Pompey's disadvantage opposite Julius Caesar. Pompey could carry out a great campaign brilliantly, but at the end of it, was never sure if he wanted absolute power enough to take it by force, or elevation by the grateful scions of Roman senatorial families, who were always too grudging and miserly to do more than pat those who served them on the head and then stand them down lest they imagine they had a right to rule rather than serve. Mark Antony was a good campaigner, but his end was to receive praise, to answer to no one else and enjoy a Bacchanalian life. Julius and Octavian Caesar wanted absolute power, were confident of their ability to take it, had no doubts of their merit, and at all times, Julius Caesar knew his military genius (whose existence he only discovered in his Spanish campaign of the early fifties) would deliver him victory, and Octavian knew his uncanny ability to calculate the correlation of political forces would always enable him to prevail. Antony was, in the company he kept, relatively guileless and excessively ambitious.

This had now happened. Antony had dishonored the most admired Roman woman, and he had ditched all the grandeur and traditions and honor and majesty of Rome for an oriental harlot in Egypt's permanent debauchery. Octavian now had Italy, Gaul and Spain, and Antony only had tyrannized, ransacked, Ptolemaic Egypt, worn-out Greece, and the seething cauldron of treachery and almost incomprehensible ambush and backbiting of Asia Minor. (Always these were as we have just seen them again: desperately dishonest people squabbling over regimes of no purpose or lasting value other than to fasten themselves onto the trade coming to Asia Minor and the Levant from all points of the compass. They must be mentioned but even the most ambitiously diligent reader would not be thankful for their more detailed recitation.)

Octavian and Mark Antony were at this point at peace, but it was hard to imagine, given the strength of Octavian's position, that having played his hand so deftly in the seven years since Julius Caesar's murder, he would not now dispose of his erratic rival and take and hold, on behalf of his late adoptive father and himself, the headship of the known world and the scepter of the known seas. They were almost within his grasp.

CHAPTER TWENTY-EIGHT

OCTAVIAN CAESAR MARK ANTONY AND CLEOPATRA, 37 B.C.-2 A.D.

Marble busts of Octavian (young), Mark Antony, and Cleopatra VII

1. Eliminating Sextus Pompeius

POMPEY'S SURVIVING son paid practically no attention to either the treaty of Brundisium or of Tarentum and the three years between them that were supposed to be a time of peace were for the most part a time of skirmishing and confrontation. Sextus Pompeius not only did not generally honor the arrangements that he made, he seemed to be incapable of cooperating on any efficient basis with other anti-Caesarian forces. He was unable to hold for long the loyalty of any prominent Romans and while his freed men won battles, he himself rarely exploited them. He never attained a stature greater than that of a guerrilla leader bearing a famous name. A dispute quickly arose over the Peloponnese: Sextus declared that it had been granted to him unconditionally and that Antony was withholding it and reducing its value by overtaxing its population. Octavian[1] took Antony's side and said that Sextus should pay over the tribute owing to him for Achaea or wait for Antony to extract a comparable amount from the Peloponnese before he left it to Sextus. With this, Pompeius sent his pirate squadrons out to prey upon Roman commerce and serious combat arose. Captured pirates confessed that they had been incited by Sextus Pompeius to attack the Roman grain supply as a priority.

Octavian published the terms of the Treaty of Misenum; Sextus' governor in Sardinia, Menas, deserted to Octavian with three legions as did the important Italian

---

[1] From now, Octavius Caesar will be called Octavian, in deference to British historical custom, until he becomes Augustus.

towns of Vibo and Rhegium, and for good measure Octavian abruptly terminated his marriage with Scribonia, pronouncing himself "utterly disgusted." (She was a dreadful woman but she and the daughter of Octavian that she was delivered of at this time, Julia, would aggravate and annoy Caesar for the remaining fifty years of his life.) Octavian replaced Scribonia with Livia, the wife of Tiberius Nero, and a woman about whom he was almost as aroused as his fellow triumvir was by the queen of Egypt. This marriage took place on January 17, 38, a busy week for the bride, three days after Livia had given birth to her second son Drusus. He and his three-year-old brother Tiberius, ultimately Octavian's successor, were to be brought up in Octavian's house. Livia was 19, beautiful, highly intelligent, discrete, and a genuine aristocrat. She had not had a happy time with Tiberius Nero, but she would bring much happiness and stability to Octavian Caesar for the entire balance of his life. It was at this point that the regrettable fiasco of Octavius requesting a meeting at Brundisium with Mark Antony and not showing up for it occurred. Sextus, who was not accustomed to complicated arrangements with serious people took this as an assurance that he could play Octavian and Antony off against each other and Octavian went to some lengths to assure the population that he and Antony were now in complete agreement.

Octavian's plan was to invade Sicily in strength. Agrippa had replaced the dishonorable Salvidiensus in Gaul and Gaius Calvisius Sabinus was appointed commander, and Octavian himself brought Lucius Cornificius' fleet from Tarentum. He declined action with Sextus' smaller force but was then surprised by a sortie by Sextus. A confused night action followed by heavy winds cost Octavian half his fleet and he had to abandon any attempt on Sicily. Sextus proclaimed himself the "Son of Neptune," but made no effort to follow-up. The year 37 went better for Octavius, as Antony pledged support and a number of Italian communities were happy to contribute to raising a new fleet for Octavian, even if Rome itself was unenthusiastic. Agrippa returned from Gaul, absolutely triumphant but declined a triumph out of deference to the difficulties of his friend. He had decisively defeated the German tribes, successfully operated on the eastern side of the Rhine, and put the Aquitanians soundly in their place. Octavian asked him to take charge of the invasion of Sicily, which he did.

In the spring of 37, Antony arrived at Tarentum with three-hundred ships seeking recruits for the Parthian campaign; he hoped to exchange ships with Octavian for soldiers for Asia Minor. Octavian was hesitant and mistrustful and had heard that Antony and Lepidus were scheming against him. He was confident that Agrippa and the newly built fleet would be more than adequate and perhaps felt somewhat embarrassed at his appeals for help the year before. Time passed and once again Octavia, concerned at a potentially explosive falling-out between her husband and her brother, arranged a meeting between them at Tarentum. The Triumvirate was extended (it had expired), and it was agreed to withhold from Sextus Pompeius what had been promised to him and a further mutual assistance agreement was negotiated. This was when Antony offered one-hundred and twenty ships and Octavian promised four legions. Menas, exasperated being under Sabinus and then under Agrippa, redefected to Sextus, which gave Octavian the pretext he needed to replace

Sabinus as fleet commander with Agrippa. A very complicated invasion plan was devised by Octavian by which he would come with over one-hundred ships from Puteoli, Statilius Taurus would simultaneously arrive with over one-hundred ships from Tarentum, Lepidus would transport sixteen legions and five-thousand horse from Africa and against this vast armada Sextus had at most three-hundred warships and ten legions.

All three assaults upon Sicily were launched on July 1. (Always somewhat superstitious, Octavian had deferred action until the month that had given its name to his adoptive father.) Lepidus landed his legions safely, blockaded much of Sextus's land force into Lilybaeum and overran the Western half of Sicily. On July 3, a tremendous storm burst over southern Italy and Sicily and Taurus returned to his base, but Octavian's fleet met the full force of the storm and was seriously depleted. Octavian maintained his steely resolve, sent his survivors back to man twenty-eight ships that did not have crews at Tarentum, such had been the zeal of his shipbuilding plan, and he himself scoured the colonies and the veterans while Maecenas went to Rome to assure the population that Sextus was not favored by the gods, and that Octavian would prevail. Sextus Pompeius himself again, inexplicably did not attempt to exploit his advantage, causing Menas disgustedly to defect for the third time.

Octavian resumed the attack in mid-August. The new plan was that Agrippa would attack Sicily from the north and lure Sextus towards him while Octavian and Valerius Masella Corvinus and Taurus transported their legions to Leucopetra, then Tauromenium, and then join with Lepidus coming from the west and attack Massana.

Sextus, a military leader of very uneven ability, was as cunning in defense as he was complacent in following up on victory, and he guessed his opponent's plans. He joined the battle against Agrippa but then detached himself as Octavian seized the opportunity to cross the empty straits ferrying three of his legions from Leucopetra. Sextus snapped the trap closed and Octavian risked a sea battle, staking a great deal in an area where Sextus was much more skillful than he. Sextus Pompeius inflicted a severe defeat on Octavian and many of his ships were lost. He himself barely escaped, reaching the mainland in a skiff and spending the night with only one of his staff. Had he been captured it would have been the end of his career and probably of his life. It has been generally alleged historically that he was so demoralized by the shattering defeat that he asked his one companion to kill him. He was in extreme peril as he couldn't be sure of Lepidus, Cornificius was isolated, and he had no idea how Agrippa was managing. But with daybreak, friendly forces arrived and he was conducted to Masella. Agrippa had been successful and Cornificius and his three legions joined Agrippa. With these developments, Sextus Pompeius was doomed: he was trapped in the northeastern corner of Sicily, and Lepidus and Octavian blockaded Massana, the towns that provided Sextus' manpower. The climactic battle occurred on September 3, 37, off Nolauchus, three-hundred ships on each side with the armies watching from the shore.

It was a long battle, but Agrippa's invention, the harpax, a superior form of catapulted grappling device, facilitating the boarding of enemy ships, was decisive; by the evening it was clear that Octavian had won; Sextus' fleet was almost completely destroyed or captured. Sextus Pompeius shed his admiral's blue cloak and regalia and dressed as a civilian; he fled in one of the few ships he had left, planning to hurl himself on the mercies of Antony. He interrupted even this mission to pillage the temple of Hera at Cape Lacinium. In perfect conformity with his usual methods, Sextus Pompeius had also sent messages to Antony's enemies among the Media and to the king of Parthia, which were intercepted by Antony. He proceeded on to Asia Minor and reopened operations as a pirate and brigand on land and sea, but after a few months Antony's legate Titius, captured and executed him. The name of Pompey still bore sufficient weight and veneration that Titius was forever after an unpopular figure in Rome.

Octavian had won another brilliant victory, not by his military prowess, which was not conspicuous and was never his forte, but by the loyalty of the friends and allies that he attracted and in whom he had placed his faith, by the soundness of his strategic planning, and particularly by the force of his own character and determination which though strained momentarily, did not desert him.

He was not to be carefree for a time, however. It seems that Lepidus, who had long simmered with resentment at his junior status, though he was not remotely as formidable, well-placed, or in any way talented as the other two triumvirs, apparently considered his movement of twelve legions to Sicily to be the beginning of a coup. When Plinius offered the surrender of Messana, Agrippa advised waiting for the arrival of Octavian, but Lepidus, as a triumvir, overrode him and accepted the surrender himself. He then, with Sextus' legions, plundered Messana, an act of treason by a member of the Triumvirate. This night of license and satiation had briefly bound the sixteen legions to him and when Octavian arrived on the next day, Lepidus with twenty-two legions behind him demanded the restoration of his status as a coequal triumvir and ordered Octavian to leave Sicily.

Octavian did not depart but made overtures to the component elements of Lepidus' revolutionary force. The Sextians deserted to Octavian as soon as he showed his disdain for Lepidus, and Octavian could assure their safety and Lepidus could not, and with this, half of Lepidus' own forces also quit. With this example before them, the rest of Lepidus's legionaries followed suit, as they had not been impressed by their commander's lassitude and inactivity while Antony and Octavian reordered the world. A few days after the outbreak of his revolt, Lepidus begged for mercy and Octavian permitted him to remain as Pontifex Maximus in exile at Circeii, but demanded and received his resignation as a triumvir. As far as is known, he did not return to Rome and was completely finished as a political force. He is generally regarded by history as a cipher, far out of his depth with Antony and Octavian. He lived tranquilly on for forty-nine years, dying in Sicily in 12 A.D., aged seventy-six.

There were now forty legions in the northeastern corner of Sicily, a polyglot assembly of Sextian and Lepidean, and Caeserean elements, all clamoring for peace and reward. Octavian moved among and between them judiciously reminding them of their oath and making promises of tangible benefit, and mysteriously arranging the disappearance of a few ringleaders, and after a good deal of toing and froing, he negotiated the disbandment of twenty-thousand legionaries who had fought at Mutina and Philippi, gave bounties to all the rest and promised early demobilization. Tribunes and centurions were given the rank of decurion in their native towns and Agrippa, who had rendered magnificent service and was always victorious, was awarded a Corona Rostrata—a golden crown adorned with ships prows, an honor never bestowed before in the history of Rome. Octavian arranged for the settlement of the territories that he had won: Sardinia, Sicily and in the African provinces—many of his soldiers were placed in the colonies that Octavian immediately began constructing there.

Octavian returned to Rome on November 13, 37; his progress through Italy was a triumph and on his arrival, he received the ovatio that the Senate had decreed. Nolauchus was deemed to be a festival day, a triumphal arch and a golden statue were to be erected to Octavian with an inscription celebrating the restoration of peace after long disturbances. He was awarded an official residence near the temple he had promised to build for his patron deity Apollo. Like Julius Caesar, he was given the right to wear the laurel wreath of the conqueror and most importantly, he was granted a sacrosanctity similar to that enjoyed by the tribunes. His person was thus hallowed and eminent, and this tribunician inviolability foreshadowed the potestas tribunicia which would be one of the great props of the coming principate that he would institute and maintain for decades. In the coming days, Octavian delivered a number of addresses to the Senate and to the people containing a long schedule of debt forgiveness, tax reductions, vacation of acts of vengeance and severity that had been made during the Civil Wars, and he broadly hinted that the Republican Constitution would be restored when Antony returned from his Parthian campaign. He spoke for an almost unanimous public spirit in saying that the Romans had too long fought each other that the time to turn against the insolent barbarians had come. This was a message for the whole Roman world and it was circulated throughout Italy and beyond. A return to complete public security was promised, to normalcy, undistracted commerce and to a time when there would be no concern about the availability and affordability of the food supply. Caesar's murder had been avenged and his last enemies had been routed.

There is no question that Octavian's success in this long struggle had confirmed his view that his fate was to complete the work of Julius Caesar and bring peace and unity to the whole Roman world and endow it with institutions that would preserve the best of what had arisen in the extraordinary growth of Rome from the days of its rustic kings, but adapted to a jurisdiction of unheard-of size and variety. The solidification of his own confidence and ambition, though never publicly communicated in quite those terms, drew a great many people to him.

> This consciousness and this singleness of purpose explain the devotion that he was able to inspire in his peers; the ordinary soldier might be fascinated by the magic of a splendid name, but it was something high and essential in the man himself that bound men of the caliber of Agrippa and Maecenas in such unquestioning and selfless loyalty or gained the respect and service of the Republican Meseala Corvinus, or of Statilius Taurus and others who were won over to his side. Because he stood for something more than mere ambition, he

could draw a nation to him in the coming struggle.[2]

The Civil War was over, but everyone can see that one great struggle remained: the entire Roman world was in the hands of two men; the statutory Triumvirate was now a crude geographic division of spheres of influence between two quite different claimants to the mantle of Julius Caesar. In influencing Mark Antony, Octavia's benign and inspired placatory influence would now give way to the inscrutable but unscrupulous designs of Cleopatra.

The war-weary legionaries of the Roman world were little interested in risking their all for the ambitions of commanders; what was needed was a cause and a rallying cry that would move the heavy weight of mass opinion. This final phase in the consolidation of the powers of Rome would now be conducted on a field where Octavian had every advantage and where Antony, by abandoning Rome and Octavia and embracing the perceived degeneracy and harlotry of the East, was absent altogether. Octavian was offering peace, justice, prosperity, order, and reform. Antony was concerned with his own pleasure, a perfectly legitimate preoccupation but not one that impressed the Senate and people of Rome or the rest of the Roman world. He had ceased to be a viable alternative to his endlessly cunning and fiercely determined rival.

2. The Invasion of Parthia

Mark Antony is generally reviled in history for a terrible mistake in evicting Octavia and marrying Cleopatra. There is much truth to this view, but his conduct was not contemptible. Fulvia loved him and if he had stayed with her he could probably have stabilized a joint rule with Octavian. Octavia apparently loved him or at least was so distinguished in her behavior that she acted as if she did and if he had remained with her, she could almost certainly have assured a smooth sharing of power in the Roman world between her husband and her brother. But Antony ditched her for Cleopatra, because he loved Cleopatra, even though Cleopatra did not love him. He did not marry Cleopatra for the wealth of Egypt, because he could easily have taken it for himself without such personal inconvenience and he never touched the wealth of Egypt, which gives the lie to the modern historical interpretation that his interest in the Egyptian queen was pecuniary. His theory was that he could conduct his invasion of Parthia successfully and raise himself unambiguously to the status of rightful heir to Julius Caesar, marry the woman he loved and live opulently and serenely as he wished, and he was perfectly content to leave Italy and the West to Octavian. If, in that scenario, Octavian had challenged him, he had seen Octavian's limitations as a military commander and was confident that he would prevail. Thus, Antony affronted Rome and Rome's most admired lady in order to do Rome's work in Parthia because of his unrequited love for the Queen of Egypt, who did not approve of the campaign in Parthia, and presumably married him for political reasons, and if she had kept her distance from him would probably have reigned a good deal longer than she did in Alexandria. (Shakespeare comes closer to the facts with

---

2 CAH, X, p. 65 (W.W. Tarn, M.P. Charlesworth).

Antony and Cleopatra than he did with his bunk about the nobility of Brutus; George Bernard Shaw is fairly accurate in *Caesar and Cleopatra*—Shaw is chiefly interested in portraying the omniscient leader with the popular touch—Caesar according to GBS, was the Stalin of his time.)

Cleopatra overplayed her hand from the beginning, demanding the empire of her predecessor Ptolemy II as a wedding present. Antony executed Lysanius in 40 and gave her his kingdom of Chalcis as well as most of Syria, and he gave her most of the coast of Palestine and Phoenicia, as well as Cyprus and Cilicia Tracheia, thus denying her only Judea, Galilee, and the one-time Ptolemaic part of Nabataea. She lobbied fiercely for Herod's kingdom, but Antony absolutely refused and all she got was Herod's hatred, though Antony did give her Herod's Balsam Gardens of Jericho and the bitumen fishery in the Dead Sea. Antony was popular in Alexandria where he was remembered as having rescued the Alexandrian prisoners from Ptolemy Auletes, and Cleopatra began a temple to him, which was unfinished when she died and was turned into one to Augustus instead. Antony and Cleopatra put their own heads on their own coinage and were presented as divine, as was expected in the Hellenistic East. To the Greeks, they were Dionysus and Aphrodite and to the Egyptians Osiris and Isis. There has been a great deal of historical speculation about the use of names and titles to encroach upon the status of the Parthian king, Phraates, and to insinuate Antony's credentials as the continuator of Alexander the Great. Of course, this was really an elaborate and vulnerable charade looked upon with some bemusement by the chief spectator in Rome.

Antony spent the winter of 37-36 at Antioch with Cleopatra, but in strenuous preparation for the long-promised Parthian campaign. He also reorganized Asia Minor, which was in desperate need of it, and had never detained the attention of the greatest Roman leaders for long—Sulla, Pompey, and Caesar (who declared he had conquered after three days); all left prematurely, but for more important objectives in Rome. Antony based his administration on three valued and capable individuals—Amyntas, Archelaus, and Polemo. Amyntas was ruler of Western Pisidia and Phrygia, who was also made king of Galatia, Lycaonia, and part of Pamphylia. This placed the whole central part of Asia Minor in his hands. Antony seized and executed Ariarathes of Cappadocia and replaced him with Archelaus, a cultured young man, and his third main protégé was Polemo: Antony had given away to Cleopatra his domain of Cilicia Tracheia but replaced it with Pontus which he added to his parts of Bithynia and Armenia and the wardenship of the upper Euphrates. These three associate monarchs and Herod would all prove highly successful and all but Amyntas, who was killed in action in 25 B.C., would have very long reigns. Asia Minor was in serviceable condition at last and Mark Antony deserves great credit for it. Herod had defeated and outwitted the Hasmonaeans in Judea, the party of his famously beautiful wife Mariamne. This faction was assisted by Cleopatra, and when the mother of the Hasmonaean pretender began agitating for his recognition and rumor spread that Herod was about to take severe measures, the would-be queen mother, Alexandria, asked Cleopatra's aid and Herod killed the child-pretender, a profoundly unpopular act in Judea and with Cleopatra. Antony eventually had a strained interview with Herod but took no reprisals.

In 37, Orodes, still king of Parthia, terribly saddened by this death of his son Pacorus, had elevated another son, Phraates IV, as his heir, but the king was so inconveniently tenacious of life that Phraates murdered him and seized the crown, causing a good deal of further violence around the royal family. It was a country unusually riven by jealousy, as the lethal reward meted out to Surenas for his decisive victory over Marcus Crassus had demonstrated. There were also social distinctions between the noble cataphract-wielders and the horse-archers. The nobles, having been badly defeated by Ventidius, intended to rely on the horse archers against Antony. Phraates started by recruiting the warden of the western marches and great Mesopotamian landlord, Monaeses, as his commander and Monaeses employed the first trick in the Parthian playbook of fleeing to Antony claiming to be in danger of his life and offering his services, with a view to discovering his plans and deserting. Antony gave him the small kingdom of Alchaudonius and promised him the throne of Parthia. It isn't clear whether Antony was actually deceived, but in any case, in 36, Monaeses returned to Parthia and accepted the command of Phraates' forces. Whatever, if anything, Antony had told him about his own deployments, would not be of any use to him now.

Antony claimed to have Caesar's plans for a Parthian campaign but there is no evidence that he did have anything more than fragmentary preliminary ideas. Caesar would never have left so unreliable and opportunistic a government in Armenia between his combat front and the base of his activities—not even Crassus did that. Then in late 37, Antony sent Quintus Dellius to conquer Armenia, apparently in emulation of Alexander the Great's winter campaigns in that area. Dellius did persuade the Armenian king Artavasdes and the king professed to submit to Antony, but he gave no guarantees, conceded no towns or hostages and there were no garrisons left behind. Few governments in the then known world could be more thoroughly unreliable than the one from which Antony apparently accepted an assurance of benign nonintervention. Phraates roused the Medians, under King Media (though his real name was Media Atropatene), and a number of the other lesser states of the area had formed a reasonably solid rank of local animosity to further Roman advance. The spread of Rome had reached a traditional point that it had not previously seriously gone beyond. However, Antony was a skilled general and he had a fine army including sixteen seasoned legions totaling about sixty-thousand men, ten-thousand Gallic and Spanish horse, thirty-thousand auxiliaries, among them sixteen-thousand Armenian cavalry who could not be considered reliable, and he had brought in a huge siege train including an eighty-foot ram, as he was operating in an unforested place. His first major objective was the Median capital of Phraaspa on his way to Ecbatana, and he was assuming a campaign of at least two years.

It began badly, as Antony sent his best units forward and left the others with his huge baggage train advancing at a slow pace; at the obvious moment the Armenians deserted, and Monaeses attacked and annihilated two legions. Polemo was captured by the Medes, the siege train was burned, and the food destroyed or carried off; it was a decisive victory and Antony found himself in mid-August impotent and running down on rations before Phraaspa, a strong and well garrisoned fortress.

But he was Mark Antony and he declined to retreat. He attempted to pierce the wall of Phraaspa, but without success and he soon ran short of food; finally, Antony offered battle and Monaeses accepted, but the discipline and courage of the Roman legions prevailed. Antony had no adequate methods of pursuit and no siege weapons, and the Parthians simply retired again inside their fortress. It was now October and Antony had no choice but to retire. An enemy deserter guided the Romans back safely by a different way; Antony was correct to accept the advice but was taking a considerable chance given the habitual Parthian recourse to false claims of defection. Antony successfully adapted to the Parthian showers of arrows that had defeated Crassus and had severely discountenanced Antony himself. His men moved into tightened squares and held shields over themselves as well as on all sides, like a giant tortoise. The Parthians thought Roman morale had collapsed and attacked en masse and were repulsed with heavy losses. Thus did the Romans successfully complete their withdrawal.

The retreat to Armenia lasted all of October. Antony marched in squares with Monaeses harassing his rear and cutting down all stragglers and foraging parties and frequently attacking on the flanks. The Roman slingers distinguished themselves and though they suffered disease, thirst, hunger, and almost inedible rations, the veterans behaved like Roman legionaries, and it was the Antony of Mutina, the indefatigable leader who shared every privation and never evinced a moment of discouragement. On one occasion his army seemed to get out of hand, and he prepared for suicide but he regained control the next day. When the Roman army, bloodied but intact neared the frontier, the victorious Parthians shouted a tribute to the courage of their enemies and withdrew.[3] The invincibility of Parthia would continue for another one-hundred and thirty years until the arrival of the Emperor Trajan. After a period of refreshment and return to a sustainable diet, the Romans resumed their retreat from Armenia. Like Napoleon remaining with his army leaving Russia until Smolensk, Antony stayed with his until he was satisfied that they were not under mortal threat and that there was nothing more that his physical presence could accomplish; he had no idea how conditions might have deteriorated in Asia Minor.

He managed to get a message through to Cleopatra and she met him at the Syrian village of Leuke Kome. Cleopatra managed the difficult winter sail and brought masses of clothing and provisions for Antony's troops, as he had requested, and they belatedly moved into winter quarters in reasonably good condition. Cleopatra did not, however, bring any money and effectively communicated that she was not prepared to subsidize harebrained Roman schemes, having never approved of the Parthian operation. Antony had lost twenty-two thousand veteran legionaries. His losses were not quite as heavy as those of Xenophon on his retreat from Cunoxa to Trapezus, but it was an irreparable blow to Antony's prestige; he would get no more seasoned troops and he could not be sure of the continuing enthusiasm of the grim survivors of this recent ill-considered endeavour. While all this was going on, Octavian had disposed of Sextus Pompeius and Lepidus, and was sitting in absolute and untroubled control of Italy, Gaul, Spain, Africa, and had forty-five fully manned and provisioned, battle-hardened, and loyal legions: the contented bulk of the Ro-

---

3 Alan Roberts, *Mark Antony*, op. cit., p. 259.

man world celebrating peace and he was a popular and capable leader. Suddenly, the young Caesar just twenty-seven, held almost all the cards. Antony's position was tenuous.

3. Preparing for the Showdown

Antony and Cleopatra returned to Alexandria and contemplated the unpromising political landscape. Antony initially hoped, though probably with no great optimism, that Octavian would unwind the arrangement by which Antony advanced him four legions in exchange for one-hundred and twenty ships. But instead, he kept the legions and sent back the ships that remained (about seventy), revealing his strategy of allowing time to pass in order to inexorably increase his advantage in the correlation of forces between them. The Western Roman world was composed, prospering, and unthreatened, and Octavian was a popular and almost omnipotent ruler of it. Greece was exhausted and quarrelsome as always, Asian Minor was a seething mass of treachery and corruption, as always. The Parthians didn't aspire to push the Romans completely out of Asia Minor but were now somewhat addicted to humiliating them from time to time. And Egypt had some grievances against Rome, but Cleopatra made common cause with Antony, not from passion, but because she had devised a commendably audacious strategy for outsmarting Rome by manipulating Roman political personalities. She had had a peerless introductory course from the great Caesar who fluffed up his reputation with the ribald soldiery and the Roman masses by impregnating the Queen of Egypt on their first night together but relegated her to the role of an occasional divertissement in a cottage on his estate and directed Rome's affairs with no regard to her interest.

She must have known that in taking up with Mark Antony against the second Caesar, and being blamed, fairly or otherwise, for causing Mark Antony to desert Octavia, she was placing all her bets on the anti-Caesareans who had lost almost every round for over twenty years. But this was now her only option and she made the case to Antony that the Parthians were neither here nor there, that all that counted was the rivalry between him and Octavian, and that though he was underdog, he was a better general and he was still a contender.

The always admirable Octavia did not consider that her husband's ostensible marriage to a foreign woman demoted her from her status as his wife and in March 35, she went to Athens with a large quantity of clothing and other necessaries for his army and two-thousand veterans selected for him by Octavian himself. She found an unsentimental message from Antony asking her to send on the men and supplies but to return to Rome. She did so, bringing with her the sympathy and respect of almost all of Roman opinion, but she rejected her brother's request that she move out of Antony's house in Rome. She remained there and continued to take care of their children (two daughters) and of her step-children from Fulvia (two sons).

Octavian was not invincible, as Julius had been, but he did not take risks as Julius had, and he had aggregated his own considerable achievements on top of the power of Julius Caesar; he had won, and his strategy clearly was cautious. There was no force compelling Octavian to risk anything in the East. But Mark Antony smarted under the humiliation he suffered and was now bound to be influenced by the impetuosity of his wife, whose wealth and renown and notoriety comprised one of Antony's few strong assets.

Cleopatra may have thought, as some Romans feared, such as Virgil, that she could rouse a racial and religious Eastern revolt, mustering all the former Alexandrine territories as far as Bactria and the gates of India, into a mighty crusade of vengeance against the arrogant heathen Romans. But as far as can be deduced, this was a myth confected and harbored by Romans who did not know much about the East—it never managed anything of the kind even against the authors of the prolonged bloodbath of the wars of Alexander's succession who slew and oppressed them. They were unlikely to get very far against Rome, whose presence in Asia Minor and the Near East had been a chapter of comparatively enlightened rulership. Furthermore, unsuccessful as it was, Antony's military performance opposite the Parthians in which they could not win in direct battle against him even with every advantage, was hardly an experience to incite the fantastic notion that the motley of barbaric and tyrant-ridden peoples and tribes of the East were in any position to challenge the incumbency of the united Roman world.

The first order of business had to be to punish Armenia for its treachery; even in Antony's depreciated condition, no Roman leader could allow such provocation to pass without chastisement. He was unable to act in 35, as his Syrian legions under Titius were chasing and hunting Sextus Pompeius, and did kill him, though in his current efforts to rebuild his forces and broaden his coalition, Antony accepted the co-murderers of Caesar, Turullius and Cassius of Parma into his ranks. He rested his forces but worked strenuously to strengthen them.

He had thirty legions though some were very depleted, seven in Macedonia, thirteen in Syria, including one at Jerusalem, two in Bithynia, three taken over from Sextus, and five rather randomly assembled. He exchanged his strongest Macedonian legions for the more disparate Asiatic ones so that his very best forces were closest to him. He also began a very advanced shipbuilding program and issued coins bearing the number of his thirty legions and on the reverse his flagship. Antony also began a campaign of ethnic self-ingratiation, by marrying Antonia, his daughter from his first wife, to the prominent Greek Pythodorus of Tralles.

The Parthians appeared to be operating on an eccentric cycle by which they beat off the Romans and then engaged in violent internecine strife. Phraates seems to have disappeared in the infighting from 36 to 34 as the Parthians and Medes squabbled and skirmished over what they had plundered, and the Median king proposed alliance to Antony. He accepted although he had no interest in an early resumption of hostilities with Parthia. But in order to represent his late Parthian excursion as having been more successful than it really was, Antony confirmed an alliance with Media. On January 1 of 34, Antony retired as a Roman consul, and invaded Armenia, quickly overrunning the country, and he captured King Artavasdes and his sons Tigranes and his own namesake, though the eldest son, Artaxes,, escaped and after failing to provoke a popular uprising fled to the beleaguered Phraates. Antony tried to put a little skin on the bones of his Median alliance by giving the Median king a section of Armenia and betrothing the son of a local ally to the Median ruler's infant daughter.

With Armenia officially a Roman province, Roman subjects (though few of them were actually Roman) flooded into the country and milked its commerce. Antony left several legions to winter there and returned to Alexandria bringing Artavasdes and his sons and a great deal of accumulated loot, including the solid gold statue of Anaitis from her temple in Acilisene. His intentions were clear to Octavian and although his self-defined "victory" over the Parthians had been celebrated, his conquest and incorporation as a province into the Roman world of Armenia were not officially mentioned. Both sides were preparing for confrontation.

To chase down the Median sideshow for the next couple of years before returning to the main narrative, Antony responded to an urgent message and visited the Median king at his frontier with Parthia where he expected an imminent attack. He gave his share of the lost Roman Eagles to Antony who took a prominent Median hostage back with him and gave him some military assistance but did not withdraw his legions from Armenia until the autumn. But the Median king sought greater security by an alliance with Phraates' renegade general Tiridates. But Phraates, a hardy survivor, chased off both the king of Media and Tiridates to Syria and Phraates seized all of Media and for good measure Armenia as well, as Antony had withdrawn his legions, and Artaxes was restored to the Armenian throne. His first act was to massacre all the Roman traders in Armenia, a popular initiative locally but with obvious international complications, and for a time, the house of cards of any Roman influence in Armenia or Media collapsed. All of this occurred while more important events unfolded in the larger Roman world.

In the autumn of 34, Antony staged a Roman triumph in Alexandria, something that had almost never been done outside Rome. Cleopatra presided on a golden throne elevated to considerable height and Antony entered the city in a triumphal extended chariot followed by his Armenian prisoners whom he ceremoniously presented to Cleopatra. The Jupiter Optimus Maximus of the capitol was the presiding deity which Romans took as an elevation of Cleopatra to a quasi-deified status in Rome, at least in Antony's opinion. This was presuming a great deal, but Antony must have realized that he would be seriously offending Roman sensibilities. Many also concluded, almost certainly mistakenly, that Antony intended to shift the capitol of the Roman world to Alexandria. One relatively humane feature of his celebration was that unlike what would normally have happened in a similar Roman proceeding, the treacherous Armenian king, Artavasdes was not put to death.

The even more remarkable ceremony was what became known as the Donations of Alexandria. They caused a huge mass of people to be gathered together in the great sports grounds of the gymnasium, and above them Antony and Cleopatra in traditional Egyptian royal attire sat side-by-side on thrones and beneath them their three children and Ptolemy Caesar. Antony delivered a forceful oration in which he said that Caesar and Cleopatra had undergone a Macedonian marriage, that Ptolemy Caesar was Caesar's legitimate son, and that he would honor Caesar's memory. He declared Cleopatra Queen of Kings and Ptolemy Caesar King of Kings, joint monarchs of Egypt and Cyprus and the territories of Cleopatra's other children. He then solemnly announced the delivery to the legitimate rule of their children of all the other territories that he could plausibly claim to direct. His own position was not precisely defined because for his Roman supporters and legionaries he must remain Marcus Antonius, a Roman magistrate. But to the Greeks and Asiatics he was a divine Hellenistic monarch, Antony Dionysus, consort of Cleopatra Isis, Queen of Egypt and Queen of Kings. Documents of the time indicate that Antony's contention was that he gained all these titles when he married Cleopatra in 37. He was neither the king of Egypt, that was Ptolemy Caesar, nor King of Kings, as that was a title that he was able to give to others. The inference is incited that he was describing himself as the Roman Emperor and implicitly Cleopatra was the Roman empress, and her official oath now included the phrase: "so surely as I shall one day give judgment in the Capitol."

Antony could scarcely have conceived of a more certain method of uniting Roman opinion behind Octavian in the necessity of shattering this imposture and reassuring Rome that under no circumstances would it be Egyptified in any way or ever subordinated to the claims of the preposterous Cleopatra. To Rome, from the old senatorial families to the rabble of the Aventine, Egypt reeked of the primitive, corrupt, vulgar, superstitious Oriental peasantry, idolatrous and dominated by a ghastly bureaucracy of eunuchs, harlots, conjurers, and palace assassins. (This was far from an entirely unjust caricature.)

It has been widely claimed that Cleopatra drove Antony into this and obviously it would not have occurred without her concurrence and encouragement. But Antony had had the habit of declaring ambitions to be already achieved, as in his claim to have conquered Armenia and Media. We cannot now be confident of exactly what his and Cleopatra's thinking was, but to have gone through such a ceremony, they must have at least been united in a consensus of how to proceed. Their conduct would indicate that a showdown with Octavian was inevitable; that he would marshal Roman opinion so there was no point trying to placate it, and that Antony's chances of victory depended on rallying the Roman legions now under his command and on his superior credentials as a combat army commander. Had Antony professed only to be a Roman governor it would have been much more difficult for Octavian to rally Roman opinion behind a policy to eliminate Antony and Cleopatra. After this grandiose dispatch of the most provoking possible formulation of Antony's Eastern ambitions, he was affronting everything that he supposedly represented and handing Octavian Caesar a blank check to lead a united Roman world to the destruction of Antony and Cleopatra.

From Cleopatra's standpoint, at least she had convincingly acted the role of Queen of the known world, and her husband had a fighting chance to bring it to pass; if it really happened, that would be serendipitous, but even if it didn't, she had raised the challenge, lived the fantasy, and carried the battle directly to the Caesars. She would win everything or be remembered forever as someone who made a mighty, highly imaginative, and unforgettably spectacular lunge for a preeminence no woman had ever remotely achieved before. She was even holding herself out, as a Macedonian, as the continuator of the great universal commonwealth of Alexander the Great. It had a certain logic, and an evident grandeur, but in this battle, for which Antony and Cleopatra were posturing and staging, their adversary was relentlessly building the odds in his favor.

Nor had Octavian been idle; he was giving effect every week to the unification of Italy as a Roman-centered country of Latin-speaking fellow citizens who with their emissaries and local allies around the Mediterranean increasingly directed a united and peaceful world. This too was a great vision, and as it was visibly and tangibly coming into being every day, it required no levitation of hopefulness to attract belief and faith. To complete the defensive redoubt of Italy now required the subjugation of the mountain tribes and the establishment of a line between the mountain peaks as the northern boundary of Italy, and the suppression of the remaining Adriatic Pirates and of the still troublesome and frequently belligerent Illyrian tribes.

Not only was a military operation necessary to accomplish this goal, it was also necessary to burnish Octavian's slightly unprepossessing status as a military leader. It was generally recognized that Antony's long-promised punitive campaign against the Parthians had been a fiasco but a moral success. Even if a carefully selected and not overly challenging campaign such as in the Alps and Illyria, would help sway opinion among the legionaries and possibly weaken the fidelity of Antony's legions, who could be assumed not to be straining at the leash to go forth and elevate Cleopatra.

Octavian had devised another complicated offensive: the fleet was to come from Southern Italy and while legions advanced east from Aquillia to Amona (Ljubljana), he would lead the balance of his army southeast into the interior and to the side of a river. This was essentially the conquest of what is now Croatia, but it was then very savage country. The historian Dio recounted the severity of the climate and the barrenness of the land and attributed the courage and vehemence of the local tribes to the fact that they could find nothing that made life worth living: "I know, for I have been a governor there myself."[4] This plan was entirely successfully executed in 35 and the fleet swept away a good many of the pirates and extracted the submission of many coastal communities. Octavian had taken for himself the most difficult part of the campaign, starting from Tergeste (Trieste) and it reached its conclusion in the siege of the capitol of the Iapudes, Metulum. The defenders had captured some Roman anti-siege equipment and successfully undermined many earthen approaches that the Romans built up against the wall of their capital. Finally, when the crisis of the siege came over the single entry that the Romans had made to the defenders' city, Octavian rushed down from the tower where he had been directing the assault, seized a shield and charged across, the standard method of rallying troops, often employed by his late adoptive father. With this, his army rallied and crowded in behind and even when the gangway collapsed and Octavian himself was seriously injured, he resumed his position in the frontline and led his forces forward. The city was overwhelmed and its more fervent occupants burned it down.

This was a legitimate victory for Octavian: his plan had succeeded entirely and he had demonstrated his personal bravery and talents as a commander. He returned to Rome for most of the winter and resumed his southeastern march in the spring capturing Senodium about halfway down the eastern shore of the Adriatic and was again wounded, and returned to Rome in late 34 to serve as consul for 33. His campaign had been thoroughly successful in conception and execution and Octavian

---

4 Dio xlix, 36; CAH, X, p. 85 (Tarn and Charlesworth).

had been justly rewarded in public and legionary opinion for his military competence and his physical courage.

In the circumstances created by the antics of Antony and Cleopatra, Octavian laid down his consulship on its first day, as Antony had done the year before, and he returned to conduct operations in Dalmatia in the spring of 33. He completely erased the regrettable history of Gabinius in this area and repossessed the standards that he had lost.

Octavian had already instituted a broad campaign throughout Italy to build monuments and theatres, broaden streets, and teach a heroic version of Roman and Italian history. He was in nation-building mode and steadily strengthened the common interest of all Italy as well as Italian colonies throughout the Roman world and an increasing number of local enthusiasts for the Roman connection, which as an article of policy, Rome generally made an important feature of its commerce with, and relatively gentle taxation of, all the areas where it was the occupant or the suzerain. Octavian's educational and religious policy treated the Greek traditions with respect but more or less explicitly banned the Asiatic, Syrian, and Egyptian rites other than in their places of origin. In 33, Octavian published edicts that expelled astrologers, fortune-tellers, and magicians from Rome. With the help of Virgil and Horace and others, Octavian was welding a Roman world of common or at least reconcilable traditions and beliefs and endowing it with a mission to govern benignly. It was a vast enterprise undertaken and executed with its architect's customary thoroughness. The break between Octavian and Antony and the supreme test that would follow were now imminent.

On learning of Antony's Donations in early 33, Octavian sent Antony a sternly worded letter in which he reproached his ill-treatment of his sister Octavia, his liaison with a foreign queen, and his attempted elevation of her son with Julius Caesar to a status that implicitly vacated Caesar's assertion that Octavian was his successor. Antony replied that Cleopatra was his wife and reminded Octavian that he was prepared to marry his daughter Julia to a Dacian and inquired of Octavian's own romantic waywardness. He assailed Octavian for ignoring the provisions of the Treaty of Brundisium that entitled Antony to half the recruits levied in Italy and allotments for his veterans, and he asked where his promised legions were and said that Octavian alone stood in the way of the restoration of the Republic. It will be recalled that instead of restoring the legions that he had promised, Octavian sent back seventy of the one-hundred and twenty ships he had borrowed, none of which Antony requested or wanted. Octavian's position was that the insult inflicted upon his sister suspended the operation of their prior agreements. He gratuitously added that Antony should find the land he offered his veterans from his conquests in Parthia.

This convinced Antony that he must seek the approval of the Senate in the conflict that was now inevitable. The support of the Senate hadn't done much good to anyone who enjoyed it for some time, and with Octavian in control in Rome, it would not be easy to obtain it. Antony sent the Senate a dispatch seeking the ratification of his acts including the Donations and indicating his willingness to lay down the powers of a triumvir if Octavian would also. (It was still referred to as a Triumvirate, though Lepidus had been expelled and not replaced.) The Triumvirate officially expired on the last day of 33, Antony kept the title but Octavian did not. The new consuls for 32, Gaius Sosius and Gnaeus Domitius Ahenobarbus, were supporters of Antony. Octavian had discreetly withdrawn from Rome this time and the consuls would have felt able to read to the Senate the message from Antony except that they feared the impact of the recitation of the gifts and titles showered upon Cleopatra would inflame Roman public opinion. Instead, Sosius, a forceful and theatrical orator, harangued the Senate in place of Antony and would have proceeded to a motion critical of Octavian had the Tribune Noni us Bulbus not interposed his veto. Octavian swiftly returned to the Senate though enveloped by a bodyguard of friends and soldiers. He defended his own acts and attacked Antony and Sosius in grave terms, offering to prove with documentary evidence the justice of his own cause. No one dared to utter or hear a word of reply and the meeting was adjourned and before the date fixed for the production of Octavian's evidence arrived, both consuls and four-hundred senators departed Rome for the East.

On the arrival of the consuls in the East in early 32, and with the return of his army from Armenia, Antony made vigorous preparations for war. He and Cleopatra wintered at Ephesus, and he set up a counter-Senate there. He removed many works of art from Asia Minor to Alexandria and gave Cleopatra the library of Pergamon in compensation for the books inadvertently burned by Caesar when he was defending her as well as himself in 47 (though there is no evidence this gift was effected). This was the bellicose course that Cleopatra had advocated, and she honorably supported it with all her resources, contributing twenty-thousand talents and an undertaking to pay for the army and navy and provide half of the three-hundred transports and a large force of oarsmen. Antony exacted an oath of allegiance from the client kings except for Polemo and Herod. Herod did come to Ephesus, but his quarrel with Cleopatra was resumed and Herod advised Antony that the path to success was to kill Cleopatra and annex Egypt: obviously, that advice was not followed, though, dispassionately, it was probably good advice.

Antony's entourage was riven with dissent over the status of Cleopatra. Antony could as a Roman lead Romans against other Romans, but he could not do so as a Hellenistic Greek and the husband-consort of the queen of Egypt. Some of Antony's lieutenants, such as Canidius and Turullius, would follow him anywhere. Domitius Ahenobarbus was one of many who would follow him if he approved of what he was doing. There were many opportunists like Titius, who just wanted to be on the winning side, and the devil take any matters of principle. And there were many whose only real loyalty was to Rome, and they would support whomever, as time went by, best advanced the Roman interest. At one point, the anti-Cleopatrans prevailed, and Antony felt obliged to send her away. She refused and as a practical matter, the fact that she was basically bankrolling the expedition made it impossible to continue a policy of conflict with Octavian without indulging Cleopatra as much as she wished. Cunning as she was, she might have been expected to realize more clearly the difficulty of maintaining unity in what was effectively a revolt against the Roman government. But this was so much her initiative, she devoted herself through replication in Athens, where Antony moved his headquarters, of the banquets and entertainments and other festivities that she had lavished upon Antony at the florid height of their relations to console him for the necessity of defying the advice of much of his entourage. When Antony and Cleopatra arrived in Athens in May 32, the Athenians conferred upon her the same honors and distinctions that they had formerly conferred upon Octavia. When a powerful contingent of Antony's Italian supporters sent a delegation urging him to rid himself of Cleopatra, her influence was such that the messenger was dismissed and sent home without a reply. That Cleopatra conceived the extraordinarily audacious plan of the moribund, long despised decrepit kingdom of Egypt effectively gaining control of much of the known world by selecting and influencing prominent personalities of the Roman government and pushed it as far as she did was an astounding accomplishment. But once having fastened on that objective and that strategy, she should have remained further in the background to facilitate Antony extending the largest tent he could over the broadest church of anti-Octavians he could assemble. Her determination to fight as co-leader of the Antonian school of Caesareans was understandable in the circumstances, but a grave tactical error. (They had Cesarean credentials: he was Caesar's chief lieutenant, and she was the mother of Caesar's only known son.)

Octavian was now thoroughly in control of the capitol and he convened what was now virtually a puppet Senate to which he delivered a comprehensive defense of his position and attacked Antony's conduct, especially the Donations, and he acerbically compared his successful actions in Illyricum and Pannonia with Antony's sanguinary fiasco in Parthia. In order to deal with what was now called an insurrectionist crisis, Octavian imposed an income tax on all citizens of twenty-five percent and a capital levy of one eighth on all freedmen, and a mighty propaganda effort was conducted to save the Roman world from this terrible malignancy. Octavian quietly backed a movement among the towns and municipalities of Italy to pass votes of confidence in Octavian as the public relations campaign representing Antony as a bemused puppet of a foreign sorceress and harlot was intensified. Antony played into his opponent's hand by sending Octavia a formal letter of divorce and expulsion from his house in Rome. For over two years she had remained, faithfully conducting his business and mothering his children including from an earlier marriage, and the spectacle of his messengers expelling her weeping from the house with those children was both a public relations and a tactical disaster for Antony.

Plancus and Titius, opportunists to be sure, went over to Octavian bringing with them a lot of privileged information including the fact that Antony had recently drawn up a will and had entrusted it to the Vestal Virgins. Convinced that that document would prove to all Italy everything that Octavian had alleged about Antony's disloyalty to Rome, Octavian demanded it. The Vestals rightly declined to surrender to his demand for the will and brushing aside the opprobrium of an act of force against such a revered institution, Octavian simply seized it and read it to the Senate. It included a clause that Ptolemy Caesar, Julius Caesar's son by Cleopatra, was the true son and heir of the late dictator and it distributed great Roman legacies to Antony's children with Cleopatra and further directed that he should be buried beside her in Alexandria. This provision was widely, though not convincingly, taken to mean that Antony intended to transfer the Capitol to Alexandria, a project that Octavian's extensive propaganda machine greatly amplified.

Antony was widely reviled as a traitor, but Cleopatra was assaulted by one of the most overwhelming and effective campaigns of defamation in history: she was accused of being a witch who had entranced and suborned Antony with oriental drugs and harlotry, of being a worshiper of beast gods, a Queen of eunuchs, a drunkard, as well as an assassin, a traitor, and a coward. As this campaign of vilification raged throughout Italy the initial discontent which led to rioting and arson in some areas over Octavian's new taxes, subsided, and town after town throughout Italy joined a solemn oath of allegiance to Octavian and a crusade against the menace in the East. Through the autumn of 32, this great public oath-taking extended through Sicily, Sardinia, Gaul, Spain, and Africa. Octavian then had Antony deprived of his triumviral power and of his right to hold the consulship in 31 and he himself as priest of the Roman people went through the formidable and ancient ritual of the theological proclamation before the Temple of Bellona of a just war. Octavian had the war proclaimed against Cleopatra alone, partially because he had announced the end of the civil wars in 36, but mainly because opinion would be firm against a foreign enemy, and it was indeed her war—she was the enemy paymaster and co-strategist-in-chief.

As 31 began, Antony and his fleet and army were in Greece; Octavian's fleets were at Brindisi and Tarentum, diplomatic interchanges had ceased though propaganda continued at a deafening level. The legalities were not entirely clear but didn't much matter as it was now a bare-knuckled battle for supremacy in the known world. Octavian had the advantage, and it would be Antony's task to assert his superior military experience and success to counter the advantage that natural forces, Antony's own tactical errors, and Octavian's unfaltering ingenuity had enabled the still young Caesar (at thirty-two) to accumulate. The propaganda war plumbed disgusting depths of malice and fiction: Antony posed as Dionysus and Octavian as Apollo; Antony was portrayed as a drunken lunatic and Octavian a coward: there were many political crimes alleged as well as sexual depravities. This tremendous fury of invective affected a great deal of historical writing down to modern times and the conventional portraits of Antony as a drunken lout departing Cleopatra's embraces only for disastrous military campaigns, and of Octavian as a cruel and treacherous coward, are almost entirely false. At the beginning of 31, Octavian became consul and in Antony's place was Marcus Valerius Masella Corvinus. Maecenas was put in charge of Italy; naval squadrons protected the western provinces, and Cornelius Gallus was sent to guard Africa. As soon as the spring of 31 permitted navigation, Octavian's gigantic fleet crossed the Adriatic.

All members of all factions were now Caesareans; those who had thought to build popularity on the assassination of Caesar had been obliterated. The Caesarean who inherited some of his combat stature and swordsman-like qualities, was facing in mortal combat the Caesarean of legitimacy, cunning and political astuteness. Mark Antony and Octavian Caesar would finally settle accounts and determine the political future of the world, a Rome tempered and accentuated with the attractions, practices, debauchery, and mysteries of the Near East, faced a renovated and relatively disciplined and austere Republic.

4. Actium

Antony had assembled a gigantic fleet, the largest in the history of the world at the time, over five-hundred warships, bearing crews of up to one-hundred and fifty thousand men. (The gigantic U.S. Pacific Fleet in 1945 carried just four-hundred thousand men to sea.) Antony had noted the heavy ship advantage that Octavian had had over Sextus Pompeius, and had over-built him, many had squared timber covered in iron to defeat ramming, and up to nine men per oar. His army was less over-powering: nineteen legions, many under-strength but almost all experienced Roman soldiers, about seventy-thousand infantry and twelve-thousand cavalry, about half of those from the client-kings. Sparta, under Eurycles, whose father Antony had executed, defected to Octavian, as did parts of Crete.

Antony labored under the fundamental strategic problem that he could not invade Italy with Cleopatra as it would have united the entire Italian Peninsula against him, and as Cleopatra was paying for most of the enterprise and absolutely refused to cease to accompany Antony, presumably for fear that he would reach another agreement with Octavian under his first wife's—Octavian's sister's— influence at Cleopatra's expense. Thus, he mustered a mighty force but remained on the defensive.

Octavian too had an immense force: over four-hundred warships, most of them heavily timber-armed and equipped with catapults for firing Agrippa's harpax for grappling ships. His army had eighty-thousand infantry and twelve-thousand horse, almost all of them battle-seasoned Roman and Italian legionaries. He did not have a field commander as accomplished as Mark Antony, but Agrippa was very capable and as naval commander, was superior to anyone on Antony's side. Octavian also had extensive manpower reserves. Octavian crossed to Greece in early 31, while Antony's army was in winter quarters. Agrippa was his fleet commander and with half his ships attacked the Peloponnese, stormed ashore in several places, and killed Bogud, the former Mauretanian co-king who had been chased out by his brother Bocchus. It was under cover of this diversionary activity that Octavian landed his army in Epirus and moved southward quickly, trying to surprise Antony's fleet from the land. He was unsuccessful in this, but seized a good position on high ground on one of the promontories which enclosed the Gulf of Ambracia.

Antony gathered his forces and deployed them to strangle or assault Octavian's army, but by the time he did so, Octavian had fortified his position and connected it by walled roads to the harbors of Comarus, while Agrippa stormed Leucas and blockaded the Ambracian Gulf, preventing the entry of grain-ships. Agrippa then took Patrae and Corinth and cut Antony off from the Peloponnese, repulsing an attempted sortie of part of Antony's fleet. Antony camped opposite Octavian and shipped troops up the Gulf and sent his cavalry around it and then in a combined attack tried to jam Octavian into a tighter territory and cut him off from his water supply. Octavian frustrated this attempt by defeating Antony's cavalry in the course of which action Rhoemetalces of Thrace, and the well-travelled Deiotarus of Paphlagonia defected to Octavian, who said darkly to Rhoemetalces: "I like treason to my benefit, but I don't like the traitors."[5] Antony attempted to recruit more cavalry and personally led a second attempt to cut Octavian off from his water source. Amyntas, a man Antony had virtually created as a serious chief, deserted to Octavian in mid-action with his two-thousand Galatian horse. Antony's effort was a fiasco and he retreated, personally defeated. Amyntas and the other dynasts did not like their treatment in Antony's Donations, and their allegiance was to Rome and not to him and Amyntas apparently indicated when he arrived in Octavian's camp that he expected him to be the victor and believed he would be judged to have played a role at a decisive point in determining the outcome of the action. Antony recognized that he had lost the battle on land though his forces were still substantial and in good order, and he must now shift focus to the sea, where apart from the superior talent of Agrippa, Antony still possessed certain advantages, but had forfeited his advantage as Rome's foremost combat general.

His forces had suffered from some debilitating diseases transmitted in marshy conditions and his rations were short as Agrippa had cut him off from their source. Food had to be brought in by man on mountain passes. (Among those press-ganged into the human chain was Plutarch's grandfather, which goes some lengths to explain his lack of sympathy for Antony.) Antony was starting to suffer increased numbers of desertions including from some higher ranks, which he attempted to stop by severe repression, including the execution of the commander of Emesa (Lamblichus), and a Roman senator. But this only accelerated the defections and even Domitius Ahenobarbus, suddenly desperately ill, deserted to Octavian to die, followed by Dellius, in better health, and Antony called a council of war. Canidius wanted to abandon the fleet and fight on land on open ground. Cleopatra insisted on using the fleet and technically was correct as on paper Antony still possessed a slight advantage at sea. But Octavian had the better admiral in Agrippa and where no principles are at stake and only ambition, the loyalty of the losing side is often very vulnerable, as the wholesale desertion of Lepidus's legions illustrated. Where the issue was the ambitions of the commanders rather than matters of culture or nationality, loyalties were very fluid and at this point were clearly running in Octavian's favor. Antony's troops were unwell and demoralized and saw the defections of officers. Antony agreed with his wife, they had to decide the issue at sea (as Octavian was shortly advised by deserters). Antony was under no illusions about the erosion of his position but believed in the end that the Roman legionaries would follow him, even though they were uneasy about serving the queen of Egypt also.

At that part of the Greek coast the wind generally blows in from the sea in the morning and changes direction altogether at mid-day and Antony developed a plan in which he would try to exploit the change of wind direction to outflank Octavian's fleet and separate it from Octavian's camp. As oarsmen could not pursue for very far, he took his sails on board, which had the additional potential of permitting a flight to Egypt in the event of defeat. To prepare for this eventuality, Cleopatra had already shipped her treasury home secretly. It was an interesting plan but since Antony didn't explain the purpose of the sails to his men, many of them feared that it was in contemplation of defeat more than pursuit of the enemy and that the fall-

---

5   CAH, X, p. 103 (Tarn and Charlesworth).

back plan was that Roman legionaries would be transported involuntarily to Egypt to fight for Antony as consort of the Egyptian queen. The implications of this for the morale of his men may be imagined.

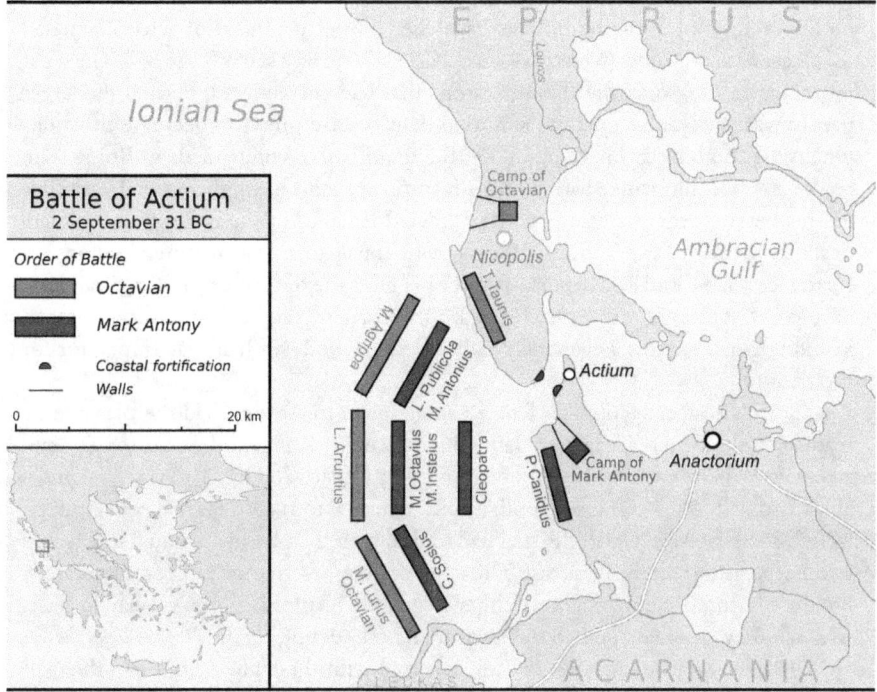

Battle of Actium

On the day, September 2, 31 B.C., off Actium, both sides came out, but the wind died and both sat on their oars. Cleopatra's squadron was deemed the most reliable and was in the rear to head off any premature desertions. Antony himself held the far right, hoping to lead the envelopment of Octavian's fleet. When the wind finally shifted Antony and Agrippa rushed to turn each other's flanks and the ends of their lines. There was skirmishing and Antony ultimately lost about ten ships and his flagship was grappled; Agrippa lost some vessels also, but the number is not known. At this point, whether from weak leadership, general demoralization, or confusion, the three squadrons of Antony's center and left, sixty percent of his ships, backed water and returned to harbor unassailed. The two inner squadrons of Antony's right, prevented by Cleopatra from following the centre, raised their oars and surrendered to Agrippa. Antony was left with only his own squadron on the extreme right, which was engaged, and Cleopatra's which was isolated well out to sea. He signaled to Cleopatra to carry out their contingency plan and she hoisted sail and stood southwards for Egypt. Antony was unable to extricate his flagship; he transferred himself on a launch to the first warship that was not directly engaged and with the rest of the squadron, about forty ships, and followed Cleopatra. He boarded her flagship and sat on the prow dejectedly staring at the sea. He was finished; no one would follow him. His extraordinary and often distinguished life was ending in disastrous failure.

Octavian was at first incredulous and remained at sea and up all night, though on the evening of September 2, he dispatched a brief summary of what happened to Maecenas in Rome (which was the basis of Horace's ninth *Epode*). The next morning, he took over the five squadrons that had surrendered, burned the larger part as was the Roman custom, and used their bronze prows to decorate the monument that he built at his camp and at the temple of Divinus Julius in Rome. The rest of the fleet ultimately formed the squadron at Frejus in southern Gaul. Canidius did his best to urge the army overland toward Egypt, but the bulk of the soldiers declined to move, and various officers were engaged in informal negotiations of surrender terms. Finally, Canidius fled for his life to rejoin Antony in Egypt and the balance of Antony's army surrendered. Octavian executed a few, pardoned most, including Sosius, and was generally rather clement, and was hailed as Imperator for the sixth time.

Cicero's son, reflecting his father's antagonism to Antony, had the pleasure of reading to the Senate Octavian's letter announcing Antony's defeat. Antony's grain stores were distributed to the grateful hungry of Greece and his legions were honorably dissolved. The veterans of both armies returned to Italy. Octavian sent Agrippa to Italy to assist Maecenas, who had had to deal with the plot by Lepidus' son as well as other manifestations of unrest. The news of Caesar's victory had a settling effect, but the returning legionaries were either disgruntled Antonians or Octavian loyalists who felt they had been denied the pleasure of plundering Egypt.

Octavian went to Athens. He was received with the highest honors—the evolution of "violet-crowned" Athens from the proudest of all cities to one routinely garlanding the latest conqueror had been a long and dismal arc. Octavian went on to Samos, but Agrippa urgently requested his return and at serious personal risk from winter storms, he went to Brundisium and on to Rome and distributed what money he could and took land for his own troops from communities that had favored Antony. Some of the dispossessed were resettled at Dyrrhacchium and Philippi. Octavian settled down the problems with a formal promise to pay both troops and landowners in full from the treasures of the Ptolemies. His credibility was deservedly high, and the wealth of Egypt was renowned. He returned to Asia secure in his vast acquests and conquests, as long as he was able to ship an adequate mountain of loot back to his conditional and avaricious supporters in Italy. The Caesars had achieved a mighty, epochal, and almost universal triumph, subject only to tying up a few loose ends.

5. The End of Antony and Cleopatra

While Antony was completely shattered in contemplation of how far he had fallen, Cleopatra was of unshaken determination and merely thrust back to where she had started; a Roman client queen, albeit one who had severely blotted her ledger opposite the master of Rome. She had her ships decked as if in victory and sailed into Alexandria harbor standing prominently forward on her flagship, her head erect. The news of what had really happened had not yet arrived and this gave her the few hours she needed to seize and execute without any pretense of due process those who might, she calculated, be tempted to rise against her. Antony advanced on Cyrenaica but instead of giving battle to Gallus, Octavian's proconsul, his legions deserted, and Antony went on to Alexandria. Cleopatra presented various alternatives to him including trying to emulate Sertorius in Spain or founding a new kingdom on the Indian ocean beyond Rome's reach. With this in mind, she had some ships taken over the isthmus but Malchus (king of the Nabataeans), attacked and burned them. She executed Artavasdes to secure the Median alliance, but all of her plans depended on Antony, as she would not abandon him and he was completely dejected, living alone in a modest house on the Mediterranean shore. She did partially restore his spirits with a new round of festivities and amusements, but he had no will even to try to collect his remaining legions and defend Egypt along the formidable boundary of the Nile. His units kept drifting away to the other side as he had no answer nor will to reply to Octavian's enticements. Nor could he bring himself to emulate Cato and Brutus and commit suicide. His fortunes had truly bottomed out: he would not commit suicide while Cleopatra wished to live, and Cleopatra could not pursue any serious new initiative while Antony was merely a broken reed waiting to die but unable to undertake the task himself. Cleopatra knew that she could not now resist Octavian's conquest of Egypt, but if she acted as client monarchs had in such circumstances, though none were obviously exactly comparable, but as Deiotarus and Herod had done, and given her crown to Octavian, there was a chance that he might pass it on to one of her sons. Accordingly, when many of the elders of Egypt offered to rise on her behalf she ostentatiously forbade it, saying that she would not inflict useless suffering on her people.

In the summer of 30, Octavian advanced upon Egypt via Syria while Gallus closed in from the west and occupied Paraetonium. Antony went to Paraetonium to make a show of strength and possibly to resist but his forty remaining ships deserted. He sent envoys to Octavian offering to kill himself and save him that inconvenience if he would spare Cleopatra; Octavian did not answer. Cleopatra sent Octavian her scepter and diadem, asking him to crown one of her sons. Publicly he ordered her to disarm but secretly assured her that she had nothing to fear. Cleopatra realized she had one big card left to play. Octavian had departed Rome promising to return with enough of the storied treasures of Egypt to satisfy both the merits and the greed of his followers. Octavian had a record of generally honorably upholding his side of cynical arrangements of life and death and treasure, although some of the antics of Antony and Cleopatra and especially the treatment of Octavian's sister, had induced in him something less than fervor as a specific performance co-contractant in recent years. It was the only play Cleopatra had left.

No effort was made to bar Octavian's way into Egypt and Cleopatra shut herself up in the upper part of the mausoleum that she had largely built for herself near the Temple of Isis but had not completed, and in the lower areas all of her treasure: precious metals, gems, ivory, spices, all were piled up adjacent to inflammable kindling. Her plan was to torch everything in a mighty pyre if Octavian did not promise to crown one of her sons. The advance Roman cavalry reached Alexandria on July 31, 30, and Antony determined on one last fight, fell on Octavian's advance guard and drove it out of Alexandria. Folklore has it that that night there was a loud, inexplicable noise which was later interpreted as the God Dionysus leaving Antony. The next morning his forces, including his cavalry and Cleopatra's ships which were manned by mercenaries all went over to Octavian, and Antony, returning alone to the city heard that Cleopatra was already dead. With that he stabbed himself but did not die at once and when he heard that she was alive, begged to be taken to her. This was done and he died in Cleopatra's arms. A few hours later, Octavian entered Alexandria without resistance. It was the first day of the month that would be named after him as he was about to attain to the dignity of Augustus-emperor. He ordered that Cleopatra be taken alive if possible and while Gallus detained her in conversation through a window, Proculeius, whom Octavian had entrusted with this mission, made his way through the mausoleum with a few of his men and although Cleopatra tried to stab herself, they captured her and carried her off to the palace where Octavian had installed himself. The mausoleum treasure house was heavily guarded and means of inflammation were disposed of, and Octavian shipped the treasures at once to Rome and decreed a reduction in official interest rates from twelve percent to four percent. Sufficient wealth was yielded for him to satisfy all military and landowners' claims, a heavy program of public works to embellish Rome as it ascended to an unheard-of status as a world capital, and the distribution of a large surplus to the entire population.

Octavian Caesar had won everything: the treasures of Egypt, the person of the queen of Egypt, and the self-inflicted death of his rival. Octavian permitted Cleopatra to bury Antony and he only executed four men: Turullius and Cassius of Parma who were among Caesar's murderers, Ovinius, a senator and manager of Cleopatra's wool-mill, and Canidius. But he also killed two of Cleopatra's sons: the young Antony, as his father's designated successor, and Ptolemy Caesar, technically Julius Caesar's son and Octavian's stepbrother (though it was a rickety connection). Cleopatra tried to send him to the Indian ocean for safety. Octavian held that the world must not have two Caesars: "It was the final brutality of a brutal age, and he meant it to be final; if the world was to have peace, he had to make an end of all who might yet trouble it."[6]

Though he was comparatively civilized, like his adoptive father, Octavian was not altogether averse to utterly ruthless homicide. But he appeared to draw the line at the murder of a woman or even complicity in her suicide. Cleopatra went on a hunger strike when imprisoned in her palace and she only stopped when Octavian threatened to kill her children. Yet Octavian realized that she had to die: her memoirs could not be published or even uttered and repeated. The key was for her to kill herself in a manner in which he was not blameworthy. Cleopatra was determined that she would not be frog-marched through Rome in her victorious enemy's triumph and shamed before the Roman mob as her sister Arsinoe had been.

While not every detail of the last days of Cleopatra is a matter of certainty, it

---

6 CAH, X, p. 109 (Tarn and Charlesworth).

seems that Octavian arranged for someone to tell her as if as a favor that in three days she would be removed forcibly to Rome for his triumph and she then asked to be able to visit Antony's grave that she might drink a libation and say a prayer at the grave of Mark Antony. This was agreed and an asp, the royal snake carried on the crown of Egypt, was brought to her by a servant in a bowl of figs and she enabled the snake to bite her lethally on her breast, which in Egyptian custom was an ennobling form of death. Her attendants, Iras and Charmian, chose to die with her. Cleopatra was thirty-nine and had reigned twenty-two years. Octavian followed through on granting her wish to be buried beside Antony and their tomb remains covered over by the modern city of Alexandria, undisturbed. Octavian put up statues of her brave hand-maids in front of the tomb. Octavia adopted her three surviving children and brought them up as her own. Mark Antony's name was publicly repressed for a time but obviously resuscitated eventually and among his and Octavia's descendants were the Roman emperors Caligula, Claudius, and Nero.

One of the colossal human dramas of world history was over, though it had just begun to infatuate and enthrall the human imagination. Though Antony's death was in some respects miserable, it was brave, and it was largely caused by the impact upon his strategic sense of passionate romantic love for one of history's most famous and remarkable women. Antony remains a hero of the Gallic Wars who took the place of the talented turncoat Labienus, was for a time indispensable to Caesar, and maintained his preeminence in Rome while Caesar was mopping up Asia and Africa. A rough soldier, Mark Antony yet composed and delivered one of the greatest and most important addresses in all of history at Caesar's funeral. Without his rallying the pro-Caesar forces while Octavian was still on his way back from the Greek islands, the murderers might actually have, at least for a time, put together a tentative and criminal regime. Antony won the day at Philippi and assured the Caesarean victory. He was not a good politician and he underestimated Octavian, and his treatment of Octavia was abominable. But he was a vital and admirable figure in a decisive moment of Roman and world history and his subsequent failings were at least palliated and even mitigated by the allowance history and nature traditionally make for disinterested romantic passion.

Cleopatra was hideously defamed and has been ludicrously caricatured. She was above all an ambitious mother and patriotic dynast and she had the imagination and intelligence to devise a plan for overturning centuries of Egyptian eclipse by inflaming the hearts and asserting a preeminent influence over the minds of leading Roman statesmen. She only amused and pleasured Julius Caesar and was too successful for her own good with Mark Antony, the wrong horse in a match race where she had no ability to influence the winner. It was a grandiose plan for a grand objective for a not ignoble motive; she came close. Even in defeat she had the victory of capturing the imagination of the world and of posterity. And in the eight-hundred years between Brennus' siege of the Capitoline Hill in 391 B.C. and Alaric and the Visigoths' sack of Rome in 410 A.D., she was, along with Hannibal, the only person Rome truly feared. (Rome feared the Teutons, whom Marius annihilated in 101 B.C., but their leaders were not distinctive personalities.)

There is no shame or embarrassment for either of them in having been defeated by so extraordinarily competent an opponent as Octavian Caesar. Even two-thousand years later, Cleopatra's life and ambitions remain one of the greatest dramas in human history, not eclipsed by anything in the Bible other than the life of Christ Himself. Yet it was still not sufficient to dim or obscure the ensuing rule of Octavian Augustus Caesar. He moved with astounding surefootedness, ignoring even the advice of his own parents, taking the place of his assassinated great uncle and adoptive father. Though only nineteen when he began to assert his claim to succession, he made an asset of being underestimated and moved with such swiftness and finesse that he almost always had the upper hand until all the rivals and all the skeptics were removed or converted. Immense though the drama that elevated him to the headship of the known world was, it did not remotely make an anti-climax of the forty-five years of the Augustan Empire that were to come.

6. The Triumph of Octavian

Octavian annexed Egypt as a so-called "gift to the Roman people," but in fact, retained the personal governance of it through an equestrian prefect, i.e., direct control by Octavian rather than a provincial government headed by a senatorial proconsul. Egypt's history, wealth, and huge grain production (wheat) gave it a particular importance. Octavian respected the Egyptian religion, though he overthrew Antony's famous Donations. In protocol terms, Octavian effectively replaced the house of Ptolemy.

He returned to Rome via Syria and Asia Minor and restored most of the art that had been plundered by Antony as a gift to Cleopatra. Cyprus and Cyrenaica again became Roman provinces and only two petty dynasts were executed: Adiatorix of Heraclea for massacring Romans and Alexander of Emesa for inciting Antony to kill his brother Lamblichus. Most of the dynasts in Asia Minor rallied to Octavian in time to save their thrones, subordinated to Rome as they were. Deiotarus of Paphlagonia, like Rhoematalces of Thrace retained their positions and Cleon, former chief of the pirates and brigands of Mysia, was made priest-king of Zeus Abrettenios. (Piracy and the priesthood were sometimes complementary activities.) The priest king of Comana was dethroned. Events in Antony's principal kingdoms remained fairly stable: Amyntas had defected to Octavian and his kingdom was enlarged with Isaura and Cilicia Tracheia. Archelaus remained as he was and Polemo was left as king of Pontus. For technical reasons Octavian relieved him of Armenia Minor but compensated him with a right of expansion to the northeast. In Greece, Octavian granted full freedom to Lappa and Cydonia in Crete, which had declared for him prior to Actium, and he rewarded his one Greek ally Sparta, with an enlargement of territory and the award of the conduct of the Actian Games. In Syria the Phoenician cities regained their freedom as did several others that had revolted from Cleopatra before Actium. In Emesa, Octavian eventually elevated Lamblichus' son. Chalcis became a free city. In Judea, where Hyrcanus had foolishly returned from Parthia and Herod killed him, Herod had made no submission even after Actium and Octavian summoned him; like Cleopatra, Herod placed his diadem before Octavian and wisely made no excuses: he said that he had been faithful to his benefactor

Antony and if Octavian would allow him, he would be equally faithful to him. Octavian was impressed with his frankness and returned his diadem, restored his balsam gardens and gave him Cleopatra's Galatian bodyguard and all of Palestine except Ascalon. The philosopher and historian Nicolaus of Damascus, who had been the tutor of Cleopatra's children, went to Herod and demonstrated with his pen the zeal of conversion.

Octavian at this point had almost no interest in what was beyond the Euphrates; he exacted no revenge on Artaxes of Armenia for his massacre of Romans other than detaining his brothers as hostages. Parthia could keep her Eagles and when the pretender Tiridates fled to him in 30, he gave him asylum in Syria but refused to support him and gave a friendly reception to envoys from King Phraates. He also received Antony's friend the Median king with kindness and restored his daughter to him and gave him Armenia Minor to guard that distant border of the Roman world.

While the great struggle between Octavian and Antony unwound, Octavian's lieutenants in important positions around the Roman world kept things in pretty good order. Maecenas was in charge of Italy and broadly speaking the West and was a competent and vigilant administrator. In spite of Agrippa's successful campaign in Gaul in 39, disturbances arose in the north and west and the Morini and the Swabians who crossed the Rhine and the Aquitanians in 28 B.C. all needed to be batted down and they were by Nonius Gallus, Gaius Carrinas and Messalla Corvinus. Spain was restructured on new provinces governed in a more enlightened manner in 38 but within a decade the northwestern tribes had revolted and were crushed by the efficient Statilius Taurus. There was thus a series of triumphs through this period for successes on the fringes of the Roman world. And there was continuous road-building and in Rome impressive public works continued to transform Rome into a more evidently important world center.

The most important of these frontier actions were those conducted by Octavian's associate consul in his fourth consulship in 30: Marcus Licinius Crassus, who in the opportunistic tradition of his family had gone from Pompey to Sextus Pompeius to Antony but then to Octavian comfortably before Actium. In the summer of 30, he was dispatched with at least four legions to Macedonia whose northern boundary was exposed to attack. There were various Thracian and Getic tribes and chieftains, and more important was the migrating Gallic tribe the Bastarnae, who thirty years before had appeared in the lower Danube and inflicted a serious defeat upon the unlucky Gaius Antonius. The Romans were not much concerned when barbarians attacked other barbarians but when they attacked Rome's Denthelete Thracian allies, whose blind king Sitas was a well-tested Roman ally, Rome was wise to intervene forcefully. In 29, Crassus drove the Bastarnae out of Sitas' territory, and when they sent Crassus an embassy, he borrowed a trick from Caesar and plied the emissaries with drink while encircling and then annihilating the enemy's main force. All through 28, Crassus was almost constantly and successfully in action hammering the Bastarnae and finally recovering the Eagles that Antonius had lost, when Crassus badly defeated the Getic chiefs Dapyx and Zyraxes and smashed the Moesi. He was accorded a rich triumph on July 4, 27. The frontier barbarians were learning that even though they were a long way from Rome, Rome's frontier forces were capable of dealing heavy blows to them whenever it felt the urge.

On January 1, 29, Octavian entered his fifth consulship at his winter headquarters in Samos. He landed in the early summer at Brindisi, rested for some days in Campania, suffering as he often did, from the stress of his office. Virgil recited the *Georgics* to him, and he arrived in good health in Rome, celebrating his mighty triple triumph from August 13-15 for Illyricum, Actium, and Egypt. A few days later came the dedication of the temple of Divus Julius and the opening of the Curia Julia. The treasures of Egypt and Asia Minor festooned the great public works underway including the modernization and extension of the Via Flaminia and the reconstruction of eighty-two temples and on the Palatine Hill, the white marble temple of Apollo, Octavian's Guardian Deity with its adjoining libraries for Greek and Latin books. The thirty-five tribes of Rome had offered him a thousand pounds of gold each as a special gift; Octavian not only refused it but made of it a handsome donation prorated to the public while endowing lavish games and expanding fourfold the distribution of free grain. He also excused all arrears of taxation and publicly destroyed any evidence of the debt. He assisted impoverished senators and former supporters of Antony were reassured by his statement that all incriminating correspondence had been burned. Rome was always stoical and determined. Rome had been shaken by many years of civil war and all classes and factions were grateful to Octavian Caesar for working assiduously for the restoration of prosperity and for his evenhanded and efficient measures that assured everyone he would not abuse his powers and would lead Rome entirely out of the civil war of twenty years but easily traceable in its frequent outbursts for thirty years prior to that. In the years immediately following 30 B.C., Octavian disbanded more than one-hundred thousand legionaries, fully paid and happily established either in old or recent colonies.

Sixty legions were reduced to thirty and all the resulting colonies of demobilized soldiers were strategically placed where they could be best used for a frontier defense or suppression of disorder among occupied peoples. Even many of the active forces were used in public works projects such as deepening canals and road improvements and aqueduct construction.

Octavian was now in a position comparable to, but even stronger than, the status of dictator enjoyed by Sulla and by Caesar. He could control the state though he was very diplomatic and careful in the exercise of his authority, frequently giving people who, in fact, had no influence at all, the impression that both their counsel and their positions were taken very seriously. Two interesting innovations in 30 were that the Senate enacted that priests and the people should offer prayers for the Savior of the state and that libations in favor of the individual designated Savior of the state, namely Octavian Caesar, should be made at all banquets. Another reform which appeared to come spontaneously from Octavian's supporters was that the six years of Tribunician sacrosanctity granted him was transformed into the power and competence equal to the tribunes in almost all respects and greater indeed as it extended one mile beyond the city boundary. The tribunes had been the only official institution that effectively opposed Caesar, and he was now and without controversy placed at the head of the tribunes and beyond their reach, and extraordinary powers could now be conferred on individuals and not just occupants of positions.

On January 1, 29, the Senate approved all Octavian Caesar's acts. Octavian was officially deemed to have saved the Roman state, which was nothing less than the truth, and was a fact much memorialized in Roman monuments. In Octavian's triumphs, for the first time the magistrates followed the triumphator into the city rather than leading him in and showing the way. In 28, Octavian was consul for the sixth time and his associate consul was his faithful and talented associate Agrippa, and for the first time in many years they were almost never away from Rome. Octavian was ever mindful of the piling up of honors upon his adoptive father which was a process accompanied by miserable consternation about what was to become of the Republic. Octavian was very careful to avoid any problems of this kind and went through extravagant acts of consultation in all directions. He also slimmed the Senate down from a thousand to eight-hundred members, it having been generally agreed that this was a meritocratic adjustment. And Octavian himself was accorded the title of Princeps Senatus, as well as the dignity of the title of Imperator. It was both the restoration of the Republic but not exactly and not only that. Octavian had both an official status as principal senator and the unique honorific of being styled effectively the head of the state, but the constitutional norms of the Republic were generally adhered to and he left no doubt of his modest official appetite compared to the great figures of the recent past: Marius, Sulla, Pompey, and even in some respects, Caesar.

Octavian could have continued indefinitely re-electing himself consul and with his unfailing judgment of how much firmness and gentleness to apply to the levers of office, guiding a modified Republic through the digestion of Rome's expanded domains. An obscure incident caused him to become more explicit about Rome's political institutions. His fellow consul Crassus was so successful in his campaigns against the Bastarnine King Deldo and other barbarians, he claimed the right to deposit spolia opima in the Temple of Jupiter Feretrius on the Capitol. This was an honor traditionally granted only to Romulus, Cornelius Cossus, and Claudius Marcellus, the hero of Clastidium. An ordinary soldier might be awarded spolia opima for killing an enemy leader but the privilege of dedicating the spoils in the temple of Feretrius had been customarily reserved for those generals who were fighting under their own auspices. The problem with the claim of Crassus was that it would create a rivalry between Crassus and Octavian, and Crassus could claim that Cossus was merely a military tribune and not an independent commander when he was granted this privilege. However, as the modernization of the temple proceeded, documentary evidence was uncovered that in fact Cossus had been a consul and thus he was under no one else's command, which enabled Octavian to have the application of Crassus denied.

This apparently absurd minuet over honorific formalities generated a broader discussion of the institutions of Roman government. It had already been agreed that in 27 Octavian would be consul for the seventh time, again accompanied in that distinction by Agrippa. Octavian opened the era of constitutional reform with an edict that all illegal acts committed under the second Triumvirate, including by himself alone, were annulled and of no validity after the end of his sixth consulship. He had wiped the slate clean and was ready to produce his reforms. He had effectively the same power as Sulla and his adoptive father had enjoyed and Sulla's reforms were not durable, and Caesar's were not comprehensive. Octavian had incited great hope for restoration of the Republic and for reforms that would spare the Republic the prolonged and terrible decline that it had suffered in the preceding century.

7. The Imperial Republic

Octavian orchestrated an intricate preparation for his reforms; he arranged for Agrippa and Maecenas, his two closest, most trusted, and most talented colleagues to conduct between themselves a debate in the Senate, Agrippa reciting all the well-known Greek authors in favor of accountable democracy while Maecenas spoke in favor of greater powers for the executive officials and a less frequent and authoritative recourse to senatorial ratification, but all within a civil and scholarly framework. Many senators were astounded to hear such a cavalcade of learned arguments from men who had not been previously known for dwelling so painstakingly on such fine points of government.

According to Dio, when Octavian appeared before the Senate at the beginning of his seventh consulship, he announced his intention of laying down the supreme power that he held, and according to Dio, he recounted that while Caesar had refused the monarchy that was offered to him, he, Octavian, was giving back to the Senate the great power that he already exercised and thus "transcended the deeds of man." That he actually used these words is a proposition that should be treated with caution, but there seems to be no doubt that he spoke in these general terms and that his words, whether by prearrangement, or pretense, or in complete sincerity, had a mixed reception between those who applauded him with gratitude, and those who urged upon Octavian the retention of the powers he was renouncing. Octavian did place at the disposal of the Senate the government of all of the provinces. Historically, these provinces were held as pro-consulships by the most powerful and ambitious figures in Roman public life as points of self-enrichment, relaunch towards the consulship, or as positions from which to conduct invasions of neighboring territory to expand and make more secure the frontiers of the Roman world. In the mid-50s, at the height of the first Triumvirate, Caesar had the northern command of Gaul, Pompey the western command of Spain, and Crassus the eastern command of Syria. Under this proposed change, all was in the disposition of the central Roman government represented by the leader of the Senate, the princeps, and it was agreed that the incumbent princeps, Octavian Caesar, should delegate legates to exercise this responsibility in the different provinces but retain the ultimate responsibility and more importantly the command of the entire Roman army himself, for a period of ten years.

In his *Res Gestae* (*Of Government*), published shortly before his death forty years after these events, Octavian published this summary: "In my sixth and seventh consulships, when I had put an end to the civil wars, having acquired supreme power over the Empire by universal consent, I transferred the Republic from my own authority to the free disposal of the Senate and People of Rome."[7] What was called the

---

7 *Res Gestae*, 34; CAH, X, p. 129 (Sir Henry Stuart-Jones).

"restoration of the Republic" occurred in the formal adoption of these changes by the Senate on January 13, 27 B.C. Three days later, the Senate compensated Octavian for his self-disposition of these powers with the conferral of various honors upon him. The official tone of this elaborate public relations exercise was captured in the official imposition of a carved Laurel of oak leaves over the door of his house, of the kind accorded a soldier who had saved a comrade's life in combat—here as on the coinage, Octavian was deemed to preserve the civic life of his fellow citizens, and a golden shield was placed in the Senate extolling Octavian's "valor, clemency, justice, and piety." In these same enactments he was designated "Augustus," as Sulla had been "Felix" (the Fortunate), and Pompey had been "Magnus" (the Great). The meaning of this word was never precisely defined, but it was generally taken to imply that the bearer was more than human. And though it was sometimes proposed that it effectively become an office as well as a description of the holder of the office that Octavian exercised, and it emerged that Augustus communicated "auctoritas"—his decisions and opinions on matters of state policy carried greater weight than those of anyone else or any group, but they were never defined as being legally binding, though in practice they almost always were. This nebulous arrangement was a masterpiece as long as it was Augustus himself, in all his governmental sophistication, who was exercising it. A resolution of the Senate always had "auctoritas," but was only legally binding when ratified by a majority making it a "consultum." When this was blocked by a tribunician veto, the resolution had only the authority that the Senate was deemed to possess by the people to whom the resolution applied. An assertion by Augustus was vested with something like this: it wasn't binding, but it had the authority of the most influential person or organ of the state, who also possessed the ability to enforce it if he so chose.

This has become known to posterity as the start of the Roman Empire with Octavian's reign as the Augustan Empire, but officially the Republic continued. (When Napoleon restored the Empire in 1815, France was proclaimed a Republic, though within the Empire.) Augustus modified the Republic by the durable addition of his own authority to its direction but did not create any office or title that specifically included that enhanced authority; rather he incorporated Augustus in his name and referred to himself officially as Princeps, the premier senator. Octavian and his supporters implicitly claimed that his prestige alone conferred upon him a distinction that provided the stability necessary to rescue the old Republic from its weaknesses and divisions. There was some truth to this, but in fact, like modern statesmen such as Richelieu and Bismarck, he devised a system that worked well while he himself was there to direct it but was seen to require further modification once it passed into the less capable hands of his successors. Of course, Richelieu and Bismarck served monarchs who delegated to them their constitutional authority, where Augustus purported to take his authority from the Senate of which he was the permanent chief member, but all three, and many others, adapted an unworkable system that only really became efficient because they were there to operate it. Rome was a long way from a constitutional system that assured continuity and its own survival even in periods of incompetent leadership.

Some historians have claimed that Augustus did revive the Republic, others that he founded the Empire. Both assertions are somewhat true. Eminent German classicist Theodor Mommsen coined the expression "dyarchy" for Augustus' regime. But the fundamental point of his rule was that it was never intended by him to allow the enhanced powers he gained to be relinquished. He produced accretions of power to a position he defined as the Princeps, and there was no dyarchy: he resolved the contest between a sovereign Senate and a sovereign executive by creating a powerful executive and representing it as a mere protocol headship of the still-preeminent Senate. In this, Augustus somewhat presaged Charles de Gaulle, who reconciled the long dispute between French monarchists and republicans in 1958, by creating a monarchy and calling it the Fifth Republic.

Augustus wasted no time before launching the physical renovation of his battered country; he took personal responsibility for the reconstruction of the Via Flaminia, the great northern road to Arminium and all of the major Roman roads were extensively modernized. In late 27, he conducted the first of countless expeditions of inspection, visited Gaul accompanied by his stepson Tiberius and his nephew M. Claudius Marcellus, the son of Octavia by her first marriage. Both boys had ridden beside Octavian in the great triumph of 29 B.C. In his absence the conduct of affairs in Rome was left to Agrippa who was succeeded as consul on January 1, 26, by Statilius Taurus, another of Augustus' most loyal and competent subalterns. On news of uprisings in northwestern Spain, the princeps and his party proceeded on to Tarraco as he entered upon his eighth consulship. They were not too far advanced when Cornelius Gallus, who had been promoted from governor of Africa to prefect of Egypt, bit the dust of his new country. He had commissioned a number of statues of himself and inscribed paeans of praise to his performance as Roman proconsul in Africa on the Pyramids. This was too much for the princeps who continued to observe a commendable public modesty. Augustus revoked his appointment and expelled him from Egypt, while the Senate unanimously voted "that he should be condemned in the courts, deprived of his estate and exiled." Gallus outperformed his critics and committed suicide. A more convincing demonstration of Augustus' practically unlimited power would be hard to imagine.

With the Spanish uprising apparently suppressed as well as a revolt by the Salassi in the Western Alps, Augustus, who was now 37, had another of his periodic illnesses, and he betrothed his daughter Julia, whose mother was Scribonia, to his stepson Marcellus. He recovered quickly and returned to Rome early in 25 and determined to distribute four-hundred sesterces to every Roman citizen but declined to publish the edict until the Senate had approved it, another of his frequent ornate gestures to collegiality. The Senate responded by giving him a general liberation from any obligation to observe the law, though this must even in what was now becoming a stilted comity of accountable government have imposed some constraints on that freedom from the law. Marcellus received from the Senate permission to be elected aedile beneath the normal age in 23 B.C., as well as the right to become a consular candidate ten years before the normal age. At the same time, Tiberius was permitted to stand for public office five years before legal requirements and was in consequence elected quaestor the following year. There was apparently an attempted coup against Augustus in 23, led by Terrentius Varro Murena (who had suppressed the

Salassi revolt and was Maecenas' brother-in-law), and Fannius Caepio. They were exiled, and Augustus had a very serious bout of his illness but was revived by the cold water treatment of the Greek physician, Antonius Musa, and at the celebration of the Latin Games, Augustus resigned the consulship. He was replaced by Cicero's friend, Sestius Quirinalis, a great and public admirer of Brutus. Augustus was going to unusual lengths to demonstrate his sportsmanship. Although he had retired as chief magistrate, the Senate set about restoring to him everything that was necessary to exercise the powers that he previously had ex officio. Special enactments restored his authority as a named individual rather than officeholder.

Augustus was empowered to bring forth one item of business at each meeting of the Senate and the right to intervene in the proceedings of the Senate whenever it pleased him to do so. His preeminence as princeps restored what he might have lost in retiring from the consulship and he took over from the consuls the right to summon the Senate. In 19 B.C., he was granted the right to sit between the consuls of the year attended by twelve lictors. In 23, the principate was confirmed by popular vote of its proponents and Augustus was deemed to share the provinces of the Empire with the people. He also had the right to make peace and war, conduct foreign relations in general and the Senate bestowed upon him "the right and power to do all such things as he may deem to serve the interest of the Republic and the dignity of all things divine and human, public and private."[8] Agrippa, Marcellus, and Tiberius, all emerged as his apparently joint successors should anything befall Augustus, after 17 B.C. The Princeps maintained the actual succession in a shroud of secrecy.

In 23, Octavian's talented and predestined nephew, Marcus Claudius Marcellus, died of the same illness that almost carried Octavian away earlier in the year, and shortly after, the Tiber freakishly overrode its banks damaging a great many crops and producing an immediate shortage of bread in Rome, always the trigger for massive unease. Popular superstition considered both developments a chastisement of the city for permitting Augustus to stand down from the chief magistracy and he received repeated embassies including large numbers of common people beseeching him to reassume his powers, to become dictator, and threatening the Senate if they did not exalt Augustus. For once we may be confident that these were spontaneous demonstrations that he was not promoting or encouraging himself. Marcellus' death was immortalized by Virgil in the *Aeneid*.[9] Augustus declined to become dictator, life consul, or censor. It all seems hokey at this distance, especially as Augustus clearly possessed all the power he needed, but there has never been any suggestion he incited these demonstrations and agitations in favor of supreme power for himself. The whole upper reaches of the Roman state were now packed with his henchmen, some of whom were former enemies. In 21, Egnatius Rufus, on laying down his aedileship, issued an edict in which he boasted that he handed the city over unimpaired and intact to his successor. Augustus transferred the duties of the fire brigade which Egnatius had formed from his own slaves to a core of six-hundred public slaves and told the praetors to celebrate the games which had been held under the auspices of the aediles. Egnatius was not easily rebuffed even by Augustus and in 19 he ran as

---

8 CAH, X, p. 141 (Stuart-Jones).
9 *Aeneid*, VI, 860-885.

a candidate for the consulship when, as in 21 only one consul was in office. (Again, the second place had been left unfilled in the hope that Augustus would consent to be elected, as Agrippa was obliged to leave Rome at the end of 20 in order to quell disturbances in Gaul and on the Rhine and then in Spain.) Saturninus was left in a position of grave responsibility and proved to be fully equal to them and declared that Egnatius was not eligible to be consul and he would not recognize his election if it apparently occurred. There were riots and bloodshed and the Senate voted an armed guard for the protection of the consul, which he declined. It was resolved to send envoys to Augustus who was now starting to return from the East. He nominated Lucretius Vespillo to fill the vacant consulship. Another attempt to assassinate Augustus came to light in which Egnatius played the principal part. The ringleaders were imprisoned and executed. (Egnatius was a meteoric presence in Roman history.) A large deputation from the Senate came out to Campania to welcome Augustus back from the East. Augustus declined a triumphal entry into the city and slipped in through the Portal Capena on October 12 and Romans were startled and thankful to find the princeps in residence the next morning. Augustus formally designated Agrippa as his successor in 19 as he had some reason to fear assassination. He retained the confidence of the senators and traditionalists in a way that his adoptive father did not, though it is unlikely that he had any more regard for them than Julius Caesar did.

In the autumn of 23, Augustus went to Sicily in order to assert changes in Rome's food supply to make consternation about potential famines less likely. At the end of the year, he asked Agrippa to return from the East and take control and to set aside his marriage with Augustus' niece Marcella in order to become the husband of Julia, with the prospect of securing the succession for the direct descendants of the princeps—Gaius, who was born the following year and Lucius, born in 17 B.C. With these matters straightened away, Augustus departed for the East to complete the settlement of the always simmering questions in that hotbed of political tortuosity and bloodletting and particularly to negotiate durable arrangements with the king of Parthia.

In 17 B.C., Julia bore Agrippa a second son, Lucius, who, together with his elder brother Gaius, was adopted at once by Augustus, putting them next to his stepsons Tiberius, twenty-five, and a praetor, and Drusus, twenty-three and a quaestor. In 16, Augustus, accompanied by Tiberius departed Rome for three years to deal with rumblings of discontent in Gaul and nasty skirmishing on the Rhine with the Teutonic tribes. T. Statilius Taurus became the Prefect of Rome, and executed that position with distinction, while Tiberius and Drusus were extremely successful in quasi-independent command positions in Gaul and Germany. The Augustan Empire was taking shape: the Republic was restored but with authoritarian guidance, and while Augustus declined any monarchical trappings, he retained powers practically as great as dictators by being the princeps and while he eschewed monarchical succession, it was understood that the succession would be among his stepsons and adopted sons. It was also clear more than twenty-five years after the assassination of Julius Caesar, that Augustus possessed a profound ability to placate former opponents and enlist their adherence, attract and retain fierce loyalties of able people, and astutely select the key personnel of his administration with a perceptive judgment unlike any of his contemporaries. In this he was superior even to the talents of his adoptive father, who was, after all, more comprehensively betrayed by his intimates from Labienus to Brutus, than any remotely comparable personality in history.

The princeps was thus to be meritocratic but quasi-hereditary, draped in republicanism but almost dictatorial, and comport the legitimacy of monarchy without its trappings or vocabulary. Again, it was a perfect system for someone providentially endowed with the qualities necessary to operate it. And again, in this respect, it somewhat presaged the great ministers of enabling monarchs of the nation state such as Richelieu (1624-1642), Walpole (1721-1742), Metternich (1809-1848), and Bismarck (1862-1890), and even outright republican, democratically elected and sustained leaders such as Franklin D. Roosevelt (1933-1945), and Charles de Gaulle (1958-1969).

In 13 B.C., Drusus became a legate for the three Gauls and Agrippa returned from a very successful operation in the East and for the third time refused the triumph that he had earned for his settlement of the kingdom of the Bosporus. Tiberius was by now a consul and presided in the Senate when the honors to be conferred upon Augustus upon his return from the West were also voted. The princeps himself accepted only the erection in the Campus Martius of an arch to the Augustan peace (which was far from complete) and the first five-year term of the Augustan imperium (the combined powers allocated to him as princeps and Augustus) was renewed for another five years. At the same time, Agrippa was continued as a tribune associated with Augustus in the powers of oversight and intervention that they both enjoyed over all of the provincial governors.

Troubles arose on the northeast frontier, and after the briefest respite in Rome, Agrippa repaired to Pannonia to deal with them. When the former triumvir, Lepidus, died and Augustus, who had tolerated his continuation as Pontifex Maximus despite his egregious political conduct, accepted the doubtless spontaneous demand that he replace him, saying: "I refused to be created Pontifex Maximus in the place of my colleague during his lifetime, though the people offered me that priesthood, which my father (as he invariably referred to Julius Caesar) had held. A few years later when the man who, taking advantage of civil strife, had seized that priesthood was dead, I accepted it; and so great was the multitude that flocked to my election from all Italy that no such gathering of Rome had heretofore been recorded."[10] Augustus thus assumed the headship of the state religion, having worked hard to rebuild its dignity and practice. Future emperors (as Augustus was generally now known) would adhere to the example of seeking popular election to the chief pontificate, an office that would survive and vastly transcend the secular offices of Rome. (The various frontier actions mentioned here will be described more thoroughly in the next chapter.)

In the spring of 12 B.C., Agrippa, having settled Pannonia down with his customary efficiency, returned to Italy and went to Campania for rest. However, his condition worsened and in the third week of March, Augustus was presiding over a games festival and was advised that Agrippa was critically ill. He hastened to Cam-

---

10 CAH, X, p. 152 (Stuart-Jones).

pania but found his most intimate and talented colleague had died a few hours before his arrival. Augustus delivered the eulogy at Agrippa's mighty state funeral in the Forum, and he had his closest friend and collaborator laid to rest in his own mausoleum. Agrippa had made the Emperor his principal heir bequeathing to him his great estates including the Thracian Chersonese, and the large team of slaves which he had formed to maintain his buildings in Rome. Agrippa bequeathed his baths and gardens to the Roman people. Tiberius was now betrothed to Julia, widow of Agrippa and widow for the second time and shortly to become the mother of a son named Agrippa Postumus. In order to enter this marriage, Tiberius had had to divorce Vipsania, Agrippa's daughter—these dynastic Roman marriages treated generational jumps, forwards and backwards, with contempt. Both Tiberius and Drusus continued their military victories and when Drusus was consul in 9 B.C., he led the Roman army to the Elbe and both the Emperor's stepsons were styled Imperator and Triumphator.

The imperium of Augustus was renewed in 8 B.C. for the third time, but on this occasion for ten years. And in 6, Tiberius was elevated to replace Agrippa as co-imperial tribune. In 5 B.C., Augustus was elected consul for the twelfth time and his quasi grandson and stepson Gaius, was elected consul for five years later, and was invited to attend meetings of the Senate and the Roman knights proclaimed him Princeps Iuventutis. In 2 B.C., Lucius was accorded the same treatment and Gaius became a member of the council of pontiffs and Lucius of the augurate.

As it appeared to Tiberius, Augustus intended to put Gaius and Lucius ahead of him in the succession, he declined to comply with Augustus's request that he go and sort out the shambles in Armenia and asked to be released from the burden of public life. Despite the objections of Augustus and Livia, he retired to Rhodes for seven years and engaged mainly in literary pursuits, and in the study of astrology, which apart from the naming of stars had become a fashionable and pseudoscientific exercise for charlatans. In Tiberius' absence, Augustus' grandsons Gaius and Lucius moved upwards in the Emperor's councils. In 2 B.C., the Senate, knights, and people of Rome conferred upon Augustus the title Pater Patriae: he was now Augustus, Pater Patriae, Princeps Senati, Pontifex Maximus, Supreme Tribune, commander of the Roman army and censor. If he had required that those titles be conferred upon him as soon as Antony and Cleopatra died, there would have been great Republican disaffection. But by going through the democratic niceties, packing the higher rungs of Roman public life with his supporters, and being thoroughly successful in virtually every initiative, Octavian bent popular opinion gradually until it set aside its bias against the semblances of monarchy and only Augustus' sure judgment prevented his more ambitious courtiers from foisting some monarchical title upon him.

Also in 2 B.C., it finally came to the notice of Augustus, though it had been a notorious matter for some years, that his daughter had been guilty of flagrant moral outrages. It was impossible, in the circumstances, for Augustus, as author of the anti-adultery law, to attempt to conceal these facts or fail to enforce his own law: Julia was banished to the island of Pantateria; lovers were exiled; except for Iullus Antonius, Mark Antony's son, who committed suicide. Augustus delayed for a time granting Tiberius the right to return to Rome, but he did permit this eventually, but when his powers as princeps (imperium) were renewed for ten years in 3 A.D., he did not appoint Tiberius regent. Augustus' plans were confounded however in that Lucius died at Marseilless in 2 A.D. on his way to Spain and on February 21, 4 A.D., his brother Gaius died from a wound received in Armenia. Faced with no serious alternative, Augustus designated Tiberius as his chosen successor and four months after the death of Gaius he adopted him by the solemn ceremony of Lex Curia as his son.

He also adopted his only surviving grandson Agrippa Postumus, the last child of Agrippa and Julia, but he proved to be completely deficient and depraved and was summarily executed as soon as Augustus died (like Stalin's assistant, Poskrebyshev, who was dismissed, and police minister, Beria, who was executed). Tiberius was again invested with full tribunician powers for a decade and was sent back to the Rhine frontier where he had been so successful in past campaigns. He continued to be highly successful there and in A.D. 13, as Augustus received the fifth and final extension of his imperium for ten years, supposedly against his will,[11] and Tiberius was awarded by a vote of the Senate on the motion of his adoptive father equal rights to Augustus in the governance of the provinces and the command of the armies as well as in the conduct of the census and the office of censor. This was where things stood in the last days of Augustus.

---

11 Ibid., p. 158.

CHAPTER TWENTY-NINE

THE AUGUSTAN EMPIRE, 27 B.C.-14 A.D.

Bust of Augustus wearing the civic crown

Bust of Virgil at the entrance to his crypt

1. Restructuring the Roman State

WE CAN SEE CLEARLY Augustus' intricate plan for reviving Republican phraseology and parliamentary manners and outward deferences to the prerogatives of the Senate while making the princeps of the Senate a figure of overriding governance in all of the provinces, and, cumulatively in the case of Augustus and Tiberius, the chief judicial officer through the tribunate, the high priest of Rome as Pontifex Maximus, and head of the executive by the practical and moral authority conferred upon him as Augustus, Imperator, and father of the nation as well as censor, commander of the army: a package voted for him as his imperium five consecutive times by the Senate as princeps, even as he served an undreamt-of thirteen terms as consul. The system would require great adaptation in future, some of it abrupt and violent, but it functioned well for the last forty-five years of Augustus' life, a time when Rome assumed a prosperity, unruffled governance, and domestic tranquility for a longer time and over a wider area than had ever been achieved before, vastly exceeding in size and political sophistication any regime that had ever been seen before in the Western world, or in the whole world.

The Senate had been formally chosen by the censors; Sulla had made a prior quaestorship obligatory to be a senator and Augustus added military service and also determined that the princeps issued commissions and controlled promotions throughout the civil service and the military ranks. He also required that before becoming a quaestor and entering on the cursus honorus career-ladder, someone had to have held one of the lesser magistracies of which there were twenty, including supervisor of police, controller of the currency, public works, and building clearance, and a variety of sinecures that would today be ministries without portfolio. Elections continued to be by the comitia, but in practice, the influence of the emperor was determining. Augustus also simplified the system for informing the tribes of his electoral wishes and he caused two of the quaestors to be what became known as candidate Caesaris, who were secretaries to the Emperor and read his messages to the Senate when he was absent. He limited the number of praetors to ten and required that quaestors had to be aediles or tribunes before becoming praetors. Augustus fixed the salary of senators at one-million sesterces in 13 B.C. In addition to the high court of the Senate, and on top of it, Augustus placed within his imperium his status as a personal high court that independently judged all appeals he consented to hear. The existing system of first instance being courts of comitia, voting citizens, was retained. The emperor's right of review was not greatly different to the right of pardon still exercisable by the British and Canadian monarch, and the presidents of the United States and France and other countries. In foreign affairs, the emperor took unto himself and designated officials the authority previously practiced by the Senate when competing claims from other regions were argued before the Senate by delegates of the protagonists, cap in hand. They were doubtless, if anything, even more humble in the presence of the emperor or people designated by him than they had been before the Senate. Tacitus commented that "Augustus gradually absorbed into himself the functions of Senate, magistrates, and laws."[1] The German classicist Gustav Hirschfeld wrote that Augustus counted on cooperation between the princeps and the Senate but: "[W]e cannot acquit him of the grave reproach of having willed the impossible and set up the impermanent."[2] It wasn't impossible when well managed and almost all governmental systems are impermanent; that of Augustus lasted longer than most, albeit with substantial modifications. (A German is not a logical source for disparagements of defective political institutions.)

Augustus' administrative reforms included reconstituting the ordo equestor, the knights, into bodies of men who would specialize in providing particular services to provincial governors and would serve a term with them. This soon became a highly talented and specialized series of prominent citizens available to assure that Roman government was better organized and more efficient than whatever the local administration was that it succeeded. It was something of a civil service. Where tax collecting had been in the hands of the highly unpopular publicans, private sector contractors who were notoriously often heavy-handed and corrupt, Augustus handed direct taxes to his provincial Procurators who answered to him and simultaneously informed the governors, but indirect taxes, which are a good deal more complicated to collect, remained with the publicans, who caused angry revolts and uprisings from

---

1 Tacitus, *Annals*, I.
2 CAH, X, p. 181 (Sir Henry Stuart-Jones).

time to time. But Augustus did radically clean up the standard of administration by provincial governors who could be abruptly withdrawn at any time if the Emperor so decided and rarely governed for more than a year. The machinery for bringing complaints to Rome was much improved and once such a complaint got to Rome it could not be fiddled through political influence as it had been in previous times. He made extensive progress in reconciling the tribes of Gaul to the payment of tribute and he generally placated opinion by his undoubtedly generous disposition of vast amounts of treasure that he had inherited from his real and adoptive father and from friends such as Agrippa as well as the spoils of confiscations in Egypt and after the death of Antony and Cleopatra. He may have spent as much as a billion denarii in benefits to veterans, the Roman plebeians, and deserving provincial groups. The central treasury was known as Aerarium, and Augustus oversaw it with great circumspection. In A.D. 6, he set up a military branch of the Aerarium, which was a sophisticated system of administering veterans' benefits. This had the additional benefit of binding to his own person the loyalty of a large number of former legionaries still capable of being mobilized quickly into a defense or public security force.

Augustus gradually took control of the coinage also; under Sulla, the Senate had lost control of the money supply: the leading generals saw fit to issue coins themselves with their own likenesses upon them. Augustus quickly stopped this practice which had obvious potential to disrupt and undermine the authority of the central state, as well as inflating and debasing the Roman currency generally. He compromised with the Senate in that he retained the authority to issue gold and silver coins and left it to the Senate, which in any case he controlled in all important matters, to issue copper and bronze coins.

It is generally agreed that Augustus radically reduced the level of corruption and oppression by provincial governors, lowered taxation for everyone, recalibrated to focus more on those capable of bearing the burden of taxation and generally ran throughout the Roman world a substantially more efficient and less expensive state than the inhabitants of every region had had before, whether from Roman occupiers or local regimes. Rome's finances were stable and secure and were not afflicted by inflation in the last forty years of Augustan rule.

As the jurisdiction governed and influenced by Rome grew, the governance of the city itself became more haphazard until Augustus created the vicomagistri, who were effectively like aldermen. In 7 B.C., the city was divided into fourteen regions holding the two-hundred and sixty-five wards which elected the vicomagistri. Augustus' interventions were gradual and over a long period, as he assigned specific policy areas such as water and sanitation, public works, fire extinguishing, etc. to different prefects, generally selected from the vicomagistri. The firefighters themselves were gathered into the seven cohorts of the vigilant seven-thousand men prepared to put out fires. Something similar was devised to maintain public order and three urban cohorts of three-thousand men were set up in the 30s B.C. to prevent continued activity by mob-manipulators emulating Clodius, Catiline, or Milo, simply causing mayhem, beating people up miscellaneously, and assaulting political opponents in their homes. Only political leaders of high military rank such as Pompey and Caesar could maintain personal security units sufficient to beat off any of the instigators of the mobs. Augustus moved quickly to end this and began the introduction in Roman affairs of the praetorian guard, which answered not to the praetors but to the emperor himself and although it was only formalized under Tiberius, the last half of Augustan rule was ultimately fortified at the summit of its activities by thousands of highly trained military and public security officials. Thus, in Augustus' time did Rome pass from a disorderly to a very secure city.

An even more urgent challenge was the food supply of Rome. We have seen how aggravated conditions became in 57 B.C., when Pompey was put in charge of it. Julius Caesar created two new aediles cereales to assure the flow of grain. The threatened famine of 23 caused Augustus, at his own expense, to raise the grain ration and he took over distribution himself which had a benign and reassuring effect within a few days. From A.D. 6, when there was a new acute concern, a special prefecture was created for amassing an adequate grain supply and a second prefecture for distributing it, but the emperor himself, then and thereafter, assumed responsibility for assuring that Romans would eat. Caesar had fixed the number of recipients of public grain assistance at one-hundred and fifty thousand, but by 5 B.C., it had risen to three-hundred and twenty thousand, but was back down to two-hundred thousand in 2 B.C.

A comparable problem was the condition of the water supply, including the unpredictable problem of the flooding of the Tiber. Under the Republic this whole question was entrusted to the censors, but under Augustus, Agrippa took direct charge of it and constructed two new large aqueducts and a body of specially trained slaves was assigned to the maintenance of the entire apparatus of water and sewage control. He bequeathed this to the Emperor when he died in 12 B.C. With the approval of the Senate, Augustus appointed a board of three equatorial curators who were senators and were presided over by a former consul. Masala held this position for twenty-five years and, in this way, long range plans could be developed and executed, and substantial public works efforts were dedicated to raising the piers along the Tiber and to developing channels into which overflows could be diverted. There were comparable senatorial committees to deal with roads, including roads all around Italy, public works, temples, and other places of worship. In all of these matters, Augustus waited until there was a universal recognition of the necessity to act, and then demonstrated his readiness to entrust work to senators or the equestrian orders including many who had not begun their public careers as supporter of his. In all cases, he transferred authority from amateurs to professionals and imposed serious cost discipline.

The principate was as welcome in Italy as in Rome itself, and Virgil, a fervent Italian Unionist whom Augustus effectively named poet Laureate of the Roman Empire, celebrated the settlement of colonies of veterans around Italy and indicated that they played a useful role in suppressing thieves and kidnappers in rural areas. As we have seen, Augustus himself repaired the Via Flaminia but this was the beginning of a pan-Italian maintenance administration for all the major roads. Augustus considered his first duty to whip up pan- Italian patriotism and to suppress Rome's long-standing hostility to its rural neighbors. As a matter of policy, Julius and Augustus Caesar treated Italy generously in matters of taxation, communications, and maintenance of a law-abiding society. Caesar's extension of the rights of citizenship all the way to the Alps was part of a larger policy that his adoptive son continued. Julius Caesar advocated a full Roman franchise for all Italians and Mark Antony professed to find in his papers the support of full citizenship for Sicilians. As the extent of Roman rule grew, the technique for this was to set up colonies of retired and semi-retired Roman soldiers all around the provinces, endow them at once with full rights of citizenship and spread those rights out from there. Caesar not only distributed Roman honors to protégés around the Mediterranean but established communities populated in part by veterans' service centers of Romanization in the areas where they served. Augustus radically accelerated this policy when it became his task to provide colonies for three-hundred thousand soldiers whom he demobilized at the end of the Civil War. Where Caesar's colonies had been rather diverse in their composition, Augustus settled mainly soldiers and their families. Augustus adjusted provincial government to accommodate, as much as was possible, the customs of the local populations. Gaul and Spain were not organized towns or municipalities, but along tribal lines and Augustus conformed to that and distributed munificence through the loyal tribal chiefs and handsomely incentivized their cooperation as individuals. The sniggering at rough Gallic emissaries and proconsuls gave way quickly to embrace of these valorous allies in Rome's civilizing mission. Cities themselves, where they existed or were developed, were on levels of gradation at which the highest were free cities of Roman citizens immune from tax, though these were rare and essentially confined to "hero cities" of great past service to Rome. Amongst these grades was spread a range of different levels of eligibility and ease of obtaining Roman citizenship.

In the East, the franchise was given less freely to cities as Augustus won his victory over Antony as the champion of the West and wished his empire to have a Latin character. There were some parallels between Augustus' Latinization and Alexander the Great's Hellenization; both were incentivized promotions of more civilized life and greater uniformity. In parts of Egypt and Asia Minor, that were substantially Hellenized, the Latinisers found themselves in the unaccustomed and disagreeable role of fighting a tendency to look down upon them as comparatively uncivilized. In general, laws became more standardized and the use of the Latin language spread. Religious differences were treated with great indulgence unless, as with Druidism, the religion included politically unacceptable notions. The worship of Augustus as a deity, as has been mentioned, took root early in the East where such practices were commonplace, but it spread and in general was welcomed not particularly by Augustus himself as by those responsible for governing distant provinces where such a religious veneration of the Roman Emperor made the burdens of government a good deal less onerous. The provinces that Augustus ruled directly through legates were Gaul, Spain, Egypt, Syria, and the more backward parts of Asia Minor while the Senate dealt with the other provinces. These arrangements would change if barbarian invasions required shifts of greater manpower to be made from other areas under Rome's direction. Augustus inherited the system by which governors were named by the Senate of those who had just retired as consuls. Pompey modified this by creating an interval of five years between the consulship or praetorship and a provincial government, as he sought the system in which important commands can be held by the same individual for a long period of time without building local power centers that endangered the state. Augustus made a city magistracy essential to becoming a provincial governor in the lesser provinces, and in the larger provinces it remained a necessary qualification for a governor to have been a consul or praetor. This formula assured an adequate number of candidates and vastly enlarged the narrow confines of eligible candidates that had prevailed under previous leaders. In the case of the comparatively civilized provinces, the selection of the governor was often by a draw from the names of the people deemed competent to rule these less-challenging jurisdictions. For the more difficult positions, the Emperor would select whomever he believed to be the best qualified candidate.

Augustus retained under the rule of client kings those areas which, while within the Empire, were not appropriate for annexation as provinces. In this category were Armenia, Judea until 6 A.D., Thrace, Mauretania, and Cappadocia. Augustus' reforms were entirely advantageous: standards of administration both in efficiency and integrity were sharply improved and administration was adapted to the circumstances and practices of each province. Taxation was everywhere reduced and more equitably distributed, and the revenue was seen to go to the treasury of Rome and not the pockets of its representatives. The process of selecting governors was approached with much more care, was open to a wider range of people but a more highly qualified range of candidates. The method of bringing complaints to Rome was reformed and charges of extortion which would now be heard by the Senate that was afraid of the wrath of the Emperor would be much more clearly heard than they had been by the senatorial chums of the sticky-fingered governors. Roads were so sharply improved and extended that messages could go throughout the Empire more quickly than ever and certainly well ahead of any competing channel of information. Over several centuries, this expedited contact between all of the areas that Rome governed and influenced a much more homogeneous civilization and an immensely amplified trade within the Empire and outside it.

Military organization was another place where Augustus affected widespread and much-needed reforms. Under the Republic, there was almost no standing army and if trouble arose in a distant province, Rome was at a disadvantage for a prolonged period until it could collect and deliver its forces. We have seen in one place after another, whether against Philip of Macedonia, Antiochus, or Mithridates, even with Carthage, Rome's enemy struck quickly and generally with the benefit of surprise and had come a long way forward before Rome was capable of responding at all. Admittedly the interim tended to induce complacency in the enemy and cause it to be overextended and built Roman determination and the spirit of revenge to an ultimately unstoppable point. As we have also seen, Rome attempted to humble its enemies and then allow them to govern themselves in the Roman interest and retired. But especially with Caesar in Gaul and in Spain, the will to conquest and outright expansion asserted itself. Generally, Rome tried to govern moderately and more justly and efficiently than whatever regime it had replaced and at a lower level of tax but as its jurisdictions grew and extended, the need for a standing army became undeniable and it was first Julius and then Augustus Caesar that addressed that need.

Similarly, Rome could not go forth with the consul of the year irrespective of his qualifications as a general. In the requirement for a professional army was included the need for professional commanders. As we have seen, the Republic only staggered through its last century because outstanding generals arose: Marius, Sulla, Pompey, and Caesar, who saved the Republic but took it over. Augustus did succeed in creating a system of generating commanders whose forces would be loyal to Rome rather than to the man who commanded them, and whom they would then encourage to take Rome over and deliver an ample share of its treasure to them. Again, we have seen how dependent Octavian himself was on availing himself of the treasures of Egypt to pay down his weary and greedy soldiers. Roman military service was also top-heavy with Italians. Under the Republic, Roman provincial rule, while it generally avoided revolts or at least crushed them with some finality, was often sufficiently unpopular that the government did not dare to arm the provincials even to defend their own homes against invasion. There were many specialist troops: cavalry, archers, and slingers, from some provinces, but not until the Civil War between Pompey and Caesar did provincials turn up in significant numbers in the legions and usually only then because of heavy casualties within the ranks of the Italians.

Augustus determined in 13 B.C. that legionaries had to have served sixteen years and members of the praetorian guard twelve years before they could claim discharge and a definite gratuity. These requirements were moved upwards in 5 A.D. to sixteen years for the praetorians and twenty years for the legionaries and their allowances were fixed respectively at twenty-thousand and twelve-thousand sisterces. These changes more than anything else transformed the Roman army into a body of long-serving and therefore experienced and generally reliably loyal troops. Augustus' standing Roman army was twenty-eight legions from six-thousand to ten-thousand soldiers each, and there were approximately as many auxiliaries, special forces, and retired soldiers, who constituted a formidable militia. The usual disposition of the legions was three in Spain, eight on the Rhine, seven in the Danubian provinces, four in Syria, two in Egypt, and one in Africa. Soldiers billeted in the provinces often settled and inter-married there and were a force for local stability and informal Roman espionage. Officers were well-trained and generally had some administrative experience even in their garrison roles and had a promising future when they retired from the army, usually only in their mid to late thirties.

The auxiliaries were accumulated guard units from the provinces with some previous military service and reasonable assurance of their loyalty. In practice and as their name implies, they were mobilized only with the regular army, and were rarely entrusted with autonomous missions; they were generally trained up and adequately equipped to be at least the equivalent of an enemy soldier. They were always located near where they lived so that the eight legions along the Rhine, and their auxiliaries were largely composed of Gauls preparing to defend their country against the hated Teutonic enemy; such conditions produced a fervent alliance and community of ambition with the Romans, no longer an occupier and much more of a protector. When Augustus died, he had twenty-five legions, not having replaced the three lost in Germany (mentioned later in this chapter), and due to the relaxed times, all somewhat under-manned and totaling only one-hundred and fifty thousand men, but the auxiliaries still totaled another one-hundred and fifty thousand and the conscription and volunteer pool of recent soldiers would be at least another one-hundred and fifty thousand men. The fact that this was not a large number to defend and assure the safety and loyalty of such a vast enterprise as the Roman Empire had become at the beginning of the Christian Era, is another testimony to Augustus' administrative and fiscal skill as an Emperor.

There remain a couple of exotic units: Rome's seven-thousand "vigilant cohorts," who comprised the municipal police but were subject to orders from the praetorian guard. And finally, the German bodyguard that Augustus assembled and provided his ultimate personal protection and that of his family. It was recruited from tribes on the fringe of the Roman Empire of the Germanic people who had somehow proved their uncompromising devotion to Rome. They were deemed to be a miraculous combination of the highest virtues of both peoples: the ingenuity and loyalty of the Roman princeps whom they served, and the indomitable courage and fighting endurance that was their birthright.

The Roman Navy had an extraordinary history as even in Augustan times, little distinction was made between the qualities required of admirals and generals and of soldiers and sailors. It will be recalled that when Rome recognized the need for a navy to do battle with Carthage, it built the ships quickly and placed Gaius Duilius, who had no seafaring background, in charge of its fleet and he won an overwhelming victory at Mylae in 260 that enabled Rome to win the first Punic War. Augustus was the first Roman leader to recognize the need for a permanent fleet and while he did not entirely grasp that the talents required to win naval battles were not identical to those needed for victory on land, he did see that it was necessary to have a permanent core of competent naval officers with advantageously placed fleets of ships to protect the general Roman interest. At this time, the principal bases for the Roman Navy were at Mysenum on the Bay of Naples and at Ravenna near the mouth of the Po. As in so many other things, Augustus was assisted in his understanding of the importance of naval power by Agrippa, the Victor of Actium and Naulochus.

The organization of the army and navy, of the auxiliaries, and the deployment of the retired soldiers were all part of the comprehensive plan developed by Augustus and his advisors to assure the defense of the whole Empire. The Army and Navy both facilitated and spread Romanization. The provincials themselves assumed most of the constant burden of defense and understood that service in the Army was a means of acquiring Roman citizenship and often of attaining high positions in the government of their provinces. Rome almost never aimed at adding to its territory and generally did so in responding to unanticipated and unprovoked aggressions (apart, up to a point, from Caesar's attack on Gaul), and was able to deploy most of its army along its northern and eastern frontiers. Whatever misgivings the Gauls and Pannonians (Hungarians) and others might have had about being governed by Rome or indeed by themselves under Roman supervision, the tribes across the Rhine and the Danube frightened them into a state not only of solidarity with Rome, but also of comparative belligerence in their resistance to incursions by their neighbors.

2. The Roman Frontiers in the Late Augustan Years I: Egypt, Syria, and Armenia

Egypt was the most defensible appendage of the Roman domain, bounded as it is by the Nile, Red Sea, Qatara depression, and Mediterranean; generally, the Arabian and Libyan deserts. The south was open to the Ethiopian tribes, but they were rarely adequately formidable to threaten Egypt below the second cataract of the Nile. Gaius Cornelius Gallus was generally in command of the western and southern defenses of Egypt and had to suppress two local uprisings, at Thebes in the South and in the Western Delta. The Romans were just a substitute for other foreigners and the issue apparently was the comparative efficiency of Roman taxation. Gallus had no difficulty stamping out these uprisings. He then proceeded to deal with the southern border with a mandate in the Roman custom to "impose the friendship of the Roman people" on the Ethiopians. Gallus put on a display of military strength which motivated the Ethiopian leaders to propose that the territory between the first cataract in the second cataract at Wadi Halfa become a Roman dependency and effectively a buffer zone between Roman rule in Egypt and the Ethiopians to the south. Gallus accepted this, proclaimed it an astonishing victory and put up statues to himself around Egypt. He was duly charged with theft and profligacy and renounced by the Senate, as was mentioned in Chapter 27. In his resulting crestfallen condition, Gallus, who had been competent but increasingly egomaniacal, committed suicide in 26 B.C.

In 25, when Aelius Gallus had taken most of the Roman legionaries in Egypt on an expedition to Arabia, the Ethiopians overpowered the garrisons that he had left on the border of the buffer zone and pillaged several small cities, removing statues of Augustus as trophies and enslaving the local inhabitants. The governor of Egypt, Gaius Petronius, soon appeared with ten-thousand infantry and eight-hundred cavalry and chased the Ethiopians to the south and decisively defeated their poorly organized army which had shields of ox-hide and axes and pikes. Petronius took numerous prisoners and the stolen statues of Augustus and retired to the former frontier. The Ethiopians were led by their Queen, another of these singular figures who always seemed to hover on the fringes of the Roman world, remembered by the Romans as "a one-eyed lady of masculine character." This was enough to stabilize the southern border of Egypt, where a garrison of medium strength was retained. But given the wealth and agricultural production of Egypt, Augustus left twenty-three thousand legionaries and auxiliaries in Egypt and a substantial fleet sailing from Alexandria which swept for pirates and convoyed grain fleets to and from Italy. Augustus also set up Nile River patrols a long way south on the river. There was no further actual fighting in Egypt for two-hundred and fifty years and assignment to the garrison of that country was regarded as notoriously comfortable and unthreatening. "The conditions of service and of recruitment were not calculated to maintain a high standard of military efficiency in the Army of Egypt."[3]

Rome's Arabian dalliances grew out of its direct control of Egypt. The campaign that Augustus had entrusted to Aelius Gallus was a departure from his cus-

---

3 Ibid., p. 247 (J.G.C. Anderson).

tomary policy of avoiding conflict that was not essential to the security of the vital frontiers of the Roman world. The attraction was the legendary kingdom of Sheba of the Bible, which was the southern half of what is now Yemen. It had been famous in the Mediterranean world for a long time as the richest and most powerful state in Arabia. It was a feudal kingdom, and its prosperity came from the production and export of aromatic substances—frankincense, myrrh, cinnamon, and cassis—highly valued in the ancient world for religious ceremonial and for the preparation of opulent fragrances, spices, and medicines. The population of Sheba traded some of this production for gold, gems, and pearls. The whole trade was a matter of considerable lore and speculation, which must be the principal justification for Augustus varying his usual rules of engagement in commissioning the expedition to Arabia. Sheba was the link between India and the Mediterranean and carried on an active trade both overland with armed caravans and by sea to the northern Red Sea ports. Augustus had his eyes set on this wealth and on taking over direct trade with India and transferring all transshipment to shipping on the Red Sea, thus dispensing with the hazard and cost of moving such valuables across the desert.

Aelius Gallus had about ten-thousand soldiers to accomplish his mission. Gallus decided to transport his men from near Suez to the southernmost area of Nabatia, a friendly regime where he would still have nine-hundred miles of desert separating him from the Sheban capitol, Mariaba. He built a fleet of eighty warships before intelligence confirmed to him that his enemy had no war fleet and he then constructed one-hundred and thirty transports. The coastal waters in the Red Sea are so treacherous he lost many ships and a disturbing number of sailors. When he finally arrived near his destination, scurvy and palsy fiercely attacked his forces and he was obliged to spend the rest of the steaming summer where he landed. He finally started on his march in the spring of 24 and eventually, having had to carry water by camel-back, he reached the land of Aretas, where he was cordially received but the only food available was coarse grain, dates, and butter.

A very challenging march of fifty days of heat and barren desert brought his force within the borders of Sheban Arabia. The king fled and Gallus took and destroyed several small cities. After another six days of skirmishing, he came to a river where the Arabs were prepared to give battle. They had not faced a serious adversary for a long time and Strabo claims that Gallus inflicted ten-thousand casualties on them for only two Romans. Gallus captured and garrisoned several more towns and eventually arrived at Mariaba. Here, after six days of siege and assault, lack of water compelled him to retire. He covered in sixty days the return southern march that had taken six months and shipped and marched and again shipped the final leg down the Nile back to Alexandria. Gallus got almost all of his forces back safely, but the expedition was abortive, having been planned in complete ignorance of the conditions that would be encountered. It did, however, hasten swiftly-escalating maritime trade from India to Sheba to Egypt and on to the whole Roman empire. It would not be long before the patterns of the monsoons were recognized, and it became possible to sail directly from the Red Sea to northern India. It would be almost another century before Roman fleets were active in the Red Sea and the Indian Ocean.

The Nabatians took their obligations as a client state of Rome rather casually and annexed Aretas when King Obodas died in 9 B.C., without consulting Rome. Augustus was not prepared to tolerate this, especially after the Nabatian vizier Syllaeus fomented a revolt against King Herod. The Roman governor of Syria supported Herod and Syllaeus embarked for Rome to plead his case in the well precedented way. Herod, with the approval of local Roman officials, attacked Arabia, which Syllaeus used to his advantage in lobbying Augustus. But when it came to light that Syllaeus had murdered the principal Roman tax collector within his reach, Augustus, who had never lost the ability to act with sudden and terminal severity, had Syllaeus executed. Herod died of natural causes in 4 B.C. and this may have motivated Augustus to send a mission of pacification and stabilization under the young Gaius Caesar in 1 B.C.

Augustus had come to Syria in 30 B.C., and it was generally assumed that he would organize the next and most strenuous assault upon Parthia and Armenia. But like Caesar and Antony before him, he stayed only briefly, made provisional arrangements, and departed for Africa and then returned to Rome to plan a more general reorganization of the Empire. (It was only a year after Actium.) There was a great deal of enthusiasm in Rome for a punitive mission against Parthia and for the whole project of matching Alexander the Great's progress to the gates of India and even in the expansive imaginations of the most adventurous Roman commentators, proceeding beyond India to what was dimly known from the traffic along the Silk Road and through the Bosporus or the Levant to the Mediterranean, as China. Augustus certainly recognized that Parthia had to be dealt with, but he was always ultra-logical in his compilation of the relative desirability of objectives. He was only 33 in 30 B.C., and this was the time to reorganize the Empire, its personnel, and to begin reshaping its principal institutions. A major offensive across the Euphrates would be necessary, but it was not the most urgent need now. He left five legions and an approximately equal number of auxiliaries in and around Syria, which was more than enough to deter impetuosities by the locals.

Peace and stability in the essential parts of the Roman Empire were the priority; Augustus (as he became in three years), even less than Julius Caesar, was not beguiled in the slightest by a replication of the dreams of Alexander the Great. Italy was, after all, to the west of Macedonia, in the center of the Mediterranean world and was little impressed or influenced by anything beyond the Euphrates except what could perhaps be better obtained in free commerce by sea, avoiding most of the avaricious and barbarous populations that Alexander encountered in his great march to India. The feud with Parthia was really initiated by Pompey and aggravated by the ill-considered aggression of Crassus. Rome wished Armenia as an important piece of its frontier, despite its lack of any cultural connection to Rome. But apart from vengeance and prestige, it had no quarrel with Parthia, a poor and remote country filled with savage people. With that said, Parthia was not really a strong country: it was poorly organized on the basis of loyalty to individual squabbling princes, had no standing army, and given the ferocity of its soldiers, it was not worth the evidently considerable trouble of taking it over. In this sense it somewhat resembled a modern Afghanistan.

It was in 23 B.C. when Augustus sent Agrippa with proconsular authority and a staff of legates and the standing of vice-regent in the East. This prompted envoys from the Parthian king to be sent to Rome asking for the surrender of King Phraates' rival Tiridates, who had sought refuge in Syria, having kidnapped the Parthian king's son Phraates, whose safe return he naturally also requested. Augustus declined to hand over Tiridates, though he said he would not assist or tolerate any attempt by him to destabilize the Parthian king, and he did offer to return the king's son in exchange for the Roman Eagles and prisoners of war left behind by Crassus and Antony. Phraates agreed.

The Euphrates was a natural eastern frontier of the Roman world. Beyond that lay the vast, incomprehensible, and absorbent Orient. Parthia had agreed to return the survivors and trophies of the unfortunate expeditions of Crassus and Antony, but in the usual abrasive Parthian manner, nothing actually happened. Augustus finally became somewhat exasperated and in 20 B.C., he commanded Tiberius, who had shown his mettle as a commander on the Rhine and was now 21, to bring a large force of legions, mainly composed of units of the armies of Macedonia and Illyricum, overland to Armenia. The Roman faction in Armenia supported King Artaxes' brother Tigranes, who had been living in Rome for ten years. Artaxes was pro-Parthian and it was assumed that Tiberius would be entrusted with overthrowing him and installing his brother to govern in the Roman interest. These moves had the desired effect of rattling the Parthian king, the elder Phraates. He finally honored the previous agreement and handed over the captured eagles and the prisoners of war and Augustus was acclaimed Imperator for the ninth time. It was a bloodless victory much celebrated in Rome and widely recognized in the Near East. This very successful diplomatic-military initiative was topped out by the convenient murder of Artaxes by members of his own family, just before Tiberius entered the country, which he did at the head of five legions unopposed. Tiberius crowned Tigranes king of Armenia. A province that Artaxes had taken over for Armenia, Media Atropatene, asked Augustus to choose them a king and he appointed Ariobarzanes, son of the former King Artavasdes. These names kept repeating themselves for centuries as we have seen, and usually came and went in the same abrupt and violent manner.

In order to foreclose any disappointed war sentiment in Rome, Augustus, with typical prudent caution, made a statement to the Senate in 10 B.C., in which he declared that any further extension of the Empire at that time was undesirable and an unjustifiable use of resources for, it was implied, the acquisition by force of people and territory that would be useless to and a drain on Roman resources. He implicitly claimed that he had won all the glory of victory bloodlessly and had spared Rome both casualties and more to the point with his senatorial audience, increased taxation. A year later, Phraates reinforced Augustus' argument by entrusting all four of his legitimate sons to the Roman governor of Syria and sending all of their young families to an opulent exile in Rome. Rome officially explained that they were sent as pledges of friendship. The historian Strabo claimed that Phraaates realized that no one could replace him without an alliance with a treacherous member of his family and this move made that impossible.

The historian Josephus, from a different perspective, claimed that Phraates was setting up the succession for his illegitimate son by an Italian slave girl sent to him by

Augustus himself and whom he intended to legitimize. This was a typical Asia Minor dénouement: treachery by almost all parties, obscurity and confusion throughout, a permanent inability to deduce motives and sequences and even important alleged facts, and no fixed strategic realities or reliable people other than what Rome could justify imposing from without. Yet the assignment of these princes and their families was a huge asset to Rome's strategic position, which was measurably strengthened by the emperor's cool-headed patience and the minor expense of bringing Tiberius eastwards at the head of what would have been, if tested, an invincible army. Augustus showed off his royal hostages to great public enthusiasm at a prodigious gladiatorial combat.

Augustus sent Agrippa back to the East in 16 B.C. to devise and impose yet another comprehensive settlement of all the disputes and rivalries of the provinces and vassal states in Asia Minor. An area of particular concern was the Bosporan Kingdom, wedged between the Scythians of Crimea on the west and on the north and east by the Sarmatian tribes of the south Russian steppes as far east as the Dniester. The Bosporan Kingdom was the only bulwark against Iranian domination of the area east and south of the Black Sea. This remote state was a delicate balance of Iranian, Russian, Hellenic, and Roman influences and was a comparatively stable hereditary monarchy but one where the king might succumb at any time to the blandishments of Rome's rivals. It was the main source of food supplies from northern Asia Minor and the Aegean and when Rome sent armies to Asia Minor, they were generally provisioned by the Bosporans. The cooperation of the Bosporan government was also necessary to assure that politically undesirable elements did not infest the Black Sea and particularly to keep a rod on the back of the imperishable and savagely rapacious Black Sea pirates.

Since the death of Julius Caesar, the Bosporan throne had been occupied by Asander, apparently a half-Greek who had overthrown Pharnaces and won popular support by marrying the late king's daughter, Dynamis. He defeated Caesar's protégé, Mithridates of Pergamon, and after three years as archon, he succeeded in being recognized by Antony and generally styled a king. He had been sufficiently emollient to be recognized by Octavian also and enrolled in the generally un-spontaneous fraternity of Friends of the Roman People. He had over many years kept the Scythians and pirates disarmed and at bay. However, an adventurer named Scribonius, claiming to be a grandson of the original Mithridates, raised a revolt against him and as Asander saw it gaining strength he went on a hunger strike to protest against the infidelity of his subjects and died in 17 B.C. at the age of ninety-three. Scribonius represented himself as having been selected by Augustus and married Asander's much younger widow (Dynamis), whom history has suspected of being a conspirator against her late husband.

Agrippa declined to recognize the new claimant to the Bosporan throne and incentivized Polemo, King of Pontus, to attack Scribonius, promising him the throne and arranging that he too should marry the much sought after former and present Queen Dynamis. The plan of Agrippa and Augustus was that in this way the two parts of the old Mithridatic kingdom would be united under a competent and reliable vassal of Rome. Before Polemo reached his new kingdom, Scribonius had been murdered by his ostensible subjects. The hope of the authors of this regicide was that it would be sufficient to deter the Romans from meddling further in their irregular succession process. They were disappointed in this ambition and resisted Polemo for several years until Agrippa himself arrived by sea and threatened dire repression. The Bosporans submitted and Agrippa required of them regular contributed units to the Roman army and reunited the Bosporan kingdom with the city of Chersonese, near Sebastopol, Crimea. Polemo took the throne accompanied by the resourceful Dynamis and Augustus judged Agrippa's achievement worthy in itself of a triumph, which as was his practice, Agrippa politely declined.

As could have been foreseen, the marriage of Polemo and Dynamis was a rocky one. They separated after a year, and Polemo married Pythodoris, daughter of a rich Bosporan. Dynamis fled to the Sarmatians, and was taken to wife by Aspurgus, son of Sarmatian tribal king Asandrochus. Dynamis proved to be no mean hell-raiser and she and her new mate kept the rebellion against Polemo going for three years. Like almost everyone else in the area, Polemo eventually had recourse to trickery and tried to infiltrate the newlywed royals' camp but was discovered and murdered by them in 8 B.C. The irrepressible Dynamis had won, conditional upon Augustus and Agrippa accepting. Her success came as Augustus was dealing with the assault of the Pisidian mountaineers in Asia Minor (described later in this chapter), new problems in Armenia, and the usual intermittent rumblings on the Rhine and parts of Gaul and Spain. In keeping with his attitude to Parthia, Augustus did not want to become too preoccupied with remote areas, though the Black Sea's commercial and grain traffic were of much greater strategic significance to Rome than anything that occurred east of the Euphrates. In all of the circumstances, and again resolutely refusing to feel provoked, the emperor allowed that he would recognize Dynamis as queen on the condition that she accepted all the obligations of a Roman vassal client monarch. She did so and adhered to her promise and became yet another "Friend of the Roman people." She died, apparently of natural causes after a couple of years, and after a further period of conditionality, the patient Aspurgus finally acceded to the kingship in A.D. 10 and became a valued Roman ally and capable king. He adopted the name of his benefactor, Tiberius Julius, and ruled contemporaneously with Tiberius, dying shortly after him in A.D. 38. He apparently defeated and even "subdued" the Scythians. Augustus achieved his goal of stable and cooperative rule over the Black Sea without Rome having to deploy significant forces or economic subsidies there.

This was the essence of the Roman grand strategy that was perfected by Augustus: only extend Roman influence as necessary to protect valuable components of the Empire even if their value lies in keeping them out of the hands of potential enemies, or to cut potential rivals down to size before they become too threatening. Rome acted preemptively against Antiochus and Philip; it seized Spain to cut off Carthage's revenue. In this process, to the maximum degree possible, reliable allies should be placed on the outer fringes of the Empire as a buffer zone against more formidable and dangerous enemies beyond. The allies would need Roman support to maintain themselves, assuring their dependence on Rome, without requiring Rome to occupy these states. Obviously, any such strategy pursued by such a vast jurisdiction as the Roman Empire had now become, had trouble spots at almost all times and it was a constant challenge to avoid unnecessary drains on resources and manpower maintaining the integrity of the vitals of the Empire. These were Italy, Gaul, and Spain for their positive value, as well as Egypt, for its wealth and agrarian abundance, and parts of Asia Minor, the Hellenic world and the Black Sea for commercial and defensive reasons.

The belligerence of the Pisidian mountaineers referred to above, attacking south toward Pamphylia, about at the centre of what is now the southern coast of Turkey, was a serious threat to the area. Amyntas, the king of Galatia, had tried diligently to suppress these lawless and fierce mountaineers and succeeded in attacking successfully and razing most of their heavily walled fortresses, and even slew their chief, but Amyntas was lured into an ambush by the chief's widow and was killed. Augustus determined he had no choice but to annex the kingdom and focus the might of the Empire on suppressing this enemy, apparently concluding that leaving it to the sons of Amyntas was an invitation to endless conflict. In 19 B.C., he founded a garrison colony at Antioch called Colombia Caesarea and comprised of veterans of the Vth (Gallic) and VIIth (Macedonian) legions. The purpose of the camp was to defeat and stop the raids of the mountain tribes.

The principal offenders were the Homanades, and Augustus determined to deal with them thoroughly and entrusted this task to P. Sulpicius Quirinius, a self-made soldier who had been advanced entirely on his merits in combat. He was consul in 12 and shortly after was assigned this task and given adequate forces to accomplish it. He attacked from the north besieging and starving one fortress town after another, driving the Homanades out of forty-four such fortresses and taking all able-bodied male prisoners to the plains of Asia Minor and settling them in small numbers amongst the cities and towns across a broad swath of what is now Turkey. The challenging operation was a complete success and Quirinius was awarded a triumph. Augustus planted five colonies of veteran soldiers around Antioch to assist in the maintenance of order and developed a relatively sophisticated road system through the formerly intractable domains of the mountaineers. Notwithstanding this conspicuous success, in A.D. 6 the neighboring Isaurians erupted in brigandage, but this too was stamped out and removed root and branch. Some irreducible mountainous factions remained but did not disturb the Romans again for a long time.

Armenian affairs reared their awkward head again: Tigranes II died in 6 B.C., and then as Augustus wrote, Armenia "revolted and rebelled:" the anti-Roman faction placed Tigranes III on the throne with his daughter, whom he married in the eastern fashion, and Augustus commissioned Tiberius to extinguish the problem. This was the occasion when Tiberius, offended by the promotion of his step-brothers, declined and instead retired to Rhodes, and Augustus ordered the installation of Artavasdes, a younger brother of the late king who had been living in Rome. In 3 or 2 B.C. he was driven out by forces aided by the Parthians and some Roman soldiers who mutinied, and Tigranes III returned to the throne. This was a serious affront to the emperor and as Tiberius declined the task, he sent Tiberius' stepson, the young Gaius Caesar (Agrippa's son), as proconsul and heir to Agrippa with instructions to pacify the province of Galatia.

Augustus assigned M. Lollius, an eastern specialist, as an advisor, and he aggravated differences between Gaius and Tiberius. Gaius and his entourage stopped at Athens, Samos (where he had a cool encounter with Tiberius), and Egypt, before going to Syria. The regional political calm, such as it ever was there, was riled in 2 B.C. by a palace revolution in Parthia where King Phraates was murdered after thirty-five years on the throne and replaced by his son Phrataces. This was the handiwork of the slave girl that Augustus had sent Phraates, Musa, whose lowly origins were unacceptable to the Parthian nobility. On learning of the approach of Gaius, Phraataces asked Augustus to return his four half-brothers from Rome. Augustus naturally declined and dismissed Phraataces as a usurper and ordered him to withdraw from Armenia where he had intervened in favor of the anti-Roman party. The Parthian sent an obnoxious reply to Augustus, always a hazardous tactic, and his supposed Armenian ally, the young Tigranes, abruptly shifted sides to Rome (not a difficult call in selecting the likely eventual winner of the contest). This was enough to give Phraataces a change of heart and he abandoned his request for the return of his half-brothers and offered to refrain from interference in Armenia. This caused a distinct improvement in the atmosphere and in the following spring, Gaius met with the Parthian king on an island in the Euphrates.

While Rome clearly got the better of the exchange, it was generally considered to be an achievement for the Parthian king to be acknowledged as a sovereign neighboring power. They had an exchange of banquets on each side of the Euphrates and on the second night when Tigranes was the host, he confided that Lollius was a notorious recipient of bribes from various Middle Eastern rulers. Gaius had this investigated, and it was confirmed, and within a few days Lollius was dead; it was never stipulated whether it was suicide or execution. He was replaced by the eminently qualified Sulpicius Quirinius. Tigranes perished in some action with the barbarians to the north and his wife abdicated. It was at this point that Augustus had Gaius give the crown to Ariobarzanes, king of Media. The pro-Parthian faction revolted, and Gaius suppressed it. While attacking a fortress near Ararat, he was lured into a conversation with the commandant of the fort he was besieging and was critically wounded in a treacherous ambush. He resumed the siege, crushed the revolt, but did not recover from his wound; he died on his passage home to Italy in Lycia on February 21, 4 A.D.

Ariobarzanes died after a couple of years, from uncertain causes, though foul play has generally been suspected. He was succeeded by his son, yet another Artavasdes, who was murdered after a couple of years, and Augustus then declared Tigranes IV to be the king; the Parthian faction quickly deposed him and the new monarch was Queen Erato, wife of Tigranes III, who was also expelled after a few months. Revolving door monarchs succeeded each other in Armenia in a blur of coups and murders. It wasn't much better in Parthia where Phraataces was overthrown and replaced by Orodes, who was soon assassinated. The interim Parthian government then sent emissaries to Rome to ask for the return of the eldest of the sons of Phraates IV, Vonones. They were sent on to see Tiberius in Germany, who did recommend his elevation, but the Parthian nobility objected to his lack of interest in hunting as well as his servile ancestry and deference to Rome. He was disposed of and replaced by Artabanus. Augustus and the Roman government lost patience with Armenia and lost faith in the policy of trying to put a Romanized Prince on an eastern throne. In Armenia and in Parthia the only method by which Rome could assure itself of a regime that it found amenable was to impose it and maintain it by overwhelming force. Rome could certainly do this but so astute a ruler as Augustus could not justify such a costly and durable intervention for so remote, poor, and inhospitable a region.

Syria remained the key to Rome's defense of the eastern frontier. At the beginning of his principate in 27 B.C., Augustus installed a legate of consular rank as the governor of Syria and Cilicia, and four legions were stationed there. Once relations with Parthia had reached a sort of stasis, based on Parthian internecine exhaustion and Rome's boredom with the teeming treachery of Oriental politics, Rome kept only modest forces on the Euphrates and most of the legionaries and auxiliaries, perhaps fifty-thousand men, were engaged in assuring orderly administration. This was the state of the eastern frontier at the end of the long reign of Augustus.

3. Judea

At this late stage in this volume, an exploration of the politics of Judea could be especially challenging, but it cannot conscientiously be avoided altogether. Shortly before he was murdered, Caesar had reaffirmed his faith in the high priest Hyrcanus II and his Idumaean minister Antipater. He allowed them to rebuild the walls of Jerusalem and reduced the amount of tribute due to Rome. Cassius had scarcely taken possession of Syria before the Judean government promised to help him, largely under the influence of Antipater's son Herod. He had had to relinquish the governorship of Galilee but took advantage of Caesar's murder to persuade his father and Hyrcanus to support the Republicans. He then persuaded Cassius to give him the task of collecting the large, extraordinary tribute imposed on Palestine which was due from Galilee, and apparently took considerable pleasure in extracting confiscatory taxation from the people that had expelled him three years before. Cassius was so impressed that he put him in charge of the general collection of funds for the Civil War in the entire province and named him Warden of the armories of Judea, entailing the general supervision of all stores of arms, which meant assuring them for the Republican cause. The rise of Herod, who now was more prominent than his elder brother Phasael, governor of Jerusalem, upset the balance that Caesar had created between Hyrcanus II and Antipater.

Herod was able to use the Roman conviction that he had inspired that he was indispensable for the support of the Republicans in Palestine to advance the interests of his family. Jewish affairs have never ceased to be complicated but they became particularly tangled after the assassination of Julius Caesar, as Judean and Roman politics conjoined. The Judeans didn't like the heavy taxation, especially as the most resistant cities like Gophna and Emmaus, were effectively enslaved. There was anti-Roman feeling generally, especially in support of Antigonus, son of the dispossessed Aristobulus and there was great additional ill-will between Malchus, a friend of Hyrcanus, and Antipater. Malchus achieved the assassination of Antipater and in refusing to charge him, Hyrcanus was suspected of being a conspirator in the murder. Herod, as devious as he was intelligent, if not more so, deployed his own bands of thugs and with Cassius' approval he secured the murder of Malchus and the destruction of his party. It was an almost completely poisonous political atmosphere in the holy city of Jerusalem, soon to experience the most storied events in all of history.

Herod was Hyrcanus' only protection from the partisans of Antigonus. Herod restrained Antigonus. leaving Hyrcanus no option but to give Herod a crown and to betroth to him one of his granddaughters, Maryamne, one of history's legendary beauties and heroines. Herod dismissed but did not divorce his first wife, who had borne him a son naturally named Antipater. This alliance with two branches of the Hasmonean family effectively gave Herod a legitimate claim to the succession although he was widely hated by Jews as a pawn of foreigners and a boot-licker of the Romans. The death of Cassius at Philippi did not disturb his protégé, contrary to the hopes of his very numerous Judean opponents, who twice sent embassies to Antony denouncing Herod. This commotion confirmed Antony in the widespread view in Roman governing circles that a full-blooded Jew could not govern Judea peaceably, a view that facilitated the claims of the house of Antipater. Antony, no less then Cassius and Caesar himself, came to see Herod as the ideal ruler of Judea: he was competent to govern and so unpopular with the Jews, he would be entirely dependent upon Rome to be sustained in power. To muddy the waters further in a way not typical of Antony, he promoted the rivalry between Herod and Phasael by naming the latter a tetrarch. Like almost everything else in this region and especially in Judea, the implications of that appointment are now too obscure to discern.

The Jews had just begun what promised to be an intense campaign of rioting and insurrection which was suppressed with considerable bloodshed when Antigonus called for assistance from the Parthians in 40 B.C. The Parthians were considered the heirs to the Persians who treated Judea gently and in any case the Parthians were automatically popular for opposing the Romans. Their invasion raised Antigonus and once again sent Herod to flight and Phasael committed suicide. Herod, though he was only thirty-three, was worldly enough to realize that there was no possibility that Parthia would be able to dislodge or supplant Rome as an influence in Judea. He strengthened the renowned fortress of Masada and deposited his relatives, his fiancée and future mother-in-law and the band of devoted followers and the treasure of his family there and departed to mother-Rome in haste. As was mentioned in Chapter 28, he was instantly recognized in Rome as the automatic leader of the pro-Roman faction in Judea and was declared to be the King of Judea and Samaria and received his coronation at the temple of Jupiter Capitolinus, an unspeakable rabbinical heresy that revealed how cavalier Herod's attitude was to Jewish religious traditions. He was obliged to conquer his kingdom with mercenaries as Rome would not do it for him; he relieved Masada but did not make much real progress until he gained an interview with Antony and persuaded him to lend him two legions under Sosius. This was a replication of Pompey's experience in Judea as even then, a Roman army was needed to elevate one of the factions grasping and slashing at each other's throats in what passed for Judean politics.

With two Roman legions, Herod was able to subdue his subjects in 38 and 37. He had to besiege Jerusalem, which resisted desperately. Even though the governing classes were generally favorable to Rome, the danger of a non-Jewish king alarmed them profoundly and they ignored two of the most famous Pharisees, Shemaya and Abtalyon, who warned that resistance to Rome was futile. It was reckoned at the time that Herod's decision to marry Maryamne in Samaria extended the siege of Jerusalem for nearly six months, but surrender it did to Herod and the Roman legions in July 37. Antigonus' partisan bands were massacred en masse and Antigonus himself was executed by Antony, but Herod managed to spare the city from being sacked to its basements and to bustle the legions back to Syria without further bloodshed or destruction. Emerging from this dreadful cavalcade of events, Herod assumed the resident kingship of the Jews.

Herod was clever and perceptive, cynical and ruthless, and specialized in judging how much Rome was likely to tolerate before severing its connection with him, upon which he was completely dependent, even if Rome's ability to be confident of Judean stability was equally dependent upon its treacherous protégé. His challenge was to operate successfully as both a gentile and Jew; he could do that but was never comfortable in either role. In all his cynicism, he felt as almost all Jews do, a profound attachment to being an ethnic if not a religious Jew, yet he aspired to the opulence and elegance of a royal gentile. In a word, he aspired to be a fine exemplar of both but was prevented by the duality of his nature and disposition from achieving either. It must be said that his goals appeared to be based entirely on ambition and not any thoughtful appreciation of the values of either Judaic or Greco-Roman civilization. He wished to be seen as the protector of the Jews and to raise it to the status of the greatest of Rome's client kingdoms. To do this, he had to secularize it and emancipate it from the clerisy and promote Hellenization as the only real cultural alternative that could be thought superior. He was thus forced to pursue simultaneously the contradictory ambitions of Hellenizing the Jewish state and of enhancing the political prestige of Judaism. His forerunners are said to have been the sons of Tobiah, who were Judaized rather than Jewish. Judging Herod by the extent to which he actually achieved his complicated ambitions, he completely failed to transform the Jews as many more formidable leaders have, and he failed equally to make it a stable and leading member of the group of Roman client states.

Herod's initial goal was to smash the aristocracy that had always opposed him and confirmed their animosity during the siege. He killed forty-five leading members of the Sanhedrin and packed it with docile cyphers. He conducted a virtual reign of terror of murders and confiscations but had to be more cautious about the high priest. This involved relations with his in-laws as well as with Antony and Cleopatra. He was ineligible to be high priest himself as his claims to be a religious Jew were not credible. He looked upon the high priest as a rival to his secular authority; what he needed was a compliant high priest from the Zadokite family, which had held that office before the Hasmoneans and would give him an appearance of legitimacy. Herod found the person he was looking for in Ananel, a priestly member of the Babylonian diaspora. His Hasmonean relatives objected strenuously, and Herod was wary of opposing them, having sought their alliance. He had extracted Hyrcanus from prison in Parthia to make himself more acceptable to lofty Jewish opinion. His position was complicated by the success of his future mother-in-law Alexandra in involving Cleopatra in Judean affairs and in particular in the promotion of her sixteen-year-old son Aristobulus to the vacant high priesthood. Cleopatra had persuaded Anthony to strip Jericho away from Herod's kingdom and give it to her, and even his future in-laws took his part in that uneven exchange. In all of the circumstances, Herod conceded the high priesthood to the young Aristobulus and with the connivance of Cleopatra she arranged for Aristobulus to flee into exile, hoping to create such agitation that he would be welcomed back to the theosophical throne of Israel. She was no match for Herod in such scheming and Herod arranged for the high priest to be drowned. Antony summoned him to Laodicea to explain himself and Herod rose to the occasion with a formidably self-righteous assertion of his innocence. Antony let it go, in no need to immerse himself in Judea this time.

The issue of the high priesthood was resolved as Herod was henceforth able to name them for prescribed periods and he generally reserved the position for those aristocrats who had supported him. The death of Aristobulus did break the alliance with the Hasmoneans and his feud with that family continued throughout his reign, their lack of rapport reaching a crescendo in the murder of Hyrcanus in 30, and in the following year the execution of Maryamne. She was a famously beautiful woman who had borne him five sons and she went to her fate with magnificent and universally admired dignity. The following year, Herod had a mob kill his mother-in-law, Alexandra. This didn't stir up the opprobrium one might have expected as the Judean masses didn't much care about the ebb and flow of the swells.

His political position was reinforced by his perceptive insight that Octavian was likely to win the great struggle with Antony and he was able to make a number of interventions immediately after Actium that helped reinforce Octavian's victory. In the end, Octavian had no reason not to confirm Herod as Rome's man in Judea. There as elsewhere the goal was to have a client-king strong enough to assure order but not so strong as to be independent of Rome. As Herod demonstrated with successive Roman leaders, he could adapt to the situation and fitted perfectly into the Augustan strategy of assisting the locals to maintain the security of the frontiers. Augustus conferred repeated benefits on Herod, and the king, in his zeal to assure the power of the secular state, systematically assaulted the theocracy. Herod did have a commendable record in his Hellenization efforts, writing his memoirs in Greek and tirelessly building theaters and hippodromes designed for spectacles despised by the Jews, and he always welcomed eminent Greeks and cultivated itinerant or resident Greeks, most famously Nicolaus of Damascus, Herod's historian.

Herod's army was composed of Greek mercenaries; there was no room for Palestinian Jews in it, though there were diaspora Jews, especially Babylonians. Most of the soldiers were Celts, Thracians, Germans, Greeks, and Idumaeans. Augustus gave Cleopatra's Celtic bodyguard to Herod. Herod's loyalty to Rome was conspicuous and genuine, if entirely opportunistic. It grated on his subjects and reached its apogee with the construction of the fine Mediterranean port of Caesarea, and in the building of a splendid temple to Augustus in Samaria. There were opulent public displays of reciprocal affection: Agrippa visited Jerusalem in 15 B.C. and his schedule was replete with occasions where Rome's gratitude and regard for Herod was much emphasized. This followed a state visit by Herod to Rome with full pomp and panoply in 17 B.C.

Whatever his spiritual and moral shortcomings, Herod was popular by the commercial and avaricious yardsticks that generally have some importance in Jewish communities. He profited from the patronage of Rome and saw to it that Rome's munificence in Judea was gratefully absorbed by the entire society. Roads, public works and entertainments, and the general acceleration of commerce, all generated a widespread prosperity, which if it did not banish public dislike for Herod, at least ameliorated it.

Herod had a total of ten marriages and the resulting competitions between heirs greatly complicated the intense political maneuvering that never stopped in Herod's court. As his wives were of different social strata and ethnic groups, the resulting rivalries were particularly intense and intricate. Having stoked up a fierce competition for the succession to himself, Herod was unable to de-escalate the skirmishing and it finally fell to Augustus at Herod's request to employ his mighty power and prestige to try to pacify Judea's conditionally ruling house. It was finally agreed that the three principal competitors for the succession would all be kings of something. But the whole business sickened Augustus, who despite his Job-like patience and unfailing calculation, found the royal politics of Asia Minor and the Middle East endlessly tiresome and unrewarding. It all broke down in recrimination and violence and Augustus famously said that he would "rather be Herod's pig than his son."[4] The Pharisees staged a revolt in 17 B.C., and when Herod imposed a fine on them for refusing to take the oath to himself, members of his own family paid the fines. His regime was becoming tattered and torn and scraped a new low in the animosity that arose between Herod and Antipater, which ended with a special court that included Roman officials concluding in a trial of Antipater for plotting Herod's overthrow that he was guilty and approved his execution. This was carried out only a few days before the death from the ailments of old age of Herod himself in April 4 B.C. In response to this news, the celebratory antics of a number of Pharisees resulted in them being accidentally burned alive. There was a great deal of lobbying of Augustus immediately following the death of Herod, as the factional scheming and striving was almost beyond description or belief even for this part of the world, where political skullduggery was the constant occupation of much of the population. Jerusalem itself became an armed camp of contending factions in pitched battles. It was all so exasperating that in 6 A.D., when Jewish and Samaritan embassies came to Rome seeking the abolition of the monarchy, Augustus agreed, declared Judea to be a Roman province and stationed a legion there to suppress disorder with evenhanded firmness. The legacy of Herod's long reign was that the people he ruled and who never accepted him as one of them decided that their only escape from his hated and chaotic dynasty was to demand the direct rule of Romans, whom they ardently disliked but did not hate as they had hated Herod, and whom they respected in a way that they could not respect a corrupt and brutal client of Rome. Appropriately, a Herodian party also arose and the struggle among the Jews continued. It continues

---

4 Ibid., p. 335 (A. Momigliano).

yet.

4. Spain, Africa, and Northern Frontiers

Between the Rhine and the Black Sea where the greatest pressure from barbarians moving west and south was applied, Rome had only two dependent kingdoms as buffer states: Noricum and Thrace. Apart from those, it was a ragged and porous frontier, and it was one of Augustus' principal objectives to rationalize the borders of the Roman Empire, geographically reestablishing them on the strongest defensible lines and making the entire Roman world as well insulated as possible from the vagaries of barbarian activity. Although, fatefully, he did not greatly extend Roman rule in Germany, Augustus did add in Western and Central Europe as great a territory and population as his adoptive father had with the conquest of Gaul. Octavian devoted his attention after Actium, as we have seen, to the consolidation and pacification of an empire that had been wracked by war intermittently for decades. Once that was accomplished and the principate had been established, he retained for his own direct rule Italy, Spain, Gaul, and Syria including Alysia and Cyprus, essentially the same provinces held by Pompey, Caesar and Crassus except that Cisalpine Gaul was not among them. The Senate retained for its proconsuls Africa, Illyricum, and Macedonia.

As princeps he turned first to Spain which had proved extremely difficult to pacify. Geographically, Spain is closer to Asia Minor than to Gaul as it is mountainous, and its rivers are rarely useful for navigation. The population is split up into many local divisions all of them resistant to outsiders and war there, even up to modern times, the Napoleonic invasion and the Civil War of 1936 to 1939, descended quickly into outright scorched earth, total war on both sides. In the time of the Caesars a small army would gradually be reduced to nothing by the inhospitability of the terrain, the weather, and the people, and a large army would starve. Augustus himself directed the Cantabrians in the campaign of 26 and 25 B.C., starting from Segestum forty miles south of Santander. Amphibious operations took place as a preferable means of supply to the Roman army and also to provide a pincers against resistance in Aquitania as the Spanish were attacked simultaneously front and rear. The Romans were constantly victorious but against a stubborn and elusive enemy that never became so engaged that it could be destroyed altogether. The rugged conditions brought on another of Octavian's then frequent and sometimes dangerous bouts of ill-health and he retired to Tarraco, near the present Barcelona.

The campaign of 25 was conducted by his deputy commanders, Antistius and Carisius, in Asturias and Callaecia in the northwest of the Iberian Peninsula. The Roman armies again approached from both sides simultaneously and systematically crushed the defenders. This part of the war was now assumed to be over, many soldiers were demobilized, the ceremony of the closing of the great gate of Janus in Rome was conducted and Augustus, after his convalescence, returned to Rome in 24. It appeared that in two years he had achieved more than Scipio or Pompey had in Spain but by the time he had returned to Rome war had flamed up again and raged in different places around Spain. The Cantabrians, having been sold into slavery, escaped to the interior and raised the tribes of much of Spain against the invader. Agrippa was dispatched to Spain in 19 B.C. He conducted a war of eighteen years in which, though a normally civilized commander, he felt militarily obliged to massacre large numbers of people, including, as happens in guerrilla warfare, many ostensible civilians, but he did finally subdue the Cantabrians.

Augustus and his generals often engaged in comprehensive enslavement and massacre as the only sure methods of ending guerrilla resistance, but they also discovered that large numbers of savage Spaniards could be shipped to the ends of the Empire and handsomely rewarded for their fighting prowess, deployed on behalf of the conquerors of their homeland, and Spanish units appeared with increasing frequency and always high effectiveness on the Rhine and in Illyricum, among other places. In *Res Gestae*, Augustus grandly observed that his preference was not to wipe tribes out entirely if they could be safely spared.[5] In all of these conquered areas, the native populations were incentivized or coerced into leaving their mountain strongholds and settling in new towns.

In Africa, Caesar converted the kingdom of Numidia into the province of Africa Nova and after the death of Bocchus in 33 B.C., all of Mauretania came into the hands of Rome. If all of this were taken as a single province from the Atlantic to what is now Libya, there would be an exposure of nearly a thousand miles to the Sahara; a client king was necessary and Augustus recruited the young prince Juba, who had become a considerable intellect, learned in science and letters. In 25, Augustus made him king of Mauretania, including much of the kingdom his father had ruled. In Africa as elsewhere, settled agricultural populations, though they were rarely enthused to have the Romans around, were relatively docile and prosperous and even appreciative that the Romans kept nasty intruders away. Infinitely more challenging were the peoples of the mountains, the steppes, and the desert, who tended to be obtrusive, crafty, brutal, and intractable. The trusty and versatile P. Sulpicius Quirinius was required to subdue Cyrenaica. There were several Gatulian wars about two-hundred miles south of what is now Algiers in the first years of the new millennium and King Juba needed two legions to assist him in suppressing extensive assaults from neighboring bands and some disaffected subjects around the same time. After 6 A.D., there were normally only one or two legions in Africa.

In the second decade of the Augustine principate, he began to stretch out and rationalize the northern borders of the Empire. The subjugation of the Alpine regions was the natural place to begin. In 16 B.C. he came to Gaul and began his rationalization of that province which had been in Roman hands for a whole generation by then. This had begun in 25 with the Little and the Great St. Bernard Passes through the Alps which were closed by fierce local inhabitants both to armed and commercial transit. These were the tribes of the Vallis Poenina and the Salassi and they were severely uprooted and defeated by Terentius Varro, who killed thousands of the Salassi and sold forty-four thousand more into slavery at the slave market of Eporedia in 17 B.C., P. Silius Nerva, proconsul of Illyricum, hammered the tribes of the valleys from Como to Lake Garda in the upper Adige. While he did so, Pannonian raiders descended upon Istria, which was the pretext for the establishment of

---

5   Ibid., p. 345 (Ronald Syme).

the kingdom of a Noricum which soon followed. In the next phase of its activities, Rome moved north of the Alps into the northern valleys, subdued the Raetians and Vindelicians of the Tirol and eastern Switzerland and Bavaria and took over all the land that descends gradually to the Danube. In 15 B.C., Tiberius made his way into Bavaria, having defeated a confederation of tribes on the shores of Lake Constance, and his brother Drusus came from Gaul and northern Italy to the Valley of the Inn, seized the Brenner Pass, and entered Bavaria, joined with Tiberius and the two advanced together to the Danube. This opened up the entire Alpine region, banished hostile tribes and ended many centuries of harassment and brigandage conducted from the mountain tribes against northern Italy. Cisalpine Gaul was integrated into Italy. These were celebrated victories at the time.

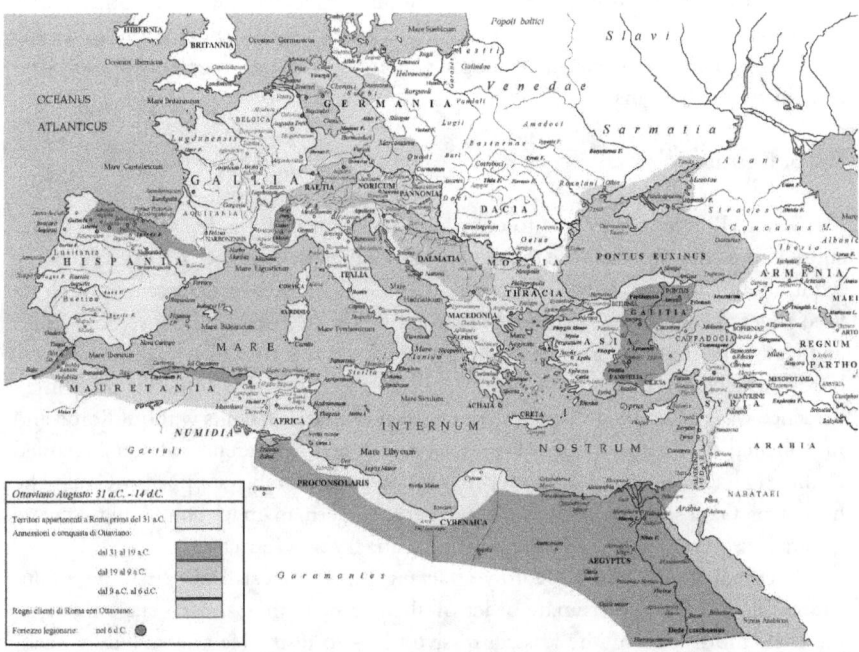

Extent of the Roman Empire under Augustus; the lightest areas represent the extent of the Empire in 31 BC, the darker shades represent gradually conquered territories under the reign of Augustus, and light grey areas on the outskirts represent client states. (credit: Cristiano64, W.H.E.)

The year of transition from consolidation and pacification to the rearrangement of frontiers and systematic strengthening of Imperial Defense was 13 B.C. With little unrest in Spain and Gaul, there were about fifteen legions available to reset the northern and eastern frontiers of the Roman Empire in Europe. In the same year, military regulations were also updated so that Rome had a standing army; the veterans had been settled in colonies and henceforth legionaries would receive a bounty of land and/or money at the end of their period of service. The era of angry veterans holding the whole state to ransom, which even Octavian had faced when he chased Antony and Cleopatra to Egypt, was over; the Senate decreed construction of the altar of Pax Augusta in Rome in 13 B.C. Drusus was in Gaul ready to move eastwards and Agrippa and Vinicius were in Illyricum and launched the Pannonian (Hungarian) war.

This war, 13-9 B.C., and the reassertion of Roman authority over the same terrain suppressing the Pannonian and Dalmatian revolt of A.D. 6-9, was conducted along the Sava River valley through Croatia and into Bosnia. (No invasion of those territories launched from the Adriatic shore has ever been successful.) These operations added the entire territory from the Adriatic to the Danube to the Roman Empire, vastly thickening and strengthening the connection of the Western Empire of Gaul and Italy with the Balkans, Macedonia, and Greece. In the actions commenced in 13 B.C., the Romans did not directly encounter the most powerful Pannonian tribe, the Breui, but brushed past them. Tiberius advanced eastwards and then south on Bosnia, where many of the less numerous and ferocious tribes soon found the not overly onerous suzerainty of Rome preferable to the savage and unprovoked assaults of the Dacians.

5. Germany

Where Roman policy was to cultivate client states, where the leaders could be shored up by minor assistance that would assure their dependence on Rome without requiring the costs of outright occupation (as with Herod, troublesome though he was) in less populous areas, they sought a cushion of reasonably peaceable tribes and clans to whom the Romans were preferable to the savage Russian and Asiatic hordes which surged irregularly out of the East, as in Bosnia. To the Gauls, Rome's presence was preferable to facing the periodic Germanic assaults without Rome and thus incited the Gauls to some loyalty to Rome, and the serenity of Gaul enabled Rome to attack Germany, a project that incited considerable support in Gaul. The history of Gaul and Germany furnished endless German attacks on Gaul that were generally repulsed eventually, but few Gallic attacks on Germany.

Caesar had conquered Gaul by attacking the strongest tribes first and subjugating them in the approximate order of their ferocity thus at each stage reducing the likely motivation of the less aggressive tribes to resist. He systematically occupied all of the major crossroads in the byways of Gaul and skillfully exploited and at times promoted conflicts between the different tribes. Almost two generations later, Drusilla concluded that the subjugation of Aquitania in West Gaul was acceptable to the Aquitanians because they were generally appreciative of the enhanced commercial market that Rome provided and of Rome's protection then against the Germans. And it was from a stable and reliable Gaul that Drusus invaded Germany in 12 B.C. Germany was centuries behind Gaul in refinement of their civilization and material culture, though they were not nomads and in their vast forests they had also cleared areas of agriculture. But it was a comparatively cold and forbidding land unenriched by the olive and the grape and one that Gauls and Italians found uncongenial in the same measure that the Germans were and remained endlessly attracted to France and Italy.

The problems of military invasion were far greater in Germany because of the heavy forestation and the necessity of transporting the armies' food rather than counting on finding it on the route of march, and because of very inferior roads, dense forests, and fiercer local populations. Gauls could be brought to battle to defend their towns and property; in Germany the invader not only had to make his own roads and bring his own supplies; when confronted, the Germans would vanish into the forests unless they were confident of victory. For all of these reasons, Drusus' plan to advance from the Rhine to the Elbe had to be executed by a smaller army than could assure a thorough conquest. His initial penetration was from the Rhine about seventy-five miles east to Cassel, almost halfway to the Elbe. Drusus built auxiliary forts along the Rhine and into the German interior and even a canal linking the Rhine through the Dutch lakes to the Atlantic. He planned for possible amphibious operations from the northern ocean.

His campaign opened when he detected that the Sugambri tribe and its allies attempted to wrongfoot him with a sneak attack across the Rhine; he was advised of their action and fell upon them as they were trying to cross the river. He mauled them badly and then ravaged much of Westphelia. Later in 12, he won over the Frisians with a naval expedition in the North Sea. In 11 B.C., he subdued the Usipetes north of the Lippe which runs into the Rhine about one-hundred miles from the North Sea. He proceeded east through the territory of the Sugambri. This would be quite close to the route ultimately followed by Charlemagne nearly eight-hundred years later in his first campaign against the Saxons. When Drusus returned towards the Rhine, the Sugambri were awaiting him and attacked him in a narrow defile, but over-hastily, and the Romans beat them off. Drusus attacked the Chatti and Marcomanni, large and bellicose tribes, in 10 B.C., and proceeded north and east to the Elbe. As he was returning, Drusus suffered an accident and died after approximately a month. Augustus gave him the postnominal "Germanicus" and Tiberius took his place.

The Sugambri persistently challenged the Romans and were severely defeated. Most of their able-bodied male survivors were transported across the Rhine and subordinated to the Gauls. At this point open resistance had almost ceased in the parts of Germany with which Rome was in touch and Tiberius departed in 7 B.C. to enjoy his triumph and prepare for the campaign in the East. It is possible that the Romans were suffering from some overconfidence at this point; Drusus, an able general at the head of a small and maneuverable army of elite soldiers had crisscrossed Western and Central Germany and defeated or intimidated many tribes between the Rhine and the Elbe but these were essentially raids; the process of subjugation had not begun and Roman parties of settlement or garrison were not left in Germany through the winter.

Following the second decade of Augustus' principate after 7 B.C., the period of ambitious conquests gave way to a time of consolidation. The stately pace of Augustus' Imperial plan was one of its strengths, in this it could not have been more different from the hectic and driven pace of Alexander the Great or less creditable figures of the future hurrying recklessly forward on accelerated timetables, such as Hitler. This was when Tiberius departed to Rhodes, depriving his adoptive father of a first-class general and trustworthy colleague. Augustus had been ruler or joint ruler of the Roman Empire for thirty-seven years in 7 B.C. and he was weary and somewhat disappointed, a condition aggravated by the death of Agrippa and Drusus and the morose self-rustication of Tiberius.

Drusus' last campaign against the Marcomanni was in the valley of the Main River, and in the aftermath of this encounter, the unusually talented young tribal notable, Maroboduus, rose to power in that tribe and persuaded it to migrate to Bohemia to avoid the encirclement and subjugation of south Germany which he correctly saw to be the likely objective of Roman policy. In this fertile and relatively civilized country with an abundance of forests and mountains, the Marcomanni, long one of the most prominent Swabian tribes, installed themselves with vindictive thoughts. Maroboduus had been to Rome and would probably have served in Roman armies and he set out to build a well-organized kingdom with a powerful army in his mountain redoubt. Before long, he extended his authority over Saxony, Brandenburg, and Silesia, and was much deferred to by neighboring tribes. His position soon developed into something analogous to Pyrrhus or Antiochus and closer to Rome. Some sort of collision was inevitable as it was part of Augustus' plan to annex Bohemia. Between 7 and 2 B.C., Rome launched three substantial expeditions beyond the Danube; Domitius Ahenobarbus first crossed the Danube and went as far as the Elbe, and he encountered the Hermunduri, and some other tribes and was exploring the best routes between the Danube and the Elbe and ascertaining the whereabouts of potentially sizable points of opposition. He and a successor expedition under Vinicius identified the danger of an alliance between Bohemia and Transylvania. Ahenobarbus and Vinicius both took advantage of the disorganized state of the Dacians following the murder of their leader and a good deal of fragmentation. The Bastarnaee and the Scythians were both active alongside the Dacians and they showed a propensity to cooperate with Rome, having encountered its forces and diplomats elsewhere. The main work with the Dacians and the others was conducted by Cornelius Lentulus.

These were exploratory missions as Rome prepared for its assault upon Bohemia. Ahenobarbus built a famous causeway over marshy lands between the Rhine and the Ems and Silvanus who followed him had to deal with a serious uprising. There was great relief when Tiberius left his self-imposed exile in Rhodes and returned to take charge of developments in Germany and Bohemia in 4 A.D., Tiberius fought his way to the Weser more than halfway from the Rhine to the Elbe and received the submission of a number of northwestern tribes. He passed the winter in Germany and in 5 A.D. conducted a great combined expedition by sea and land and defeated the Langobardi and reached the Elbe again where he was met by a fleet that had explored the northern seas as far as Jutland. Tiberius was receiving the submissions of numerous tribes as he proceeded and was now ready to attack the kingdom of Maraboduus in Bohemia—the Romans had befriended the Hermunduri in the west and cut Maraboduus off from the Dacians in the east and had removed some other allies from Maraboduus.

Tiberius attacked with twelve legions in 6 A.D. from four different directions. Tiberius had prepared a brilliant and carefully reconnoitered plan and executed it with extraordinary competence. This was to be Augustus' greatest military achievement. Maraboduus was the only organized resistance left in Germany; practically everything else had come over to the Roman side, however opportunistically, or was cowering in silent neutrality. Tiberius was about to complete the execution of his attack when word arrived of a massive uprising in Illyricum. It is not clear who took the initiative but Tiberius and Maraboduus came quickly to terms by which Maraboduus was recognized as King of Bohemia and the latest friend of the Roman people and promised to do no harm to Roman interests. Tiberius turned southwards with his entire force of over one-hundred thousand men including the auxiliaries.

As some of the tribal allies of Rome were preparing to join the campaign against Maraboduus, there was an apparently spontaneous recognition of the collective power that they held, and the possibility presented of attacking Rome. When it would least suspect it, the Dalmatians and Pannonians led the revolt which spread widely and required more than two years to suppress. Roman merchants and travelers and small military detachments were massacred. Both the Pannonians and the Dalmatians had a general named Bato, and if they had cooperated adequately, they might have inflicted a stinging defeat on several Roman garrisons especially at Sirmium. The Romans were able to relieve that garrison and the Dalmatian Bato squandered valuable time laying about him when he could have invaded Italy. But when he turned in that direction, Tiberius was hastening from Bohemia and the Roman forces got the better of their opponents in a series of large skirmishes. Tiberius had managed to put five legions between the insurgents and the roads and passes to Italy; he held a strong blocking position and awaited reinforcements.

Rhoemetalces, the King of Thrace, performed admirably near Sirmium, as the Dacians and Sarmatians forced Caecina Severus, legate of Moesia, to fall back, and this precarious condition was held through the winter, as Tiberius slowly and cautiously began to encircle the main forces of the enemy. This sudden turn of events revealed that while Augustus had thoroughly stabilized the Western Empire and the frailties of Asia Minor were notorious, at the hinge between East and West along the Rhine and the Danube there were serious vulnerabilities; this was the greatest crisis Augustus had faced in the thirty-five years since the defeat of Antony and Cleopatra. Now nearly seventy, and nearly fifty years at the summit of the Roman state, Augustus was said to have been composed but severely shaken by contemplating that if Maraboduus suddenly broke his peace with Tiberius, an event for which there were many precedents; if Thrace defected or the Dacians threw in all the force they could, Italy itself could be in some danger. The exposure of such a weakness in a unique Empire that had known nothing but victory for many decades was a shocking turn of events for everyone and for no one more than the emperor. However, tormented he may have been, his reactions were completely rational: veterans were recalled, emancipated slaves were enrolled and several legions were withdrawn from the East where fortunes were notoriously fluid and lost ground could always be regained. With the army at Sirmium substantially reinforced and led by Caecina Severus and Plautius Silvanus, it advanced against the two Batos, but they had deployed very advantageously on higher ground beside the narrow area where the Roman army had to advance. The Batos fell upon the Romans suddenly and with full force and beat off the Thracian cavalry and scattered many of the auxiliaries, but the Roman legions held and fought back to a narrow victory. This was the Battle of the Volcaean Marshes, which though it came close to being one of the greatest disasters in Roman history, was instead one of its more bracing victories. When the Roman forces united at Siscia, they were a mighty army: ten legions eighty auxiliary regiments, ten-thousand veterans, perhaps ten-thousand so-called volunteers and ten-thousand of the Thracian cavalry. Tiberius spread them carefully as winter closed in and prepared for a decisive victory in the spring of 8 A.D. A combination of Tiberius' skirmishing, famine, and subornation of enemy units caused the Pannonians to capitulate altogether before the action was rejoined in the spring. The Dalmatian Bato tried to rouse the Pannonians but was crushed by Silvanus. Tiberius executed his strategy over the next year and successively defeated and captured practically all of the enemy units, it was a great victory in the end, a great credit to Tiberius and his nephew Germanicus. Tiberius spared Bato, when he finally surrendered; Tiberius was not gentle but knew how to encourage compliance from his defeated enemies. The last embers of the revolt were stamped out.

Immediately on the heels of this great victory came the greatest military disaster of Roman history. The grandnephew of the Emperor, Varus, commanded three legions on the Weser near Minden, approximately seventy miles east of the Rhine. The wily Cherusci commander, Arminius, fomented an apparent revolt approximately twenty miles away and Varus led his three legions with a large food and replenishment train into thickly forested intervening country. There they were set upon from all sides by swarms of German warriors, lifelong habitués of the forest and bearers in full measure of the legendary ferocity of the German warrior. Varus and his men fought bravely to the end. Varus committed suicide; most of his officers were slain in battle and practically no one in the three legions escaped. It was a little like the destruction of General Edward Braddock's force by the French and Indians in Pennsylvania in 1755.

Tiberius had to forgo his triumph for Pannonia and hastened to the Rhine. Once again the Empire freed slaves who were prepared to enroll, conscripted and induced veterans and pushed them forward to serve Tiberius who with these and other reinforcements commanded eight legions and large supporting contingents. Four legions were withdrawn from Spain and the recently quieted Illyricum. A.D. 10 and 11, Tiberius and Germanicus trained up their forces and did some raiding and destruction across the Rhine but were essentially preparing for a greater game.

It was clear that Augustus and even to some extent Tiberius, who was the all-time champion of Roman generals in Germany, had underestimated the task of pacifying the Germans. They were not only ferocious, they were also so much more primitive than the Gauls that they were under-impressed by the refinements of the Romans, including the sophistication of its legions, and they had not had the experience the Spanish had suffered of being largely enslaved by foreigners for centuries. And Germany was heavily forested, very little urbanized, and almost trackless. The Roman high command had not taken all these factors into consideration and as a result, although Drusus' son and Tiberius' nephew, Germanicus, succeeded in pushing them around a bit, reestablishing Rome's composure and military self-esteem and erecting a grave at the grim site of Varus' annihilation in the Teutoburg Forest in 9

A.D., they only narrowly bested Arminius, who was clearly a commander of great intelligence and courage, although they did in another action capture Arminius' wife.

Rome regained its position in western Germany and reverted to a policy of armed neutrality and tactical intervention between the German tribes. This was a policy essentially devised by Tiberius, which exploited the fact that the decentralization of Germany, which made its conquest difficult, was the product of a complete lack of any national spirit between the Germans, unlike the Gauls and the Spanish, and this was a political condition that Roman generals with diplomatic experience could easily exploit and did, while Germany joined Parthia as a matter to be resolved later. In a few years, Arminius was dead and Maroboduus was in exile, and the German tribes were snarling and scrapping at each other with Rome, under Tiberius, putting a finger on the scale as appropriate. In the meantime, Augustus' central plan of taking complete control of the Alps and their passes and approaches, suppressing the Illyrians and Pannonians and moving the frontier of the Empire to the Danube was a great achievement that not only added as much to the Empire as the conquest of Gaul had done, but was strategically vital to the future of the Roman Empire. Augustus was personally distressed and briefly almost depressive that such a vulnerability as the Pannonian and Illyrian rebellions and the inflexible resistance of the Germans would embarrass Augustus after more than fifty years at the head of Roman affairs, but his morale swiftly recovered and the esteem in which he was held throughout the known world did not waver. (At no time were Rome's fortunes remotely as precarious as they had been when Marius, alone and outnumbered, stood between an immense Gallic and Teutonic force and Rome itself, one-hundred and ten years before.) Augustus passed his last years in comparative serenity and retained his faculties to the end.

6. Commerce and Integration of the Roman Empire in the Augustan Era

In earlier chapters we saw the development of Rome from an agricultural market town to one that took advantage of the fact that it had an excellent port only twenty miles away at Ostia, and as the power of Rome grew in the Mediterranean its commercial classes grew in wealth and numbers. Italian merchants were numerous in the Levant and the Greek islands, in Gaul and even in Germany and Britain. The New Men, as they were called, like parvenus of all ages, built elaborate country homes for themselves and particularly clustered at the Bay of Naples where there was a sophisticated oyster farming operation and many of the opulent villas, like the homes of the American robber barons at Newport, Rhode Island, or Palm Beach were fantastic structures, some on piers stretching out into the Bay of Naples, and some even had wood-fired, heated swimming pools. Not just the austere scions of traditional Rome like Cato, but the elevated members of the rural bourgeoisie like Cicero tended to despise these people in a way that is familiar to most advanced societies. But as in other times and places, they made their way. In some respects, Marcus Crassus, though his family was well known, had the ambitions and attitudes of this group though he was more talented and determined than almost any Roman capitalist.

The landed gentry were intermittently protected by laws against production of wine or olive oil in the provinces, and the large group of knights who were tax farmers were also influential and sometimes favored by factions in the Senate. The Roman habit of regarding imports as essentially a matter of plundering other countries endured for a surprisingly long time. But Augustus' Pax Romana and his homogenization of all Italy created larger and more sophisticated economic units and commerce flourished unprecedentedly in the prolonged peace such as the Western world had not seen before. The road system steadily expanded and was improved and kept in very good order. The state postal service was efficient, and people could travel from what are now Portugal to Greece in reasonable safety. Stability was popular and there were no more compulsory carve-outs of public land or oppressions of political factions or overregulation.

Generally, people were free and adequately prosperous and as the decades passed, respect for the emperor grew steadily. Romans knew what had preceded him and knew what an achievement it was to have fifty years of peace throughout most of the Western Empire. Augustus struck what proved to be the right balance between gradual reforms, such as requiring that at least a third of farm laborers be freedmen rather than slaves, and avoidance of the sort of authoritarian reforming government that made people uncomfortable and evasive. Private enterprise reigned supreme, and unlike Egypt and many states in Asia Minor and some of the Greek states, Rome was never in favor of state ownership, only occasionally state capitalism if the project was large enough to require it. Individual prosperity was not regarded with animosity or suspicion. Augustus also provided one of the rare moments in all the history of Italy when the currency was stable and of sound value.

Augustus favored the bourgeoisie; this was the real growth area of the economy and of the population, and this also conformed to Augustus' own tastes. Though he managed his relations with all groups very astutely, he considered the landed provincial aristocracy pretentious and passé; they were the greatest enemies of his predecessor and he considered that many of them claimed a distinction for themselves based on the achievements of their ancestors. He did have a reverence for the ancient Roman families for tactical and historic reasons. He did not subscribe to Julius Caesar's professed love of the masses and his flamboyant manipulation of popular opinion, though he did care for their economic condition and did not want any desperate people in Rome. He made countless provisions for them, many from his own resources and earned the respect, even moderate affection as far as can be discerned, of the poorer people of the Aventine. Augustus did not like huge and expensive spectacles, especially those devoted to grotesque orgies of bloodletting, whether of great beasts or gladiators. As an orator, he was effective, fluent and precise and cogent, but not surpassingly elegant or galvanizing like Cicero or Julius Caesar. He spoke with the knowledge and authority of his position and from his return to Rome after the assassination of his great uncle his position grew steadily stronger and for the last forty-five years of his life, he was the unchallenged head of the Roman world. He never capriciously or arrogantly asserted that fact, but everyone knew it and as the decades passed and he governed with competence and dignity and where appropriate with compassion, he gradually built a cult of overwhelming respect. To be swayed by neither a very long sequence of victories and accomplishments nor periodic challenges of great gravity never seemed to alter the thoughtful but authoritative manner in which he conducted the vast concatenation of his powers and positions that comprised the auctoritas and imperium of his principate.

Augustus adopted a policy of tariffs for certain commodities entering and leaving the Roman Empire, and where necessary, these were reinforced militarily. As always occurs when the profit motive is allowed to operate without undue interruption, businessmen became more and more ingenious at bringing raw materials from a great distance and fabricating them in different ways in other places. The components of luxury furniture for example, often came from the Greek islands that were assembled principally in Capua. The majority of the workforce in almost all areas was in fact slaves, as slavery by this time in Rome was generally a gentler version of it than what historians of the modern slave trade have chronicled. Often, it meant only the absence of citizenship.

Italy naturally was the most advanced section of the Roman Empire economically; it not only had natural resources and political cohesion but the perquisites of victory. It was not only assured a heavy flow of the fruits of martial success from all parts of the Roman Empire, it also participated in capital formation for projects elsewhere in the Empire and for aggressive exporting within the Empire. All industries—iron, glass, all manner of wooden products, building materials, pottery—flourished and grew quickly and was ever more sophisticatedly manufactured and marketed in the Augustan era. The Roman provinces were of widely varying economic success. Spain continued to produce gold and silver and the Romans ran the mines more humanely than the Carthaginians had. North Africa was a granary, and Egypt slowly deteriorated, an exhausted people and obsolescent social structure and a political system that had long since become self-destructively corrupt. There was great wealth in Asia Minor but indifferent economic management and the compulsive scheming and war-making of the region retarded its development. The great port of Alexandria became the center of the world's commerce and all of the principal Mediterranean ports, Piraeus, Genoa, Marseilless, constantly hummed with the intense activity and variety of commercial activities linking not only the entire littoral of the Mediterranean but extending to Britain, to India and even indirectly to China.

The commerce of the Empire caused great movements of people who would otherwise have been unaware of each other: Anatolians, Syrians, Alexandrians, even Palmieris with their carpets, silks, fruits, glass, cosmetics, spices, were in large numbers in port cities and all over Italy, Gaul, and on the Rhine, in the Alps, in Britain and in Spain. Once again, the Carthaginians were all around the Mediterranean. There were trade exchange buildings all over the Roman Empire and fairly extensive money exchange operations also. Guilds and professional associations arose. Rome's achievement in Augustus' time in extending Roman citizenship to all Italy and in getting all of the ethnicities of the Mediterranean basin circulating amongst each other in an orderly and ever more prosperous manner was an astounding step forward for Western man. In a single generation, Rome and Italy made a leap that Greece never accomplished until it was liberated from the Turks in the Nineteenth Century A.D. Augustus inaugurated an age of mobility, Romanization, and peace.

Augustus focused on uniting all Italians by teaching them all a proud and somewhat embellished and united Roman and Italian history, and in blending the population together and inciting the manumission of slaves. The number of slaves emancipated in Italy between 50 and 20 B.C. is reckoned at approximately half a million. Large numbers of people were continuously being effectively graduated from slavery to freed men just by their own economic and social progress and the emancipation of slaves became a very popular charitable act to the point where Rome itself was being slightly destabilized socially by men who came as indentured labor and relatively quickly were able to fend for themselves. Augustus was no particular admirer of slavery and had a humanitarian objection to its abuses but he was a zealous guardian of the identity and fraternity of Italians. He was happy to assimilate these generally highly motivated people but concerned that they should aspire to be Italians in language and social conditions and not disrupt the homogeneity of the society that he was building. This subject led to a complicated series of legislative attempts to reconcile liberality towards ex-slaves with strenuous protection of the Italian nationality.

There was little sense of any community of interest embracing and uniting all Italy at the beginning of the Augustan era, and very little familiarity of countries that were not close neighbours. The Mediterranean world had remained a sea that separated those who lived on its shores but after the Augustan transformation, all the Mediterranean peoples had developed some familiarity with each other, jostled somewhat together despite ignorance, suspicion, and rivalry, by the fact of being in the same entity under the oversight of the same emperor.

7. Augustan Social Policy

Augustus was a reforming social traditionalist; he legislated to strengthen marriage and punish depraved morals and flagrant adultery. He preferred the traditional Roman aristocracy, the authentic culture and society that had lived in and governed Rome for centuries, to the newly rich, and he conferred many preferments upon the great Roman families and assisted them in replenishing their finances as part of what must be considered a political arrangement to help them back on their feet and to their high places in Roman government and society in exchange for the unquestioned confirmation of his legitimacy. It was precisely the absence of any such bargain as this that contributed so vitally to the fear and then the hostility that the same factions had for Julius Caesar, and which ultimately conducted them to the monstrous evil of his assassination: a personal and general tragedy that was only redeemed by the astonishing success of his chosen heir.

Augustus legislated the removal of unnecessary restrictions on marriage and amendments to the laws of inheritance to incentivize parenthood, and the stimulation of childbearing in the upper classes by the systematic distribution of privileges in public life to the fathers of large families. It was, as in so much else of Augustus as legislator, a combination of reform and conservatism. In his championship of marriage and the bearing of children as the chief object of marriage, Augustus anticipated Christendom.

Augustus presided over the first period in centuries when any substantial western jurisdiction presented a coherent, focused, and consistent elaboration of public policy in every area over a period of decades. Under the Republic the yearly changes of consul, the complicated interaction between consuls, censors, and tribunes, and the factionalism of the Senate were designed to prevent tyranny, not to promote thoughtful and innovative government. And Augustus was the first Roman leader to focus directly on making Rome itself a city as physically and aesthetically imposing as the fact of its great and incomparable power in the world. The boulevards, temples, aqueducts, public works, great buildings, and impressive residential areas practically obliterated the early Roman narrow streets and cramped neighborhoods; he was a particular champion of the poor and watched carefully that the public issue of food was always adequate to their needs. He never attempted to whip them up and transform them into a political force dedicated to him as Julius Caesar had done, but he came to be revered by them as one who saw at least to their basic welfare, intervened to prevent their brutal exploitation, and never attempted to use or manipulate them. On great occasions, there were lavish distributions of cash and food much of it from his own resources.

Part of Augustus' traditionalism and conservatism was his revival of Roman religion. After the death of Lepidus, Augustus succeeded him as Pontifex Maximus in 12 B.C. He moved that title forward amongst the many that he held and he restored a religious character to many public ceremonies, requiring senators to open sessions with incense. He was not so much pious as he was a respecter of the concept that Rome was selected by Providence for unique greatness.

Rome adopted some of the Greek tendency to blur the distinction between man and God at certain points. This conformed to the ancient idea that the gods of popular worship were men who were deified by grateful people and it was generally believed that the soul of an exceptional person was in some sense divine. These were not concepts that conferred a theological distinction on individuals. Piety in antiquity consisted chiefly of votive offerings. Roman gods were not a hero cult, unlike the Greeks, and the Roman conception of deities was much less anthropomorphic than that of the Greeks. The practice of conferring divine honors on eminent Romans really began with those who achieved great distinction in the East where this was commonplace.

Julius Caesar was proclaimed Divus Julius after he died and it was not long before Octavian was Divi Filius. Starting in 30 B.C., the celebration of his birthday as a public holiday began and this gained in solemnity. The following year, his name was coupled with those of the gods in hymns. He was accorded the title of Augustus in 27 B.C., a dignity formerly attached only to deities. When he became the princeps, he was placed between a citizen and a king. Such worship as there was of Augustus was in complicated liturgies mixing the terrestrial and the divine and not in acts of physical submission to him personally. To judge from his conduct, he had no interest in such a pagan spectacle as that would have been, but only wished to adorn his office with as much natural authority as it could bear without it becoming a ludicrous imposture, as so many modern dictators and petty monarchs have become, Ruritanian fops or even absurdly histrionic figures, such as the later Mussolini.

Jesus Christ was born on December 25, 1 B.C. in Bethlehem, Judea. He was unlikely to have been identified to Augustus, and upholders of the Roman religion were naturally hostile to monotheism and profoundly sceptical of messianism, with which Judea had been simmering for some time. Rendering unto Caesar and unto God would become much more complicated as the power of this new, humanistic, universal, and monotheistic religion quickly slipped the bonds of Judaism and spread unstoppably across the world. But Augustus would not see this.

8. Death, Legacy, and Assessment of Augustus Octavian Caesar

Augustus' health declined in the spring and summer of 14 A.D. and he went to his country estate at Nola, where his parents had lived. Tiberius was summoned and arrived in time to converse for much of a whole day quietly with his adoptive father, with whom his relations had often been strained, but were finally cordial. Augustus died peacefully on August 19, the month named after him and a month short of his seventy-seventh birthday. There were the customary rumors that he had been poisoned by his wife Livia with whom he had had a superbly happy marriage, either by agreement, or in order to advance a candidate of Livia's for part of the succession. This is mere speculation (Tacitus and Dio) and there is no reason to believe that he did not die of natural causes. His last public words were announced as "I found Rome a city of clay and left it a city of marble." This was meant to apply both to its political structures and social legislation and to its monumental extent and appearance of, as it became known, "the Eternal City." The last words he uttered to Tiberius and Livia were alleged to have been: "Have I not acted the part well? Please applaud as I exit." An immense host joined his funeral procession back to Rome. Tiberius and his son Drusus gave the funeral orations and the late emperor's corpse in a plain coffin was burned on a mighty funeral pyre. As the fire began a large Eagle was released from the pyre and flew heaven-wards allegedly carrying the soul of the deceased who was deemed then to join the company of the gods. The ashes were placed in his mausoleum which had been awaiting them for some time and stands yet, though heavily overgrown with vines and moss. On September 17, the Senate decreed that he should be referred to officially as Divus Augustus and be accepted as one of the Gods of the State. Never, while he lived or when he was dead, were any powers attributed even to the divine Augustus except those of a man. Roman Gods were not necessarily omnipotent, or even superhuman. Numerius Atticus swore that he had seen Augustus rising to heaven, as Proculus had seen Romulus in the same act. This was a prelude, if not an inspiration, for the alleged physical ascension of Christ nineteen years later.

It is clear from the letters of personalities of the time that during the principate of Augustus, it was widely believed that a new age had begun in the history of mankind. In the provinces of the Hellenistic East the principate brought good government and peace. After Actium and Octavian's conquest of Egypt, it was not clear that the East's yearning for new leadership was going to be satisfied by Rome, but satisfied it was. The Hellenistic East was able to live as it wished with security and self-respect; Greek laws and culture were undisturbed though the Roman culture became steadily more competitive, but not oppressive. Freedom of religion was unmolested, the seas and roads were free of pirates and thugs; there were enemies beyond the Danube and the Euphrates but within those broad confines Rome protected everyone. To the more urbanized people of Spain and Gaul, Romanization was attractive, and Rome was credited with suppressing the savage and warlike tribes of the remoter regions of Spain and Gaul who frequently disturbed the more urban areas of those provinces. The process of Romanization was helped by large numbers of Italian settlers who were more or less easily assimilated, and the Roman auxiliaries offered a career to the many young men of high military aptitude in both Spain and Gaul. The attractiveness of Rome was heightened in Gaul as the principal protection from what had historically been the implacable challenge of defense against fierce periodic German invasions.

"Rome had divided in order to conquer; now she united in order to rule."[6] To all Roman citizens including those who lived outside Italy, the principate meant something different to anything Romans had felt before.

> Civil wars, the proscriptions and requisitions, the dread some men had of an autocrat, the dismay some felt when the removal of the autocrat brought no more than the name of freedom as a losing battle cry, the fear that Rome itself was to yield pride of place to a queen from the East with a Roman as her led-Captain—all these had induced a sense of guilt and insecurity. The Romans felt the stirring of a new emotion, doubt of themselves and despair of the Republic. In such moments, a people will turn with unquestioning and almost savage loyalty to a man who sets himself to exorcise these emotions. Whatever Octavian may have been, however ruthless and self-seeking, he stood for Rome, and all else was forgotten. Caesar had embodied faith in his own star and his own genius; Octavian stood for faith in Rome. At the Ilerda, Pharsalus, Thapsus, Munda, it was Caesar who had conquered; at Actium it was Rome and Italy. Caesar had pardoned his enemies; Octavian had watched them perish, and now could honestly declare that he had no enemies among Romans who held by Rome.[7]

The Augustan order restored Roman self-confidence, but it was not an ungrateful nationalism. The value of Greek thought and letters was acknowledged and honored, but as having become a part of the Roman-led world. Rather than be worshiped himself, Augustus was the devout leader of the practice of the Roman religion that thanked Providence for the greatness and honor of Rome and required the loyalty and patriotic devotion of all Romans and Italians. Faith in Rome's past generated faith in her future and the horrors and bloodshed of the sixty years that preceded Octavian emphasized the strength of the serenity and modestly asserted confidence of Augustus. He was seen to respect and preserve the best qualities of the Republic while transporting them to a more autocratic state made infinitely more successful by the application of his own firm but rarely oppressive personality. He realized that Rome needed and he himself needed the service of the best of the

---

6 Ibid., p. 585 (F.E. Adcock).
7 Ibid.

aristocracy. This level of collegiality, though it did not compromise his authority, furnished the state a group of trusted and proven senior administrators and legislators and reassured Rome that it was not being directed entirely by the whims and caprices of a single individual.

> The courage to dare (of Octavian) was transmuted into the courage to endure (of Augustus). More and more he displayed the hard-headed tenacity, the caution, the faith in the past together with the cool appreciation of the present that marked out the most solid parts of the Roman and Italian character.
>
> It may be argued that apart from native shrewdness and painstaking thoroughness, his guiding motives were negative; reaction from the dangerous sides of Caesar and of Antony, the ineffective side of Cicero, the impractical side of Cato, the blind side of Pompey. But this interpretation does Augustus less than justice: his statecraft is not to be explained as dictated by tradition, or the mere avoidance of refuted policies and expedients. It was the natural expression of his character, so far as we can discover what his own character was and became.[8]

This explanation labors the somewhat tiresome British practice of distinguishing between Octavian the opportunist who was on balance perhaps somewhat less continuously acting in good faith than was his rival Antony, and the majestic Emperor with whom it is difficult to find fault. The first was necessary to afford the luxury of the second and it is not for any historian, especially at the removal of more than twenty centuries, to give tactical career lessons to a statesman so overwhelmingly and durably successful.

Augustus' ability to rally and retain the loyalty of many of the most talented people in the Roman Empire for decades speaks eloquently not only of his judgment of the abilities and character of men, but of his ability to retain the loyalty of even the most talented and ambitious for decade after decade. In his forty-six years as essentially the sole ruler of the Roman Empire, there were almost no purges, though many people retired as their abilities declined or ceased to be necessary. Having taken great risks in his climb to supreme office, once installed there, he was rather risk-averse. Once he had much to lose, he looked upon those who ventured everything to win something inessential to be like a man who fished with a hook of gold: if they lost it, they would be poor. He did not possess the genius of Alexander the Great, or Julius Caesar, or Napoleon, world-historic conquerors, but he possessed a very high intelligence and almost completely unwavering judgment. He was more indispensable to the world than those three great conquerors and rendered much greater service to the world than they did. And he was ultimately more successful, other than to the extent that Julius Caesar may be credited for naming Octavian as his heir. Augustus inspired Virgil and Horace to lyricize his Romanization of the whole Mediterranean, and in most respects, except for the imbroglio in Germany, the last decade of the Augustan era was one of gently aging serenity.

Augustus' strategic policy was very successful: the advance to the Danube has

---

8 Ibid., p. 591. (Adcock).

already been adequately summarized as essential and of lasting importance to the security of the Empire. His decision to intervene in the East only in supporting Tiberius and Gaius succeed in settling Armenia was justified. Playing skillfully upon the dynastic ambitions and schemes of the various contending potentates kept the region relatively peaceful and unthreatening to Rome, and productive of large tax revenues without oppressing the local populations. This policy left him with a sustainable military budget and enough legions to deal with the Rhine and the Danube and minor risings in Spain or Gaul.

As the founder of a governmental system that was vastly more sophisticated and extensive than any that had been devised before in the West, Augustus was immensely successful. To have provided the known world with forty-five years of general peace and relative prosperity was also a great achievement. To have created a system of government which essentially continued for fifteen centuries until the end of the Eastern Roman Empire, and as the renovator of the position of Pontifex Maximus, which, albeit unrecognizably altered, retains great importance today; for all of this, Augustus must rank as one of the most important and most successful statesmen in the entire history of the world.

CHAPTER THIRTY
❧
CONCLUSION

The Christ Pantocrator of St. Catherine's
Monastery at Sinai, Sixth Century

The Apostle Saint Peter
by Peter Paul Rubens, 1610-1612

READERS WILL EASILY have followed the profound progress of political organization from the primitive tribal kingdoms of ancient Mesopotamia, which were more or less continued by the many peoples that surged and drifted across the Eur-asian land-mass throughout the period covered and eventually pressed quite consistently on or near the frontiers of the Roman world along the Rhine and Danube, and what are now northeastern Turkey, Iran, and India.

Informal and generally arbitrary authority in clans and tribes, often with the prerogatives of the high priest contested between chiefs or kings and officials claiming clerical aptitudes and insights, gradually spread into administration and planning, taxation, and rudimentary systems of justice, especially once the peoples became more urbanized and permanent capitals were established. The Greeks and Romans developed notions of rights and even a popular consultation of property-owning male adult citizens in the selection of some officials and the adoption of some laws and other measures. Notions of rights slowly took hold in many of the Greek city states and in Rome.

Rome developed beyond what Greece had accomplished in law courts and the uniformity of legal systems, weights and measures, coinage, and language around the Mediterranean world. Education was advanced by Egypt, though to a small and carefully selected class of students, and was extended somewhat in Greece and ultimately through much of the Roman Empire. The Greek cultural fermentation was more vigorous than Rome's, but the Romans had a gift for logical and strategically well-planned expansion, and a gift for public administration that they learned to assist them in conciliating and pacifying peoples that they ruled or dominated. Roman proconsuls, such as the original Tiberius Gracchus in Spain and Quinctius Flamininus in Greece were brilliantly effective and fully equal to the great figures of modern empires, such as Samuel de Champlain in New France (Quebec), and Robert Clive and Warren Hastings in India.

Welfare consisted mainly, at first, in stabilizing the food supply (grain, which was normally wheat), but once Rome became an immense metropolis with masses of drifters, displaced rural workers, undischarged slaves, and migrants from all over the known world, there were periodic efforts to carve out arable property in colonies around Italy and the Mediterranean, which alleviated the congestion and inherent instability of the Roman mob, and became useful building blocks of expansion for the Greek and Roman worlds. As, in Roman times after the rise of the political generals, starting with Marius, these were essentially veterans of Rome's wars; communities that were dispersed in this way around the Roman world proved valuable in the repulse of barbaric incursions and in the suppression of local unrest.

The Roman movement toward liberalization led by the Gracchi was brutally suppressed by the Senate and the Gracchus brothers, as described in Chapter 21, were murdered. Thereafter, until Augustan times, Rome was defended and its domains expanded by outstanding generals who arranged for their veterans to be granted land and allowances. This was an uneven method of assuring that the city of Rome was not overwhelmed and rendered chaotic and uninhabitable by the masses of urban denizens who crowded into it.

As the Roman Empire spread, there was an immense movement of cosmopolitanism, of the interchange of cultures, of ever larger and more intricate trading and commerce. A very sophisticated road system linked the whole Empire and facilitated its defense. Travelers could move with reasonable swiftness and security from what is now Cadiz, to what is now Istanbul, and all along the northern coast of Africa and in the Middle East. Pirates were periodically suppressed and the Augustan Empire was a coherent community of over fifty million people with a unitary government.

From the middle of the Punic wars on, all the peoples bordering Roman territory were in the habit of petitioning and being heard by the Roman Senate in resolving local disputes. Rome ruled, and when it saw the approach of a threat, it acted preveniently to neutralize the threat. It granted a good deal of autonomy to its component parts, apart from Gaul, Spain, Italy, and at times Greece, Britain, and Egypt, and allowed local chiefs like King Herod of Judea to govern, and assured their loyalty by providing, as necessary, the support they needed to sustain themselves, often because of the distaste of their countrymen for their substantial subservience to Rome.

Within the Roman government, there was a lengthy tug-of-war between the Senate, largely populated by the old families and the most prodigiously successful of the "new men," and the masses. These were generally represented by the tribunate, which could veto or at least delay measures adopted by the Senate. It was far from a perfect system, but it did provide a pressure valve that spared Rome serious popular uprisings for several centuries. Because senatorial government failed and the Republic was effectively replaced by military direction of the civil government—the multiple consulates of Marius, the dictatorship of Sulla, the preeminence of Pompey, the first Triumvirate, dictatorship of Caesar, Second Triumvirate, and the principate and Empire of Octavian Augustus, Rome was steadily trying to devise a durable constitutional formula for imperial government.

Rome was not as successful in this as Athens, but the two are hardly comparable, as Athens was really just a city, with an adjacent port, and a modest parcel of territory. Rome's government of its far-flung domains was reasonably steady and successful though there were always intermittent problems with corruption among governors. At the point where this volume ends, there is no real test of the Augustan system. As we have seen, and as recurs throughout history, any system may be made to work very well by a brilliant ruler; the litmus test is how it works under less inspired leadership.

Augustus gradually accumulated in his own hands the positions and dignities of Father of the People, president of the Senate, commander of the Roman army, chief Tribune, Pontifex Maximus, direct governor of several important components of the Empire, was thirteen times consul and was elected to five consecutive ten-year terms as repository of overwhelming authority, but never incited the fear or resentful envy that struck down his adoptive father, as he always treated the Senate and the administration personnel with conspicuous courtesy and often a pretended deference. He was that rare phenomenon: a visionary strategist and policy executor, and a master of the machinery of government, and a master of popular, legislative and clerical psychology. Thus did he rule in Rome, and thereby much of the world, for fifty-eight years.

His system, updated, would be successfully led by his talented successors, over the next four-hundred years, but would come apart quite badly under successive inadequate claimants to his laurel and scepter. But he left a government that was the most advanced that had ever been devised, easily exceeding anything in China or India. Rome had much less of the envious back-biting of Athens, and Roman policy sought to avoid war rather than plunge into it constantly as the Greeks did. Rome created a commonwealth where nationalist sentiment was usually a less powerful motivation than the facts that Rome kept order and generated a prosperous economy at lower tax rates than the previous local regimes had imposed, and with much more reliable and durable conditions of peace.

Nationalism was trumped by peace, prosperity, better justice, lower taxes, and the generous promotion by Rome of meritorious locals to the heady reaches of the Senate and imperial office. Particular arrangements were made for the character of individual peoples, especially the Greeks and the Jews. Rome had a subtlety of governance that completely eluded the Persians and Greeks, and was much more practical, and based on elaborated notions of political science, than anything in contemporary China or India.

It was seven-hundred and fifty years since the Trojan War, and perhaps fourteen centuries since the greatest Pharaohs, but Rome had a comprehensive administration that had at least made a good start at conciliating the plebeians and the patriciate, assured the food supply, and intermittent colonization that avoided explosions of rabble-violence in Rome and other cities, and had the entire Mediterranean littoral and Near East cooperating with an official integrality that would have been utterly astounding prior to the time of Alexander the Great three-hundred years before. And of course, it proved much more durable and institutionally solid than Alexander's brilliant but evanescent vision of Hellenization and Greco-Persian integration. Rome was a unifying force and an ever more accomplished and sophisticated civilization.

As we have seen, Rome was much reformed from earlier times, but it would remain vulnerable to faction, revolt, and instability. (Most of Augustus' successors as emperor would die violently.) So great was the scale of Roman governance, it would survive periods of terrible incompetence and official venality and would be revived, century after century, by the genius of renewal and improvisation, and by the momentum of its achievements and incumbency.

As the Augustan era passed away, the world was ready for an onrush of humanism, for something to sanctify life and make it less violent, a de-escalation of acts of inhumanity parallel to the progress that had been achieved in public administration. Philosophically and theologically, Rome was in arrears of its grasp of political science and imperial strategy. Augustus greatly promoted Roman history and the Latin language, and religion, not as a fetishistic cult of superstition (always a Roman vulnerability), but as a racially proud and unifying cult of Roman achievements and distinction.

The pinnacle of the power of the Caesars quietly passed: centuries of Rome's preeminence awaited. And the tortured but miraculous dawn of the Christian Era was at hand. Rome would unite Western man's secular and ecclesiastical destinies with unforeseeable durability.

Rome's gods were fading and a Messiah was already perceptible to a few in Israel. For a moment, man was alone, and the ancient world was still, but about to enter upon its most storied years and earth-shaking events.

INDEX

A

Aaron 31, 34
Abdi-milkutti 123
Abel 26
Abeshu 108
Abgar 938
Abimelech 36, 37
Abner 41, 42
Abraham 26, 31, 33, 52-54, 554, 693
Abram 24
Abronichus 263
Absalom 43, 44
Abtalyon 1066
Abu Simbel 201
Abydos 80, 352, 397, 532
Abyssinia 84
Acanthus 320
Acarnania 281, 308, 341, 387, 391, 470, 477, 576, 713, 714, 721, 746, 747, 767
Acarnanian(s) 315, 320, 323, 385, 391, 533, 554, 715, 716, 721, 746, 753, 758, 795
Acerrae 666
Acestorides 436
Achaea 197, 280, 285, 304, 399, 400, 470, 526, 568, 577, 586, 716, 719, 720, 722, 723, 727, 747, 750, 752, 766, 774, 796, 1011
Achaean League 765, 776, 779, 780, 790, 794, 795, 796
Achaean(s) 22, 111, 168-170, 172, 399, 457, 586, 713-717, 721-723, 752, 753, 757, 759, 764, 766, 771, 784, 796, 797
Achaemenid Empire 147
Achaemenes 227
Achaemenidae 228
Achaeus 22, 721, 730, 734, 735
Achillas (murderer of Pompey) 964
Achilles 170-173, 293, 481, 514, 518, 655, 797
Achoris 407 *See also* Hakori
Acragas 257, 258, 260, 333, 340, 414, 415, 435, 436, 438, 441, 443, 633, 644
Acrocorinth 719, 752
Acropolis 184, 187, 189, 198, 199, 207, 209, 247-251, 253, 254, 262, 288, 295, 320, 323, 329, 350, 353, 361, 364, 504, 525, 526, 720, 721, 868
Acrotatus 438
Ada 488
Adab 58
Adad-Nirari I 114, 131, 132
Adam 24, 31, 53
John Adams 46, 291
F.E. Adcock 192-194, 295, 306, 936, 945, 961, 977, 983, 1083
Adeia Eurydice 536
Adherbal 652, 839, 840
Adiatorix of Heraclea 1036
Admetus 269
Adonijah 43, 44
Adrammelech 123
Adranodorus 686
Adranum 431
Adrianople 483
Adriatic 179, 325, 420, 466, 521, 576, 623, 625, 631, 666, 669, 676, 680, 681, 700, 712-720, 725, 742, 761, 775, 784, 785, 809, 874, 953-959, 978, 998, 1024, 1028, 1072
Adys 649
Aeacides 549
Aeantides 198
aedile(s) 602, 617, 667, 695, 804, 813, 833, 835, 1042, 1043, 1049, 1051
curile aediles 617
Aedui 839, 921-923, 929, 931-933
Aegean(s) 37, 38, 47, 79, 82, 85, 94, 97, 98, 101, 110, 111, 116, 168, 169, 170, 173, 174, 175, 176, 177, 178, 179, 180, 184, 185, 195, 196, 197, 209, 215, 219, 225, 226, 233, 234, 259, 267, 282, 283, 285, 286, 287, 292, 294, 295, 311, 313, 345, 347, 349, 350, 353, 376, 384, 385, 387, 388, 390, 391, 401, 405, 425, 447, 468, 469, 475, 476, 495, 552, 553, 560, 576, 692, 717, 725, 726, 729, 732, 742, 743, 744, 766, 768, 769, 770, 771, 772, 773, 861, 862, 865, 866, 1060
Aegina 180, 198, 209, 240, 241, 243, 247,

276, 277, 278, 279, 280, 286, 302, 335, 350, 530, 722
Aeginetans 301, 318
Aegisthus 184
Aeglea 239
Aegospotami 382, 386, 391, 546
Aemilius 615, 621, 629, 633, 650, 665, 666, 681, 682, 717, 718, 747, 769, 781, 798, 817, 834, 835, 838, 954. *See also* L. Aemilius Paullus
Aeneas 596
Aenus 777, 778
Aeolian(s) 22, 174, 175, 203, 219, 374, 405, 477, 609
Aeolic invasion 171
Aeolis 234
Aeolus 22
Aequi 606, 607, 613-615, 620-622
Aerae 343
Aerarium 954, 1050
Aeschines 185, 461, 462, 463, 464, 465, 466, 468, 470, 473, 527, 528
Aeschylean trilogy 293
Aeschylus 184, 239, 293, 294, 366, 526, 581, 583
Aesernia 858, 859
Aethiopis 173. *See also The Epic Cycle*
Aetna 416, 418, 435, 645
Aetolia 315, 483, 484, 531, 533, 538, 575-577, 582, 589, 716, 721-725, 728, 743, 747, 753, 764, 765, 767-769, 771, 773
Aetolian(s) 315, 320, 532, 533, 539, 549, 554, 575, 586, 589, 670, 713, 714, 716-719, 722, 723, 725, 733, 742, 750, 751, 752, 754, 758, 759, 760, 761, 763-768, 771, 776, 777, 795
Afghanistan 61, 141, 145, 150, 164, 221, 226, 374, 503-505, 507, 557, 560, 569, 1058
Afranius 955, 956, 961, 971, 972
Africa 22-24, 45, 69, 72, 78, 82, 84, 98, 110, 140, 170, 205, 206, 226, 255, 256, 294, 295, 322, 374, 414, 420, 424, 426, 439-445, 526, 557, 639, 640, 642, 648, 649, 651, 655, 657, 658, 671, 672, 674, 678, 688, 698, 701-703, 706, 709, 725-727, 740, 768, 773, 793, 809, 826, 827, 830, 836, 841-844, 846, 849, 860, 861, 875, 876, 878, 902, 903, 918, 956-959, 964, 968-974, 978, 996, 1000, 1001, 1003, 1013, 1019, 1028, 1035, 1042, 1054, 1058, 1069, 1070, 1079, 1087
Africa Nova 973, 1070
Agade 59, 60, 62
Agamemnon 168-173, 184, 186, 293, 297, 383
Agathocleia 743, 744
Agathocles I 411, 413, 435, 436-446,
Agathocles II 628-630, 632, 633, 638-641, 653, 660, 671, 678
Agathocles (Regent of Ptolemy V)) 713, 736, 737, 743, 744
Agathocles (son of Lysimachus) 574, 576, 579, 582-584
Agema 485
Age of Reason 365
Ager Gallicus 626, 642
Ager publicus populi Romani 821
Agesilaus II 382, 383, 384, 385, 387, 389, 391, 392, 395, 396, 397, 400, 401, 402, 407, 434
Agidus 607
Agis 315, 329, 330, 343, 353, 355, 359, 449, 526, 527, 529, 531
Agrarian Law 825
Agrianian 485, 514, 515
agriculture 27, 72, 74, 76, 99, 107, 121, 131, 140, 144, 146, 156, 158, 160, 163, 174, 304, 314, 346, 350, 426, 595, 609, 803, 820, 830, 843, 846, 897, 1002, 1072
Agrigentum 645, 646, 648, 651, 687, 688, 689
Marcus Agrippa 988, 989, 1000, 1004, 1012-1015, 1029-1032, 1036, 1039, 1040, 1042-1044-1047, 1050, 1051, 1055, 1058, 1060-1062, 1067, 1070, 1072, 1074,
Agron 713, 714, 716
Q. Servilius Ahala 613, 615
Cn. Domitius Ahenobarbus 770, 839, 852, 854, 875, 883, 919, 920, 944, 953, 961, 966, 969, 970, 998, 1003, 1004, 1006, 1026, 1030, 1074
Ahmose 74, 76, 77, 78, 80
Ahura-Mazda 227, 229
Ajax 169, 194

Ajax (son of Oeleus) 169
Ajax (son of Telemon) 169
Akhetaton 88
Akhuni 134
Akkad 62, 63
Akki 60
Akshak 27, 28, 59
Alalia 257, 258, 423, 424
Alazir 204
Alba Longa 598
Alban Hills 595, 606
Alban Lake 607
Lucius Postumius Albinus 714, 715, 717, 859
Spurius Albinus 840, 841
Alcaeus 203
Alcetas 538, 539, 541, 542
Alchaudonius 938, 1018
Alcia 445
Alcibiades 182, 274, 324, 327-339, 343, 345-350, 352-355, 358, 360, 362, 366-368, 440, 442
Alcidas 311, 313
Alciphron 329
Alcmaeon 193
Alcmaeonid 236, 241, 328
Alcmaeonidae 189, 198, 199, 206, 271, 274, 302
Aleppo 37, 81, 91, 92, 103, 111, 131, 134
Alesia 910, 932, 933, 942, 943, 972
Alesion 330
Aletrium 622
Alexander (grandson of Cassander) 574
Alexander II 393, 898, 903
Alexander IV 535, 540, 544, 549, 550, 553, 556, 558, 568
Alexander of Corinth 730
Alexander of Emesa 1036
Alexander of Epirus 150, 434, 435, 444, 478, 518, 536, 560, 627, 728
Alexander of Pherae 393, 394, 402, 448, 454
Alexander's ladder 483
Alexander (son of Cassander) 573
Alexander (son of Polyperchon) 554
Alexander the Great 17, 55, 83, 95, 132, 137, 138, 147-151, 216, 222, 223, 233, 235, 251, 270, 354, 378, 381-383, 393, 398, 401-411, 422, 434, 440, 444, 448, 454, 459, 481-522, 525, 526, 529, 530, 533-536, 540, 541, 543, 545, 548-560, 566, 568-571, 574-580, 584, 587, 591, 612, 618, 625, 627-630, 634, 642, 643, 645, 647, 651, 653-655, 671, 674, 675, 695, 698, 707, 711, 713, 720, 721, 725, 726, 730, 731, 732, 738-742, 761, 762, 769, 772, 780, 783, 848, 849, 862, 887, 896, 898, 899, 901, 907, 909, 935, 983, 986, 1006, 1016-1018, 1023, 1052, 1057, 1058, 1072, 1073, 1084, 1089
Alexandra (Herod's mother-in-law) 1067
Alexandra (Hyrcanus' daughter) 1005
Alexandria 18, 277, 497, 504, 506, 509, 511, 515, 516, 518, 519, 538, 553, 558, 572, 583, 736, 737, 738, 743, 748, 759, 791, 896, 897, 898, 918, 964, 965, 966, 967, 968, 969, 984, 1002, 1005, 1016, 1017, 1020, 1022, 1026, 1027, 1033, 1034, 1035, 1056, 1057, 1079
Alexandria-the-Farthest 506
Alexandridas and Ariston (Spartan kings) 184
Alexarchus 551
Algidus Mountains 607
Ali Baba and the Forty Thieves 83
Alicante 661
Allia 609, 693
Allobroges 673, 839, 932
Quintus Fabius Maximus Allobrogicus 832
Alps 663, 666, 673, 680, 681, 699, 809, 838, 845, 846, 848, 885, 898, 930, 993, 1024, 1042, 1052, 1070, 1071, 1077, 1079
Alyattes 200, 202
Amadocus 448, 454, 455
Amalekites 40
Amarna letters 113
Amasis 128, 188, 219, 220
Amazons 175
amber 127, 256
Ambiorix 929, 930
Ambracia 468, 470, 477, 483, 576, 1029
Ambraciotes 308, 315
C. Fabius Ambustus 614
M. Fabius Ambustus 614
Amel-Marduk 129

Amenemhab 83
Amenemhet I 70, 72
Amenemhet II 71
Amenemhet III 70, 71
Amenemhet IV 71
Amenhotep, high priest of Amon 100
Amenhotep I 78
Amenhotep II 83, 84
Amenhotep III 84
Amenhotep IV 87, 88
Amenmeses 96
North America 178, 286, 334
Americans 23, 98, 129, 259, 276, 421, 427, 657, 730, 834
Amestris 376, 569, 570, 573
Amid 133
Ammon 23, 31, 35, 36, 497, 509, 514, 519, 538
Ammonites 39
Amnon 43
Amon 81, 87, 97, 99, 100, 101, 409
Amon-Re 409
Amorgos 532
Amorites 64, 91
Amos 46, 112
Amphictyonic Board 244
Amphictyonic League 188, 266, 451, 452, 464, 477
Amphilochia 315, 576
Amphilochians 323
Amphipolis 297, 300, 321-325, 328, 332, 448, 449, 450, 460-463, 466, 468, 483, 550, 578, 782, 783, 963
Amphissa 473, 474
Amphissean War 473, 476, 477
Amphitrites 514
Amphoterus 488, 526
Amurru 103
Amyclaeum 323
Amynander 750, 752
Amyntas 308, 391, 393, 448, 449, 492, 501, 504, 536, 1007, 1017, 1030, 1036, 1062
Amyrtaeus 281, 282, 406
Amyrtaeus (grandson) 406
Amytis 376
anabasis 439, 442
Anabasis 387
Analects 157
Anapus 688

Anatolia 64, 72, 73, 120, 121, 132, 168, 175, 242, 726, 729, 773, 861, 862
anatomy 25, 85
Anaxagoras 274, 298, 365, 366
Anaxagoras of Clazomenae 274
Anaxandridus 184, 186
Anaxandridus II 186
Anaxibius 380
Anaxilas of Rhegium 259
Anaximander 201
Anaximines 201
Anaxinus 470
Anaxippus 503
Anchimolius 209
The Ancient Constitution 361
Ancus Marcius 596
Andalusia 256, 424, 655
J.G.C. Anderson 1056
Andocides 386, 387
Andriscus 784, 807
Androcles 335, 336, 337, 346, 347
Andromachus 431, 734, 737, 738, 939
Andromeda 168
Livius Andronicus 636
Andros 287, 353, 355, 560, 731
Angora 490
Anhwei 161
Anio 606, 612
Anixalas 260
Ankara 489, 490
Anshan 64, 216, 227, 228
Antalcidas 386, 387, 388, 398, 407
Antander 435, 443
Antiates 615
Antigone 576, 582
Antigonus Doson 713, 716, 717, 723, 726-734
Antigonus Gonatas 150, 523, 529-591, 862
Antigonus (Mattathias) 1005-1008
Antigonus (son Aristobulus) 1064-1066
Antilcidas 387
Antioch 25, 123, 572, 585, 728, 730, 731, 732, 734, 736, 738, 749, 940, 970, 1005, 1009, 1017, 1062
Antiochis 741
Antiochus Epiphanes 51, 791
Antiochus I 149, 507, 726, 729, 730
Antiochus II 150, 729, 731-734, 862
Antiochus III (the Great) 712, 734, 736, 755, 862

Antiochus IV 780, 782
Antiochus VIII 897
Antiochus IX Cyzicenus 897
Antiochus (son of Antiochus the Great) 753, 755
Antiochus the Hawk 733
Antiochus XIII, Asiaticus 894
Antipater (Philip's general) 462, 472, 474, 482
Antipater (Alexander's general) 482, 485, 514, 515, 517, 518, 524-527, 529, 530-547, 550, 552, 554, 558, 571, 574, 578, 579, 581-585, 589, 590
Herod Antipater 895, 896, 967, 1006, 1064, 1065, 1068
Antipater (Cassander's grandson) 574
Antiphilus 532
Antiphon 347, 350, 351
Antiphon (Mecedonian spy) 468
Antium 603, 613-617, 989
Gaius Antonius 903, 904, 958, 995, 1037
Lucius Antonius 989, 1000, 1001
Marcus Antonius 873, 890, 902, 903, 1023
Marc Antony 451, 951-975, 1050, 1054, 1059, 1060, 1065-1067, 1070, 1074, 1084
Antullius 832
Anytus 367, 368
Aornos 505, 512
Aous Pass 588
Apama 383, 507, 586, 730
Apamea 772, 773
Apella 183
Apennines 619, 626, 627, 663, 676, 700, 809, 856, 919, 978
Apocalypse Now 884
Apollo 171, 172, 187, 188, 198, 201, 264, 302, 306, 319, 322, 370, 393, 415, 452, 455, 458, 461, 467, 473, 479, 509, 589, 780, 897, 1015, 1028, 1038
Apollocrates 430
Apollodorus 460, 588
Apollonia 715, 717, 719, 720, 767, 771, 981, 986, 987, 989
Apopi III 74
Appian 990
Appian Way 617, 887, 941
Apries 128, 201, 256
Apsinthians 254

Apsus River 959
Apulia 620, 621, 622, 679, 680, 683, 691-694, 856, 858, 859, 953
Apulian(s) 664
Apustius 750
Aquae Sextiae 838, 849
aqueducts 17, 45, 205, 456, 615, 635, 814, 919, 1051, 1081
Aquilius 648, 837, 866
Arab(s) 21, 23, 34, 48, 51, 124, 129, 216, 220, 408, 737, 938, 1057
Arabia 23, 36, 44, 45, 126, 132, 140, 226, 278, 374, 403, 405, 408, 519, 537, 541, 726, 1056, 1057, 1058
Arabian Desert 103
Arabian Peninsula 21, 60, 61, 109, 121
Arabian Sea 141
Arachosia 504, 514
Arakha 223
Aramaean(s) 21, 22, 23, 31, 34, 79, 116, 125, 131-135, 137
Ararat 119, 133, 1063
Aratta 514
Aratus 719, 720, 721, 894
Aratus III 894
Arausio 847, 856
Arbela 132, 223, 500, 501
Arcadia 178, 180, 184, 186, 397-400, 467, 484, 526, 553, 568, 577, 586, 717
Arcadian League 396
Arcadian(s) 174, 184, 396-399, 466, 477, 531
Arcesilas the Cruel (II) 204
Archagathus 441, 442, 443
Archagathus II 445
Archedice 198
Archelaus 366, 389, 448, 865, 867-870, 899, 1017, 1036
Archestratus 300, 359
Archias 533
Archidamus 272, 285, 300, 301, 305, 306, 309, 315, 392, 398, 434, 627
Archidamus II 305
Archimedes 687, 689
Archinus 364
archons 187, 192, 193, 194, 241, 273, 288
Archytas 428
Arciselas III 204
Ardumanish 222
Ardys 753

Areopagus 186, 187, 189, 192, 247, 273, 288, 289, 528, 529, 533, 563
Areus of Sparta 586
Arganthonius 257, 424
Argilus 321
Arginusae Islands 356
Argistis I 136
Argives 180, 182, 195, 210, 251, 252, 306, 329, 332, 340, 344, 385, 388, 397-400, 466, 467, 477
Argive War 240
Argo 168
Argolid 175, 586
Argonauts 168, 178
Argos 168, 170, 172, 175-180, 186, 196, 197, 210, 240, 243, 251, 269, 270, 273, 276, 282, 304, 322, 325-332, 362, 384, 386, 387, 396, 403, 457, 467, 469, 526, 577, 586, 720, 722, 728, 752, 759, 760, 795, 796
Aria 503, 504, 505
Ariabignes 250
Ariarathes 537, 538, 728, 762, 769, 772, 780, 790, 837, 864, 865, 868, 1017
Ariarathes IV 762, 790
Ariarathes V of Cappadocia 837
Ariarathes VII Philometor 864
Aricia 598, 619
Ariminum 665, 675-677, 809
Ariobarzanes (of Phrygia) 395, 397, 402, 403, 407
Ariobarzanes (of Persis) 862, 864, 865, 871, 899, 969,
Ariobarzanes (son of Artavasdes) 1059, 1063
Ariomandes 267
Ariovistus 921, 922, 923, 970
Aristagoras 230-234
Aristeus 301
Aristides 241, 251, 253, 262-265, 271, 288, 291, 318
Aristion 867, 868
Aristobulus 516
Aristobulus II 894, 895, 1005
Aristobulus (young, Judea) 1064, 1067
Aristodemus 461, 553, 554
Aristodemus (of Cumae) 598
Aristodicus of Tanagra 273
Aristogeiton 198
Aristomenes 758, 759

Ariston 184, 340
Aristonicus 837, 863
Aristonous 535, 539, 550
Aristophanes 292, 294, 314, 318, 322, 358
Aristophon 456
Aristotle 180, 186, 192, 193, 199, 206-208, 290, 351, 366, 459, 466, 469, 481, 485, 497, 502, 508-510, 516, 519, 525, 526, 529, 531, 536, 545, 549, 550, 551, 563, 639, 871
Ark 34, 38, 45, 57
Armageddon 16, 80, 201
Armenas 760
Armenia 21, 23, 60, 114, 223, 226, 379, 393, 395, 399, 401-403, 537-539, 541, 557, 579, 721, 741, 773, 776, 863-865, 891-894, 914, 936-938, 969, 1007, 1008, 1017, 1018-1026, 1036, 1037, 1043, 1044, 1046, 1047, 1053, 1056, 1058, 1059, 1061, 1062-1064, 1085
Arminius 933, 1076, 1077
Armistice of 1918 360
Arpad 133
Arpinum 622, 835
Arretium 626, 676, 677, 952, 992
Arrhabaeus 321
Arrhidaeus 448, 457-460, 534, 540, 541, 543, 545, 546, 590
Arrian 508
Arsaces 377, 732, 734. *See also* Artaxerxes II
Arsamosata 741
Arses 404, 494
Arshikhand 64
Arsinoe, Orestes' nurse 184
Arsinoe (Ptolemy's daughter) 573, 583, 585
Arsinoe(s) (Ptolemy II's wife and his sister) 727, 730, 737, 738, 743
Arsinoe (sister of Cleopatra) 966, 967, 974, 1002, 1034
Arsites 377, 486
Arstarchus 202
Artabanus 375, 1064
Artabazus 250, 269, 403, 404, 406, 453, 454, 490, 503, 505
Artaphernes 201, 230
Artatama 84, 114
Artavardiya 223

Artavasdes 937, 940, 1007, 1018, 1021, 1022, 1033, 1059, 1062, 1063
Artaxata 891, 893, 940
Artaxerxes (king of Persia) 50, 51, 270, 276
Artaxerxes II 375-379, 381-388, 393-395, 398, 401-407 *See also* Arsaces
Artaxerxes III Ochus (pharoah of Egypt) 453, 457, 458, 467-469, 475, 477, 494, 505, 511
Artaxes 1021, 1022, 1037, 1059
Artayctes 254
Artemesium 245, 246, 248, 250
Artemis 202, 688
Artemisia, Queen of Halicarnassus 249
Artetaurus 779
Arthashastra ("Science of Material Gain") 148
Arvad 81
Arverni 838, 839, 921, 923, 931, 933
Arx 600
Aryan Age 142
Aryandes 224
Aryans 73, 143, 144, 146, 215
Asander (0f Lydia) 539
Asander (Bosporan king) 970, 1060
Asculum 631, 856, 858, 953
Ashina 222
Ashod 176
Ashoka 149, 150, 151
Ashur 107, 114, 115, 118, 127, 131-136
Ashurbanipal 117, 123-127, 220, 230
Ashur-dan 136
Ashur-danin-apal 135
Ashur-narari V 136
Ashur-nasir-pal 132, 133
Ashur-rabi 131
Ashur-Resh-Ishi I 115
Ashur-Uballit 114
Asia Minor 23, 36, 37, 94, 109, 110, 116, 117, 119, 121, 124, 168, 169, 172-182, 185, 190, 196, 198-205, 217, 219, 226, 230, 233, 234, 247, 254, 259, 263, 266-268, 276, 277, 282, 296, 343-345, 349, 353-358, 376, 381, 383-388, 404, 405, 413, 414, 420, 448, 456, 468, 469, 477, 478, 482, 483, 485, 489, 493, 494, 504, 515, 528, 530, 537, 539, 541, 543, 545, 547, 552, 556, 559, 571, 572, 579, 581, 583-585, 587, 589, 590, 591, 612, 614, 624, 626, 635, 673, 721, 722, 726, 729, 731-736, 739, 742, 743, 753, 755, 756, 759, 762, 764, 767, 769-772, 774, 792, 793, 809, 810, 819, 835, 837, 860-863, 866, 869-871, 892-894, 898-901, 959, 961, 969, 970, 980, 995, 1000, 1001, 1003, 1005, 1009, 1012, 1014, 1017, 1019, 1020, 1021, 1026, 1036, 1038, 1052, 1060-1062, 1068, 1069, 1075, 1078, 1079
Cornelius Asina (Donkey) 648, 651 *See also* Cornelius Scipio
Askalon 95
Asopus River 253
Aspasia 298, 366
Aspendus 349, 387, 737
Aspis 440, 649, 650
Aspurgus 1061
H.H. Asquith 371
Assaceni 511, 512
Assinarus River 342
Assyria 21, 22, 82, 93, 103, 110, 111, 113-127, 131, 132, 134-137, 200, 215, 220, 223, 810
Assyrian(s) 21, 28, 38, 47, 49, 64, 92, 94, 98, 103-105, 109, 110, 113-119, 122, 124, 125, 127, 129, 131-134, 137, 149, 150, 156, 172, 174, 200, 216, 219, 224, 225, 256, 371, 408, 422, 612
Astapa 697
astronomy 25, 59, 74, 85, 366
Astyages 128, 216
Astyochus 344, 345, 346, 347, 349
Atarneus 469, 470
Kemal Ataturk 254
Ateus 472
Athamania 723
Athena 195, 247, 269, 293, 295, 298, 486, 564, 567, 574
Athenaeus 772, 778
Athenagoras 203, 337, 338
Athenian Confederacy 390, 391, 402
Athenian Conservative Party 269
Athens 18, 28, 150, 158, 159, 169, 177, 178, 180, 181, 184-199, 202, 203, 206-210, 230, 232, 235-255, 258-365, 367-369, 371, 373, 377, 378, 380-407, 413-417, 420, 421, 426-428,

431, 433, 434, 447- 479, 482-489,
495, 497, 500, 501, 503, 504, 516,
517, 519, 520, 524-534, 546, 548,
552, 553, 555, 556, 563, 564, 566,
567, 569, 570-579, 581, 584, 586,
591, 599-603, 614, 616, 618, 626,
637, 638, 640, 712, 714, 715, 716,
726-729, 746, 747, 749, 750, 752,
771, 792-794, 808, 809, 814, 815,
819, 867, 868, 978, 995, 1002, 1004,
1007, 1008, 1020, 1025-1027, 1032,
1063, 1088
Atia 989, 990
Marcus Atilius 799
Atossa 227
Atrapatene 537
Atrapates 537
Atreus 168
Attalus (associate of Perdiccas) 540, 541, 542, 584
Attalus (brother of Eumenes) 772, 780
Attalus II 744, 745, 746, 747, 752, 754, 763, 792, 796
Attalus III 822, 830, 836
Attalus (Macedonian general) 477, 478, 482
Attalus of Pergamum 699, 721, 722, 723, 726, 733, 734
Attica 174, 186-192, 198, 209, 239, 242, 243, 246, 247, 251-254, 258, 259, 263-265, 273, 278-280, 283, 304-307, 309-311, 315, 316, 318, 322, 325, 326, 328, 329, 337, 338, 340, 341, 346, 350, 355, 358, 362, 364, 384, 385, 388, 389, 460, 464, 473, 474, 532, 567, 728, 746, 749, 750, 867
Atticans 174, 207
Attic poets 173
Numerius Atticus 1082
Attila (the Hun) 774, 898
attribute (tax plan) 819
Atuatuca 929
Audoleon of Paeonia 578
Auerstadt 753
Aufidus River 681
Tiberius Minucius Augurinus 622
Augustus 83, 94, 117, 164, 216, 268, 422, 423, 478, 519, 583, 635, 660, 705, 734, 774, 802, 811, 835, 845, 851,
855, 879, 888, 909, 981, 986, 1011, 1017, 1034, 1036, 1041-1085, 1088, 1071 *See also* Octavius/Octavian
Aulis 567, 870
Austanes 508, 509
Austerlitz 484, 673, 681, 682
Australia 88, 178, 256, 604
Austria 197, 669
Autocles 318
Automata 432
Autophradates 387, 407
auxilium 602
Avaricum 931
ayatollahs 50

B

Baasha of Issachar 49
Babbar 59
Babel 26
Babylon 18, 22, 26, 27, 38, 50, 64, 73, 79, 82, 85, 103-109, 111, 113-116, 118, 120, 122-125, 127-129, 131, 134-138, 204, 216, 218, 219, 222, 227-229, 375, 376, 378, 501, 517-519, 522, 534, 535, 538, 541, 546, 551, 552, 555, 556, 559, 568-570, 584, 586, 810, 895
Babylonia 21, 26, 54, 61, 68, 73, 79, 103, 108-110, 113-115, 118, 120-131, 134, 137, 150, 217, 218, 220, 222-224, 250, 256, 501, 546, 551, 552, 735, 938, 1005
Babylonian(s) 21, 47, 73, 108, 109, 110, 125-129, 135, 149, 200, 215, 219, 221-224, 229, 242, 256, 315, 501, 556, 1067
The Babylonians 314
Bactria 141, 164, 221, 223, 375, 499, 502-505, 507, 509, 510, 511, 527, 531, 534, 537, 539, 541, 551, 727, 731, 732, 735, 741, 1021
Bactrian(s) 128, 500
Gaius Baebius 840
Baghdad 27, 59
Bagoas 404, 494
Bagradas River 705, 707
Bahrein 123
Balacrus 492, 538
Alexander Balas 791
Balearic Islands 424, 685, 703

Balikh 134
Balkans 24, 94, 203, 425, 483, 588, 754, 762, 775, 779, 836, 838, 956, 957, 958, 1072
Baluchistan 140
Bangladesh 140, 150, 637
Barak 36
Baranamtarra 58
barbarians 24, 92, 102, 115, 142, 155, 160, 165, 176, 177, 225, 390, 419, 424, 425, 434, 485, 486, 504, 506, 624, 627, 628, 630, 642, 666, 716, 724, 725, 734, 738, 741, 749, 750, 754, 758, 761, 762, 772, 783, 809, 837, 847, 882, 926, 974, 1015, 1035, 1037, 1039, 1063, 1069
Cornelius Scipio Barbatus 623
Barberini 599
Aemilius Barbula 621, 629
Barca 204, 221, 414, 653, 662, 695, 696, 699, 706, 790
Barcid party 656, 658
Bardia 221, 222, 223, 224, 242
Bardylis 449
Bar-Hadad 135, 136
Barras 190
Barsaentes 502, 503
Barsine 383, 404, 517
Basileus 189, 192
Basra 27, 108
Caecilius Bassus 980, 995
Quintus Caecilius Bassus 980
Bastarnae 1037
Bathsheba 40, 43, 44
Bato 750, 1075, 1076
Battle of Actium 1029-1032, 1036-1038, 1054, 1055, 1058, 1067, 1069, 1082, 1083
Battle of Alalia 257, 258
Battle of Alesia 910, 932-935, 942, 943, 972
Battle of Aricia 598
Battle of Austerlitz 484, 673, 681, 682
Battle of Beresina 92, 379, 579
Battle of Britain 248, 250
Battle of the Champions 186, 270
Battle of Chaeronea 434, 474
Battle of Citium 394
Battle of Clastidium 686
Battle at Corupedium 584

Battle of Cos 730
Battle of Cyzicus 352
Battle of Gabiene 551
Battle of Gaugamela 498-503, 505, 527, 537, 543, 738
Battle of Gettysburg 248, 681
Battle of Granicus 487
Battle of the Great Plains 705, 707
Battle of Himera 416
Battle of Issus 378, 481, 490, 491, 493, 497, 498, 499, 502, 526, 556, 559, 738
Battle of Lake Regillus 605
Battle of Leipzig 691, 731
Battle of Leuctra 450
Battle of Marathon 195, 215, 235-250, 267, 268, 354, 458, 528
Battle of Megalopolis 527
Battle of Mount Gilboa 40, 41
Battle of Orchomenus 869
Battle of Panion 748
Battle of Plataea 254
Battle of Pydna 782, 790
Battle of Raphia 738
Battle of Salamis 247, 266
Battle of Stalingrad 396, 700
Battle at Tanagra 280
Battle of Thapsus 972
Battle of Thermopylae 243, 244-246, 248
Battle of Trafalgar 263, 279
Battle of Marathon 195, 215, 235, 237-242, 247, 250, 267, 268, 354, 458, 528
Battle of the Metaurus 804
Battle of the Plains of Abraham 693
Battle of the Trebbia 630
Battle of Vicksburg 700
Battle of the Volcaean Marshes 1076
Battus I 204
Battus III (the Lame) 204
Bay of Biscay 925
Bay of Naples 17, 849, 859, 1055, 1077
Bay of Pagasae 470
bazaars 79
Beas River 513, 514
Bedouins 23, 26, 71, 90, 91, 114, 126
Bee-Hive Tomb Dynasty 167
Beersheeba 31
Beethoven 313
Being There 104
Beirut 79
Belgic Confederacy 923

Belgium 566, 846
Belli 800
Bellovaci 923, 933
Belshazzar 129
P.V.M. Benecke 793
Benefactors 504
Beneventum 634, 635, 679, 692, 996
Bengal 145
Benjamin (tribe) 33, 36, 38, 40, 41
Berbers 95, 98, 426, 736
Berenice (wife of Ptolemy) 559, 561, 573, 582, 585
Berenice (daughter of Ptolemy II) 730, 731, 733, 736, 743
Berenice (daughter of Ptolemy VIII, Lathyrus) 898
Beresina 92, 379, 579
Bergamo 665
Lavrenti Beria 536
Berisades 448, 449, 450, 451
Berlin 44, 181, 725
Marshal Bernadotte 202, 449
Bessus 499, 500, 502, 503, 504, 505
Lucius Calpurnius Bestia 840
Bethel 31, 32, 36, 40
E.R. Bevan 895
Bibracte 922, 932
M. Calpurnius Bibulus 912, 913, 917, 940, 941, 958, 959
Bimbisara 145
Bindusara 149
Otto von Bismarck 268, 367, 419, 468, 487, 570, 626, 729, 1041, 1045
Bit Adini 134
Bithynia 382, 493, 557, 572, 584, 586, 589, 723, 773, 776, 779, 780, 790, 792, 837, 862-865, 870, 877, 892, 899, 1002, 1003, 1017, 1021
Bithynian(s) 169, 381, 722
Bituitus 839
Bizerte 441, 654
Black Sea 79, 142, 168, 170, 175, 179, 185, 190, 196, 201, 203-205, 221, 225, 226, 234, 266, 304, 306, 352, 353, 358, 374, 379, 387, 390, 456, 458, 472, 490, 528, 552, 554, 566, 570, 571, 573, 581, 588, 727, 733, 742, 861-863, 886, 893, 894, 1060-1062, 1069
Cornelius Blasio 636

blood feuds 189
Claire Bloom 404
Blossius 825
Blossius of Cumae 837
Bocchus (brother of Bogud) 1029, 1070
Bocchus of Mauretania 842, 843, 844, 971, 973,
boeotarch 397
Boeotia 187, 198, 278, 279, 280, 281, 282, 283, 303, 310, 315, 319, 323, 325-328, 362, 364, 384, 385, 387, 392, 455, 457, 458, 473, 474, 476, 484, 532, 533, 555, 567, 575, 577, 578, 586, 723, 728, 752, 757, 766, 797, 867-869, 870
Boeotian League 198, 278, 281, 283, 325, 390, 392, 780
Boeotian(s) 169, 209, 243, 253, 304, 315, 319, 320, 323, 326, 327, 334, 335, 385, 388, 392, 400, 453, 458, 461, 530, 531, 552, 555, 575, 589, 757, 766, 795
Boges 266
Bogrud 971
Bogud 1029
Boii 626, 664, 665, 673, 809, 846, 922, 931
Bokhara 506
Bola 614, 622
Bolgius 588, 589
Simon Bolívar 933
Bologna 637, 664, 665, 676, 809
Bolognese 595
Bolsheviks 224
Bomilcar 439, 441, 688, 689, 696, 840, 841
Bonaparte 90
Book of History 157, 159
Book of Odes 158
Book of Songs 157
Book of the Portals 78
Book of What is in the Nether World 77
books of knowledge 142
John Wilkes Booth 982
Rodrigo Borgia 156
Bosporan Kingdom 1060
Bosporus 147, 170, 175, 178, 225, 226, 233, 234, 250, 254, 262-264, 266, 268, 297, 353, 371, 375, 383, 456, 474, 476, 545, 555, 728, 870, 891, 970, 1045, 1058
botanists 482

Georges Ernest Boulanger 917
Boulogne 484, 927
bows and arrows 72
Brachyllas 757
Brahmans 143, 144, 145, 512, 514
Brahmin 145, 146, 148
Branchidae 235
Marlon Brando 884
Brasidas 285, 305, 309, 313, 316, 319-324, 339, 363
Brazil 88, 420
J.H. Breasted 83, 97
Brenner Pass 848, 1071
Brennus 422, 588, 589, 609, 612, 616, 619, 636, 693, 731, 733, 774, 1035
Breui 1072
Brihadratha 145
Brindisi 420, 936, 1004, 1006, 1007, 1009, 1028, 1038
Briseis 172
Britain 47, 122, 201, 218, 225, 226, 230, 241, 248, 250, 257, 263, 271, 275, 276, 288, 289, 291, 346, 375, 384, 388, 420, 424, 425, 433, 461, 465, 684, 714, 719, 727, 751, 775, 776, 802, 839, 924, 927, 928, 934, 942, 1077, 1079, 1087
British 39, 122, 126, 129, 142, 187, 204, 207, 218, 227, 230, 236, 250, 257, 275, 276, 278, 286, 289, 296, 304, 366, 371, 384, 404, 408, 424, 427, 450, 460, 479, 507, 510, 636, 637, 655, 657, 668, 684, 714, 729, 751, 769, 832, 834, 863, 927, 928, 934, 954, 973, 985, 986, 990, 1011, 1049, 1084
British Commonwealth 218
British Raj 408
British Reform Acts 289, 820
  First Reform Act of 1832 207, 291
Brittany 256, 424, 924, 925
Brogitarus 916
bronze 72, 73, 80, 102, 103, 115, 120, 142, 152, 153, 169, 257, 424, 443, 447, 467, 481, 562, 599, 600, 611, 710, 1032, 1050
Bronze Age 168, 595
John Brown 370
Brundisium 714, 875, 911, 953, 957-959, 991, 1000, 1003, 1004, 1011, 1012, 1025, 1032
Bruttians 433-435, 445, 518, 627-629, 631, 636
Marcus Brutus 451, 600, 601, 882, 904, 914, 985, 987, 988, 991, 992, 993, 994, 995, 997, 998, 999, 1017, 1033, 1043, 1045
Decimus Brutus 925, 958, 981, 983, 989, 992, 993, 994, 995
Junius Bubulcus 622
Bucephalus 513
Buddha 139, 145, 146, 149, 150
Buddhism 145, 146, 150, 153
Nikolai Bukharin 241
Noni us Bulbus 1026
Bulgaria 174, 483, 726
bull 67, 107, 220, 257, 258, 426, 720
Jacob Burckardt 887
Burmese mountains 140
Bur-Sin 64
Richard Burton 404
J.B. Bury 174, 421
Byblos 23, 74, 78, 79, 98, 101, 133, 135
Byblos-farers 23
Lord Byron 121, 126, 271, 289
Byzantium 180, 201, 204, 233, 234, 263, 264, 266, 269, 297, 349, 353, 375, 380, 381, 383, 385, 387, 390, 402, 406, 448, 451, 453, 455, 468, 470, 471, 472, 476, 477, 555, 570, 585, 590, 723, 726, 729, 733, 744, 762, 779, 830, 870

C

Cacus 596
Cadez 424
Cadiz 256, 696, 1087
Cadmea 452, 555
Cadmus 259, 261
Caelius 968
Fannius Caepio 1043
Q. Servilius Caepio (son) 856, 857
Quintus Servilius Caepio 800, 847, 856, 857, 858
Caere 614
Julius Caesar 17, 44, 92, 95, 117, 164, 216, 225, 227, 268, 273, 281, 401, 419, 422, 423, 434, 446, 478, 479, 485, 501, 507, 510, 519-521, 571, 583, 590, 627, 635, 663, 673, 676, 705,

708, 749, 774, 776, 800, 802, 811,
823, 834, 835, 838, 845, 847, 849,
852, 855, 858-860, 871, 872, 877,
882, 884, 885, 887-890, 892, 895-
999, 1001-1006, 1009, 1011, 1012,
1015-1023, 1025-1028, 1032, 1034-
1040, 1043-1045, 1051-1054, 1058,
1060, 1062, 1064, 1065, 1069, 1070,
1072, 1078, 1080-1084, 984
L. Julius Caesar (no relation) 858
Lucius Caesar 906
Octavius Caesar 982, 983, 986, 994, 995,
1011 See also Augustus and Octavi-
an/Octavius
Sextus Caesar 896, 970, 980
Caesarea 1062, 1067
Caeserus 798
Cain 26
Cairo 68, 71, 78, 262, 406
Cairo Museum 68, 71
Calagurris 883, 884
Calatia 620, 621
Atilius Calatinus 648, 651
Calauria 533
Calchas 172
Caleb 52
Calenus 971, 992, 1001, 1006
Calicinus 781
Calippus 430, 586
Calistratus 401
Callias 276, 376, 461, 470
Callibius 361
Callicrates of Leontium 795
Callicratidas 355, 356, 357
Callimichus 237
Callisthenes 268
Callisthenes of Olynthus 485, 507, 509,
510, 545
Callistratus 391, 392, 398, 401, 402, 450,
456, 457
Callium 589
Callius 301
Calor River 635
Domitius Calvinus 883, 961, 969, 1004
Sextius Calvinus 838
Camarina 258, 259, 260, 313, 336, 415,
441, 443, 650, 651
Cambridge Ancient History (CAH) 18,
22, 23, 25, 26, 33, 58, 69, 71, 74,
78, 83, 97, 104, 113, 114, 122-124,

127, 174, 178, 183, 188, 192-194,
197, 204, 209, 222, 230, 270, 286,
342, 363, 381, 402, 405, 407, 421,
434, 446, 455, 483, 529, 569, 573,
655, 675, 687, 700, 709, 719, 743,
747, 753, 755, 793, 870, 872, 876,
884, 892, 897, 912, 934, 961, 977,
983, 990, 991, 997, 999, 1016, 1024,
1030, 1034, 1040, 1043, 1045, 1049
Cambyses 202, 204, 215, 216, 219, 220-
228, 242
camel 72, 141, 1057
L. Furius Camillus (Marcus' son) 613-616,
619
Marcus Furius Camillus 422, 595, 607,
610, 849, 973
Campania 597, 598, 613, 615, 616, 619-
621, 640, 679, 680, 682, 691, 692,
856, 858, 859, 872, 875, 879, 919,
938, 944, 953, 968, 970, 989, 1001,
1038, 1044, 1045
Campi Rudii 848
Canaan 22, 31, 36, 46, 48, 112
Canaanite 22, 41, 43, 73
Canaanite(s) 23, 32, 37, 38, 43, 44, 73, 78,
79, 414
Canada 88, 256, 375, 604, 826
Canadian Confederation 259
canalization 27, 121, 144
Canidius 1026, 1030, 1032, 1034
Cannae 681, 682, 684-686, 690, 700, 702,
703, 705, 707, 709, 710, 719, 816,
894
Cannicus 886
John Canning 126
Cantabrians 1069, 1070
Caius Canuleius 608
Cape Bon 439, 440
Cape Ecnomus 649
Cape Nao 661
Cape Palinurus 651
Cape Palos 661
Caphtor 112
Capitoline Hill 422, 596, 601, 606, 610,
611, 626, 636, 733, 849, 853, 854,
871, 1035
Manlius Capitolinus 422, 611, 616, 733
Al Capone 436
Cappadocia 64, 108, 110, 132, 135, 136,
142, 217, 242, 377, 378, 394, 395,

402, 486, 490, 537, 538, 541, 542, 551, 552, 554, 572, 728, 731, 733, 762, 769, 776, 780, 790, 837, 861-865, 891, 899, 969, 1002, 1007, 1017, 1053
Metellus Caprarius 838, 853
Capua 440, 617, 619, 620, 631, 658, 681, 683, 691-693, 699, 885, 887, 907, 917, 996, 1079
Caranus 482

C. Papirius Carbo 826, 835
Gnaeus Carbo 846, 874, 875, 876, 877, 903
Carchemish 37, 103, 127, 128, 134, 136, 137
Cardia 235, 463, 468-470, 535, 540
Cardians 469
Carduchians 379
"Cargoes" 147
Caria 175, 233, 234, 265, 310, 344, 377, 386, 387, 393, 395, 402, 451, 476, 478, 488, 539, 541, 551, 554, 555, 573, 729, 733, 734, 744, 745, 770, 772, 792, 793, 866, 1006
Thomas Carlyle 371
Carmania 504, 514-516, 551
Carmel 78
Carneades 794
Carnutes 928, 930
Carpathus 386
Carpetani 662
Carrhae 507, 938, 939, 940, 970, 986, 1006, 1007
Gaius Carrinas 1037
Johnny Carson 90
Cartagena 661
Carthage 151, 169, 255-258, 260-262, 333, 338, 401, 413-428, 431-446, 598, 603, 616, 619, 625, 632-634, 638-664, 667-672, 674-679, 683-690, 692, 694-712, 715-718, 720, 721, 724, 725, 727, 728, 739, 740, 742, 745, 746, 748, 749, 760, 763, 765, 768, 773, 779, 790, 797, 798, 802-808, 811, 817, 818, 829, 830, 831, 837, 839, 842, 844, 846, 849, 863, 883, 973, 979, 1053, 1055, 1061
Carthalo 651, 652, 803
Sp. Carvilius 624
M. Cary 188, 222, 230, 388, 446, 897, 899, 903, 912
Carystus 237, 266, 267, 460
Casilinum 691
Caspian Gates 502
Cassander 445, 482, 523, 530, 534-536, 541, 544-546, 548-579, 581, 583, 585, 586, 589, 713
Cassandra 184
Cassandreia 550, 553, 578, 586, 588, 590, 750
Gaius Cassius 451, 836, 840, 846, 865, 866, 885, 937, 938, 939, 940, 947, 961, 970, 982, 986, 989, 991, 992, 993, 995, 997, 998, 1002, 1005, 1064, 1065
Quintus Cassius 947
Spurius Cassius 603, 605, 615
Cassius of Parma 1021, 1034
Cassivelaunus 928
Castor 1002
Castus 886
cat 141, 222, 234, 404, 503, 574, 793, 794, 894
Catana 258, 336, 337, 341, 416, 430, 432, 433, 633
Catanes 508, 509
cataphracts 742, 744, 1007
Catherine the Great 425, 466, 626, 863
L. Sergius Catilina (Catiline) 859, 901, 902, 903, 904, 905, 906, 907, 908, 910, 947, 954, 1050
L. Porcius Cato 858
Marcus Cato (great grandson) 904, 908, 909
Marcus Porcius Cato 767, 789, 791, 792, 796, 798, 799, 804, 805, 808, 810, 811, 812, 813, 815, 816, 817, 818, 838, 854, 911-913, 915, 916, 920, 926, 935, 936, 941-943, 964, 971, 973, 974, 977, 979, 1004, 1033, 1077, 1084
cattle 77, 99, 107, 126, 151-153, 238, 472, 511, 615, 680, 840, 928
Lutatius Catulus 654, 656, 660, 709
Quintus Lutatius Catulus 848, 881, 882, 892
Quintus Catalus (consul) 873
Caucasus 110, 175, 226, 379, 483, 511, 741, 893, 980
Cadius Caudex 643

Caudine Peace 620
Caudium 620, 621
Caulonia 419, 427, 429, 627
Caunus 297, 383, 793
cedar 27, 62, 70, 80, 98, 116, 553
Celaenae 489, 557
Celtiberians 425, 426, 703, 705, 728, 739, 797-800, 882, 883
Celtic League 664
Celts 21, 173, 424, 425, 483, 588, 609, 623, 632, 637, 642, 645, 655, 665, 675, 681, 699, 849, 920, 921, 1067
Cenchreae 717
Cenomani 664, 665, 809
censor(s) 608, 610, 617, 643, 667, 668, 675, 691, 804, 817, 818, 819, 820, 873, 878, 903, 915, 1043, 1046, 1047, 1048, 1051, 1081
L. Marcius Censorinus 806
census 99, 165, 563, 597, 608, 611, 653, 660, 854, 1047
Fulvius Centumalus 693, 714
Cephallania 341
Cephisodotus 448
Cephisophon 471
Cerasus 380
Cerethrius 588, 590
Cerretani 1004
Cersobleptes 448, 454-457, 463, 466, 468, 469
Cornelius Cethegus 689, 809
Cetriporis 451
Chabrias 390, 391, 395, 448, 451
Chaerephon 367
Chaeron 795
Chaeronea 283, 319, 434, 453, 457, 458, 472, 474, 475, 482, 524-527, 532, 869
Chaeronia 283
Chalcedon 180, 353, 387, 585, 744, 870
Chalcideus 343
Chalcidian League 389, 391, 402
Chalcidian revolt 301
Chalcidian(s) 209, 300, 306, 308, 320, 326, 327, 330-332, 385, 392
Chalcidice 750
Chalcidic League 459
Chalcis 284, 453, 468, 470, 477, 531, 555, 575, 752, 765, 766, 767, 774, 869, 1002, 1017, 1036

Chaldeans 120, 122, 125, 131, 135
Chalybes 380
Neville Chamberlain 459
Samuel de Champlain 1087
Chandragupta Maurya 147, 149, 513
Chang Ch'ien 164
Chao Kao 160, 161
Chares 451, 453, 456, 459, 470, 471, 474, 475
Charicles 529
Charidemus 447, 448, 457, 458, 460, 475
chariot 72, 81, 91, 92, 98, 116, 120, 124, 133, 143, 180, 195, 230, 333, 368, 421, 489, 492, 564, 852, 915, 975, 981, 1022
Charitimides 281, 286
Holy Roman Emperor Charles V 149, 193
M.P. Charlesworth 990, 991, 997, 999, 1016
Charles X 934
Charmides 367
Charoeades 314
Charondas 258
Cheirisophus 379
Chenab River 513
Ch'en Sheng 161
Cheops 68, 69 *See also* Khufu
Chersonese 196, 198, 203, 225, 233-236, 265, 287, 448, 455, 461-463, 465, 466, 469, 470, 471, 476, 758, 773, 777, 838, 863, 1046, 1061
Lord Cherwell 365
Ch'i 155, 156, 159
chicken 141
chiliarch 435, 436, 518, 541
Chilon 183
Ch'in 155, 156, 159-165
Chin 155
China 17, 23, 24, 73, 79, 93, 129, 139, 140, 145, 146, 150-166, 216, 218, 219, 225, 226, 379, 408, 409, 422, 489, 511, 566, 626, 1058, 1079, 1088, 1089
Chinese 15, 17, 18, 22, 151-166, 168, 216, 408, 546, 626
Chinese Communist Party 165
Chios 175, 233-235, 263, 268, 269, 287, 341, 343-345, 353, 355, 357, 386, 390, 451, 453, 469, 471, 492, 495, 497, 722, 746, 772, 869

Jacques Chirac 667
Chola 150, 155
Chorienes 508
Chosen People 38
Duke of Chou 153
Chou Hsin 153
Chow 152
Chremonidean War 728
Chremonides 727
Christ 17, 33, 46, 102, 227, 370, 371, 409, 895, 986, 1036, 1082, 1086
Christian 17, 18, 23-25, 31, 43, 64, 77, 88, 99, 110, 116, 145, 150, 153, 162, 173, 183, 256, 293, 294, 404, 474, 590, 885, 1055, 1089
Christian Era 17, 24, 64, 145, 162, 173, 1055, 1089
Christianity 24, 25, 49, 72, 157, 590
Chrysa 172
Chryses 172
Ch'u 155, 156, 158, 159
chun tzu 157
Winston Churchill 16, 73, 201, 218, 242, 265, 270, 274, 275, 265, 269, 20, 278, 365, 371, 397, 459, 465, 467, 523, 683, 702
Church of England 187
Ch'u Yuan 158
Marcus Tullius Cicero 16, 598, 602, 814, 817, 822, 824, 829, 831, 833, 842, 845, 860, 876, 881, 884, 887, 888, 889, 891, 892, 901-904, 906-920, 928, 929, 933-936, 939, 941, 944, 952-955, 962-964, 967, 969, 972, 974, 976, 977, 982, 985-995, 997, 999, 1032, 1043, 1077, 1078, 1084
Cidus 386
Cilbiceni 655
Cilicia 110, 176, 282, 402, 492, 495, 500, 531, 535, 538, 541, 552, 559, 573, 578-581, 729, 744, 878, 890, 891, 892, 899, 958, 965, 966, 970, 1002, 1005, 1006, 1016, 1017, 1034, 1036, 1064
Cilician Gates 490
Cilicia Tracheia 1017, 1036
Cimbri 846, 848, 849, 892, 920, 921, 985
Cimmerian Bosporus 297
Cimmerians 120, 124, 200
Cimon 208, 252, 255, 265-275, 280-282, 286, 287, 291, 292, 309, 325, 336, 366, 386, 405
L. Quinctius Cincinnatus 606, 804, 815, 831, 879
Cineas 628, 631, 633
Lucius Cornelius Cinna 861, 871-874, 876-888, 890, 989
Gaius Helvius Cinna 988, 989
circumcision 32
Circus Flaminius 602
Cirrha 473
Cirta 840-843
Cirte 705
Cisalpine Gauls 420, 422, 809
Cistauric Asia 772
Citium 282, 394
Citrantakhma 223
City of the Sun 837
Cius 557, 585, 744
Civilian Conservation Corps 290
Clastidium 666, 668, 686, 809, 1039
Appius Claudius Caesus 606, 615, 617, 631, 632, 633, 642, 643, 644, 667, 684, 686, 692, 778, 796, 825, 872
Marrcus Claudius Marcellus 666, 667, 686, 691, 692, 693, 695, 699, 701, 747, 749, 755, 778, 796, 809, 825, 856, 858, 872, 885, 944, 1001, 1035, 1039, 1042, 1043
Attius Clausus. *See* Appius Claudius Caesus
Clazomenae 274, 343
Cleander 259, 381, 516
Cleandridas 284
Clearchus 353, 379
Clearidas 324, 325
Cleigenes 354
Cleippides 310
Cleisthenes of Sicyon (law-giver) 167, 181-183, 185, 193, 195, 198
Cleisthenes (son of Cleisthenes of Sicyon) 206-209, 211, 236, 241, 271, 274, 287
Cleitus 483, 487, 507, 508, 532, 543, 545, 546
Georges Clemenceau 467, 702, 771
Cleombrotus 392
Cleomenes 184, 186, 198, 199, 206, 207, 208, 209, 210, 232, 240, 241, 258
Cleomenes of Naucratis 537, 540

Cleomenes of Sparta 716, 717, 734, 736, 743
Cleon 291, 311, 314-318, 320-322, 327, 328, 331, 402, 1007, 1036
Cleonymus 435, 445, 627, 628
Queen Mother Cleopatra 790
Cleopatra (daughter of Antiochus the Great) 758
Cleopatra (daughter of Mithridates Eupator, wife of Tigranes) 864
Cleopatra (daughter of Phillip) 478
Cleopatra Eurydice 478, 482
Cleopatra II 896
Cleopatra III 896, 897, 898
Cleopatra IV 897
Cleopatra Tryphaena 897
Cleopatra VII 583, 964-969, 1002, 1011-1047 1050, 1066, 1067, 1070
Cleophon 352, 353, 357, 358, 359, 360, 361, 387, 456
cleruchies 287, 296, 297, 386
Robert Clive 1087
Gnaeus Lentulus Clodianus 885
Clodius 903, 911, 914, 915, 916, 917, 918, 919, 921, 930, 935, 941, 1050
P. Clodius 903, 911
Cluentius 859
Clupea 649
Clusium 608, 609, 610, 665
Clytaemnestra 168, 183, 184, 293
Cnemus 308, 309
Cnidus 345, 383, 387
Cnossus 167, 168
Coenus 507
coinage 129, 150, 159, 180, 183, 185, 191, 197, 437, 451, 453, 457, 503, 520, 551, 557, 558, 568, 637, 660, 710, 727, 732, 742, 855, 856, 981, 1017, 1041, 1050, 1087
Cold War 296, 573
College of Augurs 817, 944
Colline Gate 875, 876
Colombia Caesarea 1062
Colossus of Rhodes 567
Comas 202
Comimium 624
comitia 598, 599, 600, 601, 602, 1049
comitia centuriata 600
comitia curiata 599
comitia tributa populi 602

Commagene 115, 899, 1008
Commandments 34
Committee of Public Safety 361
Commius 927, 930, 933, 934
Lake Como 809
Companions 485, 487, 499, 500, 502, 506, 510, 514, 547
Concilium Plebis 821, 822, 827-831, 833, 855, 903, 905, 906, 908, 912, 917
condottiere 387, 723
Confederation of Delos 196, 264, 265, 281 *See also* Delian Confederation
Confucianism 153, 157, 158, 163
Confucius 139, 156-158, 163 *See also* K'ung fu-tzu
Congress of Berlin 725
Congress of Corinth 477, 483
Congress of the Amphictyony 193
Conon 355, 356, 358, 359, 382-386, 391, 406, 407, 546
Consentia 434
consilium plebis tributum 602
Consolitanus 665
consuls 601, 602, 608, 611, 614, 616, 620, 623, 624, 631, 633, 634, 638, 639, 645, 648-653, 659, 660, 665, 666, 667, 669, 671, 675, 681, 691, 693, 699, 700, 703, 710, 714, 715, 717, 718, 754, 801, 802, 806, 807, 820, 824, 826, 829, 839, 841, 843, 845, 853-855, 858, 860, 861, 874, 875, 877, 878, 882, 885, 902, 905, 915, 918, 936, 943, 944, 946, 947, 953, 954, 957, 971, 992, 993, 994, 1004, 1026, 1043, 1052, 1081
Continental Congress 50
conventio 598
S.A. Cook 22, 25, 26, 113
copper 46, 71, 72, 84, 96, 103, 115, 155, 256, 356, 424, 597, 655, 783, 862, 1050
Copts 70
Coracesium 753, 892
Corcyra 259, 269, 298, 299, 304, 308, 312, 313, 315, 316, 318, 325, 335, 336, 341, 353, 391, 445, 470, 576, 670, 686, 714, 715, 721, 722
Corinth 169, 178-182, 185, 186, 189, 196-198, 203, 209, 210, 232, 243, 248, 259, 276, 278, 279, 283, 285,

286, 296-302, 304, 305, 307-309,
312-315, 323, 325-330, 333, 364,
384-388, 396, 398-400, 418, 421,
431, 432, 436, 470, 477, 482-484,
487, 492, 493, 495, 497, 501-503,
517, 523, 531, 544, 552, 555, 557,
558, 561, 565, 568, 572, 575-578,
580, 586, 712, 713, 716, 728-731,
752, 759, 760, 766, 772, 795-798,
811, 829, 830, 979, 1029
Isthmus of Corinth 243
Corinthians 179, 209, 278, 298-301, 304,
318, 332, 338, 360, 399, 431, 568,
716, 753, 757
Corinthian War 384, 397
Coriolanus 606
Corneille 293
Cornelia 802, 823, 824, 827, 828, 831, 833,
888, 889, 890
Gaius Cornelius 889, 901, 1056
Lucius Cornificius 1012
Coronea 283, 385
Corregidor 767
Correus 933
Corsica 423, 424, 648, 658, 659, 660, 748,
809, 817, 878, 1004
Lucius Coruncanius 714
corvee 107
Valerius Messella Corvinus 995
M. Valerius Corvus 613
Cos 203, 451, 453, 454, 471, 559, 730, 866,
898
cosmic 35, 76, 87, 293
cosmos 26, 34, 35
Cossaean(s) 546
Cossaean tribe 518
A. Cornelius Cossus 607, 614, 615, 1039
Cornelius Cossus 1039
C. Aurelius Cotta 860
Gaius Aurelius Cotta 884
Lucius Aurelius Cotta 889
cotton 72, 121, 141
Cotys 447, 448, 450
Council of Athens 207
Council of Demiurges 752
Council of Elders 599
Council of Five Hundred 252
Council of Four Hundred 192, 347
Council of Friends 557
Council of Ten 363

Council of the Four Hundred 192
Court of One-Hundred and Four 749
Covenant 31, 34, 43, 46, 503, 524, 526
craftsmen 76, 77, 127, 128, 148, 194, 291,
307, 619
Crannon 532
Marcus Licinius Crassus 507, 701, 702,
817, 825, 833, 835, 837, 839, 854,
860, 875, 878, 884-887, 889, 896,
898, 902-911, 913, 914, 917, 919,
920, 923, 927, 929, 935-941, 944,
954, 970, 980, 986, 1006, 1018,
1019, 1037, 1039, 1040, 1058, 1059,
1069, 1077
P. Licinius Crassus 701, 817, 825, 833, 860,
875, 886, 910, 1037
Publius Crassus 923, 924, 937, 938, 939
Craterus 488, 509, 510, 512, 513, 514, 515,
516, 517, 518, 531, 532, 534, 535,
537, 538, 539, 540, 541, 543, 547,
578
Cratesipolis 561
Creation 26, 35, 366
Cremera River 607
Cremona 666, 676, 808, 996
Crenides 450, 451
Cretan(s) 79, 112, 278, 424, 514
Crete 23, 71, 78, 79, 112, 167-169, 173,
174, 176, 177, 182, 183, 186, 187,
243, 278, 309, 464, 485, 513, 516,
723, 742, 751, 752, 758-760, 772,
793, 899, 958, 1029, 1036
Crimea 204, 297, 390, 863, 899, 1060, 1061
Crimisus River 433
Crisa 188, 193
T. Qinctius Crispinus 699
Critias 360, 361, 362, 363, 367
Crito 369, 370
Critolaus 794, 796, 797
Crixus 885
Croesus of Hercules 119
Crommyon 318
Cromnus 399
Oliver Cromwell 388, 591, 668, 884
Croton 204, 205, 258, 420, 627, 628, 630-
636, 706
Crotonian(s) 201, 636
Crusaders 112, 129
Ctesias 382
Ctesiphon 461, 527, 528, 735

Cuban Missile Crisis 648
Quintus Terentius Culleo 749
Cultural Revolution 161
Cunaxa 378, 382
Quintus Fabius Maximus Cunctator 668
cuneiform 79, 110, 115, 116, 229
curia/curiae 598, 599
Gaius Curio 868
Scribonius Curio 914, 944
Manius Curius 626, 634
Manius Curius Dentatus 634
Lucius Papirius Cursor 621
Papirius Cursor the Younger 636
cursus 813, 1049
Fulvius Curvus 622
Cush 22
Cyaxares 127, 222, 223
Cybebe 233
The Cyclades 167, 175, 176, 177, 203, 231, 236, 239, 243, 248, 250, 391, 402, 554, 557, 565, 571, 572, 717, 731, 867
Cydonia 309, 1036
Cylon 189, 190, 193, 207
Cynegirus 239
Cypria 173. *See also The Epic Cycle*
Cyprus 49, 60, 82, 119, 123, 190, 220, 233, 234, 263, 267, 268, 277, 282, 359, 382, 384, 387, 388, 403, 405, 458, 459, 468, 495, 526, 538, 539, 541, 559, 564-566, 568, 572, 573, 583, 725, 730, 744, 791, 897, 916, 935, 1017, 1022, 1036, 1069
Cypselus of Corinth 181
Cyrenaica 204, 220, 221, 440, 707, 727, 730, 736, 744, 791, 839, 1033, 1036, 1070
Cyrene 128, 204, 421, 438, 440, 554, 561
Cyrrhestice 735, 1007
Cyrus I 49, 383
Cyrus II (the Great) 129, 185, 186, 200, 215, 216, 217, 218, 219, 220, 221, 222, 223, 224, 225, 226, 227, 228, 229, 247, 504, 516
Cyrus (son of Darius II) 354, 355, 356, 357, 358, 377, 378, 381, 382, 383, 403, 405
Cyrus (son of Pharnabazus) 354
Cythera 318, 341
Cyzica 899, 900

Cyzicus 352, 353, 891, 897
Czar 560, 888

D

Dacian(s) 1072, 1074, 1075
Dadarshi 223
Stephanie Dalley 128
Dalmatian(s) 784, 1075
Damades 476, 524, 530, 532, 533
Damas 435, 445
Damascus 22, 31, 42, 85, 112, 118, 131, 134-137, 491, 493, 497, 538, 571, 572, 726, 727, 731, 894, 895, 1037, 1067
Damasias 193
Damdamusa 133
Damisthymus 249
Damon 298
Damonides 274, 365, 366
Dan 32, 36, 37, 38, 45
Dante 168
Danton 354
Danube 225, 226, 230, 297, 469, 483, 520, 575, 590, 838, 846, 849, 898, 1037, 1055, 1071, 1072, 1074, 1075, 1077, 1083-1086
Daphnae 204
Dapyx 1037
Dardanelles 168, 188, 190, 194, 196, 198, 266, 352, 388, 485, 486, 488-490, 495, 497-499, 502-506, 508, 509, 512, 532, 539, 552, 555, 563, 568, 569, 570, 585, 589, 747, 769, 862, 863
Dardanians 169, 588, 713, 714, 716, 750, 753, 754
Darius I (the Great) 147, 186, 200, 201, 202, 215, 216, 221-236, 239, 240, 242, 246, 247, 251, 343, 345, 354, 358, 375, 377, 404, 406, 484-506, 511, 517, 526, 537, 576, 675, 738
Darius II 343, 377 *See also* Ochus
Darius III 404, 498, 505
Dascylium 269
Dasteira 893
Datames 394, 395, 402, 407
dates 57, 104, 141, 152, 174, 516, 596, 605, 612, 1057
Datis 238, 239
David 31, 32, 36-46, 51, 112, 150, 158, 576,

702, 771
Davidic dynasty 48
Davidic Zerubbabel 49
Marshal Louis Nicolas Davout 753
Dead Sea 22, 1017
Decalogue 34
Decelea 340, 343, 353, 357, 359
Deidameia 568, 570, 572
Deinocrates 443-446, 461, 463, 497
Deiotarus 899, 916, 970, 1002, 1007, 1029, 1033, 1036
Delian Confederacy 265, 266, 267, 268, 280, 287
Delian Confederation 264 See also Confederation of Delos
Delium 319, 320, 321, 325, 329, 766
Quintus Dellius 1018, 1030
Lucius Metellus Delmaticus 835, 838, 841 See also Lucius Metellus
Delminium 784
Delos 196, 236, 264-268, 270, 281, 287, 333, 370, 386, 387, 391, 409, 458, 467, 476, 557, 581, 730, 731, 742, 776, 779, 793, 867
  Synod of the League of Delos 287
Delphi 182, 187, 188, 193, 198, 199, 209, 243, 244, 246, 261, 266, 283, 302, 306, 322, 323, 393, 397, 452, 453, 455, 457, 458, 464, 465, 469, 473, 474, 486, 497, 509, 576, 589, 607, 690, 779, 782, 868
Delphians 322
Delphic Oracle 188, 189, 240, 244, 247, 266, 302, 451, 452 See also Oracle of Delphi
Demades 476, 525, 529
demagogues 193, 205, 259, 270, 289, 291, 292, 301, 335, 346, 351, 396, 564, 811, 822, 825, 833, 845, 851, 854, 874
Demagogues 290
Demaratus 209, 240, 482
Demaratus of Corinth 482
demarch 207
deme 207
Demeter 293, 418, 577
Demetrias 575, 580, 586, 723, 752, 765, 766, 768
Demetrius 445, 510, 529, 532, 536, 541, 547, 548, 551, 554, 555, 556, 559, 562, 563, 564, 565, 566, 567, 568, 569, 570, 572, 573, 574, 575, 576, 577, 578, 579, 580, 581, 582, 583, 584, 585, 586, 713, 714, 715, 716, 717, 718, 719, 720, 730, 731, 734, 741, 742, 754, 776, 778, 779, 784, 791, 862, 895
Demetrius III Eukairos 895
Demetrius II (son of Antigonas Gonatas) 713
Demetrius of Phalerum 532, 548, 563, 564
Demetrius Pharos 715, 716, 717, 719, 720
Demetrius Poliorcetes 445
Demetrius (sone of Euthydemus) 741
Demetrius (son of Antigonus) 541
Demetrius (son of Philip V) 778
Demochares 563, 568, 586
Demodocus 318
Demophantus 354
Demosthenes 315-320, 340-342, 401, 447, 450, 454, 456, 457, 459, 460-468, 470, 471, 473-477, 479, 480, 482, 484, 486, 488, 516, 524-531, 533, 563, 568, 575, 584, 586, 721, 728, 750
  First Philippic 459
  Third Philippic 470
  Fourth Philippic 471
denarius 637
Dercyllidas 382
Derdas 300
Dertosa 684
Deuteronomic Law 51
Deuteronomy 26, 32-34, 45, 48, 51, 52, 53
Thomas E. Dewy 884
Diadochi 148, 444, 536, 543, 548, 550, 551-553, 557, 562, 567-569, 571, 572, 579, 580-584, 586, 588, 591, 635, 711, 726, 732
Wars of the Diadochi 523-592
  First War of the Diadochi 536, 584
  Second War of the Diadochi 543, 548
  Third War of the Diadochi 55-553, 557, 562
  Fourth War of the Diadochi 562, 568
  Fifth War of the Diadochi 572, 580
  Sixth War of the Diadochi 581
Diaeus 796, 797
Diagoras 333
Dicaearchus 742

Dickensian 404
T. Didius 838
Dimale 717, 720
Dinocrates 518
Dio 918, 975, 1024, 1040, 1082
Diocles 413, 414
Roman Emperor Diocletian 149, 193
Diodorus 267, 268, 609, 657
Diodotus 311, 732, 735
Diodotus II 732
Diogenes 735, 794
Diognetus 737
Diomede of Argos 170
Diomedon 348
Dion (son in law of Dionysius I) 426, 427, 428, 429, 430, 431, 432
Dion of Syracuse 370
Dionysius I 234, 385, 387, 391, 397, 411, 413, 415, 416, 417, 418, 419, 420, 421, 422, 423
Dionysius II 426-437, 444-446, 508, 713
Dionysius of Phocaea 234
Dionysius of Halicarnassus 569, 597, 601, 603, 605, 612, 616, 619, 627, 641, 653, 660, 687, 688
Diopeithes 469, 470
Diophantus 863
Dipaea 270
Discord 173
Benjamin Disraeli 266, 291, 371, 468, 521, 725
dithyrambic poetry 197
Diviciacus 922, 923
Divicus 847
divination 25, 597
Djibouti 45
Docimus 541, 542, 555, 569
Dodecanese 203
dog 126, 141, 396, 578, 584
Corneius Dolabella 626, 884, 957, 969, 971, 995
Dolonci 196, 204
Dolopian 266
dolphin 187
Gnaeus Domitius 770, 839, 852, 854, 875, 883, 919, 920, 944, 953, 961, 966, 969, 970, 998, 1003, 1004, 1006, 1026, 1030, 1074
Don 225, 714
Donations of Alexandria 1022

donkeys 39, 73, 83, 96, 110, 595
Don Pacifico Affair 714
Dorcis 264
Doreius 206
Dorian(s) 22, 116, 168, 172, 174-180, 182, 184, 187, 203, 205, 219, 240, 241, 246, 279, 295, 313, 374, 402, 405, 609 See also Dymanes, Hylleis and Pamphylians
Dorian/Doric invasion 168, 172-174, 176, 177, 279
Dorian Sparta 174
Dorieus 258
Dorimachus 721, 743
Doriscus 266
Dorus 22
Antigonus Doson 716
Dowry of Mary 68
Draco 50, 106, 167, 186, 189-194, 196
Drappes 933
Dreadnaughts 296
Drepana 652, 654, 656
Dromichaetes 575
drums 143
C. Linius Drusus 808
M. Livius Drusus 828, 830, 831, 836, 838, 855, 856, 859, 865
M. Livius Drusus (the Younger) 855, 913, 1012, 1044, 1045, 1046, 1071, 1072, 1073, 1074, 1076, 1082
Dryopians 266
Drypetis 517
Dudu 58
Gaius Duilius 625, 647, 648, 650, 709, 1055
Dumnorix 922, 927
Dungi 63, 64
durbar 506
Dur Sharrukin 120
Dymanes 174 See also Dorians
Dynamis 1060, 1061
Dynasty of the Sea-Country 108
Dyrrhachium 714, 715, 717, 720, 959-964, 979, 998

E

Eannatum 57
Eastern Chou 154-156
East India Company 142, 637
Eber 22

ebony 81, 82
Ebro Treaty 662
Eburones 929, 930
Ecbatana 127, 216, 222, 223, 228, 501, 502, 505, 741, 1018
ecclesia 187, 192
Echetla 644
ecumenism 45
Edom 23, 42, 52, 83, 112
Edomites 34, 40, 52
Edwardian England 573
Edward VII 93
Egypt 17, 21, 22, 23, 26, 31, 33, 34, 36, 37, 43, 47, 48, 51, 60, 65, 67-100, 101, 110-115, 116, 119, 121-129, 131, 135-137, 140, 150, 151, 167, 168, 174, 176, 179, 181, 188, 190, 199-206, 215-221, 224, 229, 232, 240, 242, 277-282, 286, 294, 345, 376, 371, 375, 376, 382, 384, 392, 394, 395, 439, 402-409, 458, 492, 468, 469, 492, 493, 497, 509, 511, 516, 518, 519, 537, 538, 540, 541, 543, 545, 550-558, 564-567, 573, 582-585, 587-591, 596, 669, 609, 612, 624, 684, 707, 711, 713, 722, 725-732, 734-744, 748, 753, 758, 759, 762, 773, 776, 790, 791, 803, 807, 865, 866, 895, 896, 897, 898, 903, 904, 905, 916, 919, 963-969, 972, 974, 995, 1002, 1003, 1006, 1007, 1009, 1012, 1016, 1019, 1020, 1023, 1026, 1027, 1030-1036, 1038, 1040, 1042, 1050, 1052-1056, 1062, 1063, 1071, 1078, 1079, 1080, 1082, 1087
Egyptian(s) 21, 37, 45, 50, 69, 72-77, 79, 81, 84, 87, 88, 92, 93, 98, 99, 100-102, 108-111, 113, 119, 127, 129, 149, 166, 169, 179, 203, 204, 220, 224, 242, 245, 277, 366, 373, 405, 408, 497, 612, 634, 688, 718, 727, 736-738, 741, 748, 756, 966, 1017
Egyptian Dynasties
 First Dynasty 67, 108
 IInd Dynasty 67
 IIIrd Dynasty 67, 68
 IVth Dynasty 68
 VIth Dynasty 69
 XIth Dynasty 70

XIIth Dynasty 26, 70, 71
XIIIth Dynasty 71, 73
XVth and XVIth Dynasties 73
XVIIIth Dynasty 74, 409
XXXth Dynasty 407
Eion 266, 321
Dwight D. Eisenhower 263, 265, 290, 417, 673, 676, 783
Elaeus 352
Elah 49
Elam 27, 59, 61, 104, 105, 118, 120, 122, 125, 126, 216
Elamites 60, 61, 64, 103, 104, 110, 114, 115, 118, 122, 125, 135
Elatea 473, 567
Elba 351, 422, 521, 597, 708
Elder Daughter of the Church 68
Eleans 180, 181, 329, 330, 397, 399
Electra 184
Elegies of Ch'u 158
El Elyon 43
elephant(s) 82, 83, 141, 498, 511-516, 534, 541-543, 546, 547, 549, 550, 552, 555, 565, 568-570, 578, 580, 590, 648, 651, 677, 740, 752, 765, 767, 770, 772, 727, 737, 740, 752, 765, 767, 770, 772, 790, 804, 841, 934, 970, 972, 974
Eleusis 335, 336, 362-364
Eleutheria Festival 253
Eliashib 51
Elis 180, 181, 328, 330, 331, 336, 381, 396, 397, 399, 400, 464, 468, 484, 526, 586, 721, 727, 728
Queen Elizabeth I 93, 298, 371, 626
Elohim 53, 54
Elon 297
El Shaddai 53
Elymais 776
Elymians 255
Elysia 92
Emancipation Proclamation 554
embalming 72, 96
Embatum 453
embezzlement 46, 148, 309, 312, 314, 387, 660, 748, 913
Endius 353
Endor 40
Duke d'Enghien 504
Engidu 107

engineering 65, 74, 85, 151, 202, 242, 845, 848, 927
England 39, 68, 187, 279, 573, 616, 647, 668
Enkidu 27
Enlil-Ibni 104
Enlil-Narari 114
Enna 416
Enos 24
Entemena 57, 58, 59
Epaminondas 373, 392, 394, 396-398, 400-402, 415, 419, 449, 475
ephebate 525
Ephesus 175, 200-203, 233, 270, 343, 353, 358, 385-387, 543, 569-573, 579, 729, 733, 760, 763, 767-770, 772, 866, 869, 871, 1002, 1026
ephetae 187, 189
Ephialtes 208, 271-273, 276, 279, 280, 289, 291
Ephorate 183
Ephraim 32, 36, 37, 38
Ephraimite 52
Epicrates 384
The Epic Cycle 173. *See also Aethiopis* and *Cypria*
Epicurus 564
Epicydes 686-688
Epidamnus 298
Epidaurus 306, 318, 328-331, 348, 350, 868
Epigenes 354, 735
Epirus 150, 434, 435, 444, 445, 458, 477, 478, 482, 518, 536, 549-552, 555-557, 560, 567, 568, 570, 575, 577, 581, 582, 587, 627-629, 632, 634, 639, 721, 728, 731, 747, 751, 783, 784, 796, 1006, 1029
equites 600, 608, 685, 690, 832, 971 *See also* knights
Lucius Equitius 852, 853
Eratosthenes 168, 736
Erech 27, 58, 59, 63, 104, 107
Erechtheum 353
Eretria 195, 232, 460, 468
Eridu 57
Erigon 750
Erigyius 505
Eritrea 45
Erymnon 443
Erythrae 343, 386, 492

Eryxo 204
Esarhaddon 123-125, 220, 256
Esau 26, 40, 52
Esquiline 596, 600
Esther 50, 375
ethics 259, 274, 481, 597, 836
Ethiopia 22, 36, 44, 45, 71, 76, 201, 205, 220, 225, 226, 404, 443, 469, 511
Ethiopian(s) 408, 1056
Etrurians 258, 595, 597, 614, 621, 646, 875
Etruscan League 609, 610
Etruscans 95, 215, 257, 258, 423-425, 518, 597, 598, 606, 608, 609, 612-614, 616, 618-623, 626, 627, 646, 663, 664
Euboea 266, 283, 284, 286, 305, 343, 350, 351, 353, 390, 402, 460, 463, 468, 470, 531, 555, 567, 575, 577, 723, 752, 869
Euboeans 350, 384, 450, 531, 757
Eubulus 456, 457, 459-463
Eucles 318, 320, 321
Euclid 583
Eucrates 291
Eudicus 454
Eudoxus of Cyzicus 897
Euergetes of Pontus 837
Euergetes (nephew of Philopator) 863
Euetion 532
Eulaeus 791
Eumachus 441
Eumenes 523, 534, 535, 536, 537, 538, 539, 540, 541, 542, 543, 544, 545, 546, 547, 548, 551, 553, 556, 560, 569, 571, 579, 728, 729, 733
Eumenes (king of Pergamon) 754, 762, 763, 768, 769, 770, 772, 773, 777, 778, 779, 780, 781, 790, 791, 792, 822, 835, 837
Eunomia, Spartan law 182
Eunus 821
Euphrates 27, 45, 57-60, 65, 78-85, 93, 107, 108, 111, 113-116, 122, 127, 131, 133, 134, 222, 378, 483, 497, 498, 518, 741, 862, 865, 893, 894, 899, 938, 940, 980, 1006, 1007, 1017, 1037, 1058, 1059, 1061, 1063, 1064, 1083
Eurasia 82, 126, 140, 579
Euremydon 313

Euripides 184, 294, 333, 357, 366, 526, 940
Euro-Americans 23
Europa 482
Europe 17, 21-24, 36, 73, 75, 79, 98, 110, 116-118, 126, 131, 141-143, 153-155, 160, 164, 169, 178, 196, 210, 215, 225, 226, 256, 257, 259, 262, 266-268, 274, 286, 294, 334, 342, 366, 374, 375, 408, 425, 426, 443, 451, 463, 466, 468, 478, 506, 517, 523, 526, 534, 537, 541, 542, 545, 546, 554, 556, 582, 585, 588, 590, 605, 627, 647, 670, 673, 698, 708, 755, 756, 758, 759, 768, 769, 771, 772, 775, 793, 848, 849, 870, 899, 930, 1069, 1071
   Western Europe 17, 21, 73, 75, 142, 160, 226, 256, 257, 334, 408, 673
Euryalus 688
Eurybiades 245, 248, 250
Eurydice 448, 475, 478, 482, 536, 538, 540, 541, 543, 546, 549, 550, 559, 573, 574, 579, 582, 585, 588, 590
Eurydice (wife of Phillip III) 538
Eurydice (wife of Ptolemy) 538
Eurylochus 315, 765
Eurymedon 267, 268, 314, 315, 316, 340, 341
Eurymedon River 267
Eusebius 181
Euthydemus 741
Evaenetus 244
Evagoras 51, 382, 383, 384, 386, 387, 394, 406
Evander 596
Exodus 33, 34, 53
extortion 83, 90, 148, 152, 660, 801, 902, 903, 913, 1053
Eye 88, 90, 530
Ezekiel 23, 52, 54, 216
Ezra 49, 50, 51, 113, 229, 376

F

Quintus Fabius 498, 546, 622, 623, 658-711, 720, *See also* Quintus Fabius Maximus
   Quintus Fabius' son 692
Fabius Maximus (brother of Scipio Aemilianus) 804, 832, 839, 978, 982

Fabricaria 827
Fabricius 628, 631-633
Faisabad 508
Falerii 614, 660
Gaius Fannius 829
Far East 139, 219, 894
Felsina 609
the Fens 281, 282
Ferdinand and Isabella 727
Ferentinum/Ferentium 607, 614, 622
W.S. Ferguson 342
Fertile Crescent 23
feted corpse(s) 75
Leon Feuchtwanger 445
Gaius Marcius Figulus 784
Gaius Flavius Fimbria 870, 871
Finland 566
five elements 158
Five Years' Truce 283
Lucius Valerius Flaccus 873, 877
Marcus Fulvius Flaccus 826, 827, 832, 838
Norbanus Flaccus 998
Q. Horatius Flaccus 995, 998
Quintus Flavius Flaccus 692, 692, 694, 699, 701
flamines 599
Flaminian meadows 602
Via Flaminia 623, 679, 699, 700, 952, 1038, 1042, 1051
T. Quinctius Flamininus 740, 751, 752, 753, 754, 755, 756, 757, 758, 759, 760, 761, 763, 764, 765, 766, 767, 768, 772, 774, 776, 779, 783, 790, 795, 804, 809, 813, 867, 1087
Gaius Flaminius 663, 665, 668, 675
Lex Flaminius 663
Lucius Flavius 912
Flood 26, 27, 57, 140
Aquilius Florus 648
flutes 143
Ferdinand Foch 265, 360
Foedus Cassianum 605
Tiberius Fonteius 690
Gerald Ford 357
Forum Boarium 690
Four Years' War 567
Charles James Fox 266
France 68, 73, 98, 100, 175, 194, 195, 197, 202, 205, 206, 254, 263, 277-280, 354, 360, 361, 384, 387, 388, 424,

425, 433, 461, 487, 567, 588, 598,
599, 603, 605, 647, 667, 672, 673,
683, 684, 693, 719, 733, 775, 794,
801, 802, 808, 809, 815, 838, 934,
935, 1005, 1041, 1049, 1071, 1072,
1087
Francisco Franco 111, 850
Franco-German wars 111
T. Frank 639
Benjamin Franklin 16, 46, 73, 192, 290,
291, 367, 375, 425, 523, 676, 1045
Fravartish 222, 223
Frederick the Great 132, 304, 428, 446,
475, 520, 570, 614, 626, 887
Frederick William III 753
Fregellae 620, 621, 827, 832
French 22, 40, 129, 131, 204, 220, 224, 225,
236, 256, 257, 286, 288, 289, 293,
348, 359, 361, 366, 367, 390, 396,
422, 466, 521, 524, 534, 535, 581,
743, 766, 769, 794, 863, 917, 932,
934, 935, 985, 1042, 1076
French Academy 367, 794
French Third Republic 348, 359
Lucius Fufidius 882
Fulvia 1000, 1001, 1002, 1003, 1016, 1020
Gnaeus Fulvius Centumalus 623, 650, 693,
694, 714, 715, 717
M. Fulvius Nobilior 771, 773, 774
L. Fulvius 619
Servius Fulvius 650
Fundi 619
Publius Furius 854
Sp. Furius 615

G

A. Gabinius 889
Gades 424, 425, 661, 696-698, 703
Gaesylus 430
Galatia 772, 837, 863, 864, 893, 899, 916,
969, 1002, 1005, 1007, 1017, 1062
Sulpicius Galba 693, 722, 944
Gallic Wars 608, 920-941, 1035
Gallipoli 168, 387, 402, 558
Aelius Gallus 1056, 1057
C. Lucretius Gallus 781
Cornelius Gallus 1028, 1042, 1056
Gandara 226
Gandash 109
Gandhara 147

Gandhi 88, 146
Ganges 140, 143, 145, 148, 511
Ganymedes 966, 967
R. Gardner 876
Garonne Valley 846
Gashnu 50
Gath 41
Gauda 844
Gaul(s) 21, 131, 419-422, 431, 433, 588-
590, 605-616, 619-626, 636, 637,
641, 642, 645, 646, 662-669, 672-
677, 682, 691, 693, 699, 700, 703,
716, 717, 732-734, 739, 762, 800,
808-812, 836, 838, 839, 849, 878,
885, 906, 907, 910-930, 932, 934,
939, 957, 977, 1004, 1006, 1045,
1054, 1055, 1072, 1073, 1076, 1077
Charles de Gaulle 16, 184, 242, 275, 325,
328, 362, 369, 425, 535, 626, 649,
676, 702, 719, 749, 835, 836, 850,
934, 1042, 1045
Gaumata 221-224, 226, 242
Sidhartha Gautama 139, 145, 146
Gaza 21, 32, 37, 38, 48, 52, 80, 112, 118,
119, 137, 220, 103, 197, 554, 555,
736, 737, 744, 748
Gedrosia 504, 514
L. Geganius 615
Gela 259, 314, 319, 415, 436, 438, 443
Gelo 686
Gelon 259, 260, 261, 262
Gnaeus Servilius Geminus 675
General Plenipotentiary 437, 443, 444
Genesis 22, 26, 32, 33, 34, 53, 54
Genghis Khan 216, 521, 887
Genoa 205, 637, 703, 704, 706, 809, 1079
Genthius 782, 784
Gentiles 52
L. Genucius 614
geographers 482
King George VI 93
Gergovia 931, 932, 942
German(s) 21-24 73, 90,, 93, 104, 111,
129, 131, 201, 225, 250, 278, 286,
348, 422, 466, 487, 524, 648, 673,
684, 701, 729, 730, 809, 846, 847,
849, 855, 863, 884, 921-927, 931,
932, 933, 935, 967, 971, 985, 1012,
1042, 1049, 1055, 1067, 1072, 1073,
1076, 1077, 1083

1114

Germania 44
Germanicus 1073, 1076
Germany 22, 225, 230, 241, 270, 279, 346, 359, 360, 361, 367, 425, 426, 451, 461, 588, 625, 673, 704, 719, 725, 775, 776, 784, 846, 925, 927, 1044, 1055, 1063, 1069, 1072-1077, 1084
Gerontes 183
Gerousia 183
Getae 469, 483, 575
Gibbeonites 36
Gibeah 39
Gibeon 32, 40
Gibeonites 40
Gibraltar 199, 256, 259, 296, 424, 425, 443, 655, 661, 695, 799, 802
André Gide 41
Gideon 36
Gilead 32, 36
Gilgal 32, 36
Gilgamesh 27
Epic of Gilgamesh 107
Gimil-Sin 64
Girraimaiti 104
Rudolph Giuliani 884
Gizeh 68
Gaius Claudius Glabera 885
Marcus Acilius Glabrio 767, 889
William Ewart Gladstone 266, 271, 289, 291, 371
glass-blowing/making 72, 85
Gaius Servilius Glaucia 852
Glaucias of the Taulantii 483, 554, 567, 713
Glaucon 578, 727
Glaucus 260
Glorious Revolution 216
T. R. Glover 521
goat 141, 293
Gobryas 222
Joseph Goebbels 348
Hermann Goering 725
Johann Wolfgang von Goethe 168, 313, 366
gold 45, 64, 72, 74, 80-82, 84, 96, 101, 120, 147, 185, 228, 295, 298, 356, 424, 451, 457, 486, 488, 514, 519, 525, 527, 574, 583, 631, 655, 669, 672, 684, 696-698, 738, 740, 761, 783, 797, 802, 803, 831, 832, 844, 847, 853, 866, 883, 902, 954, 1022, 1038, 1050, 1057, 1079, 1084
golden apple 173
Golden Calf 34
Golden Fleece 168
Goliath 40, 43, 613
Mikhail Gorbachev 89, 307, 350, 365
Gordian Knot 16, 501, 509
Gordium 354, 489
Gordius 489, 864, 865
Gorgias 313
Gorgo 232
Gorgobina 931, 932
Gorgon 168
Goshen 32, 33
Gaius Gracchus 815, 817, 822, 825-835, 838, 845, 852, 855, 860, 909, 979
Tiberius Sempronius Gracchus 426, 691, 692, 798, 801, 802, 809-811, 816-827, 829, 830, 832, 834-836, 852, 874, 890, 904, 1087
Tiberius Gracchus (nephew of the elder, father of the brothers) 816
Tiberius Gracchus (the elder) 816
grain 58, 72, 77, 95, 115, 125, 164, 190, 191, 196, 221, 242, 266, 296, 297, 304, 306, 310, 314, 345, 351, 352, 358, 390, 407, 432, 439, 458, 470, 471, 476, 528, 558, 564, 574, 581, 604, 645, 655, 659, 660, 727, 792, 798, 803, 829, 852, 863, 872, 876, 878, 884, 890, 891, 903, 906, 915, 921, 961, 977, 991, 995, 1002, 1004, 1011, 1029, 1032, 1036, 1038, 1051, 1056, 1057, 1061, 1087
Grande Armee 484
Granicus River 487
Ulysses S. Grant 673, 683, 693, 708
Robert Graves 184
G.H. Gray 222, 230
Great Burning of Books 159
Great Dionysia 322
Great Gallic Revolt 930
Great King of Persia 49, 50, 83, 147, 197, 198, 200-202, 204, 209, 217, 218, 223-236, 239, 241-243, 246, 247, 250, 251, 253, 254, 259, 261, 263, 264, 265, 267, 269, 270, 272, 275, 276-279, 281, 282, 288, 296, 297, 303, 304, 307, 309, 311, 343, 344,

347, 353, 354, 357, 358, 362, 374-378, 381-383, 387, 388, 393-396, 398, 401, 403-407, 468, 469, 471, 484, 486, 489, 490-495, 497, 499, 501-503, 505-507, 509, 511, 513, 515, 517, 519, 584, 590, 637, 711, 715, 723, 724, 726, 728, 735, 741, 755, 758, 759, 762-770, 772
Great Pyramid 17, 68
Great Samnite War 620
Great Wall of China 160
Greece's Age of Illumination 365
Andrei Gromyko 68
Guadalcanal 231
Guadalquivir River 256, 424, 655
Guadiana 662
Gudea 62, 63
Guercino 31
guillotine 100
Gula-Bau-Ninkharsag 64
Gulashkird 515, 516
Gulf of Antioch 123
Gulf of Aqaba 32
Gulf of Corinth 276, 283, 286, 307, 308, 309, 313, 329, 398
Gulf of Salamis 246, 247
Gulussa 805, 807, 839, 840
Gutium 62, 63
Gyges 124
Gylippus 338-341
Gymnetes 655
Gytheum 280

H

Habron 564
Hadrumetum 707, 708
Hagnonides 529, 533, 548
Hakori 407 *See also* Achoris
Halcyoneus 728
Haliartus 384
Halicarnassus 203, 220, 249, 451, 487, 488, 585, 755
H.R. Hall 69, 71, 124, 405
Halliesis 279
B. L. Hallward 675, 687, 700, 709
Halonnesus 468, 470
Halus 462
Halycus River 434
Halys River 128, 216
Ham 22

Haman 50
Hamath 118, 119, 134, 136
Hamilcar 261, 262
Hamilcar Barca (father of Hannibal) 646, 648, 653, 654, 656, 658-664, 668, 669, 700, 702, 706, 805
Hamilcar Gisgo 414, 431, 433, 438, 439, 442, 443,
Hamilcar (son of Gisgo) 438
Alexander Hamilton 46, 266, 291
Hammurabi 26, 103-108, 114, 115, 150, 576
Hampsicoras 685
Han 155, 156, 158-165
Han Dynasty 161
Han Fei 158, 160
Han Hsin 162
Hanigalbat 111, 132
Hannibal (the Great) 414, 424, 485, 498, 520, 546, 571, 630, 631, 654, 658-709, 666, 668-711, 717-722, 738, 748, 749, 760-763, 765, 767, 768, 769, 771, 773, 774, 790, 801, 804, 808, 809, 810, 811, 816, 820, 846, 848, 849, 883, 884, 887, 898, 955, 963, 979, 1035
Hannibal (defender of Agrigentum) 646-648
Hannibal the admiral 640, 641, 644
Hanno (1) 425, 439, 441
Hanno (2) 653, 654, 658, 659, 661, 672, 673, 675, 683, 688, 689, 692, 696, 703
Hanno (son of Hannibal the admiral) 644, 646
Victor Davis Hanson 289
Harappa 140, 141
harem 40, 43, 44, 94, 100, 110, 266, 375, 403, 895, 899
Harmhab 87, 89-92
Harmodius 198
Harpalus 242, 502, 512, 516, 528, 529, 537
harpax 1013, 1029
Harran 127, 129
Harris Papyrus 100
Hasdrubal (1) 426, 433
Hasdrubal (2) 651, 652
Hasdrubal (3) 803, 804, 805, 806, 807, 808
Hasdrubal Barca 662, 664, 669, 672, 684, 689, 695-697, 699

Hasdrubal Gisgo 700, 703, 704, 705, 717
Hasdrubal the Bald 685
Hasdrubal the Fair 662
Hasmonaeans 51, 1017
Warren Hastings 1087
'1Makere-Hatshepsut 80, 83
Hattic people 110
Hattushil 92, 93
Hattushil III 111
Baron Georges-Eugene Haussmann 667
Hazael 134, 135
Hebrews 21, 23
Hebron 31, 32, 41, 52
Hecataeus 231
Hecatomnus 387
Hector 173, 421
Hegesianax of Alexandria in the Troad 758
Hegesippus 468
Hegesistratus 196
Heggai 49
Helen 168, 170, 173, 189
Helenus 634
Helepolis 566
Heliopolis 68, 82, 95
Helladic period 167
Hellene 22, 198, 242, 278, 279, 286, 325, 333, 394, 766
Hellenic League 470, 519, 532, 572, 716, 752
Hellenization 167, 172, 175, 177, 180
Hellespont 168, 169, 176, 203, 215, 233, 235, 242, 248, 250, 253, 265, 296, 297, 343, 352, 358, 375, 448, 458, 470, 471, 541, 747, 752, 758, 765, 768, 769, 998
Helmund River 504
Heloris 419
helots 174, 185, 196, 252, 268, 269, 272, 316, 317, 318, 326, 396
Helvetii 921, 922
Hephaestion 510, 511, 514, 517, 518, 534, 536, 550
Hephaestus 173
Heptastadium 967
Heraclea 185, 380, 384, 385, 428, 569, 570, 572, 573, 583, 585, 627, 632, 633, 644, 646, 648, 687, 729, 796, 899, 1036
Heraclea Minoa 428

Heracleans 380
Heracleides 428-430, 435-437, 518, 742, 743
Heracleopolis 70
Heracleopolites 70
Heracles 481, 494, 512, 514, 558, 559, 692
Heraclitus 203
Herbessus 416
Herbita 416
Hercules 119, 168, 174, 178, 199, 425, 486, 596
Appius Herdonius 606
Hermae 360
Hermaean Point 650
Carian Hermeias 735
Hermeias 469, 470
Hermione 172
Hermocrates 314, 337-340, 342, 344, 349, 413-415
Hermolaus 510
Mt. Hermon 32, 134
Hermunduri 1074
Hernici 606, 613-615, 620, 622, 646
Herod (the Great) 896, 899, 1002, 1005, 1006, 1008, 1017, 1026, 1033, 1036, 1037, 1058, 1064, 1065, 1066, 1067, 1068, 1072, 1087
Herodotus 49, 68, 70, 147, 168, 174, 176, 177, 181, 184, 186, 195, 199, 200, 202, 206, 207, 209, 220, 229, 230, 232, 237, 246, 249, 250, 252, 256, 262, 424, 511, 597
Heroic Age of Greece 168, 186
Hezekiah of Judah 122
Hicetas 431, 432, 433
Hiero 625, 641-647, 653, 656, 659, 660, 674, 683, 686, 689, 698, 703, 708
Hieronymous of Cardia 540
Hieronymus 575, 686
C. Hignett 934
Himalayas 140, 146, 509
Himera 260, 261, 336, 339, 413, 414
Himeraeans 339
Himeras River 689
Himilco 414, 415, 417, 418, 425, 687-689
Paul von Hindenburg 360
Hindu Kush 140, 505, 511, 741
Hindustan 511
hipparch 507, 534, 723
Hipparchus 197, 198, 208, 241

Hipparinus 430
Hippias 197-199, 206, 208-210, 230, 232, 236, 238, 241
Hippo 433, 654
Hippocrates 259, 260
Hippocrates (Pericles' nephew) 318-321
Hippocrates (Cartheginian envoy/Syricusan gneral) 686, 687
Hipponax 202, 203
Hipponicus 276
Hipponium 419, 627, 628
Hippo of Messana 433
Hippos 191, 192
Hiram of Tyre 45
Gustav Hirschfeld 1049
Hirtius 946, 993
Hirtuleius 883
Histiaeus of Miletus 226
Adolf Hitler 16, 44, 78, 82, 90, 93, 121, 160, 201, 216, 224, 225, 229, 230, 236, 242, 250, 268, 275, 286, 303, 304, 325, 341, 342, 346, 348, 360, 375, 415, 451, 466, 510, 521, 570, 673, 804, 1073
Hittites 21, 22, 37, 46, 47, 60,-64, 73, 82-86, 88-95, 98, 103, 108-116, 128, 129, 169, 171-174, 223, 224, 371, 422, 861, 862
H.M.S. Hood 487
Ho Chi Minh 362, 771
David George Hogarth 23
Tom Holland 868
Maurice Holleaux 719, 743
Holy Alliance 197, 210
Holy Roman Empire 279, 849
Holy See 77
Homanades 1062
Homer 167, 168, 171-175, 177, 184, 186, 188, 194, 293, 452, 551, 713
Honan 151, 152, 155
honey 41, 77
J. Edgar Hoover 68
Hophra 128, 201
hoplite(s) 179, 191, 192, 304, 311, 867
Horace 199, 653, 1025, 1032, 1084
Horatio 605
M. Horatius 615
Horatius Pulvillus 601
Hortensian Law 638, 643, 667, 710
Hortensius 868, 889, 892, 944

Lucius Hortensius 868
Horus 75
Hotepsekheumi 67
Sam Houston 688
Hsia dynasty 152
Hsiang Yu 161
Duke Hsiao 156
Hsien-yang 159
Hsiung-nu 160, 164
Hsun Ch'ing 157
Duke of Huan 155
Huang Ti 152
Victor Hugo 934
human sacrifice 426
Hungnu 408
Huns 160
Hupei 152
King Hussein of Jordan 449
Aldous Huxley 203
Hybla 336
Hydarnes 222, 223, 245, 246, 345, 383
Hydaspes River 147, 512
Hyksos 28, 72-83, 95, 98, 101, 110, 172, 174, 219, 408, 606, 612
Hylleis 174 *See also* Dorians
hymns 88, 144, 600, 1081
hypaspists 495, 514, 515, 518, 540, 541, 737
Hyperbolus 314, 328, 331, 348
Hypereides 475, 524, 529, 530, 532, 533
Hyrcania 223, 503, 735, 741
Hyrcanian Sea 518
Hyrcanus 895, 970, 1002, 1005, 1036, 1064-1067
Hysiae 179
Hystaspes 221-223, 228, 375, 406

I

Iago 427
Iberia 256, 424, 425, 639, 670, 689, 800-802, 883
Iberian(s) 424-426, 661, 802
Ibi-Sin 64
Ibiza 424
Ides of March 976, 982, 987
idolatry 45
Idrieus 488
Ikhnaton 25, 47, 87-90, 93, 94, 96, 97, 111, 113, 114
The Iliad 171-173, 194, 481

Ilici 661, 662
Ilium 170, 486, 557, 772, 984
Illyria 420, 451, 466, 478, 483, 554, 556, 576, 586, 669, 670, 681, 685, 686, 692, 712, 713, 715, 716, 718, 719, 720, 725, 728, 747, 750, 752, 782, 783, 784, 838, 1006, 1024
Illyrian(s) 451, 483, 588, 713, 714, 715, 716, 771, 1006, 1077
Illyricum 963, 1003, 1027, 1038, 1059, 1069, 1070, 1072, 1075, 1076
Iluma-ilu 108
Ilus 170
Imbros 386, 388, 451, 458, 476, 581
Imhotep 67
Immortals 245, 246, 251
Imperial University 163
Inachus Valley 178
Inaros 277, 281, 376, 405, 406
Inchon 440
India 17, 22, 23, 24, 45, 79, 88, 129, 139-155, 163, 164, 165, 166, 219, 225, 226, 227, 228, 408, 409, 422, 425, 483, 501, 503, 507, 509-511, 513-516, 518, 521, 537, 539, 587, 590, 637, 669, 673, 711, 726, 739, 741, 897, 1021, 1056-1058, 1077, 1079, 1086-1089
Indian Ocean 61, 85, 98, 140, 226, 511, 514, 515, 897, 1057
Indibilis 690, 695, 698, 703
Indigetes 655
Indochina 165
Indo-European 22, 23, 25, 142, 164
Indortes 661
Indus River 140, 226, 511
Industrial Revolution 47, 603
Indutiomarus 929
Ineni 80
infamia 608
The Influence of Sea Power on History 672
Innini 59
Instructions of King Sehetepibre 70
Insubres 609, 664, 666, 673-675
Insubrians 666, 667, 675, 808, 809
Intaphranes 222
Intef 70
Interstate Highway Program 290
Invalides 254, 360
Ion 22

Ionian Confederacy 232
Ionian League 557
Ionian migration 175
Ionian Rebellion/Revolt 201, 230
Ionians 22, 174, 176, 196, 203, 219, 232, 233, 235, 236, 259, 263, 264, 313, 374, 402, 405, 609
Ionian Sea 713, 714
Iphicrates 385, 387, 391, 394, 396, 402, 407, 447, 448, 453
Ipsus 570, 572, 575, 577, 584
Iran 21, 23, 60, 61, 64, 79, 108, 110, 118, 119, 121, 216, 239, 374, 502, 503, 557, 568, 569, 726, 732, 1086
Iraq 21, 47, 120, 131, 278, 569
Ireland 190, 256, 424
iron 37, 143, 154, 160, 162, 165, 169, 264, 379, 380, 426, 508, 535, 555, 565, 597, 599, 611, 653, 655, 783, 825, 862, 874, 886, 1029, 1079
Iron Age 47, 151, 167, 168, 596, 609, 862
Iron Gate 589
irrigation 27, 65, 71, 116, 120, 121, 144, 154, 162
Isaac 31
Isaac of Antioch 25
Isagoras 206, 207
Isaiah 46, 52, 53, 54, 122
Isfahan 547
Ishbaal 42
Ishbi-Girra 104
Ishtar 60, 107
Isin 27, 103, 104, 106, 108
Alexander Isios 743
Isis 74, 80, 113, 409, 1017, 1033
Islam 24, 46, 49, 72
Islamabad 147
Isocrates 292, 390, 466, 485, 493, 509
Isodemus 181
Isodice 265
Israel 17, 21, 22, 25, 26, 31-49, 52, 53, 54, 55, 112, 94, 102, 111, 118, 121, 127, 129, 134, 137, 176, 151, 194, 196, 258, 556, 639, 688, 726, 895, 896, 1067, 1065
Israelites 26, 32, 37, 47, 48
Istanbul 82, 204, 383, 1087
Isthmian Festival 387, 757
Isthmian games 716, 758
Istolatius 661

Istrians 809
Italian(s) 22, 205, 257, 278, 417, 419, 420, 431, 434, 441, 444, 524, 598, 607, 609, 616, 619, 623-625, 627, 628, 634-636, 639, 640, 642, 647, 656, 661, 663, 666, 672, 675, 678, 679, 691, 702, 705, 706, 713, 714, 721, 761, 765, 772, 809, 819, 820, 826, 827, 828, 831, 834, 836, 838, 840, 841, 843, 855, 856, 866, 875, 877, 883, 891, 893, 954, 955, 958, 968, 996, 1011, 1012, 1025, 1027, 1029, 1051, 1059, 1077, 1080, 1083, 1084
Italica 698, 883
Ithaca 170, 173, 175
ius 600
Ius Provocationis 193
ivory 45, 82, 141, 147, 295, 298, 424, 1033
Iwo Jima 231, 318

J

Andrew Jackson 46, 291
Jacob 26, 31, 33, 34, 40, 51-53, 887
Jacobins 286
Jainas 146
Jalalibad 511
Janicular Hill 906
King James I 39
Janiculum hill 600
Jannaeus 895
Japan 146, 149, 241, 471, 489, 626, 704, 784
Japanese 408, 471, 729, 767
Japheth 22
Jason and the Argonauts 168
Jason of Pherae 391, 393
Jason of Thessaly 393
Jauf 568
Jaxartes River 506
Jebusites 32, 36, 41
Thomas Jefferson 46, 266, 274, 291
Jehoiachin 128
Jehoiakim 128
Jehovah 17, 22, 24, 31, 32, 34, 36-41, 43, 44, 52-54, 68
Jehu 49, 134
Jena 753
Jenkins' Ear 170, 628
Jeremeel 52
Jeremiah 46, 52, 54, 128, 204

Jeroboam 48, 49
Jerusalem 32, 33, 36, 41, 43, 45, 46, 48-54, 111, 118, 121-123, 128, 228, 376, 497, 572, 894, 895, 937, 970, 973, 1005, 1008, 1021, 1064-1068
Jesse 40, 41
Jesus Christ 33, 46, 370, 895, 986, 1082
Jethro 31
Jews 17, 21, 22, 24, 25, 31-38, 40-53, 55, 65, 102, 108, 112, 113, 115, 116, 124, 126-129, 149, 150, 167, 168, 178, 179, 183, 185, 201, 203, 204, 224, 228, 229, 271, 293, 376, 423, 523, 576, 596, 862, 866, 895, 896, 969, 988, 994, 995, 1002, 1005, 1008, 1065-1068, 1088
Jhelum 512, 514
Joab 42, 44
Joan of Arc 369, 695
Job 53, 1068
Dr. Samuel Johnson 366
Jonathan 40, 41, 46
Sir William Jones 142
Jonestown, Guyana 403
Jordan 21-24, 32, 34, 40, 42, 49, 50, 78, 81, 82, 90, 294, 449, 726, 737, 895
Jordan River 32, 40, 50, 90
Jordan Valley 78
Joseph 16, 36, 40, 77, 1006
Josephus 1059
Joshua 32, 34, 36, 48, 51, 52
Josiah 204
Jotham 37
Juba 955-957, 964, 971-974, 1070
Judah 32, 33, 36-38, 42, 112, 40-46, 48-52, 54, 111, 112, 121-123, 126, 128, 201
Judaism 18, 24, 25, 32, 41, 49, 50, 52, 54, 55, 376, 1066, 1082
Judea 33, 48, 51, 896, 970, 1006, 1007, 1008, 1017, 1036, 1053, 1064, 1065, 1067, 1068, 1082, 1087
judgeships 77
Jugurtha 839-844, 849
Jugurthine War 841, 844, 845, 847
Junius Brutus 600, 601, 882
Junonia 831, 839, 979
Justin 147
Justinian 106
Jutland 279, 423, 648, 729, 1074
Juvenal 381

K

Kablinu 127
Kabul 505, 511, 569, 572, 741
Kadashman-Kharbe 114
Kadashman-Turgu 114
Kadesh 34, 79, 80, 81, 83, 91, 92, 110, 111, 169, 988
Kaiser 888
Kalakh 133
Kalinga 149
Kamenev 241
Kames 74
Kandahar 504, 505
Kansu 154, 160
Immanuel Kant 203
Kaoshan Pass 511
Kao-Tsu 162, 163, 165 See also Liu Pang
Kapilavastu 145
Karkar 134
Karnak 70, 80-82, 84, 90, 93, 98
Karos 801
Kash 111
Kashmir 150, 512, 541, 557
Kashtiliash III 115
Kassites 22, 73, 107-110, 114, 115, 174
Kautilya 148
Kazakhstan 508
John F. Kennedy 190, 834
Kerala 150
Keraunos 582-586, 588-590
Khafre 68
Khalkin Gol 471
Imran Khan 190
Khasekhemui 67
Khayub Pass 505
Kheta 84
Khinani 133
Khindanu 132
Khingans 408
Khufu 68 See also Cheops
Khumbaba 27
Khutouire Ugafa 71
Kinabu 132
Mackenzie King 192
King's Peace 388-390, 394, 395, 398, 405, 407, 421, 761
Kirgizstan 508
Kirkuk 62
Kish 27, 28, 39, 57-60, 63, 104, 108

Kishon 36
Henry Kissinger 357
K.M. Bismarck 487
knights 191, 192, 359, 620, 685, 817, 820, 823, 832, 852, 860, 938, 941, 997, 1046, 1049, 1078 See also equites
The Knights 318
kolekktretai 187
Königsberg 203
Koprates 546
Korean Peninsula 440
Kosala 145
Jerzy Kosinski 104
Kshatriyas 143
Kuan Chung 155
kung 155
K'ung fu-tzu 156 See also Confucius
Kurigalzu III 114
Kush 78, 84, 91, 101, 140, 505, 511, 741
General Mikhail Kutuzov 371
Kwangsi 160
Kwangtung 159, 160
Kyinda 545

L

Labashi-Marduk 129
Labici 607
Titus Labienus 905, 924, 929-932, 946, 952, 954, 955, 959, 960, 962, 968, 971, 973, 978, 987, 1005-1007, 1035, 1045
Lacedaemon 169, 174
Lacedaemonian(s) 197, 262, 279 322, 323, 329
Lacedes 180
Lacetani 978
Lachares 573, 574
Laches 314, 329, 330
Laconia 174, 180, 350, 385, 396, 477, 723, 760, 764, 774
Laelius 703, 704, 705, 707
Laemedon 543
L. Aemilius Paullus 681, 781 See also Aemilius
Gaius Popillius Laenas 613, 801, 829, 846
Valerius Laevinus 630, 689, 693, 694, 699, 703, 720, 721
Lagash 57, 58, 59, 62, 64
Laki 132, 133
Lamachus 335, 336, 338, 339

La Mancha 800
Lamblichus of Emesa 1002
Lamia 531, 567, 722
Lamian War 531, 560
Lampsacan(s) 196, 198
Lampsacus 235, 265, 358, 366, 486, 491, 492, 564, 568, 569, 755, 756, 759, 762, 765, 769
Lanassa 445, 576, 633
Stephen H. Langdon 58, 60, 61, 62, 63
Lanuvium 619
Laodice 730, 732, 733, 736, 779, 862, 864
Lao Tzu 157
Larak 57
Larinum 680
Larissa 454
Larsa 59, 103-106
Larsan(s) 104
Las 350, 774
Hugh Last 872, 884
Lateran Palace 84
Latian 595
Latin 22, 142, 195, 420, 421, 425, 595-598, 605-612, 614, 615, 619, 621, 622, 631, 636, 637, 641, 655, 657, 664, 688, 691, 694, 803, 810, 831, 836, 854, 903, 935, 980, 983-985, 997, 1024, 1038, 1043, 1052, 1089
Latin League 603, 605, 606, 611, 615
Lauriston Hills 518
Laurium 241
Laus 434
law code 105
T.E. Lawrence 394
League of Aeolian cities 557
League of Corinth 482, 484, 487, 492, 493, 495, 497, 501-503, 517, 523, 557, 561, 568
League of Islanders 557
League of Nations 181
League of Nuceria 620
Leah 34
Lebadea 475
Lebanese 25, 52, 70, 80, 83, 84, 98, 116, 256, 553
Lebanese cedar 80, 98, 116, 553
Lebanon 21, 32, 37, 38, 48, 60, 62, 79, 90, 94, 97, 116, 133, 294, 572, 573, 726
Lebedus 343
Robert E. Lee 683, 693, 708, 982
Legalists 158
Thomas Leland 479
lembi 713-715, 717-720
Lemnos 171, 386, 388, 451, 457, 458, 476, 564, 581
Nicholas Lempière 731
Vladimir Lenin 44, 241, 361, 535, 733
Lucius Cornelius Lentulus 634, 703, 755, 758, 759, 885, 907, 918, 920, 944, 953, 958, 1074
Leochtydas 254
Leocrates 527
Leon 184, 344, 348, 367, 445
Leon and Agesicles (Spartan kings) 184
Leonidas 245-247
Leonnatus 531, 532, 534, 535, 536, 537, 538, 539, 560
Leontini 296, 313, 334, 415-417, 429, 431-433, 443, 444, 644, 686, 687
Leosthenes 530-532
Leotychidas 240, 254, 262-264
M. Aemilius Lepidus (senatorial legate) 746, 747
Marcus Lepidus (the elder, consul) 859, 881-884
Marcus Aemilius Lepidus (triumvir) 954, 957, 958, 977, 981, 985-987, 989, 992-996, 998-1003, 1012-1014, 1019, 1024, 1025, 1029, 1030, 1032, 1043, 1045, 1081
Lepini Mountains 606
Lepreum 329
Leptines 418, 420, 421, 432, 641
Leptis Magna 706
Lesbos 171, 173, 174, 190, 203, 232, 234, 235, 263, 269, 287, 310, 343, 355, 391, 448, 490
Leucas 315, 468, 470, 1029
Leucimne 298
Leuctra 392, 393, 396, 400, 419, 450
Levant 51, 112, 115, 116, 119, 128, 137, 175-179, 190, 196, 254, 256, 261, 350, 371, 405, 491, 526, 590, 614, 726, 732, 736, 772, 966, 1009, 1058, 1077
Levi 33
Levites 34, 52
Leviticus 33, 53
Lex Claudia 675, 710
Lex Frumentaria 835

Lex Julia 858
Lex Licinia Mucia 854
Lex Orchi 804
Lex Plautia Papiria 858
Lex Sempronia Agraria 821
Lex Voconia 804
Liaoning 154
Libyans 78, 91, 95-98, 110, 168, 277, 408, 433, 439, 440, 442, 518, 737
Libys 363
Lichas 345
Licinian Law 611, 616
Marcus Licinius 792, 875, 886, 910, 1037
Ligurians 424, 433, 645, 663, 809
Lilybaeum 433, 633, 642, 644, 650, 652, 656, 674, 703, 1013
Abraham Lincoln 46, 242, 275, 554, 683, 888
Charles Lindbergh 375
Lindus 234, 503
Lingayen Gulf 561
lions 46, 85, 115, 935, 974
Lipara 647, 648
Lipari Islands 656
Li Ssu 160, 161
literature 25, 36, 46, 52, 62, 69, 75, 83, 85, 142, 143, 151, 159, 163, 168, 183, 370, 409, 424, 576, 657, 713
Liternum 749
Litylene 386
Liu Pang 161, 162 See also Kao-Tsu
Livia 1001, 1012, 1046, 1082
Livy 445, 598, 600-603, 605, 609, 610, 612, 613, 617, 618, 628, 670, 676, 700, 777, 780, 783, 816
Li Wang 154
David Lloyd George 702, 771
Locri 431, 627, 630, 633-636, 654, 685, 699, 702
Locrians 169, 245, 304, 383, 384, 452, 471, 473, 702, 757
Loire 425, 925, 930, 932, 933
Lombardy 664, 848
Lomello 674
London 28, 82, 126, 192, 258, 479, 520, 521, 817, 988
Longanus River 641
Lucius Cassius Longinus 836, 840, 846, 937
Longula 622

Tiberius Sempronius Longus 671
Lot 31
Louis Philippe 934
Louis XIV 85, 94, 250, 286
Louis XVIII 934
Lu 156, 157, 159, 161, 163
Empress Lu 163
Luca 919, 920, 924, 935, 936, 941
Lucania 623, 628, 630, 631, 633-635, 682, 683, 691, 694, 856, 858
Lucanians 419, 434, 435, 518, 619, 623, 626-629, 646, 664
Lucera 621
Luceres 598
Lucterius 930, 931, 933
Lucius Lucullus 799, 801, 867, 868, 871, 875, 883, 886, 891-894, 900, 913, 914, 916, 975
Lucumo 598
Erich Friedrich Wilhelm Ludendorf 360
Lugalzaggisi 58-61
Lung-shan (Shantung) 151
P. Rutilius Lupus 856
Lu Pu-wei 159
Gaius Annius Luscus 882
Lusitania 798, 801
Lusitanians 798-800, 882
lutes 143
Luxor 70, 84, 85, 88, 98, 159
Lycia 268, 310, 451, 488, 489, 495, 537, 744, 792, 793, 866, 899, 998, 1002, 1063
Lycian coast 176
Lycophron 454, 457
Lycurgus 182, 183, 194, 195, 474-476, 525-529, 564, 722, 775
Lydia 110, 115, 116, 124, 128, 129, 180, 181, 185, 187, 196, 200, 202, 209, 216, 217, 219, 220, 224, 229-233, 235, 353, 377, 382, 383, 385-387, 393, 395, 402, 486, 487, 539, 541, 543, 569, 730, 734, 763, 837
Lygdamis 196
Lyncestis 488
Jack Lynch 190
lyres 352
Lysander 354, 355, 357, 358-363, 373, 374, 383, 384, 385, 398, 420, 546
Lysander (aircraft) 384
Lysandra 573, 574, 583, 585

1123

Lysias 421, 791
Lysicles 291, 309, 311, 475, 525
Lysimacheia 558, 590, 744, 758, 763, 769, 773, 777
Lysimachus 535, 536, 537, 539, 546, 550, 552, 554-560, 563, 566, 568-575, 577-586, 590, 727, 729, 731, 736, 743
Lysimaetus 530

M

General Douglas MacArthur 231, 328, 440, 561, 673, 719, 767, 783, 843, 850
Thomas Babington Macaulay 271, 289
Maccabees 51, 54
Macedon 251, 270, 297, 331, 332, 335, 393, 403, 415, 422, 444, 447, 455, 460, 465, 479, 481, 491, 493, 502, 505, 535, 543, 578, 581, 582, 591, 611, 654, 670, 690, 712, 717, 719, 724-727, 738, 741, 753, 756, 774, 776, 784, 816
Macedonian Empire 148, 532, 544, 553, 566, 567, 712
Macedonian(s) 129, 170, 197, 199, 236, 271, 297, 320, 322, 363, 392, 393, 404, 450-455, 463, 466, 467, 485, 486, 491, 492, 495, 498, 499, 504, 509, 510, 516-518, 523-525, 531, 536-541, 544, 547, 550, 555, 568, 570, 571, 588, 590, 609, 612, 622, 686, 710, 711, 716, 726-728, 738, 745, 749-752, 755, 757, 767, 777, 778, 781-784, 790, 792, 862, 867
Machanidas 722, 723
Machares 894
Niccolo Machiavelli 148
Harold MacMillan 122, 192, 271
James Madison 46, 106, 291
Maeandrius 202
Sp. Maelius 617
Maer 28
Magadha 145-147
Magas 561, 727, 730, 736, 743
magister equitum 679, 977
magistrates 106, 183, 269, 351, 413, 599, 608, 617, 637, 639, 660, 668, 719, 826, 827, 830, 832, 878, 889, 915, 974, 989, 996, 997, 1039, 1049

Magna Graecia 420, 423, 428, 619, 627, 636, 692, 712, 715
Magnesia 455, 716, 723, 770, 815, 890
Magnesium 768, 771
Mago (early Carthaginian leader) 258
Mago (Carthaginian leader in Sicily) 419, 420, 423, 432
Mago (Carthaginian admiral) 632, 633,
Mago (cousin of Hannibal) 675
Mago (brother of Hannibal) 682, 685, 689, 690, 695-698, 703, 704, 706, 707
Admiral Alfred Thayer Mahan 672, 679
Mahanaim 42
Prophet Mahomet 204
Maimonides 41
John Major 357
Malaga 423, 661
Malchus 258, 423, 966, 1033, 1064, 1065
Malis 589
Lucius Malleolus 792
Malli 514
malversation 306, 312
Mamercus 433
Mamertines 640-644
Mamilian Commission 852
Quintus Mamilius 645
Manasseh 36, 51
Manchuria 159
Manchus 408
A. Mancinus 792
Lucius Mancinus 807
Mandela 88
Mandonium 434
Mandonius 695, 703
Mandrocles of Samos 225
Mandubracius 928
Manishtusu 61
Mantinea 326-331, 389, 396, 397, 399, 400, 477, 568, 577, 723
Mantineans 272, 326, 389-400
Mao Tse-tung 16, 78, 325, 379, 535, 564
Mao Tse-tung's Long March 379
Mao Tun 164. *See also* Mei Tei
Maracanda 506
Marathus 493, 494
marble 93, 96, 390, 1038, 1082
Claudius Marcellus (son of Marcus Claudius Marcellus) 809
Claudius Marcellus (consul in 50 B.C.) 944, 946

Marcus Claudius Marcellus (Consul 5x, hero of Clastidium) 666, 668, 686, 687, 688, 689, 691, 692, 693, 694, 699, 709, 710, 722, 723, 749, 755, 801, 804, 813, 1039
M. Claudius Marcellus (Roman legate) 749, 755, 856, 858, 1042
M. Claudius Marcellus (nephew of Tiberius) 1043
Marcomanni 1073, 1074
Mardonius 235, 236, 250-254
Marduk 107, 129, 227
Mari 136
Mariaba 1057
Mariamne 1005, 1008, 1017
Gaius Marius 708, 811, 812, 835, 836, 841-849, 851, 851-854, 856-861, 864-868, 870-878, 880, 882, 884, 887-890, 892, 902, 906, 911, 913, 921, 935, 947, 963-965, 973, 979, 982, 985, 1035, 1039, 1054, 1077, 1087, 1088
Gaius Marius (son) 875
Marius Gratidianus (adoptive nephew of Marius) 876
Maroboduus 1074, 1077
Maronea 777, 778
Marrucini 858
Marsala 418
Marseilless 205, 206, 257, 423, 425, 669, 809, 830, 838, 941, 956, 968, 993, 1047, 1079
Marsi 622, 856, 858
Marsic Wars 856
Martiya 222
Karl Marx 885
John Masefield 147
Masistes 375
Massaga 511
Massagetae 219, 507
Massilia 205, 257, 423, 627, 664, 666, 668, 669, 670-673, 683, 710, 755, 809, 830, 838, 839, 847, 941, 955
Massiliote 655
Massinissa 689, 698, 700, 703-707, 709, 710, 748, 749, 773, 789, 803-805, 807, 808, 826, 839, 844, 863, 971, 973
Massistius 252
Massiva 840

Mastanabal 839, 844
Mastieni 655
Matarieh 71
mathematics 74, 85, 124, 151, 166, 365
Mattiwaza 142
Mattuaza 114
Mauryan Empire 148, 150
Mausolus 395, 407, 451, 454, 488
Gnaeus Mallius Maximus 847
Quintus Fabius Maximus 498, 546, 658, 668, 679, 691, 800, 804, 832, 839
  See also Quintus Fabius
mayors 71, 106
Mazaeus 500-502
John McCain 770
Medes 126, 127, 129, 200, 215-217, 223, 269, 526, 1018, 1021
Media Atropatene 1018, 1059
medicine 17, 74, 84, 85, 482
Mediolanum 666
medism 269, 278, 388, 466, 715
medist 526
Mediterranean 17, 21, 23, 32, 45, 47, 48, 50, 59, 60, 61, 74, 78, 79, 82, 97, 98, 112, 114, 116, 121, 122, 132, 133, 135-137, 139, 140, 151, 152, 166, 168, 174, 180, 202-205, 215, 217, 219, 221, 226, 233, 234, 243, 255-259, 264, 280, 286, 295-297, 299, 325, 335, 373, 395, 401, 413, 421, 423-425, 428, 440, 443, 446, 489-491, 493, 497, 521, 552, 565, 572, 580, 588, 593, 596, 615, 616, 623-625, 638, 639, 642, 647, 649, 655, 657, 658, 661, 663, 672, 689, 697, 700, 710-714, 718, 725, 734, 737, 739, 744, 745, 756, 769, 773, 775, 780, 793, 803, 805, 809, 839, 840, 843, 845, 846, 848, 849, 866, 890, 891, 892, 947, 955, 983, 996, 1000, 1024, 1033, 1052, 1056-1058, 1067, 1077, 1079, 1080, 1084, 1087, 1089
Medizers 254
Medusa 168
Megabates 231
Megabazus 226, 278, 280, 406
Megabyxus 280, 281, 376, 406
Megacles 182, 189, 193
Megacles (grandson) 194, 195, 198, 208

Megacles (3) 241
Megacles (4) 265
Megalbyxos 222
Megalopolos 397
Megara 180, 185, 189, 190, 193, 194, 204, 260, 276, 278, 280, 283, 285, 298, 299, 300, 301, 302, 305, 309, 319, 323, 325-327, 349, 350, 468, 470, 477, 531, 575, 577, 716
Megarians 301, 302, 319, 326, 327, 354
Megarid 305, 309, 319
Megasthenes 148
Megiddo 80, 81, 90, 201
Meidias 460
Christian Meier 885
Mei Tei 164 *See also* Mao Tun
Melas 202
Meleager 534, 536, 540, 588
Melesander 311
Meletus 367, 368
Meli Shipak II 115
Melissus 297
Melita 648
Melkart 494, 495
Melos 315, 333
Gaius Memmius 840, 854
Memnon (Trojan chief) 173
Memnon 485-490
Memphis 68, 69, 70, 74, 124, 159, 219, 220, 277, 281, 404-407, 497, 538, 540
Memphites 67, 68, 70
Menander (Athenian General) 358
Menander (of Lydia) 539, 541, 545
Menapii 925, 930
Menas 1011-1013
Menaus 135
Mencius 157, 163
Mende 321
Menedemus 582
Menelaus 168-172, 174
Menelaus (of Olynthus) 448, 457-460
Menelaus (brother of Ptolemy) 559, 565
Menesaechmus 529
Menetheus 453
Meng T'ien 160
Menippus 765
Menkaure 68
Mentor of Rhodes 403, 469
merchants 64, 77, 141, 155, 165, 191, 236, 714, 1075, 1077

Merneptah 94-97, 111, 168
Merneptah-Sipta 96
Merodach-baladan 118, 120, 122, 123
Lucius Cornelius Merula 872
Meryey 95, 96, 97
Mesopotamia 21, 23, 27, 28, 43, 57-60, 62-65, 104, 105, 108, 109, 111, 129, 131, 141, 142, 151, 235, 378, 556, 557, 572, 587, 892, 899, 938
Messana 314, 336, 432, 433, 437, 438, 445, 640, 1014
Messapians 434, 664
Messene 397, 447, 456, 457, 526, 718-721
Messenia 182, 184, 396-398, 401, 467, 568, 795
Messenians 182, 316, 317, 318, 326, 398, 399, 400, 466, 477, 776
Messiah 18, 25, 35, 38, 39, 46, 47, 49, 55, 74, 1089
Messina 259, 260, 314, 419, 420, 640-645, 647, 648, 674
metallurgy 121
metaphysics 481
Lucius Metellus 835, 838, 841 *See also* Metellus Delmaticus
Caecilius Metellus (consul) 626
Mettellus (Roman general) 651
Q. Caecilius Metellus (consul) 700, 702
Quintus Caecilius Metellus (consul and dictator) 784, 795, 796, 801, 835, 838, 841-844, 849, 853, 854, 860
Quintus Caecilius Metellus Pius (general) 875, 882, 879, 882, 883, 884, 900, 905, 907, 908, 909
Metellus (Pompey's father-in-law) 942, 946
Metellus (tribune) 971
Metellus Celer 907, 908
Q. Metellus Nepo 908
Methana Peninsula 318
Methone 305, 449, 454
Methydrium 329, 330
Methymna 343, 344, 390
Metropolis 380
Metternich 184, 468, 626, 704, 1045
Vardhamana Mhavira 146
Michal 43
Micipsa 839
Midas of Phrygia 119
Middle East 15, 21, 28, 38, 43, 45, 47, 73,

79, 92, 94, 109-111, 114, 116, 117,
    135, 139, 142, 143, 155, 162, 164,
    170, 172, 174, 179, 205, 215, 219,
    229, 274, 371, 373, 375, 405, 425,
    577, 603, 639, 770, 772, 775, 815,
    894, 896, 900, 1068, 1087
Middle Kingdom (Egypt) 75, 78, 80
Milan 609, 666, 809
Milesians 259, 353
Miletus 175, 176, 178, 198, 200-203, 217,
    225, 226, 230, 231, 233-235, 295,
    296, 343, 344, 349, 355, 358, 378,
    487, 555, 573, 577, 579, 581, 585,
    590, 726, 729, 772, 830, 888
millet 151
Milo (tribune) 634
T. Annius Milo 917, 918, 930, 935, 941,
    968, 977, 1050
Miltiades (Stesagoras) 196, 198,
Miltiades (tyrant of the Chersonese) 225,
    226, 234-236, 238, 239, 241, 291,
    292
Miltiades (descendant of Stesagoras) 528
Miltiades (grand-nephew of Stesagoras)
    198, 204
Miltocythes 448
Mindarus 352, 353
mining 93, 115, 121, 148, 196, 297, 450,
    639, 656, 661, 669, 672, 696, 708,
    797, 815, 819, 862
Min of Coptos 70
Minorca 698
Treaty of Misenum 1011
Mishneh Torah 41
mission creep 338
Mitanni 47, 79-82, 84, 85, 88, 89, 92, 110,
    111, 114, 142
Jessica Mitford 203
Mithridatic Empire 861-867
Mithridates VI Eupator (king of Pontus)
    731, 837, 838, 853, 860, 863, 864
    871, 873, 883, 884, 891-894, 898,
    899, 937, 964, 966, 967, 969, 970,
    1005, 1008, 1053, 1060
Mithridates (general under Antiochus)
    753
Mithridates of Cius 557
Mithridates of Pergamon 1053
Mithridates of Pontus 585, 589
Mithridates Philopator (son of Eupator)
    890
Mithridates V 837, 838
Mithridatic Citadel 862
Francois Mitterand 194, 384, 422
Mitylene 181, 193, 203, 310, 311, 312, 343,
    344, 356, 390, 490, 723, 963
Mizraim 22
Mnaseus 458
Mnemon (Artaxerxes II) 377
Moab 23, 31, 112
Moabite(s) 22, 39, 51
Moesi 1037
Moesians 169
Mohammed 113, 216
Mohammedan 23
Mohenjo-Daro 141
Moloch 439
Apollonios Molon 888
Molon 735
Molossia 269
A. Momigliano 1068
Theodor Mommsen 884, 885, 887, 1042
Monaeses 1018, 1019
monasticism 146, 158
Monastir 449
Mongolia 17
Mongols 23, 24, 142, 408
monotheism 17, 24, 25, 36, 38, 47, 55, 64,
    75, 113, 143, 229, 274, 293, 369,
    736, 1082
Monroe Doctrine 217
Montaigne 366
Monte Cimini 607, 622
Monte St. Angelo 438
Bernard Montgomery 417, 683, 693, 701,
    843
Thomas More 370
J.P. Morgan 46
Morgantia 436
Morini 924, 925, 1037
Moscow 505, 679
Moses 24, 31, 32, 34, 36, 37, 43, 49, 50, 53,
    85, 668
Robert Moses 668
mosquito 145
Mosul 120, 498
Mo Ti 158
Motya 417, 418
Jean Moulin 469
Mount Aetna 418, 645

Mount Athos 497
Mount Barbosthenes 764
Mount Gilboa 32, 40, 41
Mount Olympus 169
Mount Pangaeus 195
Mount Parnassus 453
Mt. Ecnomus 438
Mt. Istone 313
Mt. Ithome 272
Mt. Pangaeus 268
Crassus Mucianus 837
mummification 72
Lucius Mummius 796-799, 817, 867
J.A.R. Munro 243
Munychia 363, 533, 548, 563, 564, 868
Caesarean Murcus 995
Murena 891, 1042
Terrentius Varro Murena 1042
Publius Decius Mus 623
Antonius Musa 1043
Benito Mussolini 93, 350, 375, 615, 719, 978, 1081
Mutallu 91, 92
Muthes 407
Papius Mutilus 856, 858, 859
Muttines 688, 689
Mycale 254, 274
Mycenae 116, 167-169, 173, 178
Myceneans 167
Mylae 647, 648, 1055
Myrcinus 201
myrmidons 72
Myronides 252, 278, 280
Mysia 395, 403, 1036
Mysians 169
Mysore 150
Mysteries of Eleusis 335, 336
Mytistratus 648
Myus 265

N

Nabataeans 23, 52, 966, 1033
Nabis 752, 759, 760, 764, 765, 774, 795
Nabonidus 129, 218, 220
Nabonidus II 222, 223
Nabopolassar 127, 128
Nabunassar 137
Nadab 49
Nafam-Sin 62
Naif'aurud 406 *See also* Nepherites

Namrites 135
Naples 17, 619, 624, 651, 827, 849, 859, 1055, 1077
Napoleon 82, 83, 92, 95, 106, 123, 202, 216, 224, 225, 240, 242, 248, 250, 268, 275, 286, 342, 351, 355, 358, 360, 371, 379, 415, 418, 419, 421, 422, 442, 446, 449, 464, 466, 473, 475, 484, 488, 489, 504, 510, 520, 521, 570, 571, 578, 579, 582, 669, 673, 676, 679, 682, 691, 693, 704, 707, 708, 725, 730, 749, 753, 835, 849, 850, 887, 888, 960, 978, 979, 984-986, 1019, 1041, 1084
Napoleonic Wars 366
Naram-Sin 61, 62
Narbo Martius 839
Narnia 623
Naryx 458
nauarch 355
Naulochus 1055
Naupactus 286, 307-309, 313, 315, 319, 341, 468, 718, 721, 722, 768
Nausicles 455, 457
Naxalites 231
Naxos 195, 196, 230, 231, 236, 237, 239, 267, 268, 270, 287, 336, 338, 390, 417
Nazi Germany 22, 230
Nazi Panzers 73
Nazis 230, 348, 362, 693
Nazi-Soviet Pact 104, 386, 471, 619
Neapolis 619, 620, 624, 627, 631, 642
Nearchus 489, 515, 516, 519, 535, 548, 555
Nebhapetre 70
Nebuchadnezzar 49, 103, 114, 115, 126-129, 150, 204, 218, 220, 221, 230, 256, 376, 494, 519, 576
Necho 128, 201, 204, 221
Neco of Sais 124
Nectanebo II 395, 402, 403, 404, 407, 469
Neferirikere 69
Negev Desert 74
Nehemiah 49-52
Admiral Lord Nelson 263
Neneter Banantirurenebis 67
Neolithic 27, 103, 152, 595
Neoptolemus 538-540, 865
Nepete 613, 614
Nepherites 406 *See also* Naif'aurud

Nepherites II 407
Nequinum 623
Nereids 514
Neriglissar 129
C. Claudius Nero 746, 747
Gaius Claudius Nero 693-695, 699, 700, 701
Tiberius Claudius Nero 16, 1001, 1001, 1012, 1035
P. Silius Nerva 1070
Nervii 923, 924, 929, 930, 978
Nesubenebded 100
Neterkere 70
New Carthage 661, 662, 797, 802, 883
New Kingdom 74
St. John H. Cardinal Newman 371
New York 28, 77, 82, 156, 258, 259, 523, 567, 667, 675, 676, 679, 719, 868, 885
nexum 617
Nicaea 513, 538, 539, 552, 752
Nicanor (Antigonus' supporter) 545, 546
Nicanor of Stagirus 529
Nicanor (brother of Cassander) 546, 549, 551, 556
Nicanor (Macedonian commander) 747
Nicanor of Stagirus 529
Nicanor (satrap of Cappadocia) 551
Niceratus 362
Nicias 307, 314, 317, 318, 321, 327, 328, 329, 331-342, 345, 362
Nicocles 559
Nicodemes 864, 865
Nicodromus 241
Nicolaus 737
Nicolaus of Damascus 1037, 1067
Nicomedes (regent of Pleistoanax) 279
Nicomedes I of Bithynia 586, 590
Nicomedes II of Bithynia 837, 838, 864, 865, 871, 877
Nicomedes (son of Prusias) 792
Nicostratus 313, 321, 329, 330
Nicrotis 70
Nidintu-bel 222
Nile River 46, 47, 67, 69- 82, 84, 88, 91, 94, 95, 97, 101, 111, 123, 124, 176, 201, 204, 205, 220, 277, 281, 374, 401, 403-407, 483, 495, 497, 511, 540, 555, 561, 563, 565, 736, 737, 744, 757, 759, 898, 967, 968, 1033, 1056, 1057
Nile Delta 47, 73, 74, 76, 78, 82, 91, 95, 97, 176, 204, 205, 281, 405-407, 737, 744
The Inimitables 1002
Admiral Chester W. Nimitz 231
Nimrod 22
Nina 57, 58
Ninana 59
Nineveh 116, 120[124, 127, 129, 131, 133, 134, 256
Ningirsu 58
Ninurta-apal-ekur 115
Nippur 58, 59, 62, 63, 108
nirvana 146
Nisaea 194, 276, 319, 323, 325, 354
Nishtun 132
Nistaea 285
Nixon 93, 325
Richard Nixon 325
Noah 22, 26, 31, 53, 57, 107
Nobel Prize 397
M. Fulvius Nobilior 771, 801
Noble Truths 146
Nora 542, 543, 544
Norba 615
Gaius Norbanus 874
Noricum 1069, 1071
Normandie 318
North Africa 22, 23, 140, 205, 255, 256, 295, 322, 374, 420, 441, 526, 639, 640, 642, 672, 698, 701-703, 725, 793, 844, 849, 969, 1079
Northern League 585, 586
North Korea 165
North Sea 424, 1073
North Vietnam 160
Notium 312
Nova Carthago 672, 684, 695, 698, 702, 703
Nubia 68, 71, 74, 88, 96, 99, 744
Nubian(s) 74, 78, 84, 91, 96, 110
Numa 596
Numantia 801, 802, 837, 839, 840, 882
Book of Numbers 33, 34, 51, 53
Metellus Numidicus 853, 854, 860
nung 155
Nysa 864
Nysaeus 430

O

oases 21, 81, 126, 129, 165
Obedas I 895
obelisks 80, 84, 88
Obodas 895, 1058
Observatory Affair 422
Ocean (god) 514
Ochus 376, 377, 403, 404, 407, 408, 448, 453, 468, 469, 477 See also Darius II
Ocriculum 679
Octavia 944, 1004, 1007, 1008, 1009, 1012, 1016, 1020, 1025, 1027, 1035, 1042
Octavius/Octavian 17, 44, 419, 451, 507, 519, 583, 635, 811, 817, 822, 823, 828, 834, 845, 888, 904, 909, 937, 949, 981-983, 985-987, 989-1001, 1003, 1004, 1006-1009, 1011-1016, 1019, 1020, 1022, 1023-1043, 1046, 1054, 1060, 1067, 1069, 1071, 1081-1084, 1088 See also Augustus
Gnaeus Octavius (fought in Second Punic War) 703, 705
Gnaeus Octavius (supporter of Sulla) 861
Gnaeus Octavius (consul 87 B.C.) 872, 873
Marcus Octavius (tibune) 822, 890
Marcus Octavius (admiral) 957
Octavius (legate under Crassus) 939, 940
Odysseus 170, 172, 173, 175, 532
The Odyssey 172, 173, 175
Oeleus 169
Oenanthe 743
Oeniadae 281
Oenoe 387
Oenomaus 885
Oeobazus 254
Of the Laws 941
Of the Republic 941
oils 72, 77, 190, 655
oil well (first known) 506
Okinawa 231, 318
Olbia 297
Olcades 662
Old Testament 21, 24, 25, 33-35, 38, 49, 50, 51, 121, 147, 168
Olympeium 337
Olympia 180-182, 188, 205, 368, 399, 428, 451, 529, 550, 868
Olympiad 181 See also Olympic games

Olympias (mother of Alexander the Great) 434, 444, 451, 470, 478, 479, 481, 482, 509, 536, 538, 541, 543-545, 549, 550, 555, 570, 575, 627
Olympic games 181, 189. See also Olympiad
Olympiodors 567
Olympiodorus 578
Olynthia 458
Olynthians 450, 458, 459, 460, 550
Olynthic Oration 459
Olynthus 450, 459-461, 467, 485, 509, 553
Omayyad caliphate 22
Omri 49
Omride dynasty 49
Onacritus 197
Onomarchus 453-455, 457, 458, 607
Onomastus 778
Ophellas 440, 441, 445, 446
Ophir 45, 147
Lucius Opimius 832
Opimius 832, 833, 835, 840, 841
Opis 27
Oppian Law 804
Oppius 866
Oprah 36
Optimates 761, 766
Oracle of Ammon 497, 509
Oracle of Apollo 509
Oracle of Delphi 188, 209, 266 See also Delphic Oracle
Oran 581
Orchomenus 283, 319, 329, 386, 796, 869
L. Aurelius Orestes 796
Orestes (of Thebes) 281
Orestes (son of Agamemnon and Clytaemnestra) 172, 184
Orissi 662
H.A. Ormerod 870, 892, 897, 899
Oroezes 893, 894, 916
Oroites 224
Orontes 79, 92, 379, 393-395, 403, 407, 458, 537, 558, 572, 580
Orontes River 92, 580
Orontopates 488
Oropus 351, 401, 476, 533, 555, 794
Ortygia 415, 430, 431, 633, 688
Oscans 619
Osiris 72, 74, 75, 80, 113, 409, 1017
Ossa 483, 484

Ostia 603, 604, 621, 852, 872, 978, 1077
Ostracophoria 208
ostrich feathers 74
Lee Harvey Oswald 982
Manius Otacilius 645
Otanes 222, 224
Otranto 420
Ottolobus 750
Ovinian law 668
Oxus River 505
Oxyartes 508, 511, 534
Oxydracae 514
Ozymandias 71, 89

P

Paches 311, 312
Pacorus 940, 1005, 1007, 1008, 1018
Pact of Brindisi 1004
Pacuvius 988
Paeligni 856, 859
Paeonia 451, 578, 588
P. Autronius Paetus 901
Pagondas 320
Thomas Paine 390
painting 68, 85, 177, 645
Pakistan 88, 140, 147, 148, 190, 443, 637
Palermo 648, 651
Palestine 21, 26, 32, 33, 36, 37, 38, 40, 42, 47-52, 71, 74, 78, 79, 80, 81, 83, 84, 89, 90, 92, 93, 110, 111, 113, 116, 118, 121, 122, 128, 131, 178, 196, 280, 726, 736-738, 894, 898, 1006, 1017, 1037, 1064
Palestinians 25, 37, 48, 90, 91, 95, 112
Pallene 195
Palmyra 113
Paloma 425
Pammenes 449, 454, 458
Pamphylia 176, 267, 489, 537, 729, 866, 1017, 1062
Pamphylians 174 *See also* Dorians
Panactum 323, 328
panas 148
Panathenaic Festival 198
Panathenaic stadium 525
Pandosia 435
Pandya 150
Panegyricus 390
Pangaea goldfields 450
Pan-Hellenic League 470

Panion 748, 753
Pannonians 1055, 1075-1077
Panormus 648, 651
Pansa 993
Pantaleon 181, 202
Pantauchus 577
Paphlagonia 383, 395, 537, 572, 837, 861, 862, 863, 864, 870, 1029, 1036
Paphlagonians 490
Paphos 559
Papirius Cursor I 624
Lucius Papirius II 624
Papremis 406
Aemilius Papus 633
L. Aemilius Papus 665
Paratacene 547
Parauaea 576
Paris 28, 93, 181, 184, 190, 247, 254, 360, 361, 422, 505, 584, 667, 771, 932.
Paris (son of the Trojan king Priam) 170, 173
Parmenion 451, 461, 462, 482, 485, 486, 487, 488, 490, 491, 493, 497, 498, 499, 500, 501, 503, 504, 507, 516, 519
Mount Parnes 362
Paropamisadae 511
Paros 239
Parsua 216
Parthia 223, 541, 732, 734, 735, 896, 900, 901, 910, 927, 936-940, 980, 984, 999, 1005-1007, 1009, 1014, 1016, 1018, 1019, 1021, 1022, 1025, 1027, 1036, 1037, 1044, 1058, 1059, 1061, 1063-1065, 1067, 1077
Parysatis 377, 378, 383
Pasargadae 228
Pashe 115
Pasni 515
Pater Patriae 1046
patesi 57, 58, 59, 62
patesis 62, 106
Patna 148, 150
Patres 599, 982
patricians 599, 602, 608, 611, 616, 618
patriciate 155, 358, 599, 604, 606, 617, 668, 683, 820, 834, 852, 904, 1089
Patrocles 579
Patroclus (friend of Achilles) 173, 518, 728

Pattala 515
Patton 417, 843
L. Aemilius Paullus 650, 666, 681, 717, 781, 782, 783, 798, 816, 817
Paurava 512
Pausanias 252, 253, 264-266, 268-270, 302, 364, 384, 448, 478, 479, 482
Pax Romana 653, 692, 793, 935, 1078
The Peace 322
Peace of 371 395
Peace of Callias 376
Peace of Naupactus 718
Peace of Phoenice 703
Pedaritus 344
Quintus Pedius 978, 994
Pedum 613, 619
Peel 291
T.E. Peet 74
Pegae 285, 319
Peisander 335-337, 346-348
Peisander (Agesilaus' brother-in-law) 383, 384
Peisistratus 193-199, 203, 206, 208, 236, 268, 293, 415
Peithias 312
Peitholaus 457, 459
Peithon 534, 535, 537, 540, 541, 546, 551
Peleus 170, 173
Pelion 483, 484
Pella 462, 463, 473, 481, 586, 782
Pellene 397
Pelopidas 373, 391-394, 396, 397, 398, 407, 449, 865
Peloponnese 168, 174, 175, 178-182, 184-186, 197, 198, 202, 210, 243-248, 251, 258, 259, 262-264, 270, 279, 280, 285, 287, 294, 302, 304, 306-308, 310, 314, 316, 318, 323, 326, 329, 330, 331, 334, 338, 345, 391, 397, 398, 401, 447, 456-458, 466, 467, 474, 477, 524, 526, 548, 551, 552, 555, 559, 567, 568, 573, 574, 717, 720, 721, 752, 764, 766, 776, 1004, 1011, 1029
Peloponnesian League 180, 196, 209, 210, 240, 276, 279, 286, 298, 300-302, 322, 326, 332, 333, 586, 774
Peloponnesian War 255, 276, 277, 285, 291, 299, 340, 365, 367, 404, 423, 546, 670

First Peloponnesian War 276, 277, 299
Pelops 168, 722
Pelusium 220, 736, 964, 967
Pentagon 338
Pentakosiomedimni 192
Pentateuch 33, 49, 51, 53, 54
penteconters 245
Pentewere 100
Penthesilea 173
People's Republic of China 152, 159
Pepi II Neferkere 69
M. Junius Pera 690
Perdiccas 300, 301, 306, 308, 309, 320, 321, 331, 332, 335, 349, 362, 393, 402
Perdiccas (Alexander's cousin and general) 530, 532, 534, 535, 536, 537, 538, 539, 540, 541, 546, 550, 551, 552, 569, 579, 583, 585, 698
Perdiccas III 448, 449, 454, 478, 510, 511, 514
perduellio 851
Peregil 425
perfumes 77
Perialla 240
Periander 181, 190, 203
Periander of Corinth 181
Periclean Law 364
Pericles 182, 207, 208, 255, 265, 266, 268-329, 333, 346, 349, 351, 354, 357, 362, 363, 365-367, 371, 374, 375, 376, 389, 390, 401, 402, 422, 439, 448, 455-458, 471, 484, 525, 576, 607, 626, 670, 750
Perinthus 455, 470-472, 476, 477, 494, 744
Peripatetics 545, 563, 564
Juan Peron 835, 850
C. Perperna 856
Marcus Perperna 837
Commodore Matthew Perry 149
Persepolis 127, 228, 375, 501, 502, 504, 516
Perseus (of Mycenae) 168, 720
Perseus (son of Philip V) 778-784, 791-798, 816, 817
Persian Empire 49, 51, 54, 147, 154, 202, 213, 216-219, 221-230, 235, 243, 278, 307, 376-379, 381, 388, 394, 395, 398, 404-406, 434, 444, 447, 471, 487, 489, 490-493, 502, 503, 508, 509, 513, 516, 520, 541, 557,

591, 624, 740, 901
Persian Gulf 21, 26, 27, 46, 47, 59, 60, 61, 121, 122, 515, 518, 736
Persian Wars 147, 268, 294, 404
Persis 221, 516, 535, 547, 551
Perusia 1000, 1001
Philippe Petain 359, 360
L. Sulpicius Peticus 613, 614
Petra (Sicily) 651
Petreius 955, 956, 971, 973, 974
Gaius Petronius 1056
Peucestas 516, 535, 546, 547, 551
Phaedriades Cliffs 452
Phaedrus 573, 575
Phaex 314
Phaeylus 454
Phalaecus 458, 461-464, 468
phalanx 179, 362, 485, 487, 488, 491, 492, 498, 499, 500, 534, 540, 570, 611, 630, 632, 723, 737, 738, 770, 781, 782, 869
Phalaris 257
Phaleris 260
Phalerum 199, 249, 279, 532, 546, 548, 563, 564
Phanes of Halicarnassus 220
Phaon 203
pharaoh 31, 45, 76, 77, 78, 80-85, 87-101, 111, 113, 119, 128, 201, 219, 277, 969
Pharax 418, 430
Pharnabazus 353, 354, 362, 377, 382, 383, 384, 387, 391, 394, 395, 402, 407, 414, 490, 495, 540
Pharnaces 790, 862, 863, 899, 966, 969, 970, 1060
Pharnacid dynasty 383
Pharnuches 506
Pharos 686, 715-720, 742
Pharsalus 281, 385, 961-965, 967-969, 971, 982, 1083
Phasael 1002, 1005, 1064, 1065
Phaselis 489
Phaylus 457, 458
Pheia 305
King Pheidon of Argos 179
Pheidon 179, 180, 186
Pherae 391, 393, 394, 402, 448, 454, 455, 457, 459, 464
Pheretime 204

Phidias 295, 298, 574
Phila (daughter of Perdiccas) 538, 541, 547
Phila (daughter of Antipater, wife of Antigonus) 574, 578, 579, 582, 590, 731
Phila (half-sister of Antiochus) 586
Philetaerus 584
Philip (brother of Perdiccas) 300
Philip II of Macedon 393, 403, 404, 411, 415, 422, 423, 427, 444, 447-485, 488, 491, 494, 503, 505, 507, 509, 525, 526, 527, 534, 535, 536, 538, 539, 540, 541, 543, 544, 545, 546, 548, 549, 550, 551, 559, 560, 571, 572, 574, 576, 578, 584, 590, 598, 611, 626, 654, 741, 756, 774, 776, 816, 1053, 1061
Philip III 482, 534, 540, 542-546, 549, 550, 590
Philip IV (Cassander's son) 574
Phillip V 670, 686, 692, 699, 711, 712, 713, 716, 717, 718, 719, 720, 721, 722, 723, 724, 725, 738, 740, 741, 742, 743, 744, 745, 746, 747, 748, 750, 751, 752, 753, 754, 755, 756, 757, 758, 759, 760, 761, 764, 766, 767, 768, 771, 774, 775, 776, 777, 778, 779, 780, 816
Philipoemen 723, 764, 774, 794, 795
Philip of Croton 258
Philippi 451, 976, 994, 996, 998, 1000, 1001, 1005, 1014, 1031, 1032, 1035, 1065
Philippides 239
Philippines 231, 425, 561
Philippus (Alexander's physician) 490
Philippus (Harpalus' brother) 512
Philippus (satrap of Bactria and Parthia) 541
Lucius Marcius Philippus 989
Lucius Philippus 855, 875
Quintus Marcius Philippus 780, 781, 795, 796
Philiscus of Abydos 397
Philistia 112, 137
Philistine(s) 22, 32, 36-40, 45-48, 97, 101, 110, 111-113, 119, 122, 408
Philistus 421, 427-429
L. Veturius Philo 700
Q. Publilius Philo 616, 619, 621
Philochorus 729

Philocles (Athenian general) 358
Philocles (fined for embezzlement in 326) 529
Philocles (admiral of Demetrius) 581
Philocrates 462-464, 466, 468, 471, 474, 832
Philomelus 452, 453, 457
Philomelus of Ledon 452
Philon 458, 461
philosopher king 365, 582
Philotas 503, 504, 507
Philoxenus 421
Furius Philus 665, 666
Phlius 332, 389
Phocaeans 257, 423
Phocion 458, 460, 471, 472, 474, 475, 477, 524, 525, 529-533, 548
Phoenicia 36, 38, 45, 49, 51, 60, 72, 81, 83, 84, 116, 128, 131, 179, 220, 224, 227, 256, 282, 394, 402, 403, 414, 420, 458, 468, 493, 518, 532, 545, 546, 553, 555-557, 639, 729, 738, 768, 1017
Phoenician(s) 21-23, 46, 47, 48, 50-52, 70, 71, 79, 81, 82, 84, 90, 91, 110-112, 114, 121, 177, 178, 200, 205, 215, 220, 232-235, 243, 245, 247, 249, 250, 254-258, 260-262, 267, 268, 281, 282, 294, 295, 297, 347, 349, 350, 374, 406, 423, 424, 488, 495, 553, 563, 603, 639-641, 661, 692, 697, 708, 769, 1036
Phoenix 540, 569
Phormio 307, 308-310
Phraaspa 1018
Phraates (Parthian king) 892, 893, 894, 900, 1017
Phraates IV 1018, 1021, 1022, 1037, 1059, 1063
Phrataces 1063
Phrygia 110, 115, 116, 119, 353, 377, 382, 383, 397, 406, 453, 486, 488, 531, 535-537, 541-543, 545, 546, 552, 558, 559, 568, 569, 570, 589, 733, 734, 763, 772, 837, 838, 863, 871, 891, 1017
Phrygian(s) 112, 169, 861
Phrynichus 346, 347, 350
Phrynon 190, 461
Phyle 362

Ptolemy Euergetes II, Physcon 791, 896-898 *See also* Physcon
Phyton 420
Picentes 619
A.W. Pickard-Cambridge 455
Quintus Fabius Pictor 690
Piedmont 664
pig 141, 1068
pila 963, 970
Pillars of Hercules 425
pilum 620
Pindar 180, 184, 188, 484
Pindarus 202
P'ing Wang 154
Augusto Pinochet 835
Piraeus (port) 249, 264, 265, 275-277, 279, 292, 295, 297, 303-309, 335, 342, 350-352, 359, 360, 361, 363, 364, 384, 385, 389, 473, 476, 528, 531, 532, 546, 548, 563, 564, 573, 574, 581, 583, 585, 586, 747, 750, 867, 868, 978, 1079
pirates 168, 287, 318, 343, 420, 465, 468, 476, 566, 568, 590, 666, 670, 713, 714, 719, 742, 769, 771, 772, 793, 883, 888, 890-892, 901, 955, 964, 1000, 1011, 1024, 1036, 1056, 1060, 1083
Pisa 168, 180, 181, 663, 665, 684
Pisidia 488, 489, 538, 539, 541, 772, 1017
Pisidian mountaineers 1061, 1062
Pisidias 378
Calpurnius Piso 807, 821, 889, 902, 915
Pissuthnes 296, 377
Pittacus 193, 203
Pitt the Younger 266
Pixodorus 488
Placentia 666, 674-676, 695, 957
Plain of Dongola 78
Plain of Mars 600
Plain of Tegea 179
Plain of Thyrea 179
Plataea 198, 253, 254, 263, 268, 269, 303, 304, 309, 312, 325, 374, 464, 558, 849
Plataeans 303, 309, 312, 484
Plato 16, 74, 157, 188, 258, 289, 290, 365-371, 421, 426-430, 469, 519, 525, 977
Platonic Academy 426, 430

plebeians 292, 599-606, 608, 611, 616-618, 628, 643, 667, 668, 677, 831, 833, 1050, 1089
plebiscita 601, 605
Pleistarchus (underage Spartan king) 252
Pleistarchus (Cassander's brother) 570, 572, 573
Pleistoanax 279, 283, 284, 295, 315, 321, 322
Pleistorus 254
Quintus Pleminius 702
Pleuratus 726, 750
Pliny 991, 997
Plutarch 74, 147, 191, 265, 266, 267, 268, 270, 432, 434, 482, 515, 518, 564, 783, 822, 824, 828, 832-834, 869, 880, 883, 933, 940, 986, 988, 1002, 1030
Plutarchus 460
T. Quinctius Poenus 612
Point Barbara 249
Poland 422, 471, 552
Polemaeus 554, 555, 558-560
Polemarch 187, 192
Polemo 1007, 1017, 1018, 1026, 1036, 1060, 1061
Asinius Pollio 994, 996, 1003, 1006, 1007
Polybius 445, 610, 612, 613, 659, 670, 672, 679, 680, 686, 693, 708, 709, 720, 743, 746, 747, 754, 756, 776, 778, 780, 784, 792, 797, 801, 802, 816
Polycrateia 720
Polycrates 196, 197, 201, 202, 204, 220, 223, 224
polygamy 45, 478, 517, 582
Polyperchon 530, 532, 533, 535, 543-546, 548-550, 552-554, 558-561, 565, 567, 568
Polytimetus Valley 506
Polyxenidas 768, 769, 770
Polyxenus 421
Pompeii 409, 621
Gnaeus Pompeius (son of Pompeius Strabo) 856, 871, 875, 881, 917, 964, 978
Pompeius (Roman commander) 800, 801
Sextus Pompeius 838, 973, 978, 992, 993, 998, 999, 1000, 1001, 1003, 1004, 1011, 1012, 1013, 1014, 1019, 1021, 1029, 1037

Pompeius Magnus, Pompey the Great 507, 708, 811, 856, 859, 876-878, 881-884, 886-906, 908-921, 924, 930, 934-937, 939, 941-947, 951-971, 973, 974, 976-982, 985-987, 991, 997, 1005, 1009, 1014, 1017, 1037, 1039-1041, 1050-1052, 1054, 1058, 1065, 1069, 1084, 1088
Pontifex Maximus 596, 600, 602, 701, 824, 826, 836, 852, 854, 875, 887, 905, 911, 914, 980, 989, 1014, 1045, 1046, 1048, 1081, 1085, 1088
Pontine Marshes 978
Pontus 196, 395, 537, 572, 585, 731, 773, 776, 790, 837, 860, 862, 863, 865, 891-894, 969, 970, 974, 1017, 1036, 1060
Pope Alexander VI 156
M. Popillius 609
populus 601
Po River 609, 637, 848
Portugal 420, 424, 798, 830, 912, 1078
Portuguese 22, 257, 425
Porus (king og Paurava) 512-514, 537, 546-548
Poseidon 171, 261, 271, 272, 514, 515, 529, 533, 695, 805
Alexander Poskrebyshev 536
Lucius Postumius 645, 714
Sp. Postumius 620
Agrippa Postumus 1046, 1047
potestas tribunicia 1015
Pothinus 964, 966
Potidaea 251, 300, 301, 302, 306, 307, 321, 366, 402, 450, 468, 550
Potsdam 428
pottery 57-59, 67, 72, 141, 150, 151, 167, 176, 177, 189, 190, 208, 297, 435, 730, 1079
pottery wheel 151
Enoch Powell 271
Praeneste 606, 615, 907
praetor(s) 601, 608, 617, 659, 667, 677, 686, 689, 692, 699, 710, 764, 798, 799, 804, 808, 813, 840, 876, 878, 885, 886, 901, 902, 907, 917, 941, 947, 954, 957, 971, 989, 992, 1043, 1044, 1049, 1051, 1053
praetorian guard 1051, 1054, 1055
praetor peregrinus 667

Prepalaus 569
Priam 170, 173
Priene 296, 579
princeps 1040, 1042-1045, 1047-1049,
    1055, 1069, 1081
principate 823, 1015, 1043, 1051, 1064,
    1069, 1070, 1073, 1079, 1082, 1083,
    1088
L. Tarquinius Priscus 596
Proculeius 1034
C. Plautius Proculus 614
Promised Land 36, 54
Prophetic Revolt 39
Propontis 175, 234
Propylaea 295
prorogatio imperii 616
Prosopis 406
Protagoras 333
Protestantism 309
Proxenus 462, 463, 474
Prusias 773, 779, 790, 792
Prussia 197, 451, 625
prytanys 208
Psammetichus I (Egypt) 124, 127, 201,
    376, 405
Psammetichus II 201, 219
Psammetichus III 201, 220, 224
Psammetichus (king of Libya) 296
Psyttaleia 249
Ptahshepses 68
Pteria 217
Ptolemaeus 488, 585, 586, 588, 590, 727,
    729,
Ptolemaeus of Chalcis 1002
Ptolemais 558, 573, 579, 737
Ptolemy Auletes 898, 916, 918, 964, 967,
    968, 1017
Ptolemy Caesar 1022, 1023, 1027, 1034,
    1036
Ptolemy Epiphanes 790
Ptolemy Eurgetes II 791, 896 *See also*
    Physcon
Ptolemy I Soter 440, 485, 504, 505, 512,
    514, 519, 530, 535, 536, 537, 538,
    539, 540, 541, 543, 544, 545, 547,
    550, 551, 552, 553, 554, 555, 556,
    557, 558, 559, 560, 561, 562, 563,
    564, 565, 566, 568, 569, 570, 571,
    572, 573, 574, 577, 578, 579, 581,
    582, 583, 584, 585, 587, 590, 591,
    739, 753, 758
Ptolemy II 150, 559, 582, 583, 712, 726,
    727, 728, 729, 730, 731, 732, 733,
    1017
Ptolemy III 727, 730, 732, 733, 736
Ptolemy Keraunos 582, 583, 584
Ptolemy IV, Philopator 736, 737, 738, 739,
    741, 742, 743
Ptolemy V 743, 744, 755, 758, 762, 773,
    780
Ptolemy VI Philometor 790, 791, 896
Ptolemy VIII (Lathyrus) 897
Ptolemy IX Alexander I 866, 896, 897, 898
Ptolemy X Alexander II 898, 903
Ptolemy of Aloru 393, 402
Ptolemy of Lagos 485
Ptolemy of Megalopolis 743
Ptolemy Philadelphus 635
Ptolemy (son of Sosibius) 743
Lucius Gellius Publicola 885
Valerius Publicola 601, 602
Appius Claudius Pulcher 686, 692, 872
P. Claudius Pulcher 652
L. Junius Pullus 652
Punicus 798
Punic Wars 640, 712, 790, 797, 809, 810,
    815
Punjab 140, 511, 521, 549
Rajah Puru 147
Pydna 450, 550, 782, 790, 792, 816, 817
Pylaemenes of Paphlagonia 837
Pylos 316, 318, 321, 323, 326, 327, 354,
    399
Great Pyramid at Giza 17
Pyrenees 424, 425, 662, 673, 696, 802, 839,
    849, 955
Pyrrhic victory 16, 630, 632
Pyrrhus 189,
Pyrrhus (king of Epirus) 435, 444, 445,
    567, 568, 570, 573-582, 584, 585,
    587, 622, 625, 628-637, 639-643,
    670, 671, 713, 716, 727, 728, 731,
    809, 1074
Pyrrhus Tyrant of Pisa 181
Pythagoras 204
Pythagoras (Argive Noble) 760
Pytheas 529, 531
Pythia Aristonice 244
Pythian festival 188
Pythian games 465, 576

Pytho 187, 188
Pythodoris 1061
Pythodorus 314, 1021
Python of Byzantium 468

Q

quadrumvirate 552-556, 568, 572, 935
Quadruple Alliance 329, 330, 331
quaestors 617, 748, 813, 878, 1049
Queen of Sheba 45
Quintus Cicero (brother) 929
Sestius Quirinalis 1043
P. Sulpicius Quirinius 1062, 1070

R

Gaius Rabirius 906
Rachel 34
Raecelus 195
Raetians 1071
Raja 143
Ramenses 598
Ramses I 90
Ramses II 67, 91-97, 111, 169, 230
Ramses III 47, 97-101, 111
Ramses IV 100
The Ransom of Hector (*Iliad*) 421
Rape of the Sabine Women 596
Raphia 737, 738, 742, 748
Rapikum 104
"ravens" 647, 649
Re (Sun God) 68, 221, 227, 409
Rededef 68
Red Sea 32, 45, 48, 72, 76, 82, 96, 726, 897, 900, 1056, 1057
L. Aemilius Regillus 769
M. Atilius Regulus 442, 648-650, 653, 657, 671, 680, 681
Rehoboam 46, 49
Rei 502
Reign of Terror 190, 354, 396, 445, 584
Remi 923, 929, 932
Remus 595, 596
Reneb Kakau 67
Guido Reni 31
Res Gestae (Of Government) 1040, 1070
revanchisme 360
Revelation 22, 34, 38
Rex 984
Rex Sacrarum 596

Rheims 228, 923
Rhesus 172
Rhine River 358, 647, 839, 846, 920-927, 930, 932, 942, 1012, 1037, 1044, 1047, 1054, 1055, 1059, 1061, 1069, 1070, 1073-1076, 1079, 1085, 1086
rhinoceros 140
Rhodes 174, 176, 203, 234, 263, 265, 346, 353, 355, 383, 385, 386, 387, 390, 403, 451, 453, 454, 469, 471, 495, 497, 526, 528, 541, 554, 565, 566, 567, 718, 722, 724, 742, 744, 747, 752, 753, 769-773, 775, 776, 780, 782, 792, 793, 818, 866, 871, 887, 888, 890, 900, 1002, 1046, 1062, 1073, 1074
Rhoemetalces 1029, 1075
Rhomos 596
Rhône River 206, 425, 666, 673, 674, 683, 848
rice 141
Keith Richardson 817
Richard Wagner 61, 108, 173
Cardinal Richelieu 98, 184, 220, 268, 367, 388, 419, 468, 479, 570, 626, 1041, 1045
Louis Riel 370
Rig 142, 143, 596
Rim-Sin 104, 105
Rimush 61
Alan Roberts 988, 1019
J.M. Roberts 176
Maximilien Robespierre 78, 354, 361, 445, 884
Robin Hood 362, 887
Nelson Rockefeller 357
Rock of Offense 189
Witold Rodzinski 156
Roman Catholic Church 68, 150
Roman Federation 625, 627, 635, 637, 638, 640, 657, 660, 663-665, 672, 676, 682, 683, 685, 694, 701, 725
Romanian 22
Romanovs 224
Roman Republic 151, 596, 597, 601, 668, 693, 705, 787, 812, 818, 860, 861, 874, 899, 912, 945, 946, 973, 980, 996
Roman world 17, 678, 793, 810, 818, 843, 845, 876, 878, 879, 896, 909, 934,

940, 944, 947, 955, 981, 984, 986, 996, 1003, 1004, 1006, 1007, 1015, 1016, 1019-1023, 1025, 1027, 1037, 1040, 1050, 1056, 1057, 1059, 1069, 1078, 1086, 1087
Erwin Rommel 683, 693, 701, 843, 967
Romulus 595, 596, 598, 613, 849, 935, 942, 973, 1039, 1082
Franklin D. Roosevelt 16, 73, 93, 190, 192, 242, 275, 290, 375, 425, 523, 676, 1045
Lucius Roscius 954
Jean-Jacques Rousseau 289
Roxanne 508, 517, 534, 535, 550, 553, 558
Royal Squadron 510
Rubicon 273, 868, 910, 947, 952, 953, 964
Egnatius Rufus 1043
Minucius Rufus 679, 680
P. Rutilius Rufus 841, 847
P. Sulpicius Rufus 860
Quintus Pompeius Rufus 860
Salvidienus Rufus 989, 1004
Vibullius Rufus 959
Quintus Fabius Rullianus 621, 623
P. Servilius Rullus 904
P. Rupilius 821
Lord John Russell 371
Russia 17, 22, 120, 123, 142, 197, 225, 226, 242, 250, 297, 342, 361, 379, 425, 466, 489, 566, 579, 673, 725, 815, 894, 898, 1019
Russian(s) 129, 422, 471, 546, 648
Publius Rutilius 855
C. Marcus Rutilus 614
Alexei Rykov 241

S

Sabellians 619
Sabines 606, 607, 621, 624, 664
Gaius Calvisius Sabinus 1012
Quintus Sabinus 924, 929, 1012, 1013
Sabutai 887
Sacred Band 433, 475
Sacred Hearth 144
Sacred Wars 188, 198, 282, 403, 434, 451, 453, 454, 456-458, 461, 465, 469
 First Sacred War 188, 451, 453
Sadat 262
Sadocus 321
Safure 69
Sagalassus 489
Sagartia 223
Saite dynasty 201
Salaethus 311
Salamis 169, 184, 185, 188, 190, 194, 215, 244, 246-252, 254, 266-268, 282, 293, 294, 351, 367, 374, 375, 393, 394, 419, 565-567, 849
Salassi 1042, 1043, 1070
salii 599
Livius Salinator 666, 699, 703, 717, 768
Sallust 836, 839, 883, 902, 970, 1006
Salome Alexandra 895
Salonika 174, 175
Salt Desert 504
Samaritans 33, 46, 49, 50, 51, 54
Samarkand 505, 506, 507
Samarra 61
sambuca 866
Samians 234, 259
Sammu-ramat 135
Samnites 434, 616, 619-624, 626, 628, 630, 631, 646, 664, 856, 875, 903
Samnite Wars 445
Samnium 620, 622-624, 628, 631, 633-635, 679, 682, 691, 693, 856, 876
Samos 175-178, 194, 196, 197, 200, 201, 202, 220, 225, 232, 234, 235, 251, 254, 263, 287, 295, 296, 297, 344, 346-349, 355, 359, 385, 387, 402, 451, 473, 476, 526-529, 533, 565, 729, 744, 754, 755, 769, 1032, 1038, 1063
Samosata 1008
Samothrace 586, 730, 782, 805, 890
Samsideramus 894
Samson 32, 36, 37, 38, 112
Samsu-ditana 108
Samsu-iluna 108
Samuel 32, 36-41, 43, 112, 1087
Samuel of Ephraim 32, 37
Sandrocotus 147
Sanduarri 123
San Jacinto 688
Sanskrit 142, 151
Sans Souci 428
Sappho 203
Sarah 31
Sardes 22, 197, 200, 209, 217, 224, 233, 236, 243, 250, 296, 352, 355, 375,

383, 386, 388, 539, 560, 569, 579, 584, 606, 721, 728
Sardinia 258, 423, 424, 441, 639, 642, 648, 650, 656, 658, 659-661, 663, 665, 667, 669, 670, 676, 685, 686, 688, 690, 691, 695, 699, 703-705, 707, 725, 740, 748, 804, 809, 812, 816, 875, 878, 882-884, 918, 955, 956, 996, 1000, 1004, 1011, 1015, 1028
Sardoris 137
Sarduris II 136
Sargon 59-61
Sargon II 117-121, 122
Saronic Gulf 190, 329
Sassanians 129
Satibarzanes 502, 503, 505
Saticula 620, 621
Satricum 614, 615, 621
Sattagydia 226
Lucius Apuleius Saturninus 848, 852, 853, 854, 906, 909, 913, 1044
Saudi Arabia 45, 408
Saul 32, 36, 38-43, 45, 46, 150
Decidius Saxa 998, 1005
Publius M. Scaevola 824
Scamander River 170
Scarpheia 797
Vettius Scato 857-859
Aemilius Scaurus 835, 838
Scerdilaidas 716-720, 726
scientific technique 481
scimitars 73
Scione 321, 328
Scipio Aemilianus (son of Paullus, became Numantinus) 783, 800, 801, 805, 807, 818, 825, 826, 833, 835, 837, 839, 852, 997
Cornelius Scipio (Asina) 647, 648 *See also* Cornelius Asina
Cornelius Scipio Barbatus (consul) 623
Gnaeus Cornelius Scipio 666, 671, 673, 683-685, 689, 690, 693
Lucius Cornelius Scipio (brother of Scipio Asina) 648
Lucius Scipio Asiaticus 815, 874
Lucius Scipio (brother of Publius Scipio Africanus) 697
Metellus Scipio 942, 946, 958, 961
Publius Scipio Africanus the Elder 426, 446, 485

Publius Cornelius Scipio (father of Africanus) 674, 675, 676, 678, 679, 681, 684, 685, 689, 690, 693
Publius Cornelius Scipio Africanus 694, 695-698, 700-710, 712, 720, 749, 760, 762, 767-771, 782-785, 797, 800-805, 807-809, 816-818, 821, 823-826, 830-833, 835, 837, 839, 852, 860, 871, 874, 875, 889, 913, 942, 946, 958, 961, 971-974, 997, 1069
Scipio Nasica 782, 784, 785, 805, 809, 818, 824, 826, 832, 837
Scopus 721
Scordisci 838, 846
Scotland 39, 443
Angus Scott 797
Scribonia 1001, 1012, 1042
Lucius Scribonius 957
Scribonius (claimant to Bosporan throne) 1060
sculpture 68, 70, 85, 151, 597
Scyros 265-267, 386, 388, 476
scythed chariots 498, 499, 970
Scythia 201, 225, 230, 233
Scythian archers 195
Scythian(s) 127, 129, 224-226, 472, 506, 863, 1060, 1061, 1074
Scyths 408
Red Sea 32, 45, 48, 72, 76, 82, 96, 726, 897, 900, 1056, 1057
Sea of Marmara 168, 226, 383, 391
Queen Sebuknefrure 71
secession 46, 69, 265, 268, 310, 312, 343, 602, 774, 776, 795
Second Syrian War 729
Second Triumvirate 507, 996, 997, 1088
Sedan 111
Segeda 800, 801
Segesta 333, 334, 336-338, 433, 444, 633
Segura Valley 697
Seine River 422, 425, 932
Sekenenre I 73
Sekenenre III 74
Seleucia 558, 735-737, 937, 970
Seleucid Empire 507, 585, 727, 731, 732, 733, 738, 741, 758, 862
Seleucus Nikator 148, 149, 507, 513, 535, 537, 540, 541, 546, 551, 552, 554, 556-560, 562, 563, 566, 568-573,

577-585, 726, 728, 729
Seleucus II 730, 731, 732, 733, 734, 862
Seleucus III 734
Seleucus (son of Antiochus) 586, 587, 753, 768, 769, 779, 791, 894
Selinus 261, 333-336, 414, 633
Peter Sellers 104
Selymbria 477
Semiramis 135
Semites 21, 23-26, 28, 52, 53, 62-65, 79, 109
Semitic 22, 23, 25-28, 48, 57, 59, 60, 63, 71, 103, 109, 112, 131, 639, 714
Sempronia 817, 821, 827, 852
Tiberius Sempronius 653, 671, 674-678, 690, 691, 725, 726, 747, 809, 885. *See also* Tiberius Sempronius Longus
Sena Gallica 699
Roman Senate 523, 527, 599, 601, 617, 618, 620, 624, 628, 631-633, 636, 638, 642-647, 649, 653, 654, 659, 662, 663, 665-671, 674-676, 683, 685, 690, 691, 693-695, 700-702, 704-706, 709, 710, 712, 714, 720, 721, 725, 726, 745, 746, 748-750, 752, 754, 756-758, 760, 762, 768, 769, 771-774, 778, 783, 789, 790, 791-796, 799, 800, 801, 805-808, 810, 811, 817-819, 822-843, 845, 848, 851-855, 859, 860, 861, 864, 865, 870, 872-875, 877, 878, 882-889, 891, 892, 896, 898, 899, 902-904, 907, 909, 911-919, 921, 922, 935, 941, 942, 944-947, 951-954, 968, 969, 971, 981-983, 985-990, 992-998, 1004, 1006, 1015, 1016, 1025-1027, 1032, 1038, 1039, 1040-1053, 1056, 1059, 1069, 1071, 1078, 1081, 1082, 1087, 1088
Senatus Consultum Ultimum 832, 908, 992
Sennacherib 117, 121-123, 126, 129, 216
Senones 422, 626, 627, 930, 931
Sens 627
Gaius Sentius 866
Senusret I 71
Senusret III 70, 71
Sepeia 210, 240
Septimius Severus 519

Septimuleius 833
Sequani 921, 922
serfs 85, 93, 154, 185, 272, 396, 486, 837, 862
A. Atilius Serranus 764
Quintus Sertorius 426, 800, 802, 881-885, 890, 921, 1033
Servile Wars 885
  First Servile War 821
Fabius Maximus Servilianus 800
Gnaeus Servilius 651, 653, 675, 677, 678, 679, 681, 684, 749
Paulus Servilius 958, 968
Q. Servilius 613, 615, 617
Sesta 254
Sestos 254, 262, 358, 402, 451
Set 74, 75
Seti 90, 91, 92, 96
Setnakht 97, 98
Seuthes 308, 321, 381
Seven Wonders of the World 128, 451
Seven Years' War 280
Caecina Severus 1075
L. Sextius 611, 616
Shaft Grave Dynasty 167
Shagshag 58, 59
Shah 50
William Shakespeare 158, 168, 172, 173, 293, 298, 371, 451, 560, 606, 909, 985, 986, 988, 1016
Shalmaneser I 93, 11, 113, 114, 115
Shalmaneser III 133, 135
Shalmaneser IV 136
Shalmaneser V 117, 118, 119, 120, 133, 134, 135, 136
Shamash-erba 375
Shamash-Mudammik 131
Shamash-shum-ukin 124, 125
Shamgar 32
Shamshi-adad 135
Shamshi-adad V 135
shang 155
Shang 151-154
Shang Yang 156
Shansi 152
Shantung 151, 152, 156
Sharezer 123
Shargalisharri 62
Sharuhen 74
George Bernard Shaw 564, 1017

Sheba 45, 1057
Shechem 31, 32
sheep 27, 107, 126, 141, 151, 230, 461, 595
Shem 22
Shemaya 1066
Shemesh-Edom 83
Shensi 153, 155, 159-162
Shepsekaf 68
William Tecumseh Sherman 95
shih 155
Shih Huang 159, 160
Shiloh 36, 38, 40
shipbuilding 148, 307, 391, 451, 577, 1013, 1021
Shiva 141
Shubbiluliuma 111, 114
Shudras 143
Shuruppak 57
Sian 162
Sibylline Books 918
Sicans 255
Sicel(s) 255, 259, 419, 435
Siciliotes 435
Sicily 176, 179, 180, 203, 205, 215, 255-262, 287, 292, 293, 295, 304, 313-315, 318, 319, 322, 332, 333-342, 346, 374, 397, 401, 411, 413-420, 423, 426-435, 437, 438, 441-446, 604, 619, 625, 626, 632-634, 637-654, 656-661, 670, 671, 674, 676, 683, 685-695, 699, 701, 702, 704, 705, 707, 710, 712, 722, 725, 740, 748, 765, 792, 820, 821, 856, 876, 878, 885, 886, 889, 918, 953, 955, 956, 971, 991, 996-998, 1000, 1001, 1003, 1004, 1012-1015, 1028, 1044
Sicinnus 249
Diodorus Siculus 657
Sicyon 181, 182, 185, 193, 195, 206, 274, 320, 397, 457, 561, 577
Sidhartha Gautama 145
Sidon 22, 51, 79, 116, 123, 133, 134, 256, 257, 403, 407, 468, 494, 495, 518, 572, 573, 581, 737, 748, 753
siege-towers 485, 494
Sierra Morena 655, 661
Sierra Rhonda 800
Sigeum 190, 196, 199, 203, 210
Marcus Junius Silanus 841, 846
Turpilius Silanus 841

silk 151, 162, 164, 511, 936, 975
Silk Road 164, 165, 1058
silkworm 156
Q. Pompaedius Silo 856, 859
silver 45, 61, 62, 64, 80, 82, 120, 141, 148, 191, 195, 196, 241, 256, 356, 424, 451, 529, 546, 548, 632, 633, 637, 639, 652, 653, 655, 669, 672, 684, 696, 697, 710, 748, 780, 783, 797, 800-803, 816, 817, 844, 847, 862, 902, 935, 954, 1050, 1079
Silver-man 257
Silver Shields 541, 544, 545, 547
Simeon 36
Simus 454
Simyra 79, 81, 114
Sinai 21, 32, 43, 68, 71, 72, 124, 753, 1086
Sinaitic laws 53
Sind 140, 511, 551
Sinkiang 165
Sin-muballit 104
Sin-shar-ishkun 127
Siphae 319, 320
Sippar 57
Siptah 96, 97
Siptah II 97
Sisera 36
Sitalces 297, 306, 307, 308, 320, 321, 516
Sium 62
Siwah 497, 519
Six Hundred 435, 437
slave revolt 74, 341
slavery 74, 97, 106, 129, 144, 162, 163, 165, 190, 312, 313, 328, 333, 342, 359, 366, 418, 420, 421, 444, 460, 465, 470, 475, 476, 484, 495, 604, 637, 646, 648, 694, 709, 722, 744, 761, 772, 808- 810, 818, 871, 922, 924, 925, 1069, 1070, 1079, 1080
slaves 31, 69, 74, 82, 85, 93, 99, 100, 106, 128, 144, 152, 154, 162, 163, 165, 171, 182, 185, 188, 208, 241, 262, 266, 272, 313, 316, 323, 344, 346, 356, 360, 374, 415, 472, 475, 524, 532, 554, 563, 566, 588, 599, 606, 617, 618, 659, 663, 690, 692, 777, 802, 810, 817, 818, 820, 821, 858-861, 869, 870, 872, 873, 876, 884-887, 907, 921, 958, 977, 996, 997, 1000, 1043, 1046, 1051, 1075, 1076,

1078, 1079, 1080, 1087
Slavs 112, 173
Sidney Smith 122, 123
Smyrna 200, 558, 755, 756, 759, 762, 765, 769, 772, 847, 855, 869, 995
Snefru 68
Sochoi 491
socialism 183, 185
Socrates 157, 324, 328, 357, 360, 362, 364, 366-371, 377, 378, 386, 401, 428
Socrates (of Bithynia) 865
Sogdiana 499, 505-508
Sogdian Rock 508
Sogdianus 376
Solomon 25, 31-33, 41, 43-48, 141, 146, 147, 149, 150, 230, 374, 576
Solomon Islands 729
Solon 167, 186, 190-196, 199, 202, 204, 258, 351, 533, 563, 600, 602
Solygeia 318
Somalia 45, 69
Song of Deborah 36
Sophanes 461
Sophene 776
Sophocles 293, 294, 346, 526
Sophocles (Athenian commander) 314-316
Sophonisba 703, 705
sorcery 106
Sosibius 736-738, 742-744
Sosistratus 435-438, 633
Gaius Sosius 1008, 1026, 1032, 1065
Sosthenes 589, 590
Marshal Soult 263
South Asia 139, 373, 655
South Sudan 69
Soviet Politburo 241
Soviet Union 93, 104, 201, 278, 286, 471, 523, 704
Spain 22, 23, 199, 203, 205, 206, 256, 257, 277, 279, 295, 374, 414, 421-426, 441, 461, 639, 642, 649, 654-656, 660-664, 669, 671-679, 683-686, 689, 690, 691, 693-700, 702-708, 710, 717-720, 724, 725, 727, 728, 740, 754, 755, 761, 763, 797-805, 809, 811, 812, 817-821, 825, 826, 833, 835, 837, 839, 874-877, 881-887, 889-902, 952, 921, 934, 935, 951, 952, 954-958, 960, 961, 967-969, 971, 973, 977-979, 986, 987, 994, 996, 998, 999-1004, 1007, 1009, 1028, 1033, 1037, 1040-1042, 1044, 1047, 1052-1054, 1060-1062, 1069, 1070, 1071, 1076, 1079, 1080, 1082, 1083, 1085, 1087
Spanish 22, 170, 257, 279, 414, 424, 425, 433, 467, 655, 661, 662, 669, 672, 677, 682, 684, 686, 688, 690, 695-697, 705, 706, 708, 727, 748, 798, 800-802, 803, 815-818, 821, 833, 835, 859, 882-884, 886, 902, 955, 978, 981-983, 994, 1009, 1018, 1042, 1069, 1070, 1076, 1077
Spanish Armada 279
Spanish Civil War 467
Sparta 24, 144, 161, 162, 169-172, 174, 176-180, 182-186, 188, 196-199, 202, 206, 209, 210, 217, 218, 230, 231, 232, 235-240, 243, 244-247, 251, 252, 255, 258, 259, 262-265, 267, 268, 269, 270, 271, 272, 273, 276-280, 282-287, 294, 295, 297-302, 304-308, 310, 311, 315-318, 320-333, 335-338, 340-365, 369, 373, 374, 377-402, 404, 406, 407, 413, 418, 420-422, 434-436, 438, 447, 451, 452, 456, 457, 461, 463, 465-467, 469, 474, 477, 484, 487, 491-494, 498, 500, 501, 503, 524, 526, 527, 531-533, 553, 556, 568, 575, 586, 603, 618, 627, 637, 670, 715-717, 721-723, 726, 727, 752, 759, 760, 764, 765, 774, 776, 790, 794-796, 844, 1004, 1029, 1036
Spartacus 885-887
Spartan League 251
Spartan(s) 181-184, 186, 197, 199, 209, 210, 217, 238, 240, 243, 246, 248, 249, 251-254, 262, 263, 265, 273, 278, 279, 280, 283, 301, 302, 305-308, 310, 312, 316-319, 321, 322, 326, 329-333, 339, 340, 341, 343-347, 349-353, 356-361, 383-385, 387, 390-392, 395, 397, 399, 400, 406, 407, 430, 457, 461, 462, 487, 493, 527, 614, 723, 774
Albert Speer 44
Speusippus 427, 428
Sphacteria 316-318, 322, 326

Sphodrias 389
Lentulus Spinther 918, 953
Spitamenes 506, 507, 586
Spithridates 487
spolia opima 1039
Spring and Autumn 154, 155, 157
Spring and Autumn Annals 157
Sri Lanka 150, 637
Ssu-ma Ch'ien 156
Stagirus 459, 529
Joseph Stalin 16, 44, 78, 121, 160, 241, 249, 275, 325, 425, 445, 466, 510, 521, 523, 534-536, 564, 570, 626, 733, 743, 887, 1017, 1047
Stalingrad 396, 700
Stasander 541, 551
Stasnor 541
Statira 378
Statue of Liberty 259, 567
Stesagoras 198
Sthelaidas 302
Stobi 754
C. Licinius Stolo 611, 614
Stone of Implacability 189
St. Paul 157
St. Peter 44, 258
St. Peter's Basilica 44
St. Petersburg 361
Gnaeus Pompeius Strabo 856, 857, 858, 859, 862, 872, 875, 888
Strabo (Greek astronomer) 59,
Strabo (historian) 181, 612, 1057, 1059
Stradella 675
Straits of Hormuz 516
Straits of Messina 314, 419, 420, 674
strategos autokrator 208, 242, 415
Strategus of Syracuse 641
Stratocles 475, 529, 564, 567, 568
Stratonice 573, 586, 734
Stratoniceia 793, 837, 1005
Strymon River 266, 297
Henry Stuart-Jones 1040, 1049
stupas 150
Subartu 103, 104
Succusant 600
Suetonius 979, 981, 985
Suez 17, 68, 76, 98, 119, 121, 1057
Suez Canal 17, 221, 226, 278
Sufete 748
Sugambri 927, 1073

Sugunia 133
General Suharto 835
Sukhu 133
Faustus Sulla 895, 971, 973
P. Cornelius Sulla (nephew) 901
Lucius Cornelius Sulla 601, 708, 811, 835, 843, 844, 845, 847, 851, 852, 858-861, 865, 867-884, 887-892, 894, 898-903, 905-909, 911, 913, 919, 935-937, 941, 947, 954, 958, 961, 963, 964, 965, 976-980, 982, 985, 1005, 1017, 1038-1041, 1048, 1050, 1054, 1088
P. Sulpicius 631, 693, 860, 1062, 1070
Sulpicius 613, 614, 631, 648, 693, 722, 723, 747, 750, 751, 856, 860, 861, 875, 944, 1062, 1063, 1070
Sumeria 58, 61-64, 103-106, 141
Sumerian law codes 65
Sumerian(s) 23, 26, 27, 62, 63, 65, 103, 105, 109
Sumu-la-ilum 104
L. Tarquinius Superbus 596
Quntus Bruttius Sura 867
Surenas 937-940, 1018
Susa 22, 26, 27, 50, 60, 63, 64, 126, 201, 216, 220, 227, 228, 237, 239, 247, 250, 270, 276, 353, 354, 375, 377, 378, 398, 407, 469, 501, 516, 517, 541, 546, 735
Susiana 222, 224, 516, 535, 541, 546, 551, 556
Sutrium 613, 621
Swat 511
Sybaris 201, 204, 205, 296
Sybota 299, 312
Syllaeus 1058
Syloson 202, 224
Ronald Syme 1070
Synod of the League of Delos 287
Synoikismos 186
Syracuse 179, 243, 258-262, 296, 311, 312-314, 319, 333-342, 346, 370, 413-422, 425-445, 447, 514, 567, 575, 576, 612, 616, 619, 624, 632, 633, 640-645, 653, 678, 683, 686-689, 692, 693, 698, 699, 703, 708, 720, 728, 729, 830
Syriac 22
Syrians 21, 50, 73, 84, 89, 137, 500, 767,

768, 769, 817, 1079
Szechuan 156, 161

T

Taanach 36
Tabal 121
Tabernacle 34
Tachos 395, 407, 408
Tacitus 112, 604, 1049, 1082
Tagus River 662, 695, 883
Taker of Cities 566
Talleyrand 68, 419
Tammanai 131
Tamos 378
Tamynae 460
Tanagra 273, 279, 280, 281, 320
Tao 157
Taranto 205, 436, 438, 445, 636, 809, 810
Tarentum 428, 434, 435, 438, 445, 627, 628, 630-634, 636, 642, 649, 688, 692, 694, 720, 1008, 1011-1013, 1028
Treaty of Tarentum 1008
W.W. Tarn 381, 483, 529, 569, 572, 573, 937, 1016
Tarpeian Rock 616
Tarqua 124
Tarquinii 614
Tarquinius Priscus 596, 597, 600
Tarquinius Superbus 596, 597, 598, 601
Tarracina 607
Tarshish 256, 257
Tarsus 135, 490, 491, 528, 970, 998, 1002
Tartessians 424, 655, 661, 662
Tartessus 424, 425
Tashkent 505, 506
Taulantini 483, 713
Taurani 664
Taurisci 846
Tauromenium 418, 419, 430, 431, 821, 1013
Statilius Taurus 1013, 1015, 1037, 1042, 1044
Taurus Mountains 731, 769, 772, 1006
Taurus River 590
Taurus tribes 1005, 1007
tax collectors 72, 77, 497, 911, 998
Taxila 147, 512
Taxiles 511, 513, 537
Tegea 179, 270, 326, 327, 329-331, 384,

394, 396, 400, 549
Telemon 169
Telesphorus 555
Telmessus 773, 792
Temanus 179
Temini 414
Tempe 244, 777, 781
temple harlots 107
Temple of Ammon 519, 538
Temple of Anaitis 741
Temple of Apollo at Delphi 198
Temple of Athena 247
Temple of Bellona 1028
Temple of Fides 824
Temple of Hera 420
Temple of Jerusalem 54, 895
Temple of Jupiter 874
Temple of Jupiter Feretrius 1039
Temple of Mars 978
Temple of Melkart 495
Temple of Persephone 634
Temple of Poseidon 533
Tempti-Khumma-inshushinak 125
Tenaerum 528
Tencteri 925, 936
Tennes 403
Tennessee Valley Authority 290
Teres 297
Terillus 260
Terituchmes 377
Termessus 542
Tet offensive 688
Teuta 713-717, 775
Teutoburg Forest 1076
Teuton(s) 112, 131, 846, 848, 849, 885, 920, 921, 924, 933, 935, 985, 1035
textiles 77
Thais 501
Thales 201
Juventius Thalna 784
Thapsacus 498, 518
Thasos 268, 270, 353
Theagenes 189, 190
Thearidas 421
Theban(s) 70-74, 198, 209, 245, 246, 280, 303, 312, 360, 384, 385, 388, 389, 391-394, 398, 399, 401, 402, 450, 452, 457, 458, 461, 463, 464, 467, 474, 476, 484, 493, 517
Thebes 70, 71, 73, 77-82, 84, 85, 88, 91, 93,

98, 101, 124, 167, 195, 196, 198, 209, 240, 278-281, 283, 302-304, 309, 312, 319, 325, 362, 364, 373, 384, 386-403, 413, 421, 422, 447, 449-452, 454, 456-458, 461-465, 467-469, 473, 474, 476, 477, 483, 484, 523, 531, 553, 555, 558, 564, 567, 575, 576, 578, 731, 752, 754, 898, 1056

Thebez 37

Themistocles 215, 241-251, 254, 263-266, 269, 270, 274-276, 279, 281, 287, 291, 292, 309, 343, 351, 362, 401, 415, 419, 429, 532, 750

Theodotus 736, 964, 965

Theophiliscus 744, 745

Theophrastus 510, 551, 563, 564

Theopompus 174, 177, 179

Theoric Fund 456, 460

Theramenes 344

Thermae 435, 444, 648

Thermidoreans 390

Thermopylae 243, 244-246, 248, 453, 455, 456, 461, 462, 464, 473, 531, 549, 567, 589, 731, 733, 767, 774, 804, 868

Thermus 870, 877

Theron 260, 261, 414

Theseus 266

Thessalian League 483

Thessalian(s) 243, 244, 385, 392, 394, 455, 466, 477, 493, 499, 500, 533, 549, 757, 777, 784

Thessalonice 550, 574

Thessalus 195

Thessaly 175, 177, 180, 187, 188, 193, 195, 198, 240, 243-245, 250, 251, 262, 263, 273, 276, 281, 282, 320, 385, 391, 393-395, 397, 448, 451, 454, 455, 459, 462, 466, 474, 483, 531-533, 543, 549, 552, 555, 568, 575, 577, 581, 589, 750-752, 754, 766-768, 781, 867-869, 961

Thessaly (son of Ciimon) 336

Thetes 191, 192, 289

Thetes. 191

Thetis 172, 173

Thibron 381, 387

Adolphe Thiers 90, 190

Third Great Council of Buddhism 150

Third Samnian War 623

Third Syrian War 730, 732, 736

The Thirty 284, 285, 286, 294, 299, 300, 301, 307, 361, 362, 363, 364, 367, 390, 809, 838, 1086

Thirty Years Peace 284-286, 294, 299, 300, 301, 307

Thirty Years' War 809

Thithrausetes 386

Thoas of Trichonium 764

Thoenon 633

R. Campbell Thompson 104, 114, 127

Henry David Thoreau 158

Thrace 175, 201, 225, 226, 234, 236, 242, 250, 265, 266, 268, 282, 287, 296, 297, 307, 308, 319-322, 325, 326, 332, 349, 355, 373, 375, 382, 448, 454, 455, 458, 463, 466, 469, 474, 485, 494, 526, 527, 533, 537, 546, 552, 556, 557, 568, 572, 575, 581, 585-588, 590, 605, 729, 744, 747, 753, 755, 758, 759, 762-764, 769, 771, 778, 784, 867, 998, 1029, 1036, 1053, 1069, 1075

Thracian Empire 297

Thracian Phrygians 112

Thracian(s) 170, 234, 297, 322, 355, 389, 433, 447, 448, 463, 485, 729, 754, 758, 778, 837, 885, 1067

Thraso 686

Thrasybulus 201, 348, 349, 352, 358, 362-364, 384, 387

Thrasyllus 329, 348, 352, 353, 357

The Three Thousand 362

Thucydides 174, 177, 183, 186, 237, 256, 264, 266, 269, 273, 279, 281, 291, 292, 295, 298, 304, 306, 308, 313, 318, 320, 321, 342, 351, 366, 421, 709

Thucydides of Melesias 269, 295

"Thunderbolt" *See also* Ptolemy Keranus 582-585, 588

Thurii 434, 627-630, 641, 642, 968

Thutmose I 78, 79-81

Thutmose III 67, 80, 82, 83, 91

Thutmose IV 84

Thyrea 179, 186, 318, 332

Tiber River 596, 606, 607, 609, 738, 832, 833, 863, 943, 987, 1043, 1051

Tiberius (Caesar) 801, 802, 809-812, 815-

830, 832, 832-836, 845, 852, 874, 890, 904, 1001, 1012, 1042-1048, 1051, 1059-1063, 107-1077, 1082, 1085, 1087
Tibet 160
tiger 140, 458
Tiglath Pileser I 101
Tigranes 864, 865, 891, 892-894, 916, 917, 937, 1021, 1059
Tigranes II 1062
Tigranes III 1062, 1063
Tigranes IV 1063
Tigris River 27, 58, 59-61, 65, 107, 108, 116, 120, 122, 131, 134, 135, 137, 222, 378, 379, 483, 498, 518, 546, 558, 569, 862, 980
Tigurini 847-849
Tikhsi 83, 84
Timarchus 466, 729
timocracy 192
Timocrates 384, 429
Timoleon 399, 411, 430-437, 442, 445, 619, 653
Timophanes 399
Timotheus 391, 401, 402, 453, 456
tin 141, 256, 424, 425
Tios 584, 585
Tiribazus 386-388, 394
Tiridates 1022, 1037, 1059
Tirigan 63
Tissaphernes 344, 345, 347, 349, 350, 352, 353, 354, 362, 377-379, 382, 383, 386, 391
Titienses 598
Titius 854, 1014, 1021, 1026, 1027
Josip Tito 850
Titus Tatius 598
Tlepolemus 744
Tobiah 50, 1066
Toledo 662
Tolmides 280, 283
Leo Tolstoi 371
Tombos 78
Tomeros River 515
Tomsky 241
Torah 33, 41, 50, 51
Torone 321
T. Manlius Torquatus 612, 685
Tragia 296
Trajan 1019

Trapezus 379, 380, 1019
Lake Trasimene 677-679, 684, 690, 718
Treaty of Brundisium 1025 *See also* Pact of Brundisium
Trebellius 969
Trebia 681, 690
Gaius Trebonius 955
Trebonius 955, 956, 983, 989, 995
Trerus River 606
Triballi 472, 483
Triballians 321
tribune(s) 602, 604, 608, 611, 615, 617, 626, 667, 782, 798, 799, 801, 811, 813, 820, 823, 825, 828, 829, 838, 840, 852, 853, 854, 861, 878, 884, 889, 914, 915, 917, 936, 941, 945, 947, 957, 984, 990, 1015, 1038, 1026, 1046, 1049, 1081, 1088
Tribunus Celerum 600, 601
Trifanum 619
Triparadeisus 540
Tripodiscus 319
Tripoli 133, 440, 491-493
triremes 235, 241, 245, 247, 261, 267, 282, 284, 296, 298, 299, 304-306, 308-310, 313-316, 318, 335, 340-342, 344, 346, 356, 358, 360, 363, 418, 429, 430, 431, 456, 531, 647, 742
First Triumvirate 910, 912, 914-920, 941, 968
Second Triumvirate 507, 996, 997, 1088
Troad 168, 240, 269, 448, 728, 871
Trocmi 916
Troezen 247, 318
Trojan Horse 83, 170, 261, 267, 268, 473
Trojans 169, 170, 172
Trojan War 168, 169, 175, 177, 1089
Trosezen 285
Leon Trotsky 241
Troy 116, 168-177, 187, 189, 240, 269, 297
Truceless War 659, 664
Donald J. Trump 314, 836
Tso Commentary 159
Tsou Yen 158
Tu-Chi 408
P. Sempronius Tuditanus 725, 747
Sempronius Tuditanus 653
Tukulti-Ninurta 115, 132
Tukulti-Ninurta II 132
Tullia 597

Servius Tullius 596, 597, 600, 604, 611
Tullius Hostilius 596, 598
Volcacius Tullus 902
Tung Chung-shu 163
Tunis 439, 440, 442, 649, 706
Tunisia 215, 256, 374, 413, 441, 649, 650, 740, 803
Turdetanians 798
Turin 664, 674
Turkey 21, 23, 47, 64, 88, 94, 108, 109, 119, 132, 168, 189, 190, 242, 490, 726, 732, 772, 830, 860, 1062, 1086
Turkomen 506
Turks 23, 129, 362, 366, 1079
turquoise 71, 141
Turullius 1021, 1026, 1034
Tuscan 595, 677
Tusculum 607, 611, 615, 976
Tushratta 84, 89, 111, 114
Tutankhamon 90
Twelve Labours of Hercules 178
Twelve Tables 603, 604
twelve tribes of Israel 46
Tymphaea 576
Tyndaris 648, 651
tyrant 58, 153, 180, 190, 193, 194, 196-199, 201-204, 206, 210, 225, 230, 231, 257, 260, 261, 274, 362, 393, 399, 416, 420, 430, 432, 433, 436, 437, 445, 446, 463, 469, 487, 510, 588, 598, 633, 641, 727, 729, 742, 824, 983, 986, 1021
Tyre 45, 51, 79, 128, 133, 134, 137, 256, 257, 415, 423, 424, 494, 495, 497, 502, 553, 554, 572, 573, 581, 726, 736, 737, 749, 830, 1005

U

Ulm 484
Umbria 606, 617, 623, 683, 690, 700, 702, 856, 858
Umma 58, 59, 61
Unheralded War 239
Union Sacree 359
United Kingdom 218, 227
United Nations 181, 440, 523
United States of America 46, 77, 98, 99, 104, 122, 149, 175, 201, 218, 226, 241, 275, 288, 289, 291, 346, 374, 376, 401, 408, 420, 426, 427, 465, 523, 567, 604, 625, 648, 666-668, 704, 708, 751, 802, 825, 826, 1049
Universal Love 158
Upanishad 144, 145
Ur 27, 28, 57-59, 61-64, 103, 104, 108
Urals 17
Urarti 119, 120, 133, 134, 136, 225
Urartus 118
Ur-bau 62
Ur-Engur 63, 64
Uriah the Hittite 40, 43, 44
Ur-Nina 57, 58
Uruk 108
Urukagina 58, 59
U.S. Civil War 248, 259, 670, 673, 720
Userkaf 68
Usipetes 925, 936, 1073
U.S.S.R. 218
Uta-Naphistim 107
Utica 659, 703-706, 806, 808, 830, 876, 956, 973
Utukhegal 63
Uxii 501
Uzbekistan 505, 507, 569

V

Lake Vadimo 626
Vahyazdata 223
Vaishyas 143
Vakhash River 509
Manius Valerius 645
P. Valerius 614, 615
Valerius Publicola 601, 602, 604, 605, 607, 608, 612, 613
Valley of the Kings 80, 84
Vallis Poenina 1070
Lake Van 134, 891
Vargunteius 937, 939
C. Terrentius Varro 681, 682, 710, 955, 956, 978, 1042, 1070
P. Attius Varus 956, 973, 978, 1076
P. Vatinius 913, 914, 919, 920, 963, 971, 980, 995
Vaumisa 223
Spurius Cassius Vecellinus 603, 605
Rig Veda 142, 143
Vedas 142
Veientanes 607
Veii 597, 605, 607, 609, 610, 613, 616
Velia 624

Velitrae 607, 614, 615
Veneti 924, 925
Venetians 664, 665
P. Ventidius 859, 991, 996, 1006, 1007, 1008, 1018
Venus Genetrix 974, 980
Venusium 699
Vercellae 848, 849
Vercingetorix 930-934, 974
Veriathus 798
Verres 889
T. Verturius 620
Verulae 622
Lucretius Vespillo 1044
Vestal Virgins 600, 836, 852, 981, 1027
Vestini 856, 858
Vetilius 799, 800
Lucius Vettius 914
Vibnium 679
Vichy 348
vicomagistri 1050
Queen Victoria 93
Vidacilius 858
Vipsania 1046
Virdumaras 666
Virgil 596, 1000, 1004, 1021, 1025, 1038, 1043, 1048, 1051, 1084
Virgin Birth 61
Viriathus 799, 800, 817, 884
VIth Dynasty 69
viziers 72, 76, 77
Volga 82, 225
Volsci 606, 607, 613, 614, 615, 620
Volscian Wars 606
Volsinii 626, 631, 637
Volterra 597
Lucius Volumnius 622
Vulci 626, 627, 631
L. Manlius Vulso 648

W

H.T. Wade-Gery 178, 183
Wadi Halfa 71, 1056
Richard Wagner 61, 108, 173
Richard Wagner's Ring Cycle 108, 173
Frank Walbank 731
Lech Walesa 88
E.M. Walker 209, 239, 270, 286
Robert Walpole 668, 1045
War Between Han and Chu 161

War of Eumenes 728
War of Spanish Succession 170
War of the Austrian Succession 304
War of the Brothers 730, 732, 734
War of the Gladiators 884, 885, 888
The Way and the Power 157
Warring States 154, 155
Warsaw Ghetto 54
George Washington 46, 50, 193, 291, 676, 688, 729, 749, 850, 879
water buffalo 141
Weimar Germany, 359
Wellington 263, 693, 708, 719, 850
Wen Wang 153
Duke Wen of Chin 155
Emperor Wen 164
Emperor Wu-ti 164
Western Civilization 21, 26, 34, 176, 203, 776
Western Desert 94
Western Europe 17, 21, 72, 73, 75, 142, 158, 160, 226, 256, 257, 334, 408, 673
Western Roman Empire 23, 577
Westminster 228
Weygand 360
"wheel of the law" 146
White Castle 281
wild boar 85
Wilhelm II 93, 286
William III 216, 753
Woodrow Wilson 591, 771
wine 22, 25, 26, 72, 77, 106, 143, 148, 149, 169, 178, 179, 190, 191, 196, 311, 422, 464, 507, 514, 655, 961, 972, 974, 1078
Stanley Wolpert 141
Field Marshal Garnet Wolseley 843
World War I 168, 241, 248, 259, 296, 299, 359, 702, 771
World War II 16, 22, 115, 231, 241, 248, 305, 318, 384, 425, 469, 523, 524, 605, 702, 784, 843
Wu 153, 155, 161, 164, 165
Wu Kuang 161
Wu-ti 164, 165
Wu Wang 153

X

Xanthippus 208, 241, 251, 252, 254, 271,

274, 291, 650
Xenodicus 443
Xenoetas 735
Xenophanes 719, 720
Xenophon 181, 373, 377-382, 400, 1019
Xerxes 50, 215, 226, 227, 242, 243, 244, 245, 246, 247, 248, 249, 250, 251, 254, 259, 261, 264, 266, 267, 270, 272, 345, 349, 371, 374, 375
Xerxes II 376, 403, 405, 457, 459, 494, 501, 557
Xerxes (king of Armenia) 727, 741, 745

Ziboetes 584, 586
ziggurat 59
Zimri 49
Zinoviev 241
Zion 53
Ziudsudu 57
Zoippus 686
zoologists 482
Zoroaster 229
Zoser 67
Zugagi 114
Zyraxes 1037

Y

Yahweh 22, 26, 31, 39, 43, 45, 46, 52-54
Yahwism 37
Yang-shao 151
Yangtze 154
Yellow River 152
Yemen 45, 1057
Yen 156, 158, 159
Yin and Yang 158
Yom Kippur War 688
Emperor Yu 152
Yueh 155, 164
Yueh-chih 164
Yu Wang 154

Z

Zab 378
Zacynthus 307, 308, 341, 391, 721, 723
Zadok 44, 52
Zadracarta 503
Zama 703, 707, 748, 773, 803, 805, 816, 972, 973
Zancle 259, 261
Zechariah 49
Zedekiah 128
Zelea 492
Zeno 366, 563, 580, 582, 727, 732
Zeugitae 289
Zeugites 191, 192
Zeus 26, 169, 172, 180, 181, 188, 253, 257, 312, 418, 509, 517, 520, 529, 727, 805, 1036
Zeus-Belus 26
Zeus Stratios 862
Georgy Zhukov 263
Ziaelas 734

ACKNOWLEDGEMENTS

I would like to thank my wife, Barbara, for her Job-like patience with me for the inconvenience my attention to this book has caused her, and also for her always helpful and important editorial advice, and our executive assistants, Danella Connors and Julie Fredette, for their invaluable help in editing and reorganizing the material. My IT advisor Jorge Vargas has been heroic, both in his unfailing skill as the material has been reorganized and blocks of text moved around, and in his good humor even when I have reluctantly disturbed him at all hours and during holidays. Thanks are also due to Victor D. Hanson, Henry Kissinger, and Bill Ross for having read parts of the manuscript and made useful comments about it. Most conspicuously, I must profoundly thank the Publisher, who doubled as editor and composer of the egregiously large index, Rebecca Bynum of the New English Review Press, for her tireless and diligent work and unshakeable optimism, ingenuity and encouragement, and to Doug Pepper of Random House Penguin (Canada) for his suggestions, and to my British agent Caroline Michel, for her wisdom and suavity, acquired from her vast experience with books and authors. I am grateful to all of those named, and they are blameless in any shortcomings that may be found in this narrative.

www.ingramcontent.com/pod-product-compliance
Lightning Source LLC
Chambersburg PA
CBHW070751300426
44111CB00014B/2373